Notes: Risk management includes actuarial science, insurance and health care.
Accounting includes tax.
Finance includes banking.
Management includes human resources, in particular, compensation and salary.
Political science includes voting studies.
Social studies means social studies other than geography, political science, economics and business.
General means generic data sets, often constructed to illustrate specific statistical issues.

DATA ANALYSIS USING REGRESSION MODELS

DATA ANALYSIS USING REGRESSION MODELS

The Business Perspective

Edward W. Frees
University of Wisconsin–Madison

 Prentice Hall, Upper Saddle River, NJ 07458

Library of Congress Cataloging-in-Publication Data

Frees, Edward W.
   Data analysis using regression models: the business perspective/Edward W. Frees.
     p. cm.
   Includes bibliograpical references and index.
   ISBN 0-13-219981-5
   1. Regression analysis. 2. Social science Statistical methods.
I. Title.
HA31.3.F74 1996
300'.1'519536—dc20   95-12629
                                                    CIP

Acquisitions editor: Tom Tucker
Assistant editor: Diane Peirano
Production supervision: Maryland Composition
Cover design: Bruce Kenselaer
Manufacturing buyer: Marie McNamara

Published by Prentice-Hall, Inc.
A Simon & Schuster Company/A Viacom Company
Upper Saddle River, New Jersey 07458

Printed in the United States of America
10 9 8 7 6 5 4 3 2

ISBN 0-13-219981-5

PRENTICE-HALL INTERNATIONAL (UK) LIMITED, *LONDON*
PRENTICE-HALL OF AUSTRALIA PTY. LIMITED, *SYDNEY*
PRENTICE-HALL CANADA INC., *TORONTO*
PRENTICE-HALL HISPANOAMERICANA, S. A., *MEXICO*
PRENTICE-HALL OF INDIA PRIVATE LIMITED, *NEW DELHI*
PRENTICE-HALL OF JAPAN, INC., *TOKYO*
SIMON & SCHUSTER ASIA PTE. LTD., *SINGAPORE*
EDITORA PRENTICE-HALL DO BRASIL, LTDA., *RIO DE JANEIRO*

For establishing my foundations:
To my mother, Mary Frees, and the memory of my father, William Frees

For giving me support and friendship:
To my wife, Deirdre

For inspiring me to develop a vision of and hope for the future:
To my children, Nathan and Adam

Brief Table of Contents

Additional Materials

Contents

Technical Supplements Contents

Preface

Statistics is a comfortable yet exciting subject. It is comfortable because it has a solid foundation in mathematics. As a branch of applied mathematics, statistics has its roots firmly grounded on the most basic of the sciences. As a branch of science, statistics is considered neither fuzzy nor ephemeral; it is a discipline that yields logical conclusions based on certain assumptions, models and data.

Statistics is exciting because of its usefulness in other scientific disciplines. These disciplines grow and evolve via the "scientific method:" postulating a theory, gathering data to support the theory and confirming or modifying the theory in light of the data. Statistics is a general theory about data. As such, it can be used to confirm and suggest relationships from other disciplines. Statistics plays an important supporting role in the development of modern-day science. The real excitement of statistics is that it can be used as a (sometimes deciding) argument in favor of or against a theory in another discipline.

Regression analysis, the topic of this book, is one of several applied statistical methods. If statistics as a whole is valuable because it is useful, then regression analysis is very valuable because its use is so widespread, especially in studies of business and economics.

This book introduces the reader to the theory and practice of regression analysis. To set the stage, we now consider whom this book is for, what it is about and how it delivers its message.

WHO IS THIS BOOK FOR?

This book is designed for a second course in business statistics. Specifically, in designing this book, several assumptions were made about: (1) what readers would like to learn about regression analysis, (2) readers' quantitative and business background knowledge, (3) how deeply readers would like to understand the material and (4) the types of applications that would interest readers. Here are the details of the design criteria adopted in this book.

Reader's Goals

This book provides readers with a *working knowledge* of regression analysis. It is expected that all readers will agree with the position of H.G. Wells who succinctly stated that, "Statistics will become vital for a well-informed citizen . . ." This book is written in a fashion to encourage, and help, the reader to become a critical consumer of statistics. The text is designed to make you proficient in handling the analysis of small data sets. Further, it will prepare you to be an effective member of a team charged with understanding a large data set. That is, most readers of this text are not preparing themselves to become professional statisticians. They may, however, be part of a team that includes a data base professional, a financial analyst, a statistician, a marketing professional and a general manager.

Reader's Background

The quantitative background required for the main body of the text is equivalent to a one-semester or one-quarter course in the fundamentals of statistics. Although readers will find calculus and matrix, or linear, algebra helpful, these are not required prerequisites for reading this text. Still, there is a wide variety of topics presented in a first course. Further, for many graduate students, it is often many years in between their first course and their study of this book. Thus, Chapter 2 presents the fundamentals of statistics needed for the later chapters.

This text does not require a background in business. In many undergraduate and graduate programs, statistics is often treated as a "tool" course. As such, it comes early in the program before all students have acquired an extensive exposure to business problems. This course is used in the program's later courses as one tool to make business decisions. However, an interest in business and management problems is important for reading this text. Almost every example and case study comes from business. Therefore, unless you find this orientation relevant, regression may seem dry and boring.

Level of Reader

Different readers are interested in understanding statistics at different levels. This book is written to accommodate the "armchair reader," that is, one who passively reads and does not get involved by attempting the exercises in the text. Consider an analogy to football, or any other game. Just like the armchair quarterback of football, there is a great deal that you can learn about the game just by watching. However, if you want to sharpen your skills, you have to go out and play the game. The Role of Exercises section describes several types of exercises that are contained in this text to help you sharpen your regression analysis skills. Still this text is written by interweaving examples with the basic principles. Thus, even the armchair reader can obtain a solid understanding of regression techniques through this text.

Business Perspective

This book is for readers interested in business applications. As we will see, this drives our treatment of some regression topics. This perspective has heavily influenced the choice of data sets selected to illustrate the practice of regression. In preparing the data sets, a broad perspective of the notion of "business" is taken. In the text, you will find examples from education, political science, economics and a wide variety of social sciences. These broad-based examples are not here at the expense of illustrations from more traditional business areas. Rather, there are examples from each of the major functional areas of business including accounting, finance, management, marketing and risk management. Several minor areas of business are also heavily represented. In particular, real estate pricing applications, such as renting an apartment or buying a house, lend themselves readily to regression methodology and are of immediate relevance to most readers. Further, you will find several examples of quantifying health care costs, a timely business problem in the current political environment.

WHAT IS THIS BOOK ABOUT?

The Table of Contents provides an overview of the topics covered in this book. However, in the list of references in the Appendix, you will also find over 25 current texts on regression analysis. To get a better sense as to how this book differs from those in the literature, consider: (1) the role of data and its interaction with corresponding models, (2) how modern computational resources have affected not only the practice, but also the theory, of regression analysis, (3) the choice of topics selected for this book and (4) how we communicate what we have learned from an analysis of data using regression methods.

Data and Models

Statistics is about summarizing data and making decisions using data. You will find that the data sets drive the development of the book. Nearly all the data sets are original in that they were suggested to the author either through consulting and research or through projects done by students in regression

courses. The data sets were not obtained by canvassing academic journal articles or other statistics books; these sources can be far removed from situations
that readers can appreciate. Although the data sets are original, in most cases
the sources of the data are publicly available and accessible. In this way, readers can find related sources of data for their own projects.

Statistics is about the construction of a theory to match a set of data. This
book describes the interaction between data analysis and regression models
used to represent the data. Before taking a course on regression analysis, students of business and other social sciences have had exposure to, and are comfortable with, analyzing data. They have manipulated figures from financial
statements in their beginning accounting courses or discussed election polling
data in political science courses. Further, these students have had many
courses in using models, particularly in mathematics and other science
courses. In an elementary algebra course, students have only experience in
solving an equation, not in specifying a reasonable equation to represent reality. In geometry classes, students learn to construct lines perpendicular to a
curve at a particular point. However, they take the curve as a given and not an
issue for discussion. This text will help students not only analyze regression
data and understand regression models, but also learn how to specify an appropriate model to represent a data set.

Role of Computers

The history of regression is barely over 100 years old. However, only in the last
30 years has there been tremendous activity in the development of regression.
This activity is mainly due to the growing availability of inexpensive computing power. This growing availability means that the number of users has
grown. Further, because calculations have been mechanized, techniques of calculation, such as matrix algebra, do not play the same critical role that they did
15 years ago. Because of the computer, knowledge of matrix algebra is no
longer necessary for every student of regression.

Modern-day computing power has allowed the practice of statistics to become more interactive. For example, it is now straightforward to examine data
graphically prior to the formal model specification. Calculation of statistics
that were considered impractical because of their computational complexity,
such as best subsets in regression, is now routine.

Changes in teaching practice have occurred due to events in the computing environment. Computing has become universally accessible for students,
thus allowing them to get "hands-on" experience with data analysis. As a result, teachers can now use real data sets to illustrate theory. This trend will continue as packages improve in both their data handling capabilities and user
interface. Because of the wide variety of computing systems and software
packages, it is not viable to tie a text to a particular software configuration.
However, readers will find examples of several of the most popular packages
in this text for illustrative purposes.

Finally, although modern-day computing provides increased flexibility, it also offers increased opportunities for abuses of statistics. This is the focus of the Communication section that follows.

Choice of Topics

There are many different topics, and types of emphasis, that can be presented in a text on regression analysis. Our business perspective drives the choice of topics in this text, along with my desire to produce a text that can be used in a one-semester or two-quarter course, not an encyclopedia. Some important features of the text include the treatment of cross-sectional regression, longitudinal data models and logistic regression. In the interest of length, this text excludes a detailed treatment of experimental design material.

Cross-Sectional Regression. After the Foundations chapter (Chapter 2), the text begins with six chapters on cross-sectional regression analysis. This set of techniques helps us to understand relationships between variables, an important issue in the social sciences. Cross-sectional regression has been taught in social science programs for several decades; the pedagogy of regression is a proven product. Further, the techniques that we will use, such as plotting data and least squares estimation, are useful in other contexts including longitudinal data analysis.

Longitudinal Data Models. A distinguishing feature of this book is that over one quarter of this text is on longitudinal data models. Of the 25 currently available competing texts, only one other offers this blend, the 1977 book by Miller and Wichern. Why have this unusual feature? The reasons are simple, yet compelling: most accounting, financial and economic data become available over time. Although cross-sectional inferences are useful, business decisions need to be made in real time with currently available data. The dynamic analyses of longitudinal data models give us important tools for use at the firm level. This is particularly true in the context of modern quality management that deals predominantly with time series problems. The recent text by Roberts (1990) made this point eloquently, and with great force.

Logistic Regression. Logistic regression allows us to discriminate among classes of populations. This provides another application of regression analysis, one that is particularly useful in the social sciences. Logistic regression is perhaps the most widely used special case of a nonlinear regression model. Traditionally, use of nonlinear regression models was limited due to the prohibitive amount of computation required to fit these models. However, the widespread availability of powerful, inexpensive computers has addressed this concern.

Experimental Design. This text excludes a detailed treatment of material on experimental design, the study of controlling explanatory variables in a regression study. It has become evident that most data in business arise in the context of observational studies, where data are not the result of a controlled, well-designed experiment. However, the text does not ignore the study of categorical explanatory variables nor the study of ill-behaved explanatory variables. Indeed, these topics are addressed in Chapters 5 and 6, respectively. Still, the text omits material on experimental design in the interest of space and of developing a consistent theme of handling observational data throughout the text.

Communication

As described in the opening paragraphs of this preface, in order for statistics to succeed it must assist in the advancement of other disciplines. A regression analysis of data in and of itself is rarely of interest in the world of business. It must be communicated to others, generally as a part of a larger package.

Because of the desire to see the results of a statistical analysis communicated effectively, an important feature of this text is two chapters on communication. Chapter 12 on Report Writing reminds readers what the end result should emphasize. Chapter 13 on Presenting Data is more innovative. Presenting data, either as part of text, in tabular form, or graphically, has long been an important part of statistics. However, with computer-aided graphical packages, there is a tendency for students to become preoccupied with graphical form and lose sight of the underlying substance. Chapter 13 reviews design principles and issues in statistical graphical perception.

HOW DOES THIS BOOK DELIVER ITS MESSAGE?

Readers will find several aspects of the writing in this book make the material accessible. Several original examples and case studies reinforce the material. Instructors will appreciate the modular aspects of the book allowing them to design their own course; some suggestions can be found below.

Writing

Writing means many things to different people. Consider writing in terms of the audience, orientation and the development.

Student Orientation. The several features of the text design show that the text was written for students. Each chapter begins with an overview to foreshadow future topics. Each chapter ends with a summary to provide continuity between chapters. Throughout the text, you will find numbered lists of procedures. These lists are not meant to provide a cookbook of statistical procedures; they make the mechanics routine so that you can appreciate, and use, the statistical ideas. The notes in the margin summarize key aspects of the development. End-of-chapter keywords emphasize important terms; a glossary summarizes the technical language used in statistics.

Teaching Orientation. The main body of the text explains concepts in the context of data analysis. Thus, the principles are introduced when they are needed by readers for analyzing data. The organization of the main body of the text differs from the organization of the technical supplements. On one hand, the technical supplements develop the theory in a step-by-step fashion, building on each concept in a crisp, mathematical fashion. On the other hand, the main body of the text develops the material from a user's viewpoint. Principles are introduced as needed for applications, not simply because they follow as the next logical step in a mathematical development.

Chapter Development. Each chapter has several examples interwoven with theory. In chapters where a model is introduced, we begin with an example and discuss the data analysis without regard to the theory. This analysis is presented at an intuitive level, without reference to a specific model. This is straightforward, because it amounts to little more than curve fitting. The theme is to have students summarize data sensibly without having the notion of a model obscure good data analysis. Then, an introduction to the theory is provided in the context of the introductory example. One or more additional examples follow that reinforce the theory already introduced and provide a context for explaining additional theory. In Chapters 6 and 7, which do not introduce models but rather techniques for analysis, we begin with an introduction of the technique. This introduction is then followed by an example that reinforces the explanation. In this way, the data analysis can be easily omitted without loss of continuity, if time is a concern.

Exercises

An important distinguishing feature of this text is the number and quality of exercises. Exercises provide an essential tool for sharpening understanding of statistics. The exercises are in congruence with the teaching orientation of this text. They reinforce points made in the text and occasionally provide alternative points of view.

Real Data. Most of the exercises ask the reader to work with real data. The need for working with real data is well documented; for example, see Hogg (1972), Moore and Roberts (1989) or Singer and Willett (1990). Some criteria of Singer and Willett for judging a good data set include: (1) authenticity, (2) availability of background information, (3) interest and relevance to substantive learning and (4) availability of elements with which readers can identify. Of course, there are some important disadvantages to working with real data. Data sets can quickly become outdated. Further, the ideal data set to illustrate a specific statistical issue is difficult to find. This is because with real data, almost by definition, several issues occur simultaneously. This makes it difficult to isolate a specific aspect.

Many texts on the market today work extensively with data sets that come from real problems, but are limited in size (often, around 20 observations). One distinguishing feature of this text is that we work with primarily moderate and large size data sets (generally, a sample size of at least 50). The motivation for occasionally working with small data sets is that specific statistical principles can be easily illustrated. Larger data sets generally have a lot more going on than simply the specific statistical issue being discussed. However, when 90% of the data sets in a text are small, this gives the reader a jaded perspective on the uses of regression analysis. For small data sets of only 20 observations, a set of complex summarization techniques such as regression has limited value. Certainly, for observational data sets with a sample size of only 10 observations, use of regression techniques is suspect. One of the principal applications of regression lies in summarizing data and, the more information to be summarized, the more useful is the technique.

Types of Exercises. This text contains several different types of exercises designed to sharpen different aspects of a reader's statistical skills. In the early chapters, there are several end-of-section exercise sets. The end-of-section sets allow the reader to practice the tools and techniques learned immediately following one or two sections. These are focused problems that generally ask the reader to do a short calculation or provide an interpretation of a statistical issue. The need for hand calculations has been advocated by Khamis (1990). Many teachers have found it useful to practice the mechanics in order to provide a solid foundation. With this foundation, we can get on to the real business, interpreting data using statistical principles.

At the end of each chapter, the exercises are more integrated than the end-of-section problems. Generally, each exercise has several parts, designed to follow the same logic that an analyst might use to understand a data set. You also will find that some data sets are followed over two or more chapters. In this way, students can work with the development of statistical principles on a fixed problem.

At the end of several chapters, you will find algebra and computer exercises. Especially in the early chapters, some instructors find it useful to develop the algebraic calculations in detail. This is one of the important reasons for splitting off regression with one explanatory variable as a special topic. (The other is graphical.) The instructor may choose to work these problems for the class, or assign them as out-of-class exercises.

Different Exercises for Different Readers. How deeply the reader understands statistics often depends on the effort put forth in working with a book. The different types of exercises allow the reader to achieve different levels of expertise in regression analysis. Here are several types of readers that will benefit from the exercises:

1. The armchair reader. As discussed in the Level of Reader section, this book is for the reader who, in fact, reads only and is interested in understanding the basic ideas of principles of regression analysis.
2. The person who reads the text and attempts several exercises without use of the computer. Although the working presumption that a computer is readily accessible to the data analyst, you will find that the computer output was generated for most of the problems. This allows the reader to spend more time thinking, and less time pushing buttons.
3. The person who reads the text and attempts several exercises with and without use of the computer. There is no better teacher than experience. With a statistical package, the many data sets provided with this text allow the reader to produce his or her own output. Although more time consuming than sitting at a library desk, generating output makes the reader feel in control and more comfortable with statistics.
4. The person who reads the text and attempts several exercises with and without use of the computer and also develops intuition by doing the algebra problems. For some students, algebra problems are so frustrating that they are actually counterproductive. For other students with the appropriate quantitative background, exercises using algebra can sharpen issues that otherwise may appear vague.

Modular Aspects

Several aspects of the text are modular in design to allow an instructor flexibility in designing a regression course. Here, we consider how the chapters relate to one another, how the technical supplements can be used and the assumptions made concerning the use of matrix algebra.

Chapter Sequencing. Chapters 12 and 13 are mutually independent and independent of the rest of the book. They can be read at any time. To illustrate, they can be assigned as out-of-class readings that are not tied to lecture.

Chapters 2 and 3 establish the foundation for the rest of the book. The Chapter 2 material is contained in most introductory courses in statistics and is thus optional. With the basic material in Chapter 3, the reader can either go through the cross-sectional data models materials or directly to the longitudinal data models materials. For example, readers primarily interested in quality management will want to go directly to the longitudinal data materials in Chapters 9 through 11. Chapters 9 through 11 should be read in sequence. Some of the advanced topics in Sections 10.5, 10.6, 11.3 and 11.4 require Chapter 4 material.

A more traditional reading course is the study of cross-sectional material in Chapters 4 through 8 first, followed by a less intense reading of the longitudinal data materials. Chapters 4 through 8 should be read in sequence, although Chapter 5 is not required for Chapters 6 and 7.

Technical Supplements. The technical supplements reinforce and extend the results in the main body of the text by giving a more formal, mathematical treatment of the material. This treatment is in fact a supplement because the applications and examples are described in the main body of the text. Therefore, the reader will find the technical supplements contain a concise version of the main results.

The main body of the text stresses application and interpretation of results in applied statistical methods. For readers with sufficient mathematical background, the supplements provide additional material that the reader will find useful in communicating with technical audiences. By "sufficient mathematical background," we mean that a knowledge of multivariate calculus is presupposed. Later technical supplements, including Chapter 4 and on, also presume a working knowledge of matrix algebra. However, for readers without a background in matrix algebra, an appendix provides a brief introduction.

The technical supplements provide a deeper, and broader, coverage of applied regression analysis for the mathematically inclined reader. The main body of the text states many of the results so that these are not repeated in the technical supplements. Other results are repeated, but are restated in technical language in order to stress their importance and to provide the insights that mathematical expressions can provide. Still other results can be found only in the Technical Supplements and are not in the main body of the text. These results, although not the dominant theme of the development in the main body of the text, serve to broaden the treatment and suggest additional applications of regression methods.

The technical supplements provide the reader with reference material for additional topics.. Generally, these topics will be omitted from the first reading of the material. Further, the technical supplements provide a menu of optional items that an instructor may wish to cover.

Use of Matrices. This text handles the use of matrix algebra in regression analysis at four different levels:

1. No knowledge of matrix algebra. For the course that does not use matrices, use the main body of the text.
2. Knowledge of *matrix notation* only. Here, the goal is to recognize and define a vector of responses, coefficients and errors and the matrix of explanatory variables. Only the basic definitions, and what matrix notation is about, are used.
3. Knowledge of basic matrix algebra. The goal is to add, subtract and multiply vectors and matrices. Knowledge of an inverse, as well as computing an inverse for a matrix of dimension 2 by 2, is also required.

4. Knowledge of some advanced concepts in matrix algebra. This level includes basic matrix algebra plus some advanced concepts, including determinants and inverses of block diagonal matrices.

For students with business experience but with little formal education in mathematics, the introduction of matrix notation takes little time and provides several benefits. Students have seen spreadsheet packages and are familiar with the idea of columns of numbers. This idea is then translated into a vector, which in turn leads to the concept of a matrix, and so on. Matrix notation allows students to read journal articles that are written using the language of matrix algebra and to gain insights into collinearity, leverage and standard error ideas. A special section (Section 4.7) introduces matrix notation only, not computational aspects. A more traditional approach is to present matrix calculations up through, and including, computation of a 2 by 2 inverse. For instructors who are comfortable with this approach, an appendix that introduces matrix algebra is provided.

Chapters 4 through 6 of the technical supplements actively use matrix algebra principles such as might be found in a one-semester course in linear algebra. The technical supplements to Chapters 5 and 6 also use some advanced concepts in matrix algebra that are provided in the technical supplements. Geometric representations of least squares projections are not done here. From the viewpoint presented in this text, these advanced concepts are more suited to a second course in regression analysis.

Suggested Courses

There are a wide variety of topics that can go into a regression course. The main text is the list of standard items. The technical supplements provide a list of optional items. The optional items are additional topics that an instructor may wish to emphasize or expand upon. Here are some suggested courses.

Audience	Nature of Course	Suggested Chapters
Undergraduate business students who have with a one-semester background in business statistics	Survey of regression and time series models	Chapters 1–7, 9–10, 12, 13, main body of text only, omit Sections 4.7, 5.3, 5.4 and 10.6
Graduate business students who have a one-semester background in business statistics	Survey of regression and time series models	Chapters 1–10, 12, 13, main body of text only, omit Sections 5.3, 5.4 and 10.6
Graduate business students who have a one-semester background in business statistics plus other quantitative courses (such as finance or marketing research)	Introduction to regression and time series models	Chapters 1–13, include selected portions of technical supplements
Social science students who have a two-semester background in mathematical statistics and a background in matrix algebra	Introduction to regression and time series models	Chapters 1–13, include technical supplements for Chapters 2–8

This book is for business and other social science students. The topics are ordered in a fashion so that you can go through the book sequentially. Naturally, some instructors may wish to reorder the material. The text's modular design accommodates this desire. However, instructors will find that the default ordering will produce a lively pace for their classes, as well as providing the fundamental tools that colleagues expect students to have.

ACKNOWLEDGMENTS

Many people contributed, directly or indirectly, to the development of this text. I would like to thank some of these valuable contributors.

Most of my colleagues in statistics and actuarial science, here at the University of Wisconsin, have helped me learn about the interaction between the theory and practice of statistics. Some provided detailed comments on the text while it was in manuscript form, notably Jim Hickman and Margorie Rosenberg. Detailed comments were also provided by Raja Velu of the University of Wisconsin–Whitewater. Valuable comments were also made by several reviewers over the years, comments that helped shape the text's development. These additional reviewers include Chung Chen, Syracuse University; Askar H. Choudhury, University of Alaska–Anchorage; Merwyn L. Elliott, Georgia State University; Ali S. Hadi, Cornell University; Kenneth D. Lawrence, New Jersey Institute of Technology; Ananda Sen, Oakland University; Patrick A. Thompson, University of Florida; and Robert W. Van Cleave, University of Minnesota–Minneapolis.

The text was also reviewed by several generations of regression classes here at the University of Wisconsin. I was fortunate to have the Axum statistical graphics package to help me provide a professional looking manuscript as the text evolved. The students in my classes contributed a tremendous amount of input into the text, as well as ideas for many of the data sets. Their input drove the text's development far more than they realize.

Of course, a book does not get written unless an author has a support system. My support system is my family. My extended family, which consists of brothers and their spouses, cousins, aunts, uncles, nephews, nieces and in-laws, is too numerous to mention individually. It's great to have them in the background. My immediate family heard me grumble about writing almost every day. Perhaps they realize how much I appreciate their support, but it never hurts to say it. I dedicate this book to them.

Books are living things, and I hope that this one continues to grow. Change in statistics education is inevitable, particularly with the continuing evolution of the Information Age. To grow, this book needs feedback from its customers, including students, professors and professionals. Please do not hesitate to write me care of the Business Statistics Editor at Prentice-Hall, or directly via electronic mail at "jfrees@bus.wisc.edu".

Edward W. (Jed) Frees

About the Author

Edward W. (Jed) Frees is a Professor of Business and Statistics at the University of Wisconsin–Madison and is holder of the Time Insurance Professorship of Actuarial Science. Professor Frees received his Ph.D. in mathematical statistics in 1983 from the University of North Carolina at Chapel Hill. He became a Fellow of the Society of Actuaries in 1986. Prior to being at Chapel Hill, he was employed by M & R Services (a Seattle actuarial and software consulting firm), John Eriksen's & Partners (a New Zealand actuarial consulting firm), and the United Kingdom's Government Actuaries Department. In addition, in 1989–1990 he was a Visiting Principal Researcher at the U. S. Bureau of the Census. Since 1983, he has been at Madison, teaching courses in statistics and actuarial science.

Professor Frees has contributed to business education through his work in professional societies. He has been an academic instructor and past Course Chairperson for the Society of Actuaries's intensive seminar on applied statistical methods, Course 121. He has served as a council member and chairperson of the Society's Education and Research Section. In 1988, he was a co-host of the third conference "Making Statistics More Effective in Schools of Business."

Professor Frees has also contributed to business education through his research. He has won the Society of Actuaries's Annual Prize for best paper published by the Society and the Actuarial Education and Research Fund's Halmstad Prize for best paper published in the actuarial literature in a year. He has written several articles that have appeared in the leading refereed academic journals. In business and economics, he has published articles in *Management Science, Journal of Finance, Insurance: Mathematics and Economics, Journal of Econometrics, Journal of Insurance Issues and Practices, Journal of Risk and Insurance, ASTIN Bulletin: Journal of the International Actuarial Association, Transac-*

tions of the Society of Actuaries and *Environment and Planning, Series A.* In theoretical and applied statistics, his articles have appeared in the *Journal of the American Statistical Association, Journal of Business and Economic Statistics, Annals of Statistics, Sequential Analysis, Stochastic Processes and Their Applications, Journal of Nonparametric Statistics, Journal of Statistical Planning and Inference, Naval Research Logistics Quarterly, Scandinavian Journal of Statistics, Sankhya* and *Statistica Sinica.*

1

Introduction

Chapter Objectives

To introduce the study of regression analysis as part of the discipline of statistics. To differentiate regression from other applied statistical methods by discussing types of applications and data that can be studied using regression analysis.

Chapter Outline

1.1 STATISTICS AND REGRESSION

Statistics is about collecting, summarizing, analyzing and making decisions using data.

Statistics is about data. It is the discipline concerned with the collection, summarization and analysis of data to make statements about the real world. When analysts collect data, they are really collecting information that is quantified, that is, transformed to a numerical scale. There are easy, well-understood rules for reducing the data, using either numerical or graphical summary measures. These summary measures can then be linked to a theoretical representation, or model, of the data. With a model that is calibrated by data, statements about the world can be made.

Using a variety of applied statistical methods, statisticians have had a major impact on a wide range of disciplines. In the area of data collection, the careful design of *sample surveys* is crucial to market research groups such as A. C. Nielsen and to the auditing procedures of accounting firms.

Experimental design is a second subdiscipline devoted to data collection. The focus of experimental design is on constructing methods of data collection that will extract information in the most efficient way possible. This is especially important in fields such as agriculture and engineering where each observation is expensive, possibly costing millions of dollars.

Other applied statistical methods focus on managing and predicting data. *Process control* deals with monitoring a process over time and deciding when intervention is most fruitful. *Forecasting* is about extrapolating a process into the future.

Regression analysis is an applied statistical method used to analyze data. As we will see, the distinguishing feature of this method is the ability to make statements about variables after having controlled for values of known "explanatory" variables. A *variable* is a measurement that may change, or vary, from observation to observation.

Regression is one of many applied statistical methods. Others include sample survey, experimental design, process control and forecasting.

Important as these methods are, it is regression analysis that has been most influential. To illustrate, an index of business journals, ABI/INFORM, lists over 22,000 articles using regression techniques over the period 1960–1990. And these are only the applications that were considered innovative enough to be published in scholarly reviews!

Regression analysis of data is so pervasive in modern business that it is easy to overlook the fact that the methodology is barely over 100 years old. Scholars attribute the birth of regression to the 1885 presidential address of Sir Francis Galton to the anthropological section of the British Association of the Advancement of Sciences. In that address, described in Stigler (1986), Galton provided a description of regression and linked it to normal curve theory. His discovery arose from his studies of properties of natural selection and inheritance.

To illustrate a data set that can be analyzed using regression methods, Table 1.1 displays some data included in Galton's 1885 paper. This table displays the heights of 928 adult children, classified by an index of their parents'

C1_GALTN

TABLE 1.1   Galton's 1885 Regression Data

Height of adult child in inches	Height of midparent in inches											
	<64.0	64.5	65.5	66.5	67.5	68.5	69.5	70.5	71.5	72.5	>73.0	Totals
>73.7	—	—	—	—	—	—	5	3	2	4	—	14
73.2	—	—	—	—	—	3	4	3	2	2	3	17
72.2	—	—	1	—	4	4	11	4	9	7	1	41
71.2	—	—	2	—	11	18	20	7	4	2	—	64
70.2	—	—	5	4	19	21	25	14	10	1	—	99
69.2	1	2	7	13	38	48	33	18	5	2	—	167
68.2	1	—	7	14	28	34	20	12	3	1	—	120
67.2	2	5	11	17	38	31	27	3	4	—	—	138
66.2	2	5	11	17	36	25	17	1	3	—	—	117
65.2	1	1	7	2	15	16	4	1	1	—	—	48
64.2	4	4	5	5	14	11	16	—	—	—	—	59
63.2	2	4	9	3	5	7	1	1	—	—	—	32
62.2	—	1	—	3	3	—	—	—	—	—	—	7
<61.7	1	1	1	—	—	1	—	1	—	—	—	5
Totals	14	23	66	78	211	219	183	68	43	19	4	928

Source: Stigler (1986)

height. Here, all female heights were multiplied by 1.08, and the index was created by taking the average of the father's height and rescaled mother's height. Galton was aware that each column could be adequately approximated by a normal curve. In developing regression analysis, he was able to provide a single model for the entire data set.

Table 1.1 shows that much of the information concerning the height of an adult child can be attributed to, or "explained" in terms of, the height of the parents. Thus, we use the term *explanatory variable* for measurements that provide information about a variable of interest. Regression analysis provides a methodology to determine the relationship between a variable of interest and an explanatory variable.

Of course, although this relationship is of interest in the study of heredity, it is hard to imagine the management implications. The important point is that the methodology used to study the data in Table 1.1 can also be used to study business problems. For example, in Chapter 4 we will study monthly apartment rents. Here, we will show that much of the information in rents can be explained in terms of the size of the apartment and "location, location, location." (When real estate managers are asked the three most important characteristics of a property, the standard response is "location, location and location.") In this way, knowledge of the explanatory variables can help establish the pricing structure of apartment units.

Another application of regression analysis involves investigating determinants of the returns from stock prices. Stock price returns, from a financial market such as the New York Stock Exchange, are important because they indicate how capital markets evaluate a firm. A typical regression application is to try to explain the return variable in terms of an accounting measure of a firm, such as debt per equity. This differs from the rental application in that we now have to reconcile our statistical model with a model based in financial economics. In many applications, the data are known to be influenced by a fundamental theory from disciplines such as economics, psychology or physics. The challenge here is to select a statistical model that is in congruence with the data *and* the underlying fundamental theory. In this way, statistical methods can be used to support and, in some cases, redirect the development of theory from other scientific disciplines.

Statistics can be used to support, and re-direct, theory from other scientific disciplines.

Regression analysis can also be used to forecast future values of a process. Often, the best predictor of this month's sales is the previous month's sales. Another useful predictor is the sale from the same month in the previous year, such as using sales from last January to predict this January's sales. To link this idea with the regression techniques, Chapters 9-11 will argue that a reasonable explanatory variable is a previous, or *lagged,* value of a variable. The amount of lagging will depend on the application at hand.

1.2 CATEGORIES OF DATA

Regression analysis has enjoyed tremendous popularity among data analysts because the methodology can be applied to many different types of data. Not surprisingly, the conclusions from regression are driven by the type of data that is input to the analysis. There is a variety of ways to collect information in the form of data and, having done so, several ways to classify data. For the purposes of this text, it is useful to think of data as a result of a designed study or not (experimental versus observational) and as ordered by time or not (longitudinal versus cross-sectional).

In a designed study, data are under the control of the analyst.

In the latter part of the nineteenth century and early part of the twentieth century, statistics was beginning to make an important impact on the development of experimental science. Experimental sciences often use *designed studies,* where the data are under the control of an analyst. Designed studies are performed in laboratory settings, where there are tight physical restrictions on every variable that a researcher may think is important. Designed studies also occur in larger field experiments, where the mechanisms for control are different than in laboratory settings. Agriculture and medicine use designed studies. Data from a designed study are said to be *experimental data.*

Statistics can be used to compare observations and make statements about the comparisons. In regression analysis problems, we focus on one measurement of observations that is of interest and call this the *dependent,* or *response, variable.* Other measurements associated with observations are the *ex-*

planatory, or *independent, variables.* A goal is to compare differences in the dependent variable in terms of differences in the independent variables.

To illustrate, a classic example is to consider the yield of a crop such as corn, where each of several parcels of land (the observations) are assigned various levels of fertilizer. The goal is to ascertain the effect of fertilizer (the explanatory variable) on the corn yield (the response variable). Although researchers attempt to make parcels of land as much alike as possible, differences inevitably arise. Agricultural researchers use *randomization* techniques to assign *treatments,* a type of explanatory variable, to each parcel of land. In this way, analysts can explain the overall variation in corn yields in terms of the variation due to different levels of fertilizer and due to different parcels of land. By randomization techniques, we mean the use of probability methods that will be described in Chapter 2.

Through the use of randomization techniques and assignment of treatments, researchers using designed studies can infer that the treatment has a *causal effect* on the response. By controlling the levels of several variables, effects of changes in other variables can be shown to cause a change in a response. Thus, in designed studies, data can be used to show that a variable has a causal effect on a response.

In an observational study, data are not under the control of the analyst.

In the middle part of the nineteenth century, statistics, as a discipline, was being used more and more by social science researchers trying to understand social and economic phenomena. The Galton study described in Section 1.1 illustrates the type of data analysis done at this time. Social science researchers then, and today, generally work with *observational data.* Observational data are not under control of the analyst.

To illustrate, in Chapter 4 we will study a sample of refrigerators to establish a relationship between the price and the annual cost of operating the refrigerator. Because the interest is in the effect that the operating cost has on the price, we will consider the price to be our response and the operating cost to be our explanatory variable. Other things being equal, we would expect that consumers would be willing to pay more for a refrigerator that is less expensive to maintain. Thus, we expect a negative relationship between the response and the explanatory variable. However, when we examine the data, it will turn out that this relationship is positive! The reason is that the relationship between price and cost fails to consider a third variable, the refrigerator size. Larger refrigerators tend to have higher prices and they also tend to be more expensive to operate. Thus, we will argue that the positive relationship between operating costs and price is really due to an omitted variable, size, and not bad economics.

In observational studies, analysts may not assign treatments to variables. Thus, we cannot readily infer causal effects when using observational data.

With observational data, although we can use regression techniques to make comparisons, we can not readily infer causal effects of variables using only statistics. When examining the refrigerator data, we could only observe refrigerator prices and operating costs. There was no ability to assign an explanatory variable to a refrigerator. Thus, even though we could examine prices "controlled for" the effects of operating costs, we could not exclude the possibility of omitting important information.

With observational data, because we cannot infer causal relationships, we cannot use the data to determine which variable responds to other variables. To illustrate, in the Galton data, we can compare a typical child's height for "tall" parents to a corresponding height for "short" parents, where definition of tall and short depends on the point to be made. However, we cannot infer causality from the data. For example, there may be another variable, such as family diet, that causes both variables. The demographics make it clear that if causality exists, the parents' height causes the children's height. We will examine other data sets, such as the relation between gross domestic product (GDP) and the prime interest rate, where the *direction of causality* is not clear. For this example, even if there is a strong relationship between GDP and prime rate, it is not clear if changes in GDP cause changes in prime rate, or vice versa. Economics provides no clear indication as to the direction of causality between GDP and prime rate. Statistics will rarely, if ever, help determine the direction of causality. With observational data, this determination must come from the functional field that is associated with the data.

With observational data, the interest of the study dictates which variable is the response and which may be explanatory variables.

Cross-sectional data are observations that are not time ordered. For example, there is no natural time ordering of the 928 family heights in the Galton data example. The term "cross-sectional" is meant to suggest that the data are a subset of some larger collection of entities. However, the data may also be the result of a set of processes such as the investment earnings from a collection of mutual funds. For cross-sectional data, the set of processes are not related through time.

Longitudinal data have some elements of time ordering involved. Longitudinal data are generally thought of as arising from time sequences of processes, such as the investment earnings from mutual funds. A single sequence of data that is time ordered is called a *time series*. When developing models for longitudinal data, we will face the same complications as with cross-sectional data; devising strategies to control for the effects of one or more variables. Further, with longitudinal data we will have the additional variable time to accommodate into our models. Thus, in this text, we will first develop cross-sectional models and then use this development to address the more complex longitudinal data models.

1.3 THE NATURE OF STATISTICS

Here is a list of broad principles on the nature of statistics to keep in mind as you go through this text. As you develop maturity in handling data, refer back to these principles. You will find these principles useful, not when learned by rote, but when learned through experience.

Statistics as a Science/The Art of Statistics

Statistics is both an art and a science. It is the science of summarizing data and the art of making useful inferences about the behavior of the world from data. Although statistics as a discipline is appreciated by many, other individuals view statistics with suspicion. Many people take an extreme position with respect to statistical evidence. Some feel that such evidence should be completely disregarded although others feel that, as long as the data source is trustworthy, statistical evidence can be regarded as the final word on a topic. This text is designed to encourage a thought process that encompasses a middle ground between these two extreme positions. A more moderate position is that statistical evidence should be viewed with a healthy skepticism and that such evidence should be a part of a larger decision making process. *Statistical thinking* is a willingness to actively summarize numerical information that is available in order to understand the several complex processes that constitute any business environment.

Purposes of Modeling

A *model* is a theoretical representation of the real world and is often expressed in the language of mathematics. Because a model is expressed using mathematics, it may be viewed as complex. However, as complex as models may appear, the real world is much more intricate. Models are simplifications of the real world designed to understand relationships among variables or to evaluate performance of an observation. With enough well-behaved data, a model may not be crucial for understanding relationships or performance evaluation. However, regardless of the data set available, a model is crucial for forecasting, or predicting outside the data set.

Data Summarization and Data Modeling

Summary measures of data serve a dual role: they describe the data in an intuitive way and they suggest a link to a candidate model. You will see that both graphical summaries and numerical summaries, *statistics,* are useful tools for communicating features of data. With modern statistical software that is available, it is easy to generate as many statistics as there are observations! Thus, an important goal is to create a link between the summarization of data and the model used to represent data.

Managerial Attitude

Statistical models are much like any other set of mathematical models, all too often one can be dazzled (confused?) by mathematical niceties and lose sight of the underlying purpose of the modeling efforts. In this text, a "managerial attitude" is taken toward applied statistical models. The phrase "managerial attitude" is meant to suggest that the emphasis will be on making these models work on real data sets in lieu of spending a vast proportion of time on the capabilities of the models. Although the study of properties and capabilities of models is important, equally important is an ability to know when and how to fit models to a particular data set.

Importance of Graphing Data

When viewing statistical methods from a managerial perspective, the following is an important rule: graphical analysis is the first and last thing that the data analyst should do. The old adage about a picture being worth a thousand words is especially important when dealing with statistics, the science of summarizing data. Pictures inevitably aid communication of final results and recommendations which result from quantitative models.

An often overlooked fact is that producing graphical summary measures, such as histograms and plots, should be the first thing the data analyst should do. This is because the world is nonlinear but our models are only linear, or at least nonlinear in a narrowly defined way. To provide an adequate fit of the data to the model, we must be aware of violations of the model conditions. Because these violations may occur in a nonlinear fashion, graphical methods are the easiest method of detection.

1.4 OVERVIEW OF THE TEXT

The purpose of this text is to provide you with an overview of applications of regression analysis. However, this is not simply a survey of existing statistical methods. This text develops regression from the foundations. Many of the mathematical techniques are given relatively light treatment in this text compared to standard reference books such as those written by Draper and Smith (1981) and Neter, Wasserman and Kutner (1989). However, the statistical ideas are not short-changed, but are emphasized through graphical interpretations and the development in the context of "real-world" data.

You can develop experience handling data by reading the text and doing the exercises. The text is designed to make you proficient in handling the analysis of small data sets. Further, it will prepare you to be an effective member of a team charged with understanding a large data set. That is, most readers of this text are not preparing themselves to become professional statisticians. You may, however, be part of a team that includes a data base professional, a financial analyst, a statistician, a marketing professional and a general manager. Although not in the context of commercial applications, it was the famous science fiction author H. G. Wells who said, "Statistical thinking will one day be as necessary for efficient citizenship as the ability to read and write."

This book is split into four parts: Preliminaries, Cross-Sectional Data Models, Longitudinal Data Models and Statistics in a World of Business. This chapter and a second chapter form the first part. The second chapter, entitled Foundations, reviews the basic material in statistics that is required to develop the more complex models that are in the remainder of the book. The Foundation chapter also establishes the style and notation for the remainder of the book.

Cross-Sectional Data is the subject of Part 2. Chapter 3 introduces regression in the context of one independent variable. Although just a special case of the many independent variable set-up of Chapter 4, by using just one variable it is easy to provide graphical insights into what makes regression work. Further, by focussing on one variable, many statistics in this chapter can be expressed using only algebra. The model presented in Chapter 4 is then an extension of the work of Chapter 3. The focus of Chapter 4 is on interpreting the regression model with many independent variables in the context of multidimensional data. Chapter 5 shows how to apply the model in an extended setting, where one or more variables may be *categorical,* that is, nonmetric. With little additional work, this chapter broadens the scope of potential applications. Bringing together the data and the models in a systematic fashion is the subject of Chapter 6, Regression—Selecting a Model. This chapter addresses several common difficulties of applying regression methods directly to data. Chapter 7 provides a detailed discussion of how to interpret regression results to managers. Much of this discussion is in the context of a case study involving the cost effectiveness of risk managers. The last chapter of this part focuses on using regression when the dependent variable is a special type of categorical variable, a binary (0-1) variable. This chapter provides another opportunity to broaden the arena of potential applications of regression. Further, Chapter 8 illustrates problems with heteroscedasticity (introduced in Chapter 6), another method of estimation (called maximum likelihood estimation), and explicitly uses economic, in addition to statistical, criteria when determining a model.

Longitudinal Data is the subject of Part 3. This part begins with an introduction to random processes and random walks in Chapter 9. This chapter also introduces a special type of stability, called *stationarity.* Using ideas introduced in Chapter 6, there is also a discussion of how to transform a nonstationary series into a stationary series. Chapter 10 then shows how to use regression models to uncover subtle patterns in stationary series. The technique is to use lagged dependent variables as explanatory variables. Not surprisingly, this technique is referred to as an *autoregressive* model, because one is doing a regression of the series on itself. Chapter 11 contains additional techniques for handling longitudinal data, some of which are not directly related to the regression methodology but are useful in practice.

Part 4 addresses two topics on how statistics relates to the world of business. Communication of results from an analysis of a data set almost inevitably comes in written form. When writing a statistical report there are usually several audiences, of varying technical backgrounds, that a writer must address. Chapter 12 on report writing provides some tips for structuring a statistical report. Finally, communicating numerical information graphically is the subject of Chapter 13. A carefully constructed graph was once only in the purview of professional graphic artists. With today's modern software, it is easy to generate high resolution, sophisticated graphs that have a professional look and feel. This chapter provides some basic ideas on designing a graph with a special emphasis on communicating information concisely, without losing the message.

Statistics is about data and there are several data sets described and analyzed throughout the text. These data sets are from a variety of different functional areas of business. Hopefully, this text will suggest other applications to you.

1.5 SUMMARY

This chapter introduced a classic example of regression analysis; using the heights of two parents to predict the height, at maturity, of their son. Although not directly related to business applications, the example illustrates an important purpose of regression analysis: to determine a relationship so that we can use one variable (parents' height) to predict another (son's height).

Section 1.1 introduced regression analysis in the broader context of statistics by describing several types of applied statistical methods. We saw that the conclusions, or output, that we draw from regression analysis depend on the data, or input. Thus, Section 1.2 discussed the different types of data that we will encounter in our study of regression analysis. Section 1.3 introduced several broad principles that you will find useful as you develop your ability to analyze data using regression models. Finally, the brief overview of the text in Section 1.4 provides a road map for our future study of regression.

KEY WORDS, PHRASES AND SYMBOLS

After reading this chapter, you should be able to define each of the following important terms, phrases and symbols in your own words. If not, go to the page indicated and review the definition.

statistics, 2
sample surveys, 2
experimental design, 2
process control, 2
forecasting, 2
regression analysis, 2
variable, 2

explanatory variable, 3
lagged variable, 4
designed study, 4
dependent variable, 4
experimental data, 4
response variable, 4
independent variable, 5

randomization, 5
treatment, 5
causal effect, , 5
observational data, 5
direction of causality, 6
cross-sectional data, 6
longitudinal data, 6
time series, 6

statistic, 7
statistical thinking, 7
categorical variable, 9
stationarity, 9
autoregression, 9

2

Foundations

Chapter Objectives

To provide the techniques to analyze and model a single important variable. To illustrate, we will consider:

- a student's monthly apartment rents,
- an employee's hospital costs, and
- a pension plan's asset growth.

Chapter Outline

2.1 IDENTIFYING AND SUMMARIZING DATA

Statistical thinking is the process of identifying a problem, and collecting, organizing and interpreting data to understand or solve the problem. Throughout this text, we will discuss business problems, as well as situations that you may encounter in your personal life, and show how to use data to understand or solve them. Let's begin by looking at some data.

C2_RNT93

Suppose that a student has just moved to Madison and needs to rent a two-bedroom apartment. Although new to town, the student locates a public service center that maintains information on local apartment units. For each apartment unit, information is available concerning location, size of units available, whether laundry facilities are available, and so on. To organize the data, begin by focussing on monthly rents for two-bedroom unfurnished apartments. Table 2.1 lists these rents.

Identify the collection of entities under consideration.

Although you may not need to look for an apartment in Madison, the situation can be used to illustrate how to approach a problem using statistical thinking. To understand this process and do it more efficiently, let's identify some key steps. The first step is to identify the problem, which is to locate suitable living quarters. The next step is to gather data relevant to the problem. To do this, we define a *collection of entities*, also called the *units of observation*, to be objects that contain relevant information. In our case, these are two-bedroom apartments. A numerical measurement taken from a unit of observation is called a *characteristic*. For each apartment, the characteristics include the location, laundry facilities and so on. Although we lose some nonquantifiable elements, such as the charm of an apartment, in taking measurements, we hope to recover them before making our decisions.

Sets of data can quickly become complex, so let's identify some of the basic elements. A *variable* is a measurement that can change from observation to

TABLE 2.1 Listing of Monthly Rents, in Dollars, of 29 Apartments

750	610	675	630	565	625	650	780	600
600	777.5	870	750	720	600	600	650	625
675	700	700	620	750	695	735	850	750
600	805							

observation. If only a single variable is used, then the data set is called *univariate data*. Two variables correspond to *bivariate data*, and more than two correspond to *multivariate data*.

Having represented each apartment by a set of numerical quantities, we are now in a position to organize and interpret the information. In this chapter we focus on univariate data. For example, even though we can take several measurements on each apartment, we now look at only the rent. One justification of this logic is that, in some problems, a single numerical characteristic may dominate all the others to the point that we have said everything that is important about the entity through this measurement. For example, rent may be the overriding consideration in a search for an apartment. In other problems, there is a variety of numerical characteristics that are of importance. Thus, using this chapter's techniques, we will be able to study each variable in isolation of the others. In subsequent chapters, we will face the problem of summarizing several variables jointly.

Univariate data information can be graphically conveyed using a dotplot.

Univariate data may be organized as a list which collects the data into one place and reveals general patterns. For example, Table 2.1 shows the highest and lowest rents were \$870 and \$565, respectively, with many rents falling in the \$600–700 range. To represent this information graphically, we can construct a *dotplot* (Figure 2.1).

The dotplot allows us to visualize the entire distribution of rents. A variable's *distribution* lists each possible outcome of the variable and the frequency of each outcome. We can approximate each apartment's rent by looking at the scale values of the dotplot. Thus, although we lose exact numerical values for each observation, the dotplot allows us to see various aspects of the distribu-

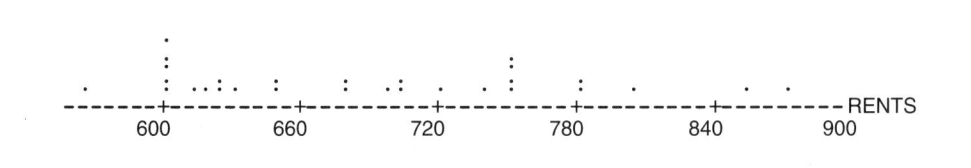

FIGURE 2.1 Dotplot of rents. Each dot represents the rent of a two-bedroom apartment. The dotpot shows the distribution of the list in Table 2.1.

tion more quickly than examining the list of data. The dotplot is a basic graphical way to represent univariate data.

If rent is the variable of interest, then with only 29 observations, further data manipulation may not be needed. Yet, if rent is one of many numerical variables, then we may need to summarize the data further. A *statistic* is a numerical summary measure. Here are several basic statistics:

1. The *mean* is the average number, that is, the sum of the numbers divided by the number of units.
2. The *median* is the middle number when the numbers are ordered by size. That is, it is the number at which 50% are below it (and 50% are above it).
3. The *standard deviation* is a measure of the spread of the distribution. It will be discussed in detail in Section 2.4.
4. A *percentile* is a number at which a specified fraction of the numbers is below it, when the numbers are ordered by size. For example, the 25th percentile is that number so that 25% are below it.

For example, refer to the rents data in Table 2.2. According to the Table 2.2, the average rent for the 29 apartments is $688.20. Fifty percent of the apartments rent for $675 or less. The lowest and highest rents are $565 and $870, respectively. Twenty-five percent of the apartments rent for $615 or less. The 25th and 75th percentiles are also referred to as the first and third quartiles, respectively.

TABLE 2.2 Summary Statistics of Monthly Rents

	Number	Mean	Median	Standard deviation	Minimum	Maximum	25th percentile	75th percentile
RENTS	29	688.2	675.0	81.8	565.0	870.0	615.0	750.0

Univariate data may also be graphically summarized by a *histogram.* The histogram differs from the dotplot by grouping data into categories, known as *cells.* By grouping, we lose the individual observations and thus, categorization serves as another way to summarize data. To illustrate, Figure 2.2 shows that there is one apartment whose rent falls in the $550–600 category, ten apartments in the $600–650 category, and so on. The histogram can provide a visual impression of several summary measures, including the mean, median, and the smallest and largest observations. However, it cannot provide information about individual entities.

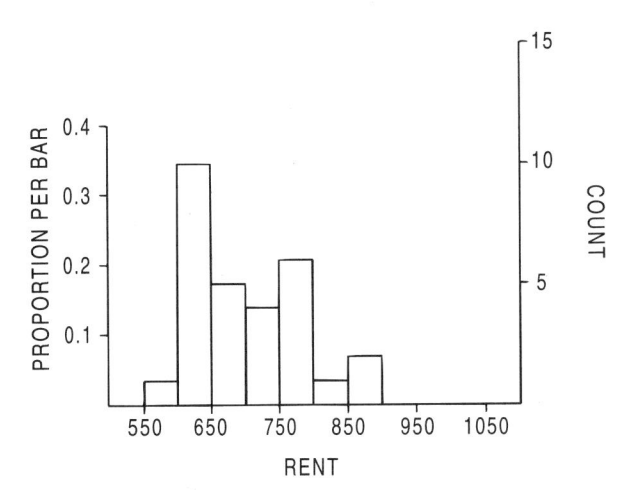

FIGURE 2.2 Histogram of rents. This histogram is a graphical summary of the list of data in Table 2.1.

To recap, there are four basic methods of presenting data. For small univariate data sets, you may wish to retain the information in individual observations. Here, a list of data and a dotplot provide the numerical and graphical methods for presenting the data. For other data, summarizing the information in the observations is preferred. Here, statistics and histograms provide the numerical and graphical presentation methods. Table 2.3 summarizes these data presentation methods.

TABLE 2.3 Types of Univariate Data Presentations

Level of presentation	Numerical	Graphical
Individual observations	List of data	Dotplot
Summarized observations	Statistic	Histogram

Numerical summaries of data by themselves are called *descriptive statistics*. As described by Fienberg (1992), an early example of descriptive statistics was John Graunt's *Observations on Bills of Mortality* (1662). This work studied births and deaths in London and outlying areas over a 60 year period. Graunt looked at ratios of males to females, age at death and the influence of the plague, to estimate of the number of men of fighting age in London. A more complete analysis of births and deaths by age was later conducted by Edmund Halley in his Breslau Life Tables (1693). These tables offered the first systematic way of computing annuity values, a cornerstone of the modern life insurance industry.

2.2 IDEALIZED HISTOGRAMS AS REPRESENTATIONS OF DATA

A theoretical *model* is an abstraction of a component of the real world and is an important tool for understanding the world's behavior. An important fact to keep in mind is that we work with models because of their simplicity. As com-

*Models are ab-
stractions of the
real world. By
studying the be-
havior of models,
we hope to learn
something about
the behavior of the
real world.*

plex as a model may appear, the real world is even more complex. Models are constructed so that their behavior can be studied. If the model is a good approximation to reality, then we can use our understanding of the model's behavior to make some reasonable statements about the corresponding behavior of the real world.

Many students ask, "Why do we need models to keep track of data when we have computers?" In principle, computers could organize and store all the data ever produced. However, businesses and other groups usually store only the data for which they have an immediate need and discard the rest. Secondly, the data may be so voluminous that conclusions are elusive. Finally, models can be used to hypothesize about behavior that we have not yet observed.

*An idealized his-
togram is a model
of the real world
as realized
through a set of
data.*

In statistics, a basic model to represent data uses a mathematical function that we call an *idealized histogram*. These functions are also called *probability density* or *mass functions* due to historical reasons and their usefulness in probability theory. A function is an idealized histogram if it is nonnegative and if the area under the function is equal to one.

Idealized histograms can be motivated by theoretical reasoning from specific disciplines, such as physics or economics, or by appealing to the classical theory of games of chance. As an example of the latter, when we toss a fair coin, classical probabilists argue that the probability of getting a head is one half because there are two equally likely sides. Idealized histograms can be also motivated using the so-called "frequentist theory." Here, the mathematical functions are defined to be the histograms that would arise if we could see more and more data. To illustrate, under the frequentist theory of probability, we imagine tossing a fair coin an enormous number of times. The probability of heads is one half because this is the number that the fraction of heads converges to as the number of tosses gets larger and larger.

An idealized histogram may also be a histogram of data. For a data histogram, the nonnegativity requirement is automatically satisfied. The second requirement can be satisfied by rescaling the vertical axis. For example, Figure 2.2 shows the vertical axis to be both the number and the fraction of observations in the cell. We can always multiply the vertical scale by a number so that the area under the curve is one.

An idealized histogram may also be a continuous curve. For example, Figure 2.3 shows a continuous curve approximating a discrete histogram. We will often use continuous curves because they are simpler to work with than discrete histograms.

*The normal curve
is an important
idealized his-
togram. It is a
continuous curve,
indicating that
realizations from
this curve may
take on any value.*

The leading example of a continuous idealized histogram is the *normal curve*. The normal curve was first used as an approximation to histograms of data around 1835 by Adolph Quetelet, a Belgian mathematician and social scientist. Like many good things, the normal curve had been around for some time, since about 1720 when Abraham de Moivre derived it for his work on

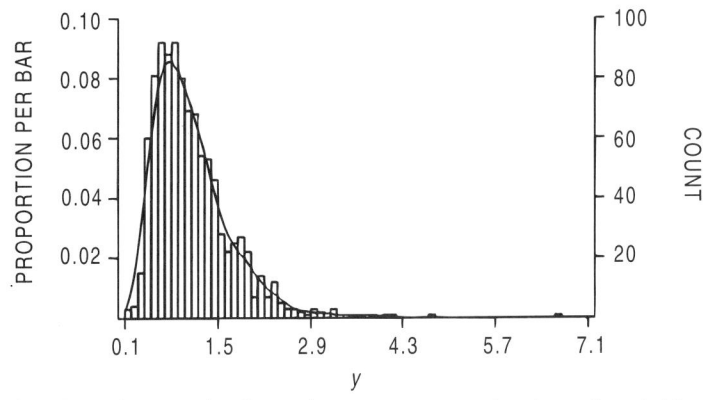

FIGURE 2.3 An example of a continuous curve approximating a discrete histogram.

modeling games of chance. The normal curve is popular because it is easy to use and has proved to be successful in many applications.

Figure 2.4 provides an example of a normal curve. This is a special normal curve called "standard" for reasons that will be discussed in Section 2.5. Like all idealized histograms, the vertical axis of the normal curve is rescaled so that the area under the curve is equal to one. Thus, it is not important to provide the vertical scale for this curve and, indeed, this scale is generally omitted.

A normal curve has several appealing properties. It is continuous and symmetric. By symmetric, we mean that if the curve was cut along the vertical axis at a point, then the two halves could be folded onto each other for a perfect match. These properties are easy to see in the standard normal curve in

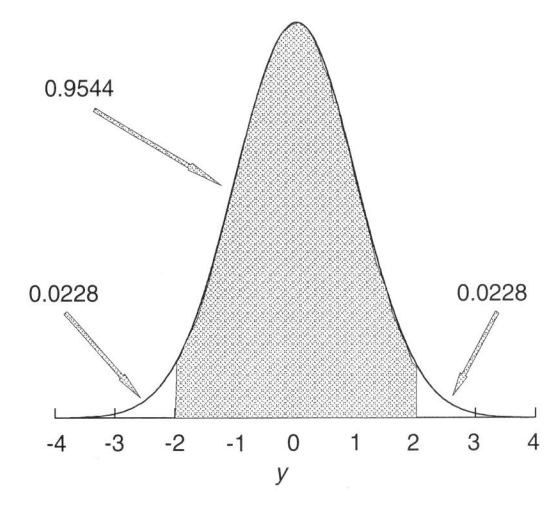

FIGURE 2.4 The standard normal curve. This idealized histogram can be described as a "bell-shaped curve." The area under the curve between -2.00 and 2.00 is 0.9544.

Figure 2.4. However, Figure 2.4 does not show that the distribution ranges over all values, from −∞ (negative infinity) to ∞ (infinity). Even though there is very little area under the curve greater than 3 and less than −3, there is some positive area. This is because the height of the curve never becomes zero, but does get closer and closer to it as we move farther and farther from the center of the curve.

Instead of adding up counts or frequencies, Section 2.3 will use the notion of the area under the curve to express ideas of probability. Because the form of the curve is not amenable to the usual techniques of integration in calculus, tabled values of the area under the curve appear in the appendix. In this table, the convention is to present the area under the curve to the left of a particular point. (The motivation for this type of presentation is due to conventions in mathematical statistics that are not of concern here.)

Tabled values of areas under the curve of continuous idealized histograms present all of the information that is important about the distribution. Unfortunately, this information is not always in a convenient form. For example, in later sections we will see that an important rule of thumb for us is that the area under the standard normal curve between −2 and 2 is 0.9544, or about 95%. To determine this from the Normal Curve Table, we:

1. Go to the table to see that the area under the curve to the left of 2.00 is 0.9772.
2. Because the total area under the curve is one, by subtraction the area under the curve to the right of 2.00 is $1.0000 - 0.9772 = 0.0228$.
3. The curve is symmetric about zero. Thus, the area to the right of 2.00 equals the area to the left of −2.00, which is 0.0228.
4. The area between −2.00 and 2.00 can be expressed as (i) the area under the curve to the left of 2.00 minus (ii) the area to the left of −2.00. Thus, by subtraction, the area between −2.00 and 2.00 is $0.9772 - 0.0228 = 0.9544$.

Figure 2.4 summarizes this procedure. Note that we did not have to worry about the probability of being exactly equal to 2.00. This is because the area under the curve when y is equal to 2.00 is zero.

2.3 DRAWING AN INDIVIDUAL ENTITY "AT RANDOM"

Histograms and Probability

Probability may be defined using a nonpredictable mechanism to draw a realization from a population.

The basic ideas from probability come from the framework of drawing an individual entity from an idealized histogram. To make this framework more concrete, think of the idealized histogram as representing a set of outcomes that we call the *population*, or *universe*. As in Sections 2.1 and 2.2, this universe may be either a list of data or data summarized by either a discrete or continuous histogram. The universe is the set of all possible outcomes of the draw.

Under this framework, the key ingredient for defining probabilities is the idea that a nonpredictable mechanism is used to select an entity from our universe. Although we cannot predetermine whether an entity is selected, probabilities determine the likelihood of it being selected. For any given set in the universe, the *probability* that the entity selected belongs to the set is given by the area under the curve over the set. Thus, through the weightings of the relative frequencies in the idealized histogram, we allow for the fact that some entities are more likely to be selected than others. If we cannot determine the outcome of the draw in advance but can determine the likelihood, then we say that the draw has been made *at random.*

To see how this works in the discrete case, consider the apartment example and suppose that the universe that we draw from is the Table 2.1 list. For simplicity, we assume that the chance of each apartment being selected is equally likely. Thus, for example, we can take our set to be the apartment that rents for $565. With this choice, the probability of selecting one that rents for $565 is $1/29 \approx 3\%$. Suppose instead we take the universe to be the data summarized by the Figure 2.2 histogram. Here, we have lost specific dollar amounts through the grouping process. We can say, however, that the probability of selecting a unit that falls in the cell with the $625 midpoint is $10/29 \approx 34.5\%$, if each apartment is equally likely to be selected. For discrete histograms, we can use a single entity as our set and still get a positive probability of the entity selected belonging to the set.

For continuous histograms such as the normal curve, probability is defined using the area under the curve between two specified points. When we draw from a population represented by a continuous histogram, the situation is more complex. To get a positive probability of a set, we must use intervals for our sets. For example, in the standard normal curve example above, a randomly drawn entity has probability 0.9544 of falling in the interval between -2.00 and 2.00. However, the probability of being *equal* to 2, or any specific number, is zero. This is a consequence of using area under the curve to represent probability.

We use the symbol y to denote a randomly selected entity before it is drawn from the parent population. The notation $\text{Prob}(a < y < b)$ means the probability of a randomly selected entity falling between a and b. See Figure 2.5 for a graphical representation of $\text{Prob}(a < y < b)$ for a continuous idealized histogram.

Expectations

The next important idea in probability theory is the notion of an *expected value.* Before the random selection of the entity, we do not know the value of y. This is called the *ex ante,* or before the fact, value of y. In the same way, the *ex post,* or after the fact, value is simply the realization of y. We can make statements about the probability that the ex ante value of y will attain certain values. We

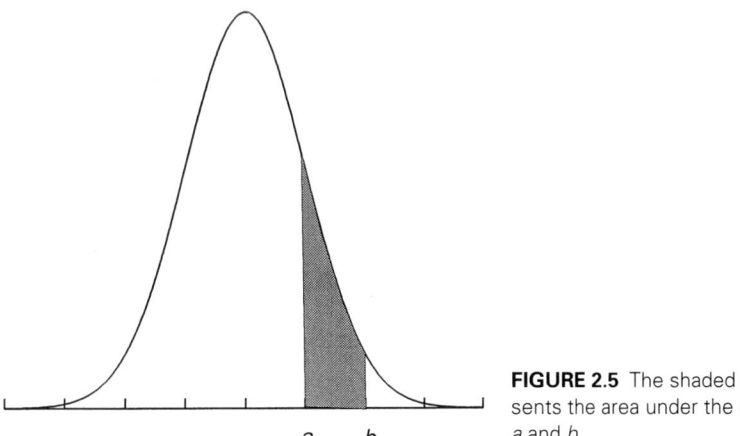

FIGURE 2.5 The shaded area represents the area under the curve between a and b.

also can state what we *expect* to be a likely occurrence of y. The expected value is not the "most likely occurrence." It is the sum of all possible occurrences, each weighted by the probability of occurring.

Here are some examples of the expected value of y using our three types of universe.

The expected value is not the "most likely occurrence." It is the sum of all possible occurrences, each weighted by the probability of occurring.

1. Pick a rent at random from the universe listed in Table 2.1. Before the draw, we expect it to be

$$750 \, \frac{1}{29} + 610 \, \frac{1}{29} + ... + 805 \, \frac{1}{29} = 688.2.$$

This calculation assumes that each rent is equally likely to be chosen. Because there are 29 apartments, each entity has a 1 out of 29 chance of being selected. Thus, the expected value is constructed as a weighted average of rents, where the weights equal the chance of being selected.

2. Pick a rent at random from the universe given by the Figure 2.2 histogram. We expect the rent to be

$$575 \, \frac{1}{29} + 625 \, \frac{10}{29} + 673 \, \frac{5}{29} + 725 \, \frac{4}{29} + 775 \, \frac{6}{29} + 825 \, \frac{1}{29} + 875 \, \frac{2}{29}$$

$$= 709.5.$$

This calculation also assumes that each rent is equally likely, so that the cell frequency determines the probability of a cell being selected. For example, there is one observation in the first cell with midpoint 575. Thus, there is 1 chance out of 29 of selecting this cell. When selecting a cell, it is not always clear what the best point to represent the cell is. Generally, the midpoint is an adequate approximation. Because this calculation is complex, it is useful to express the formula for this weighted average as:

$$y_1f(y_1) + y_2f(y_2) + y_3f(y_3) + y_4f(y_4) + y_5f(y_5) + y_6f(y_6) + y_7f(y_7)$$

$$= \sum_{i=1}^{7} y_if(y_i).$$

Here, $y_1 = 575$, $y_2 = 625$, and so on, is a list of each possible midpoint, and $f(y_1) = \frac{1}{29}$, $f(y_2) = \frac{10}{29}$, and so on, is a list of the corresponding probabilities of selection. The large sigma (Σ) is shorthand notation for *summation*. The letter i provides an *index* for values in the sum.

Under the expectation (E) operator, we sum all possible occurrences of a given function of the observation, where each occurrence is weighted by its respective probability.

3. Pick a rent at random from the data set represented by a continuous histogram. Let us label this curve by the function $f(y)$. The *expected value* is a weighted average, this time using the height of the continuous curve as the weight function. [If you have had calculus, note that the expected rent is $\int y \, f(y) \, dy$.] For the standard normal curve, this weighted average turns out to be zero, because of the symmetry of the curve about zero.

In each of the three cases, we use the notation "E" to denote the expectation operation. The Greek lower case "m" is called mu and is denoted by μ. We use this symbol for the expected value, or *mean*, of the unobserved value of the randomly selected entity. Formally, we have that

$$\mu = E \ y. \tag{2.1}$$

The notion of expectation is an important tool for summarizing information about the behavior of y.

Another important summary measure is the *variance* of y, denoted by σ^2. The Greek lower case "s" is called *sigma* and is denoted by σ. This symbol suggests the idea of *scatter*, or spread, of the distribution. The idea here is that, before the draw, $(y - \mu)^2$ is a measure of the scatter, or deviation, of y from the mean. Using the expectation operator, we can formally define the variance as

$$\sigma^2 = \text{Var} \ y = E(y - \mu)^2. \tag{2.2}$$

Thus, σ^2 is a quantity that can be calculated knowing only the idealized histogram.

The *standard deviation* is the positive square root of the variance, that is, $\sigma = (\sigma^2)^{1/2}$. In probability theory, the variance is more useful than the standard deviation because the former can be calculated directly using the expectation operator. In data analysis, the standard deviation is more useful. One reason is that this parameter is in the same units as the randomly selected entity and the mean. Thus, if the randomly selected entity is measured in dollars, then so is the mean and the standard deviation. Naturally, the variance can be directly calculated from the standard deviation, and vice versa.

Standardizing Draws from a Normal Curve

Suppose y repre-
sents a random
draw from a nor-
mal curve with
mean μ and vari-
ance σ². Then, z
= (y − μ)/σ may
be treated as a
draw from a
standard normal
curve.

Means and standard deviations can be defined for almost every idealized histogram. (There are some exceptions but these are of limited practical importance and are not discussed here.) For example, the normal curve in Figure 2.4 is called *standard* because this histogram has a mean $\mu = 0$ and standard deviation $\sigma = 1$. In general, a normal curve may have any mean μ and positive standard deviation σ.

An innocuous, yet useful, result in the theory of mathematical statistics is the following. Suppose y represents a random draw from a normal curve with mean μ and standard deviation σ. Then, we may treat the rescaled version, $z = (y − \mu)/\sigma$, as if it comes from a standard normal curve. We call z the standardized draw from a normal curve. Example 2.1 shows how to use this rescaling device.

Example 2.1: Quality of Metal Pieces

As part of a manufacturing process, two holes are drilled in a flat piece of metal. A key measure of quality, denoted by y, is the distance between the centers of the holes. Historical data has established that the distance between holes can be represented using a normal curve with mean $\mu = 3$ inches and standard deviation $\sigma = 0.02$ inches (Figure 2.6).

With this information, we can make statements about the probability of a randomly selected piece having a distance either too small or too large. For example, suppose that a piece is defective if the distance between holes is either greater than 3.04 inches or less than 2.96 inches. Graphically, we have:

	Defective	Acceptable	Defective
Inches	2.96	3.00	3.04
Units	$\mu - 2\sigma$	μ	$\mu + 2\sigma$
Standard units	−2	0	2

Thus, if a randomly selected observation (y) is greater than 3.04, then it is greater than $\mu + 2\sigma$. In this case, the observation is said to be more than two standard deviations above the mean. This is equivalent to the stan-

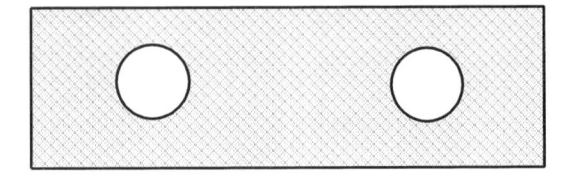

FIGURE 2.6 A piece of metal with two holes drilled into it. Manufacturing specifications require that the distance between hole centers be close to 3 inches.

dardized observation $[z = (y - \mu)/\sigma]$ being greater than 2 (in standard units). Algebraically, this can be expressed as

$$\{y > 3.04\} = \{y > \mu + 2\sigma\} = \{(y - \mu)/\sigma > 2\} = \{z > 2\}.$$

The advantage of the final expression is that this probability is easy to compute. For example, in Figure 2.4 we established that $\text{Prob}(z > 2) = 0.0228$ and $\text{Prob}(z < -2) = 0.0228$. To summarize, we have that

$$\text{Prob(drawing a defective)} = \text{Prob}(z < -2 \text{ or } z > 2) = 0.0456.$$

2.4 COMPARING SAMPLES AND POPULATIONS

The population is the entire collection of entities under consideration.

The population is the entire collection of entities under consideration. The statistical usage of this term is broader than the common usage. That is, the population need not refer to people or even living entities. Indeed, in business and economics, we often work with a collection of firms, or a stage in a manufacturing process. The characteristic of each member of the population defines our universe, the list of all possible outcomes of the draw. Because we consider only one measurement on an entity, we use the terms population and universe interchangeably.

In some situations, the population can be completely enumerated. Such a complete listing of observations is called a *census.* For example, the Constitution requires a census of the U.S. population every ten years.

Using the histogram, we can model situations where the population is finite or infinitely large.

In situations where complete enumeration is not possible, our data will consist of a *sample,* which is a subset of the population. The population's distribution can be represented using an idealized histogram instead of a complete enumeration. Using idealized histograms, we can model situations where the population is either finite or infinite.

In surprisingly many situations, a complete census of the population is impractical. For example, accounting firms regularly use sampling techniques in their audits of client firms. The purpose of these audits is to assess the accounting accuracy of a firm's financial statements. As another example, the U.S. Bureau of the Census regularly uses sampling techniques to assess the quality of its decennial census of the U.S. population. Because of the accuracy of the population estimates produced by sampling techniques, the Bureau has considered using sampling estimates instead of the traditional method of a complete enumeration.

Summary Measures

The population represents all possible outcomes of interest. In a problem, we generally focus on one or more measures that summarize some aspect of the population's distribution. A summary measure of the population's distribution is a *parameter.* A statistic is the corresponding sample summary measure.

Because the entire population cannot be observed by the analyst, parameters are unknown. However, samples are available and thus statistics are known. We use statistics to approximate parameters. The rationale is that, if the sample is representative of the population, then the statistic should be a reasonable approximation of the parameter. An important goal of statistics as a discipline is to quantify the quality of this approximation.

To illustrate, consider the Section 2.1 rents example. Here, the population of interest may be all two bedroom apartments located in the city of Madison but we have available only a sample provided by the Campus Assistance Center. For the entire population, the mean rent is denoted by the parameter μ with corresponding standard deviation σ. Because we do not have available the entire population of apartments, we cannot determine μ and σ.

Use $y_1, \ldots, y_n$ to represent the observations from the sample, where n is the sample size. Summary measures calculated from the sample, such as $\bar{y}$ and s_y, are statistics.

We denote the sample by $y_1, y_2, \ldots, y_n$, where n is the sample size. The ellipses (...) mean continue the pattern until the last entity is reached. For our example, the first rent is $y_1 = 750$, the second rent is $y_2 = 610$, and so on. From a sample, we can compute means and standard deviations. These are:

$$\bar{y} = \frac{y_1 + y_2 + \ldots + y_n}{n} = \frac{\sum_{i=1}^{n} y_i}{n} \tag{2.3}$$

and

$$s_y = \sqrt{\frac{\sum_{i=1}^{n} (y_i - \bar{y})^2}{n-1}}. \tag{2.4}$$

The average $\bar{y}$ and standard deviation s_y are summary measures from the sample, that is, statistics.

Table 2.4 provides the relationships between samples and populations and their respective summary measures. When important, we distinguish $\bar{y}$ and μ by calling them the sample mean and population mean, respectively. When the context is clear we will drop the adjective and refer to each of them simply as the mean. This convention also holds for standard deviations and other summary measures.

TABLE 2.4   Summary Measures of Samples and Populations

Data	Summary measures	Mean	Standard deviation
Sample	Statistics	$\bar{y}$	s_y
Population	Parameters	μ	σ

Normal Curve Approximations

In addition to numerical summary measures, another way to summarize the sample is through a histogram. In Section 2.1 we saw how to create a histogram by grouping the data into cells. Further, as we saw in Section 2.2, we can use a continuous histogram, such as the normal curve to approximate a discrete histogram. It is convenient to use a normal curve to approximate the distribution of a sample. To make this approximation, we use a normal curve with mean equal to $\bar{y}$, the sample mean, and standard deviation equal to s_y, the sample standard deviation. Figure 2.7 shows the histogram of monthly rents with this normal curve superimposed.

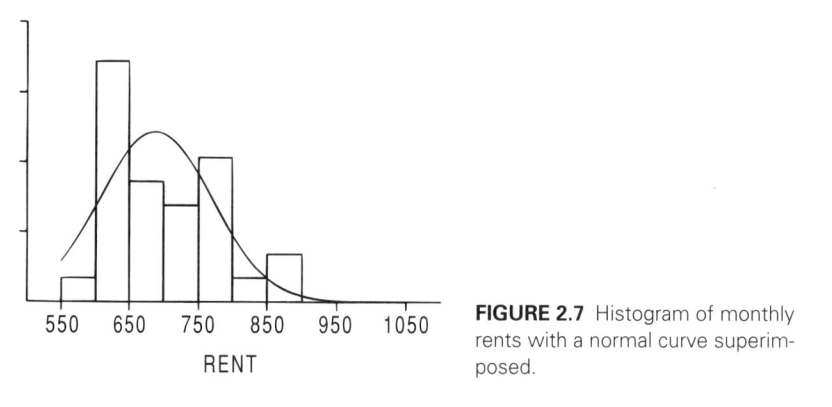

FIGURE 2.7 Histogram of monthly rents with a normal curve superimposed.

The normal curve approximation is a smooth histogram that is determined by the data. It can be created by knowing only two numbers, the mean and standard deviation. In contrast, to create a data histogram, one has to know each cell count. Thus, an important advantage of the normal curve approximation when compared to data histograms is its simplicity; only two numbers are required to approximate the entire distribution.

Having made a normal curve approximation, we will need to calculate other summary measures, such as percentiles. As described in the subsection Standardizing Draws from a Normal Curve, we convert the units of observation to standard units and treat the standard units as draws from a standard normal curve. Denoting the units of observation by y, then standard units can be expressed as $z = (y - \bar{y})/s_y$.

To illustrate, suppose that we would like to calculate the 75th percentile from our rents sample using the normal curve approximation. Figures 2.8 and 2.9 graphically depict our question and solution. The standard normal curve table shows that 0.675 is the 75th percentile of the standard normal curve. Thus, in units we have $\bar{y} + 0.675\, s_y = 688.2 + 0.675\,(81.8) = 743.4$ is the 75th percentile in units, or dollars, using the normal curve approximation. As be-

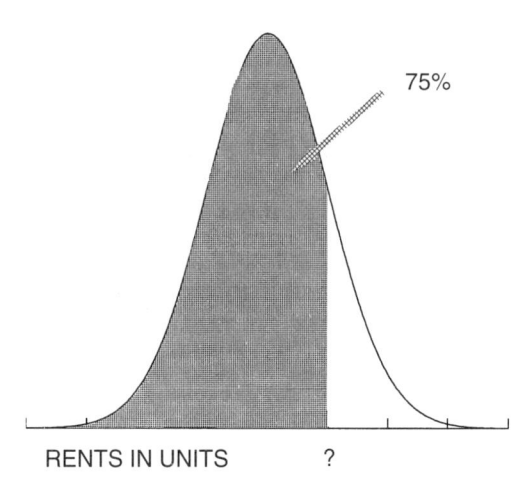

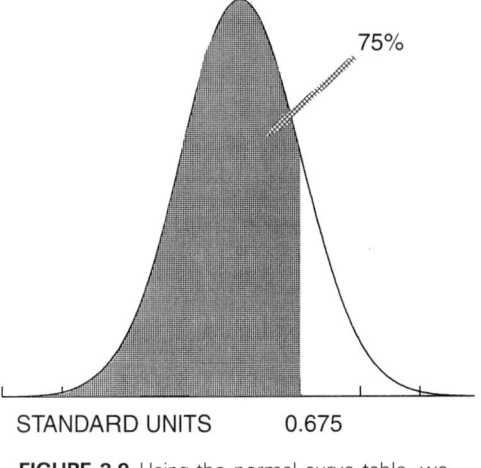

RENTS IN UNITS   ?   STANDARD UNITS   0.675

FIGURE 2.8 Under the normal curve approximation, what rent is at the 75th percentile?

FIGURE 2.9 Using the normal curve table, we see that 0.675 is the 75th percentile of the standard normal curve.

fore, this is because the set $\{z < 0.675\}$ is equivalent to the set $\{y < 743.4\}$, as seen by:

$$\{z < 0.675\} = \{(y - \bar{y})/s_y < 0.675\} = \{y < \bar{y} + 0.675\, s_y\} = \{y < 743.4\}.$$

When we summarize information, we introduce the possibility of losing important information. The normal curve approximation provides another way to summarize the sample and yet, this summarization can be inadequate. To illustrate, in the rents example we now have two estimates for the 75th percentile: 743.4, which was calculated using the normal curve approximation and 750.0, which was calculated using the entire data set. The latter estimate is more accurate because we did not need to make the additional assumption that the normal curve is a reasonable approximation. The former estimate is more convenient because only two numbers, the sample mean and standard deviation, were required to compute it. We will find both approaches useful. In cases where there is close agreement we will favor the normal curve approximation because of its simplicity. In other cases, such as illustrated in Figure 2.10, the normal curve is not adequate and we will need other devices to approximate the distribution.

The Logic of Statistics

Statistics, by its very nature, is an inferential discipline. Unlike much of mathematics that uses processes of *deduction*, statistics relies primarily on the process of *induction*. In deductive disciplines like mathematics, one works

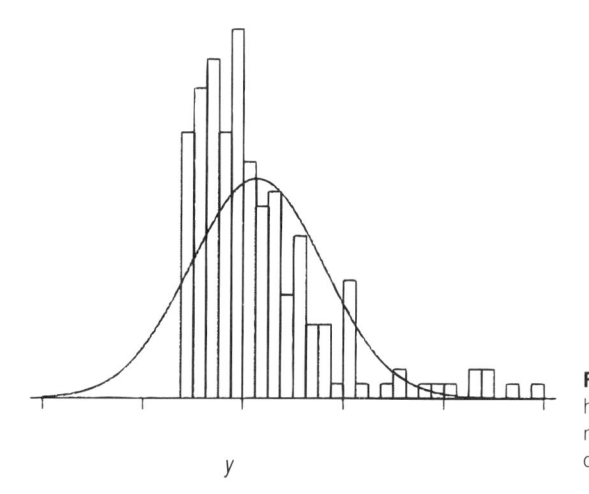

FIGURE 2.10 The sample distribution is heavily skewed to the right. The symmetric normal curve does not provide a desirable approximation.

y

from the general to the specific. For example, one could point out that all university students have high school degrees and that swim team members are university students. Therefore, all swim team members have high school degrees. This is the process of deduction, going from the larger to the smaller. In statistics, one works from the specific to the general. For example, one could point out that thirty percent of swim team members own a microcomputer and that swim team members are university students. Therefore, as an approximation, we might infer that about 30% of university students own a microcomputer (Figure 2.11). This is the process of induction, going from the smaller to the larger.

The sample must be representative of the population in order to make reasonable decisions about the population using the information in the sample. Subsets may not represent the larger population adequately. To illustrate, it may be that several swim team members are on scholarship and thus, a per-

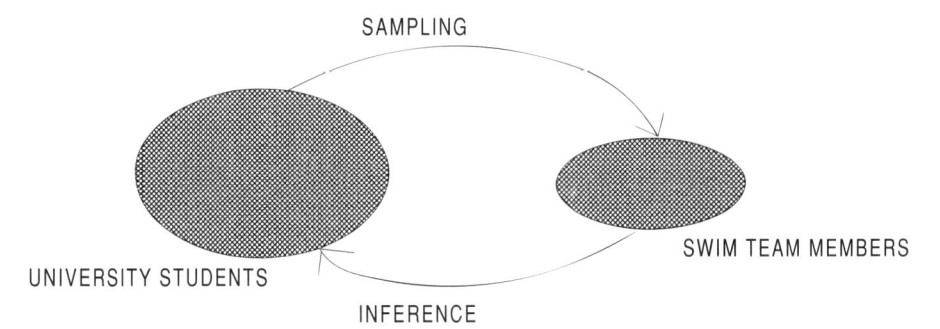

FIGURE 2.11 Swim team members form a subset of university students. We use information about a subset to infer behavior about all university students.

centage own a microcomputer when compared to the larger population of university students (Figure 2.11). There is a variety of distortions that can arise when collecting data. We will discuss these potential pitfalls in more detail in Chapter 7.

Statistics relies on the process of induction.

Making a statement about the whole from a subset introduces the possibility of error. This possibility of error is quantified by using a random mechanisms to select a representative sample, the subject of Section 2.5.

2.5 RANDOM SAMPLING

A random sample is a subset of the population that is determined using a non-predictable, or random, mechanism. By using a random mechanism, we have some assurances that the sample is representative of the population. Further, we will show how to use probabilistic arguments to quantify the degree of reliability when using statistics to approximate parameters. We define *random sample* as a sample chosen so that:

1. Each draw from the population is selected randomly.
2. The draws are unrelated to one another.

The random sampling model has proved to be useful because it is easy to work with and because it reasonably represents our knowledge of reality.

As with all model assumptions, you will find that random sampling assumptions are nearly impossible to satisfy precisely in practice. Consider a classic example, flipping a coin ten times. In this example, the random sampling model assumptions are that the probability of either head or tails occurs with equal likelihood and that the outcomes of flips are unrelated. Alternatively, we might posit a deterministic model using the laws of physics. For example, a physicist could predict the outcome of the flip using variables such as the angular velocity of the flip, the wind currents, height of the toss and distance to the floor, and so on. With perfect muscular control and constant climatic conditions, our physicist should be able to replicate perfectly the outcomes of previous tosses. In practice, there is enough variability in the world so that the deterministic model is rarely used. The random sampling model has proved to be useful because it is easy to work with and because it reasonably represents our knowledge of reality.

Sampling Distributions

To introduce sampling distributions, let's continue the example of flipping a coin 10 times. Suppose that the fraction of heads is the key statistic of interest. For each toss, let's label $y = 0$ to represent a tail and $y = 1$ to represent a head. Flipping a coin 10 times results in a sample $y_1, y_2, \ldots, y_{10}$. This sample is summarized by $\bar{y}$, which we interpret to be the fraction of heads. For example, here are the results from three illustrative samples:

Sample	Outcomes	Statistic ($\bar{y}$)
First ten flips	1, 0, 1, 1, 1, 0, 0, 0, 1, 1	0.6
Second ten flips	0, 1, 1, 1, 0, 1, 1, 0, 1, 0	0.6
Third ten flips	0, 0, 0, 0, 0, 1, 1, 0, 1, 1	0.4

Although there are only two possible outcomes of each coin flip, there are 11 possible outcomes of the statistic $\bar{y}$. That is, when we flip a coin 10 times, we could get either zero, one, two, or up to 10 heads. This results in 0.0, 0.1, 0.2, or up to 1.0 as the fraction of heads.

What are the probabilities associated with each outcome of the statistic? It is instructive to discuss the probability calculations in this particularly simple example. To begin, let's ask the question: What is the probability of getting 10 heads in a row? If the flips are unrelated and the probability of heads is 1/2, then elementary probability theory tells us that the probability is $(1/2)^{10}$. Using the notation $\bar{y}$ for the fraction of heads, this can be expressed as Prob($\bar{y} = 1.0$) = $(1/2)^{10}$. Similarly, Prob($\bar{y} = 0.0$) = $(1/2)^{10}$, that is, the probability of getting 10 tails in a row is $(1/2)^{10} \approx 0.000977$. From an introductory probability course, these ideas can be extended. For the purposes of this text, we do not need to go into the mechanics of the calculations. Yet, the results of the calculations are important and are in Table 2.5.

TABLE 2.5 Probability Distribution for the Sample Average of 10 Coin Flips

outcome	0.0	0.1	0.2	0.3	0.4	0.5
Prob ($\bar{y}$ = outcome)	0.000977	0.009766	0.043945	0.117188	0.205078	0.246094
outcome	0.6	0.7	0.8	0.9	1.0	
Prob ($\bar{y}$ = outcome)	0.205078	0.117188	0.043945	0.009766	0.000977	

Table 2.5 provides the probability distribution of $\bar{y}$. The probability distribution of a statistic is called a *sampling distribution*. Graphically, this distribution can be expressed as an idealized histogram, as shown in Figure 2.12.

Unlike an idealized histogram of random draws from a population, the Figure 2.12 idealized histogram represents the distribution of possible outcomes of a statistic. With the idealized histogram, we can compute means and variances of this distribution. For example, the mean of $\bar{y}$ is

$$E\,\bar{y} = \sum_{k=0}^{10} \frac{k}{10}\,\text{Prob}\left(\bar{y} = \frac{k}{10}\right)$$

$$= 0\,\text{Prob}(\bar{y}=0) + 0.1\,\text{Prob}(\bar{y}=0.1) + \dots + 0.9\,\text{Prob}(\bar{y}=0.9)$$

$$+ 1.0\,\text{Prob}(\bar{y}=1.0)$$

$$= 0.5.$$

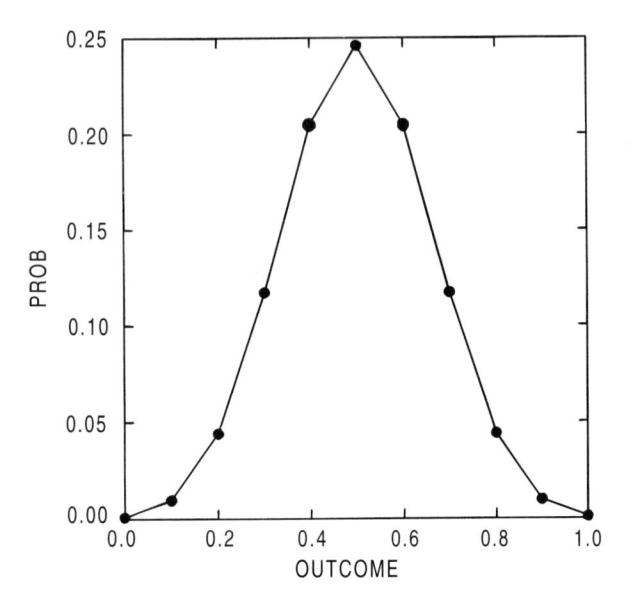

FIGURE 2.12 Idealized histogram of the sampling distribution of the average of 10 flips of a coin. Like all distributions, the sum of probabilities is one.

(Alternatively, the symmetry in Figure 2.12 shows immediately that $\mathrm{E}\,\bar{y} = 0.5$.) Similarly, the variance of $\bar{y}$ is

$$\mathrm{Var}\,\bar{y} = \mathrm{E}(\bar{y} - 0.5)^2 = \sum_{k=0}^{10} \left(\frac{k}{10} - 0.5\right)^2 \mathrm{Prob}\!\left(\bar{y} = \frac{k}{10}\right)$$

$$= (0 - 0.5)^2\,\mathrm{Prob}(\bar{y} = 0) + (0.1 - 0.5)^2\,\mathrm{Prob}(\bar{y} = 0.1) + \ldots$$

$$+ (0.9 - 0.5)^2\,\mathrm{Prob}(\bar{y} = 0.9) + (1.0 - 0.5)^2\,\mathrm{Prob}(\bar{y} = 1.0)$$

$$= 0.025.$$

The mean and variance of $\bar{y}$ turn out to be important quantities and it will be convenient to introduce simpler rules for calculating them. We have seen that calculations using the definitions can be tedious because they involve (i) determining the sampling distribution of $\bar{y}$ and (ii) calculations using an expectation operator such as in equations (2.1) and (2.2). Some simpler rules are:

$$\mathrm{E}\,\bar{y} = \mu = \mathrm{E}\,y \tag{2.5}$$

and

$$\mathrm{Var}\,\bar{y} = \frac{\sigma^2}{n} = \frac{\mathrm{Var}\,y}{n}. \tag{2.6}$$

For our fair coin example, using equation (2.1) we have that

$$\mathrm{E}\,y = 0\,\mathrm{Prob}(y = 0) + 1\,\mathrm{Prob}(y = 1) = 1/2.$$

This verifies equation (2.5) for this illustration, because $E\, y = 1/2 = E\, \bar{y}$. Similarly, using equation (2.2),

$$\sigma^2 = E(y - \mu)^2 = (0 - 1/2)^2 \operatorname{Prob}(y = 0) + (1 - 1/2)^2 \operatorname{Prob}(y = 1) = 1/4.$$

This verifies equation (2.6) for this illustration, because $(\operatorname{Var} y)/n = 0.25/10 = 0.025 = \operatorname{Var} \bar{y}$.

From equation (2.5), we see that the expected value of the sample mean is equal to μ, which is the expected value of a single draw. From equation (2.6), we see that the variance of the sample average is considerably less than the variance of a single draw. This is because some observations in the sample fall above the mean, others below and these deviations from the mean tend to cancel. The factor $1/n$ is the right amount of reduction of the variance as established using the theory of mathematical statistics.

Central Limit Theorem

For practical applications, it is not crucial that the population be normally distributed. The reason for this is an important result concerning sampling distributions, called the *Central Limit Theorem*. The statement of this result is:

Suppose $y_1, y_2, \ldots, y_n$ represent a random sample from a population having mean μ and standard deviation σ. Then $\bar{y}$ is approximately normally distributed with mean μ and standard deviation $\sigma/\sqrt{n}$. The approximation improves as n grows larger.

A desirable feature of the central limit theorem is that it reduces the need to make the assumption that the observations come from a normal distribution.

A related result is that if the parent population of $y_1, \ldots, y_n$ is normally distributed with mean μ and variance σ^2, then the distribution of $\bar{y}$ is *exactly* normally distributed with mean μ and standard deviation $\sigma/\sqrt{n}$. In contrast, a strength of the central limit theorem is that the type of distribution of the population of draws does not matter. In the "limit," or as the sample size gets larger, the distribution of $\bar{y}$ is approximately normal. By reducing our reliance on the normality assumption, the procedures that we are developing are applicable in more situations than if we had restricted our consideration to solely those populations that closely resemble a normal curve.

The more symmetric the population's distribution is, the smaller the sample size needs to be for the normal curve to adequately approximate the distribution of $\bar{y}$.

A second related result, called an *Edgeworth* expansion, states that the more symmetric the population's distribution is, then the closer is the distribution of $\bar{y}$ to the normal distribution. Thus, an important rule of thumb is that the more symmetric the distribution is, the smaller the sample size needs to be for the approximation to be effective. For most parent distributions that are not strongly *skewed*, or asymmetric, 25 observations are sufficient for the normal curve to be adequate approximation for the distribution of $\bar{y}$.

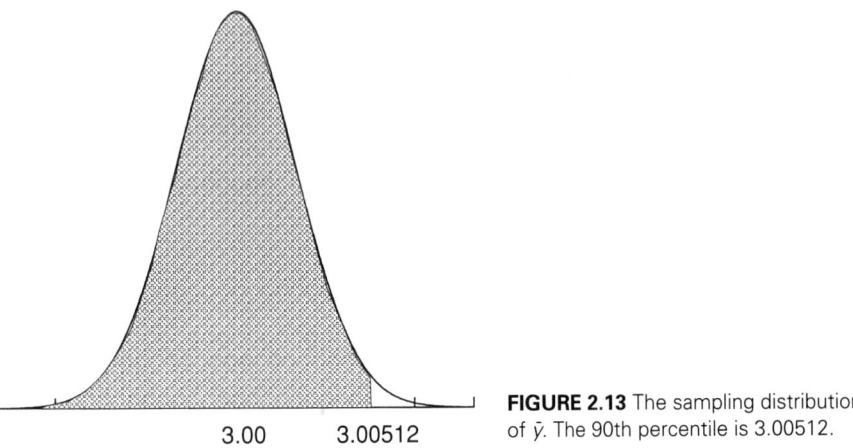

3.00   3.00512

FIGURE 2.13 The sampling distribution of $\bar{y}$. The 90th percentile is 3.00512.

Example 2.1: Quality of Metal Pieces—Continued

Questions about the sampling distribution of $\bar{y}$ such as finding the 90th percentile distance can be solved in the following manner. Randomly select 25 metal pieces from a normally distributed population with mean μ = 3 inches and standard deviation σ = 0.02 inches. The standard normal table shows that the 90th percentile of the standard normal curve is 1.28. This means that for any normal curve, the mean plus 1.28 standard deviations is the 90th percentile. Because $\bar{y}$ is approximately normal with mean 3.00 inches and standard deviation $0.02/\sqrt{25} = 0.004$, we have that the 90th percentile for $\bar{y}$ is

$$3.00 + 1.28(0.004) = 3.00512.$$

Note that the 90th percentile for $\bar{y}$ is much smaller than the 90th percentile for a single, randomly selected piece [which is $3.00 + 1.28(0.02) = 3.0256$]. This is because the variance of the sample average, σ^2/n, is much smaller than the variance of a single piece, σ^2.

The *t*-Distribution

Using equation (2.6), we have seen that the standard deviation of $\bar{y}$ is $\sigma/\sqrt{n}$. In Sections 2.6 and 2.7, we will encounter situations where it is desirable to assume that the variability parameter, σ^2, is not a known quantity. It seems reasonable to use the sample standard deviation computed, s_y, as an estimate for the population standard deviation, σ. The estimate of the standard deviation of $\bar{y}$ is called the *standard error* of $\bar{y}$ and is denoted by

$$se(\bar{y}) = \frac{s_y}{\sqrt{n}}.$$

The term *standard error* refers to the *estimated standard deviation of a statistical quantity*.

Replacing σ by s_y, our standard units are now $(\bar{y} - \mu)/se(\bar{y})$. When we replace the known quantity σ by the random quantity s_y, there is greater uncertainty in our resulting standard units. We account for this additional uncertainty by introducing another idealized, continuous histogram called the *t-distribution*. It is similar in appearance to the standard normal curve in that it is bell-shaped and symmetric about zero. As a definition, we first suppose y_1, y_2, ... , y_n represents a random sample from a normal distribution having mean μ and standard deviation σ. Then, the *t-ratio*

$$t(\bar{y}) = \frac{\bar{y} - \mu}{se(\bar{y})}$$

has a *t*-distribution with degrees of freedom $df = n - 1$. Although we do not need the details, the idealized histogram can be expressed as a function that is called a *t-curve*. Tables for this idealized histogram are in the appendix. The phrase "degrees of freedom" refers to a parameter that characterizes the *t*-distribution.

Example 2.1: Quality of Metal Pieces—Continued

Suppose that we again wish to calculate the 90th percentile of $\bar{y}$ based on a randomly selected batch of 25 pieces of metal from a normal distribution with mean $\mu = 3$ inches. We now do not assume that σ is known but rather compute the sample standard deviation, $s_y = 0.03$ inches. From the *t*-table with $df = 24$ $(= 25 - 1)$ degrees of freedom, we have that the 90th percentile of a *t*-ratio is 1.318. See Figure 2.14. Thus, the 90th percentile of $\bar{y}$ is 1.318 standard errors above the mean, or

$$3.00 + (1.318)(0.03/\sqrt{25}) = 3.007908.$$

The *t-value* 1.318 is larger than the corresponding normal value 1.28. An interpretation of this is that the *t*-distribution assumes less knowledge of the population's distribution and thus allows for greater uncertainty.

The *t*-distribution was developed by William S. Gossett (1908) in connection with his work at Guiness Brewery in Dublin. At the turn of the twentieth century, beer was a major portion of Ireland's exports and thus played a key role in the Irish economy. For most of the 1700 and 1800s, the brewing quality of beer was identified mainly by examining qualitative aspects of the main ingredients—barley and hops. By the beginning of the twentieth century, chemists were quantifying the quality of beer by looking at components such as the nitrogen content of barley and the amount of soft resin in the hops.

Gosset's experiments involved limited amounts of data; for example, he analyzed barley experiments on four farms, each growing a plot of each variety of barley. Working with such limited amounts of data meant a much

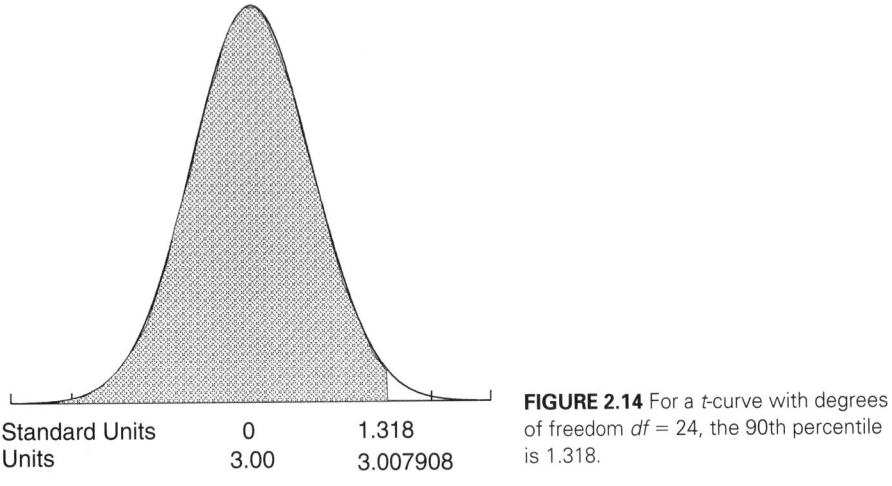

Standard Units   0   1.318
Units   3.00   3.007908

FIGURE 2.14 For a *t*-curve with degrees of freedom *df* = 24, the 90th percentile is 1.318.

greater amount of uncertainty, not only in the sample averages but also in estimates of the variability. Before this time, data analysts used such large samples that it made little difference whether or not one used the standard deviation from the sample, s_y, or a known standard deviation, σ. That is, with large samples, there is generally little estimation error when using s_y, as an estimate of σ. The turn of the twentieth century was the time of the beginning of scientific experimentation, where large samples are generally not available.

Gosset, a master chemist himself, derived the *t*-distribution and used the corresponding tables to analyze and interpret several data sets. It is interesting to note that Gosset worked under similar constraints facing scientists in industry today. Fearing that they might be giving up a competitive advantage, the owners of Guiness did not allow Gosset to publish his results under his own name. Thus, Gosset published the derivation of the *t*-distribution under the pseudonym *Student* (1908).

2.6 INTERVAL ESTIMATION

Statements about a population of interest based on a sample are called *inferences*. Generally, these statements focus on either an explanation of model behavior or the validity of predictions that arise when using a model. Section 2.8 introduces model-based predictions. Explanation of behavior is either in terms of estimates of model parameters, described in this section, or in terms of tests of hypotheses concerning model parameters, described in Section 2.7.

A population's distribution is summarized through parameters. A statistic used to approximate a parameter is called a *point estimate*. The difference between the point estimate and the parameter is called the *estimation error*. For example, $\bar{y}$ is a point estimate of the parameter μ and the estimation error is $\bar{y} - \mu$.

Interval estimates provide a range of reliability of an estimate. They are constructed by inverting probability statements.

When making inferences, the analyst cannot calculate the estimation error directly because the parameter is not known. However, the likely size of the error can be measured through the estimator's distribution. An important aspect of statistics is to give an interval about the point estimate as a measure of the estimate's reliability. This *interval estimate* is also called a *confidence interval*. We provide this interval by "inverting" the probability statements that we can make about the estimate. To illustrate this principle, let's assume again that $y_1, \ldots, y_n$ is a random sample from a normal distribution and that we use $\bar{y}$ to estimate μ. To be concrete, consider the application in Example 2.2.

C2_HOSP

Example 2.2: Hospital Costs

Managers need to be able to estimate health care costs and to measure how reliable their estimates are. Suppose that you are the risk manager for a large corporation and are trying to understand the cost of one aspect of health care, hospital costs. You decide to look at a small, homogeneous group of claims, the charges for female patients, aged 30–49 who were admitted to the hospital for circulatory disorders. Figure 2.15 displays the distribution of 1989 charges for 33 patients at a Wisconsin hospital. These data are also analyzed in Frees (1994). Table 2.6 displays the summary statistics for these charges.

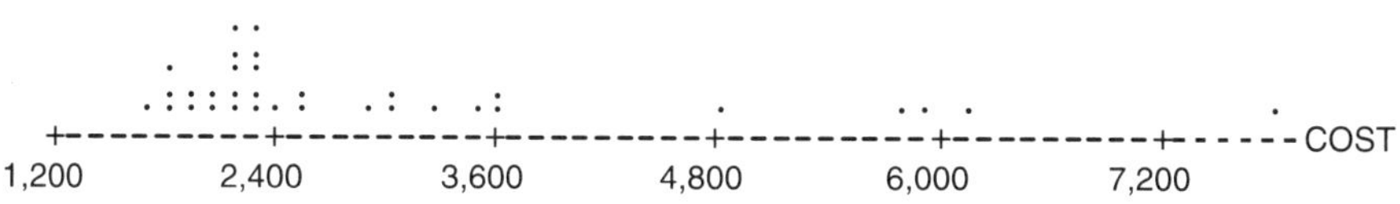

```
                      . .
                      : :
              . : : : : : . :   . :  . . :           .           . . .              .
      +---------+---------+---------+---------+---------+---------+-----COST
    1,200     2,400     3,600     4,800     6,000     7,200
```

FIGURE 2.15 Dotplot of hospital costs. Each dot represents the 1989 charges for 33 patients at a Wisconsin hospital. Each patient was female, aged 30–49 and admitted for circulatory disorders. *Source: Frees (1994)*

Table 2.6 shows that your point estimate for the cost of claims for this group is $2,955. You also can calculate an estimated standard deviation for this point estimate, $se(\bar{y}) = s_y / \sqrt{n} = 1481/(33)^{1/2} = 257.8$. To understand the relationship between these two numbers, we now introduce a confidence interval for μ.

TABLE 2.6 Summary Statistics for Hospital Costs

Number	Mean	Median	Standard deviation	Minimum	Maximum	25th percentile	75th percentile
33	2,955	2,315	1,481	1,642	7,787	2,094	3,308

From Section 2.5 we know that $t(\bar{y}) = (\bar{y} - \mu)/se(\bar{y}) = (\bar{y} - \mu)/(s_y/\sqrt{n})$, follows a t-distribution with $n - 1 = 32$ degrees of freedom. Thus, from the t-table, we have that

$$\text{Prob}[-2.036 < t(\bar{y}) < 2.036] = 0.9500.$$

Replacing $t(\bar{y})$ by $(\bar{y} - \mu)/(s_y/\sqrt{n})$, after a couple of lines of algebra, we have

$$\text{Prob}\left(\bar{y} - \frac{2.036s_y}{\sqrt{n}} < \mu < \bar{y} + \frac{2.036s_y}{\sqrt{n}} \right) = 0.95. \tag{2.7}$$

Thus, we interpret the interval $(\bar{y} - 2.036\, s_y/\sqrt{n}, \bar{y} + 2.036\, s_y/\sqrt{n})$ to be a 95% *confidence interval* for μ. As shorthand notation, we write $\bar{y} \pm 2.036\, s_y/\sqrt{n}$ for this interval. The confidence interval provides a range of reliability for the point estimate $\bar{y}$. The number 2.036 depends on the specified level of confidence and on the sample size, n. For example, if we replace 2.036 by 1.711, then this yields a 90% confidence interval. In general, we call 2.036 a *t-value*. Table 2.7 provides t-values at the 95% confidence level for some selected degrees of freedom. Because of the two-sided nature of interval estimates, these t-values are actually 97.5th percentiles.

TABLE 2.7 95% Confidence Interval t-values for Some Selected Degrees of Freedom

t-value	2.571	2.228	2.086	2.060	2.042	2.000	1.980	1.960
df	5	10	20	25	30	60	120	infinity

To summarize, we have that the general form of the confidence interval is

$$\bar{y} \pm (t\text{-value}) \frac{s_y}{\sqrt{n}}. \tag{2.8}$$

Here, the t-value is a percentile from the t-distribution with $df = n - 1$ degrees of freedom.

To interpret equation (2.8), we return to the hospital cost illustration. The point estimate is $\bar{y} = 2{,}955$ with standard error $se(\bar{y}) = 257.8$. Then, we say that our point estimate of μ is \$2,955 and the corresponding 95% confidence interval for μ is

$$2955 \pm (2.036)(257.8), \quad \text{or } 2955 \pm 525.$$

The parameter μ is a fixed, yet unknown number. Thus, this number is either within the interval 2955 ± 525 or it is not. Now, before the observations are drawn, from equation (2.7) the interval $\bar{y} \pm 2.036\, s_y/\sqrt{n}$ has a 95% chance of covering μ. After the observations are drawn, the confidence interval can be computed, and either covers μ or does not but we remain uncertain about whether this event has occurred. Thus, we can interpret a 95% confidence interval to be a procedure that is valid 95% of the time.

Another interpretation of equation (2.7) involves the frequentist interpretation of probability. With this interpretation, we suppose that we could take many samples of observations, each of size 33. For each sample, we would compute the sample mean, sample standard deviation, and using equation (2.8), the sample confidence interval. If we had used t-value = 2.036, then we would expect that about 95% of our sample confidence intervals contain the true unknown parameter μ.

As the degree of freedom increases, the t-distribution approaches the standard normal distribution.

The width of the confidence interval generally becomes smaller as the sample size, n, increases. This is primarily because of the scaling factor, $n^{-1/2}$. From Table 2.7 we see that the sample size also affects the t-value. However, as the sample size increases, t-values become closer to values from the standard normal curve. Further, sample standard deviations become closer to the population standard deviation. Thus, as the sample size increases, the changes in t-values and sample standard deviations become smaller and the scaling factor, $n^{-1/2}$, becomes the dominant term.

It is interesting that, as the sample size increases, each percentile, and thus the entire distribution, of the t-distribution approaches the standard normal distribution. For example, as n approaches infinity, we see that the 97.5th percentile of the t-curve approaches 1.96, the 97.5th percentile from the standard normal curve. The idea here is that, for sufficiently large samples, there is little estimation error in using s_y as a measure of variability. Thus, we can use the normal curve as an approximation to the t-curve. Indeed, the reader may wish to compare the tabled distributions in the appendix. Beginning with a percentile in the t-table, by going down the rows, you will eventually find the df =infinity row. This same percentile can be found in the standard normal curve table.

This discussion raises an important issue for the data analyst: "Should I use the normal curve or the t-curve?" Here are the guiding rules of thumb to address this issue.

1. For large sample sizes, because the t-curve is approximately equal to the normal curve, the choice is not important.
2. In the rare occasions when the true standard deviation σ is known, we do not need to account for the extra variability produced by the estimation of σ. Thus, we may use the normal curve.
3. For small and moderate sample sizes, the choice is generally a t-curve, with some caveats. The t-curve provides the theoretical adjustment to the normal curve needed when replacing σ by s_y. However, the definition of the t-curve is based on the fact that the observations come from a normal distribution. Use of the normal curve can be justified when the observations come from a normal distribution or from a moderately symmetric distribution.

Based on points (1)–(3), we will generally use a *t*-value in lieu of a value from the normal curve for our inference procedures, such as providing confidence intervals. In regression analysis, the true standard deviation is almost never known and most of our applications will involve samples sizes of at least twenty. Further, techniques for identifying the distribution, such as the *normal probability plot* in Section 3.5, will be introduced. These techniques will be helpful in deciding whether the population's distribution can be approximated by a normal curve.

2.7 WHAT IF? THE ROLE OF TESTING HYPOTHESES

Model ideas are summarized using parameters.

We now examine some propositions, or *hypotheses*, about the real world. The first step is to translate a real world concern into a hypothesis about a model that is described using parameters. The second step, which is more mechanical, is to test the hypothesis about the model parameters. The third step is to relate the results of the model parameter test to any implications about the real world. In this chapter, we examine the parameter μ. In subsequent chapters, the same techniques will be used to test parameters that summarize relationships between variables.

To illustrate, a manufacturer claims that its luxury cars achieve 18 miles per gallon (mpg) when tested under typical highway conditions. Suppose a sample of $n = 36$ automobiles is tested with a result of $\bar{y} = 17.2$ and $s_y = 1.8$ mpg. If we were part of a consumer advocacy group, this data would give us reason to suspect the manufacturer's claim. Although the average from our sample is only 0.8 mpg less than the claim, remember that the standard error of the sample average is $s_y/\sqrt{n}$ that, in this case, is $1.8/\sqrt{36}$, or 0.3. Thus, the sample average is 2.667 standard errors below the hypothesized value of 18 mpg. We formalize this idea with the *t*-ratio

$$t(\bar{y}) = \frac{17.2 - 18}{\dfrac{1.8}{\sqrt{36}}} = -2.667.$$

Hypothesis testing procedures might establish a real difference between a sample and a claim about model parameters, not the reason why.

We can see that this result is extremely unlikely by comparing this result to the theoretical *t*-curve using 35 degrees of freedom. In fact, the probability of getting a *t*-ratio as small or smaller than -2.667 is about 0.6%, pretty unlikely! The implications? Does this mean that the manufacturer has misstated the car's performance and should be sent to jail? Not necessarily. The procedure does mean that there is a significant difference between the manufactuer's claim and the results of the testing procedure. It could be that the consumer advocate's interpretation of "typical driving conditions" differs from the manufacturer. It could mean that the sample selection procedure was inappropriate and that an unrepresentative sample was drawn. Or it could mean that the manufacturer's claims were based on a series of engineering relationships established in the laboratory that were not adequately road tested. The sampling procedure establishes a real difference between the manufacturer's claim and the sample drawn by the consumer advocacy group, not the reason why.

Identifying Hypotheses

The claim about model parameters is called the null hypothesis.

We implicitly make decisions constantly when reasoning this data, so let's formalize the procedure. We call the claim about the parameter the *null hypothesis,* or *hypothesis of no effect.* We use the notation, $H_0: \mu = \mu_0$, to state succinctly that the null hypothesis (H_0) is that the parameter, μ, is equal to a specific value. In this case, the specific value is 18; more generally, we use μ_0 to denote this specific value. Hence, μ_0 is called the *hypothesized mean.*

The null hypothesis is $H_0: \mu = \mu_0$. An alternative may be either (i) $H_a: \mu < \mu_0$, (ii) $H_a: \mu > \mu_0$ or (iii) $H_a: \mu \neq \mu_0$. The hypotheses are made prior to examining the data.

When deciding whether or not a null hypothesis is reasonable, we compare it to an *alternative hypothesis.* That is, it is difficult to examine a proposition and decide whether or not it is plausible model of reality. It is much easier to compare it to a competing hypothesis and decide which of the two is in greater accordance with the data. Because we often wish to establish the validity of the alternative hypothesis, it is also called the *research hypothesis.* In the above example, we could use the notation, $H_a: \mu < 18$ to express the idea that we are comparing the manufacturer's claim (H_0) to the alternative idea that the true mean μ is less than 18. Because the consumer advocacy group is really interested in the fact that the true mean is less than 18, this alternative hypothesis is important. As another example, consider the marketing manager who wishes to publicize certain features of this luxury automobile. This manager may be interested in the alternative hypothesis $H_a: \mu > 18$. Similarly, the president of the manufacturing company needs to be aware of all aspects of public relations and may be interested in the alternative hypothesis $H_a: \mu \neq 18$.

To test the claim, the evidence from the data is summarized using the test statistic.

To examine this statement about a specific parameter, we look at the corresponding estimate, $\bar{y}$. To get a more meaningful picture of the estimate, the estimate is rescaled so that it corresponds to a theoretical reference curve. Above, the rescaling was done by subtracting the hypothesized mean and dividing by the standard error of $\bar{y}$. The rescaled value, called the *test statistic,* is the *t*-ratio that we may interpret using the *t*-curve as our reference distribution. That is, our test statistic is $(\bar{y} - \mu_0)/se(\bar{y})$.

Probability (*p*) Values

A p-value is the probability of observing the test statistic or a value more unlikely.

The choice of the alternative hypothesis is important. In the above example, because $\bar{y} = 17.2$ and $\mu_0 = 18$, the marketing manager would have little reason to suspect that the alternative hypothesis, $H_a: \mu > 18$, is true. The consumer advocacy's group should be very concerned that their research hypothesis is true ($H_a: \mu < 18$) and the president should be moderately concerned ($H_a: \mu \neq 18$).

We quantify this level of concern with the notion of a probability value, or p-value. A *p-value* is defined to be the probability, computed assuming the null hypothesis is true, of observing the realized test statistic or a value even more unlikely. The probability of observing the test statistic is equal to zero under a continuous idealized histogram such as the normal or the t-curve. That is why the p-value is defined as the probability of observing the test statistic or a value more unlikely. The phrase "more unlikely" implicitly means in the direction of the alternative that we are considering.

To illustrate, for testing H_a: $\mu < 18$, the p-value is

$$\text{Prob}(\bar{y} \le 17.2) = \text{Prob}(t(\bar{y}) \le -2.667) = 0.006.$$

Under the alternative hypothesis of $\mu \le 18$, "more unlikely" than 17.2 means less than or equal to 17.2. Note that in the quantity $\text{Prob}(\bar{y} \le 17.2)$, the $\bar{y}$ refers to a random occurrence of the average of the sample *before* the sample is taken (*ex ante*) and the 17.2 refers to a realization of the average *after* the sample is taken (*ex post*).

For testing H_a: $\mu \ne 18$, we are looking for "unlikely" values either above or below 18. In this case, the p-value is

$$\text{Prob}(|\bar{y} - 18| > |17.2 - 18|) = \text{Prob}(\bar{y} < 17.2 \text{ or } \bar{y} > 18.8) =$$

$$\text{Prob}(|t(\bar{y})| \ge 2.667) = 2(.006) = .012.$$

See Figure 2.16. Again, $|\bar{y} - 18|$ is the ex ante distance between the sample average and the hypothesized value of 18, and $|17.2 - 18|$ is the corresponding ex post distance.

Table 2.8 summarizes p-value calculations. In this table, use t to denote a random variable having a t-distribution with $df = n - 1$ degrees of freedom. The test statistic is the ex post value of $(\bar{y} - \mu_0)/(s_y / \sqrt{n})$, a number that can be computed based on the available sample.

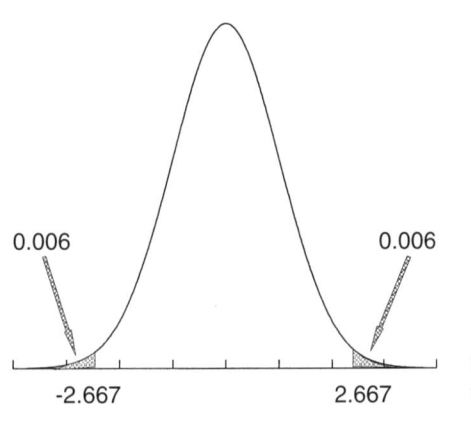

0.006   0.006

-2.667   2.667

FIGURE 2.16 The shaded area is the p-value for H_0: $\mu = 18$ versus H_a: $\mu \ne 18$.

TABLE 2.8 Calculation of Probability Values for Testing H_0: $\mu = \mu_0$

Alternative hypothesis	H_a: $\mu > \mu_0$	H_a: $\mu < \mu_0$	H_a: $\mu \neq \mu_0$
p-value	$\text{Prob}(t > \text{test statistic})$	$\text{Prob}(t < \text{test statistic})$	$Prob\,(|t| > |\text{test statistic}|)$

Testing Hypotheses

The significance level is the probability of declaring the null hypothesis invalid when it is actually true. A commonly used value is 5%.

Hypotheses are ideas and, as decision makers, we must act based on the accumulated facts to make our decisions. In a narrow sense, we may either declare the null hypothesis to be invalid or accept it as truth. In the latter case, we generally hedge our recommendations by saying that we do not have enough information to declare the null invalid. Examining the probability of making certain types of mistakes allows us to calibrate the decision-making process. The common practice is to quantify the process by using a so-called *significance level*, defined to be the probability of declaring the null hypothesis invalid when it is true. We do not deal here with other types of errors in this decision-making process, the most notable one being declaring the null hypothesis valid when it is false.

The significance level is prescribed before the data is examined. A commonly used significance level is 5%. The intuition here is that if the null hypothesis is true, then the investigator is willing to declare falsely it to be invalid 1 time in 20. The choice of the significance level depends on the application. In the life and physical sciences a smaller choice, such as 1% or 0.5%, is not uncommon. In the social sciences, higher significant levels, such as 10%, are acceptable. The 5% level is widely used and is adopted in this text for notational simplicity.

Having specified a significance level, there are two procedures for deciding between the null and alternative hypotheses. Under the first procedure, one computes the *p*-value and then declares the null hypothesis invalid if the *p*-value is less than or equal to the significance level. If the *p*-value is greater than the significance level, then the null hypothesis cannot be disproved.

Under the second procedure, so-called *critical regions* are constructed using a process similar to the one for *p*-values. If the ex post test statistic falls in the region, then one declares the null hypothesis invalid. For example, first consider H_0: $\mu = 18$ versus H_a: $\mu < 18$ with significance level 5%. The critical region is $\{t(\bar{y}) < -1.69\}$ and is illustrated in Figure 2.17. The idea here is that, ex ante, the $t(\bar{y})$ follows a *t*-curve with 35 degrees of freedom. From the *t*-table, the probability of the *t*-ratio being less than -1.69 is 5%, our prespecified significance level. If the significance level was 10%, we would use a critical region $\{t(\bar{y}) < -1.306\}$. Because $t(\bar{y}) = (\bar{y} - 18)/se(\bar{y})$, it is also acceptable to write the critical region as $\{\bar{y} < 18 - 1.306\,se(\bar{y})\}$. That is,

$$\{t(\bar{y}) < -1.306\} = \{\bar{y} < 18 - 1.306\,se(\bar{y})\}.$$

Thus, if the sample mean falls 1.306 standard errors below the hypothesized mean, then reject the null hypothesis. In our example, $\bar{y} = 17.2$ and $s_y = 1.8$,

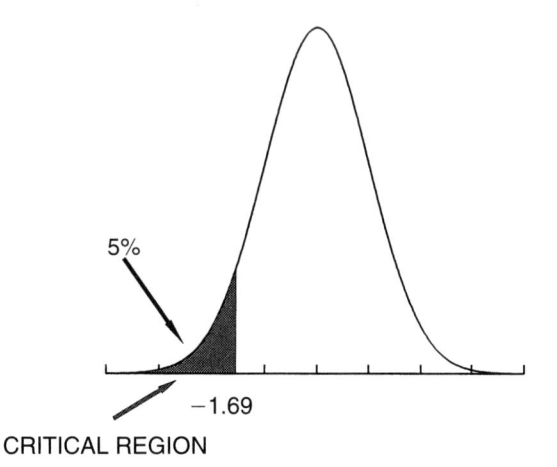

5%

−1.69

CRITICAL REGION

FIGURE 2.17 The shaded area is the critical region for a one-sided test using a *t*-curve with 35 degrees of freedom. The significance level is 5%.

leads to a *p*-value $= 0.006$ and a $t(\bar{y}) = -2.667$. Thus, both criteria lead to rejection of the null hypothesis because *p*-value $= 0.006 < 0.05$ and $t(\bar{y}) = -2.667$ < -1.69, at the 5% significance level.

The critical region for the case of $H_0: \mu = 18$ versus $H_a: \mu \neq 18$ is different. Recall that the *t*-ratio is the difference between the sample and hypothesized mean, rescaled by the standard error of the sample average. Thus, "large" values of the *t*-ratio, either positive or negative, lead to rejection of the null hypothesis. Equivalently, if the absolute value of the *t*-ratio, $|t(\bar{y})|$, is large, then reject H_0. With a 5% significance level, the critical region is $\{|t(\bar{y})| > 2.03\}$. Here, $\text{Prob}(t(\bar{y}) > 2.03) = 0.025$ and $\text{Prob}(t(\bar{y}) < -2.03) = 0.025$. Thus, half the significance level (2.5%) is spent looking for large positive values, and half is spent looking for large negative values. (See Figure 2.18.) We also could

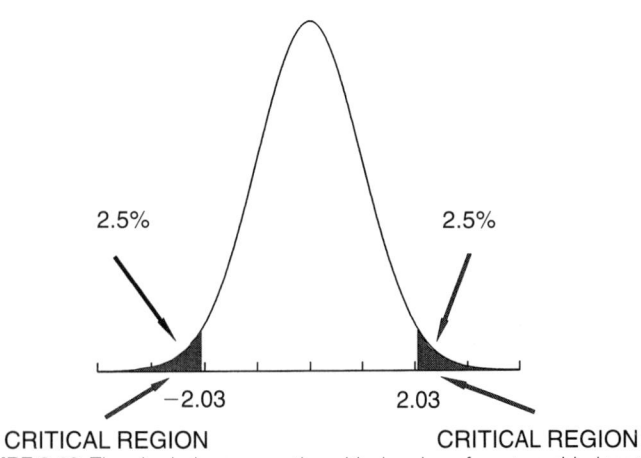

2.5%   2.5%

−2.03   2.03

CRITICAL REGION   CRITICAL REGION

FIGURE 2.18 The shaded areas are the critical regions for a two-sided test using a *t*-curve with 35 degrees of freedom. The significance level is 5%.

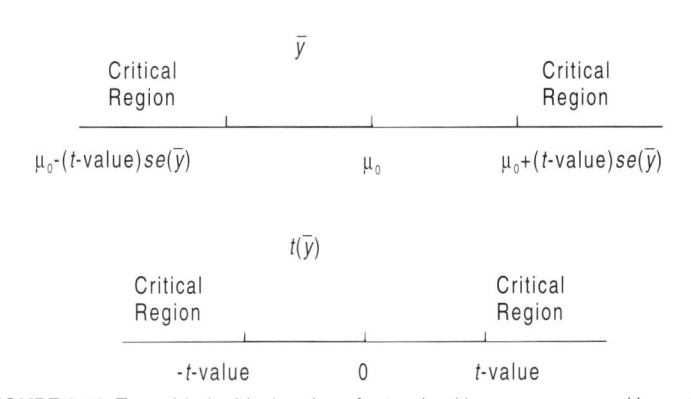

FIGURE 2.19 Two-sided critical regions for testing H_0: $\mu = \mu_0$ versus H_a: $\mu \neq \mu_0$. Critical regions may be expressed in terms of $\bar{y}$ units, or in the standardized version, $t(\bar{y})$, units.

write the critical region as $\{|\bar{y} - \mu| > 2.03\, se(\bar{y})\}$, that is, we reject H_0 if the sample average is more than 2.03 standard errors from the hypothesized mean. This is illustrated in Figure 2.19.

Table 2.9 summarizes the decision-making procedures for testing the null hypothesis H_0: $\mu = \mu_0$ versus any one of the three alternative hypotheses.

TABLE 2.9 Decision-making Procedures for Testing H_0: $\mu = \mu_0$

Alternative Hypothesis (H_a)	The *t-value* is a percentile from the *t*-curve using $df = n - 1$ degrees of freedom. The percentile is:	Procedure: Reject H_0 in favor of H_a if	
		$t(\bar{y})$ units	$\bar{y}$ units
$\mu > \mu_0$	1 − significance level	$t(\bar{y}) > t$-value	$\bar{y} > \mu_0 + (t\text{-value})\, se(\bar{y})$
$\mu < \mu_0$	1 − significance level	$t(\bar{y}) < -(t\text{-value})$	$\bar{y} < \mu_0 - (t\text{-value})\, se(\bar{y})$
$\mu \neq \mu_0$	1 − (significance level)/2	$|t(\bar{y})| > t$-value	$\bar{y} > \mu_0 + (t\text{-value})\, se(\bar{y})$ or $\bar{y} < \mu_0 - (t\text{-value})\, se(\bar{y})$

Example 2.2: Hospital Costs—Continued

Before examining the data, identify H_0: $\mu = 2{,}900$, H_a: $\mu > 2{,}900$ and a 5% significance level.

Suppose that hospital charges for circulatory disorders had been stable for many years. As the risk manager of a large corporation, in 1988 you do a small "trend analysis" and forecast, after adjusting for inflation, the average costs for females, aged 30–49, admitted for circulatory disorders, to be $\mu = \$2{,}900$. You suspect that the hospital has changed their fiscal procedures and is now charging significantly more than historically. Thus, you wish to prove H_a: $\mu > \$2{,}900$ compared to the historically valid hypothesis H_0: $\mu = \$2,900$. Based on the 1989 data, you now calculate

$$t(\bar{y}) = \frac{(\bar{y} - \mu_0)}{\left(\dfrac{s_y}{\sqrt{n}}\right)} = \frac{(2,955 - 2,900)}{\left(\dfrac{1,481}{(33)^{1/2}}\right)} = 0.213.$$

At the 5% level of significance, with $df = 32$, for a one-sided test we have t-value $= 1.693$. Thus, because $t(\bar{y}) < t$-value, we cannot reject the null hypothesis in favor of the alternative. Stated another way, this year's average claims were only 0.213 standard errors above the hypothesized value. Although $\bar{y}$ represents an increase in charges, the amount of increase is statistically insignificant, at the level of significance selected by the risk manager.

2.8 THE CONCEPT OF RANDOM ERROR

Instead of saying that $y_1, y_2, \dots, y_n$ is a random sample from a population with mean μ, we could express the observations by

$$y_i = \mu + e_i, \qquad i = 1, \dots, n.$$

This is shorthand notation for the n equations:

$$y_1 = \mu + e_1$$
$$y_2 = \mu + e_2$$
$$\cdot \quad \cdot$$
$$\cdot \quad \cdot$$
$$\cdot \quad \cdot$$
$$y_n = \mu + e_n.$$

The response (y) equals a deterministic component (μ) plus a random component (e).

Here, e_i, defined by $y_i - \mu$, is the *error*, or deviation of the response for the mean μ. Note that μ is common to all observations. The important new idea is to decompose the response (y) into a deterministic component (μ) and a random component (e). This decomposition is a key idea in regression analysis and will be described further in Chapters 3 and 4.

The idealized histograms from which $\{y_i\}$ and $\{e_i\}$ are drawn are identical, apart from the location shift of μ. In particular, because the shapes of these histograms are identical, their variances are the same, that is, $\mathrm{Var}(y_i) = \mathrm{Var}(e_i)$. In fact, for any model in which we decompose the response into a deterministic component and a random component, we:

With E e = 0, we have E y = μ. With Var μ = 0, we have Var y = Var e.

1. Assume that the random component has expected value zero, so that the expected value of the response is the deterministic component.

2. Assume that there is no uncertainty in the deterministic component, so that the variance of the response is the same as the variance of the random component.

Predicting the Next Draw from a Distribution

As a first application of the concept of random error, consider the problem of *predicting* an additional observation. Suppose that we have observed the random sample $y_1, y_2, \ldots, y_n$ and wish to predict the additional observation $y_* = \mu + e_*$ It seems reasonable that a respectable point estimate is $\bar{y}$. We write the *prediction error* as

$$y_* - \bar{y} = \qquad \mu - \bar{y} \quad + \qquad e_*$$

prediction error = estimation error + random error.

We have seen that the standard deviation of the estimation error, $\sigma/\sqrt{n}$, becomes smaller as our sample size increases. However, the standard deviation of the random error, σ, is not affected by the sample size. It represents the natural variation associated with the additional observation that we are trying to predict.

Because of the natural variation of the response, the width of prediction intervals is not dramatically reduced by increasing the sample size.

A 95% *prediction interval* of the next observation is

$$\bar{y} \pm (t\text{-value})\, s_y \sqrt{1 + \frac{1}{n}} \qquad (2.9)$$

where t-value is the 97.5th percentile from the t-curve with $n - 1$ degrees of freedom. As with confidence intervals for the mean, for prediction intervals we think of the interval width as a measure of the prediction's reliability. There are two sources of error in our predictions. The first comes from the estimation of μ. The second comes from the intrinsic, or natural, variation in the response. Unlike confidence intervals, the width of prediction intervals is not dramatically reduced by increasing the sample size. To reduce the interval width, we will look to reducing the uncertainty associated with the process. For us, this will mean looking for variables to explain patterns in the random error, thus reducing our summary measure of the variability, σ^2.

Case Study: Public Employee Retirement Systems

C2_PERS

Suppose that you are on the Board of Directors of your local public employee retirement system (PERS). A PERS is a financial security system for employees of local governments either at the state, city or county level. The benefits provided by a PERS are primarily retirement benefits although death, disability and small ancillary benefits are usually also available. Because each PERS provides retirement benefits, there is typically a considerable accumulation of assets to provide for the eventual payout of these benefits. As a member of the Board, you are concerned that your PERS has accumulated a reasonable amount of assets in the most recent year. To provide a complete answer to this concern, an actuary could be called upon to project the longevity of each potential beneficiary and then match projected cash in-flows to projected benefit payments. Another way of looking at the problem is to compare the asset accumulation of your PERS to that of other PERS having similar characteristics. In this way, the performance of all PERS can be summarized and unusual performances can be identified.

To study the characteristics of the growth of assets of PERS, we use data from the U.S. Bureau of the Census. Specifically, historical asset information was abstracted from the Census Bureau's "Employee Retirement Systems of State and Local Governments" annual publications that list financial information of individual PERS. This publication contains listings from approximately 1,000 of the 2,500 PERS. (There are 2,414 active PERS according to the 1987 Census of Governments that was released in December of 1989.) This sample is not random but is drawn from a rotating panel, with the largest PERS always remaining in the panel. The randomness in the modeling comes from unknown future values of assets, not the drawing of systems from an infinite "universe." We drew the 103 largest PERS for this study. These 103 systems held about $541 billion in assets as of June 30, 1989 that constitutes approximately 87% of all PERS assets. The characteristics reported below were part of a larger study. In that study, it turned out that four PERS displayed unreliable reporting tendencies, and therefore were discarded from the sample. Because this sample constitutes such a large percentage of assets, the summary statistics for this sample may be of interest to the financial community.

The variable of interest is the increase in asset growth from 1986 to 1987. For example, the Wisconsin Retirement System grew from $10,148,191,000 in 1986 to $11,718,424,000 in 1987 for a growth rate of 0.1547, or roughly 15.5%. How typical is this growth rate? To respond to this question, in Figure 2.20 is a dotplot and in Table 2.10 are the summary statistics of the sample PERS growth rates.

From the Figure 2.20 dotplot and the summary statistics in Table 2.10, we see that a growth rate of 15.5% was typical for this sample of public employee retirement systems. We also note that the highest and lowest of the systems have unusual growth rates when compared to others in the sample. For example, the largest growth rate, 76.34%, is 4.35 $[=(0.7634 - 0.1726)/0.1358]$ standard deviations above the average! There may be special reasons why these values occurred. The advantage of this cursory look at the data is that we are immediately alerted to these potential problems. If we had only looked at sum-

TABLE 2.10   Summary Statistics of 1986–1987 Asset Growth of 99 PERS

	Number	Mean	Median	Standard deviation	Minimum	Maximum	25th percentile	75th percentile
ASST8687	99	0.1726	0.1499	0.1358	−0.3958	0.7634	0.1188	0.1925

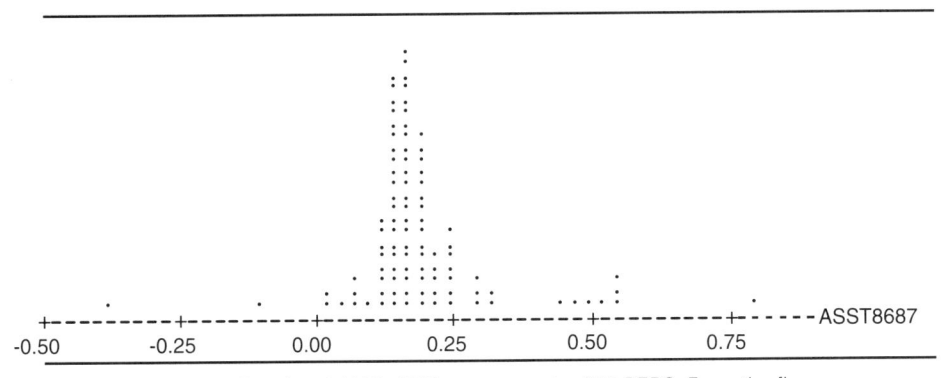

FIGURE 2.20 Dotplot of 1986–1987 asset growth of 99 PERS. From the figure, we can see that several PERS have unusually large and small growth rates.
Source: U.S. Census Bureau's "Employee Retirement Systems of State and Local Governments"

mary statistics such as the mean and standard deviation we might have never known about these unusual values.

For the sake of illustration, suppose that we decide that all values in our sample are valid and that we wish to estimate the mean growth rate. From the estimation ideas introduced in Section 2.6, our point estimate is $\bar{y} = 17.26$ percent. An approximate 95% confidence interval of the mean is

$$0.1726 \pm 1.98 \, \frac{0.1358}{\sqrt{99}} = (0.1455, 0.1997).$$

An approximate 95% prediction interval for the rate increase for a randomly selected PERS is

$$0.1726 \pm (1.98)(0.1358) \sqrt{1 + \frac{1}{99}} = (-0.095, 0.44).$$

The prediction interval is always wider than the corresponding confidence interval. The confidence interval provides a measure of reliability for estimating a parameter and thus only needs to account for estimation error. The prediction interval provides a measure of reliability for the prediction of an observation. Thus, the prediction interval needs to account for estimation error as well as the natural variability of a single observation.

2.9 SUMMARY

This chapter introduces the idea of a statistical model, and how to use the model in conjunction with a set of data. At the foundations level, the model is for univariate data only; in subsequent chapters we will consider regression models of multivariate data. Prior to the introduction of the statistical model, we first introduced some techniques of data analysis and concepts from probability theory. Section 2.1 introduced several data analysis techniques for summarizing data analytically and graphically. These techniques not only are sensible summaries of the data, they also provide approximations of parameters used in the model introduced in the latter sections. Sections 2.2 and 2.3 introduced the key ideas from probability theory, including the representation of either a data set or theoretical population using a histogram and the drawing of an entity from this histogram.

We introduced sampling, the link between data analysis and probability theory, in Section 2.4. Here we also discussed the inferential nature of statistics. Before presenting three specific types of inferences in Sections 2.6 through 2.8, in Section 2.5 we looked at a special kind of sample called a random sample. This type of sample is convenient because it allows us to easily compute the distribution of statistics of interest. For example, we showed how to standardize the sample mean to get the t-distribution.

As noted previously, statistical inference techniques are the subject of Sections 2.6 through 2.8, Section 2.6 introduced us to interval estimates, also known as confidence intervals, that provide us with ranges of reliability for our estimates of parameters. Section 2.7 introduced a method for making decisions about the nature of parameters. Finally, in Section 2.8, we showed how to predict a new observation. The prediction problem leads itself naturally to the introduction of the concept of random error. This concept is a stepping stone for the introduction of both the cross-sectional regression models in Chapter 3 and the longitudinal data models in Chapter 9.

KEY WORDS, PHRASES AND SYMBOLS

After reading this chapter, you should be able to define each of the following important terms, phrases and symbols in your own words. If not, go the page indicated and review the definition.

CHAPTER 2 EXERCISES

Section 2.2

2.1 Find the area under the standard normal curve that is:
  a. less than 1.5
  b. less than -1.0
  c. greater than 1.28
  d. greater than -1.96
  e. between -1.28 and 1.28
  f. between -1.28 and 1.96.

2.2 Find the area under the standard normal curve that is:
  a. between -1 and 1
  b. between -0.1 and 0.1
  c. between -0.01 and 0.01
  d. between -0.001 and 0.001
  e. Provide an interpretation for your results.

2.3 Find the area under the standard normal curve that is:
  a. between 1 and 2
  b. between 1 and 1.1
  c. between 1 and 1.01
  d. between 1 and 1.001
  e. Provide an interpretation for your results.

2.4 Find the following percentiles of the standard normal distribution:
  a. 50th percentile
  b. 97.5th percentile
  c. 80th percentile
  d. 95th percentile
  e. 20th percentile
  f. 10th percentile.

2.5 In a tough statistics course, scores are known to follow a normal distribution with mean $\mu = 60$ and standard deviation $\sigma = 10$. Find the score that a student needs to get to be at the:
  a. 90th percentile
  b. 80th percentile
  c. 40th percentile.

2.6 For Galton's data in Table 1.1, the average height of adult children is 68.093 inches and the standard deviation is 2.543 inches. Approximately, what is the probability of drawing a child's adult height larger than 72.8 inches using:
  a. the histogram given in Table 1.1
  b. the normal curve approximation.

Sections 2.3–2.4

2.7 Consider the following set of five observations $\{10, 6, 11, 3, 9\}$. Compute the sample variance s_y^2 using equation (2.4) in Section 2.4 and the formula given in part (c) of Exercise 2.30. Which method is easier?

C2_GLIFE

2.8 Consider the following set of five observations $\{10, 6, 10, 6, 8\}$. Compute the sample variance s_y^2 using equation (2.4) in Section 2.4 and the formula given in part (c) of Exercise 2.30. Which method is easier?

2.9 During the 1990–1991 policy year, the University of Wisconsin Insurance Association Group Life Insurance Plan paid thirty death claims. The number and amount of claims are listed in Table E2.9.
   a. Are these data cross-sectional or longitudinal?
   b. Provide a histogram of claims.
   c. From the entire data set, calculate the mean and standard deviation of claims.
   d. How many standard deviations above the mean are the two largest claims?
   e. How many standard deviations below the mean is the lowest claim?
   f. Calculate the interval defined by the mean plus or minus two standard deviations. What percentage of claims falls within the interval?

TABLE E2.9

1 for $3,150	2 for 7,350	1 for 36,300
2 for 3,500	1 for 8,050	1 for 42,350
2 for 4,375	1 for 11,025	2 for 48,650
1 for 5,250	3 for 16,975	1 for 73,500
1 for 5,775	2 for 19,600	2 for 89,600
1 for 6,125	1 for 26,250	2 for 95,550
1 for 6,825	2 for 36,050	

2.10 Suppose that a group life insurance policy paid the following claims:

50 for $10,000	100 for 25,000	10 for 50,000

   a. Calculate the mean of the claims.
   b. Calculate the median of the claims.
   c. Calculate the standard deviation of the claims.

2.11 Consider the following data set $\{42, 58, 26, 34\}$.
   a. Represent the data set using a histogram with cell width five and the first cell starting with midpoint 25.
   b. Represent the data set with a normal curve. To specify the normal curve, give the mean and standard deviation that you would use with your curve.
   c. What is the probability of drawing an observation 50 or larger from
      i. the original data set
      ii. the histogram constructed in part (a)
      iii. the normal curve constructed in part (b).

2.12. Consider the following data set of 1987 monthly rents for two-bedroom apartments. (See Tables E2.12a and b and Figure E2.12.) Approximately what is the probability of drawing an observation 373.7 or larger from:
   a. the original data set
   b. the histogram given
   c. the normal curve approximation.

C2_RNT87

TABLE E2.12a Listing of 1987 Monthly Rents

400	455	365	510	480	330	400	395	355	425
500	400	400	385	420	393	425	450	450	314
429	425	500	435	365	369	370	405	335	425
424	605								

Source: Campus Assistance Center, Madison, WI

TABLE E2.12b Summary Statistics of 1987 Monthly Rents

	Number	Mean	Median	Standard deviation	Minimum	Maximum	25th percentile	75th percentile
RENTS	32	416.8	412.5	59.1	314.0	605.0	373.7	446.3

C2_RNT87

2.13. In Exercise 2.12, the 32nd observation is $605. Use the following steps to calculate the effect of the largest observation on the standard deviation.

   a. How many standard deviations above the mean is 605?

   b. Using the normal curve approximation, what is the probability of drawing an apartment with rent ≥ 605?

   c. From the summary statistics, verify that

$$\sum_{i=1}^{32} y_i = 13{,}337.6 \quad \text{and} \quad \sum_{i=1}^{32} y_i^2 = 5{,}667{,}388.7.$$

[Hint: Use the relationship $(n-1) s_y^2 = \sum_{i=1}^{n} y_i^2 - n \bar{y}^2$ established in Exercise 2.30.]

   d. Use part (c) to calculate $\sum_{i=1}^{31} y_i$ and $\sum_{i=1}^{31} y_i^2$.

   e. Use part (d) to calculate the mean and standard deviation of the data having deleted the 32nd observation.

   f. Use the calculation in part (e) to provide an interpretation of the percentage change in the standard deviation.

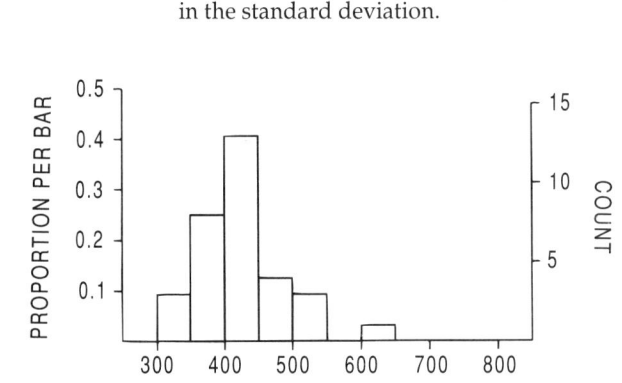

FIGURE E2.12 Histogram of rents.

C6_NFL

2.14 Consider the 1990 salaries of professional entertainers playing in the National Football League (NFL). In Table E2.14a is a sample of 198 players, with starting salaries at the beginning of their 1990 season. These data are described in more detail in the Section 6.7 Case Study.

  a. Summary statistics of the player's salaries are given in Table E2.14a. Use these summary statistics and the dotplot (Figure E2.14a) to say, approximately, what percentage of the players are in the interval.

    i. $\bar{y} \pm s_y$

    ii. $\bar{y} \pm 2s_y$

    iii. $\bar{y} \pm 3s_y$

TABLE E2.14a   Summary Statistics of NFL Players' Salaries

	Number	Mean	Median	Standard deviation	Minimum	Maximum	25th percentile	75th percentile
SALARY	198	353,788	280,000	265,297	75,000	1,500,000	165,000	456,250

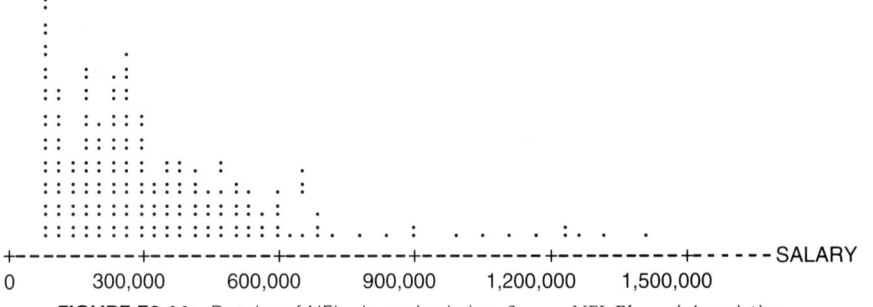

FIGURE E2.14a Dotplot of NFL players' salaries. *Source: NFL Players' Association*

  b. Summary statistics of the natural logarithm of player's salaries are given in Table E2.14b. (We will discuss in Section 6.7 why this is a useful transformation.) Use these summary statistics and the dotplot (Figure E2.14b) to say, approximately, what percentage of the players are in the interval.

    i. $\bar{y} \pm s_y$

TABLE E2.14b   Summary Statistics of the Logarithm of NFL Players' Salaries

	Number	Mean	Median	Standard deviation	Minimum	Maximum	25th percentile	75th percentile
LOGSAL	198	12.538	12.543	0.693	11.225	14.221	12.014	13.031

```
                          :
                .      : :
                .    : :: .  . : .       .
      :   :     : :: . :::: ::: : :.. .
      :::::::.:  .  .: :: ::::::.:::::: .::::: :
   :.:::::::.:.:::::::.:::::::.:::::::.:::::::.:.  .:.....:  .
   -----+---------+---------+---------+---------+---------+-LOGSAL
       11.40     12.00     12.60     13.20     13.80     14.40
```

FIGURE E2.14b Dotplot of the logarithm of NFL players' salaries.

        ii. $\bar{y} \pm 2s_y$
        iii. $\bar{y} \pm 3s_y$
   c. For the standard normal curve, calculate the area under the curve in the interval
        i. $(-1, 1)$
        ii. $(-2, 2)$
        iii. $(-3, 3)$.
   d. Using the results of parts (a), (b) and (c), say whether salaries or logged salaries are more suitably fit using a normal curve. Justify your response.

Section 2.5

2.15 Two continuous idealized histograms are shown in the figure. One is a solid curve and the other is a dashed curve. These curves represent the normal curve and a t-curve with two degrees of freedom. Identify the t-curve and specify why you have selected your choice.

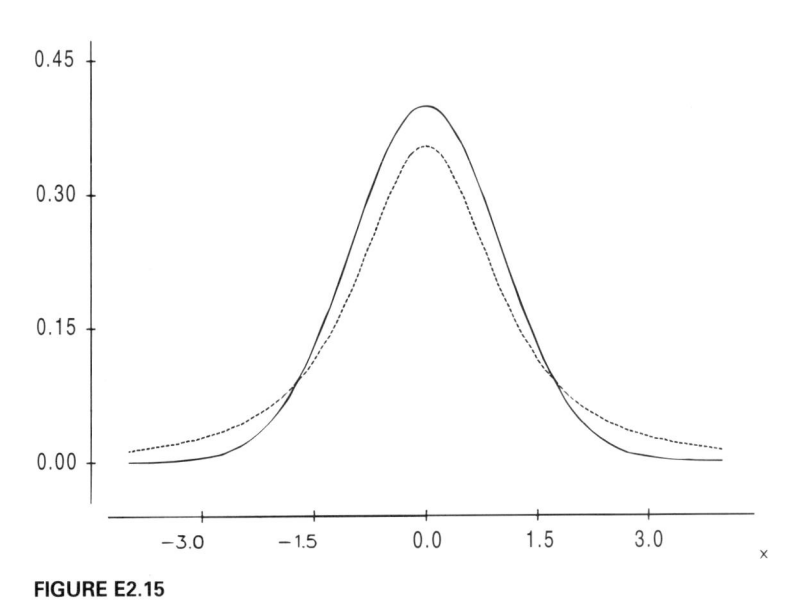

FIGURE E2.15

2.16 Approximate the area under a t-curve with 2 degrees of freedom that is:
   a. less than 1.5   **d.** greater than -1.96
   b. less than -1.0 **e.** between -1.28 and 1.28
   c. greater than 1.28   **f.** between -1.28 and 1.96.

2.17 Approximate the area between -2 and 2 for a t-curve with:
   a. 1 degree of freedom   **d.** 30 degrees of freedom
   b. 5 degrees of freedom   **e.** 60 degrees of freedom
   c. 25 degrees of freedom   **f.** degrees of freedom equal to infinity.

2.18 Approximate the area greater than 3 for a *t*-curve with:
- **a.** 1 degree of freedom
- **b.** 5 degrees of freedom
- **c.** 25 degrees of freedom
- **d.** 30 degrees of freedom
- **e.** 60 degrees of freedom
- **f.** degrees of freedom equal to infinity.

2.19 Specify the symmetric interval that corresponds to a 0.95 area under a *t*-curve with:
- **a.** 1 degree of freedom
- **b.** 5 degrees of freedom
- **c.** 25 degrees of freedom
- **d.** 30 degrees of freedom
- **e.** 60 degrees of freedom
- **f.** degrees of freedom equal to infinity.

Sections 2.6–2.7

2.20 You have diversified your company's pension plan fund to include over 50 fund managers. Suppose that each manager is expected to earn $\mu = 3\%$ over the risk-free rate with a standard deviation of $\sigma = 10\%$. For simplicity, assume that you have given an equal amount to each manager and that the manager's performances are independent. Use the Central Limit Theorem to approximate the probability that your overall return in excess of the risk-free rate, $\bar{y}$, is
- **a.** greater than 13%
- **b.** greater than 4%
- **c.** less than 1%.

C6_NFL

2.21 Consider the sample of natural logarithms of 1990 salaries of NFL payers (y), described in Exercise 2.14.
- **a.** From Exercise 2.14, the sample average is $\bar{y} = 12.538$, in terms of natural logarithms of dollars. Express this estimate of the population mean in terms of dollars.
- **b.** Compute a 95% confidence interval of the mean salary in terms of natural logarithms of dollars.
- **c.** Compute a 99% confidence interval of the mean salary in terms of natural logarithms of dollars.
- **d.** For the confidence intervals computed in parts (b) and (c), which is wider? Interpret your result.
- **e.** Express each interval endpoint of your 95% confidence interval computed in part (b) in terms of dollars.
- **f.** Is the confidence interval computed in part (e) symmetric about the estimate of the population mean computed in part (a)? Interpret your result.

C4_TAX

2.22 The data used in this analysis was randomly selected individual tax returns for 1990 prepared by a local branch of a national tax preparation service. Total income for the 65 returns selected ranged from a low of $368 to $65,627. The data collected from each return includes total income (TOTALINC), as well as a number of other variables of interest. (See Figure E2.22 and Table E2.22.)

TABLE E2.22 Summary Statistics of the Total Income for Taxpayers

	Number	Mean	Median	Standard deviation	Minimum	Maximum	25th percentile	75th percentile
TOTALINC	65	30,085	29,360	16,324	368	65,627	17,903	41,767

```
           . .      . :      .
...:. ..  ..::. :.:. :::.:....:: :  :.: :::   ... . :  . .
+---------+---------+---------+---------+---------+------ TOTALINC
    0    12,000    24,000    36,000    48,000    60,000
```

FIGURE E2.22

a. Suppose that you are interested in estimating the mean of your population of clients.
   i.   Provide a point estimate of population mean.
   ii. Provide a 95% confidence interval for your estimate of the mean.
b. Before collecting the data, you have developed several ideas about the mean total income of your population of clients. Suppose that you are interested in testing some ideas about the population mean.
   i.   Your boss is convinced that your clients have a mean income of $35,000. Test the null hypothesis that the expected value of TOTALINC is 35,000 versus the alternative that it is not 35,000. State your null hypothesis, alternative hypothesis, and all components of the decision-making rule. Use a 5% level of significance.
   ii. From the summary statistics, you note that the average from the sample is $\bar{y} = 30,085$. Assuming that the true mean is 35,000, what is the probability of getting 30,085 or smaller? You may use the assumption of normality in computing this p-value.

C2_FARM

2.23 Net income, as a percentage of equity, is a measure of a rate of return. In Figure E2.23 is net income divided by equity for farms on a state by state basis. (See Table E2.23 for summary statistics.)
   a. Identify a population that this data may be a sample of.
   b. Wisconsin is ranked third on the list of 50 states. What percentile is that?
   c. How many standard deviations is Wisconsin above the mean?
   d. Using a normal curve approximation, what percentile is Wisconsin?
   e. Economic theory has lead us to believe that the true net income per unit of equity at the state level is 10%. Test the null hypothesis that $H_0: \mu = 0.10$ versus $H_a: \mu \neq 0.10$ at the 5% level of significance.
   f. A farm lobbyist has used the Total U.S. Farm Income divided Total U.S. Farm Equity as a approximation to the mean rate of return. Explain the difference between this approximation and $\bar{y}$ to the lobbyist and why these two ideas may result in different results.

0.15176	0.13437	0.13268	0.13113	0.128859	0.12539	0.12094
0.11444	0.11322	0.11138	0.10697	0.103905	0.10220	0.09682
0.09248	0.08916	0.08882	0.08821	0.084141	0.08320	0.08129
0.08107	0.07855	0.07668	0.07392	0.070444	0.06733	0.06603
0.06332	0.06213	0.06118	0.06019	0.058727	0.05855	0.05826
0.05771	0.05712	0.05333	0.04973	0.049189	0.04874	0.04670
0.04661	0.03698	0.03685	0.03464	0.034202	0.02784	0.01379
0.01164						

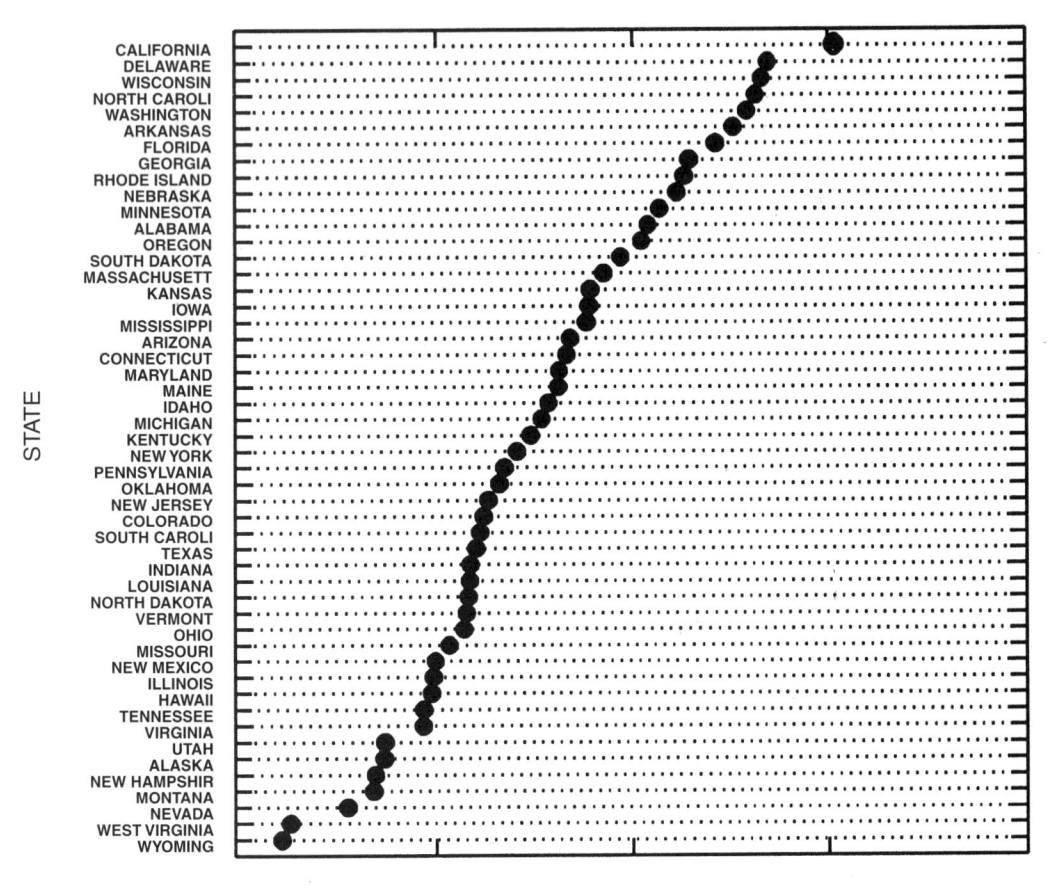

FIGURE E2.23 Dot chart of net income as a proportion of equity (by state). *Source: Wisconsin Blue Book, 1989–1990*

TABLE E2.23   Summary Statistics for Net Income per Equity

Number	Mean	Median	Standard deviation	Minimum	Maximum	25th percentile	75th percentile
50	0.07645	0.0722	0.0333	0.0116	0.1518	0.0524	0.1026

Section 2.8

2.24 Refer to Section 2.6

Consider the data introduced in Example 2.2, the hospital costs of 33 female patients admitted for circulatory disorders.

C2_HOSP

a. Assume that the responses are realizations from a normal distribution. Use this assumption and the summary statistics to arrive at a 95% prediction interval for a new observation.

b. As an alternative to part (a), do the following.

   i. Using the dotplot in Figure 2.15, find the approximate 97.5th percentile.

  ii. Using the dotplot in Figure 2.15, find the approximate 2.5th percentile.

 iii. Use parts (i) and (ii) to get an approximate 95% prediction interval for a new observation.

End-of-Chapter Exercises

2.25 Consider the following fictitious data set {42, 58, 26, 34}. Assume that the data are realizations from a normally distributed population.

  a. Calculate $\bar{y}$ and s_y.

  b. Provide a 95% confidence interval for the mean of the population, μ.

  c. Suppose that you wish to verify whether or not the true mean μ is 35. Perform a formal test of the null hypothesis $H_0: \mu = 35$ versus $H_a: \mu \neq 35$ at the 5% level of significance.

  d. Provide a 95% prediction interval for an additional observation.

C2_MIGRT

2.26 A state's net internal migration is defined to be the number of people that enter minus the number that exit a state from or to another state. The corresponding *net internal migration rate* (NETMIGRN) is the net internal migration divided by the state's population. Table E2.26 summarizes the 1987 net migration rates for the 50 states plus the District of Columbia. The data are from the U.S. Bureau of the Census and are analyzed in Frees (1992, 1993). (See Figure E2.26.)

  a. Suppose that you are interested in another region and are willing to assume that the preceding data is from the same population as the region that you are interested in. Provide a 95% prediction interval for the additional region.

  b. Because *internal* migration considers only movers from one state to another, total U.S. internal migration is equal to zero by definition. That is, because each person who exits a state enters another state, the sum over all states must equal zero. (Here, we are excluding *external* migration, or movers either to or from a foreign country.) However, the average net migration given in the above summary statistics is -0.0013. Can this only be a calculation error or do you have another explanation?

  c. Use the observation in part (b) to comment on the dependence of the observations.

TABLE E2.26 Summary Statistics of 1987 Net Migration Rates

	Number	Mean	Median	Standard deviation	Minimum	Maximum	25th percentile	75th percentile
NETMIGRN	51	-0.0013	-0.0028	0.0116	-0.0320	0.0326	-0.0069	0.0072

```
                              .
                        : .:   .    .      :  .
   .     .        . .... ::..:::.::::.. :.:.:    :  .
------+---------+---------+---------+---------+---------+--------- NETMIGRN
   -0.024     -0.012     0.000      0.012     0.024     0.036
```

FIGURE E2.26 Dotplot of 1987 net migration rates. *Source: U.S. Census Bureau*

C2_MFUND

2.27 For long-term capital appreciation, many financial advisors recommend a mutual fund, a portfolio of financial securities. Table E2.27b lists 40 of the largest General Equity mutual funds. This list was taken from the September 29, 1991 issue of *The New York Times*, the original source being *Lipper Analytical Services, Inc.* The assets are given in millions of dollars and are valued as at June 30, 1991. There are three basic ways in which sales expenses are charged to a customer and the type of sales charge is indicated in the LOAD column. The EXP RAT is the expense ratio of the fund, defined to be the ratio of a fund's expenses to its average net assets. Expenses include management, operating and marketing fees. The variable TYPE indicates the type of investment philosophy which dictates the fund's investment strategy. To evaluate the fund performance, 5YR RET and 1YR RET are the five year and one year historical returns that were earned by the fund, given in percentages. (See Figure E2.27 and Tables E2.27a and b.)

a. What are the total assets of the 40 mutual funds?
b. If the largest fund, *Fidelity Magellan,* is eliminated, then for the 39 remaining funds, find the mean and median amount of assets.
c. Does the one year return variable appear to be normally distributed? Give reasons why or why not.
d. Suppose that I decide to examine one mutual fund in detail. I randomly select one of the 40. What is the probability of drawing a no-load fund (that is, load = 3, a fund without a sales charge)?
e. Assume, for the expense ratio variable, that the sample is representative of the larger population of all mutual funds and may be modeled as a random sample.

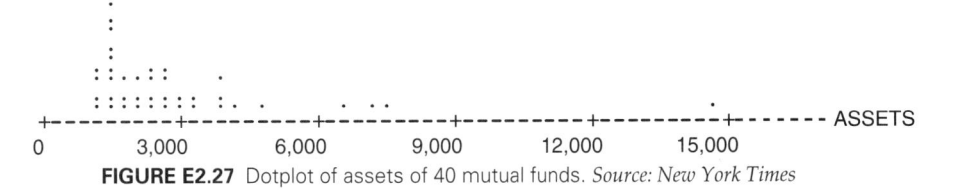

FIGURE E2.27 Dotplot of assets of 40 mutual funds. *Source: New York Times*

TABLE E2.27a Summary Statistics of Mutual Funds' Financial Variables

	Number	Number missing	Mean	Median	Standard deviation	Minimum	Maximum	25th percentile	75th percentile
LOAD	40	0	1.825	1.000	0.931	1.000	3.000	1.000	3.000
EXP RAT	40	0	0.7607	0.7700	0.2564	0.2100	1.5100	0.6075	0.8800
TYPE	40	0	3.250	4.000	1.316	1.000	5.000	2.000	4.000
ASSETS	40	0	3,012	2,372	2,568	1,193	15,252	1,501	3,332
5YR RET	39	1	87.58	83.64	22.48	56.44	136.68	68.69	99.54
1YR RET	40	0	32.64	31.11	8.44	16.82	52.30	26.55	37.24

TABLE E2.27b   Listing of Mutual Funds' Financial Variables

Fund	LOAD	EXP RAT	TYPE	ASSETS	5YR RET	1YR RET
Fidelity Magellin	2	1.06	2	15,251.8	117.37	44.90
Windsor Funds	3	0.37	4	7,708.8	62.81	37.13
Investment Co of America	1	0.55	4	7,642.7	92.03	30.22
Washington Mutual Inv	1	0.77	4	6,791.9	81.47	32.80
Fidelity Puritan	2	0.65	5	4,789.8	62.37	27.68
Fidelity Equity-Inc	2	0.70	5	4,089.1	56.44	31.32
Pioneer II	1	0.75	4	3,999.0	61.10	24.55
American Mutual	1	0.60	4	3,899.4	72.48	23.88
Twentieth Cent:Select	3	1.00	2	3,761.3	89.36	27.39
Affiliated Fund	1	0.50	4	3,379.4	67.40	26.61
Dean Witter Divid Gro	3	1.51	4	3,188.2	79.74	34.29
Vanguard Index: 500 Port	3	0.22	4	3,044.0	94.74	32.52
Windsor Funds II	3	0.52	4	2,922.8	77.97	34.05
Mutual: Shares	3	0.85	4	2,700.6	79.76	24.18
Income Fund of America	1	0.67	5	2,660.1	66.01	25.21
Growth Fund of America	1	0.79	2	2,562.6	108.12	39.24
Twentieth Cent: Growth	3	1.00	1	2,550.1	133.87	50.18
Dreyfus Fund	3	0.77	4	2,465.8	68.69	26.06
Fidelity Growth & Income	2	0.87	4	2,433.0	117.32	44.77
Putnam Growth & Income	1	0.89	4	2,395.3	83.91	26.75
Amer Cap Pace	1	0.88	2	2,348.9	74.19	32.16
Amcap Fund	1	0.79	2	2,201.4	92.48	44.07
Fidelity Destiny I	1	0.53	2	2,023.9	111.57	52.30
Janus Fund	3	1.02	1	1,959.9	133.41	37.28
United: Income	1	0.68	5	1,894.9	99.54	33.69
Nicholas Fund	3	0.81	2	1,715.0	83.64	45.45
AIM Equity: Weingarten Eq	1	1.30	2	1,700.0	136.68	45.00
Del Gr Decatur: I	1	0.70	5	1,642.4	61.67	24.67
T. Row Price: Growth	3	0.76	2	1,576.8	62.28	30.90
Pioneer Fund	1	0.78	4	1,533.0	69.07	25.79
Merrill Basic Value: A	1	0.58	4	1,490.7	68.06	29.88
Fidelity Retirement Gr	3	0.98	1	1,454.4	91.58	35.71
IDS Stock	1	0.63	4	1,417.6	94.73	26.53
Shearson Appreciation	1	0.80	2	1,410.4	94.40	26.82
Oppenheimer Equ Income	1	0.79	5	1,392.6	71.36	16.82
Mass Investors Trust	1	0.47	4	1,384.3	99.85	28.10
Fidelity Capital Apprec	2	1.14	1	1,338.8	*	20.79
IDS New Dimensions	1	0.88	2	1,316.4	133.25	45.77
Fidelity Fund	3	0.66	4	1,256.9	84.07	28.06
Ge S & S Prgrm: Mutual Fund	3	0.21	2	1,192.9	80.79	32.16

Here, LOAD = 1 means sales charges > 4.5%,

       LOAD = 2 means sales charge 4.5% or less and

       LOAD = 3 means no sales charge.

Here, TYPE = 1 means capital appreciation,

       TYPE = 2 means growth oriented,

       TYPE = 3 means small company growth oriented,

       TYPE = 4 means growth and income oriented, and

       TYPE = 5 means equity income oriented.

Provide a point estimate of the mean expense ratio for this larger population. Give the corresponding 95% confidence interval for this estimate.

f. Use the assumptions of part (e). An investment manager is convinced that the true expense ratio has increased from the traditional level of 0.75%. Use the test of hypothesis machinery to decide formally whether the expense ratio of the larger population has stayed at 0.75% or has increased. Be sure to identify all the elements of the decision making process, including the significance level that you use.

C2_BOSS

2.28 In their May 11, 1992 issue, *Forbes* magazine provided their estimates of compensation for the chief executive officers (CEOs) of 50 large U.S. based corporations. In Table E2.28b are estimates of 1991 salary plus bonus (SALARY91) and 1991 total compensation (COMP91). The total compensation figure includes salary, bonuses, and other compensation devices such as stock options, pension contributions and so on. Dotplots and summary statistics can be found in Figure E2.28. Also given, in Table E2.28a, are summary measures for a variable called FRINGES, defined by FRINGES = 1 − SALARY91/COMP91. Interpret FRINGES to be the proportion of total compensation that is not attributable to salary and bonuses.

a. Use the summary statistics to cite the average 1991 Total compensation received by the 50 CEOs. Use this to calculate the sum of all (total) compensation received by the 50 CEOs.

b. Richard L. Gelb, CEO of Bristol-Meyers Squibb, was the top-paid CEO of the 50 companies in 1991. He received $12,788,000 in total compensation, about $9 million of which was from stock gains. Calculate the sum of all (total) compensation received by the remaining 49 executives. Calculate the average 1991 Total compensation of the remaining 49 CEOs.

c. This is a good group to belong to, but someone has to be at the bottom of the totem pole. This person turned out to be Laurence Tisch, CEO of Loews, who received $394,000 in total compensation in 1991. How many standard deviations below the mean is this?

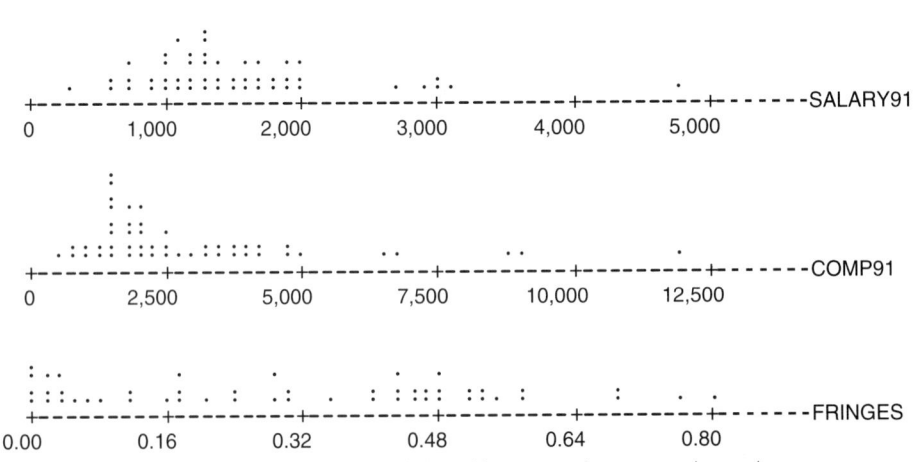

FIGURE E2.28 Dotplots of 1991 salary and bonus, total compensation and fringes. *Source: Forbes Magazine*

TABLE E2.28a Summary Statistics of 1991 Salary and Bonus, Total Compensation and Fringes

	Number	Mean	Median	Standard deviation	Minimum	Maximum	25th percentile	75th percentile
SALARY91	50	1,640	1,449	822	339	4,973	1,110	1,922
COMP91	50	3,038	2,166	2,429	394	12,788	1,551	3,886
FRINGES	50	0.3328	0.3259	0.2415	0.0000	0.8396	0.0807	0.5189

TABLE E2.28b Compensation for CEO'S of 50 Large U.S. Companies

Row	Company	Chief executive officer (CEO)	1991 salary + bonus (thousands of dollars)	1991 total compensation (thousands of dollars)
1	Bristol-Myers Squibb	Richard L. Gelb	2,051	12,788
2	Merrill Lynch	Daniel P. Tully	4,973	9,514
3	Exxon	Lawrence G. Rawl	1,813	9,358
4	RJR Nabisco	Louis V. Gerstner Jr	3,179	6,970
5	Anheuser-Busch Cos	August A. Busch III	1,879	6,685
6	General Electric	John F. Welch Jr	3,207	5,101
7	Mobil	Allen E. Murray	2,040	4,743
8	Coco-Cola	Roberto C. Goizueta	3,142	4,657
9	JP Morgan & Co	Dennis Weatherstone	2,060	4,133
10	ITT	Rand V. Araskog	2,800	4,129
11	Sara Lee	John H. Bryan	1,751	4,039
12	BankAmerica	Richard M. Rosenberg	1,600	4,016
13	Atlantic Richfield	Lodwrick M. Cook	1,674	3,842
14	Waste Management	Dean L. Buntrock	1,100	3,842
15	NationsBank	Hugh L. McColl Jr	2,000	3,538
16	Texaco	James W. Kinnear	1,667	3,415
17	Merc	P. Roy Vagelos	3,344	3,350
18	Hewlett-Packard	John A. Young	1,535	3,144
19	American Tel & Tel	Robert E. Allen	2,061	2,935
20	Bell Atlantic	Raymond W. Smith	1,453	2,776
21	Southwestern Bell	Edward E. Whitacre Jr	1,380	2,547
22	Sears, Roebuck	Edward A. Brennan	980	2,464
23	Joynson & Johnson	Ralph S. Larsen	1,253	2,417
24	Federal National Mortgage	James A. Johnson	1,080	2,353
25	Ameritech	William L. Weiss	1,270	2,227
26	Pacific Telesis Group	Sam Ginn	1,114	2,106
27	Procter & Gamble	Edwin L. Artzt	1,684	2,056
28	American Intl Group	Maurice R. Greenberg	1,950	1,950
29	PepsiCo	D. Wayne Calloway	1,912	1,916
30	GTE	Charles R. Lee	1,416	1,895
31	Chevron	Kenneth T. Derr	1,386	1,794
32	American Express	James D. Robinson III	1,625	1,781

(Table Continued)

(Table Continued)

Row	Company	Chief executive officer (CEO)	1991 salary + bonus (thousands of dollars)	1991 total compensation (thousands of dollars)
33	Philip Morris Cos	Michael A. Miles	1,777	1,777
34	Cigna	Wilson H. Taylor	1,342	1,646
35	Nynex	William C. Ferguson	1,215	1,639
36	Amoco	H Laurance Fuller	1,302	1,616
37	Xerox	Paul A. Allaire	1,083	1,608
38	Kmart	Joseph E. Antonini	1,546	1,577
39	Pacific Gas & Electric	Richard A. Clarke	1,444	1,471
40	US West	Richard D. McCormick	660	1,435
41	BellSouth	John L. Clendenin	1,356	1,403
42	El du Pont de Nemours	Edgar S. Woolard Jr	1,356	1,383
43	Minnesota Mining & Mfg	Livio D. DeSimone	685	1,381
44	Dow Chemical	Frank P. Popoff	1,069	1,331
45	Boeing	Frank A. Shrontz	1,188	1,228
46	Southern Co	Edward L. Addison	972	1,034
47	SCEcorp	John E. Bryson	810	938
48	Aetna Life & Casualty	Ronald E. Compton	779	809
49	Wal-Mart Stores	David D. Glass	710	747
50	Loews	Laurence A. Tisch	339	394

d. Suppose that, for the variable FRINGES, the sample is a reasonable approximation to a larger population of executives. Provide a 95% interval estimate of the population mean FRINGES amount.

e. Calculate a 95% prediction interval for the variable FRINGES. Discuss the value that you get for the lower bound of the interval. In particular, say whether you would quote this number to a consumer of your data analysis.

C2_STOCK

2.29 In their April, 1992 issue, *Forbes* magazine provided financial summary measures of 500 large U.S. based corporations. The companies listed are publicly traded U.S. based firms that are largest by sales, net profits, assets and market values. We consider below several of this financial variables for a sample of 50 of these firms. These variables include:

STKPRICE   stock price of a share as of December 31, 1991, in dollars
EPS   most recent earnings per share, in dollars
AS/SHARE   total assets per share, in dollars per share
NETPROF   1991 net profits, in millions of dollars
SALES   1991 sales, in millions of dollars
NETPRMRG   net profit margin, defined as net profits divided by sales

Attached are dotplots and summary statistics (Figure E2.29 and Table E2.29) for each variable. From the dotplot and summary statistics, you will see that for one company,

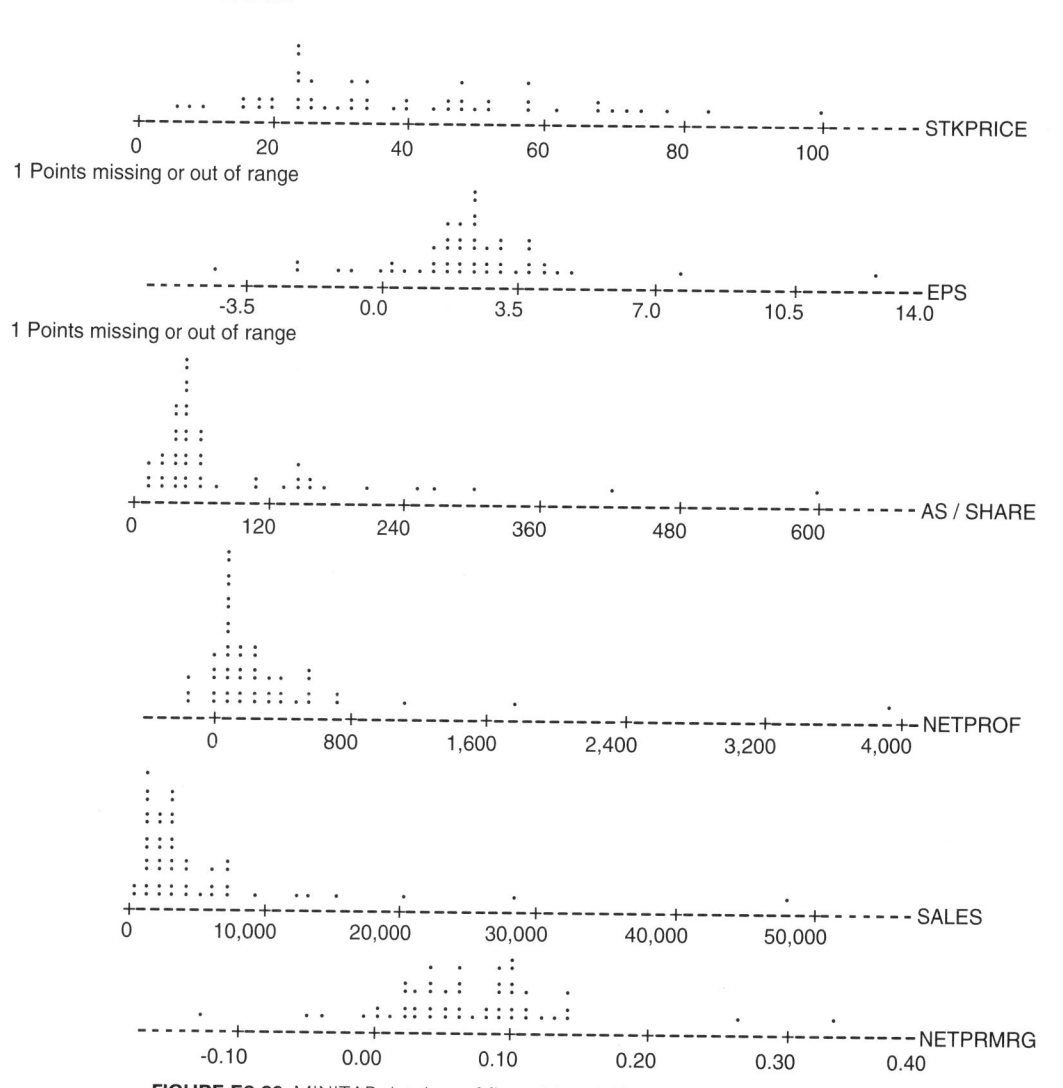

FIGURE E2.29 MINITAB dotplots of financial variables. *Source: Forbes Magazine*

TABLE E2.29 Summary Statistics of Financial Variables

	Number	Number missing	Mean	Median	Standard deviation	Minimum	Maximum	25th percentile	75th percentile
STKPRICE	50	0	40.21	33.87	21.39	5.12	100.50	23.97	53.75
EPS	49	1	2.338	2.370	2.480	−4.260	12.540	1.390	3.315
AS/SHARE	49	1	96.1	51.5	110.5	6.5	599.9	37.6	135.2
NETPROF	50	0	317.8	143.5	615.9	−186.9	3927.0	51.8	372.8
SALES	50	0	5,316	2,732	8,066	376	48,064	1,488	5,687
NETPRMRG	50	0	0.06379	0.06325	0.06483	−0.12671	0.33013	0.02750	0.09897

the Public Service of New Hampshire (PCNHQ), certain financial figures were not available from the *Forbes* publication.

a. Consider the earnings per share (EPS) variable.

    i. Using the table of summary statistics, identify the percentile that 3.315 is associated with.

    ii. Suppose that, for a larger population of firms, it is known that the mean EPS is $\mu = 3$ and the true standard deviation is $\sigma = 2.5$. Use a normal curve approximation to calculate the percentile associated with 3.315.

b. From Table E2.29, you observe that the average net profit margin is not equal to the average net profits divided by the average sales.

    i. Use x_i to denote the net profits for the *i*th firm and z_i to denote the sales for the *i*th firm. With this notation, write down the average net profit margin, the average net profits, and the average sales.

    ii. Explain why the average net profit margin is not equal to the average net profits divided by the average sales.

c. To understand the variability in earnings per share, suppose that you are interested in predicting EPS for a randomly selected company.

    i. Using the sample of 49 firms, identify the smallest and largest values of EPS from your sample of 49 firms.

    ii. Provide a 95% prediction interval for EPS.

d. An economist had hypothesized that the most recent earnings per share for 1991 would be 2.00. Based on your sample of 49 firms, does this seem to be a reasonable hypothesis? To respond to this question, test the null hypothesis that the expected value of EPS is 2.00 versus the alternative that it is not 2.00. State your null hypothesis, alternative hypothesis, and all components of the decision-making rule. Use a 5% level of significance.

Appendix

2.30 Follow the following steps to develop a formula to simplify the computation of $\sum_{i=1}^{n} (y_i - \bar{y})^2$.

a. Expand the square to get

$$\sum_{i=1}^{n} (y_i - \bar{y})^2 = \sum_{i=1}^{n} y_i^2 - 2 \sum_{i=1}^{n} y_i \bar{y} + \sum_{i=1}^{n} \bar{y}^2.$$

b. Show that

$$\sum_{i=1}^{n} y_i \bar{y} = n\bar{y}^2 \quad \text{and that} \quad \sum_{i=1}^{n} \bar{y}^2 = n\bar{y}^2.$$

c. Use parts (a) and (b) to confirm that

$$s_y^2 = \frac{\sum_{i=1}^{n} y_i^2 - n\bar{y}^2}{n - 1}.$$

2.31 Suppose that y may be only a 0 or 1, corresponding to a tail and a head in the flip of a coin. The probability of getting a head when the coin is flipped is $p = \text{Prob}(y = 1)$, which is a number between 0 and 1. Use the calculations in Section 2.3 to show:

a. that $\mu = E\, y = p$

b. that $\sigma^2 = \text{Var}\, y = p(1 - p)$

c. In the case that $p = 0.5$, the coin is said to be fair. Use the results of parts (a) and (b) to check that, for a fair coin, we have $\mu = 0.5$ and $\sigma = 0.5$.

3

Regression Using One Independent Variable

Chapter Objectives

To introduce regression analysis in the simplest context: relating a single independent variable to a dependent variable. To illustrate, we will consider relating:

- a buyer's earnings to the purchase price of a car,
- amount of experience to a pitcher's salary, and
- stock market returns to the returns of an individual stock.

Chapter Outline

This chapter considers regression in the case of only one independent variable. Despite this seeming simplicity, most of the deep ideas of regression can be developed in this framework. By limiting outselves to the one variable case, we will be able express most of the necessary calculations using simple algebra. This will allow us to develop our intuition about regression techniques by reinforcing it with simple calculations. Further, we will see how to illustrate the relationships between two variables graphically because we are working in only two dimensions. Graphical tools will prove to be important for developing a link between the data and a model to represent the data.

3.1 IDENTIFYING AND SUMMARIZING DATA

Statistical thinking, the process of actively using data to understand or solve a problem, begins with identifying the collection of entities of interest. There are generally several numerical characteristics that one could measure on any entity in the collection. In this chapter, we study two characteristics of an entity. By using two characteristics, we can discuss their relationship and whether one can be used to explain the other.

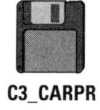

C3_CARPR

Suppose that you are the sales manager of a Ford dealership and that you wish to understand the relationship between personal characteristics of car buyers and expenditure on a new car. Understanding this relationship would aid the sales force in identifying target markets for automobiles in various price ranges and would aid the dealership management in establishing inventory levels. As sales manager, you have available a sample, taken over the months of September and October, 1990, of accepted credit applications for financing of new car purchases. Although there are alternative means of financing a new car purchase, such as cash payments and bank loans, sales through credit applications is an important part of the domestic automobile industry.

For the Ford dealership sales manager, the collection of entities of interest is the population of people that have applied for credit to purchase a new automobile and have had their credit application accepted. The sample consists of individuals whose applications were accepted in September and October, 1990. There are many quantitative measurements that could be taken for each individual; for example, their height, weight, time in a 40 yard dash, and so on. However, we are particularly interested in characteristics that may be related to the price of the automobile purchase. It turns out, for this example, that the applicant's income is the most relevant. (In Chapter 4, we will discuss techniques for handling the effects of additional personal characteristics including the applicant's sex, education level, marital status and size of the family.)

An observation represents the information collected from a single entity even though it consists of two numbers.

Having identified each variable of interest, we now attach labels to each variable. Use y to represent the purchase price variable and x to represent the income variable. In this sample, there are 62 applicants. We use subscripts to identify each applicant. For example, $y_1 = 7,200$ is the purchase price for the first applicant in the sample who has income $x_1 = 15,000$. Call the ordered pair $(x_1, y_1) = (15,000, 7,200)$ the first *observation*. This observation represents the information collected from a single individual even though it consists of two numbers. Extending this notation, the entire sample containing 62 observations may be represented by $(x_1, y_1), (x_2, y_2), \ldots, (x_{62}, y_{62})$. Recall that the ellipses $(\ldots)$ mean that the pattern is continued until the final object is encountered. We will often speak of a generic member of the sample. To do this, we refer to (x_i, y_i) as the ith observation.

For cross-sectional observations, there is no natural ordering of the data.

Table 3.1 lists the sample. The data are arranged so that the income variable is in increasing order. However, recall that for cross-sectional data, there

TABLE 3.1　Purchase Price and Income (Data are Listed in Hundreds of Dollars)

i	x_i INCOME	y_i PRICE	i	x_i INCOME	y_i PRICE	i	x_i INCOME	y_i PRICE	i	x_i INCOME	y_i PRICE
1	150	72	16	300	110	31	400	148	47	560	167
2	165	105	17	320	146	32	419	136	48	610	185
3	168	78	18	330	118	33	420	180	49	610	189
4	180	140	19	330	140	34	438	152	50	625	188
5	210	132	20	335	128	35	440	145	51	630	148
6	230	150	21	335	130	36	440	189	52	650	185
7	235	110	22	335	127	37	440	98	53	650	218
8	235	112	23	336	104	38	450	185	54	710	160
9	248	84	24	340	120	39	460	145	55	710	240
10	250	75	25	350	120	40	478	167	56	750	280
11	265	115	26	350	108	41	480	162	57	810	225
12	270	130	27	360	145	42	520	210	58	819	218
13	270	109	28	370	126	43	520	145	59	859	260
14	280	75	29	390	155	44	520	186	60	938	268
15	280	109	30	400	136	45	530	152	61	960	225
						46	540	164	62	1,020	230

is no natural ordering in the observations. Often you will find that data analysts sort various aspects of the data to make them appear more organized. There is nothing magic about sorting by increasing income. One could also sort the data by decreasing income or by purchase price. The important point is that the models and statistics for cross-sectional data do not rely on the order in which the observations are presented.

Recall from Chapter 2 that we begin to understand the data set by working with each variable separately. As Figure 3.1 shows, dotplots give a quick visual impression of each variable's distribution in isolation of the other. Further, as Table 3.2 shows, basic summary statistics give useful ideas of the structure of key features of the data. After we understand the information in each variable in isolation of the other, we can begin exploring the *relationship* between the two variables.

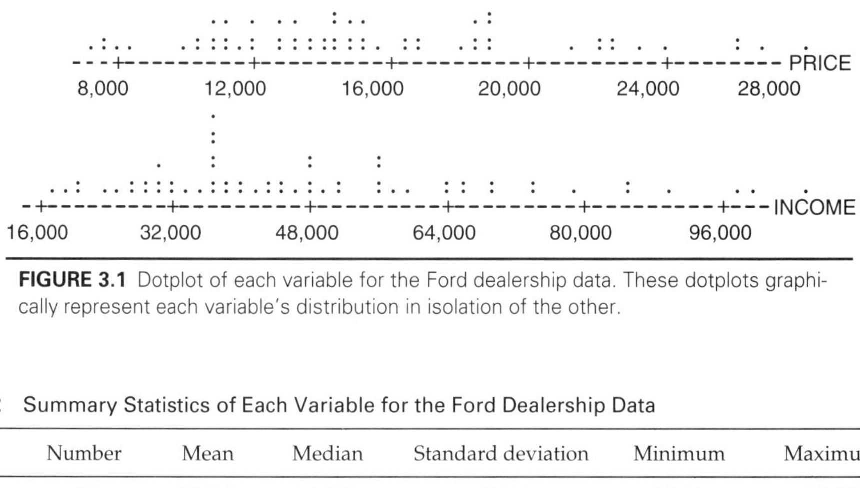

FIGURE 3.1 Dotplot of each variable for the Ford dealership data. These dotplots graphically represent each variable's distribution in isolation of the other.

TABLE 3.2 Summary Statistics of Each Variable for the Ford Dealership Data

	Number	Mean	Median	Standard deviation	Minimum	Maximum
PRICE	62	15,416	14,500	5,040	7,200	28,000
INCOME	62	45,190	40,950	20,873	15,000	102,000

Scatter Plot—A Basic Graphical Tool

We use a scatter plot as the basic graphical tool to investigate the relationship between the two variables.

The basic graphical tool used to investigate the relationship between the two variables is a *scatter plot.* Figure 3.2 graphically represents the data presented in Table 3.1. In this figure, there are sixty-two plotting symbols, each corresponding to an observation. For each symbol, we can approximate the purchase price and income by reading the values from the horizontal and vertical scales. For example, in Figure 3.3 the 56th observation is marked.

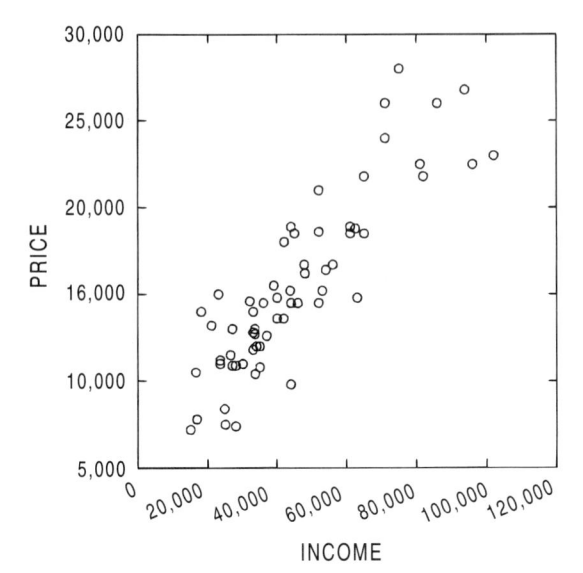

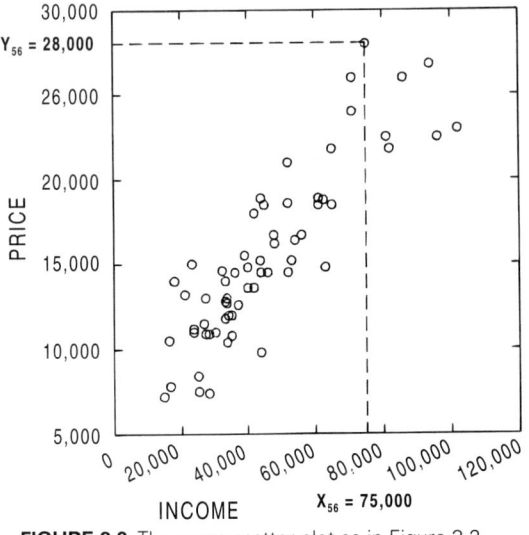

FIGURE 3.2 A scatter plot of the Ford dealership data. Each of the 62 plotting symbols corresponds to an individual in the study.

FIGURE 3.3 The same scatter plot as in Figure 3.2, with the 56th observation highlighted. This individual has an income of $75,000 and purchased a car priced at $28,000.

By graphing data we lose the exact values of the observations. What we gain is a visual impression of the relationship between purchase price and income.

Although we may lose the exact values of the observations in graphing data, we gain a visual impression of the relationship between purchase price and income. From Figure 3.2 we see that applicants with higher incomes tend to purchase more expensive cars. How strong is their relationship? Can knowledge of someone's income help us anticipate the price of a car that an applicant is interested in? We explore these two questions in the following.

Correlation Coefficient—A Basic Summary Statistic

The (ordinary) correlation statistic is a measure of the linear relationship between two variables.

One way to summarize the strength of the relationship between two variables is through a *correlation* statistic. The most useful correlation statistic is the *ordinary*, or *Pearson, correlation coefficient*. It is a measure of the linear relationship between two variables. This correlation coefficient is calculated in the following three steps.

1. Consider the first observation that is highlighted with a bold plotting symbol in Figure 3.4. From Table 3.1, we know that the income associated with the first observation, $x_1 = 15,000$, is less than the average income, $\bar{x} = 45,190$. Similarly, the purchase price corresponding to the first observation, $y_1 = 7,200$, is less than the average, $\bar{y} = 15,416$. Hence, both deviations from the means, $(x_1 - \bar{x})$ and $(y_1 - \bar{y})$, are negative. Thus, the cross-product of deviations, $(x_1 - \bar{x})(y_1 - \bar{y})$, is positive.

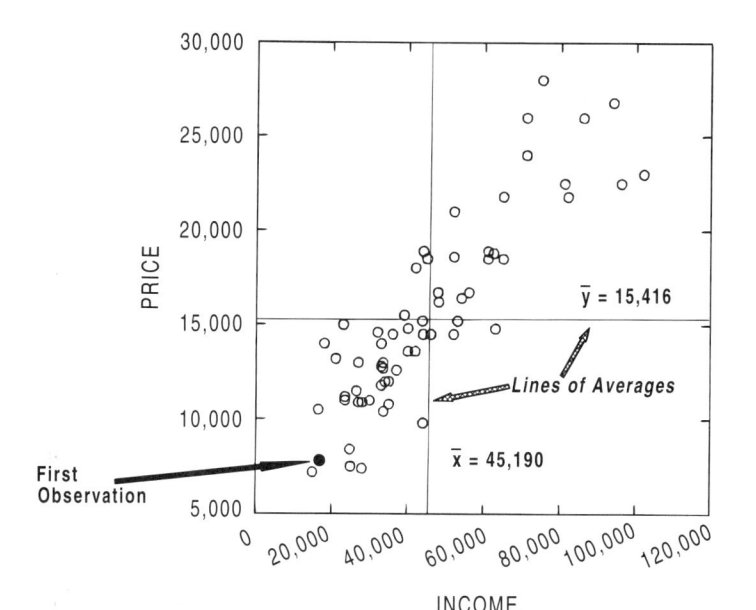

FIGURE 3.4 The same scatter plot as in Figure 3.2, with lines of averages superimposed. These lines of averages help us to visualize the relationship between income and price.

2. For each observation in the lower left hand quadrant of Figure 3.4, the product $(x_i - \bar{x})(y_i - \bar{y})$ is positive, just as with the first observation. The idea is that small values of x_i (small compared to $\bar{x}$) tend to imply small values of y_i (small compared to $\bar{y}$). Similarly, for each observation in the upper right hand quadrant, the product $(x_i - \bar{x})(y_i - \bar{y})$ is positive. For these points, large values of x_i imply large values of y_i. If an observation is either in the upper left or lower right hand quadrants, then the product $(x_i - \bar{x})(y_i - \bar{y})$ is negative. To see whether the entire data set has a tendency to be in the lower left/upper right or the upper left/lower right quadrant, we sum over the cross-products of deviations. In Figure 3.4, a visual inspection of the data tells us that lower incomes tend to imply a lower purchase price and higher incomes tend to imply a higher purchase price. Not surprisingly, when we compute the sum *of cross-products of deviations,*

$$\sum_{i=1}^{n} (x_i - \bar{x})(y_i - \bar{y}),$$

this sum turns out to be positive. This indicates that most points are in the lower left and upper right hand quadrants.

3. The larger the sum of cross-products of deviations, the greater is the tendency for the points to be in the lower left and upper right hand quad-

rants. How large is large? Unfortunately, the answer to this question depends on the units that y and x are measured in, such as dollars, hundreds of dollars, and so on. In order to compare this sum among different data sets, we standardize it by (i) dividing by a correction for the number of observations and (ii) dividing by corrections for scatter, or variation. With the goal of determining a standardized measure, we define the ordinary correlation coefficient as

$$r = \frac{\sum_{i=1}^{n} (x_i - \bar{x})(y_i - \bar{y})}{(n-1)s_x s_y} . \tag{3.1}$$

Here, as in equation (2.4), $s_y^2 = (n-1)^{-1} \sum_{i=1}^{n} (y_i - \bar{y})^2$ and similarly for $s_x^2 = (n-1)^{-1} \sum_{i=1}^{n} (x_i - \bar{x})^2$. These are measures of *scatter* of y snd x, respectively. The standard deviations, s_y and s_x, are defined by taking positive square roots. The reasoning for division by $n-1$ in lieu of n was described in Section 2.4 on sampling. The motivation is that we don't really care what the averages are because all the calculations are done in terms of deviations from the average. Thus, we lose one "degree of freedom."

If the correlation statistic, r, is positive, the variables are said to be (positively) correlated.

Although there are other correlation statistics, the correlation coefficient in equation (3.1) that was devised by Pearson (1895) has several desirable properties. One of the most important properties is that, for any data set, r is bounded by -1 and 1, that is, $-1 \le r \le 1$. If r is greater than zero, the variables are said to be *positively correlated*. If r is less than zero, the variables are said to be *negatively correlated*. The larger the coefficient is in absolute value, the stronger is the relationship. In fact, if $r = 1$, then the variables are perfectly correlated. Thus, all of the data lie on a straight line that goes through the lower left and upper right hand quadrants. If $r = -1$, then all of the data lie on a line that goes through the upper left and lower right hand quadrants. The coefficient r is a measure of linear relationship between variables.

The correlation statistic is unaffected by scale and location changes of either, or both, variables.

The correlation coefficient is *location* and *scale invariant*. Thus, each variable's center of location does not matter in the calculation of r. For example, if we add \$1,000 to the purchase price of each car, each y_i will increase by 1,000. However, $\bar{y}$, the average purchase price will also increase by 1,000 so that the deviation $y_i - \bar{y}$ remains unchanged, or *invariant*. Further, the scale of each variable does not matter in the calculation of r. For example, suppose we divide each income by 100 so that x_i now represents income in hundreds of dollars, as listed in Table 3.1. Thus, $\bar{x}$ is also divided by 100 and you should check that s_x is also divided by 100. Thus, the *standardized version* of x_i, $(x_i - \bar{x})/s_x$, remains unchanged, or invariant. Many statistical packages compute a standardized version of a variable by subtracting the average and dividing by the standard deviation. Now, let's use $y_i^* = (y_i - \bar{y})/s_y$ and $x_i^* = (x_i - \bar{x})/s_x$ to be the standardized versions of y_i and x_i, respectively. Thus, we can express the correlation coefficient as

$$r = \frac{\sum_{i=1}^{n} x_i^* y_i^*}{n-1} .$$

Because the correlation coefficient does not depend on units of measure, it is a statistic that can readily be compared across different data sets.

     The correlation coefficient is said to be a *dimensionless measure*. This is because we have taken away dollars, and all other units of measures, by considering the standardized variables x_i^* and y_i^*. Because the correlation coefficient does not depend on units of measure, it is a statistic that can readily be compared across different data sets.

     In the world of business, the term "correlation" is often used as synonymous with the term "relationship." For the purposes of this text, we use the term correlation when referring only to *linear* relationships. The classic nonlinear relationship is $y = x^2$, a *quadratic* relationship. Consider this relationship and the fictitious data set for x, $\{-2\ 1\ 0\ 1\ 2\}$. Now, as an exercise, produce a rough graph of the data set:

i	1	2	3	4	5
x_i	-2	-1	0	1	2
y_i	4	1	0	1	4

The correlation coefficient for this data set turns out to be $r = 0$ (check this). Thus, despite the fact that there is a perfect relationship between x and $y\ (= x^2)$, there is a zero correlation between x and y. Recall that location and scale changes are not relevant in correlation discussions, so we could easily change the values of x and y to be more representative of a business data set.

Correlation coefficients take up less space to report than a scatter plot. Scatter plots help us understand the strength of association between variables as well as other aspects of the data.

     It is useful to develop a sense of the relationship between the graphical representation and its corresponding correlation coefficient. Figure 3.5 shows scatter plots of several fictitious data sets with their corresponding correlation coefficients. Correlation coefficients take up less space to report than a scatter plot and are often the primary statistic of interest. Scatter plots provide information about the strength of association between variables. Further, scatter plots help us understand other aspects of the data, such as the range, and also provide indications of nonlinear relationships between variables.

     How strong is the relationship between income and purchase price? Graphically, the response is a scatter plot, as in Figure 3.2. Numerically, the main response is the correlation coefficient which turns out to be $r = 0.875$ for this data set. We interpret this statistic by saying that Price and Income are (positively) correlated. The strength of the relationship is strong because $r = 0.875$ is close to one. Thus, we may describe this relationship by saying that there is a strong correlation between INCOME and PRICE.

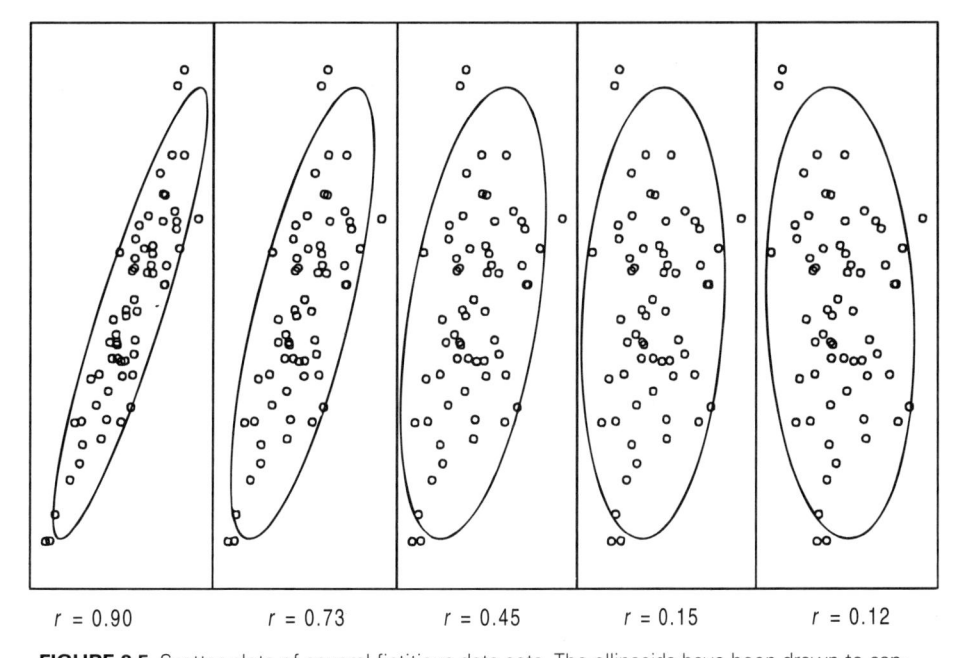

r = 0.90   r = 0.73   r = 0.45   r = 0.15   r = 0.12

FIGURE 3.5 Scatter plots of several fictitious data sets. The ellipsoids have been drawn to capture the broad tendencies of the data.

Fitting with an Independent Variable

Identify one variable to be the response, or dependent, variable and the other variable to be the explanatory, or independent, variable.

Now we begin to explore the question, "Can knowledge of income help us understand purchase price?" To respond to this question, we identify purchase price as the *response,* or *dependent,* variable. The income variable, which is used to help understand price, is called the *explanatory,* or *independent,* variable.

Suppose that we have available the 62 purchase prices (y_i) and your job is to predict the purchase price of a randomly selected individual. Without knowledge of the income variable, from Section 2.6 the best predictor is simply $\bar{y} = 15{,}416$, the average of the available sample. If however, you also have knowledge of income, then can this estimate be improved? If so, then by how much?

We begin this line of thought by supposing that you have imprecise, but still some, knowledge of income. For example, suppose that income is known to be between 80,000 and 100,000. From Figure 3.6, we see that there are five individuals in this income range. It turns out that the average purchase price of these five is 23,900 (get out your calculator and check this using Table 3.1). Not surprisingly, for a higher income category our new prediction (23,900) is higher than for the overall sample. As another example, suppose that you know that income is between 20,000 and 40,000. Again, in Figure 3.6 there are

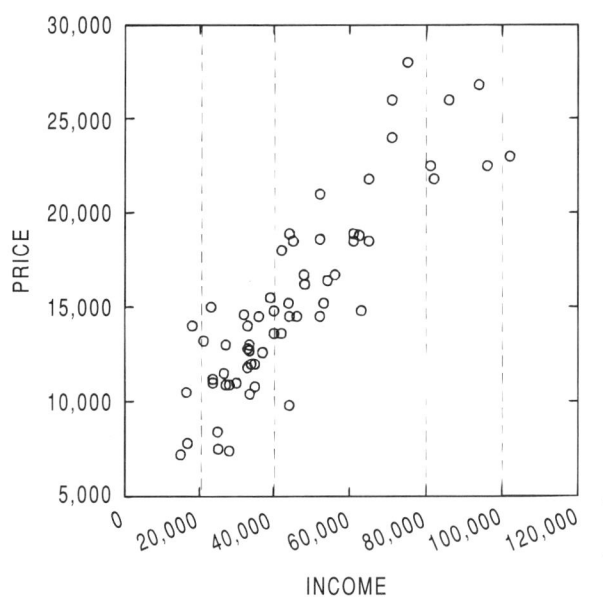

FIGURE 3.6 The same scatter plot as in Figure 3.2, with two sets of lines superimposed that help group the data based on income. For the five individuals with income in the 80,000–100,000 range, the average purchase price is $23,900. For the 24 individuals with income in the 20,000–40,000 range, the average purchase price is $11,908.

two superimposed vertical lines that separate the 24 individuals in that income range. In this income range, the average is 11,908. For a lower income range, our prediction is lower than the prediction for the overall average.

Suppose now that a new customer comes in with an income of 80,000 and we would like to predict the purchase price for this customer. In our available sample of 62, no customer has an income of 80,000. One customer, the 57th one, has an income of 81,000 ($= x_{57}$). This is the closest and we might use the corresponding purchase price ($22,500 = y_{57}$) as our predictor. However, we might also use the average of the two observations with incomes above and below 80,000 or perhaps all observations with incomes in the 75,000 to 85,000 range. Using only one, or a few, nearby observations leaves us susceptible to the large variation in estimators that are based on a limited number of observations.

So that our predictions are not overly determined by one or two observations, we now fit a line using the entire data set. The estimate can then be computed to be the height of the line at an income of $80,000. The idea is that by fitting a line to the data set we use the information in all 62 of our observations. To implement this idea, let's first review the technical details of a line.

Defining a Line

One way to define a line is by connecting two non-identical points.

There are three ways of defining a line that are useful in statistics. The first is from geometry where we learned that by connecting two observations (that are not the same), we define a line. Occasionally, more than two observations fall on a line and are said to be *collinear*. In general, however, it is not possible to fit a single line to more than two observations, as is the case in Figure 3.1 with 62 observations. This gives rise to the natural question, "Where do we put the line?", that will be addressed in the following subsection.

The second way of defining a line is through an algebraic equation such as

$$y = b_0 + b_1 x.$$

A line may also be defined as the vertical height (y) equals the intercept (b₀) plus the slope (b₁) times the horizontal distance (x).

Figure 3.7 graphically presents this line. The quantity b_0 is the *intercept,* the value of y when x is zero. Often there is no useful interpretation of this number because we are not usually concerned with purchase price of a car for an individual who submits a credit application having zero income! The intercept may be positive, negative or zero. It serves to set the height of the line. The quantity b_1 is the *slope,* the "rise over the run" or the change in y per unit change in x. The slope may be positive, negative or zero. See Figure 3.8 for examples of lines with different intercepts and slopes. For example, the line $y = 15,000 + 0.15x$ has slope $b_1 = 0.15$. For this line, if income goes up by 10,000, then price increases by $(10,000)(b_1) = 1,500$. It makes no difference if income goes from 20,000 to 30,000 or 80,000 to 90,000, the increase in price is still 1,500. The appealing property of a line is that this ratio of changes does not depend on the value of x.

The third way of defining a line is by specifying a point and a slope. We pursue this idea further below.

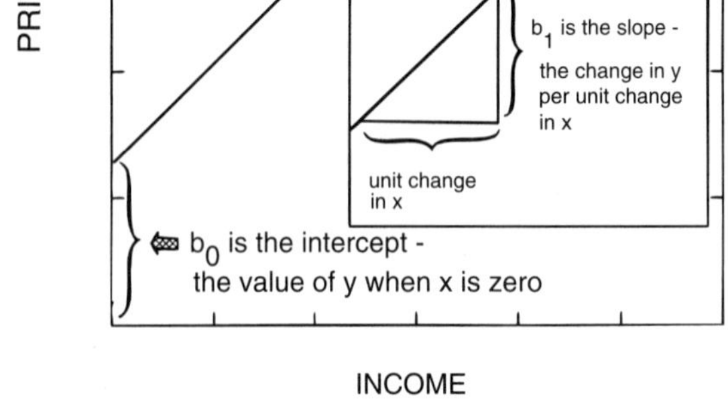

FIGURE 3.7 A geometric interpretation of a line.

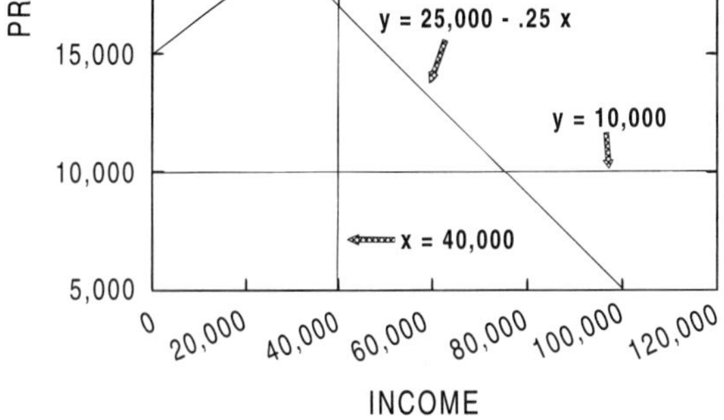

FIGURE 3.8 Here are examples of several lines.

Method of Least Squares

The regression line is fit to the observations using the method of least squares.

To fit a line to our data set, we use a technique called the *method of least squares.* We need a general technique so that, if different analysts agree on the data and agree on the fitting technique, then they will agree on the line. When different analysts fit a data set using an eyeball approximation, in general they will arrive at different lines, even using the same data set.

The process of producing a line using the method of least squares can be described in three steps:

1. Start with the line, $y = b_0^* + b_1^* x$, where the intercept and slope, b_0^* and b_1^*, are merely generic values. Because we have not yet picked b_0^* and b_1^* to satisfy any kind of criteria, call this our "candidate" line. Such a line might appear as in Figure 3.9.

2. Consider the *i*th observation, (x_i, y_i), a generic point in the data set. For this observation, the height of the candidate line is $b_0^* + b_1^* x_i$. Using this candidate line and knowledge of x_i, our prediction of y_i is $b_0^* + b_1^* x_i$. The quantity

$$y_i - (b_0^* + b_1^* x_i)$$

represents the deviation of the actual observation from the height of the candidate line. In Figure 3.10, a line segment connects each observation

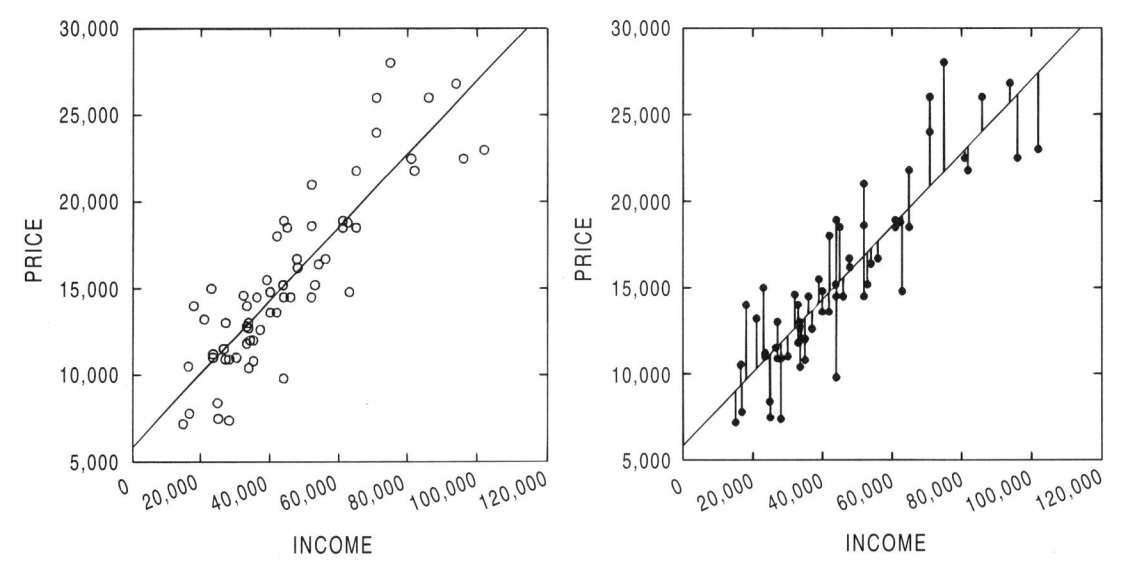

FIGURE 3.9 The same scatter plot as in Figure 3.2, with the regression line superimposed. The equation of this line is $\hat{y} = 5{,}881 + 0.211x$.

FIGURE 3.10 The vertical distance from each observation to the regression line is marked.

with the height of the line at each level of x. The length of the line segment is the size of the deviation. If the observation is below the line, the deviation is negative. If the observation is above the line, the deviation is positive.

3. The quantity

$$SS(b_0^*, b_1^*) = \sum_{i=1}^{n} (y_i - (b_0^* + b_1^* x_i))^2$$

represents the sum of squared deviations for the candidate line specified by the intercept b_0^* and slope b_1^*. With this quantity, we summarize the distances from the line to each observation. The *least squares method* of determining a fitted regression line is simply to determine the values of b_0^* and b_1^* that minimize $SS(b_0^*, b_1^*)$ for the intercept and slope. This is an easy problem that can be solved using either calculus or other analytic techniques.

The least squares estimates of the slope and intercept are, respectively, $b_1 = r\, s_y/s_x$ and $b_0 = \bar{y} - b_1 \bar{x}$.

The method of least squares produces the estimates

$$b_1 = r\, \frac{s_y}{s_x} \quad \text{and} \quad b_0 = \bar{y} - b_1 \bar{x}. \tag{3.2}$$

Recall from equation (2.4) that s_y is defined as $s_y^2 = (n-1)^{-1}\sum_{i=1}^{n}(y_i - \bar{y})^2$, and similarly s_x. We have dropped the asterisk, or star, notation because b_0 and b_1 are no longer "candidate" values for the slope and intercept. The quantities b_0 and b_1 are called the *least squares intercept* and *slope estimates.* The line that they determine, $\hat{y} = b_0 + b_1 x$, is called the *estimated,* or *fitted, regression line.*

The regression line is defined by $\hat{y} = b_0 + b_1 x$.

Does this procedure yield a sensible line for our Ford dealership sales manager? From the basic summary statistics in Table 3.2, we have $s_y = 5,040$ and $s_x = 20,873$. Earlier we computed $r = 0.875$. Together, these yield

$$b_1 = (0.875)(5,040/20,873) = 0.211.$$

With $\bar{y} = 15,416$ and $\bar{x} = 45,190$, we have

$$b_0 = 15,416 - (0.211)45,190 = 5,881.$$

This yields the fitted regression line

$$\hat{y} = 5,881 + 0.211x.$$

The carat, or "hat," on top of the y reminds us that this y, or PRICE, is an estimated value. One application of the regression line is to estimate a purchase price for a specific income say, $x = 80,000$. The estimate is the height of the regression line at this value of x, which is $5,881 + (0.211)(80,000) = 22,761$.

3.2 BASIC LINEAR REGRESSION MODEL

In the linear regression model with one variable, the expected response is a linear function of the independent variable, that is, E y = β₀ + β₁ x. The observed response is a linear function of the independent variable plus a random error term.

The Chapter 2 model assumed that the expected value of the response is the mean, that is, $E\,y = \mu$. In this chapter, we use the additional knowledge from an independent variable x and assume that the expected value of the response is a linear function of x. That is, we assume

$$E\,y = \beta_0 + \beta_1 x.$$

The intercept and slope quantities, β_0 and β_1, are the unknown parameters that determine the line. Recall from Chapter 2 that, as a notation convention, Greek letters such as σ and β (beta) are used to specify unknown parameters of the model and the corresponding roman letters such as s and b are meant to represent statistics calculated from the data.

When introducing the concept of random error in Section 2.8, we represented each response as a mean plus a random deviation from the mean, that is, $y_i = \mu + e_i$. Replacing the constant mean μ by the linear function of x, we define the *basic linear regression model* as:

$$y_i = \beta_0 + \beta_1 x_i + e_i, \qquad i = 1, ..., n. \tag{3.3}$$

Again, this shorthand notation for the n equations:

$$y_1 = \beta_0 + \beta_1 x_1 + e_1$$
$$y_2 = \beta_0 + \beta_1 x_2 + e_2$$
$$. \; . \; .$$
$$. \; . \; .$$
$$. \; . \; .$$
$$y_n = \beta_0 + \beta_1 x_n + e_n.$$

The quantity e_i is the random deviation, or error, of the ith response y_i from the height of the line at x_i. We assume the random errors $\{e_1, e_2, ..., e_n\}$ form a random sample from an unknown universe of errors.

Figure 3.11 illustrates some of the assumptions of the basic linear regression model. The data (x_1, y_1), (x_2, y_2) and (x_3, y_3) are observed and are represented by the circular opaque plotting symbols. According to the model, these observations should be close to the regression line $E\,y = \beta_0 + \beta_1 x$. Each deviation from the line is random. We will often assume that the distribution of deviations may be represented by a normal curve, as in Figure 3.11.

Because errors are assumed to be drawn from a common distribution, in Figure 3.11 we see that the shape of each curve is the same. In particular, the errors have common expected value zero and common variance σ^2. Because the model is

response = nonrandom regression line + random error,

the variance of each response is equal to σ^2, which is the variance of each error. In particular, under the basic model, the assumption is that the responses

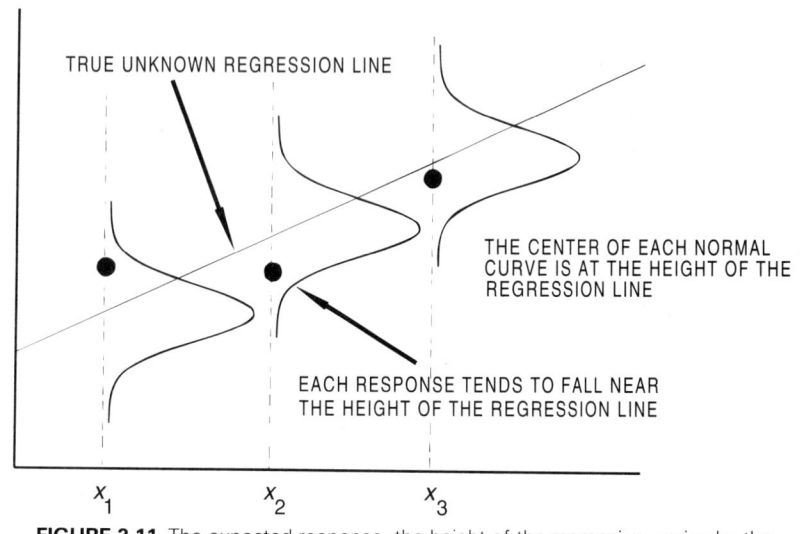

TRUE UNKNOWN REGRESSION LINE

THE CENTER OF EACH NORMAL CURVE IS AT THE HEIGHT OF THE REGRESSION LINE

EACH RESPONSE TENDS TO FALL NEAR THE HEIGHT OF THE REGRESSION LINE

x_1 x_2 x_3

FIGURE 3.11 The expected response, the height of the regression, varies by the level of the independent variable. The distribution of deviations from the line is common to all observations.

are *homoscedastic*, that is, of the "same scatter." An important model violation that we will address in Chapter 6 is the case where different observations appear to have a different amount of variability. This type of data set is called *heteroscedastic*, for "different scatter."

The basic linear regression model, specified by equation (3.3) and the random sampling assumption on the errors, provides a representation for a population of data. Table 3.3 highlights the idea that this population can be summarized by the parameters β_0, β_1 and σ^2. In Section 3.1, we discussed ways of summarizing data from a sample. In particular, we introduced the statistics b_0 and b_1 that correspond to the parameters β_0 and β_1. In Section 3.3, we will introduce s^2, the statistic corresponding to the parameter σ^2.

The Table 3.3 statistics are point estimates of the corresponding parameters and can be interpreted as such. To illustrate, consider our Section 3.1 car price example where the fitted regression line is $\hat{y} = 5{,}881 + 0.211x$, with $\hat{y}$ as the fitted price paid for a car and x as an individual's annual income. From the

TABLE 3.3 Summary Measures of the Population and Sample

| Data | Summary measures | Regression line | | Variance |
		Intercept	Slope	
Population	Parameters	β_0	β_1	σ^2
Sample	Statistics	b_0	b_1	s^2

equation $E\,y = \beta_0 + \beta_1 x$, the parameter β_1 can be interpreted as the expected change in y per unit change in x. Thus, to interpret $b_1 = 0.211$, consider comparing two customers. If the customers are similar except that one earns \$1 more in income, then we expect that customer to spend an additional \$0.211 for the purchase of a car. By the linearity of the regression equation, if one customer earns \$1,000 more than another, then we expect the customer to spend an additional \$211 on the purchase.

This interpretation is not meant to suggest a cause and effect relationship. It merely states that, when comparing two customers, on average the parameter β_1 will capture differences in spending due to income. The statistic b_1 is our estimate of this effect. Statistics as a discipline may be used to confirm cause and effect relationships, such as the introduction of a drug to reduce mortality due to an infectious disease such as AIDS. However, statistics by itself can only establish relationships between variables, not the causal nature of the relationship.

3.3 IS THE MODEL USEFUL? SOME BASIC SUMMARY MEASURES

Although statistics is the science of summarizing data, it is also the art of arguing with data. In this section, we develop with some of the basic arguments used to justify the basic linear regression model. To illustrate these justifications, we continue to examine the usefulness of income in understanding purchase price for our auto price example. The graphs in Section 3.1 provide strong evidence that income does influence purchase price. Developing numerical evidence will enable us to quantify the strength of the relationship. Further, numerical evidence will be useful when we consider other data sets where the graphical evidence is not so compelling.

Partitioning the Variability

Interpret the Total Sum of Squares, Total SS, to be the total variation in the response. In Chapter 2, we argued that squared deviations, $(y_i - \bar{y})^2$, provide us with a measure of the spread of the data. The idea is that, if we have to estimate the ith observation, then $\bar{y}$ is an appropriate estimate and $y_i - \bar{y}$ represents the deviation of the estimate. In this section, it is convenient not to standardize by the number of observations and thus we define

$$\text{Total SS} = \sum_{i=1}^{n} (y_i - \bar{y})^2.$$

The notation Total SS stands for the *total sum of squares*, or the total variation in the response.

Suppose now that we also have knowledge of x, an independent variable. From the data set we can compute $\hat{y} = b_0 + b_1 x$, the estimated regression line.

Using the estimated regression line, for each observation we can compute the corresponding *fitted value*,

$$\hat{y}_i = b_0 + b_1 x_i.$$

The fitted value is our estimate *with knowledge of the independent variable.* As before, the difference between the response and the fitted value, $y_i - \hat{y}_i$, represents the deviation of this estimate. We now have two "estimates" of y_i, $\hat{y}_i$ and $\bar{y}$. Presumably, if the regression line is useful, then $\hat{y}_i$ is a more accurate measure than $\bar{y}$. To judge this usefulness, we algebraically decompose the total deviation as:

$$y_i - \bar{y} \quad = \quad y_i - \hat{y}_i \quad + \quad \hat{y}_i - \bar{y}. \tag{3.4}$$
$$\textit{total deviation} = \textit{unexplained} + \textit{explained}$$
$$\textit{deviation} \qquad \textit{deviation}$$

Interpret this equation as "the deviation without knowledge of the independent variable equals the deviation with knowledge of the independent variable plus the deviation explained by the independent variable." Figure 3.12 is a geometric display of this decomposition. In the figure, an observation

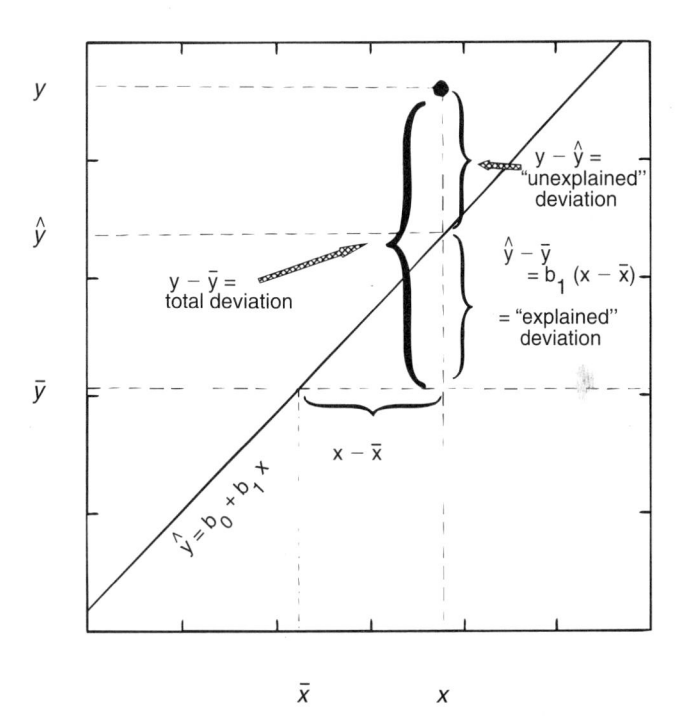

FIGURE 3.12 Geometric display of the deviation decomposition. The total deviation equals the unexplained deviation plus the deviation explained by the regression line.

above the line was chosen, yielding a positive deviation from the fitted regression line, to make the graph easier to read. A good exercise is to draw a rough sketch corresponding to Figure 3.12 with an observation below the fitted regression line.

Now, from the algebraic decomposition in equation (3.4), square each side of the equation and sum over all observations. After a little algebraic manipulation, this yields

$$\sum_{i=1}^{n} (y_i - \bar{y})^2 = \sum_{i=1}^{n} (y_i - \hat{y}_i)^2 + \sum_{i=1}^{n} (\hat{y}_i - \bar{y})^2.$$

We rewrite this as

$$\text{Total SS} = \text{Error SS} + \text{Regression SS}$$

where SS stands for sum of squares. We interpret:

1. Total SS as the total variation without knowledge of x,
2. Error SS as the total variation remaining after the introduction of x, and
3. Regression SS as the difference between the Total SS and Error SS, or the total variation "explained" through knowledge of x.

When squaring the right hand side of the deviation decomposition, we have the cross-product term $2(y_i - \hat{y}_i)(\hat{y}_i - \bar{y})$. With the "algebraic manipulation," one can check that the sum of the cross-products over all observations is zero. This result is not true for all fitted lines but is a special property of the least-squares fitted line.

Interpret the coefficient of determination, R^2, to be the proportion of variability explained by the regression line.

In many instances, the variability decomposition is reported through only a single statistic, the *coefficient of determination*. The coefficient of determination is denoted by the symbol R^2, called "R-square" and defined as

$$R^2 = \frac{\text{Regression SS}}{\text{Total SS}}.$$

We interpret R^2 to be the proportion of variability explained by the regression line. In one extreme case where the regression line fits the data perfectly, we have Error SS = 0 and $R^2 = 1$. In the other extreme case where the regression line provides no information about the response, we have Regression SS = 0 and $R^2 = 0$.

The Typical Error: *s*

Understanding the size of deviations is an important aspect of partitioning the variability. Here, we clarify some aspects of deviations and their many properties.

In the basic linear regression model, we assume the existence of a random error,

$$e_i = y_i - (\beta_0 + \beta_1 x_i).$$

The (unobserved) random error is the response minus the height of the true regression line. The (observed) residual is the response minus the height of the estimated regression line.

Although y_i and x_i are observed, the parameters β_0 and β_1 are not. Thus, although we assume various properties of e_i, such as being unrelated to one another, the errors themselves are not observed. We can, however, calculate an "estimated error" called a *residual*. The residual, $\hat{e}_i$, is defined as the response minus the corresponding fitted value:

$$\hat{e}_i = y_i - \hat{y}_i.$$

As with fitted values, the carat, or "hat," on top of e_i reminds us that this is an estimate of an unobserved quantity.

The residual, $\hat{e}_i$, should be close to the true error, e_i. The idea here is that, if b_0 and b_1 are close to β_0 and β_1, respectively, then

$$\hat{e}_i = y_i - (b_0 + b_1 x_i)$$

is close to

$$y_i - (\beta_0 + \beta_1 x_i) = e_i.$$

Thus, if the fitted regression line is close to the true regression line, then the residuals should be close to the true errors. In this case, the residual should inherit the properties of the true errors.

The variance of the error σ^2, is estimated using s^2. Interpret s, its square root, to be an estimate of the size of a typical error.

We now show how to use the residuals to estimate $\sigma^2 = \text{Var } e$, the variability of errors. In Chapter 2, we saw that a good estimate of $\sigma^2 = \text{Var } e$ is $(n-1)^{-1} \sum_{i=1}^{n} (e_i - \bar{e})^2$. Unfortunately, in the basic linear regression model setup, the errors $\{e_i\}$ are unobserved. As a close relative, we use as an estimator of σ^2 the *mean square error*,

$$s^2 = \frac{\sum\limits_{i=1}^{n} \hat{e}_i^2}{n-2}. \tag{3.5}$$

The positive square root $s = (s^2)^{1/2}$ is called the *residual standard deviation*.

Comparing the definitions of s^2 and s_y^2 in equation (2.4), you will see two important differences. First, in defining s^2, we have not subtracted the average residual from each residual before squaring. This is because the average residual is zero, which is a special property of least squares estimation. This result can be shown using algebra and is guaranteed for all data sets.

Second, in defining s^2, we have divided by $n-2$ instead of $n-1$. It turns out that dividing by either n or $n-1$ tends to underestimate σ^2. The reason is that, when fitting lines to data, we need at least two observations to determine a line. For example, we must have at least three observations for there to be any variability about a line. How much "freedom" is there for variability about a line? We will say that the *error degrees of freedom* is the number of observations available, n, minus the number of observations needed to determine a line, 2. However, as we saw in the least squares estimation subsection, we do not identify two actual observations to determine a line. The idea is that if an analyst knows the line and $n - 2$ observations, then the remaining two observations can be determined, without variability.

We can also express s^2 in terms of the sum of squares quantities. That is,

$$s^2 = \frac{\sum_{i=1}^{n} (y_i - \hat{y}_i)^2}{n - 2} = \frac{\text{Error SS}}{n - 2}.$$

The ANOVA table is a bookkeeping device used to keep track of the sources of variability. The acronym ANOVA stands for analysis of variance.

This leads us to the *analysis of variance*, or *ANOVA*, table (Table 3.4). The ANOVA table is merely a bookkeeping device used to keep track of the sources of variability. The mean square column figures are defined to be the sum of square (SS) figures divided by their respective degrees of freedom (*df*). In particular, the mean square for errors (Error MS) equals s^2 and the regression sum of squares equals the regression mean square. That is,

$$\text{Error MS} = \frac{\text{Error SS}}{n - 2} = s^2 \quad \text{and} \quad \text{Regression MS} = \text{Regression SS}.$$

This latter property is specific to the regression with one variable case; it is not true where we consider more than one independent variable.

TABLE 3.4   ANOVA Table

Source	Sum of Squares	df	Mean Square
Regression	Regression SS	1	Regression MS
Error	Error SS	$n - 2$	Error MS
Total	Total SS	$n - 1$	

The error degrees of freedom in the ANOVA table is $n - 2$. The *total degrees of freedom* is $n - 1$, reflecting the fact that one observation is used to center the data. The single degree of freedom associated with the regression portion means that the slope, plus one observation, is enough information to determine the line. This is because it takes two observations to determine a line and at least three observations for there to be any variability about the line.

The ANOVA table is produced routinely by most statistical software packages; Section 3.7 provides several examples. See the ANOVA table (Table 3.5) for the auto price data in hundreds of dollars. From this table, you can check that $R^2 = 76.6\%$ and $s = 24.59$ (hundred dollars).

Is the Independent Variable Important?: The *t*-Test

We respond to the question of whether the independent variable is important by investigating whether or not $\beta_1 = 0$. The logic is that if $\beta_1 = 0$, then from

TABLE 3.5   ANOVA Table (Data in Hundreds of Dollars)

Source	Sum of Squares	df	Mean Square
Regression	118,689.216	1	118,689.216
Error	36,285.171	60	604.753
Total	154,974.387	61	

equation (3.3) the model is $y = \beta_0 + e$, which is the model discussed in Chapter 2. Thus, we translate our question of the independent variable's importance into a narrower question that can be answered using the hypothesis testing framework. This narrower question is, is $H_0: \beta_1 = 0$ valid? We respond to this question by looking at the test statistic:

$$t\text{-ratio} = \frac{estimator - hypothesized\ value\ of\ parameter}{standard\ error\ of\ estimator}.$$

For our case of $H_0: \beta_1 = 0$, we examine the t-ratio

$$t(b_1) = \frac{b_1}{se(b_1)}$$

because the hypothesized value of β_1 is 0. From mathematical statistics, it turns out that the standard error of b_1 is

$$se(b_1) = \frac{s}{\sqrt{\sum_{i=1}^{n}(x_i - \bar{x})^2}} = \frac{s}{s_x \sqrt{n-1}}. \tag{3.6}$$

This is the appropriate standardization because, under the null hypothesis and the model assumptions described in Section 3.2, the sampling distribution of $t(b_1)$ can be shown to be the t-distribution with $df = n - 2$ degrees of freedom.

As in the hypothesis testing Section 2.7, this enables us to construct tests of hypotheses such as:

1. Test the null hypothesis H_0 against the alternative $H_a: \beta_1 \neq 0$. We reject H_0 in favor of H_a if

$$|t(b_1)|\ \text{exceeds}\ t\text{-value}.$$

   Here, this t-value is a percentile from the t-distribution using $df = n - 2$ degrees of freedom. The percentile is $1 - $ (significance level)$/2$.

2. Test the null hypothesis H_0 against the alternative $H_a: \beta_1 > 0$. We reject H_0 in favor of H_a if

$$t(b_1)\ \text{exceeds}\ t\text{-value}.$$

Here, this t-value is a percentile from the t-distribution using $df = n - 2$ degrees of freedom. The percentile is $1 -$ (significance level).

3. Test the null hypothesis H_0 against the alternative H_a: $\beta_1 < 0$. We reject H_0 in favor of H_a if

$$t(b_1) \text{ is less than } -(t\text{-value}).$$

Here, this t-value is a percentile from the t-distribution using $df = n - 2$ degrees of freedom. The percentile is $1 -$ (significance level).

Making decisions by comparing a t-ratio to a t-value is called a t-test. Alternatively, one can construct p-values, such as those defined in Section 2.7, and compare these to given significant levels. Further details of this procedure will be provided in Chapter 7.

The standard error of b_1, $se(b_1)$, is our measure of the reliability of the slope estimator, b_1. Using equation (3.6), we see that $se(b_1)$ is determined by three quantities, n, s and s_x, as follows:

1. If we have more observations so that n becomes larger, then $se(b_1)$ becomes smaller, other things being equal.
2. If the observations have a greater tendency to lie closer to the line so that s becomes smaller, then $se(b_1)$ becomes smaller, other things being equal.
3. If values of the independent variable become more spread out so that s_x increases, then $se(b_1)$ becomes smaller, other things being equal.

Other things being equal, smaller values of $se(b_1)$ result in larger values of $t(b_1)$. Thus, smaller values of $se(b_1)$ offer a better opportunity to detect relations between y and x. Figure 3.13 illustrates these relationships. Here, the scatter plot on the right has the smallest value of $se(b_1)$. Compared with the upper left plot, the right-hand plot has a smaller value of s, and thus $se(b_1)$. Compared with the lower left plot, the right-hand plot has a larger s_x, and thus smaller value of $se(b_1)$.

Another interesting way of addressing the question of the importance of an independent variable is through the correlation coefficient. Remember that the correlation coefficient is a measure of linear relationship between x and y. Let's denote this statistic by r_{yx}. This quantity is unaffected by scale changes in either variable. For example, if we multiply the x variable by the positive number b_1, then the correlation coefficient remains unchanged. Further, correlations are unchanged by additive shifts. Thus, if we add a number, say b_0, to each x variable, then the correlation coefficient remains unchanged. Using a scale change and an additive shift on the x variable can be used to produce the fitted value $\hat{y} = b_0 + b_1 x$. Thus, using notation, we have $r_{yx} = r_{y,\hat{y}}$. We may thus interpret the correlation between the responses and the independent variable to be equal to the correlation between the responses and the fitted values. This leads then to the following interesting algebraic fact:

$$R^2 = r^2,$$

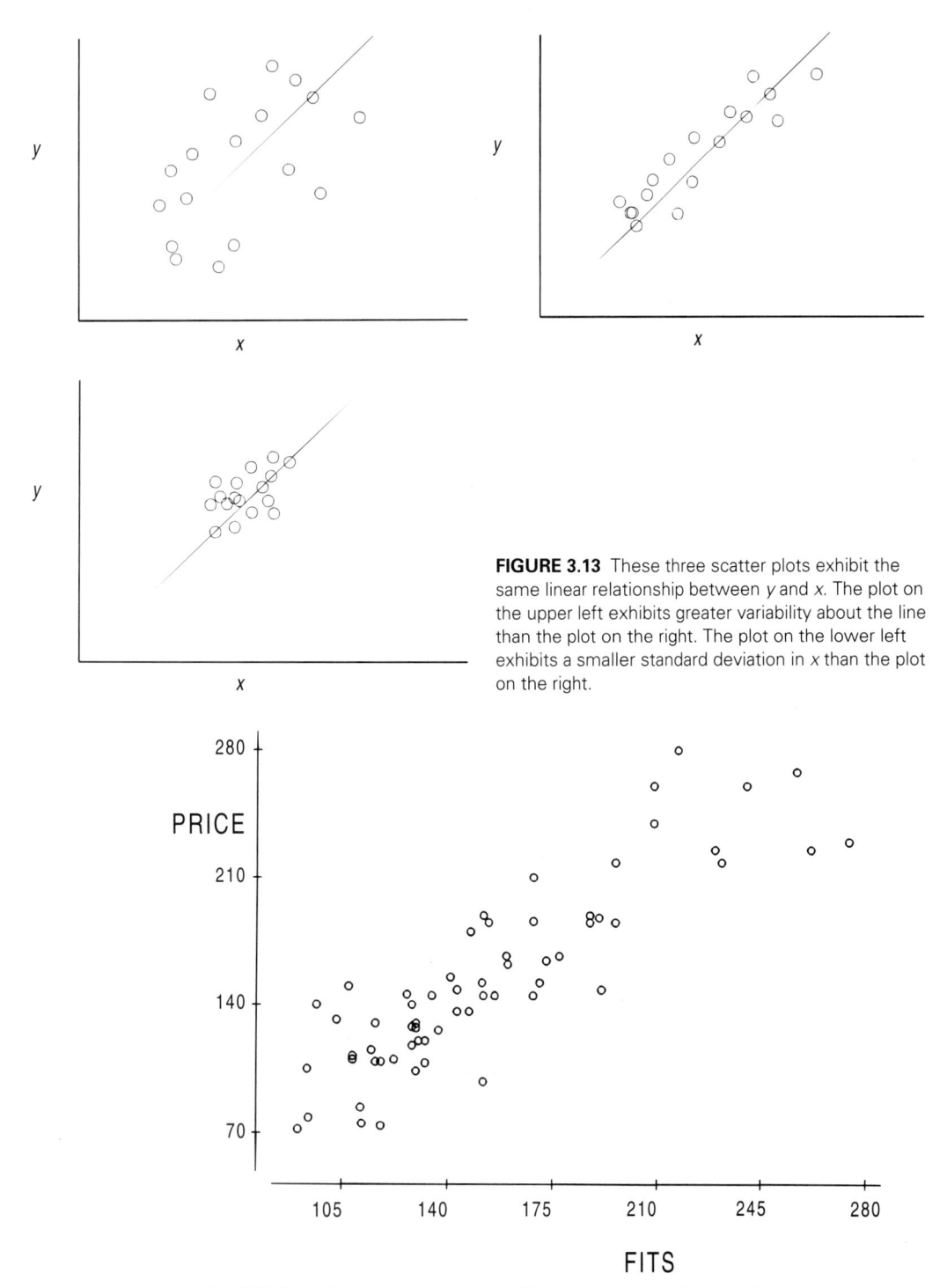

FIGURE 3.13 These three scatter plots exhibit the same linear relationship between y and x. The plot on the upper left exhibits greater variability about the line than the plot on the right. The plot on the lower left exhibits a smaller standard deviation in x than the plot on the right.

FIGURE 3.14 Plot of observed versus fitted responses for the car price example.

that is, the coefficient of determination equals the correlation coefficient squared. This is much easier to interpret if one thinks of r as the correlation between observed and fitted values. See Figure 3.14.

3.4 WHAT THE MODELING PROCEDURE TELLS US

The modeling procedure contributes to our understanding and to our ability to predict subsequent behavior of the real world.

Having fit a data set to a model, we can make a number of important statements. Generally, it is useful to think about these statements in two categories: (i) those contributing to our understanding of the real world and (ii) those useful in predicting the subsequent behavior of the real world.

Interval Estimates

An important type of statement is one already discussed in Section 3.3, "Does the explanatory variable have a *real* influence on the response?" Investigators often cite the formal hypothesis testing mechanism to respond to this type of question. A natural follow-up question is "To what extent does x affect y?" To a certain degree, one could respond using the size of the t-ratio or the p-value. However, in many instances a confidence interval for the slope is more useful.

To introduce confidence intervals for the slope, recall that b_1 is our point estimate of the true, unknown slope β_1. We argued in Section 3.3 that this estimate has standard error $se(b_1)$ and that $(b_1 - \beta_1)/se(b_1)$ follows a t-distribution with $n - 2$ degrees of freedom. When introducing interval estimates in Section 2.6, we saw that probability statements can be inverted to yield confidence intervals. Using the same logic, we have the following confidence interval for the slope β_1,

$$b_1 \pm (t\text{-value})\, se(b_1). \tag{3.7}$$

For a 95% confidence interval, use the 97.5th percentile from the t-distribution.

Here, the t-value is a percentile from the t-distribution with $df = n - 2$ degrees of freedom. Because of the two-sided nature of confidence intervals, the percentile is $1 - (1 - \text{confidence level})/2$. In this text, for notational simplicity we generally use a 95% confidence interval, so the percentile is $1 - (1 - 0.95)/2 = 0.975$. The confidence interval provides a range of reliability that measures the usefulness of the estimate.

In Section 3.1, we established that the least squares slope estimate for the auto price example is $b_1 = 0.211$. The interpretation is that if an individual's income differs by \$1,000, then we expect the purchase price to differ by \$211.

How reliable is this estimate? It turns out that $se(b_1) = 0.01508$ and thus an approximate 95% confidence interval for the slope is

$$0.211 \pm (2.000)(0.01508),$$

or $(0.208, 0.214)$. Similarly, if income differs by $1,000, a 95% confidence interval for the expected change in the purchase price is $(208, 214)$. Here, the t-value is approximately 2.000 because there are 60 $(= n - 2)$ degrees of freedom. For a 95% confidence interval, the t-value is the 97.5th percentile from the t-distribution.

To assess our ability to detect relationships between INCOME and PRICE, the form of the standard error in equation (3.6) has an interesting interpretation. If we could sample more and more automobile customers, the numerator of $se(b_1)$, s, would become closer approximation to σ, then the true variability of PRICE after controlling for INCOME. Similarly, the quantity s_x would be a closer approximation of the natural variability in customer's incomes. However, $se(b_1)$ approaches zero because the number of customers, n, increases. In this case, our ability to detect relationships between PRICE and INCOME improves and confidence intervals become more narrow. Thus, other things being equal, larger samples provide a greater ability to detect relationships and improve the accuracy of the estimates.

Other things being equal, larger samples provide a greater ability to detect relationships and provide more reliable estimates.

Prediction Intervals

In Section 3.1, we showed how to use least squares estimates to predict the purchase price for an individual, outside of our sample, having an income of $80,000. Because prediction is such an important application of statistics, we formalize the procedure so that it can be used on a regular basis.

To predict an additional observation, we assume that the level of explanatory variable is known and is denoted by x_*. To illustrate, in our previous auto price example we used $x_* = 80,000$. We also assume that the additional observation follows the same linear regression model as the observations in the sample. Thus, we can write

$$y_* = \beta_0 + \beta_1 x_* + e_*$$

as a model for the new observation.

Using our least square estimates, our point prediction is

$$\hat{y}_* = b_0 + b_1 x_*,$$

the height of our fitted regression line at x_*. As in prediction portion of Section 2.8, we can decompose the prediction error into two parts:

$$
\begin{array}{cccc}
y_* - \hat{y}_* & = \beta_0 - b_0 + (\beta_1 - b_1)x_* + & & e_* \\
\text{prediction error} = & \text{estimation error} & + & \text{random error}
\end{array}
$$

The estimation error is due to the deviation of the fitted from the true regression line. The random error is due to the natural sampling variability associated with making predictions about an individual. It can be shown that the standard error of the prediction is

$$se(pred) = s\sqrt{1 + \frac{1}{n} + \frac{(x_* - \bar{x})^2}{(n-1)s_x^2}}.$$

As with $se(b_1)$, for larger sample sizes n, the terms n^{-1} and $(x_* - x)^2/((n-1)s_x^2)$ become close to zero. In this case, we have that $se(pred) \approx s$. This simply reflects that, for large n, the estimation error becomes negligible and the random error becomes the entire source of uncertainty.

Our prediction interval is

$$\hat{y}_* \pm (t\text{-value})\, se(pred) \tag{3.7}$$

where t-value is the same as used for the confidence interval. For example, the point prediction at $x_* = 80,000$ is

$$\hat{y}_* = 5,881 + 0.211(80,000) = 22,761.$$

The standard error of this prediction is

$$se(pred) = 2,459\sqrt{1 + \frac{1}{62} + \frac{(8,000 - 45,190)^2}{(62-1)(20,873)^2}} = 2,534.$$

With a t-value close to 2.000, this yields an approximate 95% prediction interval

$$22,761 \pm (2)(2,534) = 22,761 \pm 5,068 = (17,713, 27,829).$$

We interpret these results by first pointing out that our best estimate of purchase price for an individual with an $80,000 annual income is $22,761. Our 95% prediction interval represents a range of reliability for this prediction. If we could see many individuals, each with an $80,000 income, on average we expect about 19 out of 20, or 95%, would purchase a car price between $17,713 and $27,829. It is interesting that this range covers about the top 30% of purchase prices in our sample.

3.5 IMPROVING THE MODEL THROUGH RESIDUAL ANALYSIS

If the residuals are related to a variable or display any other recognizable pattern, then we should be able to take advantage of this information and improve our model specification. Recall that, if our model is appropriate, then the residual, $\hat{e}_i$, should be close to the random error, e_i. Therefore, the residuals should contain little or no information and represent only natural variation from the

If the residuals are related to a variable or display any other recognizable pattern, then we should be able to use this information to improve our model specification.

sampling that cannot be attributed to any specific source. *Residual analysis* is the exercise of checking the residuals for patterns.

Much of residual analysis is done by examining a *standardized residual*, a residual divided by its standard error. An approximate standard error of the residual is s; in Chapter 6 we will give a precise mathematical definition. There are two reasons why we often examine standardized residuals in lieu of basic residuals. First, if errors are from a normal curve, then standardized residuals are approximate realizations from a standard normal curve. This provides a reference distribution to compare values of standardized residuals. For example, if a standardized residual exceeds two in absolute value, this is considered unusually large and the observation is called an *outlier*. Second, because standardized residuals are dimensionless, we get carryover of experience from one data set to another. This is true regardless of whether the normal reference curve is applicable.

Checking Normality

Calculations involving the normal curve are implicit in all of our confidence and prediction intervals. The central limit theorem essentially states that, for samples of moderate to large size, we may approximate the distribution of the sample average using the normal curve. There are other versions of the central limit theorems for weighted averages, not merely simple arithmetic averages. This is important because it is possible to express least squares regression estimates as weighted averages. Thus, we may also use the normal curve to approximate the distribution of the least squares regression estimates. Now, as with the central limit theorem for simple averages, this approximation performs better the closer the parent population is to a normal one. In particular, for sample sizes ranging from 25 to 50, it is important to check the normality of the error distribution.

A direct way of checking normality is to create a dotplot or histogram of the standardized residuals. Because the residuals are close to the true errors, this histogram should be close to the idealized standard normal histogram. The histogram of standardized residuals should not be lopsided but rather be bell-shaped, or at least symmetric. Further, from the standard normal curve, we expect about two-thirds (68%) of the observations to be between -1 and 1, about 95% between -2 and 2, and very few observations beyond three in absolute value. That is, to compare distributions we can compare the percentiles of the residuals to the percentiles of the theoretical normal curve.

The normal probability plot is a graphical device for comparing percentiles from a data set to the corresponding percentiles from a standard normal curve.

Another, more sophisticated approach to compare percentiles is through a *normal probability plot*. The procedure to create this plot is as follows. For the ith standardized residual, $i = 1, ..., n$, let R_i be the corresponding *rank*. (Thus, if the ith standardized residual is the smallest, then $R_i = 1$ and so on up to the case where it is the largest, when $R_i = n$.) The rank is a useful intermediate concept; for the ith standardized residual, R_i/n is the fraction less than or equal to that standardized residual. So that things work out in the extremes, or *tails*, of the distribution, define

$$p_i = (R_i - 3/8)/(n + 1/4)$$

to be the proportion of the ith standardized residual. For example, if $p_i = 0.975$, we expect roughly 97.5% of the standardized residuals to be smaller than the ith standardized residual. Define the corresponding *normal score* to be that number from the normal table so that it is the p_i-percentile. For example, if $p_i = 0.975$, then the corresponding normal score is 1.96. The normal score for $p_i = 0.50$ is zero. (We defined our largest standardized residual to have a percentile slightly less than 100% because the normal score corresponding to 100% is infinity.) To summarize, for each observation we:

1. Define R_i to be the rank of the ith standardized residual.
2. Define $p_i = (R_i - 3/8)/(n + 1/4)$ to be the corresponding proportion.
3. Define the normal score to be the percentile from the standard normal curve corresponding to the p_i-proportion.

We now compare the normal scores to the standardized residuals. A *normal probability plot* is a plot of the normal scores on one axis with the standardized residuals on the other axis. If the plot forms a reasonably straight line, then the standardized residuals may be said to be approximately normal. It is also useful to use the correlation between the normal scores and standardized residuals to summarize the linearity.

To illustrate, we return to the auto price example introduced in Section 3.1. Using PRICE as the response variable and INCOME as the explanatory variable, the regression model was fit and standardized residuals calculated. The calculation of the normal scores for the first five standardized residuals is in Table 3.6. For example, the fifth standardized residual, -1.50792, turned out to be the sixth smallest, resulting in $R_5 = 6$. The proportion for this observation is $p_5 = (6 - 3/8)/(62 + 1/4) = 9.04$ percent. Using the normal curve table, find the normal score to be -1.338. Figure 3.15 illustrates the normal curve lookup procedure. This process was done for each of the 62 standardized residuals.

TABLE 3.6 Normal Scores Calculation for the Standardized Residuals of the First Five Observations of the Auto Price Regression Example

i	Standardized residual	Rank (R_i)	Proportion (p_i)	Normal score
1	-0.29503	26	0.41165	-0.22234
2	0.47773	45	0.71687	0.57153
3	1.80070	60	0.95783	1.72852
4	1.33594	56	0.89357	1.24513
5	-1.50792	6	0.09036	-1.33846

The results are summarized in Figure 3.16 with a scatter plot of normal scores versus standardized residuals, our normal probability plot. The relationship is nearly linear, indicating that the distribution of the standardized residuals is close to a normal curve.

Outliers and High Leverage Points

Another important part of residual analysis is the identification of unusual observations in a data set. Because regression estimates are weighted averages

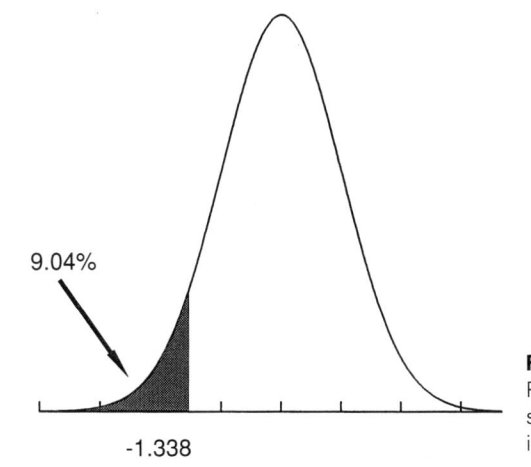

FIGURE 3.15 Normal score for the Car Price example. The percentile of the 5th standardized residual was 9.04%, resulting in a normal score of −1.338.

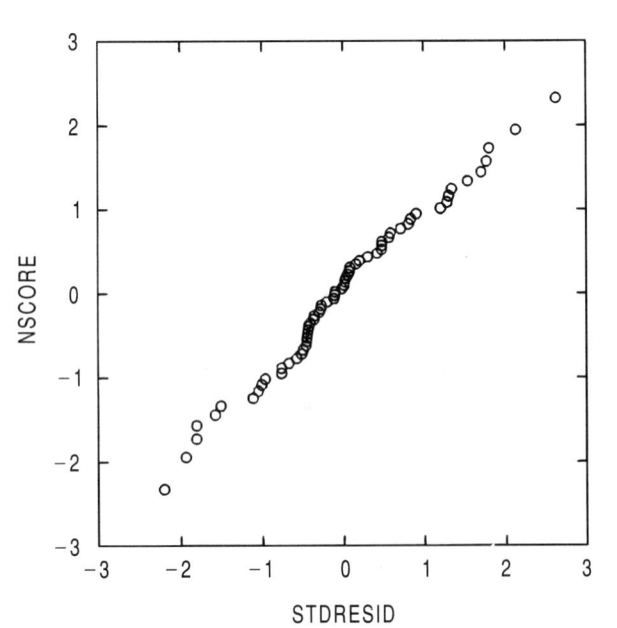

FIGURE 3.16 Scatter plot of normal scores (NSCORE) versus corresponding standardized residuals (STDRESID). Residuals are from a regression of PRICE on INCOME. The correlation coefficient is 0.991, indicating that the distribution of standardized residuals is close to a normal curve.

where the weights vary by observation, some observations are more important than others. This weighting is more important than most users of regression analysis realize. In fact, Example 3.1 demonstrates that a single observation can have a dramatic effect in a large data set.

If an observation is unusual in the vertical direction, then it is called an outlier. If it is unusual in the horizontal direction, then it is called a high leverage point.

There are two directions in which a data point can be unusual, the horizontal and vertical directions. By "unusual," we mean that an observation under consideration seems to be far from the majority of the data set. An observation that is unusual in the vertical direction is called an *outlier*. An observation that is unusual in the horizontal direction is called a *high leverage point*. An observation may be both an outlier and a high leverage point.

C3_OUTLR

Example 3.1: The Effect of Outliers and High Leverage Points

Consider the fictitious data set of 19 points plus three points, labeled A, B, and C, given in Figure 3.17 and Table 3.7. Think of the first 19 points as "good" observations that represent some type of phenomenon. We want to investigate the effect of adding a single aberrant point.

TABLE 3.7 19 Base Points Plus Three Types of Unusual Observations

	19 base points																			A	B	C
x	1.5	1.7	2.0	2.2	2.5	2.5	2.7	2.9	3.0	3.5	3.8	4.2	4.3	4.6	4.9	5.0	5.1	5.2	5.5	4.3	9.5	9.5
y	3.0	2.5	3.5	3.0	3.1	3.6	3.2	3.9	4.0	4.0	4.2	4.1	4.8	4.2	5.1	5.1	5.1	4.8	5.3	8.0	8.0	2.5

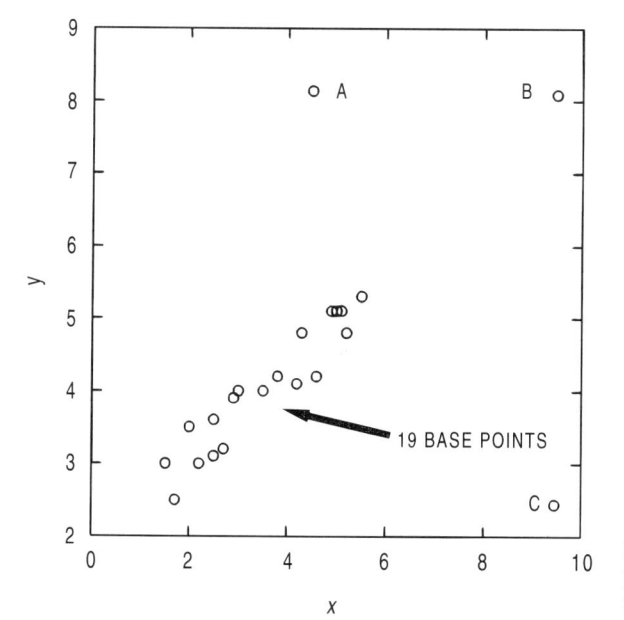

FIGURE 3.17 Scatter plot of 19 base plus 3 unusual points, labeled A, B and C.

To investigate the effect of each type of aberrant point, run four separate regressions. The first regression is for the 19 base points. The other three regressions use the 19 base points plus each type of unusual observation. Table 3.8 summarizes the results of the regressions runs.

TABLE 3.8 Regression Results

Data	b_0	b_1	s	$R^2(\%)$	$t(b_1)$
19 Base Points	1.869	0.611	0.288	89.0	11.71
" " + A	1.750	0.693	0.846	53.7	4.57
" " + B	1.775	0.640	0.285	94.7	18.01
" " + C	3.356	0.155	0.865	10.3	1.44

We see that a regression line provides a good fit for the 19 base points. The coefficient of determination, R^2, indicates about 89% of the variability has been explained by the line. The size of the typical error, s, about 0.29, is small compared to the scatter in the y-values. Further, the t-ratio for the slope coefficient is large.

When the outlier point A is added to the nineteen base points, the situation deteriorates dramatically. The R^2 drops from 89% to 53.7% and s increases from about 0.29 to about 0.85. The fitted regression line itself does not change that much even though our confidence in the estimates has decreased.

An outlier is unusual in the y-value, but "unusual" here means with respect to x. To see this, keep the y-value of Point A the same, but increase the x-value and call the point B. When the point B is added to the 19 base points, the regression line provides a *better* fit. Point B is close to being on the line of the regression fit generated by the 19 base points. Thus, the fitted regression line and the size of the typical error, s, do not change much. However, R^2 increases from 89% to nearly 95%. If we think of R^2 as 1 − (Error SS)/(Total SS), by adding point B we have increased Total SS, the total squared deviations in the y's, even though leaving Error SS relatively unchanged. Point B is not an outlier, but it is a high leverage point.

To show how influential this point is, drop the y-value considerably and call this the new point C. When this point is added to the 19 base points, the situation deteriorates dramatically. The R^2 coefficient drops from 89% to 10%, and the s more than triples, from 0.29 to 0.87. Further, the regression line coefficients change dramatically.

Most users of regression at first do not believe that 1 point in 20 can have such a dramatic effect on the regression fit. The fit of a regression line can always be improved by removing an outlier. If the point is a high leverage point and not an outlier, it is not clear whether the fit will be improved when the point is removed.

Simply because you can dramatically improve a regression fit by omitting an observation does not mean you should always do so! The goal of data analysis is to understand the information in the data. Throughout the text, we will encounter many data sets where the unusual points provide some of the most interesting information about the data. The goal of this subsection is to recognize the effects of unusual points; Chapter 6 will provide a set of options for handling unusual points in your analysis.

All quantitative disciplines, such as accounting, economics, linear programming, and so on, practice the art of *sensitivity analysis*. Sensitivity analysis is a description of the global changes in a system due to a small local change in an element of the system. Examining the effects of individual observations on the regression fit is a type of sensitivity analysis.

Quadratic Regression

Another important goal of residual analysis is to improve the specification of the model. We will do this by using residuals from an initial model fit to search for relationships with other variables or other types of patterns. Residuals are approximations of random errors and random errors should display no patterns. Our goal is to recognize any patterns that the residuals exhibit and use these patterns to improve the model formulation. In this subsection, this process is illustrated using the *quadratic regression* model.

By a quadratic regression model, we mean a basic linear regression model, with a squared, independent variable added:

$$y_i = \beta_0 + \beta_1 x_i + \beta_2 x_i^2 + e_i \qquad i = 1, \ldots, n.$$

The deterministic portion of the model, $E\, y = \beta_0 + \beta_1 x + \beta_2 x^2$, can be used to represent a gently sloping curve in x.

As a first example, consider the artificial data in Figure 3.18. Here, we see a definite increasing trend; that is, as x increases, so does y. However, the rate of increase seems to level off. Although Figure 3.18 clearly indicates the in-

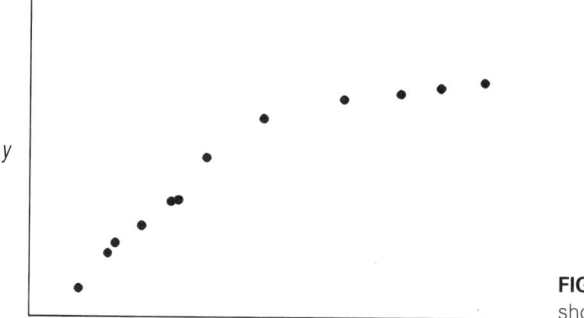

y

x

FIGURE 3.18 This plot of y versus x shows an increasing trend, although the trend may be leveling off.

creasing trend, it does not provide conclusive evidence as to whether or not the trend is constant as x changes.

A regression using the independent variable x was fit and residuals were calculated. Figure 3.19 shows a plot of the residuals versus x. This plot shows a definite quadratic relationship between the residuals and the independent variable. A residual can be interpreted to be a response, controlled for the linear effect of x. By removing the linear effect, the visual impact of the quadratic curve is more apparent.

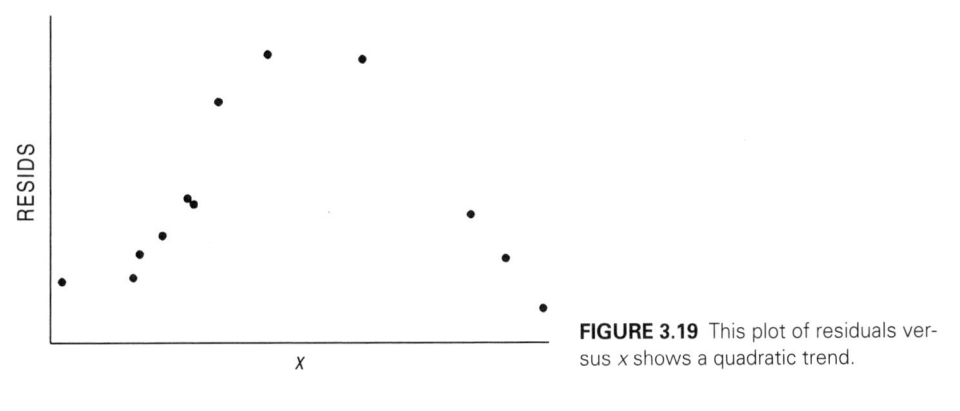

FIGURE 3.19 This plot of residuals versus x shows a quadratic trend.

Example 3.2: Major League Baseball Pitchers

To illustrate further the use of the quadratic regression model, consider a sample of 82 major league baseball pitchers. Figure 3.20 shows a scatter plot of the players' salary (y) versus years of experience (x). The salary

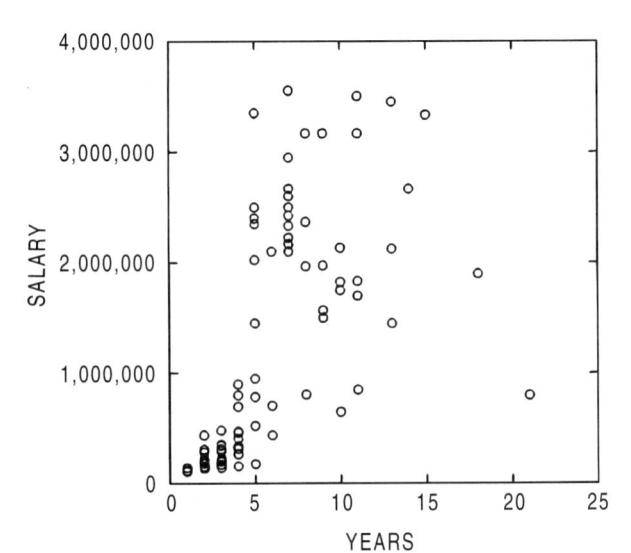

FIGURE 3.20 Scatter plot of salary versus years of experience for 82 pitchers. *Source: April 18, 1991 issue of USA Today.*

figures were taken from the April 8, 1991 issue of *USA Today*. The years of experience, and other performance-related independent variables such as earned run average, strikeouts and so on, were available from a variety of baseball almanacs and cards. The goal is to establish a model of salary using several independent variables. This model would be useful for, among other things, salary arbitration. The model would allow us to predict salary controlling for values of the independent variables. In this section, the only independent variable considered is years of experience. It turns out that this characteristic explains most of the variability.

From Figure 3.20, we see that the maximum salary is roughly $3.5 million per year. It turns out that, due to league rules, the minimum salary is $100,000. Years of experience ranges from 1 to 21 years. Note that two observations stand out when examining years of experience, one at 18 and the other at 21 years. So that this discussion is not about high leverage points, the analysis here excludes these two senior pitchers.

Before presenting a formal analysis of the residuals, we first demonstrate the effect of grouping the number of years variables and taking average salaries within groups. The purpose of this informal demonstration is the same as with Figure 3.6, to show how the behavior of the average value of y within a category should be close to the theoretical expected value of y, E y. Table 3.9 is our table of averages, with the results graphically displayed in Figure 3.21. The plot in Figure 3.21 suggests a quadratic relationship in years of experience. Remember that, when looking at this plot, we give greater weight to age groups having more observations, other things being equal.

To begin the more formal analysis of the individual observations (without grouping), Figure 3.22 is a scatter plot of salary versus years of experience. Here, the estimated regression line is superimposed. The two high leverage points were excluded, resulting is a horizontal scale different from the plot in Figure 3.20. A careful inspection of this plot reveals,

TABLE 3.9 Number and Average Salaries of Players by Experience

Experience group	Number of players	Average salary
1–2	14	201,143
3–4	21	372,905
5–6	13	1,520,000
7–8	14	2,415,927
9–10	8	1,820,927
11–12	5	2,210,000
13–14	4	2,423,000
15–16	1	3,333,000
17–18	1	1,900,000
19–22	1	800,000

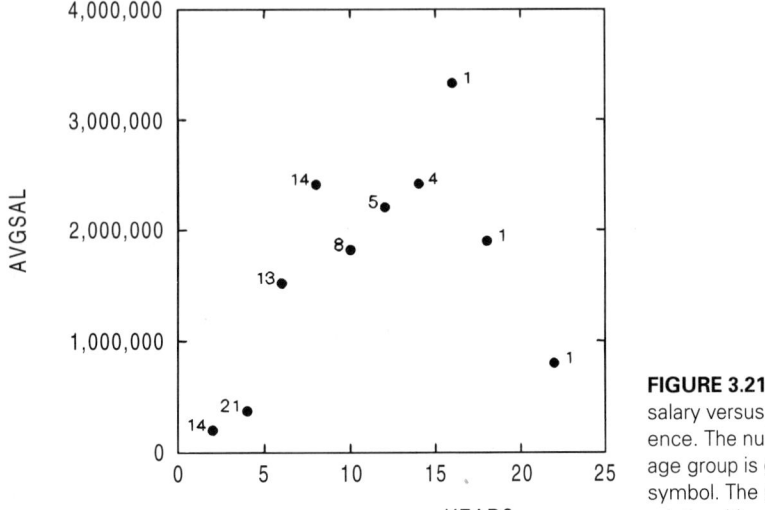

FIGURE 3.21 Scatter plot of average salary versus grouped years of experience. The number of players in each age group is given next to the plotting symbol. The plot suggests a quadratic relationship.

for most of the pitchers with 1–4 years of experience, that the actual salary is below the fitted regression line. This is also true for most of the pitchers with 12–15 years of experience. For most of the pitchers with 5–8 years of experience, the actual salaries are above the fitted regression line.

These subtle patterns are more evident in Figure 3.23, a scatter plot of the residuals from the regression of salary on years of experience. A

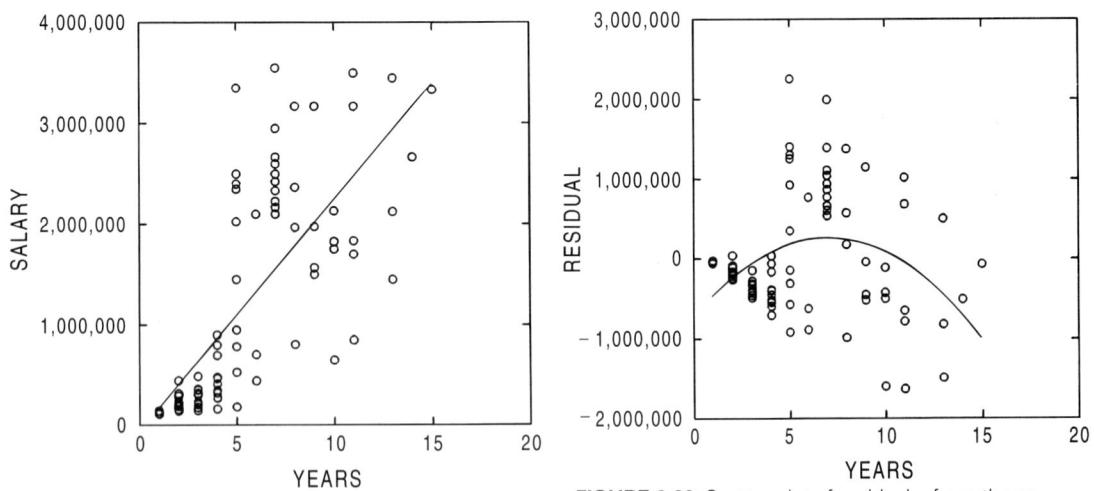

FIGURE 3.22 Scatter plot of salary versus years of experience for 80 pitchers with the estimated regression line superimposed.

FIGURE 3.23 Scatter plot of residuals, from the regression of salary on years of experience, versus years of experience. A quadratic curve has been superimposed.

quadratic curve is superimposed to emphasize this pattern. These patterns are present in the original plot of the data. However, by examining the residuals, we have controlled for the linear trend in years of experience, thus making the quadratic trend more apparent.

The residual plot not only detects patterns in the residuals, a violation of model assumptions, but also provides a suggestion as to how to improve the model specification. The fact that the residuals are related to x^2 suggests adding the term x^2 into the specified model, resulting in the quadratic regression model. Using techniques to be discussed in Chapter 4, a quadratic regression model was fit to the data. The estimated regression is

$$\text{SAL\^{A}RY} = -776{,}000 + 510{,}800 \text{ YEARS} - 19{,}950 \text{ YEARS}^2 .$$

This turned out to significantly improve the model fit. Figure 3.24 is a scatter plot of the data with the final quadratic curve superimposed. The patterns noted in Figure 3.22 seem to have been reduced. Plots of the residuals from the quadratic regression model revealed no serious violation of model assumptions.

The model is useful for salary arbitration. Given only years of experience, the model can predict salary and provide a measure of reliability for that prediction. For example, it turns out that for someone with 10 years of experience, the model predicts the salary to be SAL\^{A}RY = 2,337,000. The size of the typical error is $s = \$732{,}000$. Thus, if you have 10 years of experience and are offered \$650,000, you should be suspicious because your peers are making much more. Of course, there may be sev-

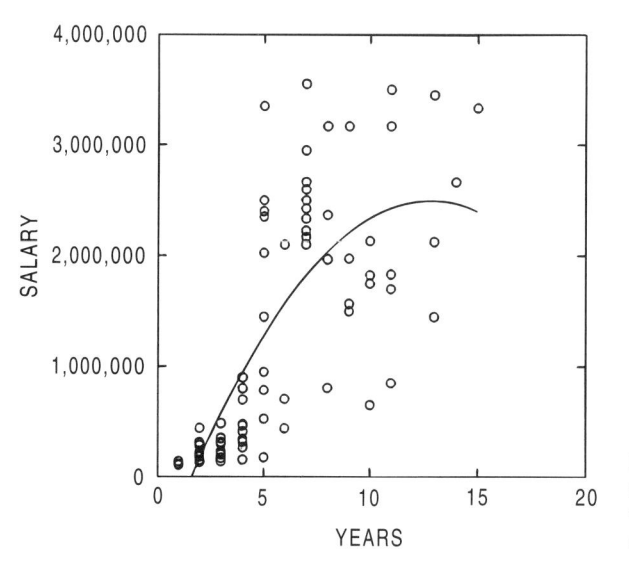

FIGURE 3.24 Scatter plot of salary versus years of experience for 80 players with the estimated quadratic regression curve superimposed.

eral good reasons that such a low offer was made. These reasons would be a part of the natural variation in the data.

The model does not suggest a causal relationship between years of experience and salary. In competitive sports, there is a strong selection process that takes place every year that a player needs to survive merely to be included in the population of interest. Further, salary figures are influenced not only by a player's ability, but also market forces such as the player's appeal to sports fans. Perhaps levels of experience are related to ability or marketability, or perhaps there are other unsuspected causal variables that influence salary. The statistical analysis establishes definite relationships, not the reasons for these relationships.

Finally, the quadratic regression model was fit to the full sample of 82 pitchers. The fitted model turns out to be

$$\text{SAL\^ARY} = -811,500 + 525,800 \text{ YEARS} - 21,090 \text{ YEARS}^2.$$

with $s = 723,000$, see Figure 3.25. It is interesting that the addition or deletion of these two points did not have a large effect on the fit of the model. High leverage points have the potential to affect the model fit, but do not necessarily do so.

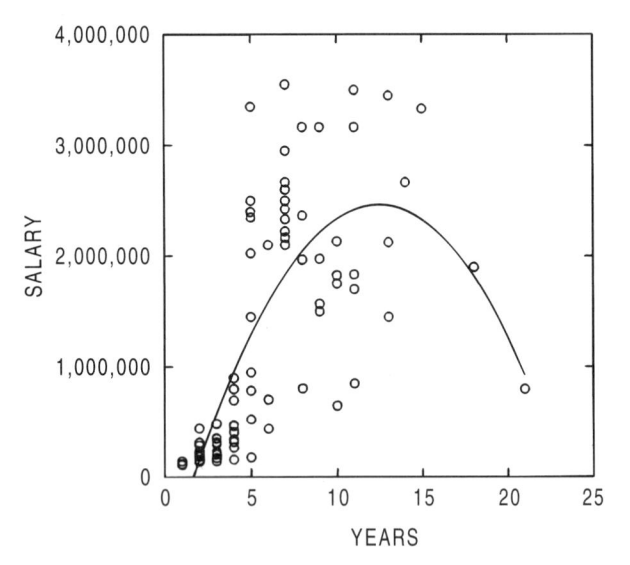

FIGURE 3.25 Scatter plot of salary versus years of experience for the 82 pitchers. A fitted quadratic regression line is superimposed.

3.6 CASE STUDY: CAPITAL ASSET PRICING MODEL

In this section, we study the use of regression analysis in the context of financial economics. A particularly useful application is the *Capital Asset Pricing Model*, often referred to by the acronym CAPM. This application is useful in that it is suggested by the theory of financial economics and confirmed by the evidence from the data. By "evidence from the data," we mean the statistical methodology introduced in the first five sections of Chapter 3.

The Capital Asset Pricing Model (CAPM) is an economic model of a security's returns.

The name Capital Asset Pricing Model is something of a misnomer in that the model is really about *returns* based on capital assets, not the prices themselves. The types of assets that we examine are equity securities that are traded on an active market, such as the New York Stock Exchange. For a stock on the exchange, we can relate returns to prices through the following expression:

return=

$$\frac{\text{price at the end of a period} + \text{dividends} - \text{price at the beginning of the period}}{\text{price at the beginning of the period}}.$$

The idea here is that, if we can estimate the returns that a stock generates, then knowledge of the price at the beginning of a generic financial period allows us to estimate the value at the end of the period (ending price plus dividends). Thus, we follow standard practice and attempt to model returns of a security.

The relationship between the performance of a security and the market is modeled by CAPM.

An intuitively appealing idea, and one of the basic characteristics of the CAPM model, is that there should be a relationship between the performance of a security and the performance of the market. One rationale is simply that if economic forces are such that the market improves, then those same forces should act upon an individual stock, suggesting that it also improve. As noted above, we measure performance of a security through the return. To measure performance of the market, several market indices exist that summarize the performance of each exchange. As an illustration, in the example below we use the "equally-weighted" index of the Standard & Poor's 500. The Standard & Poor's 500 is the collection of the 500 largest companies traded on the New York Stock Exchange, where "large" is identified by the Standard & Poor's company, a financial services rating organization. The equally-weighted index is defined by assuming a portfolio is created by investing one dollar in each of the 500 companies.

Another rationale for a relationship between security and market returns comes from financial economics theory. This is the CAPM theory, attributed to Sharpe (1964) and Lintner (1965) and based on the portfolio diversification ideas of Harry Markowitz (1959). Other things equal, investors would like to select a return with a high expected value and low standard deviation, the latter being a measure of riskiness. One of the desirable properties about using standard deviations as a measure of riskiness is that it is straight-forward to calculate the standard deviation of a portfolio, a combination of securities. One only needs to know the standard deviation of each security and the correlations among securities. A notable security is a risk-free one, that is, a security that theoretically has a zero standard deviation. Investor's often use a 30-day U.S. Treasury bill as an approximation of a risk-free security, arguing that the probability of default of the U.S. government within 30 days is negligible. Positing the existence of a risk-free asset and some other mild conditions, under the CAPM theory there exists an efficient frontier called the securities market line. This frontier specifies the minimum expected return that investors should demand for a specified level of risk. To estimate this line, we can use the equation

$$r = \beta_0 + \beta_1 r_m + e$$

where r is the security return and r_m is the market return. We interpret β_1 as a measure of the amount of security return that is attributed to the behavior of the market.

The CAPM theory is about cross-sectional relationships among returns. It can only be estimated using returns over time.

Testing economic theory, or models arising from any discipline, involves collecting data. The CAPM theory is about ex ante (before the fact) returns even though we can only test with ex post (after the fact) returns. Before the fact, the returns are unknown and there is an entire distribution of returns. After the fact, there is only a single realization of the security and market return. Because at least two observations are required to determine a line, CAPM models are estimated using security and market data gathered over time. In this way, several observations can be made.

There are a number of potential measurement problems when estimating CAPM models. One source of concern with data gathered over time is that the relationship between the security and the market may change over time. For this reason, data collection is often limited to a relatively short time period such as five years. Another issue is how frequent one should measure returns, the usual options being daily, weekly, monthly, quarterly or annually. If one samples often, such as on a daily basis, many more observations will be available over a five year period than if one uses monthly returns. However, if we analyze daily returns of a security, we are subject to some of the many so-called *market imperfections.* Market imperfections can be thought of as reasons why returns do not follow the theory from economic reasoning and, from a data analyst's perspective, why data do not follow the "ideal" regression model set-up. These reasons include the fact that stocks are typically traded discretely, for example in eighths of a dollar on the New York Stock Exchange. Another example is that, on several exchanges, we do not observe the true price of a stock, only the last traded price of the day. The last traded price of the day may be either a *bid* price (the price if an investor wishes to sell a stock) or an *ask* price (the price if an investor wishes to buy a stock). Although for most actively traded issues these prices are usually close (within one half dollar), the concept of the "true" price of a stock is an issue of discussion in the financial economics literature. See Cohen et al. (1986) for a discussion of this and other market imperfections. For the purposes of our discussions, we follow standard practice in the securities industry and examine monthly prices.

There are other sources of concern when using regression techniques to represent longitudinal data. Regression analysis can give misleading results when there are relationships between the explanatory variable and error terms or when there are relationships among the errors over time. These types of relationships are often evident in longitudinal data. Thus, we will consider modeling longitudinal data as a separate topic in Chapters 9 to 11. Fortunately, because of so-called *market efficiencies,* data analyzed using CAPM theory typically does not justify these concerns. Thus, we may continue and use our regression techniques even though the data are longitudinal.

C3_CAPM

To illustrate, consider monthly returns over the 5-year period from January 1986 to December 1990, inclusive. Specifically, we use the security returns from the Lincoln National Insurance Corporation as the dependent variable (y) and the market returns from the index of the Standard & Poor's 500 Index as the explanatory variable (x). The Lincoln is a large, multi-line, insurance company that is headquartered in the midwest of the United States, specifically in Fort Wayne, Indiana. Because it is well-known for its prudent management and stability, it is a good company to begin our analysis of the relationship between the market and an individual stock.

We begin by interpreting some basic summary statistics, in Table 3.10, in terms of financial theory. First, an investor in the Lincoln will be concerned that the 5-year average return, $\bar{y} = 0.00510$, is below the return of the market, $\bar{x} = 0.00741$. Students of interest theory recognize that monthly returns can be converted to an annual basis using geometric compounding. For example, the annual return of the Lincoln is $(1.0051)^{12} - 1 = 0.062946$, or roughly 6.29%. This is compared to an annual return of 9.26% $= [100\{1.00741\}^{12} - 1]$ for the market. A measure of *risk*, or volatility, that is used in finance is the standard deviation. Thus, interpret the fact that $s_y = 0.0859 > 0.05254 = s_x$ to mean that an investment in the Lincoln is riskier than that of the market. Another interesting aspect of Table 3.8 is that the smallest market return, -0.22052, is 4.338 standard deviations below its average $[(-0.22052 - 0.00741)/0.05254 = -4.338]$. This is highly unusual with respect to a normal curve.

We next examine the data over time, as is given graphically in Figures 3.26 and 3.27. These are scatter plots of the returns versus time, called *time series plots* in Chapter 9. In Figure 3.27, one can clearly see the smallest market return and a quick glance at the horizontal axis reveals that this unusual point is in October 1987, the time of the famous market crash. The effect of the market crash on Lincoln's return is also clearly evident in Figure 3.26. Also in Figure 3.26, we can see an unusually low return in October 1990 and a high return for the month of November. We return to this point in the following.

TABLE 3.10 Summary Statistics of the Full Data Set

	Number	Mean	Median	Standard deviation	Minimum	Maximum
LINCOLN	60	0.0051	0.0075	0.0859	−0.2803	0.3147
MARKET	60	0.00741	0.01423	0.05254	−0.22052	0.12749

Source: Center for Research on Security Prices, University of Chicago

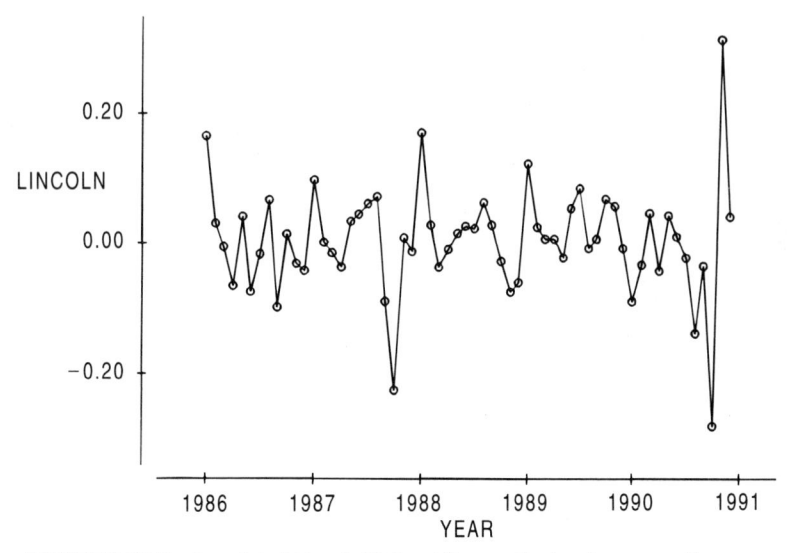

FIGURE 3.26 Scatter plot of Lincoln National Corporation's returns over time. There are 60 monthly returns over the period January 1986 through December 1990.

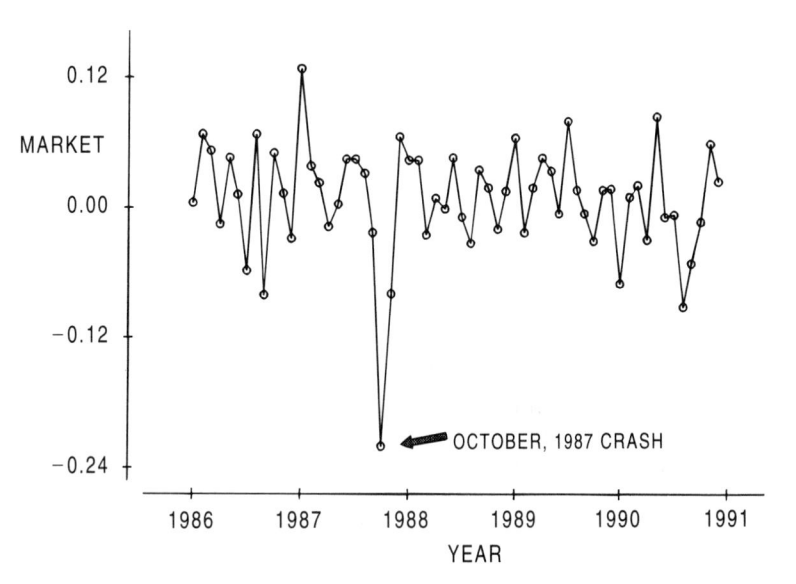

FIGURE 3.27 Scatter plot of Standard & Poor's returns over time. There are 60 monthly returns over the period January 1986 through December 1990.

From the two plots over time, it is difficult to see the relationship between Lincoln's return and the return of the market. To this end, Figure 3.28 gives a graphical summary of this relationship. The market crash is clearly evident in

Figure 3.28 and represents a high leverage point. With the regression line (described below) superimposed, the two outlying points that we noted in Figure 3.26 are also evident. Despite these anomalies, the plot in Figure 3.28 does suggest that there is a real relationship between Lincoln and market returns.

To summarize the relationship between the market and Lincoln's return, a regression model was fit. The estimated regression is

$$\widehat{\text{LINCOLN}} = -.00214 + 0.973 \text{ MARKET}.$$

The resulting estimated standard error, $s = 0.0696$ is lower than the standard deviation of Lincoln's returns, $s_y = 0.0859$. Thus, the regression model explains some of the variability of Lincoln's returns. Further, the t-ratio associated with the slope b_1 turns out to be $t(b_1) = 5.64$, which is significantly large. One disappointing aspect is that the statistic $R^2 = 35.4\%$ can be interpreted as saying that the market explains only a little over a third of the variability. Thus, even though the market is clearly an important determinant, as evidenced by the high t-statistic, it provides only a partial explanation of the performance of the Lincoln's returns.

In the context of the market model, we may interpret the standard deviation of the market, s_x, as *nondiversifiable* risk. Thus, the risk of a security can be decomposed into two components, the *diversifiable* component and the market component, which is nondiversifiable. The idea here is that by combining sev-

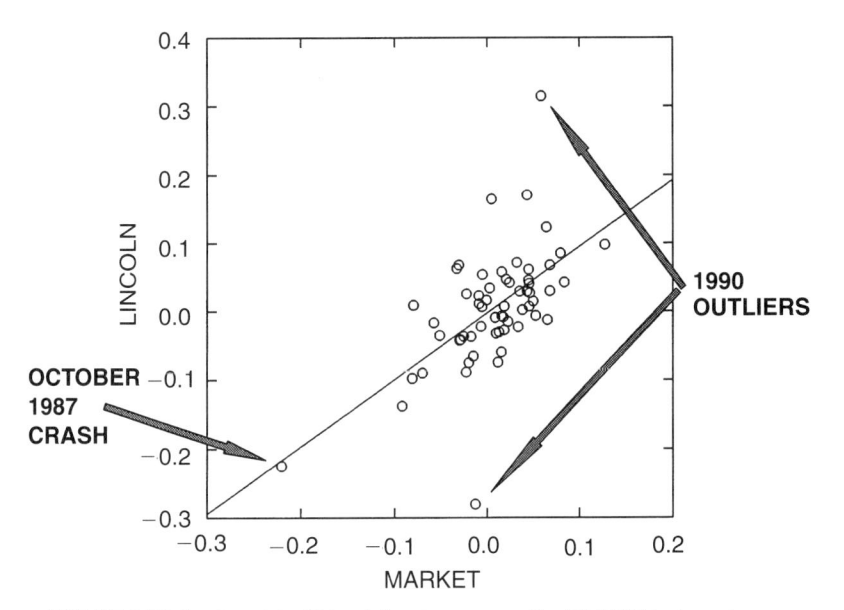

FIGURE 3.28 Scatter plot of Lincoln's return versus the S&P 500 Index return. The regression line is superimposed, enabling us to identify the market crash and two outliers.

eral securities we can create a portfolio of securities that, in most instances, will reduce the riskiness of our holdings when compared with a single security. Again, the rationale for holding a security is that we are compensated through higher expected returns by holding a security with higher riskiness. To quantify the relative riskiness, it is not hard to show that

$$s_y^2 = b_1^2 s_x^2 + s^2 \frac{n-2}{n-1} \ .$$

The riskiness of a security is due to the riskiness of the market plus the riskiness of a diversifiable component.

The riskiness of a security is due to the riskiness due to the market plus the riskiness due to a diversifiable component. Note that the riskiness due to the market component, $b_1^2 s_x^2$, is larger for securities with larger slopes. For this reason, investors think of securities with slopes b_1 greater than one as "aggressive" and slopes less than one as "defensive."

This summarization immediately raises two additional issues. First, what is the effect of the October 1987 crash on the fitted regression equation? We know that unusual observations, such as the crash, may potentially influence the fit a great deal. To this end, the regression was re-run without the observation corresponding to the crash. The motivation for this is that the October 1987 crash represents a combination of highly unusual events (the interaction of several automated trading programs operated by the large stock brokerage houses) that we do not wish to represent using the same model as our other observations. Deleting this observation, the estimated regression is

$$\widehat{\text{LINCOLN}} = -0.00181 + 0.956\ \text{MARKET},$$

Unusual points represent an opportunity because they allow the data analyst to observe the relationship between variables over broader ranges than otherwise possible.

with $R^2 = 26.4\%$, $t(b_1) = 4.52$, $s = 0.0702$ and $s_y = 0.0811$. We interpret these statistics in the same fashion as the fitted model including the October 1987 crash. It is interesting to note, however, that the proportion of variability has actually *decreased* when excluding the influential point. This illustrates an important point. High leverage points are often looked upon with dread by data analysts because they are, by definition, unlike other observations in the data set and require special attention. However, when fitting relationships among variables, they also represent an *opportunity* because they allow the data analyst to observe the relationship between variables over broader ranges than otherwise possible. The downside is that these relationships may be nonlinear or follow an entirely different pattern when compared to the relationships observed in the main portion of the data.

Regression analysis serves to identify unusual points. However, it does not provide information about the special causes that makes these points unusual.

The second question raised by the regression analysis is what can be said about the unusual circumstances that gave rise to the unusual behavior of Lincoln's returns in October and November of 1990. The useful feature of regression analysis is to identify and raise the question; it does not resolve it. Because the analysis clearly pinpoints two highly unusual points, it suggests to the data analyst to go back and ask some specific questions about the sources of the data. In this case, the answer is straightforward. In October of 1990, the Travelers' Insurance Company, a competitor, announced that it would take a large write-off in their real estate portfolio due to an unprecedented number of mortgage defaults. The market reacted quickly to this news, and investors assumed that other large stock life insurers would also soon announce large write-offs. Anticipating this news, investors tried to sell their portfolios of, for example, Lincoln's stock, thus causing the price to plummet. However, it turned out that investors overreacted to this news and that Lincoln's portfolio of real estate was indeed sound. Thus, prices quickly returned to their historical levels.

3.7 REGRESSION ANALYSIS COMPUTER OUTPUT FOR SEVERAL SELECTED STATISTICAL PACKAGES (OPTIONAL)

Computers, and statistical software packages that perform specialized calculations, play a vital role in modern-day statistical analyses. Inexpensive computing capabilities have allowed data analysts to focus on relationships of interest. Specifying models that are attractive merely for their computational simplicity is much less important than before the widespread availability of inexpensive computing. An important theme of this text is to focus on relationships of interest, and to rely on widely available statistical software to estimate the models that we specify.

With any computer package, generally the most difficult parts of operating the package are the (i) input, (ii) using the commands, (iii) generating output and (iv) interpreting the output. You will find that most modern statistical software packages accept spreadsheet or text-based, such as ASCII, input files, making input of data relatively easy. Most microcomputer statistical software packages have menu-driven command languages with easily accessible on-line help facilities. Thus, you will find that, once you decide what to do, finding the right commands is relatively easy. Generating output seems to be a problem that is site-specific; for example, this depends on whether or not you would like paper output, whether the output is to be routed through a word-processor, and so on. Although an easy problem for each site, it is difficult to give general rules for all sites and all statistical software packages.

This section provides some guidance in interpreting the output of statistical packages. Specifically, you will find that most statistical packages generate similar output. Below, four examples of standard statistical software packages, MINITAB, SYSTAT, SPSS and SAS are given. The annotation symbol "[.]" marks a statistical quantity that is described in the legend. Thus, this section provides a link between the notation used in the text and output from some of the standard statistical packages.

MINITAB Computer Output

The regression equation is [a]
PRICE = 58.7 + 0.211 INCOME

Predictor	Coef	Stdev	t-ratio	P
Constant	58.663[b]	7.498[d]	7.82[f]	0.000[h]
INCOME	0.21132[c]	0.01508[e]	14.01[g]	0.000[i]

s = 24.59[j]   R-sq = 76.6%[k] R-sq(adj) −76.2%[1]

Analysis of Variance

SOURCE	DF	SS	MS	F	P
Regression	1[m]	118689[p]	118689[s]	196.26[u]	0.000[v]
Error	60[n]	36285[q]	605[t]		
Total	61[o]	154974[r]			

Unusual Observations

Obs.	INCOME	PRICE	Fit	Stdev. Fit	Residual	St.Resid	
11[w]	750[x]	280.00[y]	217.16[z]	5.47[A]	62.84[B]	2.62R	[C]
15	1020	230.00	274.21	9.12	-44.21	-1.94 X	
39	710	260.00	208.70	4.99	51.30	2.13R	
41	938	268.00	256.89	7.97	11.11	0.48 X	
49	960	225.00	261.53	8.28	-36.53	-1.58 X	
62	440	98.00	151.65	3.13	-53.65	-2.20R	

R denotes an obs. with a large st. resid. [D]
X denotes an obs. whose X value gives it large influence.[E]

SYSTAT Computer Output

DEP VAR: PRICE   N: 62   MULTIPLE R: 0.875[F] SQUARED MULTIPLE R: 0.766[k]
ADJUSTED SQUARED MULTIPLE R: .762[1]   STANDARD ERROR OF ESTIMATE: 24.592[J]

VARIABLE	COEFFICIENT	STD ERROR	STD COEF	TOLERANCE	T	P(2 TAIL)
CONSTANT	58.663[b]	7.498[d]	0.000	·	7.824[f]	0.000[h]
INCOME	0.211[c]	0.015[e]	0.875[G]	.100E+01	14.009[g]	0.000[i]

ANALYSIS OF VARIANCE

SOURCE	SUM-OF-SQUARES	DF	MEAN-SQUARE	F-RATIO	P
REGRESSION	118689.215[p]	1[m]	118689.215[s]	196.261[u]	0.000[v]
RESIDUAL	36285.172[q]	60[n]	604.753[t]		

SPSS Computer Output
          * * * *   M U L T I P L E   R E G R E S S I O N   * * * *

Listwise Deletion of Missing Data
Equation Number 1   Dependent Variable··   PRICE
Block Number 1· Method: Enter   INCOME

Variable(s) Entered on Step Number
   1··   INCOME

Multiple R   .87514[F]
R Square   .76586[k]
Adjusted R Square   .76196[l]
Standard Error   24.59172[j]

Analysis of Variance
                  DF   Sum of Squares   Mean Square
Regression   1[m]   118689.21521[p]   118689.21531[s]
Residual   60[n]   36285.17178[q]   604.75286[t]

F =   196.26069[u]   Signif F =   .000[v]

-----------------Variables in the Equation ----------------------

Variable   B   SE B   Beta   T Sig T

INCOME   .211324[c]   .015085[e] .875136[G]   14.009[g] .0000[i]
(Constant) 58.663339[b] 7.498144[d]   7.824[f] .0000[h]

SAS Computer Output
                            The SAS System

Model: MODEL1
Dependent Variable: PRICE

                        Analysis of Variance

                          Sum of   Mean
    Source   DF   Squares   Square   F Value   Prob>F

    Model   1[m]   118689.21531[p] 118689.21531[s] 196.261[u] 0.0001[v]
    Error   60[n]   36285.17178[q]   604.75286[t]
    C Total   61[o]   154974.38710[r]

        Root MSE   24.59172[j]   R-square   0.7659[k]
        Dep Mean   154.16129[H]   Adj R-sq   0.7620[l]
        C.V.   15.95194[I]

                        Parameter Estimates

                  Parameter   Standard   T for H0:
    Variable   DF   Estimate   Error   Parameter=0   Prob > |T|

    INTERCEP   1   58.663339[b]   7.49814406[d]   7.824[f]   0.0001[h]
    INCOME   1   0.211324[c]   0.01508454[e]   14.009[g]   0.0001[i]

| *Annotation* | *Definition* |
Symbol	
[a]	The fitted regression equation $\hat{y} = b_0 + b_1 x$.
[b]	The estimated intercept b_0.
[c]	The estimated slope b_1.
[d]	The standard error of the intercept, $se(b_0)$.
[e]	The standard error of the intercept, $se(b_1)$.
[f]	The t-ratio associated with the intercept, $t(b_0) = b_0 / se(b_0)$.
[g]	The t-ratio associated with the slope, $t(b_1) = b_1 / se(b_1)$.
[h]	The p-value associated with the intercept; here, p-value $=$ Prob($|t| > |t(b_0)|$), where $t(b_0)$ is the realized value (7.82 here) and t has a t-distribution with $df = n - 2$.
[i]	The p-value associated with the slope; here, p-value $=$ Prob($|t| > |t(b_1)|$), where $t(b_1)$ is the realized value (14.01 here) and t has a t-distribution with $df = n - 2$.
[j]	The residual standard deviation, s.
[k]	The coefficient of determination, R^2.
[l]	The coefficient of determination adjusted for degrees of freedom, R_a^2. (This term will be defined Chapter 4.)
[m]	Degrees of freedom for the regression component. This is one for one independent variable.
[n]	Degrees of freedom for the error component, $n - 2$, for regression with one independent variable.
[o]	Total degrees of freedoms, $n - 1$.
[p]	The regression sum of squares, Regression SS.
[q]	The error sum of squares, Error SS.
[r]	The total sum of squares, Total SS.
[s]	The regression mean square, Regression MS $=$ Regression SS/1, for one independent variable.
[t]	The error mean square, $s^2 =$ Error MS $=$ (Error SS)$/(n - 2)$, for one independent variable.
[u]	The F-ratio $=$ (Regression MS)/(Error MS). (This term will be defined in Chapter 4.)
[v]	The p-value associated with the F-ratio; here, p-value $=$ Prob($F > F$-ratio), and F has an F-distribution with $df_1 = 1$ and $df_2 = n - 2$ degrees of freedom. (This term will be defined in Chapter 7.)
[w]	The observation number, i.
[x]	The value of the independent variable for the ith observation, x_i.
[y]	The response for the ith observation, y_i.

[z]   The fitted value for the ith observation, $\hat{y}_i$.

[A]   The standard error of the fit, $se(\hat{y}_i)$. See the Technical Supplements for a definition of this quantity.

[B]   The residual for the ith observation, $\hat{e}_i$.

[C]   The standardized residual for the ith observation, $\hat{e}_i/se(\hat{e}_i)$. The standard error $se(\hat{e}_i)$ will be defined in Chapter 6.

[D]   Points with a large standardized residual are marked by an "R". Minitab marks points if the standardized residual exceeds two in absolute value.

[E]   Points with high leverage are marked with an "X". Minitab marks a point if the leverage exceeds three times the average leverage. (Leverage will be defined in Chapter 6.)

[F]   The multiple correlation coefficient is the square root of the coefficient of determination, $R = (R^2)^{1/2}$. This will be defined in Chapter 4.

[G]   The standardized coefficient is $b_1 s_x/s_y$. For regression with one independent variable, this is equivalent to r, the correlation coefficient.

[H]   The average response, $\bar{y}$.

[I]   The coefficient of variation of the response is $s_y/\bar{y}$. SAS prints out $100\, s/\bar{y}$.

3.8 SUMMARY

This chapter extended the groundwork laid in Chapter 2 to the regression model. That is, in both chapters, we focused on (i) presenting reasonable statistics that describe the data, (ii) introducing a model to represent the data and (iii) showing how to use the model to make important decisions. These decisions focused on understanding aspects of the available data and making predictions about future data.

In this chapter, we considered the regression model in the simplest context; using only one independent variable. We began with Section 3.1, which provides the structure for summarizing the data. Section 3.2 introduced a model for the data and Section 3.3 provided several quantities for deciding whether there is a reasonable match between the data and the model. Assuming that the match is reasonable, Section 3.4 summarized some of the things that we have learned from the model. Assuming that the match is not reasonable, Section 3.5 discussed how to improve the model specification. Section 3.6 presented an important application in finance, the Capital Asset Pricing Model (CAPM).

Chapter 4 will extend our regression techniques by allowing for several explanatory variables. The chapter development will mimic Chapter 3: we will present some reasonable statistics, a model and then rules for making decisions using the model. By considering several variables, we will considerably enlarge our scope of potential applications.

KEY WORDS, PHRASES AND SYMBOLS

After reading this chapter, you should be able to define each of the following important terms, phrases and symbols in your own words. If not, go to the page indicated and review the definition.

observation, 68
(x_i, y_i), 68
scatter plot, 69
correlation, 70
ordinary (Pearson) correlation coefficient, 70
sum of cross-products of deviations, 71
r, 72
positively, negatively correlated, 72
location invariant, 72
scale invariant, 72
standardized versions, 72
dimensionless measure, 73
linear relationship, 73
quadratic relationship, 73
response variable, 74
dependent variable, 74
explanatory variable, 74

independent variable, 74
collinear, 75
b_0, 76
intercept, 76
b_1, 76
slope, 76
method of least squares, 77
least squares estimate, 78
estimated (fitted) regression line, 78
$\hat{y}$, 78
β_0, β_1, 79
basic linear regression model, 79
homoscedastic, 80
heteroscedastic, 80
total sum of squares, 81
fitted value, 82
total sum of squares (Total SS), 83
error sum of squares (Error SS), 83

regression sum of squares (Regression SS), 83
coefficient of determination, (R^2), 83
residual $(\hat{e})$, 84
mean square error (s^2), 84
residual standard error (s), 84
error degrees of freedom, 84
analysis of variance (ANOVA) table, 85
degrees of freedom (df), 85
error mean square (Error MS), 85
regression mean square (Regression MS), 85
t-test, 85
$t(b_1)$, 86
$se(b_1)$, 86

$se(pred)$, 91
residual analysis, 91
standardized residual, 92
outlier, 92
normal probability plot, 92
rank (R_i), 92
tail of the distribution, 93
normal score, 93
high leverage point, 95
sensitivity analysis, 97
quadratic regression, 97
Capital Asset Pricing Model (CAPM), 102
market imperfections, 104
bid (ask) stock price, 104
market efficiencies, 105
diversifiable (non) risk, 107

CHAPTER 3 EXERCISES

Sections 3.1–3.2

3.1 Consider the data set

i	1	2	3	4
x_i	−1	2	4	6
y_i	0	1	5	8

a. Give a rough scatter plot of the data.
b. Calculate the slope coefficient using
   i. the formula in the text,
   ii. part (b) of Exercise 3.34 and
   iii. part (c) of Exercise 3.34.
c. Which of the three methods is easiest to compute?

3.2 Consider the data set

i	1	2	3	4
x_i	0	1	5	6
y_i	1	2	4	5

a. Give a rough scatter plot of the data.
b. Calculate the slope coefficient using
   i. the formula in the text.
   ii. part (b) of Exercise 3.34 and
   iii. part (c) of Exercise 3.34.
c. Which of the three methods is easiest to compute?

3.3 A scatter plot of final exam scores (FINAL) and midterm scores (MIDTERM) is given for 300 students. Each exam score is rescaled so that the total course score (TOTAL) is computed as the midterm exam plus the final exam, that is,

$$\text{TOTAL} = \text{MIDTERM} + \text{FINAL}.$$

The correlation between MIDTERM and FINAL for the 300 students turns out to be only 0.016. The instructor decides to further analyze the performance of the those students with a TOTAL score below the 25th percentile which turned out to be 68.

a. Give a rough scatter plot of the performance of the original 300 students in terms of their MIDTERM and FINAL exam performance.
b. Superimpose a line on your scatter plot which would serve to divide the group of 75 students selected for further analysis from the remaining 225 students.
c. Qualitatively describe what you would expect the correlation coefficient to be for the group of 75 students (that is, is it close to 1, -1, 0, and so on).

3.4 For a fixed (constant) interest yield of $i = 10\%$, the present value of \$1 that will be paid in x years is currently worth $y = 1/(1 + i)^x$ dollars. An insurance salesperson makes the statement that the present value of \$1 (y) is perfectly negatively correlated to the time of payment (x). That is, the later the payment of \$1 is in time, the smaller the present value of its worth. Further, the salesperson states that correlation is unaffected by multiplying by any fixed number, so that the present value of \$1,000 paid in x years is perfectly negatively correlated to x.

a. Define the use of the word 'correlation' in the statistical sense and compare this definition to the concept used by the salesperson.
b. Describe why, or why not, the second argument concerning multiplying by \$1,000 is valid for each definition.

C3_GALTN

3.5 Refer to the Galton Data in Chapter 1
Regression analysis of data is so pervasive in modern business that it is easy to overlook the fact that the methodology is barely over 100 years old. Scholars attribute the

birth of regression to the 1885 presidential address of Sir Francis Galton to the anthropological section of the British Association of the Advancement of Sciences. In that address, Galton provided a statistical description of regression. His discovery arose as the result of his studies of properties of natural selection and inheritance. Table 1.1, in Chapter 1, is a display of the data included in Galton's 1885 paper.

a. For those children whose midparents height is less than 64 inches, give a rough sketch of a histogram of the heights of the adult children.

b. Using the data in Table 1.1, calculate an approximate average height of the adult children for:

   i.   those children whose midparents height is less than 64 inches and,

   ii. those children whose midparents height is greater than 73 inches.

c. The data in Table 1.1 has been summarized with the following results. The average and standard deviation of the heights of the adult children are 68.093 and 2.543 inches, respectively. The average and standard deviation of the heights of midparents are 68.303 and 1.812 inches, respectively. The correlation between these two measures is 0.460.

   i.   Calculate the least squares regression line, using the midparents height to predict the height of an adult child.

   ii. Use the least squares regression line to predict the height of an adult child for a midparents height of 63.5 inches.

   iii. Use the least squares regression line to predict the height of an adult child for a midparents height of 73.5 inches.

3.6 For each of the scatter plots in Figures E3.6a–e, say whether the correlation coefficient is close to $-1, 0$ or 1. Explain briefly your reasoning.

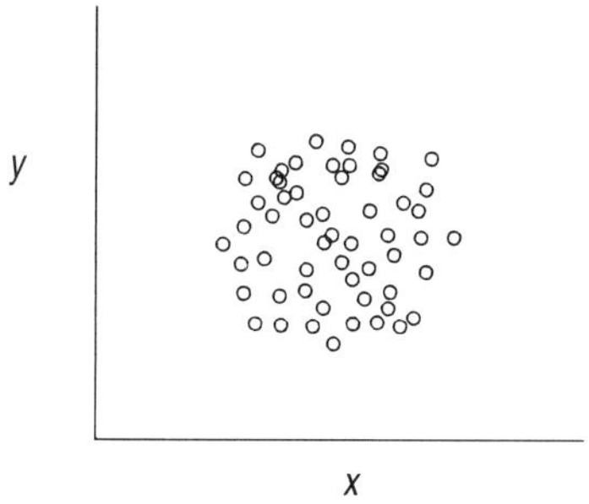

FIGURE E3.6a

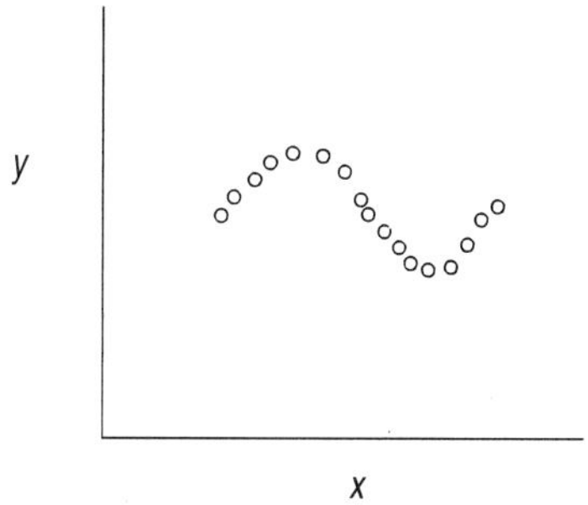

FIGURE E3.6b

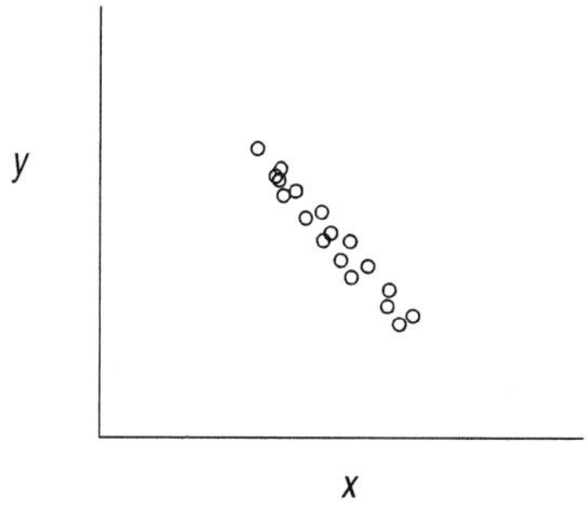

FIGURE E3.6c

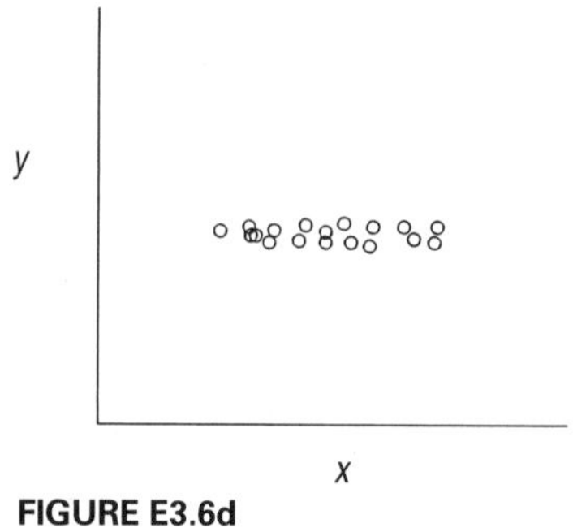

FIGURE E3.6d

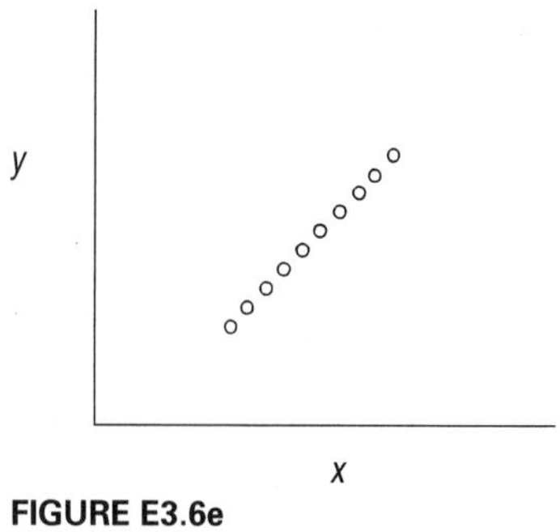

FIGURE E3.6e

3.7 a. Produce a rough scatter plot of the data:

i	1	2	3	4	5
x_i	−2	−1	0	1	2
y_i	4	1	0	1	4

b. Compute the correlation coefficient for this data.
c. Note the perfect relationship between the variables in that $y = x^2$. Discuss why and why not one might expect the correlation coefficient to be one.

3.8 Consider the eight observations in Figure E3.8. Establish that the least squares line passes through the point

$$\left(\frac{x_1 + x_2}{2}, \ \frac{3}{7}y_1 + \frac{4}{7}\bar{y}\right).$$

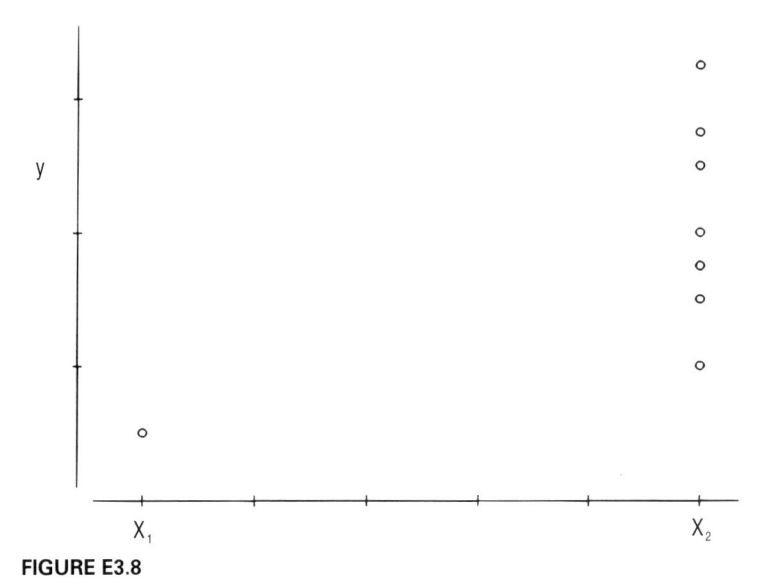

FIGURE E3.8

3.9 Consider the following three scatter plots of a fictitious data set in Figure E3.9.
a. The scatter plot on the upper left of Figure E3.9 has a fitted regression line superimposed.
  i. Define heteroscedasticity.
  ii. Describe the heteroscedasticity that is evident in the scatter plot on the upper left of Figure E3.9.
b. The scatter plot in the upper right of Figure E3.9 also has free-hand lines drawn to capture the broad tendencies of the data. Describe how these free-hand lines help us to see the heteroscedasticity.
c. The scatter plot on the lower left of Figure E3.9 also has several normal curves superimposed at each level of the independent variable. Describe how the changing shape of the curves help us to describe the heteroscedasticity in the data.

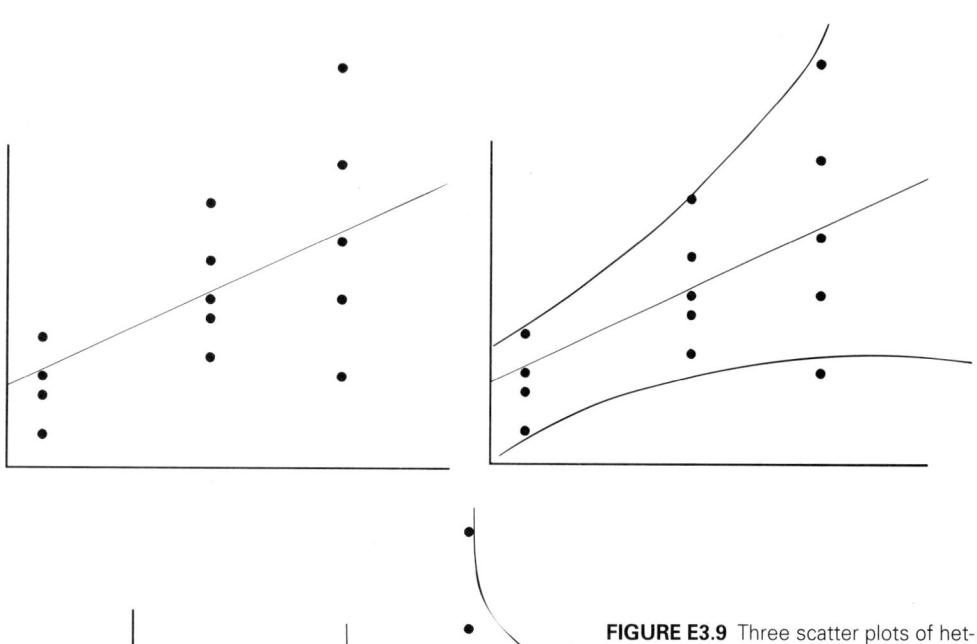

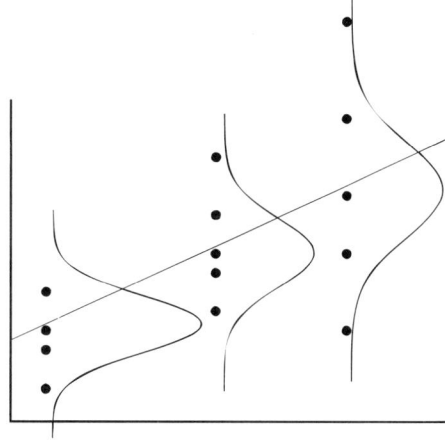

FIGURE E3.9 Three scatter plots of heteroscedastic data. The scatter plot on the upper left has a fitted regression line superimposed. The scatter plot on the upper right has a fitted regression line superimposed and free-hand lines drawn to capture the broad tendencies of the data. The scatter plot on the lower left has a fitted regression line superimposed and several normal curves to show how the distribution varies at each level of the independent variable.

Section 3.3

3.10 You are analyzing a data set of size $n = 100$. You have just performed a regression analysis using one explanatory variable and notice that the residual for the 10th observation is unusually large.

    a. Suppose that, in fact, it turns out that $\hat{e}_{10} = 8\,s$. What percentage of the error sum of squares, Error SS, is due to the 10th observation?

    b. Suppose that $\hat{e}_{10} = 4\,s$. What percentage of the error sum of squares, Error SS, is due to the 10th observation?

    c. Suppose that you reduce the data set to size $n = 20$. After running the regression, it turns out that we still have $\hat{e}_{10} = 4\,s$. What percentage of the error sum of squares, Error SS, is due to the 10th observation?

3.11 In a large class of 360 students, the results of a 40 point true–false exam have just been tallied. A diligent teaching assistant has recorded the number of correct answers (y)

and the number of incorrect answers (x) for each student. Suppose that a regression model $y = \beta_0 + \beta_1 x + e$ is fit to the data. What is b_0, b_1 and R^2? Is this a sensible model to fit to the data?

3.12 Consider the small, fictitious data set in Table E3.12.

   a. Provide a rough scatter plot for the data and verify that the intercept is $b_0 = 1$ and the slope is $b_1 = 3$. Superimposed the line on the scatter plot.

   b. Complete the table to calculate the error sum of squares and s^2. Verify that the average of the observations equals the average of the fitted values and that the average of the residuals is zero.

TABLE E3.12

y	x	$\hat{y}$	$\hat{e}$	$\hat{e}^2$
4.5	1			
9	3			
10	3			
15	4			
14.5	5			

3.13 You are given that the slope $b_1 = 2$ and that the point of averages, $(\bar{x}, \bar{y}) = (3, 6)$. Use this information to write down the equation of the fitted regression line. Interpret this result.

3.14 You are given three observations with $x_1 = -2$, $x_2 = 14$ and $x_3 = 6$. Suppose that $\hat{e}_1 = 1$, $b_0 = -1$ and $b_1 = 2$. Determine y_1, y_2 and y_3.

3.15 Suppose that, for a sample size of $n = 3$, you have $\hat{e}_2 = 24$ and $\hat{e}_3 = -1$. Determine $\hat{e}_1$.

3.16 Draw a rough sketch corresponding to Figure 3.12 with an observation below the fitted regression line.

3.17 Suppose that $r = 0$, $n = 15$ and $s_y = 10$. Determine s.

3.18 A student runs a regression with y measured in dollars and x measured in years since 1960. The regression yields $b_0 = 10$, $b_1 = 2$, $s = 10$, and $r = 0.850$. However, you have determined that it is more meaningful to report the statistical results in terms of y measured in thousands of dollars and x measured in years since 1970.

   a. Write down the relationship between the old and new values of y, and similarly for x.

   b. Provide values of b_0, b_1, s, and r using these new values of y and x.

C6_STINS

3.19 A financial analyst is investigating the performance of a stock life insurance company in the second quarter of its fiscal period in 1991. Because of a series of abnormal charges, second quarter earnings are atypical for this company. The analyst would like to determine what the "normal" earnings for this company would have been in the absence of these abnormal charges. To do this, the analyst selects a sample of size $n = 36$ stock insurance companies and compares the relationship between their 1991 second quarter earnings per share to their 1990 earnings per share. A graph of that relationship is given in Figure E3.19.

     The graph shows a strong relationship between the 1991 second quarter earnings per share, EPS (y), and the 1990 earnings per share, EPS90 (x). The average values of y and x were, respectively, $\bar{y} = 0.985$ and $\bar{x} = 3.671$. The corresponding standard de-

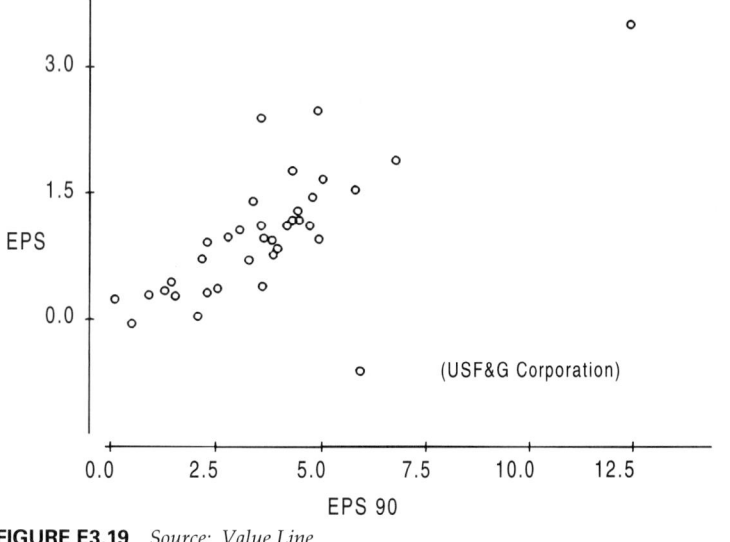

FIGURE E3.19   *Source: Value Line*

viations were $s_y = 0.784$ and $s_x = 2.155$. If fact, the correlation between the two was $r = 0.717$. The fitted regression equation turned out to be

$$y = 0.028 + 0.261x$$

with an estimated standard deviation of $s = 0.5541$.

After the financial analyst had completed these calculations, the unusual performance of the company (USF&G) in the second quarter of 1991 was noted in the graph. The analyst would like to have available the summary statistics previously described without USF&G, which happened to be the 30th observation. Specifically, we have $y_{30} = -0.62$ and $x_{30} = 5.90$. Now, suppose that USF&G has been deleted from the data set and that you are now working with $n = 35$ companies.

a. Calculate the new values of $\bar{y}$ and $\bar{x}$.
b. Calculate the new values of s_y and s_x. [Hint: Use the relationship $(n-1)s_y^2 = \sum_{i=1}^{n} y_i^2 - n\bar{y}^2$ and use the result in part (a).]
c. Calculate the new value of r. [Hint: Use the relationship $\sum_{i=1}^{n}(x_i - \bar{x})(y_i - \bar{y}) = \sum_{i=1}^{n} x_i y_i - n\bar{x}\bar{y}$.]
d. Use parts (b) and (c) to complete the ANOVA table.
e. What is the percentage change in the standard deviation s between the original data set analyzed and the data set with USF&G deleted?
f. What is the percentage change in the coefficient of determination between the original data set analyzed and the data set with USF&G deleted?

3.20 You have just completed a study using sales of a company to predict salaries of the companies' chief executive officer (CEO). You have determined values of r, b_1 and R^2. You ask an assistant to independently replicate your study. Unfortunately, the assistant mistakenly has used CEO's salaries to predict company sales. Explain to the assistant which of the quantities

1. r,
2. b_1
3. R^2

remains the same and which are different. Further, go over with the assistant the reasons why these quantities are different.

Section 3.4

3.21 Consider a data set consisting of 20 observations with the following summary statistics:

$$\bar{x} = 0, \bar{y} = 9, s_x = 1 \quad \text{and} \quad s_y = 10.$$

You run a regression using one variable and determine that $s = 7$. Determine the standard error of a prediction at $x_* = 1$.

3.22 You have run a regresssion using one variable on a data set with 6 observations and obtained the least square estimates:

$$b_0 = 2 \quad \text{and} \quad b_1 = 3.$$

Unfortunately, the data set has been partially erased. You still have available

i	1	2	3	4	5	6
x_i	0	2	4	6	8	10
y_i	2.7	7.3	11.5	14.8	*	*

Here, the asterisk, or star ('*') represents a missing value. Determine y_5 and y_6.

3.23 **Refer to Exercise 2.29**

C2_STOCK

Suppose that you are interested in relating the accounting variable EPS to the market variable STKPRICE. Figure E3.23 is a scatter plot of the stock price, STKPRICE, versus earnings per share, EPS. The corresponding fitted equation is $\hat{STKPRICE} = 30.396 + 4.381$ EPS. The figure and scatter plot summarizes information for 49 firms; Public Service of New Hampshire (PCNHQ) was excluded because no information is available on the earnings per share.

a. From the figure, we see that the Polaroid Company is very unusual. An examination of the data reveals that the earnings per share for this company is $EPS_{19} = 12.54$ and the stock price is $STKPRICE_{19} = 29.75$

   i.   Calculate the fitted value for this company.

   ii. Calculate the residual for this company.

b. For the 31st company, Public Service of New Hampshire (PCNHQ), no earnings per share figure is available. However, the stock price of the company is available, and is $STKPRICE_{31} = 19.125$.

   i.   Use this stock price and the table of summary statistics to calculate the average stock price for the 49 companies, excluding PCNHQ.

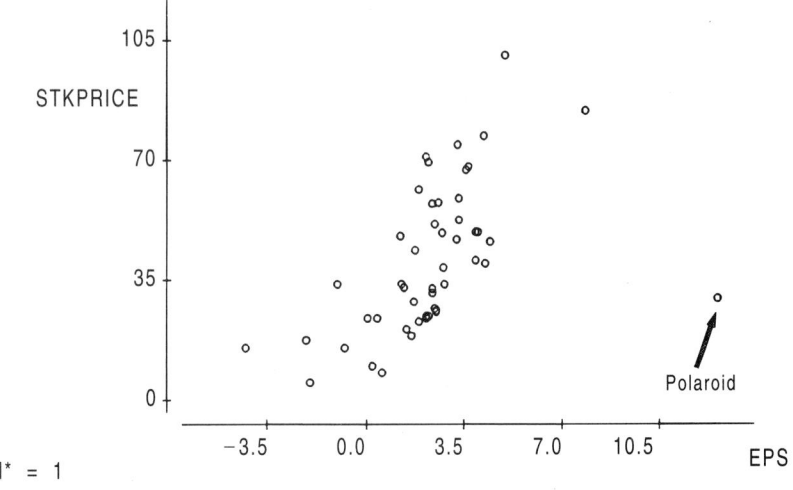

FIGURE E3.23 Scatter plot of stock price versus earnings per share. *Source: Forbes Magazine*

  ii. Use this stock price and the table of summary statistics to calculate the standard deviation of stock price for the 49 companies, excluding PCNHQ. [Hint: Use the relationship $(n - 1) s_y^2 = \Sigma_{i=1}^{n} y_i^2 - n\bar{y}^2$ and use the result in part (i).]

  iii. Use the standard deviation calculated in part (ii) to calculate the correlation coefficient between EPS and STKPRICE for the 49 companies, excluding PCNHQ.

C3_MLS

3.24 What are the factors that influence the selling price of a home? Suppose that a new real estate agent, working on the West Side of Madison, Wisconsin, wants to quickly gain some experience on pricing residential real estate properties. Value of a property is a difficult thing to measure. One of the best measures is what the market is willing to pay for a property. To this end, she collects a sample of 81 homes that were sold in three neighborhoods during 1991. This data was easy for her to get, because it was available from the Multiple Listing Service, compiled by the Madison Realtor Association. The information from this database includes the actual selling price of the home (PRICE) in thousands of dollars, size of the home in terms of the exposed square feet (EXSQFT), size of the home in terms of the total square feet (TOTSQFT, which equals exposed square feet plus unexposed square feet, that is TOTSQFT = EXSQFT + UNEXSQFT), the number of bedrooms (BEDROOM), the number of bathrooms (BATHROOM), the age of the house in years (AGE) and the neighborhood (13, 14 or 15).

  After some preliminary analysis of the data, it turns out that the size of the house, as measured by EXSQFT, is an important determinant of the selling price. Some summary statistics of these two variables are given in Table E3.24a and a scatter plot is also given (Figure E3.24). A fitted regression equation produced PRICE = 2.98 + 0.0652 EXSQFT with a correlation coefficient $r = 0.7955$.

  a. From the summary statistics and the fitted regression line, calculate the coefficient of determination, R^2.

  b. Complete the analysis of variance (ANOVA) table (Table E3.24b).

TABLE E3.24a Summary Statistics of House Price and Size

	Number	Mean	Median	Standard deviation	Minimum	Maximum
PRICE	81	94.51	86.20	36.48	36.90	277.50
EXSQFT	81	1,404.3	1,328.0	4,45.1	676.0	3,100.0

TABLE E3.24b ANOVA Table

Source	Sum of Squares	df	Mean Square
Regression			
Error			
Total			

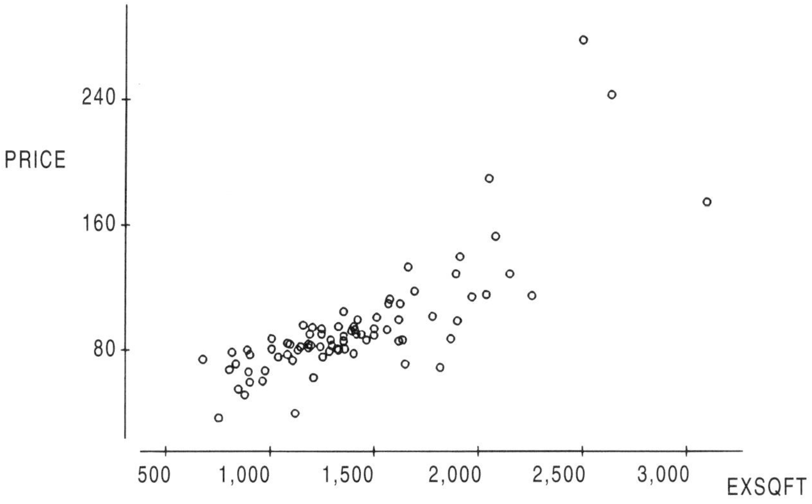

FIGURE E3.24 *Source: Madison Realtors Association*

    c. For the first observation, we have $PRICE_1 = 277.5$ and $EXSQFT_1 = 2,500$.

        i. Calculate the corresponding residual, $\hat{e}_1$.

        ii. How many multiples of s is the residual $\hat{e}_1$ away from 0?

        iii. What percentage of the error sum of squares, Error SS, is due to the first observation?

Section 3.5

3.25 A standard residual was the sixteenth smallest out of a sample size of 100, so that it is the $(16 - 3/8)/(100 + 1/4) = 0.15586$, or 15.586% percentile.

    a. Define the normal score.

    b. Compute the normal score for the sixteenth observation.

    c. Define the normal probability plot.

3.26 The data in Table E3.26 is due to Anscombe (1973). The purpose of this exercise is to demonstrate how plotting data can reveal important information that is not evident in numerical summary statistics. For this data set:

    a. Compute the average and standard deviation for each column of data. Check that the averages and standard deviations of each of the x columns are the same, within two decimal places, and similarly for each of the y columns.

    b. Run four regressions.

        i. y_1 on x_1

        ii. y_2 on x_1

        iii. y_3 on x_1

        iv. y_4 on x_2

    Verify, for each of the four regressions fits, that $b_0 \approx 3.0$, $b_1 \approx 0.5$, $s \approx 1.237$ and $R^2 \approx 0.677$, within two decimal places.

    c. Produce scatter plots for each of the four regression models that you fit in part (b).

    d. Discuss the fact that the fitted regression models produced in part (b) imply that the four data sets are similar although the four scatter plots produced in part (c) yield a dramatically different story.

TABLE E3.26 Anscombe's (1973) Data

Observation number	x_1	y_1	y_2	y_3	x_2	y_4
1	10	8.04	9.14	7.46	8	6.58
2	8	6.95	8.14	6.77	8	5.76
3	13	7.58	8.74	12.74	8	7.71
4	9	8.81	8.77	7.11	8	8.84
5	11	8.33	9.26	7.81	8	8.47
6	14	9.96	8.10	8.84	8	7.04
7	6	7.24	6.13	6.08	8	5.25
8	4	4.26	3.10	5.39	8	5.56
9	12	10.84	9.13	8.15	8	7.91
10	7	4.82	7.26	6.42	8	6.89
11	5	5.68	4.74	5.73	19	12.50

Section 3.6

C3_CAPM

3.27 Consider monthly returns over the five year period from January 1986 to December 1990, inclusive. Specifically, use the security returns from the American Family Corporation as the dependent variable (y) and the market returns from the index of the Standard & Poor's 500 Index as the explanatory variable (x). A scatter plot for the variables is given in Figure E3.27 as well as the results of a regression model fit. (Tables E3.27a and b.)

    a. An analyst is concerned as to what extent the returns of American Family follow the returns of the market. Provide a point estimate of the slope and a 95% confidence interval.

    b. Suppose that you found the relationship between returns of American and the mar-

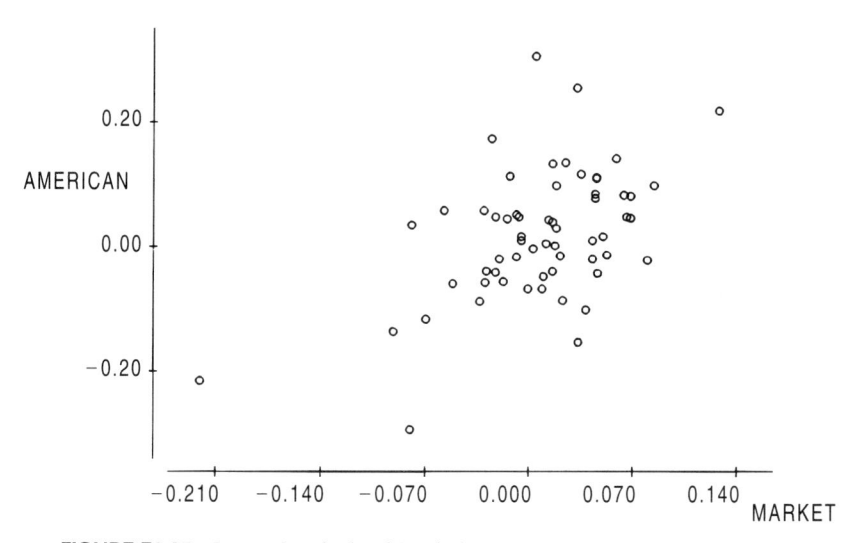

FIGURE E3.27   *Source: Standard and Poor's Compustat*

ket depressingly low. As an alternative to the coefficient of determination, calculate the correlation coefficient. Say which of the two measures is larger, and explain why.

c. Define the terms *outliers* and *high leverage points*. Use the scatter plot in Figure E3.27 to identify visually:

   i.   the two points that are most likely to be outliers and
   ii. the two points that are most likely to be high leverage points.

Regression Fit of American Returns on Market Returns

TABLE E3.27a   Coefficient Estimates

Explanatory variable	Coefficient	Standard error	*t*-ratio
Constant	0.00968	0.01181	0.82
MARKET	1.0017	0.2245	4.46

TABLE E3.27b   ANOVA Table

Source	Sum of Squares	*df*	Mean Square
Regression	0.16338	1	0.16338
Error	0.47608	58	0.00821
Total	0.63946	59	

Unusual Observations

Obs.	MARKET	AMERICAN	Fit	Residual	Std residual
1	0.005	0.3032	0.0144	0.2888	3.21
9	−0.081	−0.2945	−0.0713	−0.2232	−2.55
13	0.127	0.2163	0.1374	0.0790	0.92
20	0.032	0.2539	0.0419	0.2120	2.36
22	−0.221	−0.2164	−0.2112	−0.0052	−0.07
27	−0.025	0.1712	−0.0158	0.1870	2.09
41	0.034	−0.1552	0.0434	−0.1986	−2.22

C3_NCRAT

3.28 The purpose of this problem is to analyze an offer made by one firm to buy another firm. On December 2, 1990, American Telephone and Telegraph Company (AT&T) made a public offer to buy out the National Cash Register Company (NCR). NCR's reaction was a flat rejection. Still fighting AT&T's hostile intentions in March 1991, NCR took out a full page ad in *The New York Times* newspaper hoping to persuade its immediate stockholders that holding on to NCR's stock was the best thing to do. By using several statistical graphs, NCR's goal was to convince its stockholders and the general public that its stock, if given time, will on its own reach the level of AT&T's bidding price. Hence, there would be no need for the owners to sell their shares at that point in time for the purpose of gaining a quick profit. In NCR's eyes, the expected growth of NCR should be enough to insure the stability of the company as a whole and the reliability of the sure-to-increase stock value. If left alone, NCR's stock would reach that same value, if not greater, and benefit everyone with an interest in NCR to a much greater extent than the buyout would. To analyze the problem, we have available weekly observations of the price of NCR's stock and the Dow Jones Industrial Average (DOWJONES). Each column contains 61 observations. These observations are of Friday closing stock prices from January 1990 to February 1991. The first 49 weeks are prices before AT&T's offer. (See Figure E3.28a.)

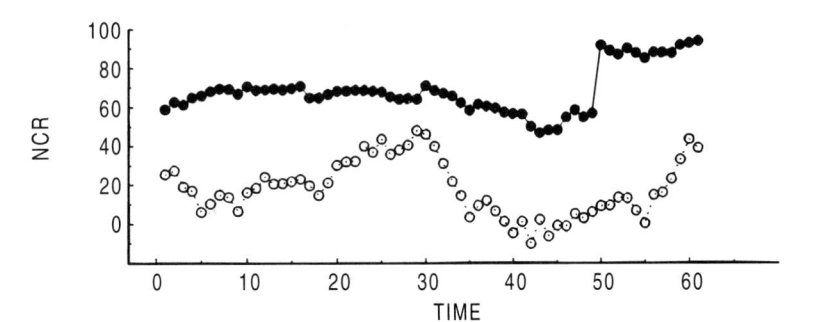

FIGURE E3.28a Weekly closing prices of NCR (opaque plotting symbol) and Dow Jones (standardized, circular transparent plotting symbol) over 61 weeks, from January 1990 to February 1991. *Source: Standard and Poor's Compustat*

a. Prices have been converted to returns and are plotted in Figure E3.28b. Use this figure to identify the outlying observation that corresponds to AT&T's offer.

b. Consider now the returns in the 48 weeks available before AT&T's offer. Figure E3.28c is a scatter plot of NCR's returns versus the returns from the market, using the Dow index. The correlation between these two variables is 0.368. Interpret the strength of the relationship between weekly NCR returns and the Dow index returns.

c. Consider fitting a regression model, using the Dow index returns to explain the behavior of NCR returns. Following are the statistics (Tables E3.28a and b) summarizing this regression fit. Describe whether or not this model is useful.

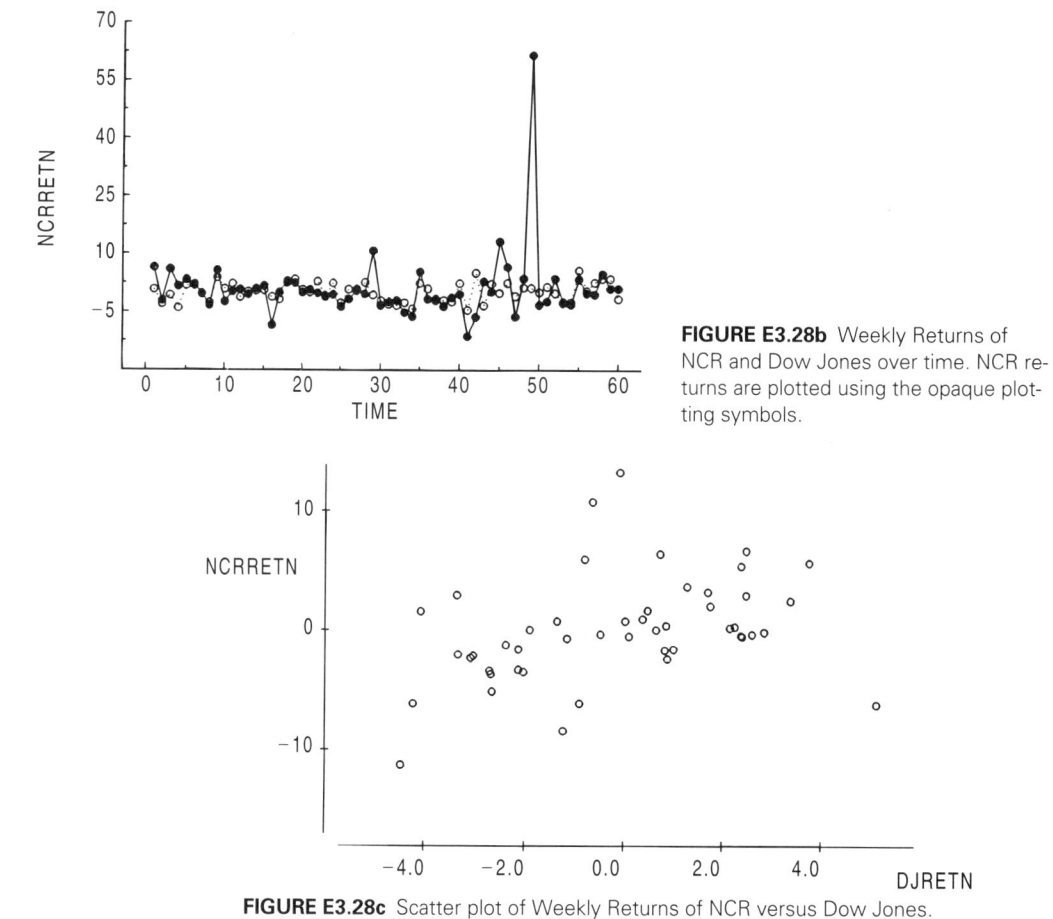

FIGURE E3.28b Weekly Returns of NCR and Dow Jones over time. NCR returns are plotted using the opaque plotting symbols.

FIGURE E3.28c Scatter plot of Weekly Returns of NCR versus Dow Jones.

TABLE E3.28a Coefficient Estimates

Explanatory variable	Coefficient	Standard error	t-ratio
Constant	0.1089	0.6109	0.18
DJRETN	0.7008	0.2608	2.69

TABLE E3.28b ANOVA Table

Source	Sum of Squares	df	Mean Square
Regression	129.00	1	129.00
Error	821.62	46	17.86
Total	950.62	47	

Unusual Observations

Obs.	DJRETN	NCRRETN	Fit	Residual	Std residual
29	−0.64	10.721	−0.339	11.061	2.65
41	−4.49	−11.308	−3.035	−8.273	−2.06
42	5.12	−6.250	3.697	−9.947	−2.52
45	−0.09	13.178	0.046	13.132	3.14

d. Following are the returns based on the Dow Jones Index in the 13 weeks immediately preceding and following AT&T's takeover offer (read across the rows):

1.28282   1.18963   0.14324   1.53635   −0.16897   −2.40071   −2.51745   5.80814
0.47718   2.68029   3.66207   3.67260   −1.54328.

With the model estimated in part (c), use these 13 returns to "predict" what the NCR returns would have been in absence of the AT&T offer.

e. The final NCR price available before the takeover offer is 56.75. Use this price and the predicted returns to estimate the NCR price as at the end of February 1991. Use this result to discuss whether or not NCR's claim is valid.

End-of-Chapter Exercises

3.29 For executives "on the go," small, portable microcomputers called *notebooks* are becoming an important tool in today's business world. In their August 1991 issue, *PC Magazine* compared a sample of the leading notebooks on the market at that time. All notebooks compared were 386 SX generation IBM-compatible machines. The comparisons included a number of *benchmark* tests as well as other factors such as price and speed of the processor. A benchmark test is simply a standard series of exercises that a computer is asked to perform so that a fair comparison can be made among competing brands. Table E3.29a contains the names of the 27 notebooks that *PC Magazine* reported on testing in this issue, together with their list price (LISTPRIC), the results of six benchmark tests, and the speed of the processor used in Megahertz (16 or 20). For the processor (PROCESSR), MEMORY, DISK and VIDEO benchmark tests, the results are given in seconds. The smaller is the result of the test, the more quickly the machine moved through the test and the better is the performance of the machine. For the BATTERY benchmark, this was a test as to how long the machine's internal battery lasted. This result is given in minutes, and the larger is the results of the battery test, the better is the machine.

a. Say whether the data is cross-sectional or longitudinal, and why.

b. A technical consultant who travels extensively was particularly interested in the relationship between the PROCESSR and BATTERY benchmark tests. To understand this relationship, a regression analysis was run using PROCESSR to understand BATTERY. (See Tables E3.29b and E3.29c.) Use the evidence from this output to decide whether PROCESSR has an important effect on BATTERY. Because this is an important decision, formally state the assumptions concerning the sample that one needs to make to use the formal test of hypothesis machinery.

c. Refer to part b. A colleague has argued that to understand the relationship between PROCESSR and BATTERY, the regression analysis should have been run using BATTERY to understand PROCESSR. What is the proportion of variability explained for this alternative regression analysis?

d. A notebook would be handy for working while traveling, for example, either by plane or by train. Presumably, many customers would find having longer batteries desirable and that this feature would be reflected in the pricing structure of the machines. (See Tables E3.29d and E3.29e.) To investigate this we:

    i. Give a rough scatter plot of the list price versus the BATTERY benchmark, assuming that knowledge of this benchmark will be used to understand the list price.

TABLE E3.29a Listing of Computer Variables

Manufacturer	LISTPRIC	PROCESSR	MEMORY	DISK	VIDEO	MHz	BATTERY
ALR Ventura	2,795	4.18	0.61	92.74	4.78	16	118
AST Premium Exc	2,995	3.44	0.58	67.05	3.68	20	158
Automated Comp Tech	2,845	4.17	0.72	73.23	4.34	16	157
Bitwise Notebook	1,995	4.23	0.66	70.48	5.22	16	118
Commax Notebook	2,994	4.17	0.61	67.98	4.78	16	130
Compaq LTE 30	4,399	3.09	0.44	68.85	1.54	20	154
CompuAdd Companion	2,999	3.78	0.55	73.14	4.01	20	125
Dataworld NB	2,650	3.75	0.53	87.02	3.96	20	102
Dell System 320N	3,548	3.53	0.58	67.11	2.81	20	181
Epson NB3s	4,298	4.10	0.66	72.58	3.18	16	62
Everex NB3s	3,299	4.18	0.72	72.43	4.39	16	158
IBM PS/2 L40	6,654	3.59	0.74	67.59	2.15	20	112
Leading Tech PC Partner XL	2,495	3.25	0.47	85.43	4.18	20	113
Micro Express NB5620	2,224	3.16	0.44	71.63	4.12	20	128
Micro Telesis NBa	1,699	4.11	0.64	73.14	5.27	16	120
Modern Computer Walkom NP-903	3,500	4.17	0.80	72.73	8.02	16	172
NMS Notebook	1,874	4.23	0.66	72.41	5.22	16	135
Northgate SlimLite	3,299	3.30	0.58	72.55	4.89	20	92
Samsung NoteMaster	3,698	4.24	0.60	73.27	3.73	16	143
Sanyo MBC-18NB	4,274	4.17	0.74	73.24	4.34	16	142
Tandon	3,495	3.27	0.55	67.02	2.58	20	111
Tangent 320N	2,183	3.16	0.44	72.21	4.12	20	101
TI TravelMate 3000	4,199	3.79	0.55	73.53	4.01	20	106
Toshiba T2000SX	4,999	4.76	0.66	83.44	1.38	16	188
Twinhead Supernote	3,495	4.76	0.69	83.44	5.38	16	110
Veridata Execulite	4,185	3.34	0.66	88.04	2.36	20	128
Zeos Notebook	3,014	4.16	0.75	73.33	4.33	16	156

Source: PC Magazine

TABLE E3.29b Coefficient Estimates

Explanatory variable	Coefficient	Standard error	t-ratio
Constant	77.02	45.06	1.71
PROCESSR	13.84	11.60	1.19

TABLE E3.29c ANOVA Table

Source	Sum of Squares	df	Mean Square
Regression	1167.6	1	1167.6
Error	20508.7	25	820.3
Total	21676.3	26	

TABLE E3.29d Summary Statistics of Computer Variables

	Number	Mean	Median	Standard deviation	Minimum	Maximum
LISTPRIC	27	3,337	3,299	1,070	1,699	6,654
PROCESSR	27	3.8548	4.1000	0.4842	3.0900	4.7600
MEMORY	27	0.6159	0.6100	0.0998	0.4400	0.8000
DISK	27	74.65	72.73	7.07	67.02	92.74
VIDEO	27	4.029	4.120	1.366	1.380	8.020
MHz	27	17.926	16.000	2.037	16.000	20.000
BATTERY	27	130.37	128.00	28.87	62.00	188.00

TABLE E3.29e   Table of Correlation Coefficients

	LISTPRIC	PROCESSOR	MEMORY	DISK	VIDEO	MHz
PROCESSR	0.026					
MEMORY	0.294	0.690				
DISK	−0.068	0.225	−0.008			
VIDEO	−0.565	0.338	0.329	0.027		
MHz	0.137	−0.883	−0.679	−0.099	−0.440	
BATTERY	0.092	0.232	0.284	−0.145	−0.060	−0.219

ii. Identify the correlation between the list price and the BATTERY benchmark. Use this and other information from the Minitab output to estimate the regression line. Superimpose a rough graph of the line on your scatter plot.

e. A notebook would be very handy for using the computer to illustrate ideas graphically. Suppose that a professor is particularly interested in the VIDEO benchmark as a measure of how low it takes the machine to build a complex image. Tables E3.29f and E3.29g show a regression analysis of using the VIDEO benchmark to understand the list price.

TABLE E3.29f   Coefficient Estimates

Explanatory variable	Coefficient	Standard error	t-ratio
Constant	5,119.5	549.1	9.32
VIDEO	−442.4	129.3	−3.42

TABLE E3.29g   ANOVA Table

Source	Sum of Squares	df	Mean Square
Regression	9,494,477	1	9,494,477
Error	20,280,774	25	811,231
Total	29,775,252	26	

Unusual Observations

Obs.	Video	LISTPRIC	Fit	Residual	Std residual
12	2.15	6654	4168	2486	2.93
16	8.02	3500	1571	1929	2.69

i. Is the VIDEO benchmark a reasonable predictor of list prices? Respond using only basic statistical arguments (evidence).

ii. One notebook that achieves a time of 4.00 seconds on the VIDEO benchmark lists for $2,999. Is this list price above or below what would have been expected using the regression line fit? Explain your answer.

iii. Suppose that, on the VIDEO benchmark, that notebooks are expected to get faster by one half a second. Assuming that the regression model is valid, what is the change in the expected list price of notebooks? Provide a 95% confidence level for this estimate.

iv. *Modern Computer Walkom* performed particularly poorly on the VIDEO benchmark. (This was due to its slow 8-bit video circuitry.) Discuss the effects of including this point in the regression. What would the regression have looked like without including this machine?

3.30 How much does it cost a major insurance company to complete an information systems computer project? To answer this, a large insurance company has developed an *automated* cost estimation system. This system includes 24 variables used in determining estimated costs. Management would like to understand the relationship between the estimated cost of a project and the projects' actual cost. To this end, a sample of 51 projects was collected. The data are cross-sectional. Additional information, not discussed here, was also collected of the types of programs and number of each type needed in each project. (See Figures E3.30a and b and Table E3.30.) The correlation between the ESTIMATE and ACTUAL is 0.941.

a. Fit the model $y = \beta_0 + \beta_1 x + e$ to these data.
b. Find R^2.
c. Provide a full analysis of variance table.
d. Test $H_0: \beta_1 = 0$ at the 5% level of significance using a t-statistic.
e. At a specified cost estimate of $x_* = 50{,}000$, do these things:
    i. Find the predicted value of y.
    ii. Obtain the standard error of the prediction.
    iii. Obtain a 95% prediction interval for your prediction.

TABLE E3.30 Summary Statistics of Costs

	Number	Mean	Median	Standard deviation	Minimum	Maximum
ESTIMATE	51	26,896	16,200	28,484	4,300	132,300
ACTUAL	51	27,999	14,792	33,506	1,793	148,266

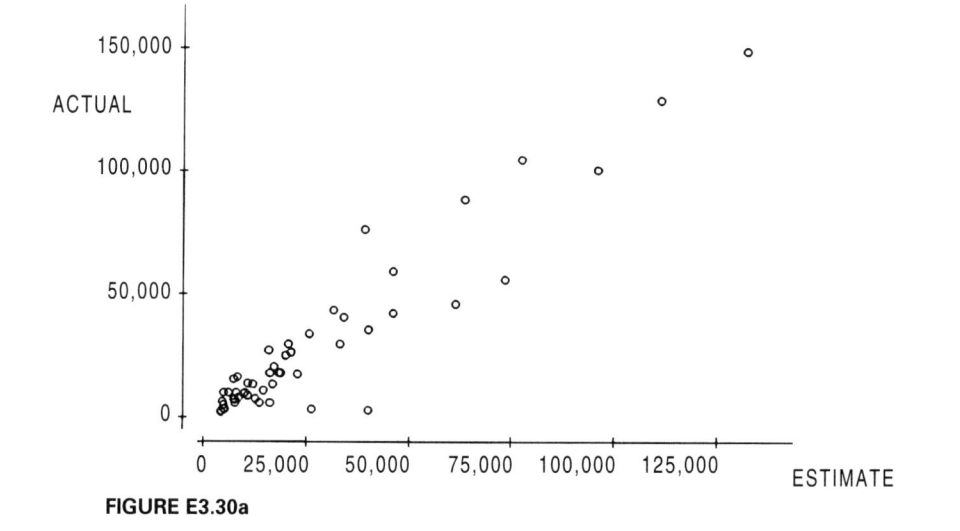

FIGURE E3.30a

```
: .
: :
::: .:: .                .
:::::::: ...  :. :  :        :       . .      .      .              .
+---------+---------+---------+---------+---------+------ ESTIMATE
0        25,000    50,000    75,000    100,000   125,000
```

```
. : .
: : :
::: . :
:::::::: .. : :.. . :.        . .     .    .     . .       .         .
+---------+---------+---------+---------+---------+------ ACTUAL
0        30,000    60,000    90,000    120,000   150,000
```

FIGURE E3.30b Dotplots of each cost variable.

3.31 Suppose that a true model is based on a variable $\{Z\}$ and two unrelated random error variables $\{e_1\}$ and $\{e_2\}$. However, we observe $\{y\}$ and $\{x\}$ defined by

$$y = Z + e_1 \quad \text{and} \quad x = Z + e_2.$$

To illustrate this, 10 observations follow.

Z	-25	-20	-15	-10	-5	0	5	10	15	20
e_1	-4	-4	-24	-5	1	3	16	7	9	1
e_2	17	9	-6	2	-2	-12	-10	16	-7	-12
x										
y										

a. Compute y and x.
b. Plot y versus Z and x versus Z.
c. Plot y versus x.
d. Use least squares to fit the line $\hat{y} = b_0 + b_1 x$.
e. Is there a statistically significant relationship between y and x?
f. How would your results in parts (a)–(e) change if you added 25 to each value of Z?
g. If you are using a computer, divide the original Z by 5 and re-do parts (a)–(e).
h. If you are using a computer, multiply the original Z by 10 and re-do parts (a)–(e).

3.32 Refer to Exercises 2.29 and 3.23
You decide to examine the relationship between STKPRICE (y) and EPS (x), after excluding the two companies, Public Service of New Hampshire and the Polaroid Company. Following is the computer output from your fitted regression.

C2_STOCK

```
The regression equation is
STKPRICE = 25.0 + 7.44 EPS

Predictor          Coef        Stdev       t-ratio          P
Constant          25.044       3.326          7.53       0.000
EPS                7.445       1.144          6.51       0.000

s = 15.73         R-sq =47.9%              R-sq (adj) = 46.8%

Analysis of Variance

SOURCE            DF           SS            MS           F          P
Regression         1         10475         10475       42.35      0.000
Error             46         11377           247
Total             47         21851

Unusual Observations
Obs.      EPS      STKPRICE       Fit        Residual     St. Resid
  8      7.86        84.25       83.56          0.69        0.05 X
 27      4.98       100.50       62.12         38.38        2.52R
 34     -4.26        15.37       -6.67         22.05         160 X

R denotes an obs. with a large st. resid.
X denotes an obs. whose X value gives it large influence.
```

FIGURE E3.32 Minitab computer output.

a. Use the computer output to calculate the correlation coefficient between EPS and STKPRICE.
b. You are interested in the effect that a marginal change in EPS has on the expected value of STKPRICE.
   i. Suppose that there is a marginal change in EPS of $2. Provide a point estimate of the expected change in STKPRICE.
   ii. Provide a 95% confidence interval corresponding to the point estimate in part (i).
c. Use the computer output to identify the high leverage points. That is, give the EPS and STKPRICE for these points. From the dotplots in Exercise 2.29, what is each point's rank in terms of EPS?

C3_USEDC

3.33 Suppose that you have just taken a position as an assistant marketing manager of local chain of used automobile dealers. Although there is a substantial amount of knowledge to be acquired through experience on pricing strategies for used cars, you are interested in finding out pricing behavior for similar, yet competing, markets. An important marketplace that competes with your dealerships is represented by private resales that are advertised in your local newspaper. Thus, for our analysis, we have data collected from the Sunday, November 14, 1993 issue of the *Wisconsin State Journal*, a local newspaper. Data for 212 listed automobiles were collected, in particular the asking price for a car (ASKPRICE). Information was also gathered on the automobile manu-

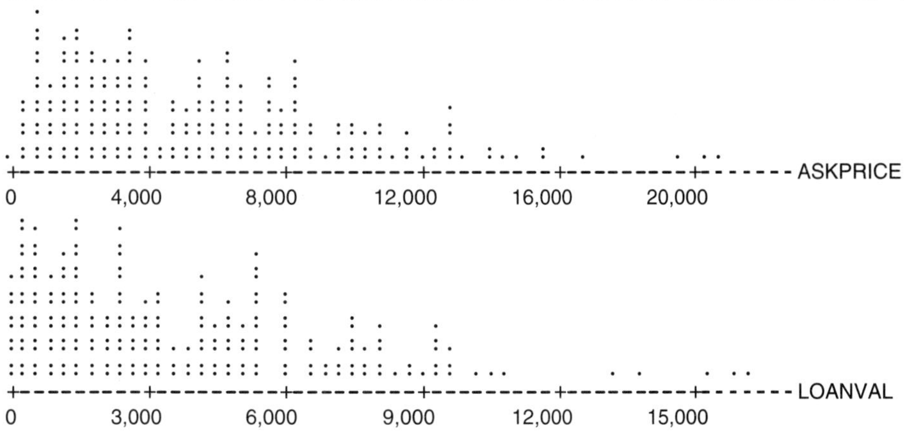

FIGURE E3.33a

facturer, the model type, the model year, the number of options beyond standard equipped power steering and brakes and the odometer mileage reading. This additional information was used with the National Automobile Dealers' Association *Resale Price Guide for the Central Region of the U.S.* to determine LOANVAL, the average amount a bank or finance company will finance. (Table E3.33a.)

The objective is to develop a model to understand the determinants of asking prices for used automobiles, ASKPRICE. Supporting summary measures follow. (Tables E3.33a through 3.33c.)

TABLE E3.33a   Summary Statistics for Automobile Price and Loan Value

	Number	Mean	Median	Standard deviation	Minimum	Maximum
ASKPRICE	212	5,648	4,935	4,179	150	20,995
LOANVAL	212	3,803	2,888	3,251	0	16,050

Source: Wisconsin State Journal and National Automobile Dealers' Association Resale Price Guide for the Central Region of the U.S.

TABLE E3.33b   Coefficient Estimates

Explanatory variable	Coefficient	Standard error	t-ratio
Constant	1,080.9	158.3	6.83
LOANVAL	1.20080	0.03167	37.92

TABLE E3.33c   ANOVA Table

Source	Sum of Squares	df	Mean Square
Regression	3,215,781,632	1	3,215,781,632
Error	469,602,816	210	2,236,204
Total	3,685,384,448	211	

a. Based on the regression output that follows, you instruct your dealers that a good rule of thumb for determining asking price (in the private resale market) is to "multiply the loan value by 120% and add $1,000." Your boss has questioned your rule.
   i.   To begin your explanations, use the computer output to calculate the correlation between ASKPRICE and LOANVAL.
   ii. Now defend your recommendation by interpreting the fitted regression equation.
   iii. As you explain to your boss, the fitted regression line is not perfect. What is your estimate of σ, the "natural variability" or deviation from the line?

b. Figure E3.33b is a plot of ASKPRICE versus LOANVAL.
   i.   Indicate on the plot the observations that are likely to have the highest leverage.
   ii. Do the observations that have the highest leverage appear to be outliers? Explain your reasoning.

Unusual Ovservations

Obs.	LOANVAL	ASKPRICE	Fit	Residual
1	9,200	7,500	12,128	−4,628
7	13,325	15,500	17,082	−1,582
24	5,875	12,400	8,136	4,264
27	8,700	15,500	11,528	3,972
29	13,700	16,900	17,532	−632
30	16,050	20,995	20,354	641
34	5,175	12,900	7,295	5,605
35	15,750	20,500	19,994	506
61	2,425	7,200	3,993	3,207
85	3,750	10,500	5,584	4,916
126	15,250	19,500	19,393	107
141	10,375	9,500	13,539	−4,039
169	3,175	8,800	4,893	3,907
179	7,575	13,900	10,177	3,723
193	5,300	11,000	7,445	3,555
194	4,175	3,000	6,094	−3,094
196	7,425	5,500	9,997	−4,497

c. Your estimates are of interest to a bank loan officer, who happens to be an old college classmate of yours. Your old classmate is interested in the relationship between the LOANVAL and prices that are actually asked for in the marketplace.
   i.   Other things being equal, if the LOANVAL of a car increases by $1,000, what does your model predict the value of the ASKPRICE to be?
   ii. In order to provide a range of reliability, provide a 95% confidence interval for your estimate in part (i).

d. Another old classmate of yours has heard about your work. She is interested in selling her 1991 Chevrolet Cavalier, that is loaded with options but has 76,000 miles on it. Through your car dealership connections, you find that the LOANVAL for her car is $5,175.

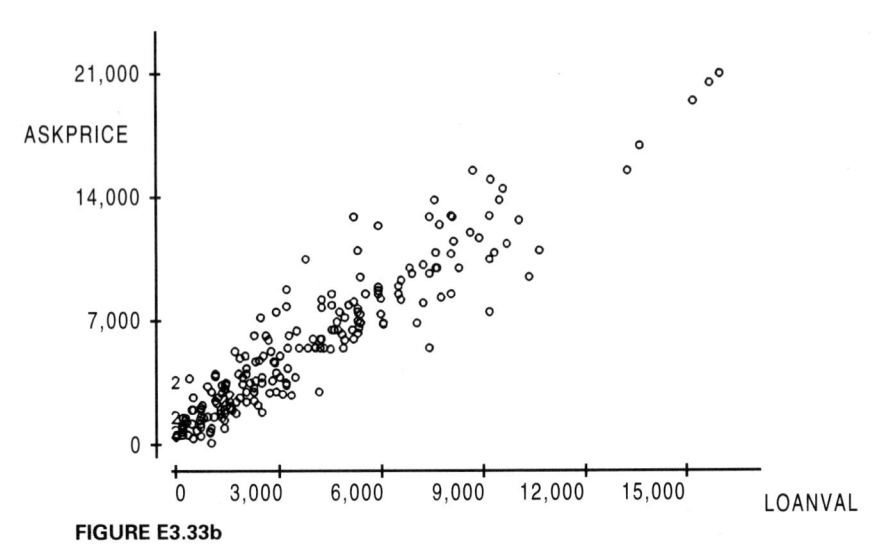

FIGURE E3.33b

    i.   Using the fitted regression equation, predict how much she would ask for her car in the private resale market.

    ii. Provide a 95% prediction interval for her.

Appendix

3.34 a. In Exercise 2.30 of Chapter 2, we developed the computational formula $\sum_{i=1}^{n}(y_i - \bar{y})^2 = \sum_{i=1}^{n} y_i^2 - n\bar{y}^2$. Follow the same steps to show

$$\sum_{i=1}^{n}(x_i - \bar{x})(y_i - \bar{y}) = \sum_{i=1}^{n} x_i y_i - n\bar{x}\bar{y}.$$

    b. Show that

$$b_1 = \frac{\sum_{i=1}^{n}(x_i - \bar{x})(y_i - \bar{y})}{\sum_{i=1}^{n}(x_i - \bar{x})^2}.$$

    c. Use the results of parts (a) and (b) to show

$$b_1 = \frac{\sum_{i=1}^{n} x_i y_i - n\bar{x}\bar{y}}{\sum_{i=1}^{n} x_i^2 - n\bar{x}^2}.$$

3.35 Use the following steps to show that r is bounded by -1 and 1 (These steps are due to Koch, 1990).

a. Let a and b be generic constants. Verify

$$0 \leq \frac{1}{n-1} \sum_{i=1}^{n} \left(a \frac{x_i - \bar{x}}{s_x} - b \frac{y_i - \bar{y}}{s_y} \right)^2 = a^2 + b^2 - 2abr.$$

b. Use the result in part (a) to show

$$2\,ab\,(r - 1) \leq (a - b)^2 .$$

c. By taking $a = b$, use the result in part (b) to show $r \leq 1$.

d. By taking $a = -b$, use the results in part (b) to show $r \geq -1$.

e. Under what conditions is $r = -1$? Under what conditions is $r = 1$?

3.36 Consider two variables, y and x. Do a regression of y on x to get a slope coefficient which we call $b_{1,x,y}$. Do another regression of x on y to get a slope coefficient that we call $b_{1,y,x}$. Show that the correlation coefficient between x and y is the geometric mean of the two slope coefficients up to sign, that is, show that

$$|r_{yx}| = \sqrt{b_{1,y,x}\, b_{1,x,y}} .$$

3.37 Use the following steps to establish a relationship between the coefficient of determination and the correlation coefficient.

a. Show that

$$\hat{y}_i - \bar{y} = b_1 (x_i - \bar{x}) .$$

b. Use part (a) to show that

$$\text{Regress SS} = \sum_{i=1}^{n} (\hat{y}_i - \bar{y})^2 = b_1^2\, s_x^2\, (n - 1) .$$

c. Use part (b) to establish

$$R^2 = b_1^2\, \frac{s_x^2}{s_y^2} = r^2 .$$

3.38 a. Establish that an alternate formula for a point prediction at x_* is

$$\hat{y}_* = \bar{y} + b_1 (x_* - \bar{x}).$$

b. Provide an interpretation for the formula given in part (a).

3.39 a. Show that $\sum_{i=1}^{n} \hat{e}_i = 0$.

b. Use part (a) to argue that the average residual is zero.

3.40 Consider as generic sequence of pairs of numbers $(x_1, y_1), (x_2, y_2), \ldots, (x_n, y_n)$.

a. Check that if

$$r(x,y) = \frac{\sum_{i=1}^{n} (x_i - \bar{x})(y_i - \bar{y})}{(n - 1)s_x\, s_y} = 0$$

then

$$\sum_{i=1}^{n} (x_i - \bar{x})(y_i - \bar{y}) = 0$$

and vice versa.

b. Suppose that either $\bar{x} = 0$ or $\bar{y} = 0$ or both $\bar{x}$ and $\bar{y} = 0$. Then, check that if $r(x, y) = 0$, then

$$\sum_{i=1}^{n} x_i y_i = 0$$

and vice versa.

c. Use part (a) of Exercise 3.37 to show that

$$\sum_{i=1}^{n} \hat{e}_i \hat{y}_i = 0.$$

d. Use parts (b) and (c) and Exercise 3.39 to show that $r(\hat{e}, \hat{y}) = 0$.

e. Use arguments analogous to those in parts (b) and (c) to show that

$$r(\hat{e}, x) = 0.$$

f. Follow the previous steps to show that, in general,

$$r(\hat{e}, y) \neq 0.$$

g. Provide interpretations of results in parts (d), (e) and (f) when performing residual analysis.

3.41. a. Use Exercise 3.39 and part (c) of Exercise 3.40 to show that

$$\sum_{i=1}^{n} (y_i - \bar{y})^2 = \sum_{i=1}^{n} (y_i - \hat{y}_i)^2 + \sum_{i=1}^{n} (\hat{y}_i - \bar{y})^2.$$

b. Use part (a) to show that

$$s_y^2 = b_1^2 s_x^2 + s^2 \frac{n-2}{n-1}.$$

3.42 a. Use algebra to show that

$$R^2 = 1 - \frac{n-2}{n-1} \frac{s^2}{s_y^2}.$$

b. Use part (a) to establish the following quick computational formula for s

$$s = s_y \sqrt{(1 - r^2) \frac{n-1}{n-2}}$$

c. Use part (b) to show that

$$t(b_1) = \sqrt{n-2} \sqrt{\frac{r^2}{1 - r^2}}.$$

3.43 Suppose that x_i only takes on the values 0 and 1. Out of the n observations, n_1 take on the value $x = 0$. These n_1 observations have an average y value of $\bar{y}_1$, the remaining $n - n_1$ observations have value $x = 1$ and an average y value $\bar{y}_2$. Use part (c) of Exercise 3.34 to show that

$$b_1 = \bar{y}_2 - \bar{y}_1.$$

3.44 Consider the model

$$y_i = \beta_1 x_i + e_i \, ,$$

that is, regression with one independent variable *without* the intercept term. This model is called *regression through the origin* because the true regression line $E \, y = \beta_1 x$ passes through the origin [the point $(0, 0)$ where both x and y are 0]. For this model, the least squares estimate of β_1 is that number b_1 that minimizes the sum of squares

$$SS(b_1^*) = \sum_{i=1}^{n} (y_i - b_i^* x_i)^2 \, .$$

a. Verify that

$$b_1 = \frac{\sum_{i=1}^{n} x_i \, y_i}{\sum_{i=1}^{n} x_i^2} \, .$$

[HINT: you can use calculus and minimize $SS(b_1^*)$ by taking the derivative and setting this equal to zero. Alternatively, if your calculus is rusty, show that $SS(b_1) \leq SS(b_1^*)$, for all candidate estimators b_1^*.]

b. Consider the model

$$y_i = \beta_1 z_i^2 + e_i \, ,$$

a quadratic model passing through the origin. Use the result of part (a) to determine the least squares estimate of β_1.

4

Regression Using Many Independent Variables

Chapter Objectives

To relate the effects that several independent variables have on a dependent variable. To illustrate, we will consider:

- how an apartment's rent relates to its size and distance from the city center and,
- how a refrigerator's price relates to its size, annual energy cost and the number of exotic features offered.

Chapter Outline

4.0 AN ITERATIVE APPROACH TO DATA ANALYSIS AND MODELING

Chapter 3 examined the data graphically, hypothesized a model structure and compared the data to the candidate model in order to formulate an improved model. Box (1980) describes this as an *iterative* process which is shown in Figure 4.1.

The iterative process provides a good recipe for approaching the task of specifying a model to represent a set of data. The first step, the model formulation stage, is accomplished by examining the data graphically and using prior knowledge of relationships, such as from economic theory. The second step in the iteration is based on the assumptions of the specified model. These assumptions must be consistent with the data to make valid use of the model. The third step, *diagnostic checking,* is also known as *data and model criticism;* the data and model should be verified before any inference about the world is made. Diagnostic checking is an important part of the model formulation; it will reveal mistakes made in previous steps and will provide ways to correct those mistakes.

Diagnostic checking not only reflects symptoms of mistakes made in the previous steps but also provides avenues to correct those mistakes.

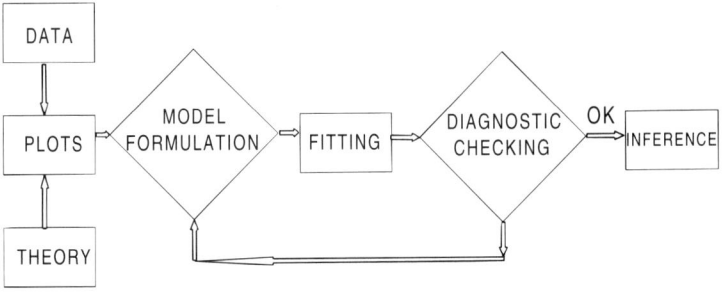

FIGURE 4.1 The iterative model specification process.

The iterative process emphasizes the skills you need to use data to make inferences about how the world works. First, you need a willingness to summarize information numerically and portray this information graphically. Second, it is important to develop an understanding of model capabilities. You should understand how a theoretical model behaves in order to match a set of data to it. Theoretical properties of the model are also important for inferring behavior of the world from behavior of the data.

Chapter 4 provides the important background information on model capabilities. With this background, in Chapters 6 and 7 we will be able to pursue a more detailed examination of the iterative model selection process.

4.1 IDENTIFYING AND SUMMARIZING DATA

The focus of Chapter 3 was on how a response may depend on a single explanatory variable. We now extend the logic of that chapter and study how a response may depend on several explanatory variables.

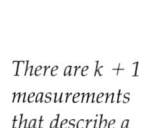

C4_RENT

Suppose an investor is interested in the income potential of several rental properties near downtown Madison. The investor needs to relate rental prices to one or more explanatory factors. Our analysis of the problem will focus on three variables. We know from the real estate literature that, for investors, prices per square foot are more important than rents. Thus, for each apartment, the monthly rent per square foot (RENT_SFT) is the dependent, or response, variable. The notation y represents RENT_SFT. The independent, or explanatory, (x) variables include the distance from the center of the city, measured in miles (MILES), and the size of the apartment, measured in square feet (FOOTAGE). A subscript for each x variable serves to differentiate the explanatory variables. For example, use x_1 for the distance from the city center and x_2 for the size of the apartment. There are 36 apartments available in the sample.

There are $k + 1$ measurements that describe a single observation.

In general, we will consider data sets where there are k independent variables and one dependent variable in a sample of size n. That is, the data consist of:

$$(x_{11}, x_{12}, \cdots, x_{1k}, y_1)$$
$$(x_{21}, x_{22}, \cdots, x_{2k}, y_2)$$
$$\cdots$$
$$\cdots$$
$$\cdots$$
$$(x_{n1}, x_{n2}, \cdots, x_{nk}, y_n)$$

The ith observation is denoted by $(x_{i1}, x_{i2}, ..., x_{ik}, y_i)$. For the general case, we take $k + 1$ measurements on each entity. For the apartment example, $k = 2$ and the data consists of $(x_{11}, x_{12}, y_1), (x_{21}, x_{22}, y_2), ..., (x_{n1}, x_{n2}, y_n)$. That is, we use three measurements on each of the $n = 36$ apartments.

Summarizing the Data

Begin the analysis by examining each variable in isolation of the others. We begin the analysis of the data by examining each variable in isolation of the others. Figure 4.2 presents dotplots of each of the three variables. These dotplots provide the location, range and distribution for each variable. This information is reinforced by some basic summary statistics, provided in Table 4.1.

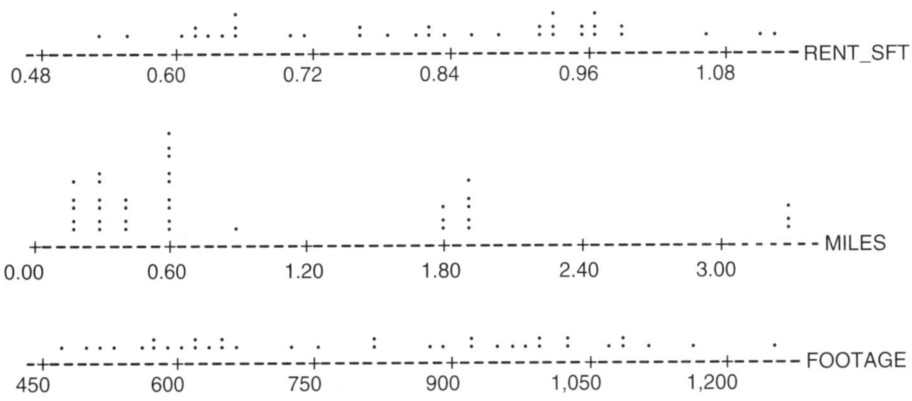

FIGURE 4.2 Dotplots of each variable for the 36 apartments in downtown Madison. These dotplots provide each variable's distribution, in isolation of the others.

The next step is to measure the effect of each x on y. To quantify the effect graphically, scatter plots of the response versus each independent variable help us understand this relationship (see Figures 4.3 and 4.4).

The data considered here are multivariate in the sense that several measurements are taken on each observation. It is difficult to produce a graph of

TABLE 4.1 Summary Statistics for Each Variable for the 36 Apartments in Downtown Madison

	Mean	Median	Standard deviation	Minimum	Maximum
RENT_SFT	0.8052	0.8139	0.1613	0.5189	1.1000
MILES	0.986	0.600	0.939	0.200	3.300
FOOTAGE	791.0	800.0	221.1	450.0	1,225.0

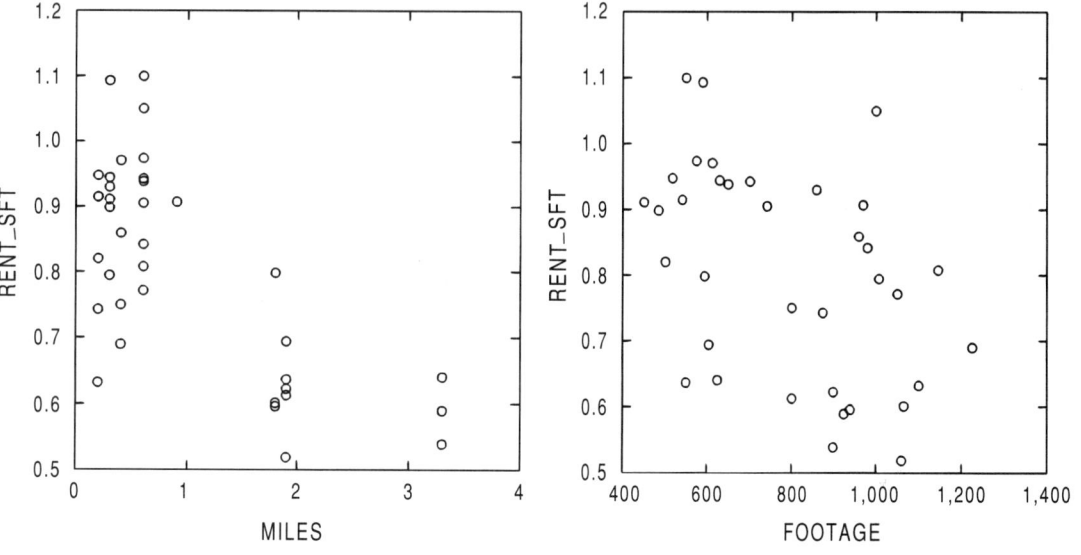

FIGURE 4.3 Scatter plot of rent per square foot versus the distance to city center in miles.

FIGURE 4.4 Scatter plot of rent per square foot versus the area of each apartment in square feet.

A scatterplot matrix shows the effect of each independent variable on the response and relationships between pairs of independent variables.

objects in three or more dimensions on a two-dimensional platform, such as a piece of paper, that is not confusing, misleading or both.

The best way to summarize graphically multivariate data in regression applications is with the *scatterplot matrix*. Figure 4.5 shows the plots in Figures 4.3 and 4.4 in the lowest row and the first and second columns, respectively, of the matrix. Each square represents a simple scatter plot of one variable versus another. For each square, the row variable gives the units of the vertical axis and the column variable gives the units of the horizontal axis. The matrix is sometimes called a *half* scatterplot matrix because only the lower left elements are presented. For example, the plot of RENT_SFT on the horizontal axis and MILES on the vertical axis need not appear because its mirror image appears in the lower left corner.

A correlation matrix numerically summarizes a scatterplot matrix, just as the correlation coefficient numerically summarizes a scatter plot.

The scatterplot matrix can be numerically summarized using a *correlation matrix* (Table 4.2). For each square, the extent of the relationship between two variables is summarized through an ordinary correlation coefficient. Remember that the correlation coefficient merely measures the extent of the linear relationship and, unlike regression, is not concerned with the distinction between a dependent and independent variable. Therefore, only half of the matrix is presented.

The scatterplot and correlation matrices capture only relationships between pairs of variables and can not detect relationships among several variables.

The scatterplot matrix and corresponding correlation matrix are useful devices for summarizing multivariate data. They are easy to produce and to interpret. Still, each device captures only relationships between pairs of variables and cannot quantify relationships among several variables. Therefore, we now study the relationship between the response and combinations of explanatory variables.

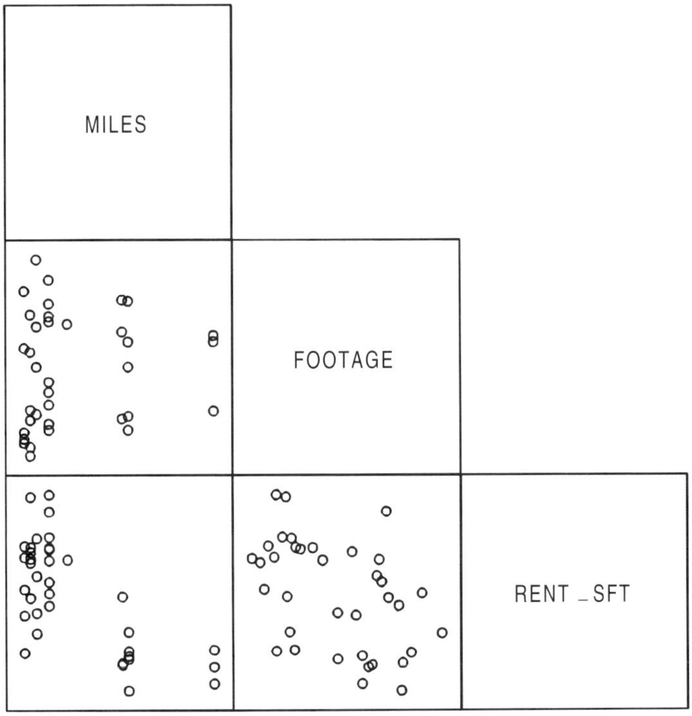

FIGURE 4.5 Half scatterplot matrix of three variables. Each off-diagonal square is a scatter plot.

Fitting the Data with a Plane

Consider the question: Can knowledge of an apartment's distance from the city center (MILES) and an apartment's size (FOOTAGE) help to predict the rent per square foot (RENT_SFT)? The correlations in Table 4.2 and the graphs in Figures 4.3 and 4.4 suggest that each variable, MILES and FOOTAGE, is a useful explanatory variable of RENT_SFT when taken individually. It seems reasonable to investigate a model that considers the joint effect of both variables on a response.

To see the effects of the explanatory variables, let's try to estimate RENT_SFT with and without MILES and FOOTAGE. If we are trying to predict

TABLE 4.2 Correlation Matrix

	MILES	FOOTAGE
FOOTAGE	0.107	
RENT_SFT	−0.696	−0.456

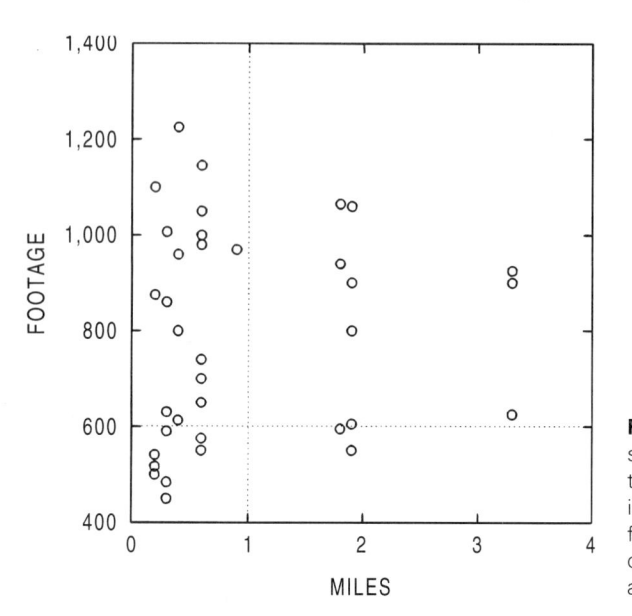

FIGURE 4.6 Scatter plot of area in square feet (FOOTAGE) versus distance to city center (MILES). Lines are superimposed to separate small apartments from larger ones and to separate inter city apartments from those in outlying area.

the rent per square foot without knowledge of MILES or FOOTAGE, then the best predictor is $\bar{y} = 0.805$. However, as seen in Figure 4.3, if we are interested in an apartment closer to the city center, then we expect to pay a higher rent. For example, for the 25 apartments that are within one mile, the average rent per square foot is 0.886. Similarly, as seen in Figure 4.4, if we select a smaller apartment, then we expect the rent per square foot to be higher. For example, for the ten apartments that are smaller than 600 square feet, the average rent per square foot is 0.909. For the joint effect of distance and size, from Figure 4.6 we see that out of the ten apartments that have less than 600 square feet of living space, eight are within one mile of the city center. For these eight apartments, the average rent per square foot is 0.958. This information is summarized in Table 4.3.

Thus, it seems that the smaller are the MILES and FOOTAGE variables, the larger is the rent per square foot. This is not only true when the variables

TABLE 4.3   Average Rent per Square Foot for Certain Categories of the Independent Variables

Category	All apartments	Apartments within one mile	Apartments smaller than 600 square feet	Apartments within one mile and smaller than 600 square feet
Sample size	36	25	10	8
Average rent per square foot	0.805	0.886	0.909	0.958

are taken one at a time but also when considered jointly. We established this by forming groups of apartments by arbitrarily selecting apartments smaller than 600 square feet and within one mile of the city center. For a more systematic approach that does not involve the arbitrary categorization of variables, we now fit smooth linear combinations of these variables by using the notion of a *plane*.

One way to define a plane in p dimensions is to connect p points that do not lie on a plane in p − 1 dimensions.

The geometric concept of a plane is used to explore the linear relationship between a response and several explanatory variables. A plane is the extension of the concept of a line to more than two dimensions. One way to define a plane is by connecting nonidentical points. Recall that for two dimensions (one response variable and one explanatory variable), two nonidentical points determine a line simply by connecting the points. For three dimensions, three points that do not lie on a straight line are enough to determine a plane. Extending this line of thought, the general rule is that a plane in p dimensions is determined by p points that do not lie on a plane in $p − 1$ dimensions. For $p = 3$, a "plane" in two ($= 3 − 1$) dimensions is simply a line.

Alternatively, a plane may be defined through an algebraic equation such as

$$y = b_0 + b_1 x_1 + b_2 x_2 + ... + b_k x_k.$$

This equation defines a plane in $p = k + 1$ dimensions. Figure 4.7 is a graphical presentation of a plane in three dimensions. For this figure, there is one response variable, RENT_SFT, and two explanatory variables, MILES and FOOTAGE. It is difficult to graph more than three dimensions in a meaningful way.

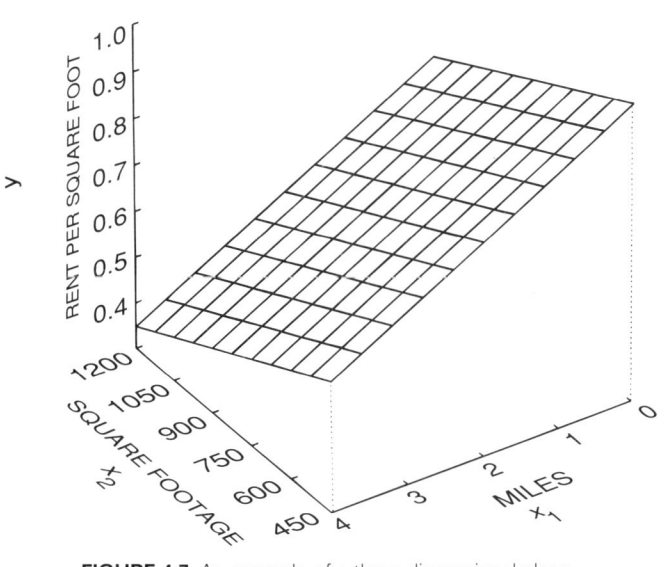

FIGURE 4.7 An example of a three-dimensional plane.

We need to specify a way to determine the plane based on the data. The difficulty is that in most regression analysis applications, the number of observations, n, far exceeds the number of observations required to fit a plane, $k + 1$. Thus, it is generally not possible to find a single plane that will fit all n observations. As in Chapter 3, we use the *method of least squares* to determine the plane from the data.

The process of fitting a plane using the method of least squares can be described in three steps:

1. Start with a plane, say, $y = b_0^* + b_1^* x_1 + b_2^* x_2 + \ldots + b_k^* x_k$. The quantities $b_0^*, b_1^*, \ldots, b_k^*$, are merely generic values that determine a candidate plane.

2. Consider the ith observation, $(x_{i1}, x_{i2}, \ldots, x_{ik}, y_i)$, a generic point in the data set. For this observation, the height of the candidate plane is $b_0^* + b_1^* x_{i1} + b_2^* x_{i2} + \ldots, b_k^* x_{ik}$. The quantity

$$y_i - (b_0^* + b_1^* x_{i1} + b_2^* x_{i2} + \ldots + b_k^* x_{ik})$$

represents the deviation of the actual observation from the height of the candidate plane.

3. The quantity

$$\text{SS}(b_0^*, b_1^*, \ldots, b_k^*) = \sum_{i=1}^{n} (y_i - (b_0^* + b_1^* x_{i1} + b_2^* x_{i2} + \ldots + b_k^* x_{ik}))^2$$

represents the sum of squared deviations for the candidate plane. This quantity summarizes the deviations from the plane over all observations. The method of least squares is simply to determine the values of $b_0^*, b_1^*, \ldots, b_k^*$ that minimize this quantity. To denote these best values, we drop the asterisk, or star, notation and use $b_0, b_1, \ldots, b_k$. If the explanatory variables are not linear combinations of one another, then there is a unique set of parameter estimates that minimize SS.

With these best values, define the *least squares, or fitted, regression plane* as

$$\hat{y} = b_0 + b_1 x_1 + b_2 x_2 + \ldots + b_k x_k. \tag{4.1}$$

Minimizing $\text{SS}(b_0^*, b_1^*, \ldots, b_k^*)$ is a straightfoward exercise using either calculus or numerical analytic techniques. It is difficult, however, to write down the resulting least squares estimates using a simple formula unless one resorts to matrix notation. An explicit formula for the estimates can be found in Section 4.7 where an introduction to matrices is provided. Fortunately, these formulas have been programmed into a wide variety of statistical and spreadsheet software packages. The fact that these packages are readily available allows us to concentrate on the ideas of the estimation procedure instead of focusing on the details of the calculation procedures.

As an example, a regression plane was fit to the apartment data. Two explanatory variables, x_1 for MILES and x_2 for FOOTAGE, were used. The resulting fitted regression plane is

$$\hat{y} = 1.14 - 0.122x_1 - 0.000281x_2.$$

4.2 LINEAR REGRESSION MODEL

The notion behind linear regression models is to decompose the response into a deterministic, or nonrandom, function of known variables and an unknown random error. The *linear regression model* is

response = nonrandom regression plane + random error

or, symbolically,

$$y = \beta_0 + \beta_1 x_1 + \ldots + \beta_k x_k + e.$$

The expected response is a linear combination of the independent variables, that is, $\beta_0 + \beta_1 x_1 + \ldots + \beta_k x_k$. The observed response is the expected response plus a random error term.

The quantities $\beta_0, \ldots, \beta_k$ are unknown, yet nonrandom, parameters that determine a plane in $k + 1$ dimensions. The quantity e represents the random deviation, or error, of an individual response from the plane. We assume that the expected value of each error is zero so that the expected response is given by the regression plane, that is,

$$\mathrm{E}\, y = \beta_0 + \beta_1 x_1 + \ldots + \beta_k x_k.$$

Further, because the regression plane is random, the variability of the response can be measured through the variability of the random error, denoted by σ^2. Thus,

$$\mathrm{Var}\, y = \mathrm{Var}\, e = \sigma^2.$$

To represent a data set of n observations, we may express the model as

$$y_i = \beta_0 + \beta_1 x_{i1} + \ldots + \beta_k x_{ik} + e_i, \qquad i = 1, \ldots, n. \qquad (4.2)$$

As in Section 3.2 for the one explanatory variable model, this is shorthand notation for n equations, one for each observation. The errors $\{e_1, e_2, \ldots, e_n\}$ are assumed to be a random sample from an unknown population of errors. Thus, the draws from this population are unrelated and have common mean zero and variance σ^2. The random errors are not observed by the analyst. Because there may be many explanatory variables, the model in equation (4.2) is called the *multiple linear regression model*.

If the jth variable is continuous, then we interpret β_j as the expected change in y per unit change in x_j, assuming all other variables are held fixed.

The expected response is determined by the parameters $\beta_0, \beta_1, \ldots, \beta_k$. We initially assume that x_j varies continuously and is not related to the other independent variables. Then, we interpret β_j using the idea of *partial changes*. That is, interpret β_j as the expected change in y per unit change in x_j, *assuming all other independent variables are held fixed*. [If you have had recent exposure to calculus, you will recognize that β_j can be interpreted as a partial derivative, that is, $\beta_j = (\partial/\partial x_j) \, \mathrm{E} \, y$.]

Further, each regression coefficient, β_j, is estimated by the corresponding statistic, b_j, and can be interpreted using partial changes. To illustrate, in Section 4.1 we discussed the estimated regression plane $\hat{y} = 1.14 - 0.112 \, x_1 - 0.000281 \, x_2$, where x_1 = MILES from the city center, x_2 = apartment size in square feet (FOOTAGE), and $\hat{y}$ is the fitted rent per square foot. We interpret $b_1 = -0.112$ to mean, other things being equal, that the rent per square feet would increase by \$0.112, or 11.2¢, if distance from the city center decreased by one mile. Similarly, if the apartment size increased by 100 square feet, then rent per square foot would decrease by 2.81¢. It is important to remind ourselves that statistical models, in and of themselves, do not suggest cause and effect relationships. For example, it would be imprudent to suggest that we could charge an extra 11.2¢ per square foot by merely moving an apartment building one mile closer to the city center. Many other factors, such as proximity to public transportation, parking and so on, come into play when determining rents. The regression estimate simply states that, if two apartments are similar except for distance from city center, on average this difference will be captured by the β_{MILES} coefficient.

To interpret $b_0 = 1.14$, we note that this is the fitted value when we are $x_1 = 0$ miles from the city center and have an apartment that is $x_2 = 0$ square feet large! These values of the explanatory variables are outside the range of our sample and are not of interest to us. Thus, the value of b_0 is not important when interpreting the model; it merely serves to set the height of the fitted regression plane. Similarly, it is often true in social science data sets that the parameter β_0 is of less interest than the other regression coefficients.

The interpretation of β_j as a partial change is valid when x_j varies continuously and is not related to the other explanatory variables. Section 4.5 and Chapter 5 will provide several examples of explanatory variables that are categorical and do not vary continuously. In Section 3.5, we introduced quadratic regression, a case where one continuous explanatory variable is related to another. In this case, we had $k = 2$, $x_1 = x$ and $x_2 = x^2$, so that $\mathrm{E} \, y = \beta_0 + \beta_1 \, x + \beta_2 \, x^2$. Here, the partial change in $\mathrm{E} \, y$ per unit change in x depends on x, in addition to the parameters β_1 and β_2. [If you have had a recent exposure to calculus, you will recognize that $(\partial/\partial x) \, \mathrm{E} \, y = (\partial/\partial x)(\beta_0 + \beta_1 x + \beta_2 x^2) = \beta_1 + 2 \beta_2 x$]. In this case, it is not possible to hold x_2 fixed while measuring changes in $\mathrm{E} \, y$ per unit changes in x_1.

4.3 BASIC CHECKS OF THE MODEL

Section 4.1 described the statistics used to summarize the data and Section 4.2 described the parameters used to summarize the model. In Section 4.3, we now describe the basic statistics that we can use to check how well the model represents the data. To this end, we (i) decompose the variability, (ii) introduce a direct check of model adequacy and (iii) examine the importance of an individual explanatory variable. We close this section by pointing out some relationships between regression and correlation.

The Variability

Algebraically, partitioning the variability of the data for regression using many variables is similar to the case of using only one variable. Unfortunately, when dealing with many variables, we do lose the easy graphical interpretation such as in Figure 3.12.

Begin with the total sum of squared deviations, Total SS $= \Sigma_{i=1}^{n} (y_i - \overline{y})^2$, as our measure of the total variation in the data set. For the ith observation, define the *fitted value* to be

$$\hat{y}_i = b_0 + b_1 x_{i1} + b_2 x_{i2} + \dots + b_k x_{ik}.$$

The algebraic decomposition is the same whether one uses one or more than one independent variables. The geometric version of this decomposition, such as in Figure 3.12 for one variable, is not useful in the many variable case.

As in equation (3.4), we may then interpret the equation

$$y_i - \overline{y} = y_i - \hat{y}_i + \hat{y}_i - \overline{y}$$

$$\begin{array}{ccc} total & = unexplained + & explained \\ deviation & deviation & deviation \end{array}$$

as the "deviation without knowledge of the explanatory variables equals the deviation with knowledge of the explanatory variables plus deviation explained by the explanatory variables." Squaring each side and summing over all observations yields

$$\text{Total SS} = \text{Error SS} + \text{Regression SS}$$

where Error SS $= \Sigma_{i=1}^{n} (y_i - \hat{y}_i)^2$ and Regression SS $= \Sigma_{i=1}^{n} (\hat{y}_i - \overline{y})^2$. As in Section 3.3 for the one explanatory variable case, the sum of the cross-product terms turns out to be zero.

A statistic that summarizes this relationship is the *coefficient of determination*,

$$R^2 = \frac{\text{Regression SS}}{\text{Total SS}}.$$

Interpret the coefficient of determination, R^2, to be the proportion of variability explained by the regression plane.

We may interpret R^2 as the proportion of variability explained by the regression plane. Alternatively, we can express R^2 as $1 - (\text{Error SS})/(\text{Total SS})$, and interpret it to be one minus the proportion of unexplained variability.

The variability decomposition is also summarized using the analysis of variance (ANOVA) table (Table 4.4). As in Section 3.3, the mean square column figures are defined to be the sum of squares figures divided by their respective degrees of freedom. To understand the degrees of freedom column, we first

TABLE 4.4 ANOVA Table

Source	Sum of Squares	df	Mean Square
Regression	Regression SS	k	Regression MS
Error	Error SS	$n - (k + 1)$	Error MS
Total	Total SS	$n - 1$	

must recall the distinction between random errors and their estimated versions, residuals.

From the linear regression model in equation (4.2), the random errors can be expressed as

$$e_i = y_i - (\beta_0 + \beta_1 x_{i1} + \ldots + \beta_k x_{ik}).$$

Because the parameters $\beta_0, \ldots, \beta_k$ are not observed, the errors themselves are not observed. Instead, we examine the "estimated errors," or *residuals*, defined by

$$\hat{e}_i = y_i - \hat{y}_i.$$

If the regression parameter estimates are close to the true parameters, then

$$\hat{e}_i = y_i - (b_0 + b_1 x_{i1} + \ldots + b_k x_{ik})$$

is close to

$$y_i - (\beta_0 + \beta_1 x_{i1} + \ldots + \beta_k x_{ik}) = e_i.$$

As discussed in Section 2.4 on sampling, a desirable estimate of $\sigma^2 =$ Var e is $(n - 1)^{-1} \sum_{i=1}^{n} (e_i - \bar{e})^2$. Because the errors are unobserved, we define the estimator of σ^2 to be

$$s^2 = \frac{\sum_{i=1}^{n} \hat{e}_i^2}{n - (k + 1)}. \tag{4.3}$$

This expression generalizes the definition in equation (3.5), which is valid for $k = 1$.

The denominator in equation (4.3) is $n - (k + 1)$ instead of n because of certain dependencies among the residuals. One dependency is due to the algebraic fact that the average residual is zero. Further, there must be at least $k + 2$ observations for there to be variation in the fit of the plane. If we have only $k + 1$ observations, we could fit a plane to the data perfectly, resulting in no variation in the fit. For example, if $k = 1$, because two observations determine a line, then at least three observations are required to observe any deviation from the line. Because of these dependencies, there are really only $n - (k + 1)$ free, or unrestricted, residuals.

In our ANOVA table, we use the term *error degrees of freedom* to denote the number of unrestricted residuals. It is this number that we use in our definition of the "average," or *mean, square error*. That is, we define

$$\text{Error MS} = \frac{\text{Error SS}}{n - (k + 1)} = s^2.$$

The square root of the mean square error, s, is our estimate of σ. Because it is based on residuals, we refer to s as the *residual standard deviation*. The quantity s is a measure of our "typical error." For this reason, s is also called the *standard error of the estimate*.

When an explanatory variable is added to the model, R^2 does not decrease.

When discussing the coefficient of determination, it can be established that whenever an explanatory variable is added to the model, R^2 never decreases. This is true regardless of how useless the added variable is. We would like a measure of fit that decreases when useless variables are entered into the model as explanatory variables. To circumvent this anomaly, a widely used statistic is a coefficient of determination *adjusted* for degrees of freedom, defined by

$$R_a^2 = 1 - \frac{\dfrac{\text{Error SS}}{n - (k + 1)}}{\dfrac{\text{Total SS}}{n - 1}} = 1 - \frac{s^2}{s_y^2}.$$

As the model fit improves, as measured through s, the adjusted R^2 becomes larger and vice versa.

To interpret this statistic, note that $SS = \sum_{i=1}^{n} (y_i - \bar{y})^2$ does not depend on the model nor the model variables. Thus, s and R_a^2 are equivalent measures of model fit. As model fit improves, then R_a^2 becomes larger and s becomes smaller, and vice versa.

To illustrate, Table 4.5 displays the summary statistics for the regression of RENT_SFT on MILES and FOOTAGE. From the degrees of freedom column, we remind ourselves that there are two explanatory variables and 36 observations. As measures of model fit, we have that the coefficient of determination is $R^2 = 63.15\%$ (=0.5748/0.9102) and the residual standard deviation is $s = 0.101$ [=$(0.0102)^{1/2}$]. If we were to attempt to predict rent per square foot without knowledge of MILES or FOOTAGE, the size of the typical error would be $s_y = 0.1613$ [=$(0.9102/35)^{1/2}$]. Thus, by taking advantage of our knowledge of FOOTAGE and MILES, we have been able to reduce the size of the typical error. We now argue that this reduction is significant in a well-defined sense.

TABLE 4.5   ANOVA Table for a Regression of RENT_SFT on MILES and FOOTAGE

Source	Sum of Squares	df	Mean Square
Regression	0.5748	2	0.2874
Error	0.3354	33	0.0102
Total	0.9102	35	

Is the Model Adequate? The *F*-Test

We translate the question, "Is the model adequate?" into a narrower question with regard to the validity of the hypothesis H_0: $\beta_1 = \beta_2 = ... = \beta_k = 0$. By doing this translation, we may use the hypothesis testing machinery to aid our decision making process.

From the linear regression model,

$$y = \beta_0 + \beta_1 x_1 + \beta_2 x_2 + ... + \beta_k x_k + e,$$

if each slope parameter, $\beta_1, ..., \beta_k$, is zero, then the model is

$$y = \beta_0 + e.$$

Because the random error term is unrelated to other variables, we can interpret this simpler model to mean that the explanatory variables are expected to have no effect on the response y. Thus, we translate the question "Is the model adequate?" into the narrower question "Are the slope parameters zero?" This narrower question can be restated using the hypothesis testing framework as

$$H_0: \beta_1 = \beta_2 = ... = \beta_k = 0.$$

We would like to compare this hypothesis against the alternative that at least one of the slope parameters if not equal to zero.

To address this narrower question, recall that the total sum of squares can be decomposed into sum of squares due to the regression fit and due to the error. Thus, the larger is the ratio of regression sum of squares to the error sum of squares, the better is the model fit. A similar argument is used to justify the usefulness of R^2. If we standardize this ratio by the respective degrees of freedom, then we get the so-called "*F*-ratio."

$$F\text{-ratio} = \frac{\dfrac{\text{Regression SS}}{k}}{\dfrac{\text{Error SS}}{n - (k + 1)}} = \frac{\text{Regression MS}}{\text{Error MS}} = \frac{\text{Regression MS}}{s^2}.$$

Both R^2 and the F-ratio are useful for summarizing model adequacy. R^2 may be interpreted as the proportion of variability explained by the model. The exact sampling distribution of the F-ratio is known, at least under the null hypothesis.

The *F*-ratio and R^2 share similar duties and, indeed, their exact relationship is pointed out in equation (4.4). The coefficient of determination, R^2, is used because of the natural interpretation associated with it, as the proportion of variability explained by the model. The *F*-ratio is used because the exact theoretical sampling distribution is known, at least when the errors are normally distributed and the null hypothesis is true. This sampling distribution is called the *F*-distribution. Both the statistic and the theoretical distribution are named for R. A. Fisher, a renown scientist and statistician who did much to advance statistics as a science in the early half of the twentieth century.

Like the normal and the *t*-distribution, the *F*-distribution is a continuous idealized histogram. The *F*-distribution is the sampling distribution for the *F*-ratio and is proportional to the ratio of two sum of squares, each of which is positive or zero. Thus, unlike the normal distribution and the *t*-distribution, the *F*-distribution takes on only nonnegative values. Recall that the *t*-distribution is indexed by a single degree of freedom parameter. The *F*-distribution is indexed by two degree of freedom parameters: one for the numerator, df_1, and one for the denominator, df_2. Figure 4.8 is a graph of an F-curve. Tables of the 95th percentile for several F-curves are in the appendix.

Declare H_0 to be invalid if F-ratio exceeds an F-value. The F-value is computed using a significance level with $df_1 =k$ and $df_2 = n - (k + 1)$ degrees of freedom.

Our first application of the F-distribution will be to use the data to test the null hypothesis $H_0: \beta_1 = \beta_2 = \ldots = \beta_k = 0$. The fact from mathematical statistics that we use is that, assuming that the errors are normally distributed and that H_0 is true, then the F-ratio has an F-distribution with $df_1 = k$ and $df_2 = n - (k + 1)$ degrees of freedom. We use a prespecified significance level, such as 5%, to determine the F-value, that number so that the area under the curve to the right of it is 5%. Because the area under the curve to the left of F-value is 0.95, it is the 95th percentile of the F-distribution. Then, the procedure is to declare the null hypothesis invalid if the F-ratio is "large," that is, if the F-ratio exceeds the F-value. This procedure is called the F-test. Because we are only searching for large values of the F-ratio, the testing procedure is "one-sided." Thus, the percentile that we use is $1 -$ significance level.

To illustrate, consider the data summarized in the ANOVA Table 4.4 and assume a significance level at 5%. From Table 4.4, the F-ratio is $0.2874/0.0102 = 28.18$. From the table in the appendix, with $df_1 = 2$ and $df_2 = 33$, we have that the F-value is approximately 3.30. This leads us to reject the notion that the MILES and FOOTAGE variables are not useful in understanding rent per square foot, reaffirming what we learned in the graphical and correlation analysis. Any other result would be surprising.

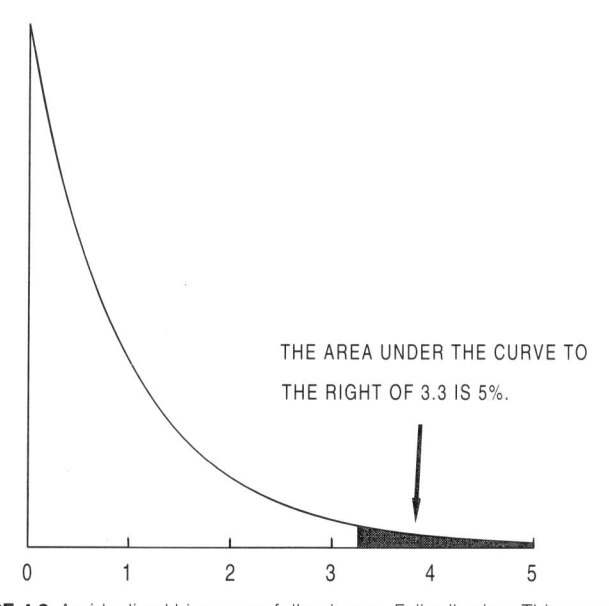

THE AREA UNDER THE CURVE TO THE RIGHT OF 3.3 IS 5%.

0　1　2　3　4　5

FIGURE 4.8 An idealized histogram following an F-distribution. This curve is indexed by $df_1 = 2$ and $df_2 = 33$ degrees of freedom. For this distribution, the 95th percentile is 3.3.

Is an Independent Variable Important? The *t*-Test

In many applications, by using theory from another scientific discipline, the researcher identifies several independent variables that may affect the response simultaneously. The *F*-test is well-suited to test this proposition. In other applications, the researcher may be primarily interested in the effect of a single explanatory variable on a response and has included other explanatory variables to control for additional sources of variation in the response. To illustrate, we might be interested in the effect that the explanatory variable education level has on the response variable, an individual's income. In our analysis, we could include other explanatory variables such as an individual's sex, type of occupation, age and so on. By including these additional explanatory variables, we hope to control for these variables and thus gain a better understanding of the relationship between education level and income.

As in Section 3.3, we now respond to the question "Is x_j important?" by investigating whether or not the corresponding slope parameter, β_j, equals zero. The question whether β_j is zero can be restated in the hypothesis testing framework as "Is $H_0: \beta_j = 0$ valid?"

We need to examine the proximity of b_j to zero in order to determine whether or not β_j is zero. Because the units of b_j depend on the units of y and x_j, we would like to standardize this quantity. For standardization, we use the standard error of b_j, $se(b_j)$, which is the estimated standard deviation of b_j. A mathematical definition of $se(b_j)$ will be given in Section 4.7. For now, you may assume that $se(b_j)$ can be found as output from your statistical software package.

To test $H_0: \beta_j = 0$, we examine the *t*-ratio,

$$t(b_j) = \frac{b_j}{se(b_j)} .$$

We can interpret $t(b_j)$ to be the number of standard errors that b_j is from zero. This is the appropriate quantity because the sampling distribution of $t(b_j)$ can be shown to be the *t*-distribution with $df = n - (k + 1)$ degrees of freedom. This enables us to construct tests of the null hypothesis such as the following procedure, called a *t-test*.

Declare H_0 invalid in favor $H_a: \beta_j \neq 0$ if $|t(b_j)|$ exceeds a *t*-value. Here, this *t*-value is a percentile from the *t*-distribution using $df = n - (k + 1)$ degrees of freedom. The percentile is $1 - $ (significance level)$/2$.

As a rule of thumb, we will interpret a variable to be important if it's t-ratio exceeds two in absolute value.

In many applications, the sample size will be large enough so that we may approximate the *t*-value by the corresponding percentile from the standard normal curve. At the 5% level of significance, this percentile is 1.96. Thus, as a rule of thumb, we can interpret a variable to be important if it's *t*-ratio exceeds two in absolute value.

Alternatively, one can construct *p*-values and compare these to given significant levels. Further discussion of this, and one-sided alternatives, will be presented in Section 7.1.

*A useful conven-
tion when report-
ing the results of a
statistical analysis
is to place the
standard error of a
statistic in paren-
thesis below that
statistic.*

A useful convention when reporting the results of a statistical analysis is to place the standard error of a statistic in parenthesis below that statistic. Thus, for example, in our regression of rent per square foot (RENT_SFT) on MILES and FOOTAGE, the estimated regression equation is:

$$\widehat{\text{RENT\_SFT}} = 1.14 - 0.112 \text{ MILES} - 0.000281 \text{ FOOTAGE} .$$
$$\textit{std error} \quad (0.064) \quad\quad (0.0183) \quad\quad\quad (0.0000775)$$

Using our general notation, the parameter estimates are $b_0 = 1.14$, $b_1 = -0.112$ and $b_2 = -0.000281$. The corresponding standard errors are $se(b_0) = 0.064$, $se(b_1) = 0.0183$ and $se(b_2) = 0.0000775$. With this information, we can immediately compute t-ratios to check to see whether an individual variable is significantly different from zero. For example, the t-ratio for the MILES variable is $t(b_1) = -0.112/0.0183 = -6.12$. The interpretation is that b_1 is over six standard errors below zero and thus x_1 is an important variable in the model. More formally, we may be interested in testing the null hypothesis that $H_0: \beta_1 = 0$ versus $H_a: \beta_1 \neq 0$. At a 5% level of significance, the t-value is 2.03, because $df = 33$. We thus reject the null in favor of the alternative hypothesis, that distance from the city center (MILES) is important in determining rent per square feet.

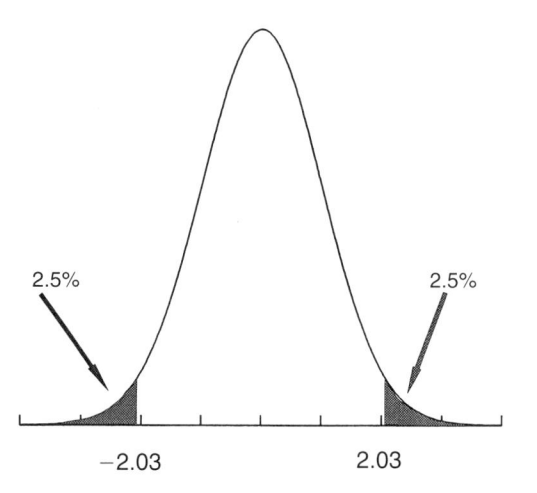

*For regression
with one indepen-
dent variable, the
F-ratio is equal to
the t-ratio
squared. The F-
test has the ad-
vantage that it
works for more
than one predic-
tor. The t-test has
the advantage that
we can consider
one-sided alterna-
tives.*

If $k = 1$, which do we use, a t- or an F-test? This answer is either, in that they are equivalent. It turns out that the square of a t-ratio has an F-distribution with $df_1 = 1$ and $df_2 = n - 2$ degrees of freedom. The square of the t-value for the two-sided test equals the F-value with $df_1 = 1$ and $df_2 = n - 2$ degrees of freedom. The F-test has the advantage that it works for more than one predictor. The t-test has the advantage that one can consider one-sided alternatives, described in Section 3.4. Thus, both tests are considered useful.

Some Relationships Between Correlation and Regression

Because it can be interpreted as the correlation between the response and the fitted values, R is called the multiple correlation coefficient.

If the model is a desirable one for the data, one would expect a strong relationship between the observed responses and those "expected" under the model, the fitted values. As a matter of fact, in time series analysis, the fitted values are called the "smoothed values" because the natural variation has been removed. An interesting algebraic fact is the following: if one squares the correlation coefficient between the responses and the fitted values, we get the coefficient of determination, that is,

$$R^2 = (r_{y, \hat{y}})^2.$$

Both F-ratio and R^2 are measures of model fit. Because of an algebraic relationship, we know that as R^2 increases, so does the F-ratio.

As a result, R, the positive square root of R^2, is called the *multiple correlation coefficient*. It can be interpreted as the correlation between the response and the best linear combination of the explanatory variables, the fitted values.

Because both F-ratio and R^2 are measures of model fit, it seems intuitively plausible that they be related in some fashion. Indeed, there is an exact algebraic relationship between these two statistics, given by:

$$F\text{-ratio} = \frac{R^2}{1 - R^2} \frac{n - (k + 1)}{k} . \tag{4.4}$$

An important consequence of this relationship is the fact that as R^2 increases, so does the F-ratio and vice versa. To repeat what was pointed out above, the F-ratio is used because its sampling distribution is known under a null hypothesis and R^2 is used because of the easy interpretations associated with it.

4.4 ADDED VARIABLE PLOTS

To represent multivariate data graphically, we have seen that a scatterplot matrix is a useful device. However, the major shortcoming of the scatterplot matrix is that it only captures relationships between pairs of variables. When data can be summarized using a regression model, a graphical device that does not have this shortcoming is an *added variable plot*. The added variable plot is also called a *partial regression plot* because, as we will see, it is constructed in terms of residuals from certain regression fits. We will also see that the added variable plot can be summarized in terms of a *partial correlation coefficient,* thus providing yet another link between correlation and regression. To introduce these ideas, we work in the context of Example 4.1.

Example 4.1: Refrigerator Prices

What characteristics of a refrigerator are important in determining its price (PRICE)? We consider here several characteristics of a refrigerator, including the size of the refrigerator in cubic feet (R_CU_FT), the size

C4_REFRG

of the freezer compartment in cubic feet (F_CU_FT), the average amount of money spent per year to operate the refrigerator (E_COST, for "energy cost"), the number of shelves in the refrigerator and freezer doors (SHELVES) and the number of features (FEATURES). The features variable includes shelves for cans, see-through crispers, ice makers, egg racks and so on.

Both consumers and manufacturers are interested in models of refrigerator prices. Other things being equal, consumers generally prefer larger refrigerators with lower energy costs that have more features. Due to forces of supply and demand, we would expect consumers to pay more for these refrigerators. A large refrigerator with low energy costs that has several features is considered desirable by the consumer. Similarly, manufacturers are interested in pricing models of refrigerators. Manufacturers have to make production decisions and need to make cost versus revenue decisions. For example, manufacturers may wish to estimate from their production processes the additional cost of adding two cubic feet to their freezer compartment. How much extra would the consumer be willing to pay for this additional space? A model of market prices for refrigerators provides some insight into this question.

To this end, we analyze data from 37 refrigerators. The data were obtained from the July 1992 issue of *Consumer Reports* in an article entitled, "Refrigerators: A Comprehensive Guide to the Big White Box." Table 4.6 provides basic summary statistics for the response variable PRICE and the five explanatory variables. From this table, we see that the average refrigerator price is $\bar{y} = \$626.40$, with standard deviation $s_y = \$139.80$. Similarly, the average annual amount to operate a refrigerator, or average E_COST, is $70.51.

TABLE 4.6 Summary Statistics for Each Variable for 37 Refrigerators

	Mean	Median	Standard deviation	Minimum	Maximum
E_COST	70.51	68.00	9.14	60.00	94.00
R_CU_FT	13.400	13.200	0.600	12.600	14.700
F_CU_FT	5.184	5.100	0.938	4.100	7.400
SHELVES	2.514	2.000	1.121	1.000	5.000
FEATURES	3.459	3.000	2.512	1.000	12.000
PRICE	626.4	590.0	139.8	460.0	1,200.0

Source: Consumer Reports, July 1992.

To analyze relationships among pairs of variables, Figure 4.9 provides a scatterplot matrix of the six variables. This scatterplot matrix is summarized in the Table 4.7 matrix of correlation coefficients. From the figure and table, we see that there are strong linear relationships between PRICE and each of freezer space (F_CU_FT) and the number of FEA-

TABLE 4.7   Matrix of Correlation Coefficients Corresponding to the Scatter Plot Matrix in Figure 4.9

					FEATURES
PRICE	0.522	−0.024	0.720	0.400	0.697

TURES. Surprisingly, there is also a strong positive correlation between PRICE and E_COST. Recall that E_COST is the energy cost; we would think that higher priced refrigerators should enjoy lower energy costs.

A regression model was fit to the data. The fitted regression is:

$$\widehat{PRICE} = -798 - 6.96 \text{ E\_COST} + 76.5 \text{ R\_CU\_FT} + 137 \text{ F\_CU\_FT}$$

std errors   (271.4) (2.275)   (19.44)   (23.76)

t-ratios   [−2.9] [−3.1]   [3.9]   [5.8]

$$+ 37.9 \text{ SHELVES} + 23.8 \text{ FEATURES}$$

(9.886)   (4.512)

[3.8]   [5.3]

(4.5)

with $s = 60.65$ and $R^2 = 83.8$ percent. The explanatory variables seem to be useful predictors of refrigerator prices. Together, these variables account for 83.8% of the variability. For understanding prices, the typical error has dropped from $s_y = \$139.80$ to $s = \$60.65$. Using the relationship in equation (4.4), from $R^2 = 0.838$, we have F-ratio = 32.1. Thus, you should check that the formal F-test indicates model adequacy. Indeed, the *t*-ratios for each of the explanatory variables exceeds two in absolute value, indicating that each variable is important on an individual basis.

What is somewhat surprising about the regression fit is the negative coefficient associated with energy cost. Remember, we can interpret $b_{E\_COST} = -6.96$ to mean that, for each dollar increase in E_COST, we expect the PRICE to decrease by $6.96. This negative relationship conforms to our economic intuition. However, it is surprising that the same data set has shown us, in Figure 4.9 and Table 4.7, that there is a positive relationship between PRICE and E_COST. This seeming anomaly is because correlation only measures relationships between pairs of variables although the regression fit can account for several variables simultaneously. To provide more insight into this seeming anomaly, we now introduce the *added variable plot*.

Another useful convention when reporting the results of a statistical analysis is to place the t-ratio of a statistic in square brackets below that statistic.

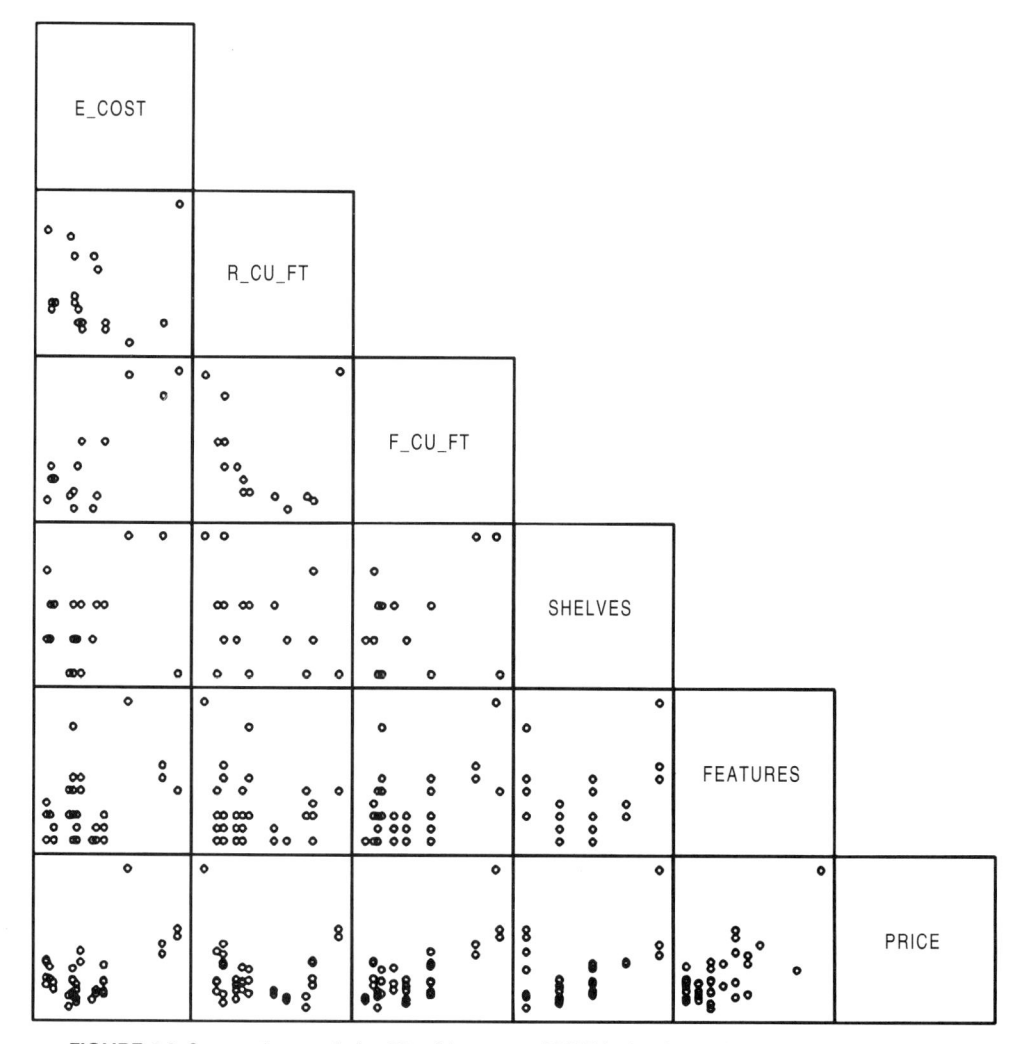

FIGURE 4.9 Scatterplot matrix for 37 refrigerators. PRICE is the dependent variable, and there are five independent variables.

Producing an Added Variable Plot

The added variable plot provides additional links between the regression methodology and more fundamental tools such as scatter plots and correlations. We work in the context of the refrigerator price illustration to demon-

$\hat{e}_2$.

3. Plot $\hat{e}_1$ versus $\hat{e}_2$. This is the added variable plot of PRICE versus E_COST, controlling for the effects of the R_CU_FT, F_CU_FT, SHELVES AND FEATURES. This plot appears in Figure 4.10.

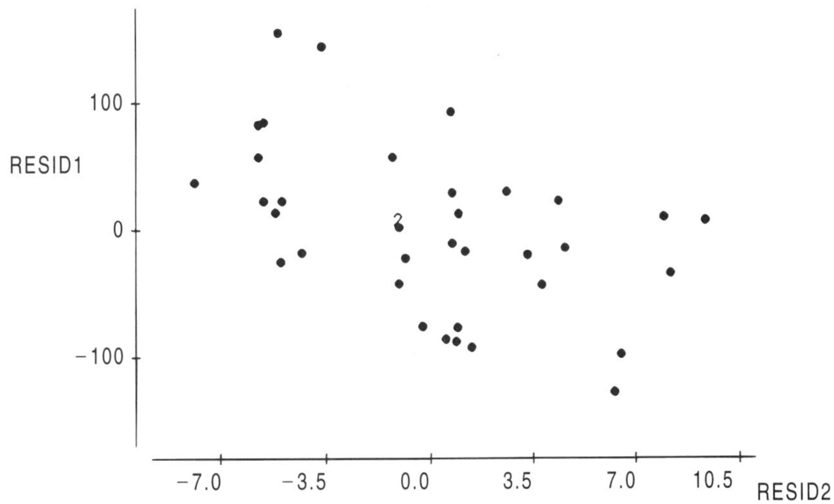

FIGURE 4.10 An added variable plot. The residuals from the regression of PRICE on the explanatory variables, omitting E_COST, are on the vertical axis. On the horizontal axis are the residuals from the regression fit of E_COST on the other explanatory variables. The correlation coefficient is −0.48.

When we introduced the concept of random errors in Section 2.8, we noted that e could be interpreted as the quantity due to the natural variation in a sample. In many situations, this natural variation is small compared to the patterns evident in the nonrandom regression component. Thus, it is useful to think of the error, $e = y - (\beta_0 + \beta_1 x_1 + \ldots + \beta_k x_k)$, as the response after controlling for the effects of the explanatory variables. In Section 4.3, we saw that a random error can be approximated by a residual, $e \approx \hat{e} = y - (b_0 + b_1 x_1 + \ldots + b_k x_k)$. Thus, in the same way, we may think of a residual as the response after "controlling for" the effects of the explanatory variables.

We may think of a residual as the response after controlling the effects of the independent variables.

With this in mind, we can interpret the vertical axis of Figure 4.10 as the refrigerator PRICE controlled for effects of R_CU_FT, F_CU_FT, SHELVES and FEATURES. Similarly, we can interpret the horizontal axis as the E_COST controlled for effects of R_CU_FT, F_CU_FT, SHELVES and FEATURES. The plot then provides a graphical representation of the relation between PRICE and E_COST, after controlling for the other explanatory variables. For comparison, the scatter plot of PRICE and E_COST in Figure 4.9 does not control for other explanatory variables. Thus, it is possible that the positive relationship between PRICE and E_COST is not due to a causal relationship but rather one or more additional variables that cause both variables to be large. For example, in Figure 4.9 and Table 4.7, we see that the freezer size (F_CU_FT) is positively correlated with both E_COST and PRICE. It certainly seems reasonable that increasing the size of a freezer would cause both the energy cost and the price to increase. If this is the case, then the positive correlation between E_COST and PRICE is due to the fact that we have not controlled for F_CU_FT. That is, large values of E_COST do not cause large values of PRICE, as suggested by the positive correlation between E_COST and PRICE. Rather, the positive correlation may be due to the fact that large values of F_CU_FT mean large values of both E_COST and PRICE.

Variables left out of a regression are called *omitted variables.* To illustrate, suppose that large values of F_CU_FT mean large values of both E_COST and PRICE. Further suppose that, because of this, we observe a positive correlation between E_COST and PRICE when there is actually a negative relationship between E_COST and PRICE, holding F_CU_FT fixed. Now consider the implications of running a regression of PRICE on E_COST, that is, inadvertently omitting F_CU_FT. Because of the positive correlation between PRICE and E_COST, we know that the regression coefficient would be positive, from the relationships between regression and correlation discussed in Chapter 3. This result could cause a serious problem in regression model fit; the regression coefficient could be not only strongly significant when it should not be, but it may also be of the incorrect sign. To see the true relationship, we should regress PRICE on E_COST and F_CU_FT. In this way, we can investigate the relationship between PRICE and E_COST after controlling for F_CU_FT. Selecting the proper set of variables to be included in the regression model is an important task; it is the subject of Chapter 6.

Omitted variables may seriously bias our regression fits.

To summarize, the general recipe for added variable plots begins with a response y and k explanatory variables, $x_1, ..., x_k$. Omit the jth explanatory variable and get the residuals $\hat{e}_1$ by running a regression of y on the remaining explanatory variables, that is, $x_1, ..., x_{j-1}, x_{j+1}, ..., x_k$. Similarly, get the residuals $\hat{e}_2$ by running a regression of x_j on the remaining explanatory variables. The plot of $\hat{e}_1$ versus $\hat{e}_2$ is our *added variable plot.*

Added variable plots help to isolate the contribution of a variable to understanding the effects on the response in the presence of the other explanatory variables. With this plot, we can detect linear as well as nonlinear relationships between the variables. In Chapter 6, we will argue that this is an important tool for model selection.

lation between y and x_j, in the presence of the other explanatory variables. To illustrate, the correlation between PRICE and E_COST in the presence of the other explanatory variables is -0.48.

The partial correlation coefficient can also be calculated using

$$r(y, x_j \mid x_1, \ldots, x_{j-1}, x_{j+1}, \ldots, x_k) = \frac{t(b_j)}{\sqrt{t(b_j)^2 + n - (k + 1)}}. \qquad (4.6)$$

Here, $t(b_j)$ is the t-ratio for b_j from a regression of y on $x_1, \ldots, x_k$. An important aspect of equation (4.6) is that it allows us to calculate partial correlation coefficients running only one regression. For example, from equations (4.5) and (4.6), the partial correlation between PRICE and E_COST in the presence of the other explanatory variables is $(-3.1)/((-3.1)^2 + 37 - (5 + 1))^{1/2} \approx -0.48$.

Partial correlation coefficients can be quickly calculated using the relationship with the t-ratio. However, these correlations can fail to detect nonlinear relationships that would be evident in an added variable plot.

Calculation of partial correlation coefficients is quicker when using the relationship with the t-ratio, but may fail to detect nonlinear relationships. The expression in equation (4.6) allows us to calculate all five partial correlation coefficients in the refrigerator price example after running only one regression. The three-step procedure for producing added variable plots requires ten regressions, two for each of the five explanatory variables. Of course, by producing added variable plots, we can detect nonlinear relationships that are missed by correlation coefficients.

Partial correlation coefficients provide another interpretation for t-ratios. Equation (4.6) shows how to calculate a correlation statistic from a t-ratio, thus providing another link between correlation and regression analysis. Moreover, from equation (4.6) we see that the larger is the t-ratio, the larger is the partial correlation coefficient. That is, large t-ratios mean that there is a large correlation between the response and the explanatory variable, controlling for other explanatory variables. This provides a partial response to the question that is regularly asked by consumers of regression analyses, "Which variable is most important?"

4.5 SOME SPECIAL INDEPENDENT VARIABLES

The linear regression model introduced in Sections 4.1 through 4.4 provides the basis for a rich family of models. In this section, we provide several examples to illustrate the richness of this family. These examples demonstrate the use of (i) indicator variables, (ii) transformation of independent variables and

(iii) interaction terms. This section also serves to underscore the meaning of the adjective linear in the phrase "linear regression model"; the model is linear in the parameters but may represent a highly nonlinear function of the explanatory variables.

Linear regression models are linear in the parameters but may represent a highly nonlinear function of the explanatory variables.

Indicator Variables

Categorical variables provide a numerical label for measurements of observations that fall in distinct groups, or categories. Because of the grouping, categorical variables are and generally take on a finite number of values. We begin our discussion with a categorical variable that can take on one of only two values. Further discussion of categorical variables is in Chapter 5. For concreteness, we return to the Apartment Rents example introduced in Section 4.1. Here, we use RENT_SFT for the response variable (y), and MILES (x_1) and FOOTAGE (x_2) for the explanatory variables.

An indicator variable indicates the presence, or absence, of an attribute.

We now define $x_3 = 0$ if an apartment has one bedroom and $x_3 = 1$ if it has two bedrooms. The variable x_3, labelled TWOBED, is said to be an *indicator* variable, because it indicates the presence, or absence, of two bedrooms in an apartment. We could use 0 and 100, or 20 and 36, or any other distinct values for the two possible values of x_3. However, 0 and 1 are convenient for the interpretation of the parameter values, discussed in the following. To streamline the discussion, we now present a model using only x_3 and x_1 (MILES) as explanatory variables.

For our 36 apartments, 19 have two bedrooms and the remaining 17 have one bedroom. To see the relationships among y, x_1 and x_3, Figure 4.11 intro-

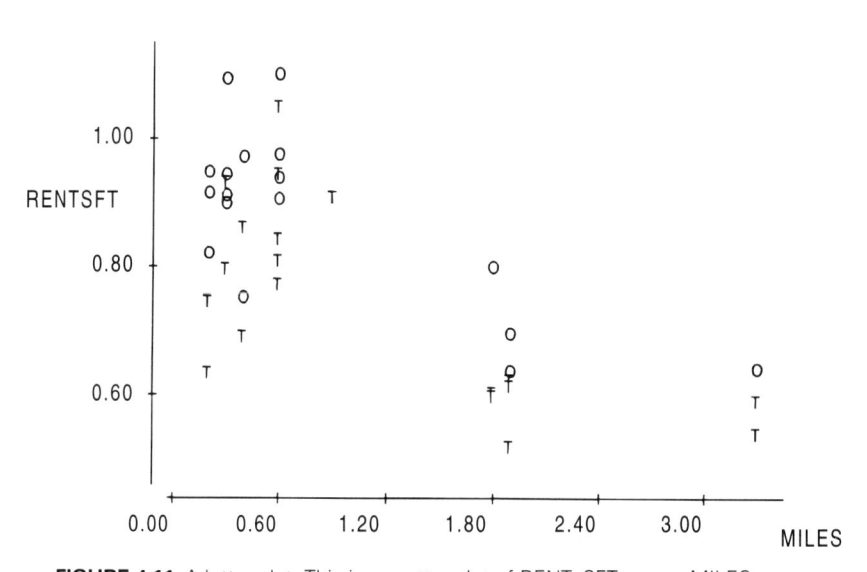

FIGURE 4.11 A letter plot. This is a scatter plot of RENT_SFT versus MILES, with the letter code 'O' for one bedroom and 'T' for two bedroom apartments.

bedroom and `1` for two bedroom were selected because they remind the reader of the nature of the coding scheme. Regardless of the coding scheme, the important point is that a letter plot is a useful device for graphically por-

traying three or more variables in two dimensions. The main restriction is that the additional information must be categorized, such as with indicator vari- ables, to make the coding scheme work.

Figure 4.11 suggests that RENT_SFT is higher for one-bedroom apart- ments than two-bedroom apartments. Thus, we now consider a regression model of RENT_SFT on MILES and TWOBED. We examine the model

$$y = \beta_0 + \beta_1 x_1 + \beta_3 x_3 + e.$$

The nonrandom portion of this model is $E\, y = \beta_0 + \beta_1 x_1 + \beta_3 x_3$. This can be rewritten as:

$$E\, y = (\beta_0 + \beta_3) + \beta_1 x_1 \qquad \text{for two-bedroom apartments}$$
$$E\, y = \beta_0 + \beta_1 x_1 \qquad \text{for one-bedroom apartments.}$$

The interpretation of the model coefficients is dramatically different from the continuous variable case. For continuous variables such as x_1, we inter- preted β_1 as the expected change in y per unit change in x_1, holding other vari- ables fixed. For indicator variables such as x_3, we interpret β_3 as the expected increase in y when going from the base level of x_3 ($=0$) to the alternative level. Thus, although we have one model for our apartments, we can interpret the model using two regression equations, one for each type of apartment. By writ- ing a separate equation for each apartment, we have been able to simplify a complicated multiple regression equation. Sometimes, you will find it easier to communicate a series of simple relationships compared to a single, complex re- lationship.

In Sections 4.2 and 4.3 we discussed the least squares method of calculat- ing the regression coefficient estimators, and their resulting theoretical prop- erties. Both the calculations and resulting properties are still valid when using indicator variables as explanatory variables. To illustrate, the fitted version of the above model is

$$\hat{y} = 0.969 - 0.110 x_1 - 0.104 x_3,$$
$$std\ error \qquad (0.030) \quad (0.019) \quad (0.036)$$

with $s = 0.1065$ and $R^2 = 58.9\%$. To interpret $b_3 = -0.104$, we say that we expect the rent per square foot to be smaller by $0.104, or 10.4¢, for a two-bedroom apartment as compared to a one-bedroom apartment. This assumes that other things, such as distance from the city center, remain unchanged. For a graphical interpretation of this fit, in Figure 4.12 is a letter plot with the two fitted regression lines superimposed.

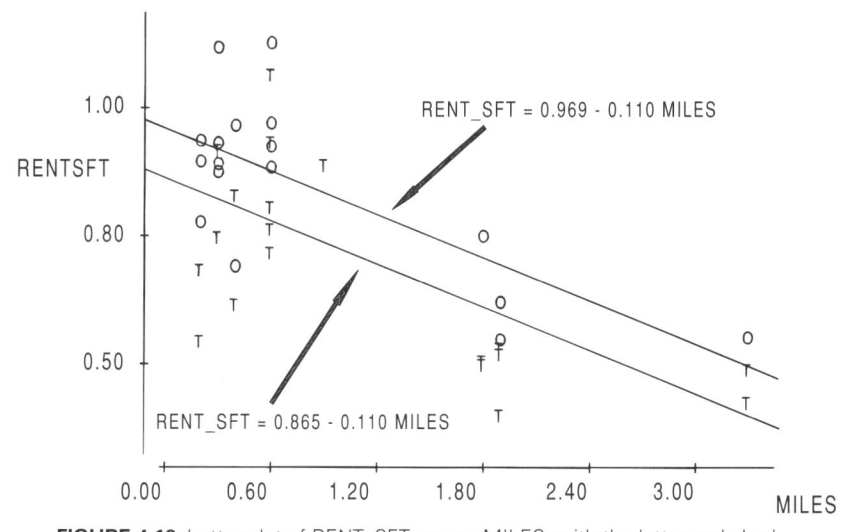

FIGURE 4.12 Letter plot of RENT_SFT versus MILES, with the letter code bedroom. The fitted regression lines have been superimposed. The upper line is for one-bedroom and the lower line is for two-bedroom apartments.

Transforming Independent Variables

Regression models have the ability to represent complex, nonlinear relationships between the expected response and the explanatory variables. For example, we have seen how to incorporate a squared term in x, thus producing a gently sloping curve in x, as in Figure 4.13. Early regression texts, such as Plackett (1960, Chapter 6) devote an entire chapter of material to *polynomial regression*,

$$\text{E } y = \beta_0 + \beta_1 x + \beta_2 x^2 + \ldots + \beta_p x^p. \tag{4.7}$$

Here, the idea is that a pth order polynomial in x can be used to approximate general, unknown nonlinear functions of x. Figure 4.14 is an example of a cubic regression function ($p = 3$).

The modern day treatment of polynomial regression does not require an entire chapter because the model in equation (4.7) can be expressed as a special case of the linear regression model. That is, with $\text{E } y = \beta_0 + \beta_1 x_1 + \beta_2 x_2 + \ldots + \beta_p x_k$, we can choose $k = p$ and $x_1 = x, x_2 = x^2, \ldots, x_p = x^p$. Thus, sometimes the curve might bend more sharply, sometimes it would need a higher maximum turnover of x.

We can use the same properties of x in our choice of transformations. For example, the model $Ey = \beta_0 + \beta_1 x + \beta_2 x^2$ in x as in Figure 4.13, provides another way to represent a quadratic relationship in x. This model can be written as a special case of the multiple regression model using $x_1 = x$, $x_2 = x^2$, where x_1 is x and x_2 is the second power of x.

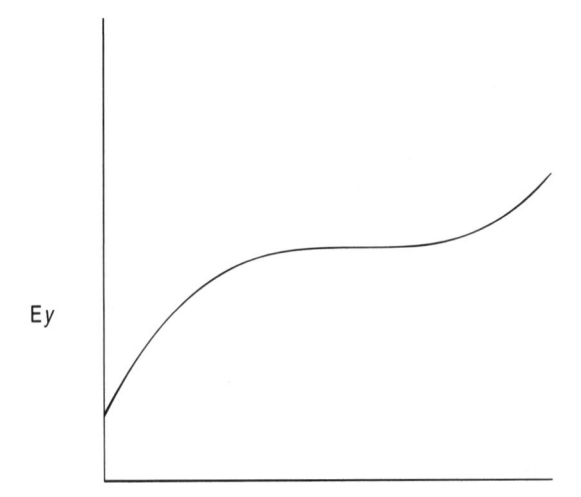

FIGURE 4.13 Plot of E $y = \beta_0 + \beta_1 x + \beta_2 x^2$ versus x.

FIGURE 4.14 Plot of E $y = \beta_0 + \beta_1 x + \beta_2 x^2 + \beta_3 x^3$ versus x.

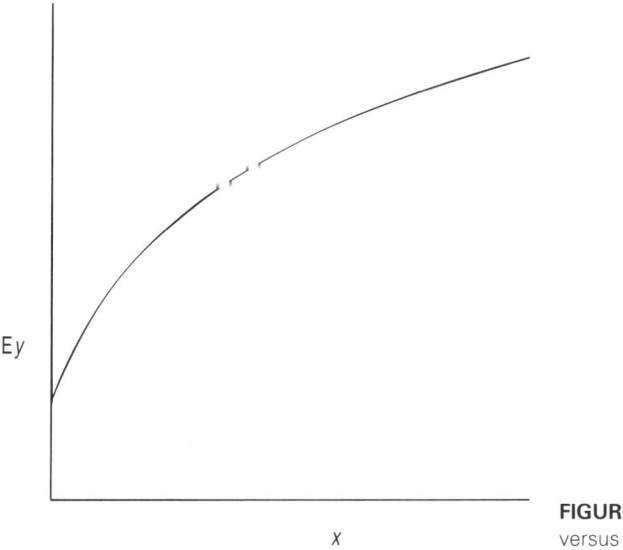

Ey

x

FIGURE 4.15 Plot of E $y = \beta_0 + \beta_1 \ln x$ versus x.

Transformations of independent variables need not be smooth functions. To illustrate, in some applications, it is useful to categorize a continuous explanatory variable. For example, suppose that x represents the number of years of primary school attended for a sample of senior citizens and we are trying to understand y, the highest annual salary earned. Here, x may vary from 0 to 13, with 13 meaning that the person completed kindergarten and 12 years of grades 1 to 12. Assume that we also have information available to control for sex, industry, type of occupation, and so on, but that the real interest is in the relationship between education and salary. If we are relying on information self-reported by our sample of senior citizens, there may be a substantial amount of error in the measurement of x. We could elect to use a less informative, but more reliable, transform of x such as x^*, an indicator variable for finishing 13 years of school (finishing high school). Formally, we would code $x^* = 1$ if $x = 13$ and $x^* = 0$ if $x < 13$.

Thus, there are several ways that nonlinear functions of the explanatory variables that can be used in the regression model. For the linear regression model,

$$\mathrm{E}\, y = \beta_0 + \beta_1 x_1 + \beta_2 x_2 + \ldots + \beta_k x_k,$$

The linear regression model is linear in the parameters β_0, $\beta_1,\ldots,\beta_k$.

we expect the deterministic portion E y to be linear in the regression coefficient parameters β_0, β_1, ..., β_k. An example of a nonlinear regression model is

$$y = \beta_0 \exp(\beta_1 x) + e.$$

Nonlinear regression models are discussed in, for example, Bates and Watts (1988). Chapter 8 addresses a special case of a nonlinear regression model.

when compared to low values of x_2. One way to model this simply is to create an *interaction variable* $x_3 = x_1 x_2$ and consider the model

$$\mathrm{E}\, y = \beta_0 + \beta_1 x_1 + \beta_2 x_2 + \beta_3 x_3.$$

With this model, the change in the expected y per unit change in x_1 now depends on x_2. To see this, suppose that x_1 moves from x_1 to $x_1 + 1$, so that

$$change = \mathrm{E}\, y_{\text{new}} - \mathrm{E}\, y_{\text{old}} = (\beta_0 + \beta_1(x_1 + 1) + \beta_2 x_2 + \beta_3 (x_1 + 1)x_2)$$

$$- (\beta_0 + \beta_1 x_1 + \beta_2 x_2 + \beta_3 x_1 x_2) = \beta_1 + \beta_3 x_2.$$

[Alternatively, if you have had a recent exposure to calculus, note that $(\partial / \partial x_1)$ $\mathrm{E}\, y = \beta_1 + \beta_3 x_2.$] In this way, we may allow for more complicated functions of x_1 and x_2. Figure 4.16 illustrates this complex structure. From this figure and the above calculations, we see that the partial changes of $\mathrm{E}\, y$ due to movement of x_1 depend on the value of x_2. In this way, we say that the partial changes due to each variable are not unrelated but rather "move together."

More generally, an *interaction term* is a variable that is created as a nonlinear function of two or more explanatory variables. These special terms, even though permitting us to explore a rich family of nonlinear functions, can be

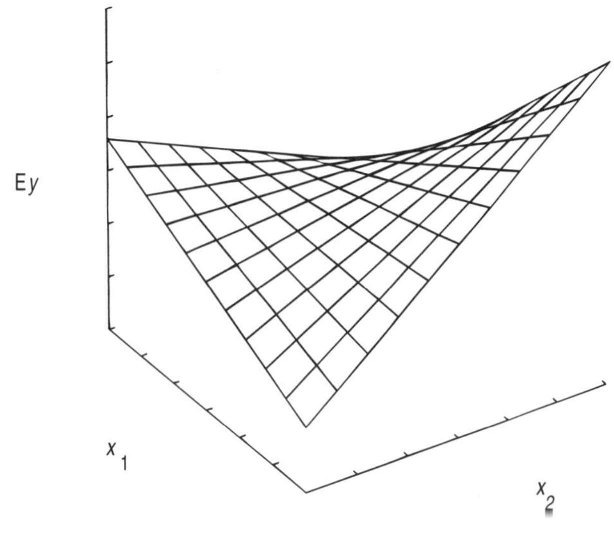

$\mathrm{E}y$

x_1

x_2

FIGURE 4.16 Plot of $\mathrm{E}\, y = \beta_0 + \beta_1 x_1 + \beta_2 x_2 + \beta_3 x_1 x_2$ versus x_1 and x_2.

cast as special cases of the linear regression model. To do this, we simply create the variable of interest and treat this newly created term as another explanatory variable. Of course, not every variable that we create will be useful.
In some instances, the created variable may be so similar to variables already in
our model that it will provide us with no new information. Fortunately, we can
use t-tests, described in Section 4.3, to check whether the new variable is useful. Further, in Section 4.6, we will introduce a test to decide whether a group
of variables is useful.

The function that we use to create an interaction variable must be more
than just a linear combination of other explanatory variables. For example, if
we use $x_3 = x_1 + x_2$ in the model $E\, y = \beta_0 + \beta_1 x_1 + \beta_2 x_2 + \beta_3(x_1 + x_2)$, we will
not be able to estimate all of the parameters. In Section 6.3, we will introduce
some techniques to help us avoid situations when one variable is a linear combination of the others.

To give you some exposure to the wide variety of potential applications
of special explanatory variables, we now present a series of short examples.

Example 4.2: Combining an Indicator and a Continuous Variable

Consider the apartment rent example described in the Indicator
Variable subsection above with y as rent per square foot, x_1 as miles from
the city center and x_3 as an indicator of two bedrooms in an apartment. In
addition, consider using the interaction $x_1 x_3$ in the linear regression
model. The deterministic portion of the model

$$y = \beta_0 + \beta_1 x_1 + \beta_3 x_3 + \beta_4 x_1 x_3 + e$$

can be written as:

$$E\, y = (\beta_0 + \beta_3) + (\beta_1 + \beta_4)x_1 \qquad \text{for two-bedroom apartments}$$

$$E\, y = \beta_0 + \beta_1 x_1 \qquad\qquad\qquad \text{for one-bedroom apartments.}$$

Figure 4.17 presents these two regression lines, one for each bedroom
size. By adding the interaction term $\beta_4 x_1 x_3$, we have been able to model
nonparallel lines.

By fitting a single regression model to the entire data set, we are implicitly assuming a common variability parameter for the one- and two-
bedroom apartments. Alternatively, we could fit a regression model to
the one-bedroom apartments and another model to the two-bedroom
apartments. With this approach, we not only have different fitted regression lines for each apartment size but also different estimates of the variability.

C4_TAX

Example 4.3: Combining an Indicator and Several Continuous Variables

Consider a sample of randomly selected individual tax returns for
1990 prepared by a local branch of a national tax preparation service. The
data collected from each return include:

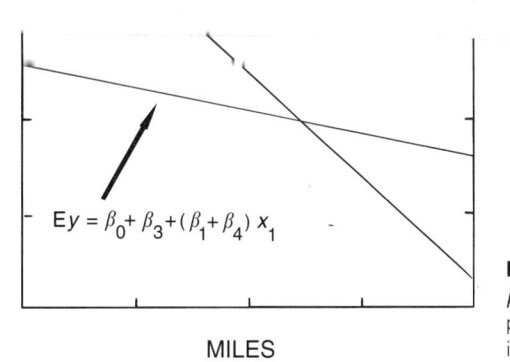

FIGURE 4.17 The model $E\,y = \beta_0 + \beta_1 x_1 + \beta_3 x_3 + \beta_4 x_1 x_3$ can be interpreted as two nonparallel lines when x_3 is an indicator variable.

x_1 = total income (TOTALINC)
x_2 = earned income (EARNDINC),
x_3 = federal itemized or standard deductions (DEDUCTS),
x_4 = marital status (MARRIED, = 1 if married, = 0 if single) and
y = total tax paid as a percent of total income (TAXPERCT).

By definition, total income is the sum of earned plus other income (TOTALINC = EARNDINC + OTHERINC).

We can combine the indicator variable, x_4, with each of the other explanatory variables to get the model

$$y = \beta_0 + \beta_1 x_1 + \beta_2 x_2 + \beta_3 x_3 + \beta_4 x_4 + \beta_{14} x_1 x_4 + \beta_{24} x_2 x_4 + \beta_{34} x_3 x_4 + e.$$

The deterministic portion of this model can be written as:

$$E\,y = (\beta_0 + \beta_4) + (\beta_1 + \beta_{14})x_1 + (\beta_2 + \beta_{24})x_2 \qquad \text{for married filers}$$
$$+ (\beta_3 + \beta_{34})x_3$$

$$E\,y = \beta_0 + \beta_1 x_1 + \beta_2 x_2 + \beta_3 x_3 \qquad\qquad\qquad \text{for single filers.}$$

The labeling of the higher order parameters, such as β_{14}, is merely for notation convenience. You may use β_5, if you find it easier.

The model that we use for estimating parameters has six explanatory variables. However, we can interpret the expected response as two three-variable regression models, one for married filers and one for single filers. As previously noted, although equivalent representations, you may find the series of simpler expressions easier to explain and interpret than the longer, single expression.

Example 4.4: Curvilinear Response Functions

We can expand the polynomial functions of an explanatory variable to include several explanatory variables. For example, the expected response, or response function, for a second order model with two explanatory variables is

$$E\, y = \beta_0 + \beta_1 x_1 + \beta_2 x_2 + \beta_{11} x_1^2 + \beta_{22} x_2^2 + \beta_{12} x_1 x_2.$$

Figure 4.18 illustrates this response function. Similarly, the response function for a second-order model with three explanatory variables is

$$\begin{aligned}
E\, y = {}& \beta_0 + \beta_1 x_1 + \beta_2 x_2 + \beta_3 x_3 \\
& + \beta_{11} x_1^2 + \beta_{22} x_2^2 + \beta_{33} x_3^2 + \beta_{12} x_1 x_2 + \beta_{13} x_1 x_3 + \beta_{23} x_2 x_3.
\end{aligned}$$

When there is more than one explanatory variable, third and higher order models are rarely used in applications.

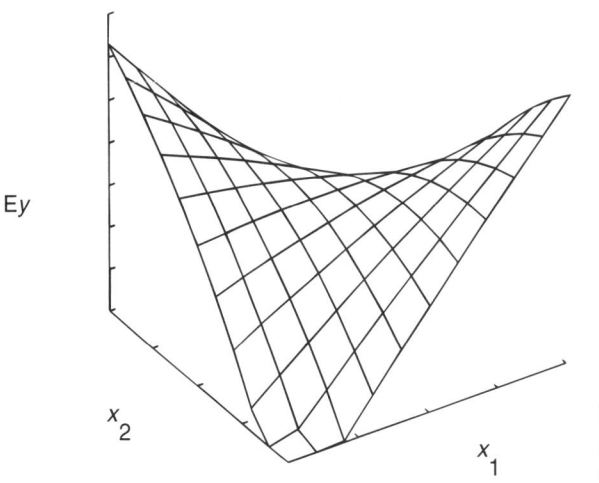

Ey

x_2

x_1

FIGURE 4.18 Plot of $E\, y = \beta_0 + \beta_1 x_1 + \beta_2 x_2 + \beta_{11} x_1^2 + \beta_{22} x^2 + \beta_{12} x_1 x_2$ versus x_1 and x_2.

Example 4.5: Nonlinear Functions of a Continuous Variable

In some applications, we expect the response to have some abrupt changes in behavior at certain values of an explanatory variable, even if the variable is continuous. For example, suppose that we are trying to model an individual's charitable contributions (y) in terms of their wages (x). For 1992 data, a simple model we might entertain is given in Figure 4.19.

A rationale for this model is that, in 1992 individuals paid 6.2% of their income for Social Security taxes up to $55,500. No social security taxes are excised on wages in excess of $55,500. Thus, one theory is that,

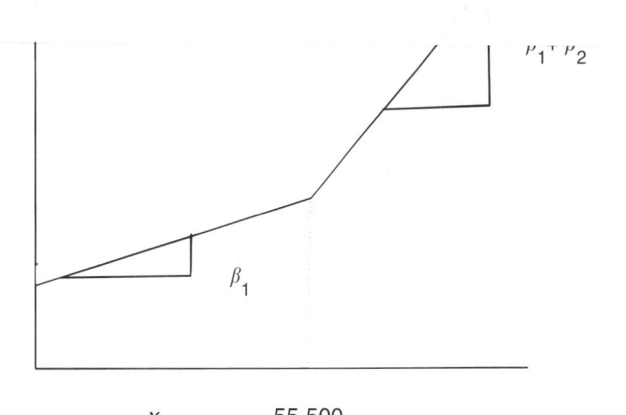

FIGURE 4.19 The marginal change in E y per unit change in x is different from values of x below \$55,500 compared to values above \$55,500. The parameter β_2 represents the difference in slopes.

for wages in excess of \$55,500, individuals have more disposal income per dollar and thus should be more willing to make charitable contributions. Under this theory, we expect β_2 to exceed zero.

To model this relationship, define the indicator variable z to be zero if $x < 55,500$ and to be one if $x \geq 55,500$. Define the response function to be E $y = \beta_0 + \beta_1 x + \beta_2 z(x - 55,500)$. This can be written as:

$$\text{E } y = \beta_0 + \beta_1 x_1 \qquad\qquad\qquad \text{for} \quad x < 55,500$$

$$\text{E } y = \beta_0 - \beta_2(55,500) + (\beta_1 + \beta_2)x_1 \qquad \text{for} \quad x \geq 55,500.$$

To estimate this model, we would run a regression of y on two explanatory variables, $x_1 = x$ and $x_2 = z(x - 55,500)$.

This example is an illustration of *piecewise linear regression*. The sharp break in Figure 4.19 at $x = 55,500$ is called a "kink." We have linear relationships above and below the kinks and have used an indicator variable to put the two pieces together. We are not restricted to one kink. For example, if we instead had considered federal taxable income for 1992 single filers, the marginal tax rate below \$21,450 is 15%, above \$51,900 is 31%, and in between is 28%. For this example, we would use two kinks, at 21,450 and 51,900.

Further, piecewise linear regression is not restricted to continuous response functions. For example, suppose that we are studying the commissions

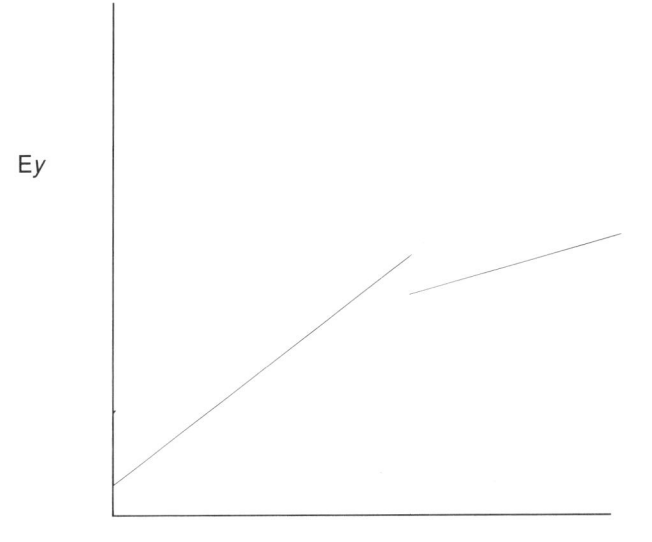

FIGURE 4.20 Plot of expected commissions (E y) versus number of shares traded (x). The break at $x = 100$ reflects savings in administrative expenses. The lower slope for $x \geq 100$ reflects economies of scales in expenses.

paid to stockbrokers (y) in terms of the number of shares purchased by a client (x). We might expect to see the relationship illustrated in Figure 4.20. Here, the discontinuity at $x = 100$ reflects the administrative expenses of trading in *odd lots*, as trades of less than 100 shares are called. The lower marginal cost for trades in excess of 100 shares simply reflects the economies of scale for doing business in larger volumes. A regression model of this is

$$y = \beta_0 + \beta_1 x + \beta_2 z + \beta_3 zx + e$$

where $z = 0$ if $x < 100$ and $z = 1$ if $x \geq 100$. The regression function depicted in Figure 4.20 is

$$\mathrm{E}\, y = \beta_0 + \beta_1 x_1 \qquad\qquad \text{for}\quad x < 100$$
$$\mathrm{E}\, y = \beta_0 + \beta_2 + (\beta_1 + \beta_3) x_1 \qquad \text{for}\quad x \geq 100.$$

4.6 IS A GROUP OF INDEPENDENT VARIABLES IMPORTANT? THE PARTIAL *F*- TEST

In many applications, it is useful to examine a group of several independent variables to see whether they are important in the formulated model. We have already seen in Section 4.3 how to test the importance of a single independent variable using a *t*-test. Also in Section 4.3, we saw how to examine the importance of all the independent variables using an *F*-test. In this section, we now examine subsets of independent variables using the so-called *partial F-test*.

Examining groups of subjects of variables is particularly important when considering models that are built using complicated functions of variables used in the function. For example, an analyst may be considering a second-order model with two explanatory variables such as

$$y = \beta_0 + \beta_1 x_1 + \beta_2 x_2 + \beta_{11} x_1^2 + \beta_{22} x_2^2 + \beta_{12} x_1 x_2 + e$$

However, the analyst may be concerned that the second order terms make the model unnecessarily complicated. To consider removing the second order terms x_1^2, x_2^2 and $x_1 x_2$, the analyst would wish to entertain the hypothesis $H_0: \beta_{11} = \beta_{22} = \beta_{12} = 0$.

As another example, we will work with the model presented in Illustration 4.3,

$$y = \beta_0 + \beta_1 x_1 + \beta_2 x_2 + \beta_3 x_3 + \beta_4 x_4 + \beta_{14} x_1 x_4 + \beta_{24} x_2 x_4 + \beta_{34} x_3 x_4 + e. \tag{4.8}$$

Here, recall that x_1 represents total income, x_2 is earned income, x_3 is federal itemized or standard deductions, x_4 is marital status and y represents total tax paid as a percent of total income. In Section 4.5, we saw that this model had the useful interpretation that there are separate regression functions for married and single filers. However, the analyst may be concerned that having different regression coefficients for x_1, x_2 and x_3 is needlessly complex. The analyst may be interested in the null hypothesis $H_0: \beta_{14} = \beta_{24} = \beta_{34} = 0$. Under this hypothesis, the model is

$$y = \beta_0 + \beta_1 x_1 + \beta_2 x_2 + \beta_3 x_3 + \beta_4 x_4 + e \tag{4.9}$$

which is much simpler.

We now address both of these examples by introducing a test of hypothesis for a general situation. To this end, consider what we call a *full* model,

$$y = \beta_0 + \beta_1 x_1 + \ldots + \beta_k x_k + \beta_{k+1} x_{k+1} + \ldots + \beta_{k+p} x_{k+p} + e.$$

Here, think of the first k explanatory variables, $x_1, \ldots, x_k$, as our base variables. The additional p variables $x_{k+1}, \ldots, x_{k+p}$, are the ones that we are considering dropping. Formally, we consider the full model and wish to test the null hypothesis, $H_0: \beta_{k+1} = \beta_{k+2} = \ldots = \beta_{k+p} = 0$. The alternative hypothesis is that at least one of these beta coefficients is not zero. This test, called the *partial F-test*, can be performed using to the following four steps.

We can test whether a group of independent variables is important using a partial F-test.

1. Run the full regression and get the error sum of squares, which we label (Error SS)$_{full}$.

2. Compare this model to what we call a *reduced* model,

$$y = \beta_0 + \beta_1 x_1 + \ldots + \beta_k x_k + e.$$

Run a regression with this model and get the error sum of squares, which we label (Error SS)$_{reduced}$.

3. Calculate

$$F\text{-ratio} = \frac{\dfrac{(\text{Error SS})_{reduced} - (\text{Error SS})_{full}}{p}}{\dfrac{(\text{Error SS})_{full}}{n - (k + p + 1)}}. \qquad (4.10)$$

This is the change in the error sum of squares, rescaled so that it can be compared to an idealized histogram, as follows.

4. Reject the null hypothesis in favor of the alternative if the *F*-ratio exceeds an *F*-value. The *F*-value is a percentile from the *F*-distribution with $df_1 = p$ and $df_2 = n - (k + p + 1)$ degrees of freedom. The percentile is one minus the significance level of the test.

Example 4.3—Continued

Before discussing the logic and the implications of the partial *F*-test, let's illustrate the use of it. Consider our taxpayer example, described in Example 4.3. Suppose that we are examining a 1990 sample of $n = 65$ returns prepared by a local branch office of a national tax preparation service. We are working with the full regression model in equation (4.8) and wish to compare it to the reduced regression model in equation (4.9). According to step 1, we begin by running the full regression model and get $(\text{Error SS})_{full} = 401.61$. In this regression run, we also get the statistics $s_{full} = 2.654$ and $R^2_{full} = 84.6\%$. As described in step 2, we next run the reduced regression model to get $(\text{Error SS})_{reduced} = 504.88$, $s_{reduced} = 2.901$ and $R^2_{reduced} = 80.6\%$. To implement step 3, we first identify the number of explanatory variables in the reduced model to be $k = 4$. The number of variables that we consider dropping is $p = 3$. Thus, the test statistic is

$$F\text{-ratio} = \frac{\dfrac{504.88 - 401.61}{3}}{\dfrac{401.61}{65 - (4 + 3 + 1)}} = 4.886.$$

Finally, in step 4, using a 5% level of significance, the 95th percentile from an *F*-distribution with $df_1 = 3$ and $df_2 = 57$ is approximately *F*-value ≈ 2.766. Thus, we reject the null hypothesis $H_0: \beta_{14} = \beta_{24} = \beta_{34} = 0$. This suggests that it is important to have separate regression functions for married and single filers.

To understand the logic of partial *F*-tests, recall that the error sum of squares for the full model is determined to be the minimum value of

$$SS(b_0^*, b_1^*, \ldots, b_{k+p}^*) = \sum_{i=1}^{n} (y_i - (b_0^* + b_1^* x_{i1} + b_2^* x_{i2} + \ldots + b_{k+p}^* x_{i,k+p}))^2.$$

Here, $SS(b_0^*, b_1^*, ..., b_{k+p}^*)$ is a function of $b_0^*, b_1^*, ..., b_{k+p}^*$ and $(\text{Error SS})_{full}$ is the minimum over all possible values of $b_0^*, b_1^*, ..., b_{k+p}^*$. Similarly, $(\text{Error SS})_{reduced}$ is the minimum over all possible values of $b_0^*, b_1^*, ..., b_k^*$. Because we are taking a minimum over more arguments in $(\text{Error SS})_{full}$, we have that $(\text{Error SS})_{full} \leq (\text{Error SS})_{reduced}$. Stated another way, when adding variables to a regression model, the error sum of squares never goes up (and, in fact, usually goes down). Thus, when adding variables to the reduced model to get the full model, we expect a drop in the error sum of squares.

How large a decrease in the error sum of squares is necessary to warrant the additional complexity of including these additional variables? To respond to this, we first divide the drop in the error sum of squares by the number of variables excluded to get $[(\text{Error SS})_{reduced} - (\text{Error SS})_{full}]/p$. This quantity is in y units squared. Thus, we divide it by our best estimate of the variance term, the s^2 from the full model, $(\text{Error SS})_{full}/(n - (k + p + 1))$. Based on some results from mathematical statistics, under the assumptions of independence, the normality of errors and the null hypothesis, it turns out that this quantity has an F-distribution with $df_1 = p$ and $df_2 = n - (k + p + 1)$ degrees of freedom. This allows us to compare it to a percentile from the F-distrtibution to see if the test statistic is unusually large under the null hypothesis.

By dividing the numerator and denominator by Total SS, the test statistic can also be written as:

$$F\text{-ratio} = \frac{\dfrac{R_{full}^2 - R_{reduced}^2}{p}}{\dfrac{1 - R_{full}^2}{n - (k + p + 1)}}. \tag{4.11}$$

The interpretation of this expression is that the F-ratio measures the drop in the coefficient of determination, R^2.

The partial F-test is closely related to the tests of hypotheses introduced in Section 4.3. Here are some additional facts about the F-test for collections of explanatory variables.

1. Suppose $k = 0$. Then $(\text{Error SS})_{reduced} = \text{Total SS}$. This leads to our first test of model adequacy, described in Section 4.3.
2. Suppose $p = 1$. Then the null hypothesis is $H_0: \beta_{k+1} = 0$. We can already test this null hypothesis using the t-ratio test. In this special case, it turns out that $(t\text{-ratio})^2 = F\text{-ratio}$. Thus, these tests are equivalent for testing $H_0: \beta_j = 0$ versus $H_a: \beta_j \neq 0$. The partial F-test has the

advantage that it works for more than one predictor. The *t*-test has the advantage that one can consider one-sided alternatives, the mechanics of which are described in Section 7.1. Thus, both tests are considered useful.

Using the relationship Regression SS = Total SS − Error SS, we can also express the test statistic as

$$F\text{-ratio} = \frac{(\text{Regression SS})_{full} - (\text{Regression SS})_{reduced}}{ps_{full}^2} \; .$$

where

$$s_{full}^2 = (\text{Error SS})_{full}/(n - (k + p + 1)),$$

$$(\text{Regression SS})_{full} = \text{Total SS} - (\text{Error SS})_{full}, \text{ and}$$

$$(\text{Regression SS})_{reduced} = \text{Total SS} - (\text{Error SS})_{reduced}.$$

The interpretation of this expression is that the test statistic is a measure of the increase in the regression sum of squares due to the introduction of the additional variables $x_{k+1}, \ldots, x_{k+p}$.

The numerator of this expression, $(\text{Regression SS})_{full} - (\text{Regression SS})_{reduced}$, is called the *extra sum of squares* for $x_{k+1}, \ldots, x_{k+p}$. It is the regression sum of squares due to $x_{k+1}, \ldots, x_{k+p}$ in the presence of $x_1, \ldots, x_k$. You will find that many statistical software packages allow you to compute this quantity directly in a single regression run. The advantage of this is it allows the analyst to perform a partial *F*-test using a single regression run, instead of two regression runs as in our four-step procedure previously described. Remember that the additional variables do not need to be the last p in your regression run. Dropping $x_{k+1}, \ldots, x_{k+p}$ is for notational convenience only. From a list of $k+p$ variables $x_1, \ldots, x_k, x_{k+1}, \ldots, x_{k+p}$, you may drop any p variables that you deem appropriate.

The partial *F*-test is available whenever you can express one model as a subset of another. For this reason, it is useful to think of it as a device for comparing "smaller" to "larger" models. However, the smaller model must be a subset of the larger model. For example, the partial *F*-test cannot be used to compare the regression functions $E\,y = \beta_0 + \beta_7 x_7$ versus $E\,y = \beta_0 + \beta_1 x_1 + \beta_2 x_2 + \beta_3 x_3 + \beta_4 x_4$. This is because the former, smaller function is not a subset of the latter, larger function. Section 6.5 will introduce some techniques for addressing this comparison.

4.7 EXPRESSING THE MODEL IN MATRIX NOTATION (OPTIONAL)

One can go a long way in understanding the ideas of regression analysis without developing complex mathematical notions such as a *matrix*. However, if we do the extra work of understanding these notions, there are several rewards. Some of these rewards include:

1. A facility with this notation is useful when reading journal articles on the latest findings. Many researchers have been schooled in matrix notation and find it a natural way to express ideas. As a result, this notation is used extensively in scholarly journals.
2. The notation provides insight into expressions of some complex statistical ideas, such as standard errors for slope coefficients and for residuals.
3. The notation is useful in the discussion of how important an outlying observation is, particularly the notion of a high leverage point, that will be described in Chapter 6.

A vector is a mathematical way of representing columns of numbers.

To begin the discussion, we start with the notion of a *vector*. As an important example, we use

$$\mathbf{y} = \begin{bmatrix} y_1 \\ y_2 \\ \cdot \\ \cdot \\ \cdot \\ y_n \end{bmatrix}$$

to be the *vector of dependent variables*. A vector is merely a mathematical way of representing a column of numbers, for example, as you might see in a spreadsheet. A convention for denoting a vector is to use a bold-faced letter (or to use a curly underscore when writing it on the blackboard). There are n rows in the vector $\mathbf{y}$ and one column. Similarly, some other important examples of a vector include the vector of parameters

$$\boldsymbol{\beta} = \begin{bmatrix} \beta_0 \\ \beta_1 \\ \cdot \\ \cdot \\ \cdot \\ \beta_k \end{bmatrix},$$

and the vector of errors

$$\mathbf{e} = \begin{bmatrix} e_1 \\ e_2 \\ \cdot \\ \cdot \\ \cdot \\ e_n \end{bmatrix}.$$

Now, recall from equation (4.2), that the regression model is:

$$y_1 = \beta_0(1) + \beta_1 x_{11} + \beta_2 x_{12} + \ldots + \beta_k x_{1k} + e_1$$

$$y_2 = \beta_0(1) + \beta_1 x_{21} + \beta_2 x_{22} + \ldots + \beta_k x_{2k} + e_2$$

$$\cdot \cdot \cdot$$

$$\cdot \cdot \cdot$$

$$\cdot \cdot \cdot$$

$$y_n = \beta_0(1) + \beta_1 x_{n1} + \beta_2 x_{n2} + \ldots + \beta_k x_{nk} + e_n.$$

Matrices are special ways of organizing numbers. A matrix is formed simply by putting several vectors together side-by-side. We can represent the explanatory variables using a *matrix*. A matrix is formed by putting several vectors together side-by-side. *The matrix of explanatory variables* is

$$\mathbf{X} = \begin{bmatrix} 1 & x_{11} & x_{12} & \cdots & x_{1k} \\ 1 & x_{11} & x_{12} & \cdots & x_{2k} \\ \cdot & \cdot & \cdot & \cdots & \cdot \\ \cdot & \cdot & \cdot & \cdots & \cdot \\ 1 & x_{n1} & x_{n2} & \cdots & x_{nk} \end{bmatrix}.$$

The matrix $\mathbf{X}$ has n rows and $k + 1$ columns. The first column of $\mathbf{X}$ is a vector of ones, corresponding to the intercept term. Note that a vector is a special kind of matrix; that is, a vector is a matrix with one column.

Matrices (the plural of matrix) are simply special quantities for organizing numbers. Just as with numbers, we have special rules for adding, subtracting, multiplying and "dividing" matrices. This field of study is called, not surprisingly, *matrix algebra*. We do not go into these rules here, but suffice it to say that an equivalent way of writing the general regression model is

$$\mathbf{y} = \mathbf{X}\boldsymbol{\beta} + \mathbf{e}.$$

This is a shorter expression of the regression model than presented in equation (4.2). It is well-defined once you have gone through the rules to multiply $\mathbf{X}$

time $\boldsymbol{\beta}$ to get:

$$\mathbf{X}\boldsymbol{\beta} = \begin{bmatrix} \beta_0 + \beta_1 x_{11} + \beta_2 x_{12} + \dots + \beta_k x_{1k} \\ \beta_0 + \beta_1 x_{21} + \beta_2 x_{22} + \dots + \beta_k x_{2k} \\ \dots \\ \dots \\ \beta_0 + \beta_1 x_{n1} + \beta_2 x_{n2} + \dots + \beta_k x_{nk} \end{bmatrix}.$$

Note that there are n rows but only one column in the expression for $\mathbf{X}\boldsymbol{\beta}$.

A useful concept in the manipulation of matrices is the concept of a *transpose*, defined to be the "mirror image" of a matrix and denoted by $\mathbf{X}'$. When reading the latest findings, you will find that, to save space, a journal will use $\mathbf{y} = (y_1, y_2, \dots, y_n)'$ to define a vector $\mathbf{y}$. Another useful feature of the concept of the transpose is with respect to matrix multiplication. To multiply $\mathbf{X}$ by itself, we first take the transpose, for example, $\mathbf{X}'\mathbf{X}$. This matrix has $k + 1$ columns and $k + 1$ rows and is termed a "square" matrix.

There is no real concept of "division" in matrix algebra. Instead we multiply by the reciprocal, or inverse, of a matrtix. For example, $(\mathbf{X}'\mathbf{X})^{-1}$ is the inverse of the matrix $\mathbf{X}'\mathbf{X}$.

We now apply these ideas to the estimation aspects of Chapter 4 and begin with the method of least squares. The vector of least squares slope estimates, $\mathbf{b} = (b_0, b_1, b_2, \dots, b_k)'$, is defined to be the solution of the so-called *normal equations*,

$$\mathbf{X}'\mathbf{X}\mathbf{b} = \mathbf{X}'\mathbf{y}.$$

This is a set of $k + 1$ equations with $k + 1$ unknowns written in matrix notation. This set of equations can be solved by "dividing each side by $\mathbf{X}'\mathbf{X}$," or more precisely, multiplying by the inverse of $\mathbf{X}'\mathbf{X}$, to get

$$\mathbf{b} = (\mathbf{X}'\mathbf{X})^{-1}\mathbf{X}'\mathbf{y}.$$

This provides an explicit expression for $\mathbf{b}$, the *vector of least squares estimates*. Using $\mathbf{b}$, it is straightforward to define the *vector of fitted values* $\hat{\mathbf{y}} = \mathbf{X}\mathbf{b}$.

In addition to being used to find the least squares estimates $\mathbf{b}$, there are two additional applications of the matrix $(\mathbf{X}'\mathbf{X})^{-1}$. First, the standard error of the slope coefficients that can be expressed using this matrix. It turns out that $se(b_j)$ is equal to s times the square root of the element in $(j + 1)$st row and $(j + 1)$st column of $(\mathbf{X}'\mathbf{X})^{-1}$. That is,

$$se(b_j) = s\sqrt{(j+1)\text{st }\textit{diagonal element of }(\mathbf{X}'\mathbf{X})^{-1}}.$$

As a second application of the matrix $(\mathbf{X}'\mathbf{X})^{-1}$, we introduce the so-called *projection matrix*. Define $\mathbf{H} = \mathbf{X}(\mathbf{X}'\mathbf{X})^{-1}\mathbf{X}'$ to be the matrix that projects, or transforms, the observations into the fitted values, that is, $\hat{y} = \mathbf{H}\mathbf{y}$. The vector of residuals is $\hat{e} = \mathbf{y} - \hat{\mathbf{y}}$. The number in the ith row and ith column of $\mathbf{H}$, denoted by h_{ii}, is called the ith *leverage*. This is an important concept associated with high leverage points and will be discussed in Chapter 6.

Example 4.6: Apartment Rents

To illustrate the matrix formulation of a regression problem, consider the apartment rent example introduced in Section 4.1. We use y to represent the rent per square feet, x_1 to represent the distance from the city center and x_2 to represent the size of each apartment in square feet. Thus, there are $k = 2$ explanatory variables and $n = 36$ apartments. The vector of responses and the matrix of explanatory variables are:

$$\mathbf{y} = \begin{bmatrix} y_1 \\ y_2 \\ y_3 \\ y_4 \\ \cdot \\ \cdot \\ \cdot \\ y_{35} \\ y_{36} \end{bmatrix} = \begin{bmatrix} 0.58919 \\ 0.64000 \\ 0.53889 \\ 0.61250 \\ \cdot \\ \cdot \\ \cdot \\ 0.90541 \\ 0.80786 \end{bmatrix} \qquad \mathbf{X} = \begin{bmatrix} 1 & x_{11} & x_{12} \\ 1 & x_{21} & x_{22} \\ 1 & x_{31} & x_{32} \\ 1 & x_{41} & x_{42} \\ \cdot & \cdot & \cdot \\ \cdot & \cdot & \cdot \\ \cdot & \cdot & \cdot \\ 1 & x_{n-1,1} & x_{n-1,2} \\ 1 & x_{n1} & x_{n2} \end{bmatrix} = \begin{bmatrix} 1 & 3.3 & 925 \\ 1 & 3.3 & 625 \\ 1 & 3.3 & 900 \\ 1 & 1.9 & 800 \\ \cdot & \cdot & \cdot \\ \cdot & \cdot & \cdot \\ \cdot & \cdot & \cdot \\ 1 & 0.6 & 740 \\ 1 & 0.6 & 1145 \end{bmatrix}.$$

For the least squares estimates and the standard error of the estimates, we need the $(\mathbf{X}'\mathbf{X})^{-1}$ matrix. This matrix, with preliminary calculation of $\mathbf{X}'\mathbf{X}$, is given below.

$$\mathbf{X}'\mathbf{X} = \begin{bmatrix} 1 & 1 & 1 & \cdots & 1 \\ 3.3 & 3.3 & 3.3 & \cdots & 0.6 \\ 925 & 625 & 900 & \cdots & 1145 \end{bmatrix} \begin{bmatrix} 1 & 3.3 & 925 \\ 1 & 3.3 & 625 \\ 1 & 3.3 & 900 \\ \cdot & \cdot & \cdot \\ \cdot & \cdot & \cdot \\ \cdot & \cdot & \cdot \\ 1 & 0.6 & 1145 \end{bmatrix}$$

$$= \begin{bmatrix} 36 & 35.5 & 28477 \\ 35.5 & 65.9 & 28863 \\ 28477 & 28863 & 24237268 \end{bmatrix}$$

$$(\mathbf{X}'\mathbf{X})^{-1} = \begin{bmatrix} 0.406254 & -0.0204882 & -0.000452921 \\ -0.0204882 & 0.032780 & -0.000014963 \\ -0.000452921 & -0.000014963 & 0.000000591 \end{bmatrix}$$

We are now in a position to present the vector of least squares estimates, **b**. This is given below with the preliminary calculation of $\mathbf{X'y}$. From this display, we see that $b_0 = 1.14$, $b_1 = -0.112$ and $b_2 = -0.00028$.

$$\mathbf{X'y} = \begin{bmatrix} 1 & 1 & 1 & \cdots & 1 \\ 3.3 & 3.3 & 3.3 & \cdots & 0.6 \\ 925 & 625 & 900 & \cdots & 1145 \end{bmatrix} \begin{bmatrix} 0.58919 \\ 0.64000 \\ 0.53889 \\ \cdot \\ \cdot \\ \cdot \\ 0.80786 \end{bmatrix} = \begin{bmatrix} 28.986 \\ 24.892 \\ 223600 \end{bmatrix}$$

$$\mathbf{b} = \begin{bmatrix} b_0 \\ b_1 \\ b_2 \end{bmatrix} = (\mathbf{X'X})^{-1}\mathbf{X'y}$$

$$= \begin{bmatrix} 0.406254 & -0.0204882 & -0.000452921 \\ -0.0204882 & 0.032780 & -0.000014963 \\ -0.000452921 & -0.000014963 & 0.000000591 \end{bmatrix} \begin{bmatrix} 28.986 \\ 24.892 \\ 223600 \end{bmatrix}$$

$$= \begin{bmatrix} 1.14 \\ -0.112 \\ -0.00028 \end{bmatrix}$$

Quantities useful in the decomposition of the variance are the vector of fitted values $\mathbf{\hat{y}}$ and the vector of residuals $\mathbf{\hat{e}}$. These calculations follow:

$$\mathbf{\hat{y}} = \mathbf{Xb} = \begin{bmatrix} 1 & 3.3 & 925 \\ 1 & 3.3 & 625 \\ 1 & 3.3 & 900 \\ \cdot & \cdot & \cdot \\ \cdot & \cdot & \cdot \\ \cdot & \cdot & \cdot \\ 1 & 0.6 & 1145 \end{bmatrix} \begin{bmatrix} 1.14 \\ -0.112 \\ -0.00028 \end{bmatrix} = \begin{bmatrix} 0.50726 \\ 0.59152 \\ 0.51328 \\ \cdot \\ \cdot \\ \cdot \\ 0.74917 \end{bmatrix}$$

$$\mathbf{\hat{e}} = \mathbf{y} - \mathbf{\hat{y}} = \begin{bmatrix} 0.58919 \\ 0.64000 \\ 0.53889 \\ \cdot \\ \cdot \\ 0.80786 \end{bmatrix} - \begin{bmatrix} 0.50726 \\ 0.59152 \\ 0.51328 \\ \cdot \\ \cdot \\ 0.74917 \end{bmatrix} = \begin{bmatrix} 0.08893 \\ 0.04848 \\ 0.02461 \\ \cdot \\ \cdot \\ 0.05869 \end{bmatrix}$$

For example, we can use the vector of residuals to compute $s^2 = (n - (k + 1))^{-1} \sum_{i=1}^{n} \hat{e}^2$. The matrix version of this formula is as follows.

$$s^2 = \frac{\hat{e}'\hat{e}}{n - (k + 1)}$$

$$= \frac{1}{36 - 3} [0.08893 \quad 0.04848 \quad 0.02461 \quad \cdots \quad 0.05869] \begin{bmatrix} 0.08893 \\ 0.04848 \\ 0.02461 \\ \cdot \\ \cdot \\ \cdot \\ 0.05869 \end{bmatrix}$$

$$= 0.01016$$

However, we don't really need matrix algebra for expressions in the ANOVA table because ordinary algebraic expressions, such as the expression for s^2 above, work just fine. The matrix formulation is required for the standard errors of regression coefficients, $se(b_j)$. For our illustration, we have $s = (0.01016)^{1/2} = 0.1008$ and

$$se(b_0) = (0.1008)\sqrt{0.406254} = 0.06425$$

$$se(b_1) = (0.1008)\sqrt{0.032780} = 0.01825$$

$$se(b_2) = (0.1008)\sqrt{0.000000591} = 0.00007751.$$

Another important quantity needed is the projection matrix, **H**. In general, this matrix has n rows and n columns which, in our example, is a 36 $\times$ 36 matrix. The calculation of the **H** matrix is illustrated in the following:

$$\mathbf{H} = \mathbf{X}(\mathbf{X}'\mathbf{X})^{-1}\mathbf{X}'$$

$$= \begin{bmatrix} 1 & 3.3 & 925 \\ 1 & 3.3 & 625 \\ 1 & 3.3 & 900 \\ \cdot & \cdot & \cdot \\ \cdot & \cdot & \cdot \\ \cdot & \cdot & \cdot \\ 1 & 0.6 & 1,145 \end{bmatrix} \begin{bmatrix} 0.406254 & -0.0204882 & -0.000452921 \\ -0.0204882 & 0.032780 & -0.000014963 \\ -0.000452921 & -0.000014963 & 0.000000591 \end{bmatrix}$$

$$\times \begin{bmatrix} 1 & 1 & 1 & \cdots & 1 \\ 3.3 & 3.3 & 3.3 & \cdots & 0.6 \\ 925 & 625 & 900 & \cdots & 1,145 \end{bmatrix}.$$

We generally only use elements on the diagonal which are expressed as h_{ii}. As an example, h_{11} is the element in the first row and column of $\mathbf{H}$ and is presented below.

$$h_{11} = [1\ 3.3\ 925] \begin{bmatrix} 0.406254 & -0.0204882 & -0.000452921 \\ -0.0204882 & 0.032780 & -0.000014963 \\ -0.000452921 & -0.000014963 & 0.000000591 \end{bmatrix} \begin{bmatrix} 1 \\ 3.3 \\ 925 \end{bmatrix}$$

$$= 0.204619.$$

4.8 SUMMARY

In this chapter, we extended our discussion of the regression model from the one variable case, introduced in Chapter 3, to situations involving many independent variables. Through this extension, we implicitly introduce the problem of selecting the appropriate variables. Selection of the appropriate regression model to represent a data set is a complex issue. In the preliminary Section 4.0, we outlined an iterative procedure for model selection. Most of the discussion of how to fit a model to a particular data set and some of the difficulties one might encounter will be discussed in Chapter 6.

The goals of this chapter are much more modest. These goals are merely to identify the data suitable for regression analysis, define the regression model, and discuss ways in which the model summarizes features of the data. These issues were addressed in Sections 4.1, 4.2 and 4.3, respectively. Added variable plots are the subject to Section 4.4. These plots and their corresponding partial correlation coefficients are useful devices for interpreting the results of fitted regression models. Some special models were described in Section 4.5. Section 4.6 introduced a test for examining portions of the model, another useful device for interpreting the results from a fitted regression model. The techniques for fitting a specified model to a data set does not receive a good deal of attention, although it was described in the matrix formulation of the model in Section 4.7.

Chapter 4 introduces the linear regression model. Chapter 5 will enlarge the scope of potential applications by showing how to include categorical variables into the linear regression model. As previously stated, Chapter 6 is devoted to model selection. Chapter 7 will summarize the linear regression model inference possibilities, the final stage in the iterative analysis process.

KEY WORDS, PHRASES AND SYMBOLS

After reading this chapter, you should be able to define each of the following important terms, phrases and symbols in your own words. If not, go the page indicated and review the definition.

CHAPTER 4 EXERCISES

Sections 4.1–4.3

4.1 50 observations have been generated from an F-distribution with $df_1 = 1$ and $df_2 = 40$ degrees of freedom (Figure E4.1).
  a. From the following dotplot of realized observations, find the approximate 90th and 98th percentiles.
  b. Find the 90th and 98th percentiles from the theortical distribution (you do not need these percentiles from an F-table).

```
MTB > random 50 c1;    # MINITAB commands to create 50 realizations from an
SUBC. f 1 40.          # F-distribution with 1 and 40 df
MTB > dotp c1
```

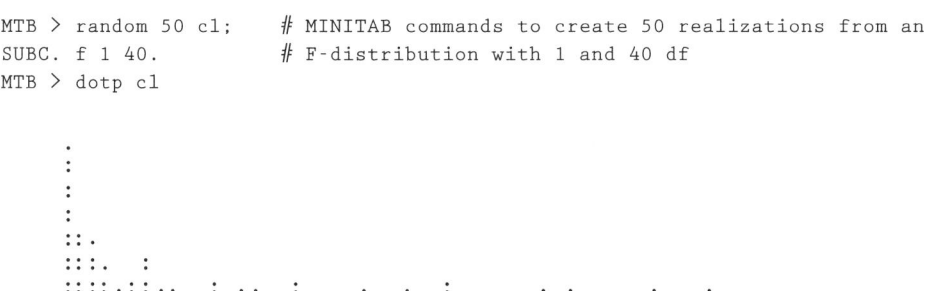

FIGURE E4.1

4.2 Find the 95th percentile for an F-distribution with each of the following choices of degrees of freedom:

a. $df_1 = 1$ and $df_2 = 2$
b. $df_1 = 2$ and $df_2 = 1$
c. $df_1 = 1$ and $df_2 = 20$
d. $df_1 = 1$ and $df_2 = 60$
e. $df_1 = 1$ and $df_2 = \text{infinity}$

f. $df_1 = 2$ and $df_2 = 20$
g. $df_1 = \text{infinity}$ and $df_2 = 2$
h. Find the 97.5th for a t-distribution with $df = 2$ Check your answer by squaring the result and see if it agrees with your answer in part (a).

4.3 Consider a fictitious data set of $n = 100$ observations with $s_y = 100$. We run a regression with three independent variables to get $s = 50$.

a. Calculate the adjusted coefficient of determination, R_a^2.
b. Complete the ANOVA table. (Table E4.3.)
c. Calculate the (unadjusted) coefficient of determination, R^2.

TABLE E4.3

Source	Sum of Squares	df	Mean Square	F-ratio
Regression				
Error				
Total				

C4_VOTE

4.4 There is a great deal of concern among political leaders about the lack of involvement of citizens in their country's political process. In particular, in the last ten years, the United States has exhibited one of the lowest voter turnout rates among electoral democracies. Voter turnout rates are useful measures of public involvement in the political process. Thus, it is of interest to study the voter turnout rate and various factors that may influence it. To this end, data from each of the 50 states in the Union plus the District of Columbia was gathered for the 1988 presidential election. For each "state," the voter turnout rate (TURNOUT) was measured, together with a number of potential explanatory variables. The variables that we consider initially are the percentage of voting age population that is non-Caucasian (MINOR), the percentage of voting age population that completed 4 year high school or more (%HISCH), and the percentage of voting age population that is registered to vote (%REG). (See Tables E4.4a, E4.4b and E4.4c.)

a. In the attached output, a regression model was fit using three independent variables. Summarize the fit of this model by calculating the square root of the mean square error, s, the coefficient of determination, R^2, and its adjusted version, R_a^2.

b. Is %HISCH a statistically significant variable? To respond to this question, use a formal test of hypothesis. State your null and alternative hypotheses, decision making criterion, and your decision making rule.

c. Wisconsin is known to have a relatively high TURNOUT of 61.0, a high %HISCH of 81.1 and a low MINOR of 7.8. Unfortunately, the value %REG was not available in the data base for Wisconsin and one other state, resulting in two missing observations for the regression fit. A researcher suggests that you estimate the value of %REG for Wisconsin by using the fitted regression equation.

TABLE E4.4a   Summary Statistics of Basic Variables

	Number	Number missing	Mean	Median	Standard deviation	Minimum	Maximum
MINOR	51	0	16.61	15.90	10.35	1.40	39.20
%HISCH	51	0	77.651	78.000	6.142	63.200	88.200
TURNOUT	51	0	51.914	52.600	6.351	39.000	65.500
%REG	49	2	72.88	71.59	9.53	54.48	94.16

Correlation Matrix

	MINOR	%HISCH	TURNOUT
%HISCH	−0.355		
TURNOUT	−0.277	0.565	
%REG	−0.411	0.125	0.715

Regression of TURNOUT on Three Explanatory Variables

TABLE E4.4b   Coefficient Estimates

Explanatory variables	Coefficient	Standard error	t-ratio
Constant	−0.765	6.850	−0.11
%HISCH	0.38479	0.06957	5.53
%REG	0.35100	0.04684	7.49
MINOR	−0.18256	0.04551	−4.01

TABLE E4.4c   ANOVA Table

Source	Sum of Squares	df	Mean Square
Regression	1,479.10	3	493.03
Error	357.98	45	7.96
Total	1,837.07	48	

    i. Write down the fitted regression equation, substitute the known values of the explanatory variables and solve to get an estimated value of %REG for Wisconsin.

   ii. Another data analyst, over lunch, suggests that it might be easier to run a regression using %REG as the dependent variable and TURNOUT, %HISCH and MINOR as independent variables. Describe whether or not these two procedures would arrive at the same conclusion. In general, do we get the same regression fit if we interchange the role of y and an x?

Sections 4.4–4.6

C4_VOTE

4.5 Refer to Exercise 4.4

Suppose that you are convinced that %HISCH is an important explanatory variable when describing the dependent variable TURNOUT. Do the variables %REG and MINOR add significantly to your ability to explain the response TURNOUT? Given that %HISCH is in the model, test whether %REG and MINOR are jointly important explanatory variables for understanding TURNOUT. State your null and alternative hypotheses, decision making criterion, and your decision making rule. Use a 5% level of significance.

C4_RENT

4.6 Using 36 observations, we fit the regression model $\widehat{RENT\_SFT} = 1.14 - 0.112$ MILES $- 0.000281$ FOOTAGE, where the t-ratio associated with the FOOTAGE variable was $t(b_2) = 3.63$. Calculate the partial correlation coefficient between RENT_SFT and FOOTAGE.

C3_MLS

4.7 Refer to Exercise 3.24
The analysis done in Exercise 3.24 suggests that the exposed number of square feet is an important determinant of Price. This is intuitively appealing in that the larger a house is, the higher is the selling price that it commands. However, a cagey veteran suggests to the young rookie agent that it is not the exposed number of square feet, but rather the total number of square feet that is important. Recall that the difference between the total and exposed square feet is the unexposed square feet. To investigate this issue, correlation and regression analyses using (i) TOTSQFT and (ii) TOTSQFT and EXSQFT are presented in Tables E4.7a through E4.7d.

   a. Do you think that TOTSQFT is an important determinant of the selling price of a house?

      i. Use Figure E4.7 to justify your response.

      ii. Use the regression with only TOTSQFT as the independent variable and a formal test of hypotheses to justify your response. State your null hypothesis, alternative hypothesis, and all components of the decision making rule.

TABLE E4.7a Coefficient Estimates

Explanatory variables	Coefficient	Standard error	t-ratio
Constant	10.988	8.667	1.27
TOTSQFT	0.055505	0.005476	10.14

TABLE E4.7b ANOVA Table

Source	Sum of Squares	df	Mean Square
Regression	60,175	1	60,175
Error	46,264	79	586
Total	106,439	80	

The regression fit also yields $s = 24.20$, $R^2 = 56.5\%$ and $R_a^2 = 56.0\%$.

   b. Both EXSQFT and TOTSQFT seem to be related to PRICE, as illustrated by the following correlation matrix. To decide which variable to use, you decide to run a regression using both explanatory variables. (See Tables E4.7c and E4.7d.)

      i. To investigate the usefulness of TOTSQFT, you decide to use a formal test of hypotheses. When conducting this test, state your null hypothesis, alternative hypothesis, and all components of the decision making rule.

      ii. Explain why it appears that your results in part (i) are a contradiction (an "anomaly") to the results in the following correlation matrix.

   c. To explain the anomaly in part (b):

      i. Calculate the partial correlation coefficient between PRICE and TOTSQFT, given EXSQFT.

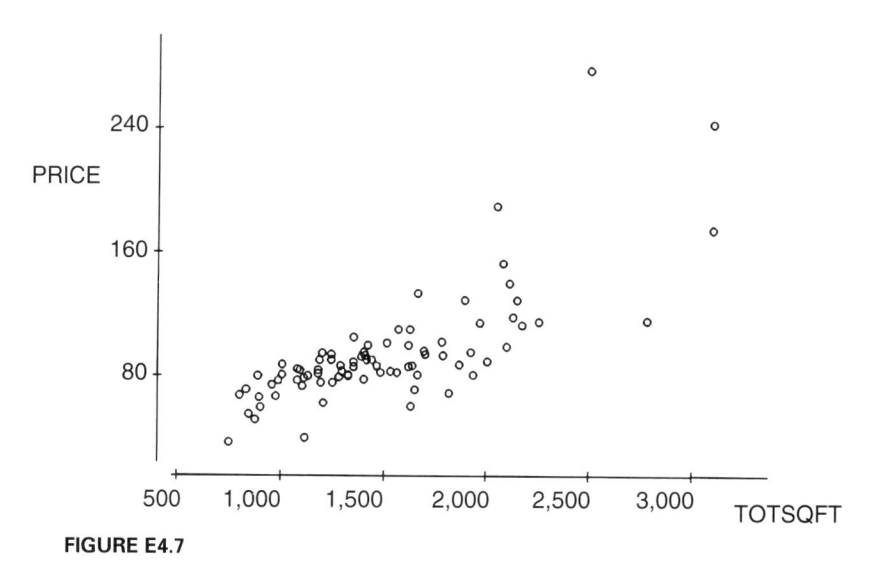

FIGURE E4.7

   ii. Interpret your result.
  d. Suppose that instead of using TOTSQFT as the second explanatory variable, you decide to use UNEXSQFT. Calculate the fitted regression equation.

Correlation Matrix Between PRICE, EXSQFT and TOTSQFT

	PRICE	EXSQFT
EXSQFT	0.795	
TOTSQFT	0.752	0.918

TABLE E4.7c Coefficient Estimates

Explanatory variables	Coefficient	Standard error	t-ratio
Constant	2.243	8.298	0.27
EXSQFT	0.05492	0.01416	3.88
TOTSQFT	0.01006	0.01276	0.79

TABLE E4.7d ANOVA Table

Source	Sum of Squares	df	Mean Square
Regression	67,676	2	33,828
Error	38,783	78	497
Total	106,439	80	

C4_TAX

The regression fit also yields $s = 22.30$, $R^2 = 63.6\%$ and $R_a^2 = 62.6\%$.

4.8 Refer to Exercise 2.22

The data used in this analysis were randomly selected individual tax returns for 1990 prepared by a local branch of a national tax preparation service. Total income for the 65 returns selected ranged from a low of \$368 to \$65,627. The data collected from each return includes total income (TOTALINC), earned income (EARNDINC), other in-

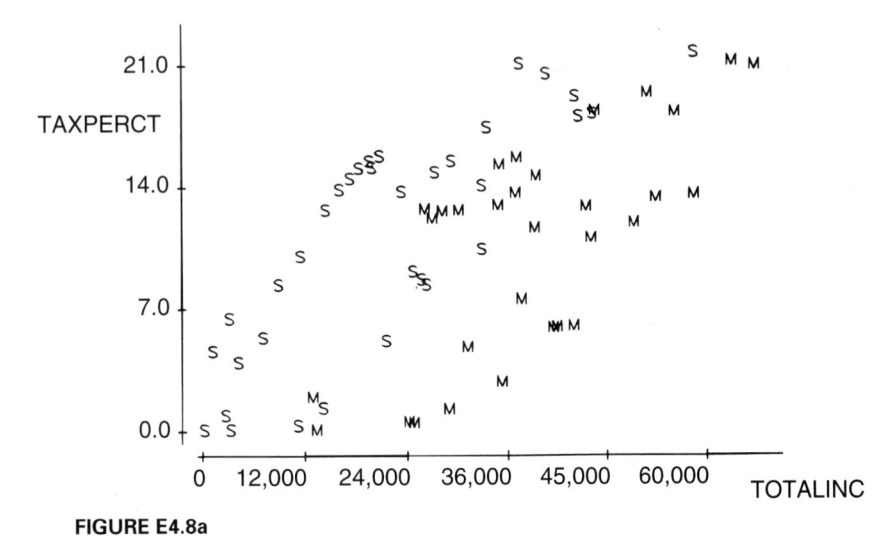

FIGURE E4.8a

come (OTHERINC), federal itemized or standard deductions (DEDUCTS), marital status (MARRIED, $= 1$ if married, $= 0$ otherwise) and total tax paid as a percent of total income (TAXPERCT). By definition, total income is the sum of earned plus other income (TOTALINC = EARNDINC + OTHERINC).

a. In Figure E4.8a, a scatter plot of TOTALINC versus TAXPERCT is shown. Here, different plotting symbols have been used to identify marital status (M means MARRIED $= 1$ and S means MARRIED $= 0$, or single). Sketch two parallel lines on the plot, one for married and one for single. These lines suggest a regression model that has TAXPERCT as the dependent variable and 2 independent variables.

b. Based on several plots similar to those in part (a) and corresponding summary statistics, you decide to estimate a 4 variable regression model for TAXPERCT. The resulting fit is summarized in Tables E4.8a and E4.8b. Use this information to test the adequacy of the model. State your null hypothesis, alternative hypothesis, and all components of the decision making rule. Use a 5% level of significance. The regression fit also yields $s = 2.901$, $R^2 = 80.6\%$ and $R_a^2 = 79.3\%$.

c. Suppose that, for presentation purposes, you decide to use the fitted model but replace the variable TOTALINC with the variable OTHERINC. Without refitting the

TABLE E4.8a   Coefficient Estimates

Explanatory variables	Coefficient	Standard error	t-ratio
Constant	4.7372	0.8495	5.58
TOTALINC	0.00032617	0.00003049	10.70
EARNDINC	0.00017410	0.00002402	7.25
DEDUCTS	−0.0006867	0.0001443	−4.76
MARRIED	−6.0425	0.8632	−7.00

TABLE E4.8b   ANOVA Table

Source	Sum of Squares	df	Mean Square
Regression	2101.54	4	525.38
Error	504.88	60	8.41
Total	2606.42	64	

model, write down the fitted model in part (b) and the new fitted model with this replacement.

d. To illustrate the importance of DEDUCTS, and investigate potential nonlinearities, you decide to make an added variable plot. You do this by first fitting a regression equation of TAXPERCT on TOTALINC, EARNDINC and MARRIED. The resulting fitted equation is

$$\widehat{\text{TAXPERCT}} = 2.98 + 0.000276 \text{ TOTALINC} + 0.000157 \text{ EARNDINC}$$

$$- 6.79 \text{ MARRIED}.$$

The residuals from this fitted equation are denoted by RESIDY2. You then fit a regression equation of DEDUCTS on TOTALINC, EARNDINC and MARRIED. The resulting fitted equation is:

$$\widehat{\text{DEDUCTS}} = 2613 + 0.0727 \text{ TOTALINC} + 0.0255 \text{ EARNDINC} + 1094 \text{ MARRIED}.$$

The residuals from this fitted equation are denoted by RESID12. The added variable plot, that is, the scatter plot of RESIDY2 versus RESID12, is in Figure E4.8b.

i. Provide an interpretation of this added variable plot.

ii. Use the regression output from the main model to calculate the correlation coefficient between RESIDY2 and RESID12.

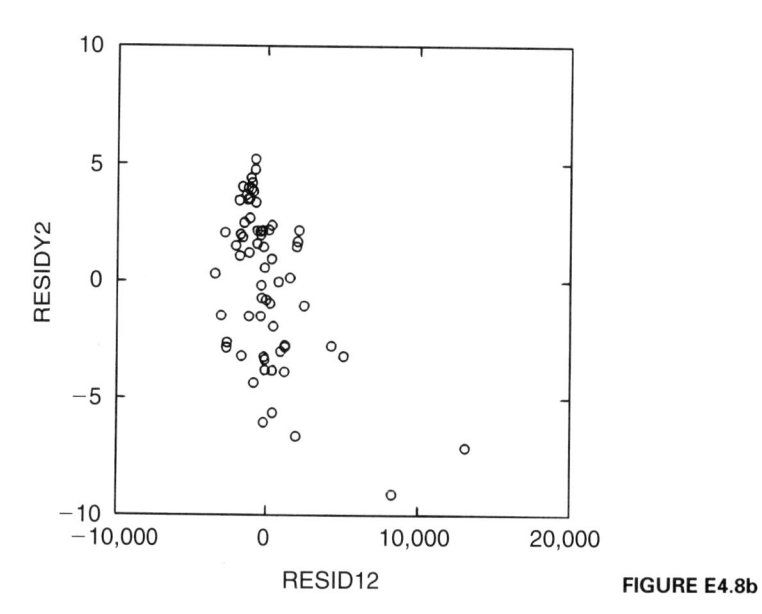

FIGURE E4.8b

C3_CARPR

Section 4.7

4.9 You have information on 62 purchasers of Ford automobiles. In particular, you have the amount paid for the car (y) in hundreds of dollars, the annual income of the individuals (x_1) in hundreds of dollars, the sex of the purchaser $(x_2, 1 = \text{male and } 0 = \text{fe-}$

male), and whether or not the purchaser graduated from college (x_3, 1 = yes and 0 = no). After examining the data and other information available, you decide to use the following regression model:

$$y = \beta_0 + \beta_1 x_1 + \beta_2 x_2 + \beta_3 x_3 + e.$$

The data are listed in matrix form in the following. Also additional summary measures are available and are listed.

$$y = \begin{bmatrix} 136 \\ 105 \\ 140 \\ 180 \\ \cdot \\ \cdot \\ \cdot \\ 145 \\ 98 \end{bmatrix} \quad X = \begin{bmatrix} 1 & 400 & 1 & 0 \\ 1 & 165 & 0 & 1 \\ 1 & 180 & 1 & 1 \\ 1 & 420 & 1 & 1 \\ \cdot & \cdot & \cdot \\ \cdot & \cdot & \cdot \\ \cdot & \cdot & \cdot \\ 1 & 460 & 0 & 1 \\ 1 & 440 & 1 & 0 \end{bmatrix}$$

$$(X'X)^{-1} = \begin{bmatrix} 0.109564 & -0.000115 & -0.035300 & -0.026804 \\ -0.000115 & 0.000001 & -0.000115 & -0.000091 \\ -0.035300 & -0.000115 & 0.102446 & 0.023971 \\ -0.026804 & -0.000091 & 0.023971 & 0.083184 \end{bmatrix}$$

$$X'y = \begin{bmatrix} 1 & 1 & 1 & \cdots & 1 \\ 400 & 165 & 180 & \cdots & 440 \\ 1 & 0 & 1 & \cdots & 1 \\ 0 & 1 & 1 & \cdots & 0 \end{bmatrix} \begin{bmatrix} 136 \\ 105 \\ 140 \\ \cdot \\ \cdot \\ \cdot \\ 98 \end{bmatrix} = \begin{bmatrix} 9,558 \\ 4,880,937 \\ 7,396 \\ 6,552 \end{bmatrix}$$

a. Identify the price paid for the car, income, sex and educational status for the third individual in the sample.

b. It turns out the mean square error for the model is $s^2 = 30106$. Compute the standard error for b_2, the coefficient associated with the sex variable.

c. If you have studied matrix algebra, then do the following:
   i. Compute the least squares estimates of beta coefficients for the above model.
   ii. Suppose that a female purchaser newly arrives on the scene. Her annual income is $80,000, although she has not completed college. Provide a prediction for the amount spent to purchase a car.

End-of-Chapter Exercises

4.10 Does advertising have an important effect on the choice of vacation destination? To address this issue, Johnson and Messmer (1991) examined the effects of advertising on visitations to Colonial Williamsburg in Virginia, a restored historical site. To examine these effects, the country was partitioned into 55 geographic markets of interest to the Colonial Williamsburg Foundation (which owns and operates the restoration). For each market, the following measures were available:

A: Advertising ependitures per 1,000 households, in thousands of dollars
E: Per capita income, in thousands of dollars
D: Driving distance from Williamsburg, Virginia, in thousands of miles
W: An indicator variable for markets more than 900 miles from Williamsburg,
       Virginia
I: Telephone inquiries per 1,000 households

It is known that there is a strong relationship between telephone inquiries and actual visits, so we use I for our response variable. It is also known that, from past data, that visitors to Williamsburg typically have above average incomes. Thus, E was investigated as a possible important effect. The Mississippi River is approximately 900 miles from Williamsburg, suggesting that W may be an important explanatory variable. The following regression model was fit to the data.

$$\hat{I} = 0.0168 - 0.498A + 0.00326E + 0.0543AE - 0.108D(1 - W)$$

$$+ 0.0585D^2(1 - W) - 0.0524W$$

$R^2 = 0.88, n = 55$.

a. Determine the F-ratio for testing the model adequacy from the above information.
b. Use the above information and the results in part (a) to test the adequacy of the model. Be sure to state your null hypothesis, alternative hypothesis, and decision-making rule. Use a 5% level of significance.
c. The standard error associated with the coefficient of A is 0.12456. Use this information to calculate the t-ratio for this variable. Is A important?
d. The preceding fitted regression equation can be simplified if it is known that the metropolitan area is more than 900 miles from Williamsburg. Write down the fitted regression equation in this case.
e. Suppose that $D = 0.300$ thousandths of miles. Write down the fitted regression equation.
f. For your fitted regression in part (e), calculate the fitted inquiries for advertising expenditures = 0, 50, 100, 150, and 200. Plot these fitted values versus advertising expenditures and connect the plotted points with a line. Use $E = 13.751$ ($000), the per capita income that was two standard deviations above the mean.
g. Repeat part (f) using $E = 8.716$ ($000), the per capita income that was two standard deviations below the mean. Use the same plot as in part (f).
h. The coefficient associated with A is negative. Interpret this result. Be sure to include a discussion of your work in parts (f) and (g).

4.11 Does the perceived ethical behavior of a salesperson enhance the trust and satisfaction that a salesperson can establish with a client? Lagace, Dahlstrom and Gassengeimer (1991) studied this and related issues by conducting a survey of 90 physicians regarding their relationships with pharmaceutical salespersons. There are over 25,000 pharmaceutical salespeople, known as detailers, in the United States. Using previous literature as a guide, Lagace, Dahlstrom and Gassengeimer asked a number of questions from which they were able to construct measures of trust of a salesperson (TRUST), satisfaction with the exchange (SATISFACTION), perceived ethical behavior of the salesperson (ETHICAL) and the perceived expertise of the salesperson (EXPERTISE). Expertise is important since these salespeople carry information about drugs to physicians and often provide key information when a busy physician decides whether or not to adopt a drug. Also available is the duration of the relationship between the salesperson and physician (DURATION), the number of meetings between these parties (FREQUENCY), and information about the physician in terms of years of practice. Other physician information, such as specialty and number of prescriptions per week, turned out to be not important and is not discussed further here. Some of the analysis done by Lagace, Dahlstrom and Gassengeimer is summarized in the two regression analyses in Tables E4.11a and E4.11b.

TABLE E4.11a Correlation Matrix

	EXPERTISE	DURATION	FREQUENCY	ETHICAL	SATISFACTION
DURATION	0.13				
FREQUENCY	0.05	0.04			
ETHICAL	0.41	0.05	0.16		
SATISFACTION	0.55	0.04	0.16	0.43	
TRUST	0.65	0.15	−0.20	0.43	0.52

Source: Lagace, R. R., Dahlstrom, R. and Gassengeimer, J. B. (1991). The relevance of ethical salesperson behavior on relationship quality: The pharmaceutical industry. *Journal of Personal Selling & Sales Management*, 11, (4), 39-47.

TABLE E4.11b Two Regression Analyses—with Estimated Beta Coefficients

	Dependent variables	
Independent variables	TRUST	SATISFACTION
ETHICAL	0.209**	0.212***
EXPERTISE	0.554***	0.450***
FREQUENCY	−0.270***	0.098
DURATION	−0.064	−0.031
Years in practice	0.128	0.093
Adjusted R^2	50.2%	32.2%
F-statistic	18.73***	9.36***

** p-value; < 0.05; *** p-value < 0.01

a. Suppose that your boss is more comfortable with the coefficient of determination, R^2, than the adjusted version. Calculate R^2 for each regression.

b. Consider the regression using TRUST as the dependent variable. According to Lagace, Dahlstrom and Gassengeimer, the F-statistic is statistically significant at the 1% significance level. Does this mean it is significant at the 5% significance level? Perform a test of model adequacy using the 5% significance level. Be sure to write down your null and alternative hypotheses and your decision-making procedure.

C4_MURD

4.12 Suppose that we are interested in the relationship between violent crimes and various demographic and socioeconomic factors. As a measure of violent crimes, we use the number of murders per 100,000 persons (MURDER_HT) in a given state. Also at the state level, we have data concerning the percentage of people in poverty (POVERTY), percentage of people living in urban areas (PCNT_URB), size of the population in millions (POPLN), number of people per square mile (POP_MILE), percentage of people completing a 4-year high school (HIGHSCL) and the state's per capita income (PCNT_PCI), as a percentage of the United States' per capita income. In the analysis below, it turns out that Nevada has an unusually high murder rate, presumably because of the presence of organized crime in Las Vegas.

The data summarized in Tables E4.12a and E4.12b are for each of the 50 states. The figures are 1980 data, and were collected from a variety of publications. These publications include the *Statistical Abstract of the U.S.*, U.S. Department of Justice (1980) *Crime in the United States,* U.S. Department of Justice (1985) *The Nature and Patterns of American Homicide,* and U.S. Bureau of the Census (1986) *State and Metropolitan Area Data Book.*

TABLE E4.12a   Summary Statistics of Crime and Socioeconomic Variables

	Number	Mean	Median	Standard deviation	Minimum	Maximum
MURDR_HT	50	8.183	8.356	4.509	0.727	19.992
POVERTY	50	12.298	11.200	3.494	7.000	23.900
PCNT_URB	50	66.94	67.10	14.40	33.80	91.30
POPLN	50	4.494	3.033	4.690	0.400	23.533
POP_MILE	50	154.4	78.7	221.4	0.7	986.2
HIGHSCL	50	67.47	67.95	7.57	53.10	82.50
PCNT_PCI	50	96.28	97.05	13.58	69.70	137.00

TABLE E4.12b   Correlation Matrix of Crime and Socioeconomic Variables

	POVERTY	PCNT_URB	POPLN	POP_MILE	HIGHSCL	PCNT_PCI	NEVADA
PCNT_URB	−0.365						
POPLN	0.004	0.456					
POP_MILE	−0.249	0.479	0.218				
HIGHSCL	−0.732	0.358	−0.133	−0.102			
PCNT_PCI	−0.686	0.618	0.263	0.343	0.620		
NEVADA	−0.149	0.184	−0.114	−0.096	0.153	0.190	
MURDR_HT	0.505	0.338	0.430	−0.088	−0.378	0.030	0.378

a. Use the summary statistics and the histograms to describe the shape of each variable's distribution. In particular, state which explanatory variable is the most skewed.

b. As mentioned, in 1980 Nevada had the highest murder rate of the 50 states (the District of Columbia was not included in this study because the portions of the data were unavailable from the sources cited. Identify the location of Nevada on the scatter plots (Figure E4.12). The population in Nevada in 1980 was 800,312. Estimate the number of murders in Nevada in 1980.

c. A regression model was estimated using all seven explanatory variables (the six basic variables plus a variable to indicate the presence or absence of Nevada). Complete the ANOVA table (Table E4.12c).

TABLE E4.12c   ANOVA Table

Source	Sum of Squares	df	Mean Square	F-ratio
Regression	888.51			
Error				
Total	996.02			

d. Use the results of part (c) to calculate R^2, R_a^2 and s. In terms of the coefficient of determination, does this seem like a reasonable model to you?

e. For the same regression fit as described in part (c), perform an F-test to check the adequacy of the model. Provide a formal statement of the null and alternative hypotheses, your test statistic and your decision criteria. Use a 5% level of significance.

f. For the same regression fit as described in part (c), the estimated regression equations is:

$$\widehat{MURDR\_HT} = -8.33 + 0.810 \text{ POVERTY} + 0.156 \text{ PCNT\_URB} + 0.134 \text{ POPLN}$$

$$- 0.00756 \text{ POP\_MILE} - 0.270 \text{ HIGHSCL} + 0.153 \text{ PCNT\_PCI} + 10.9 \text{ NEVADA}.$$

Interpret the signs of the coefficient of each variable. Do they seem reasonable?

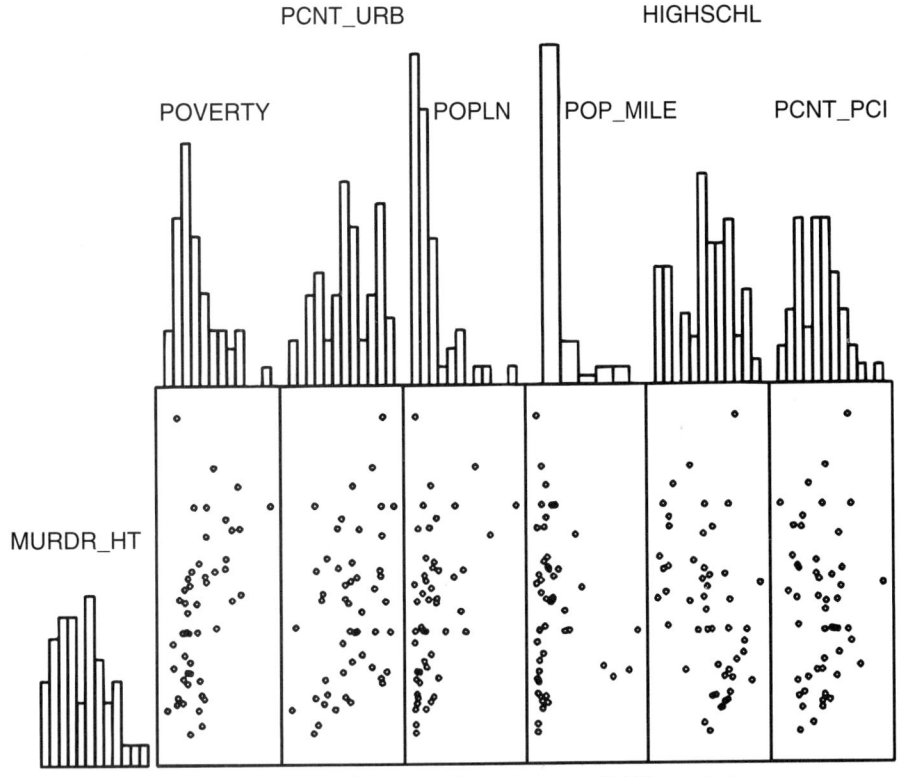

FIGURE E4.12 Scatter plot of number of murders per 100,000 population versus various explanatory variables.

g. For the same regression fit as described in part (c), the following are the standard errors of the coefficients. Based on this model, suppose that you wanted to make a statement about the importance of education. Perform a formal test of the hypothesis to check whether the high school variable is important. Provide a formal statement of the null and alternative hypotheses, your test statistic and your decision criteria. Use a 10% level of significance.

Predictor	Coefficient	Standard error	Predictor	Coefficient	Standard error
Constant	−8.325	4.895	POP_MILE	−0.007555	0.001546
POVERTY	0.8099	0.1178	HIGHSCL	−0.26987	0.06189
PCNT_URB	0.15551	0.02653	PCNT_PCI	0.15260	0.02960
POPLN	0.13412	0.06446	NEVADA	10.903	1.787

h. Suppose that you wanted to make a case that Wisconsin is a nice place to live despite the fact that, in 1980, there were 2.9054 murders per hundred thousand people living in Wisconsin. Here is the information that you have about Wisconsin for 1980: PROVERTY = 8.7, PCNT_URB = 64.2, POPLN = 4.6089, POP_MILE = 86.5, HIGHSCL = 69.6, PCNT_PCI = 98.6. Calculate the "predicted" murder rate under the estimated model and compare that to the actual result. Interpret the deviation.

C4_AIR

4.13 Air traffic congestion is a serious concern of U.S. airline passengers. In addition to sheer inconvenience of congested air routes, consumers, air traffic controllers and governmental regulation agencies such as the Federal Aviation Agency are concerned with safety issues associated with air traffic congestion. Further, these and other parties are concerned with environmental aspects of over-crowded air highways.

To begin an exploration of the air traffic congestion issue, data were collected from the *1988 U.S. Statistical Abstract* on a state by state basis. In particular, we analyze two explanatory variables of air traffic congestion, INC_PC, the state income per capita, and AUTO_PC, the number of automobiles per capita. The measure of air traffic is LNPGR_PC, the number of passengers carried by scheduled air carriers, in natural logarithm units. This measure is our dependent variable.

The following questions are about a regression model of LNPGR_PC on INC_PC and AUTO_PC that was fit; the computer output follows.

a. Use this fitted regression model to decide whether or not the number of autos per capita signficantly affects LNPGR_PC. State your null hypothesis, alternative hypothesis, and all components of the decision-making rule. Use a 5% level of significance.

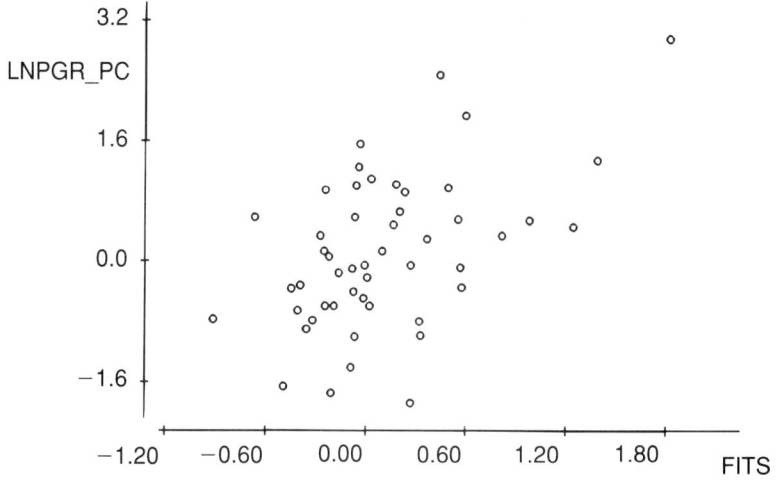

FIGURE E4.13 Scatter plot of responses versus fitted values. *Source: 1988 U.S. Statistical Abstract*

    b. Calculate the correlation between LNPGR_PC and AUTO_PC, after controlling for effects of INC_PC, that is, the partial correlation coefficient. Compare this result to the ordinary correlation between LNPGR_PC and AUTO_PC.

    c. **i.** Use the ANOVA table to calculate s, R^2 and R_a^2.

        ii. Figure E4.13 shows a scatter plot of LNPGR_PC versus its fitted values. Calculate the corresponding correlation coefficient.

```
            MINITAB computer output for airline travel question

                                                    CORRELATION MATRIX

           LNPGR_PC  INC_PC
INC_PC      0.414
AUTO_PC    -0.188    0.238

                                               FITTED REGRESSION MODEL

The regression equation is
LNPGR_PC = -0.36 + 0.000155 INC_PC - 3.75 AUTO_PC


50 cases used 1 cases contain missing values


Predictor        Coef         Stdev       t-ratio
Constant        -0.365        1.014        -0.36
INC_PC       0.00015541    0.00004147       3.75
AUTO_PC         -3.754        1.609        -2.33


Analysis of Variance
SOURCE          DF          SS            MS
Regression       2       12.9811        6.4906
Error           47       37.4938        0.7977
Total           49       50.4749


Unusual Observations
Obs.   INC_PC  LNPGR_PC    Fit   Residual   St.Resid
  7    24683    -0.348    0.581   -0.928     -1.18 X
  9    23491     2.949    1.822    1.127      1.47 X
 12    18472     2.476    0.441    2.034      2.31R
 30    20267    -1.882    0.270   -2.151     -2.50R
```

C3_USEDC

4.14 **Refer to Exercise 3.33**

Suppose that you have just taken a position as an assistant marketing manager of a local chain of used automobile dealers. Although there is a substantial amount of knowledge to be acquired through experience on pricing strategies for used cars, you are interested in finding out pricing behavior for similar, yet competing, markets. An important marketplace that competes with your dealerships is represented by private resales that are advertised in your local newspaper. Thus, for our analysis, we have data collected from the Sunday, November 14, 1993 issue of the *Wisconsin State Journal*, a local newspaper. Data for 212 listed automobiles were collected, including the asking price for a car (ASKPRICE). Information was also gathered on the automobile manufacturer, the model type, the model year, the number of options beyond standard equipped power steering and brakes and the odometer mileage reading. This additional information was used with the National Automobile Dealers' Association *Resale Price Guide for the Central Region of the U.S.* to determine LOANVAL, the average amount a bank or finance company will finance, and NEWPRICE, the price of the car when new. You also consider MILEAGE, the odometer mileage reading in thousands of miles.

The objective is to develop a model to understand the determinants of asking prices for used automobiles, ASKPRICE. Supporting computer output follows.

a. A regression of ASKPRICE on LOANVAL, MILEAGE and NEWPRICE was fit. The computer output follows. Figure E4.14a is a plot of ASKPRICE versus the fitted values from the fitted model. To understand the relationship between observed and fitted values:

i. Determine s, the size of the typical error.
ii. Determine the correlation between the observed and fitted values.

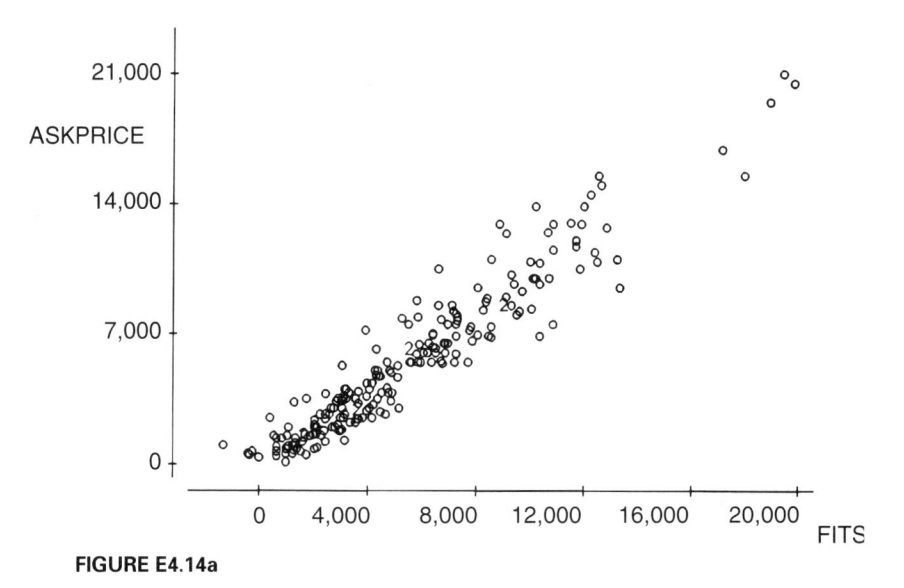

FIGURE E4.14a

b. A regression of ASKPRICE on LOANVAL, MILEAGE and NEWPRICE was fit. The computer output follows. An old classmate of yours has heard about your work. She has tried to sell her 1991 Chevrolet Cavalier, that is loaded with options but has 76,000 miles on it. Because of your car dealership connections, you find that the LOANVAL for her car is $5,175 and the price when new was NEWPRICE = $9,265.

i.   Determine the predicted asking price under the fitted model.
ii. It turns out that she actually asked for ASKPRICE = $5,995. Determine the deviation of the actual asking price from that expected under the fitted model.
iii. Suppose that you find later that the odometer reading was actually 67,000 miles; the six and the seven were transposed. What is the change in the fitted value due to this change? You may assume that LOANVAL remains constant.

c. You have decided to compare your regression of ASKPRICE on LOANVAL, MILEAGE and NEWPRICE to the simpler model, a regression of ASKPRICE on

LOANVAL. Perform a partial *F*-test to decide whether or not to include the variables MILEAGE and NEWPRICE in your regression equation. State your null hypothesis, alternative hypothesis, and all components of the decision making rule. Use a 5% level of significance.

MINITAB computer output for the used automobile question

SUMMARY STATISTICS

	N	MEAN	MEDIAN	STDEV	MIN	MAX
ASKPRICE	212	5598	4836	4154	150	20995
MILEAGE	212	67.37	65.00	35.43	4.00	196.00
NEWPRICE	212	11393	10164	5916	1566	53000
LOANVAL	212	3766	2875	3247	0	16050

CORRELATION STATISTICS

	ASKPRICE	MILEAGE	NEWPRICE
MILEAGE	-0.671		
NEWPRICE	0.654	-0.209	
LOANVAL	0.934	-0.561	0.689

REGRESSION WITH ONE INDEPENDENT VARIABLE

The regression equation is
ASKPRICE = 1099 + 1.19 LOANVAL

Predictor	Coef	Stdev	t-ratio
Constant	1098.6	156.9	7.00
LOANVAL	1.19474	0.03158	37.83

s = 1489   R-sq = 87.2%   R-sq(adj) = 87.1%

Analysis of Variance

SOURCE	DF	SS	MS	F
Regression	1	3174942464	3174942464	1431.23
Error	210	465849472	22188331	
Total	211	3640792064		

REGRESSION WITH THREE INDEPENDENT VARIABLES

The regression equation is
ASKPRICE = 3179 + 0.931 LOANVAL - 28.3 MILEAGE + 0.0719 NEWPRICE

Predictor	Coef	Stdev	t-ratio
Constant	3179.3	305.0	10.43

```
LOANVAL      0.93126    0.04562      20.41
MILEAGE      -28.320    3.101        -9.13
NEWPRICE     0.07193    0.02120      3.39


s = 1263        R-sq = 90.9%    R-sq(adj) = 90.8%


Analysis of Variance
SOURCE        DF           SS            MS         F
Regression     3     3308896768    1102965632    691.23
Error        208      331895200       1595650
Total        211     3640792064
```

d. Attached is an added variable plot (Figure E4.14b) of ASKPRICE versus MILEAGE, controlling for the variables LOANVAL and NEWPRICE.
  i. Describe the purpose of an added variable plot.
  ii. Determine the partial correlation coefficient between ASKPRICE and MILEAGE, controlling for the variables LOANVAL and NEWPRICE.
  iii. From the computer output, write down the usual correlation between ASKPRICE and MILEAGE. Interpret the difference between this correlation and the correlation that you calculated in part (ii).
e. Figure E4.14c suggests a nonlinear relationship between ASKPRICE and MILEAGE. Thus, a regression of ASKPRICE on LOANVAL, MILEAGE, NEW-PRICE and MILEAGE squared (C25) was fit. The computer output follows. Suppose that you need to decide whether or not the MILEAGE squared vari-

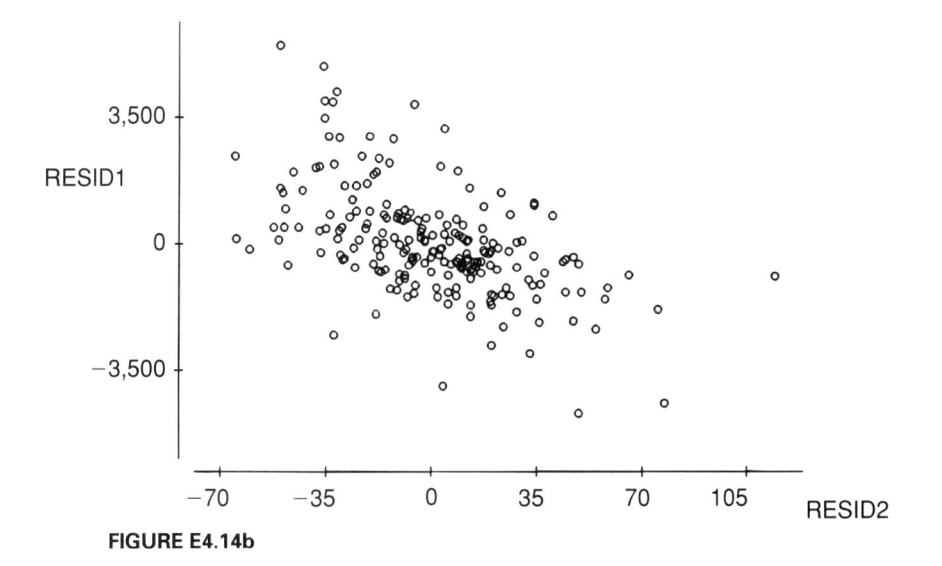

FIGURE E4.14b

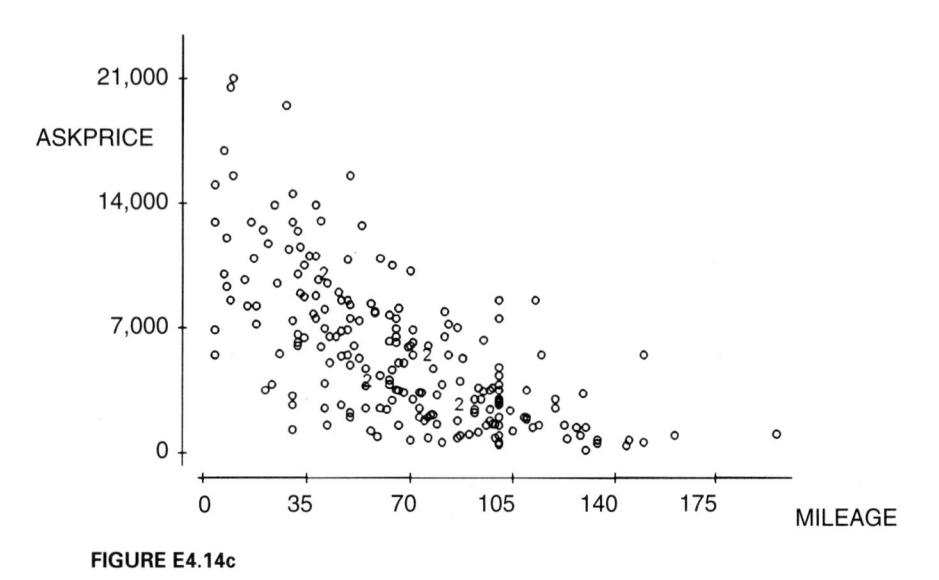

FIGURE E4.14c

able belongs in the regression equation. Because this is an important decision, you decide to use a formal hypothesis decision-making procedure. State your null hypothesis, alternative hypothesis, and all components of the decision-making rule. Use a 5% level of significance.

```
                MINITAB computer output for the used automobile question

                                    REGRESSION WITH FOUR INDEPENDENT VARIABLES
The regression equation is
ASKPRICE = 3894 - 50.3 MILEAGE + 0.0826 NEWPRICE + 0.893 LOANVAL + 0.137 C25

Predictor        Coef        Stdev     t-ratio
Constant        3893.8       409.0        9.52
MILEAGE         -50.320      9.062       -5.55
NEWPRICE        0.08258      0.02133      3.87
LOANVAL         0.89269      0.04744     18.82
C25             0.13677      0.05303      2.58

s = 1246      R-sq = 91.2%    R-sq(adj) = 91.0%

Analysis of Variance
SOURCE      DF         SS          MS          F
Regression   4   3319229952   829807488   534.17
Error      207    321561824     1553439
Total      211   3640791808
```

C4_HOSP3

4.15 The growth of health care expenditures in the United States has accelerated at an alarming rate in recent years. For example, health care expenditures grew from 5.3% of the gross domestic product in 1969 to 12.2% in 1990. This data set was gathered to understand some of the determinants of health care expenditures at the state level, so that there are 50 observations. As a measure of the hospital utilization level of each state, the 1991 annual revenue of community hospitals on a per capita basis is used as the response variable of interest, labelled HOSPEXPN.

Several potential explanatory variables were gathered from a variety of databases, including the Health Insurance Association of America's *Source Book of Health Insurance Data 1991,* The National Data Bank's *Statistical Abstract of the U.S. (1991),* and the *State and Metropolitan Area Data Book 1991* from the U.S. Bureau of the Census. The potential explanatory variables include the average annual per capita income (AVGINCOM), percent of residents complete at least four years of high school (HIGH-SCHL), the birth rate per 1,000 population (BRTHRATE), population density defined by the number of state residents per square mile (POPSQ), percent of residents age 65 years and over (OVER65YR), number of physicians and dentists per 1,000,000 population (PHYDENT), number of hospital beds per 1,000 population (BEDPOP), percent of residents below the poverty level (PVRTRATE), and a variable to indicate whether 50% of the state population live in a metropolitan area (MTROAREA). (See Table E4.15a)

a. The relationships between HOSPEXPN and BEDPOP and between HOSPEXPN and PHYDENT are presented graphically in Figure E4.15 and numerically in the correlation matrix table (Table E4.15b). Interpret these relationships. In particular, discuss the sign, strength and linearity of the relationships.

b. The variables BEDPOP and PHYDENT turn out to be important determinants of HOSPEXPN and are graphed in Figure E4.15. Another important explanatory vari-

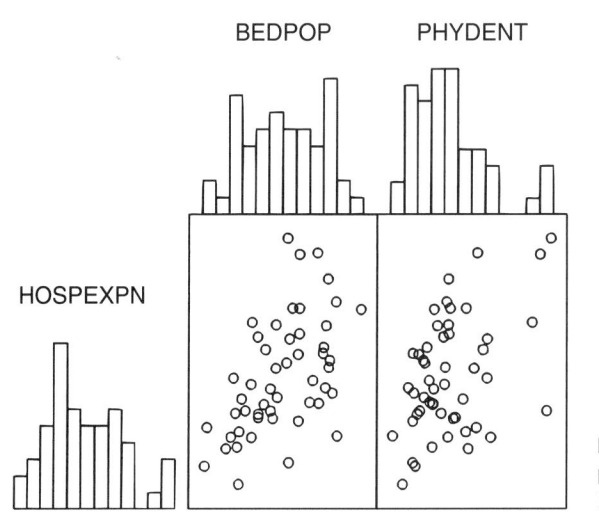

FIGURE E4.15 Histograms and scatter plots of HOSPEXPN, BEDPOP and PHYDENT.

TABLE E4.15a   Summary Statistics of Dependent and Independent Variables

	Mean	Median	Standard deviation	Minimum	Maximum
HOSPEXPN	791.7	769.0	130	548.2	1103.4
AVGINCOM	14202	13939	2447	10102	20687
HIGHSCHL	67.47	67.95	7.57	53.10	82.50
BRTHRATE	15.66	15.20	1.829	12.00	22.000
POPSQ	166.1	77.1	235.2	1.0	1042.0
OVER65YR	12.37	12.60	2.100	4.100	18.000
PHYDENT	246.3	238.2	54.62	160.8	398.20
BEDPOP	3.491	3.492	0.764	1.929	5.089
PVRTRATE	12.49	11.60	3.460	7.900	23.900
MTROAREA	0.700	1.000	0.463	0.000	1.0000

Source: Health Insurance Association of America's Source Book of Health Insurance Data 1991, The National Data Bank's Statistical Abstract of the U.S. (1991), and the State and Metropolitan Area Data Book 1991 from the U.S. Bureau of the Census.

TABLE 4.15b   Correlation Matrix of Dependent and Independent Variables

	HOSPEXPN	AVGINCOM	HIGHSCHL	BRTHRATE	POPSQ	OVER65YR	PHYDENT	BEDPOP	PVRTRATE
AVGINCOM	0.265								
HIGHSCHL	−0.318	0.405							
BRTHRATE	−0.250	0.093	0.355						
POPSQ	0.465	0.631	−0.098	−0.177					
OVER65YR	0.477	−0.151	−0.305	−0.662	0.227				
PHYDENT	0.436	0.702	0.219	−0.059	0.668	0.109			
BEDPOP	0.528	−0.419	−0.524	−0.449	−0.076	0.579	−0.273		
PVRTRATE	−0.044	−0.636	−0.727	0.010	−0.286	0.074	−0.470	0.405	
MTROAREA	0.329	0.413	−0.021	0.145	0.375	−0.022	0.426	−0.259	−0.314

able is MTROAREA. Use the table of summary statistics and the table of correlations to provide a rough scatter plot of HOSPEXPN versus MTROAREA.

c. Based on a number of steps, a final model was specified. This is a regression model using BEDPOP, PHYDENT and MTROAREA as explanatory variables. The fitted regression model appears in Display 2.

    i. Is MTROAREA a statistically significant variable? To respond to this question, use a formal test of hypothesis. State your null and alternative hypotheses, decision-making criterion, and your decision-making rules.

    ii. Test whether BEDPOP, PHYDENT and MTROAREA are jointly important explanatory variables for understanding HOSPEXPN.

    iii. You are interested in estimating HOSPEXPN when it is known that BEDPOP = 3.491, PHYDENT = 246.29 and MTROAREA = 1. Calculate a fitted value for these variables.

    iv. An enthusiastic statistics student notes, for Question c (iii), that if MTROAREA = 0.70, then each explanatory variable would be equal to its average, and hence, the fitted value is equal to the average. That is, the fitted value of HOSPEXPN turns out to be 791.7 (with rounding). Discuss whether or not this seems reasonable. Use your knowledge of one variable regression to guide your intuition.

    v. What is the adjusted coefficient of determination for this fitted regression?

d. To make sure that you have not eliminated any important variables, you decided to run a regression using all nine independent variables. The fitted regression model appears in Display 3.

    i. Has the coefficient of determination increased from the three variable regression model to the nine variable model? Does this mean that the model is improved or does it provide little information? Explain your response.

    ii. To state formally whether one should use the three or nine variable model, use a partial *F*-test. State your null and alternative hypotheses, decision-making criterion, and your decision-making rules.

    iii. Similarly, decide whether one should use the one or three variable model using a partial *F*-test. State your null and alternative hypotheses, decision-making criterion, and your decision-making rules. The one variable fitted model appears in Display 1.

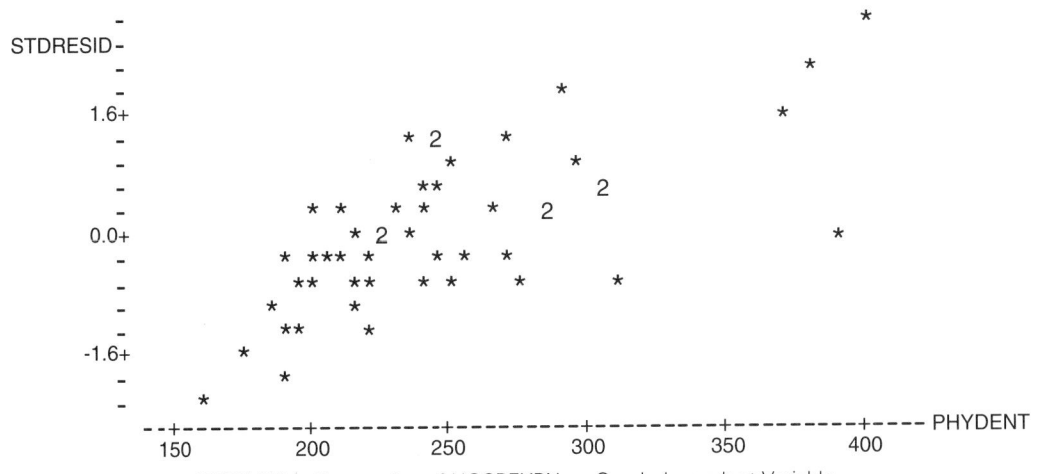

The regression equation is HOSPEXPN = 478 + 89.9 BEDPOP

Table. Correlations between STDRESID and the Dependent and Independent Variables

HOSPEXPN	AVGINCOM	HIGHSCHL	BRTHRATE	POPSQ	OVER6 5YR	PHYDENT	BEDPOP	PVRTRATE	MTROAREA
0.849	0.571	-0.049	-0.016	0.593	0.203	0.682	0.000	-0.306	0.550

Figure. Scatter plot of STDRESID versus PHYDENT

DISPLAY 1. Regression of HOSPEXPN on One Independent Variable.

Coefficient Estimates

Explanatory variables	Coefficient	Standard error	t-ratio
Constant	−9.75	77.72	−0.13
PHYDENT	1.2111	0.2102	5.76
BEDPOP	126.95	14.08	9.01
MTROAREA	85.75	24.71	3.47

ANOVA Table

Source	Sum of Squares	df	Mean Square
Regression	592,624	3	197,547
Error	234,919	46	5,107
Total	827,561	49	

The regression fit also yields $s = 71.46$ and $R^2 = 71.6\%$.

DISPLAY 2. Regression of HOSPEXPN on Three Independent Variables.

Coefficient Estimates

Explanatory variables	Coefficient	Standard error	t-ratio
Constant	−25.7	291.7	−0.09
AVGINCOM	0.013746	0.007733	1.78
HIGHSCHL	−5.688	3.107	−1.83
BRTHRATE	19.286	9.005	2.14
POPSQ	−0.02153	0.07252	−0.30
OVER65YR	10.463	7.785	1.34
PHYDENT	0.9089	0.2927	3.11
BEDPOP	121.11	19.54	6.20
PVRTRATE	−7.851	6.464	−1.21
MTROAREA	42.18	29.79	1.42

ANOVA Table

Source	Sum of Squares	df	Mean Square
Regression	636,976	9	70,775
Error	190,584	40	4,765
Total	827,561	49	

The regression fit also yields $s = 69.03$, $R^2 = 77.0\%$ and $R_a^2 = 71.8\%$.

DISPLAY 3. Regression of HOSPEXPN on Nine Independent Variables.

C4_DIVOR

4.16 This exercise requires the use of a computer

In the file 'C4_DIVOR' are data describing the divorce rate in each state. In addition, there are other socioeconomic state variables that may be related to the divorce rate. In particular, data concerning the number of marriages and births, unemployment and crime rates, and AFDC (Aid to Families with Dependent Children) payments are available. In this file, data are available for the years 1965, 1975 and 1985. In this exercise, we consider only the data for year 1985. The information provided by this study is potentially useful for governing agencies in budgeting for social needs such as judicial and welfare services which are affected by divorce.

The data for the study were collected from various *U.S. Statistical Abstracts*. Divorce rate is defined as the number of divorces and annulments per 1,000 population per state. The independent variables include the number of marriages and live births per 1,000 population, the total unemployment rate as percent of total work force, the average monthly AFDC payments per family, and the total number of criminal offenses known to the police (murder, rape, robbery, aggravated assault, burglary, larceny and motor vehicle theft). Some of the data points contain missing observations due to unavailability, and Nevada was eliminated due to its uniquely high and unrepresentative marriage and divorce rates.

a. Provide dotplot and summary statistics of the dependent variable 'DIVRCE85'. Check to see whether there are any unusually large observations. Identify the row number of these observations. To see the effect of these observations, delete them and re-do the dotplot and summary statistics. Comment on the decrease in the standard deviation.

b. Working with the full data set, suppose that you wish to understand the relationship between the dependent variables and the explanatory variables 'BIRTH85', 'MARRG85', 'UNEMP85', 'CRIME85' and 'AFDC85'. Provide scatter plots of the dependent variable versus each of the independent variables. Examine the scatter plot of 'DIVRCE85' versus 'MARRG85'. Identify the row number of one observation that seems to be unusual with respect to the others.

c. Summarize these scatter plots with a correlation matrix. Interpret the correlations between the dependent variable and the independent variables with particular attention to the sign of the coefficient. To see the effect of outliers, delete the aberrant observation noted in part (b) and re-calculate the correlations.

d. With the full data set, run a regression using all five of the independent variables.
   i. Describe the coefficient of determination and discuss the percentage change in the estimate of the variability in the data.
   ii. Perform an F-test to determine the significance of the regression.
   iii. Interpret each coefficient in the fitted regression model.
   iv. Suppose that you are considering deleting one of the variables from the model. Which variable would you eliminate? Give your justification.

e. Suppose that you are interested in predicting the divorce rate for one of the states where the divorce information was not available. You do, however, have the following information concerning the explanatory variables: 'BIRTH85' = 18.2, 'MARRG85' = 8.8, 'UNEMP85' = 11.5, 'CRIME85' = 55.64 and 'AFDC85' = 168. Give a point estimate for this state.

f. Re-run the regression analysis that you did in part (d) after deleting the unusual observation noted in part (b).
   i. Discuss the percentage change in the variability of the data.
   ii. Would you eliminate any variables from the model? Give your justification.
   iii. Provide a point estimate for the state discussed in part (e).

5

Regression Using Categorical Independent Variables

Chapter Objectives

To introduce three types of regression models for including categorical independent variables: regression using indicator variables, the classical analysis of variance models and the general linear model. To illustrate, we will consider:

- explaining the price of a car in terms of its horsepower and the categorical variable, the type of car,
- explaining hospital costs in terms of utilization and the categorical variable, admission type, and
- explaining a machine's performance in terms of the categorical variables the machine type and machine operator type.

Chapter Outline

5.1 INTRODUCTION

Categorical variables provide a numerical label for observations that fall in distinct groups, or categories.

Categorical variables provide a numerical label for observations that fall in distinct groups, or categories. In Section 4.5, we considered *indicator* variables; these indicate the presence, or absence, of an attribute. As an example, to label a voter's political party affiliation, we might construct a variable to be one if the voter is Democrat, and zero otherwise. Categorical variables provide an extension of the idea of indicator variables. For example, we could get more information about a voter's political party affiliation by investigating the categorical variable constructed so that the variable is one if a voter is Democrat, two if Republican, three if Libertarian, four if Socialist, five if a member of Ross Perot's United We Stand party, and six otherwise.

For categorical variables, there may or may not be an ordering of the groups. As an example of a categorization that displays ordering, we might consider the age of an apartment building as new, intermediate or old. Any continuous variable, such as age, can be grouped into distinct categories and be treated as a categorical variable. As an example of a categorization that does not display ordering, in the section, we will discuss the type of the car. Another interesting example is the political party affiliation example previously cited. For some studies, one might argue that there is an ordering of political philosophies, for example, from strongly conservative to strongly liberal. For other studies, it may be difficult to make this argument. In our treatment, we do not make use of the ordering of categories within a factor. *Factor* is another term used for a categorical, independent variable.

Factor is another term used for a categorical, independent variable.

Historically, factors were used primarily to represent grouped continuous variables. By categorizing a continuous variable, the precision of measuring the variable is less of an issue than if an exact measurement was used. Models using only factors became so widely used in experimental research that a separate literature has been developed called the study of *ANOVA models* (for analysis of variance). Leading researchers in statistics, such as R. A. Fisher, realized that ANOVA models could be written as a special case of regression models. However, because of the lack of readily available computing prior to 1960, regression analysis was not a widely used tool and this connection was not appreciated by many researchers.

An important theme of this chapter is that traditional ANOVA models can be expressed using the regression model.

An important theme of this chapter is that traditional ANOVA models can be expressed using the regression model. A consequence of this theme is that the inferences, introduced in Chapter 4 and further described in Chapter 7, are also available in the ANOVA model set-up. Still, it is useful to present ANOVA models separately for at least two reasons. First, in the ANOVA context, the formulas for parameter estimates and partitioning the variability can be done directly using only averages and sums of squares. In particular, no matrix manipulations are required. Second, even though we are able to write ANOVA models in the regression set-up, the details can be cumbersome. Interpretations of the estimation formulas and the model coefficients are more intuitive in the ANOVA set-up.

5.2 REGRESSION USING INDICATOR VARIABLES

The most direct way of handling categorical variables in regression is through the use of indicator variables. A categorical variable with c levels can be represented using c indicator variables, one for each category. In regression analysis with an intercept term, we use $c - 1$ of these indicator variables. The remaining one enters implicitly through the intercept term. Consider the following example.

Example 5.1: Car Prices

C5_CARPR

Motor Trend's *1993 New Car Buyer's Guide* provides information on 173 new cars, including the price, horsepower and the type of car. Here, we consider LN_PRICE, the natural logarithm of the car price, as the response variable of interest. We use H/P, the car's horsepower, as a continuous explanatory variable. Presumably, consumers are willing to pay more for more powerful cars, and H/P is a standard industry measure of a car's power. We also consider CLASS_CD, the car class, where there are $c = 5$ different types of cars. The variable CLASS_CD is categorical, where 0 means convertible, 1 means coupe, 2 means hatchback, 4 means sedan and 5 means mini-van.

We begin by summarizing each continuous variable in Table 5.1. We know all the possible outcomes of the categorical variable CLASS_CD, so it need not be examined in isolation of the other variables.

TABLE 5.1 Summary Statistics of Each Continuous Variable

	Number	Mean	Median	Standard deviation	Minimum	Maximum
LN_PRICE	173	9.80	9.70	0.60	8.81	11.612
H/P	173	147	134	60	55	400

The next step is to display the distribution of the continuous variables. So that we can use it later in a more complex setting, we now introduce a graphical method for displaying a variable's distribution called the *box plot*. For examining larger data sets, analysts have found this to be a useful graphical form. Figure 5.1 illustrates the box plot for the logarithm of car price. Here the box captures the middle 50% of the data and the so-called "whiskers" capture the middle 80%. By using the box and whiskers to capture the majority of the data, the viewer can get a quick sense of the distribution and important summary statistics without examining individual observations. (For comparison with a normal curve in some statistical packages, you will also see the box and whiskers defined in relation to percentiles from a standard normal curve.)

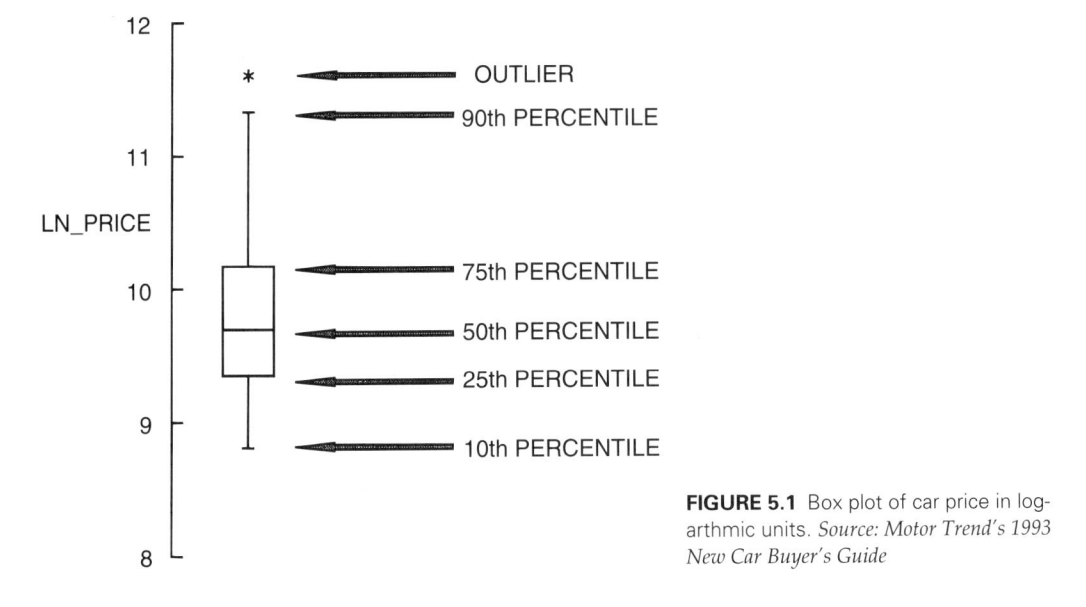

FIGURE 5.1 Box plot of car price in logarithmic units. *Source: Motor Trend's 1993 New Car Buyer's Guide*

To summarize the categorical variable and its relation to the response variable, Table 5.2 provides summary statistics by car type. Here,

TABLE 5.2 Summary Statistics of Logarithmic Price by Car Type

	CLASS_CD	Number	Mean	Standard deviation
Convertible	0	10	10.46	0.77
Coupe	1	46	9.89	0.67
Hatchback	2	19	9.29	0.47
Sedan	4	79	9.83	0.53
Mini-Van	5	19	9.63	0.23
ALL		173	9.80	0.60

we see that most observations are sedans and coupes and that these car types have similar average prices. The mini-vans are priced similarly to the sedans and coupes, yet display relatively little variation in price. The convertibles display the highest average and variability of prices. Many of these observations can also be seen in Figure 5.2 which is a box plot of logarithmic price by car type.

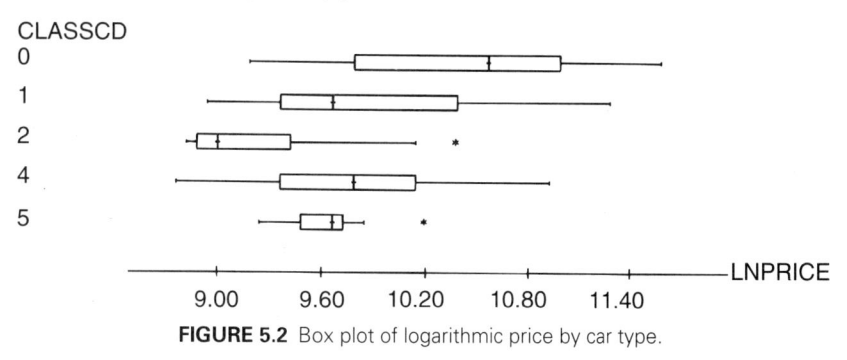

FIGURE 5.2 Box plot of logarithmic price by car type.

Both Table 5.2 and Figure 5.2 show that the type of car seems important for explaining price. Is this also true of horsepower? Figure 5.3 shows the answer to be a resounding "Yes!" by exhibiting a strong relationship between LN_PRICE and H/P. The correlation coefficient turns out to be 87.2%.

Also in Figure 5.3 you will notice that a letter coding was used as plotting symbols. In this way, we are able to look at the three variables si-

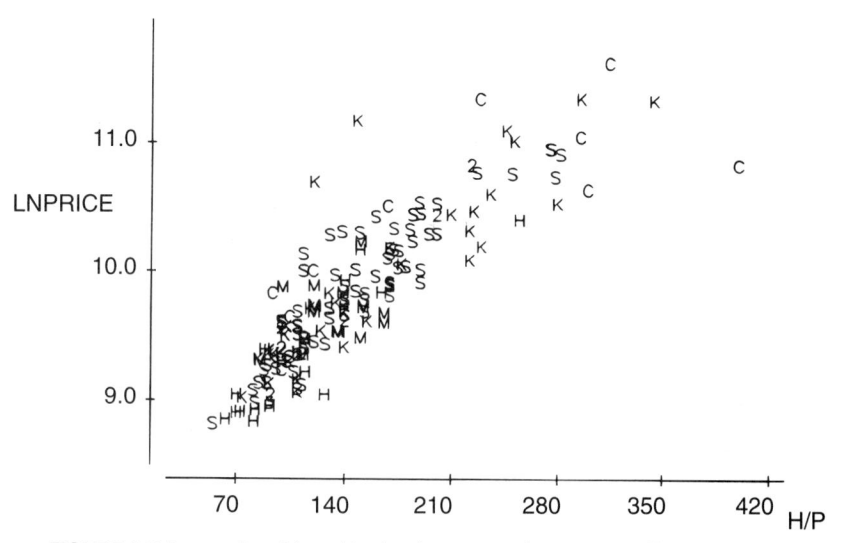

FIGURE 5.3 Letter plot of logarithmic prices versus horsepower. Here, the letter codes are 'C' for convertible, 'K' for coupe, 'H' for hatchback, 'S' for sedan and 'M' for mini-van.

multaneously. Unfortunately, for this application, adding the letter coding produced little additional information. The letter coding does show that the high priced cars are convertibles and coupes. You should be aware of the potential for using more sophisticated graphing techniques such as letter plots and also realize that they do not always succeed.

Are the continuous and categorical variables jointly important determinants of response? To answer this, a regression was run using LN_PRICE as the response, H/P as an explanatory variable and four indicator variables of the car class. Here, we define C to be an indicator variable for convertibles so that C = 1 if the car is a convertible and C = 0 for the other car types. Similarly, define the indicator variables K for coupe, H for hatchback, S for sedan and M for mini-van.

Display 5.3 summarizes the results of a regression run using H/P, C, K, H and S as explanatory variables. From the ANOVA Table, we see that the independent variables explain a good deal of the price variability. For example, the proportion of variability explained is R^2 = 48.0304/62.1070 = 77.3%. Further, the t-ratios for H/P show that it is a significant explanatory variable because $t(b_{H/P})$ = 21.2 is very large.

ANOVA Table

Source	Sum of Squares	df	Mean Square
Regression	48.0304	5	9.6061
Error	14.0765	167	0.0843
Total	62.1070	172	

Coefficient Estimates

Explanatory variable	Coefficient	Standard error	t-ratio
Constant	8.55326	0.08383	102.04
H/P	0.008379	0.0003954	21.2
C	0.124	0.118	1.05
K	0.033	0.080	0.41
H	−0.180	0.094	−1.90
S	0.042	0.745	0.57

DISPLAY 5.3 ANOVA table and coefficient estimates for Example 5.1

From Display 5.3, we see that the fitted regression equation is

$$\hat{y} = 8.55326 + 0.008379 \text{ H/P} + 0.124 \text{ C} + 0.033 \text{ K} - 0.18 \text{ H} + 0.042 \text{ S}.$$

Thus, for example, for a convertible with H/P − 200, we would predict the logarithmic price to be

$$\hat{y} = 8.55326 + 0.008379(200) + 0.124(1) + 0.033(0) - 0.18(0) + 0.042(0)$$

$$= 10.35306,$$

which corresponds to $e^{10.35306}$ = $31,353. If, however, the car were a mini-van with H/P = 200, we would predict the logarithmic price to be

$$\hat{y} = 8.55326 + 0.008379(200) + 0.124(0) + 0.033(0) - 0.18(0) + 0.042(0)$$

$$= 10.22906.$$

The difference between these two estimates is 0.124, the coefficient associated with convertibles. Thus, we may interpret $b_C = 0.124$ to be the estimated expected price difference between a convertible and a mini-van.

Similarly, we may interpret the regression coefficient of each indicator variable to be the estimated expected difference between the variable being indicated and the one being dropped. For a variable with c categories, we only use $c - 1$ indicator variables. The reasons will be discussed in greater detail in Sections 5.2 and 6.3. Because no assumption is made regarding the ordering of the categories, it does not matter which variable is dropped with regard to the fit of the model. However, as we have seen, it does matter for the interpretation of the regression coefficients.

To illustrate, the regression model was re-run with H/P as a continuous explanatory variable and C, K, S and M as indicator explanatory variables. The analysis of variance table is the same as given in Display 5.3. The coefficient estimates are given in Table 5.3. Unlike Display 5.3, we see that almost all of the t-ratios of the indicator variables are now statistically significant, in that they exceed two in absolute value. Does this mean that the car type is now much more important by retaining these four indicator variables?

No, the t-ratios in Table 5.3 are for comparing each of the variables with the omitted hatchback variable. The significant t-ratios mean that each car type is priced significantly higher than the hatchback. This is to be expected from our preliminary examination of the data in Table 5.2, that indicates that hatchbacks were the least expensive type of car. Further, Table 5.2 also shows that mini-vans are close to being in the middle of the price range. Thus, when we examined the summary of the regression fit in Display 5.3, we saw that some car types were more highly priced, some lower, but none were significantly different than the mini-van type.

TABLE 5.3 Coefficient Estimates of a Regression of Car Price on Horsepower, and Indicators of Convertible, Coupe, Sedan and Mini-van

Explanatory variable	Coefficient	Standard error	t-ratio
Constant	8.37338	0.07950	105.3
H/P	0.008379	0.0003954	21.2
C	0.304	0.121	2.53
K	0.219	0.082	2.62
S	0.222	0.076	2.94
M	0.180	0.094	1.90

All indicator variables are significantly different from the hatchbacks, the omitted indicator variable.

5.3 ONE FACTOR ANOVA MODEL

C5_HOSP

To illustrate a one factor ANOVA model, we now study the impact of various explanatory variables on hospital charges in the state of Wisconsin. Identifying explanatory variables of hospital charges can provide direction for hospitals, government, insurers and consumers in controlling these factors that in turn leads to better control of hospital costs. The data for the year 1989 were obtained from the Office of Health Care Information, Wisconsin's Department of Health and Human Services. Cross-sectional data are used, which details the 20 diagnosis-related group (DRG) discharge costs for hospitals in the state of Wisconsin, broken down into nine major health service areas and three types of payer (fee for service, HMO, and other). Even though there are 540 potential DRG, area and payer combinations ($20 \times 9 \times 3 = 540$), only 526 combinations were actually realized in the 1989 data set. Other explanatory variables included the logarithm of the total number of discharges (NO DSCHG) and total number of hospital beds (NUM BEDS) for each combination. The response variable is the logarithm of total hospital charges per number of discharges (CHG_NUM).

As before, we use the symbol y to denote the response variable. Not surprisingly, it turns out that the diagnosis-related group (DRG) is an important determinant of costs. In this section, we focus our analysis on this categorical variable. Thus, we use the notation y_{ij} to mean the ith observation of the jth DRG. For this data set, j may be 1, 2, ..., or 20. For the jth DRG, we assume there are n_j observations. There are $n = n_1 + n_2 + ... + n_c$ observations. The data are:

Data for DRG 1	y_{11}	y_{21}	$\cdots$	$y_{n_1,1}$
Data for DRG 2	y_{12}	y_{22}	$\cdots$	$y_{n_2,2}$
.	.	.	$\cdots$	.
Data for DRG c	y_{1c}	y_{2c}	$\cdots$	$y_{n_c,c}$

Because each level of a factor can be arranged in a single row (or column), another expression for this type of data is a one way classification.

where $c = 20$ is the number of *levels* of the DRG factor. Because we do not assume an ordering of the levels, any system of ordering of the DRGs is fine. Because each level of a factor can be arranged in a single row (or column), another term for this type of data is a *one way* classification. Thus, a *one way model* is another term for a one factor model.

Summarizing the Data: Hospital Charges Case Study

An important summary measure of each level of the factor is the sample average. We use

$$\bar{y}_j = \frac{1}{n_j} \sum_{i=1}^{n_j} y_{ij}$$

to denote the average from the jth DRG.

A plot of the response versus the average by level, as in Figure 5.4, helps us to see a number of features of the data.

To get an idea of cost by level of the factor, Figure 5.4 is a scatter plot of $\{y_{ij}\}$ versus $\{\bar{y}_j\}$. This plot illustrates features of the data. These are:

1. First, it is clear that the average cost varies by type of DRG. For example, it turns out that *angina pectoris*, chest pains, normal newborns and chemotherapy are relatively inexpensive diagnosis-related groups. On the other hand, major joint and limb reattachment and psychoses are expensive DRGs.

2. We see that the variability is about the same for each DRG. Note that we have controlled for the frequency by working on a per discharge basis. Further, working in logarithmic units evens out the variability (see Section 6.6 for more discussion on this point).

3. As emphasized by Levin, Sarlin and Webne-Behrman (1989), when the horizontal and vertical axes are on the same scale, the data are centered about a 45 degree line. This aids in interpreting the graph. In particular, the scatter plot makes it easy to identify the outlier for the group with average cost about 8.5. For this particular combination of medical treatment, health service area and type of payer, there were only two patients discharged in 1989, compared to an average of 509 discharges. Thus, although unusual, this point represents a relatively small amount of information about hospital costs and should not have an undue influence in driving the model selection.

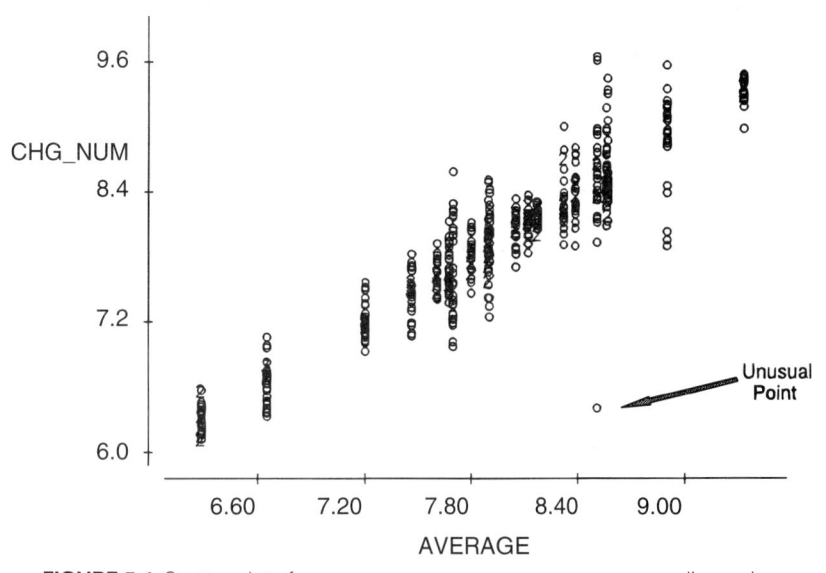

FIGURE 5.4 Scatter plot of responses versus average response over diagnosis-related group (DRG). *Source: Wisconsin Department of Health and Human Services*

Model Assumptions and Analysis

When introducing the concept of random error in Section 2.8, we decomposed the response as

response (y) = deterministic component (μ) + random error (e).

In this section, each part of the decomposition is allowed to vary by the level of the factor, denoted by j. We can express this model as

$$y_{ij} = \mu_j + e_{ij} \quad i = 1, \dots, n_j, \quad j = 1, \dots, c.$$

This is shorthand notation for $n_1 + n_2 + \dots + n_c = n$ equations, one for each observation. The random errors $\{e_{ij}\}$ are assumed to be a random sample from an unknown population of errors. Because we assume the expected value of each error is zero, we have $\mathrm{E}\, y_{ij} = \mu_j$. Thus, we interpret μ_j to be the expected value of the response y_{ij}. Similarly, because we assume that the random errors have variance σ^2, we have $\mathrm{Var}\, y_{ij} = \sigma^2$. Thus, we interpret σ^2 to be the true, unknown variance of the response. This variance is assumed to be common over all factor levels.

To estimate the parameters $\{\mu_j\}$, as with regression we use the *method of least squares*, introduced in Section 3.1. That is, let $\hat{\mu}_j^*$ be some candidate estimate of μ_j. The quantity

$$\mathrm{SS}(\hat{\mu}_1^*, \dots, \hat{\mu}_c^*) = \sum_{j=1}^{c} \sum_{i=1}^{n_j} (y_{ij} - \hat{\mu}_j^*)^2$$

The least squares estimate of μ_j is $\bar{y}_j$.

represents the sum of squared deviations of the responses from these candidate estimates. From straightforward algebra, the value of $\hat{\mu}_j^*$ that minimizes this sum of squares is $\bar{y}_j$. Thus, $\bar{y}_j$ is the *least squares estimate* of μ_j.

To understand how reliable the estimates are, we can partition the variability as in the regression case, presented in Sections 3.3 and 4.3. The minimum sum of squared deviations is called the *error sum of squares* and is defined to be

$$\text{Error SS} = \mathrm{SS}(\bar{y}_1, \dots, \bar{y}_c) = \sum_{j=1}^{c} \sum_{i=1}^{n_j} (y_{ij} - \bar{y}_j)^2.$$

The total variation in the data set is summarized by the *total sum of squares*, Total SS $= \sum_{j=1}^{c} \sum_{i=1}^{n_j} (y_{ij} - \bar{y})^2$. The difference, called the *factor sum of squares*, can be expressed as:

$$\text{Factor SS} = \text{Total SS} - \text{Error SS}$$

$$= \sum_{j=1}^{c} \sum_{i=1}^{n_j} (y_{ij} - \bar{y})^2 - \sum_{j=1}^{c} \sum_{i=1}^{n_j} (y_{ij} - \bar{y}_j)^2 = \sum_{j=1}^{c} \sum_{i=1}^{n_j} (\bar{y}_j - \bar{y})^2$$

$$= \sum_{j=1}^{c} n_j (\bar{y}_j - \bar{y})^2.$$

The last two equalities follow from algebraic manipulation. The Factor SS plays the same role as the Regression SS in Chapters 3 and 4. The variability decomposition is summarized in the analysis of variance (ANOVA) table (Table 5.4).

As with regression, the analysis of variance table is a useful bookkeeping device for keeping track of the sources of variability.

TABLE 5.4 ANOVA Table for One Factor Model

Source	Sum of Squares	df	Mean Square
Factor	Factor SS	$c - 1$	Factor MS
Error	Error SS	$n - c$	Error MS
Total	Total SS	$n - 1$	

The conventions for this table are the same as in the regression case. That is, the mean squares column is defined to be the sum of squares column divided by the degrees of freedom (df) column. Thus, Factor MS $\equiv$ (Factor SS)/$(c - 1)$ and Error MS $\equiv$ (Error SS)/$(n - c)$. We use

$$s^2 = \text{Error MS} = \frac{\sum_{j=1}^{c} \sum_{i=1}^{n_j} \hat{e}_{ij}^2}{n - c}$$

to be our estimate of σ^2, where $\hat{e}_{ij} = y_{ij} - \bar{y}_j$ is the residual. The variability in the ANOVA table is often summarized by $R^2 = $ (Factor SS)/(Total SS), the coefficient of determination, or its adjusted version, $R_a^2 = 1 - s^2/s_y^2$, where $s_y^2 = $ (Total SS)/$(n - 1)$.

Example 5.2: Machine Run Times

Before continuing, we consider a small, hypothetical, data set to illustrate the computational issues. Suppose that we have measured the time it takes for three types of machines to run a given benchmark test. The run times are presented in Table 5.5.

Recall that the notion y_{ij} means the ith run from the jth machine. For example, $y_{21} = 12$ and $y_{23} = 10$. The average run times are computed as $\bar{y}_j = (\sum_{i=1}^{4} y_{ij})/4$. Note that Machine 3, with average run time $\bar{y}_3 = 8$, is the fastest. The issue is, based on the data, can we be confident that there is a real difference in machines or could this difference be due to sampling variability, that is, chance?

TABLE 5.5 Hypothetical Run Times for Three Machines

Machine	Run times	Average run time
1	14, 12, 10, 12	$\bar{y}_1 = 12$
2	9, 16, 15, 12	$\bar{y}_2 = 13$
3	8, 10, 7, 7	$\bar{y}_3 = 8$

To this end, we first construct the ANOVA table. You should check that

$$\bar{y} = \frac{\left(\sum\limits_{j=1}^{3}\sum\limits_{i=1}^{4} y_{ij}\right)}{12} = 11 \quad \text{and} \quad \text{Total SS} = \sum\limits_{j=1}^{3}\sum\limits_{i=1}^{4} \frac{(y_{ij} - \bar{y})^2}{(12-1)} = 100.$$

Further, we have

$$\text{Factor SS} = \sum\limits_{j=1}^{3} n_j(\bar{y}_j - \bar{y})^2 = 4(12-11)^2 + 4(13-11)^2 + 4(8-11)^2 = 56.$$

Table 5.6 summarizes these calculations. From this table, we can compute $R^2 = 56\%$ and $s = (\text{Error MS})^{1/2} = (4.89)^{1/2} = 2.21$.

TABLE 5.6 ANOVA Table for Hypothetical Run Times for Three Machines

Source	Sum of Squares	df	Mean Square
Machine	56	2	28.00
Error	44	9	4.89
Total	100	11	

We translate the question, "Is the factor important?" into a narrower question regarding the validity of the hypothesis H_0: $\mu_1 = \mu_2 = \ldots = \mu_c$.

To make a formal decision as to whether the differences among machines are real, we introduce a test of hypothesis in the one factor model framework. The null, or working, hypothesis, is no difference among the levels of the factors, denoted by H_0: $\mu_1 = \mu_2 = \ldots = \mu_c$. This notation states that the null hypothesis is the equality of the means. The alternative hypothesis is that at least one of the means differ from another. As in regression, we examine the test statistic F-ratio = (Factor MS)/(Error MS). The procedure is to reject the null hypothesis in favor of the alternative if

$$F\text{-ratio} > F\text{-value}.$$

Here, F-value is a percentile from the F-distribution with $df_1 = c - 1$ and $df_2 = n - c$ degrees of freedom. The percentile is one minus significance level of the test.

To interpret this test, recall that under H_0, we have equality of the means so that all means μ_j are equal to one another and are equal to, say, μ. The sample averages are approximations to the true means. Thus, under H_0, we expect the sample means to be close to one number, $\bar{y}$. To examine their separation, we look at squared differences, $(\bar{y}_j - \bar{y})^2$. To give levels with more observations greater weight and look at all separations together, we examine

$$\sum\limits_{j=1}^{c} n_j(\bar{y}_j - \bar{y})^2 = \text{Factor SS}.$$

The larger that Factor SS is, the less likely we will be to believe in the null hypothesis H_0. Dividing Factor SS by $(c-1)$ and by $s^2 =$ Error MS is the right standardization so that we can compare it to the reference distribution, the F-distribution.

In example 5.2, we have realized average run times of $\bar{y}_1 = 12$, $\bar{y}_2 = 13$ and $\bar{y}_3 = 8$. Is there a real difference? We hypothesize H_0: $\mu_1 = \mu_2 = \mu_3$, no difference among the true run times. From Table 5.6, we calculate F-ratio $=$ (Factor MS)/(Error MS) $= (28.00)/(4.89) = 5.726$. Is this large? Looking to the F-table, at the 5% level of significance with $df_1 = c - 1 = 2$ and $df_2 = n - c = 9$, we have F-value $= 4.256$. Because the F-ratio exceeds the F-value, we reject the null hypothesis and declare that there does seem to be a real difference among the run times. The data does not provide us with an indication as to the cause of this difference, only that it is unlikely that the difference can be ascribed to mere sampling variability.

As another example, consider the Hospital Charges example. From Figure 5.4, it seems clear that costs differ by DRG. To make a formal statement using our test of hypothesis machinery, some straightforward calculations yield the results of Table 5.7. From this table, we note that DRGs have explained $R^2 = 260.09/296.63 = 0.877$, or 87.7%, of the variability. The "typical" error is $s = $ (Error MS)$^{1/2} = 0.27$. To conduct the test of the null hypothesis, H_0: $\mu_1 = \mu_2 = \ldots = \mu_{20}$, we have F-ratio $= 13.69/0.0722 = 189.6$. From the F-table, with $df_1 = 19$, $df_2 = $ infinity and, at the 5% level of significance, we have F-value $= 1.590$. Because F-ratio $> F$-value, we reject the null hypothesis in favor of the alternative, that there is some difference among costs of different diagnosis-related groups.

TABLE 5.7 ANOVA Table for Hospital Charges

Source	Sum of Squares	df	Mean Square
DRG	260.09	19	13.69
Error	36.54	506	0.0722
Total	296.63	525	

The confidence interval, $y_j \pm (t\text{-value})\, s/(n_j^{1/2})$, provides an interval estimate for μ_j.

Although comforting, this hypothesis test does not really tell us anything that is not clearly evident in Figure 5.4. To supplement this information, it is useful to give estimates, and ranges of reliability, of the cost summary measures. To this end, we use $\bar{y}_j$ as our *point estimate* of the parameter μ_j. To provide a range of reliability, the corresponding interval estimate is

$$\bar{y}_j \pm (t\text{-value})\, \frac{s}{\sqrt{n_j}}.$$

Here, the t-value is a percentile from the t-distribution with $n - c$ degrees. The percentile is $1 - (1 - \text{confidence level})/2$.

To illustrate, we consider costs for the psychoses DRG, the highest cost of the medical treatment groups. This was the $j = 10$th DRG, and we have $\bar{y}_{10} = 9.3267$ and $n_{10} = 26$. Thus, a 95% confidence interval for μ_{10} is

$$9.3267 \pm (1.96)(0.27)/(26)^{1/2} = 9.3267 \pm 0.1038, \text{ or } (9.2229, 9.4305).$$

Note that these estimates are in natural logarithmic units. In dollars per discharge, our point estimate is $e^{9.3267} = \$11,234$ and our 95% confidence interval is $(e^{9.2229}, e^{9.4305})$, or ($\$10,188$, $\$12,463$).

Link with Regression and Reparameterization

As described in Section 5.1, an important feature of the tests of hypotheses and confidence intervals is the ease of computation. Although the sum of squares appears complex, it is important to note that no matrix calculations are required. Rather, all of the calculations can be done through averages and sums of squares. This has been an historically important consideration, before the age of readily available desktop computing. Further, it also provides for direct interpretation of the results.

In this subsection, we show how a one factor ANOVA model can be rewritten as a regression model. The regression model relies on more general, yet more cumbersome, estimation methodologies. However, using the regression formulation, we already have introduced many of the important statistical inference results. For example, with this rewriting we will be able to show that the test of equality of means is a special case of the regression test of model adequacy. Thus, justifications of the tests and intervals estimates need only be done in the regression case and need not be repeated in the ANOVA context. Further, the remedies for model inadequacy that we will present in Chapter 6 and the additional inference techniques in Chapter 7 will be available for both the regression and ANOVA models.

By using c indicator variables, we can express the one factor ANOVA model as a regression model. To this end, for a categorical variable with c levels, define c indicator variables, $x_1, x_2, \ldots, x_c$. Here, x_1 is a one if the observation falls in the first level and is zero otherwise. Similarly, x_2 is an indicator variable for an observation falling in the second level, and so on. Thus, x_j indicates whether or not an observation falls in the jth level.

With these variables, we can rewrite our one factor ANOVA model

$$y = \mu_j + e$$

as

$$y = \mu_1 x_1 + \mu_2 x_2 + \ldots + \mu_c x_c + e. \tag{5.1}$$

The regression model in equation (5.1) includes c independent variables but does not include an intercept term, β_0. To include an intercept term, define $\tau_j = \mu_j - \mu$, where μ is an, as yet, unspecified parameter. Because each observation must fall into one of the c categories, we have $x_1 + x_2 + \ldots + x_c = 1$ for each observation. Thus, using $\mu_j = \tau_j + \mu$ in equation (5.1), we have

$$y = \mu + \tau_1 x_1 + \tau_2 x_2 + \ldots + \tau_c x_c + e. \tag{5.2}$$

Thus, we have re-written the model into what appears to be our usual regression format, as in equation (4.2).

We use the τ in lieu of β for historical reasons. ANOVA models were invented by R. A. Fisher in connection with agricultural experiments. Here, the typical set-up is to apply several *treatments* to plots of land in order to quantify crop yield responses. Thus, the greek t, τ, suggests the word treatment, another term used to described levels of the factor of interest.

A simpler version of equation (5.2) can be given when we identify the level of the factor. That is, if we know an observation falls in the jth level, then only x_j is one and the other x's are 0. Thus, a simpler expression for equation (5.2) is

$$y_{ij} = \mu + \tau_j + e_{ij}. \tag{5.3}$$

For overparameterized models, we must restrict the movement of parameters.

Comparing equations (5.1) and (5.2), we see that the number of parameters has increased by one. That is, in equation (5.1), there are c parameters, $\mu_1, \ldots, \mu_c$, even though in equation (5.2) there are $c + 1$ parameters, μ, and $\tau_1, \ldots, \tau_c$. The model in equation (5.2) is said to be *overparameterized*. To make these two expressions equivalent, we now present two ways of *restricting* the movement of parameters in (5.2).

The first type of restriction, usually done in the regression context, is to require one of the τ's to be zero. This amounts to *dropping* one of the explanatory variables. For example, we might use

$$y = \mu + \tau_1 x_1 + \tau_2 x_2 + \ldots + \tau_{c-1} x_{c-1} + e, \tag{5.4}$$

The first type of restriction on the parameters is dropping one of the explanatory indicator variables. With this restriction, it is easy to fit the data using standard regression statistical software.

dropping x_c. With this formulation, it is easy to fit the model in equation (5.4) using regression statistical software routines because one only needs to run the regression with $c - 1$ explanatory variables. However, one needs to be careful with the interpretation of parameters. To equate the models in (5.1) and (5.4), we need to define $\mu \equiv \mu_c$ and $\tau_j = \mu_j - \mu_c$ for $j = 1, 2, \ldots, c - 1$. That is, the regression intercept term is the mean level of the category dropped, and each regression coefficient is the difference between a mean level and the mean level dropped. It is not necessary to drop the last level c, and indeed, one could drop any level. However, the interpretation of the parameters does depend on the variable dropped. With this restriction, the fitted values are $\hat{\mu} = \hat{\mu}_c = \bar{y}_c$ and $\hat{\tau}_j = \hat{\mu}_j - \hat{\mu}_c = \bar{y}_j - \bar{y}_c$. Recall that the carat (^), or "hat," stands for an estimated, or fitted, value.

The second type of restriction, from the ANOVA context, is to interpret μ as a mean for the entire population. To this end, the usual requirement is $\mu \equiv (1/n) \sum_{j=1}^{c} n_j \mu_j$, that is, μ is a weighted average of means. With this definition, we interpret $\tau_j = \mu_j - \mu$ as a treatment difference between a mean level and the population mean. Another way of expressing this restriction is $\Sigma_{j=1}^{c} n_j \tau_j = 0$, that is, the (weighted) sum of treatment differences is zero. The disadvantage of this restriction is that it is not readily implementable with a regression routine, and a special routine is needed. The advantage is that there is a symmetry in the definitions of the parameters. There is no need to worry about which variable is being dropped from the equation, an important consideration. With this restriction, the parameter estimates are

$$\hat{\mu} = (1/n) \sum_{j=1}^{c} n_j \hat{\mu}_j = (1/n) \sum_{j=1}^{c} n_j \bar{y}_j = \bar{y} \quad \text{and} \quad \hat{\tau}_j = \hat{\mu}_j - \hat{\mu} = \bar{y}_j - \bar{y}.$$

To illustrate, consider the hypothetical machine run time data described in Illustration 5.1. The estimate of the mean levels are $\hat{\mu}_1 = \bar{y}_1 = 12$, $\hat{\mu}_2 = \bar{y}_2 = 13$ and $\hat{\mu}_3 = \bar{y}_3 = 8$. To apply the first restriction, we could drop, for instance, the third category. The resulting regression equation would be $E\,y = \mu + \tau_1 x_1 + \tau_2 x_2 = \mu_3 + (\mu_1 - \mu_3)x_1 + (\mu_2 - \mu_3)x_2$. The corresponding fitted equation would be

$$\hat{y} = 8 + 4x_1 + 5x_2.$$

If you have a regression package available, use the data in Table 5.5 and verify that this is the correct fitted equation.

The second restriction yields $\mu \equiv (1/n)\Sigma_{j=1}^{c} n_j \mu_j = (1/c)\Sigma_{j=1}^{c} \mu_j$, because there are an equal number of observations in each cell. Here, c is 3, so $\mu = (\mu_1 + \mu_2 + \mu_3)/3$. The estimate is $\hat{\mu} = \bar{y} = 11$. The estimated differences are

$$\hat{\tau}_1 = \bar{y}_1 - \bar{y} = 12 - 11 = 1, \quad \hat{\tau}_2 = \bar{y}_2 - \bar{y} = 13 - 11 = 2 \quad \text{and}$$

$$\hat{\tau}_3 = \bar{y}_3 - \bar{y} = 8 - 11 = -3.$$

The model remains the same regardless of our choice of restriction on parameters. Because the model is the same, all predictions and other inferences are the same. To illustrate, suppose that we are interested in getting a point estimate for the first machine. For an observation at the first level, we have $x_1 = 1$ and $x_2 = 0$. Thus, using the estimated regression equation from our first restriction, we have $\hat{y} = 8 + 4(1) + 5(0) = 12$. Using the model express with the second restriction, our fitted value is $\hat{\mu} + \hat{\tau}_1 = 11 + 1 = 12$. The two methods produce equivalent fitted values, as anticipated.

5.4 TWO FACTOR ANOVA MODEL

Suppose that we now wish to consider two independent categorical variables, or factors. To be specific, we again consider the hypothetical machine run time example introduced in Example 5.1. In this example, the response of interest is the length of time it takes a machine to complete a certain benchmark test. The explanatory variable previously considered was the type of machine. Suppose that we now have additional information available on another factor, the type of person operating the machine. For convenience, think of the operator as either experienced or inexperienced (a rookie). We refer to the operator as Factor 1 and the type of machine as Factor 2, although these designations are interchangeable. Table 5.8 presents the data for the run times.

TABLE 5.8 Hypothetical Run Times of Three Machines by Two Operators

Machine (Factor 2)	Operator (Factor 1)		Machine averages
	Rookie	Experienced	
1	14, 12	10, 12	$\bar{y}_{.1.} = 12$
2	15, 16	9, 12	$\bar{y}_{.2.} = 13$
3	8, 10	7, 7	$\bar{y}_{.3.} = 8$
Operator averages	$\bar{y}_{1..} = 12.5$	$\bar{y}_{2..} = 9.5$	$\bar{y}_{...} = 11$

Extending the notation introduction in Section 5.3, we use y_{ijk} to denote the kth observation of the ith operator of the jth machine. We suppose that there are $K = 2$ observations for each combination of the $I = 2$ types of operators and $c = 3$ types of machines. Thus, there are $n = IcK = 2(3)2 = 12$ observations in total.

As in Section 5.3, an important issue that can be addressed with this data is whether the (population) mean run times differ among machines types. To this end, we define the average for each machine, $j = 1, 2, 3$, using

$$\bar{y}_{.j.} = \frac{1}{IK} \sum_{i=1}^{I} \sum_{k=1}^{K} y_{ijk} .$$

Here, the notation $\{\cdot j \cdot\}$ in the subscript means sum over $i = 1, \ldots, I$, leave j fixed, and sum over $k = 1, \ldots, K$. Extending the example in Section 5.3, one goal of this section is to explain part of the unknown variability in terms of the type of operator. To this end, we can define the average for each operator, $i = 1, 2$, using

$$\bar{y}_{i..} = \frac{1}{cK} \sum_{j=1}^{c} \sum_{k=1}^{K} y_{ijk} .$$

It is also convenient for subsequent analyses to define the average over each combination of operator and machine

$$\bar{y}_{ij.} = \frac{1}{K} \sum_{k=1}^{K} y_{ijk} .$$

Based on an examination of the data in Table 5.8, it appears that there may be a difference between the two types of operators as well as the three types of machines. Are the differences in sample mean run times due to sampling variability or are they due to differences in population mean run times? How does accounting for the type of operator help understand the performance of different machine types? To respond to these and related questions, we now introduce two models of variability.

Model Assumptions and Analysis—Additive Model

The basic approaches for combining categorical variables are the additive and interaction models.

If we wish to put two categorical, or attribute, variables together in one model, there are two basic approaches. These are call *additive* and *interaction* models, respectively. To illustrate these two approaches, we begin with the simpler additive model.

Using the one factor formulation in equation (5.3), we interpret the parameter μ to be the population mean and τ_j to be the difference due to the jth level of Factor 2. Similarly, we introduce the parameter β_i to be interpreted as the difference due to the ith level of Factor 1. With these parameters, the two factor additive model is

$$y_{ijk} = \mu + \beta_i + \tau_j + e_{ijk},\qquad(5.5)$$

where $i = 1, ..., I, j = 1, ..., c$, and $k = 1, ..., K$. The errors, $\{e_{ijk}\}$, are assumed to be random, independent draws from a common population with mean zero and variance σ^2.

As with the one factor model, we again need to impose certain restrictions on the factor differences. So that all levels of each factor are treated in the same fashion, we require

$$\beta_1 + \beta_2 + ... + \beta_I = 0 \quad \text{and} \quad \tau_1 + \tau_2 + ... + \tau_c = 0.\qquad(5.6)$$

When the number of observations does not depend on the level of each factor, then the data are said to be balanced.

Note that in this section we do not use the number of observations in our restrictions as we did in Section 5.3. This is because, in this section, the data are assumed to be *balanced*. That is, for each combination of levels of Factors 1 and 2, we assume that there are an equal number, K, of observations available. This assumption is made primarily in order to simplify the presentation. It is possible to present the formulas where the number of observations may vary by combinations of levels (see, for example, Searle, 1987). Instead, in the chapter, we handle unbalanced data a special case of the general linear model that will be introduced in Section 5.5.

The least squares parameter estimates are determined by minimizing the sum of squares

$$\text{SS}(\hat{\mu}^*, \hat{\beta}^*_1, ..., \hat{\beta}^*_I, \hat{\tau}^*_1, ..., \hat{\tau}^*_c) = \sum_{i=1}^{I} \sum_{j=1}^{c} \sum_{k=1}^{K} (y_{ijk} - (\hat{\mu}^* + \hat{\beta}^*_i + \hat{\tau}^*_j))^2.$$

Here, $\hat{\mu}^*, \hat{\beta}^*_1, ..., \hat{\beta}^*_I, \hat{\tau}^*_1, ..., \hat{\tau}^*_c$ candidate estimates of $\mu, \beta_1, ..., \beta_I, \tau_1, ..., \tau_c$. Minimizing this sum of squares subject to the restrictions in equation (5.6), the least squares estimates are

$$\hat{\mu} = \bar{y}_{...}, \quad \hat{\beta}_i = \bar{y}_{i..} - \bar{y}_{...}, \quad \text{and} \quad \hat{\tau}_j = \bar{y}_{\cdot j \cdot} - \bar{y}_{....} \tag{5.7}$$

Thus, the variability still unaccounted for, after the introduction of the parameters μ, β and τ, is summarized by

$$\text{Error SS} = SS(\hat{\mu}, \hat{\beta}_1, \ldots, \hat{\beta}_I, \hat{\tau}_1, \ldots, \hat{\tau}_c) = \sum_{i=1}^{I}\sum_{j=1}^{c}\sum_{k=1}^{K} (y_{ijk} - (\hat{\mu} + \hat{\beta}_i + \hat{\tau}_j))^2$$

$$= \sum_{i=1}^{I}\sum_{j=1}^{c}\sum_{k=1}^{K} (y_{ijk} - \bar{y}_{i..} - \bar{y}_{\cdot j \cdot} + \bar{y}_{...})^2 . \tag{5.8}$$

To account for each source of the variability, consider the decomposition

$$\underset{(1)}{y_{ijk} - \bar{y}_{...}} = \underset{(2)}{(\bar{y}_{\cdot i \cdot} - \bar{y}_{...})} + \underset{(3)}{(\bar{y}_{\cdot j \cdot} - \bar{y}_{...})} + \underset{(4)}{(y_{ijk} - \bar{y}_{i..} - \bar{y}_{\cdot j \cdot} + \bar{y}_{...})} . \tag{5.9}$$

Interpret this equation as (1) the total deviation equals (2) the deviation explained by Factor 1 plus (3) the deviation explained by Factor 2 plus (4) the unexplained deviation. Squaring each side of equation (5.9) and summing over all observations yields

$$\text{Total SS} = \text{Factor 1 SS} + \text{Factor 2 SS} + \text{Error SS}.$$

Here, Error SS is defined in equation (5.8) and, with equation (5.7),

$$\text{Total SS} = \sum_{i=1}^{I}\sum_{j=1}^{c}\sum_{k=1}^{K} (y_{ijk} - \bar{y}_{...})^2,$$

$$\text{Factor 1 SS} = cK \sum_{i=1}^{I} (\bar{y}_{j..} - \bar{y}_{...})^2 = cK \sum_{i=1}^{I} \hat{\beta}_i^2 \tag{5.10}$$

$$\text{Factor 2 SS} = IK \sum_{j=1}^{c} (\bar{y}_{\cdot j \cdot} - \bar{y}_{...})^2 = IK \sum_{j=1}^{c} \hat{\tau}_j^2 .$$

For the degrees of freedom column, with our restrictions, there are I-1 free Factor 1 parameters and c-1 free Factor 2 parameters.

The variability decomposition is summarized in the following analysis of variance (ANOVA) table. Again, the mean squares (MS) column is defined by the sum of squares (SS) column divided by the degrees of freedom (df) column.

ANOVA Table for Two Factor Additive Model

Source	Sum of Squares	df	Mean Square
Factor 1	Factor 1 SS	$I - 1$	Factor 1 MS
Factor 2	Factor 2 SS	$c - 1$	Factor 2 MS
Error	Error SS	$n - (I + c - 1)$	Error MS
Total	Total SS	$n - 1$	

Thus, Factor 1 MS $\equiv$ (Factor 1 SS)/$(I - 1)$, Factor 2 MS $\equiv$ (Factor 2 SS)/$(c - 1)$ and Error MS $\equiv$ (Error SS)/$(n - (I + c - 1))$. To understand the degrees of freedom column for the errors, first note that there are $1 + I + c$ parameters, one for μ, I for β and c for τ. However, there are two restrictions on $\{\beta_i\}$ and $\{\tau_j\}$, resulting in $I + c - 1$ free parameters. Thus, the error degrees of freedom follows the same rule as all regression models, the number of observations, n, minus the number of (free) parameters, $I + c - 1$.

To illustrate, Table 5.9 presents results for the data in Table 5.8.

TABLE 5.9 ANOVA Table for Two Factor Additive Model of Hypothetical Run Times

Source	Sum of Squares	df	Mean Square
Operator (Factor 1)	27	1	27
Machine (Factor 2)	56	2	28
Error	17	8	2.12
Total	100	11	

As before, tests of hypotheses allow us to test formally for differences among levels of each factor. For example, the notation $H_0: \beta_1 = \ldots = \beta_I = 0$ stands for the null hypothesis: all Factor 1 level mean differences are equal to zero. In other words, this is the hypothesis that there is no difference among levels of Factor 1. The alternative hypothesis is that at least one mean differs from another. For this test, we examine the F-ratio = (Factor 1 MS)/(Error MS). The null hypothesis is rejected in favor of the alternative if

$$F\text{- ratio} > F\text{-value}.$$

Here, the F-value is a percentile from the F-distribution with $df_1 = I - 1$ and $df_2 = n - (I + c - 1)$ degrees of freedom. The percentile is one $-$ significance level. In our machine example, with $df_1 = 1$ and $df_2 = 8$, at the 5% significance level, we have F-value = 5.318 from the F-table. From Table 5.9, we have F-ratio = $27/2.12 = 12.74$. Because $12.74 = F$-ratio $> F$-value = 5.318, we reject the null hypothesis and conclude that there is a real difference between types of operators. This result reinforces our examination of the data in Table 5.8.

The test for differences among levels of Factor 2 is similar. To summarize, consider Table 5.10.

For example, to test differences among types of machines, we hypothesize $H_0: \tau_1 = \tau_2 = \tau_3 = 0$. To perform the test, we first calculate F-ratio = (Factor 2 MS)/(Error MS) = $28/2.12 = 13.21$. From the F-table with $df_1 = 2$ and $df_2 = 8$, at the 5% significance level, we have F-value = 4.459. Because $13.21 > 4.459$, we reject the null hypothesis that there is no difference among machines.

Recall that this was the same decision made in Section 5.3 when we examined only one factor. The advantage of introducing a second explanatory factor is that we have significantly reduced our estimate of the variability, s^2. Thus, we can be more confident in the decisions that we make.

TABLE 5.10   Tests of Hypothesis of Differences Among Levels for Two Factor Additive Model

Factor	Null hypothesis	Alternative hypothesis	Test statistic (F-ratio)	Degrees of freedom to use with the F-value
1	$H_0: \beta_1 = \ldots = \beta_I = 0$	H_a: At least one $\beta \neq 0$	(Factor 1 MS)/ (Error MS)	$df_1 = I - 1, df_2 = n - (I + c - 1)$
2	$H_0: \tau_1 = \ldots = \tau_c = 0$	H_a: At least one $\tau \neq 0$	(Factor 2 MS)/ (Error MS)	$df_1 = c - 1, df_2 = n - (I + c - 1)$

Model Assumptions and Analysis—Interaction Model

For the two factor additive model, we assumed that we could simply add together the impact of each variable, together with a population mean, to form the expected response. However, it may be that reality is better represented by examining more complicated *interactions* between the two factors. For example, in our hypothetical machine example, it may be that experienced operators run certain types of machines much faster than inexperienced operators even though, for other types of machines, experienced operators post only marginally faster run times.

To accommodate potential interactions, we use the model

$$y_{ijk} = \mu_{ij} + e_{ijk}. \tag{5.11}$$

Here, μ_{ij} represents the mean response for the ith level of Factor 1 and the jth level of Factor 2. As with equation (5.3), we would like to rewrite this model into interpretable components. To this end, define

$$\text{(a)} \quad \mu = \frac{1}{Ic} \sum_{i=1}^{I} \sum_{j=1}^{c} \mu_{ij}, \quad \text{(b)} \quad \beta_i = \left(\frac{1}{c} \sum_{j=1}^{c} \mu_{ij} \right) - \mu,$$

$$\text{(c)} \quad \tau_j = \left(\frac{1}{I} \sum_{i=1}^{I} \mu_{ij} \right) - \mu, \quad \text{and} \quad \text{(d)} \quad (\beta\tau)_{ij} = \mu_{ij} - \beta_i - \tau_j - \mu.$$

As with the additive model, μ represents the overall mean, β_i represents Factor 1 differences and τ_j represents Factor 2 differences. We use the term $(\beta\tau)_{ij}$ to represent the *interaction* between the two factors.

By substituting the expression for $(\beta\tau)_{ij}$ into (5.11), we get

$$y_{ijk} = \mu + \beta_i + \tau_j + (\beta\tau)_{ij} + e_{ijk}. \tag{5.12}$$

When comparing equations (5.11) and (5.12), we see that there are Ic linear parameters in equation (5.11) even though there are $1 + I + c + Ic$ parameters in equation (5.12). As before, certain restrictions need to be imposed on the parameters in equation (5.12) so that these models are equivalent. The restrictions adopted here are:

$$\sum_{i=1}^{I} \beta_i = 0, \sum_{j=1}^{c} \tau_j = 0, \sum_{i=1}^{I} (\beta\tau)_{ij} = 0, \quad \text{for each} \quad j,$$

$$\text{and} \quad \sum_{j=1}^{c} (\beta\tau)_{ij} = 0, \quad \text{for each} \quad i.$$

These restrictions impose $I + c + 1$ constraints, so that there are Ic free parameters in each expression.

Parameter estimation and partitioning the variability of the interaction model parallel the development of the additive model. Thus, only a brief outline is presented here. The least squares estimates of μ, β_i and τ_j are the same as presented in equation (5.6). The least squares estimate of $(\beta\tau)_{ij}$ turns out to be $\bar{y}_{ij\cdot} - \bar{y}_{i\cdot\cdot} - \bar{y}_{\cdot j\cdot} + \bar{y}_{\cdots}$. Partitioning the variability yields:

Total SS = Factor 1 SS + Factor 2 SS + Interaction SS + Error SS.

Here, Total SS, Factor 1 SS and Factor 2 SS are defined in equation (5.10) and

$$\text{Interaction SS} = K \sum_{i=1}^{I} \sum_{j=1}^{c} (\bar{y}_{ij\cdot} - \bar{y}_{i\cdot\cdot} - \bar{y}_{\cdot j\cdot} + \bar{y}_{\cdots})^2$$

$$\text{and} \quad \text{Error SS} = \sum_{i=1}^{I} \sum_{j=1}^{c} \sum_{k=1}^{K} (y_{ijk} - \bar{y}_{ij\cdot})^2.$$

These results can be summarized in the analysis of variance table (Table 5.11). We remark that the degrees of freedom for the unexplained variability, the Error Source, is the number of observations, n, minus the number of free parameters, Ic.

From the error degrees of freedom, we see that it is necessary to have more than one observation for each combination of the two factors. That is, K must be greater than one. If K equals one, then the number of observations, $n = IcK$, equals the number of parameters. In this case, the data fits the model perfectly, there is no error, and there are no degrees of freedom available for

TABLE 5.11 ANOVA Table for Two Factor Interaction Model

Source	Sum of Squares	df	Mean Square
Factor 1	Factor 1 SS	$I - 1$	Factor 1 MS
Factor 2	Factor 2 SS	$c - 1$	Factor 2 MS
Interaction	Interaction SS	$(I - 1)(c - 1)$	Interaction MS
Error	Error SS	$n - Ic$	Error MS
Total	Total SS	$n - 1$	

the error sum of squares. This is not the case in the additive model where we may have $K = 1$. This is because the error degrees of freedom, $n - (I + c + 1)$ $= IcK - (I + c + 1)$, can be greater than zero even if $K = 1$.

To test whether or not the interaction terms are important, we hypothesize H_0: all $(\beta\tau)_{ij}$'s $= 0$ versus the alternative hypothesis H_a: at least one $(\beta\tau)_{ij}$ $\neq 0$. This null hypothesis is rejected in favor of the alternative if F-ratio $=$ (Interaction MS)/(Error MS) $> F$-value, where the F-value is a $(1 -$ significance level) percentile from the F-distribution with $df_1 = (I - 1)(c - 1)$ and $df_2 = n - Ic$ degrees of freedom. To illustrate this test, consider the machine run data presented in Table 5.8. Table 5.12 presents the analysis of variance for the two factor interaction model fit of this example. To test for the presence of significant interaction terms, we compute F-ratio $=3/1.83 = 1.64$. From the F-table with $df_1 = 2$ and $df_2 = 6$ degrees of freedom, at the 5% level of significance we have F-value $= 5.143$. Thus, we cannot reject the null hypothesis that the interaction effects are significantly different from zero.

TABLE 5.12   ANOVA Table for Two Factor Interaction Model of Hypothetical Run Times

Source	Sum of Squares	df	Mean Square
Operator (Factor 1)	27	1	27
Machine (Factor 2)	56	2	28
Interaction	6	2	3
Error	11	6	1.83
Total	100	11	

It is also possible to test the hypothesis of no differences among factor levels using the interaction model. One would simply use the procedures outlined in Table 5.10 for the additive model but using the interaction model error mean squares and degrees of freedom. However, the interpretation of this decision-making procedure is not clear. Under the interaction model, the terms $(\beta\tau)_{ij}$ represent the interaction, or joint effect, of the ith level of Factor 1 and the jth level of Factor 2. With terms of this type present, it is difficult to interpret the decision that either Factor 1 or Factor 2 is not important.

Deciding whether or not a factor is important may be the main goal of the data analysis. One way to address this is to test first whether or not the interaction terms are important. If not, as in the preceding machine example, the analyst can then represent the data using the additive model where the importance of a factor can be tested. It is important to note that with this procedure, we are fitting two models to the data and that the usual caveats apply.

Link with Regression

In this subsection, we show how to connect the two factor ANOVA models to a regression model using indicator variables. To this end, for the I levels of Factor 1, define $x_{1,1}$ to be a one if the observation falls in the first level of Factor 1 and is zero otherwise. Similarly, $x_{1,2}$ is an indicator variable for an observation fall in the second level of Factor 1, and so on up to $x_{1,I}$, an indicator for the Ith level of Factor 1. Thus, we define $x_{1,i}$ to be an indicator of the ith level of Factor 1. Similarly, define $x_{2,j}$ to be an indicator of the jth level of Factor 2.

With this notation, we can re-express the two factor additive model in equation (5.5) as

$$y = \mu + \sum_{i=1}^{I} \beta_i x_{1,i} + \sum_{j=1}^{c} \tau_j x_{2,j} + e. \tag{5.13}$$

For example, for an observation falling in the third level of Factor 1 and the fourth level of Factor 2, we have $x_{1,3} = 1$, $x_{2,4} = 1$ and all other x's $= 0$. Thus, equation (5.13) reduces to $y_{34,k} = \mu + \beta_3 + \tau_4 + e_{34,k}$, as in equation (5.5).

As with equation (5.5), certain restrictions must be applied to the parameters. In the ANOVA models, the restriction is that the sum over levels of the parameters is zero. For regression routines, it is more straightforward to drop an explanatory indicator variable from each factor. Dropping the last variable of each factor yields

$$y = \mu + \sum_{i=1}^{I-1} \beta_i x_{1,j} + \sum_{j=1}^{c-1} \tau_j x_{2,j} + e.$$

Here, we interpret μ to be the mean response for the Ith level of Factor 1 and the cth level of Factor 2. The parameter β_i is interpreted to be the difference in mean responses between the ith and the Ith levels of Factor 1. Similarly, the parameter τ_j is interpreted to be the difference in mean responses between the jth and the cth levels of Factor 2. For the model fit, it does not matter which variables are dropped from the equation. However, it does matter which variables are dropped from the equation. However, it does matter when interpreting the parameters, and their resulting estimates.

The case of the two factor interaction model is similar. We can rewrite equation (5.12) as

$$y = \mu + \sum_{i=1}^{I} \beta_i x_{1,i} + \sum_{j=1}^{c} \tau_j x_{2,j} + \sum_{i=1}^{I}\sum_{j=1}^{c} (\beta\tau)_{ij} x_{1,i} x_{2,j} + e. \tag{5.14}$$

Dropping one indicator variable from each factor yields the analogous regression model

$$y = \mu + \sum_{i=1}^{I-1} \beta_i x_{1,i} + \sum_{j=1}^{c-1} \tau_j x_{2,j} + \sum_{i=1}^{I-1}\sum_{j=1}^{c-1} (\beta\tau)_{ij} x_{1,i} x_{2,j} + e. \tag{5.15}$$

Again, equation (5.14) must be estimated using restricted parameters. Equation (5.15) provides an equivalent formulation without the need to restrict the parameters. To illustrate equation (5.15), consider our machine example with $I = 2$ and $c = 3$. In this case, equation (5.15) reduces to:

$$y = \mu + \beta_1 x_{1,1} + \tau_1 x_{2,1} + \tau_2 x_{2,2} + (\beta\tau)_{11} x_{1,1} x_{2,1} + (\beta\tau)_{12} x_{1,1} x_{2,2} + e.$$

This is a multiple linear regression model with five independent variables.

5.5 REGRESSION USING CATEGORICAL AND CONTINUOUS VARIABLES

When combining categorical and continuous variable models, we use the terminology factor for the categorical variable and covariate for the continuous variable.

In Section 5.4, we introduced two ways of combining two categorical variables, additive models and interaction models. In Section 4.5, several ways of combining continuous variables were presented. In that section, we also discussed ways of modeling combinations of indicator and continuous variables. In this section, we extend that discussion by presenting ways of combining categorical and continuous variables. We initially present the case of only one categorical and one continuous variable. We then briefly present an extension called the *general linear model*. When combining categorical and continuous variable models, we use the terminology *factor* for the categorical variable and *covariate* for the continuous variable.

Combining One Categorical and One Continuous Variable

Combining categorical and continuous variables models begins with separate models for each variable. In Section 5.3 is a discussion of the one factor model:

$$y_{ij} = \mu_j + e_{ij} \qquad i = 1, \ldots, n_j, \quad j = 1, \ldots, c.$$

In Chapter 3 is a discussion of the continuous variable, or covariate, model:

$$y_{ij} = \beta_0 + \beta_1 x_{ij} + e_{ij}.$$

Table 5.13 describes several models that could be used to represent combinations of a factor and a covariate.

TABLE 5.13 Several Models that Represent Combinations of One Factor and One Covariate

Model description	Notation
One factor ANOVA (no covariate model)	$y_{ij} = \mu_j + e_{ij}$
Regression with constant intercept and slope (no factor model)	$y_{ij} = \beta_0 + \beta_1 x_{ij} + e_{ij}$
Regression with variable intercept and constant slope (analysis of covariance model)	$y_{ij} = \beta_{0j} + \beta_1 x_{ij} + e_{ij}$
Regression with constant intercept and variable slope	$y_{ij} = \beta_0 + \beta_{1j} x_{ij} + e_{ij}$
Regression with variable intercept and slope	$y_{ij} = \beta_{0j} + \beta_{1j} x_{ij} + e_{ij}$

We can interpret the regression with variable intercept and constant slope to be an additive model because we are adding the factor effect, β_{0j}, to the covariate effect, $\beta_1 x_{ij}$. Note that one could also use the notation, μ_j, in lieu of $\beta_{0,j}$ to suggest the presence of a factor effect. The regression with variable intercept and slope can be thought of as an interaction model. Here, both the intercept, β_{0j}, and slope, $\beta_{1,j}$, may vary by level of the factor. In this sense, we interpret the factor and covariate to be "interacting." The model with constant intercept and variable slope is typically not used in practice. It is included here for completeness. With this model, the factor and covariate interact through the variable slope but there is no main effect, as represented by the constant intercept. Figures 5.5 through 5.7 illustrate the expected responses of these models.

For each model presented in Table 5.13, parameter estimates can be calculated using the method of least squares. As usual, this means writing the expected response, E y_{ij}, as a function of known variables and unknown parameters. Then, for candidate estimates of the parameters, an error sum of squares can be calculated and minimized over all candidate estimates. It turns out, for the regression model with variable intercept and constant slope, that the least squares estimates can be expressed compactly as:

$$b_1 = \frac{\sum_{j=1}^{c} \sum_{i=1}^{n_j} (x_{ij} - \bar{x}_j)(y_{ij} - \bar{y}_j)}{\sum_{j=1}^{c} \sum_{i=1}^{n_j} (x_{ij} - \bar{x}_j)^2}$$

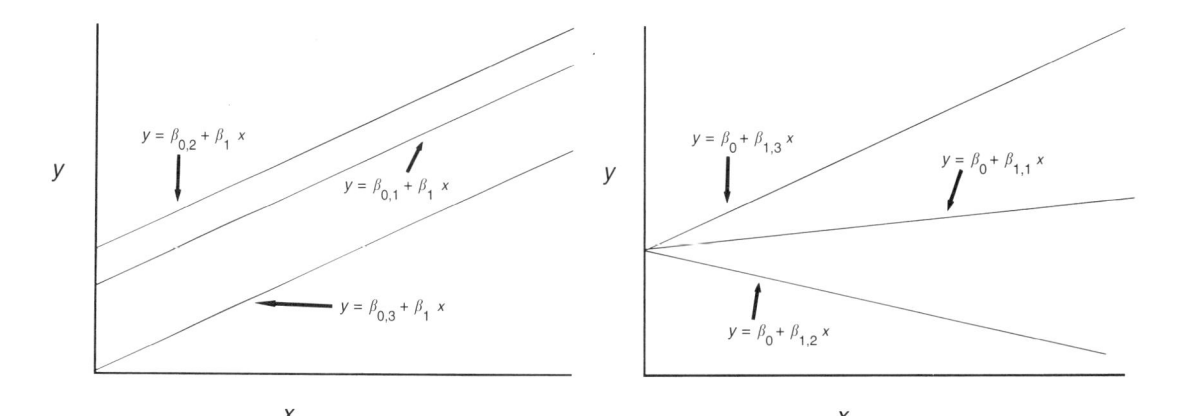

FIGURE 5.5 Plot of the expected response versus the covariate for the regression model with variable intercept and constant slope.

FIGURE 5.6 Plot of the expected response versus the covariate for the regression model with constant intercept and variable slope.

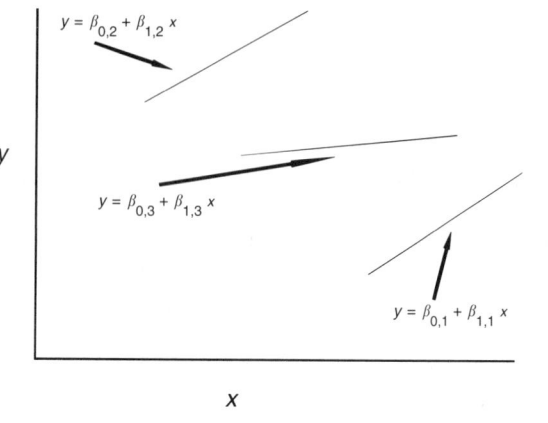

FIGURE 5.7 Plot of the expected response versus the covariate for the regression model with variable intercept and slope.

and $b_{0,j} = \bar{y}_j - b_1\bar{x}_j$. Similarly, the least squares estimates for the regression model with variable intercept and slope can be expressed as:

$$b_{1,j} = \frac{\sum\limits_{i=1}^{n_j} (x_{ij} - \bar{x}_j)(y_{ij} - \bar{y}_j)}{\sum\limits_{i=1}^{n_j} (x_{ij} - \bar{x}_j)^2}$$

and $b_{0,j} = \bar{y}_j - b_{1,j}\bar{x}_j$. With these parameter estimates, fitted values may be calculated.

For each model, the error sum of squares is defined as the sum of squared deviations between the observation and the corresponding fitted values, that is,

$$\text{Error SS} = \sum_{j=1}^{c} \sum_{i=1}^{n_j} (y_{ij} - \hat{y}_{ij})^2.$$

Fitted values are defined to be the expected response with the unknown parameters replaced by their least squares estimates. For example, for the regression model with variable intercept and constant slope the fitted values are $\hat{y}_{ij} = b_{0,j} + b_1 x_{ij}$.

C5_EXMPL

To illustrate, we now consider the Hospital Charges case study introduced in Section 5.3. To streamline the presentation, we initially consider only costs associated with three diagnostic-related groups (DRGs), DRG #209, DRG #391 and DRG #430.

The covariate, x, that we consider is the natural logarithm of the number of discharges. In ideal settings, hospitals with more patients enjoy lower costs due to economies of scale. In non-ideal settings, hospitals may not have excess capacity and thus, hospitals with more patients have higher costs. One purpose of this analysis is to investigate the relationship between hospital costs and hospital utilization.

Recall that our measure of hospital charges is the logarithm of costs per discharge (y). The scatter plot in Figure 5.8 gives a preliminary idea of the relationship between y and x. Here, we see the unusual point in the lower left hand part of the plot, corresponding to an observation with a small number of patients discharged. We also note what appears to be a negative relationship between y and x.

The negative relationship between y and x suggested by Figure 5.8 is misleading and is induced by an *omitted variable,* the category of the cost (DRG). To see the joint effect of the categorical variable DRG and the continuous variable log discharges x, in Figure 5.9 is a scatter plot of y versus x where the plotting symbols are codes for the level of the categorical variable. From this plot, we see that the level of cost varies by level of the factor DRG. Moreover, for each level of DRG, the slope between y and x is either zero or positive. The slopes are not negative, as suggested by the scatter plot in Figure 5.8.

The misleading results produced by omitting categorical variables is sometimes referred to as a problem of *aggregation of data.* The idea here is that we should be analyzing the data at the DRG level as in Figure 5.9. When we omit this factor and consider all levels of DRG simultaneously as in Figure 5.8, we look at the less complex, more "aggregate" levels of the data. As we have seen in this example, this may produce misleading results.

Each of the five models defined in Table 5.13 was fit to this subset of the Hospital case study. The summary statistics are in Table 5.14 For this data set, there are $n = 79$ observations and $c = 3$ levels of the DRG factor. For each

The scatter plot in Figure 5.8 suggests a mild negative relationship between y and x. However, when we introduce the factor effect in Figure 5.9, we get a positive relationship between y and x.

The misleading results produced by omitting categorical variables is sometimes referred to as a probiem of aggregation of data.

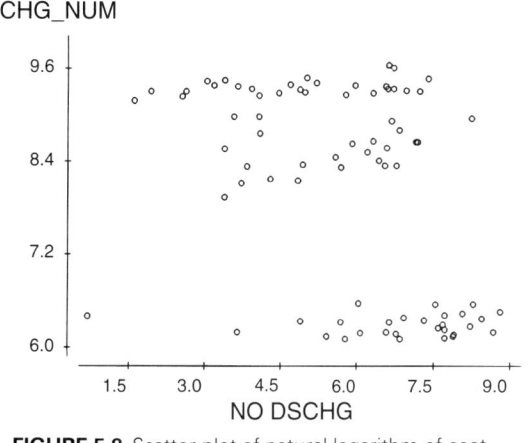

FIGURE 5.8 Scatter plot of natural logarithm of cost per discharge versus natural logarithm of the number of discharges.

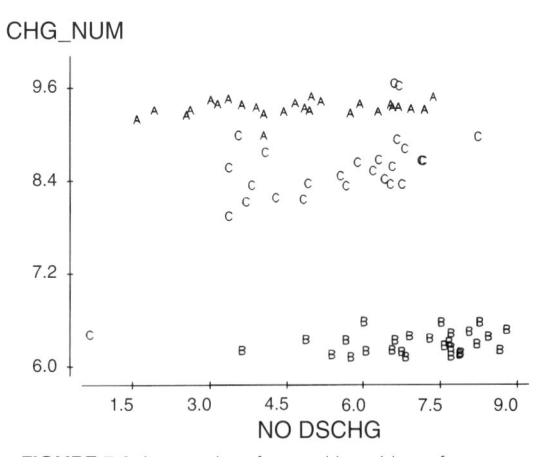

FIGURE 5.9 Letter plot of natural logarithm of cost per discharge versus natural logarithm of the number of discharges by DRG. Here, A is for DRG #209, B is for DRG #391 and C is for DRG #430.

TABLE 5.14 Degrees of Freedom and Error Sum of Squares of Several Models to Represent One Factor and One Covariate for the DRG Example

Model description	Model degrees of freedom	Error degrees of freedom	Error Sum of Squares	Coefficient of determination (%)	Error Mean Square
One factor ANOVA	2	76	9.396	93.3	0.124
Regression with constant intercept and slope	1	77	115.059	18.2	1.222
Regression with variable intercept and constant slope	3	75	7.482	94.7	0.100
Regression with constant intercept and variable slope	3	75	14.048	90.0	0.187
Regression with variable intercept and slope	5	73	5.458	96.1	0.075

model, the model degrees of freedom is the number of model parameters minus one and the error degrees of freedom is the number of observations minus the number of model parameters. The error sum of squares has already been defined. The coefficient of determination is one minus the ratio of the error sum of squares to the total of squares and the error mean square is the error sum of squares divided by the error degrees of freedom.

Using indicator variables, each of the models in Table 5.13 can be written in a regression format. Thus, we may interpret the summary statistics in Table 5.14 using the same principles that we introduced in the regression context, in Chapter 4. For example, when selecting the best model, we interpret the coefficient of determination, R^2, to be the proportion of variability explained by the model. Thus, we look for models with a high R^2. However, an algebraic fact shows that R^2 can always be increased by adding a variable to the models. The error mean square, Error MS, compensates for this. The Error MS $= s^2$ is our estimate of overall variability in the model that we would like to be as small as possible. Thus, we look for models with low Error MS.

As we have seen in Section 4.6, when a model can be written as a subset of another, larger model, we have formal testing procedures available to decide which model is more appropriate. That is, we can examine entire portions of the model to see if they should be included in our model specification. Recall that, when examining portions of a model, we call the larger model under consideration the *full* model. Thus, denote (Error SS)$_{full}$ and $(df)_{full}$ to be the error sum of squares and error degrees of freedom calculated using this model. The subset of this model under consideration is called the *reduced* model. Similarly, denote (Error SS)$_{reduced}$ and $(df)_{reduced}$ to be the error sum of squares and error degrees of freedom calculated using this model. Because the reduced model is a subset of the full model, we know that both the error sum of squares and the degrees of freedom are larger for the reduced model. We examine the test statistic

$$F\text{-ratio} = \frac{\dfrac{(\text{Error SS})_{reduced} - (\text{Error SS})_{full}}{(df)_{reduced} - (df)_{full}}}{\dfrac{(\text{Error SS})_{full}}{(df)_{full}}}$$

to see if the decrease in the error sum of squares is significant. We reject the null hypothesis H_0: Reduced Model is valid in favor of the alternative hypothesis H_a: Full Model is valid if $F\text{-ratio} > F\text{-value}$, where the F-value is a specified percentile from an F-distribution with $df_1 = (df)_{reduced} - (df)_{full}$ and $df_2 = (df)_{full}$.

To illustrate this testing procedure with our DRG example, consider the summary statistics for several models presented in Table 5.14. From this table and the associated scatter plots, it seems clear that the DRG factor is important. Further, a t-test, not presented here, shows that the covariate x is important. Thus, let's compare the full model $E\ y_{ij} = \beta_{0,j} + \beta_{1,j}x$ to the reduced model $E\ y_{ij} = \beta_{0,j} + \beta_1 x$. In other words, is there a different slope for each DRG?

To this end, from Table 5.14, for the regression model with variable intercept and slope, we have $(\text{Error SS})_{full} = 5.458$ and $(df)_{full} = 73$. For the regression model with variable intercept and constant slope, we have $(\text{Error SS})_{reduced} = 7.482$ and $(df)_{reduced} = 75$. Thus, our test statistic is

$$F\text{-ratio} = \frac{\dfrac{7.482 - 5.458}{75 - 73}}{\dfrac{5.458}{73}} = 13.535.$$

The 95th percentile from an F-distribution with $df_1 = (df)_{reduced} - (df)_{full} = 75 - 73 = 2$ and $df_2 = (df)_{full} = 73$ is approximately 3.13. Thus, this test leads us to reject the null hypothesis and declare the alternative, the regression model with variable intercept and variable slope, to be valid. (Using the data set available with the book, the reader may find it interesting to perform this test after omitting the outlying point noted previously.)

General Linear Model

In Section 5.2, we saw that we use only $c - 1$ indicator variables to represent a categorical variable with c levels. Similarly, in Section 5.3 we saw that the one factor ANOVA model could be expressed as a regression model with c indicator variables. However, if we had attempted to estimate the model in equation (5.2), the method of least squares would not have arrived at a unique set of regression coefficient estimates. The reason is that, in equation (5.2), each explanatory variable can be expressed as a linear combination of the others. For example, observe that $x_c = 1 - (x_1 + x_2 + \ldots + x_{c-1})$.

In the general linear model, we allow for the fact that some explanatory variables may be a linear combination of the others. This is not allowed in the general regression model.

The fact that parameter estimates are not unique is a drawback, but not an overwhelming one. In fact, we now introduce the *general linear model*,

$$y = \beta_0 + \beta_1 x_1 + \ldots + \beta_k x_k + e, \qquad (5.15)$$

where $\{e_i\}$ is a random sample from an unknown population with mean zero. We follow standard terminology and view the linear regression model as a special case of the general linear model. To distinguish the two sets of models, we assume that the explanatory variables are not linear combinations of one another in the linear regression model context. This restriction is not made in the general linear model case. To illustrate, the models in equations (5.2) and (5.13) are examples of general linear models that are not regression models.

In the general linear model, although parameter estimates may not be unique, fitted values are unique.

In the linear regression model case, the assumption that the explanatory variables are not linear combinations of one another means that we can compute unique estimates of the regression coefficients using the method of least squares. In the general linear model case, the parameter estimates need not be unique. However, an important feature of the general linear model is that the resulting fitted values turn out to be unique.

Specifically, suppose that we are considering the model in equation (5.15) and, using the method of least squares, our regression coefficient estimates are b_0^o, b_1^o, ..., b_k^o. This set of regression coefficients estimates minimizes our error sum of squares, but there are other sets of coefficients that also minimize the error sum of squares. The fitted values are computed as $\hat{y}_i = b_0^o + b_1^o x_{i1} + \ldots + b_k^o x_{ik}$. It can be shown that the resulting fitted values are unique, in the sense that any set of coefficients that minimize the error sum of squares produce the same fitted values.

The advantage of the regression model context is that we get unique parameter estimates. The advantage of the general linear model context is that we need not worry about the type of restrictions to impose on the parameters.

Thus, for a set of data and a specified general linear model, fitted values are unique. Because residuals are computed as observed responses minus fitted values, we have that the residuals are unique. Because residuals are unique, we have the error sums of squares are unique. Thus, it seems reasonable, and is true, that we can use the general test of hypotheses described in Section 4.6 to decide whether collections of explanatory variables are important.

To summarize, for general linear models, parameter estimates are not unique and thus not meaningful. An important part of regression models is the interpretation of regression coefficients. This interpretation is not necessarily available in the general linear model context. However, for general linear models, we may still discuss the importance of an individual variable or collection of variables through partial F-tests. Further, fitted values, and the corresponding exercise of prediction, works in the general linear model context. The advantage of the general linear model context is that we need not worry about the type of restrictions to impose on the parameters. Although not the subject of this text, this advantage is particularly important in complicated experimental designs used in the life sciences. Searle (1987) is one reference for these designs and for further details of the general linear model. The reader will find that general linear model estimation routines are widely available in statistical software packages available on the market today.

General linear model estimation routines in statistical software packages are widely available on the market today.

5.6 SUMMARY

Chapter 4 introduced the multiple linear regression model, showed how to estimate the model parameters, and provided basic inference results. Chapter 5 extends this introduction by showing how to use categorical independent variables in the regression context. Section 5.2 directly extended Section 4.5 by showing how to use indicator variables to represent categorical variables in the regression context.

An important theme of this chapter is that traditional ANOVA models can be expressed using the regression model. To illustrate this theme, in Section 5.3 we considered the ANOVA models using only one factor. Many of the details concerning analysis of data, the assumptions of the model and some of the inferences that can be made using the model were presented. Further, the link between the ANOVA and regressions set-ups were constructed in detail. By showing that ANOVA models are a special case of the regression set-up, no new theory was needed to represent ANOVA models. In Section 5.4 we considered the ANOVA model using two factors. Here, the treatment was briefer than in Section 5.3, with only the important highlights underscored. The focus was mainly on the different ways that one can combine two categorical variables. We followed the same pattern as in Chapter 4: we first introduced additive models and then added an additional level of complexity, the interaction terms. In Section 5.5 we introduced an extension called the *general linear model*. The general linear model encompasses not only categorical variables, but also continuous variables and combinations of the two types of variables. In this section, we presented an important special case, combining one categorical and one continuous variable.

As in Chapter 4, in Chapter 5 only passing references are made to issues of model selection. We take up this important topic in Chapter 6.

KEY WORDS, PHRASES AND SYMBOLS

After reading this chapter, you should be able to define each of the following important terms, phrases and symbols in your own words. If not, go to the page indicated and review the definition.

categorical variable, 211
indicator variable, 211
factor, 211
ANOVA (analysis of variance) model, 211
c, 212
box plot, 213
y_{ij}, 217
n_j, 217

level of a factor, 217
one way classification, 217
one way model, 217
μ_j, 219
Factor Sum of Squares, 219
τ_j, 224
treatment, 224

overparameterize, 224
y_{ijk}, 226
I, K, 226
$\bar{y}_{.j.}, \bar{y}_{i..}, \bar{y}_{..k}$, 226
additive two factor model, 226
β_i, 226
balanced, 226
$\hat{\mu}, \hat{\beta}_i, \hat{\tau}_j$, 227

interaction two factor model, 230
μ_{ij}, 230
$(\beta\tau)_{ij}$, 230
general linear model, 234
covariate, 234
omitted variable, 237
aggregation of data, 237

CHAPTER 5 EXERCISES

End-of-Chapter Exercises

C5_FILE

5.1 There is a widespread belief that, in the United States, parties have become increasingly willing to go to the judicial system to settle disputes. This is particularly true in the insurance industry, an industry designed to spread risk among individuals who are subject to unfortunate events that threaten their livelihoods. Litigation in the insurance industry arises from two types of disagreement among parties, breach of faith and tort. A breach of faith is a failure by a party to the contract to perform according to its terms. This type of dispute is essentially confined to issues of facts including the nature of the duties and the actions of each party. A tort action is a civil wrong, other than breach of contract, for which the court will provide a remedy in the form of action for damages. A civil wrong may include malice, wantonness oppression or capricious behavior by a party. Generally, much larger damages can be collected for tort actions because the award may be large enough to "sting" the guilty party. Because large insurance companies are viewed as having "deep pockets," these awards can be quite large indeed.

  The data that we consider is the number of FILINGS of tort actions against insurance companies (y). Here, for each of six years (TIME), the data was obtained from 19 STATEs. Thus, there are $6 \times 19 = 114$ observations available.

a. Suppose that you are interested in investigating the effect of TIME on the number of FILINGS and are willing to omit the effect of the STATE variable, for the moment. You run a one factor ANOVA (one way classification) model on FILINGS using the TIME factor. Write down the model and the null and alternative hypotheses that you want to test.

b. Complete the ANOVA table. (Table E5.1.)

TABLE E5.1

Source	Sum of Squares	*df*	Mean Square	*F*-ratio
Regression	25,383			
Error	2,096,953			
Total	2,122,336			

Source: An Empirical Study of the Effects of Tort Reforms on the Rate of Tort Filings, Unpublished Ph.D. Dissertation, Han-Duck Lee, University of Wisconsin-Madison.

c. Perform the *F*-test to decide whether there is a year effect.

d. You are interested in the theory that some states may have systems, or simply precedence, or both that encourage litigation. Suppose that you decide to test this idea by examining a one factor ANOVA (one way classification) and model on FIL-

INGS using the STATE factor. Use the Minitab output below to say whether there is an important difference among states.

e. Use the model and data output referred to part (d) to provide a point estimate and a 95% confidence interval for the expected number of FILINGS in the 19th state.

```
                MINITAB output for one way analysis of variance

ANALYSIS OF VARIANCE ON FILINGS
SOURCE          DF        SS        MS        F         P
STATE           18    1847916    102662     35.54     0.000
ERROR           95     274420      2889
TOTAL          113    2122336
                                          INDIVIDUAL 95 PCT CI'S FOR MEAN
                                          BASED ON POOLED STDEV
LEVEL           N       MEAN      STDEV   --------+---------+---------+-------
  1             6      313.95    118.65                  (- * -)
  2             6      384.20    102.57                    (- * -)
  3             6      450.38     43.75                       (-- * -)
  4             6      145.20     26.83        (- * -)
  5             6      273.85     18.31                 (- * -)
  6             6      160.68      3.63       (- * -)
  7             6      175.08     27.20       (- * -)
  8             6      174.27      7.55       (- * -)
  9             6      164.98     14.37       (- * -)
 10             6      275.35     30.35                 (- * -)
 11             6      312.35     47.20                  (-- * -)
 12             6      210.62     15.38      (-- * -)
 13             6      632.90     86.04                                (-- * -)
 14             6      217.23     65.03              (- * -)
 15             6       82.23      5.33    (- * -)
 16             6      250.93     25.23                (-- * -)
 17             6      224.75     11.42              (- * -)
 18             6       91.77     29.99    (-- * -)
 19             6      240.50     97.92                (- * -)
                                          --------+---------+---------+-------
POOLED STDEV =          53.75               200       400       600
```

---

f. Figure E5.1 is a plot of observed FILINGS versus FILINGS fit under the model described in part (d). Describe what we can learn from this plot. Is the positive slope unusual, and why or why not?

g. Suppose that you wish to fit a model using both TIME and STATE factors to explain the response FILINGS. Write down the theoretical model, be sure to label all parameters and assumptions that you use.

h. Use the model that you described in part (g) and the following ANOVA table to say whether each of TIME and STATE are important.

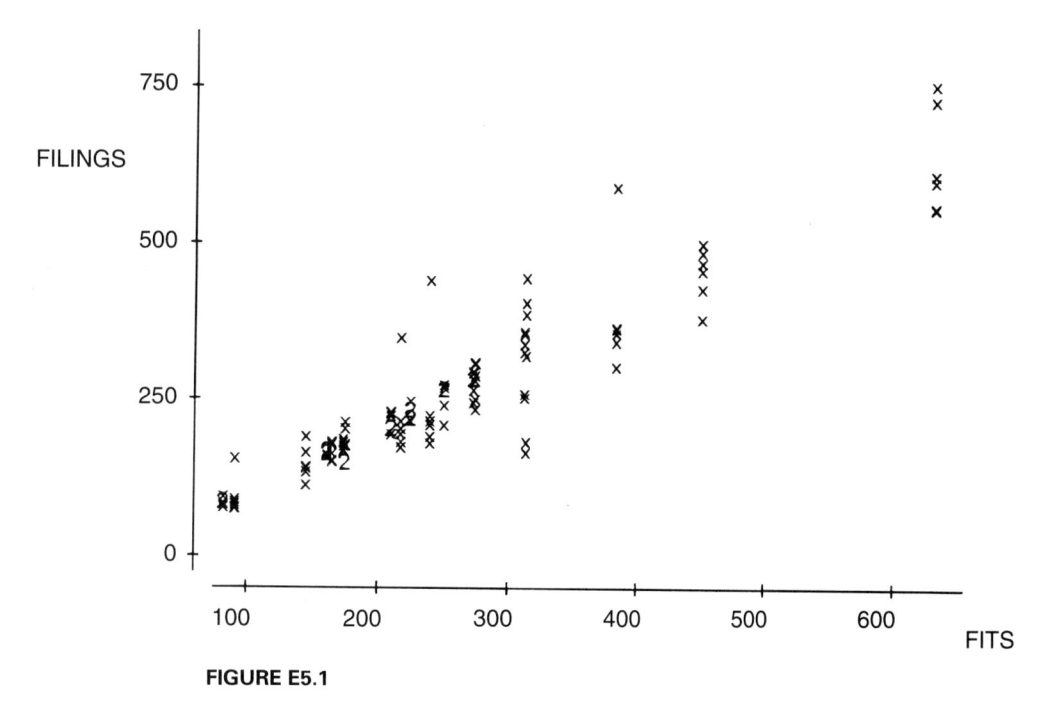

FIGURE E5.1

MINITAB output for two way analysis of variance

ANALYSIS OF VARIANCE FILINGS

SOURCE	DF	SS	MS
TIME	5	25383	5077
STATE	18	1847916	102662
ERROR	90	249037	2767
TOTAL	113	2122336	

C5_CARPR

5.2 Refer to Example 5.1

Motor Trend's 1993 *New Car Buyer's Guide* provides information on 173 new cars, including the price and the type of car. Here, we consider LN_PRICE, the natural logarithm of the car price, and CLASS_CD, the car class. The variable CLASS_CD is categorical, where 0 means convertible, 1 means coupe, 2 means hatchback, 4 means sedan and 5 means mini-van. The computer output that follows fits the model using LN_PRICE as the dependent variable and CLASS_CD as the categorical variable in a one factor model.

  a. Using the one factor estimated model:
     i. What is the point estimate of the price of a new convertible, in natural loga-
        rithmic units?
     ii. Determine the corresponding 95% confidence interval of the price of a new
        convertible, in natural logarithmic units.
     iii. Convert the 95% confidence interval of the price of a new convertible that you
        determined in part (ii) to dollars.
  b. Is CLASS_CD, the car class, an important determinant of the logarithm of price?
    Perform a test of hypothesis to respond to this question. State your null hypothe-
    sis, alternative hypothesis and all components of the decision-making rule. Use a
    5% level of significance.
  c. i. Write down a regression model, using indicator variables, corresponding to
        the one factor model. Include the convertible in this regression. Further, restrict
        the number of variables so that parameter estimates are unique.
     ii. For your regression model, provide the least squares estimate of the parame-
        ter corresponding to the convertible indicator variable.

MINITAB computer output for the car pricing question

ANALYSIS OF VARIANCE ON LN-PRICE

SOURCE	DF	SS	MS	F	P
CLASS-CD	4	10.169	2.542	8.22	0.000
ERROR	168	51.938	0.309		
TOTAL	172	62.107			

```
                                    INDIVIDUAL 95 PCT CI'S FOR MEAN
                                    BASED ON POOLED STDEV
LEVEL    N      MEAN     STDEV    --------+---------+---------+-------
   0    10    10.458     0.774                        (------*------)
   1    46     9.888     0.665                    (--*--)
   2    19     9.293     0.469    (----*----)
   4    79     9.829     0.528                  (--*-)
   5    19     9.632     0.230          (----*----)
                                    --------+---------+---------+-------
POOLED STDEV =     0.556              9.50     10.00     10.50
```

C2_HOSP

5.3 Managing health care costs was an important objective of the Clinton Administration.
Suppose that you are the risk manager for a large corporation and are trying to understand the cost of one aspect of health care, hospital costs. To get a handle on the
variability of costs, you decide to look at a small, homogeneous group of claims. You
decide to look at the charges for female patients, aged 30–49 who were admitted to the
hospital for circulatory disorders. The data on the computer output that follows displays the distribution of 1989 charges for 33 patients at a Wisconsin hospital.

In addition to the total hospital charges, you also have information on the several categorical variables available at the time of admission to the hospital. These include:

'TYP', the admission type, 1 if emergency, 2 if urgent and 3 if elective.

'SRC', the admission source, 2 if referral, 4 if transfer and 7 if emergency room.

'PAY', the type of payment, 4 if private insurance and 5 if self pay.

a. A one-way analysis of variance, using TYP as the factor, was run. The computer follows. Using this model, decide whether or not the admission type is an important factor in determining hospital charges. State your null hypothesis, alternative hypothesis and all components of the decision-making rule. Use a 5% level of significance.

b. Consider the one-way analysis of variance, using TYP as the factor. Using this model:

i. Provide a point estimate of hospital charges for an emergency room type of admission.

ii. Provide a 95% confidence interval for your point estimate in part (i).

c. A regression model using indicator variables for two levels of TYP, two levels of SRC and one level of PAY, was run. The computer output follows.

i. Explain why one level of each factor was omitted in the regression run.

ii. Compare the low levels of the *t*-ratios (for testing the importance of individual regression coefficients) and the level of the *F*-ratio (for testing model adequacy). Describe the seeming inconsistency, and provide an explanation for this inconsistency.

d. i. Write down the one-way analysis of variance model using regression notation.

ii. Use the output from the one-way analysis of variance model and the regression model using five indicator variables to test the significance of the source of admission and payment type. State your null hypothesis, alternative hypothesis and all components of the decision-making rule. Use a 5% level of significance.

MINITAB computer output for hospital cost question

Dotplot of the Cost Variable

```
                . .
                . .
            .   . .
         . . . . .    .       .       .
         . . . . . . . .    . .  . .              . .  .                  .
     +---------+---------+---------+---------+---------+---------+------COST
   1200      2400      3600      4800      6000      7200
```

Table of Summary Statistics for Hospital Costs

	N	MEAN	MEDIAN	STDEV	MIN	MAX	Q1	Q3
COST	33	2955	2315	1481	1642	7787	2094	3308

```
                  Table of Frequency Counts by Categorical Variables
        TYP     COUNT     SRC     COUNT     PAY     COUNT
         1         5       2         2        4       29
         2         6       4        24        5        4
         3        22       7         7       N=       33
        N=        33      N=        33
```

Analysis of Variance Using One Factor

ANALYSIS OF VARIANCE ON COST

SOURCE	DF	SS	MS	F	P
TYP	2	17611384	8805692	5.02	0.013
ERROR	30	52580372	1752679		
TOTAL	32	70191752			

```
                                       INDIVIDUAL 95 PCT CI'S FOR MEAN
                                       BASED ON POOLED STDEV
LEVEL       N      MEAN     STDEV     --+---------+---------+---------+----
  1         5      3505      1318         (-----------*-----------)
  2         6      4297      1826            (----------*----------)
  3        22      2465      1174     (-----*----)
                                      --+---------+---------+---------+----
POOLED STDEV =    blank              2000      3000      4000      5000
```

Regression Using Five Indicator Variables

The regression equation is

COST = 3989 + 331 TYP1 + 613 TYP2 + 1674 SRC2 - 5521 SRC4 - 1019 PAY4

Predictor	Coef	Stdev	t-ratio	P
Constant	3989	1498	2.66	0.013
TYP1	331	1343	0.25	0.807
TYP2	613.3	885.2	0.69	0.494
SRC2	1674	1500	1.12	0.274
SRC4	-552	1197	-0.46	0.648
PAY4	-1018.6	903.9	-1.13	0.270

s = 1197   R-sq = 44.95%   R-sq (adj) = 34.6%

Analysis of Variance

SOURCE	DF	SS	MS	F	P
Regression	5	31485984	6297197	4.39	0.005
Error	27	38705772	1433547		
Total	32	70191760			

C5_HOSP

5.4 Refer to Section 5.3

    a. A regression model was estimated using NO DSCHG and NUM BEDS to predict CHG_NUM. The estimated regression equation is

$$\text{CHG\_NUM} = \underset{(223.5)}{2903} - \underset{(0.01492)}{0.712 \text{ NO DSCHG}} + \underset{(0.09514)}{0.528 \text{ NUM BEDS}}$$

    std errors

For this equation, the coefficient of determination was $R^2 = 7.0\%$ and $n = 526$. Calculate the F-ratio that would be used for determining the validity of the model.

b. It was determined that the standard deviation of CHG_NUM is $s_y = 2,796$. Using the estimated regression model in part (a), calculate the resulting square root of the mean square error, s. Is this estimate smaller than s_y? Interpret your result.

c. Interpret the regression coefficients associated with the NO DSCHG and NUM BEDS variables in the final regression model. In your interpretation, be sure to discuss:

   i. the signs of each coefficient and

   ii. partial slope.

Regression fits using two continuous explanatory variables
and 19 indicator variables for
healthcare costs in the state of wisconsin

FINAL REGRESSION MODEL

Explanatory Variable	Coefficient	Standard Error	t-ratios
Constant	1705.1	250.8	6.80
NO DSCHG	-0.03800	0.08509	-0.45
NUM BEDS	0.34684	0.04428	7.83
DRG14	3251.7	333.8	9.74
DRG89	2047.5	333.8	6.13
DRG112	5459.3	337.2	16.19
DRG125	664.2	344.5	1.93
DRG127	1803.5	333.3	5.41
DRG140	53.1	330.9	0.16
DRG143	-406.1	331.3	-1.23
DRG182	361.0	330.6	1.09
DRG183	-649.8	331.0	-1.96
DRG209	8844.1	333.7	26.50
DRG215	2963.4	334.5	8.86
DRG243	-230.4	330.4	-0.70
DRG359	1118.0	330.7	3.38
DRG371	959.7	330.5	2.90
DRG373	-1003.7	349.1	-2.87
DRG390	-1633.2	330.7	-4.94
DRG391	-1812.1	353.6	-5.12
DRG410	365.7	337.4	1.08
DRG430	3289.9	330.3	9.96

ANOVA TABLE

Source	Sum of Squares	df	Mean Square
Regression	3,375,098,112	211	60,718,960
Error	727,910,656	504	1,444,267
Total	4,103,008,768	525	

The regression fit also yields $s = 1202$, $R^2 = 82.3\%$ and $R_a^2 = 81.5\%$

5.5 One of the major sources of revenue of local municipalities are property taxes, collected from commercial organizations and private homeowners. For an individual homeowner, these taxes are based on the value of the home and property, a value that is assessed by representatives of the municipality. Homeowners are thus concerned with the assessed value of their homes and, in particular, want to make sure that their assessed values are not out of line with others in their community.

In Table E5.5a are data for averaged assessed values for 89 neighborhoods in 11 areas of Madison, Wisconsin. Data are available for 1991 and 1992 assessed values, and, for each neighborhood, the assessed values are averages of single-family residential properties. The 11 AREAs are: 1 = far west, 2 = southwest, 3 = near west, 4 = west central, 5 = near south, 6 = far south, 7 = east central, 8 = near east, 9 = far east, 10 = northeast and 11 = near north. The data appeared in the April 10, 1992 issue of the *Wisconsin State Journal.*

The following data are analyzed in hundreds of dollars.

a. Is AREA an important factor in terms of the 1992 assessment? A regression model was fit using ASSESS92 as the dependent variable and AREA as a categorical independent variable.

TABLE E5.5a   Listing of Assessed Values by Neighborhood Average

Neighborhood	Assess 91	Assess 92	Area	Neighborhood	Assess 91	Assess 92	Area
Spring Harbor-Indian Hills	92,100	101,000	1	Lakeshore-Spring Harbor	198,800	198,600	1
Faircrest	118,900	137,700	1	Oakbridge	100,900	104,500	1
Mendota Beach Heights-Old Middleton Road	71,800	75,100	1	Wexford Village-Woodland Hills	153,600	167,200	1
Highlands	303,800	332,300	1	Wexford Village	129,500	138,700	1
Parkwood Hills	159,400	170,900	1	Meadowood	77,800	83,400	2
Walnut Grove/Sauk Creek	151,600	161,300	1	Orchard Ridge	99,700	107,000	2
Glen Oak Hills-Crestwood	73,000	78,200	1	Muir Field West	98,200	106,200	2
Camelot-Thorstrand-Skyline	139,200	146,700	1	Green Tree	110,000	116,800	2
				High Point Estates	205,000	285,000	2

(Continued)

TABLE E5.5a *(continued)*

Neighborhood	Assess 91	Assess 92	Area	Neighborhood	Assess 91	Assess 92	Area
Meadowood West	82,900	89,100	2	Arbor Hills-South Beltline	134,700	139,900	6
Heather Downs-Park Ridge Heights	82,900	88,400	2	Rimrock Heights-Moorland Road	70,700	76,500	6
Putnam-McKee	91,200	98,200	2	Lapham School-Breese Stevens (Square)	55,700	59,100	7
Valhalla Valley/Highland Village	96,300	104,200	2	Wil-Mar	47,700	54,500	7
Hill Farms	107,600	116,100	3	Tenney Park	65,900	71,300	7
Segoe-Mineral Point Road (Lincoln Hills)	77,500	83,200	3	Orton Park	72,400	91,800	7
				East High	51,700	55,100	7
Nakoma	136,000	150,500	3	Atwood-Winnebago	51,400	55,200	7
Westmorland	82,600	87,800	3	Fair Oaks	46,000	48,000	7
Midvale Heights-Tokay	78,500	85,100	3	North Gate-Aberg Avenue	47,700	50,600	7
Hammersley Road-West Beltline	76,100	81,400	3	Elmside-Oakridge	75,300	80,900	7
				Lakeshore-Near East	214,200	214,900	7
Midvale Heights	84,200	90,900	3	Highwood-Glendale	75,800	81,400	8
Odana-Westgate	104,400	110,800	3	Glendale	68,000	73,000	8
Midvale School-Westmorland	79,500	86,400	3	Lake Edge	61,000	65,300	8
				Olbrich	49,700	54,500	8
Findlay Park-Quarrytown	68,000	72,800	3	Eastmorland	59,100	62,800	8
Midvale Heights-Odana	87,500	93,800	3	Olbrich Park-Cottage Grove Road	54,400	58,400	8
Sunset Hills	148,500	157,400	3	East Broadway	59,700	65,200	9
West Beltline-Seminole Highway	57,900	63,600	3	Acewood	72,600	77,800	9
Sunset Village-Hilldale	75,100	80,400	3	Buckeye-Droster	74,300	79,700	9
Sunset Village	85,200	92,100	3	Rolling Meadows	71,200	76,200	9
Sunset Woods-Forest Hills	78,500	85,100	3	Mira Loma-Sunrise Meadows	84,400	90,600	9
Dudgeon-Monroe	76,300	82,000	4	Milwaukee Street I-90-94	76,400	83,000	9
Westlawn-Randall School (West High)	97,700	106,100	4	Heritage Heights	89,800	95,300	9
				East Washington-Stoughton Road	59,400	62,800	10
Vilas-Longfellow School	71,200	75,500	4	Holiday Bluff	78,200	84,100	10
University Area	63,000	68,000	4	Commercial Avenue-Lexington Park	48,200	50,900	10
Langdon Area	80,200	87,800	4				
Near West (Square)	62,900	65,800	4	Patio Gardens-Lakeview Heights	73,100	78,000	11
Near East (Square)	57,300	62,300	4				
University/Breese Terrace	91,200	97,300	4	Northport-Sherman Village	65,500	69,600	11
West High-Hoyt Park	92,200	102,300	4	Cherokee	128,900	143,100	11
University Heights	141,500	187,300	4	Mendota Hills/North Shore	88,600	93,600	11
Brittingham Park	49,300	52,500	4	Mendota Hospital-Warner Park	66,200	73,100	11
Vilas-Edgewood Avenue	105,100	114,200	4				
Waunona	73,100	74,800	5	Sherman School	50,800	55,100	11
South Madison	54,200	58,400	5	Lake Shore-Woodward	228,900	229,900	11
Burr Oaks-Lincoln School	66,500	68,400	5	Brentwood Village	79,300	83,500	11
Lake Shore-Waunona	188,400	189,000	5				

Source: *Wisconsin State Journal*

    i.   Write down the theoretical regression model.

    ii.   Determine the usefulness of the model using the summary output in the ANOVA table (Table E5.5b).

Summary Statistsics by AREA

AREA	Number	Mean	Standard Deviation
1	12	1510.2	687.4
2	9	1198.1	628.6
3	16	960.9	258.4
4	12	917.6	356.8
5	4	976.5	612.7
6	2	1082.0	448.3
7	10	781.4	501.0
8	6	659.0	98.7
9	7	811.1	98.8
10	3	659.3	168.2
11	8	1032.4	574.6

TABLE E5.5b ANOVA Table

Source	Sum of Squares	df	Mean Square
Regression	5,379,872	10	537,987
Error	16,820,728	78	
Total	22,200,600	88	

The regression fit yields s = 46438.

b. You are interested in investigating the relationship between ASSESS91 and ASSESS92. Tables E5.5c and E5.5d summarize a fit of the relationship using a linear regression model.
   i. Describe the regression relation in terms of the estimated equation and the usefulness of this equation.
   ii. Interpret the estimate of the slope parameter.
   iii. Provide a 95% confidence interval for the slope parameter.

TABLE E5.5c Coefficient Estimates

Explanatory variables	Coefficient	Standard error	t-ratio
Constant	−10.28	21.34	−0.48
ASSESS91	1.09295	0.02075	52.66

TABLE E5.5d ANOVA Table

Source	Sum of Squares	df	Mean Square
Regression	21,525,382	1	21,525,382
Error	675,219	87	7,761
Total	22,200,602	88	

The regression fit also yields $s = 88.10$, $R^2 = 97.0\%$ and $R_a^2 = 96.9\%$.

c. Is AREA an important factor in the growth of assessments from 1991 to 1992? To answer this question, a regression model was fit. Describe the regression relation in terms of the estimated equation and the usefulness of this equation. (See Tables E5.5e and E5.5f.)

TABLE E5.5e Coefficient Estimates

Explanatory variables	Coefficient	Standard error	t-ratio
Constant	−21.97	24.42	−0.90
ASSESS91	1.09960	0.02420	45.45

TABLE E5.5f ANOVA Table

Source	Sum of Squares	df	Mean Square
Regression	21,596,017	11	1,963,274.3
Error	604,585	77	7,852
Total	22,200,602	88	

Appendix

5.6 Use the following steps to derive the least squares estimate for the one factor analysis of variance model.

   a. Show that y is the least squares estimate for the model $y_i = \mu + e_i$. That is, show that

$$\sum_{i=1}^{n} (y_i - m^*)^2 \geq \sum_{i=1}^{n} (y_i - \bar{y})^2$$

   for any number m^*.

   b. Consider the model $y_{ij} = \mu_j + e_{ij}$. Use the results of part (a) to show that $\bar{y}_j$ is the least squares estimate of μ_j.

6

Regression—Selecting a Model

Chapter Objectives

To introduce the art of model selection by focusing on the choice of variables and on the critical examination of individual observations. To illustrate, we will consider:

- understanding measures that influence liquidity, in order to see how easy it is to sell a stock and
- determining a system for understanding salaries of professional football players.

When selecting a regression model, we will encounter the following questions:

- How will you decide which variables to include?
- What do you do with an observation that is "out of line" compared to the rest of your data?
- What about a variable that seems to be giving the same information as another variable?
- Is the regression fit useful when the data do not appear to satisfy the assumptions of the model?

Chapter Outline

6.1 AUTOMATIC VARIABLE SELECTION PROCEDURES

With several explanatory variables, the analyst can generate a large number of linear models and an infinite number of nonlinear ones.

In studies of business and economics, there are generally several variables that may serve as useful predictors of the response. In searching for a suitable representation of the data, there are a large number of models that are based on linear combinations of explanatory variables and virtually an infinite number of models that are based on nonlinear combinations. To search among the models based on linear combinations, several automatic procedures are available to select variables to be included in the model. These automatic procedures are easy to use, and will suggest one or more models that you can explore in further detail.

To illustrate how large the potential number of linear models is, suppose that there are only four variables, x_1, x_2, x_3 and x_4, under consideration for fitting a model to y. Without any consideration of multiplication or other nonlinear combinations of independent variables, how many possible models are there? The answer is 16. (See Table 6.1a.)

TABLE 6.1a Sixteen Possible Models

$\mathrm{E}\,y = \beta_0$			1 model with no independent variables
$\mathrm{E}\,y = \beta_0 + \beta_1\, x_i,$	$i =$	$1, 2, 3, 4$	4 models with one independent variable
$\mathrm{E}\,y = \beta_0 + \beta_1\, x_i + \beta_2\, x_j,$	$(i, j) =$	$(1,2), (1,3), (1,4),$ $(2,3), (2,4), (3,4)$	6 models with two independent variables
$\mathrm{E}\,y = \beta_0 + \beta_1\, x_1 + \beta_2\, x_j$ $+ \beta_3\, x_k,$	$(i, j, k) =$	$(1,2,3), (1,2,4),$ $(1,3,4), (2,3,4)$	4 models with three independent variables
$\mathrm{E}\,y = \beta_0 + \beta_1\, x_1 + \beta_2\, x_2$ $+ \beta_3\, x_3 + \beta_4 x_4$			1 model with all independent variables

Now suppose there were only three independent variables under consideration. Use the same logic to verify that there are eight possible models. How many linear models will there be if there are ten independent variables? The answer is 1,024, which is quite a few. In general, the answer is 2^k, where k is the number of independent variables. For example 2^3 is 8, 2^4 is 16, and so on.

Stepwise regression is an exploratory procedure for bringing explanatory variables into the model.

In any case, for a moderately large number of independent variables, there are many potential models that are based on linear combinations of independent variables. We would like a procedure to search quickly through a number of these potential models to give us more time to think about some of the more interesting aspects of the problem. One procedure for bringing explanatory variables into the model is *stepwise regression*. This procedure employs a series of *t*-tests to check the "significance" of explanatory variables entered into, or deleted from, the model. The following is a description of the basic algorithm.

Stepwise Regression Algorithm

Suppose that the analyst has identified one variable as the response, y, and several potential explanatory variables, $x_1, x_2, \ldots, x_k$.

1. Consider all possible regressions using one explanatory variable. For each of the k regressions, compute the *t*-ratio for the slope. Choose that variable with the largest absolute value of the *t*-ratio. If the *t*-ratio does not exceed a prespecified *t*-value (such as two) in absolute value, then do not choose any variables and halt the procedure.

2. Add a variable to the model from the previous step. The variable to enter is the one that makes the largest significant contribution. To determine the size of contribution, use the absolute value of the variable's *t*-ratio. To enter, the *t*-ratio must exceed a prespecified *t*-value in absolute value.

3. Delete a variable from the model from the previous step. The variable to be removed is the one that makes the smallest contribution. To determine the size of contribution, use the absolute value of the vari-

able's t-ratio. To be removed, the t-ratio must be less than a prespecified t-value in absolute value.

4. Repeat steps #2 and #3 until all possible additions and deletions are performed.

When implementing this routine, some statistical software packages use an F-test in lieu of t-tests. Recall, when only one variable is being considered, that $(t\text{-ratio})^2 = F\text{-ratio}$ and thus these procedures are equivalent.

This procedure does arrive at a candidate model quickly. There are, however, several potential drawbacks in using this search mechanism.

This algorithm is useful in that it quickly searches through a number of candidate models. However, there are several drawbacks:

1. The procedure "snoops" through a large number of models and may fit the data "too well."
2. There is no guarantee that the selected model is the best. The algorithm does not consider models that are based on nonlinear combinations of explanatory variables. It also ignores the presence of outliers and high leverage points.
3. In addition, the algorithm does not even search all 2^k possible linear regressions.
4. The algorithm uses one criterion, a t-ratio, and does not consider other criteria such as s, R^2, R_a^2, and so on.
5. There is a sequence of significance tests involved. Thus, the significance level that determines the t-value is not meaningful.
6. By considering each variable separately, the algorithm does not take into account the joint effect of independent variables.
7. Purely automatic procedures may not take into account an investigator's special knowledge.

Because the procedure is not optimal, there are some simpler variants that are available. An advantage of these variants is that they are easier to explain. These include:

1. Forward selection. Add one variable at a time without trying to delete variables.
2. Backwards selection. Start with the full model and delete one variable at a time without trying to add variables.

Many of the criticisms of the basic stepwise regression algorithm can be addressed with modern computing software that is now widely available. We now consider each drawback, in reverse order. To respond to drawback number seven, many statistical software routines have options for forcing variables into a model equation. In this way, if other evidence indicates that one or more variables should be included in the model, then the investigator can force the inclusion of these variables.

For drawback number six, in the subsection on *suppressor variables* in Section 6.3, we will provide examples of variables that do not have important individual effects but are important when considered jointly. These combinations of variables may not be detected with the basic algorithm but will be detected with the backwards selection algorithm. Becaue the backwards procedure starts with all variables, it will detect, and retain, variables that are jointly important.

When a variable enters a model, s will decrease if the variable's t-ratio exceeds one in absolute value.

Drawback number five is really a suggestion about the way to use stepwise regression. Bendel and Afifi (1977) suggest using a cut-off smaller than you ordinarily might. For example, in lieu of using a t-value = 2, corresponding approximately to a 5% significance level, consider using a t-value $\approx$ 1.645, corresponding approximately to a 10% significance level. In this way, there is less chance of screening out variables that may be important. A lower bound, but still a good choice for exploratory work, is a cut-off as small as t-value = 1. This choice is motivated by an algebraic result: when a variable enters a model, s will decrease if the t-ratio exceeds one in absolute value.

To address drawbacks number three and four, we now introduce the *best regressions* routine. Best regressions is a useful algorithm that is now widely available in statistical software packages. The best regression algorithm searches over all possible combinations of explanatory variables, unlike stepwise regression that adds and deletes one variable at a time. For example, suppose that there are four possible explanatory variables, x_1, x_2, x_3 and x_4, and the user would like to know what is the best two variable model. The best regression algorithm searches over *all* six models of the form $E y = \beta_0 + \beta_1 x_i + \beta_2 x_j$. Typically, a best regression routine recommends one or two models for each p coefficient model, where p is a number that is user specified. Because it has specified the number of coefficients to enter the model, it does not matter which of the criteria we use: R^2, R_a^2 or s.

The best regression algorithm performs its search by a clever use of the algebraic fact that, when a variable is added to the model, the error sum of squares does not increase. Because of this fact, certain combinations of variables included in the model need not be computed. An important drawback of the best regressions algorithm is that it still takes a considerable amount of time when the number of variables considered in the model is large.

Data-snooping occurs when the analyst fits a great number of models to a data set.

Users of regression do not always appreciate the depth of drawback number one, *data-snooping*. Data-snooping occurs when the analyst fits a great number of models to a data set. We will address the problem of data-snooping in the subsection on model validation in Section 6.5. Here, we illustrate the effect of data-snooping in stepwise regression.

Example 6.1: Data-Snooping in Stepwise Regression

The idea of this illustration is due to Rencher and Pun (1980). Consider n = 100 observations and y and 50 explanatory variables, $x_1, x_2, \ldots, x_{50}$. The

C6_STEP

data we consider here were simulated using independent standard normal random variates. Because the variables were simulated independently, we are working under the null hypothesis of no relation between the response and the explanatory variables, that is, $H_0: \beta_1 = \beta_2 = \ldots = \beta_{50} = 0$. Indeed, when the model with all 50 explanatory variables was fit, it turns out that $s = 1.142$, $R^2 = 46.2\%$ and F-ratio = (Regression MS)/(Error MS) = 0.84. Using an F-distribution with $df_1 = 50$ and $df_2 = 49$, the 95th percentile is 1.604. In fact, 0.84 is the 27th percentile of this distribution, indicating that the p-value is 0.73. Thus, as expected, the data are in congruence with H_0.

Next, a stepwise regression with t-value = 2 was performed. Two variables were retained by this procedure, yielding a model with $s = 1.05$, $R^2 = 9.5\%$ and F-ratio = 5.09. For an F-distribution with $df_1 = 2$ and $df_2 = 97$, the 95th percentile F-value = 3.09. This indicates that the two variables are *significant* predictors of y. At first glance, this result is surprising. The data were generated so that y is unrelated to the independent variables. However, because F-ratio > F-value, the F-test indicates that two independent variables are significantly related to y. The reason is that stepwise regression has performed many hypothesis tests on the data. For example, in Step 1, 50 tests were performed to find significant variables. Recall that a 5% level means that we expect to make roughly one mistake in 20. Thus, with 50 tests, we expect to find 50 (0.05) = 2.5 "significant" variables, even under the null hypothesis of no relationship between y and the explanatory variables.

To continue, a stepwise regression with t-value = 1.645 was performed. Six variables were retained by this procedure, yielding a model with $s = 0.99$, $R^2 = 22.9\%$ and F-ratio = 4.61. As before, an F-test indicates a significant relationship between the response and these six explanatory variables.

To summarize, using simulation we constructed a data set so that the explanatory variables have no relationship with the response. However, when using stepwise regression to examine the data, we "found" seemingly significant relationships between the response and certain subsets of the explanatory variables. This example illustrates a general caveat in model selection: when explanatory variables are selected using the data, t-ratios and F-ratios will be too large, thus overstating the importance of variables in the model.

Automatic variable selection procedures can quickly search through several candidate models. However, these procedures ignore nonlinear alternatives as well as the effects of unusual points.

A model suggested by an automatic variable selection procedure should be subject to the same careful diagnostic checking procedures as a model arrived at by any other means.

Stepwise regression and best regressions are examples of *automatic variable selection procedures*. In your modeling work, you will find these procedures to be very useful because they can quickly search through several candidate models. However, these procedures ignore nonlinear alternatives as well as the effect of outliers and high leverage points. The main point of the procedures is to mechanize certain routine tasks. This automatic selection approach can be extended and indeed, there are a number of so-called "expert systems" available in the market. For example, algorithms are available that "automatically" handle unusual points such as outliers and high leverage points. A model suggested by automatic variable selection procedures should be subject to the same careful diagnostic checking procedures as a model arrived at by any other means.

6.2 RESIDUAL ANALYSIS

Patterns in the residuals indicate the presence of additional information that we hope to incorporate into the model.

Recall the role of a residual in the linear regression model. A residual is a response minus the corresponding fitted value under the model. Because the model summarizes the linear effect of several independent variables, we may think of a residual as a response controlled for values of the independent variables. If the model is an adequate representation of the data, then residuals should closely approximate random errors. Random errors are used to represent the natural variation of the model; they represent the result of an unpredictable mechanism. Thus, to the extent that residuals resemble random errors, there should be no discernible patterns in the residuals. Patterns in the residuals indicate the presence of additional information that we hope to incorporate into the model. A lack of patterns in the residuals indicates that the model seems to account for the most important relationships in the data.

There are at least four types of patterns that can be uncovered through the *analysis of residuals.* In this section, we discuss the first two; residuals that are unusual and those that are related to other independent variables. We then introduce the third type, residuals that display a heteroscedastic pattern, in Section 6.6. In our study of longitudinal data models that begins in Chapter 9, we will introduce the fourth type, residuals that display patterns through time.

When examining residuals, it is usually easier to work with a *standardized residual,* a residual that has been rescaled to be dimensionless. As described in our first look at residual analysis in Section 3.5, we generally work with standardized residuals because we achieve some kind of carry-over of experience from one data set to another and may thus focus on relationships of interest. By using standardized residuals, we can train ourselves to look at a variety of residual plots and immediately recognize an unusual point when working in standard units.

There are a number of ways of defining a standardized residual. Using $\hat{e}_i = y_i - \hat{y}_i$ as the ith residual, here are three most commonly used ones:

$$(a)\ \frac{\hat{e}_i}{s}, \quad (b)\ \frac{\hat{e}_i}{s\sqrt{1 - h_{ii}}}, \tag{6.1}$$

and

$$(c)\ \frac{\hat{e}_i}{s_{(i)}\sqrt{1 - h_{ii}}}.$$

Here, h_{ii} is the ith *leverage*. It is calculated based on values of the explanatory variables and will be defined in Section 6.3. Recall that s is the square root of the mean square error (Error MS). Similarly, define $s_{(i)}$ to be the square root of the Error MS when running a regression after having deleted the ith observation.

Now, the first choice of definition of standardized residuals in (a) is simple and is easy to explain. An easy calculation shows that the sample standard deviation of the residuals is approximately s and, indeed, s is often referred to as the residual standard deviation. Thus, it seems reasonable to standardize residuals by dividing by s.

The second choice is presented in (b) and, although more complex, is more precise. Using theory from mathematical statistics, it turns out that the variance of the ith residual is exactly

$$\text{Var}(\hat{e}_i) = \sigma^2(1 - h_{ii}).$$

Note that this variance is smaller than the variance of the true error term, $\text{Var}(e_i) = \sigma^2$. Now, we can replace σ by its estimate, s. Then, this result leads to using the quantity $s(1 - h_{ii})^{1/2}$ as an estimated standard deviation, or standard error, for $\hat{e}_i$. Thus, we define the standard error of $\hat{e}_i$ to be

$$se(\hat{e}_i) = s\sqrt{1 - h_{ii}}.$$

Following the conventions introduced in Section 2.6, in this text we use $\hat{e}_i/se(\hat{e}_i)$ to be our *standardized residual*.

The third choice is a modification of the second and is sometimes termed a *studentized residual*. As noted in Section 3.5 and discussed further in the following, one important use of standardized residuals is to identify unusually large responses. Now, suppose that the ith response is unusually large and that this is reflected through its residual. This unusually large residual will also cause the value of s to be large. Because the large effect appears in both the numerator and denominator, the standardized residual may not detect this unusual response. However, this large response will not inflate $s_{(i)}$ because it is constructed after having deleted the ith observation. Thus, when using studentized residuals we get a better measure of observations that have unusually large residuals. By omitting this observation from the estimate of σ, the size of the observation affects only the numerator $\hat{e}_i$ and not the denominator $s_{(i)}$.

Another advantage of the third choice is that the studentized residuals can be shown to be realizations from a t-distribution with $n - (k + 1)$ degrees of freedom, assuming the errors are drawn from a normal population. This knowledge of the precise distribution allows us to assess the degree of model fit, particularly in small samples. It is this relationship with the "Student's" *t*-distribution that suggests the name "studentized" residuals.

The Role of Residuals

Outliers are observations where the residual from a model fit is unusually large.

One important role of residual analysis is to identify outliers, observations where the residual is unusually large. A good rule of thumb that is used by many statistical packages is that an observation is an outlier if the standardized residual exceeds two in absolute value. To the extent that the distribution of standardized residuals mimics the standard normal curve, we expect about only one in 20 observations, or 5%, to exceed two in absolute value and very few observations to exceed three.

Outliers provide a signal that an observation should be investigated to understand special causes associated with this point. An outlier is an observation that seems unusual with respect to the rest of the data set. It is often the case that the reason for this unusualness may be uncovered after additional investigation. Indeed, this may be the primary purpose of the regression analysis of a data set.

In performance analysis studies, the residual is the primary statistic of interest. The residual is the response, controlled for values of the explanatory variables.

Consider a simple example of so-called *performance analysis.* Suppose we have available a sample of *n* salespeople and are trying to understand each person's second-year sales based on their first-year sales. To a certain extent, we expect that higher first-year sales are associated with higher second-year sales. High sales may be due to a salesperson's natural ability, ambition, good territory and so on. First-year sales may be thought of as a proxy variable that summarizes these factors. We expect variation in sales performance both cross-sectionally and across years. What is interesting is when one salesperson performs unusually well (or poorly) in the second year compared to their first-year performance. Residuals provide a formal mechanism for evaluating second-year sales after controlling for the effects of first-year sales.

Outliers may be handled by ignoring them, deleting them or flagging them with indicator variables.

Outliers are points that are not typical when compared to other observations in the data set. When summarizing the entire data set using regression techniques, there are a number of options available for handling outliers.

1. Include the observation in the usual summary statistics but comment on its effects. An outlier may be large but not so large as to skew the results of the entire analysis. If no special causes for this unusual observation can be determined, then this observation may reflect the variability of the data.

2. Delete this observation from the data set. The observation may be determined to be unrepresentative of the population for which the sample is being used for inference. If this is the case, then there may be little information contained in the observation that can be used to make general statements about the population. This possibility means that we would

omit the observation from the regression summary statistics and discuss it in our report as a separate case.

3. Flag the observation with an indicator variable. If one or several special causes have been identified to explain an outlier, then these causes could be introduced into the modeling procedure formally by introducing a variable to indicate the presence (or absence) of these causes. This approach is similar to point deletion but allows the outlier to be formally included in the model formulation so that, if additional observations arise that are affected by the same special causes, then they can be handled on an automatic basis.

Residuals can be used to help identify additional explanatory variables that may improve the model formulation.

Another important role of residuals analysis is to help identify additional explanatory variables that may be used to improve the formulation of the model. If we have specified the model correctly, then residuals should resemble random errors and contain no discernible patterns. Thus, when comparing residuals to explanatory variables, we do not expect any relationships. If we do detect a relationship, then this suggests the need to control for this additional variable. This can be accomplished by introducing the additional variable into the regression model.

Relationships between residuals and explanatory variables can be quickly established using correlation statistics. However, if an explanatory variable is already included in the regression model, then the correlation between the residuals and an explanatory variable will be zero, by a result from matrix algebra. It is a good idea to reinforce this correlation with a scatter plot. Not only will a scatter plot of residuals versus explanatory variables reinforce graphically the correlation statistic, it will also serve to detect potential nonlinear relationships. For example, the quadratic relationship illustrated in Section 3.5 could only be detected using a scatter plot, not a correlation statistic.

If you detect a relationship between the residuals from a preliminary model fit and an additional explanatory variable, then introducing this additional variable will not always improve your model specification. The reason is that the additional variable may be linearly related to the variables that are already in the model. If you would like a guarantee that adding an additional variable will improve your model, then construct an added variable plot, as described in Section 4.4.

To summarize, after a preliminary model fit, you should:

1. Calculate summary statistics and display the distribution of (standardized) residuals to identify outliers.
2. Calculate the correlation between the (standardized) residuals and additional explanatory variables to search for linear relationships.
3. Create scatter plots between the (standardized) residuals and additional explanatory variables to search for nonlinear relationships.

Case Study: Stock Liquidity

An investor's decision to purchase a stock is generally made with a number of criteria in mind. First, the investor is usually looking for a high expected return. Second, because investors pay a premium for safety of their investment, they expect to earn higher returns for investing in stocks that are riskier. Thus, a second criterion is the riskiness of a stock that can be measured through the variability of the returns. Third, many investors are concerned with how long they are committing their capital to the purchase of a security. Many income stocks, such as utilities, regularly return portions of capital investments in the form of dividends. Other stocks, particularly growth stocks, return nothing until the sale of the security. Here, the philosophy is that the investor is better off reaping long-term profits that are hoped for in growth stocks than the immediate returns afforded by income stocks. Thus, the average length of investment in a security is another criterion. Fourth, investors are concerned with the ability to sell the stock at any time convenient to the investor. We refer to this fourth criterion as the *liquidity* of the stock. The more liquid the stock, the easier it is to sell. To measure the liquidity, in this study we use the number of shares traded on an exchange over a specified period of time (called the VOLUME). We are interested in studying the relationship between the volume and other financial characteristics of a stock.

We begin this study with 126 companies whose options were traded on December 3, 1984. The stock data were obtained from Francis Emory Fitch, Inc. for the period from December 3, 1984 to February 28, 1985. For the trading activity variables, we examine the three months total trading volume (VOLUME), the three months total number of transactions (NTRAN) and the average time between transactions (AVGT). For the firm size variables, we use the opening stock price on January 2, 1985 (PRICE), the number of outstanding shares on December 31, 1984 (SHARE) and the market equity value (VALUE) obtained by taking the product of PRICE and SHARE. Finally, for the financial leverage, we examine the debt-to-equity ratio (DEB_EQ) obtained from the Compustat Industrial Tape and the Moody's manual. The data in SHARE are obtained from the Center for Research in Security Prices (CRSP) monthly tape.

After examining some preliminary summary statistics of the data, three companies were deleted because they either had an unusually large volume or high price. They are Teledyne and Capital Cities Communication, whose prices were more than four times the average price of the remaining companies, and American Telephone and Telegraph, whose total volume was more than seven times the average total volume of the remaining companies. Based on additional investigation, the details of which are not presented here, these companies were deleted because they seemed to represent special circumstances that we would not wish to model. Table 6.1 summarizes the descriptive statistics of the stock liquidity variables based on the remaining 123 companies. For example, from Table 6.1 we see that the average time between

TABLE 6.1 Summary Statistics of the Stock Liquidity Variables

	Mean	Median	Standard deviation	Minimum	Maximum
VOLUME	13.423	11.556	10.632	0.658	64.572
AVGT	5.441	4.284	3.853	0.590	20.772
NTRAN	6436	5071	5310	999	36420
PRICE	38.80	34.37	21.37	9.12	122.37
SHARE	94.7	53.8	115.1	6.7	783.1
VALUE	4.116	2.065	8.157	0.115	75.437
DEB_EQ	2.697	1.105	6.509	0.185	53.628

Legend:	VOLUME:	Total trading volume for the entire three months in million shares.
	AVGT:	Average transaction time interval measured in minutes.
	NTRAN:	Total number of transactions for the three months.
	PRICE:	Stock price at the opening on January 2, 1985 in U.S. dollars.
	SHARE:	Number of shares outstanding on December 31, 1984 in million shares.
	VALUE:	Market value in billion dollars (PRICE × SHARE).
	DEB_EQ:	Debt-to-equity ratio at the end of 1984.

Source: Francis Emory Fitch, Inc., Standard & Poor's Compustat, and University of Chicago's Center for Research on Security Prices.

transactions is about five minutes and this time ranges from a minimum of less than a minute to a maximum of about 20 minutes.

Table 6.2 reports the correlation coefficients and Figure 6.1 provides the corresponding scatterplot matrix. If you have a background in finance, you will find it interesting to note that the financial leverage, measured by DEB_EQ, does not seem to be related to the other variables. From the scatterplot and correlation matrix, we see a strong relationship between VOLUME and the size of the firm as measured by SHARE and VALUE. Further, the three trading activity variables, VOLUME, AVGT and NTRAN, are all highly related to one another.

TABLE 6.2 Correlation Matrix of the Stock Liquidity Variables

	AVGT	NTRAN	PRICE	SHARE	VALUE	DEB_EQ
NTRAN	−0.668					
PRICE	−0.128	0.190				
SHARE	−0.429	0.817	0.177			
VALUE	−0.318	0.760	0.457	0.829		
DEB_EQ	0.094	−0.092	−0.038	−0.077	−0.077	
VOLUME	−0.674	0.913	0.168	0.773	0.702	−0.052

Figure 6.1 shows that the variable AVGT is inversely related to VOLUME and NTRAN is inversely related to AVGT. In fact, it turned out the correlation between the average time between transactions and the reciprocal of the number of transactions was 99.98%! This is not so surprising when one thinks about how AVGT might be calculated. For example, on the New York Stock Exchange, the market is open from 10:00 A.M. to 4:00 P.M. For each stock on a par-

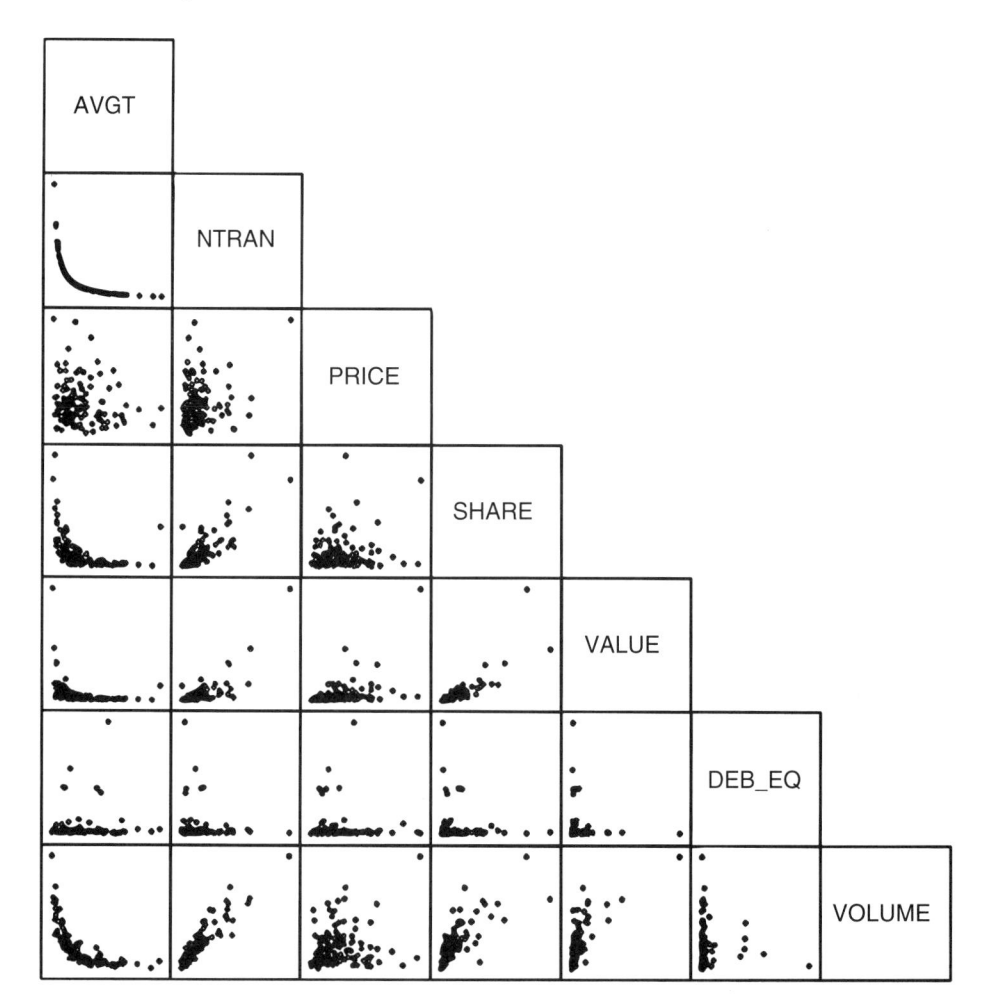

FIGURE 6.1 Scatterplot matrix for stock liquidity variables. The number of transactions variable (NTRAN) appears to be strongly related to the VOLUME of shares traded, and inversely related to AVGT.

ticular day, the average time between transactions times the number of transactions is nearly equal to 360 minutes (=6 hours). Thus, except for rounding errors because transactions are only recorded to the nearest minute, there is a perfect linear relationship between AVGT and the reciprocal of NTRAN.

To begin to understand the liquidity measure VOLUME, we first fit a regression model using NTRAN as an explanatory variable. The fitted regression model is:

$$\widehat{\text{VOLUME}} = 1.65 + 0.00183 \, \text{NTRAN}$$

$$\textit{std errors} \quad (0.0018) \quad (0.000074)$$

with $R^2 = 83.4\%$ and $s = 4.35$. Note that the t-ratio for the slope associated with NTRAN is $t(b_1) = b_1/se(b_1) = 0.00183/0.000074 = 24.7$, indicating that b_1 is about 24.7 standard errors above zero. Residuals were computed using this estimated model. To see if the residuals are related to the other explanatory variables, review Table 6.2a correlations.

TABLE 6.2a   First Table of Correlation

	AVGT	PRICE	SHARE	VALUE	DEB_EQ
RESID	−0.155	−0.017	0.055	0.007	0.078

Table 6.2a correlations between residuals and several explanatory variables. The residuals were created from a regression of VOLUME on NTRAN.

The correlation between the residual from a regression fit and another explanatory variable may indicate that there is some information in the explanatory variable about the response.

The correlation between the residual and AVGT and the scatter plot (not given here) indicates that there may be some information in the variable AVGT in the residual. Thus, it seems sensible to use AVGT directly in the regression model. Remember that we are interpreting the residual as the value of VOLUME having controlled for the effect of NTRAN.

We next fit a regression model using NTRAN and AVGT as explanatory variables. The fitted regression model is:

$$\hat{\text{VOLUME}} = 4.41 - 0.322\,\text{AVGT} + 0.00167\,\text{NTRAN}$$

$$\textit{std errors}\quad (1.30)\qquad (0.135)\qquad\qquad (0.000098)$$

with $R^2 = 84.2\%$ and $s = 4.26$. Based on the t-ratio for AVGT, $t(b_1) = (-0.322)/0.135 = -2.39$, it seems as if AVGT is a useful explanatory variable in the model. Note also that s has decreased, indicating that R_a^2 has increased.

The table (Table 6.2b) of correlations between the model residuals and other potential explanatory variables indicates that there does not seem to be much additional information in the explanatory variables. This is reaffirmed by the corresponding table of scatter plots in Figure 6.2. The histograms in Figure 6.2 suggest that although the distribution of the residuals is fairly symmetric, the distribution of each explanatory variable is skewed. Because of this, transformations of the explanatory variables were explored. Unfortunately, this line of thought provided no real improvements and thus the details are not provided here.

TABLE 6.2b   Second Table of Correlation

	PRICE	SHARE	VALUE	DEB_EQ
RESID	−0.015	0.096	0.071	0.089

Table 6.2b correlations between residuals and several explanatory variables. The residuals were created from a regression of VOLUME on NTRAN and AVGT.

Thus, the firm size variables, although strongly related to volume, are not important determinants when other trading activity variables are entered into the model as explanatory variables. In Section 6.4 we will fit a model of VOLUME without using other trading activity variables as explanatory variables.

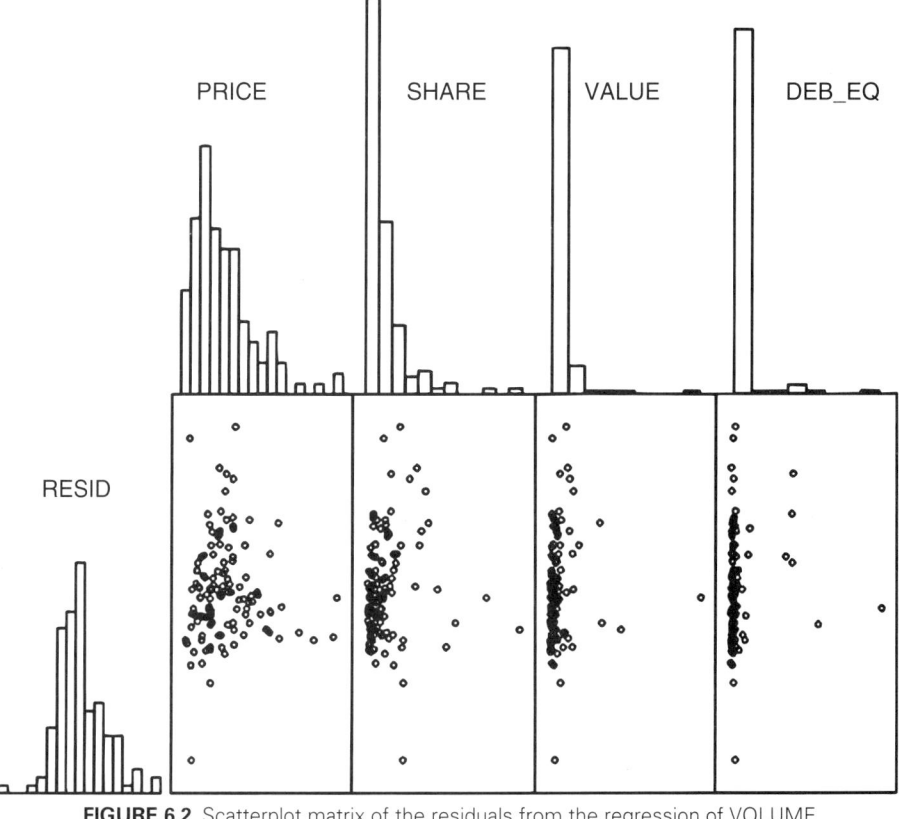

FIGURE 6.2 Scatterplot matrix of the residuals from the regression of VOLUME on NTRAN and AVGT on the vertical axis and the remaining predictor variables on the horizontal axes.

6.3 LEVERAGE

The examination of unusual observations can be decomposed into the analysis of residuals and of high leverage points. In Section 3.5, we saw that a high leverage point is an observation containing an unusual set of explanatory variables. Such a point may turn out to be *influential* because it has a disproportionate effect on the overall regression fit. To illustrate this, an example from

Section 3.5 showed how 1 observation in 20 can reduce the R^2 from 90% to 10% (point C).

The reason for this disproportionate effect is that regression slope estimates can be shown to be weighted averages of slopes, where the weights are determined by (squared Euclidean) distances between explanatory variables. This result is surprising because the regression estimates are defined as quantities that minimize the sum of squared deviations. To illustrate, recall in the case of regression using one variable that the least squares slope estimate is $b_1 = r s_y / s_x$. Using algebra, it can be checked that an alternative expression is

$$b_1 = \frac{\sum_{i=1}^{n} weight_i \; slope_i}{\sum_{i=1}^{n} weight_i}.$$

Here, we have $weight_i = (x_i - \bar{x})^2$ and $slope_i = (y_i - \bar{y})/(x_i - \bar{x})$. That is, the ith slope is the slope between (x_i, y_i) and $(\bar{x}, \bar{y})$.

When there are more than two explanatory variables, it is difficult to determine graphically whether a point is unusual. With only one explanatory variable, it is easy to determine what is "unusual" merely by examining the histogram of the explanatory variable. With more than one variable, determining an unusual point is not as straightforward. Consider the fictitious data set represented in Figure 6.3. The point marked in the upper right hand corner

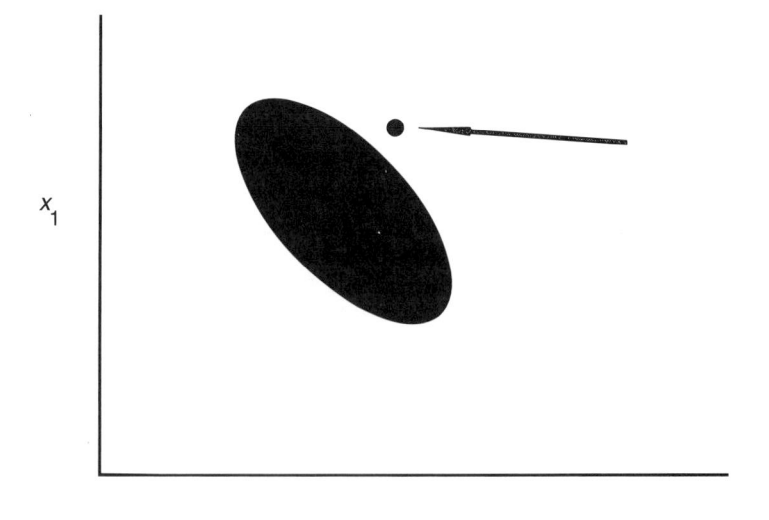

x_1

x_2

FIGURE 6.3 The ellipsoid represents most of the data. The arrow marks an unusual point.

is unusual. However, it is not unusual when examining the histogram of either x_1 or x_2. It is only unusual when the explanatory variables are considered jointly. For two explanatory variables, this is apparent when examining the data graphically. Because it is difficult to examine graphically data having more than two explanatory variables, we resort to the following numerical procedure.

Using matrix algebra, it can be shown that the fitted values can be expressed as a linear combination of responses. Thus, we have

$$\hat{y}_i = h_{i1}y_1 + h_{i2}y_2 + \ldots + h_{ii}y_i + \ldots + h_{in}y_n.$$

The values h_{ij} are calculated using only the values of the explanatory variables. If you are interested, the details of these calculations are in Section 4.7. From this expression, we see that the larger is h_{ii}, the larger is the effect that the ith response (y_i) has on the corresponding fitted value ($\hat{y}_i$). Thus, we call h_{ii} to be the *leverage* for the ith observation. Because the values h_{ii} are calculated based on the explanatory variables, the values of the response variable do not affect the calculation of leverages.

The average leverage equals the number of regression coefficients divided by the number of observations. An observation is called a high leverage point if its leverage exceeds three times the average leverage.

Large leverage values indicate that an observation may exhibit a disproportionate effect on the fit, essentially because it is distant from the other observations (when looking at explanatory variables). How large is large? Some guidelines are available from matrix algebra, where we have that

$$\frac{1}{n} \leq h_{ii} \leq 1$$

and

$$\overline{h} = \frac{1}{n} \sum_{i=1}^{n} h_{ii} = \frac{k+1}{n}.$$

Thus, each leverage is bounded by n^{-1} and one and the average leverage equals the number of regression coefficients divided by the number of observations. From these and related arguments, we use a widely adopted convention and declare an observation to be a *high leverage point* if the leverage exceeds three times the average, that is, if $h_{ii} > 3(k+1)/n$.

The options available for handling influential points are similar to those for handling outliers.

Having identified high leverage points, as with outliers it is important for the analyst to search for special causes that may have produced these unusual points. To illustrate, in Section 3.6 we identified the 1987 market crash as the reason behind the high leverage point. Further, high leverage points may be due to clerical errors in coding the data, which may or may not be easy to rectify. In general, the following options for dealing with high leverage points are similar to those available for dealing with outliers.

1. Include the observation in the summary statistics but comment on its effect. For example, an observation may barely exceed a cut-off and its effect may not be important in the overall analysis.

2. Delete the observation from the data set. Again, the basic rationale for this action is that the observation is deemed not representative of some larger population. An intermediate course of action between (1) and (2) is to present the analysis both with and without the high leverage point. In this way the impact of the point is fully demonstrated and the reader of your analysis may decide which option is more appropriate.

3. Choose another variable to represent the information. In some instances, another explanatory variable will be available to serve as a replacement. For example, in our Chapter 4 example on apartment rents, we used the indicator of two bedrooms variable to replace the square footage variable. Both variables provide information about the size of an apartment. Although an apartment may be unusually large causing it to be a high leverage point, it will only have one or two bedrooms in the sample we examined.

4. Use a nonlinear transformation of an explanatory variable, as described in Section 4.5. To illustrate, with our Stock Liquidity example in Section 6.1, we can transform the debt-to-equity DEB_EQ continuous variable into a variable that indicates the presence of "high" debt-to-equity. For example, we might code DE_IND $= 1$ if DEB_EQ > 5 and DE_IND $= 0$ if DEB_EQ ≤ 5. With this recoding, we still retain information on the financial leverage of a company without allowing large values of DEB_EQ to drive the regression fit.

To reduce the effect of outliers and high leverage points, robust estimation techniques are available.

In addition, some statisticians use "robust" estimation methodologies as an alternative to least squares estimation. The basic idea of these techniques is to reduce the effect of any particular observation. These techniques are useful in reducing the effect of both outliers and high leverage points. This tactic may be viewed as intermediate between one extreme procedure, ignoring the effect of unusual points, and another extreme procedure, giving unusual points full credibility by deleting them from the data set. The word *robust* is meant to suggest that these estimation methodologies are "healthy" even when attacked by an occasional bad observation (a germ). We have seen that this is not true for least squares estimates.

A measure of how unusual a point is that considers both the response and predictor variables is Cook's distance.

Cook's Distance

To quantify how unusual a point is, a measure that considers both the response and explanatory variables is *Cook's distance*. This distance, D_i, is defined as

$$D_i = \frac{\sum_{j=1}^{n} (\hat{y}_j - \hat{y}_{j(i)})^2}{(k+1)s^2}$$

$$= \left(\frac{\hat{e}_i}{se(\hat{e}_i)}\right)^2 \frac{h_{ii}}{(k+1)(1-h_{ii})}.$$

(6.2)

The first expression provides a definition. Here, $\hat{y}_{j(i)}$ is the prediction of the jth observation, computed leaving the ith observation out of the regression fit. To measure the impact of the ith observation, we compare the fitted values with and without the ith observation. Each difference is then squared and summed over all observations to summarize the impact.

After rescaling by $(k+1)s^2$, the second equation provides another interpretation of the distance D_i. The first part, $(\hat{e}_i/se(\hat{e}_i))^2$, is the square of the ith standardized residual. The second part, $h_{ii}/((k+1)(1-h_{ii}))$, is attributable solely to the leverage. Thus, the distance D_i is composed of a measure for outliers times a measure for leverage. In this way, Cook's distance accounts for both the response and explanatory variables.

To get an idea of the expected size of D_i for a point that is not unusual, recall that we expect the squared standardized residuals to be about one and the leverage h_{ii} to be about $(k+1)/n$. Thus, we anticipate that D_i should be about $1/n$. Another rule of thumb is to compare D_i to an F-distribution $df_1 = k+1$ and $df_2 = n - (k+1)$ degrees of freedom. Values of D_i that are large compared to this distribution merit attention.

To illustrate, we return to our outlier Example 3.1 in Section 3.5. In this example, we consider 19 "good," or base, points plus each of the three types of unusual points, labelled A, B and C. Table 6.3 summarizes the calculations.

TABLE 6.3 Measures of Unusual Points for Example 3.1

Data	Standardized residual $\hat{e}_i/se(\hat{e}_i)$	Leverage h_{ii}	Cook's distance D_i
19 Base Points plus A	4.00	.067	.577
19 Base Points plus B	.77	.550	.363
19 Base Points plus C	−4.01	.550	9.832

As noted in Section 3.5, from the standardized residual column we see that both points A and C are outliers. To judge the size of the leverages, because there are $n = 20$ points, the leverages are bounded by 0.05 and 1.00 with the average leverage being $\bar{h} = 2/20 = 0.10$. Using $3\bar{h}$ as a cut-off, both points B and C are high leverage points. Note that their values are the same. This is because, from Figure 3.12, the values of the explanatory variables are the same and only the response variable has been changed. The column for Cook's distance captures both types of unusual behavior. Because the typical value of D_i is $1/n$ or 0.05, Cook's distance provides one statistic to alert us to the fact that each point is unusual in one respect or another. In particular, point C has a very large D_i, reflecting the fact that it is both an outlier and a high leverage point. The 95th percentile of an F-distribution with $df_1 = 2$ and $df_2 = 18$ is 3.555. The fact that point C has a value of D_i that well exceeds this cut-off indicates the substantial influence of this point.

6.4 COLLINEARITY

Collinearity oc-curs when one ex-planatory variable is, or nearly is, a linear combina-tion of the other explanatory vari-ables.

Collinearity, or *multicollinearity,* occurs when one explanatory variable is, or nearly is, a linear combination of the other explanatory variables. Intuitively, it is useful to think of the independent variables as being highly correlated with one another as an indication of collinearity. With collinear data, the explana-tory variables may provide little additional information over and above the in-formation provided by the other explanatory variables. The issues are: Is collinearity important? If so, how does it affect our model fit and how do we detect it? To address the first question, consider a somewhat pathological ex-ample.

Example 6.2: Perfectly Correlated Independent Variables

Joe Finance was asked to fit the model E $y = \beta_0 + \beta_1 x_1 + \beta_2 x_2$ to a data set. His resulting fitted model was

$$\hat{y} = -87 + x_1 + 18x_2.$$

The data set under consideration is:

i	1	2	3	4
y_i	23	83	63	103
x_{i1}	2	8	6	10
x_{i2}	6	9	8	10

Source: Neter, Wasserman and Kutner (1989)

Joe checked the fit for each observation. Joe was very happy because he fit the data perfectly! For example, for the third observation the fitted value is $\hat{y}_3 = -87 + 6 + 18(8) = 63$, which is equal to the third response, y_3. Because the response equals the fitted value, the residual is zero. You may check that this is true of each observation and thus the R^2 turned out to be 100%.

However, Jane Accountant came along and fit the model

$$\hat{y} = -7 + 9x_1 + 2x_2.$$

Jane performed the same careful checks that Joe did and also got a perfect fit. Who is right?

The answer is both and neither one. There are, in fact, an infinite number of fits. This is due to the perfect relationship

$$x_2 = 5 + x_1/2$$

between the two explanatory variables.

This example serves to illustrate some important facts about collinearity.

If our data are highly collinear, fitting a model to the data and making predictions from the model may be valid. However, the estimated regression coefficients are not reliable.

1. The fact that there is high correlation (among independent variables) neither precludes us from getting good fits nor from making predictions of new observations. Note that in the example we got perfect fits.
2. Estimates of error variances and, therefore, tests of model adequacy, are still reliable.
3. In cases of serious collinearity, standard errors of individual regression coefficients are larger than cases where, other things being equal, serious collinearity does not exist. With large standard errors, individual regression coefficients may not be meaningful. Further, because a large standard error means that the corresponding t-ratio is small, it is difficult to detect the importance of a variable.

There are several useful devices for detecting collinearity. A matrix of correlation coefficients of explanatory variables is simple to create and is easy to interpret. This matrix quickly captures linear relationships between pairs of variables. A scatterplot matrix serves to provide a visual reinforcement of the summary statistics in the correlation matrix. Note that, for collinearity, we are only interested in detecting linear trends, so nonlinear relationships between variables are not an issue here. For example, we have seen that it is sometimes useful to retain both an explanatory variable (x) and its square (x^2), despite the fact that there is a perfect (nonlinear) relationship between the two.

Variance Inflation Factors

The variance inflation factor captures linear relationships among several variables.

Correlation and scatterplot matrices capture only relationships between pairs of variables. To capture more complex relationships among several variables, we use the concept of a *variance inflation factor* (*VIF*). To define a *VIF*, suppose that the set of explanatory variables is labelled $x_1, x_2, ..., x_k$. Now, run the regression using x_j as the "response" and the other x's ($x_1, x_2, ..., x_{j-1}, x_{j+1}, ..., x_k$) as the explanatory variables. Denote the coefficient of determination from this regression by R_j^2. We interpret R_j^2 as the square of the multiple correlation coefficient between x_j and linear combinations of the other x's. From this coefficient of determination, we define the variance inflation factor

$$VIF_j = \frac{1}{1 - R_j^2} \quad \text{for} \quad j = 1, 2, ..., k.$$

A larger R_j^2 results in a larger VIF_j; this means greater collinearity between x_j and the other x's. Now, R_j^2 alone is enough to capture the linear relationship of interest. However, we use VIF_j in lieu of R_j^2 as our measure for collinearity because of the algebraic relationship:

$$se(b_j) = s \frac{\sqrt{VIF_j}}{\sqrt{\sum_{i=1}^{n} (x_{ij} - \bar{x}_j)^2}} = s \frac{\sqrt{VIF_j}}{s_{x_j} \sqrt{n-1}}. \tag{6.3}$$

Here, $se(b_j)$ and s are standard errors and residual standard deviation from a full regression fit of y on $x_1, \ldots, x_k$. Further, s_{x_j} is the sample standard deviation of the jth variable x_j.

As a rule of thumb, when VIF_j exceeds ten, we say that severe collinearity exists.

Thus, a larger VIF_j results in a larger standard error associated with the jth slope, b_j. [If you studied Section 4.7, then you will recall that $se(b_j)$ is s times the $(j + 1)$st diagonal element of $(\mathbf{X'X})^{-1}$. The idea is that when collinearity occurs, the matrix $\mathbf{X'X}$ has properties similar to the number zero. When we attempt to calculate the inverse of $\mathbf{X'X}$, this is analogous to dividing by zero for scalar numbers.] As a rule of thumb, when VIF_j exceeds 10 (which is equivalent to $R_j^2 > 90\%$), we say that severe collinearity exists. This may signal a need for action.

Example 6.3: Stock Liquidity Case Study—Continued

As an example, consider a regression of VOLUME on PRICE, SHARE and VALUE. Unlike the explanatory variables considered in Section 6.2, these three explanatory variables are not measures of trading activity. From a regression fit, we have $R^2 = 61\%$ and $s = 6.72$. From Table 6.1, we saw that $s_y = 10.6$, so $s = 6.72$ represents a considerable drop in our estimate of the variability. Statistics associated with the regression coefficients are in Table 6.4.

TABLE 6.4   Statistics from a Regression of VOLUME on PRICE, SHARE and VALUE

x_j	s_{x_j}	b_j	$se(b_j)$	$t(b_j)$	VIF_j
PRICE	21.37	−0.022	0.035	−0.63	1.5
SHARE	115.1	0.054	0.010	5.19	3.8
VALUE	8.157	0.313	0.162	1.94	4.7

You may check that the relationship in equation (6.3) is valid for each of the explanatory variables in Table 6.4. Because each VIF statistic is less than ten, there is little reason to suspect severe collinearity. This is interesting because you may recall that there is a perfect relationship between PRICE, SHARE and VALUE in that we defined the market value to be VALUE = PRICE × SHARE. However, the relationship is multiplicative, and hence is nonlinear. Because the variables are not linearly related, it is valid to enter all three into the regression model.

Still, we must check that nonlinear relationships are not approximately linear over the sampling region. Even though the relationship is theoretically nonlinear, if it is close to linear for our available sample, then problems of collinearity might arise. Figure 6.4 illustrates this situation.

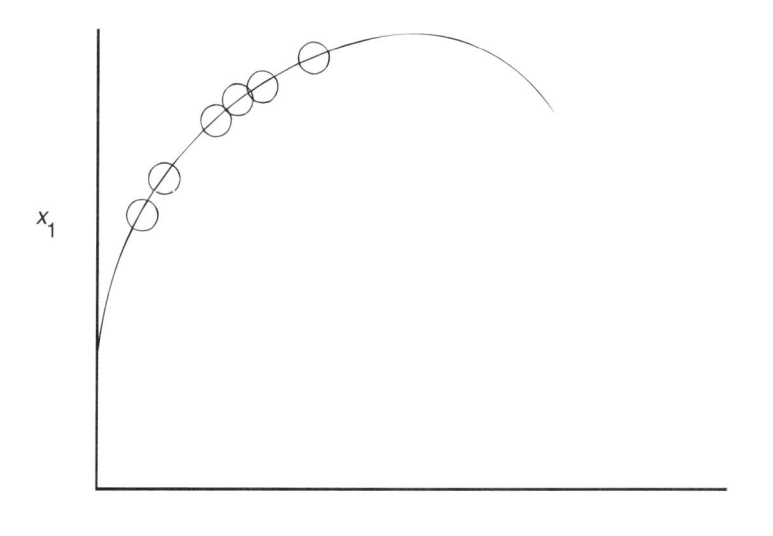

FIGURE 6.4 The relationship between x_1 and x_2 is nonlinear. However, over the region sampled, the variables have close to a linear relationship.

What can we do in the presence of collinearity? One option is to *center* each variable, by subtracting its average and dividing by its standard deviation. For example, create a new variable $x_{ij}^* = (x_{ij} - \bar{x}_j)/s_{x_j}$. Occasionally, one variable appears as millions of units and another variable appears as fractions of units. Compared to the first mentioned variable, the second mentioned variable is close to a constant column of zeroes, at least if one uses single-precision (eight significant digits) arithmetic. If this is true, then the second variable looks very much like a linear shift of the constant column of ones corresponding to the intercept. This is a problem even using double-precision arithmetic because, with the least squares operations, we are implicitly squaring numbers that can make these columns appear even more similar.

This problem is simply a computational one and is easy to rectify. Simply recode the variables so that the units are of similar order of magnitude. Some data analysts automatically center all variables to avoid these problems. This is a legitimate approach because regression techniques search for linear relationships; scale and location shifts do not affect linear relationships.

Another option is to simply not explicitly account for collinearity in the analysis but to discuss some of its implications when interpreting the results of the regression analysis. This approach is probably the most commonly adopted one. It is a fact of life that, when dealing with business and economic data, collinearity does tend to exist among variables. Because the data tend to be observational in lieu of experimental in nature, there is little that the analyst can do to avoid this situation.

The best option for handling collinearity is to remove one or more explanatory variables and to replace them by a transformed version or an auxiliary alternative.

When severe collinearity exists, often the only option is to remove one or more variables from the regression equation. In the best-case situation an auxiliary variable, that provides similar information and that eases the collinearity problem, is available to replace a variable. Similar to our discussion of high leverage points, a transformed version of the explanatory variable may also be a useful substitute. In some situations, such an ideal replacement is not available and we are forced to remove one or more variables. Deciding which variables to remove is a difficult choice. Sometimes automatic variables selection techniques, described in Section 6.1, can help determine an overall suitable model choice. When deciding among variables, often the choice will be dictated by the investigator's judgement as to which is the most relevant set of variables.

Collinearity and Leverage

Measures of collinearity and leverage share common characteristics, and yet are designed to capture different aspects of a data set. Both are useful for data and model criticism; they are applied after a preliminary model fit with the objective of improving model specification. Further, both are calculated using only the explanatory variables; values of the responses do not enter into either calculation.

Our measure of collinearity, the variance inflation factor, is designed to help us with model criticism. It is a measure calculated for each explanatory variable, designed to explain the relationships with other explanatory variables.

The leverage statistic is designed to help us with data criticism. It is a measure calculated for each observation to help us explain how unusual an observation is with respect to other observations.

Collinearity may be masked or induced by high leverage points, as pointed out by Mason and Gunst (1985) and Hadi (1988). Figures 6.5 and 6.6 provide illustrations of each case. These simple examples underscore an important point: data criticism and model criticism are not separate exercises.

The examples in Figures 6.5 and 6.6 also help us to see one way in which high leverage points may affect standard errors of regression coefficients. Recall, in Section 6.2, we saw that high leverage points may affect the model fitted values. In Figures 6.5 and 6.6, we see that high leverage points affect collinearity. Thus, from equation (6.3), we have that high leverage points can also affect our standard errors of regression coefficients.

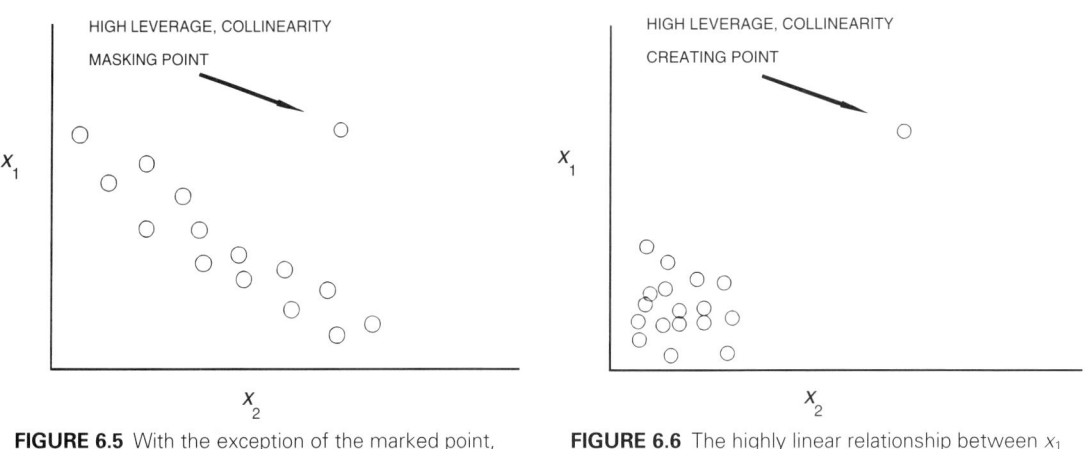

FIGURE 6.5 With the exception of the marked point, x_1 and x_2 are highly linearly related.

FIGURE 6.6 The highly linear relationship between x_1 and x_2 is primarily due to the marked point.

Suppressor Variables

As we have seen, severe collinearity can seriously inflate standard errors of regression coefficients, other things equal. Because we rely on these standard errors for judging the usefulness of explanatory variables, our model selection procedures and inferences may be deficient in the presence of severe collinearity. Despite these drawbacks, collinearity in a data set should not necessarily be viewed as a deficiency of the data set; it is simply an attribute of the available explanatory variables.

A suppressor variable is an explanatory variable that increases the importance of other explanatory variables when included in the model.

Even if one explanatory variable is nearly a linear combination of the others, that does not necessarily mean that the information that it provides is redundant. To illustrate, we now consider a *suppressor variable,* an explanatory variable that increases the importance of other explanatory variables when included in the model. Figure 6.7 shows a scatterplot matrix of a hypothetical data set of 50 observations. This data set contains a response and two explanatory variables. Table 6.5 is the corresponding matrix of correlation coefficients. Here, we see that the two explanatory variables are highly correlated. Now recall, for regression with one independent variable, that the correlation coefficient squared is the coefficient of determination. Thus, using Table 6.5, for a regression of y and x_1, the coefficient of determination is $(0.188)^2 = 3.5\%$. Similarly, for a regression of y on x_2, the coefficient of determination is $(-0.022)^2$

TABLE 6.5 Correlation Matrix for the Supressor Example Corresponding to Figure 6.7

	x_1	x_2
x_2	0.972	
y	0.188	-0.022

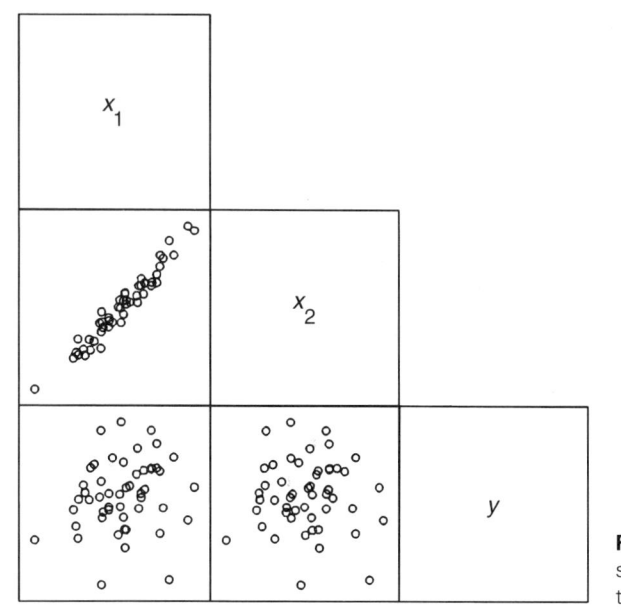

FIGURE 6.7 Scatterplot matrix of a response and two explanatory variable for the suppressor variable example.

= 0.04%. However, for a regression of y on x_1 and x_2, the coefficient of determination turns out to be a surprisingly high 80.7%. The interpretation is that individually, both x_1 and x_2 have little impact on y. However, when taken jointly, the two explanatory variables have a significant effect on y. Although Table 6.5 shows that x_1 and x_2 are strongly linearly related, this relationship does not mean that x_1 and x_2 provide the same information. In fact, in this example the two variables complement one another.

6.5 SELECTION CRITERIA

There are several criteria available for selecting models. We introduced most of the basic criteria in Chapter 4. These criteria include the coefficient of determination (R^2), an adjusted version (R_a^2), the size of the typical error (s) and the t-ratio of each slope coefficient. Here, we discuss an additional quantity, the C_p statistic. According to the iterative procedure outlined in Section 4.0, we use these selection criteria in conjunction with diagnostic checks to arrive at candidate models.

C_p Statistic

Like the automatic variable selection procedures described in Section 6.1, the C_p statistic is used in the beginning stages of developing a regression model.

To define this statistic, assume that we have available k explanatory variables $x_1, \ldots, x_k$ and we first run a regression to get s_{full}^2 as the mean square error. Now, suppose that we are considering using only $p - 1$ explanatory variables so that there are p regression coefficients. With these $p - 1$ explanatory variables, we run a regression to get the error sum of squares $(Error\ SS)_p$. Thus, we are in the position to define

$$C_p = \frac{(Error\ SS)_p}{s_{full}^2} - (n - 2p).$$

The choice of p may vary from 1 to $k + 1$. For example, in the case where $p = k + 1$, all of the variables are included. In this case, we have

$$C_{k+1} = \frac{(Error\ SS)_{k+1}}{s_{full}^2} - (n - 2(k + 1))$$

$$= (n - (k + 1)) \frac{(Error\ MS)_{k+1}}{s_{full}^2} - (n - 2(k + 1))$$

$$= (n - (k + 1)) - (n - 2(k + 1)) = k + 1,$$

because $(Error\ MS)_{k+1} = s_{full}^2$.

In general, if the model with p regression coefficients is correct, then we expect C_p to be close to p. The idea is that s_{full}^2 should be close to σ^2 and, if the model is correct, then $(Error\ MS)_p$ should also be close to σ^2. Thus,

$$C_p = (n - p) \frac{(Error\ MS)_p}{s_{full}^2} - (n - 2p)$$

$$\approx (n - p) \frac{\sigma^2}{\sigma^2} - (n - 2p) = p.$$

As a selection criterion, we choose the model with a "small" C_p coefficient, where small is taken to be relative to p. In general, models with smaller values of C_p are more desirable.

In general, we prefer a model with a small C_p coefficient such that $C_p \approx p$.

The C_p statistic measures the candidate model's mean square error relative to a full model mean square error. In general, we prefer models with a small C_p coefficient such that $C_p \approx p$. It may be, however, that the full model is poorly specified and that the resulting mean square error is inflated. In such cases, the value of C_p can be negative. This not to say that the model with the smallest C_p is poor; it merely states that the full model is poorly specified.

Model Validation

Model validation is the process of confirming that our proposed model is appropriate, especially in light of the purposes of the investigation. Recall the iterative model formulation selection process described in Section 4.0. Using this iterative procedure, we examine the basic selection criteria as well as additional diagnostic checks described in Sections 3.6, 6.1 and 6.2 to arrive at the final stage of model selection. An important criticism of this iterative process is that it is guilty of data-snooping, that is, fitting a great number of models to a single set of data. As we saw in Example 6.1 on data-snooping in stepwise regression, by looking at a large number of models we may actually overfit the data and understate the natural variation in our representation. Another drawback of the iterative fitting process is that we are implicitly using a sequence of tests of hypotheses to formulate our ideas about the candidate model. By doing a number of tests of hypothesis on a single data set, we may be working at a much higher significance level than we nominally prescribe.

With out-of-sample validation, we fit various models to one portion of the data and test, or validate, the best candidate models on a second portion of the data.

We can respond to these criticisms by using a technique called *out-of-sample validation*. The idea is to have available two sets of data, one for model development and one for model validation. We initially develop one, or several, models on a first data set. The models developed from the first set of data are called our *candidate models*. Then, ideally, the relative performance of the candidate models could be measured on a second set of data. In this way, the data used to validate the model is unaffected by the procedures used to formulate the model.

Unfortunately, rarely will two sets of data be available to the investigator. However, we can implement the out-of-sample validation process by *splitting the data set* into two subsamples. We call these the *model development* and *validation subsamples*, respectively. To see how the data-splitting process works in the linear regression context, consider the following basic out-of-sample validation procedure:

1. Begin with a sample size of n and divide it into two subsamples, called the model development and validation subsamples. Let n_1 and n_2 denote the size of each subsample. In cross-sectional regression, do this split using a random sampling mechanism. Use the notation $i = 1, ..., n_1$ to represent observations from the model development subsample and $i = n_1 + 1, ..., n_1 + n_2 = n$ for the observations from the validation subsample. (In longitudinal data, we will use the first n_1 data points to predict the subsequent n_2 observations.) Figure 6.8 illustrates this procedure.

2. Using the model development subsample, fit a candidate model to the data set $i = 1, ..., n_1$.

3. Using the model created in Step 2 and the explanatory variables from the validation subsample, "predict" the dependent variables in the validation subsample, $\hat{y}_i$, where $i = n_1 + 1, ..., n_1 + n_2$. (To get these predictions, you may need to transform the dependent variables back to the original scale. This will be discussed further in Section 6.6.)

4. Compute the *sum of squared prediction errors*

$$SSPE = \sum_{i=n_1+1}^{n_1+n_2} (y_i - \hat{y}_i)^2. \tag{6.5}$$

Repeat Steps 2 through 4 for each candidate model. Choose the model with the smallest *SSPE*.

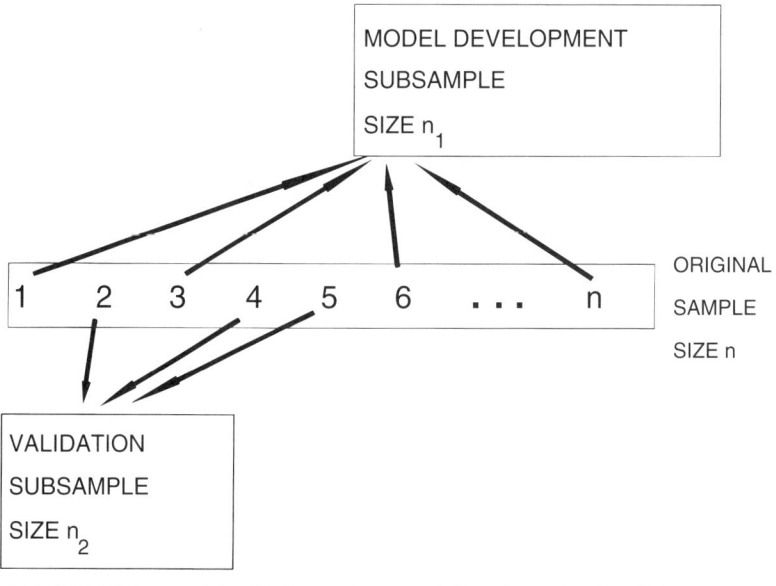

FIGURE 6.8 For model validation, a data set of size *n* is randomly split into two subsamples.

The calculation of SSPE depends on a random drawing mechanism and an arbitrary choice of relative subset size splits. Further, the calculation is labor intensive.

There are a number of criticisms of the *SSPE*. First, it is clear that it takes a considerable amount of time and effort to calculate this statistic for each of several candidate models. However, as with many statistical techniques, this is merely a matter of having specialized statistical software available to perform the steps described above. Second, because the statistic itself is based on a random subset of the sample, its value will vary from analyst to analyst. This objection would be overcome by using the first n_1 observations from the sample. In most applications this is not done in case there is a lurking relationship in the order of the observations. Third, and perhaps most important, is the fact that the choice of the relative subset sizes, n_1 and n_2, is not clear. Various researchers recommend different proportions for the allocation. Snee (1977) suggests that data-splitting not be done unless the sample size is moderately large, specifically, $n \geq 2(k + 1) + 20$. The guidelines of Picard and Berk (1990) show that the greater the number of parameters to be estimated, the greater the proportion of observations needed for the model development subsample. As a rule of thumb, for data sets with 100 or fewer observations, use about 25–35% of the sample for out-of-sample validation. For data sets with 500 or more observations, use 50% of the sample for out-of-sample validation.

Because of these criticisms, several variants of the basic out-of-sample validation process are used by analysts. Although there is no theoretically best procedure, it is widely agreed that model validation is an important part of confirming the usefulness of a model.

PRESS Statistic

The PRESS statistic is more attractive than SSPE for small sample sizes.

For small sample sizes, an attractive out-of-sample validation statistic is PRESS, the *Predicted Residual Sum of Squares*. To define the statistic, consider the following procedure where we suppose that a candidate model is available.

1. From the full sample, omit the ith point and use the remaining $n - 1$ observations to compute regression coefficients.
2. Use the regression coefficients computed in step one and the explanatory variables for the ith observation to compute the predicted response, $\hat{y}_{(i)}$. This part of the procedure is similar to steps one through three for calculating the SSPE statistic described above with $n_1 = n - 1$ and $n_2 = 1$.
3. Now, repeat this procedure for $i = 1, ..., n$, and define

$$PRESS = \sum_{i=1}^{n} (y_i - \hat{y}_{(i)})^2. \tag{6.6}$$

As with SSPE, this statistic is calculated for each of several competing models. Under this criterion, we choose the model with the smallest PRESS.

At first glance, the statistic seems very computationally intensive in that it requires n regression fits to evaluate it. However, matrix algebra can be used to establish that

$$y_i - \hat{y}_{(i)} = \frac{\hat{e}_i}{1 - h_{ii}}. \tag{6.7}$$

Here, $\hat{e}_i$ and h_{ii} represent the ith residual and leverage from the regression fit using the complete data set. This yields

$$PRESS = \sum_{i=1}^{n} \left(\frac{\hat{e}_i}{1 - h_{ii}} \right)^2, \tag{6.8}$$

which is a much easier computational formula. Thus, the PRESS statistic is less computationally intensive than SSPE.

Another important advantage of this statistic, when compared to SSPE, is that we do not need to make an arbitrary choice as to our relative subset sizes split. Indeed, because we are performing an "out-of-sample" validation for each observation, it can be argued that this procedure is more efficient, an especially important consideration when the sample size is small (say, less than 50 observations).

Because the model is re-fit for each point deleted, *PRESS* does not enjoy the appearance of independence between the estimation and prediction aspects, unlike *SSPE*. Further, out-of-sample validation is a general principle that is useful in a number of circumstances, including cross-sectional regression and time series. Although computationally attractive, the sample re-use principle that the *PRESS* statistic is based on is not as well understood for model selection purposes.

6.6 HANDLING HETEROSCEDASTICITY—TRANSFORMATIONS

When fitting regression models to data, an important assumption is that the variability is common among all observations. This assumption of common variability is called *homoscedasticity* which stands for "same scatter." Indeed, the least squares procedure assumes that the expected variability of each observation is constant and gives the same weight to each observation when minimizing the sum of squared deviations. When the scatter varies by observation, the data are said to be *heteroscedastic*. Figure 6.9 is a plot of regression data with one explanatory variable where the scatter seems to increase as the explanatory variable increases.

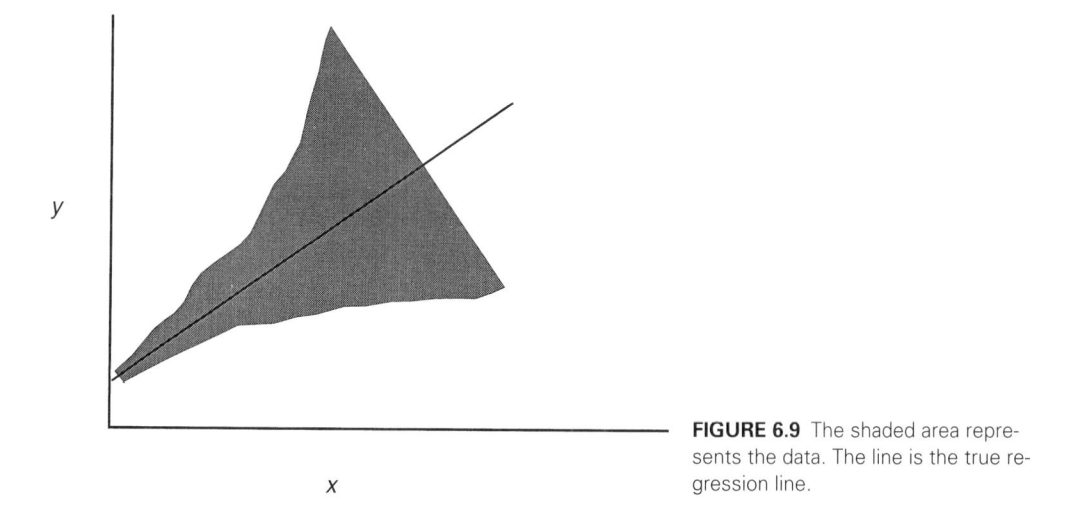

y

x

FIGURE 6.9 The shaded area represents the data. The line is the true regression line.

To detect heteroscedasticity, a good idea is to perform a preliminary regression fit of the data and plot the residuals versus the fitted values. Figure 6.10 is an example of this plot. The preliminary regression fit removes many of the major patterns in the data and leaves the eye free to concentrate on other patterns that may influence the fit. We plot residuals versus fitted values because the fitted values are an approximation of the expected value of the re-

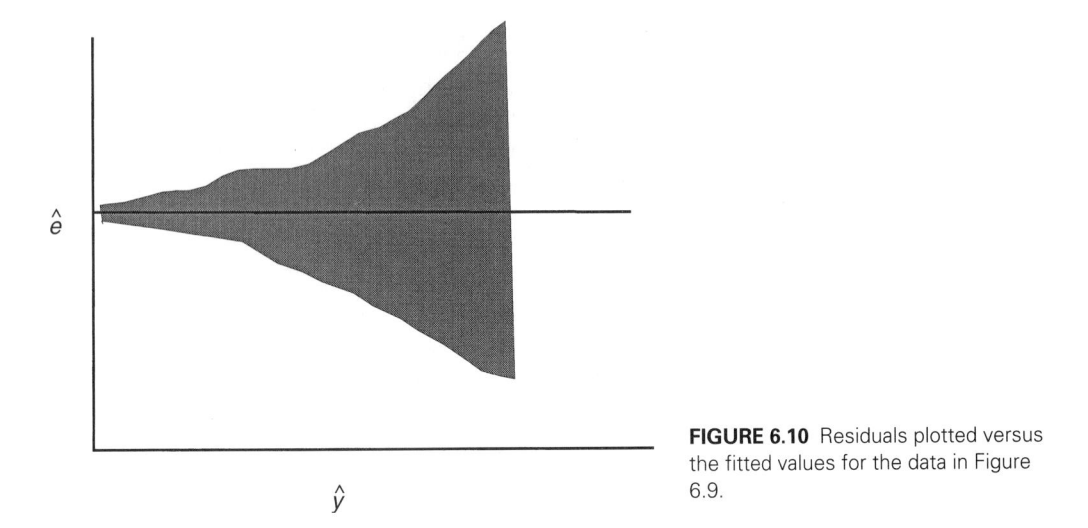

$\hat{e}$

$\hat{y}$

FIGURE 6.10 Residuals plotted versus the fitted values for the data in Figure 6.9.

sponse and, in many situations, the variability grows with the expected response.

A plot of residuals versus fitted values is useful for detecting heteroscedasticity.

Fortunately, when we perform regression fits on heteroscedastic data, it has been established that our resulting estimates are still unbiased. However, because the variability of the response differs from observation to observation, there is no common measure of variability, such as σ^2. Thus, many of our tests of hypotheses and confidence and prediction intervals are no longer valid. Further, our estimates are not as efficient as they could be, a particularly important point when the sample size is small.

When minimizing the sum of squared errors using heteroscedastic data, the expected variability of some observations is smaller than others. Intuitively, it seems reasonable that the smaller the variability of the response, the more reliable is that response and the greater weight that it should receive in the minimization procedure. We will introduce a technique, called *weighted least squares*, in Chapter 8 that accounts for this "variable variability."

A simpler device that we pursue in this section is to simply transform the response variable. Even though this device is not always available, it has proven effective for a surprisingly large number of data sets. Many of the transforms that are used in practice can be expressed as part of the *Box-Cox family of transforms*. Within this family of transforms, in lieu of using the response y, we use a *transformed*, or *rescaled* version, $y^* = y^\lambda$. That is, the new response equals the old response raised to a specified power. Here, the power λ (lambda, a greek "el") is a number that is user specified. Typical values of λ that are used in practice are $\lambda = 1, \frac{1}{2}, 0$ or -1. When we use $\lambda = 0$, we mean y^*

$= \ln(y)$, that is, the natural logarithmic transform. More formally, the Box-Cox family can be expressed as

$$y^* = \frac{y^\lambda - 1}{\lambda}.$$

Transformations may help achieve a symmetric distribution of responses.

Because regression estimates are not affected by location and scale shifts, in practice we do not need to subtract one nor divide by λ when rescaling the response. [The advantage of the above expression is that, if we let λ approach 0, then y^* approaches $\ln (y)$, from some straightforward calculus arguments.]

Transformation of the response may help to stabilize the variance and to achieve a symmetric distribution of responses, and thus of errors. To see the effects on the distribution of responses, Figure 6.11 displays the distribution of a set of responses and several transformations. The data were created by simulating 250 observations from the sum of five squared standard normal variates. As we can see from the histogram in the upper right hand of Figure 6.11, this distribution is skewed to the right. Histograms of the data transformed using the square root, logarithmic and negative reciprocal transformations are in the left hand column of Figure 6.11. We see that the square root and logarithmic transformation have served to symmetrize the distribution although the negative reciprocal transformation has produced a distribution that is skewed to the left. The three scatter plots in Figure 6.11, between y and each of $y^{1/2}$, $\ln(y)$ and $-1/y$, indicate that each of these transformations is highly nonlinear.

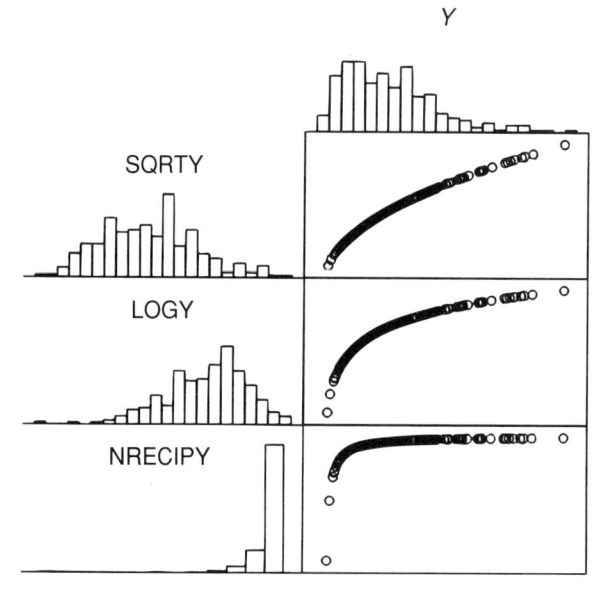

FIGURE 6.11 Effects of the square root, logarithmic and negative reciprocal transformations on the distribution of a response.

Transforming the response variable has an effect on the distribution of the response and the expected variability of the response. If the only reason for investigating a transformation is to handle a potential nonlinear relation between a response and an explanatory variable, then it is simpler to transform the explanatory variable. We introduced this topic in Section 4.5.

Values of the transformation parameter $\lambda < 1$ serve to "shrink" spread out data. There are several special cases when certain choices of λ work well. For example, when the response is a type of *count data*, then the square root transform is suggested. Here, count data refers to the number of some entity, for example, the number of people in a family.

Transforming explanatory variables, introduced in Section 4.5, is another device for handling nonlinear relationships between explanatory variables and responses.

Another example in which the use of logarithmic transformations arise naturally are in connection with *multiplicative models*. Here the general set-up is that response may be modeled as the expected response *times* the natural error, that is, $y = (\text{E } y)\, e$. For example, consider modeling the response M_{od}, the number of migrants from a specified state of origin o to a specified destination state d. The so-called "gravity model" is (see, for example, Frees, 1992),

$$M_{od} = c\, \frac{P_o P_d}{D_{od}^c} \left(\frac{I_d}{I_o} \right)^b \left(\frac{E_d}{E_o} \right)^f e_{od}$$

for migration from the oth to dth state. Here, P is state population, I is state income, E is state (un)employment, D is distance between population centroids, a, b, c and f are parameters to be estimated, and e_{od} is the multiplicative error term. This model can be easily converted to the linear model via the logarithmic transform.

If the response is in natural logarithmic units, then a per unit change can be interpreted as a proportional (or, when multiplied by 100, percentage) change in the original units of the response.

When using the natural logarithm (base e) transformation, there is a useful interpretation of the regression coefficients. Recall the idea that a partial slope is interpreted as the expected change in the response per unit change in the explanatory variable, holding other explanatory variables fixed. Thus, if the response is in natural logarithmic units, then a per unit change can be interpreted as a proportional (or, when multiplied by 100, percentage) change in the original units of the response. See the discussion toward the end of Section 6.7 for an illustration of this point.

6.7 CASE STUDY: NFL PLAYERS' COMPENSATION

In this section we report on a study of compensation of players in the National Football League (NFL). Our goal is to understand the relationship between a player's salary and various personal characteristics that may influence salary. These relationships could be useful in predicting or determining salaries of future players. This study may also be useful in salary arbitration matters. For example, based on certain characteristics of a player, the model could be used to determine an expected salary. The difference between an actual salary and that expected under the model could represent an important deviation of a player from his peers. The reason for this deviation would be the subject of arbitration—of course, our usual caveats for interpreting regression models hold. In particular, the regression model establishes the size of the deviation, not the reasons why the deviation occurs.

Data Sources and Characteristics

C6_NFL

Data for the palyers' salaries were provided by the *NFL Players' Association*. Of the 1,570 salary figures available at the beginning of the 1990 season, a random sample of 200 players was drawn. The salaries represent the response variable in this study. Also available from the Players' Association was the POSITION of the player, the round in which the player was DRAFTed and the years of experience of a player (YRS EXP). Additional personal characteristics of the players were collected from the *1990 Media Guide*. These characteristics included the number of regular season games PLAYED in the previous year and the number of regular season games STARTED in the previous year. Only one characteristic about the team that the player belongs to was investigated. This was the size of the city in which the team is domiciled (CITY POP). These data were collected from *The Statistical Abstract of the United States, 1990*. The conjecture here was that players from larger cities may have larger salaries to offset the higher cost of living compared to smaller metropolitan areas.

After a preliminary analysis of the data, it became clear that rookies (players with YRS EXP = 0) followed a different compensation market than veterans. Thus, 35 rookie players were excluded from the analysis. Further, two veteran players were unusual with respect to other players in the data set. These were Warren Moon, veteran quarterback of the Houston Oilers, and Bo Jackson, part-time player for the Los Angeles Raiders (and professional baseball's Kansas City Royals). The circumstances of each player are unusual and it was decided not to try to accommodate these unusual circumstances with the model. Thus, these players were also deleted, leaving us with a data set of size 163. Unfortunately, the media guide did not include information for three teams. For this reason, the data regarding games PLAYED and STARTED was missing for 26 veteran players.

An examination of plots and summary statistics reveals several interesting aspects of the data. To begin, Table 6.6 is a correlation matrix and Figure 6.12 displays a series of scatter plots of the response versus each of the explanatory variables. We see that games started and years of experience have a strong influence on salaries. The variable DRAFT has a strong negative effect, indicating that the lower is the round in which a player was selected into the

TABLE 6.6 Correlation Matrix

	DRAFT	YRS EXP	PLAYED	STARTED	CITYPOP
YRS EXP	−0.041				
PLAYED	−0.105	0.383			
STARTED	−0.284	0.410	0.516		
CITYPOP	−0.128	−0.015	0.186	0.156	
SALARY	−0.412	0.457	0.301	0.559	0.044

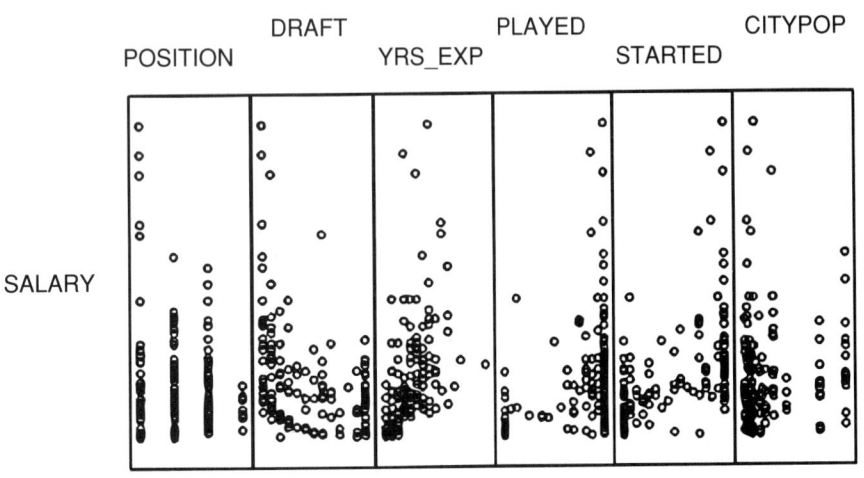

FIGURE 6.12 Scatter plots of SALARY versus several explanatory variables.
Sources: NFL Players' Association, 1990 Media Guide, and the 1990 Statistical Abstract of the U.S.

league (DRAFTed), the higher is the salary. A closer examination of the scatterplot matrix in Figure 6.12 reveals that the reciprocal of draft (1/DRAFT) may provide a better fit. The motivation for this is that there is a large difference between the first and second rounds in a draft when compared to, say, differences between the ninth and tenth rounds. This is reflected in the reciprocal of draft but not the draft variable itself.

The categorical variable POSITION was split into four indicator variables, one for offensive back (POSITION = 1), defensive back (POSITION = 2), lineman (POSITION = 3) and kicker/punter (POSITION = 4). It turned out that only the indicator for offensive back (OB) was important in the subsequent analysis. That is, once we control for other personal characteristics of a player, it did not seem to matter if the player was a defensive back, lineman or kicker/punter.

Finally, Figures 6.13 and 6.14 are histograms of the response variable SALARY. In Figure 6.13 we see that salaries are skewed to the right. Note that this is a real effect and not merely the result of one or two players earning large salaries. (Recall that we have already deleted two players with large salaries.) To "bring in" players with large salaries, we intend to argue that it is more appropriate to model the *logarithm* of the salaries as the response variable than the salary itself. Figure 6.14 is the histogram of the salaries but now the horizontal axis is on a logarithmic (base ten) scale. Using this scale, players with large salaries are still large but not as dramatically large as on the original scale.

Preliminary Regression Model

In anticipation of the model validation step, 18 observations were randomly selected. These observations were held out to be used in subsequent model val-

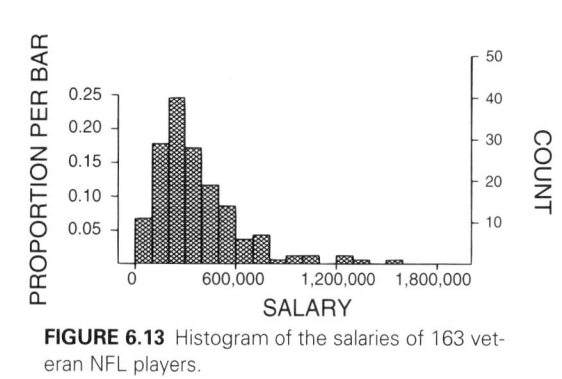

FIGURE 6.13 Histogram of the salaries of 163 veteran NFL players.

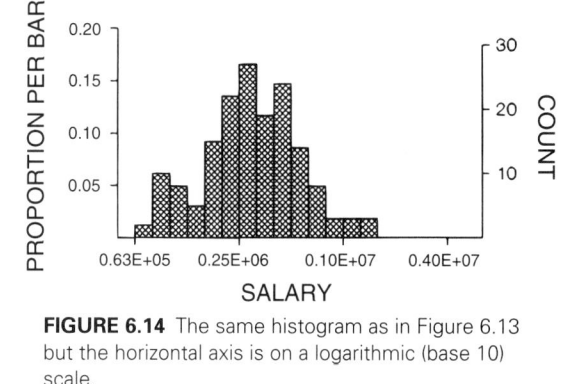

FIGURE 6.14 The same histogram as in Figure 6.13 but the horizontal axis is on a logarithmic (base 10) scale.

idation. Thus, in the preliminary model development stages, you will find 163 − 18 = 145 observations.

One way of quickly arriving at a candidate model is to use the automatic variable selection procedures described in Section 6.1. Exhibits 6.1 and 6.2 are examples of the results based on forward and backward stepwise regression

```
        FORWARD STEPWISE REGRESSION OF SALARY
            ON  7 PREDICTORS, WITH N = 121
        N(CASES  WITH MISSING OBS.)
                =  24 N(ALL CASES) = 145
```

STEP	1	2	3	4
CONTANT	209372	45145	42902	9602
1/DRAFT	418194	399961	328178	302858
T-RATIO	7.18	7.71	5.89	5.62
YRS EXP		33465	25866	26596
T-RATIO		5.68	4.14	4.44
STARTED			8867	9701
T-RATIO			2.98	3.39
OB				125901
T-RATIO				3.36
S	215257	191570	185473	177836
R-SQ	30.25	45.22	49.09	53.59

EXHIBIT 6.1 Minitab Output of the Forward Stepwise Regression Routine.

```
            BACKWARD STEPWISE REGRESSION OF  SALARY
               ON  7 PREDICTORS, WITH N = 121
          N (CASES  WITH MISSING OBS.)
                =  24 N(ALL CASES) =  145


            STEP         1          2          3          4
        CONSTANT    -34307     -29475     -40280       9602


           DRAFT      4750       4508       4629
         T-RATIO      0.77       0.74       0.77


         YRS EXP     27012      27010      26687      26596
         T-RATIO      4.37       4.39       4.44       4.44


          PLAYED     -1123      -1018
         T-RATIO     -0.29      -0.27


         STARTED      9880       9967       9627       9701
         T-RATIO      3.11       3.17       3.35       3.39


         CITYPOP    0.0008
         T-RATIO      0.24


         1/DRAFT    355802     352610     355126     302858
         T-RATIO      3.99       4.01       4.08       5.61


              OB    132132     131697     131966     125901
         T-RATIO      3.41       3.41       3.44       3.36


               S    179618     178875     178152     177836
            R-SQ     53.88      53.86      53.83      53.59
```

EXHIBIT 6.2 Minitab Output of the Backward Stepwise Regression Routine.

routines. For these routines, the criterion for adding and deleting a variable was to declare the variable unimportant if the variable's *t*-ratio is less than two in absolute value. A comforting fact is that both algorithms wind up with the same recommended model.

Based on these procedures and further examination of the data, a preliminary fit of the data was made using SALARY as the response variable and 1/DRAFT, YRS EXP, STARTED and OB as explanatory variables. The model fit well. The adjusted coefficient of determination was $R_a^2 = 52\%$ and the size of the typical error was $s \approx 178,000$, a reduction from $s_y \approx 250,000$. Figure 6.15 is a plot of the standardized residuals versus the fitted values from this regression fit. It seems that there is a tendency to make large mistakes for indi-

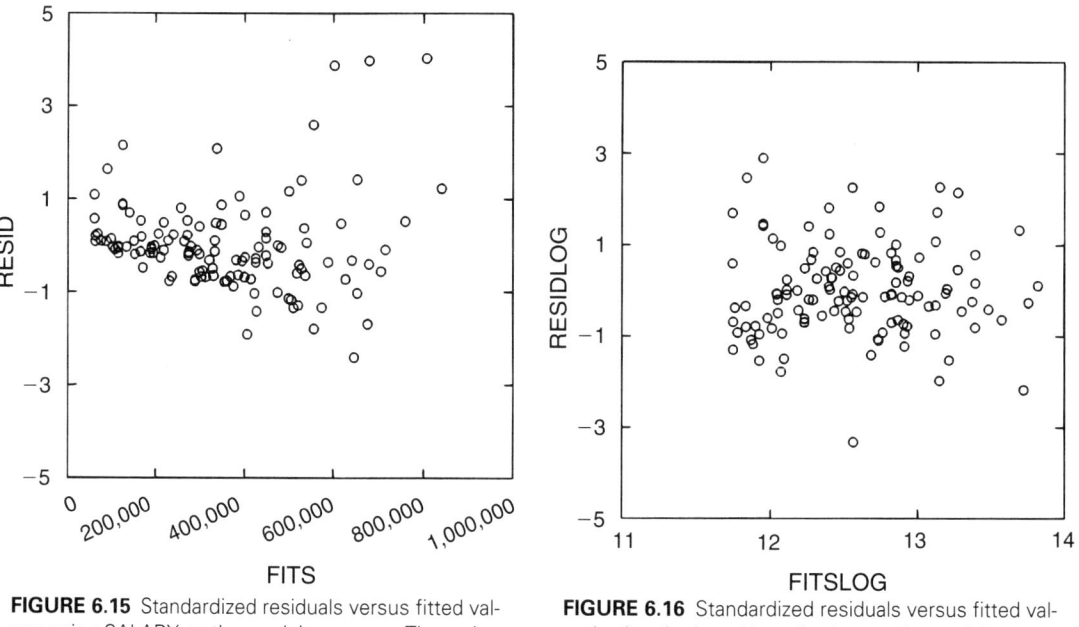

FIGURE 6.15 Standardized residuals versus fitted values using SALARY as the model response. The variability seems to increase as the fitted response increases.

FIGURE 6.16 Standardized residuals versus fitted valued using the logarithm of salary as the model response. No patterns are apparent.

viduals who have a high expected salary under the model. We call this tendency a heteroscedastic error. One way to compensate for this violation of model assumptions is to consider a transformed version of the response variable, logged salaries.

The choice of the base of the logarithm is made premised on resulting interpretation and does not affect the essential arguments for transforming the data.

Before continuing, it should be noted that the choice of *base* that one uses in the logarithm does not affect the essential arguments here. The choice of base ten has especially desirable interpretations when one deals with monetary figures; Figure 6.14 illustrates this. Demographers and other scientists often prefer base two because it is the natural scale to see how often entities, such as populations, double over time. In this text, we use the natural logarithm that uses the base $e \approx 2.7182818$.

From this discussion, the next step is to explore models using the logarithm of salary (LNSALARY) as the response. To illustrate further automatic variable selection procedures, in Exhibit 6.3 is the output of a best subsets regression procedure. Using the criteria R^2, R_a^2, s and C_p, it seems as if the best model is the one using the same four explanatory variables, 1/DRAFT, YRS EXP, STARTED and OB. This model is fit to the data. Figure 6.16 is a plot of standardized residuals of this model versus the fitted values. Based on this plot, no patterns are apparent. Further diagnostic checks were also made on the data. Although not included here, a plot of residuals versus years of

```
BEST SUBSETS REGRESSION of LNSALARY
121 cases used 24 cases contain missing values.
                          Y     S  C  1
                          R     P  T  I  /
                          D  S  L  A  T  D
                          R     A  R  Y  R
                          A  E  Y  T  P  A
             Adj.         F  X  E  E  O  F  O
Vars  R-sq   R-sq   C-p        s  T  P  D  D  P  T  B
  1   36.4   35.8   72.6   0.52227          X
  1   29.3   28.7   93.6   0.55044    X
  2   54.7   53.9   20.0   0.44260    X           X
  2   47.2   46.3   42.2   0.47757    X     X
  3   59.9   58.9    6.5   0.41819    X     X     X
  3   56.1   55.0   17.8   0.43746    X           X  X
  4   61.8   60.5    2.7   0.40967    X     X     X  X
  4   60.1   58.7    8.0   0.41908    X     X  X  X
  5   62.0   60.4    4.2   0.41043    X     X  X  X  X
  5   61.8   60.2    4.7   0.41134 X  X     X     X  X
```

EXHIBIT 6.3 Minitab Output of the Best Subsets Regression Routine.

experience indicated the potential need to include a quadratic term in years of experience. When this variable was included in the regression model, the t-ratio associated with this variable was -3.43, indicating a great deal of significance. Thus, this variable was also considered when validating our candidate models.

Model Validation

In this subsection, we consider three candidate models. The first uses SALARY as the response variable and uses 1/DRAFT, YRS EXP, STARTED and OB as explanatory variables. The second model has the same explanatory variables but uses LNSALARY as the response. The third candidate model also uses LNSALARY as the response and adds years of experience squared (EXP SQR) to the list of explanatory variables. These three models are compared based on their ability to predict the sample that was held out for validation purposes. This subset was randomly selected from the original sample. Thus, to the extent that observations are independent, any mischief that we may have inadvertently gotten into by overanalyzing the data should not affect the results of this independent validation. Of course, the drawback is that we are allowing our model choice to be driven by a small percentage of the data. One can always increase this percentage of the data, but then there are fewer observations upon which we can base our opinion as to what viable candidate models might be.

For the subset of 18 observations originally held out, it turns out that some of the media guide data were unavailable for two of the observations. Thus, only 16 observations, about 10% of the data set, were available for validation. The three fitted models are:

Model 1: $\widehat{\text{SALARY}}$ = 9,602 + 26,596 YRS EXP + 9,701 STARTED
+ 302,858 1/DRAFT + 125,901 OB

Model 2: $\widehat{\text{LNSALARY}}$ = 11.6 + 0.0907 YRS EXP + 0.0275 STARTED
+ 0.721 1/DRAFT + 0.210 OB

Model 3: $\widehat{\text{LNSALARY}}$ = 11.3 + 0.214 YRS EXP + 0.0227 STARTED
+ 0.717 1/DRAFT + 0.216 OB − 0.00932 EXP SQR.

For the values of the held-out explanatory variables, predictions were made for each model. For example, Figure 6.17 is a scatter plot of actual salaries of the 16 held-out players versus their predicted salaries based on the first model. To compare the models, predictions from Models 2 and 3 were exponentiated so that the predictions, as well as actual salaries, would be in dollars. For each model, the deviation between actual salary and predicted salary was calculated, squared and then summed over all 16 individuals. Table 6.7 presents the result of this procedure in the form of the sum of squared prediction errors (*SSPE*) statistic, which was described in Section 6.5.

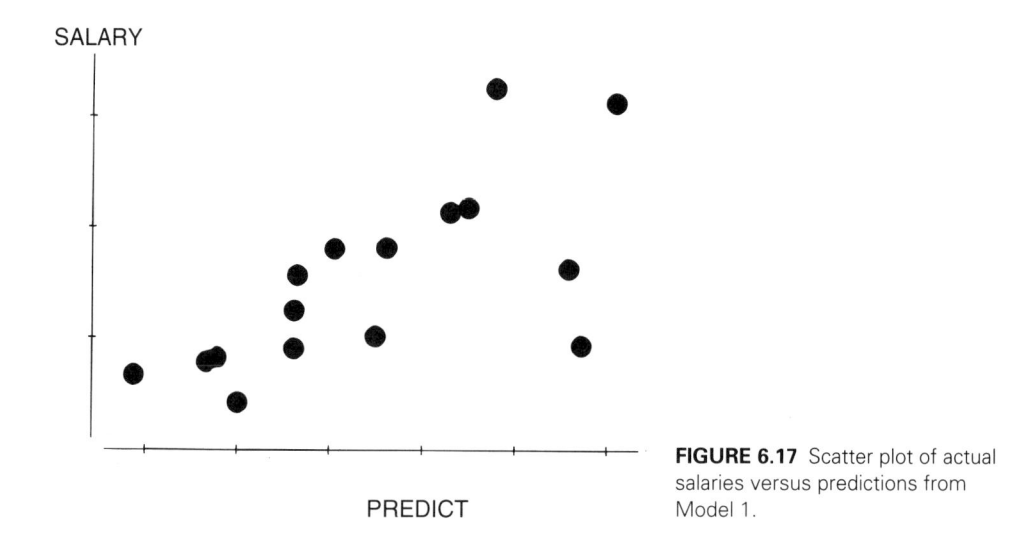

SALARY

PREDICT

FIGURE 6.17 Scatter plot of actual salaries versus predictions from Model 1.

TABLE 6.7   Sum of Squared Prediciton Errors for Three Competing Models

Model	SSPE (in Millions of Dollars Squared)
Model 1	0.2795
Model 2	0.1692
Model 3	0.2209

The *SSPE* statistics are not meaningful in and of themselves but they do allow for a meaningful comparison between models using different scales for the responses. Based on this work, it seems that Model 2 is the preferred choice.

Transformed Responses: *PRESS* and Regression Coefficient Interpretation

To complete the model validation process, the *PRESS* statistic was calculated for each model using the full data set. Because the responses are in different units, they must be converted to the same scale. That is, using equation (6.8) directly yields a *PRESS* statistic in (dollars)^2 units for Model 1 and in (logged dollars)^2 for Models 2 and 3. This conversion also needs to be done for the *SSPE* statistic. The conversion procedure for *SSPE* is similar to the one for the *PRESS* and is easier. For example, to convert the Model 2 *PRESS* statistic to (dollars)^2 units, we use the following steps:

1. Run the regression model using LNSALARY as the response. Obtain residuals LNRESID and leverages HI.
2. Using equation (6.7), compute each omit i fitted value, $LNSALARY_{(i)} = LNSALARY_i - LNRESID_i/(1 - HI_i)$.
3. Express each omit i fitted value in dollars through exponentiation, that is, define $SALARY_{(i)} = \exp(LNSALARY_{(i)})$.
4. Summarize the omit i fitted values through the *PRESS* statistic using

$$\text{PRESS} = \sum_{i=1}^{n} (SALARY_i - SALARY_{(i)})^2.$$

The results of these calculations are in Table 6.8. In this table, we provide values of the *PRESS* statistic for each of three models, for each type of unit. The *PRESS* statistic is presented in both (dollars)^2 and (logged dollars)^2 units because different results can be obtained depending on the type of unit. However, Table 6.8 shows that the third model is the best in terms of *PRESS*, regardless of the units measurement.

TABLE 6.8 Predicted Residual Sum of Squares for Three Competing Models

Model	PRESS (in Millions of dollars squared)	PRESS (in logged dollars squared)
Model 1	4.3475	31.633
Model 2	4.3373	23.041
Model 3	3.7823	21.430

From our model validation processes, Model 1 was the poorest candidate model. This model displayed the highest *SSPE* and *PRESS* statistics. This presents a strong argument for using the logarithm of salaries as the response. The choice between Models 2 and 3 is less clear; Model 2 outperforms Model 3 based on the *SSPE* although the reverse is true for the *PRESS* criterion. You might elect to choose Model 2 on the *principle of parsimony*; choosing the simplest model possible to represent the real world. Here is the result of the Model 2 estimation procedure using the full sample of observations.

$$\text{LN}\hat{\text{S}}\text{ALARY} = 11.6 + 0.0861 \text{ YRS EXP} + 0.0332 \text{ STARTED}$$

$$\textit{std errors} \quad (0.0782) \quad (0.01269) \quad\quad\quad (0.005925)$$

$$+ 0.642 \, 1/\text{DRAFT} + 0.170 \text{ OB.}$$

$$(0.1135) \quad\quad\quad (0.08074)$$

$$s = 0.3996 \quad R^2 = 62.4\% \quad R_a^2 = 61.2\%$$

This model could then be used for predicting a player's salary for arbitration purposes. The idea here is that if various characteristics about a player are known, in particular, the years of experience, number of games started in the prior year, the round selected in his first year (DRAFT) and position played, then an estimate of the player's salary can be made. This estimate is not perfect but it is interpreted as a weighted average of the many other players in the league having similar characteristics. In this way a player can be compared to his peers. We also have a measure of the natural variation in the data. That is, every player represents a special circumstance. We allow for individuality in the regression model and yet, at the same time, attempt to measure the impact of individuality through the concept of natural variation.

We have a special interpretation for the estimated coefficients when using a logarithmic response. When using the natural logarithm transformation, a per unit change can be interpreted as proportional (or, when multiplied by 100, percentage) change in the original units of the response. Thus, we can interpet the coefficient associated with YRS EXP as meaning that salary increases by 8.61% per unit change in years of experience. The idea here is that, because the logarithm of salary increases by 0.0861, then the increase in salary is (SALARY) 1.0861. That is, suppose that YRS EXP increases by one unit, causing salary to go from $SALARY_{old}$ to $SALARY_{new}$. Then, the unit increase means that the log salary increase is 0.0861, or,

$$increase = .0861 = \ln(SALARY_{new}) - \ln(SALARY_{old}) = \ln\left(\frac{SALARY_{new}}{SALARY_{old}}\right).$$

$$\text{Thus,} \quad \frac{SALARY_{new}}{SALARY_{old}} = e^{.0861} \approx 1.0861.$$

To summarize, in business and economic studies we generally use the natural logarithmic transformation. This is due to (i) the interpretation of the regression coefficients as proportional changes and (ii) the natural logarithmic transformation is a member of the Box-Cox family of transforms.

6.8 SUMMARY

Chapter 6 plays a pivotal role in our development of multiple linear regression models in Chapters 4 through 7. Chapter 4 introduced the model, with estimation and basic statistical inference ideas. Chapter 5 extended the linear regression model to include categorical independent variables. These two chapters are part of the "science" of statistics; ideas that are grounded on firm results in mathematical statistics and that are subject to relatively little disagreement among researchers. Chapter 6 provides tools and guidelines for selecting a model to represent a data set. This chapter is part of the "art" of statistics; different analysts, regardless of their diligence and thoughtfulness, will use different models to represent the same data set.

In this chapter, we discussed some of the common difficulties encountered when fitting regression models to data and provided practical suggestions for dealing with these difficulties. Unusual observations cause difficulties because regression models use weighted averages to estimate coefficients. In Sections 6.2 and 6.3, we explored two types of unusual observations, outliers and high leverage points. We think of these techniques as directed towards "data criticism" because the statistics vary at the observation level. In contrast, the techniques introduced in Sections 6.4 through 6.6 used statistics at the variable level. Specifically, the extent to which one independent variable duplicates the information contained in other variables was discussed in Section 6.4. Criteria for selecting a regression model, and procedures for arriving at candidate models were discussed in Sections 6.1, 6.4 and 6.5. Heteroscedasticity, and how to handle this model difficulty using a re-scaling, or transformation, of the response variables was addressed in Section 6.6. The case study in Section 6.7 provides an example to illustrate how to deal with the situation when several of these difficulties occur in a single data set.

Selecting a model is an inexact aspect of statistics. As such, you must carefully defend your choice of model selection. Model selection determines much of what we can say about a data set. Thus, when selecting a model, we are essentially reasoning with data. The arguments for, and against, choosing a specific model should be carefully spelled out. Chapter 7 summarizes the many lines of arguments that we can use when interpreting the results of a regression study. We will see, although the model selection formally drives the interpretation of results, that potential interpretations of results also influence our choice of a model.

KEY WORDS, PHASES AND SYMBOLS

After reading this chapter, you should be able to define each of the following important terms, phrases and symbols in your own words. If not, go to the page indicated and review the definition.

CHAPTER 6 EXERCISES

Sections 6.1–6.3

C2_STOCK

6.1 Refer to Exercise 2.29

In their April, 1992 issue, *Forbes* magazine provided financial summary measures of 500 large U.S. based corporations. The companies listed are publicly traded U.S. based firms that are largest by sales, net profits, assets and market values. We consider several of these financial variables for a sample of 50 of these firms. These variables include:

STKPRICE (y)   stock price of a share as of December 31, 1991, in dollars

Accounting Variables:

NETPRMRG	net profit margin, defined as net profits divided by sales
NALYSTS	Number of Analysts
EPS	most recent earnings per share, in dollars
SALES	1991 sales, in millions of dollars

ASSETS	1991 total assets
CASHFLOW	cashflow, in millions of dollars
NETPROF	1991 net profits, in millions of dollars
NUMSHARE	number of outstanding shares, in millions
SALES/SH	sales per share
AS/SHARE	total assets per share, in dollars per share
CASH/SH	cashflow per share
DIV	dividend.

Suppose that you are interested in relating the market variable STKPRICE (y) to the accounting variables. To begin the search for a model of STKPRICE using the accounting variables, a stepwise regression was run. The computer output follows.

a. A student has elected to use the model at stage nine of the stepwise regression procedure because this model has the largest value of R^2. Explain why this is usually not the best selection criterion.

b. Explain why there are fewer variables in the model at stage ten than in stage nine.

c. Suppose that a student wants to use stepwise regression but would like to use a t-ratio = 1.5 to enter the model (corresponding to an FENTER = 1.5^2 = 2.25). Using the attached computer output, what model would be suggested using this version of stepwise regression?

MINITAB Computer Output for Exercise 6.1

STEPWISE REGRESSION OF STKPRICE ON 12 PREDICTORS, WITH N =   48
N (CASES WITH MISSING OBS.) =   2 N(ALL CASES) =   50

STEP	1	2	3	4	5	6	7	8	9	10
CONSTANT	25.04	23.03	24.49	23.79	21.77	19.01	13.84	15.18	18.52	19.39
EPS	7.4	6.9	7.2	7.5	7.8	8.1	8.0	7.1	8.3	8.4
T-RATIO	6.51	6.12	6.46	6.71	7.08	7.25	7.15	5.79	5.65	5.88
SALES		0.00056	0.00102	0.00236	0.00253	0.00224	0.00232	0.00171	0.00057	
T-RATIO		2.02	2.83	2.44	2.67	2.32	2.43	1.66	0.44	
ASSETS			-0.00052	-0.00048	-0.00044	-0.00041	-0.00044	-0.00047	-0.00046	-0.00045
T-RATIO			-1.92	-1.77	-1.67	-1.55	-1.70	-1.81	-1.81	-1.79
CASHFLOW				-0.0125	-0.0270	-0.0269	-0.0292	-0.0350	-0.0312	-0.0285
T-RATIO				-1.49	-2.32	-2.33	-2.54	-2.92	-2.57	-2.75
NUMSHARE					0.066	0.078	0.077	0.080	0.085	0.085
T-RATIO					1.75	2.02	2.03	2.12	2.27	2.32
SALES/SH						0.032	0.036	0.038	0.036	0.038
T-RATIO						1.32	1.50	1.62	1.56	1.65
NALYSTS							0.39	0.49	0.52	0.53
T-RATIO							1.42	1.76	1.89	1.95

NETPROF								0.017	0.024	0.028
T-RATIO								1.48	1.95	2.64
NETPRMRG									-94	-112
T-RATIO									-1.43	-2.18
S	15.7	15.2	14.8	14.6	14.2	14.1	14.0	13.8	13.6	13.4
R-SQ	47.94	52.57	55.97	58.14	60.99	62.57	64.35	66.25	67.97	67.80

C2_STINS

6.2 Refer to Exercise 3.19

A financial analyst is investigating the performance of a stock insurance company in the second quarter of its fiscal period in 1991. Because of a series of abnormal accounting charges, second quarter earnings were unusual for this company. The analyst would like to determine what the "normal" earnings for this company would have been in the absence of these charges. To do this, the analyst selects a sample of size n = 36 stock insurance companies and compares the relationship between their 1991 second quarter earnings per share (EPS) with various characteristics of the company. The characteristics include: 1990 earnings per share (EPS90), total assets as a percent of common stockholders equity (TAPCE), long term debt as a percent of total capital (LDPTC), net sales in thousands of dollars (NTSLS), preferred dividends (PFDIV), common shares outstanding (CSO) and total assets as a percent of retained earnings (TAPRE). A summary of these relationships is given in Figure E6.2 and Table E6.2a.

TABLE E6.2a Summary Statistics for Exercise 6.2 Variables

	Number	Mean	Median	Standard deviation	Minimum	Maximum
EPS	36	0.985	0.945	0.784	−0.620	3.490
EPS90	36	3.671	3.595	2.155	0.090	12.450
TAPCE	36	800.4	742.8	521.8	−697.3	2479.3
LDPTC	36	24.80	21.88	18.47	0.00	75.13
NTSLS	36	4126	2602	4969	86	19020
PFDIV	36	3.66	0.00	6.08	0.00	21.22
CSO	36	54692	46992	41418	4885	212143
TAPRE	36	775	929	2671	−13505	5792

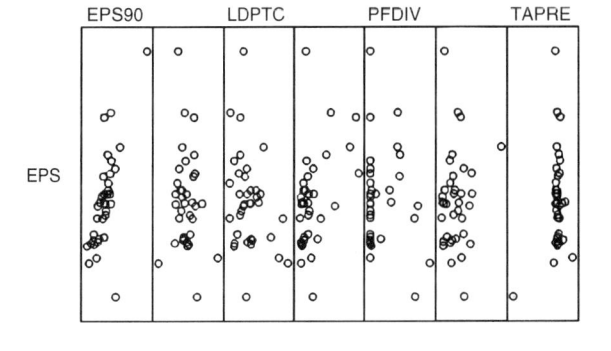

FIGURE E6.2

Correlation Matrix for Exercise 6.2 Variables

	EPS90	TAPCE	LDPTC	NTSLS	PFDIV	CSO	TAPRE
TAPCE	−0.022						
LDPTC	−0.116	0.039					
NTSLS	0.229	0.301	−0.063				
PFDIV	−0.045	−0.021	0.399	0.239			
CSO	0.159	0.173	0.182	0.666	0.263		
TAPRE	−0.246	0.146	0.133	0.038	−0.347	−0.100	
EPS	0.717	−0.091	−0.315	0.424	−0.119	0.080	0.244

a. A Preliminary Regression Model was run using all of the variables and all of the data. See Tables E6.2b and E6.2c for the details of the analysis. The t-ratio associated with the total assets as a percent of retained earnings (TAPRE) was large. Calculate the partial correlation between TAPRE and EPS. Compare this to the correlation between TAPRE and EPS. Use the scatter plots to explain why this correlation is large.

b. One company, USF&G Corporation, observation $i = 30$, had an unusually poor second quarter, $EPS_{30} = -0.620$. Use the information from the unusual observation display and the definition of the standardized residual to calculate the leverage associated with this point. What is the overall average leverage? Is this leverage unusual?

c. From the Preliminary Regression Model (Table E6.2b), use an expression for the standard error of the partial slope to calculate the variance inflation factor for EPS90. Describe what the variance inflation factor measures and say whether your statistic is large.

d. A second regression model was fit, after eliminating USF&G Corporation. The output is in the attached output under the heading "Second Regression Model." Note that the fifth observation has a large standardized residual. What percentage of the error sum of squares is due to the fifth observation?

e. Use the summary statistics and the fact that $EPS90_{30} = 5.9$ to check that the standard deviation of EPS90 after having deleted the 30th observation is $s_{EPS90,new} = 2.152$.

Preliminary Regression Model

TABLE E6.2b Coefficient Estimates

Explanatory variables	Coefficient	Standard error	t-ratio
Constant	0.2876	0.1389	2.07
EPS90	0.27852	0.02304	12.09
TAPCE	−0.00031556	0.00009262	−3.41
LDPTC	−0.013259	0.003090	−4.29
NTSLS	0.00005353	0.00001450	3.69
PFDIV	0.024033	0.009972	2.41
CSO	−0.00000320	0.00000159	−2.02
TAPRE	0.00015824	0.00002116	7.28

TABLE E6.2c ANOVA Table

Source	Sum of Squares	df	Mean Square
Regression	19.4848	7	2.7835
Error	2.0029	28	0.0715
Total	21.4877	35	

The regression fit also yields $s = 0.2675$, $R^2 = 90.7\%$ and $R_a^2 = 88.3\%$.

UNUSUAL OBSERVATIONS

Obs	EPS90	EPS	Fit	Residual	Std Resid
2	4.7	1.4400	1.9570	−0.5170	−2.44
5	3.6	2.3800	1.7484	0.6316	3.23
30	5.9	−0.6200	−0.5875	−0.0325	−0.62

Second Regression Model

TABLE E6.2d Coefficient Estimates

Explanatory variables	Coefficient	Standard error	t-ratio
Constant	0.2782	0.1414	1.97
EPS90	0.27602	0.02366	11.66
TAPCE	−0.0002231	0.0001781	−1.25
LDPTC	−0.012535	0.003343	−3.75
NTSLS	0.00005275	0.00001472	3.58
PFDIV	0.02364	0.01011	2.34
CSO	−0.00000329	0.00000161	−20.4
TAPRE	0.0001063	0.00008815	1.20

TABLE E6.2e ANOVA Table

Source	Sum of Squares	df	Mean Square
Regression	16.8624	7	2.4089
Error	1.9756	27	0.0732
Total	18.8381	34	

The regression fit also yields $s = 0.2705$, $R^2 = 89.5\%$ and $R_a^2 = 86.8\%$.

UNUSUAL OBSERVATIONS

Obs	EPS90	EPS	Fit	Residual	Std Resid
2	4.7	1.4400	1.9571	−0.5171	−2.41
5	3.6	2.3800	1.7370	0.6430	3.27

C6_ARCH

6.3 Professor Kerry Vandell studied the effects that various characteristics, called "amenities" in the regional science literature, have on the value of a building. Such amenities typically include easily measured characteristics such as age of the building, availability of on-site parking, distance to the city center, and so forth. Possibly due to the fact that it is difficult to measure, an amenity that has not received much attention in the literature is the quality of the architectural design. Assessing the contribution of architectural quality to the building's value is the primary goal of this study. Because a number of characteristics may affect the market performance, the effect of architectural design should be analyzed given the presence of these other characteristics. This is a follow-up to the study reported by Vandell and Land in the *AREUA Journal*, Vol. 17, No. 2, 1989, entitled "The economics of architecture and urban design: Some preliminary findings."

To investigate empirically these issues, cross-sectional data from 84 large office buildings in Boston, Massachusetts have been collected. Although there are a number of different measures of "market performance" of a building, this study uses rent per square foot of rentable area for the second quarter of 1990 (RENT90) as the measure of value. The objective characteristics considered here are the year the building was built (YEAR), building size in terms of number of floors, whether on-site parking is available (ONSITE), the distance to public transportation (DIS PUBL) and the distance to

The Data for this Exercise

NAME	COUNT	MISSING
ID	84	
NAME	84	
RENT90	84	4
YEAR	84	
NUMFLOOR	84	2
SQFEET	84	19
NUMPARK	84	23
ONSITE	84	3
DIS PUBL	84	2
CITY CEN	84	2
RATING	84	

the city center (CITY CEN). Also included are the size of the building in square footage and size of the parking lot. These latter two variables are characteristics routinely considered in the regional science literature but were difficult to obtain in this sample. Thus, information on several apartment buildings is missing. To assess the quality of architectural design, a survey was sent to leading "experts" in the field. There are 21 respondents to the survey, each of whom assessed the quality of architectural design for each of the 84 buildings. Each expert rated each building on a 0 to 5 scale (for example, 0 means poor design and 5 means excellent design). The variable "RATING" is the rating by building averaged over the 21 experts.

a. From Figure E6.3, give a verbal interpretation of the effect on the rent of the number of floors and the availability of on-site parking.

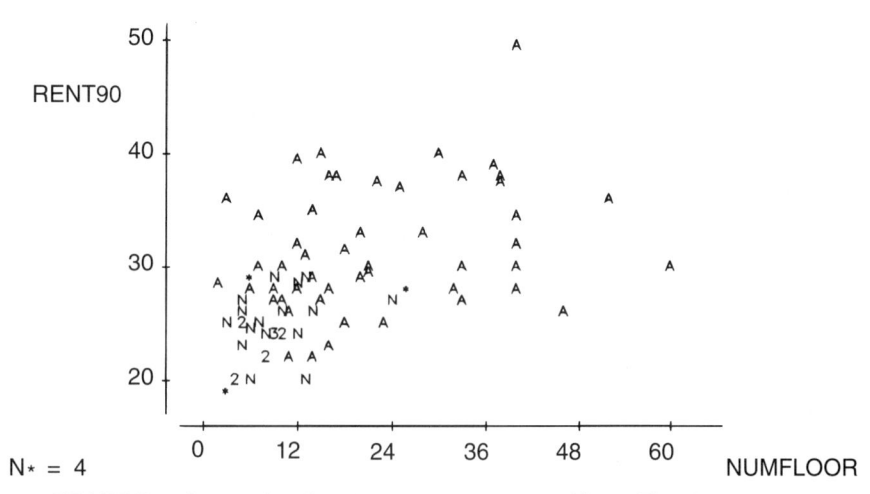

FIGURE E6.3 Scatter plot of 1990 rent versus number of floors. The plotting symbol is used to indicate the availability of onsite parking, with "A" meaning it is available and "N" meaning it is not.
Source: Vandell and Land in the AREUA Journal, Vol. 17, No. 2, 1989, entitled "The economics of architecture and urban design: Some preliminary findings."

b. For the following regression model (Tables E6.3a and b), calculate the partial correlation between the RATING variable and the RENT90 variable, in the presence of the other variables, including YEAR, NUMFLOOR, ONSITE, DIS PUBL and CITY CEN.

TABLE E6.3a Coefficient Estimates

Explanatory variables	Coefficient	Standard error	t-ratio
Constant	−267.4	136.1	−1.96
YEAR	0.14800	0.06883	2.15
NUMFLOOR	0.15679	0.04892	3.21
ONSITE	−4.913	1.683	−2.92
DIS PUBL	0.0009059	0.0009302	0.97
CITY CEN	−0.00007521	0.00009552	−0.79
RATING	0.7222	0.6259	1.15

TABLE E6.3b ANOVA Table

Source	Sum of Squares	df	Mean Square
Regression	1126.87	6	187.81
Error	1497.33	70	21.39
Total	2624.20	76	

The regression fit also yields $s = 4.625$, $R^2 = 42.9\%$ and $R_a^2 = 38.1\%$.

c. Using the output from the best subsets regression, describe which model that you prefer. Justify your response in terms of each of the four criteria provided by the best subsets routine. In your justification, define each of the four criteria.

```
Best Subsets Regression of RENT90
77 cases used 7 cases contain missing values.
```

					Y E A R	N U M F L O O R	O N S I T E	D I S P U B L	C I T Y C E N	R A T I N G
Vars	R-sq	Adj. R-sq	C-p	s						
1	28.9	28.0	14.2	4.9860			X			
1	23.9	22.9	20.4	5.1600		X				
2	36.00	34.3	7.5	4.7622		X				
2	31.4	29.5	13.2	4.9330	X		X			
3	40.9	38.4	3.5	4.6107	X	X	X			
3	38.2	35.7	6.8	4.7136		X	X			X
4	41.7	38.5	4.5	4.6090	X	X	X			X
4	41.4	38.2	4.9	4.6211	X	X	X	X		
5	42.4	38.4	5.6	4.6126	X	X	X	X		X
5	42.2	38.1	5.9	4.6233	X	X	X		X	X
6	42.9	38.1	7.0	4.6250	X	X	X	X	X	X

d. The forward and backward versions of the stepwise regression routines are presented in the following. Surprisingly, the forward version arrives at a model with a much lower R^2 than that achieved for the backward version. Even more surprising, this is true when the same model is being consider by each routine. Explain this seeming anomaly.

```
STEPWISE REGRESSION OF RENT90
   ON  8 PREDICTORS, WITH N =  47
N(CASES WITH MISSING OBS.) =  37
   N(ALL CASES) =    84
```

STEP	1	2	3	4
CONSTANT	24.91	22.69	23.55	-304.32
RATING	2.26	2.40	2.28	1.78
T-RATIO	2.54	2.81	2.68	1.98
SQFEET		0.00000	0.00000	0.00000
T-RATIO		2.22	1.91	2.32
ONSITE			-3.6	-4.5
T-RATIO			-1.34	-1.66
YEAR				0.17
T-RATIO				1.52
S	5.32	5.10	5.05	4.98
R-SQ	12.58	21.40	24.54	28.49

Forward stepwise regression.

```
STEPWISE REGRESSION OF  RENT90
    ON  6 PREDICTORS, WITH N =  77
N(CASES WITH MISSING OBS.) =   7
   N(ALL CASES) =    84
```

STEP	1	2	3
CONSTANT	-267.4	-366.1	-256.5
YEAR	0.148	0.147	0.143
T-RATIO	2.15	2.14	2.09
NUMFLOOR	0.157	0.165	0.161
T-RATIO	3.21	3.47	3.40
ONSITE	-4.9	-5.5	-4.9
T-RATIO	-2.92	-3.74	-3.76
DIS PUBL	0.00091	0.00087	
T-RATIO	0.97	0.94	

CITY CEN	-0.00008		
T-RATIO	-0.79		
RATING	0.72	0.70	0.64
T-RATIO	1.15	1.13	1.03
S	4.62	4.61	4.61
R-SQ	42.94	42.44	41.72

Backward stepwise regression.

6.4 A pilot, or preliminary, study was conducted at a local savings and loan to understand the relationship between the size of a bank loan and various characteristics. A sample of 35 loans was drawn from approximately 24,000 home mortgage loans originated from 1984 to 1988. For each sample loan, we have information concerning the initial loan amount, the age, monthly income and marital status of the lendee. Financial characteristics of the lendee include the total outstanding debt (net of the mortgage) and net worth. Characteristics of the loan include the loan to value ratio and a variable to indicate whether the loan used a fixed rate of assumed interest or was allowed to vary with the Consumer's Price Index. (See Figures E6.4a and b.) Correlations among loan amount, net worth and the logarithm of net worth follow.

	LNAMT	NETWTH
NETWTH	0.383	
LOGNETWH	0.485	0.726

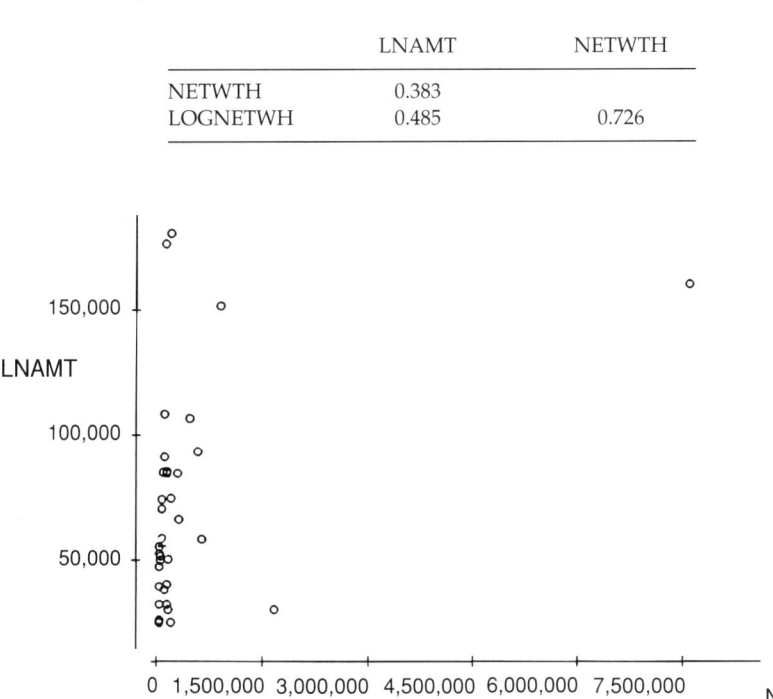

FIGURE E6.4a Scatter plot of loan amount versus net worth.

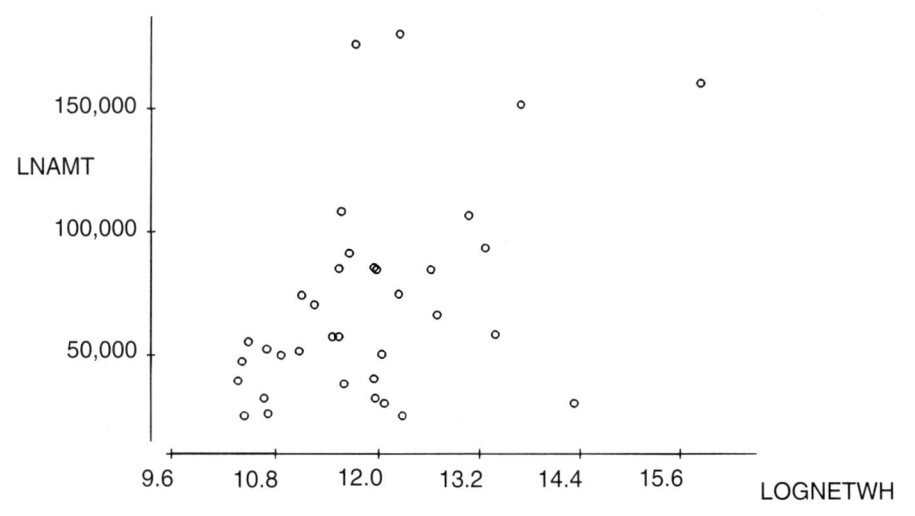

FIGURE E6.4b Scatter plot of loan amount versus the logarithm of net worth.

    a. See the scatter plots of the response, loan amount, versus net worth and the logarithm of net worth, together with the correlation coefficients. Describe which of the two measures of net worth that you consider more useful, and say why.

    b. In the following exhibits, the forward and backward version of stepwise regression was run using the same predictor variables. Unfortunately, the two algorithms recommended different models. Describe how this can happen by giving the basic set-up of each procedure. Based on these exhibits, say which model you would tentatively entertain.

```
              STEPWISE REGRESSION OF  LNAMT
              ON   9  PREDICTORS, WITH N =
              35

                   STEP          1          2
              CONSTANT        33169     -25646

              INCOME           7.8        6.9
              T-RATIO         4.78       4.68

              LTV                       90854
              T-RATIO                    3.03

              S              32854      29415
              R-SQ           40.92      54.08
```

Forward stepwise regression.

```
STEPWISE REGRESSION ON   LNAMT   ON  9 PREDICTORS, WITH N =   35

        STEP      1         2         3         4         5         6
    CONSTANT  -426167   -428580   -442400   -433002   -403557   -482774

AGE           -159
T-RATIO      -0.23

INCOME         3.5       3.3       3.5       3.4       3.2
T-RATIO       1.28      1.29      1.47      1.44      1.39

MARSTAT      -7864     -6450     -8034     -8074
T-RATIO      -0.49     -0.44     -0.59     -0.60

TOTDEBT       0.045     0.046     0.046     0.045     0.044     0.050
T-RATIO       2.65      2.72      2.79      2.79      2.77      3.26

LTV         120611    122779    125199    124823    121547    139243
T-RATIO       3.52      3.79      4.04      4.09      4.09      5.11

NETWTH       -0.104    -0.104    -0.105    -0.103    -0.098    -0.109
T-RATIO      -2.76     -2.80     -2.93     -2.93     -2.91     -3.25

FIXED         3438      3926
T-RATIO       0.27      0.32

LOGDEBT       -943      -741      -792
T-RATIO      -0.49     -0.44     -0.47

LOGNETWH     36739     36016     37359     35940     33098     40114
T-RATIO       2.86      2.94      3.31      3.35      3.47      4.88

S            27552     27046     26593     26222     25933     26328
R-SQ         68.52     68.46     68.33     68.07     67.65     65.51
```

Backward stepwise regression.

c. Suppose that you decide to estimate the model suggested by the backward stepwise regression procedure. Table E6.4a is the output from this model fitting. Describe drawbacks of this estimated model in terms of the variance inflation factor.

TABLE E6.4a Coefficient Estimates

Explanatory variables	Coefficient	Standard error	t-ratio	VIF
Constant	−403557	111339	−3.62	
INCOME	3.174	2.290	1.39	3.2
TOTDEBT	0.04396	0.01587	2.77	76.7
LTV	121547	29719	4.09	1.3
NETWTH	−0.09816	0.03377	−2.91	95.2
LOGNETWH	33099	9548	3.47	6.6

The regression fit also yields $s = 25933$, $R^2 = 67.7\%$ and $R_a^2 = 62.1\%$.

Sections 6.4–6.6

C5_ASSES

6.5 Refer to Exercise 5.5

   a. One potential criticism of the regression model fit in part (b) of Exercise 5.5 is the presence of heteroscedasticity.

   i. In Figure E6.5a below is a scatter plot of ASSESS92 versus ASSESS91. Discuss how this could be viewed as a heteroscedastic relationship.

   ii. In Figure E6.5b is a plot of the standardized residuals from the regression fit versus ASSESS91. Describe the heteroscedasticity that is evident in this plot.

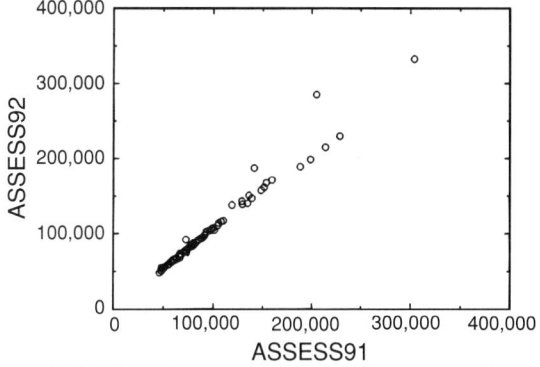

FIGURE E6.5a Scatter plot of ASSESS92 versus AS-SESS91.

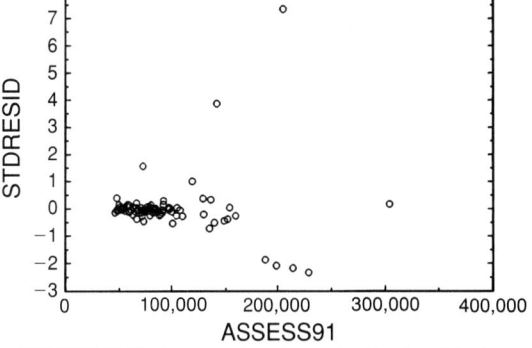

FIGURE E6.5b Scatter plot of standardized residuals versus ASSESS91. The residuals are from a regression of ASSESS92 on ASSESS91.

   b. To understand the growth in assessed values, let's look directly at the percentage change, defined by PCHANGE = 100[(ASSESS92/ASSESS91) − 1].

   i. What is a point estimate for the expected percentage change?

   ii. Discuss reasons that the point estimate in part b(i) above differs from the estimate in part b(ii) of Exercise 5.5.

   iii. Provide a 95% confidence interval for the expected percentage change. (See Table E6.5a)

TABLE E6.5a Summary Statistics for the Percentage Change

	Number	Mean	Median	Standard deviation	Minimum	Maximum
PCHANGE	89	7.963	7.322	5.353	−0.101	39.024

   c. In Figure E6.5c is a plot of the percentage change versus ASSESS91. Compare this plot to the plot of standardized residuals versus ASSESS91.

   i. Which scatter plot displays less heteroscedasticity?

   ii. Based on the comparison of the two scatter plots, write down the theoretical model that you prefer.

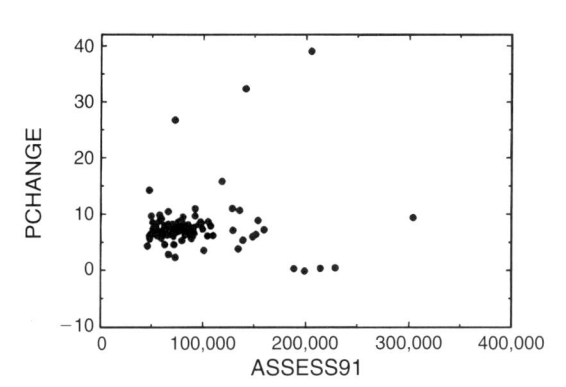

FIGURE E6.5c

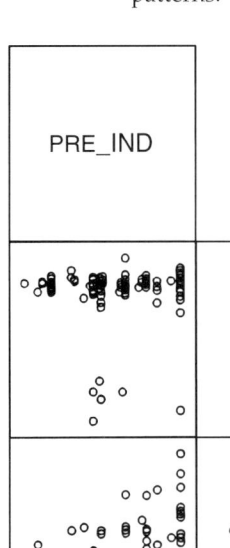

6.6 Many investors rely on predictions of a company's performance compiled by professional analysts. One such compilation is *Zach's Index*. Here, we examine a company's predicted earnings per share (PRE_EPS) and attempt to explain this in terms of a number of firm and industry variables. The industry variables include the expected industry change in EPS for the next five years (PRE_IND) and the type of industry (IND) . For this data set, four industries are considered: retail (IND = 1), manufacturing (IND = 2), life and health insurance (IND = 3) and service (IND = 4). The firm variable is the company change in EPS over the last five years (CL5Y). The data were collected from the *Disclosure Database*. From each industry, a random sample of 25 to 35 firms was used to create the full data set of 110 firms. Figures are for 1990.

    a. Figure E6.6 is a scatterplot matrix of PRE_EPS, PRE_IND and CL5Y. Describe the relationships between these variables. In particular, note the linear and nonlinear patterns.

FIGURE E6.6
Source: Disclosure Database. Originally from the U.S. Securities and Exchange Commission.

C6_EPSPR

    b. Tables E6.6a and b show a fitted regression model of PRE_EPS on PRE_IND and CL5Y. Describe the adequacy of the model.

TABLE E6.6a Coefficient Estimates

Explanatory variables	Coefficient	Standard error	t-ratio
Constant	1.456	1.990	0.73
PRE_IND	0.7789	0.1221	6.38
CL5Y	0.020163	0.006642	3.04

TABLE E6.6b ANOVA Table

Source	Sum of Squares	df	Mean Square
Regression	671.63	2	335.81
Error	1432.37	107	13.39
Total	2103.99	109	

    The regression fit also yields $s = 3.659$, $R^2 = 31.9\%$ and $R_a^2 = 30.6\%$.

    c. In our sample of 110 firms, from the preceding scatterplot matrix we can see that seven companies had particularly large downturns in their earnings per share over the last five years. Because this pattern may represent a nonlinear effect, an indicator variable for these seven firms was created and called "BADCL5Y." This variable was also included in the fitted regression model (Tables E6.6c and d). Explain the presence of the relatively large VIF statistics.

TABLE E6.6c Coefficient Estimates

Explanatory variables	Coefficient	Standard error	t-ratio	VIF
Constant	1.171	1.993	0.59	
PRE_IND	0.7774	0.1217	6.39	1.0
CL5Y	0.05004	0.02320	2.16	12.3
BADCL5Y	6.707	4.993	1.34	12.3

TABLE E6.6d ANOVA Table

Source	Sum of Squares	df	Mean Square
Regression	695.60	3	231.87
Error	1408.39	106	13.29
Total	2103.99	109	

The regression fit also yields $s = 3.645$, $R^2 = 33.1\%$ and $R_a^2 = 31.2\%$.

    d. The following dotplots of the standardized residuals from the regression model fit in part (b). These dotplots are given by level of the industry variable. Also provided are the corresponding summary statistics (Table E6.6e). Use these graphs and statistics to describe differences in the variability by industry.

```
                Dotplots of Standardized Residuals by Level of IND
IND.
1
           .:   .  . .:   ..: :.  .   .:  . .        .  :  .
       ---+---------+---------+---------+---------+---------+---C20
IND.
2              .    .... .:  .:  :.: ::  . :           .
       ---+---------+---------+---------+---------+---------+---C20
```

```
IND.                      .     .      .    .
3                      :  .:  ..::...:. :.      ..
    ---+---------+---------+---------+---------+---------+---C20
IND.                   .                .
4        .    . :   . :  .::..:    . .:::  .     ..:    ..        .
    ---+---------+---------+---------+---------+---------+---C20
       -2.0       -1.0       0.0        1.0        2.0        3.0
```

TABLE E6.6e Summary Statistics of Standardized Residuals by Level of IND

Level of IND	Number	Mean	Standard deviation
1	25	0.0002	1.1592
2	26	0.0470	0.8946
3	26	−0.2704	0.5922
4	33	0.1818	1.2028
ALL	110	0.0018	1.0063

e. To assess whether there is a difference in variability by industry, the standardized residuals are raised to the $2/3$rd power. Then, one can treat the transformed residuals as the dependent variable and use regression models to see if the categorical variable industry is important. The idea here is that, by going to the $2/3$rd's power, we are looking at the variability of the standardized residuals. (Essentially, the square converts the residuals to estimates of variability and the one third power symmetrizes the distribution.) From the regression fit, describe how we can conclude that the variability differs among industries. (Also use Tables E6.6f and g.)

```
              Dotplots of Standardized Residuals Raised to the 2/3rd Power
                             by Level of IND
IND.                          .
1        . .  .   . .  . ... :   :..  .    .     ..:.   : .
    -+---------+---------+---------+---------+---------+-----C21
IND.                      .
2          . ..:..:  ....:..  :  ..:.          .             .
    -+---------+---------+---------+---------+---------+-----C21
IND.              .            :
3      ...   :    : : :..::. ..    : :   ..
    -+---------+---------+---------+---------+---------+-----C21
IND.                     .
4        . ..   .....::..:  ::  .    ......:.   . :        .
    -+---------+---------+---------+---------+---------+-----C21
     0.00      0.40      0.80      1.20      1.60      2.00
```

TABLE E6.6f ANOVA Table

Source	Sum of Squares	df	Mean Square
IND	1.866	3	0.622
Error	18.600	106	0.175
Total	20.466	109	

TABLE E6.6g Summary Statistics of Standardized Residuals Raised to the $\frac{2}{3}$rd Power by Level of IND

Level of IND	Number	Mean	Standard deviation
1	25	0.8885	0.4758
2	26	0.7438	0.3814
3	26	0.6061	0.3312
4	33	0.9361	0.4605

f. Given the fact that we encountered heteroscedasticity among industry groups in part (e), describe a regression modeling approach that would handle this fact.

6.7 Suppose that you have completed a regression analysis of data and now wish to validate the results of your study.

   i. Define the PRESS statistic. Be sure to identify all the terms that you use.

   ii. You notice that the PRESS statistic is greater than the error sum of squares, Error SS. Using algebra, show that this is always the case.

   iii. You would like to calculate the PRESS statistic for two models, one using y as the response and the second using ln y as the response. To check your computations, you decide to do a computation by hand with only three observations. Your results are in Table E6.7.

TABLE E6.7

Model: $y = \beta_0 + \beta_1 x + e$		Model: $\ln y = \beta_0 + \beta_1 x + e$	
Response y	1, 1, 20.0855	Response ln y	0, 0, 3
Residual $\hat{e}$	3.181, −6.362, 3.181	Residual $\hat{e}^*$	.5, −1, .5
Leverage h_{ii}	.8333, .3333, .8333	Leverage h_{ii}	.8333, .3333, .8333

Calculate the PRESS statistic for each model. Express your results in original y units (squared).

END-OF-CHAPTER EXERCISES

C2_STOCK

6.8 **Refer to Exercise 6.1**

   a. Based on the stepwise regression and additional analyses, a five variable model was fit. The computer output follows.

      i. What does the variance inflation factor measure?

      ii. What constitutes a large variance inflation factor?

      iii. If a large variance inflation factor is detected, what possible courses of action do we have to address this aspect of the data?

   b. Again, examine the fit of the five variable model in the following computer output. At the bottom, several high leverage points are noted by the statistical package.

      i. Define the concept of a high leverage point.

     ii. Calculate the leverage for the sixth observation.

  c. An alternative model, using only three variables, was also fit. The computer output follows.

      i. To compare the two models, PRESS statistics were calculated. For the five variable model, the PRESS statistic is 11,592. For the three variable model, the PRESS statistic is 12,543. Define the PRESS statistic, and say which of the two models you prefer based on this statistic.

     ii. Which model do you prefer, the three or five variable model? After stating your preference, give arguments for and against your choice of models.

MINITAB Computer Output for Exercise 6.8

Five Variable Regression with VIF's

```
The regression equation is
STKPRICE = 21.8 + 7.82 EPS + 0.00253 SALES -0.000440 ASSETS - 0.0270
           CASHFLOW + 0.0662 NUMSHARE
```

```
48 cases used 2 cases contain missing values
Predictor       Coef       Stdev     t-ratio        VIF
Constant      21.774       3.467        6.28
EPS            7.823       1.105        7.08        1.1
SALES      0.0025339   0.0009505        2.67       14.0
ASSETS    -0.0004404   0.0002645       -1.67        1.9
CASHFLOW    -0.02698     0.01164       -2.32       28.4
NUMSHARE     0.06623     0.03783        1.75       11.8
```

```
s = 14.25      R-sq = 61.0%     R-sq(adj) - 56.3%
```

Analysis of Variance

```
SOURCE        DF         SS         MS          F
Regression     5     13326.1     2665.2      13.13
Error         42      8525.3      203.0
Total         47     21851.4
```

Unusual Observations

```
Obs.    EPS  STKPRICE      Fit    Residual   St. Resid
  6     1.4     32.87    45.20     -12.32     -1.29 X
 11     4.2     77.13    70.44       6.68      0.86 X
 18     4.0     49.00    38.71      10.29      1.04 X
 20     2.2     69.50    39.24      30.26      2.16 R
 28     5.0    100.50    92.03       8.47      0.79 X
```

Three Variable Regression with VIF's

```
The regression equation is
STKPRICE = 24.0 + 7.23 EPS -0.000398 ASSETS + 0.0364 NUMSHARE
```

```
48 cases used 2 cases contain missing values

Predictor        Coef       Stdev    t-ratio       VIF
Constant       23.992       3.456       6.94
EPS             7.229       1.130       6.40        1.1
ASSETS      -0.0003982   0.0002617      -1.52        1.7
NUMSHARE      0.03641     0.01499       2.43        1.7


s = 15.10        R-sq = 54.1%    R-sq(adj) = 51.0%


Analysis of Variance

SOURCE        DF          SS          MS          F
Regression     3       11819.7      3939.9     17.28
Error         44       10031.7       228.0
Total         47       21851.4


Unusual Observations
Obs.     EPS    STKPRICE      Fit   Residual   Std. Resid
   6     1.4      32.87     55.00     -22.12        -1.81
  11     4.2      77.13     69.26       7.86         0.69
  18     4.0      49.00     38.58      10.42         0.92
```

6.9 **Refer to Exercise 6.2**

C6_STINS

    a. From the Second Regression Model, use an expression for the standard error of the partial slope to calculate the variance inflation factor for EPS90. Describe what the variance inflation factor measures and say whether your statistic is large.

    b. For the company of interest to the financial analyst, suppose that EPS90 = 1.53, TAPCE = 938, LDPTC = 28, NTSLS = 870, PFDIV = 0, CSO = 105600 and TAPRE = 1275. Use the final regression model to provide a prediction for EPS. (See Tables E6.9a and b.)

Final Regression Model

TABLE E6.9a Coefficient Estimates

Explanatory variables	Coefficient	Standard error	t-ratio
Constant	0.2351	0.1194	1.97
EPS90	0.27099	0.02243	12.08
LDPTC	−0.011079	0.002930	−3.78
NTSLS	0.00005018	0.00001353	−3.71
PFDIV	0.022684	0.009464	2.40
CSO	−0.00000349	0.00000157	−2.22

TABLE E6.9b ANOVA Table

Source	Sum of Squares	df	Mean Square
Regression	16.7414	5	3.3483
Error	2.0967	29	0.0723
Total	18.8381	34	

The regression fit also yields $s = 0.2689$, $R^2 = 88.9\%$ and $R_a^2 = 87.0\%$.

6.10 Are lower prices related to higher sales volume? A response to this question is imporant to manufacturers competing in the United States automobile market, not unlike many other markets. To investigate this question, base model prices of 48 types of cars were collected from the April 1989 issue of *Consumer Reports*. Also in this issue was information on the miles per gallons (MPG) of each car, a measure of size of the car in terms of the number of passengers (2, 4, 5 or 6) and the manufacturer of each car. Manufacturers were categorized into five groups, 'FORD', General Motors (GM), 'JAPANESE', 'CHRYSLER' and 'EUROPE', respectively (see Table E6.10b). The response variable of interest was the number of autombiles sold, collected from *Automotive Weekly* and *Automotive Facts and Figures*. (See Table E6.10a.)

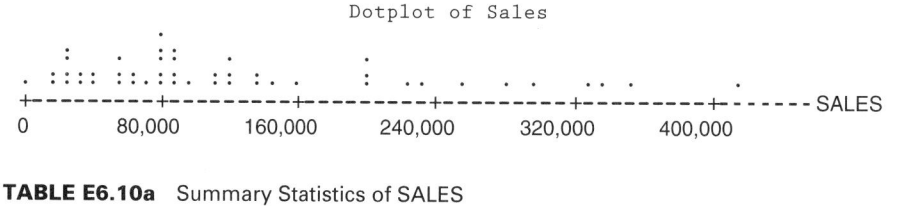

TABLE E6.10a Summary Statistics of SALES

	Number	Mean	Median	Standard deviation	Minimum	Maximum
SALES	48	123,337	85,150	101,693	2,743	416,957

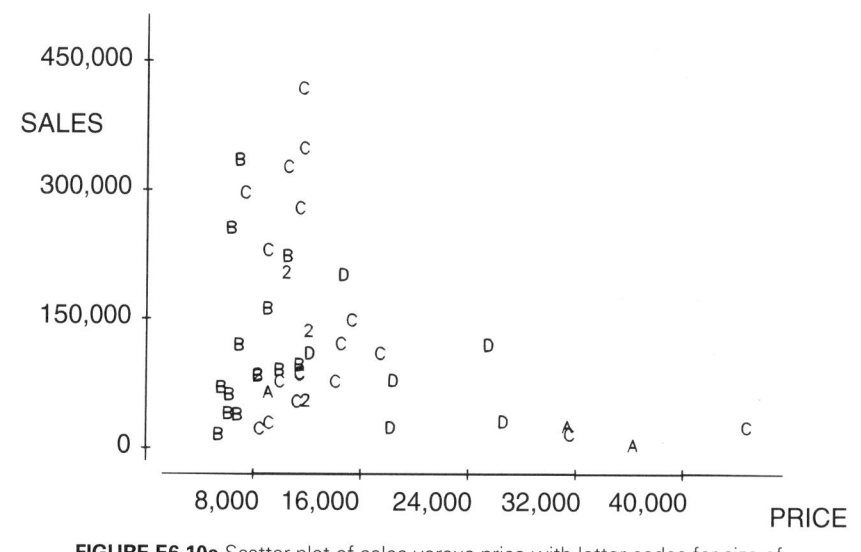

FIGURE E6.10a Scatter plot of sales versus price with letter codes for size of car. Here, 'A' is a two-passenger car and 'B', 'C' and 'D' are 4, 5 and 6 passenger cars, respectively. *Source: Consumer Reports, Automotive Weekly and Automotive Facts and Figures*

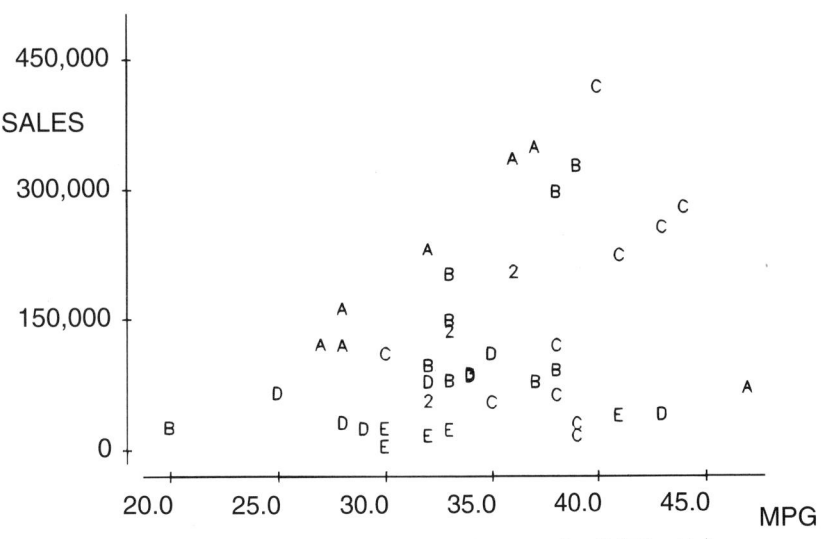

FIGURE E6.10b Scatter plot of sales versus miles per gallon (MPG) with letter codes for the category of the car's manufacturer. Here, the letter codes 'A', 'B', 'C', 'D' and 'E' represents FORD, GM, JAPANESE, CHRYSLER and EUROPE, respectively.

TABLE E6.10b   Table of SALES, PRICE and MPG by Category of Manufacturer

| Manufacturer | | SALES | | PRICE | | MPG | |
	Number	Mean	Standard deviation	Mean	Standard deviation	Mean	Standard deviation
FORD	7	197,200	109,475	11,817	6,745	33.571	7.138
GM	15	141,179	89,019	13,552	5,642	33.667	4.515
JAPANESE	10	155,760	131,838	9,690	3,637	38.700	4.001
CHRYSLER	11	69,516	27,092	11,906	5,851	32.909	4.636
EUROPE	5	19,960	12,765	25,631	17,073	33.200	4.550
ALL	48	123,337	101,693	13,375	8,346	34.479	5.182

a. Use Table E6.10a and the dotplot to describe the shape of the distribution of SALES.

b. Use the scatter plots (Figures E6.10a and b) to describe any patterns in the variability of SALES.

c. Does the type of manufacturer seem to affect levels of SALES? Use the scatter plot and Table E6.10b to address this question.

d. From the scatter plots, describe the effect that each of PRICE, MPG and size of the automobile seem to have on SALES.

e. The data was fit using the logarithm of sales (LOGSALES) as the response variable and using PRICE, MPG, size and categories of manufacturer as the explanatory variables. The output from this fit is given in the preliminary regression model.

Why was the category 'European' not fit? Describe the relationships among the explanatory variables using the variance inflation factor.

f. Two of the unusually large residuals, observations numbers 30 and 31, were from the Japanese manufacturer Mitsubishi. It turned out that these were the only observations from Mitsubishi in the data set. Use this, and Tables E6.10c, d and e to describe why an indicator variable for the presence of Mitsubishi might be a reasonable addition to the model specification.

TABLE E6.10c Coefficient Estimates

Explanatory variables	Coefficient	Standard error	t-ratio	VIF
Constant	8.727	1.285	6.79	
PRICE	−0.00003146	0.00001895	−1.66	2.4
MPG	−0.02980	0.02780	1.07	2.0
SIZE	0.2963	0.1326	2.21	1.1
FORD	1.8964	0.4911	3.86	2.9
GM	1.5825	0.4285	3.69	3.9
JAPANESE	1.2215	0.4539	2.69	3.3
CHRYSLER	0.8923	0.4737	1.88	3.9

TABLE E6.10d ANOVA Table

Source	Sum of Squares	df	Mean Square
Regression	27.6140	7	3.9449
Error	19.6096	40	0.4902
Total	47.2236	47	

The regression fit also yields $s = 0.7002$, $R^2 = 58.5\%$ and $R_a^2 = 51.2\%$.

UNUSUAL OBSERVATIONS

Obs.	LOGSALES	Fit	Residual	Std Resid
30	10.280	11.703	−1.424	−2.15
31	9.618	11.525	−1.907	−2.89
37	11.147	12.432	−1.285	−2.32

TABLE E6.10e Summary Statistics Categorized by Mitsubishi

		SALES			Standardized Residual	
	Number	Mean	Standard deviation		Mean	Standard deviation
Non-Mitsubishi	46	127739	101604		0.1017	0.8920
Mitsubishi	2	22086	9969		−2.5242	0.5227
ALL	48	123337	101693		−0.0077	1.0242

g. Based on the analysis of the preliminary regression model, an indicator variable for Mitsubishi was added. Further, the MPG variable was dropped because of it's low t-ratio. The resulting fitted model is under the Final Regression Model heading. Do you think that this is an improvement? Discuss your reasons.

h. You have asked your assistant to review your work. The assistant inadvertently runs five indicator variables in the regression. The statistical package drops one of the five variables, 'Europe.' The assistant then examines the t-ratios of the alternative model and is quite excited because these seem to be much better than your "final" model. Has the assistant discovered a better model? Explain the differences between the models and say which your prefer.

```
                 MINITAB Computer Output

             FINAL REGRESSION MODEL

The regression equation is
LOGSALES = 11.7 -0.000049 PRICE + 0.328 SIZE - 0.277 GM - 0.127 JAPANESE
          - 1.03 CHRYSLER - 1.66 EUROPE - 2.12 MITSU
```

Predictor	Coef	Stdev	t-ratio
Constant	11.7329	0.3626	32.36
PRICE	-0.00004858	0.00001214	-4.00
SIZE	0.3280	0.1064	3.08
GM	-0.2774	0.2625	-1.06
JAPANESE	-0.1270	0.2964	-0.43
CHRYSLER	-1.0260	0.2761	-3.72
EUROPE	-1.6602	0.3787	-4.38
MITSU	-2.1208	0.4525	-4.69

```
s = 0.5706     R-sq = 72.4%     R-sq(adj) = 67.6%
```

```
             ALTERNATIVE FINAL MODEL

* EUROPE is highly correlated with other X variables
* EUROPE has been removed from the equation
The regression equation is
LOGSALES = 10.1 -0.000049 PRICE + 0.328 SIZE + 1.66 FORD + 1.38 GM
          + 1.53 JAPANESE + 0.634 CHRYSLER - 2.12 MITSU
```

Predictor	Coef	Stdev	t-ratio
Constant	10.0727	0.4367	23.06
PRICE	-0.00004858	0.00001214	-4.00
SIZE	0.3280	0.1064	3.08
FORD	1.6602	0.3787	4.38
GM	1.3828	0.3319	4.17
JAPANESE	1.5332	0.3762	4.08
CHRYSLER	0.6342	0.3575	1.77
MITSU	-2.1208	0.4525	-4.69

```
s = 0.5706     R-sq = 72.4%     R-sq(adj) = 67.6%
```

6.11 Consider the problem of modeling interstate migration in terms of various economic, demographic and geographic factors. Specifically, the response variable is M_{od}, the number of migrants from state o to state d. Here, the index o stands for the state of origin, and ranges from 1 to 51 which includes the 50 states in the Union plus the District of Columbia. The index d also ranges from 1 to 51 but since intra-state moves are not counted, $o \neq d$. Thus, there are $51 \times 50 = 2{,}550$ observations.

There are four types of predictor variables available. These are:

P for state population,
I for state income,
E for state employment and
D for the distance between population centroids.

The *traditional* model for these observations is the so-called *gravity model*,

$$M_{od} = c \, \frac{P_o P_d}{D_{od}^a} \left(\frac{I_d}{I_o} \right)^b \left(\frac{E_d}{E_o} \right)^f e_{od}$$

for migration from the oth to the dth state. Here, e_{od} is the multiplicative error term and a, b, c and f are parameters to be estimated. The idea behind this model is, for example, if the ratio of state income in the dth destination state to the income in oth origin state is high, we expect the migration from that origin state to that destination state to be high.

a. To fit a linear regression model, suppose that you are considering using the logarithm of the number of migrants, $log\, M_{od}$, as the response variable. Discuss whether this would be reasonable based on:

   i. the traditional formulation of the *gravity model* and
   ii. the dotplots of the number of migrants and its logged version presented in the following computer output.

Each dot represents 97 points

Each dot represents 9 points

b. The correlation matrix of the response and explanatory variables follows. All data are in natural logarithm units. The same variables are used in the subsequent regression model (Tables E6.11a and b). The VIF statistic presented in the computer output may suggest model inadequacy. To this end:

i. Define the VIF statistic and what it measures.
ii. Say whether the statistic is high for this data set.
iii. Finally, describe how this result might have been anticipated by the correlation matrix.

Correlation Matrix

	LOGMIGNT	EMPLORIG	EMPLDEST	TPIORIG	TPIDEST	POPLORIG	POPLDEST
EMPLORIG	0.519						
EMPLDEST	0.547	-0.020					
TPIORIG	0.520	0.994	-0.020				
TPIDEST	0.547	-0.020	0.994	-0.020			
POPLORIG	0.523	0.990	-0.020	0.990	-0.020		
POPLDEST	0.544	-0.020	0.990	-0.020	0.990	-0.020	
DISTANCE	-0.423	-0.137	-0.137	-0.125	-0.125	-0.137	-0.137

TABLE E6.11a   Coefficient Estimates

Explanatory variables	Coefficient	Standard error	t-ratio	VIF
Constant	-16.3428	0.6999	-23.35	
EMPLORIG	-0.5775	0.1845	-3.13	104.7
EMPLDEST	-0.0598	0.1845	0.32	104.7
TPIORIG	0.8652	0.1756	4.93	107.5
TPIDEST	0.8608	0.1756	4.90	107.5
POPLORIG	0.4280	0.1347	3.18	57.8
POPLDEST	-0.0382	0.1347	-0.28	57.8
DISTANCE	-0.58407	0.2323	-25.14	1.1

TABLE E6.11b   ANOVA Table

Source	Sum of Squares	df	Mean Square
Regression	4136.04	7	590.86
Error	2057.87	2542	0.81
Total	6193.91	2549	

The regression fit also yields $s = 0.8997$, $R^2 = 66.8\%$ and $R_a^2 = 66.7\%$.

c. Because of the VIF and other model inadequacies in the regression fit in part (b), an automatic variable selection procedure, stepwise regression, was run on data. From the following output, the variable EMPLDEST, or E_d, was first brought into the model but eliminated in later stages. Explain how this could happen using the stepwise regression routine.

```
STEPWISE REGRESSION OF LOGMIGNT ON  7 PREDICTORS, WITH N =  2550
      STEP      1        2        3        4        5        6        7
  CONSTANT  -5.755  -18.130  -12.534  -14.386  -14.289  -15.292 -16.155

  EMPLDEST   0.862    0.879    0.816   -0.050
  T-RATIO    32.96    43.58    44.41    -0.29
  POPLORIG            0.827    0.765    0.764    0.764    0.283    0.429
```

T-RATIO		41.74	42.38	42.51	42.53	2.24	3.19
DISTANCE			-0.557	-0.570	-0.569	-0.576	-0.582
T-RATIO			-24.13	-24.65	-24.80	-25.09	-25.32
TPIDEST				0.817	0.770	0.770	0.769
T-RATIO				5.02	44.91	45.00	45.04
TPIORIG						0.46	0.86
T-RATIO						3.85	4.91
EMPLORIG							-0.57
T-RATIO							-3.12
S	1.31	1.01	0.908	0.904	0.903	0.901	0.899
R-SQ	29.89	58.37	66.12	66.45	66.45	66.65	66.77

d. A model suggested by the stepwise regression routine, using DISTANCE (D_{od}), population in the state of origin, POPLORIG (P_o), and total personal income in the state of destination, TPIDEST (I_d), as explanatory variables. This model was fit, and standardized residuals and leverages were calculated. Dotplots and descriptive statistics of these variables can be found in Tables E6.11c–e.

  i. Two points were large outliers, having standardized residuals that are -4.338 and 3.906, respectively. What percentage of the error sum of squares do these two points represent? You may assume that their leverages are equal to the average leverage in doing your calculation.

  ii. Are there any influential points that you would investigate in this data set?

  iii. A plot of the leverages versus the DISTANCE variable, (D_{od}) follows. What does this plot tell us about the relationship between the leverages and DISTANCE?

TABLE E6.11c Coefficient Estimates

Explanatory variables	Coefficient	Standard error	t-ratio
Constant	−14.2886	0.4628	−30.88
TPIDEST	0.77011	0.01715	44.91
POPLORIG	0.76429	0.01797	42.53
DISTANCE	−0.56881	0.02293	−24.80

TABLE E6.11d ANOVA Table

Source	Sum of Squares	df	Mean Square
Regression	4115.9	3	1372.0
Error	2078.07	2546	0.8
Total	6193.9	2549	

The regression fit also yields $s = 0.9034$, $R^2 = 66.5\%$ and $R_a^2 = 66.4\%$.

Each dot represents 11 points

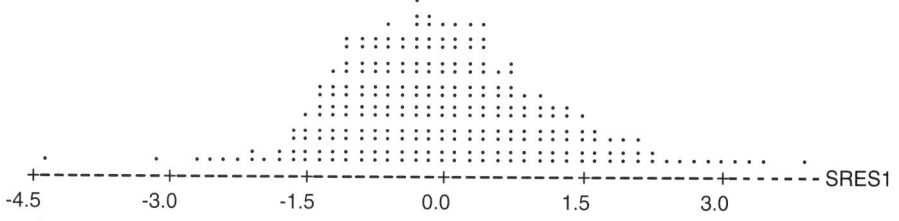

DOTPLOT OF STANDARDIZED RESIDUALS

TABLE E6.11e Summary Statistics of Standardized Residuals and Leverages

	Number	Mean	Median	Standard deviation	Minimum	Maximum
Standardized Residual (SRES1)	2,550	0.0001	−0.0998	1.0003	−4.3379	3.9058
Leverage (HI1)	2,550	0.00157	0.00136	0.00094	0.00039	0.01133

Each dot represents 22 points

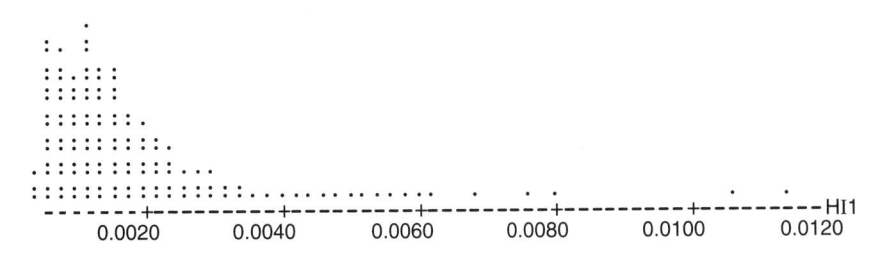

```
                      DOTPLOT OF LEVERAGES


                  .         .
               : .   :
               : : . : : :
               : : : : : :
               : : : : : : .
               : : : : : : : :
             . : : : : : : : : : .  .  .
             : : : : : : : : : : : : : . . . . . .        .    . .         .      .
           ---------+---------+---------+---------+---------+---------HI1
              0.0020    0.0040    0.0060    0.0080    0.0100    0.0120
```

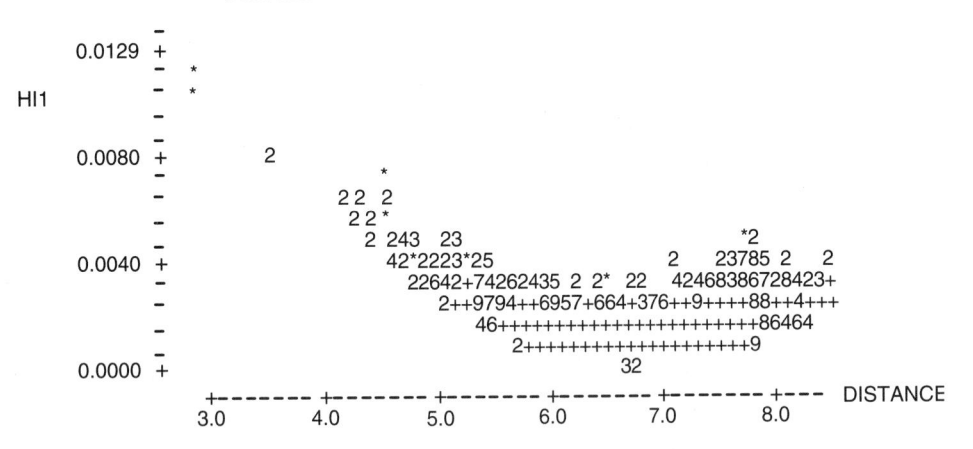

```
           SCATTER PLOT OF LEVERAGES VERSUS DISTANCE

          -
   0.0129 +
          -    *
HI1       -    *
          -
          -
   0.0080 +         2
          -                *
          -            2 2 2
          -            2 2 *
          -            2 243   23                      *2
   0.0040 +           42*2223*25           2    23785 2   2
          -           22642+74262435 2 2*  22  42468386728423+
          -           2++9794++6957+664+376++9++++88++4+++
          -           46+++++++++++++++++++++86464
          -           2+++++++++++++++++++++9
   0.0000 +                     32
          -
           +-------+-------+-------+-------+-------+--- DISTANCE
              3.0     4.0     5.0     6.0     7.0     8.0
```

C6_HELTH

6.12 Who is doing health care right? Health care decisions are made at the individual, corporate and government levels. Virtually every person, corporation and government have their own perspective on health care; these different perspectives result in a wide variety of systems for managing health care. Comparing different health care systems help us learn about approaches other than our own, which in turn help us make better decisions in designing improved systems.

Here, we consider health care systems from 40 countries throughout the world. As a measure of the quality of care, we use LIFE_EXP, the life expectancy at birth. This dependent variable, with several independent variables, are listed in Table E6.12a. From this table, you will note that although there are 40 countries considered in this study, not all countries provided information for each variable. Data not available are noted under the column "Number of observations missing."

TABLE E6.12a

Variable name	Description of variable	Number of observations missing
LIFE_EXP	Life expectancy at birth	
TEMP	Temperature, degrees fahrenheit	
URBAN %	Percent of population living in urban areas	1
POPULN	Total population, in millions	
BEDS_POP	Number of beds per thousand population	
HOSP_POP	Number of hospitals per thousand population	6
RN_POP	Number of nurses per thousand population	5
PHARMPOP	Number of pharmacists per thousand population	6
MD_POP	Number of medical doctors per thousand population	1
POPDWELL	Population per dwelling	3
GNP	Gross national product (in thousands) per population	
LNGNP	Natural logarithm of GNP	

a. Consider first a regression with all independent variables, excluding LNGNP.
  i. You are concerned that several variables, such BEDS_POP, HOSP_POP, RN_POP and so on, are all measures of different aspects of health care expenditures. Briefly explain how this concern relates to the concept of collinearity in regression analysis.
  ii. Comments on the degree of collinearity that you observe in the computer output. Describe whether or not there is serious collinearity using standard rules of thumb.
b. To search for a better regression model, you decide to use stepwise regression to explore the data. The computer output follows.
  i. How many countries are used to fit the models considered by stepwise regression?
  ii. What is a drawback of including all the variables in this regression algorithm?
  iii. The variable Population per dwelling is initially considered important by the stepwise regression algorithm but is dropped in the latter stages. Provide some intuition as to how this could happen.
c. After further exploratory work, a regression model was run with two independent variables, URBAN% and LNGNP. The computer output follows. It turns out that the nineteenth observation, corresponding to the People's Republic of China, was an unusually large residual. (See Table E6.12b–d.)
  i. Describe the options that an analyst has for dealing with unusually large residuals.
  ii. Which option would you use to deal with the observation corresponding to China?

Computer Output for Exercise 6.12

TABLE E6.12b Summary Statistics

Variable	Number	Number missing	Mean	Median	Standard deviation	Minimum	Maximum
LIFE_EXP	40	0	64.92	66.83	10.25	36.95	78.65
TEMP	40	0	61.78	61.00	13.43	36.00	85.00
URBAN %	39	1	59.07	62.10	22.95	14.00	96.00
POPULN	40	0	88.3	25.8	217.8	0.1	1134.0
BEDS_POP	40	0	5.971	4.100	4.304	0.790	15.630
HOSP_POP	34	6	0.04694	0.02954	0.04401	0.00570	0.21876
RN_POP	35	5	0.656	0.472	0.875	0.002	4.656
PHARMPOP	34	6	0.2552	0.1530	0.2463	0.0014	0.8213
MD_POP	39	1	1.034	0.789	0.825	0.046	2.854
POPDWELL	37	3	3.829	3.800	1.391	1.700	6.400
GNP	40	0	8.75	2.53	9.53	0.34	32.31
LNGNP	40	0	1.314	0.928	1.461	−1.079	3.475

Correlation Matrix

	LIFE_EXP	TEMP	URBAN%	POPULN	BEDS_POP	HOSP_POP	RN_POP	PHARMPOP	MD_POP	POPDWELL	GNP
TEMP	−0.469										
URBAN%	0.698	−0.385									
POPULN	−0.154	0.010	−0.341								
BEDS_POP	0.677	−0.603	0.553	−0.243							
HOSP_POP	0.308	−0.255	0.191	−0.089	0.646						
RN_POP	0.300	−0.181	0.042	−0.029	0.113	−0.089					
PHARMPOP	0.582	−0.681	0.296	0.161	0.694	0.537	0.253				
MF_POP	0.711	−0.611	0.551	−0.132	0.741	0.354	0.288	0.767			
POPDWELL	−0.620	0.496	−0.435	0.121	−0.737	−0.412	−0.211	−0.707	−0.684		
GNP	0.688	−0.577	0.457	−0.162	0.867	0.412	0.279	0.703	0.754	−0.721	
LNGNP	0.790	−0.556	0.671	−0.329	0.863	0.363	0.280	0.568	0.781	−0.682	0.926

MINITAB Computer Output

Regression With All Independent Variables

```
The regression equation is
LIFE_EXP = 36.9 + 0.151 TEMP + 0.131 URBAN% - 0.0121 POPULN - 0.648 BEDS_POP
         + 14.5 HOSP POP + 1.53 RN_POP - 12.2 PHARMPOP + 3.83 MD_POP
         + 0.48 POPDWELL + 1.17 GNP
22 cases used 18 cases contain missing values
```

Predictor	Coef	Stdev	t-ratio	VIF
Constant	36.93	19.80	1.86	
TEMP	0.1509	0.1123	1.34	1.9
URBAN%	0.13087	0.07664	1.71	2.9

```
POPULN                   -0.012109      0.006764     -1.79      1.5
BEDS_POP                 -0.6479        0.9077       -0.71     16.9
HOSP_POP                 14.54         42.37          0.34      4.7
RN_POP                    1.531         1.313         1.17      1.9
PHARMPOP                -12.24         10.44         -1.17      5.7
MD_POP                    3.827         2.701         1.42      4.4
POPDWELL                  0.483         2.596         0.19     14.5
GNP                       1.1679        0.3362        3.47      9.6
```

s = 4.581   R-sq = 90.1%   R-sq(adj) = 81.2%

Analysis of Variance

SOURCE	DF	SS	MS	F
Regression	10	2111.91	211.19	10.06
Error	11	230.87	20.99	
Total	21	2342.78		

Unusual Observations

Obs.	TEMP	LIFE_EXP	Fit	Residual	St.Resid
20	74.0	45.550	45.535	0.015	0.05

Initial Stepwise Regression

STEPWISE REGRESSION OF LIFE EXP ON 10 PREDICTORS, WITH N = 22
N(CASES WITH MISSING OBS.) = 18 N(ALL CASES) = 40

STEP	1	2	3	4	5	6	7
CONSTANT	90.33	76.61	59.76	48.24	45.40	33.97	35.96
POPDWELL	-6.13	-3.73	-1.77				
T-RATIO	-7.23	-2.20	-0.88				
GNP		0.44	0.58	0.79	0.70	0.80	0.84
T-RATIO		1.61	2.11	5.63	5.00	5.41	5.77
URBAN%			0.117	0.154	0.185	0.194	0.156
T-RATIO			1.62	2.69	3.27	3.56	2.65
RN_POP					2.0	2.1	2.0
T-RATIO					1.84	2.01	2.00
TEMP						0.160	0.175
T-RATIO						1.61	1.81
POPULN							-0.0093
T-RATIO							-1.47
S	5.69	5.48	5.26	5.23	4.92	4.72	4.57
R-SQ	72.32	75.64	78.75	77.85	81.36	83.82	85.75

Regression with Two Variables

TABLE E6.12c   Coefficient Estimates

Explanatory variables	Coefficient	Standard error	t-ratio	VIF
Constant	51.577	2.903	17.77	
URBAN %	0.13370	0.05712	2.34	1.8
LNGNP	4.2429	0.8940	4.75	1.8

TABLE E6.12d   ANOVA Table

Source	Sum of Squares	df	Mean Square
Regression	2802.2	2	1401.1
Error	1292.0	26	35.9
Total	4094.1	28	

The regression fit also yields $s = 5.991$, $R^2 = 68.4\%$ and $R_a^2 = 66.7\%$.

UNUSUAL OBSERVATIONS

Obs.	URBAN%	LIFE _EXP	Fit	Residual	Std Resid
4	16.1	36.950	49.153	−12.203	−2.18
19	26.2	64.550	50.862	13.688	2.40
27	84.9	54.040	65.740	−11.700	−2.09
30	62.1	60.670	72.384	−11.714	−2.04

C3_MLS

6.13 Refer to Exercises 3.24 and 4.24

The information from this database includes the number of bedrooms (BEDROOM, 2, 3, 4 or 5) and the neighborhood (13, 14 or 15). To provide further detail, BED2 is an indicator variable as to whether a house has 2 bedrooms, and similarly for BED3, BED4 and BED5. Further, W13 is an indicator as to whether the house is in neighborhood 13, and similarly for W14 and W15.

a. After some preliminary analysis, it was found that the exposed square feet, the number of bedrooms, and the neighborhood variables seem to affect the selling price of a house. Thus, in the following computer output, Tables E6.13a–e and Figures E6.13a–e are summary statistics for fitting a regression model of PRICE on EXSQFT, W13, W14, BED3, BED4, and BED5. To help explain this fitted model, Figures E6.13a has an added variable plot of PRICE versus EXSQFT, after controlling for W13, W14, BED3, BED4 and BED5.

  i.   Explain how to construct this added variable plot.

  ii. Interpret the unusual point labelled 'A' in Figure E6.13a.

  iii. Calculate the correlation coefficient to summarize the numbers presented in Figure E6.13a. What is the coefficient called?

b. From the regression model fitted described in part (a), several observations appear to be unusually large.

  i.   Identify the two unusually large residuals.

  ii. What proportion of the error sum of squares is represented by the two observations that you identified in part (i)?

  iii. Calculate the average leverage for the data set. Identify lower and upper bounds on these leverage values. Provide a rule of thumb for identifying a high leverage point.

  iv. From the regression model fitted, calculate the leverage for observation number four.

TABLE E6.13a Coefficient Estimates

Explanatory variables	Coefficient	Standard error	t-ratio
Constant	6.886	8.435	0.82
EXSQFT	0.061987	0.006700	9.25
W13	6.298	5.915	1.06
W14	15.628	6.665	2.34
BED3	−10.700	6.764	−1.58
BED4	6.820	9.699	0.70
BED5	−50.51	16.75	−3.02

TABLE E6.13b ANOVA Table

Source	Sum of Squares	df	Mean Square
Regression	76,090	6	12,682
Error	30,349	74	410
Total	106,439	80	

The regression fit also yields $s = 20.25$, $R^2 = 71.5\%$ and $R_a^2 = 69.2\%$.

UNUSUAL OBSERVATIONS

Obs.	EXSQFT	PRICE	Fit	Residual	Std Resid
1	2500	277.50	184.30	93.20	4.98
2	2639	243.00	192.92	50.08	2.70
4	3100	174.90	212.17	−37.27	−2.17
12	2255	115.00	111.78	3.22	0.23
38	1866	87.50	127.48	−39.98	−2.03
70	1649	71.00	74.22	−3.22	−0.23
71	1820	69.40	109.00	−39.60	−2.06

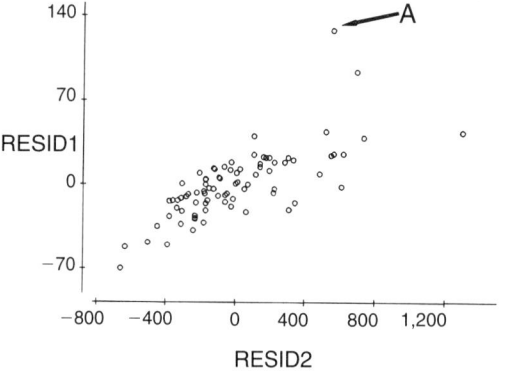

FIGURE E6.13a Added variable plot.

c. Based on the analysis above and additional investigations, the first three observations were deleted. These houses seem to be unusual with respect to the rest of the data set and follow different market forces. The model was then refit, with standardized residuals and fitted values calculated.

   i. In Figure E6.13b is a plot of standardized residuals versus the fitted values. What can we hope to learn from this type of plot?

ii. In Figures E6.13c–e are plots of standardized residuals versus the additional explanatory variables that were not included in the initial model specification. These plots are summarized in the following correlation matrix. What can we hope to learn from this type of plot?

iii. Discuss how you could use the information in this plots and the corresponding correlation matrix to improve your modeling efforts.

Regression Model of PRICE on EXSQFT, W13, W14, BED3, BED4 AND BED5 After Deleting Three Observations

TABLE E6.13c   Coefficient Estimates

Explanatory variables	Coefficient	Standard error	t-ratio
Constant	21.114	5.289	3.99
EXSQFT	0.045746	0.004342	10.53
W13	11.103	3.619	3.07
W14	10.269	4.088	2.51
BED3	−2.388	4.179	−0.57
BED4	−3.390	5.999	−0.57
BED5	−27.68	10.38	−2.67

TABLE E6.13d   ANOVA Table

Source	Sum of Squares	df	Mean Square
Regression	28730.3	6	4788.4
Error	10738.8	71	151.3
Total	39469.1	77	

The regression fit also yields $s = 12.30$, $R^2 = 72.8\%$ and $R_a^2 = 70.5\%$.

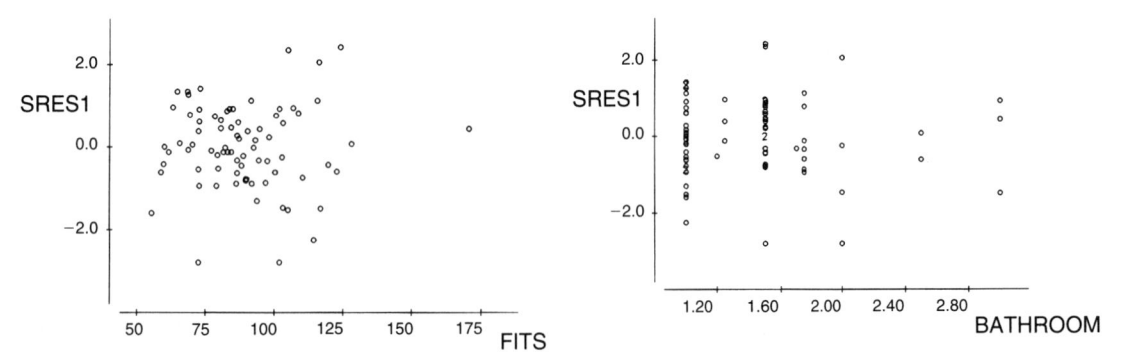

FIGURE E6.13b Plot of standardized residuals versus fitted values.

FIGURE E6.13c Plot of standardized residuals versus number of bathrooms.

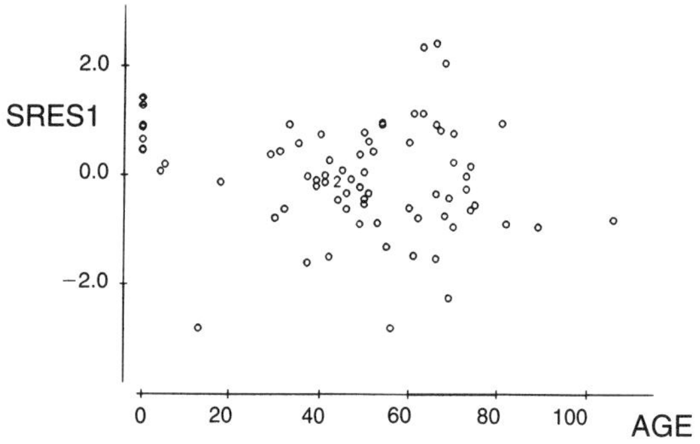

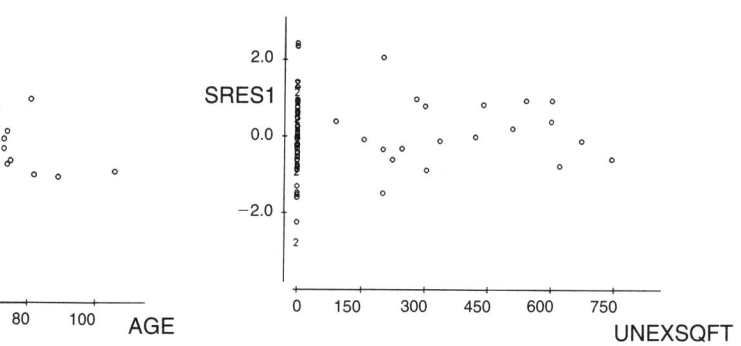

FIGURE E6.13d Plot of standardized residuals versus the age of the house.

FIGURE E6.13e Plot of standardized residuals versus the number of unexposed square feet.

TABLE E6.13e Correlation Matrix of the Standardized Residuals and Several Explanatory Variables

	SRES1	UNEXSQFT	BATHROOM	BRICK
UNEXSQFT	0.051			
BATHROOM	−0.021	0.311		
BRICK	−0.038	−0.108	−0.043	
AGE	−0.215	−0.118	−0.055	0.027

Appendix

6.14 For the model

$$y_i = \beta_0 + \beta_1 x_i + e_i,$$

the ith leverage can be simplified to

$$h_{ii} = \frac{1}{n} + \frac{(x_i - \bar{x})^2}{(n-1)\,s_x^2}.$$

a. Check that $\bar{h} = 2/n$.

b. Suppose that $h_{ii} = 3\,\bar{h}$. How many standard deviations is x_i away (either above or below) the mean?

6.15 The formula for the standard error of b_1 is

$$se(b_1) = s\,\frac{\sqrt{VIF_1}}{s_{x_1}\sqrt{n-1}}$$

where there are many predictors in the regression model. When there is only one predictor, the formula is

$$se(b_1) = \frac{s}{s_{x_1}\sqrt{n-1}}$$

Interpret the VIF_1 statistic when there is only one predictor variable in the model.

6.16 An investor invests \$100 in a mutual fund at the beginning of the year.
  a. Suppose the fund is worth \$120 at the end of the year.
    i. Calculate the logarithmic return, $\ln 120 - \ln 100$.
    ii. Compare this to the percentage return, $(120/100) - 1$.
  b. Suppose the fund is worth \$105 at the end of the year.
    i. Calculate the logarithmic return, $\ln 105 - \ln 100$.
    ii. Compare this to the percentage return, $(105/100) - 1$.

6.17 Consider a (percentage) rate of return, y, such that $-1 < y < 1$.
  a. Show that $|\ln(1+y) - y| < y^2/(2(1-|y|))$.
  b. Using result in part (a) and numerical examples, argue that if $|y| < 10\%$, then $\ln(1+y)$ is an adequate approximation to y.

7

Regression—Interpreting Results

Chapter Objectives

To summarize the interpretation of results, the final output, of a regression study. In doing so, we will also discuss aspects of data collection, the inputs, to the study. To illustrate, we will consider determining a firm's characteristics that influence its effectiveness in managing risk.

Chapter Outline

Studying a problem using regression analysis techniques involves a substantial commitment of time and energy. One must first embrace the concept of statistical thinking, a willingness to use data actively as part of a decision making process. Second, one must appreciate the usefulness of a model that is used to approximate reality. Having made this substantial commitment, there is a natural tendency to "oversell" the results of statistical methods such as regression analysis. By overselling any set of ideas, consumers eventually become disappointed when the results do not live up to their expectations. This chapter is about what we can reasonably expect to learn from the regression modeling procedures.

7.1 WHAT THE MODELING PROCESS TELLS

In most investigations, the process of developing a model tells us as much about the world as the resulting model. This process begins with the task of relating vague ideas to data that may shed light on these ideas. Statistical thinking about a problem requires collecting and analyzing data. This usually represents more effort than "arm-chair brainstorming." However, reasoning that is a result of a careful analysis of data is powerful and will often sway even determined skeptics to the position that you are advocating. Although the discipline of relating available numerical information to ideas is exacting, it also provides numerous insights. As noted by Ruskin, "The work of science is to substitute facts for appearances and demonstrations for impressions."

Model formulation and data collection form the first stage of the modeling process. Students of statistics are usually surprised at the difficulty of relating ideas about relationships between factors to available data. These difficulties include the lack of readily available data and the need to use certain data as proxies for ideal information that is not available numerically. Section 7.3 will describe several types of difficulties that can arise when collecting data. As described in Section 2.2, models are designed to be much simpler than relationships among entities that exist in the real world. A model is merely an approximation of reality. As stated by George Box (1979), "All models are wrong, but some are useful."

"All models are wrong, but some are useful."

Statistics can be thought of as the art of reasoning with data.

Model development is the next stage, as noted in Section 4.0. Developing the model, the subject of Chapter 6, is part of the art of statistics. The resulting product has certain aesthetic values and the principles of arriving at the final product are by no means predetermined. Statistics can be thought of as the art of reasoning with data. Section 7.2 will underscore the importance of model selection.

Model inference is the final stage of the modeling process. By studying the behavior of models, we hope to learn something about the real world. Models serve to impose an order on reality and provide a basis for understanding reality through the nature of the imposed order. Further, statistical models are based on reasoning with the available data from a sample. Thus, models serve as an important guide for predicting the behavior of observations outside the available sample. The remainder of this section is devoted to a more detailed discussion of the use of models for understanding and prediction.

Using Models for Understanding

The Importance of Explanatory Variables

One interpretation of the regression model,

$$y = \beta_0 + \beta_1 x_1 + \ldots + \beta_k x_k + e,$$

is that the response can be interpreted as a linear combination of the k variables, $x_1, \ldots, x_k$, plus a random error term. The parameter β_j controls the amount of the contribution of the variable x_j to the expected response. It seems reasonable to ask whether the contribution is important. This is certainly an important aspect of model selection, as discussed in Chapter 6.

The inclusion of a random error term, representing the natural variation inherent in the data, serves implicitly to limit the number of variables in the model.

Because the world is so interrelated, the number of variables x that can affect the expected response can be overwhelmingly large. The inclusion of a random error term, representing the natural variation inherent in the data, implicitly serves to limit the number of variables in the model. It does so as follows. Recall from Section 4.3 that the jth variable could be excluded if $\beta_j = 0$. To see whether the jth variable is important, we test the null hypothesis that $H_0: \beta_j = 0$ versus the alternative hypothesis $H_a: \beta_j \neq 0$. The procedure for testing this set of ideas is to reject H_0 in favor of H_a if the test statistic

$$t(b_j) = \frac{b_j}{se(b_j)}$$

exceeds a t-value in absolute value. Here, the t-value is from the t-distribution using $df = n - (k + 1)$ degrees of freedom with a two-tailed significance level. At the 5% level of significance, we have seen that t-value ≈ 2 is an adequate approximation for most degrees of freedom. The idea behind this test is that we are trying to find out whether b_j is close to zero, the hypothesized value, relative to its standard error. In Section 6.4, we expressed the standard error as

$$se(b_j) = s\frac{\sqrt{VIF_j}}{s_{x_j}\sqrt{n-1}}$$

where s_{x_j} is the standard deviation of the jth variable x_j. By expressing the standard error in this form, we see that the larger the natural variation is, as measured by s, the more difficult it is to reject H_0, other things being equal.

For large samples, we have an opportunity for detecting the importance of variables that might go unnoticed in small or even moderate size samples.

The form of the standard error is interesting and suggests an important rule of thumb. Suppose that a mechanism that is similar to draws from a stable population is used to observe the explanatory variables. Then, the standard deviation of x_j, s_{x_j}, should be stable as the number of draws increases. Similarly, so should R_j^2 and s^2. Then, the standard error $se(b_j)$ should decrease as the sample size, n, increases. This means that, for large samples, we have an opportunity for detecting the importance of variables that might go unnoticed in small or even moderate size samples. Unfortunately, it also means that variables with small parameter coefficients, that contribute little to understanding the variation in the response, can be judged to be important using our decision making procedures. This phenomenon results in declaring variables to be *statistically significant but practically unimportant.* For large samples, it may be prudent for the investigator to omit variables from the model selection when their presence is not in accord with an accepted theory, even if they are judged statistically significant.

Variables can be statistically significant even though they are practically unimportant.

The flip side of this argument is that when sample sizes are small, it may be reasonable to include variables even if their t-ratios are less than two in absolute value. The idea here is that the sampling variability may be large enough to mask important patterns. A good rule of thumb for model selection, advocated by Roberts (1990), is to omit variables if $|t(b_j)| \le 1$, include them if $|t(b_j)| \ge 2$ and weigh their importance if $1 < |t(b_j)| < 2$.

A good rule of thumb for model selection, is to omit variables if $|t(b_j)| \le 1$, include them if $|t(b_j)| \ge 2$ and weigh their importance if $1 < |t(b_j)| < 2$.

Testing Hypotheses

As in the one variable case introduced in Section 2.7, testing of hypotheses is not limited to a two-sided test nor to a hypothesized parameter value of zero. In general, we may use $\beta_{0,j}$ for the hypothesized value of the parameter, β_j. The corresponding test statistic is

$$test\ statistic = \frac{b_j - \beta_{0j}}{se(b_j)}. \tag{7.1}$$

Table 7.1a provides an outline for the decision making procedures. These procedures are for testing $H_0: \beta_j = \beta_{0,j}$ at a prescribed significance level.

Tests of hypotheses are useful in that they provide a formal, agreed-upon standard, for deciding whether or not a variable provides an important contribution to an expected response. In many applications, this may be the main reason for analyzing the data.

TABLE 7.1a Table of Decision-Making Procedures for Testing $H_0: \beta_j = \beta_{j,0}$

Alternative hypothesis (H_a)	The t-value is a percentile from the t-distribution using $df = n - (k + 1)$ degrees of freedom. The percentile is:	Procedure: Reject H_0 in favor of H_a if
$\beta_j > \beta_{j,0}$	1 - significance level	*test statistic > t-value*
$\beta_j < \beta_{j,0}$	1 - significance level	*test statistic < -(t-value)*
$\beta_j \neq \beta_{j,0}$	1 - (significance level)/2	*| test statistic | > t-value*

The end result of a test of hypothesis is only whether a hypothesis is accepted or rejected. In many instances, it is useful to supplement this information by describing the strength of the decision. As described in Section 2.7, this can be accomplished using the *p-value*, or *probability value*. To calculate a *p*-value, let *t* denote a random observation from a *t*-distribution with $df = n - (k + 1)$ degrees of freedom and assume that *test statistic* is a realized quantity, calculated from the sample. Table 7.1b provides an outline for calculating *p*-values. For this table, the *test statistic* is defined in equation (7.1).

TABLE 7.1b Table for Calculating Probability Values for Testing $H_0: \beta_j = \beta_{j,0}$

Alternative hypothesis	$H_a: \beta_j > \beta_{0,j}$	$H_a: \beta_j < \beta_{0,j}$	$H_a: \beta_j \neq \beta_{0,j}$
p-value	Prob *(t > test statistic)*	Prob *(t < test statistic)*	Prob *(|t| > |test statistic|)*

The statistic b_j is called a point estimate of the parameter β_j.

Confidence intervals.   *Confidence intervals* for parameters are another device for describing the strength of the contribution of the *j*th explanatory variable. The statistic b_j is called a *point estimate* of the parameter β_j. To provide a range of reliability, we use the confidence interval

$$b_j \pm (t\text{-value}) \; se(b_j) \tag{7.2}$$

Here, the *t*-value is a percentile from the *t*-distribution with $df = n - (k + 1)$ degrees of freedom. We use the same *t*-value as in the two-sided hypothesis test. Indeed, there is a duality between the confidence interval and the two-sided hypothesis test. For example, it is not hard to check that if a hypothesized value $\beta_{0,j}$ falls outside the confidence interval, then H_0 will be rejected in favor of H_a. Further, knowledge of the *p*-value, point estimate and hypothesized value can be used to determine a confidence interval.

Performance evaluation.   With the regression model, the expected response is

$$\mathrm{E}\, y = \beta_0 + \beta_1 x_1 + \dots + \beta_k x_k.$$

The residual can be interpreted as the response controlled for a given set of characteristics.

An interpretation of this expectation is that $\mathrm{E}\, y$ is the long-run average response if we could see many responses for a single set of characteristics x_1, x_2, $\dots$, x_k. Thus, we can interpret the corresponding error, e_i, as the deviation of the response (y_i) from that expected for a given set of characteristics $x_1, \dots, x_k$. That is, the error is the response controlled for a given set of characteristics. Similarly, we can interpret the residual $\hat{e}_i$ as the deviation of the response y_i from the estimated expected value $\hat{y}_i$ for a given set of characteristics. That is, the residual is the response controlled for a given set of characteristics.

In some investigations, the main purpose may be to determine whether a specific observation is "in line" with the others available. For example, in Section 6.7 we examined the salaries of professional football players. The main purpose of such an analysis could have been to see whether a player's salary is high or low compared to other players in the sample, controlling for characteristics such as position played and years of experience. As described above, the residual summarizes the deviation of the response from that expected under the model. The residual can then be compared to its standard error. If the residual is unusual, when compared to its standard error, we interpret this to mean that there are unusual circumstances associated with this observation. This analysis does not suggest the nature nor the causes of these circumstances. It merely states that the observation is unusual with respect to others in the sample. For some investigations, such as for litigation concerning compensation packages, this is a powerful statement.

Unusual points.   Unusual points, such as outliers and high leverage points, provide a tremendous amount of information about data that is useful for business decision making purposes. Unusual points represent circumstances that are atypical. They may represent situations that are unusually bad and to be avoided in the future. Or they may represent circumstances that are unusually favorable. In any case, these points are informative and tell a lot about the data being analyzed. Unfortunately, because these points stick out like "sore thumbs" in the analysis, students of statistics tend to ignore them or, worse yet, delete them from the analysis *without careful consideration.* By definition, unusual points do not fit neatly into a model. However, the world is not neat and tidy, either. Unusual points are informative; they should be carefully considered when describing what we learned from the modeling of data.

Using Models for Prediction

The primary motivation for many applications of cross-sectional regression modeling is the prediction of the behavior of a response outside of the data set.

Prediction, or *forecasting,* is the main motivation of most analyses of time series data, the subject of Chapters 9–11.

For prediction in the cross-sectional regression context, assume that we have available a given set of characteristics, $x_{*1}, x_{*2}, \ldots, x_{*k}$. According to our model, the new response is

$$y_* = \beta_0 + \beta_1 x_{*1} + \ldots + \beta_k x_{*k} + e_*.$$

We use as our prediction

$$\hat{y}_* = b_0 + b_1 x_{*1} + \ldots + b_k x_{*k}.$$

As in Section 3.4, we can decompose the prediction error into the estimation error plus the random error, as follows:

$$y_* - \hat{y}_* = \beta_0 - b_0 + (\beta_1 - b_1)x_{*1} + \ldots + (\beta_k - b_k)x_{*k} + e_*$$

prediction error =   estimation error   + random error .

This decomposition allows us to provide a distribution for the prediction error. We summarize this distribution using a prediction interval

$$\hat{y}_* \pm (t\text{-value})\, se(pred).$$

The standard error of the prediction, $se(pred)$, can be calculated using standard statistical software routines. [If you studied Section 4.7, the hand calculation formula, $se(pred) = s(1 + x'_*(\mathbf{X}'\mathbf{X})^{-1}x_*)^{1/2}$ is well defined. Here, x'_* is defined by $\mathbf{x}'_* = (1, x_{*1}, x_{*2}, \ldots, x_{*k})$.] This t-value is a percentile from the t-distribution using $df = n - (k + 1)$ degrees of freedom. The percentile is $1 - (\text{significance level})/2$.

A prediction interval provides a single point prediction as well as a range of reliability.

Communicating the distribution of potential errors about a point prediction is an important goal. When analyzing data, there may be several alternative prediction techniques available. Even within the class of regression models, each of several candidate models will produce a different prediction. It is important to provide a distribution, or range, of potential errors. Naive consumers can easily become disappointed with the results of predictions from regression models. These consumers are told (correctly) that the regression model is optimal, based on certain well-defined criteria, and are then provided with a point prediction, such as $\hat{y}_*$. Without knowledge of an interval, the consumer has expectations for the performance of the prediction, usually higher than is warranted by information available in the sample. A prediction interval not only provides a single optimal point prediction, but also a range of reliability.

When making predictions, the sample and the new observation follow the same model. Thus, the basic conditions should remain unchanged for the new observation.

When making predictions, there is an important assumption that the new observation follows the same model as that used in the sample. Thus, the basic conditions about the distribution of the errors should remain unchanged for new observations. It is also important that the level of the predictor variables, $x_{*1}, \ldots, x_{*k}$, be similar to those in the available sample. If one or several of the predictor variables differs dramatically from those in the available sample, then the resulting prediction can perform poorly. For example, it would be imprudent to use the model developed in Sections 3.1 through 3.3 to predict the purchase price of a car for an individual with income equal to $x_* =$ $500,000$, nearly five times the largest income in our sample. Even though it would be easy to plug $x_* = 500,000$ into our formulas, the result would have little intuitive appeal. The reason is that the regression methodology uses straight lines and planes to approximate relationships between variables. Extrapolating relationships beyond the observed data requires expertise with the nature of the data as well as the statistical methodology. In Section 7.3, we will identify this problem as a potential bias due to the sampling region.

7.2 THE IMPORTANCE OF MODEL SELECTION

On one hand, choosing a theoretical model to summarize precisely events in the real world is probably an impossible task. On the other hand, choosing a model to represent approximately the real world is an important practical matter. The closer our model is to the real world, the more accurate are the statements that we make, suggested by the model. Although we cannot get the right model, we may be able to select a useful, or at least adequate, model.

Users of statistics, from the raw beginner to the seasoned expert, will always select an inadequate model from time to time. The key question is: *How important is it to select an adequate model?* Although not every kind of mistake can be accounted for in advance, there are some guiding principles that are useful to keep in mind when selecting a model. To explore these principles, let us look at some of the mistakes that can be, and often are, made.

Overfitting the Model

When extraneous variables are included in the model specification, the model is overfit.

This type of mistake occurs when extraneous variables are included in the model specification. If only a small number of variables, such as one or two, are added, then this type of error will probably not dramatically skew most of the types of conclusions that might be reached from the model fitting exercise. For example, we know that when we add a variable to the model, the error sum of squares does not increase. If the variable is extraneous, then the error sum of squares will not become appreciably smaller either. In fact, adding an extraneous variable will increase s^2 because the denominator is smaller by one degree of freedom. However, for most data sets of reasonable sample size, the effect is minimal. Adding several extraneous variables can inflate s^2 appreciably, however. Further, there is the possibility that adding extraneous explanatory variables will induce, or worsen, the presence of collinearity.

When adding extraneous variables, our regression parameter estimates remain unbiased.

Perhaps a more important issue is that, by adding extraneous variables, our estimates remain *unbiased*. *Bias* is a technical term referring to the difference between the expected value of the estimator and the expected value under the true model. Bias is a type of error or deviation that does not cancel out. Consider the following example.

Example 7.1: Regression Using One Independent Variable

Assume that the true model of the responses is

$$y_i = \beta_0 + e_i, \quad i = 1, \ldots, n.$$

Under this true model, the level of a generic explanatory variable x does not affect the value of the response y. If we were to predict the response at any level of x, the prediction would be $\bar{y}$ which has expected value β_0. However, suppose we mistakenly fit the data using the model

$$y_i = \beta_0^* + \beta_1^* x_i + e_i^*.$$

With this model, the prediction at a generic level x is $b_0^* + b_1^* x$ where b_0^* and b_1^* are the usual least square estimates of β_0^* and β_1^*, respectively. It is not to hard to confirm that

$$Bias = \mathrm{E}\,(b_0^* + b_1^* x) - \mathrm{E}\, y = 0,$$

where the expectations are calculated using the true model. Thus, by using a slightly larger model than we should have, we did not pay for it in terms of making a persistent, long term error such as represented by the bias. The price of making this mistake is that our standard error is slightly higher than it would be if we had chosen the correct model.

Underfitting the Model

When important variables are omitted from the specified model, the model is underfit.

This type of error occurs when important variables are omitted from the model specification. This type of error is more serious than overfitting. Omitting important variables can cause appreciable amounts of bias in our resulting estimates. Further, the resulting estimates of s^2 are larger than need be. A larger s inflates our prediction intervals and produces inaccurate tests of hypotheses concerning the importance of explanatory variables. To see the effects of underfitting a model, we continue the previous example of regression using one independent variable.

Example 7.2: Regression Using One Independent Variable—Continued

We now reverse the roles of the model. Assume that the true model is

When important variables are omitted, the estimates of the regression coefficients in the specified model are usually biased.

$$y_i = \beta_0 + \beta_1 x_i + e_i$$

and that we mistakenly fit the following model to the data,

$$y_i = \beta_0^* + e_i^*.$$

Thus, we have inadvertently omitted the effects of the explanatory variable x. Using the fitted model, we would use $\bar{y}$ for our prediction at any generic level of x. Using the true model, we have $\bar{y} = \beta_0 + \beta_1 \bar{x} + \bar{e}$. The bias is

$$Bias = E\,\bar{y} - E\,(\beta_0 + \beta_1 x + e)$$

$$= E\,(\beta_0 + \beta_1 \bar{x} + \bar{e}) - (\beta_0 + \beta_1 x) = \beta_1(\bar{x} - x).$$

Thus, there is a persistent, long term error in omitting the explanatory variable x. More generally, one can check that this type of error produces biased regression parameter estimates and an inflated value of s^2.

7.3 THE IMPORTANCE OF DATA COLLECTION

When performing a regression analysis, collecting the data is the first thing an analyst must do. We have seen how to do the analyses in Chapters 3 through 6 and the first parts of Chapter 7. Having studied the process, and the outcomes, of a regression analysis, we can now discuss the inputs to the process. Not surprisingly, there is a long list of potential pitfalls that are frequently encountered in regression studies. In this section, we identify the major potential pitfalls and provide some avenues for avoiding these pitfalls.

When data are observational, inferring causal relationships among variables is never justified based on the data alone.

In this book, we assume that the data are observational in nature, that is, beyond the control of the researcher. An important implication of this is that any finding through our analysis of the data does not provide us information as to the nature of causal relations between variables. For example, if we find that one x is important, it does not mean that this x causes the response y; it merely means that there is a significant relationship between the two variables. This is somewhat counterintuitive because the data analyst has to pick one variable to be the response and use the other variables as explanatory variables. However, we have seen examples where a third (omitted) variable may be driving the relationship between two variables. If the data analyst is allowed to control aspects of the experiment, then there are many devices such as randomization to detect unseen forces. Only when the experimenter is allowed to control the circumstances under which the data are collected can statistics alone be used to say something about the causal relationships among variables. Statistics is, however, useful for making causal statements about relationships when used in conjunction with theory from an underlying discipline, such as financial economics or marketing.

Despite the explosive growth of computerized databases, getting the right kind of data for a problem at hand can be difficult.

One aspect of the widespread availability of computers is the access to data. In the twentieth century "Information Age," it is becoming easier to access more data. However, plentiful data does not necessarily mean the right kind of data for an analyst's task at hand. To put it another way, we are working with information in the form of data. However, merely having data available does not mean that we have the right kind of information. Particularly in the private sector, businesses view management information as proprietary and are often unwilling to part with data, for fear of giving competitors valuable information. As described in Chapter 2, this same problem plagued Gosset at the turn of the twentieth century. In a competitive market environment, it is not reasonable to think that managers will readily part with vital company information. Further, as pointed out by Roberts (1990), companies also do not retain data over time. In Chapters 9 through 11, we will study techniques for controlling and forecasting data over time; techniques that can be useful for planning and improving processes. Unfortunately, in a short-sighted planning environment where historical data are not retained, forecasting is reduced to gazing through a crystal ball. The important point is that, in many situations, the right data for a specific problem are simply not available.

Bias, in any statistical analysis, is a type of error or deviation that does not cancel out.

When the right data are not available, the analyst is forced to resort to proxy variables, one invitation to the problem of *bias*. Bias, in any statistical analysis, is a type of error or deviation that does not cancel out. In contrast, the error terms $\{e_i\}$ represent the natural variation associated with an observation. Because our parameter estimates are weighted averages of observations, the effect of error terms do cancel out, and become less significant as the sample size increases. Increasing sample sizes does not mitigate the problem of bias. Below is the list of problem areas that can give rise to bias.

Bias Due to Sampling Frame Error

In the end, a sample must be a representative subset of a larger population, or universe, of interest. If the sample is not representative, taking a larger sample does not eliminate bias; you simply repeat the same mistake over again and again. When taking surveys of populations, bias can arise from *sampling frame error*. As described in Section 2.4, sampling frame error occurs when the sampling frame, the list from which the sample is drawn, is not an adequate approximation of the population of interest.

Perhaps the most widely known example of sampling frame error is from the 1936 *Literary Digest* poll. This poll was conducted to predict the winner of the 1936 U.S. Presidential election. The two leading candidates were Franklin D. Roosevelt, the Democrat, and Alfred Landon, the Republican. *Literary Digest*, a prominent magazine at the time, conducted a survey of ten million voters. Of those polled, 2.4 million responded, predicting a Landon victory by a 57% to 43% margin. However, the actual election resulted in an overwhelming Roosevelt victory, by a 62% to 38% margin. What went wrong?

There were a number of problems with the *Literary Digest* survey. Perhaps the most important was the sampling frame error. To develop their sampling frame, *Literary Digest* used addresses from telephone books and membership lists of clubs. In 1936, the United States was in the depths of the Great Depression; telephones and club memberships were a luxury that only upper income individuals could afford. Thus, *Literary Digest*'s list included an unrepresentative number of upper income individuals. In previous presidential elections conducted by *Literary Digest*, the rich and poor tended to vote along similar lines and this was not a problem. However, economic problems were top political issues in the 1936 presidential election. As it turned out, the poor tended to vote for Roosevelt and the rich tended to vote for Landon. As a result, the *Literary Digest* poll results were grossly mistaken. Taking a large sample, even of size 2.4 million, did not help; the basic mistake was repeated over and over again.

Bias Due to Omitted Variables

As we have seen, omitting variables from a regression model can be an important source of bias. Section 7.2 gave a technical discussion under the subsection, Underfitting a Model. Our first data example appeared in Example 4.1 where we considered refrigerator prices. In this example, we found that a cross-section of refrigerators displayed a significantly positive correlation between price and the annual energy cost of operating the refrigerator. This positive correlation was counter-intuitive because we would hope that higher prices would mean lower annual expenditures in operating a refrigerator. However, when we included several additional variables, in particular, measures of the size of a refrigerator, we found a significantly negative relationship between price and energy costs. Again, by omitting these additional variables, there was an important bias when using regression to understand the relationship between price and energy costs.

Bias Due to Limited Sampling Region

In Chapter 6, we saw that a smaller spread of a variable, other things equal, means a less reliable estimate of the slope coefficient associated with that variable. That is, from equation (6.3), we have

$$se(b_j) = s\,\frac{\sqrt{VIF_j}}{s_{x_j}\sqrt{n-1}}\ .$$

Thus, the smaller is the spread of x_j, as measured by s_{x_j}, the larger is the standard error of b_j, $se(b_j)$. Taken to the extreme, where $s_{x_j} = 0$, we might have a situation such as illustrated in Figure 7.1. For this extreme situation there is not

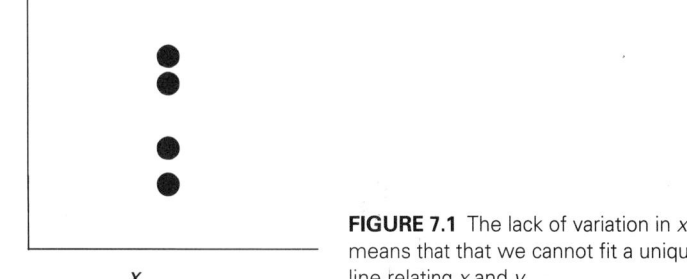

FIGURE 7.1 The lack of variation in x means that that we cannot fit a unique line relating x and y.

enough variation in x to estimate the corresponding slope parameter. This provides an illustration where the slope parameter is a nonestimable function. Estimable functions of parameters were described briefly in Section 5.4.

The other pitfall that can arise due to a limited sampling region is the potential bias that can arise when we try to extrapolate outside of the sampling region. To illustrate, consider Figure 7.2. Here, based on the data in the sampling region, a line may seem to be an appropriate representation. However, if a quadratic curve is the true expected response, any forecast that is far from the sampling region will be seriously biased.

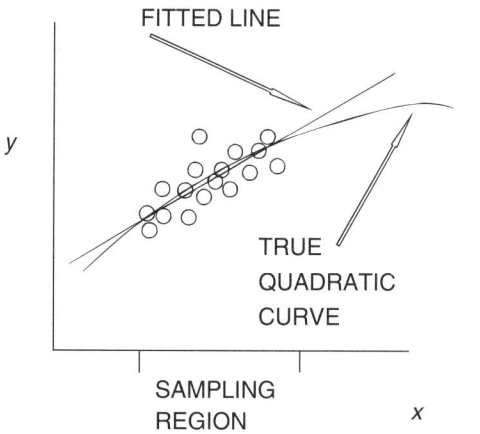

FIGURE 7.2 Extrapolation outside of the sampling region may always be biased.

Bias Due to Missing Data

In the data examples, illustrations, case studies and exercises of this text, there are many instances where certain data are unavailable for analysis, or *missing*. In every instance, the data were not carelessly lost but were missing due to real reasons associated with the data collection. For example, when we examined stock returns from a cross-section of companies, we saw that some companies did not have an average five year earnings per share figure. The reason was simply that they had not been in existence for five years. As another example, when examining voting behavior, some states simply did not report the percent registered to vote. Missing data are an inescapable aspect of analyzing data in the social sciences.

When the reason for the lack of availability of data is unrelated to actual data values, the data are said to be missing at random.

When the reason for the lack of availability of data is unrelated to actual data values, the data are said to be *missing at random*. There are a variety of techniques for handling missing at random data, none of which is clearly superior to the others. One technique is to simply ignore the problem. Hence, missing at random is sometimes called the *ignorable case* of missing data.

If there are only a few missing data, compared to the total number available, a widely employed strategy is to delete the observations corresponding to the missing data. Assuming that the data are missing at random, little information is lost by deleting a small portion of the data. Further, with this strategy, we need not make additional assumptions about the relationships among the data.

If the missing data are primarily from one variable, we can consider omitting this variable. Here, the motivation is that we lose less information when omitting this variable as compared to retaining the variable but losing the observations associated with the missing data.

Imputation strategies allow the researcher to approximate missing values and thus retain missing data.

Another strategy is to fill in, or *impute,* missing data. There are many variations of the imputation strategy. All assume some type of relationships among the variables in addition to the regression model assumptions. Although these methods yield reasonable results, note that any type of filled-in values do not yield the same inherent variability as the real data. Thus, results of analyses based on imputed values often reflect less variability than those with real data.

Specialized techniques, called the *EM algorithm* and related approaches, are also available to handle missing at random data. An advantage of these techniques is that they use all of the information in the data available. Disadvantages include the fact that additional assumptions need to be made, specialized software is required and the results of such analyses are less well-understood. See Little and Rubin (1987) for further details.

Data that are missing in a non-random fashion give rise to bias when least squares techniques are used to analyze the data.

Specialized modeling is required for data that are not missing at random. That is, researchers have identified many sample selection problems that cause data to be missing in a nonrandom fashion. Models are developed for each type of problem, and estimation of each model is accomplished on a problem specific basis. For our purposes, the important point is that data that are missing in a nonrandom fashion give rise to bias when least squares techniques are used to analyze the data.

Bias Due to Limited Dependent Variables

Bias can occur when outcomes of the dependent variable are restricted, or limited, so that the outcomes are not purely continuous.

In some applications, the dependent variable is constrained to fall within certain regions. To see why this is a problem, first recall that under the linear regression model, the dependent variable equals the regression function plus a random error. Typically, the random error is assumed to be approximately normally distributed, so that the response varies continuously. However, if the outcomes of the dependent variable are restricted, or limited, then the outcomes are not purely continuous. This means that our assumption of normal errors is not strictly correct, and may not even be a good approximation.

To illustrate, Figure 7.3 shows a plot of individual's income versus purchase price of an automobile. Unlike the example in Section 3.1, this plot includes several individuals who did not purchase a car. The sample in this plot represents two subsamples, those who purchased a car, corresponding to $y > 0$, and those who did not, corresponding to "price" $y = 0$. When we dealt with only those who purchased a car we still had the implicit lower bound of zero, that is, a car price must exceed zero. However, for the data that we considered this bound was not close to our sampling region and thus did not represent an important practical problem. By including several individuals who did not purchase a car (and thus spent $0 on a car), our sampling region now clearly includes this lower bound.

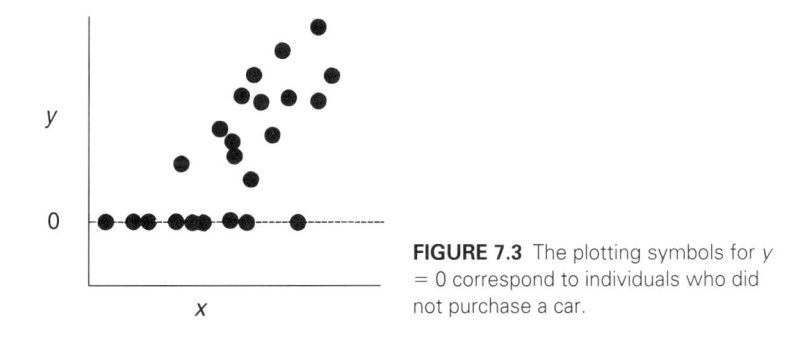

FIGURE 7.3 The plotting symbols for y = 0 correspond to individuals who did not purchase a car.

There are several ways in which dependent variables can be restricted. Figure 7.3 illustrates the case in which y is said to be *censored*, that is, the value of y may be no lower than zero. If censoring is severe, ordinary least squares produces biased results. Specialized approaches, called *censored regression models*, exist in the literature to handle this problem. See Greene (1993) for further discussion.

Figure 7.4 illustrates another commonly encountered restriction on the value of the dependent variable. For this scenario, purchases of low-priced automobiles, say, purchase price below y^*, simply do not enter the sample. In this case, the data are said to be *truncated*. Not surprisingly, *truncated regression models* are available to handle this special situation. Truncated data represent a more serious source of bias than censored data. When data are truncated, we do not have values of dependent variables and thus we are working with much less information than when the data are censored.

Chapter 8 discusses another example of a limited dependent variable, responses that are indicator variables.

Bias Due to Level of Aggregation of Data

From Section 2.4, recall the idea of a stratified random sample; a population carved up into homogeneous subpopulations, or strata, and then a random sample is taken from each strata. For regression models, we can think of each level of $(x_1, x_2, ..., x_k)$ as identifying a strata. From each level, a random sam-

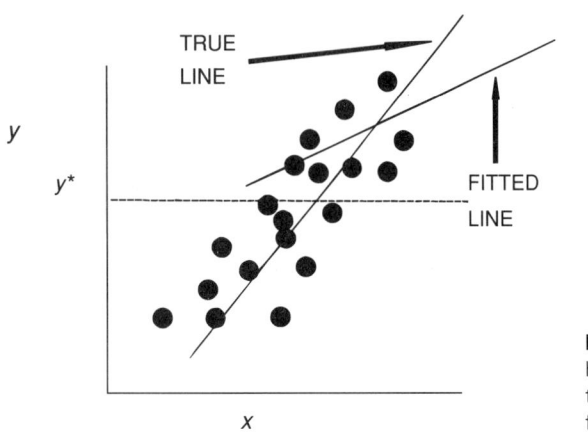

FIGURE 7.4 If the responses below the horizontal line at $y = y^*$ are omitted, then the fitted regression line is very different from the true regression line.

ple is drawn. Generally, if each explanatory variable is continuous, then the sample size from each strata is one. If the explanatory variables are categorical, we may get sample sizes larger than one.

Another source of bias occurs when explanatory variables are measured with error. For example, using incomes of individuals to explain the price paid for a car may be a source of difficulty. People are reluctant to report sensitive information such as income; often, they report an income figure larger than they actually earned. When explanatory variables are measured with error, data are classified into the wrong strata. This leads to bias.

Grouping explanatory variables may not lead to bias. For example, you may elect to categorize the continuous income variable into groups of, say, low, intermediate and high income. Or suppose you have a categorical variable that tells whether a voter is Democrat, Republican, Libertarian, Socialist, Communist or in the United We Stand party. You may elect to consider a simpler variable, such as a variable to indicate whether a voter is Democrat or not. Grouping explanatory variables does not result in bias but is an inefficient use of data. That is, more information can be gleaned from the data if it is not overly summarized. Grouping can be useful, however, when the explanatory variables are measured with error. For example, suppose that people misreport their incomes by an error of up to 10% of their income. By categorizing incomes as low, intermediate or high, most of this misreporting bias is eliminated. Only at the cut-offs for the categorization will there be misclassification. The extent of this misclassification problem will, of course, depend on the data set of interest.

Although grouping explanatory variables may lead to only small difficulties, explanatory variables that need to be considered in finer detail can also lead to serious problems. The lack of homogeneous subgroups is called a *level of aggregation* bias. For example, in Section 5.4 we saw that a plot of hospital costs versus utilization gave a surprising negative correlation. However, when we included the category of admission to the hospital, the relationship changed dramatically. In a sense, the level of aggregation bias is simply another form of omitted variable bias. With the level of aggregation bias, we inadvertently omit certain categorical variables that help to refine the detail of explanatory variables and create more homogeneous strata.

7.4 CASE STUDY: RISK MANAGERS' COST EFFECTIVENESS

This section examines data from a survey on the cost effectiveness of risk management practices. Risk management practices are simply activities undertaken by a firm to minimize the potential cost of future contingent losses, such as the event of a fire in a warehouse or an accident that injures employees. This section develops a model that can be used to make statements about cost of managing risks. Unlike Chapter 4, that presents results of a final model, in this section we stress the development of a model. The steps presented here are those that you might use when investigating a similar data set. As we pointed out in Section 7.1, the process of developing the model often tells us as much about the world as the resulting model.

An outline of the model development process is as follows. We begin by providing an introduction to the problem and giving some brief background on the data. Certain prior theories about the data will lead us to present a preliminary analysis of the data. Using diagnostic techniques, it will be evident that several assumptions of this model are not met with the data. This will lead us to go back to the beginning and start the analysis from scratch. Following an analysis of each variable in isolation of the others, we will look at the structure between pairs of random variables. Things that we learn from this examination of the data will lead us to postulate some new models. Finally, to communicate certain aspects of the new model, we will explore the use of certain devices for graphical presentation of the recommended model.

Introduction

C7_SURVY

The data for this study were provided by Professor Joan Schmit and are discussed in more detail in the paper, "Cost effectiveness of risk management practices," by J. T. Schmit and K. Roth, in *The Journal of Risk and Insurance*, vol. 57, No. 3, p. 455–470. The data are from a questionnaire that was sent to 374 risk managers of large U.S. based organizations. The purpose of the study was to relate cost effectiveness to management's philosophy of controlling the company's exposure to various property and casualty losses, after adjusting for exogenous company factors such as size and industry type.

First, some caveats. Survey data are often based on samples of convenience, not probability samples. Just as with all observational data sets, regression methodology is a useful tool for summarizing data. However, we must be careful when making inferences based on this type of data set. For this particular survey, 162 managers returned completed surveys resulting in a good response rate of 43%. However, for the variables included in the analysis (defined in the following), only 73 forms were completed resulting in a complete response rate of 20%. Why such a dramatic difference? Managers, like most people, typically do not mind responding to queries about their attitudes, or opinions, about various issues. When questioned about hard facts, in this case company asset size or insurance premiums, either they considered the information proprietary and were reluctant to respond even when guaranteed anonymity or they simply were not willing to take the time to look up the information. From a surveyor's standpoint, this is unfortunate because typically "attitudinal" data are fuzzy (high variance compared to the mean) as compared to hard financial data. The tradeoff is that the latter data are often hard to obtain. In fact, for this survey, several prequestionnaires were sent to ascertain managers' willingness to answer specific questions. From the prequestionnaires, the researchers severely reduced the number of financial questions that they intended to ask.

A measure of risk management cost effectiveness, FIRMCOST, is the dependent variable. This variable is defined as total property and casualty premiums and uninsured losses as a percentage of total assets. It is a proxy for annual costs associated with insurable events, standardized by company size. Here, for the financial variables, ASSUME is the per occurrence retention amount as a percentage of total assets, CAP indicates whether the company owns a captive insurance company, SIZELOG is the logarithm of total assets and INDCOST is a measure of the firm's industry risk. Attitudinal variables include CENTRAL, a measure of the importance of the local managers in choosing the amount of risk to be retained and SOPH, a measure of the degree of importance in using analytical tools, such as regression, in making risk management decisions.

In the paper, the researchers describe several weaknesses of the definitions used but argue that these definitions provide useful information, based on the willingness of risk managers to obtain reliable information. The researchers also describe several theories concerning relationships that may be confirmed by the data. Specifically, they hypothesize that:

1. There exists an inverse relationship between the risk retention (ASSUME) and cost (FIRMCOST). The idea behind this theory is that larger retention amounts should mean lower expenses to a firm, resulting in lower costs.

2. The use of a captive insurance company (CAP) results in lower costs. Presumably, a captive is used only when cost effective and consequently, this variable should indicate lower costs if used effectively.

3. There exists an inverse relationship between the measure of centralization (CENTRAL) and cost (FIRMCOST). Presumably, local managers would be able to make more cost effective decisions because they are

more familiar with local circumstances regarding risk management than centrally located managers.

4. There exists an inverse relationship between the measure of sophistication (SOPH) and cost (FIRMCOST). Presumably, more sophisticated analytical tools help firms to manage risk better, resulting in lower costs.

Preliminary Analysis

To test these theories, the regression analysis framework can be used. To do this, posit the model

$$\text{FIRMCOST} = \beta_0 + \beta_1 \text{ ASSUME} + \beta_2 \text{ CAP} + \beta_3 \text{ SIZELOG} + \beta_4 \text{ INDCOST}$$
$$+ \beta_5 \text{ CENTRAL} + \beta_6 \text{ SOPH} + e.$$

With this model, each theory can be interpreted in terms of regression coefficients. For example, β_1 can be interpreted as the expected change in cost per unit change in retention level (ASSUME). Thus, if the first theory is true, we expect β_1 to be negative. To test this, we can estimate b_1 and use our tests of hypotheses machinery to decide if b_1 is significantly less than zero. The variables SIZELOG and INDCOST are included in the model to control for the effects of these variables. These variables are not directly under a risk manager's control and thus are not of primary interest. As the following data shows, however, inclusion of these variables does account for an important part of the variability.

To illustrate, information from 73 managers was fit using the above regression model. The following is a summary of the fitted model.

$$\widehat{\text{FIRMCOST}} = 59.76 - 0.300 \text{ ASSUME} + 5.50 \text{ CAP} - 6.84 \text{ SIZELOG}$$

| *std errors* | (19.1) | (0.222) | (3.85) | (1.92) |
| *t*-ratios | [3.13] | [−1.35] | [1.43] | [−3.56] |

$$+ 23.08 \text{ INDCOST} + 0.133 \text{ CENTRAL} - 0.137 \text{ SOPH}$$

| | (8.30) | (1.44) | (0.347) |
| | [2.78] | [0.89] | [−0.39] |

The adjusted coefficient of determination is $R_a^2 = 18.8\%$, the F-ratio is 3.78 and the size of the typical error is $s = 14.56$. Remember, the numbers in parentheses are standard errors for the regression parameter estimates. Regression estimates are divided by standard errors to yield t-statistics, given in square brackets below the standard errors. With these statistics, we can perform formal test of hypotheses to evaluate our theories.

Based on the summary statistics from the regression model, we can conclude that the measures of centralization and sophistication do not have an impact on our measure of cost effectiveness. For each of these variables the t-ratio is low, less than 0.5 in absolute value. The effect of risk retention seems only somewhat important. The coefficient has the appropriate sign although is only 1.35 standard errors below zero. This would not be considered statistically significant at the 5% level, although it would be at the 10% level (the p-value is 9%). Perhaps most perplexing is the coefficient associated with the CAP variable. We theorized that this coefficient would be negative. However, in our analysis of the data, the coefficient turns out to be positive and is 1.43 standard errors above zero. This not only leads us to disaffirm our theory, but also to search for new ideas that are in accordance with the information learned from the data. Schmit and Roth suggest reasons that may help us interpret the results of our hypothesis testing procedures. For example, they suggest that managers in the sample may not have the most sophisticated tools available to them when managing risks, resulting in an insignificant coefficient associated with SOPH. They also discussed alternative suggestions, as well as interpretations for the other results of the tests of hypotheses.

The pristine discipline of hypothesis testing demands that the user write down the competing hypotheses, collect and analyze the data, and report out the results based on the results of the decision-making procedure. Many textbooks give numerous warnings about the dangers of data-snooping, that is, the practice of letting your data formulate not only your decision but also the decision-making procedures. These warnings are important because it is all too easy to become overconfident when using the data to formulate the procedure as well as to drive the decision.

However, it is also important to determine a model that adequately represents the data. Section 7.2 reviewed some of the dangers of working with an inadequate model. Some readers may feel uncomfortable with the model selected above because two out of the six variables have t-ratios less than 1 in absolute value and four out of six have t-ratios less than 1.5 in absolute value. Perhaps even more important, dotplots of the standardized residuals and leverages, in Figure 7.5, show several observations to be outliers and high leverage points. To illustrate, the largest residual turns out to be $\hat{e}_{15} = 83.73$. The error sum of squares is Error SS $= (n - (k + 1))s^2 = (73 - 7)(14.56)^2 = 13,987$. Thus, the 15th observation represents 50.1% of the error sum of squares ($= 83.73^2/13,987$). Further, plots of standardized residuals versus fitted values, not presented here, displayed evidence of heteroscedastic residuals. Based on these observations, it seems reasonable to look into ways of formulating a more adequate model.

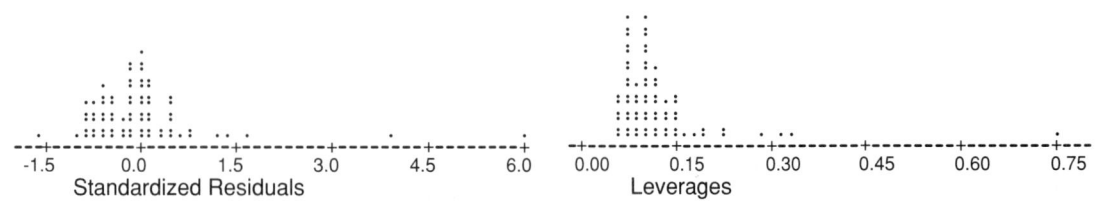

FIGURE 7.5 Dotplot of standardized residuals and leverages from a preliminary regression model fit.

Back to the Basics

To get a better understanding of the data, we begin by examining the basic summary statistics in Table 7.1c and corresponding histograms in Figure 7.6. From Table 7.1c, the largest value of FIRMCOST is 97.55, which is more than five standard deviations above the mean $[10.97 + 5(16.16) = 91.77]$. An examination of the data shows that this point is observation #15, the same observation that was an outlier in the preliminary regression fit. However, the histogram of FIRMCOST in Figure 7.6 reveals that this is not the only unusual point. Two other observations have unusually large values of FIRMCOST, resulting in a distribution that is heavily skewed to the right. The histogram, in Figure 7.6, of the ASSUME variable shows that this distribution is also skewed to the right, possibly due solely to two large observations. From the basic summary statistics in Table 7.1c, we see that the largest value of ASSUME is more than seven standard deviations above the mean. This observation may well turn out to be influential in subsequent regression model fitting. The scatter plot of FIRMCOST versus ASSUME in Figure 7.6 tells us that the observation with the largest value of FIRMCOST is not the same as the observation with the largest value of ASSUME.

TABLE 7.1c Basic Summary Statistics

	Number	Mean	Median	Standard deviation	Minimum	Maximum
FIRMCOST	73	10.97	6.08	16.16	0.20	97.55
ASSUME	73	2.574	0.510	8.445	0.000	61.820
CAP	73	0.3425	0.0000	0.4778	0.0000	1.0000
SIZELOG	73	8.332	8.270	0.963	5.270	10.600
INDCOST	73	0.4184	0.3400	0.2162	0.0900	1.2200
CENTRAL	73	2.247	2.000	1.256	1.000	5.000
SOPH	73	21.192	23.000	5.304	5.000	31.000

Source: Schmit and Roth, Journal of Risk and Insurance (1990)

From the histograms of SIZELOG, INDCOST, CENTRAL and SOPH, we see that these distributions are not heavily skewed. Taking logarithms of the size of total company assets has served to make the distribution more symmetric than in the original units. From the histogram and summary statistics, we see that CENTRAL is a discrete variable, taking on values one through five. The other discrete variable is CAP, an indicator variable taking values only zero and one. The histogram and scatter plot corresponding to CAP is not presented here. It is more informative to provide a *table of means* of each variable by levels of CAP, as in Table 7.2. From this table, we see that 25 of the 73 companies surveyed own captive insurers. Further, on one hand, the average FIRMCOST for those companies with captive insurers (CAP = 1) is larger than those without (CAP = 0). On the other hand, when moving to the logarithmic scale, the opposite is true; that is, average COSTLOG for those companies with captive insurers (CAP = 1) is larger than those without (CAP = 0).

TABLE 7.2   Table of Means by Level of CAP

	N	FIRMCOST	ASSUME	SIZELOG	INDCOST	CENTRAL	SOPH	COSTLOG
CAP=0	48	9.954	1.175	8.1965	0.39937	2.2500	21.521	1.8202
CAP=1	25	12.931	5.258	8.5920	0.45480	2.2400	20.560	1.5946
TOTAL	73	10.973	2.574	8.3319	0.41836	2.2466	21.192	1.7430

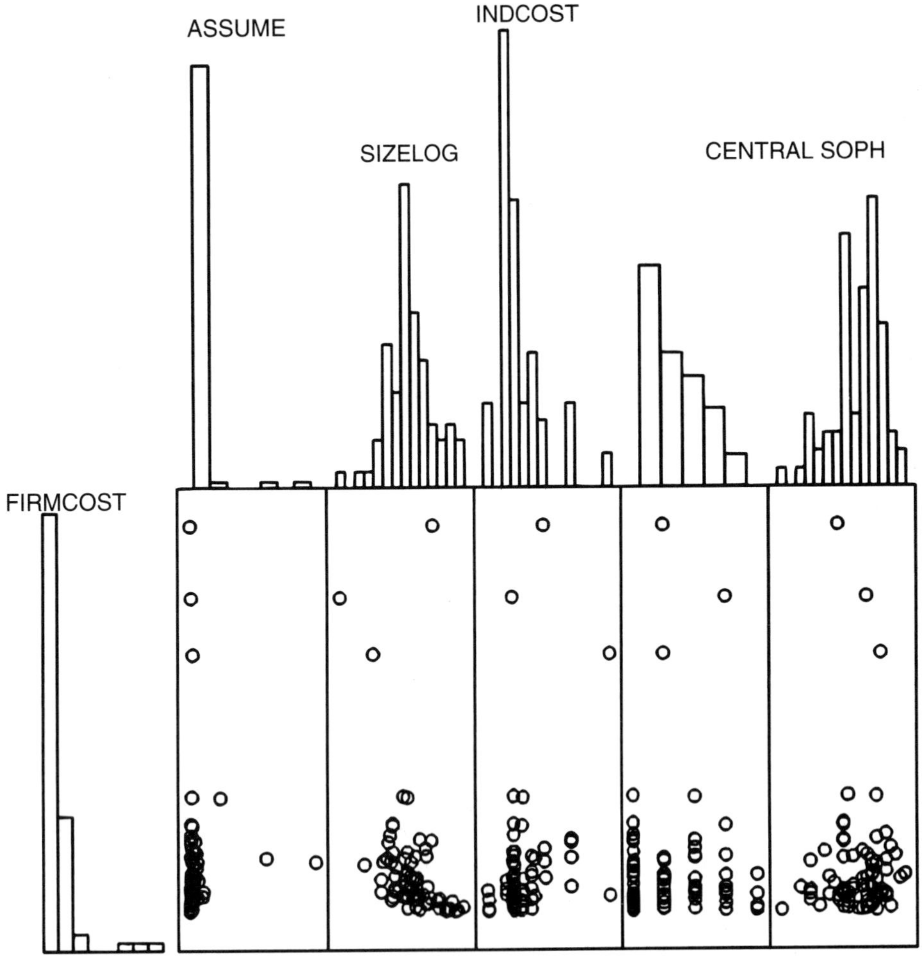

FIGURE 7.6 Histograms and scatter plots of FIRMCOST and several explanatory variables. The distributions of FIRMCOST and ASSUME are heavily skewed to the right. There is a negative relationship between FIRMCOST and SIZELOG, although nonlinear.

The correlation matrix in Table 7.3 masks a feature that is evident in the scatter plots in Figure 7.2, the effect of unusually large observations.

When examining relationships between pairs of variables, in Figure 7.6 we see some of the relationships that were evident from preliminary regression fit. There is an inverse relationship between FIRMCOST and SIZELOG, and the scatter plot suggests this relationship may be nonlinear. There is also a mild positive relationship between FIRMCOST and INDCOST and no apparent relationships between FIRMCOST and any of the other explanatory variables. These observations are reinforced by the table of correlations given in Table 7.3. Note that the table masks a feature that is evident in the scatter plots, the effect of the unusually large observations.

TABLE 7.3 Correlation Matrix

	COSTLOG	FIRMCOST	ASSUME	CAP	SIZELOG	INDCOST	CENTRAL
FIRMCOST	0.713						
ASSUME	0.165	0.039					
CAP	−0.088	0.088	0.231				
SIZELOG	−0.637	−0.366	−0.209	0.196			
INDCOST	0.395	0.326	0.249	0.122	−0.102		
CENTRAL	−0.054	0.014	−0.068	−0.004	−0.080	−0.085	
SOPH	0.144	0.048	0.062	−0.087	−0.209	0.093	0.283

Because of the skewness of the distribution and the effect of the unusually large observations, it seems like a transformation of the response variable might lead to fruitful results. Figure 7.7 is the histogram of COSTLOG, defined to be the logarithm of FIRMCOST. The distribution is much less skewed than the distribution of FIRMCOST. The variable COSTLOG was also included in the correlation matrix in Table 7.3. From this table, the relationship between SIZELOG appears to be stronger with COSTLOG than with FIRMCOST. Figure 7.8 shows several scatter plots illustrating the relationship between COSTLOG and the explanatory variables. The relationship between COSTLOG and SIZELOG appears to be linear. It is easier to interpret these scatter plots than those in Figure 7.6 due to the absence of the large unusual values of the dependent variable.

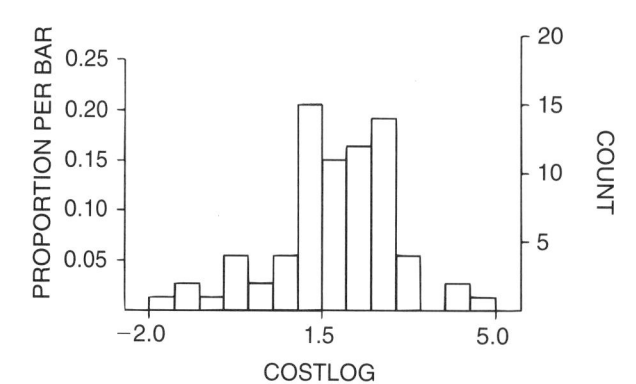

FIGURE 7.7 Histogram of COSTLOG (the natural logarithm of FIRMCOST). The distribution of COSTLOG is less skewed than that of FIRMCOST.

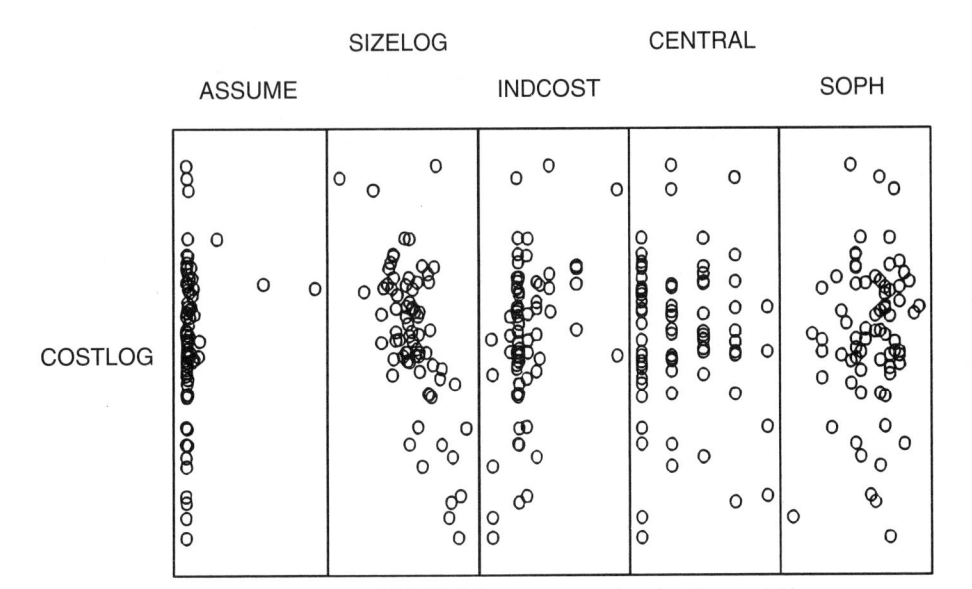

FIGURE 7.8 Scatter plots of COSTLOG versus several explanatory variables. There is a negative linear relationship between COSTLOG and SIZELOG and there is a mild positive relationship between COSTLOG and INDCOST.

Some New Models

Now, we explore the use of COSTLOG as the dependent variable. This line of thought is based on the work in the previous subsection and the plots of residuals from the preliminary regression fit. As a first step, we fit a model with all explanatory variables. Thus, this model is the same as the preliminary regression fit except using COSTLOG in lieu of FIRMCOST as the dependent variable. This model serves as a useful benchmark for our subsequent work.

$$\widehat{\text{COSTLOG}} = 7.64 - 0.008\ \text{ASSUME} + 0.015\ \text{CAP} - 0.787\ \text{SIZELOG}$$

std errors	(1.16)	(0.013)	(0.233)	(0.117)
t-ratios	[6.62]	[-0.61]	[0.06]	[-6.75]

$$+\ 1.90\ \text{INDCOST} - 0.080\ \text{CENTRAL} + 0.002\ \text{SOPH}.$$

(0.503)	(0.087)	(0.021)
[3.79]	[-0.92]	[0.12]

Here, $R_a^2 = 48\%$, F-ratio $= 12.1$ and $s = 0.882$. The dotplot of standardized residuals (Figure 7.9) is less skewed than the corresponding in Figure 7.5. The dotplot of leverages shows that there are still highly influential observations. (As a matter of fact, the distribution of leverages appear to be the same as in

Figure 7.5. Why?) Four of the six variables have *t*-ratios less than one in absolute value, suggesting that we continue our search for a better model.

To continue the search, Exhibits 7.1 and 7.2 illustrate the use of automatic variable selection techniques, specifically, best subsets regression and backward stepwise regression. The output from these search techniques, as well as the fitted regression model above, suggests using the variables SIZELOG and INDCOST to explain the dependent variable COSTLOG.

A regression was run using SIZELOG and INDCOST as explanatory variables. From Figure 7.10, we see that the size and shape of the distribution of standardized residuals are similar to that in Figure 7.9. The leverages are much smaller, reflecting the elimination of several explanatory variables from the

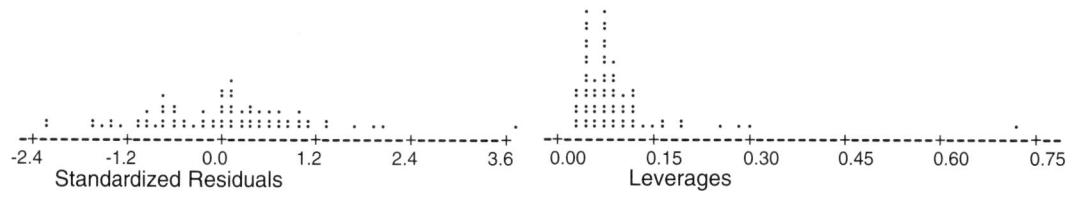

FIGURE 7.9 Dotplot of standardized residuals and leverages using COSTLOG as the dependent variable.

```
Best Subsets Regression of COSTLOG
```

		Adj.			A S S S U M E	C A P	S I Z E L O G	I N D C O S T	C E N T R A L	S O P H
Var	R-sq	R-sq	C-p	s						
1	40.5	39.7	13.4	0.94989			X			
1	15.6	14.4	47.9	1.1317				X		
2	51.5	50.1	0.2	0.86387			X	X		
2	41.6	40.0	13.8	0.94764			X		X	
3	52.1	50.0	1.4	0.86507			X	X	X	
3	51.7	49.6	1.9	0.86813	X		X	X		
4	52.3	49.5	3.0	0.86895	X		X	X	X	
4	52.1	49.2	3.4	0.87134		X	X	X	X	
5	52.3	48.8	5.0	0.87533	X		X	X	X	X
5	52.3	48.8	5.0	0.87539	X	X	X	X	X	

EXHIBIT 7.1 Best Subsets Regression. The model with SIZELOG and INDCOST has the highest R_a^2 and lowest C_p statistics.

model. Remember that the average leverage is $\bar{h} = (k + 1)/n = 3/73 \approx 0.04$. Thus, we still have three points that exceed three times the average and thus are considered high leverage points.

BACKWARD STEPWISE REGRESSION OF COSTLOG ON 6 PREDICTORS,
WITH N =   73

STEP	1	2	3	4	5
CONSTANT	7.643	7.632	7.692	7.582	7.329
ASSUME	-0.008	-0.008	-0.008		
T-RATIO	-0.61	-0.62	-0.62		
CAP	0.01				
T-RATIO	0.06				
SIZELOG	-0.79	-0.78	-0.79	-0.77	-0.76
T-RATIO	-6.75	-7.01	-7.19	-7.24	-7.20
INDCOST	1.90	1.91	1.91	1.84	1.88
T-RATIO	3.79	3.84	3.90	3.87	3.98
CENTRAL	-0.080	-0.080	-0.077	-0.073	
T-RATIO	-0.92	-0.92	-0.93	-0.90	
SOPH	0.002	0.002			
T-RATIO	0.12	0.11			
S	0.882	0.875	0.869	0.865	0.864
R-SQ	52.34	52.34	52.33	52.06	51.50

EXHIBIT 7.2 Backwards Stepwise Regression. This procedure also suggests the model with SIZELOG and INDCOST.

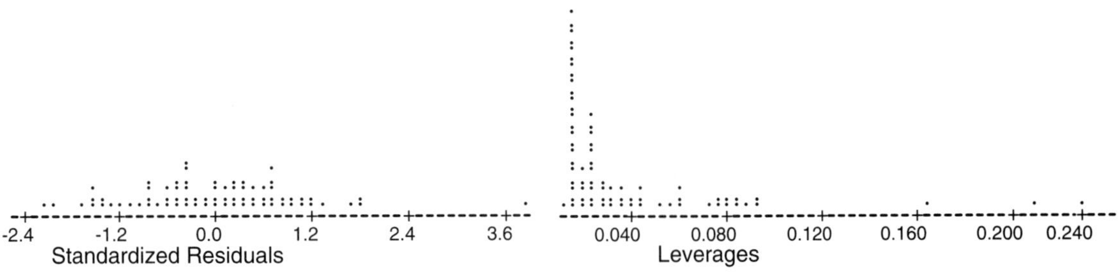

FIGURE 7.10 Dotplot of standardized residuals and leverages using SIZELOG and INDCOST as explanatory variables.

Plots of residuals versus the explanatory variables reveal some mild patterns. The scatter plot of residuals versus INDCOST, in Figure 7.11, displays a mild quadratic trend in INDCOST. To see if this trend was important, the variable INDCOST was squared and used as an explanatory variable in a regression model.

$$\text{COSTLOG} = 6.35 - 0.773\ \text{SIZELOG} + 6.26\ \text{INDCOST} - 3.58\ (\text{INDCOST})^2$$

std errors	(0.953)	(0.101)	(1.61)	(1.27)
t−ratios	[6.67]	[−7.63]	[3.89]	[−2.83]

From the t-ratio associated with $(\text{INDCOST})^2$, we see that the variable seems to be important. The sign is reasonable, indicating that the rate of increase of COSTLOG decreases as INDCOST increases. That is, the expected change in COSTLOG per unit change of INDCOST is positive and decreases as IND-COST increases.

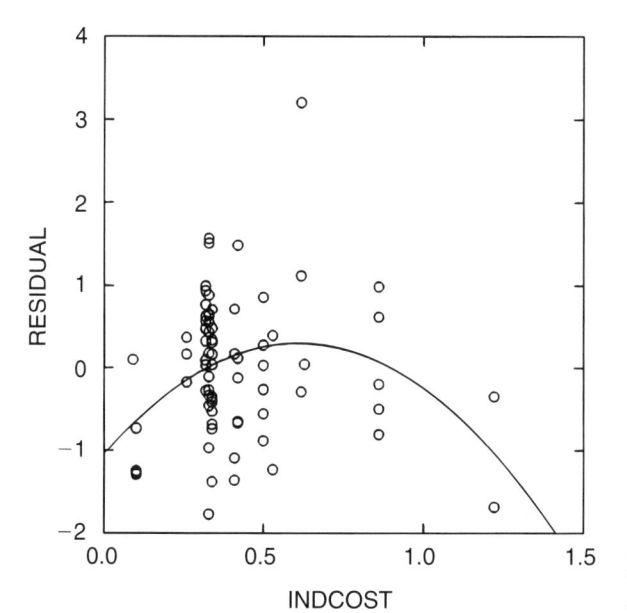

FIGURE 7.11 Scatter plot of residuals versus INDCOST with a quadratic curve superimposed.

Further diagnostic checks of the model revealed no additonal patterns. Thus, from the data available, we cannot affirm any of the four hypotheses that were introduced in the Introduction subsection. This is not to say that these variables are not important. We are simply stating that the natural variability of the data was large enough to obscure any relationships that might exist. We have established, however, the importance of the size of the firm and the firm's industry risk.

Figures 7.12 through 7.15 are graphical summaries of the estimated relationships among these variables. In particular, in Figure 7.15, we see that for most of the firms in the sample, FIRMCOST was relatively stable. However, for small firms, as measured by SIZELOG, we see that the industry risk, as measured INDCOST, was particularly important. For small firms, the fitted FIRM-COST increases as the variable INDCOST increases, with the rate of increase leveling off. Although the model theoretically predicts FIRMCOST to decrease with a large INDCOST (>1.2), no small firms were actually in this area of the data region.

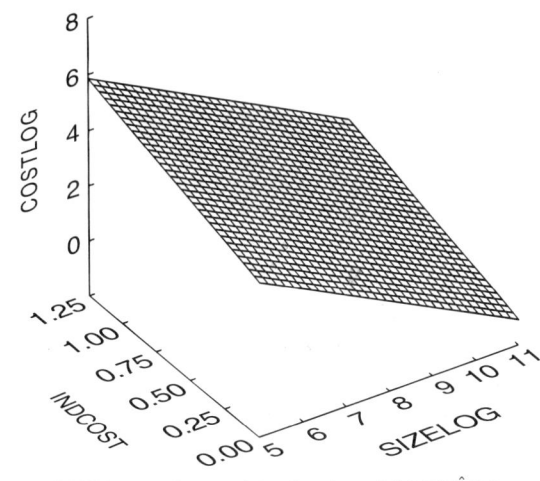

FIGURE 7.12 Graph of the fitted model $\widehat{\text{COSTLOG}}$ = 7.33 − 0.765 SIZELOG + 1.88 INDCOST. The estimated cost is larger for smaller firms with a higher industry risk. The size and industry risk has a linear effect on the logarithm of cost.

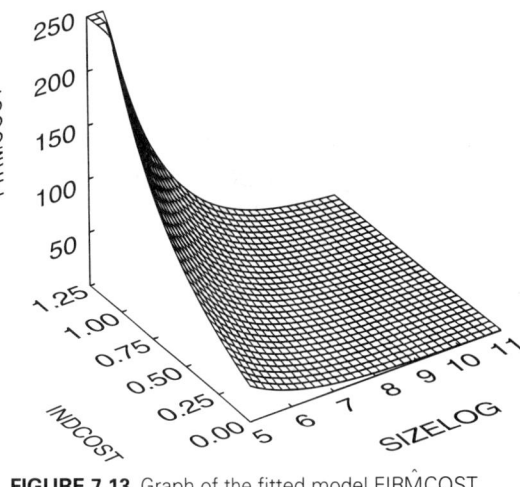

FIGURE 7.13 Graph of the fitted model $\widehat{\text{FIRMCOST}}$ = exp(7.33 − 0.765 SIZELOG + 1.88 INDCOST). The estimated cost is high for small firms that are in a risky industry.

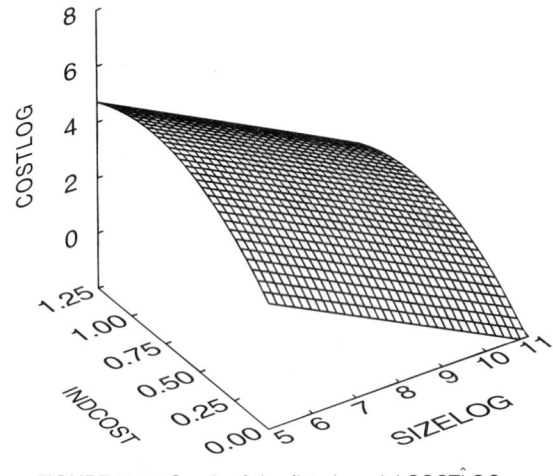

FIGURE 7.14 Graph of the fitted model $\widehat{\text{COSTLOG}}$ = 6.35 − 0.773 SIZELOG + 6.26 INDCOST − 3.58 (INDCOST)^2. Firms with a higher industry risk experience higher costs, although the rate of increase levels off.

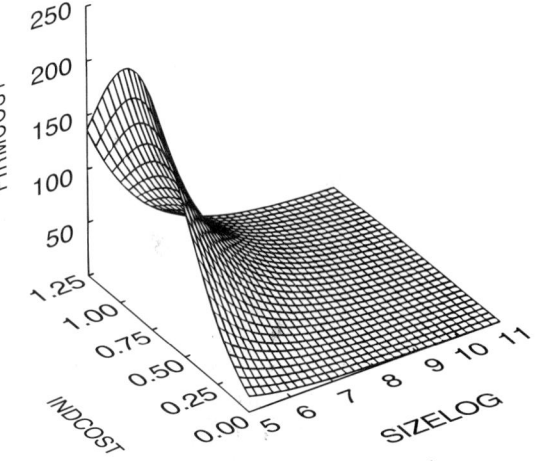

FIGURE 7.15 Graph of the fitted model $\widehat{\text{FIRMCOST}}$ = exp(6.35 − 0.773 SIZELOG + 6.26 INDCOST − 3.58 (INDCOST)^2). Small firms in risky industries exhibit high costs.

7.5 SUMMARY

We began our study of regression in Chapter 3 by focussing on the case of one independent variable. Chapter 4 extended the model to include several independent variables. Chapter 5 considered categorical variables and Chapter 6 showed how to select a model. The focus of Chapter 7 is on interpreting results from regression modeling.

Interpreting the results of a regression study means more than just examining the outputs of a study; what we learn can be imbedded in our consideration of the inputs to the study and the process of model selection. We began the chapter in Section 7.1 by examining the outputs and, in particular, interpreting models for understanding and for prediction. Interpreting the process of model selection was next discussed in Section 7.2. There, we emphasized the fact that models are approximations to reality and no model is a perfect representation. Nonetheless, Section 7.2 presents the important consequences of underfitting versus overfitting the model. Next, Section 7.3 discussed an important input to a regression study, data. Now that we have seen how data are used in regression models, we were able to discuss several known, and widely suffered, pitfalls when collecting regression data. Section 7.4 illustrated these and other issues with a data set of interest to international risk managers.

Chapter 7 concludes our study of cross-sectional linear regression. Before beginning our study of longitudinal data in Chapter 9, Chapter 8 introduces a model of cross-sectional nonlinear regression. Of course, there are many ways in which a model can be nonlinear; the logistic regression model of Chapter 8 is well-suited for handling binary dependent variables. Further, with this model we will be able to address another important application of regression techniques, the classification problem.

KEY WORDS, PHRASES AND SYMBOLS

After reading this chapter, you should be able to define each of the following important terms, phrases and symbols in your own words. If not, go to the page indicated and review the definition.

statistically significant but practically unimportant, 334
test statistic, 334
performance evaluation, 335
$se(pred)$, 337

unbiased, 338
bias, 338
sampling frame error, 341
limited sampling region, 342
missing data, 343

missing of random, 343
ignorable case of missing data, 343
impute missing data, 344
EM algorithm, 344
censored response, 345

censored regression model, 345
truncated response, 345
truncated regression model, 345
level of aggregation bias, 345

CHAPTER 7 EXERCISES

End-of-Chapter Exercises

C6_STINS

7.1 **Refer to Exercises 6.2 and 6.9**

    a. In the Second Regression Model, two variables TAPRE and TAPCE, had small t-ratios. These variables were eliminated and a third regression model was fit. The output can be found in the computer output, labeled as the "Final Regression Model." Perform a formal test of hypothesis to see whether both variables can be eliminated from the second regression model. Use a 5% level of significance. Be sure to state all elements of the procedure, including your null and alternative hypotheses, test statistic and decision making procedure.

    b. For the Final Regression Model, provide a 95% confidence interval for the coefficient associated with EPS90.

C5_HOSP

7.2 **Refer to Exercise 5.4**

    a. A FINAL REGRESSION MODEL with NO DSCHG, NUM BEDS and indicator variables for the diagnosis-related groups (DRGs), is estimated in the computer output. Here, "DRG14" stands for DRG number 14, and similarly for the others. Suppose that you decide to perform a partial F-test to check for the importance of the DRG factor. Calculate the appropriate F-ratio.

    b. For the Final Regression Model, give a 95% confidence interval for the expected change in CHG_NUM per unit change in NUM BEDS.

7.3 **Refer to Exercise 6.10**

    a. For the Final Regression Model, summarized in the computer output, interpret the coefficient associated with the price variable. Assuming that this is the correct model, do lower prices lead to higher sales volume? Justify your response in terms of a formal test of hypothesis. Use a 5% level of significance and assume that the usual regression assumptions are valid.

    b. For the Final Regression Model, interpret the coefficient associated with the price variable. Assuming that the price of a car decreases by $1,000, how much would you expect sales volume to increase? Give a point estimate and a 95% confidence interval to answer this question.

C6_CARS

    c. Does the calculation in part (b) mean that, if a manufacturer actually decreases price by $1,000, then sales will approximately increase by the amount calculated in part (b)? Explain.

7.4 **Refer to Exercise 4.11**

    {Hint: For this problem, use the relationship for one variable regression, $r = t/(t^2 + (n - 2))^{1/2}$, where $t = t(b_1)$. Under the null hypothesis $\beta_1 = 0$, t has an approximate t-distribution with $n - 2$ degrees of freedom.}

    a. When examining the correlation matrix, Lagace, Dahlstrom, and Gassengeimer state that correlations that approximately exceed 0.2 have p-values less than 0.05. How can one determine the cut-off 0.2?

    b. Referring to part (a), what is the cut-off for a p-value of 0.01?

    c. What is the approximate p-value for the correlation between DURATION and TRUST?

    d. For the regression using TRUST as the dependent variable, the p-value associated with the DURATION variable is 0.33. Use this information to calculate the t-ratio for DURATION.

e. Use the results of part (d) to compute the partial correlation between TRUST and DURATION, controlling for the effects of ETHICAL, EXPERTISE, FREQUENCY and Years in Practice.

C7_LIMIT

7.5 As an individual or owner of a business, you buy life insurance to protect against the untimely death of yourself, your loved ones or certain employees that may be vital to the operation of your business. Although beneficiaries of insurance cannot be compensated for their grief, they can be protected from negative financial consequences that would result from an untimely death. Under a standard life insurance contract, in the event of the death of the insured, the insurance company pays the beneficiary of the policy an agreed upon amount. In the same way, insurance companies may also purchase insurance from companies called *reinsurers*. For example, an insurance company may issue a $1.5 million policy which would be payable in the event of the insured's death. However, the insurance company may then buy protection from a reinsurer for a given premium. For example, the reinsurer might agree to pay the excess of claims on a single policy over, say $1 million. This limit is called the *retention limit*. Suppose instead that the insurer's retention limit were as high as $1.5 million. Then, the insurer for this policy would not purchase any protection from the reinsurer and thus would not have to pay any premiums for this protection. Thus, the insurer would earn all the profits from the policy. On the other hand, if the insurer's limit were lower, for example, $1 million, then the insurer would have to pay for the protection. Of course, the advantage of this is that if a claim does occur, then the insurer would only be liable for the first $1 million of claims. The reinsurer would have to pay for the excess over the retention limit which, in this case, is $0.5 million.

In choosing a retention limit, an insurer must balance the certain premium costs against the uncertain liabilities that may arise from a claim. There are several financial characteristics of a firm that influence the choice of an insurer's retention limit. These effects were studied by Lee, Palmer and Skipper (March, 1992, An analysis of life insurer retention limits, *Journal of Risk and Insurance*, volume 59, pages 57–71). The following data was excerpted from this article.

In particular, we examine the retention limits of 97 large U.S. insurers. The retention limits varied in size from $25,000 to $20,000,000. Here, we discuss the natural logarithm of these limits, called LOGLIM. Size of the company turns out to be an important variable. The assets of the firms in this sample range from $108 million to $31.8 billion. The variable FIRMSIZE represents the natural logarithm of each firm's assets. Other variables include ORG.FORM, an indicator variable of the organizational structure of the firm (= 1 for mutual companies and = 0 for stock companies) and LIRR. LIRR is an acronym that stands for "life insurance reserve ratio." This the ratio of life insurance reserve to total policy reserves, in percentages. Total policy reserves would include annuity and health, as well as life, insurance reserves.

a. You decide to estimate a three variable regression model for LOGLIM. The resulting fit, with basic summary statistics, is summarized in the following computer output. It has been hypothesized that having more business in annuities and health insurance should lead to greater retention levels. That is, the lower is the ratio of life insurance reserves, the greater is the need for a larger retention level. Use Tables E7.5a–b to test the null hypothesis that the regression coefficient associated with LIRR is 0 versus the alternative that it is negative. State your null hypothesis, alternative hypothesis and all components of the decision making rule. Use a 5% level of significance.

Regression with Three Independent Variables

TABLE E7.5a Coefficient Estimates

Explanatory variables	Coefficient	Standard error	t-ratio
Constant	−1.867	1.229	−1.52
FIRMSIZE	0.74358	0.05209	14.27
ORG. FORM	0.1816	0.1346	1.35
LIRR	−0.014872	0.008242	−1.80

Source: Lee, Palmer and Skipper, 1992, "An analysis of life in-surer retention limits," Journal of Risk and Insurance, volume 59, p. 57–71.

TABLE E7.5b ANOVA Table

Source	Sum of Squares	df	Mean Square
Regression	91.446	3	30.489
Error	33.367	93	0.359
Total	124.834	96	

The regression fit also yields $s = 0.5990$, $R^2 = 73.3\%$ and $R_a^2 = 72.4\%$.

b. It has been hypothesized that the regression coefficient associated with FIRMSIZE is 1. Use the model fit in part (a) to test this assumption when compared to a two sided alternative. State your null hypothesis, alternative hypothesis and all components of the decision making rule. Use a 5% level of significance.

c. You are working for a large mutual company with assets of $1 billion. Your company primarily writes life business, with a life insurance reserve ratio of LIRR =93, in percentages. To provide a benchmark figure, calculate the retention level, in dollars, for your company under the model fit in part (a). (Note that both retention levels and assets are modeled using natural logarithm units.)

d. Examining the regression output in part (a), because of low t-ratios you are not sure of whether or not to keep the variables ORG.FORM and LIRR in the model. Using the regression output (Tables E7.5c and d), perform a partial F-test to make your decision. State your null hypothesis, alternative hypothesis and all components of the decision making rule. Use a 5% level of significance.

Regression with One Independent Variable

TABLE E7.5c Coefficient Estimates

Explanatory variables	Coefficient	Standard error	t-ratio
Constant	−3.6634	0.8975	−4.08
FIRMSIZE	0.77769	0.04999	15.56

TABLE E7.5d ANOVA Table

Source	Sum of Squares	df	Mean Square
Regression	89.645	1	89.645
Error	35.189	95	0.370
Total	124.814	96	

C8_LOAN

The regression fit also yields $s = 0.6086$, $R^2 = 71.8\%$ and $R_a^2 = 71.5\%$.

7.6 A pilot, or preliminary, study was conducted at a local savings and loan to understand the relationship between the size of a bank loan and various characteristics. A sample of 35 loans was drawn from approximately 24,000 home mortgage loans originated from 1984 to 1988. For each sample loan, we have information concerning the initial loan amount (LNAMT) and the monthly income (INCOME). Financial characteristics of the lendee include the total outstanding debt (net of the mortgage, denoted by TOT-DEBT) and net worth (in natural logarithmic units, denoted by LOGNETWH). Characteristics of the loan include the loan to value ratio (LTV).

a. You decide to estimate a three variable regression model for LNAMT. The resulting fit is summarized in the following computer output. It has been hypothesized that having a higher loan to value ratio qualifies a lendee for a higher loan. Use the model fitted Tables E7.6a and b to test the null hypothesis that the regression coefficient associated with LTV is 0 versus the alternative that it is positive. State your null hypothesis, alternative hypothesis and all components of the decision making rule. Use a 5% level of significance.

Regression with Three Independent Variables

TABLE E7.6a Coefficient Estimates

Explanatory variables	Coefficient	Standard error	t-ratio	VIF
Constant	−157192	81916	−1.92	
INCOME	4.094	2.237	1.83	2.5
LTV	115211	32692	3.52	1.3
LOGNETWH	10793	6503	1.66	2.5

TABLE E7.6b ANOVA Table

Source	Sum of Squares	df	Mean Square
Regression	34,866,307,072	3	11,622,102,016
Error	25,427,339,264	31	820,236,736
Total	60,293,646,336	34	

The regression fit also yields $s = 28640$, $R^2 = 57.8\%$ and $R_a^2 = 53.7\%$.

b. It has been hypothesized that the regression coefficient associated with INCOME is 4. Use the model fit in part (a) to test this assumption when compared to a two-sided alternative. State your null hypothesis, alternative hypothesis and all components of the decision making rule. Use a 5% level of significance.

c. You are working for a client who would like to understand the size of a typical loan with the client's characteristics. Suppose that the client enjoys $150,000 in net worth, has a monthly INCOME of $12,000 and would like to work with a loan to value ratio of 0.90. To provide a benchmark figure, calculate the loan amount, in dollars, for your client under the model fit in Part (a). (Note that the net worth is modeled using natural logarithm units.)

d. A backward stepwise regression procedure has suggested an alternative model to that estimated in the regression output in part (a). The fitted model can be found in Table E7.6c. Because of the high VIF values, you decide to perform a partial F-test to make your choice between these two competing models. State your null hypothesis, alternative hypothesis and all components of the decision making rule. Use a 5% level of significance.

Regression with Three Independent Variables

TABLE E7.6c Coefficient Estimates

Explanatory variables	Coefficient	Standard error	t-ratio	VIF
Constant	−403557	111339	−3.62	
INCOME	3.174	2.290	1.39	3.2
TOTDEBT	0.04396	0.01587	2.77	76.7
LTV	121547	29719	4.09	1.3
NETWTH	−0.09816	0.03377	−2.91	95.2
LOGNETWH	33099	9548	3.47	6.6

The regression fit also yields $s = 25933$, $R^2 = 67.7\%$ and $R_a^2 = 62.1\%$.

7.7   The University of Wisconsin at Madison completed a study entitled "Gender Equity Study of Faculty Pay," dated June 5, 1992. The main purpose of the study was to determine whether women are treated unfairly in salary determinations at a major research university in the United States. To this end, the committee that issued the report studied 1990 salaries of 1,898 faculty members in the university. It is well-known that men are paid more than women. In fact, the mean 1990 salary for the 1,528 male faculty members is $54,478, which is 28% higher than the mean 1990 salary for female faculty members, which is $43,315. However, it was argued that male faculty members are in general more senior (average years of experience is 18.8 years) than female faculty members (average years of experience is 11.9 years), and thus deserved higher pay. When comparing salaries of full professors (thus controlling for years of experience), male faculty members earned about 13% more than their female counterparts. Even so, it is generally agreed that fields in demand must offer higher salaries in order to maintain a world-class faculty. For example, salaries in engineering are higher than salaries in humanities simply because faculty in engineering have many more employment opportunities outside of academia than faculty in humanities. Thus, when considering salaries, one must also control for department.

To control for these variables, the study reports a regression analysis using the logarithm of salary as the dependent variable. The independent variables included information on race, gender, rank (either assistant professor/instructor, associate professor or full professor), several measures of years of experience, 98 different categories of departments and a measure of salary differential by department. There were 109 explanatory variables in all (including 97 departmental indicator variables), of which 12 were nondepartmental variables. The analysis of variance table is given in Table E7.7b. Below that are variable definition, parameter estimates and t-ratios for the 12 nondepartmental variables (Table E7.7a).

TABLE E7.7a   Non-Departmental Variables and Parameter Estimates

Explanatory variable	Variable description	Parameter estimate	t-ratio
INTERCEPT		10.7461	261.10
GENDER	= 1 if male, 0 otherwise	0.0162	1.86
RACE	= 1 if white, 0 otherwise	−0.0291	−2.44
FULL	= 1 if a full professor, 0 otherwise	0.1859	16.42
ASSISTANT	= 1 if an assistant professor, 0 otherwise	−0.2052	−15.93
ANYDOC	= 1 if has a terminal degree such as a Ph.D.	0.0222	1.11
COHORT1	= 1 if hired before 1969, 0 otherwise	−0.1015	−4.84
COHORT2	= 1 if hired 1969–1985, 0 otherwise	−0.0456	−3.48
FULLYEARS	Number of years as a full professor at UW	0.0118	12.84
ASSOCYEARS	Number of years as an associate professor at UW	−0.0123	−8.65
ASSISYEARS	Number of years as an assistant professor or an instructor at UW	0.0015	.91
DIFYRS	Number of years since receiving a terminal degree before arriving to UW	0.0036	4.46
MRKTRATIO	Natural logarithm of a "market ratio"–defined as the ratio of the average salary at peer institutions for a given discipline and rank	0.6647	7.64

Source: "Gender Equity Study of Facility Pay," June 5, 1992, The University of Wisconsin at Madison.

TABLE E7.7b ANOVA Table

Source	Sum of Squares	df	Mean Square	F-ratio
Model	114.04847	109	1.04632	62.943
Error	29.73913	1789	0.01662	
Total	143.78761	1898		

a. Suppose that a female faculty member in the chemistry department feels that her salary is below what it should be. Briefly describe how this study can be used as a basis for performance evaluation.

b. Based on this study, do you think that salaries of women are significantly lower than men?

    i. Cite statistical arguments supporting the fact that men are not paid significantly more than women.

    ii. Cite statistical arguments supporting the fact that men are paid significantly more than women.

    iii. Suppose that you decide that women are paid less than men. Based on this study, how much would you raise female faculty members' salaries to be on par with their male counterparts?

8

Regression Using Binary Dependent Variables

Chapter Objectives

To introduce three methods of handling regression using binary, or indicator, dependent variables. There are: ordinary least squares, weighted least squares and logistic regression. To introduce the classification problem and show how to apply regression to address this problem. To illustrate, we will consider:

- determining characteristics of taxpayers who use a professional tax preparer and
- determining characteristics of bicyclists who are expert riders.

Chapter Outline

8.1 ESTIMATION USING LEAST SQUARES REGRESSION

We begin our study of regression using binary dependent variables by examining an important issue in the tax accounting literature: determining the special characteristics of taxpayers who use a professional tax preparer. Taxpayer compliance is an important issue in all industrialized nations, including the United States. Although many aspects of tax compliance are as complex as the tax forms themselves, it is known that individuals who use professional tax preparers tend to underreport income by a significant percentage when compared to what they would report if they had prepared the returns themselves. It is thus of interest from a public policy standpoint to determine what influences a taxpayer to elect to have a professional prepare the tax return. Some good background material, references and additional details can be found in a paper entitled, "Determinants of Tax Preparer Usage" by Christian, Gupta and Lin (1992).

The response is an indicator variable. For the taxpayer illustration, the response indicates whether or not a professional tax preparer was used.

To examine this issue, we analyze data from the Ernst & Young/University of Michigan Tax Research Database. Specifically, we examine the 1984 returns from 192 individuals that were randomly selected from the database. These 192 individuals represent about 2% of the 9,762 returns on the database, which is itself meant to represent a random sample of returns. For each individual, we are interested in understanding whether or not they used a professional preparer (PREP = 1 if so, and 0 otherwise) in terms of a number of explanatory variables. These variables include:

C8_PREP

marital status (MS = 1 if married, and 0 otherwise),

whether or not the taxpayer is self-employed (EMP),

(EMP = 1 if self-employed, and 0 otherwise),

whether an additional exemption for age 65 and over is claimed

(AGE 65 = 1, and 0 otherwise),

the number of dependents claimed (DEPS),

the number of schedules filed (SCHS),

the filer's marginal tax rate (MTR),

the logarithm of the total personal income (LOGTPI) and

the type of tax form filed.

Here, total positive income is the sum of all positive income line items that taxpayers are required to report. For the type of tax form filed, we use F1040 to indicate whether or not a 1040 form has been filed (F1040 = 1 if filed, and 0 otherwise) and F1040EZ to indicate whether or not an "EZ" version of the 1040 form has been filed (F1040EZ = 1 if filed, and 0 otherwise). See the paper by Christian, Gupta and Lin (1992) for further details of the definitions of these variables.

Identifying and Summarizing Variables

For indicator variables, the sample mean is the only summary statistic that should be reported.

Table 8.1 provides sample averages of indicator variables. For these variables, values of the minimum and maximum are not necessary to report because they are, by definition, zero and one, respectively. Further, for indicator variables, we may interpret the average to mean the proportion of ones. If this proportion is greater than one-half, it is easy to check that the median is one. Therefore, it is not necessary to report the median, because it can be determined by knowing the sample mean. Indeed, when the data are binary, the median is not a useful statistic because it provides little information about the distribution. Further, an easy algebraic relationship is that if y is an indicator variable, then $s_y^2 = n \, \bar{y} \, (1 - \bar{y})/(n - 1)$. Thus, for indicator variables, we only need to report out the sample average mean. Table 8.2 provides summary statistics for the other explanatory variables.

TABLE 8.1   Averages of Indicator Variables

Variable	PREP	MS	EMP	AGE65	F1040	F1040EZ
	0.453	0.484	0.115	0.083	0.688	0.135

Source: Ernst & Young/University of Michigan Tax Research Database

TABLE 8.2   Summary Statistics for Other Explanatory Variables

	Mean	Median	Standard deviation	Minimum	Maximum
SCHS	0.531	0.000	0.737	0.000	3.000
MTR	19.43	18.00	10.48	0.00	50.00
DEPS	2.469	2.000	1.365	1.000	7.000
LOGTPI	9.756	9.913	1.034	5.771	12.806

For binary variables, correlation coefficients are still useful. However, by averaging over both levels of a binary variable, correlations can mask strong relationships at one of the levels.

To investigate relationships among variables, correlation coefficients have proven to be a useful summary statistic for us. This remains true when working with binary variables, but we must use a bit more caution than when working with continuous variables. Correlation coefficients among the variables are provided in Table 8.3. In particular, note the strong correlations between the presence of a tax preparer (PREP) and the type of tax form filed, F1040 and F1040EZ. It makes a great deal of sense that there should be a relationship between the type of tax form filed and the use of a preparer. Indeed, from Table 8.4, we see that all 26 individuals that filed the "EZ" version of the 1040 form did not use a preparer. Thus, this type of information provides "perfect" information about PREP. It is perfect in the sense that if we know that F1040EZ equals one, then PREP equals zero. This type of information is masked in the correlation table but comes out clearly in Table 8.4

TABLE 8.3 Correlation Matrix

	PREP	MS	SCHS	AGE65	EMP	F1040	F1040EZ	MTR	DEPS
MS	0.227								
SCHS	0.310	0.519							
AGE65	0.066	0.009	−0.064						
EMP	0.198	0.306	0.452	−0.049					
F1040	0.456	0.406	0.380	0.081	0.243				
F1040EZ	−0.360	−0.384	−0.286	−0.119	−0.142	−0.587			
MTR	0.155	0.367	0.410	−0.023	0.085	0.389	−0.382		
DEPS	0.194	0.669	0.313	0.090	0.188	0.298	−0.427	0.216	
LOGTPI	0.250	0.562	0.489	0.034	0.188	0.515	−0.555	0.875	0.436

TABLE 8.4 Table of Counts and Average Number of Tax Preparers by Type of Tax Form Filed

	F1040EZ = 0	F1040EZ = 1	Total
F1040 = 0	34	26	60
	(.206)	(0)	(.117)
F1040 = 1	132	0	132
	(.606)	(−)	(.606)
Total	166	26	192
	(.524)	(0)	(.453)

Average Number in Parenthesis

In the following regression modeling, we follow Christian, Gupta and Lin (1992) and do not use the type of tax form nor the number of schedules filed as explanatory variables. The purpose of the data analysis is to determine the characteristics of the taxpayer that would cause that individual to hire a professional tax preparer. Thus, the type of tax form filed does not really help us with our basic goal. This provides another illustration as to how the purpose of the regression study influences the choice of the regression model.

Table 8.4 works well because each explanatory variable is discrete and, in this case, is binary. We can also get further insight into correlation analyses by providing tables of means and standard deviations by levels of the tax preparer variable. Table 8.5 provides an example. Here, we see a strong difference in the means of the marginal tax rate (MTR) and the logarithm of total positive income (LOGTPI) by level of PREP. This difference does not seem apparent in the number of dependents (DEPS). This table reinforces the information provided in the correlation Table 8.3.

TABLE 8.5   Table of Counts, Means and Standard Deviations of Variables by Level of PREP

	Number	MTR		DEPS		LOGTPI	
		Mean	Standard deviation	Mean	Standard deviation	Mean	Standard deviation
PREP = 0	105	17.952	11.126	2.2286	1.3746	9.521	1.149
PREP = 1	87	21.207	9.390	2.7586	1.3026	10.039	0.793
Total	192	19.427	10.476	2.4688	1.3649	9.756	1.034

To investigate relationships among variables, scatter plots have proven to be a useful graphical summary device for us. Figure 8.1 is a scatter plot of PREP versus LOGTPI. Because PREP is a binary variable, there is little separation among observations on the vertical scale and thus, it is difficult to discern any patterns. A better graphical device is to produce dotplots, or histograms, by level of the binary variable. Some examples are in Figure 8.2 and 8.3. Here, we can see the shape of the distribution of each explanatory variable for individuals using tax preparers (PREP = 1) and those who do not (PREP = 0).

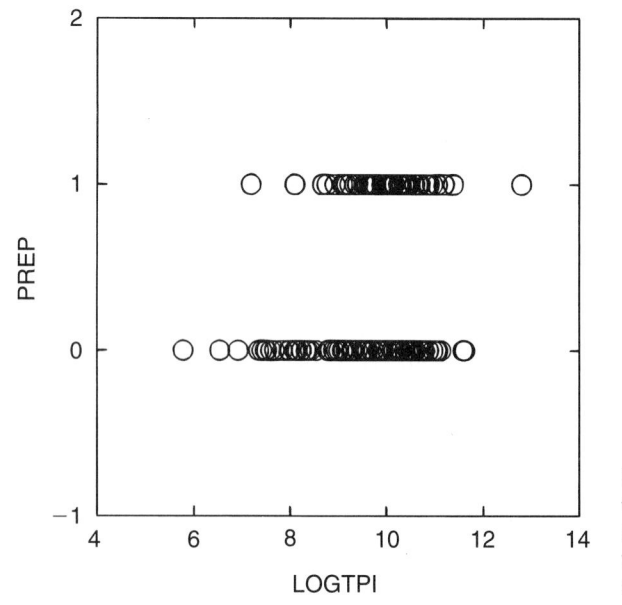

FIGURE 8.1 Scatter plot of tax preparer versus the logarithm of total positive income. It is difficult to discern patterns with scatter plots involving binary variables.

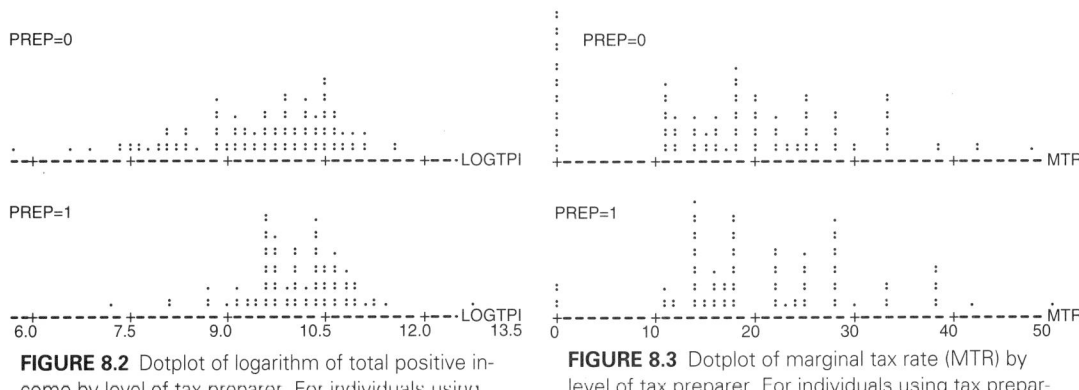

FIGURE 8.2 Dotplot of logarithm of total positive income by level of tax preparer. For individuals using tax preparers (PREP = 1), there is a tendency to have a larger income than for those not using preparers.

FIGURE 8.3 Dotplot of marginal tax rate (MTR) by level of tax preparer. For individuals using tax preparers (PREP = 1), there is tendency to have a larger marginal tax rate than for those not using preparers. Much of the difference is attributable to those individuals at the zero marginal tax rate.

Tables and plots by levels of a categorical variable are useful devices.

Scatter plots of one explanatory variable versus another are useful for understanding linear relationships among the explanatory variables. For example, Figure 8.4 is a scatter plot of the logarithm of total positive income versus the marginal tax rate. Note that, from Table 8.3, the correlation between these two variables is 0.875. From Figure 8.4, we see that for high levels of MTR and LOGTPI, these variables appear to be linearly related. However, the relationship is weaker at low levels of MTR, particularly when the marginal tax rate is zero. This indicates that although these variables are similar, they provide different types of information. Note that in Figure 8.4 we have also superimposed

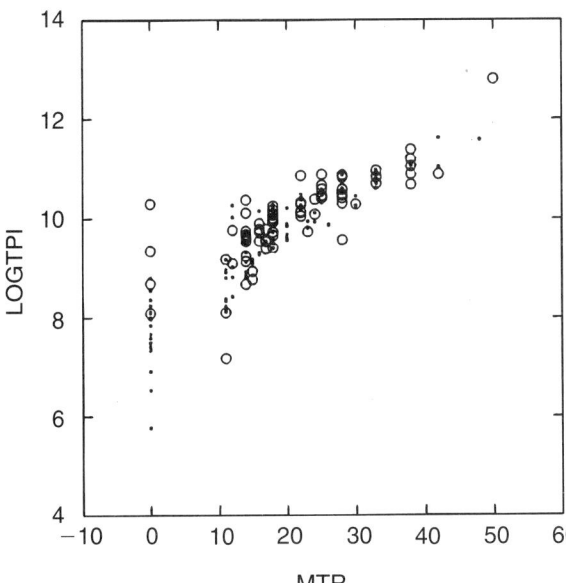

FIGURE 8.4 Scatter plot of logarithm of total positive income versus marginal tax indicating a positive, although nonlinear, relationship between the two. A large plotting symbol is used for cases with PREP = 1 and a small plotting symbol used for PREP = 0.

the tax preparer variable, PREP, through the use of different plotting symbols. This allows us to see, for example, the fact that taxpayers at the zero marginal tax rate tend to use preparers more if they enjoy a larger total positive income, an anticipated finding.

Fitting Least Squares Regression Estimates

A scatter plot of a binary y versus x reveals few discernible patterns. To assess patterns graphically, group the data using the x-value and plot ȳ versus x̄ for each group.

As pointed out in the scatter plot in Figure 8.1, there is little separation among the points which makes it difficult to detect relationships visually. Because we are trying to determine E y at a specific level of x, this suggests that if we had several responses at a level of x, we might average the responses to form an estimate of E y. In the absence of having several responses at each value of x, as an approximation we can categorize, or group, the explanatory variable x and then take averages over each group. Table 8.6 displays the result of such a categorization. Here, we have rounded the logarithm of total positive income to the nearest $1/2$ unit, counted the number in each group and calculated the average number of tax preparers in each group. From this table, we see that as the value of x increases, so does the average value of y. This observation is reinforced by the accompanying scatter plot in Figure 8.5. Next to each plotting symbol is the number of individuals in each group. When approximating any relationship between E y and x, remember that the higher the count in the average, the smaller is the variance and thus the more reliable is the point. Thus, for example, when estimating relationships, we would give low weights to the plotting symbols representing 2 and 3 individuals relative to those representing, for example, 11 and 36 individuals. The plot suggests a linear relationship between y and x, at least over the middle of the range of x.

TABLE 8.6   Table of Counts and Average Number of Tax Preparer's by Category of the Logarithm of Total Positive Income

Logarithm of total positive income	Number	Average of PREP
6	1	0.0000
6.5	1	0.0000
7	2	0.5000
7.5	6	0.0000
8	11	0.1818
8.5	7	0.2857
9	20	0.3000
9.5	36	0.5556
10	34	0.5000
10.5	49	0.5102
11	21	0.5714
11.5	3	0.3333
13	1	1.0000

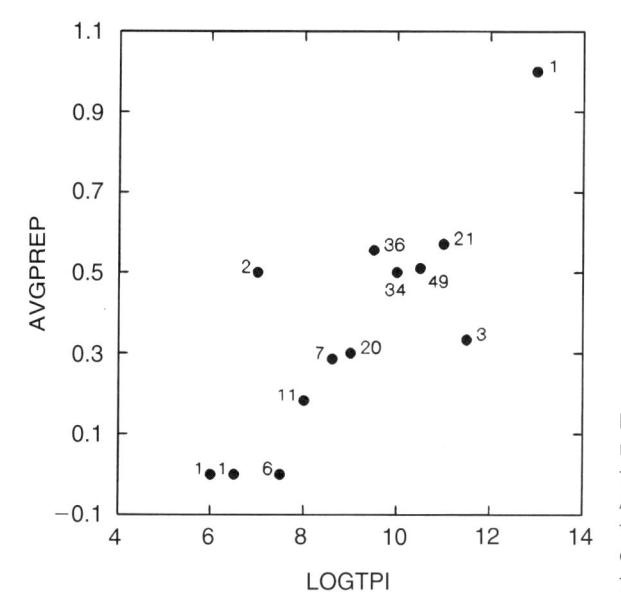

FIGURE 8.5 Scatter plot of average number of tax preparers by category of the logarithm of total positive income. After grouping, we see a positive relationship. The number of taxpayers in each age group is given next to the plotting symbol.

Additional exploratory analyses were performed using the techniques described in Chapter 6. The details are not presented here. As a result, a least squares regression model was fit, treating the response PREP as if it were a continuous response. The result of the fit is:

$$\hat{PREP} = -1.35 + 0.203 \, LOGTPI + 0.216 \, EMP - 0.0107 \, MTR \qquad (8.1)$$

std errors	(0.578)	(0.071)	(0.112)	(0.00692)
t-ratios	[−2.33]	[2.86]	[1.93]	[−1.55]

with $R^2 = 9.8\%$ and $s = 0.4779$. From our discussion of the linear regression model in Chapter 7, we would interpret the variable LOGTPI to be an important determinant of PREP. Thus, the larger is the total positive income, the larger is the likelihood of using a tax preparer. The variables EMP and MTR seem to be somewhat important. However, although the model identifies some important determinants of the use of a tax preparer, it only serves to explain a small fraction of the variability in a taxpayer's decision to use a professional tax preparer.

A criticism of least squares regression is that fitted values can lie outside the interval [0, 1]. This is undesirable because these fitted values are supposed to be estimates of probabilities that, by definition, lie within [0, 1].

Criticisms of Least Squares Regression

The model in equation (8.1) can be criticized for a low coefficient of determination and for low *t*-ratios. However, some deeper criticisms stem from the fact that the response, PREP, is binary. Because of this, from Chapter 2 we have that

$$\text{E PREP} = \text{Prob}(\text{PREP} = 1).$$

That is, the expected value of PREP is a probability. Now, probabilities are supposed to be between zero and one and fitted values are supposed to be desirable approximations of expected values. However, it is possible that the fitted values may be less than zero or greater than one, resulting in unreasonable approximations of the expected value. For example, our 27th observation represents a taxpayer with a small total positive income, a zero marginal tax rate and not self-employed. Specifically, we have LOGTPI = 5.7714, MTR = 0 and EMP = 0. Using equation (8.1), the resulting fitted value is − 0.1733. Because we know that the true expected value is at least zero, this fitted value cannot be interpreted as a reasonable approximation to the true expected value.

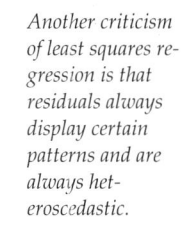

Another criticism of least squares regression is that residuals always display certain patterns and are always heteroscedastic.

Another drawback of the least squares regression model is that patterns in the residuals are always evident when the response is binary. That is, the ith residual is

$$\hat{e}_i = y_i - \hat{y}_i = \begin{cases} -\hat{y}_i & \text{when } y_i = 0 \\ 1 - \hat{y}_i & \text{when } y_i = 1. \end{cases}$$

Figure 8.6 is a scatter plot of standardized residuals versus fitted values. The two parallel lines correspond to the cases of $y = 1$ and $y = 0$, respectively. Thus,

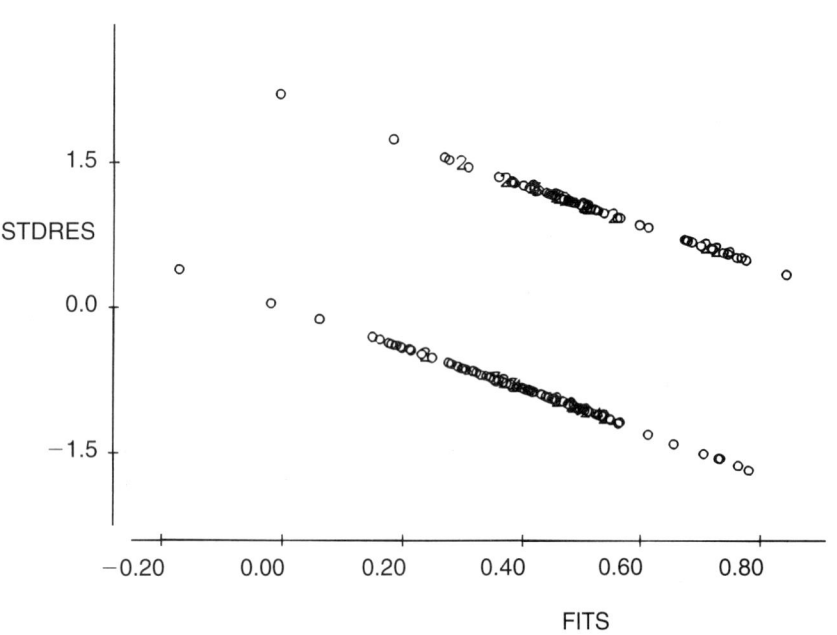

FIGURE 8.6 Scatter plot of standardized residuals versus fitted values. The patterns that are evident do not help us improve our model specification.

residual plots are much less informative than the usual case when y is continuous. The residual plots seem to indicate nonrandom patterns, but do not really help us to formulate an improved linear regression model.

Another drawback will be seen in the next section, where we argue that the binary nature of the response also induces heteroscedasticity, or variable scatter, when examining the residuals.

8.2 WEIGHTED LEAST SQUARES REGRESSION

A device for handling heteroscedasticity is transformation of y. However, transformations are not effective in the case where y is binary.

Recall from Section 6.6 that heteroscedasticity is the term used by statisticians to describe the situation where the variability of the response differs over levels of the explanatory variables. For example, a situation encountered in many applications is when the variability increases as the expected value increases, for example, Var $y_i = \sigma^2 (E\ y_i)^2$, where σ^2 is a constant. In Section 6.6, we discussed the use of a simple transformation of the response to improve our estimation procedures. In particular, the logarithmic transform is especially useful in business and economics.

However, transformations are not always available for many types of dependent variables. As an example, the logarithmic transform is not appropriate for handling situations where y is negative or the case of a binary y. An alternative approach for handling heteroscedasticity is estimation using the *method of weighted least squares*. This technique is similar to the usual least squares method in that we are trying to find the most useful linear combination of k explanatory variables, $x_1, x_2, ..., x_k$, to approximate $E\ y$. The procedure is to find the values of $b_0^*, b_1^*, ..., b_k^*$ that minimize

$$\text{WSS}(b_0^*, b_1^*, ..., b_k^*) = \sum_{i=1}^{n} w_i(y_i - (b_0^* + b_1^* x_{i1} + b_2^* x_{i2} + ... + b_k^* x_{ik}))^2. \qquad (8.2)$$

Using the method of weighted least squares, we choose slope estimates to minimize a weighted sum of squares, given in equation (8.2). Ideally, the weights selected are proportional to the reciprocal of the variances.

Here, the variable w_i is interpreted to a weight that is assumed to be known. Like least squares, weighted least square estimation routines are available in most statistical software packages.

Weighted least squares estimates are appropriate for some data using the linear regression model

$$y_i = \beta_0 + \beta_1 x_{i1} + ... + \beta_k x_{ik} + e_i, \qquad i = 1, ..., n.$$

The thing that distinguishes this model from the one considered in Chapters 3 through 7 is that the variability is allowed to vary by the case. Thus, we write Var $e_i = \sigma_i^2$ to remind ourselves that the variability term σ^2 may depend on i. Now, it seems reasonable that points with smaller variability are more reliable, and thus we would like to give them greater weight in the estimation procedure. The ideal choice of the weight in the estimation procedure is to choose w_i to be proportional to the reciprocal of σ_i^2, for example, choose $w_i = 1/\sigma_i^2$. To see this, look at the expected contribution of each point to the sum of squares. With this choice of weight, we have that

$$E \, w_i \, (y_i - (\beta_0 + \beta_1 x_{i1} + \ldots + \beta_k x_{ik}))^2 = w_i \, \mathrm{Var} \, y_i = 1.$$

Thus, each point is expected to contribute the same amount to the sum of squares, our measure of total variability.

For binary y, the variance is Var y = p (1 − p), where p = Ey is the probability of y = 1.

We now examine the method of weighted least squares when the responses are binary. The model is

$$y_i = \beta_0 + \beta_1 x_{i1} + \ldots + \beta_k x_{ik} + e_i = \mathrm{E} \, y_i + e_i.$$

In Section 8.1, we noted that $\mathrm{E} \, y_i = \mathrm{Prob}(y_i = 1)$ that we can label as p_i. Similar calculations show that $\sigma_i^2 = \mathrm{Var} \, y_i = p_i(1 - p_i) = \mathrm{E} \, y_i(1 - \mathrm{E} \, y_i)$. This calculation indicates the nature of the variable scatter of binary response data.

For feasible weighted least squares, we run a regression fit at each stage. In the first stage, we estimate the weights. In the second stage, we fit using weighted least squares where the weights are estimated in the first stage.

To implement weighted least squares, we would like to choose our weights to be of the form $w_i = 1/(p_i(1 - p_i))$. Unfortunately, values of p_i are not known. This is true because $p_i = \mathrm{E} \, y_i = \beta_0 + \beta_1 x_{i1} + \ldots + \beta_k x_{ik}$ and the regression parameters $\beta_0, \beta_1, \ldots, \beta_k$, are not known. To circumvent this difficulty, a two-stage procedure, called *feasible weighted least squares*, is often used. The binary regression procedure is:

1. In the first stage, run the usual least squares regression. Calculate regression coefficients and fitted values $\hat{y}_i$.
2. In the second stage, use the fitted values from the first stage, $\hat{y}_i$, as approximation for $\mathrm{E} \, y_i = p_i$. Use this approximation to estimate the weights $w_i = 1/(p_i(1 - p_i))$ using $\hat{w}_i = 1/(\hat{y}_i(1 - \hat{y}_i))$. Run weighted least squares using the approximate weights.

It is possible to iterate this procedure. That is, once we have better estimates of the regression coefficient in Stage 2, we could re-calculate fitted values, use these as estimated weights and re-run weighted least squares. However, evidence gathered from examining many data sets and corroborative theoretical investigations suggest that the two-stage procedure is adequate for practical purposes. See Carroll and Ruppert (1988) for a detailed discussion of this issue.

Set negative weights to zero.

To illustrate, the tax preparer data set was used to fit a weighted regression model. Equation (8.1) was used to calculate the fitted values. These fitted values were used to calculate the approximate weights. Three fitted values were less than zero, resulting in negative weights. These negative weights were set to zero. The fitted model using weighted least squares is:

Weighted least squares specifically models the heteroscedasticity. However, a drawback is that we may still obtain fitted values outside [0, 1].

$$\widehat{\mathrm{PREP}} \quad = -1.89 \; + 0.267 \; \mathrm{LOGTPI} \; + 0.189 \; \mathrm{EMP} \; - 0.0150 \; \mathrm{MTR}. \qquad (8.3)$$

std errors   (0.586)   (0.073)   (0.105)   (0.00700)

t-ratios   [−3.23]   [3.68]   [1.85]   [−2.15]

The formula for standard errors, and associated *t*-ratios, of the regression coefficients are not explicitly presented here, although they are calculated as part of most statistical software packages. The results of the fitted model are quali-tatively similar to the model fit in equation (8.1). In principle, the method of weighted least squares addresses the problem of heteroscedasticity by speci-fying weights. However, for binary regression, we are still faced with the prob-lem of fitted values potentially lying outside the interval [0,1]. This problem is addressed by the model introduced in the next section, the Logistic Regression model.

8.3 LOGISTIC REGRESSION

Use p to denote the probability of y = 1. Then, p / (1 − p) is said to give the odds of y = 1.

When the response y is binary, all of the information about the distribution can be summarized by knowing only the probability of a one, $p = \text{Prob}(y = 1)$. In some applications, a simple transformation of p has an important interpreta-tion. The lead example of this is the *odds* transformation, given by $p/(1 − p)$. For example, suppose y is an indicator variable of a horse winning a race, that is, $y = 1$ if the horse wins and $y = 0$ if the horse does not. Interpret p to be the probability of the horse winning the race and, as an example, suppose that $p = 0.25$. Then, the *odds* of the horse winning the race is $0.25/(1.00 − 0.25) = 0.3333$. We might say that the odds of winning are 0.3333 to 1, or one to three. Equiv-alently, we can say that the probability of not winning is $1 − p = 0.75$. Thus, the odds of the horse not winning are $0.75/(1 − 0.75) = 3$. We interpret this to mean the odds against the horse are three to one.

Odds have a useful interpretation from a betting standpoint. Suppose that we are playing a fair game and that we place a bet of $1 with odds of one to three. If the horse wins, we get our $1 back plus winnings of $3. If the horse loses, we lose our bet of $1. It is a *fair game* in the sense that the expected value of the game is zero because we win $3 with probability $p = 0.25$ and lose $1 with probability $1 − p = 0.75$. From an economic standpoint, the odds provide the important numbers (bet of $1 and winnings of $3), not the probabilities. Of course, if we know p, we can always calculate the odds. Similarly, if we know the odds, we can always calculate the probability p.

The log odds transformation, or logit, is defined by logit (p) = ln (p/(1 − p)).

The difficulty that we encountered in Sections 8.1 and 8.2 was that prob-abilities vary between zero and one although linear combinations of expla-natory variables can vary between $-\infty$ and ∞. Previously, we introduced a simple transformation to convert probabilities into odds. Note that as proba-bilities vary between zero and one, odds vary between zero and infinity. We now consider an additional transformation, the logarithm of the odds. With this transformation, as probabilities vary between zero and one, log odds vary between $-\infty$ and ∞, thus providing us with a match of the range for linear combinations of explanatory variables. We thus consider the log odds transformation, called the *logit*, defined by

$$\text{logit}(p) = \ln\left(\frac{p}{1-p}\right).$$

Using $p_i = \text{Prob}(y_i = 1)$, the *logistic regression* equation is defined as

$$\text{logit}(p_i) = \beta_0 + \beta_1 x_{i1} + \dots + \beta_k x_{ik}. \qquad (8.4)$$

Thus, we relate the parameter p to a linear combination of the explanatory variables. An alternative way of expressing equation (8.4) is

$$p_i = \frac{1}{1 + e^{-(\beta_0 + \beta_1 x_{i1} + \beta_2 x_{i2} + \dots + \beta_k x_{ik})}}. \qquad (8.5)$$

An important feature of this model is that, regardless of values of $\beta_0, \beta_1, \dots, \beta_k$ and $x_1, x_2, \dots, x_k$, the true probabilities p lie in the interval [0,1]. The key feature of the logistic regression equation is that we use a linear combination of explanatory variables to represent the log odds of probabilities, as compared to the expected response in ordinary least squares regression.

Another way to think of the logistic regression model is through a so-called threshold interpretation.   Another way to think of the logistic regression model is through a so-called *threshold interpretation*. Here, we assume there is an underlying linear regression model, with continuous random errors, given by

$$y_i^* = \beta_0 + \beta_1 x_{i1} + \dots + \beta_k x_{ik} + e_i.$$

The variable y_i^* is a continuous variable, although unobserved. What we observe is whether or not y_i^* passes some threshold that, for convenience, we take to be zero. We then define the observed response as

$$y_i = \begin{cases} 1 & \text{when } y_i^* \geq 0 \\ 0 & \text{when } y_i^* < 0. \end{cases}$$

For example, y_i^* may represent the propensity for a horse to win a race, such as the speed of a horse in a one mile race. We assume, however, that we only observe whether or not a horse wins the race, a binary outcome.

To link the threshold model to the logistic regression equation, assume that the distribution of the random errors can be described using *logistic distribution function*. That is, we assume

$$\text{Prob}(e_i \leq a) = \frac{1}{1 + e^{-a}}. \qquad (8.6)$$

The distribution function defined in equation (8.6) is close to the standard normal distribution. Like the idealized histogram of the standard normal, the idealized histogram of the logistic distribution is symmetric about zero. Due to this symmetry, we have

$$p_i = \text{Prob}(y_i = 1) = \text{Prob}(-e_i \leq \beta_0 + \beta_1 x_{i1} + \beta_2 x_{i2} + \dots + \beta_k x_{ik})$$

$$= \text{Prob}(e_i \leq \beta_0 + \beta_1 x_{i1} + \dots + \beta_k x_{ik})$$

$$= \frac{1}{1 + e^{-(\beta_0 + \beta_1 x_{il} + \dots + \beta_k x_{ik})}}.$$

This is the same model as given in equation (8.5).

The method of *maximum likelihood estimation* is used to determine estimates of the parameters and associated standard errors. A discussion of this estimation technique can be found in Hosmer and Lemeshow (1989). Using our convention for notation, let $b_0, b_1, ..., b_k$ denote the maximum likelihood estimates of $\beta_0, \beta_1, ..., \beta_k$. With these estimates, we can calculate fitted values as

$$\hat{p}_i = \frac{1}{1 + e^{-(b_0 + b_1 x_{i1} + b_2 x_{i2} + ... + b_k x_{ik})}} \ .$$

To illustrate, consider the tax preparer example introduced in Section 8.1. Using LOGTPI, EMP and MTR as explanatory variables, the fitted model is

$$\hat{PREP} = \frac{1}{1 + e^{-(-9.3218 + 1.0344\text{LOGTPI} + .8956\text{EMP} - .0512\text{MTR})}} \ .$$

Following our previous example, for the 27th observation, we have LOGTPI = 5.7714, MTR = 0 and EMP = 0. Thus, our estimate of the probability of using a tax preparer is

$$\hat{PREP}_{27} = \frac{1}{1 + e^{-[-9.3218 + 1.0344(5.7714) + .8956(0) - .0512(0)]}} = \frac{1}{1 + e^{3.3518}} = 0.033834.$$

Thus, unlike linear least squares, the logistic regression fitted value is constrained to lie in the interval [0,1].

Consider all individuals who are not self-employed and who are at the zero marginal tax rate, that is, EMP = 0 and MTR = 0. Our estimated probabilities are

$$\hat{PREP} = \frac{1}{1 + e^{-(-9.3218 + 1.0344\text{LOGTPI})}} \ .$$

Figure 8.7 displays a graph of these estimated probabilities. The logistic regression fits form a curve that looks like a tilted "S." From this graph, we see that estimated probabilities lie in the [0,1] interval. Further, one can also see the nonlinear relationship between the explanatory variable LOGTPI and the fitted value. Superimposed on the logistic regression fitted curve is the weighted least squares fitted line, from equation (8.3) with EMP = MTR = 0. Here, we see that these two fits are close to one another over the middle of the range of independent variable LOGTPI. The difference is in the extremes of LOGTPI, where the linear least squares fit fails to accommodate the fact that the fitted values must lie in the interval [0,1].

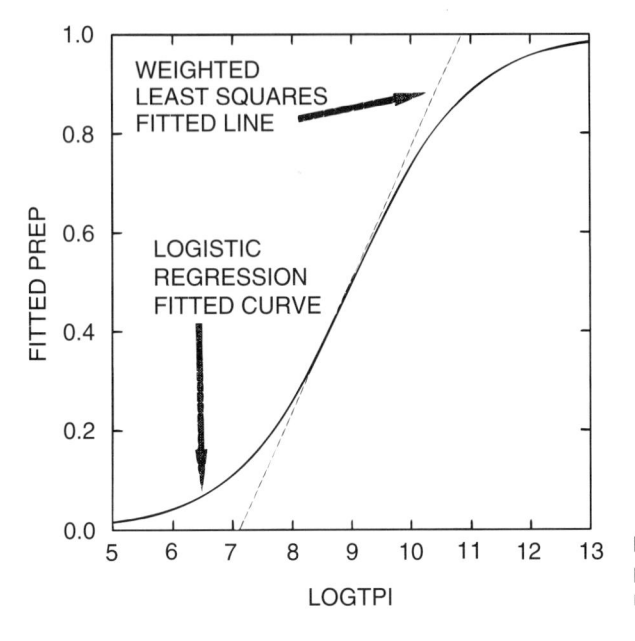

FIGURE 8.7 Comparison of estimated probabilities using the logistic and linear regression models.

8.4 CLASSIFICATION RULES

Classification Problem

Suppose that you are a loan officer working for a bank and you need to decide whether or not a loan applicant is a good credit risk. What you are really trying to do is to decide whether you think the applicant will repay the loan on a timely basis or default. Of course, because you can only permit the loan or not, there is no room for a contingent recommendation. You have available certain characteristics of the applicant and would like to use this information to *classify* the applicant as a good or poor credit risk.

Or perhaps you are the underwriter at an insurance company, and need to decide whether an insurance applicant is a good risk for an automobile or a life insurance policy. Perhaps you are the fund manager for a large pension plan and need to understand the chances of a risky company that you are investing in becoming insolvent. Possibly, as the manager of a large group of automobile salespersons, you would like to be able to classify potential customers as individuals likely to buy one of your products and thus provide those potential buyers with a bit more attention than the average window shopper.

The classification problem is about developing rules to determine whether or not an observation falls into a certain category.

In each of these situations, we would like the ability to determine whether or not an observation falls into a certain category. We approach the problem by defining a variable that indicates whether or not the observation belongs to the group. We can then use this indicator as the response in the regression framework. This is also known as the *discrimination* problem, in that we are trying to establish rules to discriminate, or differentiate, among populations. Although it is possible to consider more than two categories of the dependent variable, we limit ourselves to the case of binary responses.

To see how regression works in the classification problem, we consider how to predict whether or not the U.S. Cycling Federation classifies a bicyclist as an expert rider or not. We first develop fitted linear and nonlinear regression equations using a sample of cyclists in the following subsection entitled Expert Cyclists. We then show how to use these equations in the final subsection, Using Regression Rules to Classify.

Illustration: Expert Cyclists

Consider the problem of trying to establish an empirical rule for classifying whether a bicyclist is an "expert" rider or not. To make this determination, we rely on the opinion of the governing body of bicycle racing in the United States, the U.S. Cycling Federation (USCF). There are approximately 25,000 members in the USCF, about 13% of whom are classified as experts (road categories one and two in USCF terminology).

C8_BIKER

As part of a pilot study, a list of the nearly 500 USCF members in Wisconsin was obtained from the main headquarters of USCF, located in Colorado Springs, Colorado. From this list, a telephone survey was conducted, resulting in a sample of 33 cyclists. In the survey, demographic variables such as age, sex and educational background were collected. Also collected was data relevant to racing performance, including average weekly number of hours in training, whether or not the cyclist has a coach and average number of races participated in a season. In the following, we present summary measures of variables that turned out to be most relevant for the regression fits. These variables are TOTPLACE, the number of first through fifth places that a rider achieved in the last racing season and GRADSCHL, a variable indicating whether or not the cyclist attended graduate school. The dependent variable is EXPERT, which is one if the USCF has classified a cyclist as an expert and zero otherwise.

Tables 8.7 and 8.8 provide summary statistics for EXPERT, GRADSCHL and TOTPLACE. About one quarter of the cyclists sampled had attended graduate school and only 18.18% (or 6 out of 33) have an expert rating.

TABLE 8.7 Averages of Indicator Variables

Variable	EXPERT	GRADSCHL
Average	.1818	.2424

TABLE 8.8 Summary Statistics for the Total Number of Places

	Mean	Median	Standard deviation	Minimum	Maximum
TOTPLACE	5.61	3.00	8.89	0	36

To investigate relationships among the variables, we examine Table 8.9, which provides the basic correlation statistics. Here, we see that EXPERT is strongly related to TOTPLACE and is somewhat related to GRADSCHL. The two independent variables, TOTPLACE and GRADSCHL, are not linearly correlated. Table 8.10 provides further information on the nature of the relationship between EXPERT and GRADSCHL. Here, we see that 37.5% (3 out of 8) of the people that attended graduate school have an expert rating, compared to 12% for people that did not. Figure 8.8 provides further information about the relationship between EXPERT and TOTPLACE. Here, we see that all of the cyclists with TOTPLACE = 0 are considered to be nonexperts and the four cyclists with the highest number of places are considered to be experts. The interesting thing about this data set is that the TOTPLACE variable is not a perfect predictor of EXPERT. In Figure 8.8 we see that some expert cyclists have a relatively smaller number of total places (as small as five) and nonexpert cyclists have a relatively large number of TOTPLACEs (as large as eighteen).

TABLE 8.9 Correlations

	EXPERT	TOTPLACE
TOTPLACE	0.730	
GRADSCHL	0.283	−0.007

TABLE 8.10 Table of Counts of Experts by Graduate Education

	GRADSCHL = 0	GRADSCHL = 1	Total
EXPERT = 0	22	5	37
EXPERT = 1	3	3	6
Total	25	8	33

A least squares regression was fit, treating the response EXPERT as if it were a continuous response. The result of the fit is:

$$\hat{\text{EXPERT}} = -0.062 + 0.260 \text{ GRADSCHL} + 0.032 \text{ TOTPLACE} \qquad (8.7)$$

std errors	(0.0575)	(0.102)	(0.0050)
t-ratios	[−1.08]	[2.55]	[6.47]

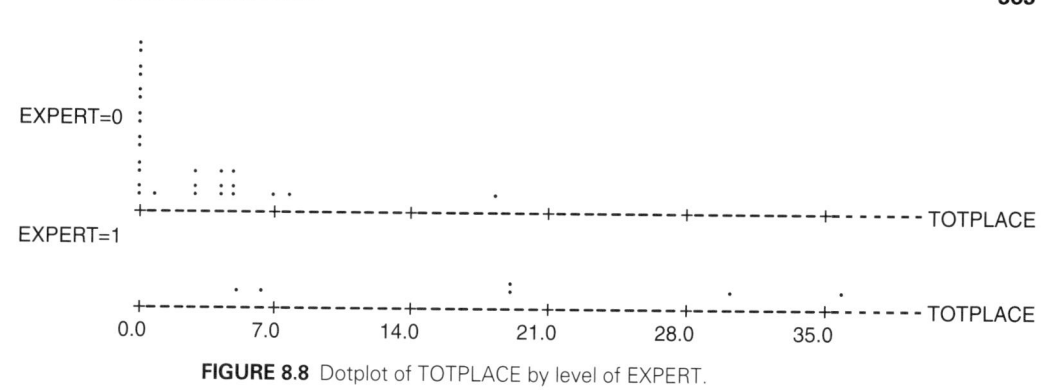

FIGURE 8.8 Dotplot of TOTPLACE by level of EXPERT.

with $R^2 = 61.6\%$ and $s = 0.251$. Further, a logistic regression model was fit, resulting in:

$$\widehat{\text{EXPERT}} = \frac{1}{1 + e^{13.873 - 9.582\text{GRADSCHL} - .750\text{TOTPLACE}}}.\qquad(8.8)$$

Using Regression Rules to Classify

If the fitted value exceeds a cut-off, we classify an observation falling into the category $(y = 1)$. If the populations are treated equally, use 0.5 for the cut-off.

Equations (8.7) and (8.8) provide a way to calculate predicted values of the response variable EXPERT. To classify observations, we judge that an observation with fitted value $\hat{y} > 0.5$ comes from the expert population $(y = 1)$ and otherwise comes from the nonexpert population. The cut-off value 0.5 comes from the fact that we are treating each population equally. Plots of the fitted values can be found in Figures 8.9 and 8.10.

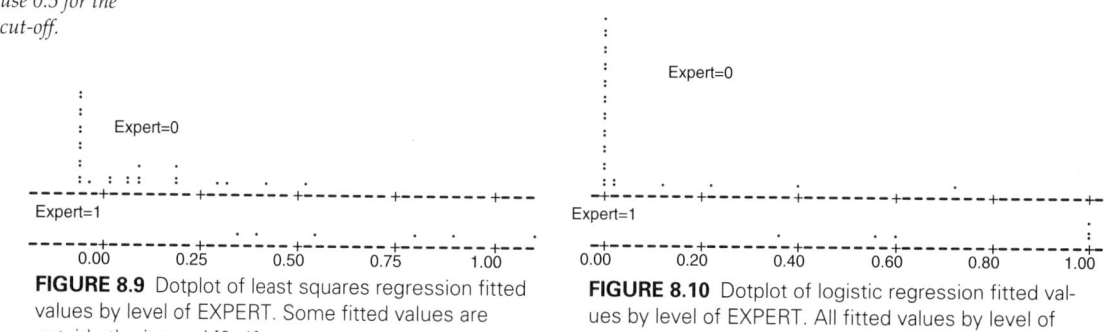

FIGURE 8.9 Dotplot of least squares regression fitted values by level of EXPERT. Some fitted values are outside the interval [0, 1].

FIGURE 8.10 Dotplot of logistic regression fitted values by level of EXPERT. All fitted values by level of EXPERT. All fitted values are inside the interval [0, 1].

Using the least squares fitted values, from the top dotplot in Figure 8.9, we see that one nonexpert cyclist would be incorrectly classified as expert. From the bottom dotplot, we see that two expert cyclists would be incorrectly

The (total) misclassification rate is the number of misclassified observations divided by the number of observations.

classified as nonexperts. This results in a *total misclassification rate* of 3 out of 33, or 9.1%. Similarly, from Figure 8.10, we have that the total misclassification rate is 2 out of 33, or 6.1%. This is due to the one nonexpert incorrectly classified, as seen in the top dotplot, and to the one expert incorrectly classified, from the bottom dotplot. As a general rule, logistic regression fits are more accurate for classification purposes than least squares fits. This is yet another reason to prefer logistic regression over least squares models for data involving binary dependent variables.

Varying the choice of the cut-off allows us to reduce the probability of one type of misclassification error, at the expense of the other.

Choice of the cut-off value, 0.5 in this case, will depend on the application at hand. For example, suppose that we use a cut-off of 0.3 with the logistic regression fits. This results in a total misclassification rate of 2 out of 33, or 6.1%, that is the same as when using a cut-off = 0.5. However, with a cut-off = 0.3, we have not misclassified any expert riders, only two nonexpert riders. If we were trying to identify really good riders, we might be somewhat reluctant to overlook an outstanding candidate on a first pass. Thus, we may choose a somewhat conservative classification rule that would produce more total errors but produce fewer errors of a certain kind. By varying the cut-off level you can decrease the rate in falsely classifying experts, or "1"s. The trade-off is that you simultaneously increase in falsely classifying nonexperts, or "0"s.

8.5 SUMMARY

Regression methods are not limited to continuous variables. In Chapters 4 and 5, we saw several techniques for incorporating categorical independent variables into the model. This chapter introduced techniques for modeling categorical, and in particular binary, dependent variables.

Section 8.1 introduced the problem of modeling binary dependent variables using ordinary regression techniques. There, we discussed ways of presenting and interpreting binary data. Further, we noted two drawbacks of using regression for binary dependent variables: heteroscedasticity and fitted values not being constrained to lie within [0,1]. Unfortunately, the transformation technique for dealing with heteroscedasticity introduced in Section 6.6 is no longer available because the responses are zeroes and ones. Section 8.2 introduced a new estimation technique to handle the heteroscedasticity problem; estimation using weighted least squares. Although weighted least squares can be easily implemented using regression routines, the second drawback is not addressed. The logistic regression model, introduced in Section 8.3, does address both drawbacks. This is our first model that is not linear in its parameters. We finished the chapter by providing yet another application of regression, the classification problem. The problem of classifying entities into groups is particularly well suited to regression models that use binary dependent variables.

This Chapter concludes the part of the book dealing with cross-sectional data and models. In Chapter 9, we turn to the problem of using regression techniques with longitudinal data.

KEY WORDS, PHRASES AND SYMBOLS

After reading this chapter, you should be able to define each of the following important terms, phrases and symbols in your own words. If not, go to the page indicated and review the definition.

CHAPTER 8 EXERCISES

End-of-Chapter Exercises

C8_LOAN

8.1 **This problem is also described in Exercises 6.4 and 7.6.**

Suppose that you are interested in predicting whether someone chooses a fixed or variable assumption for their mortgage loan based on the characteristics available. After a preliminary examination of the data, you decide to fit an ordinary least squares model using the indicator variable FIXED as the response and the continuous variable loan amount (LNAMT) and income (INCOME) as explanatory variables. The regression fit follows (Tables E8.1a and b). A plot of the standardized residuals versus fitted values (See Figure E8.1.) displays some clear patterns. Describe the nature of the patterns and say why these patterns occur.

TABLE E8.1a Coefficient Estimates

Explanatory variables	Coefficient	Standard error	t-ratio
Constant	0.3218	0.1478	2.18
LNAMT	0.00000263	0.00000229	1.15
INCOME	0.00003650	0.00002778	1.31

TABLE E8.1b ANOVA Table

Source	Sum of Squares	df	Mean Square
Regression	1.5743	12	0.7871
Error	5.9686	32	0.1865
Total	7.5429	34	

The regression fit also yields $s = 0.4319$, $R^2 = 20.9\%$ and $R_a^2 = 15.9\%$.

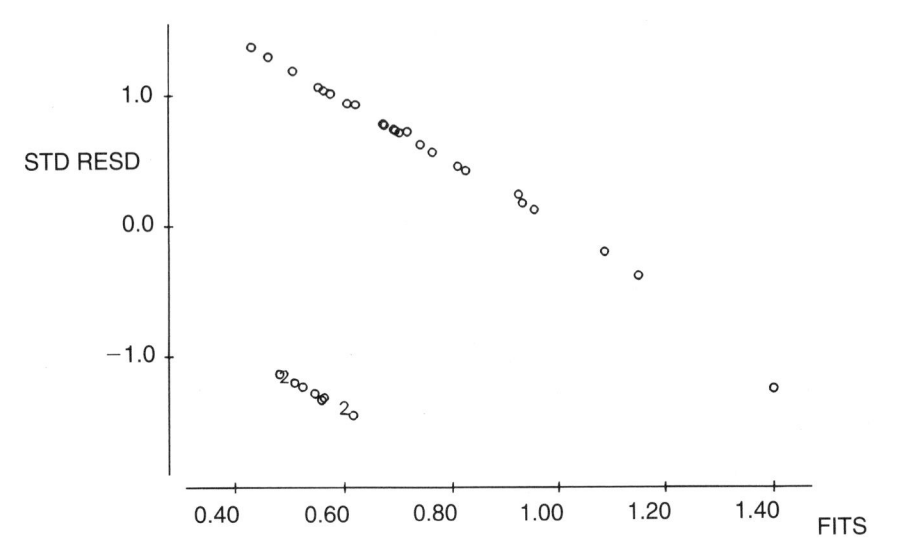

FIGURE E8.1 Scatter plot of standardized residuals versus fitted values.

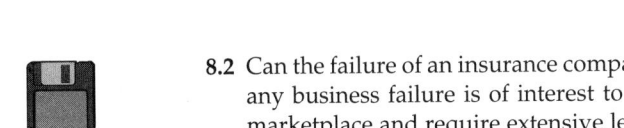

8.2 Can the failure of an insurance company be predicted? To a certain extent, prediction of any business failure is of interest to society because failures cause disruptions in the marketplace and require extensive legal fees to sort them out. Further, insurance companies are in the business of protecting their policyholders interest and thus have a higher fiduciary responsibility in the public's eye. To address the issue, information was obtained from a report entitled *Insurer Failures—Property/Casualty Insurer Insolvencies and State Guaranty Funds* in the July 1987 *Government Accountant's Office Report to Congressional Requesters.* Specifically, we consider 15 property and casualty insurers that were domiciled in the Midwest who failed during the 1983 through 1986 period. Here, "Midwest" means Wisconsin, Illinois, Michigan, Minnesota, Iowa, Indiana, Ohio, Missouri, North Dakota, South Dakota and Kansas. To compare with these insolvent companies, a random sample of 62 companies from the Midwest was taken from the 1988 edition of *Best's Insurance Reports—Property/Casualty.*

Several variables were collected on each company. These variables included number of states operating in, percentage change in assets for two most recent years of business, age of the company, structure of the company (stock or mutual), annual net (written) premiums, policyholder's surplus, percentage of commissions from direct written premiums and current liabilities. It turned out that none of these variables was very useful for explaining insolvency. The best explanatory variable was a transform of policyholder surplus, given as LOG SURP = log(1 + (policyholder surplus)/10,000,000). The logarithmic transform was used to bring some of the large companies more in line with the smaller companies. The '1' was added before taking logarithms because some insolvent companies had a negative surplus.

C8_INSOL

a. In the dotplot and Table E8.2a, information about the relation between LOG SURP and INSOLVNT is provided. Interpret the dotplots and table, and say whether there is a relationship between these two variables.

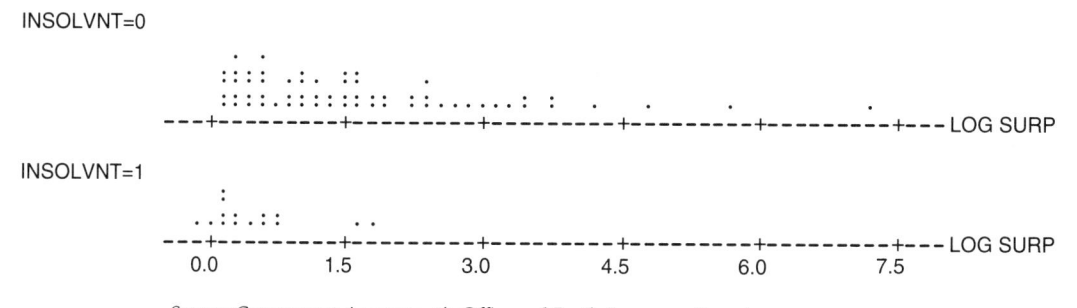

INSOLVNT=0

INSOLVNT=1

Source: Government Accountant's Office and Best's Insurance Reports

TABLE E8.2a Summary Statistics of LOG SURP by Level of INSOLVNT

	Number	Mean	Standard deviation
INSOLVNT = 0	62	1.7229	1.4344
INSOLVNT = 1	15	0.5076	0.5795
ALL	77	1.4862	1.3958

b. Table E8.2b is an ordinary least squares regression fit using LOG SURP as a predictor variable. Does LOG SURP appear to be useful? Explain in terms of the basic regression summary statistics.

TABLE E8.2b Coefficient Estimates

Explanatory variables	Coefficient	Standard error	t-ratio
Constant	0.34215	0.06287	5.44
LOG SURP	−0.09914	0.03093	−3.21

The regression fit also yields $s = 0.3763$, $R^2 = 12.0\%$ and $R_a^2 = 10.9\%$.

c. Figure E8.2 is a plot of standardized residuals versus fitted values from the preceding regression fit. There appears to be two distinct clumps of data. Has a mistake been made in fitting the regression model or do you have another explanation for the clustering of points?

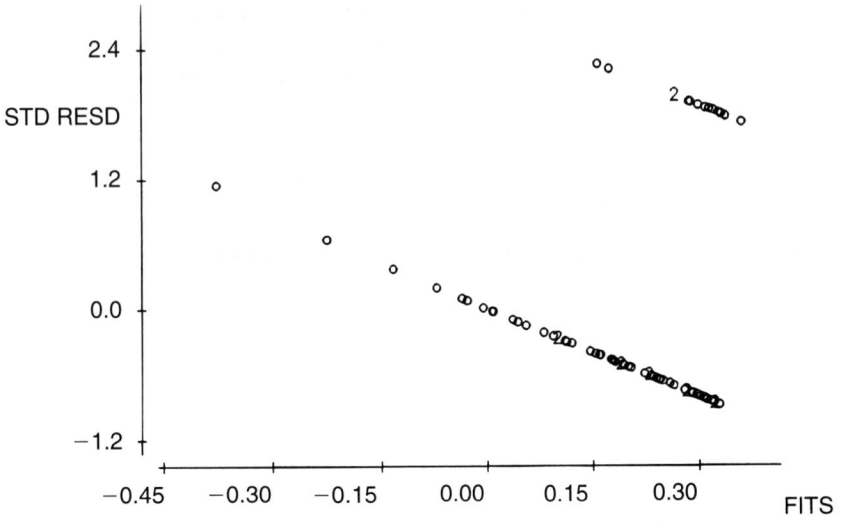

FIGURE E8.2 Scatter plot of standardized residuals versus fitted values.

d. The 62 solvent companies were taken using a random sample from *Best's* report which contains approximately 1,970 property and casualty insurers listed. Can you think of another way of taking a sample of 62 firms from this report that might provide more information about variables that affect insolvency?

e. The fitted values are summarized in the dotplots and, after being sorted, are listed in Table E8.2c. Use the dotplots and the listing to determine the misclassification rate if we use the *cut-off:*
   i.   20%
   ii. 30%
   iii. 40%.

f. Suppose instead that we are interested in the error rate defined by the number of *insolvent* companies incorrectly misclassified divided by the total number of companies. Such an error rate may be of interest to an insurance commissioner, who needs to identify *potential* insolvencies for further auditing and introducing remedial measures that may preempt insolvency. Use the dotplots and Table E8.2c to determine this error rate if we use the *cut-off:*
   i.   20%
   ii. 30%
   iii. 40%.

Dotplots of Fitted Values by Level of Insolvency

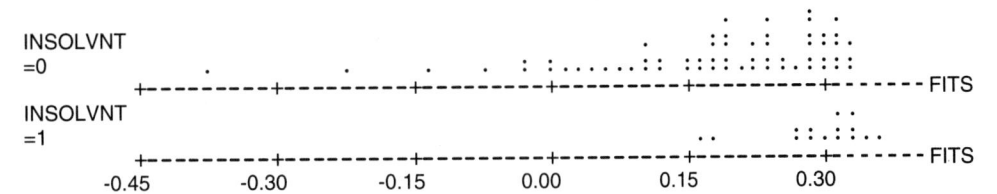

TABLE E8.2c Listing of Insolvency Indicator and Fitted Values—Sorted by Size

Row number	INSOLVNT	Fits	Row number	INSOLVNT	Fits	Row number	INSOLVNT	Fits
1	0	−0.376033	27	0	0.178724	53	1	0.288279
2	0	−0.224499	28	0	0.179298	54	0	0.288932
3	0	−0.0133120	29	0	0.181828	55	0	0.289711
4	0	−0.071905	30	0	0.191192	56	0	0.291076
5	0	−0.035789	31	0	0.191263	57	0	0.297158
6	0	−0.029023	32	0	0.193635	58	0	0.298400
7	0	−0.004967	33	0	0.195503	59	1	0.299962
8	0	0.006726	34	0	0.201071	60	0	0.301568
9	0	0.010044	35	0	0.204717	61	0	0.305559
10	0	0.037187	36	0	0.222658	62	0	0.307728
11	0	0.044446	37	0	0.229839	63	0	0.309702
12	0	0.056381	38	0	0.230281	64	1	0.309838
13	0	0.081159	39	0	0.233141	65	0	0.310751
14	0	0.094368	40	0	0.235883	66	1	0.314730
15	0	0.100358	41	0	0.240479	67	0	0.316161
16	0	0.101210	42	0	0.243427	68	1	0.319900
17	0	0.110950	43	0	0.246096	69	0	0.320815
18	0	0.113305	44	0	0.250249	70	0	0.322525
19	0	0.119423	45	0	0.258501	71	0	0.322745
20	0	0.145724	46	0	0.263566	72	0	0.328078
21	0	0.153924	47	1	0.267498	73	1	0.328406
22	1	0.157751	48	1	0.268422	74	1	0.330888
23	0	0.159149	49	0	0.278844	75	1	0.332063
24	0	0.160717	50	0	0.282998	76	1	0.338223
25	1	0.173679	51	0	0.283309	77	1	0.360874
26	0	0.175475	52	1	0.286867			

C8_HOR10

8.3 The race track is a fascinating example of financial market dynamics at work. Let's go to the track and make a straightforward investment, or wager. Suppose that, from a field of 10 horses, we simply want to pick a winner. In the context of regression, we will let y be the response variable indicating whether a horse wins ($y = 1$) or not ($y = 0$). From racing forms, newspapers and so on, there are many independent variables that are publicly available that might help us predict the outcome for y. Some candidate variables include the age of the horse, recent track performance of the horse and jockey, pedigree of the horse and so on. These variables are assessed by the investors present at the race, the betting crowd. Like many financial markets, it turns out that one of the most useful explanatory variables is the crowd's overall assessment of the horse's abilities. These assessments are not made based on a survey of the crowd, but rather based on the wagers placed by the crowd. Information about the crowd's wagers is available on a large sign at the race called the *tote board*. The tote board provides the odds of each horse winning a race. Table E8.3a is a hypothetical tote board for a race of 10 horses.

TABLE E8.3a Hypothetical Tote Board

Horse	1	2	3	4	5	6	7	8	9	10
Posted Odds	1-1	79-1	7-1	3-1	15-1	7-1	49-1	49-1	19-1	79-1

The odds that appear on the tote board are not the theoretical odds that are discussed in Section 8.3 but have been *adjusted* to provide a "track take." That is, for every dollar that has been wagered, $T goes to the track for sponsoring the race and $(1 − T) goes to the winning bettors. Typical track takes are in the neighborhood of 20%, or T = 0.20.

We can, however, readily convert the odds on the tote board to the crowd's assessment of the probabilities of winning. To illustrate this, Table E8.3b shows the hypothetical bets to win which resulted in the displayed information on the hypothetical tote board.

TABLE E8.3b Hypothetical Bets

Horse	1	2	3	4	5	6	7	8	9	10	Total
Bets To Win	8,000	200	2,000	4,000	1,000	3,000	400	400	800	200	20,000
Probability	0.40	0.01	0.10	0.20	0.05	0.15	0.02	0.02	0.04	0.02	1.000
Posted Odds	1-1	1-1/79	1-1/7	1-1/3	1-1/15	1-1/7	1-1/49	1-1/49	1-1/19	1-1/79	

For this hypothetical race, $20,000 was bet to win. Because $8,000 of this $20,000 was bet on the first horse, interpret the ratio 8,000/20,000 = 0.40 as the crowd's assessment of the probability to win. The theoretical odds are calculated as $0.4/(1 − 0.4) = \frac{2}{3}$, or a 67¢ bet wins $1. However, the theoretical odds assume a fair game with no track take. To adjust for the fact that only $(1 − T) are available to the winner, the posted odds for this horse would be $0.4/(1 − T − 0.4) = 0.4/(0.8 − 0.4) = 1$, if T = 0.20. For this case, it now takes a $1 bet to win $1. We then have the relationship *new odds* $= x/(1 − T − x)$, where x is the crowd's assessment of the probability of winning.

Before the start of the race, the tote board provides us with adjusted odds that can readily be converted into x, the crowd's assessment of winning. We use this measure to help us to predict y, the event of the horse actually winning the race.

The following is information from 925 races run in Hong Kong from September 1981 through September 1989. In each race, there were ten horses, one of whom was randomly selected to be in the sample. In Table E8.3c, use FINISH = y to be the indicator of a horse winning a race and WIN = x to be the crowd's prior probability assessment of a horse winning a race.

a. Suppose that, instead of selecting one horse randomly from a field of 10, two horses are randomly chosen.

   i. Describe the relationship between the dependent variables of the two horses selected.

  ii. Say how this violates the regression model assumptions.

b. Based on the attached summary statistics, note that the standard deviation of FINISH is higher than that of WIN, even though the sample means are about the same. For the variable FINISH, what is the relationship between the sample mean and standard deviation?

TABLE E8.3c Summary Statistics

	Number	Mean	Median	Standard deviation	Minimum	Maximum
FINISH	925	0.09514	0.00000	0.29356	0.00000	1.00000
WIN	925	0.09956	0.07997	0.08190	0.00269	0.64999

c. Based on the summary statistics by level of FINISH (Table E8.3d), the sample mean is larger for horses that won (FINISH = 1) than for those that lost (FINISH = 0). Interpret this result.

TABLE E8.3d Summary Statistics by Level of FINISH

	Number	Mean	Median	Standard deviation	Minimum	Maximum
FINISH = 0	837	0.09309	0.07537	0.07641	0.00269	0.46947
FINISH = 1	88	0.1612	0.1445	0.1044	0.0061	0.6500

d. Suppose that you simply would like to make a statement about the relationship between FINISH and WIN.
   i. From the computer output for regression with one variable (Table E8.3e–f) is there a statistically significant relationship between FINISH and WIN?
   ii. For regression with one independent variable, recall the relationship $r = t/(t^2 + n - 2)^{1/2}$, where $t = t(b_1)$. Calculate the correlation coefficient.
e. Is the regression with one independent variable a useful model? In your response, describe the roles of the coefficient of determination and the t-ratio.
f. For this estimated model, is it possible for the fitted values to lie outside the interval $[0, 1]$? Note, by definition, that the x-variable WIN must lie within the interval $[0, 1]$.
g. The fitted weighted least squares model is $\widehat{\text{FINISH}} = 0.0083 + 0.872$ WIN. The fitted logistic regression model is

$$\widehat{\text{FINISH}} = \frac{1}{1 + e^{3.184 - 7.6467 \text{WIN}}}.$$

(See Tables E8.3e–h.) For each of these models, provide fitted values at
   i.   WIN = 0
   ii. WIN = 0.01
   iii. WIN = 0.05
   iv. WIN = 0.10
   v.   WIN = 1.0.
h. Interpret WIN as the crowd's prior probability assessment of the probability of a horse winning a race. The fitted values, $\widehat{\text{FINISH}}$, is your new estimate of the probability of a horse winning a race, based on the crowd's assessment. Discuss a betting strategy that you might employ based on the difference, $\widehat{\text{FINISH}} - \text{WIN}$.

Dotplots of WIN by Level of FINISH

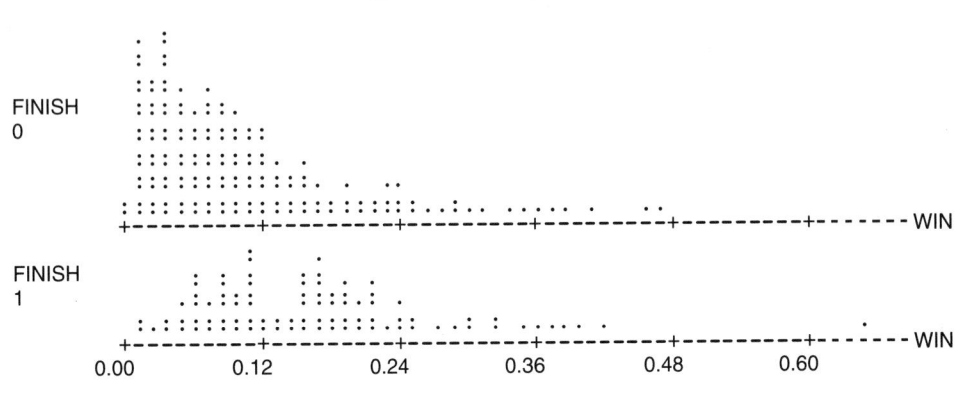

Ordinary Regression with One Independent Variable

TABLE E8.3e Coefficient Estimates

Explanatory variables	Coefficient	Standard error	t-ratio
Constant	0.00802	0.01475	0.54
WIN	0.8749	0.1144	7.65

TABLE E8.3f ANOVA Table

Source	Sum of Squares	df	Mean Square
Regression	4.7488	1	4.7488
Error	74.8833	923	0.0811
Total	79.6281	924	

The regression fit also yields $s = 0.2848$, $R^2 = 6.0\%$ and $R_a^2 = 5.9\%$.

Weighted Regression with One Independent Variable

TABLE E8.3g Coefficient Estimates

Explanatory variables	Coefficient	Standard error	t-ratio
Constant	0.00834	0.01024	0.81
WIN	0.8724	0.1280	6.82

TABLE E8.3h ANOVA Table

Source	Sum of Squares	df	Mean Square
Regression	46.702	1	46.702
Error	928.085	923	1.006
Total	974.786	924	

Logistic Regression Using SAS

```
                    The LOGISTIC Procedure


Data Set: LIB?HOR10
Response Variable: FINISH
Response Levels:  2
```

```
Number of Observations:  925
Link Function:  Logit
```

```
                          Response Profile

                     Ordered
                      Value    FINISH    Count
                        1        0        837
                        2        1         88
```

```
                 Criteria for Assessing Model Fit

                                  Intercept
                       Intercept    and
      Criterion         Only     Covariates   Chi-Square for Covariates

      AIC              583.382    541.505            .
      SC               588.211    551.164            .
      -2 LOG L         581.382    537.505     43.877 with 1 DF (p=0.001)
      Score               .          .        55.118 with 1 DF (p=0.001)
```

```
              Analysis of Maximum Likelihood Estimates

                  Parameter Standard   Wald      Pr >    Standardized
      Variable DF Estimate   Error  Chi-Square Chi-Square  Estimate

      INTERCEPT 1   3.1840   0.2004  252.3495    0.0001        .
      WIN       1  -7.6467   1.1469   44.4493    0.0001    -0.345287
```

C8_PREP

8.4 Section 8.1 introduces the problem of trying to model whether or not tax filers use a professional tax preparer (PREP = 1 if a preparer was used PREP = 0 otherwise). The explanatory variables include the logarithm of total personal income (LOGTPI), a filer's marginal tax rate (MTR) and whether or not the filer is self-employed (EMP = 1 if self-employed and EMP = 0 otherwise). In Section 8.1, the fitted least squares model presented was:

$$\widehat{PREP} = -1.35 + 0.203\,LOGTPI + 0.216\,EMP - 0.0107\,MTR.$$

In Section 8.3, the fitted logistic regression model presented was:

$$\widehat{PREP} = \frac{1}{1 + e^{-(-9.3218 + 1.034\,LOGTPI + 0.08956\,EMP - 0.0512\,MTR)}}.$$

A random sample of 50 returns was taken from the full data set of 192 returns. For each return, the fitted value for both estimated models was calculated. The results are in Table E8.4.

a. For the least squares fitted values, determine the misclassification rate if we use the *cut-off*:

  i. 30%
  ii. 50%
  iii. 70%.

b. For the logistic regression fitted values, determine the misclassification rate if we use the *cut-off*:

    i. 30%

    ii. 50%

    iii. 70%.

c. Based on your results in Parts (a) and (b), say which model is preferable.

TABLE E8.4 Sample of 50 Tax Returns

Row number	PREP	Least squares fits	Logistic regression fits	Row number	PREP	Least squares fits	Logistic regression fits
1	0	−0.018824	0.071342	26	1	0.460584	0.486819
2	0	0.213399	0.200191	27	1	0.468258	0.491453
3	0	0.230202	0.220615	28	1	0.485619	0.523751
4	0	0.237809	0.227339	29	1	0.486156	0.524432
5	0	0.248194	0.230033	30	1	0.494958	0.525382
6	0	0.290034	0.279384	31	1	0.502121	0.548864
7	1	0.298211	0.278137	32	1	0.505741	0.549196
8	0	0.300605	0.290336	33	1	0.507294	0.542692
9	0	0.315251	0.305921	34	1	0.507970	0.548623
10	0	0.316439	0.305755	35	0	0.511161	0.560221
11	0	0.340306	0.334387	36	0	0.512284	0.554894
12	0	0.346585	0.338469	37	1	0.515201	0.556028
13	0	0.357681	0.351997	38	0	0.522635	0.567856
14	0	0.370950	0.372315	39	0	0.531240	0.576065
15	0	0.380549	0.390272	40	0	0.540622	0.592628
16	1	0.380724	0.383197	41	1	0.598328	0.658836
17	1	0.400592	0.402411	42	1	0.612709	0.666791
18	1	0.409505	0.418334	43	1	0.676200	0.710334
19	1	0.423408	0.446575	44	1	0.678300	0.695458
20	1	0.441702	0.456091	45	1	0.708960	0.743384
21	0	0.447042	0.586666	46	1	0.710950	0.732135
22	0	0.450537	0.472360	47	1	0.728296	0.753544
23	1	0.454952	0.472853	48	0	0.731168	0.753087
24	0	0.457071	0.491736	49	1	0.746865	0.790556
25	1	0.459623	0.481335	50	1	0.775216	0.788966

Note: Observations are sorted by the Least Squares Fit

C7_SURVY

8.5 Refer to Section 7.4

    a. In the computer output that follows (Tables E8.5a–d), a regression was first run using FIRMCOST as the dependent variable and the other six variables as explanatory variables. Then, a regression was run using CAP as the dependent variable and the other six variables as explanatory variables. Interpret the fitted relationship between FIRMCOST and CAP in each of these two regression models.

b. Using the fitted regression model with CAP as dependent variable, fitted values were calculated and plotted by level of CAP.

   i. Use this plot to calculate the misclassification rate, using a cut-off of 0.50.

   ii. Suppose that you would like to develop a classification rule so that you were reasonably certain that no firm with CAP = 0 (without a captive insurance company) was included. Based on our sample of 73 firms, what cut-off would satisfy this constraint?

c. A colleague feels that it is important to use a least squares regression model for classification because of the ease of interpretation. Describe two major drawbacks when using ordinary least squares for classification purposes.

Regression Using FIRMCOST as the Dependent Variable

TABLE E8.5a Coefficient Estimates

Explanatory variables	Coefficient	Standard error	t-ratio	VIF
Constant	59.76	19.07	3.13	
ASSUME	−0.3004	0.2221	−1.35	1.2
CAP	5.498	3.848	1.43	1.1
SIZELOG	−6.836	1.923	−3.56	1.2
INDCOST	23.078	8.304	2.78	1.1
CENTRAL	0.133	1.441	0.09	1.1
SOPH	−0.1367	0.3468	−0.39	1.1

TABLE E8.5b ANOVA Table

Source	Sum of squares	df	Mean square
Regression	4812.2	6	802.0
Error	13987.1	66	211.9
Total	18799.2	72	

The regression fit also yields $s = 14.56$, $R^2 = 25.6\%$ and $R_a^2 = 18.8\%$.

Regression Using CAP as the Dependent Variable

TABLE E8.5c Coefficient Estimates

Explanatory variables	Coefficient	Standard error	t-ratio	VIF
Constant	−1.0318	0.6311	−1.63	
FIRMCOST	0.005457	0.003819	1.32	1.3
ASSUME	0.016422	0.006800	2.42	1.1
SIZELOG	0.15807	0.06320	2.50	1.3
INDCOST	0.0748	0.2763	0.27	1.2
CENTRAL	0.02307	0.04532	0.51	1.1
SOPH	−0.00604	0.01091	−0.55	1.1

TABLE E8.5d ANOVA Table

Source	Sum of squares	df	Mean square
Regression	2.5567	6	0.4261
Error	13.8817	66	0.2103
Total	16.4384	72	

The regression fit also yields $s = 0.4586$, $R^2 = 15.6\%$ and $R_a^2 = 7.9\%$.

Dotplots of Fitted Values by Level of CAP

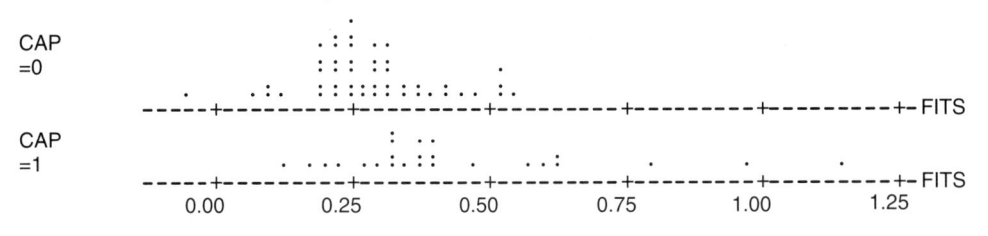

CAP =0

CAP =1

8.6 **Refer to Section 5.2 and Exercise 5.2**

C5_CARPR

To understand the role of a warranty in the automobile market, we use Motor Trend's *1993 New Car Buyer's Guide* to obtain information on 173 new cars. The best type of warranty offered on cars guarantees most parts of the automobile for at least 48,000 miles. Define WARR_48 to be an indicator variable that is one if this type of warranty is available, and zero otherwise. As explanatory variables, we consider LN_PRICE, the natural logarithm of the car price, H/P, the horsepower and PASSENGR. The variable PASSENGR indicates whether or not the car was a two passenger car. Thus, values of one mean that the car holds two passengers and values of zero mean that the car holds more than two passengers. The computer output that follows (Tables E8.6a–d) fits the model using WARR_48 as the dependent variable and LN_PRICE, H/P and PASSENGR as the explanatory variables.

a. Attached is a scatter plot of LN_PRICE versus H/P, with the letter code 'W' for a warranty of at least 48,000 miles and code 'O' otherwise (Figure E8.6).

   i.   What relationship between WARR_48 and LN_PRICE does the plot suggest?

   ii. What relationship between WARR_48 and H/P does the plot suggest?

b. A regression model of WARR_48 on LN_PRICE, H/P and PASSENGR was fit in the computer output that follows.

   i.   Interpret the relationship between WARR_48 and LN_PRICE.

   ii. Interpret the relationship between WARR_48 and H/P.

   iii. Interpret the relationship between WARR_48 and PASSENGR.

c. The fitted values from the regression model of WARR_48 on LN_PRICE, H/P and PASSENGR can be found in dotplots in the attached computer output. Determine the approximate misclassification rate if we use the *cut-off*:

   i.   25%

   ii. 50%.

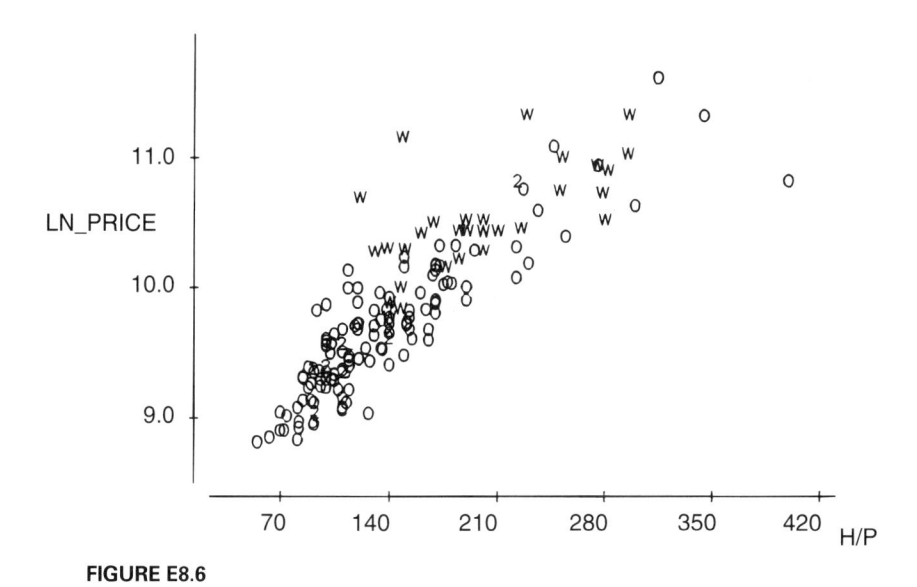

FIGURE E8.6

Computer Output for Exercise 8.6

TABLE E8.6a Summary Statistics of LN_PRICE and H/P by Level of WARR_48

Variable	WARR_48	Number	Mean	Standard deviation
LN_PRICE	0	140	9.6279	0.5034
LN_PRICE	1	33	10.533	0.396
H/P	0	140	134.26	54.42
H/P	1	33	200.94	52.35

Dotplot of LN_PRICE by Level of WARR_48

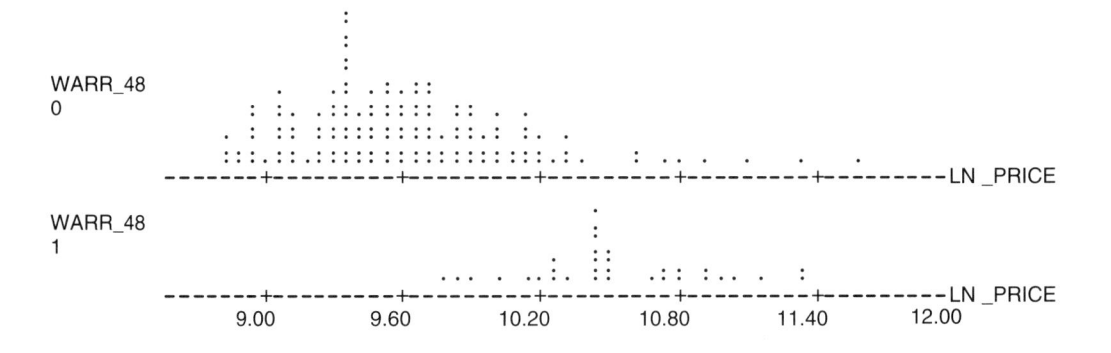

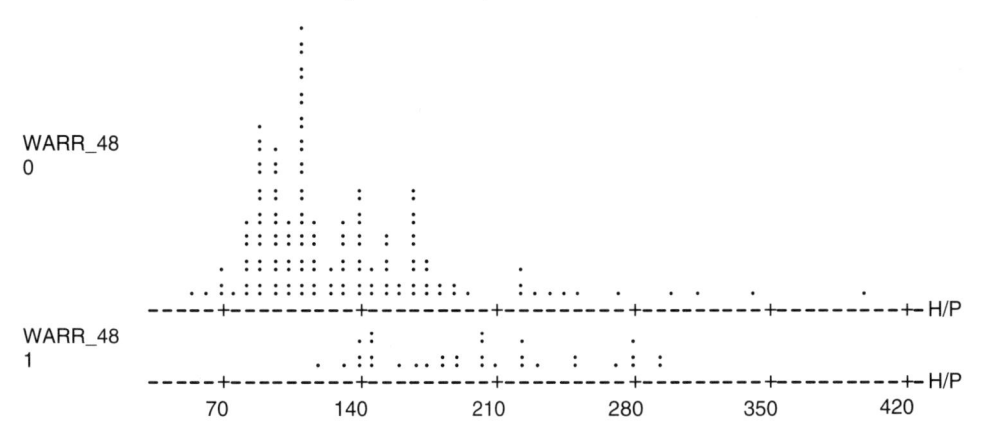

Dotplot of H/P by Level of WARR_48

TABLE E8.6b   Frequency Table by Level WARR_48 and PASSENGR

	WARR_48 = 0	WARR_48 = 1	ALL
PASSENGR = 0	116	28	144
PASSENGR = 1	24	5	29
ALL	140	33	173

Correlation Matrix

```
         LN_PRICE  PASSENGR     H/P
PASSENGR   0.261
H/P        0.872     0.322
WARR_48    0.593    -0.021   0.438
```

Regression Model

TABLE E8.6c   Coefficient Estimates

Explanatory variables	Coefficient	Standard error	t-ratio
Constant	−0.5881	0.6815	−7.47
LN_PRICE	0.56758	0.07973	7.12
PASSENGR	−0.16992	0.06621	−2.57
H/P	−0.0017364	0.0008150	−2.13

TABLE E8.6d   ANOVA Table

Source	Sum of Squares	df	Mean Square
Regression	10.7100	3	3.5700
Error	15.9952	169	0.0946
Total	26.7052	172	

The regression fit also yields $s = 0.3076$, $R^2 = 40.1\%$ and $R_a^2 = 39.0\%$.

Dotplot of Fitted Values by Level of WARR_48

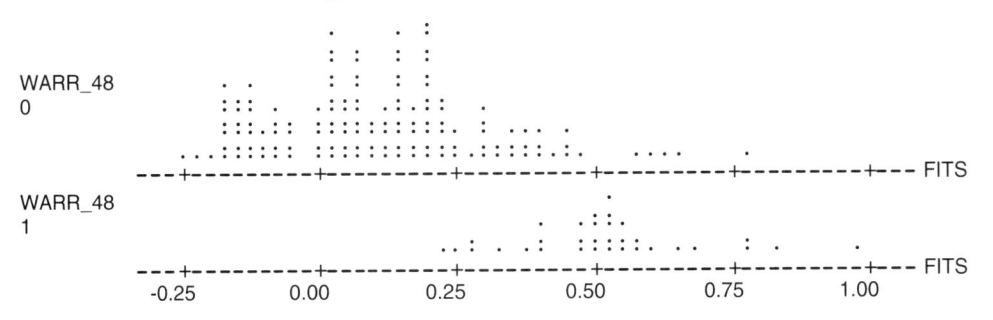

9

Stabilizing Longitudinal Data

Chapter Objectives

To identify major trends that arise in data over time, to introduce methods to stabilize the data trends, and to forecast the data into the future. To illustrate, we will consider forecasting:

- beer prices,
- the number of voters in a general election and
- an index of common stocks.

Chapter Outline

9.0 BASIC LONGITUDINAL DATA VOCABULARY

Business firms are not defined by the solid stone bank building that symbolizes financial security. Nor are they defined by space alien invader toys that propel our children to worlds of seemingly harmless mock violence. Business firms are comprised of several complex, interrelated processes. A process is a series of actions or operations that leads to a particular end.

Processes are not only the building blocks of businesses, they also provide the foundations for our everyday lives. We may go to work or school every day, play racquetball or study statistics. These are regular sequences of activities that define us.

Processes result in data and this data can be used to improve processes. We have already seen that the field of statistics relies on a numerical description of entities. Numerical descriptions of some processes are straightforward, such as the time it takes to get from home to the office each day. Many numerical descriptions of businesses are more complex; in fact, the entire field of accounting is devoted to producing comparable, useful measures of business performance.

Some processes evolve over time, such as my daily trips to work or the quarterly earnings of a firm. We use the term *longitudinal data* for numerical realizations of processes that evolve over time. But there are elements besides time that must be considered for other processes. For example, evaluating an oil-drilling project requires taking samples of the earth at various longitudes, latitudes and depths. This yields observations ordered by the three dimensions of space but not time. As another example, the study of holes in the ozone layer requires taking atmospheric measurements. Because the interest is in the trend of ozone depletion, the measurements are taken at various longitudes, latitudes, heights and times. Although we consider only processes ordered by time, in other studies of longitudinal data you may see alternatives orderings, such as spatial ones.

We measure processes to improve or manage their performance and to forecast the future behavior of the process.

A basic concern with processes that evolve over time is the stability of the process. For example: "Is it taking me longer to get to work since they put in the new stop light?" "Have quarterly earnings improved since the new CEO took over?" We measure processes to improve or manage their performance and to forecast the future behavior of the process. For either purpose, the stability of the process is a fundamental concern.

Because stability is a fundamental concern, we will work with a special kind of stability called *stationarity*. For a *stationary process*, we expect that successive samples of modest size from a process should have the same distribution. To illustrate, we could compare the histogram of the first five observations to that of the next five, the five after that and so on. For a stationary process, we expect each of these histograms of successive samples to be similar.

As a practical matter, we will be concerned with the mean and variance of our histograms of modest successive samples. In particular, for a stationary process, both the mean and variance are constant over time. Because they are constant, they are common to all observations and hence can be estimated from the data. In contrast, a nonstationary process may have a mean or a variance that is changing over time.

The distribution of the process may be defined if the process is stationary.

A distribution was described in Chapter 2 as a model using an idealized histogram to describe the relative frequency of draws from a universe. Because of the special type of stability in a stationary process, we may still use a single distribution to describe the distribution of outcomes of the process. However, we will not restrict ourselves to the case where the draws are unrelated. For nonstationary processes, the histograms of draws may change over time and we cannot represent the process's outcomes using a single distribution. Indeed, we will see examples where attempts to do so can be misleading.

9.1 IDENTIFYING AND SUMMARIZING DATA

As in the Foundations Chapter 2, in this chapter we study only one measurement. The measurement is taken on a process which yields a variable over time. The observations of this variable are denoted by y_1, y_2, ..., y_T and are called a *time series*. By convention, the number of observations is denoted by T to remind us that we observing a process over time. Similarly, we usually refer to the tth generic observation in lieu of the ith. The ordering of the longitudinal observations can be important, unlike cross-sectional observations.

Summarizing Data Graphically

To help understand the concept of stationarity, we begin with Example 9.1, a classic example of a stationary process. For contrast, Example 9.2 will provide an example of a process that is not stationary.

Example 9.1: Sum of Two Dice

A die is a six sided cube with a mark on each side going from one to six. When two dice are rolled, the sum can be 2, 3, 4, ..., or 12. A pair of dice was rolled 50 times. Table 9.1 presents the first five of 50 rolls. From Table 9.1, we see that the first observation was $y_1 = 10$, the second was $y_2 = 6$, and so on.

TABLE 9.1   First Five of the 50 Rolls

t	1	2	3	4	5
y_t	10	6	11	3	9

With time series plots, we connect adjacent points using lines to detect patterns over time.

In Figure 9.1 is a scatter plot of the entire sample of $T = 50$ rolls, that is, of $y_1, y_2, ..., y_{50}$. A scatter plot of y_t versus t is called a *time series plot*. In time series plots, the convention is to connect adjacent points using a line to help us detect patterns over time. Not surprisingly, the series appears

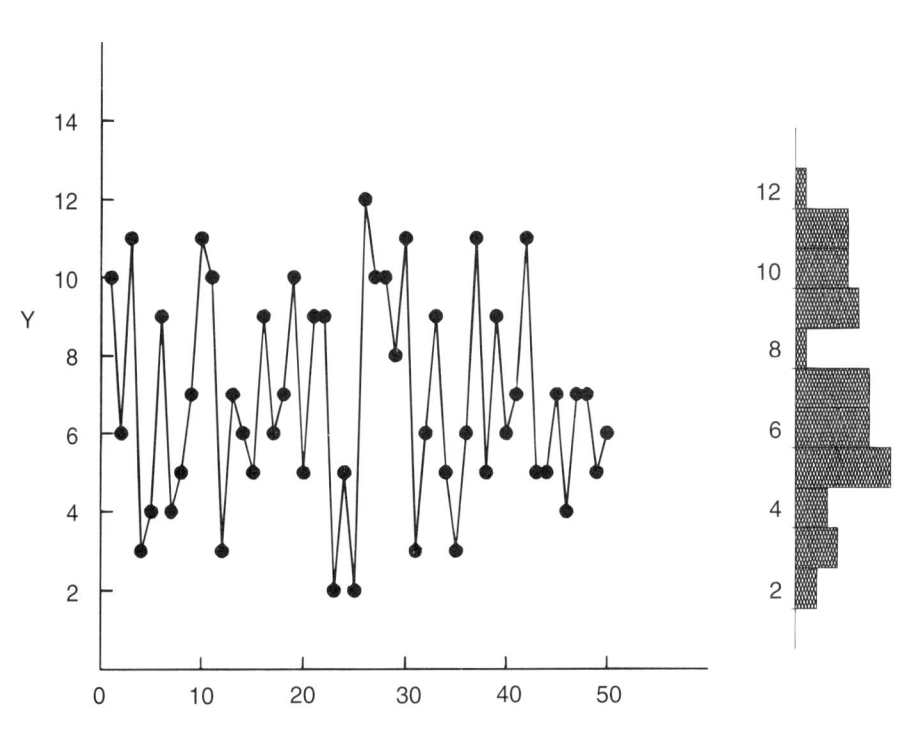

FIGURE 9.1 Time series plot of 50 throws of the sum of two dice. The histogram that appears on the right provides information on the distribution of throws. *Source:* Original

to be stable over time and thus it makes sense to discuss the distribution of rolls. The Figure 9.1 histogram summarizes this distribution graphically.

Example 9.2: Domestic Beer Prices

An important component of total domestic sales of beer is the Beer Price Index, a measure of the average price of beer. This index is compiled by the Bureau of Labor Statistics. The Beer Price Index that we consider here deflated by the Consumer Price Index, so that the price of beer can be taken relative to other goods. This adjusted Beer Price Index considered here ranges from 1952 to 1988, inclusive.

Figure 9.2 provides a time series plot of the adjusted price of beer. This plot shows a clear downward trend in the series, indicating nonstationarity. Because the data are not stationary, summary statistics of the process are not meaningful. For example, the Figure 9.2 histogram that gives the process's distribution is meaningless because it does not account for the time trend.

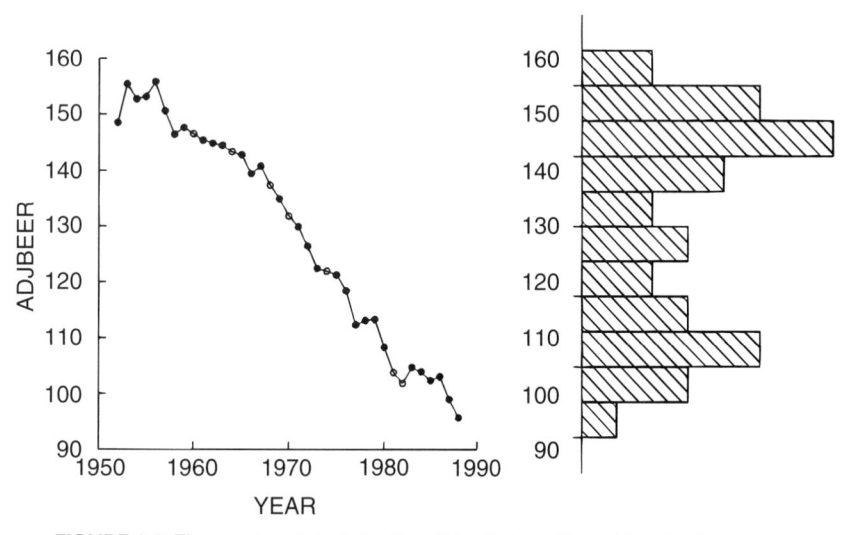

FIGURE 9.2 Time series plot of the Beer Price Index adjusted for the Consumer Price Index. The histogram that appears on the right provides no meaningful information. *Source: Bureau of Labor Statistics*

We can decompose a series into three types of patterns: trends in time, seasonal patterns and random, or irregular, patterns.

Understanding Patterns over Time

Forecasting is about predicting future realizations of a time series. Over the years, forecasters have found it convenient to decompose a series into three types of patterns: *trends in time* (T_t), *seasonal patterns* (S_t) and *random, or ir-*

regular, patterns (ϵ_t). A series can then be forecast by extrapolating each of the three patterns.

In applications, analysts typically combine these patterns in two ways: in an additive fashion,

$$y_t = T_t + S_t + \epsilon_t, \tag{9.1}$$

or in a multiplicative fashion,

$$y_t = T_t\, S_t + \epsilon_t. \tag{9.2}$$

The models in equations (9.1) and (9.2) handle series with or without seasonal components. If the seasonal component is not important, then we can use $S_t = 0$ for the additive model in equation (9.1) and $S_t = 1$ for the multiplicative model in equation (9.2). Note that if the model is purely multiplicative, that is, $y_t = T_t S_t \epsilon_t$, it can be converted to an additive model by taking logarithms of both sides of the equation, as in Section 6.6.

It is instructive to see how these three components can be combined to form a series of interest. Consider the three components in Figure 9.3. Under the additive model, the trend and seasonal components are combined to form

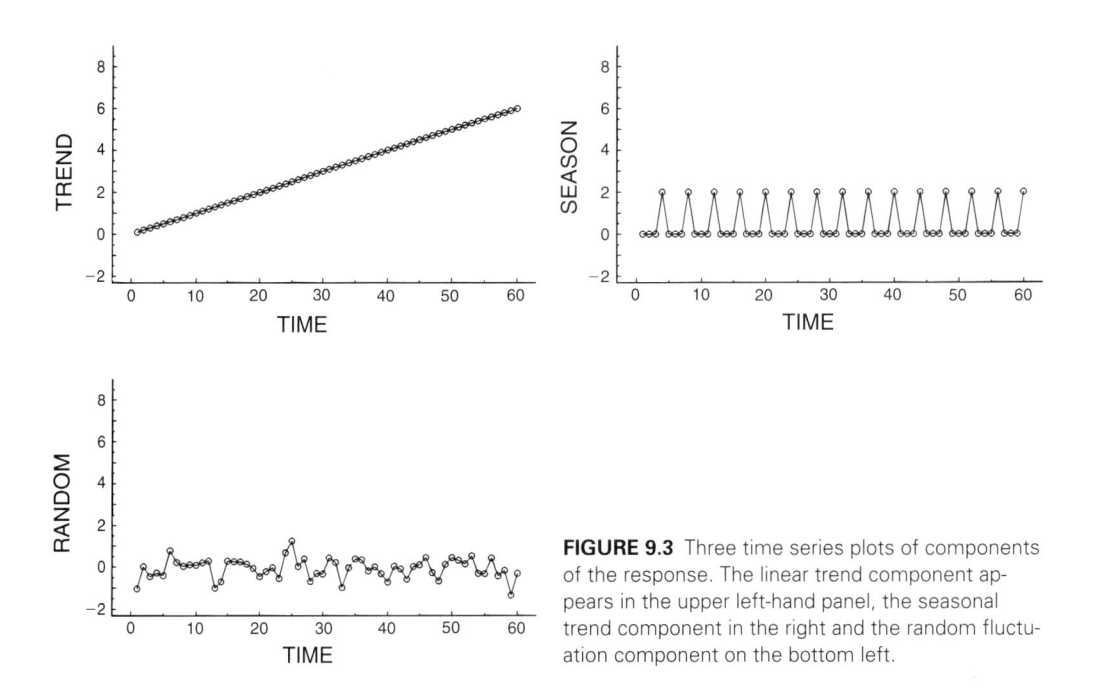

FIGURE 9.3 Three time series plots of components of the response. The linear trend component appears in the upper left-hand panel, the seasonal trend component in the right and the random fluctuation component on the bottom left.

the series that appears in the left hand plot in Figure 9.4. The addition of the random component forms the series in the right hand plot in Figure 9.4. The right hand plot in Figure 9.4 is our time series plot of the response; when analyzing data, this is the first type of plot that we will examine. We now discuss techniques for decomposing a series into these three components.

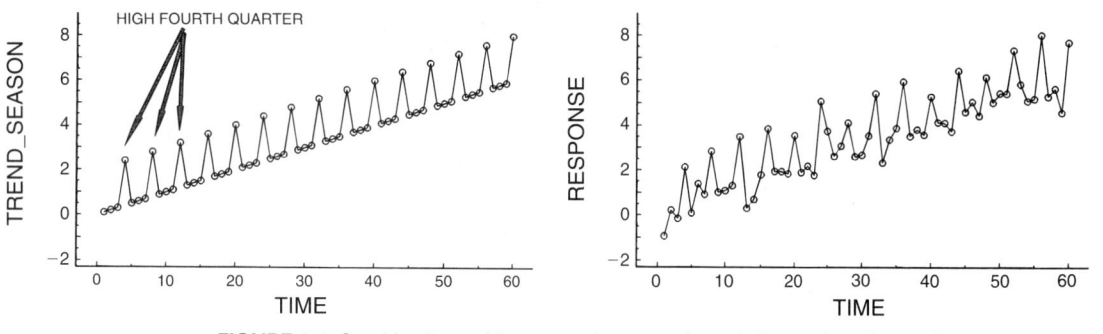

FIGURE 9.4 Combinations of linear trend, seasonal trend plus random fluctuation components. The time series plot on the left is the sum of the linear trend plus seasonal components. The time series plot on the right is the sum of all three components.

Fitting Trends in Time

The simplest type of time trend is a complete lack of trend. For example, Figure 9.1 shows little evidence of trends. Here, if each roll of the dice is unrelated to other rolls, then we expect there to be little trend. Assuming that rolls of dice are unrelated, we could use random errors for the irregular fluctuations, resulting in the model

$$y_t = \beta_0 + e_t.$$

This is the random error model that we studied in Section 2.8. There we saw, for example, that the best predictor of observations outside the data set is $\bar{y}$.

Fitting polynomial functions of time is another type of trend that is easy to interpret and to fit to the data. To fit this type of trend, we can use regression techniques using various functions of time as explanatory variables. For example, we begin with a straight line for our polynomial function of time. This yields the *linear trend in time* model:

$$y_t = \beta_0 + \beta_1 t + e_t. \tag{9.3}$$

Example 9.2: Domestic Beer Prices—Continued

To forecast this series, we consider the linear trend in time model. First note that Figure 9.2 shows a clear downward trend of the data. To handle this trend, one option is to use $t = 1, 2, \ldots, 37$, as an explanatory variable to indicate the time period. This is equivalent to using $year$ = 1952, 1953, ..., 1988, as an explanatory variable because the variables t and $year$ are perfectly related through the expression $t = year - 1951$. We use the variable t because it is easier to interpret the intercept coefficient b_0.

For our data, the fitted regression equation turns out to be:

$$\text{ADJ}\hat{\text{BEER}}_t = 161.94 - 1.7482\,t.$$

$$std\ errors \quad (1.247) \quad (0.0572)$$

The coefficient of determination is a healthy $R^2 = 96.4\%$ and typical error has dropped from $s_y = 19.28$ down to $s = 3.716$ (our residual standard deviation). Figure 9.5 shows the relationship between the data and fitted values through the time series plot of the adjusted price of beer with the fitted values superimposed.

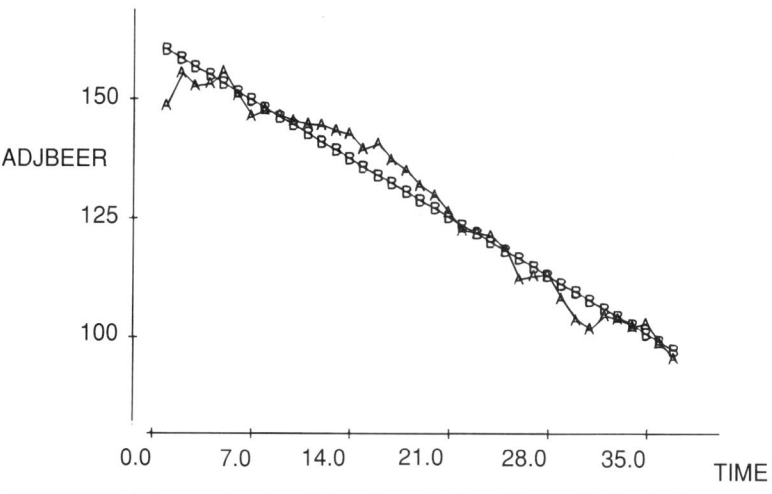

FIGURE 9.5 A time series plot of the adjusted price of beer with fitted values superimposed. Here, the fitted values are from a regression using time as an explanatory variable. The letter code "A" represents actual prices and the code "B" represents fitted values.

To apply these regression results to the forecasting problem, suppose that we wanted to predict the adjusted price of beer for 1989, or $t = 38$. Our prediction is

$$\text{ADJ}\hat{\text{BEER}}_{38} = 161.94 - 1.7482\,(38) = 95.508.$$

The overall conclusion is that the regression model using time t as an explanatory variable represents the data well. A close inspection of Figure 9.5, however, reveals that there are some slight patterns in the deviations of the fitted values from the responses. In the early and latter parts of the series, the responses seem to be consistently lower than the fitted values although in the middle part of the series, the responses seem to be consistently higher than the fitted values. These patterns suggest that we might improve upon the model specification. One way would be to introduce a higher order polynomial model in time. For example, by introducing cubic terms in time into the regression model, we could produce an "S-shaped" curve to accommodate the patterns noted previously. In Section 9.3, we will argue that the *random walk* is an even better model for this data.

Similarly, regression techniques can be used to fit other functions that represent trends in time. We have seen that equation (9.3) provides an expression for a linear trend in time model. This could be easily extended to handle a *quadratic trend in time model*,

$$y_t = \beta_0 + \beta_1 t + \beta_2 t^2 + e_t,$$

or a higher-order polynomial.

Further, other nonlinear functions of time may also be useful. To illustrate, we might study some measure of quality management over time (y_t) and be interested in the effect of a change in management practices. Define z_t to be an indicator variable that is zero before the change occurs and is one during and after the change. Consider the model,

$$y_t = \beta_0 + \beta_1 z_t + e_t. \tag{9.4}$$

Thus, using

$$\mathrm{E}\, y_t = \begin{cases} \beta_0 + \beta_1 & \text{if } z_t = 1 \\ \beta_0 & \text{if } z_t = 0 \end{cases},$$

the parameter β_1 captures the expected change in the quality due to the change in management procedures. (See Figure 9.6.)

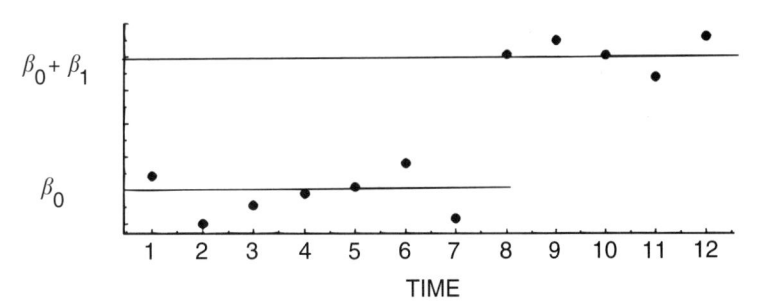

FIGURE 9.6 A time series plot of quality management over time. There is a clear shift in the quality measure due to a change in management practices. This shift can be measured using a regression model with an explanatory variable to indicate the change.

Fitting Seasonal Trends

Regular periodic behavior is often found in business and economic data. Because such periodicity is often tied to the climate, periodic trends are called *seasonal components*. Periodic trends can be modeled using the same techniques as with regular, or aperiodic, trends. Example 9.3 shows how to capture behavior using seasonal indicator variables.

Example 9.3 Trends in Voting

C9_WVTE

On any given election day, the number of voters that actually turn out to voting booths depends on a number of factors: the publicity that an election race has received, the issues that are debated as part of the race, other issues facing voters on election day and nonpolitical factors, such as the weather. Now, potential political candidates base their projections of campaign financing, and chances of winning an election, on forecasts of the number of voters who will actually participate in an election. Decisions as to whether or not to participate as a candidate must be made well in advance; generally, so far in advance that well-known factors such as the weather on election day cannot be used in generating forecasts.

We consider here the number of Wisconsin voters who participated in statewide elections over the period 1920 through 1990. Although the interest is in forecasting the actual number of voters, we consider voters as a percentage of the qualified voting public. Dividing by the qualified voting public controls for the size of the population of voters; this enhances comparability between the early and latter parts of the series. Because mortality trends are relatively stable, reliable projections of the qualified voting public can be readily attained. Forecasts of the percentage may then be multiplied by projections of the voting public to obtain forecasts of the actual voter turnout.

To specify a model, we examine Figure 9.7, a time series plot of the voter turnout as a percent of the qualified voting public. This figure displays the low voter turnout in the early part of the series, followed by larger turnout in the 1950s and 1960s, followed by a smaller turnout in the 1980s. This pattern can be modeled using, for example, a quadratic trend in time. Figure 9.7 also displays a much larger turnout in presidential elections years. This periodic, or "seasonal," component can be modeled using an indicator variable. A candidate model is

$$y_t = \beta_0 + \beta_1 t + \beta_2 t^2 + \beta_3 z_t + e_t,$$

where

$$z_t = \begin{cases} 1 & \textit{if presidential election year} \\ 0 & \textit{otherwise.} \end{cases}$$

Here, $\beta_3 z_t$ captures the seasonal component in this model.

Regression was used to fit the model. The fitted model provided a good fit on the data. Figure 9.8 shows the relationship between the fitted and actual values.

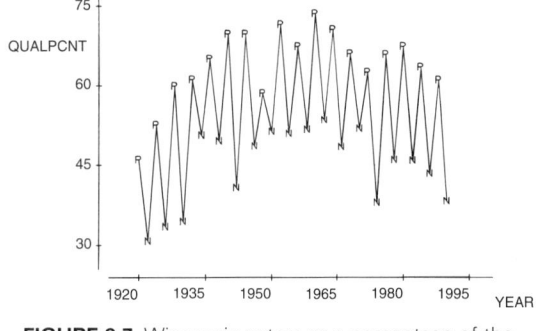

FIGURE 9.7 Wisconsin voters as a percentage of the qualified voting public, by year. The 'P' plotting symbol indicates a presidential election year, and the 'N' indicates a non-presidential election year.

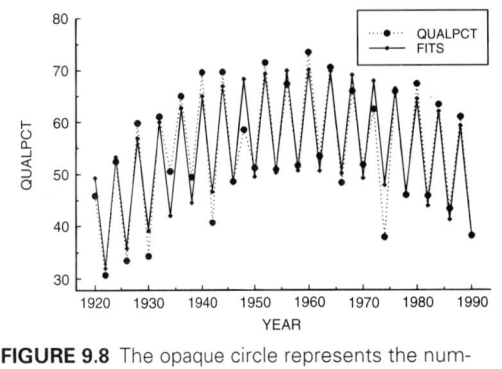

FIGURE 9.8 The opaque circle represents the number of Wisconsin voters as a percentage of the qualified voting public, by year. The solid diamond represents the fitted value, using a quadratic trend in time plus an indicator variable for presidential year.

Example 9.3 demonstrates the use of indicator variables to capture seasonal components. Similarly, seasonal effects may be also be represented using categorical variables, such as

$$z_t = \begin{cases} 1 & \text{if spring} \\ 2 & \text{if summer} \\ 3 & \text{if fall} \\ 4 & \text{if winter.} \end{cases}$$

Regression analysis estimates give the most weight to observations with large explanatory variables. Unfortunately, for time series data, this often means giving a great deal of weight to observations that occur early in the series.

Another way of capturing seasonal effects is through the use of trigonometric functions. Further discussion of the use of trigonometric functions to handle seasonal components is in Section 11.3.

Thus, regression analysis using various functions of time as explanatory variables is a simple yet powerful tool for analyzing and forecasting longitudinal data. It does, however, have drawbacks. Because we are fitting a curve to the entire data set, there is no guarantee that the fit for the most recent part of the data will be adequate. That is, for forecasting, the primary concern is for the most recent part of the series. We know that regression analysis estimates give the most weight to observations with unusually large explanatory variables. To illustrate, using a linear trend in time model, this means giving the most weight to observations at the end and beginning of the series. Using a model that gives large weight to observations at the beginning of the series is viewed with suspicion by forecasters. This drawback of regression analysis motivates us to introduce additional tools for analyzing and forecasting longitudinal data in the following sections.

9.2 RANDOM PROCESS AND RANDOM WALK MODELS

A random process is a special type of stationary process.

The link between longitudinal and cross-sectional models of data can be established through the notion of a *random process,* also called a *white noise* process. A random process is a stationary process that displays no apparent patterns through time. A random process is a special type of stationary process. It is possible for a stationary process to display patterns through time and thus not qualify as a random process. An example of a stationary process that displays patterns through time is an *autoregressive model,* which will be introduced in Chapter 10.

Time ordering is not relevant for a random process because it displays no pattern through time. Thus, a random process model is equivalent to the random error model that was introduced in Section 2.8. Because of this connection, we may use all of the inference tools introduced in Chapter 2 on a time series that has been identified as a random process. In particular, from Section 2.8, prediction intervals are readily available.

A special feature of the random process is that forecasts do not depend on how far into the future that we wish to forecast. Suppose that a series of observations, $y_1, y_2, \ldots, y_T$, has been identified as a random process. Let $\bar{y}$ and s_y denote the sample average and standard deviation, respectively. From Section 2.8, a forecast of an observation in the future, say y_{T+l}, for l *lead* time units in the future, is $\bar{y}$. Further, from equation (2.9), a 95% prediction interval is

$$\bar{y} \pm (t\text{-value})\, s_y \sqrt{1 + \frac{1}{T}}\,.$$

In time series applications, because the sample size T is typically relatively large, we use the approximate 95% prediction interval

$$\bar{y} \pm 2\, s_y\,.$$

A filter is a procedure that reduces a series to a random process. After all patterns have been filtered from the data, the uncertainty is irreducible.

Note that this prediction interval does not depend on the choice of l, the number of lead units that we forecast into the future.

Just as with the random error model, the random process model is both the least and the most important of time series models. It is the least important in the sense that the model assumes that the observations are unrelated to one another, an unlikely event for most series of interest. It is the most important because our modeling efforts are directed toward reducing a series to a random process. The procedure for reducing a series to a random process is called a *filter.* After all patterns have been filtered from the data, the uncertainty is said to be *irreducible.*

We now introduce the *random walk model.* For this time series model, we will show how to filter the data simply by taking differences. We return to Example 9.1 to play a simple game based on the rolls of the two dice. To play the game, you must pay $7 each time you roll the dice. You receive the number of dollars corresponding the sum of the two dice, y_t. We use the notation y_t^* to denote your winnings on each roll, so that $y_t^* = y_t - 7$.

Assume that you start with initial capital of $C_0 = \$100$. Let C_t denote the sum of capital after the tth roll. Note that C_t is determined recursively by $C_t = C_{t-1} + y_t^*$. For example, because you won $3 on the first roll, $t = 1$, you now have capital $C_1 = C_0 + y_1^*$, or $103 = 100 + 3$. Table 9.2 shows the results for the first five throws. Figure 9.9 is a time series plot of the sums, C_t, for the 50 throws.

TABLE 9.2   Winnings for Five of the 50 Rolls

t	1	2	3	4	5
y_t	10	6	11	3	9
y_t^*	3	−1	4	−4	2
C_t	103	102	106	102	104

A random walk process may be defined by the partial sums of a random process.

The *partial sums* of a random process define a random walk model. For example, the series $C_1, C_2, ..., C_{50}$ in Figure 9.9 is a realization of the random walk model. The phrase "partial sum" is used because each observation, C_t, was created by summing the winnings up to time t. For this example, winnings, y_t^*, are a random process because the amount returned, y_t, is a random process. In our example, your winnings from each roll of the dice is represented using a ran-

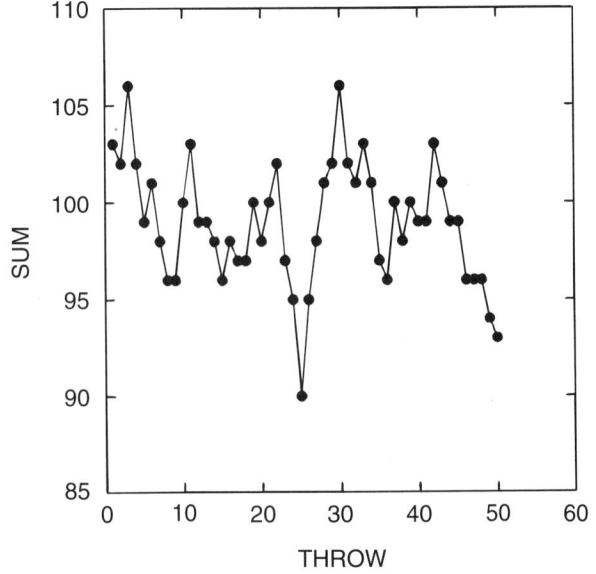

FIGURE 9.9 Time series plot of sum of capital.

dom process. Whether you win on one roll of the dice has no influence on the outcome of the next, or previous, roll of the dice. Your amount of capital at any roll of the dice is highly related to the amount of capital after the next roll, or previous roll. Your amount of capital after each roll of the dice is represented by a random walk model.

9.3 INFERENCE USING RANDOM WALK MODELS

Section 9.1 describes the statistics used to summarize the data and Section 9.2 describes two fundamental time series models. In Section 9.3, we now describe how to use the random walk model. Specifically, we first discuss the properties of the model. These properties are then used for forecasting and identifying a series as a random walk. Finally, this section compares the random walk to a competitor, the linear trend in time model.

Model Properties

To state the properties of the random walk, let's recap the some definitions. Let $y_1, y_2, y_3, \ldots, y_T$ be T observations from a random process. As before, a random walk can be expressed recursively as

$$C_t = C_{t-1} + y_t. \tag{9.5}$$

Alternatively, by repeated substitution, we have

$$C_t = y_t + C_{t-1} = y_t + (y_{t-1} + C_{t-2}) = y_t + y_{t-1} + (y_{t-2} + C_{t-3}) = \ldots$$

If we use C_0 to be an initial level, then we can express the random walk as

$$C_t = C_0 + y_1 + \ldots + y_t. \tag{9.6}$$

Using either expression, the random walk is the partial sum of a random process.

The random walk is not a stationary process because the variability, The random walk is not a stationary process because the variability, and possibly the mean, depends on the time point at which the series is observed. Although we do not go into the details here, introductory probability theory yields the mean level and variability of the random walk process:

$$\mathrm{E}\, C_t = C_0 + t\, \mu_y \qquad \text{and} \qquad \mathrm{Var}\, C_t = t\, \sigma_y^2.$$

and possibly the mean, depends on the time point at which the series is observed. Hence, as long as there is some variability in the random process, that is, $\sigma_y^2 > 0$, the random walk process is nonstationary in the variance. Further, if $\mu_y \neq 0$, then the random walk process is nonstationary in the mean.

To forecast a random walk, we first forecast the series changes. We then sum the forecast changes to get the forecast series.

Forecasting

How can we forecast a series of observations, $C_1, C_2, \ldots, C_T$, that has been identified as a realization of a random walk model? The technique we use is to forecast the *differences,* or changes, in the series and then sum the forecast differences to get the forecast series. This technique is tractable because, by the definition of a random walk model, the differences can be represented using a random process, a process that we know how to forecast.

Specifically, suppose we wish to forecast C_{T+l}, the value of the series l lead time units into the future. Let $y_t = C_t - C_{t-1}$ represent the differences in the series, so that

$$C_{T+l} = C_{T+l-1} + y_{T+l} = C_{T+l-2} + y_{T+l-1} + y_{T+l} = \ldots$$
$$= C_T + y_{T+1} + \ldots + y_{T+l-1} + y_{T+l}.$$

We interpret C_{T+l} to be equal to the current value of the series, C_T, plus the partial sum of future differences.

To forecast C_{T+l}, because at time T we know C_T, we need only forecast the differences $y_{T+1}, \ldots, y_{T+l}$. Because a forecast of a future value of a random process is just the average of the process, the forecast of y_{T+k} is $\bar{y}$ for $k = 1, 2, \ldots, l$. Putting these together, the forecast of C_{T+l} is $C_T + l\bar{y}$. For example, for $l = 1$, we interpret the forecast of the next value of the series to be the current value of the series plus the average change of the series.

Using similar ideas, we have that an approximate 95% prediction interval for C_{T+l}

$$C_T + l\,\bar{y} \pm 2\,s_y\,\sqrt{l}$$

where s_y is the standard deviation computed using the differences $y_2, y_3, \ldots, y_T$. Note that the width of the prediction interval, $4\,s_y\,(l)^{1/2}$, grows as the lead time l grows. This increasing width simply reflects our diminishing ability to predict into the future.

To illustrate, in Example 9.1 we rolled the dice $T = 50$ times. As a goal, suppose that we would like to forecast C_{60}, our sum of capital after 60 rolls. At time 50, it turned out that our sum of money available was $C_{50} = \$93$. Starting with $C_0 = \$100$, the average change was $\bar{y} = -7/50 = \$-0.14$, with standard deviation $s_y = \$2.703$. Thus, the forecast at time 60 is $93 + 10\,(-0.14) = 91.6$. The corresponding 95% prediction interval is

$$91.6 \pm 2\,(2.703)\,\sqrt{10} = 91.6 \pm 17.1 = (74.5, 108.7).$$

Differencing is the procedure (filter) that reduces a random walk to a random process.

We have seen how to do useful things, like forecasting, with random walk models. But how do we identify a series as a realization from a random walk? From our model properties, we know that if the average level of a series is trending in a linear way or if the variance grows over time, then the random walk is a good candidate model. We also know that the random walk is a special kind of nonstationary model. Section 9.4 will discuss identifying nonstationary models.

The most useful way of establishing whether a random walk is an appropriate model is to examine the changes of the series and determine whether the changes follow a random process. If there are no apparent patterns associated with the changes, then the changes can be modeled as a random process which means that the series can be modeled using the random walk. Taking differences is not very satisfying to beginning students of data analysis because there may be a clear pattern in the original series that is "lost" when examining changes in the series.

Example 9.2—Continued

To forecast the adjusted price of beer with a random walk, we begin with our most recent observation, $ADJBEER_{37} = 95.869$. We denote the change in the price of beer by y_t, so that $y_t = ADJBEER_t - ADJBEER_{t-1}$. It turns out that the average change is $\bar{y} = -1.468$ with standard deviation $s_y = 2.623$. Thus, using a random walk model, an approximate 95% prediction interval for the l step forecast is

$$95.689 - 1.468\, l \pm 5.246\, (l)^{1/2}.$$

Recall that $T = 37$ corresponds to year 1988. Thus, for example, a 95% prediction interval for 1989 is 94.221 ± 5.246, or $(88.975, 99.467)$. Figure 9.10 illustrates prediction intervals for 1989 through 1992, inclusive.

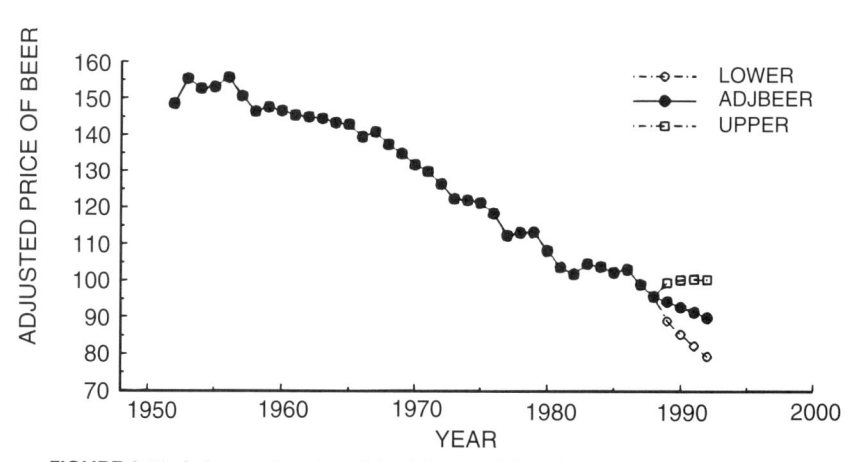

FIGURE 9.10 A time series plot of the Adjusted Price of Beer with forecast values for 1989–1992. The middle series represents the point forecast. The upper and lower series represent the upper and lower 95% prediction intervals. Data for 1952–1988 represent actual values.

Random Walk versus Linear Trend in Time Models

The adjusted price of beer example, in Example 9.2, could be represented using either a random walk or a linear trend in time model. These two models are, in fact, more closely related to one another than is evident at first glance. To see this relationship, first recall that the linear trend in time model can be written as

$$C_t = \beta_0 + \beta_1 t + e_t \qquad (9.7)$$

where $\{e_t\}$ is a random error process. If $\{C_t\}$ is a random walk, then it can be modelled as a partial sum as in equation (9.6). We can also decompose the random process into a drift term μ_y plus another random process, that is, $y_t = \mu_y + e_t$. Combining these two ideas, we see that a random walk model can be written as

$$C_t = C_0 + \mu_y t + u_t \qquad (9.8)$$

where $u_t = \Sigma_{j=1}^{t} e_j$. Comparing equations (9.7) and (9.8), we see that the two models are similar in that the deterministic portion is an unknown linear function of time. The difference is in the error component. The error component for the linear trend in time model is a stationary, random process. The error component for the random walk model is a nonstationary, partial sum of random processes. That is, the error component is another random walk model. Many introductory treatments of the random walk model focus on the "fair game" example and ignore the drift term μ_y. This is unfortunate because the comparison between the random walk model and the linear trend in time model is not as clear when the parameter μ_y is equal to zero.

9.4 DETECTING NONSTATIONARITY

For understanding, or forecasting, a series of observations over time, we must first decide whether or not the series is stationary. Recall, from Section 9.0, for a stationary process, successive samples of modest size should have approximately the same distribution. In this section, we introduce several graphical devices for deciding whether or not a series is a realization of a stationary process. We also provide some rules of thumb for deciding whether or not a series is a realization of a special kind of nonstationary process, a random walk.

A (retrospective) control chart is a time series plot with control limits (for example, $\bar{y}$ ± 3 SDs) superimposed. These control limits are useful for deciding whether or not a process is stationary.

Control Charts

A control chart is a useful graphical device for detecting the lack of stationarity in a time series. The basic idea is to superimpose reference lines called *control limits* on a time series plot of the data. These reference lines help us visually detect trends in the data and identify unusual points. The mechanics behind controls limits are straightforward. For a given series of observations, calculate $\bar{y}$ and a standard deviation (SD). Define the "upper control limit" by UCL = $\bar{y}$ + 3 SD and the "lower control limit" by LCL = $\bar{y}$ − 3 SD. Time series plots with these superimposed control limits are termed *control charts*. For example, the differenced series in Figure 9.11 lies well within the control limits, an indication of stationarity.

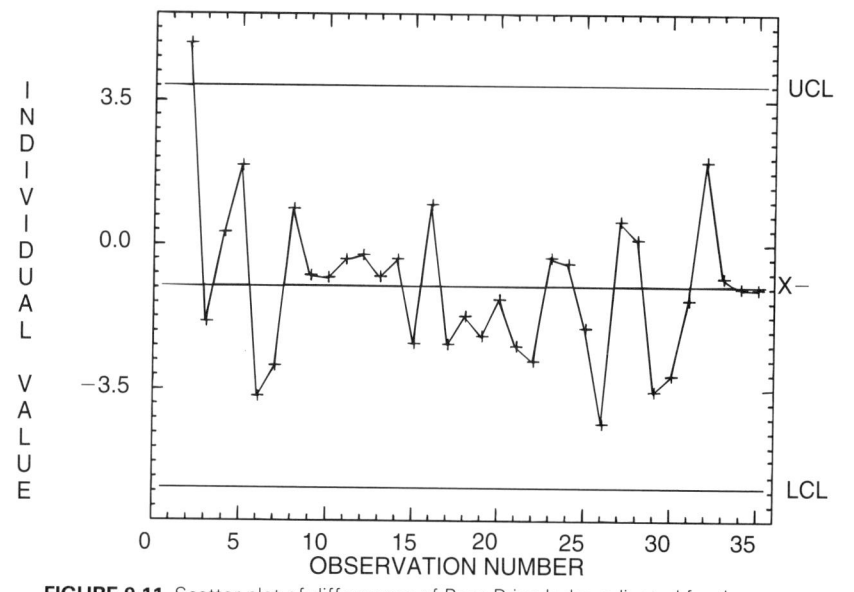

FIGURE 9.11 Scatter plot of differences of Beer Price Index adjusted for the Consumer Price Index. The upper and lower horizontal are control limits.

Sometimes the adjective *retrospective* is associated with this type of control chart. This adjective reminds the user that averages and standard deviations are based on all the available data. In contrast, when the control chart is used as an ongoing management tool for detecting whether an industrial process is "out of control," a *prospective control chart* may be more suitable. Here, prospective merely means using only an early portion of the process, that is "in control," to compute the control limits.

Control limits calculated at plus or minus three standard deviations are called *3-sigma limits*. To a certain extent, the choice of three is arbitrary but seems to be imbedded in the statistical quality control literature. If the process is stationary and if the distribution follows a normal distribution, we can calculate the probability of an observation exceeding the control limits. Using tables that are more refined than the normal table in the appendix, we have that

$$\text{Prob}(|z| > 3) = \text{Prob}(z > 3) + \text{Prob}(z < -3)$$

$$= 0.00135 + 0.00135 = 0.0027,$$

where z is a standard normal random variable. We interpret this to mean that the probability that an observation exceeds the control limits is 2.7, or roughly three, out of a thousand. Note the natural confusion that arises between the language "3-sigma" and the approximate probability three out of a thousand.

Xbar, R and *s* Charts

Modern quality improvement management is concerned with the stability of processes. Processes must be stabilized before management changes can be implemented that lead to an improved level of the process with a reduction in the variability. Control charts are important to both managers and production line workers as tools for detecting stability, or lack thereof, in a process.

As we discussed in Section 9.0, in this text we use the concept of stationarity as our measure of stability of a process. In applications, particularly in quality management applications, we look at the average and measures of variability in successive samples of modest size. If both the mean and the variability are stable over time, then the process is deemed to be stable and is said to be *in control.*

A control chart that helps us to examine the stability of the mean is the *Xbar chart.* An *Xbar* chart is created by combining successive observations of modest size, taking an average over this group, and then creating a control chart for the group averages. By taking averages over groups, the variability associated with each point on the chart is smaller than for a control chart for individual observations. This allows the data analyst to get a clearer picture of any patterns that may be evident in the mean of the series. If there are seasonal components to the series, with the appropriate choice of the size of the group, then these patterns may be masked when taking group averages. However, we can still get a picture of (nonseasonal) time trends even in the presence of seasonal components.

Two control charts that help us examine the stability of the variability are the *R chart* and *s chart.* As with the *Xbar* chart, we begin by forming successive groups of modest size. With the *R* chart, for each group we compute the *range,* which is the largest minus the smallest observation, and then create a control chart for the group ranges. With the *s* chart, for each group we compute the standard deviation, and then create a control chart for the group standard deviations. Both the range and standard deviation are measures of variability. The advantage of the standard deviation is that it is a better measure of variability based on sets of statistical assumptions or based on sets of assumptions from financial economics. The standard deviation measure is widely studied in beginning courses in statistics and finance. However, the range is much easier to compute, and is easier to interpret, particularly for production line workers, an important user group of control charts. We will employ both types of charts in this text.

By grouping observations and taking a measure of variability over successive groups, both R charts and s charts are useful for detecting changes in the variability of a process.

Example 9.3 Trends in Voting—Continued

Using Figure 9.7, we argued that there is a quadratic trend in the number of Wisconsin voters as a percentage of the qualified voting public. However, it is difficult to detect this trend in the Figure 9.7 time series plot. This is because it is obscured by (i) the natural variability in voter turnout in any particular year and (ii) the clear difference in voter turnout between presidential and nonpresidential election years. Figure 9.12 is an *Xbar* chart of this series, using two for grouping the sample averages. This *Xbar* chart helps us detect the quadratic trend in voter turnout. Figures 9.13 and 9.14 are *R* and *s* charts, respectively. The same grouping size was used. Each plot indicates little changing variability over time.

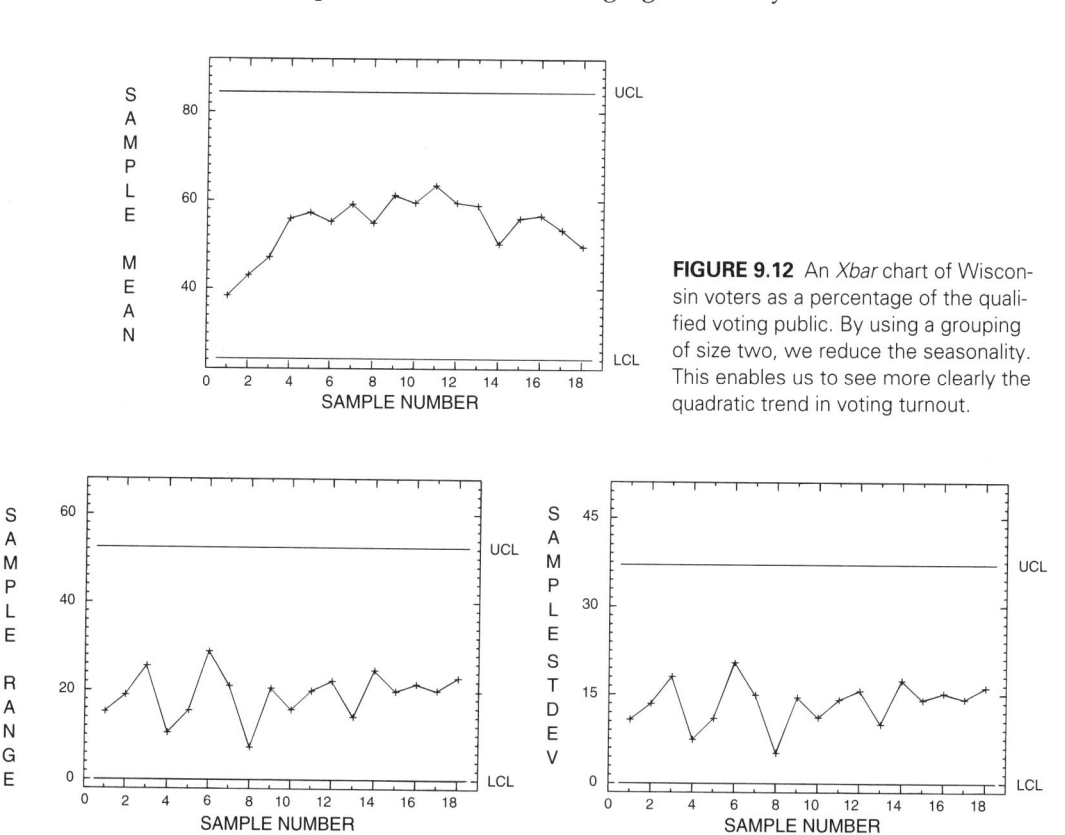

FIGURE 9.12 An *Xbar* chart of Wisconsin voters as a percentage of the qualified voting public. By using a grouping of size two, we reduce the seasonality. This enables us to see more clearly the quadratic trend in voting turnout.

FIGURE 9.13 An *R* chart of Wisconsin voter turnout. The variability appears to be stable.

FIGURE 9.14 An *s* chart of Wisconsin voter turnout. As with the *R* chart, this plot helps us see that the variability appears to be stable.

Identifying a Random Walk Model

Given that we have a series of observations, $y_1, y_2, \ldots, y_T$, how do we identify the fact that these are realizations of a random walk model? Recall that the expected value of a random walk, $\mathrm{E}\, C_t = C_0 + t\, \mu_y$, suggests that such a series follows a linear trend in time. The variance of a random walk, $\mathrm{Var}\, C_t = t\, \sigma_y^2$, suggests that the variability of a series gets larger at time t gets large. A control chart can help us to detect these patterns, whether they are of a linear trend in time, increasing variability or both.

If the original data follows a random walk model, then the differenced series follows a random process model. If a random walk model is a candidate model, then you should examine the differences of the series. In this case, the time series plot of the differences should be a stationary, random process that displays no apparent patterns. Control charts can help us to detect this lack of patterns.

Another good device for identification is to compare the standard deviations of the original series and the differenced series. Because the number of observations, T, exceeds one, we expect

$$SD(random\ walk) \approx \sqrt{T\sigma_y^2} > \sqrt{\sigma_y^2} \approx SD(differences).$$

If the series can be represented by a random walk, then we expect a substantial reduction in the standard deviation when taking differences.

Here, $SD(random\ walk)$ stands for the standard deviation of the original series and $SD(differences)$ for the standard deviation of the differenced series. Thus, if the series can be represented by a random walk, we expect a substantial reduction in the standard deviation when taking differences.

For example, first consider Example 9.1, the sum of two dice. In Figure 9.9 is the time series plot of the sum that is modeled using a random walk. The time series plot of the differences can be seen from Figure 9.1, after subtracting 7 from each roll. As noted, it turned out that the standard deviation of the rolls, and hence the differences of the sum of capital, was 2.703. For contrast, the standard deviation calculated using the sum of capital series was 3.165.

For an example where the patterns are much clearer, consider Example 9.2, the beer consumption example. The time series plot of the series in Figure 9.2 displays a clear downward trend. The time series plot of the differences in Figure 9.11 appears to be much more stable. Further, when computing differences of each series, it turned out that

$$13.05 = SD(series) > SD(differences) = 1.857.$$

In Chapter 10, we will discuss two additional identification devices. These are scatter plots of series versus a lagged version of the series and the corresponding summary statistics called autocorrelations.

9.5 FILTERING TO ACHIEVE STATIONARITY

As defined in Section 9.2, a filter is a procedure for reducing observations to randomness. In regression, we accomplished this by simply subtracting the regression function from the observations, that is, $y_i - (\beta_0 + \beta_1 x_{1i} + \dots + \beta_k x_{ki}) = e_i$. *Transformation* of the data is another device for filtering that we introduced, in Section 6.6, when analyzing cross-sectional data. We encountered

*Filters are proce-
dures for reducing
observations to a
random process.
Filters used in
this text include
subtracting the re-
gression function,
differencing and
transforming the
data.*

another example of a filter in Section 9.3. There, by taking differences of observations, we reduced a random walk series to a random process.

As in Section 4.0, an important theme of this text is to use an *iterative approach* for fitting models to data. In particular, in this chapter we discuss techniques for reducing a sequence of observations to a stationary series. By
definition, a stationary series is stable and hence is far easier to forecast than an
unstable series. This stage, sometimes known as *preprocessing* the data, generally accounts for the most important sources of trends in the data. In the next
chapter, we will discuss models that account for subtler trends in the data.

Transformations

*A transformation,
or rescaling, of ob-
servations is an-
other type of filter.*

When analyzing longitudinal data, a transformation is an important tool used
to filter a data set to reduce it to a random process. Recall that a transformation
is merely a rescaling of the data. If the data are shifted by some combination of
a scale and a shift change, then this is referred to as a *linear transformation.* Examples of scale and shift changes are, respectively, converting dollars to cents
($\$x = 100 \, x \, ¢$) and converting Celsius scale to Kelvin scale [$x \, °C = (273 + x)° \, K$].
A logarithmic transformation is an example of a nonlinear transformation that
is frequently used (the Richter scale). Because we can always convert data back
to the original scale through exponentiation, there is no loss of information
when doing this type of rescaling.

*The power family
is a useful class of
nonlinear trans-
forms.*

Using a logarithmic transformation tends to shrink "spread out" data.
This feature gives us an alternative method to deal with a process where the
variability appears to grow with time. Recall the first option discussed is to
posit a random walk model and examine differences of the data. Alternatively,
one may take a log transform that helps to reduce increasing variance through
time.

The log transform may be considered as a special case of the power family class of nonlinear transforms, introduced in Section 6.6. The two other
transforms regularly used in this class are the square root transform (data
raised to the one half power) and the negative reciprocal transform. (Negative
one times the data raised to the minus one power. The negative one is a rever-
sal of scale so that large numbers remain large, even after transformation.) If
we view the log transform as data raised to the "zero power," then the square
root transform can be viewed as intermediate between the log transform and
the original series. Thus, if the series variance increases through time but the
log series decreases through time, try a square root transform. Extending this
idea, the negative reciprocal transform can be viewed as more extreme than the
log transform. Thus, if both the series variance and log series variance increase
through time, try the negative reciprocal transform. Alternatively, from the
random walk discussion, we know that if both the series variance and log series variance increase through time, the differences of the log transform might

Differences of logs are pleasing because they can be interpreted as proportional, or percentages, changes.

handle this increasing variability. Differences of natural logarithms are particularly pleasing because they can be interpreted as *proportional*, or *percentages*, *changes*. To see this, define $pchange_t = (y_t/y_{t-1}) - 1$. Then,

$$\ln y_t - \ln y_{t-1} = \ln\left(\frac{y_t}{y_{t-1}}\right) = \ln(1 + pchange_t) \approx pchange_t.$$

Case Study: Standard & Poor's Composite Quarterly Index

C9_S&P

An important task of a financial analyst is to quantify costs associated with future events. Considerations of cash flows that occur in the future leads to present value of money concepts that in turn leads to a notion of a rate of return. We consider here funds invested in a standard measure of overall market performance, the Standard & Poor's (S&P) Composite Index. It is known that portfolios of investment funds are generally related to such a market index. In fact, the extent of that relationship can be quantified by a financial economics model known as the Capital Asset Pricing Model, discussed in Section 3.6. For now, we consider the performance of the S&P index as the performance of an investment portfolio. The goal is to describe the performance of the portfolio for discounting of cash flows.

In particular, we examine the S&P Composite Quarterly Index for the years 1936 to 1977, inclusive. By today's standards, this period may not be the most representative because the depression of the 1930s is included although the extreme volatility in rates of return of the 1980s is excluded. However, we will be able to demonstrate various statistical techniques including transformations of the data and differencing to induce stationarity. The data were taken from the "Report of the Maturity Guarantees Working Party" in the *Journal of the Institute of Actuaries*, (1980), volume 107, pp. 103–213. The purpose of this paper was to study long term behavior of investment returns from an actuarial viewpoint.

To see how graphical techniques suggest a useful transformation for reducing the data to a stationary process, we begin with a time series plot of the data in Figure 9.15. Note that the mean level and variability increases with time. To see this, the *Xbar* chart in Figure 9.16 demonstrates the increasing mean level in the index over time. The *s* chart in Figure 9.17 demonstrates the increasing level of variability in the index over time.

From our discussions in Sections 9.2 and 9.3, a candidate model that has these properties is the random walk. However, the time series plot of the differences, in Figure 9.18, still indicates a pattern of variability increasing with time. An alternative transformation is to consider logarithmic values of the series. The time series plot of logged values, presented in Figure 9.19, indicates the pattern of increasing variability is reduced but still increasing with time.

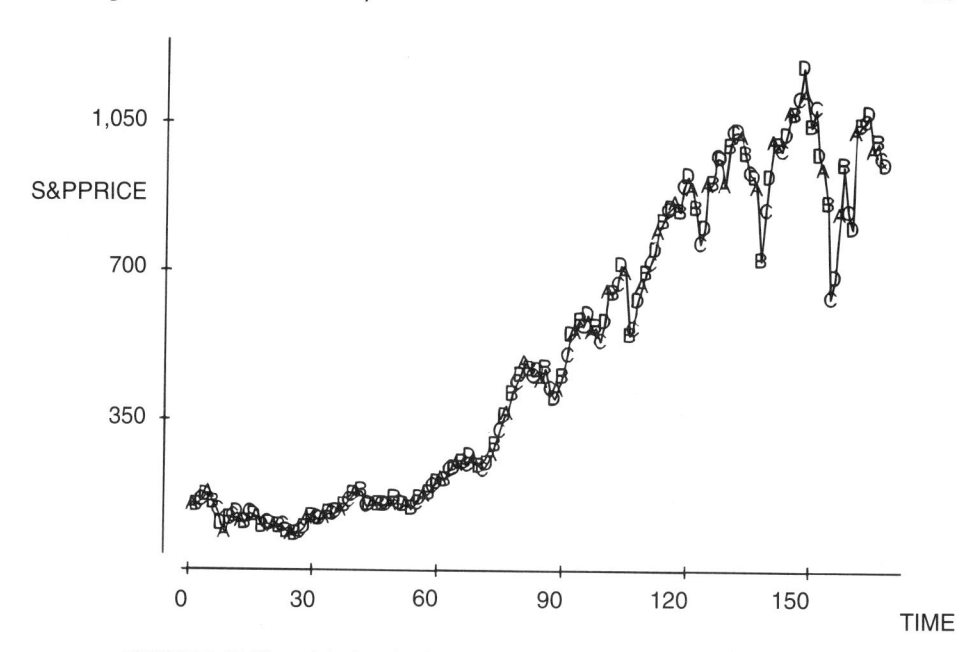

FIGURE 9.15 The original series is nonstationary in the mean and in the variability. The letter codes for plotting symbols indicate the quarter within the season.

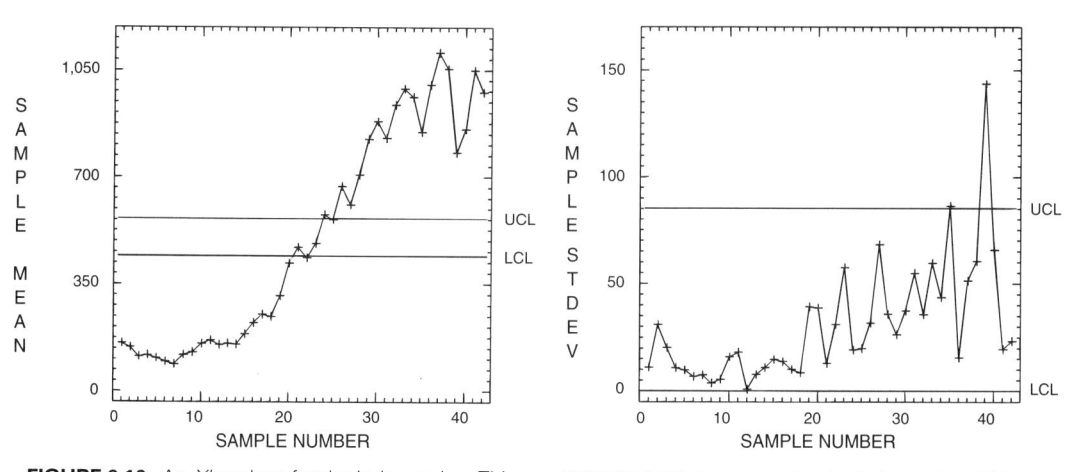

FIGURE 9.16 An *Xbar* chart for the index series. This chart indicates nonstationarity in the mean.

FIGURE 9.17 An *s* chart for the index series. This chart indicates nonstationarity in the variability.

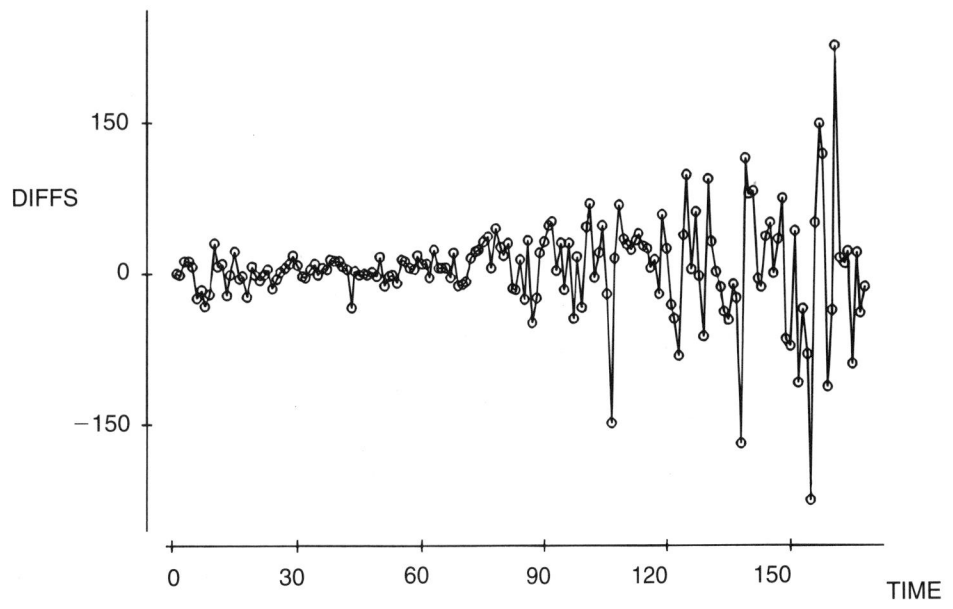

FIGURE 9.18 The differenced series is stationary in the mean, although not in the variability.

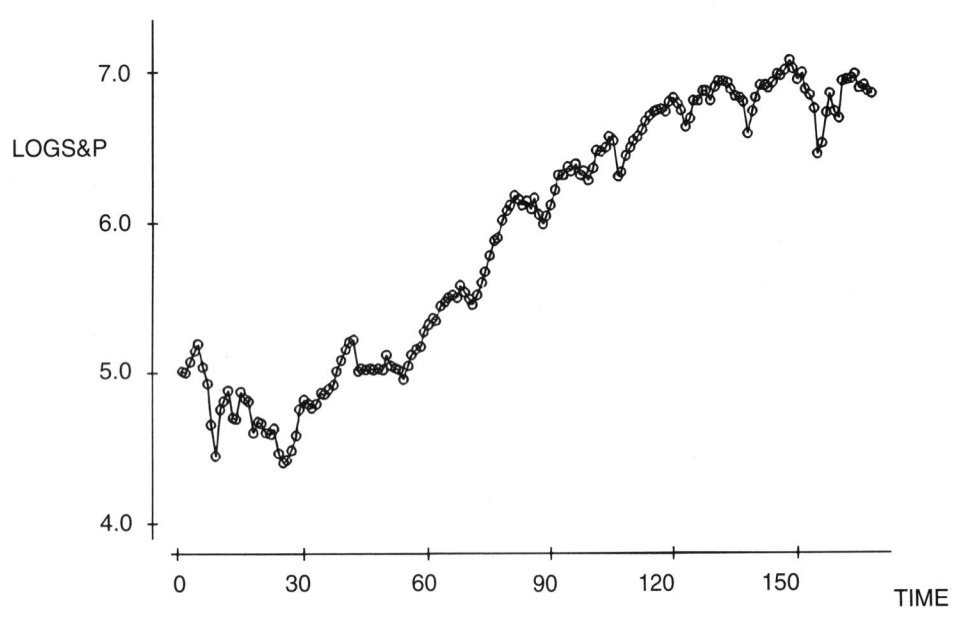

FIGURE 9.19 The logarithmic series seems to be more stationary in the variability, although not in the mean.

One approach would be to examine the reciprocal of the series. An alternative approach is to examine differences of the logarithmic series. This is especially desirable when looking at indices, or "breadbaskets," because the difference of logarithms can be interpreted as proportional changes. From the final time series plot, in Figure 9.20, we see that there are fewer discernible patterns in the transformed series, the difference of logs. This transformed series seems to be stationary. It is interesting to note that there seems to be a higher level of volatility at the beginning and end of the series. This type of *nonmonotonic* changing volatility is much more difficult to model and has recently been the subject of considerable attention in the financial economics literature (see, for example, Tsay, 1987).

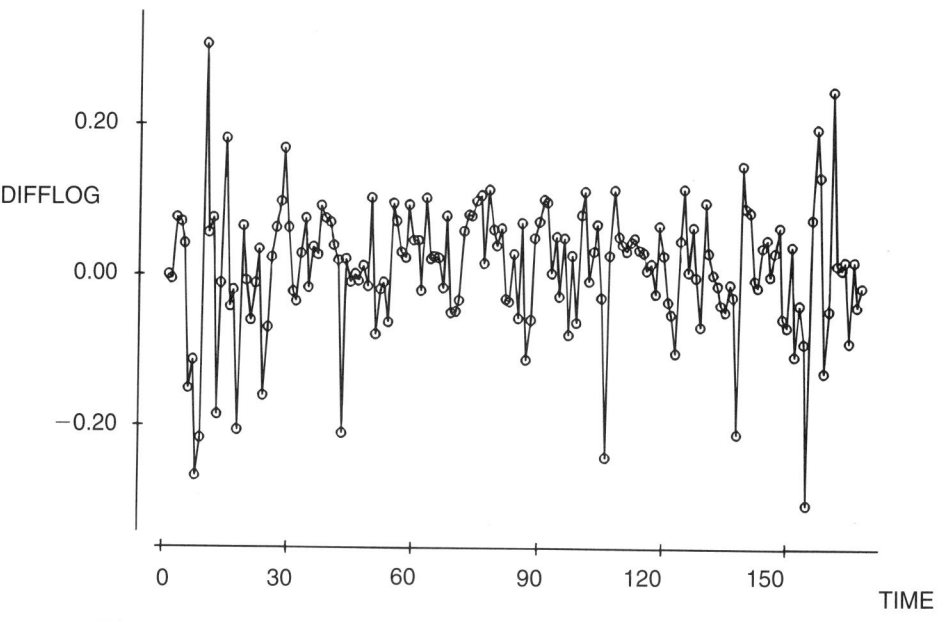

FIGURE 9.20 The differences of logarithmic series appears to be stationary in the mean and in the variability.

9.6 FORECAST EVALUATION

Judging the accuracy of forecasts is important when modeling time series data. In this section, we present forecast evaluation techniques that:

1. Help in detecting recent unanticipated trends or patterns in the data.
2. Are useful for comparing different forecasting methods.
3. Provide an intuitive and easy to explain method for evaluating the accuracy of forecasts.

Out-of-Sample Validation

In the first five sections of Chapter 9, we presented several techniques for detecting patterns in residuals from a fitted model. Measures that summarize the distribution of residuals are called *goodness-of-fit* statistics. As we saw in our study of cross-sectional models, by fitting several different models to a data set, we introduce the possibility of overfitting the data. To address this concern, we will use *out-of-sample validation* techniques, similar to those introduced in Section 6.5.

To perform an out-of-sample validation of a proposed model, ideally one would develop the model on a data set and then corroborate the model's usefulness on a second, independent data set. Because two such ideal data sets are rarely available, in practice we can split a data set into two subsamples, a model development subsample and a validation subsample. For longitudinal data, the practice is to use the beginning part of the series, the first T_1 observations, to develop one or more candidate models. The latter part of the series, the last $T_2 = T - T_1$ observations, are used to evaluate the forecasts. For example, we might have ten years of monthly data so that $T = 120$. It would be reasonable to use the first eight years of data to develop a model and the last two years of data for validation, yielding $T_1 = 96$ and $T_2 = 24$. (See Figure 9.21.)

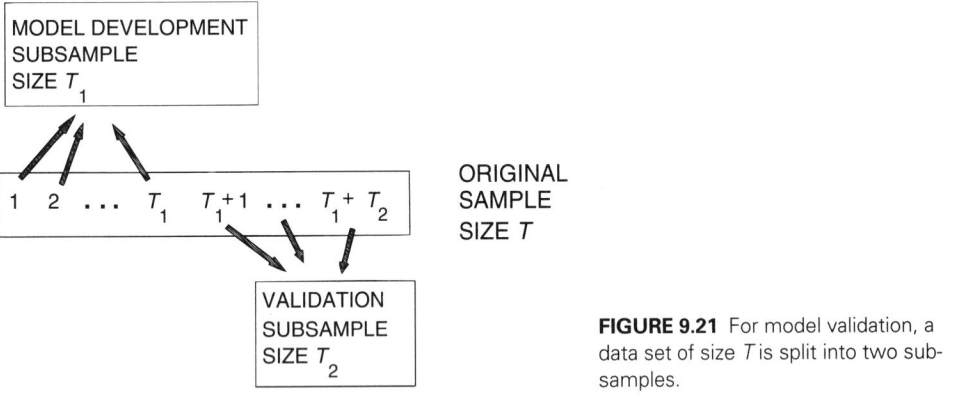

FIGURE 9.21 For model validation, a data set of size T is split into two subsamples.

Thus, observations $y_1, y_2, \ldots, y_{T_1}$ are used to develop a model. From these T_1 observations and the candidate fitted model, we can determine the residual standard deviation, s. Using the fitted model, we can determine fitted values for the model validation subsample, $\hat{y}_t$, for $t = T_1 + 1, T_1 + 2, \ldots, T_1 + T_2$. For the random walk models and other models that will be introduced in Chapter 10, these are *one-step fitted values* in that they rely on the data up to and including time $t - 1$. Taking the difference between the actual and fitted values yield *one-step forecast residuals*, denoted by

$$\hat{e}_t = y_t - \hat{y}_t.$$

These forecast residuals, together with the residual standard deviation, are the basic quantities that we will use to evaluate and compare forecasting techniques.

Evaluating Forecasts

A comparison of forecasts to actual values can be used to assess the adequacy of a candidate model using devices that are similar to in-sample measures.

To detect recent trends that were not anticipated by the model, the *mean error* statistic

$$ME = \frac{1}{T_2} \sum_{i=T_1+1}^{T_1+T_2} \hat{e}_t \tag{9.9}$$

is useful. This statistic can detect bias in our forecasts. If our candidate model is correct, then the standardized version,

$$t(ME) = \frac{ME}{s/\sqrt{T_2}},$$

approximately follows a *t*-distribution with $df = T_2 - p$ degrees of freedom. Here, p is the number of linear parameters used to fit the model. Thus, we can reject the hypothesis of no bias if $|t(ME)| > t$-value, where *t*-value is a percentile from the *t*-distribution using $df = T_1 - p$ degrees of freedom. The percentile is $1 - $ (significance level)$/2$.

The mean error test for bias will not detect several types of patterns in the forecast residuals, such as seasonal trends and heteroscedasticity. Another test for the adequacy of the model is based on

$$F\text{-ratio} = \frac{1}{T_2 \, s^2} \sum_{t=T_1+1}^{T_1+T_2} \hat{e}_t^2 \,.$$

By squaring forecast residuals, we are able to detect many more patterns. This *F*-ratio has an approximate *F*-distribution with $df_1 = T_2$ and $df_2 = T_1 - p$ degrees of freedom. Thus, we can reject a hypothesis of no patterns if *F*-ratio $>$ *F*-value, where *F*-value is a percentile from the *F*-distribution using $df_1 = T_2$ and $df_2 = T_1 - p$ degrees of freedom. The percentile is $1 - $ significance level.

Many patterns in the forecast residuals can be seen graphically using a plot of y_t versus $\hat{y}_t$, that is, actual versus one-step fitted values. Deviations of this plot from 45 degree line indicate bias. Further, unlike the tests of hypotheses, the plot may reveal the nature of the bias.

Comparing Forecasts

Out-of-sample validation can be used to compare the accuracy of forecasts from virtually any forecasting model. As we saw in Section 6.5, we are not limited to comparisons where one model is a subset of another, where the competing models use the same units for the response, and so on. To compare models, we use a four-step process similar to that described in Section 6.5.

1. Divide the sample of size T into two subsamples, a model development subsample ($t = 1, ..., T_1$) and a model validation subsample ($t = T_1 + 1, ..., T_1 + T_2$).
2. Using the model development subsample, fit a candidate model to the data set $t = 1, ..., T_1$.
3. Using the model created in Step 2 and the dependent variables up to and including $t - 1$, forecast the dependent variable $\hat{y}_t$, where $t = T_1 + 1, ..., T_1 + T_2$.
4. Use actual observations and the fitted values computed in Step 3 to compute one-step forecast residuals, $\hat{e}_t = y_t - \hat{y}_t$, for the model validation subsample. Summarize these residuals with one or more of the following comparison statistics.

Repeat Steps 2 through 4 for each of the candidate models. Choose the model with the smallest set of comparison statistics.

There are several statistics that are commonly used to compare forecasts. These include:

1. The mean error statistic defined in equation (9.9). This statistic measures recent trends that are not anticipated by the model.
2. The *mean percent error*, defined by

$$MPE = \frac{100}{T_2} \sum_{t=T_1+1}^{T_1+T_2} \frac{\hat{e}_t}{y_t}.$$

This statistic is also a measure of trend, but examines error relative to the actual value.
3. The *mean square error*, defined by

$$MSE = \frac{1}{T_2} \sum_{t=T_1+1}^{T_1+T_2} \hat{e}_t^2.$$

This statistic can detect more patterns than ME. It is the same as the cross-sectional $SSPE$ statistic, except for the division by T_2.

4. The *mean absolute error*, defined by

$$MAE = \frac{1}{T_2} \sum_{t=T_1+1}^{T_1+T_2} |\hat{e}_t| .$$

Like *MSE*, this statistic can detect more trend patterns than *ME*. The units of *MAE* are the same as the dependent variable.

5. The *mean absolute percent error*, defined by

$$MAPE = \frac{100}{T_2} \sum_{t=T_1+1}^{T_1+T_2} \left| \frac{\hat{e}_t}{y_t} \right| .$$

Like *MAE*, this statistic can detect more than trend patterns. Like *MPE*, it examines each error relative to the actual value.

Example 9.2—Continued

We can use out-of-sample validation measures to compare two models for the adjusted price of beer: the linear trend in time model and the random walk model. For this illustration, we examined the price of beer for years 1952 through 1988, inclusive. This corresponds to $T_1 = 37$ observations defined in Step 1. Data were subsequently gathered on beer prices for 1989 through 1992, inclusive, corresponding to $T_2 = 4$ for out-of-sample validation. For Step 2, we fit each model using $t = 1, ..., T_{37}$, earlier in this chapter. For Step 3, the one-step forecasts are:

$$\hat{y}_t = 161.94 - 1.7482 \, t$$

and

$$\hat{y}_t = y_{t-1} - 1.468,$$

for the linear trend in time and the random walk models, respectively. For Step 4, Table 9.3 summarizes the forecast comparison statistics. Based on these statistics, the choice of the model is clearly the random walk.

TABLE 9.3 Out of Sample Forecast Comparison for the Adjusted Price of Beer Example

	ME	MPE	MSE	MAE	MAPE
Linear trend in time model	3.30	−3.69	12.7	3.30	3.69
Random walk model	−0.43	−0.48	4.8	1.88	2.10

9.7 SUMMARY

This chapter provided an introduction to the analysis and forecasting of time series, or longitudinal, data. For understanding and forecasting time series data, it is important to identify underlying patterns in the data. Thus, in this chapter, we presented several trends that are commonly encountered in time series analysis. Further, we introduced ways of stabilizing, or de-trending, longitudinal data.

We began in Section 9.0 by introducing some of the basic terminology. Graphical examination of the data and basic trend analysis were discussed in Section 9.1 without reference to formal mathematical models. Two formal models were introduced in Section 9.2. The random process model for longitudinal data is equivalent to the random error model for cross-sectional data. The random walk model, defined as the partial sums of the random process, is an important model when considering efficient financial markets. Because of the importance of this model, in Section 9.3 we discussed some of the properties and the forecasting techniques associated with the random walk model. Sections 9.4, 9.5 and 9.6 provided some important tools for model selection. Section 9.4 introduced control charts, a basic graphical device for detecting nonstationarity. Section 9.5 presented various tools, such as transformations, for achieving stationarity. Section 9.6 introduced out-of-sample validation techniques for comparing models.

The focus of Chapter 9 has been to recognize, and account for, major trends in the data. In Chapter 10, we will focus on subtler data trends, or patterns, that we will summarize using autocorrelation statistics. These subtler trends can be represented using a class of models called autoregressive models, regression models using lagged dependent variables as predictor variables. Thus, we will be able to continue using the experience that we have accumulated in regression techniques for forecasting time series data.

KEY WORDS, PHRASES AND SYMBOLS

After reading this chapter, you should be able to define each of the following important terms, phrases and symbols in your own words. If not, go to the page indicated and review the definition.

CHAPTER 9 EXERCISES

C9_WORLD

Sections 9.0–9.1

9.1 Like the U.S. Standard & Poor's Composite Index, the London Financial Times-Stock Exchange 100 Shares Index is an important barometer of the movement of equity securities. Because of the United Kingdom's traditional strength in financial services, movements of this index are of interest to domestic (U.K.) and international investors. Further, it is of interest to understand the movements of this Index because options based on the future movement of the index, and other derivative securities, are important financial instruments for many investors.

We consider here the daily closing prices of this index over 1991; there were 253 trading days that year. Supporting computer output follows.

a. Figure E9.1a is a time series plot of the daily LONDON index for 1991.

    i. Define the concept of a stationary time series.

    ii. Is the LONDON index stationary? Use your definition in part (i) to justify your response.

b. Based on an inspection of Figure E9.1a in part (a), you decide to fit a quadratic trend model to the data. Tables E9.1a and b describe the fit; Figure E9.1b superimposes the fitted values on a plot of the series.

    i. Cite several basic regression statistics that summarize the quality of the fit.

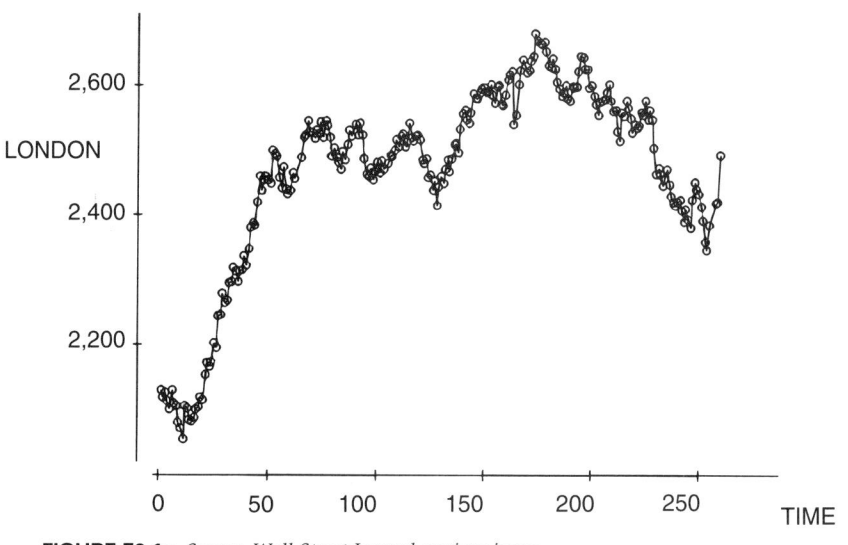

FIGURE E9.1a *Source: Wall Street Journal, various issues*

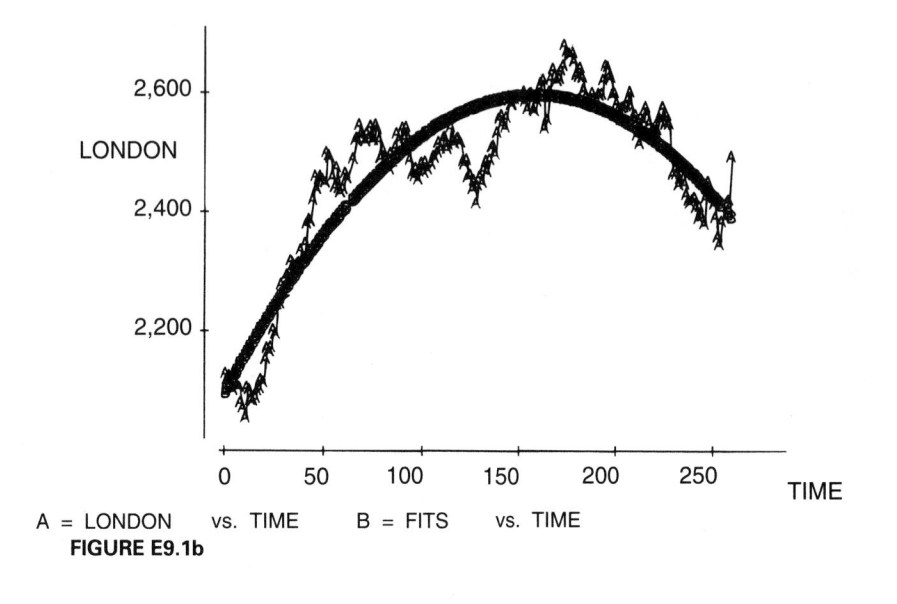

A = LONDON   vs. TIME   B = FITS   vs. TIME
FIGURE E9.1b

ii. Briefly describe any residual patterns that you observe in the attached figure.

iii. Here, TIME varies from 1, 2, ... up to 253. Using this model, calculate the two-step forecast corresponding to TIME = 255.

Computer Output for the Quadratric Trend Model

TABLE E9.1a Coefficient Estimates

Explanatory variables	Coefficient	Standard error	t-ratio
Constant	2089.87	10.95	190.91
TIME	6.3568	0.1952	32.56
TIMESQ	−0.0199865	0.0007300	−27.38

TABLE E9.1b ANOVA Table

Source	Sum of Squares	df	Mean Square
Regression	4,506,319	2	2,253,160
Error	842,629	250	3,371
Total	5,348,948	252	

The regression fit also yields $s = 58.06$, $R^2 = 84.2\%$ and $R_a^2 = 84.1\%$.

C9_NHOME

9.2 Health care financial analysts are concerned with levels of utilization of nursing home facilities. We examine monthly data, taken over the period June, 1990 through June, 1993, inclusive, of a nursing home facility. This facility is located in Wisconsin and specializes in developmentally disabled care. The measure of utilization that we examine is TOTDAYS, adjusted total daily patients days. This variable is defined to be the sum of (i) the average daily census of patients under care and (ii) a fraction (85%) of the average daily census of beds held for patients on leave or in the hospital. Beds held for patients represent a cost to the nursing home facility and thus are part of the total utilization measure. However, beds held for patients not on site at the nursing home represent a lower cost, and thus only a fraction is used in the utilization measure.

The objective is to develop a model for short term forecasts of TOTDAYS. Supporting computer output follows in Tables E9.2a–e.

   a. Figure E9.2a is a time series plot of TOTDAYS.
      i. Define the concept of stationarity of a time series.
     ii. Use the definition in part (i) and the time series plot to decide whether or not TOTDAYS is stationary. Justify your choice.
   b. A straight line in time and quadratic curve in time (Figure E9.2b) was fit to TOTDAYS.
      i. Provide some basic justifications to argue that the straight line in time is a reasonable model.

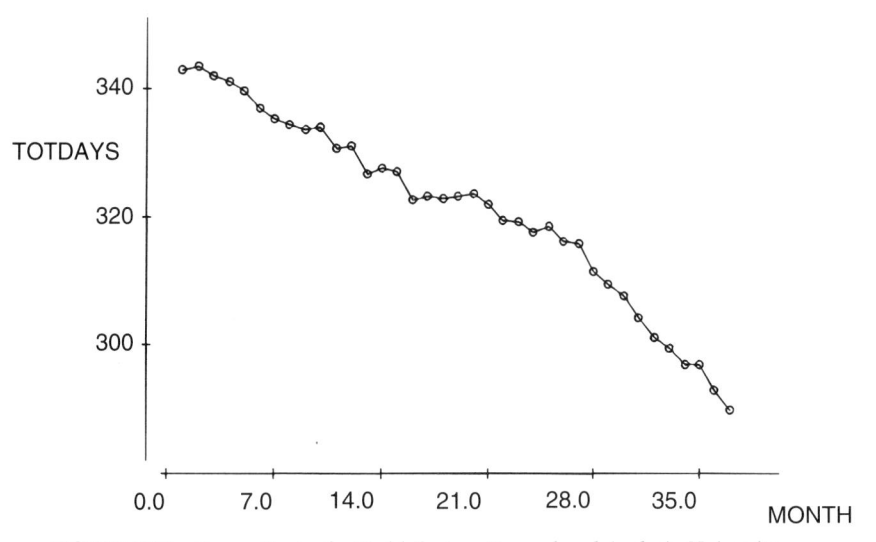

FIGURE E9.2a *Source: Center for Health Systems Research and Analysis, University of Wisconsin*

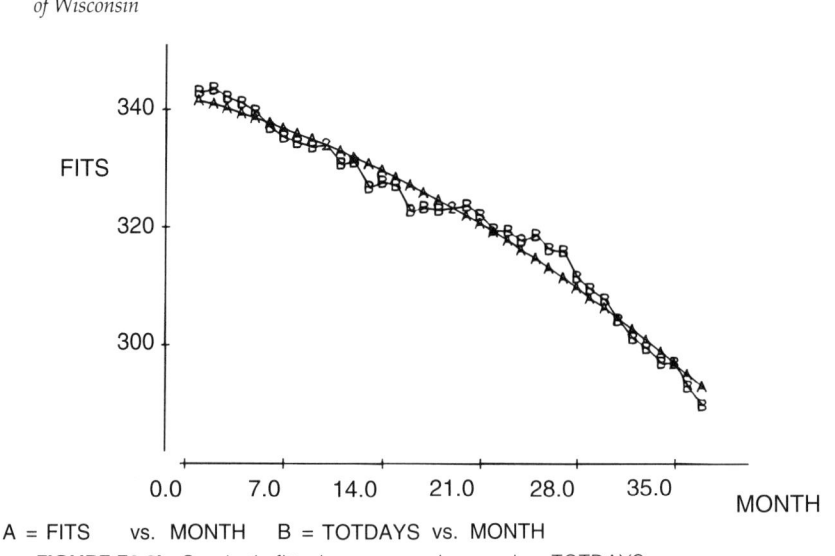

A = FITS   vs. MONTH   B = TOTDAYS vs. MONTH

FIGURE E9.2b Quadratic fitted curve superimposed on TOTDAYS.

ii.   Say whether or not you think that the quadratic curve in time is an improvement over the straight line in time model. Justify your choice.

iii. Provide a (point) forecast using the quadratic curve in time fitted model at MONTH = 38 (corresponding to August, 1993).

TABLE E9.2a   Summary Statistics for Exercise 9.2

	Number	Mean	Median	Standard deviation	Minimum	Maximum
MONTH	37	19.00	19.00	10.82	1.00	37.00
TOTDAYS	37	321.12	322.93	14.93	289.80	343.49

Computer Output for Straight Line in Time Fitted Model

TABLE E9.2b   Coefficient Estimates

Explanatory variables	Coefficient	Standard error	t-ratio
Constant	346.825	0.988	350.89
MONTH	−1.35285	0.04535	−29.83

TABLE E9.2c   ANOVA Table

Source	Sum of Squares	df	Mean Square
Regression	7719.8	1	7719.8
Error	303.6	35	8.7
Total	8023.5	36	

The regression fit also yields $s = 2.945$, $R^2 = 96.2\%$ and $R_a^2 = 96.1\%$.

Computer Output for Quadratic Curve in Time Fitted Model

TABLE E9.2d   Coefficient Estimates

Explanatory variables	Coefficient	Standard error	t-ratio
Constant	342.193	1.161	294.84
MONTH	−0.6402	0.1408	−4.55
MONTHSQ	−0.018754	0.003595	−5.22

TABLE E9.2e   ANOVA Table

Source	Sum of Squares	df	Mean Square
Regression	7854.8	2	3927.4
Error	168.6	34	5.0
Total	8023.5	36	

The regression fit also yields $s = 2.227$, $R^2 = 97.9\%$ and $R_a^2 = 97.8\%$.

C11_BEER

9.3   The brewing industry is an important aspect of the U.S. economy. Each year, billions of dollars are spent on malt beverages. These beverages are served in over 60% of American homes. To understand and forecast the demand for beer, monthly data were collected on brewery sales in the United States. Specifically, the data available are from January, 1975 to December, 1990. Each observation represents brewery sales, in millions of barrels and is denoted by DEM_BEER. The data source is *The Brewer's Almanac*.

a.   Figure E9.3a is a time series plot of DEM_BEER, with a plotting symbol used to represent the month. For example, the 'A' symbols represent January sales, the 'B' symbols represent February sales and so on.

    i. Describe whether or not the series is stationary. Provide reasons for your response.

    ii. Describe the seasonal patterns that are evident in the graph.

b. An independent categorical variable called 'MONTH' has a 1 for January, 2 for February and so on. A model using MONTH as an independent variable was fit to the data. This fitted model, with a plot of its residuals versus time, are presented in Figure E9.3b.

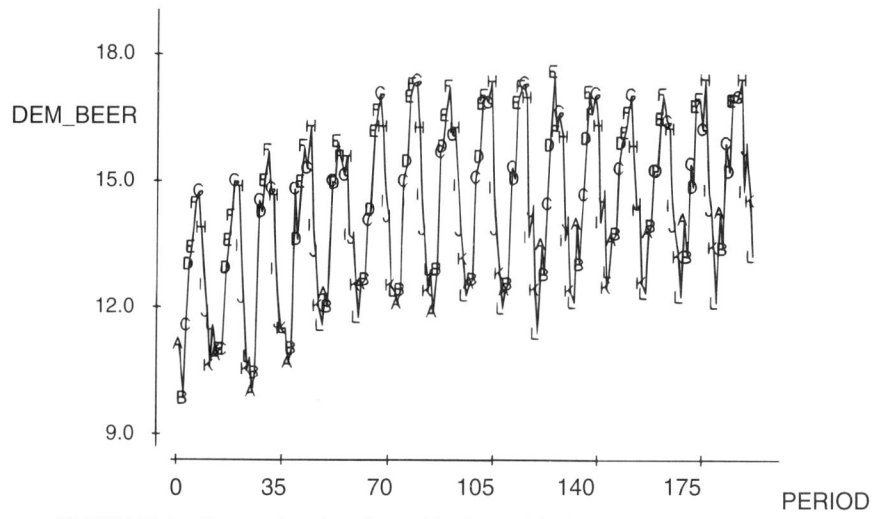

FIGURE E9.3a Time series plot of monthly demand for beer, 1975–1990. *Source: The Brewer's Almanac*

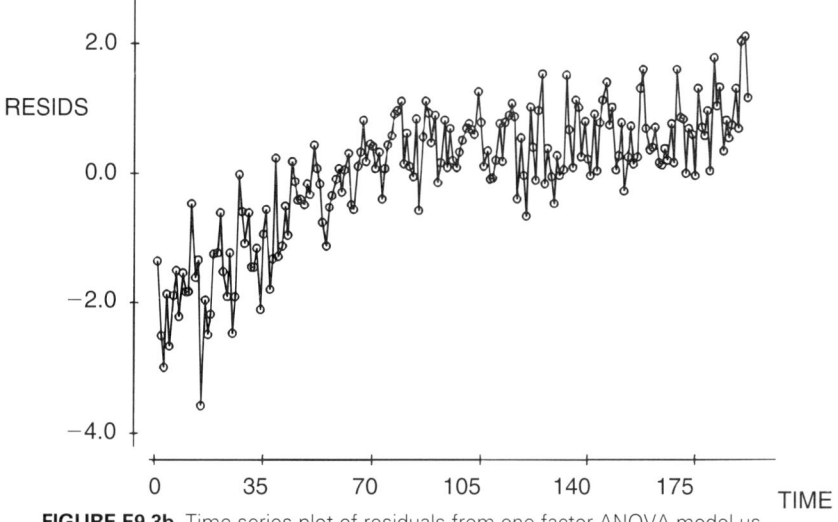

FIGURE E9.3b Time series plot of residuals from one factor ANOVA model using MONTH.

i.   Does the fitted model accommodate fixed or changing seasonality patterns?
ii. Is the MONTH factor important? Justify your response.
iii. TIME is an independent variable indicating the order of an observations. For example, the value of TIME is 1 for the first observation, 2 for the second and so on. What do we learn from the plot of residuals versus TIME?

MINITAB Output for One Way ANOVA Using MONTH Factor

ANALYSIS OF VARIANCE ON DEM_BEER

SOURCE	DF	SS	MS	F	P
MONTH	11	491.86	44.71	40.12	0.000
ERROR	180	200.60	1.11		
TOTAL	191	692.46			

```
                                   INDIVIDUAL 95 PCT CI'S FOR MEAN
                                   BASED ON POOLED STDEV
LEVEL    N      MEAN    STDEV   ----+---------+---------+---------+-
   1    16    12.486    1.328       (--+---)
   2    16    12.343    1.185       (--+---)
   3    16    14.568    1.366                   (--+---)
   4    16    14.883    0.999                      (--*---)
   5    16    16.085    1.231                           (--*---)
   6    16    16.335    0.966                            (--*---)
   7    16    16.254    0.952                            (--*---)
   8    16    16.094    0.994                           (--*---)
   9    16    14.059    0.718                  (---*--)
  10    16    13.740    1.058                  (---*--)
  11    16    12.438    0.990         (---*--)
  12    16    12.063    0.619        (--*---)
                                   ----+---------+---------+---------+-
POOLED STDEV =    1.056            12.0      13.5      15.0      16.5
```

Section 9.2

C9_DISCT

9.4 Consider the annual returns of the Salomon Brothers Bond Index for the period 1926–1985, inclusive. The data discussed below were abstracted from Ibbotson and Sinquefield (*Stocks, Bonds, Bills and Inflation,* Ibbotson Associates, 1986, Chicago). The logarithm of one plus the return is known as the *force of interest*, a quantity of importance when examining long-run behavior of returns. In Figure E9.4 is plot of the data over time.

a. Figure E9.4 is called a (retrospective, individual) control chart. Describe a control chart and its relationship to a scatter plot. Further, describe what we hope to learn from a control chart.

b. Describe the concept of stationarity of a series and different aspects of stationarity. Does the series in the figure appear to be stationary?

c. Suppose that a series is nonstationary. What can we learn by examining a histogram of a series?

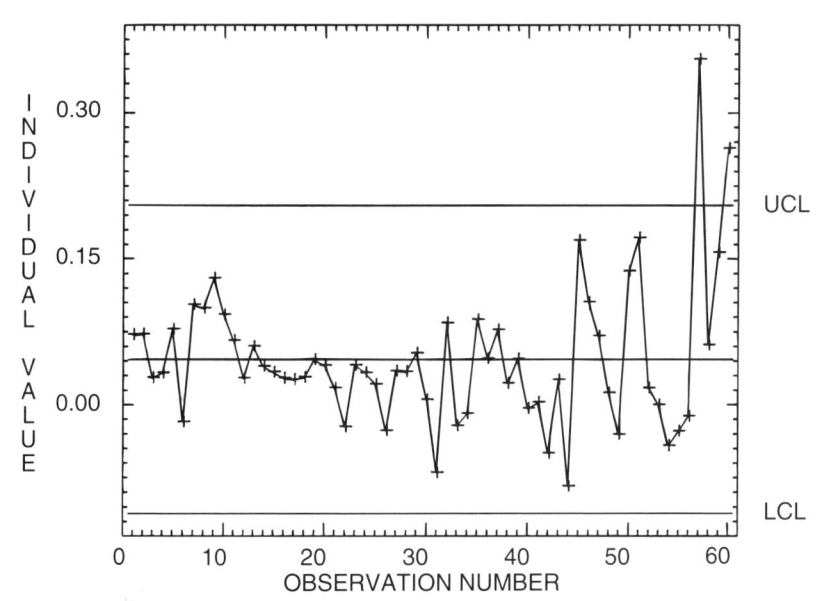

FIGURE E9.4 *Source: Ibbotson and Sinquefield, "Stocks, Bonds, Bills and Inflation," Ibbotson Associates, 1986, Chicago.*

d. Table E9.4 shows some summary statistics from the series. Suppose that you would like to estimate a random process model. Write down the theoretical model together with the fitted model.

TABLE E9.4 Summary Statistics for Exercise 9.4

	Number	Mean	Median	Standard deviation	Minimum	Maximum
LOGSALBR	60	0.04677	0.03343	0.07362	−0.08447	0.35438

Section 9.5

C9_DOW

9.5 Approximately 40% of life insurance company assets are invested in corporate bonds, according to the 1992 *Life Insurance Fact Book* (published by the American Council of Life Insurance). Thus, it is of a great deal of interest to the insurance community to study the performance of bonds over time. Here, we consider one measure of bond performance, Moody's Ten Year Bond Yields. This data was taken from the CRSP (Center for Research on Security Prices) database of economic indicators. Specifically, we study the variable BOND which contains monthly bond yields from January, 1977 to December , 1991, inclusive.

a. Figure E9.5a is a time series plot of Moody's Ten Year Bond Yields (BOND). The plot seems to indicate that the series is nonstationary.

    i. Define the concept of stationarity.

    ii. Say how the Bond Yield series is nonstationary.

b. Figures E9.5b and c are transformed versions of the Bond Yield series. Figure E9.5b is a time series plot of the differences, or changes, in monthly yields (DIFF-BOND). Figure E9.5c is a time series plot of the percentage changes in monthly yields (%BOND).

    i. What is the purpose of examining these transformed versions of the original series?

    ii. Describe which of the two series that you prefer to analyze, in accordance with the purpose that you discussed in part (i).

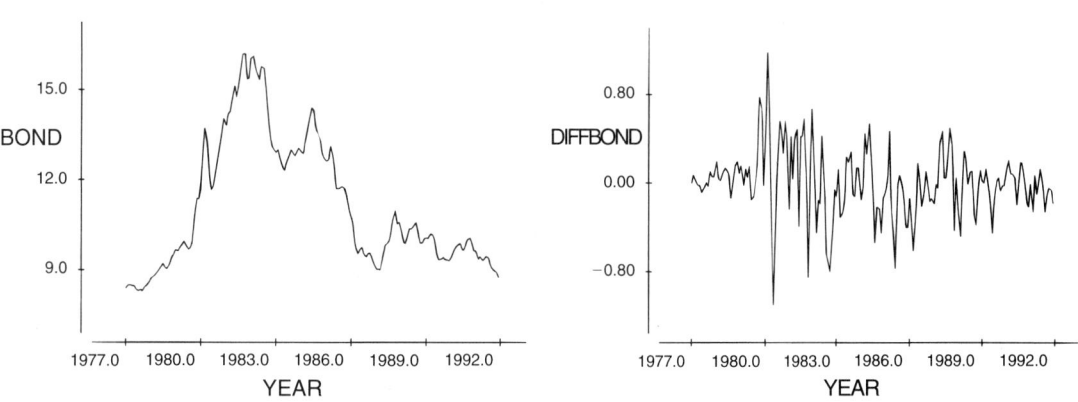

FIGURE E9.5a Time series plot of Ten Year Bond Yields (BOND). *Source: Center for Research on Security Prices, University of Chicago*

FIGURE E9.5b Time series plot of the differences, or changes, in monthly yields (DIFFBOND).

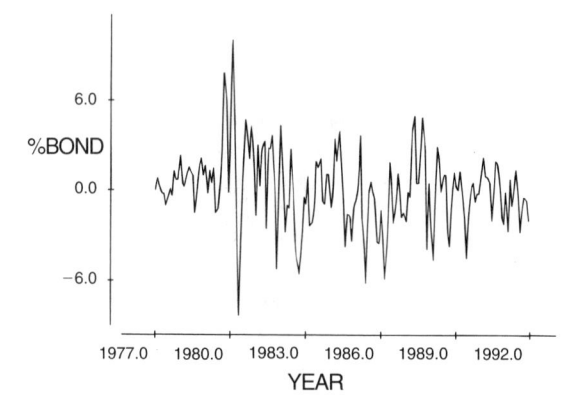

FIGURE E9.5c Time series plot of the percentage changes in montly yields (%BOND).

End-of-Chapter Exercises

C9_IMC

9.6 Figure E9.6a is a time series plot of the weekly prices of 1990 and 1991 for the IMC Fertilizer Group, a multinational corporation traded on the New York Stock Exchange. There are 105 observations in this series with the last price, at the end of 1991, being $56.75. These prices have been adjusted for dividends so that, to get weekly returns, one only needs to use the relation.

$$\text{RETURN}_t = (\text{PRICE}_t / \text{PRICE}_{t-1}) - 1.$$

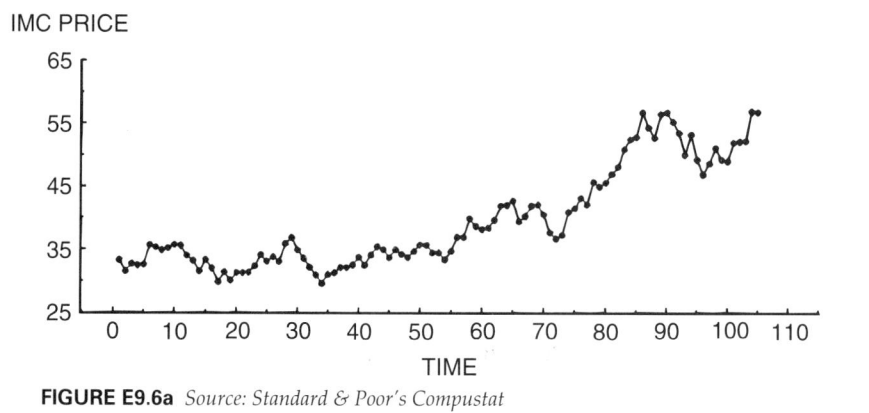

FIGURE E9.6a *Source: Standard & Poor's Compustat*

a. Several things can be learned about the characteristics of the IMC Price series by examining the time series plot in Figure E9.6a. Fill in the blanks to make the following statements true. Explain your choice.

i. The IMC Price series is not _____ data (cross-sectional or longitudinal).

ii. The IMC Price series is not a _____ process (stationary or nonstationary).

iii. A reasonable candidate model for the IMC Price series is not a _____ model (random process or random walk).

b. Suppose that you are interested in predicting the price of IMC for the first two weeks of 1992. One model you consider is a regression of PRICE using time as an explanatory variable. The fitted model turns out to be

$$\widehat{\text{PRICE}}_t = 27.3 + 0.230\, t,$$

where $t = 1, \ldots, 105$, and $R^2 = 76\%$. A second model that you consider is the random walk model. The price changes are graphed in Figure E9.6b, with an average price change of 0.226.

i. Provide point forecasts of the first two weeks of 1992 prices using the regression of price on time model.

ii. Provide point forecasts of the first two weeks of 1992 prices using the random walk model.

iii. The last two prices of the series, for December of 1991, are 56.875 and 56.75. Based on the point forecasts alone, say which of the two models you prefer. Explain your choice.

c. Yet another way to transform stock prices are to consider *returns*. In Figure E9.6c is a time series plot of weekly returns of IMC.

    i.   Assume that the returns series can be modeled as a random process. The average return for this series turns out to be 0.00632. Use this model to produce yet another set of point forecasts for the price of the IMC stock for the first two weeks of 1992.

    ii. You are assigned to select between the random process model for returns, discussed in part (i) and the random process model for changes in stock prices, discussed in part (b). Describe a graphical feature of the data that may influence your choice and the economic substance of the data that may influence your choice.

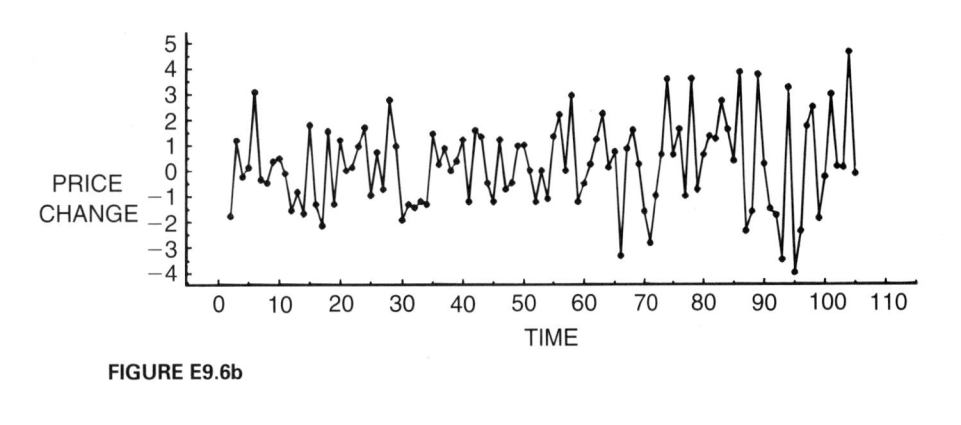

FIGURE E9.6b

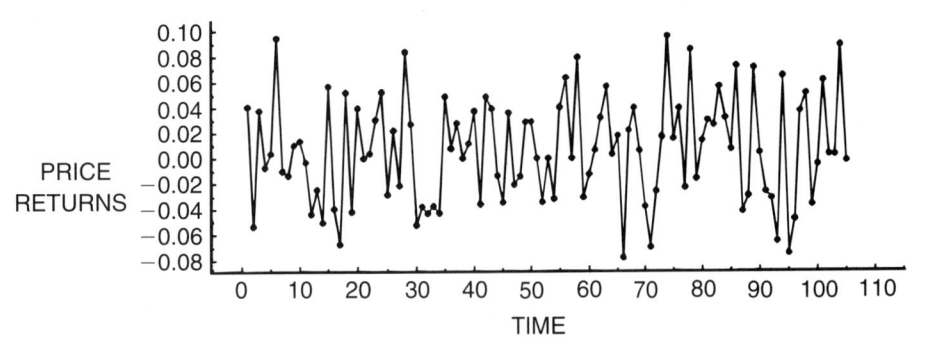

FIGURE E9.6c

C9_MILWK

9.7 As part of an effort to understand trends in violent crimes, the number of rapes in a large metropolitan area, the Greater Milwaukee area, is being studied. Over a period of 19 years, the number of rapes has more than tripled, from 116 in 1971 to 485 in 1989. The data for the period 1971–1989 were collected from the *Milwaukee Office of Justice Assistance* and are presented in Tables E9.7a and b. The series is presented using the name RAPES. The variable DIFFRAPE represents the differences, or annual changes, in the number of rapes.

TABLE E9.7a Number of Rapes in Greater Milwaukee Area

Year	Number	Year	Number	Year	Number	Year	Number
1971	116	1976	201	1981	313	1986	477
1972	116	1977	240	1982	239	1987	466
1973	219	1978	322	1983	269	1988	436
1974	218	1979	314	1984	318	1989	485
1975	173	1980	246	1985	415		

TABLE E9.7b Summary Statistics for Exercise 9.7

	Number	Mean	Median	Standard deviation	Minimum	Maximum
RAPES	19	293.8	269.0	116.3	116.0	485.0
DIFFRAPE	18	20.5	29.0	53.5	−74.0	103.0

a. Are the data cross-sectional or longitudinal?

b. Is the series stationary? Use the control charts (Figures E9.7a and b) as part of your response.

c. Assuming that the series is a random process, give a forecast for the number of rapes in 1990. Is this a sensible forecast?

d. From the summary statistics (Table E9.7b):

   i. Identify the standard deviation of the original series and of the differences of the series.

   ii. Explain how these standard deviations suggest using a random walk model.

e. Explain how the control charts of the series and the differences suggest using a random walk model for the series.

f. Assuming a random walk model for the series, provide point forecasts for 1990 through 1994, inclusive.

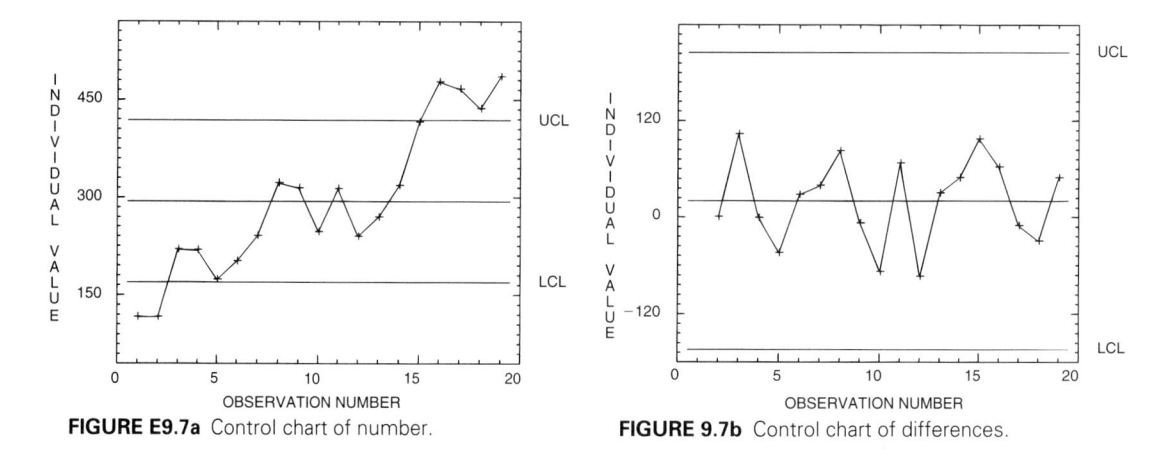

FIGURE E9.7a Control chart of number.

FIGURE 9.7b Control chart of differences.

g. Assuming a random walk model for the series, provide 95% prediction intervals for 1990 through 1994, inclusive.

h. Give a rough time series plot of the actual series for 1971–1989 with your predictions and prediction intervals for 1990 through 1994.

9.8   **Refer to Exercise 9.1**

C9_WORLD

a. You decide to investigate an alternative, the random walk model. The computer output (Table E9.8) describes summary statistics of the changes; Figure E9.8a is a time series plot of the changes.

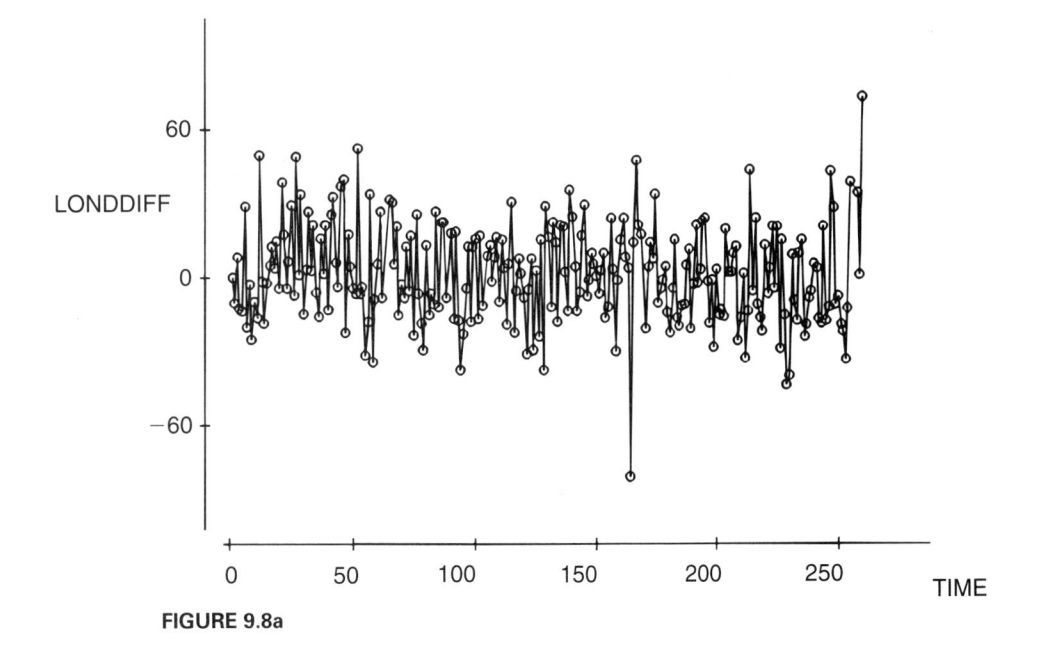

FIGURE 9.8a

i.   Based on the summary statistics of the index changes and of the quadratic trend fitted model (in part b of Exercise 9.1), which model would you prefer? Justify your response.

ii. The last value of the index is $INDEX_{253} = 2493.10$. Using the random walk model, calculate the two-step forecast of the index.

TABLE E9.8   Summary Statistics for the Index Changes

	Number	Number missing	Mean	Median	Standard deviation	Minimum	Maximum
LONDDIFF	252	1	1.45	0.95	20.27	−80.50	73.10

Correlation of DIFFLOG and PCHANGE = 1.000

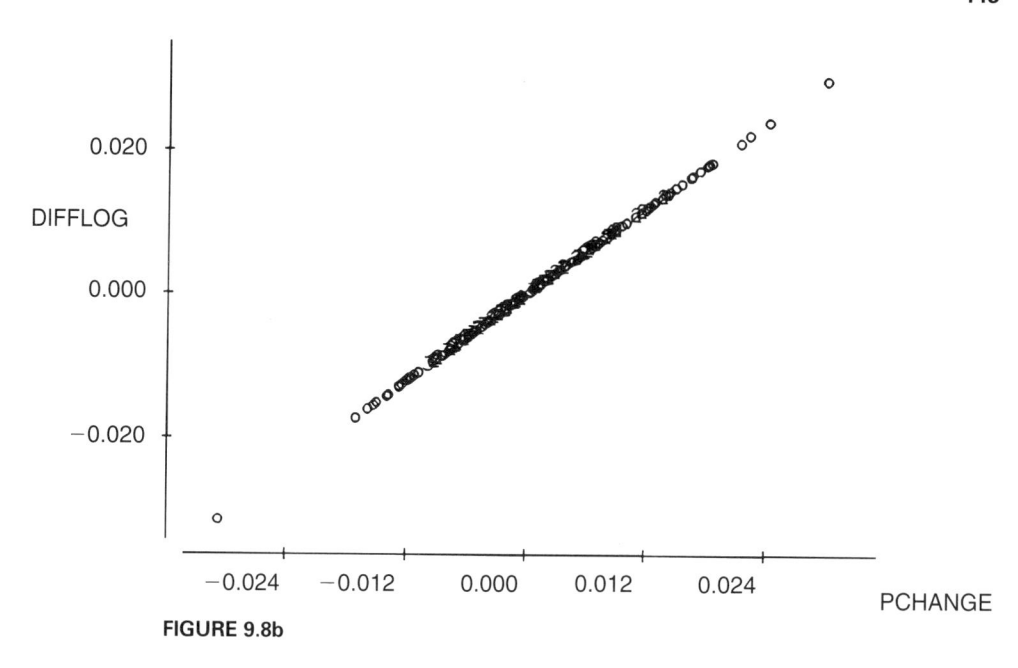

FIGURE 9.8b

  iii. Provide a 95% prediction interval for your forecast in part (ii).
 b. A financial analyst states that *proportional* changes, or returns, of the index should be used in lieu of changes. To help the analyst understand the role of transformations, you calculate the difference of the logarithmic series and proportional changes. Figure E9.8b compares the two series.
  i. Describe the similarities between proportional changes and differences of logarithms. Refer to the attached plot in your description.
  ii. When will proportional changes and differences of logarithms become different?

9.9 **Refer to Exercise 9.2**
 a. To investigate a different approach, DIFFTDAY, the difference of TOTDAYS was calculated. In Table E9.9a are the basic summary statistics and a control chart for DIFFTDAY.
  i. Describe the presence, or lack, of stationarity that is evident in the control chart (Figure E9.9).
  ii. Suppose that you decide to model DIFFTDAY as a random process. What is the name of the model for TOTDAYS?
  iii. Suppose that you decide to model DIFFTDAY as a random process. Using the summary statistics for DIFFTDAY, provide a 95% prediction interval for TOTDAYS$_{39}$. The most recent value available is TOTDAYS$_{37}$ = 289.8.

C9_NHOME

TABLE E9.9a Summary Statistics for the Index Changes

	Number	Number missing	Mean	Median	Standard deviation	Minimum	Maximum
DIFFTDAY	36	1	−1.474	−1.492	1.615	−4.480	0.855

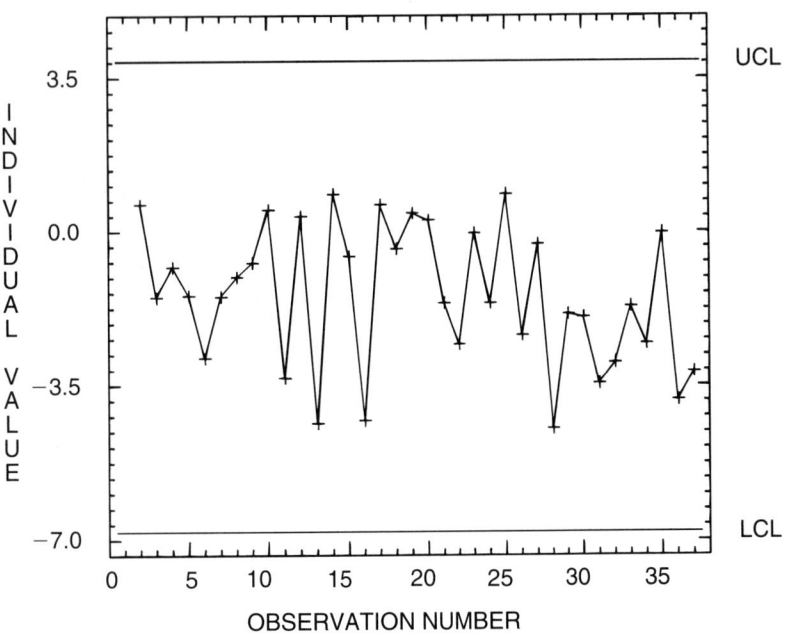

FIGURE 9.9 Control chart for DIFFTDAY.

b. You decide to perform an out-of-sample validation to choose among using the straight line in time, the quadratic curve in time and the difference model. In Tables E9.9b–c, the last four months were omitted and each model refit. Forecasts were then made for the straight line in time and quadratic curve in time models. With these omitted points, the most recent point available is $TODAYS_{33} = 299.425$. The following tables are a summary of the forecasts.

TABLE E9.9b

Month	34	35	36	37
Actual values	296.870	296.835	292.995	289.800
Straight line in time model forecasts	303.393	302.157	300.922	299.687
Quadratic curve in time model forecasts	301.326	299.726	298.105	296.463
Difference model forecasts				

i. Fill in Table E9.9b by providing forecasts for the difference model forecasts.
ii. Use the Table E9.9b to decide which of the three models provides the best out-of-sample fit to the data. Justify your choice.

TABLE E9.9c Summary Statistics for Model Development Sample

	Number	Number missing	Mean	Median	Standard deviation	Minimum	Maximum
MONTH	33	0	17.00	17.00	9.67	1.00	33.00
TOTDAYS	33	0	324.39	323.35	12.15	299.42	343.49
MONTHSQ	33	0	379.7	289.0	338.9	1.0	1,089.0
DIFFTDAY	32	1	−1.358	−1.475	1.597	−4.480	0.855

10

Autocorrelations and Autoregressive Models

Chapter Objectives

To introduce time series methods that detect subtle patterns by using lagged response variables as predictors. To illustrate, we will consider forecasting:

- the cost of transporting goods from producers to retail outlets,
- daily movements of a major stock index and
- the medical component of the Consumer Price Index.

Chapter Outline

10.1 IDENTIFYING AND SUMMARIZING DATA

This chapter continues our study of a single measurement on a process of interest. Chapter 9 introduced techniques for determining major patterns that provide a good first step for forecasting. However, in situations when pricing is competitive or investment competition is active, obtaining the best possible forecasts are economically important. Chapter 10 provides techniques for detecting subtle trends in time and models to accommodate these trends. In particular, we now introduce statistics to detect relationships between the current and past value of a series.

C10_TPOR

The data that we will use to begin this chapter is the Total Rail Freight Index, published by the *Bureau of Labor Statistics.* Semiannual values of the index, for April and October, are available for years 1977 through 1993, inclusive. Figure 10.1 presents a time series plot of the data. This index represents an important component of the relation between wholesale and retail prices of farm goods and fertilizer products. For this industry, one of the largest components of the difference between wholesale and retail prices is simply the cost of transportation that is measured by the rail freight index. Although wholesale prices of certain fertilizer products are readily available on a timely basis (*Green Markets: Fertilizer Market Intelligence Weekly,* by McGraw-Hill, is one such publication), corresponding retail prices are available on a less frequent basis. However, it is the retail prices that are of primary interest to farmers and to retail suppliers of fertilizer products. The goal is to develop an understanding of the transportation index that could be used as part of a larger study concerning the relation between wholesale and retail prices.

Summarizing Data Graphically

Economic theory suggests stabilizing indices by examining proportional changes.

The series in Figure 10.1 is clearly nonstationary. We have seen in Chapter 9 that one device for handling nonstationarity is to difference the series. However, as described in Example 9.3, when dealing with indices it often makes more sense from an economic standpoint to work with proportional changes. For this relatively short time period, it is difficult to determine that proportional changes are more useful than ordinary changes based only on the data. However, on one hand, index units are not economically meaningful quantities and thus neither are changes in index units. For example, in the early part of the series, when the index is around 60, 5 units represents $5/60 \approx 8.3\%$ of the index. In contrast, in the latter part of the series, when the index is around 100, 5 units represents only 5% of the index. If the index represents a fixed standard of living or stable "breadbasket" of goods, then the amount of goods that 5 units represents depends on its share of the index. On the other hand, proportional changes signify growth in the index and thus are economically meaningful quantities. This shows how the underlying theory (economic theory, in this case) associated with the data can be used to help determine the form of the model.

Our goal is detect patterns in the data and provide models to represent these patterns. From the Figure 10.2 time series plot of the proportional changes, it appears that many of the major trends in the series have been filtered out. The corresponding control chart in Figure 10.3 gives further credence to this argument. However, a careful inspection of the control chart reveals some subtle patterns in the proportional change series. The middle horizontal line is at height $\bar{y}$; this serves as a reference line for computing the deviations from the mean. In particular, in Figure 10.3 note that the 2nd, 3rd, ..., 10th proportional changes are all above the average, $\bar{y}$. The 11th, 12th and 13th are all below $\bar{y}$, and so on. A visual inspection of the control chart seems to imply that there are some mild patterns in the observations.

One way to think about this pattern is to reason that if an observation, y_{t-1}, is large, then there is a tendency for the next observation, y_t, to be large. Here, "large" refers to relative to the mean. One way to identify graphically

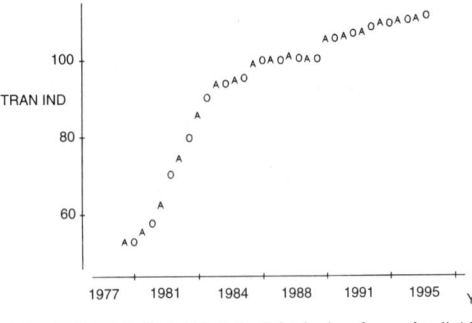

FIGURE 10.1 Total Rail Freight Index from April 1977 to October 1993. This series appears to be nonstationary. Here, "A" is for April and "O" is for October.
Source: Bureau of Labor Statistics

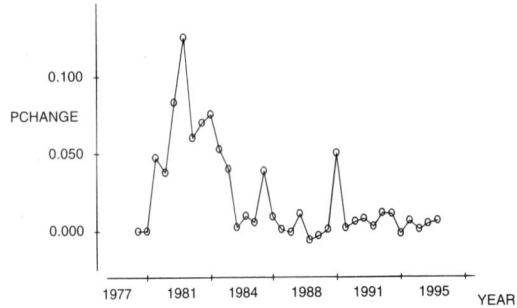

FIGURE 10.2 The proportional changes of the index appear to be stationary.

A scatter plot of the current versus immediate past value of a series helps identify trends over time.

this relationship is through the use of a scatter plot of the current versus the immediate past value of the series. As we have seen in cross-sectional data analysis, the scatter plot is a powerful tool for graphically identifying relationships between two variables. Here, the second variable is the lagged value of the first variable.

Explicitly, if the points of the proportional change of the transportation index are labeled by $y_1, y_2, \ldots, y_T$, then this scatter plot is a plot of y_2 versus y_1, y_3 versus $y_2, \ldots, y_T$ versus y_{T-1}. To illustrate, Table 10.1 lists the first five observations, together with their lagged values.

TABLE 10.1 First Five Values of the Total Rail Freight Index with Proportional Changes and Lagged Values

t	0	1	2	3	4
Index	53.0	53.0	55.5	57.6	62.4
Lagged index	*	53.0	53.0	55.5	57.6
Proportional change (y_t)	*	0	.0472	.0378	.0833
Lagged proportional change (y_{t-1})	*	*	0	.0472	.0378

Here, the asterisk (*) means that the value is missing, that is, no observation is available. From the scatter plot of this data, in Figure 10.4, we see that there is a definite linear relationship between the current and immediate past value of the proportional changes.

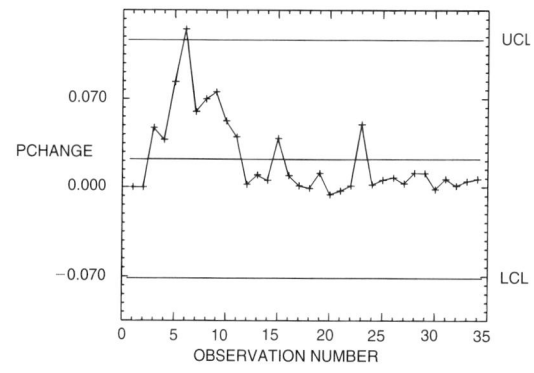

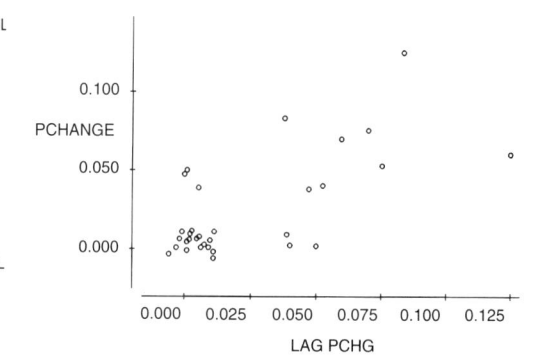

FIGURE 10.3 The control chart of the proportional changes of the index reveals some subtle patterns through time.

FIGURE 10.4 This scatter plot reveals a linear relationship between the proportional change of the index and its immediate preceding value.

Autocorrelations

An autocorrelation is the correlation between a variable and its lagged version.

Scatter plots are useful because they graphically display nonlinear, as well as linear, relationships between two variables. However, in situations such as the Standard & Poor's daily index example that will be presented in Section 10.5, no clear tendencies may be visually evident and a summary measure of some sort is required. The correlation statistic can be used to measure the relation between two variables.

Recall that when dealing with cross-sectional data, we summarized relations between a $\{y_t\}$ and an $\{x_t\}$ variable using the correlation statistic

$$r = \frac{\sum_{t=1}^{T} (x_t - \bar{x})(y_t - \bar{y})}{(T-1)\, s_x\, s_y}.$$

We now mimic this statistic using the series $\{y_{t-1}\}$ in place of $\{x_t\}$. With this replacement, use $\bar{y}$ in place of $\bar{x}$ and, for the denominator, use s_y in place of s_x. With this last substitution, we have $(T-1)\, s_y^2 = \sum_{t=1}^{T} (y_t - \bar{y})^2$. Our resulting correlation statistic is

$$r_1 = \frac{\sum_{t=2}^{T} (y_t - \bar{y})(y_{t-1} - \bar{y})}{\sum_{t=1}^{T} (y_t - \bar{y})^2}.$$

When one variable is a lagged version of the other, this statistic is referred to as an *autocorrelation*, that is, a correlation of the series upon itself. This statistic summarizes the linear relationship between $\{y_t\}$ and $\{y_{t-1}\}$, that is, observations that are one time unit apart. In general, it is also useful to summarize the linear relationship between observations that are k time units apart, $\{y_t\}$ and $\{y_{t-k}\}$. We call this summary statistic the *lag k autocorrelation* statistic, defined to be

$$r_k = \frac{\sum_{t=k+1}^{T} (y_t - \bar{y})(y_{t-k} - \bar{y})}{\sum_{t=1}^{T} (y_t - \bar{y})^2}. \tag{10.1}$$

Properties of autocorrelations are similar to correlations. Just as with the usual correlation statistic r, the denominator, $\sum_{t=1}^{T} (y_t - \bar{y})^2$, is always nonnegative and hence does not change the sign of the numerator. It is a rescaling device, included so that r_k always lies on or between -1 and 1. Thus, when we interpret r_k, a value near $-1, 0$ and 1, means, respectively, a strong negative, near null or strong positive relationship between y_t and y_{t-k}. If there is a positive relationship between y_t and y_{t-1}, then $r_1 > 0$ and the process is said to be positively autocorrelated. For example, Table 10.2 displays the first five autocorrelations for the proportional changes of the Total Rail Freight Index. These autocorrelations indicate that there seems to be a positive relationship between adjacent observations.

TABLE 10.2 Autocorrelations for the Proportional Changes of the Total Rail Freight Index

k	1	2	3	4	5
r_k	0.668	0.547	0.430	0.284	0.199

10.2 AUTOREGRESSIVE MODELS OF ORDER ONE

Model Definition and Properties

An autoregressive model of order one, AR(1), is a process that can be modeled using regression with the lagged dependent variable as the predictor variable.

In Figure 10.4 we noted the strong relationship between the current and immediate past values of the proportional changes of the transportation index. This suggests using y_{t-1} to explain y_t in a regression model. Using previous values of a series to predict current values of a series is termed, not surprisingly, an *autoregression*. When only the immediate past is used as a predictor, the model is said to be an *autoregressive model of order one* and is denoted by $AR(1)$. It is convenient to formally write the model as

$$y_t = \beta_0 + \beta_1 y_{t-1} + e_t, \qquad t = 2, \ldots, T \tag{10.2}$$

where the process $\{e_t\}$ is a random process and β_0 and β_1 are unknown parameters.

In the $AR(1)$ model, the parameter β_0 may be any fixed constant. However, the parameter β_1 is restricted to be between -1 and 1. By making this restriction, it can be established that the $AR(1)$ series $\{y_t\}$ is stationary. Note that if $\beta_1 = 1$, then the model is a random walk and hence is nonstationary. This is because, if $\beta_1 = 1$, then equation (10.2) may be rewritten as

Equation (10.2) yields a random walk model using $\beta_1 = 1$. To define an AR(1), we restrict β_1 to lie in $(-1,1)$ so that the model is stationary.

$$y_t - y_{t-1} = \beta_0 + e_t, \qquad t = 2, \ldots, T.$$

If the differences of a series form a random process, then the series itself must be a random walk.

Equation (10.2) is useful in the discussion of model properties. We can view an $AR(1)$ model as a generalization of both a random process and a random walk model. If $\beta_1 = 0$, then equation (10.2) reduces to a random process. If $\beta_1 = 1$, then equation (10.2) is a random walk.

A stationary process where there is a linear relationship between y_{t-2} and y_t is said to be *autoregressive of order 2*, and similarly for higher order processes. Discussion of these higher order processes is in Section 10.6.

Identification

We can identify an AR(1) model through its auto-correlation structure. For an AR(1) model, we have Corr· $(y_t, y_{t-k}) = \beta_1^k$.

When examining the data, how does one recognize that an autoregressive model may be a suitable candidate model? First, an autoregressive model is stationary and thus a control chart is a good device to examine graphically the data to search for stability. Second, in principle, adjacent realizations of an AR(1) model should be related. To a certain extent, this can be detected visually by a scatter plot of current versus immediate past values of the series. Third, we can recognize an AR(1) model through its autocorrelation structure, as follows.

Another useful property of the model is that the correlation between observations that are k time units apart turns out to be β_1^k. Stated another way, a mathematical result that we will use is that the theoretical lag k autocorrelation, ρ_k, defined by Corr(y_t, y_{t-k}), is equal to β_1^k for any value of t. Hence, in principle, the absolute values of the autocorrelations of an AR(1) are getting smaller as the lag time k increases. In fact, they are decreasing at a geometric rate. We remark that for a random process, we have $\beta_1 = 0$, and thus ρ_k should be equal to zero for all lags k.

To identify a sta-tionary model, we match the ob-served autocorre-lations $\{r_k\}$ to the theoretical auto-correlations $\{\rho_k\}$.

As an aid in model identification, we use the idea of matching the observed autocorrelations r_k to quantities that we expect from the theory, ρ_k. As previously noted, under the random process model, the lag k autocorrelation coefficient should be approximately zero for each lag k. Even though each r_k is algebraically bounded by -1 and 1, the question arises, how large does r_k need to be, in absolute value, to be considered significantly different from zero? The answer to this type of question is given in terms of the statistic's standard error. It turns out that, under the hypothesis of no autocorrelation, a good approximation to the standard error of the lag k autocorrelation statistic is

$$se(r_k) \approx \frac{1}{\sqrt{T}}.$$

Thus, if r_k exceeds $2\,se(r_k) = 2/T^{1/2}$ in absolute value, it may be considered to be significantly nonzero.

As an example, there are $T = 33$ proportional changes available for the Total Rail Freight Index example. Is a random process model a good candidate to represent this series? The autocorrelations are given in Table 10.2. For a random process model, we expect each autocorrelation r_k to be close to zero but note that, for example, $r_1 = 0.668$. The estimated standard error of each autocorrelation is

$$se(r_k) = \frac{1}{\sqrt{33}} = 0.174.$$

Thus, r_1 is $0.668/0.174 = 3.84$ standard errors above zero. Using normal theory as a reference distribution, this difference is significant, implying that a random process is not a suitable candidate model. Is the autoregressive model of order one a suitable choice? Well, because $\rho_k = \beta_1^k$, a good estimate of $\beta_1 = \rho_1$ is $r_1 = 0.668$. If this is the case, then under the $AR(1)$ model, another estimate of ρ_k is $(0.668)^k$. Thus, we have two estimates of ρ_k; (i) r_k, which does not depend on a parametric model and (ii) $(r_1)^k$, which depends on the $AR(1)$ model. To illustrate, see Table 10.3. Given that the estimated standard error of each autocorrelation is $se(r_k) = 0.174$, there seems to be a good match between the two autocorrelations. Because of this match, in Section 10.3 we will discuss how to fit the $AR(1)$ model to this set of data and to check to see if the representation is a good one.

TABLE 10.3 Theoretical versus Estimated Autocorrelations for the Proportional Changes of the Total Rail Freight Index

k	1	2	3	4	5
ρ_k	0.668	$0.668^2 = 0.446$	$0.668^3 = 0.298$	$0.668^4 = 0.199$	$0.668^5 = 0.133$
r_k	0.668	0.547	0.430	0.284	0.199

Meandering Process

A process is meandering if adjacent points are related to one another.

Many processes display the pattern of adjacent points being related to one another. Thinking of the process evolving as a river, Roberts (1991) picturesquely describes such processes as *meandering*. The notion of a meandering process is fundamental to the problem of forecasting future values of a process. To supplement this intuitive notion, we say that a process is meandering if the lag one autocorrelation of the series is positive. For example, from the control chart and the scatter plot in Figures 10.3 and 10.4, it seems clear that the proportional changes of the Total Rail Freight Index is a good example of a meandering series. Indeed, an $AR(1)$ model with a positive slope coefficient is a meandering process.

C9_BEER

What about the case when the slope coefficient approaches one, resulting in a random walk? Consider the Beer Price Index in Example 9.1 that can be modeled as a random walk with a downward drift. It seems clear that any point in the process is highly related to each adjacent point in the process. For example, Figure 10.5 shows that there is a strong linear relationship between the current and immediate past value of the adjusted Beer Price Index. Because of the strong linear relationship in Figure 10.5, we will use the terminology meandering process for a data set that may be modeled using a random walk.

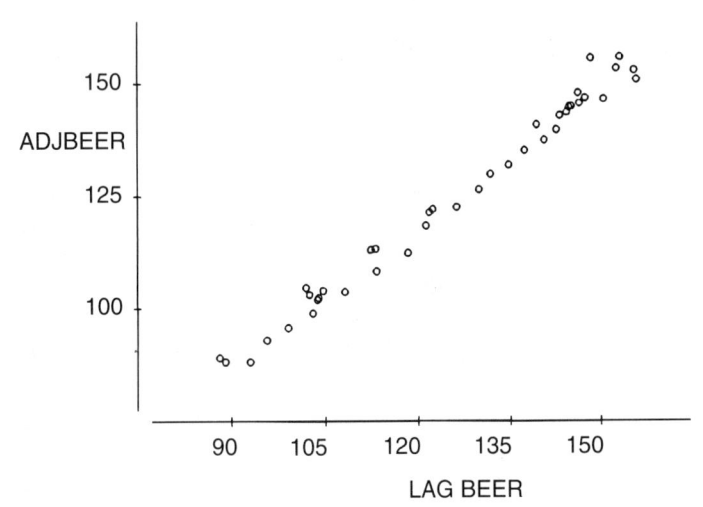

FIGURE 10.5 Current versus immediate past adjusted Beer Price Index.

In Chapter 9, we saw that the random walk is a nonstationary model. In particular, the variance, and possibly the mean, of a random walk depend on time. In the same fashion, it can be checked that the theoretical correlation between two lagged values of the series, say y_t and y_{t-k}, depends not only on the lag k but also on the time t. Thus, autocorrelations for a nonstationary series such as the random walk depend on time. However, for any series, we can always compute the observed autocorrelations from the data as if they do not depend on time. For example, Table 10.4 presents the first ten autocorrelations computed from the Beer Price Index series.

TABLE 10.4   Autocorrelations for the Adjusted Price of Beer

k	1	2	3	4	5	6	7	8	9	10
r_k	0.934	0.855	0.782	0.702	0.601	0.507	0.427	0.352	0.271	0.182

Series whose observed autocorrelations are close to one and do not decrease quickly may be nonstationary. The random walk is one such nonstationary series.

The data are clearly from a meandering process. From this table, we would entertain either an $AR(1)$ or a random walk model to represent the data. Following this line of logic, it is evident that any random walk model is a meandering process. Because the observed autocorrelations from a random walk model should be positive, this suggests another way of identifying a random walk process. First, for a random walk, each observed autocorrelation is close to one. Second, autocorrelations need not decrease geometrically. For a series whose observed autocorrelations have these two traits, one should consider using the random walk model.

10.3 ESTIMATION AND DIAGNOSTIC CHECKING

We use conditional least squares to determine estimates of the intercept and slope.

Having identified a tentative model, the task now at hand is to fit the model to the data as closely as possible, within the general structure of the model. For the $AR(1)$ model, this means determining estimates of the values of β_0 and β_1 that provide the best fit for the data. In this section, we use the method of *conditional least squares* to determine the estimates b_0 and b_1. The method of least squares was introduced in Section 3.1. Here, we are actually using the least squares principle to find estimates that provide the best fit of an observation conditional on the previous observation. Using equation (3.1), we have that some reasonable approximations of the estimates are given by

$$b_1 \approx r_1 \quad \text{and} \quad b_0 \approx \bar{y}\,(1 - r_1).$$

Residuals from the model fit can be used to verify model validity.

From equation (10.2), we know that if we have the correct model and the correct parameters β_0 and β_1, then we can compute the errors. The true errors, $e_t = y_t - (\beta_0 + \beta_1 y_{t-1})$, can be described as a random process. If we have only estimated parameters, b_0 and b_1, we can compute the residuals

$$\hat{e}_t = y_t - (b_0 + b_1 y_{t-1}).$$

Note, without further approximations, that the first residual $\hat{e}_1$, is not available because y_0 ($=y_{t-1}$ when $t = 1$) is not available. As in cross-sectional regression, the idea is that if the specified model is correct and if the estimated parameters are close to the true (unknown) parameters, then the residuals should behave similarly to a random process.

The important idea behind residual analysis is that we search for any remaining patterns in the residuals. Often times, any patterns discovered will lead us to reformulate our ideas of what the underlying model should be. In cross-sectional regression, we checked for relationships between the residuals and other predictor variables. With longitudinal data, we must also search for relationships over time.

To check that residuals closely resemble a random process, create a control chart and compute the autocorrelations of residuals.

The fact that the residuals should behave similarly to a random process can be checked by looking at a control chart and an autocorrelation function. The control chart establishes the stationarity and the autocorrelation function verifies the lack of milder patterns through time.

Residuals are also used to estimate the variability inherent in the model.

The residuals also play an important role in calculating standard errors associated with model parameter estimates. From equation (10.2), we see that the unobserved errors are driving the updating of the new observations. Indeed, in principle, if we knew the entire history of the errors, then this would provide any source of information about the current observation. Thus, it makes sense to focus on the variance of the errors and, as in cross-sectional data, we define

$$\sigma^2 = \sigma_e^2 = \text{Var}\,(e).$$

In cross-sectional regression, because the predictor variables are nonstochastic, the variance of the response (σ_y^2) equals the variance of the errors (σ_e^2). For the $AR(1)$ model, a mathematical relationship establishes $\sigma_e^2 = \sigma_y^2 (1 - \beta_1^2)$, so that $\sigma_e^2 < \sigma_y^2$. Thus, knowing β_1 and σ_e^2 is sufficient to calculate the variance of a response y.

To estimate σ_e^2, basic introductory statistics would suggest using $\Sigma_{t=1}^T$ $(e_t - \bar{e})^2 / (T - 1)$. However, the true errors $\{e_t\}$ are never observed. Thus, we use the residuals in place of the errors and define

$$s^2 = \frac{\sum_{t=2}^T (\hat{e}_t - \bar{\hat{e}})^2}{T - 3} \qquad (10.3)$$

as our estimate of σ_e^2. Note, in equation (10.3), that the first residual $\hat{e}_1$ is assumed to be not available and thus the number of residuals available is $T - 1$. Because of losing the first residual, the average of the residuals is not automatically zero and thus $\bar{\hat{e}}$ is included in the sum of squares. Further, the denominator in the right hand side of equation (10.3) is still the number of observations minus the number of parameters, keeping in mind the proviso that the "number of observations" is $T - 1$ and the "number of parameters" is two. As in the cross-sectional regression context, we refer to s^2 as the *mean square error*.

To illustrate, the proportional changes of the transportation index were fit using an $AR(1)$ model. The estimated equation turned out to be

$$\text{PCHÂNGE}_t = 0.079 + 0.674\,\text{PCHÂNGE}_{t-1}$$
$$std\ errors \qquad (0.0054) \qquad\qquad (0.134)$$

with $s = 0.0238$. The standard errors, given in parentheses, were computed using the method of conditional least squares. For example, the t-ratio for b_1 is $0.674/0.134 = 5.0$ indicting that the immediate past response is an important predictor of the current response.

Residuals were computed as $\hat{e}_t = \text{PCHANGE}_t - (0.0079 + 0.674$ $\text{PCHANGE}_{t-1})$. The control chart of the residuals in Figure 10.6 reveals no apparent patterns. Several autocorrelations of residuals are presented in Table 10.5. Recall, with 33 observations, that the approximate standard error is $se(r_k)$ $= (33)^{-1/2} = 0.174$. All autocorrelations presented are less than one standard error in absolute value. This provides another indication that there are no apparent trends in the residuals, a property of the random process.

TABLE 10.5 Autocorrelations of Residuals from the $AR(1)$ Model—Proportional Changes of the Total Rail Freight Index

k	1	2	3	4	5
r_k	−0.076	0.105	0.201	0.066	0.069

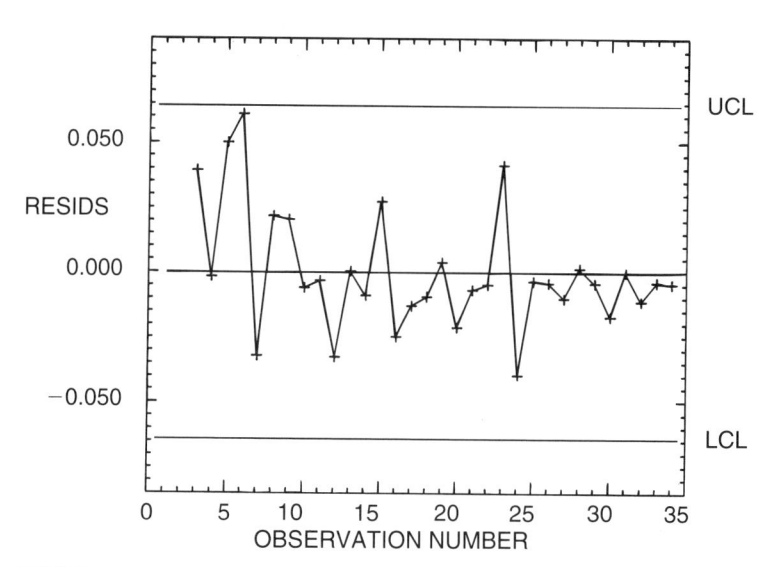

FIGURE 10.6 Control chart of residuals from the $AR(1)$ model—proportional changes of the Total Rail Freight Index.

10.4 SMOOTHING AND PREDICTION

Having identified, fit, and checked the identification of the model, we now proceed to basic inference. Recall that by inference we mean the process of using the data set to make statements about the nature of the world. To make statements about the series, analysts often examine the values fitted under the model, called the smoothed series. The *smoothed* series is the estimated expected value of the series given the past. For the $AR(1)$ model, the smoothed series is

$$\hat{y}_t = b_0 + b_1 y_{t-1}.$$

In Figure 10.7, the solid line represents the actual proportional change of the Total Rail Freight Index and the dashed line is the corresponding smoothed series. Because the smoothed series is the actual series with the estimated noise component removed, the smoothed series can be interpreted to represent the "real" value of the series. Note that the smoothed series varies less than the actual series. For contrast with cross-sectional data, recall that we often plot $\{y_t\}$ versus $\{\hat{y}_t\}$ to understand the strength of the relationship between the observed and fitted values.

The most important application of models arising from longitudinal data is the forecasting, or prediction, of future values of the series.

Typically, the most important application of time series models is the forecasting, or prediction, of future values of the series. From equation (10.2), the immediate future value of the series is $y_{T+1} = \beta_0 + \beta_1 y_T + e_{T+1}$. Because the series $\{e_t\}$ is random, our best estimate of e_{T+1} is its mean, zero. Thus, if the

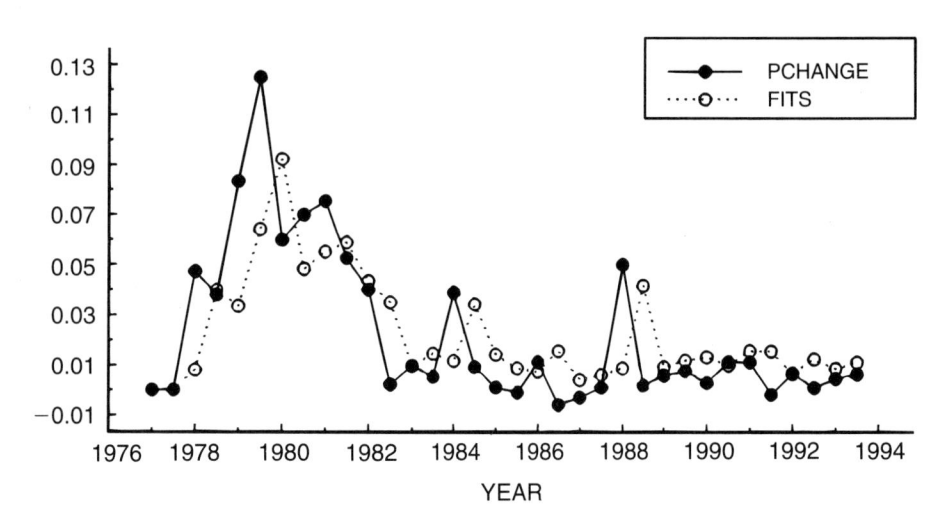

FIGURE 10.7 Smoothed proportional changes of the Total Rail Freight Index superimposed on the actual proportional changes.

estimates b_0 and b_1 are close to the true parameters β_0 and β_1, then a desirable estimate of the series at time $T + 1$ is $\hat{y}_{T+1} = b_0 + b_1 y_T$. Similarly, one can recursively compute an estimate for the series k time points in the future, y_{T+k}, using the equation

$$\hat{y}_{T+k} = b_0 + b_1 \hat{y}_{T+k-1}. \tag{10.4}$$

To get an idea of the error in using $\hat{y}_{T+1} = b_0 + b_1 y_T$ to estimate the unknown (at time T) observation y_{T+1}, we can assume that the error in using b_0 and b_1 to estimate β_0 and β_1 is negligible. With this assumption, the forecast error is

$$y_{T+1} - \hat{y}_{T+1} = (\beta_0 + \beta_1 y_T + e_{T+1}) - (b_0 + b_1 y_T) \approx e_{T+1}. \tag{10.5}$$

Thus, the variance of this forecast error is approximately Var$(e) = \sigma^2$. Similarly, it can be shown that the approximate variance of the forecast error $\hat{y}_{T+k} - y_{T+k}$ is $\sigma^2 (1 + \beta_1^2 + \ldots + \beta_1^{2(k-1)})$.

From this variance calculation and the approximate normality, we have that an approximate prediction interval for a k-step ahead forecast is

$$\hat{y}_{T+k} \pm (t\text{-value}) \, s \, \sqrt{1 + b_1^2 + \ldots + b_1^{2(k-1)}}. \tag{10.6}$$

Here, the t-value is a percentile from the t-distribution using $df = T - 2$ degrees of freedom. The percentile is $1 - (1 - \text{prediction level})/2$. For example, for 95% prediction intervals, we would have t-value ≈ 2. Thus, one and two step 95%

prediction intervals are:

one-step: $\qquad \hat{y}_{T+1} \pm 2\,s$

two-step: $\qquad \hat{y}_{T+2} \pm 2\,s\,(1 + b_1^2)^{1/2}$.

Figure 10.8 illustrates forercasts for the proportional changes of the Total Rail Freight Index.

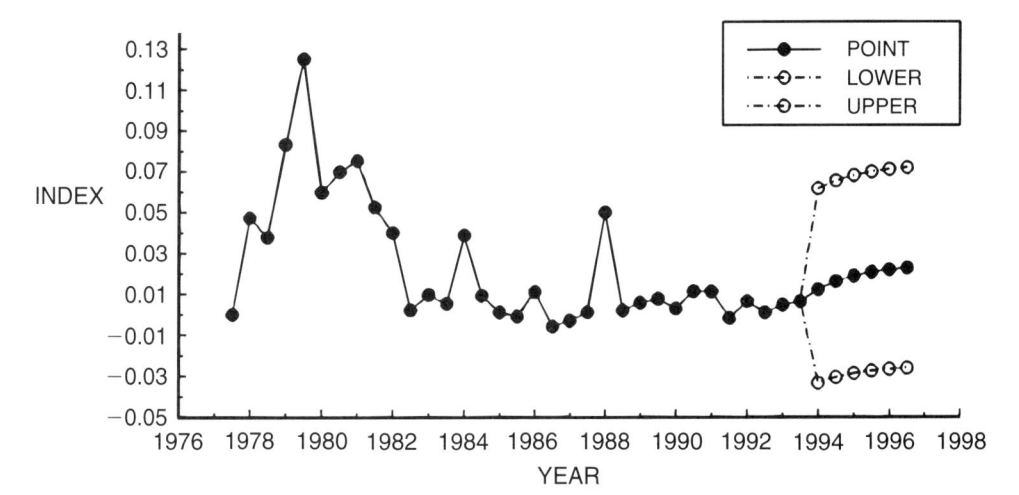

FIGURE 10.8 The Total Rail Freight Index. Values from 1977–1993 are actual. For 1994–1996, the middle series gives point forecasts using the *AR*(1) model. The upper and lower lines yield an approximate 95% prediction band.

10.5 CASE STUDY: 1986 STANDARD & POOR'S DAILY RETURNS

C10_INDX

The Standard & Poor's Index

The data for this example consists of the 253 daily returns for the calendar year 1986 of the Standard and Poor's (S&P) equally weighted index. This data set was created as follows. Out of the 365 days in calendar year 1986, there were 253 days on which the exchanges were open and stocks were traded. For each trading day an average of the closing, or last, price of various stocks was taken to form the S&P *equally weighted* index for that day. There are, of course, several indices to measure the market's overall "worth." The equally weighted index is created by assuming that $1 is invested in each stock. The return for the day is defined to be the ratio of the current day's index to the previous day's index, minus one. To calculate the return for the first trading day of the year, we used the value of the index for the last trading day of 1985.

The control chart of the series in Figure 10.9 provides some reassurance that the series is stationary. There are three points below the lower control line that warrant further consideration in the modeling. Such points are atypical and are termed outliers.

Figure 10.10 is a scatter plot of current versus immediate past returns. The horizontal and vertical lines mark the average. From the scatter plot, it is difficult to detect visually any relationship between the response and its lagged value. Because of the large number of observations, the eye has a difficult time establishing patterns that are not very strong. It is precisely in these situations that a statistic, such as an autocorrelation, is useful. Statistics numerically summarize the tendencies of the data and are not hampered by the size of the data set. It turns out that the lag one autocorrelation coefficient for this data set is $r_1 = 0.236$. Given the lack of tendencies visually detectable in the scatter plot, this is surprisingly large compared to its approximate standard error $se(r_1) = (253)^{-1/2} \approx 0.06$.

There is a concern as to whether the three outliers are causing the statistic to be much larger than would be produced by the rest of the data set. One approach is to delete these outlying observations and recalculate the statistic based on the remaining observations. However, deleting observations in a time series data set is awkward because observations, even aberrant ones, can influence adjacent, in time, observations. As an alternative, we now introduce a *nonparametric* estimate of the lag one autocorrelation.

Deleting unusual data points in time series data is awkward because each observation can affect adjacent observations.

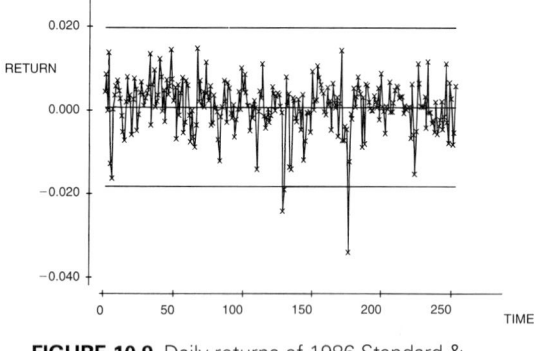

FIGURE 10.9 Daily returns of 1986 Standard & Poor's Index. Control limits are plus or minus three standard deviations. *Source: Standard and Poor's Compustat*

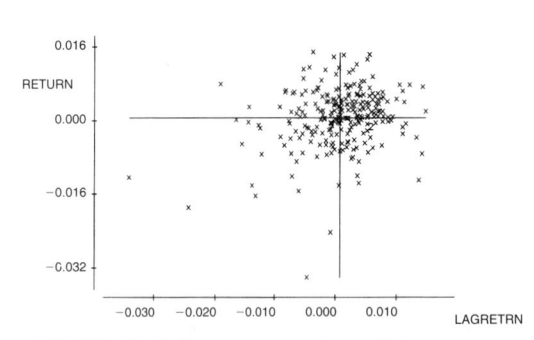

FIGURE 10.10 Current versus immediate past returns. Horizontal and vertical lines mark the average return.

A Nonparametric Autocorrelation Statistic (Optional)

The summary measure r_k is often termed a *parametric* statistic as it is closely related to the autoregressive model in equation (10.2). An alternative summary measure can be developed using the ranks of the observations. As in Section

Nonparametric statistics are constructed by statisticians so as not to rely heavily on any parametric structure. Often, these statistics are robust to model deviations, such as outliers.

3.5, we let R_t be the rank of y_t. A *nonparametric* correlation statistic can be defined using the usual correlation statistic but replacing the observations by their corresponding ranks. This nonparametric statistic is called a *Spearman's correlation* statistic, named for its inventor. Formally, define the Spearman's lag k autocorrelation statistic by

$$sr_k = \frac{\sum_{t=k+1}^{T} (R_t - \bar{R})(R_{t-k} - \bar{R})}{\sum_{t=1}^{T} (R_t - \bar{R})^2} . \tag{10.7}$$

The statistic sr_k also lies on or between -1 and 1 and the interpretation of sr_k is similar to r_k. For different data sets, r_k and sr_k may highlight different aspects of the data.

For example, for the data in Figure 10.9, it turns out that $r_1 = 0.232$ even though $sr_1 = 0.175$. Both statistics report a positive lag one autocorrelation but r_1 gives heavier weight to the three outlying points that are in the lower left hand quadrant. Both the nonparametric and parametric yield qualitatively similar information. In this way, the two different techniques strengthen and reinforce one another.

Inference Using an *AR*(1) Model

As noted, the process seems to be stationary as evidenced by the control chart. In examining the autocorrelation structure, note that the approximate standard errors for each autocorrelation is $1/(T)^{1/2} = 1/(253)^{1/2} \approx 0.06210$. The estimated lag one autocorrelation coefficient is $r_1 = 0.236$, which is almost four standard errors above zero. It turns out that the other autocorrelations are all within one half standard error from zero. Were we to entertain the random process as a model, we would expect $\rho_1 = 0$. Because r_1 is almost four standard errors above zero, the random process model does not seem to be adequate.

Now, recall that under the autoregressive model of order one, the theoretical lag k autocorrelation coefficient is $\rho_k = \beta_1^k$. Thinking of r_1 as a good estimate of β_1, we see that higher order autocorrelations are indistinguishable from zero. That is, we expect ρ_k to be about $(0.236)^k$ which is less than one approximate standard error even for $k = 2$. Thus, the fact that only the first lag autocorrelation coefficient is significant is not inconsistent with the data even though the $AR(1)$ model anticipates positive autocorrelations at all lags.

Using the autoregressive model of order one, we now may proceed to estimate this model. The fitted model is presented in equation (10.8). From the fitted values of the parameters, residuals were calculated. The residuals were plotted through time and used to calculate the autocorrelation structure to search for additional patterns. In this case, all autocorrelations of the residuals were less than $1/(T)^{1/2}$, the approximate standard error, and hence provided no evidence that there is additional autocorrelation structure in the residuals. Because there are no additional patterns, this suggests that the residuals, and hence the underlying errors, closely resemble a random process.

Having satisfied the diagnostic checks, we proceed to the inference stage. From the residuals, an estimate of the standard deviation of the errors was computed. In this case, it turns out to be approximately 0.00615. This was calculated directed from equation (10.4). It is interesting to note that, with $s_y = 0.00632$ and $b_1 = 0.233$, we have $s_y(1 - b_1^2)^{1/2} \approx 0.00615$, as anticipated. This comes from putting estimates into the theoretical relationship $\sigma_y^2(1 - \beta_1^2) = \sigma_e^2$.

To summarize, the final estimated equation turned out to be

$$\text{RET}\hat{\text{U}}\text{RN}_t = 0.000516 + 0.233 \, \text{RETURN}_{t-1} \tag{10.8}$$

$$std \; errors \quad (0.0039) \quad (0.062)$$

with $s = 0.0062$. As noted, $s_y = 0.0063$, indicating that the amount of variability reduced was small. For example, the adjusted coefficient of determination is $R_a^2 = 1 - s^2/s_y^2 = 4\%$. How do we reconcile the large t-ratio ($3.8 = 0.233/0.062$) with the small R_a^2? They are saying two different things. We interpret $R_a^2 = 4\%$ as saying that the market is largely unpredictable. Much of the variation on a day-to-day basis is unpredictable given only previous daily returns. However, over the long run, there is a significant relationship between returns that are adjacent in time.

In principle, this long run relationship should help us to forecast the behavior of the market as measured by the S&P Index. However, in practice it has been found that costs of buying and selling equities (called *transactions costs*) are large enough to prevent us from taking advantage of these slight tendencies in the swings of the market. Indeed, there exists financial economic theory that states that if the market were predictable, many investors would attempt to take advantage of these predictions, thus forcing unpredictability. For example, suppose a statistical model reliably predicted mutual fund A to increase twofold over the next 18 months. Then, the *no arbitrage* principle in financial economics states that several alert investors, armed with information from the statistical model, would bid to buy mutual fund A, thus causing the price to increase because demand is increasing. These alert investors would continue to purchase until the price of mutual fund A rose to the point where the return was equivalent to other investment opportunities in the same risk class. Thus, any advantages produced by the statistical model would disappear rapidly, thus eliminating this advantage.

Not all statistically significant relationships are practically important.

The S&P Index analysis illustrates a relationship that is sometimes called *statistically significant but not practically significant*. This is not to suggest that statistics is not practical (heaven forbid!). Instead, statistics in and of itself does not explicitly recognize factors, such as economic, psychological and so on, that may be extremely important in any given situation. It is up to the analyst to interpret the statistical analysis in light of these factors.

10.6 GENERAL AUTOREGRESSIVE MODELS

C10_MCPI

The autoregressive model of order one allows us to predict the current behavior of an observation based on its immediate past value. However, in some applications, there are also important effects of observations that are more distant in the past than simply the immediate preceding observation.

To illustrate, consider the medical component of the Consumer Price Index (CPI). The CPI is a breadbasket of goods and services whose price is measured by the Bureau of Labor Statistics. By measuring this breadbasket periodically, consumers get an idea of the change in prices over time which, among other things, serves as a proxy for inflation. The CPI itself is composed of many components, reflecting the relative importance of each component to the overall economy. Here, we study the medical component of the CPI, the fastest growing part of the overall breadbasket since 1967. The data we consider are quarterly values of the medical component of the CPI (MCPI) over a 41 year period from 1950 to 1990, inclusive. Over this period, the index rose from 47.0 to 472.9. This represents more than a tenfold increase over the 41 year period which translates roughly into a 1.4% quarterly increase.

Figure 10.11 is a time series plot of quarterly percentage changes in MCPI. Note that we have already switched from the nonstationary index itself to percentage changes. (The index is nonstationary because it exhibits such a tremendous growth over the period considered.) From this time series plot, we note that there are still some aspects of nonstationarity. This is mainly a feature of the large increases in the MCPI beginning in the late 1970s, large relative to earlier time periods. Further evidence of this nonstationarity is in the table of autocorrelations in Table 10.6. Here, we see large autocorrelations for the

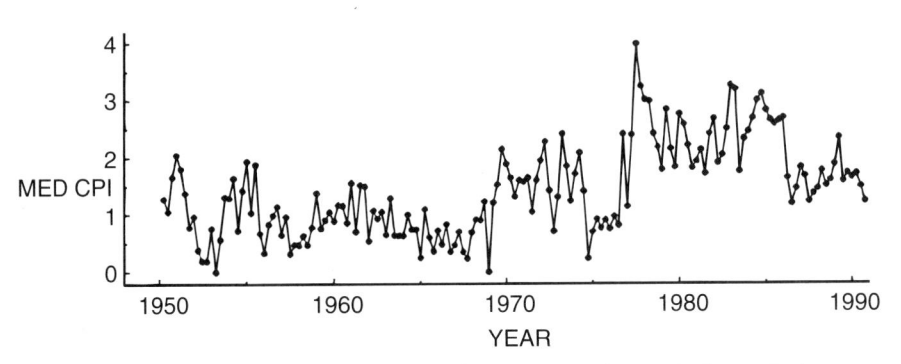

FIGURE 10.11 Time series plot of quarterly percentage changes in the medical component of the Consumer Price Index. *Source: Bureau of Labor Statistics*

TABLE 10.6 Autocorrelations of the Percentage Changes and the Differences of
Percentage Changes of MCPI

Lag	1	2	3	4	5	6	7	8	9	10
Percentage changes	0.766	0.664	0.642	0.610	0.561	0.464	0.439	0.417	0.375	0.387
Differences of percentage changes	−0.283	−0.169	0.025	0.034	0.102	−0.155	−0.006	0.040	−0.118	0.082

percentage changes that do not decrease quickly as the lag k increases. In contrast, the autocorrelations for the differences in percentage changes decrease, and although still significantly different from zero, do not indicate nonstationarity.

For the 41 years available, we have $T = 164$ quarterly observations. Thus, with the approximate standard error, $1/(T)^{1/2} \approx 0.08$, we see that the first two lags are significantly different from zero. This suggests tentatively fitting an $AR(1)$ model. The result of this tentative model identification is:

$$\hat{y}_t = 0.0015 - 0.283\, y_{t-1},$$

$$std\ errors\quad (0.041)\quad (0.076)$$

where y_t represents the difference in percentage changes. Thus, the coefficient associated with the lag one variable is strongly significant, as foreshadowed by the table of autocorrelations. However, it turns out that the residuals from this model are not devoid of patterns through time. For example, the correlation between the residuals and y_{t-2} is -0.261.

This strong relationship suggests introducing y_{t-2} into the model specification, yielding a model of the form:

$$y_t = \beta_0 + \beta_1 y_{t-1} + \beta_2 y_{t-2} + e_t.$$

This model is a special case of the general *autoregressive model of order p, AR(p)*, defined by

$$y_t = \beta_0 + \beta_1 y_{t-1} + \ldots + \beta_p y_{t-p} + e_t. \tag{10.9}$$

As a convention, when data analysts specify an $AR(p)$ model, they include not only y_{t-p} as a predictor variable, but also the intervening lags, $y_{t-1}, \ldots, y_{t-p+1}$. The exceptions to this convention are the seasonal autoregressive models that will be introduced in Section 11.3.

As described in Section 10.3, in this text we use the conditional least squares for estimating autoregressive parameters. Other techniques, often more computationally intensive, are available on computer statistical packages. For large data sets containing several hundred observations and a well-specified model, the choice of the estimation technique is not of overriding practical importance. Otherwise, there can be large differences in parameter estimates for different estimation techniques. See Abraham and Ledolter (1983, Section 5.6) for further discussions of this issue.

To illustrate, the conditional least squares estimates for the $AR(2)$ model are:

$$\hat{y}_t = -0.0010 - 0.358\, y_{t-1} - 0.271\, y_{t-2}.$$

$$\textit{std errors} \quad (0.040) \quad (0.076) \quad\quad (0.076)$$

Identification and Partial Autocorrelations

Matching a series with a particular choice of an $AR(p)$ model requires several steps. First, as emphasized in Chapter 9, the series must first be converted to stationarity. Second, the autocorrelation patterns of the series are examined. For all autoregressive series, the absolute values of the autocorrelations should become small as the lag k increases. In the case that the autocorrelations decrease approximately like a geometric series, an $AR(1)$ model may be identified. Unfortunately, for the other types of autoregressive series, the rules of thumb for identifying the series from the autocorrelations become more cloudy. One device that is useful for identifying the order of an autoregressive series is the *partial autocorrelation function.*

Just like autocorrelations, we now define a *partial autocorrelation* for specific lag k. Consider the model

$$y_t = \beta_{0,k} + \beta_{1,k} y_{t-1} + \ldots + \beta_{k,k} y_{t-k} + \epsilon_t.$$

Here, $\{\epsilon_t\}$ is a stationary error that may or may not be a random process. The second subscript on the βs, ", k", is there to remind us that the value of each β may change when the order of the model, k, changes. With this model specification, we can interpret $\beta_{k,k}$ as the correlation between y_t and y_{t-k} after the effects of the intervening variables, $y_{t-1}, \ldots, y_{t-k+1}$, have been removed. This is the same idea as the partial correlation coefficient, introduced in Section 4.4. Estimates of partial correlation coefficients, $b_{k,k}$, can then be calculated using conditional least squares or other techniques. We define $b_{k,k}$ to be the lag k partial autocorrelation. As with other correlations in this text, we use $1/(T)^{1/2}$ as an approximate standard error for detecting significant differences from zero.

Partial autocorrelations are used in model identification in the following way. First calculate the first several estimates, $b_{1,1}$, $b_{2,2}$, $b_{3,3}$, and so on. Then, choose the order of the autoregressive model to be the largest k so that the estimate $b_{k,k}$ is significantly different from zero. For example, for the medical CPI example, recall that the approximate standard error for correlations is $1/(T)^{1/2} \approx 0.08$. Table 10.7 provides the first ten partial autocorrelations for the percentage changes and for their differences for the Quarterly MCPI. Using twice the standard error as our rough cut-off rule, we see that the first two partial autocorrelations of the differences exceed $2 \times 0.08 = 0.16$ in absolute value. This would suggest using an $AR(2)$ as a tentative first model choice. Alternatively,

TABLE 10.7 Partial Autocorrelations of the Percentage Changes and the Differences of Percentage Changes of MCPI

Lag	1	2	3	4	5	6	7	8	9	10
Percentage changes	0.766	0.187	0.215	0.094	0.024	−0.137	0.052	0.014	−0.001	0.138
Differences of percentage changes	−0.283	−0.271	−0.132	−0.056	0.098	−0.092	−0.052	−0.038	−0.171	−0.028

the reader may wish to argue that because the third partial autocorrelation is $0.132/(164)^{1/2} \approx 1.69$ standard errors below zero, a better initial model identification is an $AR(3)$ model. This is not an incorrect argument. Recall that developing models for data is an art as well as a science.

Finally, the reader may be interested in what happens to partial autocorrelations calculated on nonstationary series. Table 10.7 provides partial autocorrelations for the percentage changes of MCPI. Note how large the first partial autocorrelation is. That is, yet another way of identifying a series as nonstationary is to examine the partial autocorrelation function and see a large lag one partial autocorrelation.

Residual Checking and Forecasting

Having identified and fit an $AR(p)$ model, residual checking is still an important part of determining a model's validity. With the fitted model,

$$\hat{y}_t = b_0 + b_1 y_{t-1} + \dots + b_p y_{t-p},$$

the residuals may be computed in the usual fashion, that is, as $\hat{e}_t = y_t - \hat{y}_t$. Without further approximations, note that the residuals $\hat{e}_1, \dots, \hat{e}_p$ are missing because observations before time one are missing. If the model is valid, we expect to discover no further patterns in the residuals, including patterns through time. To check for patterns, use the devices described in Section 10.3, such as the control chart to check for stationarity and the autocorrelation function to check for lagged variable relationships.

As with the $AR(1)$ model forecasts described in Section 10.4, we use the notation $\hat{y}_{T+k}$ to denote our k-step forecast of the future (at time T) observation y_{T+k}. Similar to equation (10.4), this forecast is calculated recursively using

$$\hat{y}_{T+k} = b_0 + b_1 \hat{y}_{T+k-1} + \dots + b_p \hat{y}_{T+k-p}. \qquad (10.10)$$

For observations where $k \leq p$, we have $\hat{y}_{T+k-p} = y_{T+k-p}$, because the data are known up to time T. For example, from (10.10) for $k = 1$, we have

$$\hat{y}_{T+1} = b_0 + b_1 y_T + \dots + b_p y_{T+1-p}.$$

Similarly, for $k = 2$, we have

$$\hat{y}_{T+2} = b_0 + b_1 \hat{y}_{T+1} + b_2 y_T + \ldots + b_p y_{T-p+2},$$

and so on.

The forecast error is defined as $y_{T+k} - \hat{y}_{T+k}$. Just as in equation (10.5) for the $AR(1)$ model case, the $AR(p)$ forecast error can be expressed as an approximate linear combination of future errors, $e_{T+k}, e_{T+k-1}, \ldots, e_{T+1}$. As in the $AR(1)$ case, with this linear combination of unrelated errors, it is straightforward to compute the variance of the prediction errors. Assuming approximate normality of the errors, prediction intervals can be readily computed. For example, Figure 10.12 provides 95% prediction intervals for the quarterly medical CPI series. These prediction intervals are produced by many statistical computer software packages.

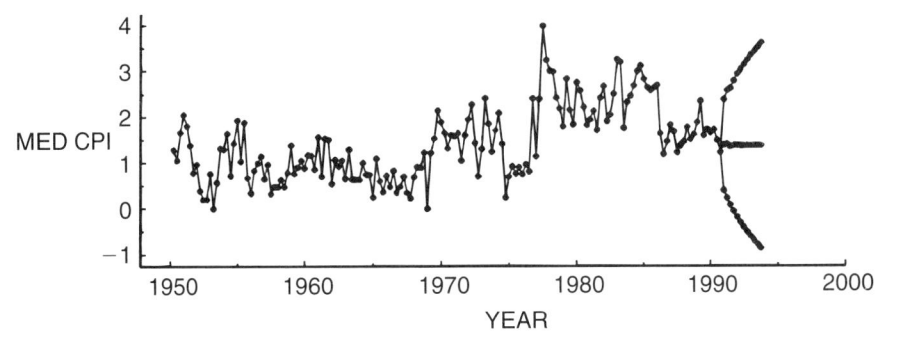

FIGURE 10.12 Time series plot of quarterly percentage changes in MCPI. Values to 1991 are actual values. For 1991–1993, the middle series yields point forecasts. The upper and lower lines yield a 95% prediction band.

10.7 SUMMARY

Having either identified a series or converted it to stationarity, the next step is to search for more subtle patterns through time. Chapter 10 provides several techniques for searching for subtle patterns through time using the regression techniques that were developed in Chapters 3 through 8. Unlike the material in Chapter 9, Chapter 10 introduces regression techniques for longitudinal data using lagged dependent variables as independent variables.

Section 10.1 discussed graphical and numerical methods for identifying subtle patterns in relations among lagged variables. The lead example appeared in Section 10.2, the autoregressive model of order one. This model can be thought of as a special case of the model presented in Chapter 3, with the lagged response as the independent variable. Section 10.2 introduced the model and its properties. Section 10.3 discussed how the model is estimated and how well the model fits. The details of how to use the model for prediction are in Section 10.4. To illustrate, an important application is in Section 10.5. Section 10.6 extended the autoregressive model to the case of several lags.

Chapter 11 will present another set of techniques for forecasting longitudinal data, including moving (running) average and exponential smoothing methods of forecasting. You will see that these techniques are simple to explain and easily interpretable. To provide a theoretical justification, we will show how these models can be also expressed as regression models, where the technique of weighted least squares is used to compute our parameter estimates.

KEY WORDS, PHRASES AND SYMBOLS

After reading this chapter, you should be able to define each of the following important terms, phrases and symbols in your own words. If not, go to the page indicated and review the definition.

autocorrelations, 450
lag k autocorrelation
   statistic (r_k), 450
autoregression, 451
autoregressive model of
   order one [$AR(1)$],
   451

autoregressive model of
   order two [$AR(2)$],
   452
meandering, 453
conditional least
   squares, 455
smoothed series, 457

parametric, 460
nonparametric, 461
Spearman's correlation
   (sr_k), 461
statistically significant
   but not practially
   significant, 462

autoregressive model of
   order p [$AR(p)$], 464
partial autocorrelation,
   465

CHAPTER 10 EXERCISES

Section 10.1

10.1 Consider the following sequence of $T = 5$ observations.
   a. Complete Table E10.1 and compute the lag one autocorrelation.

TABLE E10.1

t	1	2	3	4	5	SUM
y_t	10	6	11	4	9	
$y_t - \bar{y}$						
$(y_t - \bar{y})^2$						
$y_{t-1} - \bar{y}$						
$(y_{t-1} - \bar{y})(y_t - \bar{y})$						

   b. Compute the lag two and three autocorrelations.

10.2 Consider the following sequence of $T = 5$ observations in Table E10.2. Give a scatter plot of $\{y_t\}$ versus $\{y_{t-1}\}$ and give an approximate correlation based on the plot. Then, compute the lag one autocorrelation. Explain any differences that you note.

TABLE E10.2

t	1	2	3	4	5
y_t	10	9	8	7	6

10.3 Figure E10.3 is a time series plot of a fictitious variable $\{y_t\}$.
   i. Provide a rough scatter plot of y_t versus y_{t-1}.
   ii. Provide a rough approximation of the lag one autocorrelation (that is, is r_1 positive and close to one, negative and close to -1, or about zero).
   iii. Provide a rough approximation of the lag two autocorrelation (that is, is r_2 positive and close to one, negative and close to -1, or about zero).

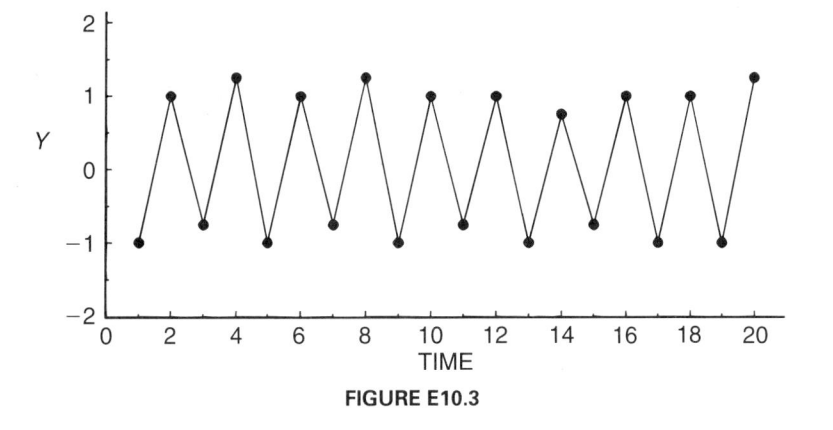

FIGURE E10.3

10.4 Refer to Exercise 9.4
Consider the annual returns of the Salomon Brothers Bond Index for the period 1926–1985, inclusive. You suspect that there may be some mild autocorrelation in the data. The correlation between the index and its lagged value turns out to be 0.155. Is this correlation large enough to make you suspect autocorrelation? In your response, provide an approximate standard error for the lag one autocorrelation coefficient.

Section 10.3

C9_DOW

10.5 Refer to Exercise 9.5
   a. Regardless of your response to exercise 9.5 (b), a student has decided to analyze the percentage change series, %BOND.

    i.   In Figure E10.5 is a scatter plot of the current value of this series versus its immediate past value (LAG%BOND). Describe the types of temporal patterns that this scatter plot reveals.

    ii. Attached is estimated autocorrelation function for the series %BOND. Which statistic serves to summarize the graphical information in Figure E10.5? Provide the value of this statistic.

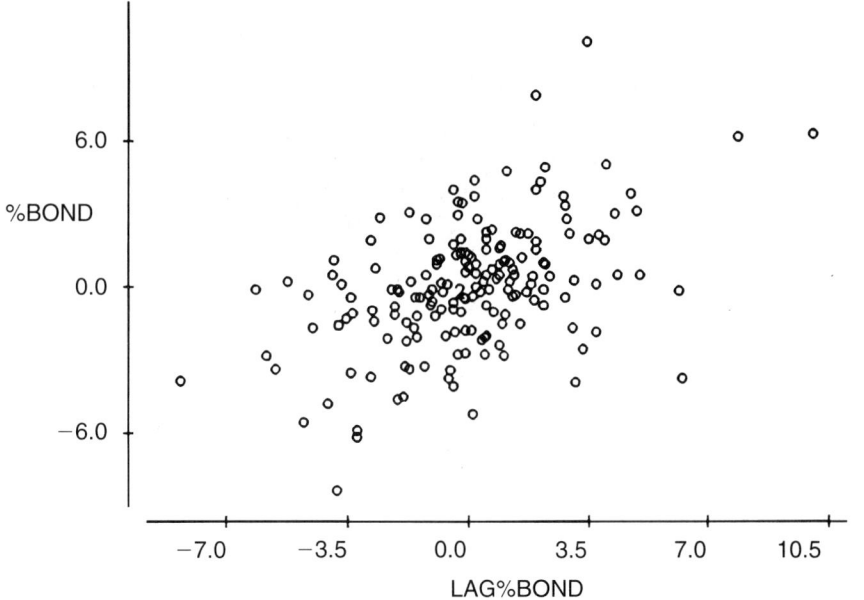

FIGURE E10.5 Scatter plot of the current value of the %BOND series versus its immediate past value (LAG%BOND).

   b. Based on the exploratory work in part (a), an $AR(1)$ model was fit to the %BOND series. Is the lag one autoregressive parameter useful? Provide a formal test of hypothesis to justify your response.

```
                 Autocorrelations of the %BOND Series

         -1.0 -0.8 -0.6 -0.4 -0.2  0.0  0.2  0.4  0.6  0.8  1.0
           +----+----+----+----+----+----+----+----+----+----+
  1   0.468                             XXXXXXXXXXXXX
  2  -0.003                             X
  3  -0.060                           XXX
  4   0.056                             XX
  5   0.129                             XXXX
  6   0.012                             X
  7  -0.025                            XX
  8   0.087                             XXX
  9   0.148                             XXXXX
 10   0.200                             XXXXXX
```

```
11   0.128                              XXXX
12   0.033                              XX
13  −0.009                              X
14  −0.039                              XX
15  −0.052                              XX
```

MINITAB Output for AR(1) Model for %BOND Series

```
Final Estimates of Parameters
Type        Estimate    St. Dev.    t-ratio
AR   1      0.4697      0.0665       7.06
Constant    0.0259      0.1710       0.15
Mean        0.0488      0.3224

No. of obs.:   179
Residuals:     SS = 925.935 (backforecasts excluded)
               MS =   5.231 DF = 177

Modified Box-Pierce chisquare statistic
Lag                12          24          36          48
Chisquare   31.4(DF=11)  42.7(DF=23)  50.2(DF=35)  57.7(DF=47)
```

Section 10.6

C9_DOW

10.6 Refer to Exercise 9.5 and Exercise 10.5

Regardless of your response to Exercise 10.5 (b), a student has decided to fit an $AR(2)$ model to the %BOND series.

   i. Figure E10.6 is a time series plot of residuals from this fitted model. What is the purpose of making this type of plot?

   ii. Write down the fitted model.

   iii. Values for the last 6 months of 1991 for the BOND series are: 9.42 (July), 9.16, 9.03, 8.99, 8.93, 9.75 (December). Use these values and the fitted model in part (ii) to forecast the values of the BOND series for January 1992.

MINITAB Output for AR(2) Model for %BOND Series

```
Final Estimates of Parameters
Type Estimate    St. Dev.    t-ratio
AR1      0.6036    0.0724       8.34
AR2     -0.2860    0.0724      -3.95
Constant 0.0359    0.1643       0.22
Mean     0.0526    0.2408

No. of obs.:    179
Residuals:     SS = 850.462  (backforecasts excluded)
               MS =   4.832  DF = 176

Modified Box-Pierce chisquare statistic
Lag                12            24            36            48
Chisquare   14.6 (DF=10)   26.0 (DF=22)   30.5 (DF=34)   40.2 (DF=46)
```

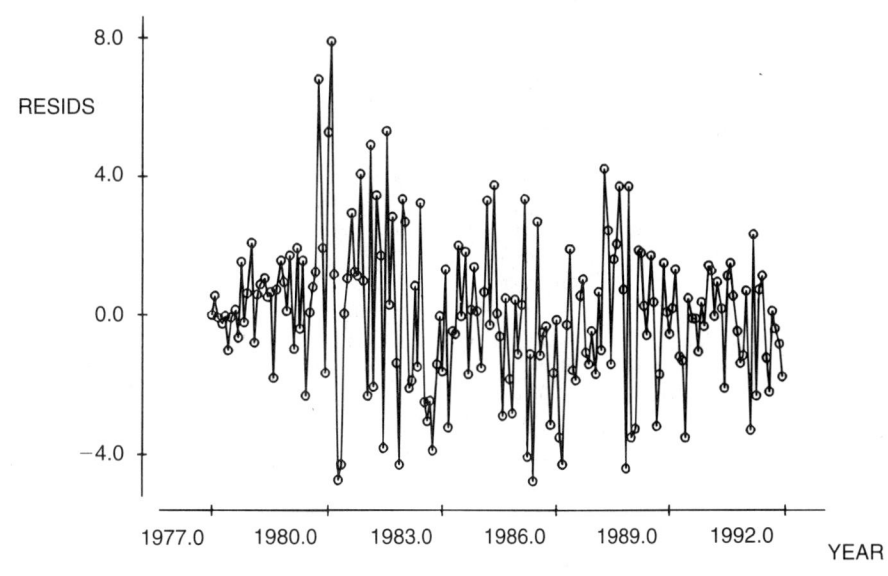

FIGURE E10.6 Time series plot of residuals from the *AR*(2) model for %BOND series.

End-of-Chapter Exercises

10.7 Governments, corporations and individuals rely on projections of populations for a wide variety of planning purposes. In addition to births and deaths, *interstate migration* is an important part of the change of the size of a population. Consider the total U.S. interstate migration rate, defined to be the total number of U.S. interstate migrants divided by the total U.S. population. The rate was multiplied by 100 so that the data is in percentage form. An interstate migrant is defined to be a person who moves from one state to another. That is, people who move within a state or who move either to or from overseas are not counted as interstate migrants. We consider the migration rate from years 1975–1987, inclusive. In Figure E10.7a is a plot of the data over time.

   a. Describe the concept of a meandering series. Say whether the series, plotted in Figure E10.7a, is meandering.

   b. Suppose that you decide to fit a random process model to the data. Use the summary statistics in Table E10.7 to compute forecasts of the migration rate for 1988 and 1989.

   c. The lag one autocorrelation coefficient turns out to be $r_1 = 0.535$. Relate this statistic to the Figure E10.7b scatter plot of the migration rate versus its lagged value.

TABLE E10.7 Summary Statistics for Exercise 10.7

	Number	Mean	Median	Standard deviation	Minimum	Maximum
MIGRANT	13	3.0105	3.0139	0.1571	2.7884	3.2736

Use these two pieces of information to say why an autoregressive model of order one may be a suitable candidate model to fit to the data.

d. An $AR(1)$ model was fit to the data using conditional least squares. Part of the computer output follows. Use this output to compute the square root of the mean square error, s.

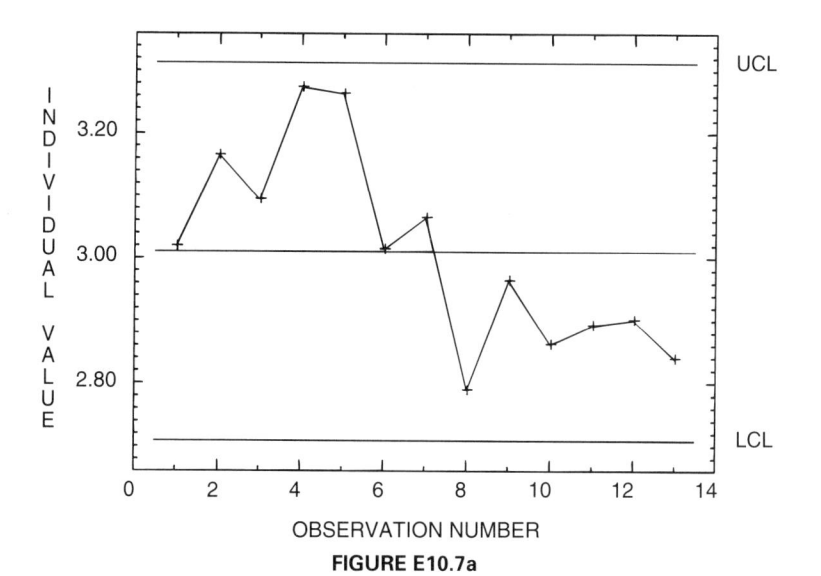

FIGURE E10.7a

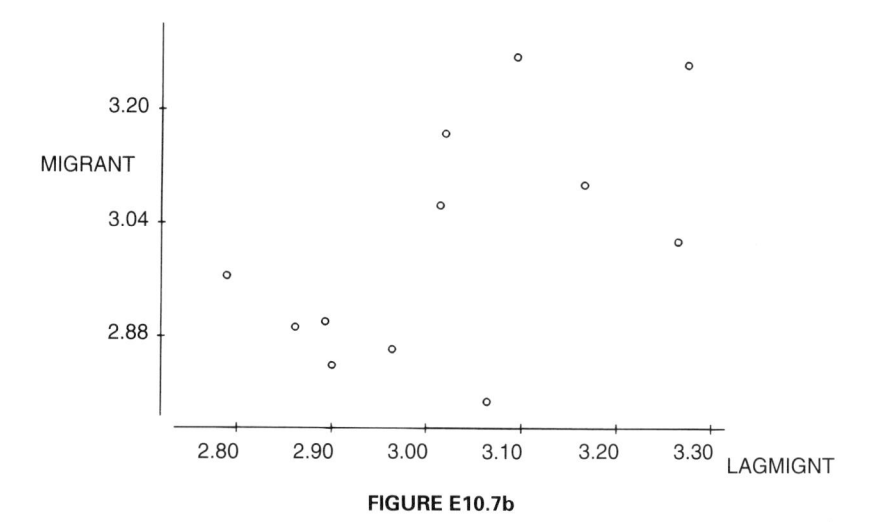

FIGURE E10.7b

The regression equation is MIGRANT = 1.19   + 0.600 LAGMIGNT

                                   (0.8352)   (0.2758)

                                   numbers in parens are standard errors

SOURCE	DF	SS	
Regression		0.09521	
Error		0.20089	Analysis of Variance
Total		0.29611	

e. The migration rate for 1987 was $MIGRANT_{13} = 2.83852$. Use this value, and the estimated $AR(1)$ equation, to provide point forecasts for 1988 and 1989. Compare these to the forecasts you made in part (b).

f. Calculate 95% forecast intervals for your point forecasts for 1988 and 1989.

C10_CRED

10.8 You are working for a large life insurance company that is interested in forecasting the size of the market for credit life insurance. For this situation, take credit insurance as life insurance for holders of loans of 10 years or shorter duration. A consulting firm that you are dealing with has presented you with a complex model for forecasting the market size over a 3–5 year horizon. To see if the consulting firm's projections are reasonable, you decide to forecast the size of the credit life insurance market in the United States. To this end, you have collected data from 1950 to 1989, inclusive, from the 1990 edition of the *Life Insurance Fact Book,* published by the *American Council of Life Insurance.* The data analyzed in Figures E10.8a–c and Tables E10.8 a–d are in millions of dollars. For the two most recent years available, 1988 and 1989, there were 251,015 and 260,107 (millions of) dollars of credit life insurance in force, respectively.

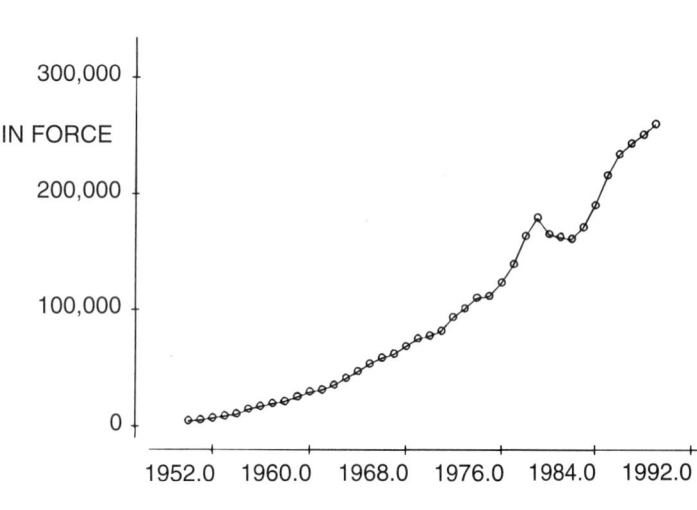

FIGURE E10.8a *Source: 1990 Life Insurance Fact Book, American Council of Life Insurance*

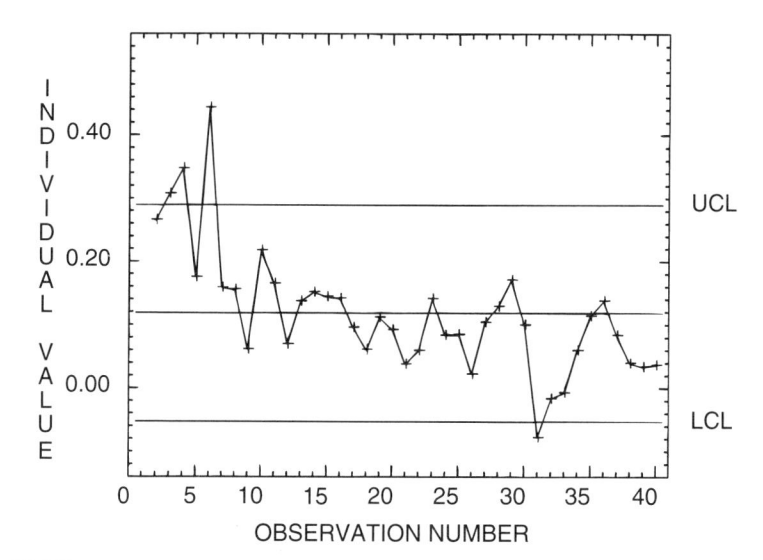

FIGURE E10.8b Time series plot of the proportional change in insurance in force.

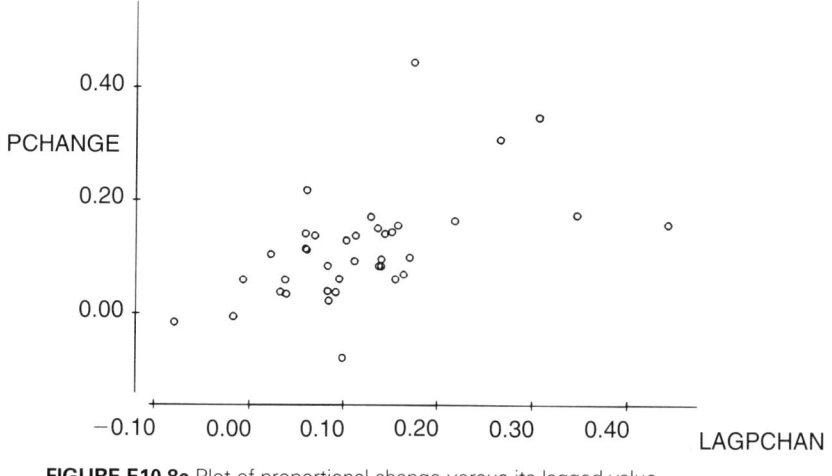

FIGURE E10.8c Plot of proportional change versus its lagged value.

TABLE E10.8a Summary Statistics for Exercise 10.8

	Number	Number missing	Mean	Median	Standard deviation	Minimum	Maximum
PCHANGE	39	1	0.118	0.1030	0.0986	−0.0783	0.4427

TABLE E10.8b Autocorrelations and Partial Autocorrelations for PCHANGE

Lag	1	2	3	4	5	6	7	8	9	10
Autocorrelation	0.525	0.441	0.219	0.293	0.162	0.174	0.214	0.162	0.127	0.056
Partial autocorrelation	0.525	0.228	−0.116	0.204	−0.056	0.012	0.196	−0.098	−0.011	−0.010

TABLE E10.8c Coefficient Estimates

Explanatory variables	Coefficient	Standard error	t-ratio
Constant	0.0498	0.02115	2.35
LAGPCHAN	0.5360	0.1365	3.93

TABLE E10.8d ANOVA Table

Source	Sum of Squares	df	Mean Square
Regression	0.10408	1	0.10408
Error	0.24297	36	0.00675
Total	0.34705	37	

The regression fit also yields $s = 0.0822$, $R^2 = 30.0\%$ and $R_a^2 = 28.0\%$.

a. i. Use the scatter plot of the insurance in force (IN FORCE) versus years to iden-tify an "unusual" period in the development of the credit market.

  ii. The Figure E10.8a scatter plot suggests that the amount of credit insurance is nonstationary. Thus, the proportional change, or growth rate, of the credit in-surance market is plotted. That is, PCHANGE$_t$ = IN FORCE $_t$/IN FORCE$_{t-1}$ − 1. Use the control chart of PCHANGE to identify the "unusual" years.

  iii. Are the "unusual" years in parts (i) and (ii) the same? Explain.

b. i. A scatter plot of PCHANGE versus its lagged value, Figure E10.8c, suggests that the PCHANGE series is meandering. Describe the meandering aspect of the series that is evident in the control chart which is referred to in question a, part (ii).

  ii. As additional model identification tools, an autocorrelation and partial auto-correlation function of PCHANGE were calculated. Use these tools to identify tentatively an ARIMA model. State your reasons for your selection.

c. Without regard to your careful selection procedures, your trainee decides to fit an autoregressive model of order one to the data. [Do not let this selection influence your specification in question b, part (ii).] Use this model to calculate a point fore-cast of the credit life insurance in force in 1992.

C10_SALE

10.9 The following data represent sales, net of discounts, of an optometric practice in Madi-son, Wisconsin. Thirty observations are available, corresponding to monthly sales be-ginning in May 1988 and ending in November 1990. The revenue figures contain professional service fees such as eye examination fees and contact lens fitting fees, and product sales such as spectacle frames, spectacle lens and contact lens. (See Table E10.9a.)

a. i. List the first five values of the series and the corresponding lagged sales.

  ii. Give a rough scatter plot of the pairs of observations in part (i).

Listing of NETSALES

(read from left to right)

207.01	239.83	223.27	224.22	207.65	192.74	193.60	210.05
217.60	186.41	184.15	175.84	202.05	243.71	229.34	270.17
254.51	185.32	167.53	210.46	265.14	248.85	267.23	229.14
266.45	234.65	298.63	268.12	175.02	222.31		

b. Using the Figure E10.9a control chart and Table E10.9b autocorrelations, describe whether or not the series is stationary.

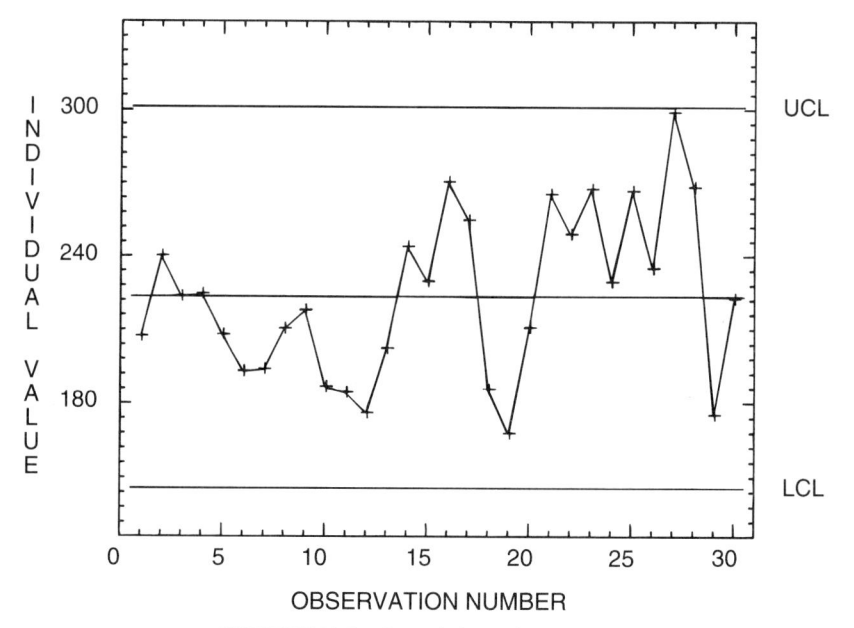

FIGURE E10.9a Control chart of net sales.

c. Assume a random process model for the series. For December of 1990, provide a:
   i. point forecast
   ii. 95% prediction interval.

TABLE E10.9a Summary Statistics for Exercise 10.9

	Number	Mean	Median	Standard deviation	Minimum	Maximum
NETSALES	30	223.37	222.79	33.79	167.53	298.63

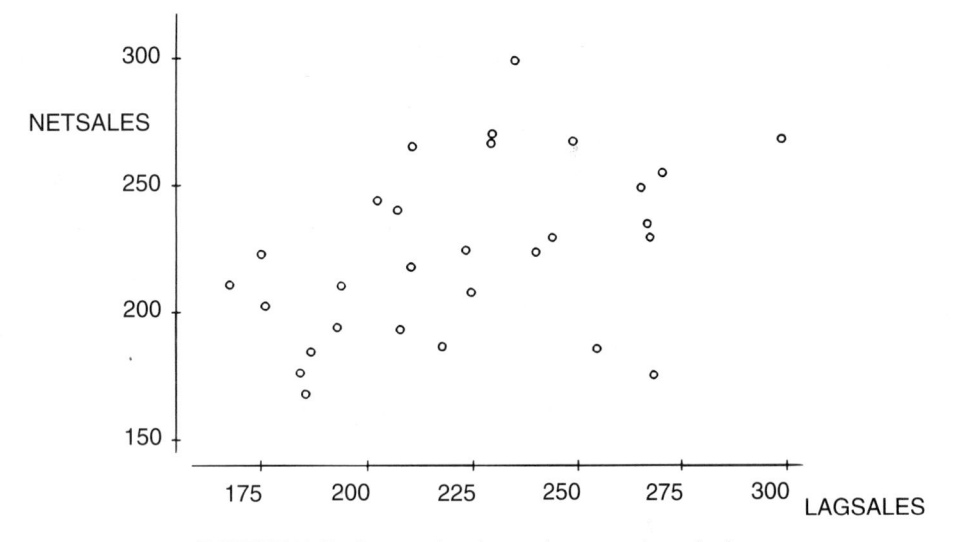

FIGURE E10.9b Scatter plot of net sales versus lagged sales.

d. What is the correlation coefficient for the scatter plot (Figure E10.9b) of net sales versus lagged sales? (See Table E10.9b.)

e. i. Calculate the standard error of each autocorrelation statistic.

   ii. How many standard errors is r_1 above 0?

   iii. Assume that the series is an $AR(1)$ model with parameter $\phi = \rho_1 = 0.421 = r_1$. What is the theoretical of ρ_2?

   iv. How far is r_2 from ρ_2 in terms of standard errors?

TABLE E10.9b Autocorrelations of NETSALES

Lag	1	2	3	4	5	6	7
Autocorrelations	0.421	0.081	−0.058	−0.040	0.111	0.139	0.133

f. An $AR(1)$ model was fit to the data. The fitted model is:

$$\text{NET}\hat{\text{S}}\text{ALES}_t = 128.3 + .4245\,\text{NETSALES}_{t-1}$$
$$\qquad\qquad (5.68) \qquad\qquad (0.171)$$

with s = 31.1. For December of 1990, provide a:

   i. point forecast, and

   ii. a 95% prediction interval.

```
                    MINITAB Output for Fitted AR(1) Model of NETSALES

        Final Estimates of Parameters

        Type      Estimate   St. Dev.   t-ratio
        AR1         0.4245    0.1710      2.48
        Constant  128.313     5.687      22.56
        Mean      222.962     9.882

        No. of obs.:   30
        Residuals:     SS = 27164.3  (backforecasts excluded)
                       MS =   970.2  DF = 28

        Modified Box-Pierce chisquare statistic
        Lag               12          24          36          48
        Chisquare   5.7(DF=11)  15.2(DF=23)   * (DF= *)   * (DF= *)
```

C10_WDOW

10.10 For this question, we examine the weekly Dow Jones Industrial Average. The following data are Friday values of this average, called DJ20, taken over the period August 2, 1990 to February 29, 1991. Percentage changes of DJ20 are called DJ PERCT.

    a. Figure E10.10a is a scatter plot of DJ PERCT versus its lagged value. In the computer output that follows are the autocorrelations of DJ PERCT.

        i. What patterns are evident in the scatter plot of DJ PERCT versus its lagged value?

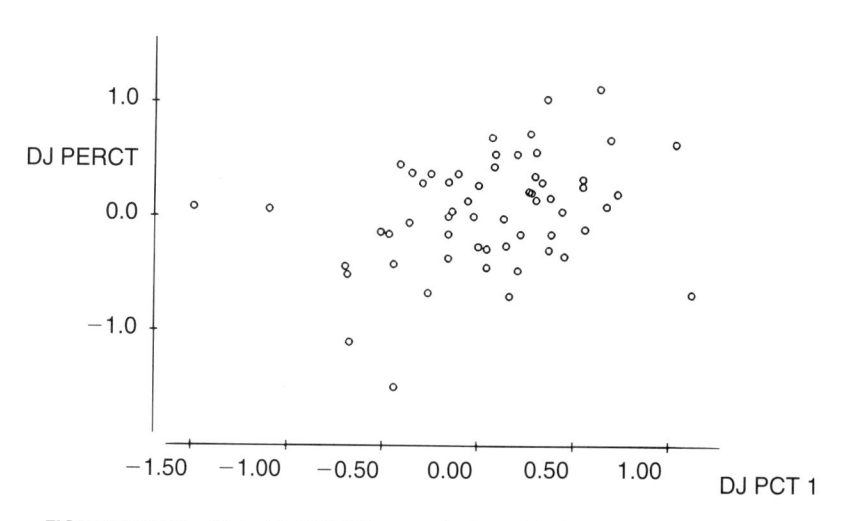

FIGURE E10.10a Plot of DJ PERCT versus its lagged value. *Source: Standard and Poor's Compustat*

ii. What statistic in the autocorrelations summarizes the graphical information in the scatter plot in part (i)?

iii. Does the statistic in part (ii) differ significantly from zero? Justify your responses.

iv. What additional information is available in the series of autocorrelations that is not available in the scatter plot?

```
        MINITAB Autocorrelations of Percentage Chages in DJ20

        -1.0 -0.8 -0.6 -0.4 -0.2  0.0  0.2  0.4  0.6  0.8  1.0
        +----+----+----+----+----+----+----+----+----+----+
  1   0.304                         XXXXXXXXX
  2   0.118                         XXXX
  3  -0.125                     XXXX
  4  -0.022                       XX
  5  -0.020                       XX
  6   0.943                       XX
  7   0.028                       XX
  8   0.072                       XXX
```

b. In Table E10.10a are summary statistics of DJ PERCT and its lagged value, DJ PCT1. Why are there differences in the mean and the standard deviation?

TABLE E10.10a Summary Statistics for Exercise 10.10

	Number	Number missing	Mean	Median	Standard deviation	Minimum	Maximum
DJ PERCT	59	1	0.0445	0.0786	0.4788	−1.4935	1.1193
DJ PCT1	58	2	0.0501	0.0837	0.4811	−1.4935	1.1193

c. You decide to fit an autoregressive model of order one to the DJ PERCT series (Tables E10.10b–d).

i. Write down the theoretical model using parameters to be estimated from the data.

ii. Using the computer output, write down the estimated model corresponding to the theoretical model in part (i).

iii. What do we learn about the acceptability of this estimated model from the autocorrelations of the residuals?

TABLE E10.10b Coefficient Estimates

Explanatory variables	Coefficient	Standard error	t-ratio
Constant	0.02519	0.06112	0.41
DJ PCT1	0.3068	0.1275	2.41

TABLE E10.10c ANOVA Table

Source	Sum of Squares	df	Mean Square
Regression	1.2421	1	1.2421
Error	12.0028	56	0.2143
Total	13.2449	57	

TABLE E10.10d Residual Autocorrelations

Lag	1	2	3	4	5	6	7
Autocorrelations	−0.010	0.093	−0.184	0.033	−0.023	0.040	−0.005

The regression fit also yields $s = 0.4630$, $R^2 = 9.4\%$ and $R_a^2 = 7.8\%$.

Unusual Observations

Obs. DJ	PCT1	DJ PERCT	Fit	Residual	Std Resid
13	−0.68	−1.1029	−0.1819	−0.9210	−2.05
14	−1.10	0.0676	−0.3132	0.3808	0.88
30	−0.44	−1.4935	−0.1100	−1.3835	−3.04
31	−1.49	0.0786	−0.4331	0.5117	1.23
56	1.12	−0.6852	0.3686	−1.0538	−2.40

    d. The last two values of the DJ20 are $DJ20_{58} = 93.64$ and $DJ20_{59} = 93.38$. Thus, the most recent percentage change is DJ $PERCT_{59} = 100(DJ20_{59}/DJ20_{58} - 1) = -0.278$.(See Figures E10.10b and c.)

        i. Compute a 95% prediction interval for the percentage change two weeks into the future, corresponding to DJ $PERCT_{61}$.

       ii. Compute the corresponding (point) forecast for the industrial average two weeks into the future, corresponding to $DJ20_{61}$.

Plots of the Weekly Dow Industrial Stock Index

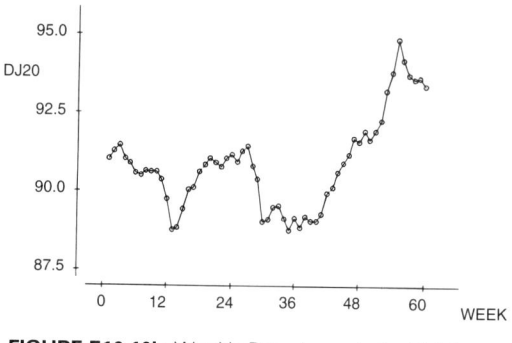

FIGURE E10.10b Weekly Dow Jones Industrial Averager (DJ20)

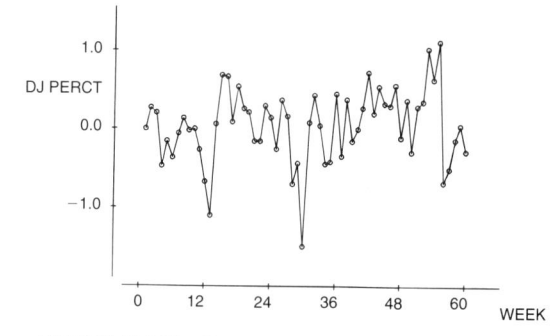

FIGURE E10.10c Percentage changes in DJ20, called DJ PERCT.

C10_SHEL

10.11 Globally, the role of ethics and heightened social responsibility has become more prominent in the 1990s than previously. One aspect of this is the plight of homeless persons in the United States, which has received increased public scrutiny. On a more local level, we examine here the number of individuals staying at the West Washington Drop-in Shelter for Men, a Madison, Wisconsin homeless shelter. The main variable of interest is HOMELESS, defined to be the number of persons actually housed in the shelter plus the number who could not be served due to space limitations. Thus, the variable HOMELESS captures the demand for shelter services. Monthly data from January 1988 through August 1993 is studied (except for February 1989, which was not available).

a. Figure E10.11a summarizes graphically the relationship between the HOMELESS and its lagged version, LAGHOME. A student computed the correlation between HOMELESS and LAGHOME, which turned out to be 0.875. Her friend computed the lag one autocorrelation of HOMELESS, which turn out to be 0.857. Although close, the numbers are not exactly the same. Write down formula for the two correlations and explain the relationship between these two statistics.

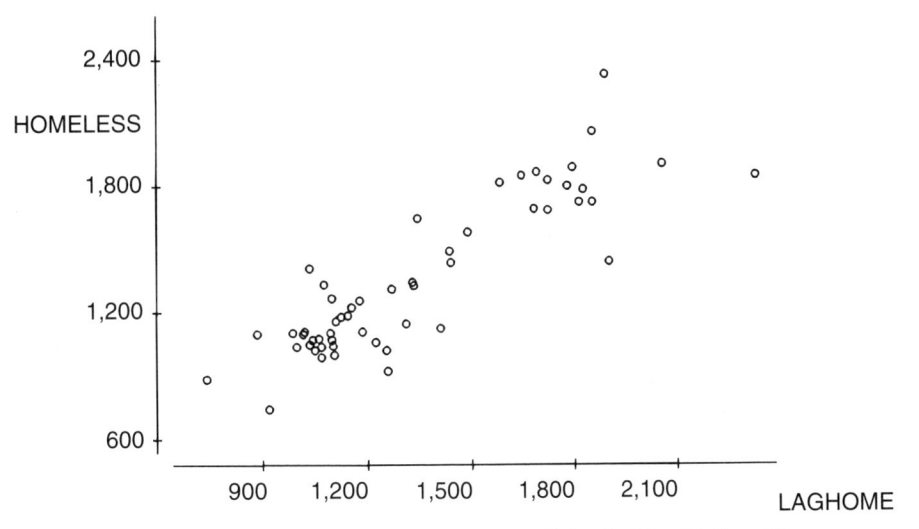

FIGURE E10.11a *Source: West Washington Drop-In Shelter for Men, Madison, Wisconsin and Wisconsin Department of Industry, Labor and Human Relations*

b. An $AR(1)$ model was fit to the HOMELESS series. The most recent value, corresponding to August 1993, is $HOMELESS_{55} = 1866$.

  i. Do the residual autocorrelations from this model appear to be statistically different from zero? Cite the approximate standard error of the residual autocorrelations to justify your response. (See Tables E10.11a–c.)

  ii. Using the fitted model, compute the one-, two-, and three-step forecasts, corresponding to forecasts of September, October and November of 1993.

  iii. Compute a 95% prediction interval for *only* the three-step forecast, corresponding to November of 1993.

Autoregressive Model

TABLE E10.11a Coefficient Estimates

Explanatory variables	Coefficient	Standard error	t-ratio
Constant	156.63	95.06	1.65
LAGHOME	0.89196	0.06838	13.04

TABLE E10.11b ANOVA Table

Source	Sum of Squares	df	Mean Square
Regression	5,269,343	1	5,269,343
Error	1,610,218	52	30,966
Total	6,879,561	53	

The regression fit also yields $s = 176.0$, $R^2 = 76.6\%$ and $R_a^2 = 76.1\%$.

Unusual Observations

Obs.	LAGHOME	HOMELESS	Fit	Residual	Std Resid
2	1257	920.0	1277.8	−357.8	−2.05
40	1903	1440.0	1854.0	−414.0	−2.43
50	1890	2329.0	1842.4	486.6	2.86
51	2329	1851.0	2234.0	−383.0	−2.38

TABLE E10.11c Residual Autocorrelations

Lag	1	2	3	4	5	6	7
Autocorrelations	−0.001	−0.140	−0.001	−0.155	−0.044	0.095	−0.040

c. The Figure E10.11b time series plot of HOMELESS reveals an increasing trend over time. In the attached computer output, the linear trend was fit and residuals auto-correlation computed. Based on this, the model was refit with a linear trend and a lagged response as independent variables. (See Tables E10.11d–h.)

  i. Describe how the autocorrelations of residuals from the linear trend model suggest an $AR(1)$ structure.

  ii. For the fitted model with a linear trend and a lagged response as independent variables, how many standard errors is the autoregressive parameter from one?

  iii. For the fitted autoregressive model (without a linear trend), how many standard errors is the autoregressive parameter from one? If the autoregressive parameter is one, what is the resulting model?

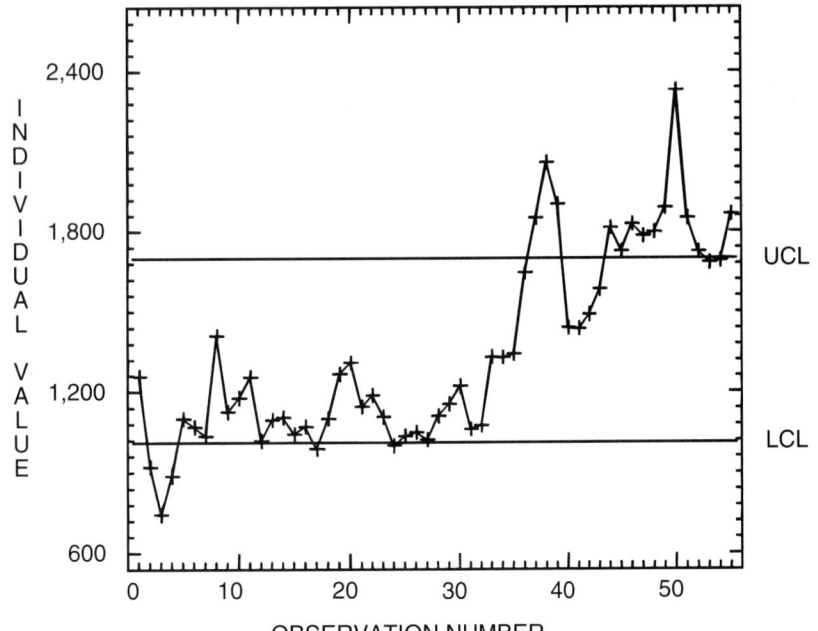

OBSERVATION NUMBER

FIGURE E10.11b

Linear Trend Regression

TABLE E10.11d Coefficient Estimates

Explanatory variables	Coefficient	Standard error	t-ratio
Constant	849.17	58.92	14.41
TIME1	17.579	1.785	9.85

TABLE E10.11e ANOVA Table

Source	Sum of Squares	df	Mean Square
Regression	4,455,040	1	4,455,040
Error	2,434,266	53	45,930
Total	6,889,306	54	

The regression fit also yields $s = 214.3$, $R^2 = 64.7\%$ and $R_a^2 = 64.0\%$.

Unusual Observations

Obs.	TIME1	HOMELESS	Fit	Residual	Std Resid
8	8.0	1410.0	989.8	420.2	2.01
38	39.0	2059.0	1534.8	524.2	2.48
50	51.0	2329.0	1745.7	583.3	2.80

TABLE E10.11f Residual Autocorrelations from Linear Trend Regression

Lag	1	2	3	4	5	6	7
Autocorrelations	0.617	0.329	0.208	0.091	0.088	0.093	0.073

Linear Trend Regression

TABLE E10.11g Coefficient Estimates

Explanatory variables	Coefficient	Standard error	t-ratio
Constant	300.89	97.67	3.08
TIME1	7.487	2.282	3.28
LAGHOME	0.6218	0.1035	6.01

TABLE E10.11h ANOVA Table

Source	Sum of Squares	df	Mean Square
Regression	5,549,986	2	2,774,993
Error	1,329,574	51	26,070
Total	6,889,306	53	

The regression fit also yields $s = 161.5$, $R^2 = 80.7\%$ and $R_a^2 = 79.9\%$.

Unusual Observations

Obs.	TIME1	HOMELESS	Fit	Residual	Std Resid
8	8.0	1410.0	1004.3	405.7	2.58
38	39.0	2059.0	1743.8	315.2	2.03
40	41.0	1440.0	1791.1	−351.1	−2.27
50	51.0	2329.0	1857.9	471.1	3.02
51	52.0	1851.0	2138.4	−287.4	−1.99

Appendix

10.12 The Durbin-Watson statistic is designed to detect autocorrelation and is defined by

$$DW = \frac{\sum_{t=2}^{T} (y_t - y_{t-1})^2}{\sum_{t=1}^{T} (y_t - \bar{y})^2}.$$

The idea behind this statistic is that if $\{y_t\}$ and $\{y_{t-1}\}$ are closely related to one another, then DW should be small. The following steps develop a realtionship between DW and r_1, the lag one autocorrelation statistic.

a. Add and subtract $\bar{y}$ to get

$$\sum_{t=2}^{T} (y_t - y_{t-1})^2 = \sum_{t=2}^{T} ((y_t - \bar{y}) - (y_{t-1} - \bar{y}))^2$$

$$= \sum_{t=2}^{T} (y_t - \bar{y})^2 - 2 \sum_{t=2}^{T} (y_t - \bar{y})(y_{t-1} - \bar{y}) + \sum_{t=2}^{T} (y_{t-1} - \bar{y})^2.$$

b. Change the index of summation to get

$$\sum_{t=2}^{T} (y_t - y_{t-1})^2 = 2 \sum_{t=1}^{T} (y_t - \bar{y})^2 - 2 \sum_{t=2}^{T} (y_t - \bar{y})(y_{t-1} - \bar{y}) - (y_1 - \bar{y})^2 - (y_T - \bar{y})^2.$$

c. Divide by $\Sigma_{t=1}^{T}(y_t - \bar{y})^2$ to get

$$DW = 2(1 - r_1) - \frac{(y_1 - \bar{y})^2 + (y_T - \bar{y})^2}{(T-1)s_y^2}.$$

d. Argue that the approximation

$$DW \approx 2(1 - r_1)$$

is useful for most data sets.

e. If DW is close to 0, what can we say about the autocorrelations for the series?

10.13 Suppose that conditional least squares is used to compute estimates of the parameters in the $AR(1)$ model. Using the expressions for regression with one variable in Chapter 3, replace $\{x_t\}$ by $\{y_{t-1}\}$ to show that

$$\hat{\phi} = r_1 s_y / s_y^*$$

$$\hat{\alpha} = \bar{y} - \hat{\phi}\bar{y}^*$$

where $\bar{y}^* = (T-1)^{-1}(y_2 + y_3 + \ldots + y_T)$ and $s_y^{*2} = (T-2)^{-1}\Sigma_{t=1}^{T}(y_t - \bar{y})^2$.

11

Forecasting and Time Series Models

Chapter Objectives

To provide an overview of the general forecasting problem, to show how the methods of Chapters 9 and 10 fit into this problem and to introduce additional forecasting techniques. To illustrate, we will consider forecasting:

- the medical component of the Consumer Price Index and
- the cost of pharmaceutical drugs.

Chapter Outline

11.0 OVERVIEW OF FORECASTING

Forecasting is about predicting the behavior of future events. As with all other aspects of this text, we are interested in *quantitative* measures of events. For example, we might be interested in a forecast of the "behavior of the weather" when we get up in the morning. With weather patterns, we are usually satisfied with a forecast of quantitative measures such as the high temperature and the likelihood of precipitation. As another example, we might be interested in forecasts of the "financial strength of a firm" for investment purposes. The financial strength is often summarized through four or five key quantitative measures such as the price of the firm's stock, recent dividend history, debt-to-equity ratio and current assets to current liability ratio. Qualitative forecasts are also important for planning purposes. To illustrate, expert opinions are valuable. An expert opinion can consist of a forecast of whether the economy will be "good" next year or whether my hockey team will be "strong" in three years. Such forecasts are useful commodities in making business decisions.

Forecasts can be qualitative or quantitative. Our focus is on quantitative forecasts.

Time Series versus Causal Models

Numerical forecasts can be described as either *time series forecasts* or forecasts from a *causal model.* Time series forecasts are extrapolations of a sequence of observations avalable over time, that is, a time series. In Sections 11.1 and 11.2, we introduce two methods of time series forecasting, using moving (or running) averages and using exponential smoothing. These methods were originally conceived based on their intuitive simplicity. They have survived the test of time not only due to their simplicity, but also because they can be justified as optimal techniques based on certain statistical models. As we have seen, the regression and autoregression models introduced in Chapters 9 and 10 also produce time series forecasts.

In our regression models, we identified one variable to be the response and the other variables as measures that may help to explain the response. A related idea is to identify one series as the main series of interest and to use the other series as predictors for the main series. This is the subject of causal models. This type of modeling is employed extensively in econometrics, where it is assumed that economic theory provides the information needed to specify the causal relationships. A brief introduction of this topic is provided in Section 11.4. For more details on causal models, the interested reader is referred to Pindyck and Rubinfeld (1991) and Harvey (1991).

Characteristics of Time Series Forecasts

Time series forecasts are also called *naive* forecasts. The adjective "naive" is somewhat ironic becuase many time series forecasting techniques are technical in nature and complex to compute. However, these forecasts are based on extrapolating a single series of observations. Thus, they are naive in the sense that the forecasts ignore other sources of information that may be available to the forecaster and users of the forecasts. Despite ignoring this possibly important information, time series forecasts are useful in that they provide an objective benchmark that other forecasts and expert opinions can be compared against.

A good projection should provide a user with a sense of the reliability of the forecast. One way of quantifying this is to provide forecasts under "low-intermediate-high" sets of assumptions. For example, if we are forecasting the national debt, we might do so under three scenarios of the future performance of the economy. Alternatively, we can calculate *prediction intervals* using many of the models for forecasting that are discussed in this text. Prediction intervals provide a measure of reliability that can be interpreted in a familiar probabilistic sense. Further, by varying the desired level of confidence, the prediction intervals vary, thus allowing us to respond to "what if" types of questions.

Forecasts become less reliable the further that we forecast into the future. Prediction intervals provide a measure of reliability.

Prediction intervals have the aditional advantage in that they serve to quantify the fact that forecasts become less reliable the further that we forecast into the future. For example, with our forecasts intervals for random walks in Chapter 9, we saw that the forecast interval is a function of l, the lead time into the future. Even with cross-sectional data, we saw that the further away we were from the main part of the data, the less confident we felt about our predictions. This is also true in forecasting for longitudinal data. It is important to communicate this to consumers of forecasts, and prediction intervals are one convenient way of doing so.

11.1 FORECASTING WITH MOVING AVERAGES

Smoothing a time series with a moving, or running, average is a time-honored procedure. This technique continues to be used by many data analysts today because of its ease of computation and resulting ease of interpretation. As we discuss here, this estimator can also be motivated as a weighted least square (WLS) estimator. Thus, the estimator enjoys certain theoretical properties.

The basic *moving, or running, average estimate* is defined by

$$\hat{s}_t = \frac{y_t + y_{t-1} + \ldots + y_{t-k+1}}{k} \qquad (11.1)$$

where k is the *running average length*. The choice of k depends on the amount of smoothing desired. The larger is k, the smoother are the *smoothed values* $\hat{s}$ because there is more averaging done. Note that the choice $k = 1$ corresponds to no smoothing.

Example 11.1 The Medical Component of the Consumer Price Index

C10_MCPI

To illustrate the effect of the choice k, consider Figures 11.1 and 11.2. These are time series plots of the quarterly index of the medical component of the consumer price index, a data set introduced in Section 10.6. In Figure 11.1, the smoothed series with $k = 4$ is superimposed on the actual series. Figure 11.2 is the corresponding graph with $k = 8$. The fitted values in Figure 11.2 are less jagged than the fitted values in Figure 11.1. This helps us to identify graphically the real trends in the series. The danger in choosing too large a value of k is that we may "over-smooth" the data and lose sight of the real trends.

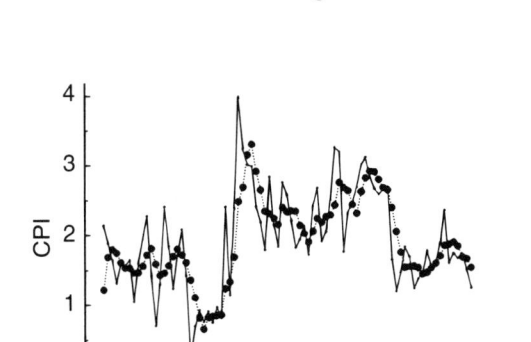

FIGURE 11.1 Time series plot of Quarterly Medical CPI from 1970 to 1991. Smoothed running average, with run length 4, is superimposed.

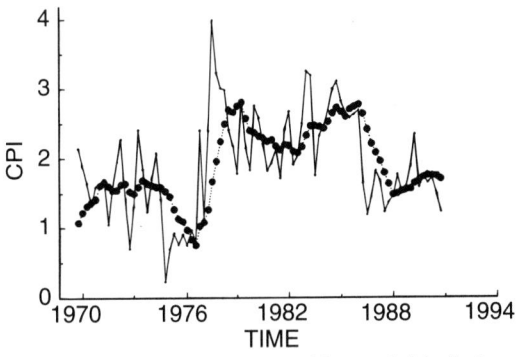

FIGURE 11.2 Time series plot of Quarterly Medical CPI from 1970 to 1991. Smoothed running average, with run length 8, is superimposed.

To forecast the series, re-express equation (11.1) recursively to get

$$\hat{s}_t = \frac{y_t + y_{t-1} + \ldots + y_{t-k+1}}{k} = \frac{y_t + k\hat{s}_{t-1} - y_{t-k}}{k}$$

$$= \hat{s}_{t-1} + \frac{y_t - y_{t-k}}{k}. \qquad (11.2)$$

If there are no trends in the data, then the second term on the right hand side, $(y_t - y_{t-k})/k$, may be ignored in practice. This yields the forecasting equation

$$\hat{y}_{T+l} = \hat{s}_T$$

for forecasts l lead time units into the future.

Several variants of running averages are available in the literature. For example, suppose that a series can be expressed as $y_t = T_t + \epsilon_t$, where T_t is included to handle the presence of a linear trend in time $T_t = \beta_0 + \beta_1 t$. This can be handled through te following *double smoothing* procedure:

1. Create a smoothed series using equation (11.1), that is $\hat{s}_t^{(1)} = (y_t + \ldots + y_{t-k+1})/k$.
2. Create a double smoothed series by using equation (11.1) and treating the smoothed series created in step (1) as input. That is, $\hat{s}_t^{(2)} = (\hat{s}_t^{(1)} + \ldots + \hat{s}_{t-k+1}^{(1)})/k$.

It is easy to check that this procedure smooths out the effects of linear trends in time. The estimate for the trend is $b_{1,T} = 2\,(\hat{s}_{(T)}^{(1)} - \hat{s}_{(T)}^{(2)})/(k-1)$. The resulting forecasts are:

$$\hat{y}_{T+l} = \hat{s}_T + b_{1,T}l$$

for forecasts l lead time units into the future. For other variations of the running average method, see Abraham and Ledolter (1983).

Weighted Least Squares

An important feature of moving, or running, averages is that they can be expressed as weighted least squares (WLS) estimates. Recall, from Section 8.2, that WLS estimates are minimizers of a weighted sum of squares. The WLS procedure is to find the values of $b_0^*, b_1^*, \ldots, b_k^*$ that minimize

$$WSS_T(b_0^*, b_1^*, \ldots, b_k^*) = \sum_{t=1}^{T} w_t(y_t - (b_0^* + b_1^* x_{t1} + b_2^* x_{t2} + \ldots + b_k^* x_{tk}))^2. \quad (11.3)$$

Here, WSS_T is the *weighted sum of squares* at time T.

To arrive at the moving, or running, average estimate we use the model

$$y_t = \beta_0 + e_t \quad (11.4)$$

with the choice of weights $w_t = 1$ for $t = T-k+1, \ldots, T$ and $w_t = 0$ for $t < T - k + 1$. Thus, the problem of minimizing WSS_T in equation (11.3) reduces to finding b_0^* that minimizes

$$WSS_T(b_0^*) = \sum_{t=T-k+1}^{T} (y_t - b_0^*)^2.$$

The value of b_0^* that minimizes $WSS_T(b_0^*)$ is $b_0 = \hat{s}_T = (y_{T-k+1} + \ldots + y_T)/k$, which is the running average of length k.

The model in equation (11.4), together with this choice of weights, is called a *locally constant mean model*. Under a *globally constant mean model*, equal weights are used and the least squares estimate of β_0 is the overall average, $\bar{y}$. Under the locally constant mean model, we give equal weight to observations within k time units of the evaluation time T and zero weight to other observations. Although it is intuitively appealing to give more weight to more recent observations, the notion of an abrupt cutoff at a somewhat arbitrarily chosen k is not appealing. This criticism is addressed using exponential smoothing, introduced in the following section.

11.2 FORECASTING WITH EXPONENTIAL SMOOTHING

Exponential smoothing estimates are weighted averages of past values of a series, where the weights are given by a series that becomes exponentially small. To illustrate, think of w as a weight number that is between zero and one and consider the weighted average:

$$\frac{y_t + wy_{t-1} + w^2 y_{t-2} + w^3 y_{t-3} + \ldots}{\dfrac{1}{1-w}}.$$

This is a weighted average because the weights $w^k(1-w)$ sum to one [that is, a geometric series expansion yields $\sum_{k=0}^{\infty} w^k = 1/(1-w)$]. Because observations are not available in the infinite past, we use the truncated version

$$\hat{s}_t = \frac{y_t + wy_{t-1} + \ldots + w^{t-1}y_1 + w^t y_0}{\dfrac{1}{1-w}} \tag{11.5}$$

to define the *exponential smoothed estimate* of the series. Here, y_0 is called the *starting value* of the series and is often chosen to be either zero, y_1, or the average value of the series, $\bar{y}$. Like running average estimates, the smoothed estimates in equation (11.5) provide greater weights to more recent observations as compared to observations far in the past with respect to time t. Unlike running averages, the weight function is smooth, giving weights using a geometrically decreasing series $\{w^k\}$. Figure 11.3 illustrates the behavior of the two weighting functions.

The definition of exponential smoothing estimates in equation (11.5) appears complex. However, as with running averages in equation (11.2), we can re-express equation (11.5) recursively to yield

$$\hat{s}_t = \hat{s}_{t-1} + (1-w)(y_t - \hat{s}_{t-1}) = (1-w)y_t + w\hat{s}_{t-1} \tag{11.6}$$

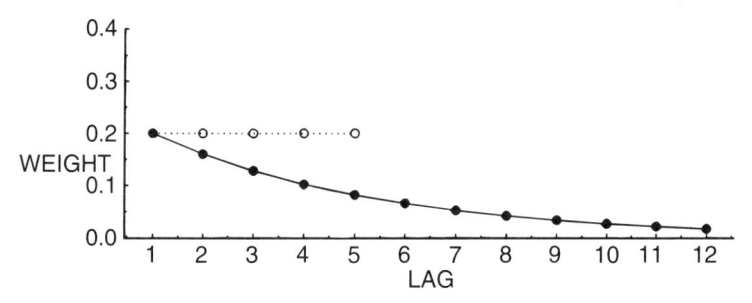

FIGURE 11.3 Weights of two time series forecasting methods. The running average weights are given by the open circles, the exponential smoothing weights are marked with the opaque circles.

The expression of the smoothed estimates in equation (11.6) is easier to compute than the definition in equation (11.5).

Equation (11.6) also provides insights into the role of w as the smoothing parameter. For example, on one hand as w gets close to zero, from equation (11.6) we see that $\hat{s}_t$ gets close to y_t. This indicates that little smoothing has taken place. On the other hand, as w gets close to one, there is little effect of y_t on $\hat{s}_t$. This indicates that a substantial amount of smoothing has taken place because the current fitted value is almost entirely composed of past observations.

Example 11.1: The Medical Component of the CPI—Continued

To illustrate the effect of the choice of the smoothing parameter, consider Figures 11.4 and 11.5. These are time series plots of the quarterly index of the medical component of the CPI, the same data that was used in Section 11.1. In Figure 11.4, the smoothed series with $w = 0.2$ is superimposed on the actual series. Figure 11.5 is the corresponding graph with $w = 0.8$. From these figures, we can see that the larger is w, then the smoother are our fitted values.

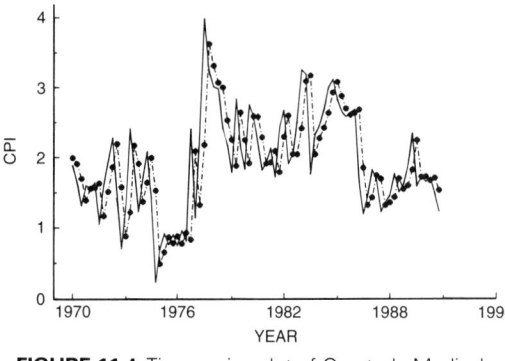

FIGURE 11.4 Time series plot of Quarterly Medical CPI from 1970 to 1990. Exponential smoothing fit, with weight = 0.2, is superimposed.

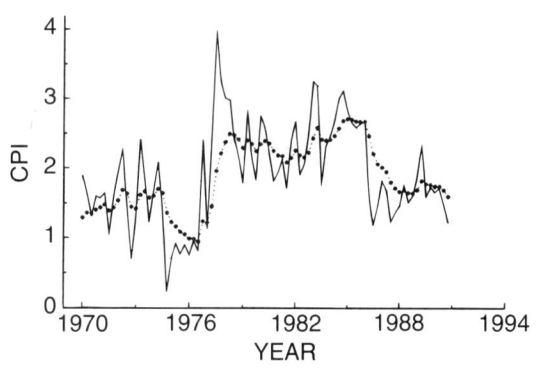

FIGURE 11.5 Time series plot of Quarterly Medical CPI from 1970 to 1990. Exponential smoothing fit, with weight = 0.8, is superimposed.

Equation (11.6) also suggests the forecasting equation,

$$\hat{y}_{T+l} = \hat{s}_T,$$

for our forecast of y_{T+l}, that is, the series at l lead units in the future. Forecasts not only provide a way of predicting the future but also a way of assessing the fit. At time $t - 1$, our "forecast" of y_t is $\hat{s}_{t-1}$. The difference is called the *one-step prediction error*.

To assess the degree of fit, we use the sum of squared one-step prediction errors

$$SS(w) = \sum_{t=1}^{T} (y_t - \hat{s}_{t-1})^2. \tag{11.7}$$

An important thing to note is that this sum of squares is a function of the smoothing parameter, w. This then provides a criterion for choosing the smoothing parameter: choose the w that minimizes $SS(w)$. Traditionally, analysts have recommended that w lie within the interval $(0.70, 0.95)$, without providing an objective criterion for the choice. Although minimizing $SS(w)$ does provide an objective criterion, it is also computationally intensive. In absence of a sophisticated numerical routine, this minimization is typically accomplished by calculating $SS(w)$ at a number of choices of w and choosing the w that provides the smallest value of $SS(w)$.

To illustrate the choice of the exponential smoothing parameter w, we return to Example 11.1. Figure 11.6 summarizes the calculation of $SS(w)$ for various values of w. For this data set, it appears a choice of $w \approx 0.30$ minimizes $SS(w)$.

As with running averages, the presence of a linear trend in time, $T_t = \beta_0 + \beta_1 t$, can be handled through the following *double smoothing* procedure:

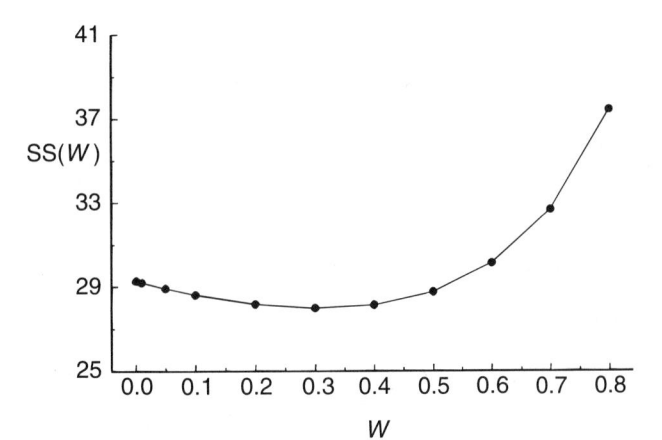

FIGURE 11.6 Plot of sum of squared one-step prediction errors, SS(w), versus the exponential smoothing parameter w.

1. Create a smoothed series using equation (11.6), that is, $\hat{s}_t^{(1)} = (1 - w)\, y_t + w\, \hat{s}_{t-1}^{(1)}$.
2. Create a doubly smoothed series by using equation (11.6) and treating the smoothed series created in step (1) as input. That is,

$$\hat{s}_t^{(2)} = (1 - w)\, \hat{s}_t^{(1)} + w\, \hat{s}_{t-1}^{(2)}.$$

The estimate of the trend is $b_{1,T} = ((1 - w)/w)\,(\hat{s}_T^{(1)} - \hat{s}_T^{(2)})$. The forecasts are given by $\hat{y}_{T+l} = b_{0,T} + l\, b_{1,T}$, where the estimate of the intercept is $b_{0,T} = 2\,\hat{s}_T^{(1)} - \hat{s}_T^{(2)}$. We will also show how to use exponential smoothing for data with seasonal patterns in Section 11.3. Other variants of exponential smoothing can be found in Abraham and Ledolter (1983).

Weighted Least Squares

As with running averages, an important feature of exponentially smoothed estimates is that they can be expressed as weighted least squares (WLS) estimates. To see this, for the model

$$y_t = \beta_0 + e_t,$$

the general weighted sum of squares in equation (11.3) reduces to

$$\text{WSS}_T(b_0^*) = \sum_{t=1}^{T} w_t (y_t - b_0^*)^2.$$

The value of b_0^* that minimizes $WSS_T(b_0^*)$ is

$$b_0 = \sum_{t=1}^{T} w_t y_t \Big/ \sum_{t=1}^{T} w_t.$$

With the choice $w_t = w^{T-t}$, we have $b_0 \approx \hat{s}_T$, where there is equality except for the minor issue of the starting value. Thus, exponential smoothing estimates are WLS estimates. Further, because of the choice of the form of the weights, exponential smoothing estimates are also called *discounted least squares estimates*. Here, the thinking is that $w_t = w^{T-t}$ is a discounting function that one might use in considering the time value of money.

11.3 SEASONAL TIME SERIES MODELS

Seasonal patterns appear in many time series that arise in the study of business and economics. Models of seasonality are predominantly used to address patterns that arise as the result of an identifiable, physical phenomenon. For example, seasonal weather patterns affect people's health and, in turn, the demand for prescription drugs. These same seasonal models may be used to model longer cyclical behavior. Example 9.3 showed how the effect of presidential elections could be accounted for using a seasonal component.

There is a variety of techniques available for handling seasonal patterns including fixed seasonal effects, seasonal autoregressive models and seasonal exponential smoothing methods. We address each of these techniques in the following sections.

Fixed Seasonal Effects

Recall that, in equations (9.1) and (9.1), we used S_t to represent the seasonal effects under additive and multiplicative decomposition models, respectively. A *fixed seasonal effects model* represents S_t as a function of time t. The two most important examples of fixed effects functions are the seasonal indicator functions and trigonometric functions. Example 9.3 showed how to use seasonal indicators and Example 11.2 will demonstrate the use of trigonometric functions. The qualifier "fixed effects" means that relationships are constant over time. In contrast, both exponential smoothing and autoregression techniques provide us with methods that adapt to recent events and allow for trends that change over time.

A large class of seasonal patterns can be represented using trigonometric functions. Consider the function

$$g(t) = a \sin(ft + b)$$

where a is the amplitude (the largest value of the curve), f is the frequency (the number of cycles that occurs in the interval $(0, 2\pi)$), and b is the phase shift. Because of the basic identity, $\sin(x + y) = \sin x \cos y + \sin y \cos x$, we can write

$$g(t) = \beta_1 \sin(ft) + \beta_2 \cos(ft),$$

where $\beta_1 = a \cos b$ and $\beta_2 = a \sin b$. For a time series with *seasonal base SB*, we can represent a wide variety of seasonal patterns using

$$S_t = \sum_{i=1}^{m} a_i \sin(f_i t + b_i) = \sum_{i=1}^{m} \beta_{1i} \sin(f_i t) + \beta_{2i} \cos(f_i t) \qquad (11.8)$$

with $f_i = 2\pi i/SB$. To illustrate, the complex function shown in Figure 11.8 was constructed as the sum of the ($m=$) 2 simpler trigonometric functions that are shown in Figure 11.7.

Consider the model $y_t = \beta_0 + S_t + e_t$, where S_t is specified in equation (11.8). Because $\sin(f_i t)$ and $\cos(f_i t)$ are functions of time, they can be treated as known explanatory variables. Thus, the model

$$y_t = \beta_0 + \sum_{i=1}^{m} \{\beta_{1i} \sin(f_i t) + \beta_{2i} \cos(f_i t)\} + e_t$$

is a multiple linear regresssion model with $k = 2m$ explanatory variables. This model can be estimated using standard statistical regression software. Further, we can use our variable selection techniques to choose m, the number of trigonometric functions. We note that m is at most $SB/2$, for SB even. Other-

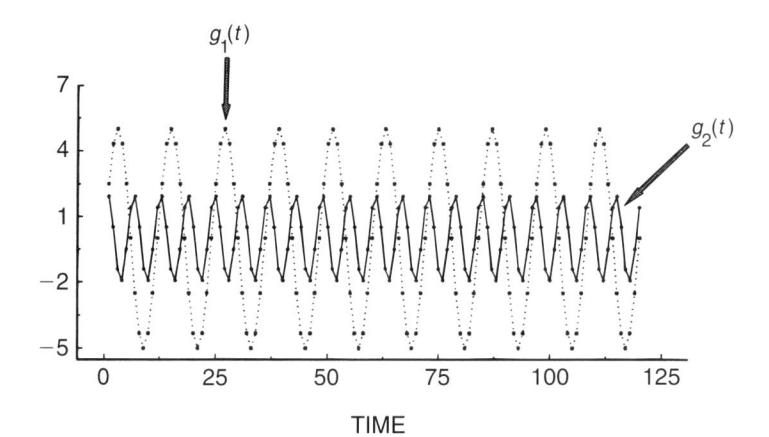

FIGURE 11.7 Plot of two trigonometric functions. Here, $g_1(t)$ has amplitude a_1 = 5, frequency $f_1 = 2\pi/12$ and phase shift $b_1 = 0$. Further, $g_2(t)$ has amplitude $a_2 = 2$, frequency $f_2 = 4\pi/12$ and phase shift $b_2 = \pi/4$.

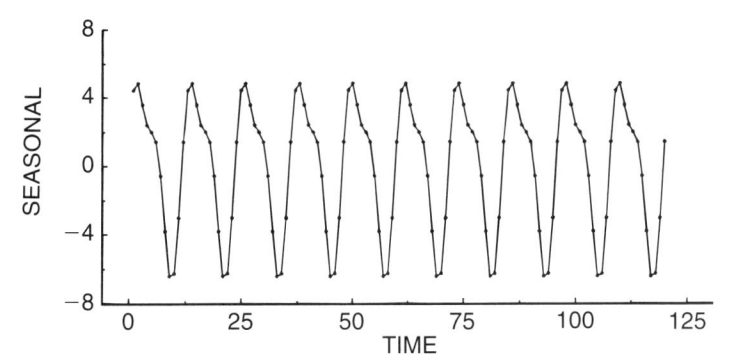

FIGURE 11.8 Plot of sum of the two trigonometric functions in Figure 11.7.

wise, we would have perfect collinearity because of the periodicity of the sine function. Example 11.2 demonstrates how to choose m less than $SB/2$.

Example 11.2: Cost of Prescription Drugs

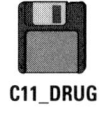

C11_DRUG

We consider a series from the State of New Jersey's Prescription Drug Program, the cost per prescription claim. This monthly series is available over the period August 1986 through March 1992, inclusive.

Figure 11.9 shows that the series is clearly nonstationary, in that cost per prescription claims are increasing over time. There is a variety of ways of handling this trend. One may begin with a linear trend in time and include lag claims to handle autocorrelations. For this series, a good approach to the modeling turns out to be to consider the percentage changes in the cost per claim series. Figure 11.10 is a time series plot of the

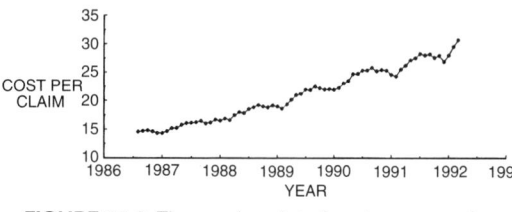

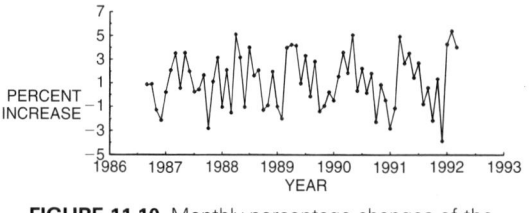

FIGURE 11.9 Time series plot of cost per prescription claim of the State of New Jersey's Prescription Drug Plan.

FIGURE 11.10 Monthly percentage changes of the cost per prescription claim.

percent changes. In this figure, we see that many of the trends that were evident in Figure 11.9 have been filtered out.

Figure 11.10 displays some mild seasonal patterns in the data. A close inspection of the data reveals higher percentage increases in the spring and lower increases in the fall months. A trigonometric function using $m = 1$ was fit to the data; the fitted model is:

$$\hat{y}_t = \quad 1.2217 \quad - 1.6956 \sin(2\pi t/12) \quad + 0.6536 \cos(2\pi t/12)$$

$$std\ errors \quad (0.2325) \qquad (0.3269) \qquad\qquad (0.3298)$$

$$t-ratios \quad [5.25] \qquad\quad [-5.08] \qquad\qquad [1.98]$$

with $s = 1.897$ and $R^2 = 31.5\%$. This model reveals some important seasonal patterns. The explanatory variables are statistically significant and an F-test establishes the significance of the model. Figure 11.11 shows the data with fitted values from the model superimposed. These superimposed fitted values help to detect visually the seasonal patterns.

Examination of the residuals from this fitted model revealed few

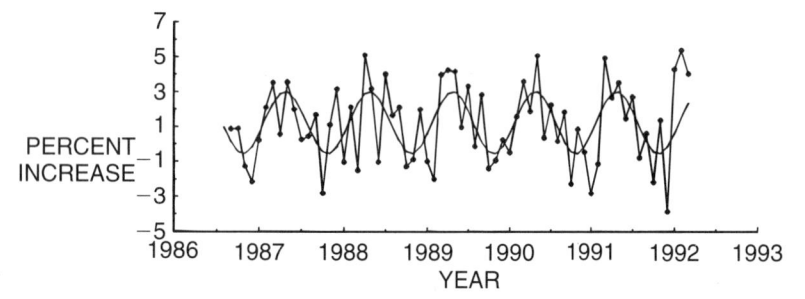

FIGURE 11.11 Monthly percentage changes of the cost per prescription claim. Fitted values from the seasonal trigonometric model have been superimposed.

further patterns. Further, the model using $m = 2$ was fit to the data, resulting in $R^2 = 33.6\%$. We can decide whether to use $m = 1$ or 2 by considering the model

$$y_t = \beta_0 + \sum_{i=1}^{2} \{\beta_{1i} \sin(f_i t) + \beta_{2i} \cos(f_i t)\} + e_t$$

and testing H_0: $\beta_{12} = \beta_{22} = 0$. Using the partial F-test, with $T = 67$, $k = p = 2$, from equation (4.10), we have

$$F\text{-ratio} = \frac{\dfrac{0.336 - 0.315}{2}}{\dfrac{1.000 - 0.336}{62}} = 0.98.$$

With $df_1 = p = 2$ and $df_2 = T - (k + p + 1) = 62$, the 95th percentile of the F-distribution is F-value = 3.15. Because F-ratio $< F$-value, we can not reject H_0 and conclude that $m = 1$ is the preferred choice.

Finally, it is also of interest to see how our model of the transformed data works with our original data, in units of cost per prescription claim. Fitted values of percentage increases were converted back to fitted values of cost per claim. Figure 11.12 shows the original data with fitted values superimposed. This figure establishes the strong relationship between the actual and fitted series.

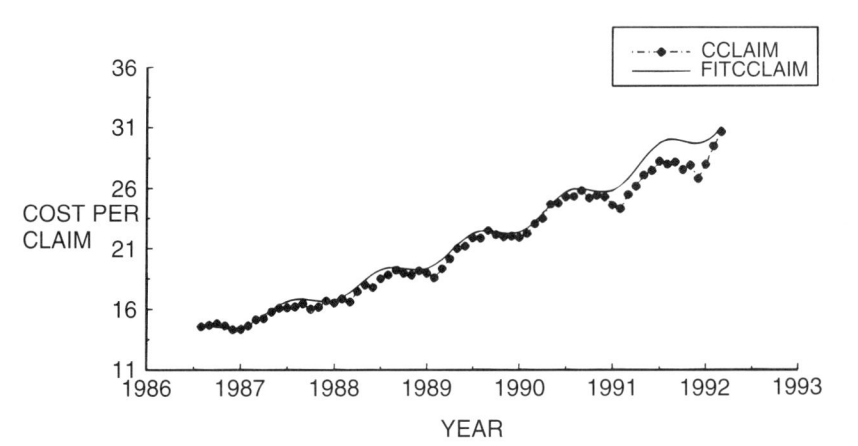

FIGURE 11.12 Monthly costs per prescription claim. Fitted values from the seasonal trigonometric model have been superimposed.

Seasonal Autoregressive Models

In Chapter 10 we examined patterns through time using autocorrelations of the form ρ_k, the correlation between y_t and y_{t-k}. We constructed representations of these temporal patterns using autoregressive models, regression models with lagged responses as explanatory variables. Seasonal time patterns can be handled similarly. We define the *seasonal autoregressive model of order P*, *SAR(P)*, as

$$y_t = \beta_0 + \beta_1 y_{t-SB} + \beta_2 y_{t-2SB} + \ldots + \beta_P y_{t-PSB} + e_t, \tag{11.9}$$

where SB is the seasonal base under consideration. For example, using $SB = 12$, a seasonal model of order one, $SAR(1)$, is

$$y_t = \beta_0 + \beta_1 y_{t-12} + e_t.$$

Unlike the $AR(12)$ model defined in equation (10.7), for the $SAR(1)$ model we have omitted $y_{t-1}, y_{t-2}, \ldots, y_{t-11}$ as explanatory variables, although retaining y_{t-12}.

Just as in Chapter 10, choice of the order of the model is accomplished by examining the autocorrelation structure and using an iterative model fitting strategy. Similarly, the choice of seasonality SB is based on an examination of the data. We refer the interested reader to Abraham and Ledolter (1983).

Example 11.2: Cost of Prescription Drugs—Continued

Table 11.1 presents autocorrelations for the percentage increase in cost per claim of prescription drugs. There are $n = 67$ observations for this data set, resulting in approximate standard error of $se(r_k) = (67)^{-1/2} \approx 0.122$. Thus, autocorrelations at and around lags 6, 12 and 18 appear to be significantly different than zero. This suggests using $SB = 6$. Further examination of the data suggested an $SAR(2)$ model. The resulting fitted model is:

$\hat{y}_t =$	1.2191	$- 0.2867\, y_{t-6}$	$+ 0.3120\, y_{t-12}$
std errors	(0.4064)	(0.1502)	(0.1489)
t–ratios	[3.00]	[−1.91]	[2.09]

with $s = 2.156$. This model was fit using conditional least squares. Note that because we are using y_{t-12} as an explanatory variable, the first resid-

TABLE 11.1 Autocorrelations of the Monthly Percentage Changes of the Cost per Prescription Claim

k	1	2	3	4	5	6	7	8	9
r_k	0.08	0.10	−0.12	−0.11	−0.32	−0.33	−0.29	0.07	0.08
k	10	11	12	13	14	15	16	17	18
r_k	0.25	0.24	0.31	−0.01	0.14	−0.10	−0.08	−0.25	−0.18

ual that can be estimated is $\hat{e}_{13}$. That is, we lose 12 observations when lagging by 12 when using least squares estimates.

The fitted model shows that the seasonal lagged variables are significant predictors of the percentage increase in costs per prescription claim. Figure 11.13 illustrates the relationship between actual costs and the fitted values under the model.

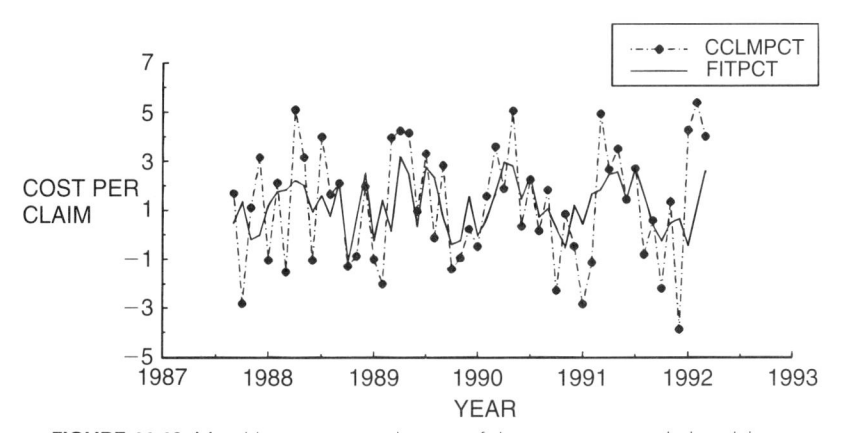

FIGURE 11.13 Monthly percentage changes of the cost per prescription claim. Fitted values from the seasonal autoregressive model have been superimposed.

Seasonal Exponential Smoothing

An exponential smoothing method that has enjoyed considerable popularity among forecasters is the *Holt–Winter additive seasonal model*. Although it is difficult to express forecasts from this model as weighted least square estimates, the model does appear to work well in practice.

The Holt procedure is a generalization of the double exponential smoothing procedure.

Holt (1957) introduced the following generalization of the double exponential smoothing method. Let w_1 and w_2 be two smoothing parameters and calculate recursively the parameter estimates:

$$b_{0,t} = (1 - w_1)y_t + w_1(b_{0,t-1} + b_{1,t-1})$$
$$b_{1,t} = (1 - w_2)(b_{0,t} - b_{0,t-1}) + w_2 b_{1,t-1}.$$

These estimates can be used to forecast the linear trend model, $y_t = \beta_0 + \beta_1 t + e_t$. The forecasts are $\hat{y}_{T+l} = b_{0,T} + b_{1,T}l$. With the choice $w_1 = w^2$ and $w_2 = 2w/(1 + w)$, the Holt procedure can be shown to produce the same estimates as the double exponential smoothing estimates described in Section 11.2. Because there are two smoothing parameters, the Holt procedure is a generalization of the doubly exponentially smoothed procedure. With two parameters, we need not use the same smoothing constants for the level (β_0) and the trend (β_1) components. This extra flexibility has found appeal with some data analysts.

Winters (1960) extended the Holt procedure to accommodate seasonal trends. Specifically, the Holt-Winter seasonal additive model is

$$y_t = \beta_0 + \beta_1 t + S_t + e_t$$

where $S_t = S_{t-SB}$, $S_1 + S_2 + \ldots + S_{SB} = 0$ and SB is the seasonal base. We now employ three smoothing parameters: one for the level, w_1, one for the trend, w_2, and one for the seasonality, w_3. The parameter estimates for this model are determined recursively using:

$$b_{0,t} = (1 - w_1)(y_t - \hat{S}_{t-SB}) + w_1(b_{0,t-1} + b_{1,t-1})$$
$$b_{1,t} = (1 - w_2)(b_{0,t} - b_{0,t-1}) + w_2 b_{1,t-1}$$
$$\hat{S}_t = (1 - w_3)(y_t - b_{0,t}) + w_3 \hat{S}_{t-SB}.$$

With these parameter estimates, forecasts are determined using:

$$\hat{y}_T(l) = b_{0,T} + b_{1,T}l + \hat{S}_T(l)$$

where $\hat{S}_T(l) = \hat{S}_{T+l}$ for $l = 1, 2, \ldots, SB$, $\hat{S}_T(l) = \hat{S}_{T+l-SB}$ for $l = SB+1, \ldots, 2SB$ and so on.

In order to compute the recursive estimates, we must decide on (i) initial starting values and (ii) a choice of smoothing parameters. To determine initial starting values, we recommend fitting a regression equation to the first portion of the data. The regression equation will include a linear trend in time, $\beta_0 + \beta_1 t$, and $SB - 1$ indicator variables for seasonal variation. Thus, only $SB + 1$ observations are required to determine initial estimates $b_{0,0}, b_{1,0}, y_{1-SB}, y_{2-SB}, \ldots, y_0$.

Choosing the three smoothing parameters is more difficult. Analysts have found it difficult to choose parameters using an objective criterion, such as the minimization of the sum of squared one-step prediction errors, as in Section 11.2. Part of the difficulty stems from the nonlinearity of the minimization, resulting in prohibitive computational time. Another part of the difficulty is that a function such as the sum of squared one-step prediction errors often turns out to be relatively insensitive to the choice of parameters. Analysts have instead relied on rules of thumb to guide the choice of smoothing parameters. In particular, because seasonal effects may take several years to develop, a lower value of w_3 is recommended (resulting in more smoothing). Cryer and Miller (1994) recommend $w_1 = w_2 = 0.9$ and $w_3 = 0.6$.

11.4 CAUSAL TIME SERIES MODELS

A *causal time series model* is a representation of a response over time, y_t, that includes one more independent variables $\{x_t\}$. To illustrate, consider the model

$$y_t = \beta_0 + \beta_1 y_{t-1} + \beta_2 x_t + \beta_3 x_{t-1} + e_t.$$

As in Chapter 10, we may use the lagged response, y_{t-1}, as a predictor variable. We have also included as a predictor variable x_t, a *contemporaneous* variable, as well as x_{t-1}, a *lagged independent* variable.

Causal models are also referred to as *econometric models*; specification of these models may be suggested by underlying economic theory as opposed to a close examination of the data. Even specifying a simple causal model such as

$$y_t = \beta_0 + \beta_1 x_t + e_t \qquad (11.10)$$

is fraught with difficulties. This is typically due to the problem of distinguishing the autocorrelations of $\{y_t\}$ and $\{x_t\}$ from the cross-sectional correlation between $\{y_t\}$ and $\{x_t\}$. Cross-sectional correlations that appear significant but are induced by autocorrelations are called *spurious* correlations.

For contrast, we have already worked with two special cases of the model in equation (11.10) in which we have had few problems estimating a model. The first special case was the CAPM model of Section 3.6, where y_t represented the return from a security and x_t represented the return from the market. For this example, it turned out that there was little autocorrelation in either the $\{y_t\}$ or in the $\{x_t\}$ series. This lack of autocorrelation allowed us to focus on the cross-sectional correlation. The second example occurred in Section 9.1 where we used x_t as a deterministic function of time, including an indicator and a linear trend variable. Because of the deterministic nature of x_t, there was no need to be concerned about autocorrelations of the $\{x_t\}$ series. This greatly reduced the impediments to specifying causal models.

In many instances, the series $\{x_t\}$ is stochastic, which causes a number of difficulties. We have already alluded to the problem of specifying the model. However, even if a model such as in equation (11.10) is correctly specified, there may still be problems using the model for inference. For example, if we wished to use the model in equation (11.10) for forecasting, then we would need to forecast a value of x. Recall that this was not a problem when x_t was a deterministic function of time, because any value of x_t could be calculated once the associated parameters were determined. If only short term forecasts are of interest, then one solution is to replace x_t by x_{t-1} to form the model

$$y_t = \beta_0 + \beta_1 x_{t-1} + e_t.$$

In this case, the variable x is said to be a *leading indicator* of y. If this model is correct, then $\hat{y}_{T+1} = b_0 + b_1 x_T$ may be a useful one-step forecast of y from time T. However, for longer term forecasts, one still needs to forecast the $\{x_t\}$ series.

Thus, there are several difficulties in specifying causal models and using these models for inference. In this section, we introduce a causal model that has enjoyed a great deal of attention in the econometric literature, the *regression model with autoregressive disturbances*. Specifically, we assume the model

$$y_t = \beta_0 + \beta_1 x_{1t} + \ldots + \beta_k x_{kt} + e_t$$

where $\qquad\qquad\qquad\qquad\qquad\qquad\qquad\qquad\qquad\qquad\qquad\qquad$ (11.11)

$$e_t = \phi_1 e_{t-1} + \ldots + \phi_p e_{t-p} + u_t.$$

Here, we assume that $\{u_t\}$ follows a random process so that the disturbance series $\{e_t\}$ follows an $AR(p)$ model. Further, we assume that the explanatory variables are either deterministic or are independent of the disturbance series. Following the development of Chapter 10, we now focus on the special case $p = 1$ so that the disturbances follow an $AR(1)$ process with mean zero. We first address the identification and specification, and then the estimation, of this model.

Regression Models with Autoregressive Disturbances—Identification

We assume, either through underlying theory, or a preliminary examination of the data, that k explanatory variables $x_1, x_2, ..., x_k$, have been specified. With these variables, ordinary least squares estimates $b_0, b_1, ..., b_k$ can be easily determined and used to calculate the residuals $\hat{e}_t = y_t - (b_0 + b_1 x_1 + ... + b_k x_k)$ in the usual manner. If the disturbances follow an $AR(p)$ process, then it turns out that the least squares method still provides reliable estimates of the regression parameters $\beta_0, \beta_1, ..., \beta_k$. Thus, we can use the residuals to approximate the disturbances. Thus, we can now present two types of methods for determining whether the disturbances follow an autoregressive model or a random process.

The first type of method begins with constructing the autocorrelations of the residual series. Specifically, we define the *lag k autocorrelation of the residuals*,

$$r_k(\hat{e}) = \frac{\sum_{t=k+1}^{T} \hat{e}_t \hat{e}_{t-k}}{\sum_{t=1}^{T} \hat{e}_t^2}. \tag{11.12}$$

This autocorrelation is the same as r_k defined in equation (10.1), except that the residuals are used as inputs. Recall that, if $\hat{e}$ is a residual from a linear regression model with an intercept, then the average residual is zero. Thus, no average residual term appears in equation (11.12). With these autocorrelations, identification of an autoregressive model for the disturbances can proceed as introduced in Chapter 10, treating the residuals as data.

The second type of method is due to Durbin and Watson (1950). They proposed the statistic

$$DW = \frac{\sum_{t=2}^{T} (\hat{e}_t - \hat{e}_{t-1})^2}{\sum_{t=1}^{T} \hat{e}_t^2}. \tag{11.13}$$

To see the relationship between *DW* and the autocorrelation statistics, we have

$$DW = \frac{\sum_{t=2}^{T} (\hat{e}_t^2 + \hat{e}_{t-1}^2 - 2\hat{e}_t\hat{e}_{t-1})}{\sum_{t=1}^{T} \hat{e}_t^2} = 2 - \frac{\hat{e}_1^2 + \hat{e}_T^2}{\sum_{t=1}^{T} \hat{e}_t^2} - 2r_1(\hat{e})$$

$$\approx 2(1 - r_1(\hat{e})).$$

In developing the approximation $DW \approx 2 (1 - r_1(\hat{e}))$, we have used the assumption that $\hat{e}_1^2$ and $\hat{e}_T^2$ are small compared to the error sum of squares, $\Sigma_{t=1}^{T} \hat{e}_t^2$. From this approximation, we see that the Durbin-Watson statistic detects only lag one relationships. This statistic does not detect relationships at higher order lags, such as might be encountered with seasonal data.

The advantage of *DW* compared to the autocorrelation statistics is that exact tables are available for testing the null hypothesis that the lag one autocorrelation of the disturbances is zero, that is, $H_0: \rho_1(e) = 0$. This table provides cut-offs that vary by T and k, and are exact assuming normality of the disturbances. Thus, in the event of a small sample size, for example $T \leq 20$, the Durbin-Watson statistic may be a useful alternative to the autocorrelation statistic. Tables of the Durbin-Watson cutoffs can be found in, for example, Box, Jenkins and Reinsel (1994).

Regression Models with Autoregressive Disturbances— Estimation

There are several methods for estimating parameters of a regression model with an $AR(1)$ disturbance. We present here the method due to Prais and Winston (1954); this turns out to be an application of the *generalized least squares* (GLS) method of estimation. The GLS method is an extension of the weighted least squares (WLS) method that was introduced in Chapter 8. As with WLS, the approach in GLS is to transform the data so that the model satisfies the assumptions of the basic linear regression model described in Chapter 4. To see how this transformation works, first assume that the autoregressive parameter ϕ_1 is known. Then, from equation (11.11) with $p = 1$, we can write for $t = 2, 3, \ldots, T$

$$y_t^* = y_t - \phi_1 y_{t-1} = (\beta_0 + \beta_1 x_{1t} + \ldots + \beta_k x_{kt} + e_t)$$

$$- \phi_1(\beta_0 + \beta_1 x_{1t-1} + \ldots + \beta_k x_{k,t-1} + e_{t-1}) \qquad (11.14)$$

$$= \beta_0(1 - \phi_1) + \beta_1 x_{1t}^* + \ldots + \beta_k x_{kt}^* + u_t$$

where $x_{jt}^* = x_{j,t} - \phi_1 x_{j,t-1}$ for $j = 1, 2, \ldots, k$. For $t = 1$, we can write

$$y_1^* = y_1(1 - \phi_1^2)^{1/2}$$

$$= \beta_0(1 - \phi_1^2)^{1/2} + \beta_1 x_{11}^* + \ldots + \beta_k x_{k1}^* + u_1^* \qquad (11.15)$$

where $x_{j1}^* = x_{j1} (1 - \phi_1^2)^{1/2}$ for $j = 1, 2, \ldots, k$ and $u_1^* = e_1 (1 - \phi_1^2)^{1/2}$. The advantage of this transformation is that now the disturbances of the transformed model $\{u_1^*, u_2, \ldots, u_T\}$ can be shown to be independent and homoscedastic. Thus, with the minor item of an intercept term that is different at time one, the transformed model follows our basic linear regression model set-up.

To implement this GLS estimation, use the following two-stage procedure:

1. Run the usual (ordinary) least squares regression routine. Determine the residuals from the regression fit and use these residuals to calculate $r_1(\hat{e})$.
2. Use $r_1(\hat{e})$ as the estimate of ϕ_1. With this estimated value, calculate the transformed model in equations (11.14) and (11.15). Run ordinary least squares on this transformed model to get parameter estimates.

As with WLS, it is possible to iterate this procedure. This is, once we have GLS regression parameter estimates from stage two, we could return to stage one, calculate residuals and a new estimate of ϕ_1. Experience and theory suggest that there is only a small gain after the first iteration. Unless the iterative procedure is automated, we recommend running only the basic two-step procedure. See Greene (1993) for further discussion of this and alternative estimation procedures for autoregressive disturbances.

11.5 SUMMARY

Chapter 11 is the last of the three chapters (9, 10, and 11) on models of longitudinal data. It provides a survey of popular forecasting techniques that are not described in Chapters 9 and 10. Among the techniques introduced in Chapter 11, each can be expressed as a regression model.

We began in Section 11.0 with an overview of forecasting and discussed qualitative versus quantitative forecasts, time series versus causal models and useful characteristics of forecasts. Sections 11.1 and 11.2 introduced two intuitively appealing and easy to compute forecasting techniques, moving averages and exponential smoothing. To connect these popular techniques with the rest of the text, we pointed out how each could be expressed as weighted least squares estimates; this provides certain theoretical underpinnings and removes some of the arbitrariness from consideration of the procedures. Section 11.3 extended our discussion of time series models to accommodate seasonal data. In particular, we extended the discussion on fixed seasonal effects that began in Section 9.1 to include trigonometric functions. As other devices for handling seasonal data, we then discussed modifications of the autoregressive models introduced in Chapter 10 and exponential smoothing methods. Finally, Section 11.4 provided a brief introduction to causal time series models that are used extensively in econometrics. Forecasting series using stochastic explanatory variables is an important subject that is fraught with potential difficulties. Section 11.4 introduced some of these difficulties and provided background for further reading, such as Harvey (1989).

KEY WORDS, PHRASES AND SYMBOLS

After reading this chapter, you should be able to define each of the following important terms, phrases and symbols in your own words. If not, go to the page indicated and review the definition.

time series forecast, 488
causal model, 488
naive forecast, 489
moving, or running, average estimate, 490
running average length (k), 490
smoothed values ($\hat{s}$), 490
double smoothing, 491
weighted sum of squares (WSS), 491
locally constant mean model, 492
globally constant mean model, 492

weight (w), 492
exponential smoothed estimate, 492
starting value of the series (y_0), 492
one-step prediction error, 494
discounted least squares estimates, 495
fixed seasonal effects model, 496
seasonal base (SB), 496
m (number of trigonometric functions), 496

seasonal autoregressive model of order P, $SAR(P)$, 500
Holt-Winter additive seasonal model, 501
causal time series model, 502
contemporaneous variable, 503
lagged independent variable, 503
econometric models, 503
spurious correlation, 503
leading indicator, 503

regression model with autoregressive disturbances, 503
ϕ_1 (autoregressive parameter of disturbance term), 503
lag k autocorrelation of the residuals ($r_k(\hat{e})$), 504
Durbin-Watson statistic (DW), 504
generalized least squares (GLS), 505

CHAPTER 11 EXERCISES

C11_BEER

Section 11.3

11.1 Refer to Exercise 9.3

    a. A regression model was fit using the independent variables TIME and MONTH. Residuals from this model were calculated and summarized using an autocorrelation function.

        i. What is the square root of the mean square error (standard error of the estimate) for this model?

        ii. Do you detect any room for model improvement in the patterns displayed by the residuals? Use the autocorrelation function to justify your response. In your response, specify the approximate cut-offs that you are using.

MINITAB Output

Regression Using TIME and MONTH as Independent Variables

DEM_BEER = −322 + 0.168 YEAR + 0.423 C50 + 0.280 C51 + 2.51 C52
           + 2.82 C53 + 4.02 C54 + 4.27 C55 + 4.19 C56 + 4.03 C57
           + 2.00 C58 + 1.68 C59 + 0.375 C60

Predictor	Coef	Stdev	t-ratio	P
Constant	−321.51	21.40	−15.02	0.000
YEAR	0.16826	0.01079	15.59	0.000
C50	0.4231	0.2438	1.74	0.084
C51	0.2805	0.2438	1.15	0.251
C52	2.5053	0.2438	10.28	0.000
C53	2.8207	0.2438	11.57	0.000
C54	4.0220	0.2438	16.50	0.000
C55	4.2728	0.2438	17.53	0.000
C56	4.1917	0.2438	17.20	0.000
C57	4.0319	0.2438	16.54	0.000
C58	1.9959	0.2438	8.19	0.000
C59	1.6775	0.2438	6.88	0.000
C60	0.3751	0.2438	1.54	0.126

R-sq = 87.7%   R-sq(adj) = 86.9%

Analysis of Variance

SOURCE	DF	SS	MS	F	P
Regression	12	607.368	50.614	106.47	0.000
Error	179	85.093	0.475		
Total	191	692.461			

Autocorrelation of Residuals from the
Regression Using TIME and MONTH as Independent Variables
```
    -1.0 -0.8 -0.6 -0.4 -0.2  0.0  0.2  0.4  0.6  0.8  1.0
      +----+----+----+----+----+----+----+----+----+----+
 1  0.431                              XXXXXXXXXXX
 2  0.372                              XXXXXXXXXX
 3  0.415                              XXXXXXXXXXX
 4  0.172                              XXXXX
 5  0.221                              XXXXXXX
 6  0.287                              XXXXXXXX
 7  0.287                              XXXXXXXX
 8  0.347                              XXXXXXXXXX
 9  0.463                              XXXXXXXXXXXX
10  0.303                              XXXXXXXXX
11  0.354                              XXXXXXXXXX
12  0.458                              XXXXXXXXXXX
13  0.189                              XXXXXX
```

b. As an alternative way of analyzing the data, suppose that we decide to look at annual differences of the data.

    i. In the dotplot of differences (Figures E11.1a and b and Table E11.1a), an unusually large point was observed. So that this point would not have undue influence on the model selection process, this point was set to zero. Explain how this procedure is equivalent to running a regression using an indicator variable as the only explanatory variable.

    ii. Compare the standard deviation of the differences with the square root of the mean square error in part a(i). Explain why this provides motivation for further examination of the annual differences.

Create Annual Differences in Demand

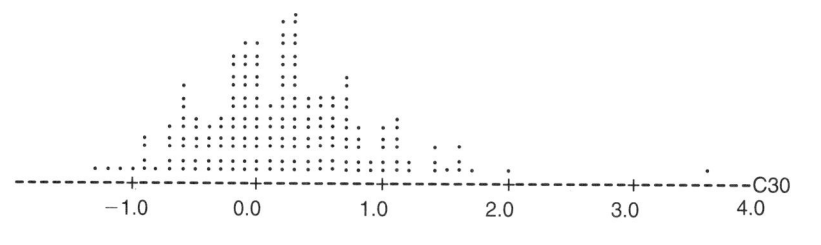

FIGURE E11.1a Dotplot with the large point.

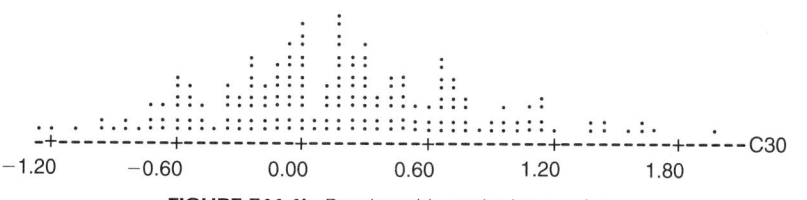

FIGURE E11.1b Dotplot without the large point.

TABLE E11.1a Summary Statistics of Difference

	Number	Number missing	Mean	Median	Standard deviation	Minimum	Maximum
DIFFERENCES	180	12	0.1835	0.1770	0.6139	−1.2668	1.9528

c. The autocorrelation of annual differences suggest that further patterns in the annual differences exist. A preliminary $AR(1)$ model was fit and residuals from this model were calculated.

    i. Does the $AR(1)$ parameter estimate differ significantly from zero? Justify your response.

    ii. Do the residuals exhibit a random pattern? Use the autocorrelation of residuals to justify your response.

    iii. What type of residual autocorrelation pattern would we expect from a random pattern?

```
                            MINITAB Output

                  Autocorrelations of Annual Differences
          -1.0 -0.8 -0.6 -0.4 -0.2  0.0  0.2  0.4  0.6  0.8  1.0
           +----+----+----+----+----+----+----+----+----+----+

      1   0.290                              XXXXXXX
      2   0.085                              XXX
      3   0.036                              XX
      4  -0.208                          XXXXXX
      5  -0.152                           XXXXX
      6   0.027                              XX
      7   0.200                              XXXXX
      8   0.238                              XXXXXXX
      9   0.264                              XXXXXXXX
     10   0.037                              XX
     11  -0.014                             X
     12  -0.210                          XXXXX
     13  -0.233                          XXXXXXX
     14   0.096                              XXX
     15   0.066                              XXX
     16   0.117                              XXXX
     17   0.163                              XXXXX
     18   0.100                              XXX


            Lag One Autoregression Model of Annual Differences

   Final Estimates of Parameters
   Type      Estimate      St. Dev.    t-ratio
   AR   1      0.2946        0.0721       4.08
   Constant   0.13031       0.04388      2.97
   Mean       0.18473       0.06221


   No. of Obs.:   180
   Residuals:    SS = 61.6881  (backforecasts excluded)
                 MS =  0.3466  DF = 178


   Modified Box-Pierce chisquare statistic
   Lag                  12          24          36          48
   Chisquare  36.4 (DF=11)  75.5 (DF=23)  93.6 (DF=35)  113.4 (DF=47)

     Autocorrelation of Residuals from the Lag One Autoregression Model
                        of Annual Differences


          -1.0 -0.8 -0.6 -0.4 -0.2  0.0  0.2  0.4  0.6  0.8  1.0
           +----+----+----+----+----+----+----+----+----+----+
```

```
 1   -0.001                              X
 2   -0.002                              X
 3    0.088                             XXX
 4   -0.210                           XXXXXX
 5   -0.124                            XXXX
 6    0.020                             XX
 7    0.152                            XXXXX
 8    0.133                            XXXX
 9    0.226                           XXXXXXX
10   -0.035                            XX
11    0.039                            XX
12   -0.171                           XXXXX
13   -0.242                          XXXXXXX
14    0.169                           XXXXX
15    0.011                            X
16    0.065                           XXX
17    0.130                           XXXX
18    0.089                           XXX
```

d. Further analysis shows that another candidate model is an autoregressive model with a lag one and a lag twelve component. That model is fit in the following computer output.

   i.   Write down the model that is being fit. Be sure to label all your terms.

  ii.   Write down the corresponding fitted version of the model.

 iii.   Recent values for 1988, 1989 and 1990 are presented in Table E11.1b. Use these values and the fitted model to forecast the next value of the series, January of 1991.

TABLE E11.1b

t	168	169	180	181	192
y_t	12.235	14.091	12.100	14.260	13.220

 iv.   Compare the square root of the mean square error with the corresponding estimates that you examined in part b(ii). Explain why this is a justification for choosing this model.

```
                          MINITAB Output

     Lags One and Twelve Autoregression Model of Annual Differences

     Final Estimates of Parameters
     Type       Estimate    St. Dev.  t-ratio
     AR   1       0.2885     0.0730     3.95
     SAR 12      -0.1825     0.0760    -2.40
```

```
Constant    0.15369    0.04326    3.55
Mean        0.18270    0.05142

No. of obs.:   180
Residuals:     SS = 59.5777  (backforecasts excluded)
               MS =  0.3366  DF = 177

Modified Box-Pierce chisquare statistic
Lag                12            14              36            48
Chisquare  31.9 (DF=10) 80.8  (DF=22)  104.0 (DF=34)  129.8 (DF=46)
```

End-of-Chapter Exercises

C11_WEMP

11.2 As a major marketer of group health insurance in Wisconsin, you are interested in forecasting the number of new business incorporations in Wisconsin. To make your forecasts, you have collected quarterly data from 1980 through 1989, inclusive, on new business incorporations (*NEWINC*) from *Wisconsin Business Indicators*. For this series, it turns out that the average number of new businesses is $\bar{y} = 579.1$ (per quarter) with a standard deviation of $s_y = 74.9$.

   a. Assuming a random process model for *NEWINC*, provide an approximate 95% prediction interval for the fourth quarter of 1990.

   b. i. Use the autocorrelation function to describe any patterns through time that you notice. In your description, specify your guidelines to identify important patterns.

   ii. In the analysis of variance of *NEWINC* by quarter, identify any patterns through time that you notice.

   iii. Describe how the time series plot in Figure E11.2 graphically supports your anawers to parts (i) and (ii).

MINITAB Output

AutoCorrelation Function of NEWINC

```
       -1.0 -0.8 -0.6 -0.4 -0.2  0.0  0.2  0.4  0.6  0.8  1.0
        +----+----+----+----+----+----+----+----+----+----+
   1   0.088                     XXX
   2   0.109                     XXXX
   3  -0.087                   XXX
   4   0.175                     XXXXX
   5  -0.055                    XX
   6  -0.039                    XX
   7  -0.171                  XXXXX
   9   0.152                     XXXXX
```

```
                   Analysis of Variance on NEWINC
       SOURCE     DF      SS      MS        F         P
       quarters    3    64039   21346     4.97     0.005
       ERROR      36   154549    4293
       TOTAL      39   218588
                                     INDIVIDUAL 95 PCT CI'S FOR MEAN
                                     BASED ON POOLED STDEV
       LEVEL      N     MEAN    STDEV   -------+---------+---------+-----
       ----
           1     10   604.00   76.27                        (--------*------
       -)
           2     10   592.50   62.46                       (--------*-------)
           3     10   609.30   75.18                       (--------*-----
       --)
           4     10   510.60   42.46       (-------*--------)
                                          -------+---------+---------+-----
       ----
       POOLED STDEV = 65.52                  500       550       600
```

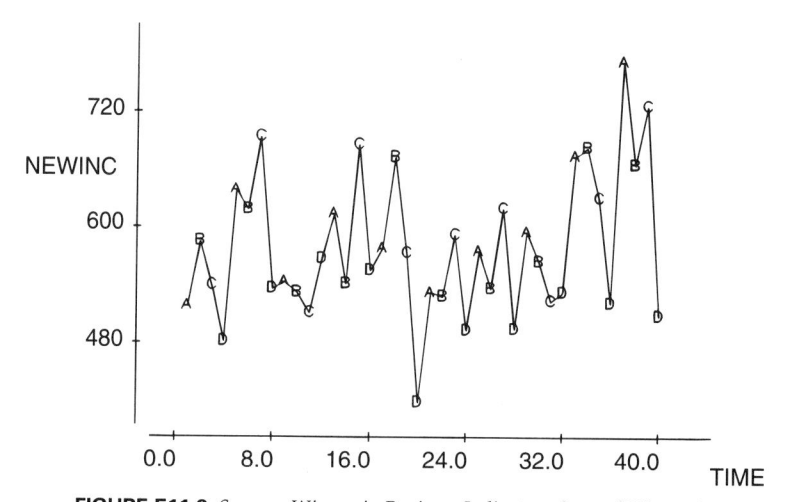

FIGURE E11.2 *Source: Wisconsin Business Indicators, State of Wisconsin*

c. You decide to use the indicator variable of the fourth quarter as an independent variable. After examining the residuals from this preliminary fit, you also include a lagged variable in the regression equation. This model is estimated in the Tables E11.2a–b. Using the estimated model:
   i. Write down the estimated model. Use this model to provide a prediction for each of the four quarters.
   ii. In the fourth quarter of 1989, the most recent data available, there were 508 new businesses incorporated. Use this and your estimated model to provide a point forecast for the fourth quarter of 1990.

TABLE E11.2a Coefficient Estimates

Explanatory variables	Coefficient	Standard error	t-ratio
Constant	475.43	79.50	5.98
LAGINC	0.2266	0.1377	1.64
Q4	−102.87	23.33	−4.41

TABLE E11.2b ANOVA Table

Source	Sum of Squares	df	Mean Square
Regression	76420	2	38210
Error	138338	36	3843
Total	214759	38	

The regression fit also yields $s = 61.99$, $R^2 = 35.6\%$ and $R_a^2 = 32.0\%$.

Unusual Observations

Obs.	LAGINC	NEWINC	Fit	Residual	Std Resid
37	521	772.00	593.47	178.53	2.95
38	772	665.00	650.34	14.66	0.27

d. The first quarter of 1989 was highly unusual. The model described in part (c) was re-fit with an indicator variable for this point. Write down the new fitted model and describe a plausible motivation for this new model.

TABLE E11.2c Coefficient Estimates

Explanatory variables	Coefficient	Standard error	t-ratio
Constant	442.49	79.50	5.98
LAGINC	0.2729	0.1224	2.23
OBS 37	187.32	56.08	3.34
Q4	−98.18	20.65	−4.75

TABLE E11.2d ANOVA Table

Source	Sum of Squares	df	Mean Square
Regression	109863	3	36621
Error	104896	35	2997
Total	214759	38	

The regession fit also yields $s = 54.75$, $R^2 = 51.2\%$ and $R_a^2 = 47.0\%$.

12

Report Writing: Communicating Data Analysis Results

Chapter Objectives

To show how to write statistical reports that inform nontechnical managers as well as technicians reviewing the report. To illustrate, we will consider a report on a study that summarizes patterns in chief executive officer (CEO) compensation.

Chapter Outline

12.1 OVERVIEW

The last relationship has been explored, the last parameter has been estimated, the last forecast has been made, and now you are ready to share the results of your statistical analysis with the world at large. The medium of communication can come in many forms: you may simply recommend to a client to "buy low, sell high" or you may give an oral presentation to your peers. Most likely, however , you will need to summarize your findings in a written report.

Communicating technical information is difficult for a variety of reasons. First, in most data analyses there is no one "right" answer that the author is trying to communicate to the reader. To establish a "right" answer, one only need establish the pros and cons of an issue and weigh their relative merits. Instead, the author is trying to communicate characteristics of the data analyzed and the relationship of the data to more general patterns, a much more complex task. Second, in principle the report containing results of a data analysis should be directed to a primary client, or audience. However, the report is often read by many others and it is important to take into consideration the characteristics of these other readers when judging the pace and order in that the material is presented. This is particularly difficult when a writer can only guess who the secondary audience may be. Third, at times, the writer who is proficient in the subject matter may be less careful in writing the report than in performing the analysis. Conversely, even for a generally effective writer, any confusion in the analysis is inevitably reflected in the report.

As noted, communication of data analysis results could be a brief oral recommendation to a client or a 500-page Ph.D. dissertation. However, a 10- to 20-page report summarizing the main conclusions and outlining the details of the analysis suffice for most business purposes. One key aspect of such a report is to provide the reader with an understanding of the salient features of the data. Enough details of the study should be provided so that the analysis could be independently replicated with access to the original data.

Following is an outline of a report, together with a discussion of the order in which ideas should appear in the report. This outline style, although not appropriate for all situations, serves as a workable framework on which to base your statistical report. Because this is a report about data, the third section describes several methods that you may use when communicating data. In the fourth section are some general guidelines for writing a report.

12.2 HOW TO ORGANIZE

Experts in writing universally agree that ideas in a report should be reported in an organized fashion with some logical flow, although there is no consensus on how this goal should be achieved. Every story has a beginning and an end, usually with an interesting path connecting the two endpoints. There are many types of paths, or methods of development, that connect the beginning and the end. For general technical writing, the method of development may be organized chronologically, spatially, by order of importance, general-to-specific or specific-to-general, by cause-and-effect or any other logical development of the issues. In this section is a discussion of one method of organization for statistical report writing that has achieved desirable results in a number of different circumstances, including the 10- to 20-page report described previously. The broad outline of the recommended format is:

1. Title and Executive Summary,
2. Introduction,
3. Data Characteristics,
4. Model Selection and Interpretation,
5. Summary and Concluding Remarks, and
6. References and Appendix.

Sections (1) and (2) serve as the preparatory material, designed to orient the reader. Sections (3) and (4) form the main body of the report while Sections (5) and (6) are parts of the ending. Each of these sections is described in the following.

Title and Executive Summary

If your report is disseminated widely (as you hope), here is some disappointing news. A vast majority of your intended audience gets no further than the title and the executive summary. Even for readers who carefully read your report, they will usually carry in their memory the impressions left by the title and executive summary unless they are experts in the subject that you are reporting on (which most readers will not be). Choose the title of your report carefully. It should be concise and to the point. Do not include deadwood (phrases like *The Study of, An Analysis of*) but do not be too brief, for example, by using only one word titles. In addition to being concise, the title should be comprehensible, complete and correct.

The executive summary is a one- to two-paragraph summary of your investigation; 75 to 200 words are reasonable rules of thumb. *The language should be nontechnical* as you are trying to reach as broad an audience as possible. This section should summarize the main findings of your report. Be sure to respond to such questions as: What problem was studied? How was it studied? What were the findings? Because you are summarizing not only your results but also your report, it is generally most efficient to write this section last.

Introduction

As with the general report, the introduction should be partitioned into three sections: orientation material, key aspects of the report and a plan of the paper.

To begin the orientation material, re-introduce the problem at the level of technicality that you wish to use in the report. It may or may not be more technical than the statement of the problem in the executive summary. The introduction sets the pace, or the speed at which new ideas are introduced, in the report. Throughout the report, be consistent in the pace. To clearly identify the nature of the problem, in some instances a short literature review is appropriate here. The literature review identifies other reports that provide insight on related aspects of the same problem. This helps to crystallize the new features of your report.

As part of the key aspects of the report, identify the source and nature of the data used in your study. Make sure that the manner in which your data set can address the stated problem is apparent. Give an indication of the class of modeling techniques that you intend to use in order to use the data to make inferences about the problem. Is the purpose behind this model selection clear (for example, understanding versus forecasting)?

At this point, things may get a bit complex for many readers. It is a good idea to provide an outline of the remainder of the report at the close of the introduction. This provides a map to guide the reader through the complex arguments of the report. Further, many readers will be interested only in specific aspects of the report and, with the outline, will be able to "fast-forward" to the sections that interest them most.

Data Characteristics

In a data analysis project, the job is to summarize the data and use this summary information to make inferences about the state of the world. Much of this summarization is done through statistics that are used to estimate model parameters. However, it is also useful to describe the data without reference to a specific model for at least two reasons. First, by using basic summary measures of the data, you can appeal to a larger audience than if you restrict your considerations to a specific statistical model. Indeed, with a carefully constructed graphical summary device, you should be able to reach virtually any reader who is interested in the subject material. Conversely, familiarity with statistical models requires a certain amount of mathematical sophistication and you may or may not wish to restrict your audience at this stage of the report. Second, constructing statistics that are immediately connected to specific models leaves you open to the criticism that your model selection is incorrect. For most reports, the selection of a model is an unavoidable juncture in the process of inference, but you need not do it at this relatively early stage of your report.

In the data characteristics section, identify the nature of data. For example, be sure to identify the component variables, and state whether each variable is longitudinal versus cross-sectional, observational versus experimental and so forth. You should present here any basic summary statistics that would help the reader develop an overall understanding of the data. It is a good idea to include about two plots. Here, emphasize scatter plots to indicate primary relationships in cross-sectional data or time series plots to indicate most important trends in longitudinal data. The plots, and concomitant summary statistics, should not only isolate the most important trends or relationships but may also serve to identify unusual points that are worthy of special consideration. Carefully choose the statistics and graphical summaries that you present in this section. Do not overwhelm the reader at this point with a plethora of numbers. The details presented in this section should foreshadow the development of the model in the subsequent section. Other salient features of the data may appear in the appendix.

Model Selection and Interpretation

This is the heart and soul of your report. The results reported in this section generally took the longest to achieve. However, the length of the section need not be in proportion to the time it took you to accomplish the analysis. Remember, you are trying to spare the reader of the anguish that you went through in arriving at your conclusions. However, at the same time you want to convince the reader of the thoughtfulness of your recommendations. Here is an outline for the Model Selection and Interpretation Section that incorporates the key elements that should appear:

1. an outline of the section,
2. a statement of the recommended model,
3. an interpretation of the model, parameter estimates and any broad implications of the model,
4. the basic justifications of the model,
5. an outline of a thought process that would lead up to this model, and
6. a discussion of alternative models.

In this section, develop your ideas by discussing the general issues first and specific details later. Use subsections (1)–(3) to address the broad, general concerns that a nontechnical manager or client may have. Additional details can be provided in subsections (4)–(6) to address the concerns of the technically-inclined reader. In this way, the outline is designed to accommodate the needs of these two types of readers. More details of each subsection are described in the following.

You are again confronted with the conflicting goals of wanting as large an audience as possible and yet needing to address the concerns of a technical audience. Start this all-important section with an *outline* of things to come. That will enable the reader to pick and choose. Indeed, many readers will wish only to examine your recommended model and the corresponding interpretations and will assume that your justifications are reliable. So, after providing the outline, immediately provide a *statement of the recommended model* in no uncertain terms. Now, it may not be clear at all from the data set that your recommended model is superior to alternative models and, if that is the case, just say so. However, be sure to state, without ambiguity, what you considered best. Do not let the confusion that arises from several competing models representing the data equally well drift over into your statement of a model.

The statement of a model is often in statistical terminology, a language used to express model ideas precisely. Immediately follow the statement of the recommended model with the concomitant *interpretations.* The interpretations should be done using nontechnical language. In addition to discussing the overall form of the model, the parameter estimates may provide an indication of the strength of any relationships that you have discovered. Often a model is easily digested by the reader when discussed in terms of the resulting implications of a model, such as a confidence or prediction interval. Although only one property of the basic model, this type of implication is important to many readers.

It is a good idea to discuss briefly some of the technical *justifications of the model* in the main body of the report. This is to convince the reader that you know what you are doing. Thus, to defend your selection of a model, cite some of the basic justifications such as t-statistics, coefficient of determination, residual standard deviation, and so forth in the main body and include more detailed arguments in the appendix. To further convince the reader that you have seriously thought about the problem, include a brief description of a *thought process* that would lead one from the data to your proposed model. Do *not* describe to the reader all the pitfalls that you encountered on the way. Describe instead a clean process that ties the model to the data, with as little fuss as possible.

As mentioned, in data analysis there is rarely if ever a "right" answer. To convince the reader that you have thought about the problem deeply, it is a good idea to mention *alternative models.* This will show that you considered the problem from more than one perspective and are aware that careful, thoughtful individuals may arrive at different conclusions. However, in the end, you still need to give your recommended model and stand by your recommendation. You will sharpen your arguments by discussing a close competitor and comparing it with your recommended model.

Summary and Concluding Remarks

This section should rehash the results of the report in a concise fashion, in different words than the executive summary. The language may or may not be more technical than the executive summary, depending on the tone that you set in the introduction. Refer to the key questions posed when you began the study and tie these to the results. This section may look back over the analysis and may serve as a springboard for questions and suggestions about future investigations. Include ideas that you have about future investigations, keeping in mind costs and other considerations that may be involved in collecting further information.

References and Appendix

The appendix may contain many auxiliary figures and analyses. The reader will not give the appendix the same level of attention as the main body of the report. However, the appendix is a useful place to include many crucial details for the technically inclined reader and important features that are not critical to the main recommendations of your report. Because the level of technical content here is generally higher than in the main body of the report, it is important that each portion of the appendix be clearly identified, especially with respect to its relation to the main body of the report.

12.3 METHODS FOR COMMUNICATING DATA

For the reader to be able to interpret numerical information effectively, the data should be presented using a combination of words, numbers and drawings that reveal its complexity. Thus, the creators of data presentations must draw on background skills from several areas including: (i) an understanding of the underlying substantive area, (ii) a knowledge of the related statistical concepts, (iii) an appreciation of design attributes of data presentations and (iv) an understanding of the characteristics of the intended audience. This balanced background is vital if the purpose of the data presentation is to inform. If the purpose is to enliven the data ("because data are inherently boring") or to attract attention, then the design attributes may take on a more prominent role. Conversely, some creators with strong quantitative skills take great pains to simplify data presentations in order to reach a broad audience. By not using the appropriate design attributes, they reveal only part of the numerical information and hide the true story of their data. To quote Albert Einstein, "You should make your models as simple as possible, but no simpler."

This section presents the basic elements and rules for constructing successful data presentations. To this end, we discuss in turn each of the three modes of presenting numerical information: (i) within text data, (ii) tabular data and (iii) data graphics. You will see that these three modes are ordered roughly in the complexity of data that they are designed to present: From the within text data mode that is most useful for portraying the simplest types of data, up to the data graphics mode that is capable of conveying numerical information from extremely large sets of data.

Within Text Data

Within text data simply means numerical quantities that are cited within the usual sentence structure. For example:

> The price of Vigoro stock today is $36.50 per share, a record high.

When presenting data within text, you will have to decide whether to use figures or spell out a particular number. There are several guidelines for choosing between figures and words, although generally for business writing you will use words if this choice results in a concise statement. Some of the important guidelines include:

1. Spell out whole numbers from one to ninety-nine.
2. Use figures for fractional numbers.
3. Spell out round numbers that are approximations.
4. Spell out numbers that begin a sentence.
5. Use figures in sentences that contain several numbers.

For example:

> There are forty-three students in my class.
> With $0.67 U.S. dollars, I can buy one German Deutschemark.
> There are about forty-three thousand students at this university.
> Three thousand, four hundred and fifty-six people voted for me.
> Those boys are 3, 4, 6 and 7 years old.

You can find further discussion of these and other guidelines in *The Chicago Manual of Style,* a well-known reference for preparing and editing written copy.

Text flows linearly; this makes it difficult for the reader to make comparisons of data within a sentence. When lists of numbers become long or important comparisons are to be made, a useful device for presenting data is the *within text table,* also called the *semitabular* form. For example:

Recent primary turnout levels, the percentage of eligible voters that actually vote, in the eighth U.S. congressional district are:

1986—12.4%
1988—18.7%
1990—15.1%
1992—16.5%

(*Source: Wisconsin Blue Book* 1987–88; 1989–1990; 1991–1992; 1993–94).

Tables

When the list of numbers is longer, the tabular form, or table, is the preferred choice for presenting data. Figure 12.1 describes the basic elements of a table.

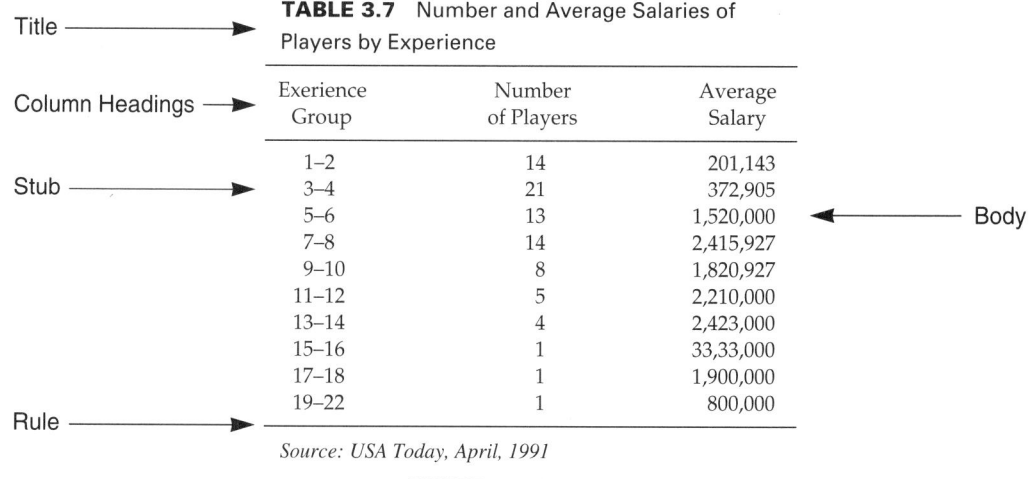

TABLE 3.7   Number and Average Salaries of Players by Experience

Exerience Group	Number of Players	Average Salary
1–2	14	201,143
3–4	21	372,905
5–6	13	1,520,000
7–8	14	2,415,927
9–10	8	1,820,927
11–12	5	2,210,000
13–14	4	2,423,000
15–16	1	33,33,000
17–18	1	1,900,000
19–22	1	800,000

Source: USA Today, April, 1991

FIGURE 12.1 Elements of a table.

These are:

1. *Title.* A short description of the data, placed above or to the side of the table. For longer documents, provide a table number for easy reference within the main body of the text. The title may be supplemented by additional remarks, thus forming a *caption.*
2. *Column Headings.* Names of the variables that are listed vertically.
3. *Stub.* The left hand vertical column. It often provides identifying information for individual row items.
4. *Body.* The other vertical columns of the table.
5. *Rules.* Lines that separate the table into its various components.
6. *Source.* Provides the origin of the data.

TABLE 12.1 Eighth U.S. Congressional District Election Results: General Election Results

		1990						1992					
		Turnout		Van Sistine (Democrat)		Roth (Republican)		Turnout		Helms (Democrat)		Roth (Republican)	
County	Voting age population (1990)	Count	Percent	Count	Percent	Count	Percent	Count	Percent	Count	Percent	Count	Percent
Brown	141,993	62,451	44	35,062	56	27,389	43.9	98,236	69.2	33,968	34.6	64,268	65.4
Outagamie (partial)	100,590 (87,111)	42,651	42.4	18,027	42.3	24,624	57.7	60,445	69.4	16,819	27.8	43,626	72.2
Marinette	29,650	12,907	43.5	5,184	40.2	7,723	59.8	19,911	67.2	4,938	24.8	14,973	75.2
Shawano	27,177	10,341	38.1	3,942	38.1	6,399	61.9	16,552	60.9	3,924	23.7	12,628	76.3
Oconto	21,995	9,170	41.7	4,251	46.4	4,919	53.6	14,701	66.8	4,502	30.6	10,199	69.4
Door	19,031	8,658	45.5	3,669	42.4	4,989	57.6	13,391	70.4	3,736	27.9	9,655	72.1
Langlade	14,302	5,975	41.8	2,047	34.3	3,928	65.7	9,483	66.3	2,212	23.3	7,271	76.7
Oneida	13,962	7,144	51.2	2,605	36.5	4,539	63.5	10,869	77.8	3,198	29.4	7,671	70.6
Vilas (partial)	13,772	7,237	52.5	2,296	31.7	4,941	68.3	10,537	76.5	2,624	24.9	7,913	75.1
Kewaunee	13,563	7,198	53.1	3,751	52.1	3,447	47.9	10,276	75.8	3,045	29.6	7,231	70.4
Forest	6,395	3,006	47	1,249	41.6	1,757	58.4	3,857	60.3	1,277	33.1	2,580	66.9
Florence	3,368	1,383	41.1	566	40.9	817	59.1	2,495	74.1	703	28.2	1,792	71.8
Calumet (partial)	2,951							1,682	57.0	485	28.8	1,197	71.2
Menominee (partial)	2,290	980	42.8	550	56.1	430	43.9	713	31.1	233	32.7	480	67.3
Manitowoc (partial)	n/a							348	n/a	128	36.8	220	63.2
Total	407,993	179,101	43.9	83,199	46.5	95,902	53.5	273,496	67	81,792	29.9	191,704	70.1

(*Source: Wisconsin Blue Book 1991–1992; 1993–94*)

As with the semitabular form, tables can be designed to enhance comparisons between numbers. Unlike the semitabular form, tables are separate from the main body of the text. Because they are separate, tables should be self-contained so that the reader can draw information from the table with little reference to the text. The title should draw attention to the important features of the table. The layout should guide the reader's eye and facilitate comparisons. Table 12.1 illustrates the application of some basic rules for constructing "user friendly" tables. These rules include:

1. For titles and other headers, STRINGS OF CAPITALS ARE DIFFICULT TO READ, keep these to a minimum.
2. Reduce the physical size of a table so that the eye does not have to travel as far as it might otherwise; use single spacing and reduce the type size.
3. Use columns for figures to be compared rather than rows; columns are easier to compare, although this makes documents longer.
4. Use row and column averages and totals to provide focus. This allows readers to make comparisons.
5. When possible, order rows and/or columns by size in order to facilitate comparisons. Generally, ordering by alphabetical listing of categories does little for understanding complex data sets.
6. Use combinations of spacing and horizontal and vertical rules to facilitate comparisons. Horizontal rules are useful for separating major categories; vertical rules should be used sparingly. White space between columns serves to separate categories; closely spaced pairs of columns encourage comparison.
7. Use tinting and different type size and attributes to draw attention to figures. Use of tint is also effective for breaking up the monotonous appearance of a large table.
8. The first time that the data are displayed, provide the source.

You can find further discussion of these and other guidelines in Ehrenberg (1977) and Tufte (1983).

Graphs

For portraying large, complex data sets, or data where the actual numerical values are less important than the relations to be established, graphical representations of data are useful. Figure 12.2 describes some of the basic elements of a *graph*, also called a *chart, illustration* or *figure*. These include:

1. *Title* and *Caption*. As with a table, these provide short descriptions of the main features of the figure. Long captions may be used to describe everything that is being graphed, draw attention to the important features and describe the conclusions to be drawn from the data. Include the source of the data here or on a separate line immediately below the graph.

2. *Scale Lines (Axes) and Scale Labels.* Choose the scales so that the data fills up as much of the data region as possible. Do not insist that zero be included; assume that the viewer will look at the range of the scales and understand them.

3. *Tick Marks and Tick Mark Labels.* Choose the range of the tick marks to include almost all of the data. Three to ten tick marks are generally sufficient. When possible put the tick outside of the data region, so that they do not interfere with the data.

FIGURE A letter plot. This is a scatter plot of RENT_SFT versus MILES, with the letter code 'O' for one-bedroom and 'T' for two-bedroom apartments

THIS CAPTION INCLUDES THE TITLE AND A SHORT DESCRIPTION.

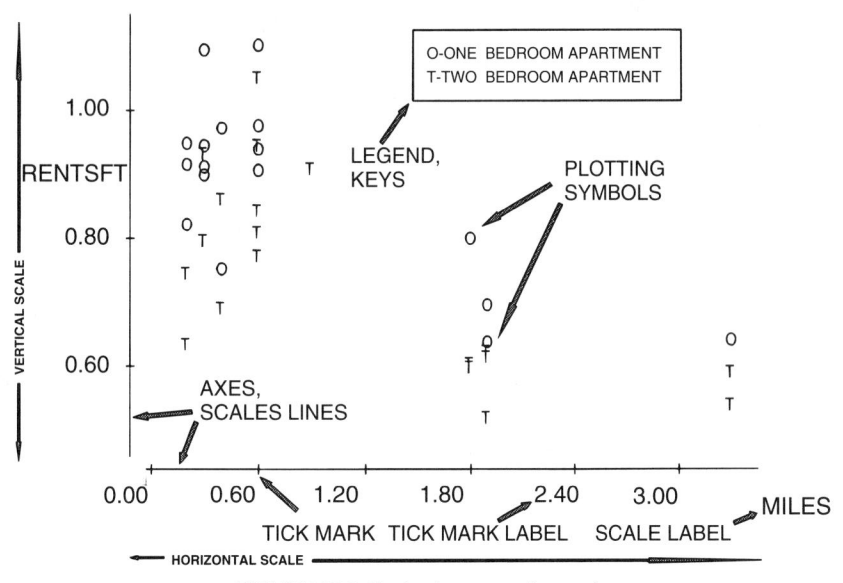

FIGURE 12.2 Basic elements of a graph.

4. *Plotting Symbols.* Use different plotting symbols to encode different levels of a variable. Plotting symbols should be chosen so that they are easy to identify, for example, 'O' for one and 'T' for two. However, be sure that plotting symbols are easy to distinguish; for example, it can be difficult to distinguish 'F' and 'E'.

5. *Legend (Keys).* These are small textual displays that help to identify certain aspects of the data. Do not let these displays interfere with the data or clutter the graph.

As with tables, graphs are separate from the main body of the text and thus should be self-contained. Especially with long documents, the tables and graphs may contain a separate story line, providing a look at the main message of the document in a different way than the main body of the text. Cleveland (1985) and Tufte (1990) provide several tips to make graphs more "user-friendly."

1. Make lines as thin as possible. Thin lines distract the eye less from the data when compared to thicker lines. However, make the lines thick enough so that the image will not degrade under reproduction.

2. Try to use as few lines as possible. Again, several lines distract the eye from the data, which carries the information. Try to avoid "grid" lines, if possible. If you must use grid lines, a light ink, such as a gray or half tone, is the preferred choice.

3. Spell out words and avoid abbreviations. Rarely is the space saved worth the potential confusion that the shortened version may cause the viewer.

4. Use a type that includes both capital and small letters.

5. Place graphs on the same page as the text that discusses the graph.

6. Make words run from left to right, not vertically.

7. Use the substance of the data to suggest the shape and size of the graph. For time series graphs, make the graph twice as wide as tall. For scatter plots, make the graph equally wide as tall. If a graph displays an important message, make the graph large.

Of course, for most graphs it will be impossible to follow all these pieces of advice simultaneously. To illustrate, if we spell out the scale label on a left hand vertical axis and make it run from left to right, then we cut into the vertical scale. This forces us to reduce the size of the graph, perhaps at the expense of reducing the message.

A graph is a powerful tool for summarizing and presenting numerical information. Graphs can be used to break up long documents; they can provoke and maintain reader interest. Further, graphs can reveal aspects of the data that other methods cannot.

12.4 FURTHER SUGGESTIONS FOR REPORT WRITING

1. Be as brief as you can although still including all important details. On one hand, the key aspects of several regression outputs can often be summarized in one table. Often a number of plots can be summarized in one sentence. On the other hand, recognize the value of a well-constructed plot or table for conveying important information.

2. Keep your readership in mind when writing your report. Explain what you now understand about the problem, with little emphasis on how you happened to get there. Give practical interpretations of results, in language the client will be comfortable with.

3. Outline, outline. Develop your ideas in a logical, step-by-step fashion. It is *vital* that there be a logical flow to the report. Start with a broad outline that specifies the basic layout of the report. Then make a more detailed

outline, listing each issue that you wish to discuss in each section. You only retain literary freedom by imposing structure on your reporting.

4. Simplicity, simplicity, simplicity. Emphasize your primary ideas through simple language. Replace complex words by simpler words if the meaning remains the same. Avoid the use of clichés and trite language. Although technical language may be used, avoid the use of technical jargon or slang. Statistical jargon, such as "Let $x_1, x_2, \ldots$ be i.i.d. random variables …" is rarely necessary. Do not use Latin phrases (e.g., i.e.) if an English phrase will suffice (such as, that is).

5. Include important summary tables and plots in the body of the report. Label all figures and tables so each is understandable when viewed alone.

6. Use one or more appendices to provide supporting details. Plots of secondary importance, such as residuals plots, and statistical software output, such as regression fits, can be included in an appendix. Include enough detail so that another analyst, with access to the data, could replicate your work. Provide a strong link between the primary ideas that are described in the main body of the report and the supporting material in the appendix.

12.5 CASE STUDY: CEO COMPENSATION

Determinants of CEO Compensation

Executive Summary

What problem was studied? How was it studied? What were the findings?

Chief executive officer (CEO) compensation varies significantly from firm to firm. This report examines a sample of firms from a survey by *Forbes Magazine* to establish important patterns in the compensation of CEOs. Specifically, the report introduces a regression model that explains CEO salaries in terms of the firm's sales and the CEO's length of experience, education level and ownership stake in the firm. Among other things, this model shows that larger firms tend to pay CEOs more and, somewhat surprisingly, that CEOs with a higher educational levels earn less than otherwise comparable CEOs. In addition to establishing important influences on CEO compensation, this model could be used to predict CEO compensation for salary negotiation purposes.

Section 1. Introduction

A chief executive officer (CEO) is a leader of a firm or organization. The CEO leads by developing and implementing a strategic policy for the firm. The CEO is in charge of a management team that is responsible for the daily firm operations, financial strength and corporate social responsibilities.

Begin with some orientation material.

The CEO also leads the firm in compensation. Generally, a CEO is the most highly paid person in a firm; CEO salaries are at the top of the pyramid. Although some industries have employees whose salaries exceed the CEO's, for example sales agents, the broad rule is that CEO salaries form an effective upper bound for employee compensation. Thus, although very few managers ever become chief executive officers, there is a great deal of interest in CEO salaries. CEO compensation indirectly influences salaries for a large portion of the firm workforce.

CEO salaries in the United States are of interest because of their relationship to salaries in international firms and to salaries of people that do not belong to Corporate America. Top managers in the United States have come under a great deal of criticism for being so highly paid compared to their international counterparts. Yet, compensation of CEOs may not be out of line compared to top professionals in other fields. For example, Linden and Machan (1992, "Put Them at Risk!" *Forbes Magazine*, p. 158) compares CEO salaries with professionals such as actors, models, surgeons, sports personalities and so on, and finds the compensation comparable.

Measuring annual compensation for a CEO is fraught with difficulties. Compensation clearly includes salary plus bonuses, that is, cash payments that may or may not be performance related. Other compensation is more difficult to measure and may include restricted stock awards and contributions to retirement, health insurance, and other insurance plans. Remuneration may also come in the form of stock gains based on the CEO's stock ownership or exercise of stock options, although we did not consider this source of income.

When describing the key aspects of the report, include sources of data.

The data for this study were drawn the May 25, 1992 issue of *Forbes Magazine* entitled "What 800 Companies Paid for their Bosses." This article provides several measures of CEO compensation, as well as characteristics of the CEO and measures of his firm's performance. We say "his" because of the 800 CEOs studied in this article, only one was a woman. The goal of this report is to study CEO and firm characteristics to determine the important factors influencing CEO compensation.

Provide a plan for the remainder of the paper.

The outline of the remainder of the paper is as follows. In Section 2, I present the most important characteristics of the data. To summarize these characteristics, in Section 3 is the discussion of a model to represent the data. Concluding remarks can be found in Section 4 and many of the details of the analysis are in the appendix.

Section 2. Data Characteristics

C12_COMP

To understand the determinants of CEO compensation, one hundred observations were randomly selected from the 800 listed in the *Forbes* article. Although the *Forbes* article did not cite the basis for a firm to be included in its survey, the 800 companies seem to represent the largest publicly traded com-

Identify the nature of the data.

panies in the United States. Our sample of one hundred CEOs and their firms represent a cross-sectional sample of America's largest corporations. In our cross-section, the CEO and firm characteristics were based on 1991 measures.

From a preliminary examination of the data, the 51st observation, had an unusually low compensation. This was Craig McCaw, CEO of McCaw Cellular, who reported a salary of $155,000 in 1991. This was despite a five-year total reported salary of over fifty-three million dollars. As founder of McCaw Cellular, Mr. McCaw received a substantial amount of remuneration outside of figures reported in 1991 and thus I omitted him from the sample.

For the remaining ninety-nine observations, Figure 1 provides the distribution of total compensation. More details are in Appendix A.3. Compensation ranges from a low of $307,000 to a high of $4,657,000, with a mean of $1,131,400. In measuring compensation, we consider the CEOs salary, bonus and other 1991 compensation. Each of these variables is available in the *Forbes* report.

Use selected plots and statistics to emphasize the primary trends. Do not refer to a statistical model in this section.

Figure 1 shows that the distribution of compensation is skewed to the right. In our subsequent analysis for understanding determinants of compensation, this skewness gives undue weight to highly compensated individuals. Figure 2 is a redrawing of Figure 1 with the data on a logarithmic scale. On this scale, we see that the distribution of compensation is much more symmetric.

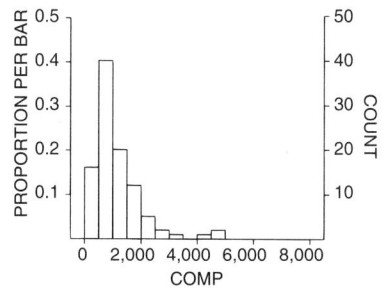

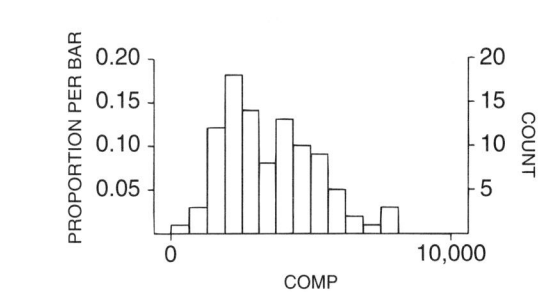

FIGURE 1 Histogram of the CEO compensation in thousands of dollars. *Source: Forbes Magazine*

FIGURE 2 The same histogram as in Figure 2 but the horizontal axis is on a logarithmic scale.

Firm characteristics studied in this report include measures of size and profitability of the firm. It was conjectured that more profitable firms may have more generous compensation packages as rewards for strong performance. Further, larger firms may have more generous compensation packages because of the greater responsibilities that CEOs must assume. Although there are several possible measures of firm size, the company's revenue as measured by 1991 sales turned out to be most relevant for this study. Figure 3 shows the relationship between compensation and sales, both on a logarithmic scale. The correlation coefficient associated with this plot, $r = 0.49$, indicates that companies with larger sales tend to provide larger compensation to their CEOs.

With basic statistics and plots, attempt to foreshadow the model developed in subsequent sections.

Other CEO characteristics considered in this study include educational background, professional background, percentage of the company's stock

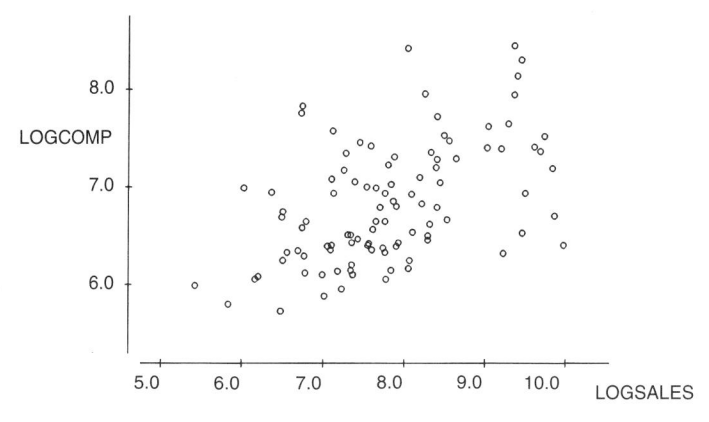

FIGURE 3 Scatter plot of compensation versus sales, both on a logarithmic basis.

owned by the CEO (PCTOWN) and the market valuation of the stock (VAL), experience as CEO measured in years (EXPER) and length of time with the firm (TENURE). Professional background of the CEO contains eleven categories, such as marketing, finance, accounting, insurance and so on. Detailed information is in Appendix A.4. Educational background was categorized into three levels: not a recipient of an undergraduate degree (NODEGR), a recipient of only an undergraduate degree (UNDERGRD) and a recipient of an undergraduate plus a graduate degree such as a Master's or Ph.D. (GRAD). To illustrate, Table 1 provides summary statistics by level of educational attainment. Interestingly, this table shows that CEOs with the highest level of educational attainment receive the lowest average compensation.

TABLE 1 Average Compensation by Educational Level

Educational level	Number	Average compensation	Average logarithmic compensation
No Undergraduate Degree (NODEGR)	7	1462.7	7.0929
Undergraduate Degree (UNDERGRD)	31	1470.8	7.0796
Graduate Degree (GRAD)	61	921.0	6.6662
TOTAL	99	1131.4	6.8258

Section 3. Model Selection and Interpretation

Section 2 established that there are real patterns between compensation and CEO and firm characteristics, despite the great variability in these variables. This section summarizes these patterns using a regression model. Following the statement of the model and its interpretation, this section describes features of the data that drove the selection of the recommended model.

As a result of this study, I recommend the following linear regression model,

$$\text{LOGCOMP} = \beta_0 + \beta_1 \text{ LOGSALES} + \beta_2 \text{ EXPER} + \beta_3 \text{ GRAD}$$

$$+ \beta_4 \text{ PERCENT5} + e. \qquad (1)$$

Start with a statement of your recommended model.

Here, the variables LOGCOMP and LOGSALES are the compensation and sales, respectively, in natural logarithmic units. The variable PERCENT5 indicates whether or not the CEO owned more than 5% of the company's stock. Under this model, the β's (betas) represent unknown parameters that can be estimated using the data.

The estimated version of the model in equation (1) is:

$$\widehat{\text{LOGCOMP}} = 4.75 + 0.28 \text{ LOGSALES} + 0.019 \text{ EXPER} - 0.35 \text{ GRAD}$$

$$- 0.64 \text{ PERCENT5}. \qquad (2)$$

This model could be used for estimating compensation for executives that are either in or not in the sample. To illustrate, in 1991 William L. Weiss had eight years of experience as CEO of Ameritech and earned $2.27 million in total compensation. Mr. Weiss received a bachelor's degree from Penn State in 1951 and owned approximately 0.05% of Ameritech stock. Ameritech did well in 1991; it had profits of $1,166 millions on sales of $10,818 millions. To estimate Mr.

Interpret the model; discuss variables, coefficients and broad implications of the model.

Weiss's compensation using equation (2), use:

$$\widehat{\text{LOGCOMP}} = 4.75 + 0.28 \log(10{,}818) + 0.019 \,(8) - 0.35 \,(0) - 0.64 \,(0)$$

$$= 7.49819.$$

This is an estimated compensation of $\exp(\widehat{\text{LOGCOMP}}) = \exp(7.49819) =$ $1,805, in thousands of dollars. Although below the actual compensation of $2,270 (thousands), the estimate was arrived at knowing only four characteristics of Mr. Weiss and Ameritech.

Equation (2) is also useful for understanding relationships between variables. In particular, we may summarize several relationships using the signs and magnitudes of the estimated regression coefficients. To begin, the negative sign associated with PERCENT5 indicates that, other things equal, CEOs with more than a 5% ownership stake are expected to have a lower compensation level than those with less than 5% ownership. Although CEOs with more than 5% ownership are undoubtably powerful individuals within the firm, they may be receiving much of their remuneration through long-term compensation packages, including stock incentives, that are not captured within the one year financial figures.

The negative sign associated with the GRAD variable is also unexpected, in that we generally think that higher levels of education do not hurt compensation levels and may even help! A number of explanations are possible; the most likely is that the average CEO is 57 years old and was climbing the corporate ladder in an era when professional qualifications were less important than they are today. Some additional conjectures concerning this interesting artifact are in the concluding remarks in Section 4.

The positive sign associated with LOGSALES was anticipated in Section 2. This coefficient indicates a positive relationship between a CEOs compensation and the firm's size, as measured through annual sales.

The positive sign associated with EXPER is also not surprising. Here, we see individuals that are more experienced in their position tend to be more highly compensated. Because of the natural logarithmic scaling of compensation, we can interpret the coefficient to mean that an extra year of experience is associated with a 1.9% increase in salary. We caution the reader that this is not a dynamic relationship; that is, we are not anticipating that compensation levels will increase by 1.9% each year. Rather, given two CEOs that are alike except that one has an additional year of experience, we expect that one to have a higher compensation level by a factor of 1.9%.

What are some of the basic justifications of the model?

The model provided a reasonable fit to the available data. The t-coefficients associated with each coefficient exceeded three in absolute value. The coefficient of determination, $R^2 = 0.43$, indicates that the model explained 43% of the variation in compensation. The coefficient of determination adjusted for degrees of freedom, $R_a^2 = 0.406$, was only slightly less. The multiple correlation coefficient, which is the correlation between compensation and the explanatory variables, was a healthy $R = 65.5\%$. The model's residual standard deviation, $s = 0.473$, which estimates the remaining variability, was much lower than the original variability in compensation levels, $s_y = 0.624$. The following display summarizes the regression fit:

$$\widehat{\text{LOG COMP}} = 4.75 + 0.28 \text{ LOGSALES} + 0.019 \text{ EXPER} - 0.35 \text{ GRAD} - 0.64 \text{ PERCENT5}$$

std errors	(0.41)	(0.049)	(0.00603)	(0.104)	(0.175)
t-ratios	[11.59]	[5.76]	[−3.19]	[−3.40]	[−3.66]

Provide a strong link between the main body of the report and the appendix.

Additional statistics supporting the final fitted model can be found in the computer output in Appendix A.6. There, the reader can check (using variance inflation factors) that there is no important collinearity in the final fitted model. Further, six unusual observations are identified by the computer software that I used, MINITAB. Five observations were high leverage points and one was an outlier. Although different, these points seemed to be only mild variations from the majority. For example, when the model was re-fit without the outlier (John Fort of Tyco Laboratories), R^2 increased from 43% to 46.5% and other summary statistics also remained essentially unchanged. Thus, these slightly unusual points were left in the final fitted model that was estimated.

There were no other major patterns between the residuals from the final fitted model and other explanatory variables. Appendix A.7 contains some of the diagnostic checks employed, including a plot of standardized residuals versus fitted values to check for heteroscedasticity. The one exception to this is the market valuation variable that is discussed in the following.

Is there a thought process that leads us to conclude the model is a useful one?

In determining the final model, the first decision made was to use logarithmic transformations of several variables. We have seen in Section 2 how the logarithmic transformation symmetrizes the distribution of compensation. Figure 3 shows a strong relationship between compensation and sales, on a logarithmic scale. When the same plot was made using the original scale (not given in this report), no such relationship was evident. A similar argument was made for market valuation (VAL).

For the categorical explanatory variables, the tables and boxplots in Table 1 and Appendix A.4 suggest that education level is an important explanatory variable although professional background is not. The binary categorical, or indicator, variable PERCENT5 is more interesting. In Appendix A.3, a histogram shows that the distribution of PCTOWN is highly skewed. A plot of compensation versus PCTOWN, not given here, showed the relationship to be highly nonlinear. After some experimentation, the continuous variable PCTOWN was reduced to the indicator variable PERCENT5. Techniques like stepwise regression, in Appendix A.8, suggested that PERCENT5 is an important explanatory variable.

A good way to justify your recomended model is to compare it to one or more alternatives.

An alternative model that requires serious consideration allows the market value of the CEO's stock (VAL) to be included as an explanatory variable. Appendix A.9 shows that when this variable is included, the fit of model improves significantly. For example, this new model results in $R^2 = 52.7\%$, an improvement from the final recommended model with $R^2 = 43.7\%$. Including VAL in the model does not increase the complexity of the model because, as suggested by the correlation matrix in Appendix A.5, VAL provides information that is similar to EXPER. When including VAL in the model, EXPER could be dropped without significant loss of explanatory power.

Some readers may prefer to select the fitted model using VAL as their preferred model. I did not because of its strong link to the source of income from stock gains based on the CEO's stock ownership or exercise of stock options. Stock gains, although an important source of income, represent remuneration for services performed over several years with the firm. To include this variable, a longitudinal study measuring CEO compensation over time would be more appropriate than the cross-sectional study that I undertook. Stock gains were not included in the response because this source of income is highly variable; stock gains may be zero for many years before a very large gain is realized and reported. For example, this was the case with Mr. McCaw of McCaw Cellular. To reiterate, this is not to say that stock gains are unimportant but rather that this variable should be studied by examining CEO compensation over time.

Section 4. Summary and Concluding Remarks

Rehash the results in a concise fashion. Discuss shortcomings and potential extensions of the work.

Although CEO compensation varies significantly, we have seen that it is possible to establish important determinants of compensation. The recommended regression model concludes that CEO salaries can be explained in terms of the firm's sales and the CEO's length of experience, education level and ownership stake in the firm.

This study was based on a cross-section of one hundred firms. Although several important determinants were established, future studies may uncover other important determinants. With our source of data, we were able to analyze several characteristics of the CEO yet relatively few characteristics of the firm. In particular, I conjecture that future studies should include a variable that captures the firm's industry. For example, compensation in relatively stable industries such as banking or insurance should be lower than growth industries such as technology firms because of the relative risk factor. However, no industry information was readily available to me when the data was gathered.

Compensation should also be studied over time. Because only a one year cross-section was examined, stock gains had to be excluded from the response because of their highly volatile nature. However, by tracking CEO compensation over time, this important source of information could be more readily compared across different CEOs and firms. Of course, examining data over time may introduce a host of new problems such as examining the present value of compensation patterns, the effect of exits and entrances of CEOs from the study, the changing social attitudes of CEO compensation, and so on. I leave this problem as an area for future research.

Appendix

Include references, detailed data analysis and other materials of lesser importance in the appendices.

A table of contents, or outline, is useful for long appendices.

APPENDIX TABLE OF CONTENTS
1. References
2. Variable Definitions
3. Basic Summary Statistics
4. Summary Statistics by Professional Background and Education Level
5. Summary Statistics Relating Compensation to Other Explanatory Variables
6. Final Fitted Regression Model—MINITAB Output
7. Checking Residuals from the Final Fitted Model—MINITAB Output
8. Stepwise Regression that Suggests the Final Fitted Model—MINITAB Output
9. Alternative Fitted Regression Model—MINITAB Output

A.1 References

LINDEN AND MACHAN (1992), "Put Them at Risk!" *Forbes Magazine,* May 25, 1992, p. 158.
"What 800 Companies Paid for their Bosses," *Forbes Magazine,* May 25, 1992, p. 182.

A.2 Variable Definitions

TABLE A.1   Variable Definitions

Variable	Definitions
COMP	Sum of salary, bonus and other 1991 compensation, in thousands of dollars. Other compensation does not include stock gains.
LOGCOMP	Natural logarithm of COMP
SALES	1991 sales revenues, in millions of dollars
LOGSALES	Natural logarithm of SALES
TENURE	Number of years employed by the firm
EXPER	Number of years as the firm CEO
VAL	Market value of the CEOs stock, in natural log units
PCTOWN	Percentage of firm's market value owned by the CEO
PROF	1991 profits of the firm, before taxes, in millions of dollars
NODEGR	Indicates that the CEO does not have an undergraduate degree
UNDERGRD	Indicates that the CEO has only an undergraduate degree
GRAD	Indicates that the CEO has a graduate degree
PERCENT5	Indicates that the CEO owns more than five percent of the firm's stock

A.3 Basic Summary Statistics

TABLE A.2   Summary Statistics of Firm and CEO Variables

	Number	Mean	Median	Standard deviation	Minimum	Maximum
COMP	99	1,131.4	809.0	851.4	307.0	4,657.0
LOGCOMP	99	6.8258	6.6958	0.6139	5.7268	8.4461
SALES	99	4,111	2,344	4,722	228	21,351
LOGSALES	99	7.809	7.760	1.003	5.429	9.969
TENURE	99	23.77	27.00	12.49	1.00	46.00
EXPER	99	8.929	6.000	8.308	0.500	35.000
VAL	99	1.340	1.281	2.116	−2.303	7.432
PROF	99	142.2	82.0	340.6	−1,086.0	1,618.0

```
Histogram of PCTOWN
Each * represents 2 observations


Midpoint      Count
       0         83    ******************************************
       4          7    ****
       8          3    **
      12          3    **
      16          2    *
      20          0
      24          0
      28          0
      32          0
      36          1    *
```

A.4 Summary Statistics by Professional Background and Education Level

TABLE A.3 Summary Statistics of Logarithmic Compensation by Type of Professional Background

Background	Number	Mean	Standard deviation
Unknown	1	6.6896	—
Technical	17	7.0640	0.7531
Insurance	3	7.1035	0.4679
Operations	13	6.9160	0.5683
Banking	13	6.6795	0.5214
Legal	12	6.5531	0.5152
Marketing	7	6.7641	0.4375
Administration	12	7.0673	0.6128
Sales	6	6.9139	0.6035
Financial	14	6.6211	0.6594
Journalist	1	5.9558	—
Total	99	6.8258	0.6139

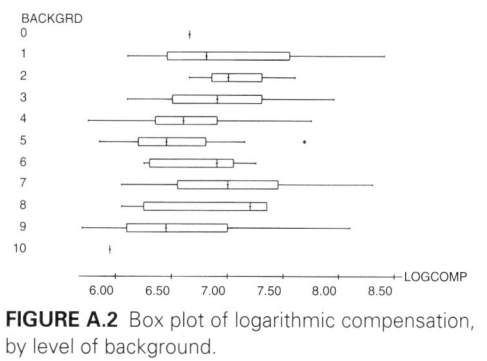

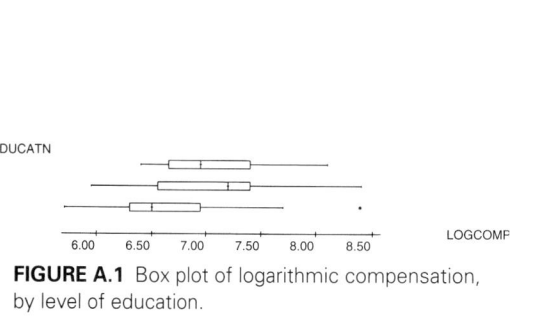

FIGURE A.1 Box plot of logarithmic compensation, by level of education.

FIGURE A.2 Box plot of logarithmic compensation, by level of background.

A.5 Summary Statistics Relating Compensation to Other Explanatory Variables

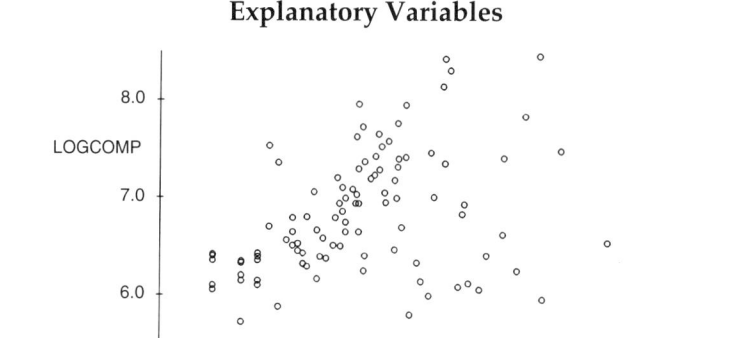

FIGURE A.3 Scatter plot of compensation versus market value, both on a logarithmic basis.

```
Correlation Matrix
           LOGCOMP  LOGSALES  TENURE   EXPER  PCTOWN    VAL
LOGSALES    0.496
TENURE      0.236     0.349
EXPER       0.216    -0.062    0.390
PCTOWN     -0.141    -0.102    0.141   0.337
VAL         0.366     0.114    0.300   0.535   0.596
PERCENT5   -0.181    -0.034    0.170   0.247   0.831   0.530
```

A.6 Final Fitted Regression Model—MINITAB Output

```
The regression equation is
LOGCOMP = 4.75 + 0.280 LOGSALES - 0.354 GRAD - 0.641 PERCENT5 + 0.0192 EXPER

Predictor       Coef      Stdev     t-ratio       p      VIF
Constant      4.7468     0.4097       11.59   0.000
LOGSALES     0.27963    0.04858        5.76   0.000      1.0
GRAD         -0.3540     0.1041       -3.40   0.001      1.1
PERCENT5     -0.6413     0.1751       -3.66   0.000      1.1
EXPER       0.019242   0.006028        3.19   0.002      1.1

s = 0.4730    R-sq = 43.0%    R-sq(adj) = 40.6%

Analysis of Variance

SOURCE        DF        SS         MS        F        p
Regression     4   15.8970     3.9742    17.76    0.000
Error         94   21.0321     0.2237
Total         98   36.9291

Unusual Observations
Obs.LOGSALES   LOGCOMP        Fit   Residual  St. Resid
  15     8.31    6.6201     6.4379     0.1821      0.42 X
  28     6.20    6.0845     6.1583    -0.0738     -0.18 X
  57     8.09    6.5338     6.5538    -0.0200     -0.05 X
  69     7.10    6.3969     6.1106     0.2863      0.66 X
  87     8.03    8.4185     6.8119     1.6066      3.43R
  95     7.23    5.9558     6.1464    -0.1906     -0.44 X

R denotes an obs. with a large st. resid.
X denotes an obs. whose X value gives it large influence.
```

A.7 Checking Residuals from the Final Fitted Model—MINITAB Output

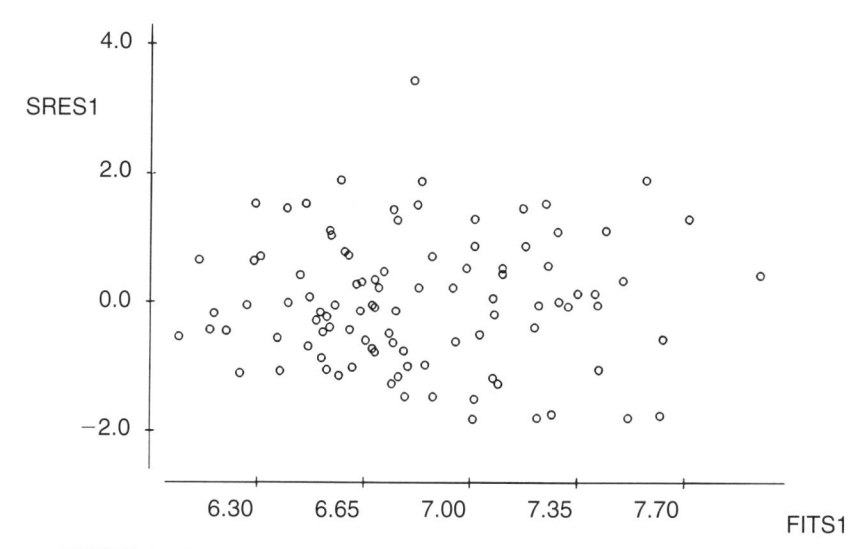

FIGURE A.4 Scatter plot of standardized residuals versus fitted values from the final model.

```
Table of Standardized Residuals
Versus Professional Background
ROWS:    BACKGRD
```

	N	MEAN	STD DEV
0	1	−0.1388	- -
1	17	0.3080	1.2583
2	3	0.1751	1.7151
3	13	−0.1602	1.0124
4	13	0.0600	0.5989
5	12	−0.3186	1.0682
6	7	−0.3269	0.7073
7	12	0.4760	1.0637
8	6	−0.1604	1.0261
9	14	−0.1901	0.8751
10	1	−0.4383	- -
ALL	99	−0.0014	1.0035

A.8 Stepwise Regression that suggests the Final Fitted Model—MINITAB Output

```
STEPWISE REGRESSION OF LOGCOMP   ON   9 PREDICTORS, WITH N = 99
N (CASES WITH MISSING OBS.) =  1 N (ALL CASES) = 100
```

STEP	1	2	3	4	5
CONSTANT	4.456	4.854	5.045	4.747	4.646
LOGSALES	0.303	0.278	0.267	0.280	0.287
T-RATIO	5.62	5.30	5.26	5.76	5.92
GRAD		−0.32	−0.41	−0.35	−0.31
T-RATIO		−3.01	−3.80	−3.40	−2.83
PERCENT5			−0.53	−0.64	−0.71
T-RATIO			−2.95	−3.66	−3.94
EXPER				0.0192	0.0189
T-RATIO				3.19	3.15
NODEGR					0.31
T-RATIO					1.50
S	0.536	0.515	0.495	0.473	0.470
R-SQ	24.57	31.10	36.87	43.05	44.38

A.9 Alternative Fitted Regression Model—MINITAB Output

```
The regression equation is
LOGCOMP = 5.00 + 0.240 LOGSALES − 0.240 GRAD − 1.02 PERCENT5 + 0.145 VAL

99 cases used 1 cases contain missing values
```

Predictor	Coef	Stdev	t-ratio	p	VIF
Constant	4.9985	0.3635	13.75	0.000	
LOGSALES	0.23998	0.04435	5.41	0.000	1.0
GRAD	−0.24009	0.09826	−2.44	0.016	1.2
PERCENT5	−1.0225	0.1792	−5.70	0.000	1.4
VAL	0.14491	0.02580	5.62	0.000	1.6

```
s = 0.4309     R-sq = 52.7%    R-sq(adj) = 50.7%
```

Analysis of Variance

SOURCE	DF	SS	MS	F	p
Regression	4	19.4757	4.8689	26.22	0.000
Error	94	17.4534	0.1857		
Total	98	36.9291			

```
Unusual Observations
Obs.LOGSALES   LOGCOMP       Fit    Residual   St. Resid
  16   6.77     6.1159     6.9627    -0.8468     -2.04R
  28   6.20     6.0845     5.7685     0.3160      0.80 X
  42   9.97     6.3969     7.3588    -0.9618     -2.32R
  58   8.09     6.5338     6.7555    -0.2217     -0.57 X
  88   8.03     8.4185     7.1840     1.2345      2.93R
  94   8.49     7.5262     6.6630     0.8632      2.04R
```

R denotes an obs. with a large st. resid.
X denotes an obs. whose X value gives it large influence.

13

Presenting Data

Chapter Objectives

To introduce principles of design and principles for perceiving data graphics, with an emphasis on data presentation within a formal report.

Chapter Outline

542

13.1 INTRODUCTION

Numerical statistics, on one hand, are potent entities because they can reduce a large, complex system of data into smaller, more comprehensible quantities. Yet, this reduction can miss important aspects of the data. Graphical methods, on the other hand, can reveal the data through a more flexible process of visual perception. However, through their flexibility, graphs can give viewers misleading impressions of the data and thus, again, miss important aspects. This chapter shows how either numerical statistics or graphical methods, when taken individually, can fail. Sound presentation of data information is based on a combination of numerical statistics and graphical methods.

On one hand, *data reduction methods* summarize the information contained in sets of data, but they do so in a way that may miss important aspects of information contained in the data. For example, we have seen that statistics from a fitted regression model summarize the linear relationship between a response and one or more explanatory variables, but may ignore information about any nonlinear relationships. On the other hand, graphical methods allow the viewer to see potential nonlinear patterns. However, graphs must be carefully constructed to highlight patterns of interest; otherwise, the overall variability in a data set can obscure patterns of interest.

Example 13.1: Anscombe's Data

Anscombe (1973) showed how data reduction methods can emphasize certain patterns in the data yet may also mask patterns that graphical methods can reveal. Anscombe constructed four small data sets of the same size. Figure 13.1 illustrates these data; they are also listed in Exercise 3.26. The response and explanatory variables have the same means and standard deviations for each of these four data sets. Further, each data set exhibits the same fitted regression coefficients, the same standard errors and the same coefficient of determination. Thus, from the viewpoint of a data reduction method, such as fitting a regression model with one explanatory variable, each of the four data sets exhibit the same information. However, Figure 13.1 reveals that the four data sets are very different. They exhibit different types of nonlinear deviations from the regression model. Thus, although the summary statistics reveal some information, the scatter plots exhibit the most important features of the data.

The method of data presentation depends on the purpose at hand. Generally, this chapter assumes that the purpose of the data presentation is for communicating the results of an analysis of data within a report. An important consequence of this assumption is that we will assume that the basic purpose of the data communication is to inform, not to entertain nor persuade. Still, you will find that the basic principles of data presentation can be applied to, for example, data graphics that you may see in a popular magazine or a presentation by a political candidate. However, with some literary works or persuasive pre-

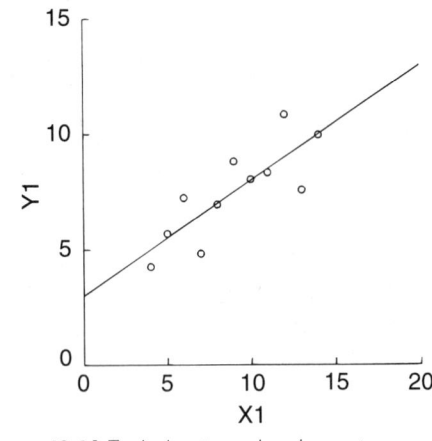

Figure 13.1A Typical pattern showing a strong, yet not perfect, relationship.

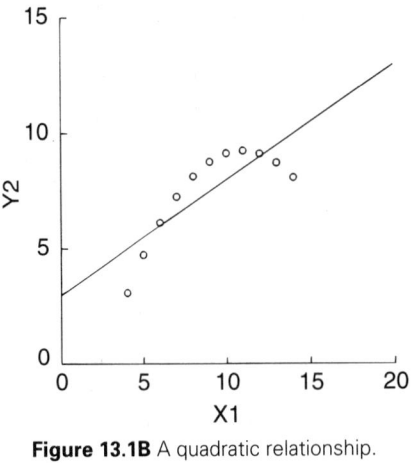

Figure 13.1B A quadratic relationship.

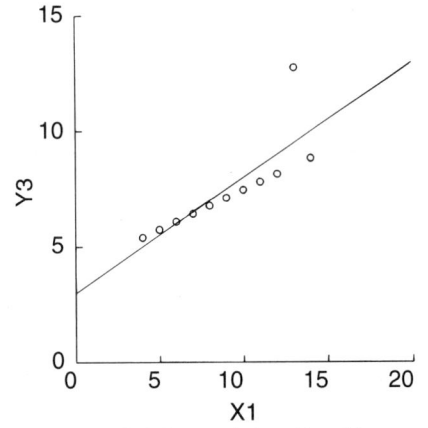

Figure 13.1C A linear relationship with an outlier.

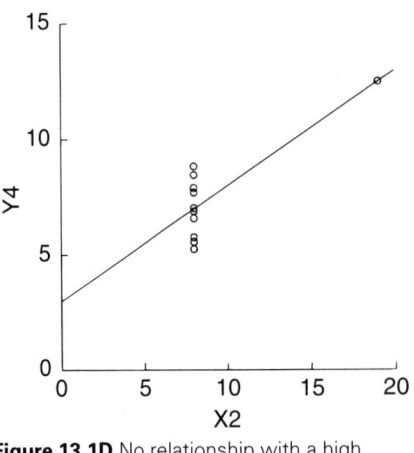

Figure 13.1D No relationship with a high leverage point.

FIGURE 13.1 Anscombe's (1973) data. The summary statistics for each of these four small data sets are nearly identical. That is, they have the same means, standard deviations, fitted slopes and coefficients of determination. However, a visual inspection of the four scatter plots reveals that they have very different features.

sentations, certain liberties may be taken to strengthen a particular point. By focusing on the basic principles, we will be able to point out instances where these liberties are taken and thus enable you to be a more critical consumer of statistics.

It is useful to compare the two purposes of data presentation: communication versus analysis. For communication purposes, data presentations are

Just as with writing, graphs that are well-constructed are the result of repeated revising and editing.

carefully constructed entities that are designed to tell a story. Just as with other aspects of report writing, discussed in Chapter 12, these presentations are the result of repeated revising and editing. For communication purposes, data presented should be constructed with an audience in mind. Conversely, for analysis purposes, data presentations are constructed to gain further insights into any patterns the data may exhibit and to corroborate and suggest further model representations of the data. Further, for analysis purposes, data presentations need only be understood by the data analyst. Generally, the data analyst (i) has a better understanding of the data than the audience of a report and (ii) has a deeper appreciation of technical models that may be used to represent a data set. Thus, data presentations for analysis purposes emphasize data exploration; they do not necessarily convey a broad message to a variety of readers that is important for data presentations in a report.

There are three basic forms of data presentation: within text, tabular and graphical.

Data can be presented in a variety of ways. Chapter 12 introduced the text, tabular and graphical modes. When considering graphical modes, we restrict our consideration to quantitative or data graphics. Graphics may also include other types of visual representations, such as those of a glamorous model extolling the lifestyles of tobacco smokers or a Salvador Dali abstraction portraying various symbols of time. However, we restrict our consideration to visual representations of data. In Section 12.3, we presented basic elements and rules for making each of the three types of data presentations. Just as with writing, there is a great deal of freedom in the selection of the mode and method for communicating data, as long as you follow basic principles of data presentation.

Example 13.2: Some Deceptive Graphs

Statistics without visual examination of the data can be misleading. Similarly, because graphical representations are flexible, when taken by themselves, they can be misleading.

To underscore the importance of methods and principles of data presentations, here is a series of statistical "lies." Mark Twain attributed the quote "There are three kinds of lies: ordinary lies, damned lies and statistics" to Benjamin Disraeli, a nineteenth-century British Prime Minister. Although every statistician is tired of hearing this quote, it carries an important message: numerical information can be used as a powerful persuasive device. Unlike other types of debating devices, a large portion of the population consider themselves to be innumerate, unable to reason quantitatively, and vulnerable to numerical demonstrations of ideas. However, just like any other debating device, data presentations can be modified (or twisted) to reinforce a chosen point of view.

Figures 13.2 through 13.5 exhibit four sets of deceptive graphs. Figure 13.2 displays a time series of monthly values of the number of people employed in Wisconsin which is called the Wisconsin labor force. The left panel, Figure 13.2A, includes zero in the vertical axis. This makes the Wisconsin labor force appear stable over time. The right panel, Figure 13.2B, shows more variation by using the data to determine limits in the

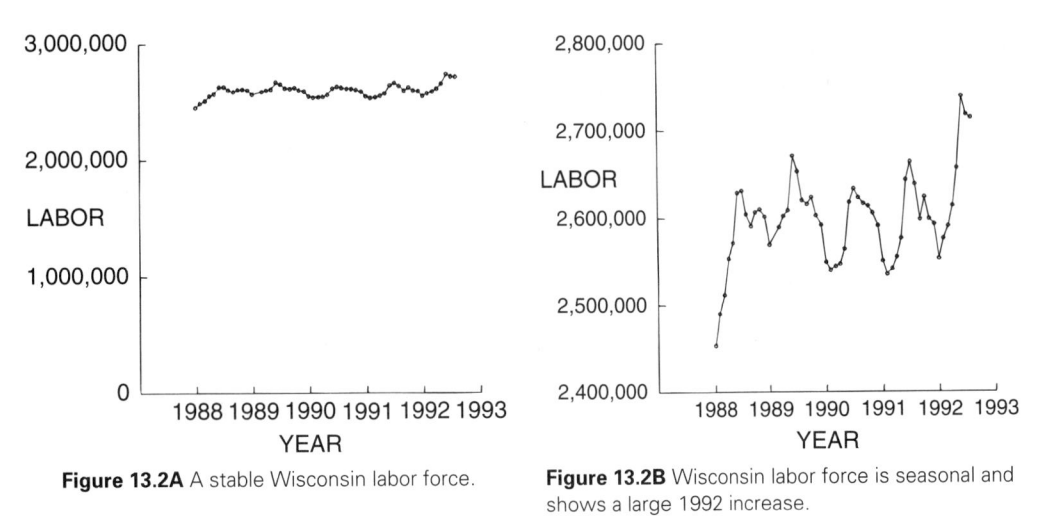

Figure 13.2A A stable Wisconsin labor force.   **Figure 13.2B** Wisconsin labor force is seasonal and shows a large 1992 increase.

FIGURE 13.2 Monthly values of Wisconsin labor force over 1988–1992, inclusive. By allowing the data to determine the scale ranges, interesting aspects of the data are revealed.

vertical scale. In particular, seasonal effects and the mild increase in 1992 employment are clearer in Figure 13.2B when compared to Figure 13.2A.

Figure 13.3 exhibits an effect of scaling. When the amount of insurance (INFORCE) is examined on a linear scale in Figure 13.3A, the U.S. credit insurance market appears to be expanding rapidly. However, Figure 13.3B shows that, when examined on a logarithmic scale, the market is levelling off. In Chapter 6 we showed that changes on a logarithmic scale can be interpreted as proportional changes. Thus, Figure 13.3A shows the market increasing rapidly and Figure 13.3B shows that the rate of increase is levelling off. These messages are not contradictory but do require that the viewer interpret each graph critically to understand the information in the data.

Figure 13.4 provides an example of the use, and misuse, of graphs that have "double vertical axes." In the two panels in Figure 13.4, the left scale gives values for the Beer Price Index (BPI) and the right scale gives values for the Consumer Price Index (CPI). In Figure 13.4A, the scales are restricted to be the same. Thus, this figure shows that the CPI is growing more rapidly than the BPI. In Figure 13.4B, the scales are determined by the data. Thus, from this figure it appears that the two indices grow at the same rate. However, because the range of the CPI is wider in Figure 13.4B than the range for the BPI, Figure 13.4B also shows that the CPI is growing more quickly than the BPI. This subtle point is easily missed by a viewer who is not looking for deceptive graphs.

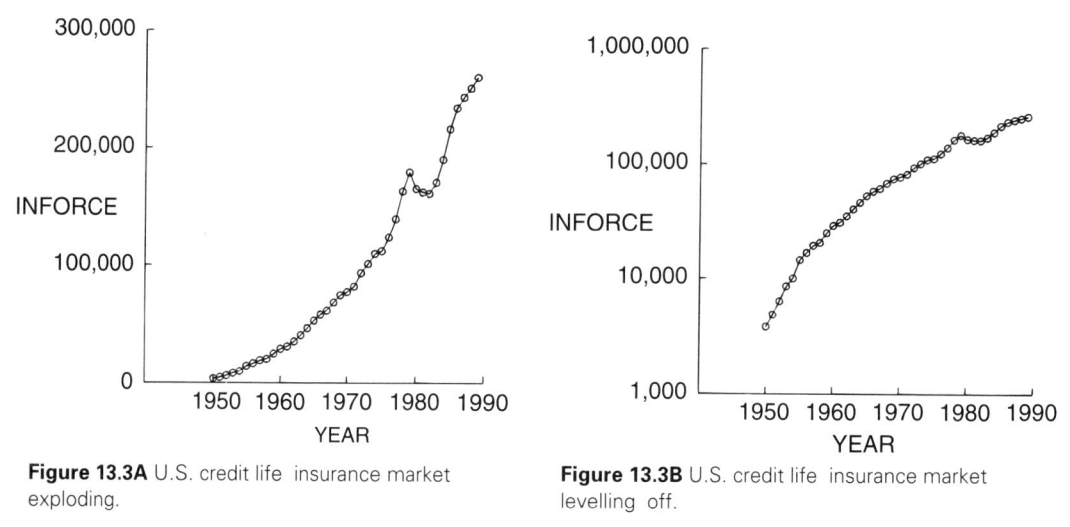

Figure 13.3A U.S. credit life insurance market exploding.

Figure 13.3B U.S. credit life insurance market levelling off.

FIGURE 13.3 Annual U.S. credit life insurance in force over 1950–1990, inclusive. Different vertical scales provide the viewer with different impressions of the rate of growth over time.

Figure 13.5 exhibits another effect of scaling. The data, introduced in Chapter 3, consists of the annual income of 62 customers of a Ford dealership and the price that they paid for a car. The left panel, Figure 13.5A, uses the data to determine the scaling limits. The right panel, Figure 13.5B, has more white space due to the increased scales. As shown by

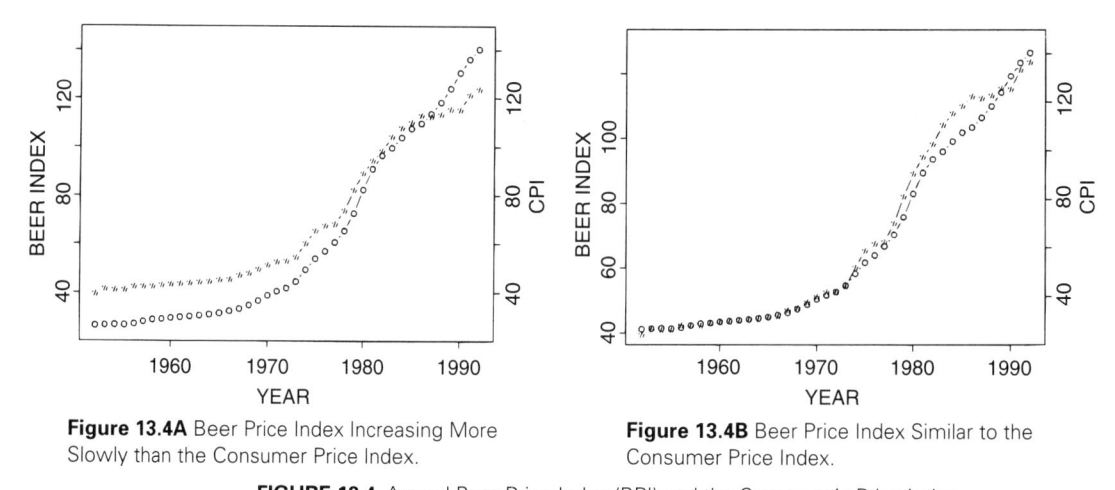

Figure 13.4A Beer Price Index Increasing More Slowly than the Consumer Price Index.

Figure 13.4B Beer Price Index Similar to the Consumer Price Index.

FIGURE 13.4 Annual Beer Price Index (BPI) and the Consumer's Price Index (CPI) over 1952–1992, inclusive. The asterisk plotting symbols represent the BPI and the open circles represent the CPI. By choosing different scale ranges we can alter the appearances of relative growth of the two series.

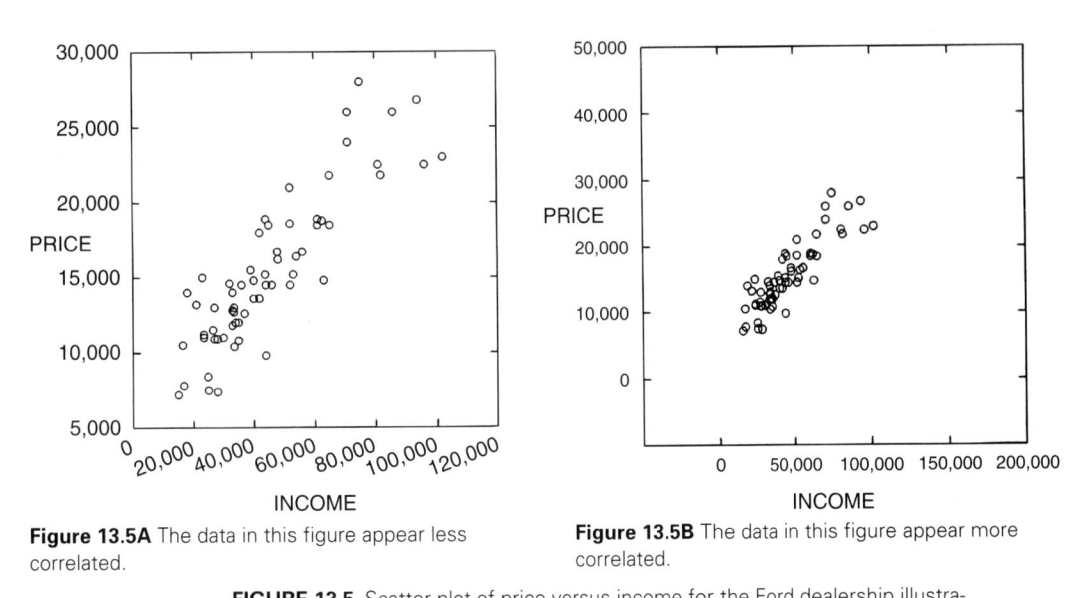

Figure 13.5A The data in this figure appear less correlated.

Figure 13.5B The data in this figure appear more correlated.

FIGURE 13.5 Scatter plot of price versus income for the Ford dealership illustration. The data represented in each figure are the same. However, the wider scales in Figure 13.5B suggest that the data are more highly correlated.

Cleveland, Diaconis and McGill (1982), this makes the left panel appear less correlated, despite the fact that the data in both panels are the same.

13.2 PRINCIPLES FOR DESIGNING DATA GRAPHICS

Section 12.3 introduced the basic forms for presenting data and methods to implement each of these basic forms. We saw that graphs provide a flexible and powerful tool for communicating numerical information. Because graphical forms are so flexible, it is difficult to judge the quality of a graph. In this section, we introduce four broad principles for designing data graphics. These principles not only lead to criteria for judging the effectiveness of a graph, but will also help you choose among graphical forms and improve graphs that you make.

Principle One: Data Talks

In a data graphic, the data contains the information and should receive the most prominent role in the graphic: "let the data do the talking." To this end, we should strive to remove elements from a graph that detract from the data and use visually prominent elements to depict the data. Just as with effective writing, unnecessary appendages on a graph should be pruned.

Unnecessary elements of a graph are called chartjunk. Less chartjunk means a greater opportunity for the data information to reach the viewer.

Tufte (1983) called unnecessary elements in a graph *chartjunk*. Chartjunk is the opposite of what Tufte termed "data-ink," the nonerasable part of a graph. That is, if we erase data-ink, then we lose some numerical information. To let the data talk, Tufte recommends maximizing the ratio of data-ink to the overall ink in a graph. This can be done by erasing nondata-ink.

Figure 13.6, a three-dimensional pie chart of data analyzed in Exercise 6.10, illustrates the presence of excessive chartjunk. To begin, note that there are only five numbers being represented in this complex graph; four if you assume that the viewer will realize that the percentages will add to 100. The third dimension, that provides so-called *perspective,* adds nothing in terms of data information. The vibrating shadings that partition the pie into different categories are distracting.

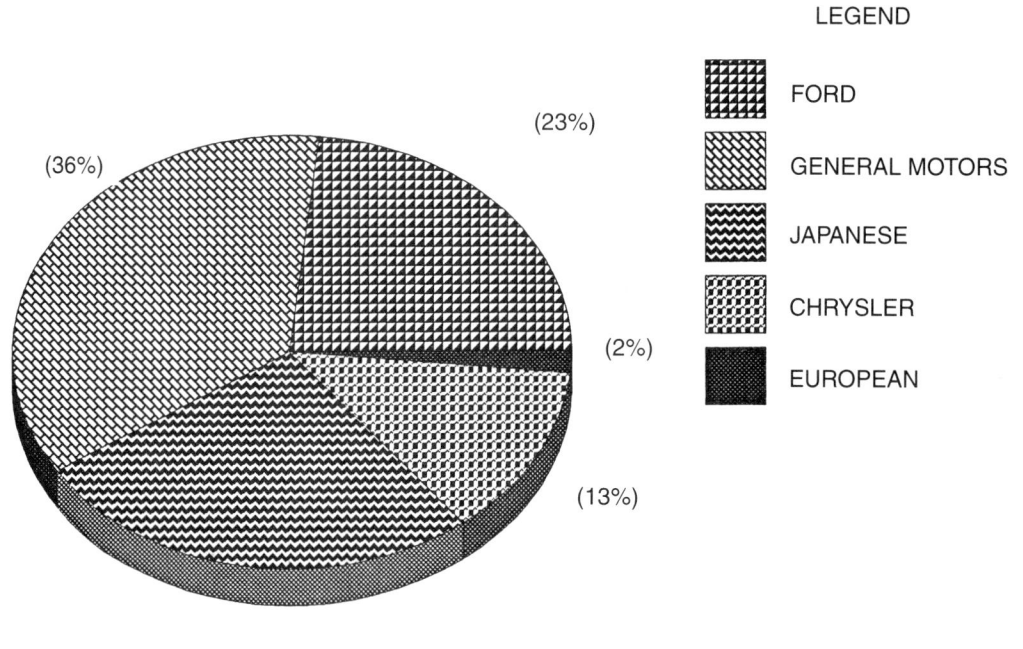

FIGURE 13.6 A pie chart of automobile sales. This complex figure represents only five numbers.

The vibrating shadings are also present in Figure 13.7, a stacked bar chart of data analyzed in Exercise 6.13. Tuftle (1983) called these shadings *moiré vibrations.* Here, the term moiré refers to a watery or wavelike appearance. Thus, moiré effects are those in which the design produces a distracting appearance of vibration and motion. Although the false perspective of a third dimension and complex shadings that produce moiré effects may be eyecatching and entertaining, they make the task of representing complex information through data graphics harder, not easier.

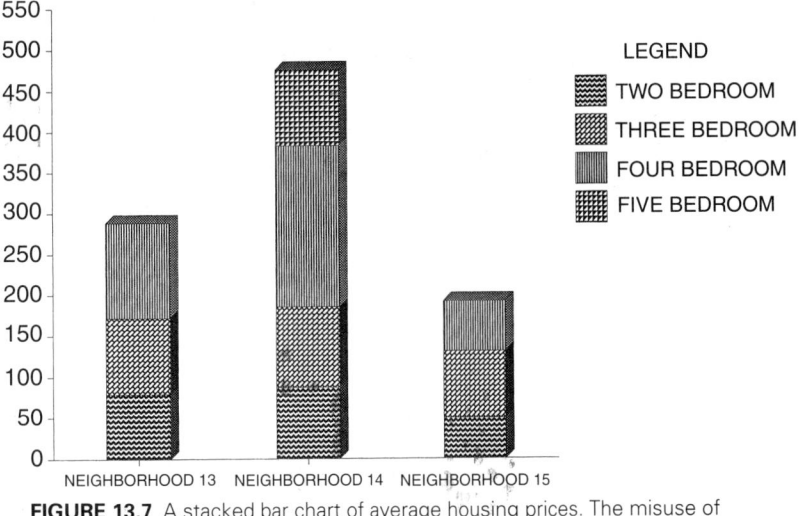

FIGURE 13.7 A stacked bar chart of average housing prices. The misuse of stacking, pseudo-perspective and moiré vibration render this figure ineffective.

Principle Two: Graph Size and Information Are Related

"How large should the graph be?" is a question that many writers ask (or at least they should). The bounds on size are clear. Graphs should not be so small that they are not clearly legible, particularly upon reproduction that degrades an image. Graphs should not be so large that they exceed a page. With large graphs, it is difficult to compare elements within the graph, thus defeating a primary purpose of graphs.

Graph size should be proportional to the information content.

Within these bounds, a graph should be proportional to the amount of information that it contains. To discuss the proportional information in a graph, Tufte (1983) introduced the *data density of a graph*. This is defined to be the number of data entries per unit area of the graph. For comparing graph size and information, the data density is a quantity to be maximized, either by increasing the number of data entries or reducing the size of the graph. By examining this density over a number of popular publications, Tufte concluded that most graphs could be effectively shrunk.

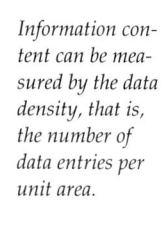

Information content can be measured by the data density, that is, the number of data entries per unit area.

For example, Figure 13.6 illustrates a chart with a low data density. This chart represents only five numbers. With an area of approximately nine square inches, this graph's data density is roughly 5/9 For comparison, Figure 11.5, redrawn here as Figure 13.8 for convenience, represents 252 (= 3 × 84) numbers. These are values of 84 quarters for the quarterly medical component of the consumer price index and for the corresponding fitted values under exponential smoothing. With an area of approximately nine square inches, this graph's data density is roughly 252/9. This is much larger that the corresponding data density for Figure 13.6.

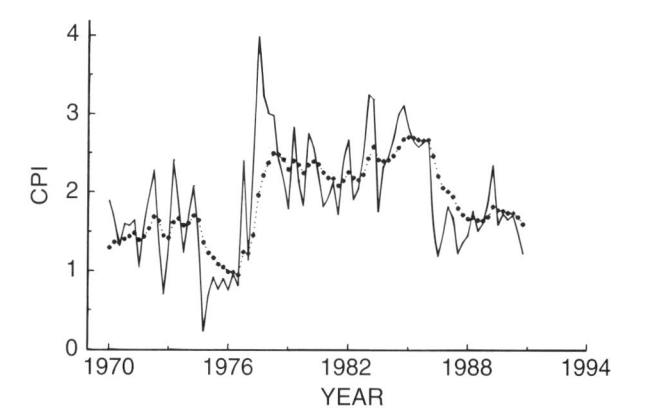

FIGURE Time series plot of Quaterly Medical CPI from 1970 to 1990. An exponential smoothing fit, with weight = 0.8, is superimposed.

FIGURE 13.8 There are 252 data elements represented in this time series plot.

Information content can also be measured by the importance of the information to the viewer.

One way to think about the information content of a graph is to consider the number of data elements that a graph represents. Another way is to consider the importance of the information to the viewer. Cleveland (1985) urges us to put major conclusions of our analyses into graphical form. Figures 7.12 through 7.15 of the Section 7.4 Risk Managers case study illustrates this. An implication of this, and Tufte's data density concept, is to make graphs proportional to their importance to the reader. For example, on one hand, Figure 7.15 illustrates the final model of an analysis. This graph could be as large as an entire page in a report because of its importance. However, on the other hand, Figure 13.9, taken from the first part of section 7.4, is part of the model checking at an early stage of the analysis. This graph is too large in relation to the message that it conveys.

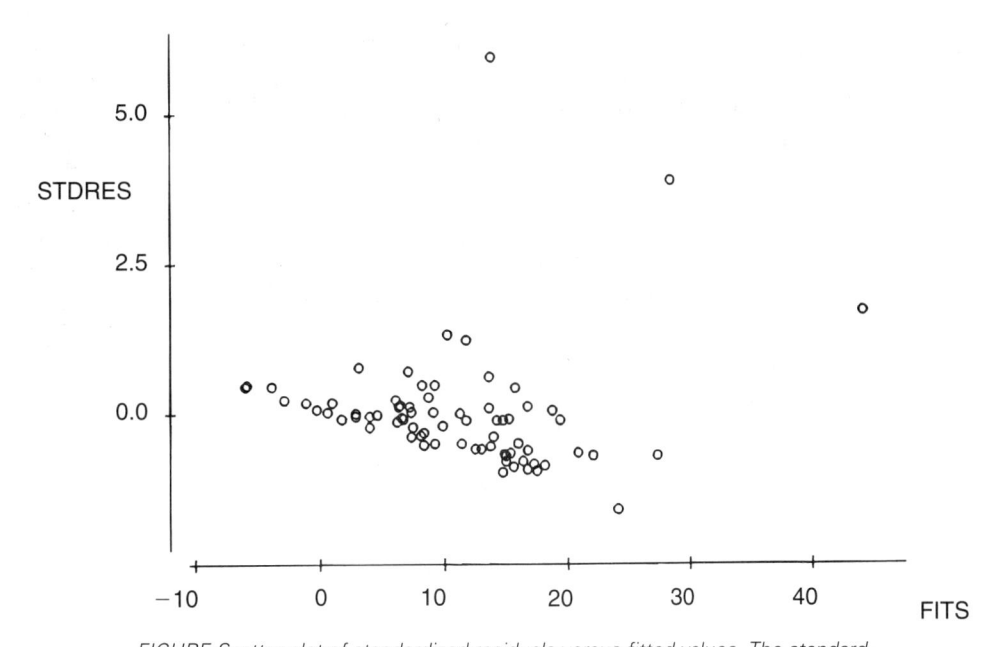

FIGURE Scatter plot of standardized residuals versus fitted values. The standardized residuals are from a fitted regression using FIRMCOST as the response.

FIGURE 13.9 Scatter plot based on a preliminary model fit of the Section 7.4
case study. Because this plot is part of a preliminary data analysis stage and not
a final model of interest to the reader, the large size of the graph is inappropriate.

Principle Three: Complex Graphs Are Okay

Many authors believe that "a graph should be immediately understood by the
viewer." There are some desirable aspects to this concept of a graph, including:
(i) you can reach a broad audience with simple graphs, (ii) simple graphs can
be shown quickly and digested immediately and (iii) you can chain several
simple graphs together to form a complex message. However, this concept is
limiting in that it precludes the notion that graphs can be used to represent
complex ideas. Complex patterns should be portrayed as simply as possible although the patterns themselves should not be unnecessarily simplified.

    One way for a graph to represent complex patterns is for some of its ba-
sic elements to serve more than one purpose. Tufte (1983) called these elements
multifunctioning. For example, in letter plots we use plotting symbols to represent not only elements corresponding to the horizontal and vertical scales but
also a level of a categorical variable. Another important example used in data
analysis is the *stem-and-leaf plot*, illustrated in Figure 13.10.

    In Figure 13.10, we see that the leading digit of the variable is used to in-
dicate the different categories. The leading digits on the left comprise the *stem*
portion of the graph. For this example, each row of the stem portion corre-

sponds to hundreds of dollars of monthly rent. Each digit listed on the right, the *leaf* portion, represents a plotting symbol for an apartment. Digits on the right give the next digit in the apartment's monthly rent, corresponding to tens of dollars.

Thus, the stem-and-leaf plot provides a graphical summary of a variable's distribution, as does the histogram. Further, by using numbers for plotting symbols, the stem-and-leaf plot not only provides a count for each category but also an indication of individual values within the category.

```
Stem-and-leaf of RENTS              N = 29
Leaf Unit = 10

  5  6
  6  0000012223
  6  55779
  7  555578
  8  0
  8  57
```

FIGURE 13.10 Stem-and-Leaf Plot. The data are the monthly rents of 29 apartments, first presented in Table 2.1.

Principle Four: Graphs Are Not Islands

Within a report, treat a graph as a paragraph.

Data graphics should be carefully integrated with the text, tables and other graphs. A caption of a graph can provide a description of the graph and its main message. However, the surrounding text develops the theme leading up to the message and discusses its impact. Although "a picture is worth a thousand words," a graph needs supporting text. Tufte (1983) encourages readers and writers to think of data graphics as paragraphs, and to be treated as such.

Data graphics may also be complemented by a tabular presentation of data. As introduced in Section 12.3, graphics can highlight relationships within the data and tables can present precise numerical descriptions of the data. Thus, the two modes may complement one another. In Chapter 12, we also saw that a good writing device is to place a graphical display in the main body of the report and to reinforce the graph with a tabular display in an appendix.

A data graphic may also be closely related to other graphs. For multivariate data, we often use more than one graph to feature various aspects of the same data set. For example, a scatterplot matrix is an excellent graphical device to see patterns with multiple graphs. More than one graph may also be used for comparisons. For example, in Figure 13.2 we used two graphs to demonstrate the effect of including zero in the vertical axis.

Graphs and models should be used to strengthen and reinforce one another.

Cleveland (1985) recommends that you "put major conclusions in a graphical form." In regression data analysis, major conclusions are about patterns in the data that are summarized using models. However, major conclusions can also be presented graphically. Graphs allow a large amount of information to be presented and retained by the viewer. Graphs can be used to communicate patterns present in the data to a viewer directly, without using a model to represent the patterns. In this way, a wider audience can be reached compared to a presentation that relies solely on a model-based interpretation of the data. Further, patterns suggested by a graph can be used to reinforce those represented by a model, and vice-versa. Thus the two tools, graphs and models, reinforce and strengthen one another.

13.3 PERCEIVING GRAPHS

You may have noticed that this text does not display a number of graphical forms that are mainstays in business publications and the popular press, such as pie charts, pictographs and stacked bar charts. In fact, we only have seen pie and stacked bar charts in Section 13.2 as examples of how *not* to draw figures. Why are these widely used graphical forms of communication not adopted in a text that emphasizes data graphics? The reasons lie in how graphical forms communicate information and how we perceive graphical information. We will demonstrate that, given how we perceive information, pie and stacked bar charts are poor communicators of numerical information.

Data graphics encode information and we, as viewers, decode this information when viewing a graph.

Data graphics encode information and we, as viewers, decode this information when viewing a graph. The efficiency of the process of this transmision can be considered in the context of cognitive psychology, the science of perception. This discipline provides a framework for distinguishing among different types of information processing that we do when decoding graphs. Identifying different types of information processing will help us decide what are effective, and ineffective, graphical forms.

Table 13.1 provides an ordered list of basic graphical perception tasks, due to Cleveland (1985). Here, the ordering is from the set of tasks that are least difficult for a viewer to perform to those that are most difficult. Thus, for example, judging position along a common scale is the least difficult for viewers and judging relative shadings of colors and density (the amount of ink) is the most difficult.

TABLE 13.1   Basic Graphical Perception Tasks, Ordered by Level of Difficulty

1. Position along a common scale
2. Position along identical, nonaligned scales
3. Length
4. Angles and slopes
5. Area
6. Volume
7. Color and density

To understand the relative difficulty of the tasks, Cleveland and McGill (1984) performed a series of tests on many experimental subjects. To illustrate, Figures 13.11 through 13.15 present a series of tests that are analogous to the first five tasks. Cleveland and McGill summarized the performance of the experimental subjects by calculating the accuracy that the subjects performed each set of tasks. Through these measures of relative accuracy, and arguments from cognitive psychology, Cleveland and McGill developed the ordering presented in Table 13.1.

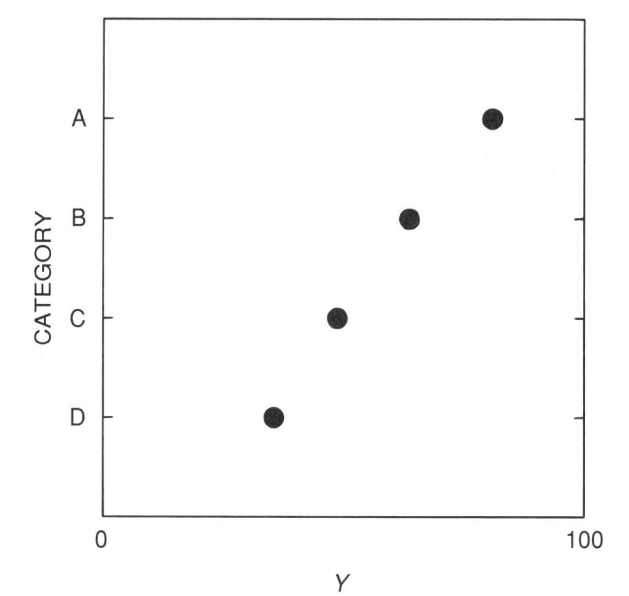

FIGURE 13.11 Experiment to judge position along a common scale. Assess the relative values of A, B. C and D along this 100 point scale.

When choosing among graphical forms, select the form that is the least difficult for the viewer to decode.

The ordered list of graphical perception tasks can help you decide on the appropriate graphical form to portray a data set. In general, when confronted with a choice of two graphical forms, select the form that is least difficult for the viewer. Other things being equal, a task that can be performed with little difficulty by the viewer means that more reliable information can be transmitted.

To illustrate, we present three examples where Table 13.1 can help you decide on the appropriate graphical form. The first example demonstrates the inadequacy of the pie chart. Figure 13.16 use the same data as in Figure 13.6. To be fair, the distracting moiré vibrations and the third dimension have been removed. Even with these improvements, it is still difficult to judge, for example, the relative percentage sales of Japanese manufacturers versus Ford. The comparison is easier in Figure 13.17, where the *dot chart* shows that Japanese manufacturers have a larger share than Ford for our sample data. This exam-

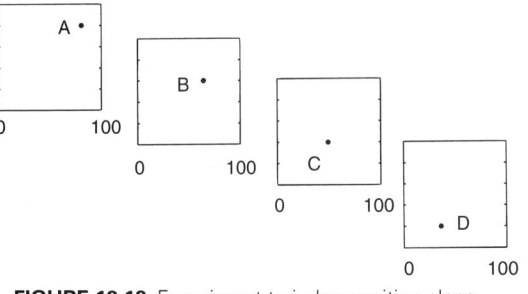

FIGURE 13.12 Experiment to judge position along identical, nonaligned scales. Assess the relative values of A, B. C and D on a common 100 point scale.

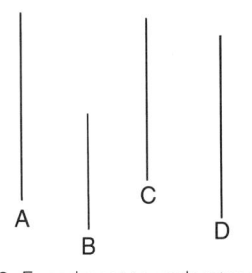

FIGURE 13.13 Experiment to understand length judgments. Suppose line A is 100 units long. Assess the relative lengths of the lines B, C and D.

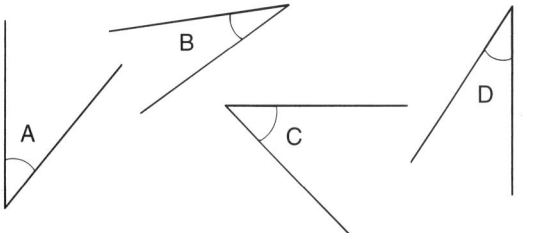

FIGURE 13.14 Experiment to understand angle judgments. Suppose angle A is 100 units. Assess the relative values of angles B, C and D.

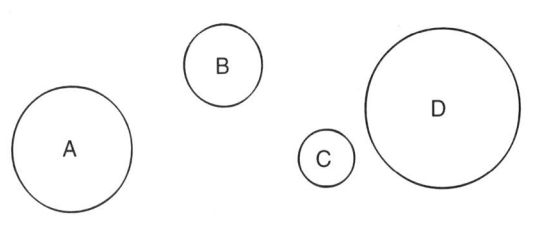

FIGURE 13.15 Experiment to understand area judgments. Suppose circle A has area 100 units. Assess the relative areas of circles B, C, and D.

ple illustrates that judgments along a common scale are less difficult, and more accurate, than judgments involving angles.

Our next example demonstrates the usefulness of residual plots in regression analysis. The data are taken from Exercise 5.5, a sample of average assessed home prices in 89 neighborhoods. Figure 13.18 displays a scatter plot of 1992 assessed values on the vertical scale versus 1991 values on the horizontal scale. Both 1991 and 1992 values are on base ten logarithmic scale. Figure 13.18 displays the strong linear relations between these two variables; the correlation is $r = 0.993$.

The angle of the slope makes it difficult to detect deviations from the line. This is partly due to the fact that assessing the deviations from the line means assessing positions along nonaligned scales. Alternatively, Figure 13.19 shows a scatter plot of the deviations from the line, the residuals, versus the 1991 valuation. This figure shows the strong pattern of increasing variability from the line, the heteroscedasticity. This pattern is evident in Figure 13.18 upon close inspection although is much more difficult to detect. In Figure 13.19 we have removed the angle of the line by examining residuals and can assess positions along a common scale. Further, by examining residuals, we can enlarge the vertical scale, thus making it easier to detect subtle patterns.

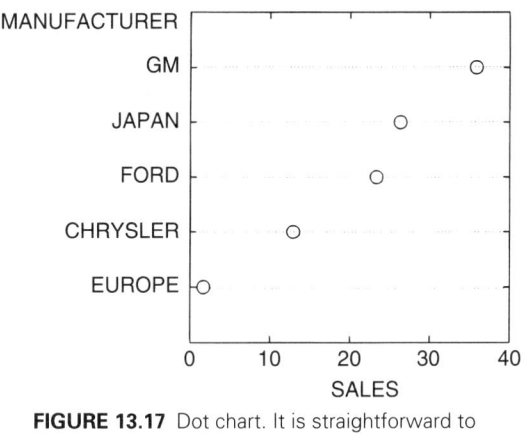

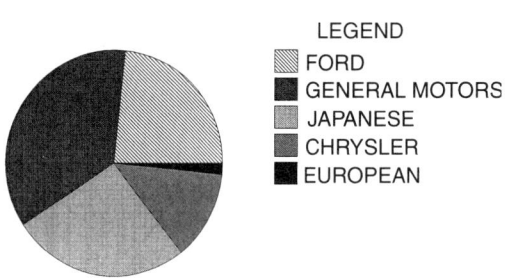

FIGURE 13.16 Pie chart. It is difficult to judge relative sizes of angles.

FIGURE 13.17 Dot chart. It is straightforward to judge relative proportions of sales volume.

Figure 13.20 is a redrawing of Figure 13.7; the moiré vibrations and the third dimension have been removed to help us focus on the data. The data, described in Exercise 6.13, are average selling prices of 78 homes in three neighborhoods, grouped by the number of bedrooms in each house. There are a number of problems with Figure 13.20. First, because of the stacking, viewers are asked to make line judgments to compare, for example, the relative prices of houses having a different number of bedrooms over the same neighborhood. Second, the stacking also implicitly adds average prices over different numbers of bedrooms over each neighborhood. If viewers use the height of

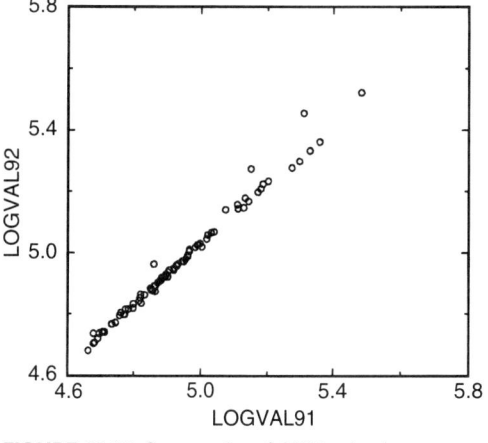

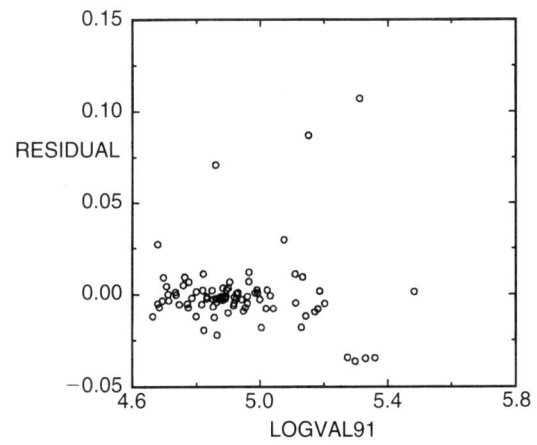

FIGURE 13.18 Scatter plot of 1992 valuation versus 1991 valuation. It is difficult to see deviations from the line.

FIGURE 13.19 Scatter plot of residuals from 1992 valuation versus 1991 valuation. It is easier to see deviations from the line.

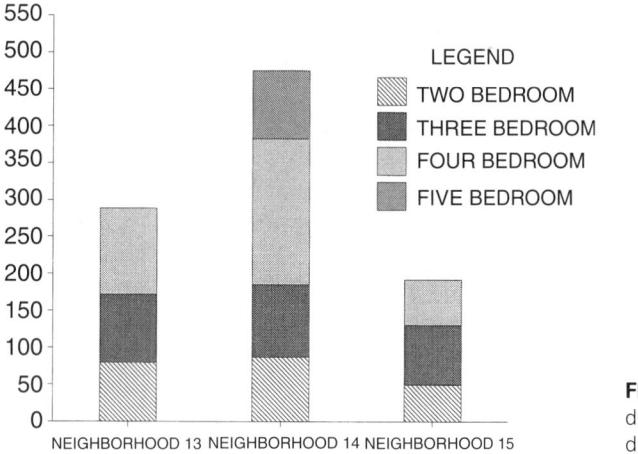

FIGURE 13.20 Stacked bar chart. It is difficult to judge relative sizes of prices due to different bedrooms.

each bar to make comparisons across neighborhoods, they are implicitly assuming that the number of houses within each category are relatively equal. This is certainly not true of five-bedroom houses because there are none of these larger houses in neighborhoods 13 and 15.

To avoid these deficiencies, an alternative to the stacked bar chart is the overlay bar chart. This widely used alternative is not presented here because in Section 13.4 we will present a better method for graphically showing the data, a two-way dot chart. However, we now emphasize the importance of tabular methods. Table 13.2 provides the same data that is illustrated in Figure 13.20. With this table, the data are accessible and comparisons, over neighborhoods and bedrooms, are easily made. Although not as colorful or as eye-catching as a graph, tables often provide an efficient way of presenting data.

TABLE 13.2   Average House Price by Neighborhood and Bedroom Size, in Thousands of Dollars

	Neighborhood 13	Neighborhood 14	Neighborhood 15
Two Bedroom	79.3	87.0	49.7
Three Bedroom	92.4	98.0	80.8
Four Bedroom	116.8	197.5	61.3
Five Bedroom	—	93.0	—

13.4 GRAPHS FOR ANALYZING DATA

This book provides a survey of regression analysis and, for many readers, an introduction to data analysis. As an introduction, the intent has been to present a minimal number of tools so that the reader has the opportunity to capture the spirit of examining data. However, for those readers interested in seeing more sophisticated data analytic graphs in action, this section provides an introduction. For an excellent discussion of modern graphical tools beyond that presented here, see Cleveland (1994). For the classic introduction to exploratory data analysis using numerical and graphical tools, see Tukey (1977).

To appreciate the wide variety of graphic tools available to the analyst, Table 13.3 presents a list of tools categorized by the type of variable being portrayed. We have already used many of these tools in this text, most being seen as useful but some disregarded as ineffective devices for examining data. This list is for analyzing data that includes at least one quantitative, or continuous, variable. When a qualitative, or categorical, variable is the only quantity being considered, generally a semitabular or tabular representation of the data is preferable to a graphical form.

TABLE 13.3 Graphical Tools for Exploring Data, Described by Type of Variable

One quantitative variable	One quantitative variable with labels
Dot plot	Dot chart
Histogram	Pie chart
Stem-and-leaf plot	Bar chart
Box plot	Pareto chart
Quantile plot	
Probability plot	

Two quantitative variables	Two variables—one quantitative and one qualitative
Scatter plot	Two-way dot chart
Time series plot	Dot plot
Quantile-quantile plot	Box plot

Three or more variables—two or more quantitative	Three or more variables—one quantitative
Letter plot	Stacked bar chart
Scatter plot with varying symbol size	Divided bar chart
Scatterplot matrix	Overlay bar chart
Multiple time series plot	Multiway dot chart
Three dimensional plot	
Added variable plot	
Coplot	

One Quantitative Variable

Because a quantitative variable is a basic unit of analysis, there are several graphical forms used to represent it. Two basic forms are the *dot plot* and *histogram*, introduced in Chapter 2. Both forms are useful for seeing the entire distribution; dot plots are suitable for smaller data sets and histograms, because they summarize data, are suitable for larger data sets. A variation of the histogram is the *stem-and-leaf plot,* a graphical form that uses the numerical value of the observation to identify the individual observations. Figure 13.10 illustrated the stem-and-leaf plot. It is useful for examining smaller data sets.

For examining larger data sets, analysts have found the *box plot* to be a useful graphical form. Figure 13.21 illustrates the box plot for the housing price data considered in Section 13.3 and introduced in Exericse 6.13. Here the box captures the middle 50% of the data and the so-called "whiskers" capture the middle 80%. By using the box and whiskers to capture the majority of the data, the viewer can get a quick sense of the distribution and important summary statistics without examining individuals observations. For comparison with a normal curve, you will also see the box and whiskers defined in relation to percentiles from a standard normal curve.

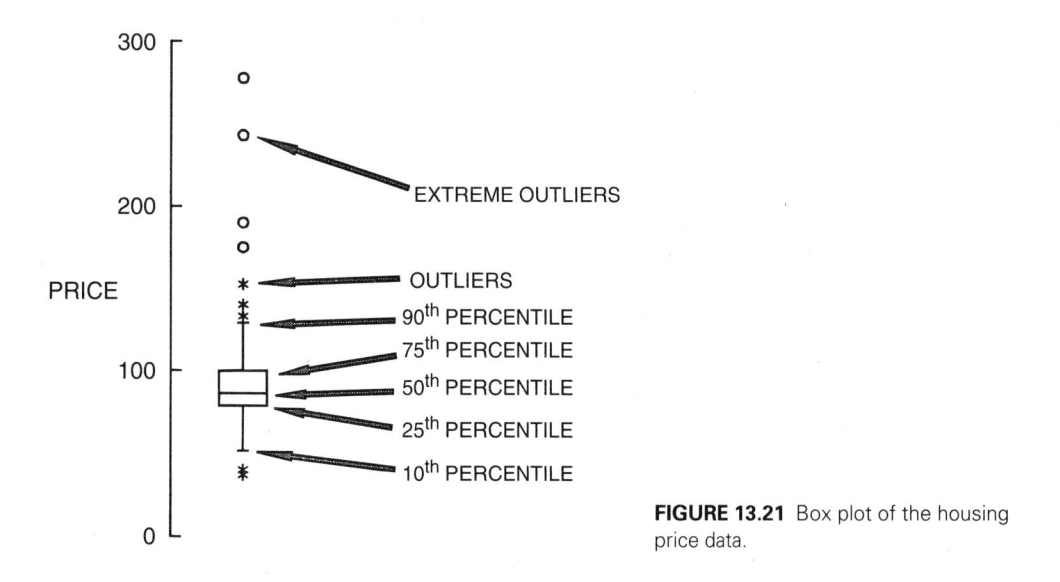

FIGURE 13.21 Box plot of the housing price data.

Two other ways of examining the distribution of a quantitative variable are through the *quantile* and *probability* plots, illustrated in Figures 13.22 and 13.23, respectively. In Figure 13.22, for each house price that we identify on the horizontal axis, the corresponding level on the vertical axis provides the quantile, or percentile, for that house. Thus, for example, we see that a house priced slightly less than $100 thousand dollars is at the 50th percentile, or median, of our distribution. The probability plot then transforms these percentiles for comparison with a known distribution. Figure 13.23 illustrates a normal probability plot. Here, each percentile is converted to an expected quantity under the standard normal curve. For example, at our house price that is slightly less than $100 thousand dollars corresponding to the median, the expected stan-

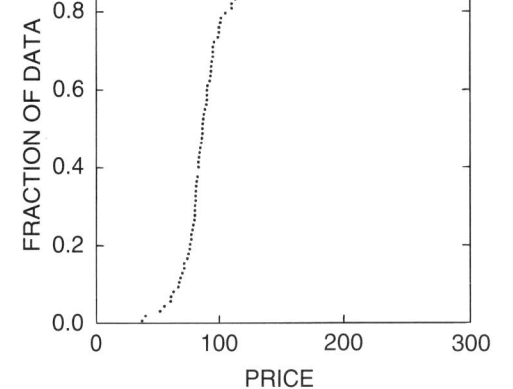

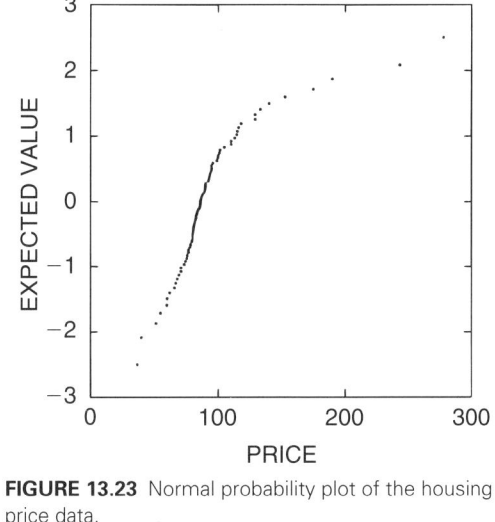

FIGURE 13.22 Quantile plot of the housing price data.

FIGURE 13.23 Normal probability plot of the housing price data.

dard normal value is zero. We first saw normal probability plots defined in Section 3.5.

One Quantitative Variable with Labels

Pie charts are not used in data analysis due to their low data density and because they require viewers to make difficult angle judgments.

For small data sets, individual observations can be identified with case identi-fiers or *labels.* When the variable can be rescaled to a percentage basis, a widely used graphical form is the *pie chart.* This is the worst type of graphical form, due to its low data density ratio and because it forces the viewer to make an-gle judgments when comparing different categories. For several decades, graphic experts have criticized pie charts as ineffective designs, see Schmid (1992, Chapter 4) for background. However, pie charts continue to be used in business presentations, probably due to their psychological appeal. For a pre-sentation that contains only a limited amount of numerical information, the weak design of a pie chart may not be a serious drawback. Because of their psy-chological appeal and because audiences are used to seeing this mode of in-formation transmittal, pie charts may be effective. However, when analyzing data, pie charts are particuarly ineffective because they do a poor job when there is a substantial amount of data information to be interpreted.

Two graphical alternatives to the pie chart are the *dot chart* and the *bar chart.* The dot chart, a variation of the dot plot, is a graphical form that also pro-vides labels to identify individual observations. We have already seen Figures 13.16 and 13.17 compare the pie chart to the dot chart. For effective communi-cation of data, dot charts are preferable to pie charts. This is because dot charts require judgments using position along a common scale compared to the more difficult angle judgments required by pie charts. For the same reason, bar charts are preferable to pie charts. Dot charts are preferred to bar charts because they have a higher data density.

A variation of the bar chart used extensively in modern quality management is the *Pareto chart*. A Pareto chart is a bar chart of a variable expressed on a percentage basis where the bars are listed in order of importance. For presentation of tabular data, in Section 12.3 we saw that an important rule for creating efficient presentations is to order the columns to facilitate comparisons. As we see with the Pareto chart, this rule can be applied to graphical as well as tabular presentation of data. Indeed, presentation rules are common to the choice of textual, tabular and graphical modes because the rules are all consequences of how we perceive data.

Two Quantitative Variables

A *scatter plot* is a method of displaying two-dimensional quantitative data using a Cartesian coordinate system. Section 3.1 introduced this graphical tool that has been used as our basic graphical form for viewing two-dimensional data. A *time series plot* is a special case of the scatter plot where one variable is a measure of time. In time series plots, by convention we connect the plotting symbols so that patterns over time can be emphasized.

For comparing distributions of two quantitative variables, a useful tool is the *quantile-quantile*, or *q-q*, plot due to Wilk and Gnanadesikan (1980). A *q-q* plot is a scatter plot of selected quantiles of one variable versus the quantiles of another variable. The quantiles, or percentiles, may either correspond to the available observations or some subset, the latter being useful for large data sets or where the number of observations differs between variables. The *q-q* plot is useful for comparing the distribution of one variable versus another. With a *q-q* plot, this is done by comparing percentiles of each distribution in lieu of the actual observations.

To compare distributions of two variables, we usually begin by comparing sample means. However, means are affected by unusual observations, a drawback that is not true of medians. The *q-q* plot allows us to compare medians, and more. For example, if we were interested in comparing the heights of infant males to infant females, from the *q-q* plot we can examine the 50th percentile from each distribution to compare a "typical" infant male to female. Similarly, we could also compare "tall" infant males to females by examining the 90th percentile from each distribution, or any other percentile of interest. The *q-q* plot reveals a great deal about the relationship between two distributions over the entire range and for selected percentiles.

Two Variables—One Quantitative and One Qualitative

Plotting data containing quantitative and qualitative variables extends the idea of plotting a quantitative variable with labels. Indeed, you may think of each data label as a unique "category." Thus, for some data sets, you may wish to use the graphical tools that are useful for quantitative variables with labels. For example, bar, pie and Pareto charts are useful tools for analyzing data having a quantitative and qualitative variable. However, with other data sets, repeated applications of plotting tools that are useful for quantitative variables, without labels, are more appropriate.

For small data sets, *two-way dot charts*, are informative. These can be arranged to compare categories and still provide individual information using labels. We will see an illustration in Figure 13.31. For larger data sets where it is not possible to provide individual case identifiers, dotplots are a useful tool. Figures 8.2 and 8.3 illustrate an application of repeated dotplots. For yet larger data sets, box plots are useful. Figure 13.24 illustrates a box plot repeated over several categories. This is an effective device for comparing distributions among categories.

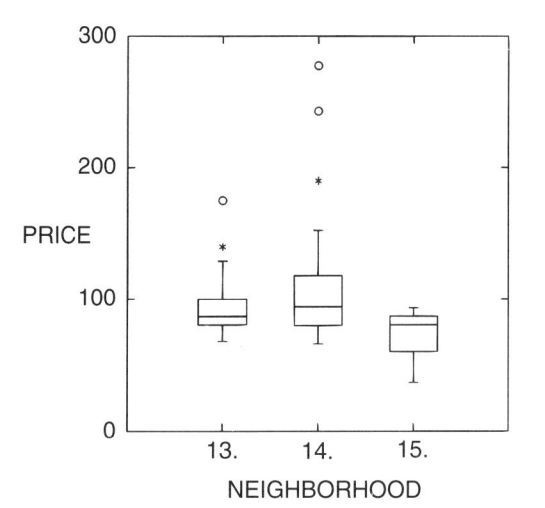

FIGURE 13.24 Box plot of the housing price data. The categories are the three neighborhoods.

Three or More Variables—Two or More Quantitative

Portraying more than two quantitative variables on a two-dimensional platform, such as a piece of paper or computer screen, is a difficult task. When one or more of the variables is categorical, the task is more tractable. For example, with two quantitative variables and one qualitative variable, data can be efficiently communicated using a *letter plot*. Figure 13.5 illustrated a letter plot, where the two quantitative variables are represented by the usual scatter plot and the third variable is encoded using a letter in the plotting symbol. Of course, using letters is only one such coding symbol. Other devices that you will see include use of different plotting symbols and colors. In particular, if you have the technology available, use of colors to represent different categories is an effective way of portraying patterns by level of the category (see, for example, Cleveland, 1985, Chapter 3).

However, when the third dimension is quantitative, use of colors is ineffective. Although the physical spectrum does present an ordering for colorings, from Table 13.1 we see that one of the most difficult tasks a viewer can be asked to do is to make judgments using color. An easier task used by some analysts involves coding the third quantitative dimension using the *size of the plotting symbol.* This can be effective for coding leverage or other diagnostic values (recall from Chapter 6 that leverage is a measure of how "unusual" is an observation). However, from Table 13.1 we see that making area judgments is still a difficult task for viewers.

For viewing multivariate data with more than two quantitative variables, an effective device is the *scatterplot matrix.* This graphical form, illustrated first in Figure 4.5, is an organized group of scatter plots. The organization is the key; the scatter plots are grouped to form a matrix having comparable scales. For k variables, there are $k^2 - k$ scatter plots in the matrix. Because we can get virtually the same information of a plot of x_1 versus x_2 as a plot of x_2 versus x_1, a useful variation is to omit half of the (redundant) scatter plots, resulting in the *half scatterplot matrix.* For a half scatterplot matrix with k variables, there are $k(k - 1)/2$ scatter plots.

For example, consider the 37 refrigerators introduced in Example 4.1. This data set includes the price (PRICE) of each refrigerator, the size measured in cubic feet of the freezer component (FCUFT), and the annual expenditure for maintaining the refrigerator called the energy cost (ECOST). Figure 13.25 shows a positive relationship between PRICE and ECOST. Further, by examining the size of the plotting symbols, we also see positive relationship between FCUFT and each of PRICE and ECOST. These pairwise relationships are more easily discernible in the scatterplot matrix in Figure 13.26.

When one of the variables is time, another way to portray multivariate data with more than two quantitative variables is the *multiple time series plot.* Figure 3.8 illustrates this plotting technique. Here, different styles of plotting lines may be used to connect the points. In addition, if you have the technology available, using different colors provides an effective way of discriminating different patterns over time.

Interactive statistical packages allow you to "rotate" plots in real time, thus allowing you to "see" three-dimensional data on a two-dimensional computer monitor.

For viewing three-dimensional quantitative data, *three-dimensional plots* can be useful. However, it takes a great deal of effort to rotate the data in exactly the right way to see data in three dimensions on a two-dimensional platform. Heretofore, three-dimensional plots were used only for communication of final model results, not for analysis to develop an understanding of the data. However, modern computational techniques are available for viewing data interactively. In particular, many statistical software packages will allow you to interactively *rotate* the data. You will find that rotating the data allows you to

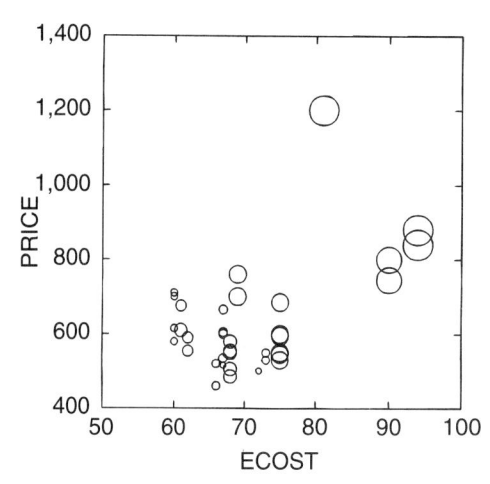

FIGURE13.25 Scatter plot of price versus energy cost (ECOST). Here, the size of the plotting symbol is used to represent a third variable, the size of the freezer in cubic feet (FCUFT).

FIGURE 13.26 Scatterplot matrix. Here it is easy to see the positive pairwise correlation among the three variables.

"see" the third dimension effectively, even on a two-dimensional platform such as a computer monitor.

Figure 13.27 illustrates a three-dimensional plot for our refrigerator data. This graph is complex, yet it does reveal many interesting aspects of the data. First, the positive pairwise association among the three variables is evident in this graph, although it is easier to see in Figure 13.26. The location of the plotting symbol provides information about ECOST and FCUFT and the length of the vertical deviation line provides information about PRICE. Sec-

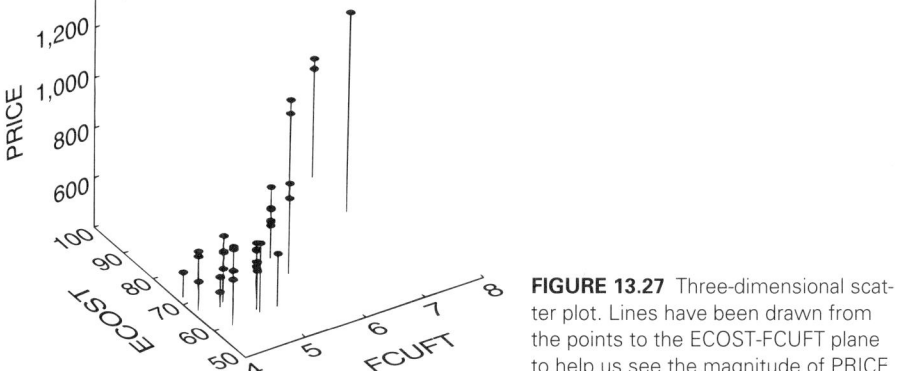

FIGURE 13.27 Three-dimensional scatter plot. Lines have been drawn from the points to the ECOST-FCUFT plane to help us see the magnitude of PRICE.

ond, upon close inspection, you will see that, if you consider a group of refrigerators within a small band of FCUFT (say, 4.5 to 5.5 FCUFT), then PRICE decreases with ECOST. On a visual basis, this is at best a very faint pattern, one that we can highlight by introducing special model structures and by introducing other graphical tools.

The paper medium limits us to two dimensions yet our everyday visual experiences are in three dimensions. Although the scatterplot matrix is a useful device that is not limited to three dimensions, it only allows us to understand the relationships between pairs of variables. For seeing more than three variables, either the data must have a special form or we must impose a special structure on it, for example, through the use of a model. For example, data representing a geographic location have a special form that can be represented using a map.

One way to impose a special structure on multivariate data is through the regression model. We have already seen, in Section 4.4, the *added variable*, or *partial regression, plot*. This plot allows us to see the relation between two variables conditional on the values of the other variables by using a linear regression function for the conditioning. Figure 13.28 illustrates an added variable plot for our refrigerator data. Section 4.4 explained the mechanics of creating an added variable plot. Essentially, we interpret the residuals from a regression as the dependent variable controlled for values of the independent variables. In Figure 13.28, we are using FCUFT as the control variable. The added variable plot is a plot of residuals from regressions using PRICE and ECOST as the dependent variables. In Figure 4.4, we used several explanatory variables as control variables.

Another graphical tool to view the conditional relationship between two variables is the *conditioning plot*, or *coplot*. Unlike the added variable plot, the

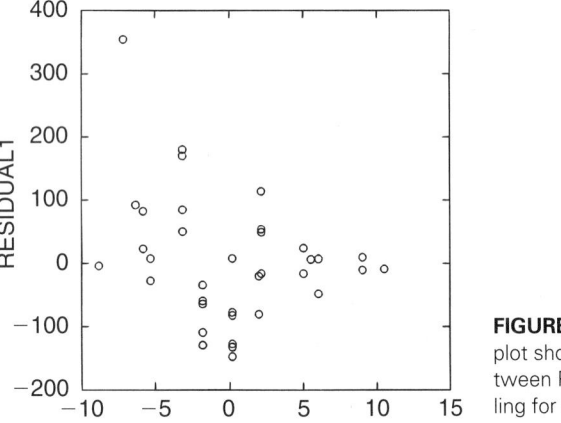

FIGURE 13.28 Added variable plot. This plot shows a negative relationship between PRICE and ECOST, after controlling for FCUFT.

coplot does not use a linear function for the conditioning. Instead, it uses a more general local averaging technique, as described in Cleveland (1994).

Figure 13.29 illustrates the coplot for our refrigerator data. The top and bottom displays are called the *given panel* and the *dependence panels.* The given panel describes values of the control variable, FCUFT in this case, that we are conditioning on. Six bands of FCUFT are graphed in the given panel and each band corresponds to a dependence panel. The correspondence is, moving from smaller to larger values of FCUFT means moving from the lower left panel to the upper right, going first from left to right and then from bottom to top. For each band in the given panel, if an observation's value of FCUFT falls within the band, then the observation is plotted in the corresponding depencence panel. In this way, we can observe the changing relationship between PRICE and ECOST over changing values of FCUFT. To help us see the changing rela-tionship, a fitted curve is superimposed on each display. This curve is fit using a local smoothing technique called *lowess,* as described in Cleveland (1994).

The main advan-tage of the more complex coplots compared to added variable plots is that we do not re-quire linear rela-tionships when controlling for ad-ditional variables.

Figure 13.29 suggests that for most values of FCUFT, the relationship be-tween PRICE and ECOST is negative. However, for some large values of FCUFT, we also see a nonlinear relationship that may be driven by two or four influential points. The main advantage of the more complex coplots compared to added variable plots is that we do not require linear relationships when con-trolling for additional variables.

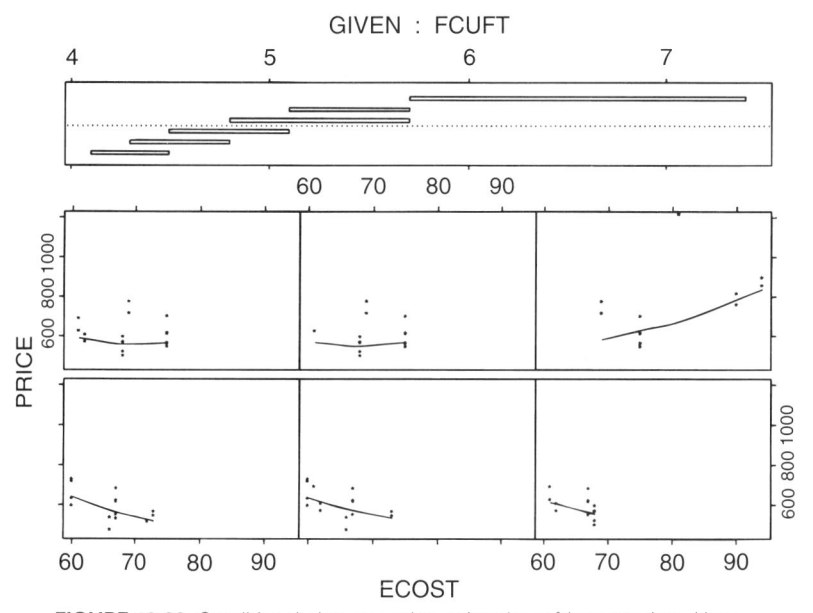

FIGURE 13.29 Conditional plot, or coplot, using the refrigerator data. Here, FCUFT is the control variable.

Three or More Variables—One Quantitative

For data with only one quantitative variable, we can use visual codes and tabular presentation methods to present effectively highly multivariate data. Indeed, an important method for exploring the data is to categorize certain quantitative variables and then use graphical and tabular tools for understanding relationships among variables.

For two or more qualitative variables, the bar chart is probably the most widely used graphical tool. We have already seen Figure 13.19 that illustrated the *stacked bar chart*. When the quantitative variable is a percentage that sums to 100 for each bar category, this is called a *divided bar chart*. A drawback of stacked and divided bar charts is that the viewer is asked to make length judgments, a relatively difficult task. Figure 13.30 presents an illustration of an *overlay bar chart* for the same data. This chart is easier for a viewer to assess because it only requires position judgments along a common scale.

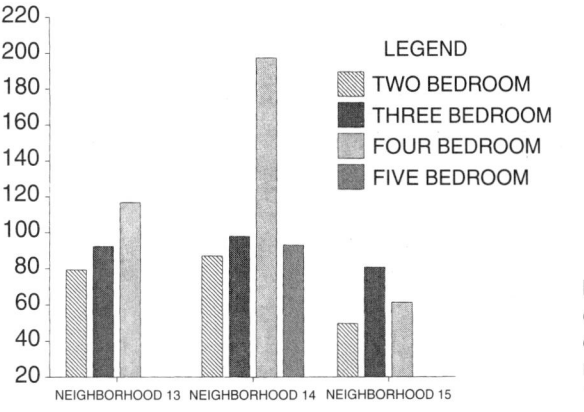

FIGURE 13.30 Overlay bar chart. It is easier to judge relative sizes of prices due to different bedrooms than the corresponding stacked bar chart in Figure 13.20.

A better graphical tool is the *multiway dot chart*. This chart is illustrated in Figure 13.31. Comparing this figure to Figure 13.30, we see that we only need to make judgements of position along a common scale, our easiest task according to Table 13.1. You may find overlay bar charts suitable for some presentation purposes. However, without further discussion of the purpose of the data presentation, we recommend using Figure 13.31 because it provides the most information for the least data-ink. That is, the data-density is higher in Figure 13.31 than Figure 13.30. This is especially important for situations with many more categories or levels within categories. Further, in choosing among graphical forms, do not forget tabular modes of presentation of data. Often, for qualitative variables, these represent more direct and effective ways of presenting data than graphical modes.

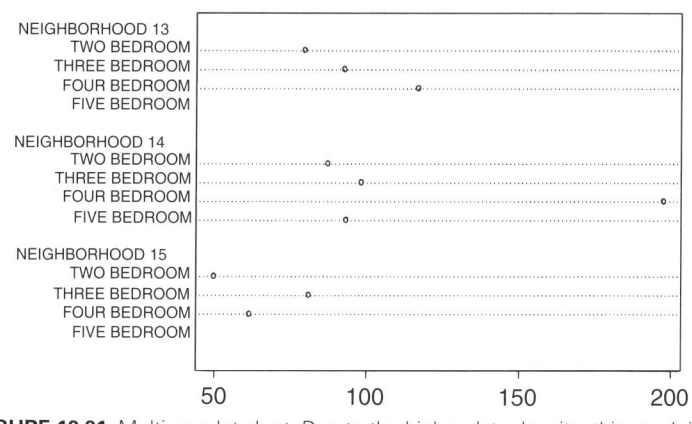

FIGURE 13.31 Multiway dot chart. Due to the higher data density, this graph is easier to use than the overlay bar chart.

13.5 SUMMARY AND CONCLUDING REMARKS

Decision makers rely on data information; data should be communicated as clearly and efficiently as possible. This chapter describes methods and principles of data presentation. These methods and principles are important; Section 13.1 illustrated that numerical statistics are not enough and that undisciplined graphical methods can be used to deceive viewers.

To understand the role of data presentations, Section 13.2 introduced four principles for designing graphical data presentations. These principles can help you understand the role of a data graphic within a presentation; specifically, when a graph is useful and when it is not. To understand the relationship between the choice of method and the data, Section 13.3 described some results from psychology on how we perceive graphs. These results turn out to be useful because they provide us with yet another set of criteria for choosing among graphical forms.

Although methods and principles are the same, this chapter is directed toward the purpose of communication of final results in the context of a report instead of the analysis of data. However, Section 13.4 provides a classification of graphical tools used by data analysts. Within each category of the classification, we discussed how to use the principles of design and perception for choosing among graphical forms.

This chapter provides only an introduction to data presentation. The goal has been to lay down the basics that can be used by a wide variety of readers. Unfortunately, this means that several useful ideas and concepts have not been presented in this chapter. Many graphical techniques are now readily available in statistical packages and are accessible to a broad audience. Readers interested in statistical graphics will not be disappointed in the works of Tufte

(1983, 1990) on design and Cleveland (1985, 1994) on perception. A historical perspective on statistical graphs can also be found in Schmid (1992).

KEY WORDS, PHRASES AND SYMBOLS

After reading this chapter, you should be able to define each of the following important terms, phrases and symbols in your own words. If not, go to the page indicated and review the definition.

data reduction methods, 543	stem-and-leaf plot, 552	Pareto chart, 562	conditioning plot, 566
chartjunk, 549	dot chart, 555	quantile-quantile (q-q) plot, 562	coplot, 566
perspective, 549	box plot, 560		given panel, 567
moiré vibrations, 549	quantile plot, 560	two-way dot charts, 563	dependence panels, 567
data density of a graph, 550	probability plot, 560	multiple time series plot, 564	stacked bar chart, 568
multifunctioning, 552	labels, 561	three-dimensional plots, 564	divided bar chart, 568
	pie chart, 561		overlay bar chart, 568
	bar chart, 561		multiway dot chart, 568

Elements of Matrix Algebra

A.1 BASIC DEFINITIONS

A *matrix* is a rectangular array of numbers arranged in rows and columns (the plural of matrix is matrices). For example, consider the income and age of 3 people.

$$
\begin{array}{cc}
& \text{Col 1} \quad \text{Col 2} \\
\mathbf{A} = \begin{array}{c} \text{Row 1} \\ \text{Row 2} \\ \text{Row 3} \end{array} & \begin{bmatrix} 6{,}000 & 23 \\ 13{,}000 & 47 \\ 11{,}000 & 35 \end{bmatrix}
\end{array}
$$

Here, column 1 represents income and column 2 represents age. Each row corresponds to an individual. For example, the first individual is 23 years old with an income of $6,000.

The number of rows and columns is called the *dimension* of the matrix. For example, the dimension of the matrix $\mathbf{A}$ is 3×2 (read 3 "by" 2). This stands for 3 rows and 2 columns. If we were to represent the income and age of 100 people, the dimension of the matrix would be 100×2.

It is convenient to represent a matrix using the notation

$$
\mathbf{A} = \begin{bmatrix} a_{11} & a_{12} \\ a_{21} & a_{22} \\ a_{31} & a_{32} \end{bmatrix}.
$$

Here, a_{ij} is the symbol for the number in the ith row and jth column of $\mathbf{A}$. In general, we work with matrices of the form

$$\mathbf{A} = \begin{bmatrix} a_{11} & a_{12} & \cdots & a_{1k} \\ \cdot & \cdot & \cdots & \cdot \\ a_{n1} & a_{n2} & \cdots & a_{nk} \end{bmatrix}.$$

Here, the matrix $\mathbf{A}$ has dimension $n \times k$.

A *vector* is a special matrix. A row vector is a matrix containing only 1 row ($n = 1$). A column vector is a matrix containing only 1 column ($k = 1$). For example,

$$\text{column vector} \rightarrow \begin{bmatrix} 2 \\ 3 \\ 4 \\ 5 \\ 6 \end{bmatrix} \qquad \text{row vector} \rightarrow [2 \quad 3 \quad 4 \quad 5 \quad 6].$$

Notice that the row vector takes much less room on a printed page than the corresponding column vector. To relate the two quantities, a basic operation that can be formed on a matrix is to take its *transpose*. The transpose of a matrix $\mathbf{A}$ is defined by interchanging the rows and columns and is denoted by $\mathbf{A}'$ (or $\mathbf{A}^{\mathrm{T}}$). For example,

$$\mathbf{A} = \begin{bmatrix} 6{,}000 & 23 \\ 13{,}000 & 47 \\ 11{,}000 & 35 \end{bmatrix} \qquad \mathbf{A}' = \begin{bmatrix} 6{,}000 & 13{,}000 & 11{,}000 \\ 23 & 47 & 35 \end{bmatrix}.$$

Thus, if $\mathbf{A}$ has dimension $n \times k$, then $\mathbf{A}'$ has dimension $k \times n$.

A.2 SOME SPECIAL MATRICES

1. A *square matrix* is a matrix where the number of rows equals the number of columns, that is, $n = k$.

2. The *diagonal* numbers of a square matrix are the numbers of a matrix where the row number equals the column number, for example, a_{11}, a_{22}, and so on. A *diagonal matrix* is a square matrix where all nondiagonal numbers are equal to 0. For example,

$$\mathbf{A} = \begin{bmatrix} -1 & 0 & 0 \\ 0 & 2 & 0 \\ 0 & 0 & 3 \end{bmatrix}.$$

3. An *identity matrix* is a diagonal matrix where all the numbers on the diagonal are equal to 1. This special matrix is often denoted by $\mathbf{I}$.

4. A *symmetric matrix* is a square matrix **A** such that the matrix remains unchanged if we interchange the roles of the rows and columns. More formally, a matrix **A** is symmetric if $\mathbf{A} = \mathbf{A}'$. For example,

$$\mathbf{A} = \begin{bmatrix} 1 & 2 & 3 \\ 2 & 4 & 5 \\ 3 & 5 & 10 \end{bmatrix} = \mathbf{A}'.$$

Note that a diagonal matrix is a symmetric matrix.

A.3 SCALAR MULTIPLICATION

Let **A** by a $n \times k$ matrix and let c be a real number. That is, a real number is a 1×1 matrix and is also called a *scalar*. Multiplying a scalar c by a matrix **A** is denoted by $c\,A$ and defined by

$$\begin{bmatrix} c\,a_{11} & c\,a_{12} & \dots & c\,a_{1k} \\ \cdot & \cdot & \dots & \cdot \\ c\,a_{n1} & c\,a_{n2} & \dots & c\,a_{nk} \end{bmatrix}.$$

For example, suppose that $c = 10$ and

$$\mathbf{A} = \begin{bmatrix} 1 & 2 \\ 6 & 8 \end{bmatrix} \quad \text{then} \quad \mathbf{B} = c\mathbf{A} = \begin{bmatrix} 10 & 20 \\ 60 & 80 \end{bmatrix}.$$

Note that $c\,\mathbf{A} = \mathbf{A}\,c$.

A.4 ADDITION AND SUBTRACTION OF MATRICES

Let **A** and **B** be matrices with dimensions $n \times k$. Use a_{ij} and b_{ij} to denote the numbers in the ith row and jth column of **A** and **B**, respectively. Then, the matrix $\mathbf{C} = \mathbf{A} + \mathbf{B}$ is defined to be the matrix with the number $(a_{ij} + b_{ij})$ to denote the numbers in the ith row and jth column. Similarly, the matrix $\mathbf{C} = \mathbf{A} - \mathbf{B}$ is defined to be the matrix with the number $(a_{ij} - b_{ij})$ to denote the numbers in the ith row and jth column. Symbolically, we write this as:

$$\text{If} \quad \mathbf{A} = (a_{ij})_{ij} \quad \mathbf{B} = (b_{ij})_{ij}, \text{ then}$$

$$\mathbf{C} = \mathbf{A} + \mathbf{B} = (a_{ij} + b_{ij})_{ij} \quad \text{and} \quad \mathbf{C} = \mathbf{A} - \mathbf{B} = (a_{ij} - b_{ij})_{ij}.$$

For example, consider

$$\mathbf{A} = \begin{bmatrix} 2 & 5 \\ 4 & 1 \end{bmatrix} \quad \mathbf{B} = \begin{bmatrix} 4 & 6 \\ 8 & 1 \end{bmatrix}.$$

$$\text{Then} \quad \mathbf{A} + \mathbf{B} = \begin{bmatrix} 6 & 11 \\ 12 & 2 \end{bmatrix} \quad \text{and} \quad \mathbf{A} - \mathbf{B} = \begin{bmatrix} -2 & -1 \\ -4 & 0 \end{bmatrix}.$$

Regression with One Independent Variable Example

Now, recall that the regression model with one independent variable can be written as n equations:

$$y_1 = \beta_0 + \beta_1 x_1 + e_1$$
$$y_2 = \beta_0 + \beta_1 x_2 + e_2$$
$$\cdot \cdot \cdot$$
$$\cdot \cdot \cdot$$
$$\cdot \cdot \cdot$$
$$y_n = \beta_0 + \beta_1 x_n + e_n.$$

We can define

$$\mathbf{y} = \begin{bmatrix} y_1 \\ y_2 \\ \cdot \\ \cdot \\ \cdot \\ y_n \end{bmatrix} \quad \mathbf{e} = \begin{bmatrix} e_1 \\ e_2 \\ \cdot \\ \cdot \\ \cdot \\ e_n \end{bmatrix} \quad \text{and} \quad \mathbf{E}\,\mathbf{y} = \begin{bmatrix} \beta_0 + \beta_1 x_1 \\ \beta_0 + \beta_1 x_2 \\ \cdot \\ \cdot \\ \cdot \\ \beta_0 + \beta_1 x_n \end{bmatrix}.$$

Thus, we can express the n equations much more compactly as $\mathbf{y} = \mathbf{E}\,\mathbf{y} + \mathbf{e}$.

A.5 MATRIX MULTIPLICATION

In general, if $\mathbf{A}$ is a matrix of dimension $n \times c$ and $\mathbf{B}$ is a matrix of dimension $c \times k$, the $\mathbf{C} = \mathbf{AB}$ is a matrix of dimension $n \times k$ and is defined by

$$\mathbf{C} = \mathbf{AB} = \left[\left(\sum_{s=1}^{c} a_{is} b_{sj} \right) \right]_{ij}.$$

For example consider the following 2×2 matrices $\mathbf{A}$ and $\mathbf{B}$.

$$\mathbf{A} = \begin{bmatrix} 2 & 5 \\ 4 & 1 \end{bmatrix} \quad \mathbf{B} = \begin{bmatrix} 4 & 6 \\ 8 & 1 \end{bmatrix}.$$

The matrix $\mathbf{AB}$ has dimension 2×2. To illustrate the calculation, consider the number in the first row and second column of $\mathbf{AB}$. By the rule presented previously, with $i = 1$ and $j = 2$, the number is $\sum_{s=1}^{2} a_{1s} b_{s2} = a_{11} b_{12} + a_{12} b_{22} = 2(6) + 5(1) = 17$. The other calculations are summarized in the following.

$$\mathbf{AB} = \begin{bmatrix} 2(4) + 5(8) & 2(6) + 5(1) \\ 4(4) + 1(8) & 4(6) + 1(1) \end{bmatrix} = \begin{bmatrix} 48 & 17 \\ 24 & 25 \end{bmatrix}.$$

As another example, consider

$$\mathbf{A} = \begin{bmatrix} 1 & 2 & 4 \\ 0 & 5 & 8 \end{bmatrix} \qquad \mathbf{B} = \begin{bmatrix} 3 \\ 5 \\ 2 \end{bmatrix}.$$

Since $\mathbf{A}$ has dimension 2×3 and $\mathbf{B}$ has dimension 3×1, this means that the product $\mathbf{AB}$ has dimension 2×1. The calculations are summarized in the following.

$$\mathbf{AB} = \begin{bmatrix} 1(3) + 2(5) + 4(2) \\ 0(3) + 5(5) + 8(2) \end{bmatrix} = \begin{bmatrix} 21 \\ 41 \end{bmatrix}.$$

For some additional examples, we have

$$\begin{bmatrix} 4 & 2 \\ 5 & 8 \end{bmatrix} \begin{bmatrix} a_1 \\ a_2 \end{bmatrix} = \begin{bmatrix} 4a_1 + 2a_2 \\ 5a_1 + 8a_2 \end{bmatrix}$$

$$[2 \quad 3 \quad 5] \begin{bmatrix} 2 \\ 3 \\ 5 \end{bmatrix} = 2^2 + 3^2 + 5^2 = 38, \qquad \begin{bmatrix} 2 \\ 3 \\ 5 \end{bmatrix} [2 \quad 3 \quad 5] = \begin{bmatrix} 4 & 6 & 10 \\ 6 & 9 & 15 \\ 10 & 15 & 25 \end{bmatrix}.$$

In general, it should be noted that $\mathbf{AB} \ne \mathbf{BA}$ in matrix multiplication, unlike multiplication of scalars (real numbers). Further, the identity matrix serves the role of "one" in matrix multiplication, in that $\mathbf{AI} = \mathbf{A}$ and $\mathbf{IA} = \mathbf{A}$ for any matrix $\mathbf{A}$, providing that the dimensions are compatible to allow matrix multiplication.

Regression with One Independent Variable Example

Define

$$\mathbf{X} = \begin{bmatrix} 1 & x_1 \\ 1 & x_2 \\ . & . \\ . & . \\ . & . \\ 1 & x_n \end{bmatrix} \qquad \beta = \begin{bmatrix} \beta_0 \\ \beta_1 \end{bmatrix}, \qquad \text{to get} \quad \mathbf{X}\beta = \begin{bmatrix} \beta_0 + \beta_1 x_1 \\ \beta_0 + \beta_1 x_2 \\ . \\ . \\ . \\ \beta_0 + \beta_1 x_n \end{bmatrix} = E\,\mathbf{y}.$$

Thus, this yields the famioliar matrix expression of the regression mode, $\mathbf{y} = \mathbf{X}\beta + \mathbf{e}$. Some other quantities that are useful are

$$\mathbf{y}'\mathbf{y} = [y_1 \quad y_2 \quad \cdots \quad y_n] \begin{bmatrix} y_1 \\ y_2 \\ . \\ . \\ . \\ y_n \end{bmatrix} = y_1^2 + y_2^2 + \ldots + y_n^2 = \sum_{i=1}^{n} y_i^2.$$

and

$$\mathbf{X}'\mathbf{y} = \begin{bmatrix} 1 & 1 & \cdots & 1 \\ x_1 & x_2 & \cdots & x_n \end{bmatrix} \begin{bmatrix} y_1 \\ y_2 \\ \cdot \\ \cdot \\ \cdot \\ y_n \end{bmatrix} = \begin{bmatrix} \sum_{i=1}^{n} y_i \\ \sum_{i=1}^{n} x_i y_i \end{bmatrix}, \text{ and } \mathbf{X}'\mathbf{X} = \begin{bmatrix} n & \sum_{i=1}^{n} x_i \\ \sum_{i=1}^{n} x_i & \sum_{i=1}^{n} x_i^2 \end{bmatrix}.$$

Note that $\mathbf{X}'\mathbf{X}$ is a symmetric matrix.

A.6 MATRIX INVERSES

In matrix algebra, there is no concept of "division." Instead, we extend the concept of "reciprocals" of real numbers. To begin, suppose that $\mathbf{A}$ is a square matrix of dimension $k \times k$ and let $\mathbf{I}$ be the $k \times k$ identity matrix. If there exists a $k \times k$ matrix $\mathbf{B}$ such that $\mathbf{AB} = \mathbf{I} = \mathbf{BA}$, then $\mathbf{B}$ is called the *inverse* of $\mathbf{I}$ and is written

$$\mathbf{B} = \mathbf{A}^{-1}.$$

Now, not all square matrices have inverses. Further, even when inverses exist, they are not easy to compute by hand. One exception to this rule are diagonal matrices. Suppose that $\mathbf{A}$ is diagonal of the form

$$A = \begin{bmatrix} a_{11} & 0 & \cdots & 0 \\ 0 & a_{22} & \cdots & 0 \\ \cdot & \cdot & \cdots & \cdot \\ 0 & 0 & \cdots & a_{kk} \end{bmatrix}, \text{ then } A^{-1} = \begin{bmatrix} \dfrac{1}{a_{11}} & 0 & \cdots & 0 \\ 0 & \dfrac{1}{a_{22}} & \cdots & 0 \\ \cdot & \cdot & \cdots & \cdot \\ 0 & 0 & \cdots & \dfrac{1}{a_{kk}} \end{bmatrix}.$$

For example,

$$\begin{bmatrix} 2 & 0 \\ 0 & -19 \end{bmatrix} \begin{bmatrix} \dfrac{1}{2} & 0 \\ 0 & \dfrac{-1}{19} \end{bmatrix} = \begin{bmatrix} 1 & 0 \\ 0 & 1 \end{bmatrix}$$

$$\mathbf{A} \qquad \mathbf{A}^{-1} \quad = \quad \mathbf{I}.$$

In the case of a matrix of dimension 2×2, the inversion procedure can be accomplished by hand easily even when the matrix is not diagonal. In the 2×2

case, we suppose

$$\mathbf{A} = \begin{bmatrix} a & b \\ c & d \end{bmatrix}, \quad \text{then} \quad \mathbf{A}^{-1} = \begin{bmatrix} \dfrac{d}{ad-bc} & \dfrac{-b}{ad-bc} \\[2mm] \dfrac{-c}{ad-bc} & \dfrac{a}{ad-bc} \end{bmatrix} = \frac{1}{ad-bc}\begin{bmatrix} d & -b \\ -c & a \end{bmatrix}.$$

Thus, for example, if

$$\mathbf{A} = \begin{bmatrix} 2 & 2 \\ 3 & 4 \end{bmatrix}, \quad \text{then} \quad \mathbf{A}^{-1} = \frac{1}{2(4)-2(3)}\begin{bmatrix} 4 & -2 \\ -3 & 2 \end{bmatrix} = \begin{bmatrix} 2 & -1 \\ -3/2 & 1 \end{bmatrix}.$$

As a check, we have

$$\mathbf{A}\mathbf{A}^{-1} = \begin{bmatrix} 2 & 2 \\ 3 & 4 \end{bmatrix}\begin{bmatrix} 2 & -1 \\ -3/2 & 1 \end{bmatrix} = \begin{bmatrix} 2(2)-2(3/2) & 2(-1)+2(1) \\ 3(2)-4(3/2) & 3(-1)+4(1) \end{bmatrix} = \begin{bmatrix} 1 & 0 \\ 0 & 1 \end{bmatrix} = \mathbf{I}.$$

Regression with One Independent Variable Example

Recall

$$\mathbf{X'y} = \begin{bmatrix} 1 & 1 & \cdots & 1 \\ x_1 & x_2 & \cdots & x_n \end{bmatrix}\begin{bmatrix} y_1 \\ y_2 \\ \vdots \\ y_n \end{bmatrix} = \begin{bmatrix} \displaystyle\sum_{i=1}^{n} y_i \\ \displaystyle\sum_{i=1}^{n} x_i y_i \end{bmatrix}, \quad \text{and} \quad \mathbf{X'X} = \begin{bmatrix} n & \displaystyle\sum_{i=1}^{n} x_i \\ \displaystyle\sum_{i=1}^{n} x_i & \displaystyle\sum_{i=1}^{n} x_i^2 \end{bmatrix}.$$

Thus,

$$(\mathbf{X'X})^{-1} = \frac{1}{n\displaystyle\sum_{i=1}^{n} x_i^2 - \left(\displaystyle\sum_{i=1}^{n} x_i\right)^2}\begin{bmatrix} \displaystyle\sum_{i=1}^{n} x_i^2 & -\displaystyle\sum_{i=1}^{n} x_i \\ -\displaystyle\sum_{i=1}^{n} x_i & n \end{bmatrix}$$

$$= \frac{1}{\displaystyle\sum_{i=1}^{n} x_i^2 - n\bar{x}^2}\begin{bmatrix} \dfrac{1}{n}\displaystyle\sum_{i=1}^{n} x_i^2 & -\bar{x} \\ -\bar{x} & 1 \end{bmatrix}.$$

This yields

$$\boldsymbol{b} = \begin{bmatrix} b_0 \\ b_1 \end{bmatrix} = (\mathbf{X}'\mathbf{X})^{-1}\mathbf{X}'\mathbf{y} = \frac{1}{\displaystyle\sum_{i=1}^{n} x_i^2 - n\bar{x}^2} \begin{bmatrix} \dfrac{1}{n}\displaystyle\sum_{i=1}^{n} x_i^2 & -\bar{x} \\ -\bar{x} & 1 \end{bmatrix} \begin{bmatrix} \displaystyle\sum_{i=1}^{n} y_i \\ \displaystyle\sum_{i=1}^{n} x_i y_i \end{bmatrix}$$

$$= \frac{1}{\displaystyle\sum_{i=1}^{n} x_i^2 - n\bar{x}^2} \begin{bmatrix} \displaystyle\sum_{i=1}^{n} (\bar{y}x_i^2 - \bar{x}x_i y_i) \\ \displaystyle\sum_{i=1}^{n} x_i y_i - n\bar{x}\bar{y} \end{bmatrix}.$$

From this expression, we see that

$$b_1 = \frac{\displaystyle\sum_{i=1}^{n} x_i y_i - n\bar{x}\bar{y}}{\displaystyle\sum_{i=1}^{n} x_i^2 - n\bar{x}^2} \quad \text{and}$$

$$b_0 = \frac{\bar{y}\displaystyle\sum_{i=1}^{n} x_i^2 - \bar{x}\displaystyle\sum_{i=1}^{n} x_i y_i}{\displaystyle\sum_{i=1}^{n} x_i^2 - n\bar{x}^2} = \frac{\bar{y}\left(\displaystyle\sum_{i=1}^{n} x_i^2 - n\bar{x}^2\right) - \bar{x}\left(\displaystyle\sum_{i=1}^{n} x_i y_i - n\bar{x}\bar{y}\right)}{\displaystyle\sum_{i=1}^{n} x_i^2 - n\bar{x}^2}$$

$$= \bar{y} - \bar{x}\, b_1.$$

These are the usual expressions for the slope b_1 and intercept b_0.

Technical Supplements

CHAPTER 2

TS 2.1 Distributions of Random Variables

Random Variables and Distribution Functions.   When considering a value of y, it is said to be *variable* if y can change from measurement to measurement. If the value of y is governed by a random draw from a large universe, or population, of measurements, then we say that y is a *random variable*. If the value of y is governed by a random, unpredictable mechanism, then we define likely occurrences of y through its distribution. In particular, we define the *distribution function*

$$F(a) = \text{Prob}(y \leq a)$$

to be the probability that the random variable y is less than or equal to the number a. Because the distribution function is defined in terms of probabilities, it is a special function. In particular, it is bounded below and above by 0 and 1, respectively. Further, it is monotonically increasing in the sense that $F(a_1) \leq F(a_2)$ for each $a_1 < a_2$.

Probability Functions.   Just as with variables, random variables can be either discrete or continuous. On one hand, a discrete (random) variable is one that takes on distinct, separate values. In this case, it is useful to talk about the probability that a random variable takes on specific values. To this end, define

$$f(a) = \text{Prob}(y = a)$$

to be the *probability mass function* of y. On the other hand, a continuous (random) variable is one that can take on any value within specified intervals. In this case, the probability mass function is not a useful device because the probability that a random variable takes on a specific value is 0. Instead, for continuous random variables, define

$$f(a) = F'(a) = \lim_{\epsilon \to 0} \frac{F(a + \epsilon) - F(a)}{\epsilon} = \lim_{\epsilon \to 0} \frac{1}{\epsilon} \text{Prob}(a < y \le a + \epsilon) \quad \text{(TS2.1)}$$

to be the *probability density function*. Essentially, f(a) is the probability that y falls in a neighborhood of a, (a, a + ε), rescaled by the length of the neighborhood. We remark that there are examples of random variables that are mixtures of discrete and continuous random variables, and other examples of continuous random variables that are not smooth enough to satisfy equation (TS2.1). These types of random variables will not be useful for the purposes of this text, and are omitted.

Properties of Probability Functions. Both versions of f, the probability mass function and the probability density function, share two mathematical properties. These two properties are that both functions are nonnegative and both "sum" to 1. That is, in the discrete case,

$$\sum_{\text{all occurrences of } y} f(y) = 1.$$

In the continuous case,

$$\int_{\text{all occurrences of } y} f(y) \, dy = 1.$$

Summary Measures of Probability Functions. Both versions of f can also be used to summarize important characteristics of the distribution. Many important summary measures can be written in terms of the *expectation operator*, E. Consider a generic function, g. For the discrete case, define

$$E \, g(y) = \sum_{\text{all occurrences of } y} g(y) \, f(y).$$

For the continuous case, define

$$E \, g(y) = \int_{\text{all occurrences of } y} g(y) \, f(y) \, dy,$$

TABLE TS2.1 Important Summary Measures

Function	Description	Symbol	Discrete case expression	Continuous case expression
$g(y) = y$	Mean	$\mu = E\,y$	$\Sigma\, y\, f(y)$	$\int y\, f(y)\, dy$
$g(y) = (y - \mu)^2$	Variance	$\sigma^2 = \operatorname{Var} y = E\,(y - \mu)^2$	$\Sigma\,(y - \mu)^2\, f(y)$	$\int (y - \mu)^2\, f(y)\, dy$
$g(y) = (y - \mu)^3$	Skewness	$\gamma = E\,(y - \mu)^3$	$\Sigma\,(y - \mu)^3\, f(y)$	$\int (y - \mu)^3\, f(y)\, dy$

where the integration is well-defined. Table TS2.1 presents the most important examples.

TS 2.2 Relationships Among Random Variables

Joint and Marginal Distribution Functions. To discuss relationships among random variables, we consider a collection of random variables, $\{y_1, y_2, \ldots, y_n\}$. The basic building block for considering collections of random variables is the *joint distribution function,* defined by

$$F(a_1, a_2, \ldots, a_n) = \operatorname{Prob}(y_1 \le a_1, y_2 \le a_2, \ldots, y_n \le a_n).$$

From the joint distribution function, the distribution function of each random variable can be derived. For example, $\operatorname{Prob}(y_1 \le a_1) = \operatorname{Prob}(y_1 \le a_1, y_2 \le \infty, \ldots, y_n \le \infty) = F(a_1, \infty, \ldots, \infty)$. Thus, we can define $F_i(a_i) = \operatorname{Prob}(y_i \le a_i) = F(\infty, \ldots, \infty, a_i, \infty, \ldots, \infty)$ to be the distribution function of y_i. It is called a *marginal* distribution function because it is constructed using the joint distribution function F. In the discrete case, define $f_i(a_i) = \operatorname{Prob}(y_i = a_i)$ to be the ith marginal probability mass function. In the continuous case, define $f_i(a_i) = F_i'(a_i)$ to be the ith marginal probability density function. In the case where $F_1 = F_2 = \ldots = F_n$, the random variables are governed by the same distribution and are said to have *identical* distributions.

Joint Probability Functions. As with one variable, we construct idealized histograms from the distribution function. In the discrete case, the *joint probability mass function* is

$$f(a_1, a_2, \ldots, a_n) = \operatorname{Prob}(y_1 = a_1, y_2 = a_2, \ldots, y_n = a_n).$$

In the continuous case, the *joint probability density function* is

$$f(a_1, a_2, \ldots, a_n) = \frac{\partial}{\partial a_1} \frac{\partial}{\partial a_2} \cdots \frac{\partial}{\partial a_n} F(a_1, a_2, \ldots, a_n).$$

Expectations Associated with Joint Probability Functions. These are the basic quantities used to define the expectations

$$\text{E } g(y_1, ..., y_n) = \sum_{\text{all occurrences of } y_1} \cdots \sum_{\text{all occurrences of } y_n} g(y_1, ..., y_n) \, f(y_1, ..., y_n)$$

$$\text{E } g(y_1, ..., y_n) = \int_{\text{all occurrences of } y_1} \cdots \int_{\text{all occurrences of } y_n} g(y_1, ..., y_n) \, f(y_1, ..., y_n)$$
$$\times \, dy_1 \ldots dy_n$$

in the discrete and continuous cases, respectively. Again, we assume that both sums and integrals are well-defined.

Properties of Expectations. A number of useful properties arise from the definition of E $g(y_1, ..., y_n)$. To illustrate, choose g to be a linear combination, $g(y_1,..., y_n) = a_1 y_1 + ... + a_n y_n$, where $a_1,..., a_n$ are known constants. Then, by the linearity of sums and integrals, we get the *linearity of expectations property*

$$\text{E } \{a_1 y_1 + ... + a_n y_n\} = a_1 \text{ E } y_1 + ... + a_n \text{ E } y_n. \qquad \text{(TS2.2)}$$

To illustrate this result, first choose $n = 2$ and g to be $g(y_1, y_2) = (y_1 - \text{E } y_1)(y_2 - \text{E } y_2)$. Then, we can define

$$\text{Cov}(y_1, y_2) = \text{E } \{(y_1 - \text{E } y_1)(y_2 - \text{E } y_2)\}$$

to be the *covariance* between y_1 and y_2. By the linearity property in equation (TS2.2), it is easy to check that $\text{Cov}(y_1, y_2) = \text{E } \{y_1 y_2\} - \text{E } y_1 \text{ E } y_2$. Thus, the covariances can be calculated as the expectation of the product minus the product of expectations. From this result, we can easily check the *linearity of covariances,*

$$\text{Cov}(a_1y_1 + a_2, a_3y_2 + a_4) = a_1a_3 \text{ Cov}(y_1, y_2) \qquad \text{(TS2.3)}$$

Using Var $(y) = \text{Cov}(y,y)$, another immediate consequence of equation (TS2.2) is

$$\text{Var}\left(\sum_{i=1}^{n} a_i y_i\right) = \sum_{i=1}^{n} a_i^2 \text{Var } y_i + 2 \sum_{i=2}^{n} \sum_{j=1}^{i-1} a_i a_j \text{ Cov}(y_i, y_j). \qquad \text{(TS2.4)}$$

The *correlation* between y_1 and y_2 is a rescaled version of covariance, defined by

$$\rho(y_1, y_2) = \frac{\text{Cov}(y_1, y_2)}{\sqrt{\text{Var}(y_1) \, \text{Var}(y_2)}}.$$

If $\rho(y_1, y_2) = 0$, then the random variables y_1 and y_2 are said to be *uncorrelated*. It is easy to see that in this case $\text{Cov}(y_1, y_2) = 0$. Indeed, if each pair of $y_1, ..., y_n$

are uncorrelated, then

$$\text{Var}\left(\sum_{i=1}^{n} a_i y_i\right) = \sum_{i=1}^{n} a_i^2 \text{Var } y_i, \tag{TS2.5}$$

that is, the variance of the sum is the sum of the variances.

Statistical Independence. Another concept of relationships among random variables is *statistical independence.* The random variables $\{y_1, \ldots, y_n\}$ are said to be statistically independent if

$$f(a_1, a_2, \ldots, a_n) = f_1(a_1)f_2(a_2) \ldots f_n(a_n).$$

Some straightforward calculations show that if $\{y_1, \ldots, y_n\}$ are statistically independent, then they are pairwise uncorrelated. Further, when $\{y_1, \ldots, y_n\}$ are statistically independent and have the same distribution, they are referred to as *i.i.d.,* an acronym which stands for *identically and independently distributed.* For *i.i.d.* random variables $\{y_1, \ldots, y_n\}$ with $\text{E } y_i = \mu$ and $\text{Var } y_i = \sigma^2$, we have

$$\text{E} \sum_{i=1}^{n} a_i y_i = \mu \sum_{i=1}^{n} a_i, \qquad \text{Var}\left(\sum_{i=1}^{n} a_i y_i\right) = \sigma^2 \sum_{i=1}^{n} a_i^2, \tag{TS2.6}$$

and

$$f(a_1, \ldots, a_n) = f(a_1) \ldots f(a_n) = \prod_{i=1}^{n} f(a_i). \tag{TS2.7}$$

Conditional Distributions. *Conditional distributions* provide another useful concept in the study of relationships of random variables. Suppose that the random variables y_1, y_2 have joint probability function f. Then, the conditional probability function of y_1 at a_1 *given* the occurrence of $y_2 = a_2$ is defined to be

$$f(a_1 \mid y_2 = a_2) = \frac{f(a_1, a_2)}{f_2(a_2)} \qquad \text{for} \quad f_2(a_2) > 0.$$

Recall that f_2 is the marginal probability function of y_2. Here, the probability functions are assumed to be mass functions for discrete ys and density functions for continuous ys. Now, $f(. \mid y_2 = a_2)$ is a real probability function in the sense that it is positive and "sums" to 1. To illustrate, consider the continuous ys case, to get

$$\int f(y \mid y_2 = a_2) \, dy = \int \frac{f(y, a_2)}{f_2(a_2)} \, dy = \frac{1}{f_2(a_2)} \int f(y, a_2) \, dy = \frac{1}{f_2(a_2)} f_2(a_2) = 1.$$

Moments can also be calculated. In particular, the expected value of y_1 given

$y_2 = a_2$ is defined by

$$E(y_1 \mid y_2 = a_2) = \int y_1 f(y_1 \mid y_2 = a_2)\, dy_1.$$

The case for discrete random variables is similar.

Conditional Distributions and Statistical Independence.   In the case that y_1 is statistically independent of y_2, then $f(a_1 \mid y_2 = a_2) = f(a_1)$, by straight-forward calculations. That is, we may disregard the distribution of y_2 when cal-culating distribution quantities related solely to y_1. To illustrate, suppose that x and e are statistically independent and that e has mean 0. From these random variables, form a new random variable $y = x + e$. If x_0 is a specific, known value of x, then we have

$$E(y \mid x = x_0) = E(x + e \mid x = x_0) = E(x \mid x = x_0) + E(e \mid x = x_0)$$

$$= x_0 + E\,e = x_0.$$

The fact that $E\,(e \mid x = x_0) = E\,e$ comes from the fact that x and e are statistically independent.

TS 2.3 Some Special Distributions

Binomial Distribution.   Perhaps the most important discrete distribu-tion is the *binomial distribution*. This distribution is described by two parame-ters, p, the "probability of success," and n, the "number of trials." We write $y \sim \text{Binomial}(n,p)$ to mean that the random variable y has a Binomial distribu-tion with parameters n and p. The probability mass function is

$$f(a) = \text{Prob}(y = a) = \binom{n}{a} p^a (1 - p)^{n-a} \qquad \text{for} \quad a = 0, 1, \ldots, n,$$

where n is a positive integer and $0 \leq p \leq 1$. Easy calculations show

$$E\,y = \sum_{y=0}^{n} y f(y) = \sum_{y=0}^{n} y \binom{n}{y} p^y (1 - p)^{n-y} = np$$

and

$$\text{Var}\,y = \sum_{y=0}^{n} (y - np)^2 f(y) = \sum_{y=0}^{n} (y - np)^2 \binom{n}{y} p^y (1 - p)^{n-y} = np(1 - p).$$

Normal Distribution.   Perhaps the most important continuous curve is the normal curve, introduced in Section 2.3. The probability density function of the normal curve is defined by

$$f(y) = \frac{1}{\sqrt{2\pi\sigma^2}} \, e^{-(y-\mu)^2/2\sigma^2}, \quad -\infty < y < \infty$$

where μ and σ^2 are parameters that describe the curve. In this case, we write $y \sim N(\mu,\sigma^2)$. Straightforward calculations show that

$$\mathrm{E}\, y = \int_{-\infty}^{\infty} yf(y) \, dy = \int_{-\infty}^{\infty} y \, \frac{1}{\sqrt{2\pi\sigma^2}} \, e^{-(y-\mu)^2/2\sigma^2} \, dy = \mu$$

and

$$\mathrm{Var}\, y = \int_{-\infty}^{\infty} (y-\mu)^2 f(y) \, dy = \int_{-\infty}^{\infty} (y-\mu)^2 \, \frac{1}{\sqrt{2\pi\sigma^2}} \, e^{-(y-\mu)^2/2\sigma^2} \, dy = \sigma^2.$$

Thus, the notation $y \sim N(\mu,\sigma^2)$ is interpreted to mean the random variable is distributed normally with mean μ and variance σ^2. If $y \sim N(0,1)$, then y is said to be *standard normal*.

Chi-Square Distribution. Several important distributions can be linked to the normal distribution. If $y_1, \ldots, y_n$ are i.i.d. random variables such that each $y_i \sim N(0,1)$, then $\sum_{i=1}^{n} y_i^2$ is said to have a *chi-square* distribution with n degrees of freedom. More generally, a random variable w with probability density function

$$f(w) = \frac{2^{-k/2}}{\Gamma(k/2)} \, w^{k/2-1} \, e^{-w/2} \qquad w > 0$$

is said to have a chi-square with k degrees of freedom, written $w \sim \chi_k^2$. Easy calculations show that for $w \sim \chi_k^2$, we have $\mathrm{E}\, w = k$ and $\mathrm{Var}\, w = 2k$. In general, the degrees of freedom parameter need not be an integer, although it is for the applications of this text.

t-Distribution. Suppose that y and w are independent with $y \sim N(0,1)$ and $w \sim \chi_k^2$. Then, the variable $t = y/(w/k)^{1/2}$ is said to have a *t*-distribution with k degrees of freedom, written t_k. The probability density function is

$$f(t) = \frac{\Gamma\left(k + \dfrac{1}{2}\right)}{\Gamma(k/2)} \, (k\pi)^{-1/2} \left(1 + \frac{t^2}{k}\right)^{-(k+1)/2}, \qquad -\infty < t < \infty.$$

This has mean 0, for $k > 1$, and variance $k/(k-2)$ for $k > 2$.

F-Distribution. Finally, suppose that w_1 and w_2 are independent with distributions $w_1 \sim \chi^2_m$ and $w_2 \sim \chi^2_n$. Then, the variable $F = (w_1/m)/(w_2/n)$ has an F-distribution with parameters m and n, respectively. The probability density function is

$$f(y) = \frac{\Gamma\left(\dfrac{m+n}{2}\right)}{\Gamma(m/2)\Gamma(n/2)} \left(\frac{m}{n}\right)^{m/2} \frac{y^{(m-2)/2}}{\left(1 + \dfrac{m}{n}y\right)^{m+n/2}}, \qquad y > 0.$$

This has mean $n/(n-2)$, for $n > 2$, and variance $\{2n^2(m+n-2)\}/\{m(n-2)^2(n-4)\}$ for $n > 4$. The χ^2, t and F are important when considering the distribution of certain sample statistics, as discussed in the next subsection.

TS 2.4 Distributions of Functions of Random Variables

Statistics and Sampling Distributions. Observations are often assumed to be realizations of random variables and functions of random variables are *statistics*. Thus, the study of distributions of function of random variables is really the study of the distributions of statistics, referred to as *sampling distributions*. An important first function to consider is the function specified by linear combinations of its arguments. Thus, suppose that $y_1, \ldots, y_n$ are mutually independent random variables with $\mathrm{E}\, y_i = \mu_i$ and $\mathrm{Var}\, y_i = \sigma^2_i$. Then, from equations (TS2.2) and TS2.5), we have

$$\mathrm{E} \sum_{i=1}^{n} a_i y_i = \sum_{i=1}^{n} a_i \mu_i, \qquad \mathrm{Var}\left(\sum_{i=1}^{n} a_i y_i\right) = \sum_{i=1}^{n} a_i^2 \sigma_i^2.$$

An important property in mathematical statistics is that, if each random variable is normally distributed, then linear combinations are also normally distributed. That is, we have the following result.

Linearity of Normal Random Variables. Suppose that $y_1, \ldots, y_n$ are mutually independent random variables with $y_i \sim N(\mu_i, \sigma^2_i)$. Then,

$$\sum_{i=1}^{n} a_i y_i \sim N\left(\sum_{i=1}^{n} a_i \mu_i, \sum_{i=1}^{n} a_i^2 \sigma_i^2\right). \tag{TS2.8}$$

There are several applications of this important property. First, it can be checked that if $y \sim N(\mu, \sigma^2)$, then $(y - \mu)/\sigma \sim N(0,1)$. Second, assume that $y_1, \ldots, y_n$ are i.i.d. $N(\mu, \sigma^2)$ and take $a_i = n^{-1}$. Then, we have

$$\bar{y} = \frac{1}{n} \sum_{i=1}^{n} y_i \sim N\left(\mu, \frac{\sigma^2}{n}\right).$$

Equivalently,

$$\sqrt{n}(\bar{y} - \mu)/\sigma \sim N(0, 1),$$

that is, $n^{1/2}(\bar{y} - \mu)/\sigma$ is standard normal. Other important applications of equation (TS2.6) arise in Chapter 3.

Thus, the important sample statistic $\bar{y}$ has a normal distribution. Further, the distribution of the sample statistics s_y^2 can also be calculated. For $y_1, \ldots, y_n$ i.i.d. $N(\mu, \sigma^2)$, we have that

$$(n - 1)s_y^2/\sigma^2 \sim \chi_{n-1}^2$$

and that s_y^2 is independent of $\bar{y}$. From these two results, we have that

$$\frac{\sqrt{n}(\bar{y} - \mu)}{s_y} \sim t_{n-1}$$

an important result in applied statistics.

TS 2.5 Approximating Sampling Distributions

Finite Sample Results.   Results providing the distributions of sample statistics are useful for providing statistical inferences such as with confidence intervals and tests of hypothesis. The results in the previous subsection are *exact* in the sense that they are available for each sample size n. For this reason, they are also called *finite sample* results. Direct application of these results is limited in the sense that they rely on some restrictive assumptions. In particular, the observations are assumed to arise from normally distributed populations. There are a number of results in mathematical statistics that demonstrate that the results are useful even when observations do not arise from a normally distributed population. Further, some of these results suggest methods for improving our procedures.

Large Sample Results.   To illustrate, consider initially the sample statistic $\bar{y}$. From the preceding subsection, we know that if $y_1, \ldots, y_n$ are i.i.d. $N(\mu, \sigma^2)$, then $\bar{y}$ is also a normal random variable. By the following theorem, this result is also approximately true even when $y_1, \ldots, y_n$ are not normally distributed.

Central Limit Theorem.   Suppose that $y_1, \ldots, y_n$ are i.i.d. with mean μ and finite variance σ^2. Then,

$$\lim_{n \to \infty} \text{Prob}\left(\frac{\sqrt{n}(\bar{y} - \mu)}{\sigma} \le x\right) = \text{Prob}(z \le x), \qquad \text{for each } x$$

where $z \sim N(0, 1)$.

The Central Limit Theorem is a limiting distribution result because it can be interpreted as meaning that the distribution $n^{1/2}(\bar{y} - \mu)/\sigma$ approaches a standard normal as the sample size, n, increases. We interpret this as meaning that, for "large" sample sizes, the distribution of $n^{1/2}(\bar{y} - \mu)/\sigma$ may be approximated by a standard normal distribution. Empirical investigations have shown that sample sizes of $n = 25$ through 50 provide adequate approximations for most purposes. For users who would like a guarantee, the following result provides a bound on the error of the approximation for all values of n.

Berry-Esséen Theorem. Suppose that $y_1, \dots, y_n$ are i.i.d. with mean μ, variance σ^2 and $E\,|y|^3$ is finite. Then,

$$\left| \text{Prob}\left(\frac{\sqrt{n}(\bar{y} - \mu)}{\sigma} \leq x \right) - \text{Prob}(z \leq x) \right| \leq \frac{33}{4} \frac{E\,|y - \mu|^3}{\sigma^3 \sqrt{n}}.$$

Thus, for most applications, using the normal curve proves to be an adequate approximation to the distribution of $\bar{y}$. There are certain devices available, however, to improve this approximation. To this end, we now present another result from mathematical statistics.

Edgeworth Approximation. Suppose that $y_1, \dots, y_n$ are i.i.d. with mean μ, variance σ^2 and $E\,|y|^3$ is finite. Then,

$$\text{Prob}\left(\frac{\sqrt{n}(\bar{y} - \mu)}{\sigma} \leq x \right) = \text{Prob}(z \leq x) + \frac{1}{6} \frac{1}{\sqrt{2\pi\sigma^2}}\, e^{-x^2/2} \frac{E\,(y - \mu)^3}{\sigma^3 \sqrt{n}} + \frac{\epsilon_n}{\sqrt{n}},$$

where $z \sim N(0, 1)$, and $\epsilon_n \to 0$ as $n \to \infty$.

This approximation is useful because it suggests that the distribution of $n^{1/2}(\bar{y} - \mu)/\sigma$ becomes close to the distribution of a standard normal curve as the skewness coefficient, $E\,(y - \mu)^3 = \gamma$, gets close to zero. Indeed, in Chapter 6 are rescaling devices that suggest *transforming* the data to achieve symmetry. One pay-off of this symmetrization is that the distribution of averages is closer to the normal curve distribution.

Each of the three limiting distribution results has been presented for the simple arithmetic average, $\bar{y}$. However, in the subsequent chapters, we will point out that regression analysis is the study of *weighted* averages. Analogous results are available for weighted averages for Central Limit Theorems, Berry-Esséen Theorems and Edgeworth approximations. See Beard, Pentikäinen and Pesonen (1984) for further discussion of Edgeworth approximations and Serfling (1980) for further information on details of the other results. Although we will not explicitly cite these results, they do provide important motivation for our assumptions of normality.

TS 2.6 Estimation and Prediction

Suppose that $y_1, \dots, y_n$ are i.i.d. random variables that represent observations. Assume that the distribution can be summarized by an unknown parameter θ. We are interested in the quality of an estimate of θ based on the data. We use

$\hat{\theta}$ to be this estimator. For example, we consider $\theta = \mu$ with $\hat{\theta} = \bar{y}$ and $\theta = \sigma^2$ with $\hat{\theta} = s_y^2$ as our leading examples in this chapter.

Point Estimation and Unbiasedness. Because $\hat{\theta}$ provides a single approximation of θ, it is referred to as a *point estimate* of θ. As a statistic, $\hat{\theta}$ is a function of the observations $y_1, \ldots, y_n$ that change from one sample to the next. Thus, values of $\hat{\theta}$ change from one sample to the next. To examine how close $\hat{\theta}$ tends to be to θ, we examine several properties of $\hat{\theta}$, in particular, the bias and consistency. A point estimate $\hat{\theta}$ is said to be an *unbiased* estimate of θ if E $\hat{\theta} = \theta$. For example, because E $\bar{y} = \mu$, $\bar{y}$ is an unbiased estimate of μ.

Finite Sample versus Large Sample Properties of Estimators. Biasedness if said to be a *finite sample* property because it is valid for each sample size n. A *limiting*, or *large*, *sample* property is *consistency*. Consistency is expressed in two ways, weak and strong consistency. An estimator is said to be *weakly consistent* if

$$\lim_{n \to \infty} \mathrm{Prob}(\,|\,\hat{\theta} - \theta\,| < \epsilon) = 1$$

for each positive ϵ. An estimator is said to be *strongly consistent* if $\lim_{n \to \infty} \hat{\theta} = \theta$ with probability one.

Least Squares Estimation Principle. In this text, two main estimation principles are used, least squares estimation and maximum likelihood estimation. For the least squares procedure, consider independent random variables $y_1, \ldots, y_n$ with means E $y_i = g_i(\theta)$. Here, g_i is a known function up to θ, an unknown parameter that indexes $\{g_i\}$. The least squares estimate $\hat{\theta}$ of θ is that value of θ^* that minimizes the sum of squares

$$SS(\theta^*) = \sum_{i=1}^{n} (y_i - g_i(\theta^*))^2.$$

Maximum Likelihood Estimation Principle. Maximum likelihood estimates are values of the parameter that are "most likely" to have been produced by the data. Consider the independent random variables $y_1, \ldots, y_n$ with probability function $f_i(a_i, \theta)$. Here, $f_i(a_i, \theta)$ is interpreted to be a probability mass function for discrete y_i or a probability density function for continuous y_i. The function $f_i(a_i, \theta)$ is assumed known up to θ, an unknown parameter. The likelihood of $y_1, \ldots, y_n$ taking on values $a_1, \ldots, a_n$ is

$$L(\theta) = \prod_{i=1}^{n} f_i(a_i, \theta).$$

The value of θ^* that maximizes $L(\theta^*)$ is denoted by $\hat{\theta}$ and is called the *maximum likelihood estimate* of θ.

Confidence Intervals. Although point estimates provide a single approximation to parameters, interval estimates provide ranges that include parameters with a certain prespecified level of probability, or confidence. A pair of statistics, $\hat{\theta}_1 < \hat{\theta}_2$ provides an interval estimate of the form $[\hat{\theta}_1, \hat{\theta}_2]$. This interval estimate is a $100(1 - \alpha)\%$ confidence interval for θ if

$$\text{Prob}(\hat{\theta}_1 \leq \theta \leq \hat{\theta}_2) \geq 1 - \alpha.$$

For example, suppose that $y_1, \ldots, y_n$ are i.i.d. $N(\mu, \sigma^2)$ random variables. Recall, in this case, that $n^{1/2}(\bar{y} - \mu)/s_y \sim t_{n-1}$. This fact allows us to develop a $100(1 - \alpha)\%$ confidence interval for μ of the form $\bar{y} \pm (t\text{-value}) \, s_y/n^{1/2}$, where t-value is the $(1 - \alpha/2)$th percentile from a t-distribution with $n - 1$ degrees of freedom. To see this, consider

$$1 - \alpha = \text{Prob}(-(t\text{-value}) \leq t_{n-1} \leq (t\text{-value}))$$

$$= \text{Prob}\left(-(t\text{-value}) \leq \frac{\sqrt{n}(\bar{y} - \mu)}{s_y} \leq (t\text{-value})\right)$$

$$= \text{Prob}\left(\frac{-(t\text{-value})s_y}{\sqrt{n}} \leq \bar{y} - \mu \leq \frac{(t\text{-value})s_y}{\sqrt{n}}\right)$$

$$= \text{Prob}\left(\frac{-(t\text{-value})s_y}{\sqrt{n}} \leq \mu - \bar{y} \leq \frac{(t\text{-value})s_y}{\sqrt{n}}\right)$$

$$= \text{Prob}\left(\bar{y} - \frac{(t\text{-value})s_y}{\sqrt{n}} \leq \mu \leq \bar{y} + \frac{(t\text{-value})s_y}{\sqrt{n}}\right) = \text{Prob}(\hat{\theta}_1 \leq \theta \leq \hat{\theta}_2).$$

Here, we have $\theta = \mu$, $\hat{\theta}_1 = \bar{y} - (t\text{-value}) \, s_y/n^{1/2}$ and $\hat{\theta}_2 = \bar{y} + (t\text{-value}) \, s_y/n^{1/2}$.

Prediction Intervals. Prediction intervals are similar in form to confidence intervals. However, confidence intervals provide ranges for parameter estimates and prediction intervals provide ranges for future values of observations. Based on observations $y_1, \ldots, y_n$, we seek to construct statistics $\hat{\theta}_1$ and $\hat{\theta}_2$ such that $\text{Prob}(\hat{\theta}_1 < y_0 < \hat{\theta}_2) \geq 1 - \alpha$. Here, y_0 is an additional observation that is independent of $y_1, \ldots, y_n$.

TS 2.7 Testing Hypotheses

Null and Alternative Hypotheses and Test Statistics. An important application of statistical procedures is verifying ideas about parameters. That is, before the data is observed, certain ideas about the parameters are formulated. In this text, we consider only two competing ideas, or *hypotheses*, although it is certainly possible to consider more complex structures. To simplify the discussion further, in this text we only consider a *null hypothesis* of the form $H_0: \theta = \theta_0$ versus an *alternative hypothesis*. We consider a two-sided alternative, $H_a: \theta \neq \theta_0$, and one-sided alternatives, either $H_a: \theta > \theta_0$ or $H_a: \theta < \theta_0$. The choice of hypotheses is based on the research question to be decided, not the data. To choose between the null and alternative hypotheses, we use a *test statistic* T_n that is typically a point estimate of θ or a version that is rescaled to conform to a reference distribution under H_0. For example, to test $H_0: \mu = \mu_0$, we often use $T_n = \bar{y}$ or $T_n = n^{1/2}(\bar{y} - \mu_0)/s_y$. Note that the latter choice has a t_{n-1} distribution, under the null hypothesis and assumptions of i.i.d. normal data.

Rejection Regions and Significance Level.   With a statistic in hand, we must now establish a criterion for deciding between the two competing hypotheses. This can be done by establishing a *rejection*, or *critical region*. The critical region consists of all possible outcomes of T_n that leads us to reject H_0 in favor of H_a. In order to specify the critical region, we first quantify the types of errors that can be made in the decision making procedure. A *Type I* error consists of rejecting H_0 falsely and a *Type II* error consists of rejecting H_a falsely. The probability of a Type I error is called the *significance level*. Prespecifying the significance level is often enough to determine the critical region. For example, suppose that $y_1, \ldots, y_n$ are i.i.d. $N(\mu, \sigma^2)$ and we are interested in deciding between $H_0: \mu = \mu_0$ and $H_a: \mu > \mu_0$. Thinking of our test statistic $T_n = \bar{y}$, we know that we would like to reject H_0 if $\bar{y}$ is larger that μ_0. The question is how much larger? Specifying a significance level α, we wish to find a critical region of the form $\{\bar{y} > c\}$ for some constant c. To this end, we have

$$\alpha = \text{Prob(Type I Error)} = \text{Prob(Reject } H_0 \text{ assuming } H_0: \mu = \mu_0 \text{ is true)}$$

$$= \text{Prob}(\bar{y} > c \text{ assuming } \mu = \mu_0 \text{ is true})$$

$$= \text{Prob}(n^{1/2}(\bar{y} - \mu)/s_y > n^{1/2}(c - \mu_0)/s_y \text{ assuming } \mu = \mu_0 \text{ is true})$$

$$= \text{Prob}(t_{n-1} > n^{1/2}(c - \mu_0)/s_y).$$

From the *t*-table with $df = n - 1$ degrees of freedom, we have that *t*-value $= n^{1/2}(c - \mu_0)/s_y$ where the *t*-value is the $(1 - \alpha)$th percentile from a *t*-distribution. Thus, solving for c, our critical region is of the form $\{\bar{y} > \mu_0 + (t\text{-value})s_y/n^{1/2}\}$.

Relationship between Confidence Intervals and Hypothesis Tests. Similar calculations show, for testing $H_0: \mu = \mu_0$ versus $H_a: \mu \neq \mu_0$, that the critical region is of the form $\{\bar{y} < \mu_0 - (t\text{-value})s_y/n^{1/2}$ or $\bar{y} > \mu_0 + (t\text{-value}) s_y/n^{1/2}\}$. Here, the *t*-value is a $(1 - \alpha/2)$th percentile from a *t*-distribution with $df = n - 1$ degrees of freedom. It is interesting to note that the event of $\bar{y}$ falling in this two-sided critical region is equivalent to the event of μ_0 falling outside the confidence interval $\bar{y} \pm (t\text{-value})s_y/n^{1/2}$. This establishes the fact that confidence intervals and hypothesis tests are really reporting the same statistical evidence with different emphasis on interpretation of the statistical inference.

p-Value   Another useful concept in hypothesis testing is the *p*-value, which is shorthand for probability value. For a data set, a *p*-value is defined to be the smallest significance level for which the null hypothesis would be rejected. The *p*-value is a useful summary statistic for the data analyst to report because it allows the report reader to understand the strength of the deviation from the null hypothesis.

CHAPTER 3

TS 3.1 Least Squares Estimates

Normal Equations.   Assume that we have the data $(x_1, y_1), \ldots, (x_n, y_n)$ available and we wish to approximate y by a linear function of x. Under the least squares estimation principle described in Section TS 2.6, we choose b_0^* and b_1^* to minimize the sum of squares

$$SS(b_0^*, b_1^*) = \sum_{i=1}^{n} (y_i - (b_0^* + b_1^* x_i))^2.$$

Minimization of this quantity is a straightforward exercise using calculus. Taking partial derivatives with respect to each argument and setting these quantities equal to zero yields

$$\frac{\partial}{\partial b_0^*} SS(b_0^*, b_1^*) = \sum_{i=1}^{n} (-2)(y_i - (b_0^* + b_1^* x_i)) = 0$$

and

$$\frac{\partial}{\partial b_1^*} SS(b_0^*, b_1^*) = \sum_{i=1}^{n} (-2x_i)(y_i - (b_0^* + b_1^* x_i)) = 0.$$

The reader is invited to take second partial derivatives to ensure that we are minimizing, not maximizing, this function. Canceling constant terms yields

$$\sum_{i=1}^{n} (y_i - (b_0^* + b_1^* x_i)) = 0$$

and

$$\sum_{i=1}^{n} x_i(y_i - (b_0^* + b_1^* x_i)) = 0$$

which are called the *normal equations*. Solving these equations yields the best values of b_0^* and b_1^*,

$$b_1 = \frac{\sum_{i=1}^{n} (x_i - \bar{x})(y_i - \bar{y})}{\sum_{i=1}^{n} (x_i - \bar{x})^2} = \frac{\sum_{i=1}^{n} (x_i - \bar{x})(y_i - \bar{y})}{(n-1)s_x^2} = r \frac{s_y}{s_x}$$

and

$$b_0 = \bar{y} - b_1\bar{x}.$$

These best values are called the *least squares estimates.*

Least Squares Estimates. The least squares estimates can be expressed as weighted sum of the responses. To see this, define the weights $w_i = (x_i - \bar{x})/\sum_{i=1}^{n}(x_i - \bar{x})^2$. Some easy algebra shows that $\sum_{i=1}^{n} w_i = 0$. Thus, we can express the slope estimate as

$$b_1 = \sum_{i=1}^{n} w_i(y_i - \bar{y}) = \sum_{i=1}^{n} w_i y_i - \bar{y}\sum_{i=1}^{n} w_i = \sum_{i=1}^{n} w_i y_i \qquad \text{(TS3.1)}$$

as a *weighted sum* of the responses. Similarly, the intercept term can also be expressed as a weighted sum of the responses, as follows:

$$b_0 = \frac{1}{n}\sum_{i=1}^{n} y_i - \left(\sum_{i=1}^{n} w_i y_i\right)\bar{x} = \sum_{i=1}^{n}\left(\frac{1}{n} - w_i\bar{x}\right)y_i. \qquad \text{(TS3.2)}$$

TS 3.2 Linear Regression Model

The basic linear regression model represents a relationship between y and x as,

$$y_i = \beta_0 + \beta_1 x_i + e_i, \qquad i = 1, \ldots, n.$$

Here, the error terms $\{e_i\}$ are assumed to be i.i.d. random variables with $E\, e_i = 0$ and $\text{Var}\, e_i = \sigma^2$. The independent variables $\{x_i\}$ are assumed to be variables, yet nonrandom. Thus, by the linearity of expectations in equation (TS2.2), the mean response is $E\, y_i = \beta_0 + \beta_1 x_i + E\, e_i = \beta_0 + \beta_1 x_i$. Further, the variance is $\text{Var}\, y_i = \sigma^2$.

We also use the assumption that the error distribution is normal, that is, $e_i \sim N$. This assumption with the above moment assumptions can be summarized using the notation, $e_i \sim N(0, \sigma^2)$. Further, by the linearity of normal random variables in equation (TS2.8), we have $y_i \sim N(\beta_0 + \beta_1 x_i, \sigma^2)$.

TS 3.3 Finite Sample Properties of Regression Coefficient Estimates

As shown in equations (TS3.1) and (TS3.2), the least squares regression coefficients estimates can be expressed as linear combinations of responses. With our model assumptions, we can easily check properties of the estimates. In this subsection, we present only exact, finite sample properties. In the next subsection, we examine approximate, large sample, properties.

Unbiasedness of the Estimates. By equation (TS3.1) and the linearity of expectations in equation (TS2.2), we have

$$\mathrm{E}\, b_1 = \mathrm{E} \sum_{i=1}^{n} w_i y_i = \sum_{i=1}^{n} w_i\, \mathrm{E}\, y_i = \sum_{i=1}^{n} w_i(\beta_0 + \beta_1 x_i) = \beta_1.$$

This is true because $\bar{x} \sum_{i=1}^{n} w_i = 0$, yielding $\sum_{i=1}^{n} w_i\, x_i = \sum_{i=1}^{n} w_i\, x_i - \bar{x} \sum_{i=1}^{n} w_i = \sum_{i=1}^{n} w_i\, (x_i - \bar{x}) = (\sum_{i=1}^{n} (x_i - \bar{x})^2)/((n-1)\, s_x^2) = 1$. Similarly, from equation (TS3.2),

$$\mathrm{E}\, b_0 = \mathrm{E} \sum_{i=1}^{n} \left(\frac{1}{n} - w_i \bar{x}\right) y_i = \sum_{i=1}^{n} \left(\frac{1}{n} - w_i \bar{x}\right)(\beta_0 + \beta_1 x_i)$$

$$= \beta_0 + \beta_1 \sum_{i=1}^{n} \left(\frac{1}{n} - w_i \bar{x}\right) x_i = \beta_0 + \beta_1 \bar{x} - \beta_1 \bar{x} \sum_{i=1}^{n} w_i x_i$$

$$= \beta_0 + \beta_1 \bar{x} - \beta_1 \bar{x} = \beta_0.$$

Thus, b_0 and b_1 are unbiased estimators of β_0 and β_1, respectively.

Variance of the Estimates.   From straightforward algebra, we have $\sum_{i=1}^{n} w_i^2 = (\sum_{i=1}^{n} (x_i - \bar{x})^2)/((n-1)\, s_x^2)^2 = 1/((n-1)\, s_x^2)$. Thus, by equation (TS2.5), we have

$$\mathrm{Var}\, b_1 = \mathrm{Var}\left(\sum_{i=1}^{n} w_i\, y_i\right) = \sum_{i=1}^{n} w_i^2\, \mathrm{Var}\, y_i = \sigma^2 \sum_{i=1}^{n} w_i^2 = \frac{\sigma^2}{(n-1)s_x^2}.$$

Similarly,

$$\mathrm{Var}\, b_0 = \sigma^2 \sum_{i=1}^{n} \left(\frac{1}{n} - w_i \bar{x}\right)^2 = \sigma^2 \left(\frac{1}{n} + \bar{x}^2 \sum_{i=1}^{n} w_i^2\right) = \sigma^2 \left(\frac{1}{n} + \frac{\bar{x}^2}{(n-1)s_x^2}\right).$$

Covariance of the Estimates.   From equations (TS3.1) and (TS3.2) and the linearity of covariances in equation (TS2.3), we have

$$\mathrm{Cov}(b_0, b_1) = \mathrm{Cov}\left(\sum_{i=1}^{n} \left(\frac{1}{n} - w_i \bar{x}\right) y_i, \sum_{j=1}^{n} w_j y_j\right)$$

$$= \sum_{i=1}^{n} \sum_{j=1}^{n} \left(\frac{1}{n} - w_i \bar{x}\right) w_j\, \mathrm{Cov}(y_i, y_j)$$

$$= \sigma^2 \sum_{i=1}^{n} \left(\frac{1}{n} - w_i \bar{x}\right) w_i = -\bar{x} \sigma^2 \sum_{i=1}^{n} w_i^2 = \frac{-\bar{x}\sigma^2}{(n-1)s_x^2}.$$

Distribution of the Estimates.   Assume, in addition, that the errors are normally distributed. Because $b_1 = \sum_{i=1}^{n} w_i y_i$ and y_i are normally distributed, we have, by (TS2.8), that b_1 is normally distributed. This is,

$$b_1 \sim N\left(\beta_1, \frac{\sigma^2}{(n-1)s_x^2}\right). \tag{TS3.3}$$

Similarly,

$$b_0 \sim N\left(\beta_0, \sigma^2\left(\frac{1}{n} + \frac{\bar{x}^2}{(n-1)s_x^2}\right)\right).$$

Standard Errors of the Estimates. Estimators of the square root of the variance are called *standard errors.* We use $s = (\text{Error MS})^{1/2}$ as our estimate of σ. Thus, the estimated square root of the variance of b_1 is the standard error of b_1

$$se(b_1) = \frac{s}{s_x\sqrt{n-1}}.$$

Similarly, the standard error of b_0 is

$$se(b_0) = s\sqrt{\frac{1}{n} + \frac{\bar{x}^2}{(n-1)s_x^2}}.$$

Distribution of Standardized Estimates. Assume that the errors are normally distributed. From Section TS2.4, we have

$$\frac{b_1 - \beta_1}{\dfrac{\sigma}{s_x\sqrt{n-1}}} \sim N(0,1)$$

and

$$\frac{b_0 - \beta_0}{\sigma\sqrt{\dfrac{1}{n} + \dfrac{\bar{x}^2}{(n-1)s_x^2}}} \sim N(0,1).$$

Replacing σ by s introduces additional variability. It can be checked that

$$\frac{b_1 - \beta_1}{se(b_1)} = \frac{b_1 - \beta_1}{\dfrac{s}{s_x\sqrt{n-1}}} \sim t_{n-2}$$

and

$$\frac{b_0 - \beta_0}{se(b_0)} = \frac{b_0 - \beta_0}{s\sqrt{\dfrac{1}{n} + \dfrac{\bar{x}^2}{(n-1)s_x^2}}} \sim t_{n-2}.$$

Linear Combinations of Estimates. Consider estimating $\theta = a_0\beta_0 + a_1\beta_1$ where a_0 and a_1 are known constants. An unbiased estimator of θ is $\hat{\theta} = a_0b_0 + a_1b_1$ because $\mathrm{E}\,\hat{\theta} = a_0\,\mathrm{E}\,b_0 + a_1\,\mathrm{E}\,b_1 = a_0\beta_0 + a_1\beta_1 = \theta$. From equation (TS2.4), we have

$$\mathrm{Var}\,\hat{\theta} = a_0^2\,\mathrm{Var}\,b_0 + a_1^2\,\mathrm{Var}\,b_1 + 2a_0a_1\,\mathrm{Cov}(b_0,b_1)$$

$$= a_0^2\sigma^2\left(\frac{1}{n} + \frac{\bar{x}^2}{(n-1)s_x^2}\right) + \frac{a_1^2\sigma^2}{(n-1)s_x^2} - \frac{2a_0a_1\bar{x}\sigma^2}{(n-1)s_x^2}$$

$$= \sigma^2\left(\frac{a_0^2}{n} + \frac{(a_1 - a_0\bar{x})^2}{(n-1)s_x^2}\right).$$

Thus, replacing σ^2 by s^2 and taking square roots, we have

$$se(\hat{\theta}) = s\sqrt{\frac{a_0^2}{n} + \frac{(a_1 - a_0\bar{x})^2}{(n-1)s_x^2}}.$$

By equation (TS3.1) and (TS3.2), we can express

$$\hat{\theta} = a_0b_0 + a_1b_1 = \sum_{i=1}^{n}\left[\frac{a_0}{n} + w_i(a_1 - a_0\bar{x})\right]y_i \qquad (\mathrm{TS3.4})$$

as a linear combination of observations. Thus, if the errors are normally distributed, then so are the observations and hence the linear combination of estimators. Further, it can be checked that

$$\frac{\hat{\theta} - \theta}{se(\hat{\theta})} \sim t_{n-2}.$$

This result subsumes the results for individual regression coefficients. For example, by taking $a_0 = 0$ and $a_1 = 1$, we have that $\theta = 0(\beta_0) + 1(\beta_1) = \beta_1$. Further, if x_* is a known quantity, by taking $a_0 = 1$ and $a_1 = x_*$, we may interpret $\theta = \beta_0 + \beta_1 x_*$ to be the *expected response* at x_*. Thus, we get

$$\frac{(b_0 + b_1 x_*) - (\beta_0 + \beta_1 x_*)}{s\sqrt{\dfrac{1}{n} + \dfrac{(x_* - \bar{x})^2}{(n-1)s_x^2}}} \sim t_{n-2}.$$

Inference for Linear Combinations of Estimates. Having identified a sampling distribution for standardized linear combinations of estimates, we can immediately write down confidence intervals and tests of hypotheses results. To begin, a $100(1 - \alpha)\%$ confidence interval for θ is

$$\hat{\theta} \pm (t\text{-value})\ se(\hat{\theta}),$$

where t-value is a $(1 - \alpha/2)$th percentile from a t-distribution with $df = n - 2$ degrees of freedom. For example, for a known value x_*, a $100(1 - \alpha)\%$ confidence interval for the expected, or mean, response at x_* is

$$b_0 + b_1 x_* \pm (t\text{-value})\ s\ \sqrt{\frac{1}{n} + \frac{(x_* - \bar{x})^2}{(n - 1)s_x^2}}\ .$$

For a two-sided hypothesis test, we consider hypotheses $H_0: \theta = \theta_0$ versus $H_a: \theta \neq \theta_0$, where θ_0 is a known value. Specifying a significance level α, the null hypothesis is rejected in favor of the alternative if

$$\left| \frac{\hat{\theta} - \theta_0}{se(\hat{\theta})} \right| > t\text{-value}$$

where t-value is a $(1 - \alpha/2)$th percentile from a t-distribution with $df = n - 2$ degrees of freedom. For example, taking $a_0 = 0$ and $a_1 = 1$, we have $\theta = \beta_1$, $\hat{\theta} = b_1$, $\theta_0 = \beta_{1,0}$, a specified value, and

$$se(\hat{\theta}) = s\ \sqrt{\frac{0^2}{n} + \frac{(1 - 0\bar{x})^2}{(n - 1)s_x^2}} = s\ \sqrt{\frac{1}{(n - 1)s_x^2}} = se(b_1).$$

That is, we reject if $|(b_1 - \beta_{1,0})/se(b_1)| > t$-value.

One-sided tests are similar. To test $H_0: \theta = \theta_0$ versus $H_a: \theta > \theta_0$, we reject H_0 if

$$\frac{\hat{\theta} - \theta_0}{se(\hat{\theta})} > t\text{-value}$$

where t-value is a $(1 - \alpha)$th percentile from a t-distribution with $df = n - 2$ degrees of freedom.

Predicting Future Values. Assume that we have the data (x_1, y_1), ..., (x_n, y_n) available and we wish to predict an additional value, say y_*, at known explanatory variable x_*. Based on the available data, the prediction is $\hat{y}_* = b_0 + b_1 x_*$. Using equation (TS2.5), the variance of the prediction error is

$$\text{Var}(y_* - \hat{y}) = \text{Var}\ y_* + \text{Var}(b_0 + b_1 x_*) = \sigma^2 + \sigma^2 \left(\frac{1}{n} + \frac{(x_* - \bar{x})^2}{(n - 1)s_x^2} \right),$$

because y_* and $\hat{y}_*$ are independent. Replacing σ^2 by s^2 and taking square roots, we have

$$se(pred) = s\sqrt{1 + \frac{1}{n} + \frac{(x - \bar{x})^2}{(n-1)s_x^2}} \, .$$

It can be checked that

$$\frac{y_* - \hat{y}_*}{se(pred)} \sim t_{n-2}.$$

This leads to our $100(1 - \alpha)\%$ prediction interval

$$\hat{y}_* \pm (t\text{-value}) \, se(pred).$$

Here, t-value is a $(1 - \alpha/2)$th percentile from a t-distribution with $df = n - 2$ degrees of freedom.

TS 3.4 Large Sample Properties of Regression Coefficient Estimates

Just as with averages of i.i.d. random variables, there exist limiting distribution results for weighted averages of independent random variables. These results are important because, as established in equation (TS3.4), we can express coefficients as weighted sums of random variables. To illustrate this, we first cite a general result on sums which can be found as a special case of a corollary in Serfling (1980, page 32).

Weighted Central Limit Theorem
Let $y_1, \dots y_n$ be independent random variables such that $E \, |y_i - E \, y_i|^3$ is uniformly finite. Further, assume that d_i are constants such that

$$\lim_{n \to \infty} \frac{\sum_{i=1}^{n} d_i^2}{\left(\sum_{i=1}^{n} d_i^2\right)^{3/2}} = 0.$$

Then,

$$\lim_{n \to \infty} \mathrm{Prob}\left(\frac{\sum_{i=1}^{n} d_i(y - E \, y_i)}{\sqrt{\sum_{i=1}^{n} d_i^2 \, Var \, y_i}} \le x\right) = \mathrm{Prob}(z \le x)$$

where $z \sim N(0,1)$.

To illustrate the use of this general result, take $y_i = \beta_0 + \beta_1 x_i + e_i$ and suppose that we are interested in establishing a central limit theorem for b_1. Then, taking $d_i = w_i = (x_i - \bar{x})/((n-1) s_x^2)$, from equation (TS3.1) we have $\Sigma_{i=1}^n d_i^2 y_i = b_1$. From Section TS 3.3, we have that, $\Sigma_{i=1}^n d_i \, \mathrm{E} \, y_i = \beta_1$ and $\Sigma_{i=1}^n d_i^2 \, \mathrm{Var} \, y_i = \sigma^2 \Sigma_{i=1}^n w_i^2 = \sigma^2/((n-1) s_x^2)$. Thus, from the weighted central limit theorem, we have a central limit theorem for b_1,

$$\lim_{n \to \infty} \mathrm{Prob} \left(\frac{b_1 - \beta_1}{\dfrac{\sigma}{s_x \sqrt{n-1}}} \leq x \right) = \mathrm{Prob}(z \leq x).$$

This is simply a limiting version of equation (TS3.3). The important point is that the limiting version holds *without assuming the normality of the errors*. To satisfy the condition of the theorem, we require that

$$\frac{\displaystyle\sum_{i=1}^n d_i^3}{\left(\displaystyle\sum_{i=1}^n d_i^2\right)^{3/2}} = \frac{\displaystyle\sum_{i=1}^n \frac{(x_i - \bar{x})^3}{((n-1)s_x^2)^3}}{\left(\dfrac{1}{(n-1)s_x^2}\right)^{3/2}} = \frac{\displaystyle\sum_{i=1}^n (x_i - \bar{x})^3}{(n-1)^{3/2} s_x^3} \to 0 \, .$$

This requirement is simply a mathematical condition for enough spread of the explanatory variables to estimate the slope, b_1, reliably.

TS 3.5 Properties of Residuals

Residuals are defined to be the observed response corrected for the fitted response under the model. Specifically, the ith residual is $\hat{e}_i = y_i - \hat{y}_i$, where $\hat{y}_i = b_0 + b_1 x_i$. The fitted value $\hat{y}_i$ is a linear combination of regression coefficients. That is, with $a_0 = 1$ and $a_1 = x_i$, we have $\hat{\theta} = (1) b_0 + (x_i) b_1 = \hat{y}_i$. Thus, from Section TS 3.3, we immediately have that $\mathrm{E} \, \hat{y}_i = \beta_0 + \beta_1 x_i$ and $\mathrm{Var} \, (\hat{y}_i) = \sigma^2 (n^{-1} + (x_i - \bar{x})^2/((n-1)s_x^2))$. Because $\mathrm{E} \, y_i = \beta_0 + \beta_1 x_i$, we have

$$\mathrm{E} \, \hat{e}_i = \mathrm{E} \, y_i - \mathrm{E} \, \hat{y}_i = 0,$$

that is, the ith residual has mean zero, like the true error e_i. Further, linear combinations of regression coefficients can be expressed as linear combinations of observations. Thus, from equation (TS3.4) with $a_0 = 1$ and $a_1 = x_i$, we have

$$\hat{y}_i = \sum_{j=1}^n \left(\frac{1}{n} + w_j(x_i - \bar{x}) \right) y_j.$$

Using equation (TS2.3) and the independence of responses yields

$$\text{Cov}(y_i, \hat{y}_i) = \text{Cov}\left(y_i, \sum_{j=1}^{n}\left(\frac{1}{n} + w_j(x_i - \bar{x})\right)y_j\right)$$

$$= \text{Cov}\left(y_i, \left(\frac{1}{n} + w_i(x_i - \bar{x})\right)y_i\right)$$

$$= \sigma^2\left(\frac{1}{n} + w_i(x_i - \bar{x})\right) = \sigma^2\left(\frac{1}{n} + \frac{(x_i - \bar{x})^2}{(n-1)s_x^2}\right).$$

Thus, using equation (TS2.4), we have

$$\text{Var } \hat{e}_i = \text{Var}(y_i - \hat{y}_i) = \text{Var } y_i + \text{Var } \hat{y}_i - 2\,\text{Cov}(y_i, \hat{y}_i)$$

$$= \sigma^2 + \sigma^2\left(\frac{1}{n} + \frac{(x_i - \bar{x})^2}{(n-1)s_x^2}\right) - 2\,\sigma^2\left(\frac{1}{n} + \frac{(x_i - \bar{x})^2}{(n-1)s_x^2}\right)$$

$$= \sigma^2\left(1 - \left(\frac{1}{n} + \frac{(x_i - \bar{x})^2}{(n-1)s_x^2}\right)\right).$$

Replacing σ^2 by s^2 and taking square roots yields the standard error of the ith residual

$$se(\hat{e}_i) = s\sqrt{1 - \left(\frac{1}{n} + \frac{(x_i - \bar{x})^2}{(n-1)s_x^2}\right)}.$$

TS 3.6 Random Explanatory Variables

Model.   In this chapter, we consider the model $y_i = \beta_0 + \beta_1 x_i + e_i$. Prior to this section, the explanatory variables have been assumed to be nonrandom variables. This allows for analyzing data where the analyst has *control* over the explanatory variables. For example, a researcher may be interested in understanding $y =$ crop yield on $x =$ an amount of fertilizer. Setting the amount of fertilizer may be within the control of the researcher. On the other hand, the researcher may be analyzing data that is randomly drawn from a population of farms and thus has no control over the independent variable. In this case, we think of (x_i, y_i) as a random draw and hence x_i is a random variable. In this subsection, we show how to interpet this model as a special case of our model that represents x as a nonrandom variable.

Correlation.   We begin by assuming that $(x_1, y_1), \ldots, (x_n, y_n)$ is an i.i.d. sample from a population. One summary measure of this population is the correlation coefficient, defined as

$$\rho = \frac{\text{Cov}(x, y)}{\sqrt{\text{Var } x \text{ Var } y}} .$$

Both r and ρ are unitless measues and both must line in the interval $[-1, 1]$. The statistic r is a useful estimate of the parameter ρ. It is consistent and nearly unbiased; for moderate sample sizes the extent of the bias is negligible. Recall that $r = b_1 (s_x/s_y)$ and that we have large sample normality results available for the slope b_1. Thus, it is reasonable to conjecture that there are large sample normality results for r, and indeed this is true. However, because both r and ρ are bounded by $[-1, 1]$, it turns out that the distribution of r is skewed for large values of $|\rho|$. This can, for example, be seen by an Edgeworth expansion. Thus, instead we present a large sample normality result for a *transformed* version of r, as follows.

Large Sample Normality for a Transformed Version of r.　Assume that $(x_1, y_1), \ldots, (x_n, y_n)$ is an i.i.d. sample with correlation coefficient ρ. Based on the sample, let r denote the correlation coefficient. Define $g(r) = 1/2 \ln((1 + r)/(1 - r))$ to be the transformed version and similarly for $g(\rho)$. Then,

$$lim_{n \to \infty} \text{Prob} \left(\frac{g(r) - g(\rho)}{1/\sqrt{n - 3}} \leq x \right) = \text{Prob}(z \leq x).$$

Thus , we have that $g(r)$ is approximately distributed as $N(g(\rho), (n - 3)^{-1})$. As a direct application of this, we have that a $100(1 - \alpha)\%$ confidence interval for $g(\rho)$ is $g(r) \pm (z\text{-value})/(n - 3)^{1/2}$. Here, the z-value is a $100(1 - \alpha/2)$th percentile from a standard normal curve. This can be easily converted to a $100(1 - \alpha)\%$ confidence interval for ρ, as follows. First, note that the inverse function of g is $g^{-1}(a) = (\exp(2a) - 1)/(\exp(2a) + 1)$. That is, easy calculus shows that $g^{-1}(g(a)) = a$. From the approximate normality and applying g^{-1} to each side of the inequality, we have

$$1 - \alpha \approx \text{Prob} \left(g(r) - \frac{z\text{-value}}{\sqrt{n - 3}} \leq g(\rho) \leq g(r) + \frac{z\text{-value}}{\sqrt{n - 3}} \right)$$

$$= \text{Prob} \left(g^{-1} \left(g(r) - \frac{z\text{-value}}{\sqrt{n - 3}} \right) \leq \rho \leq g^{-1} \left(g(r) + \frac{z\text{-value}}{\sqrt{n - 3}} \right) \right)$$

Thus, a $100(1 - \alpha)\%$ confidence interval for ρ is

$$\left(g^{-1} \left(g(r) - \frac{z\text{-value}}{\sqrt{n - 3}} \right), g^{-1} \left(g(r) + \frac{z\text{-value}}{\sqrt{n - 3}} \right) \right)$$

To illustrate, suppose that $r = 0.90$, $n = 67$ and $\alpha = 0.05$. Then $g(r) = g(0.9) = 1/2 \ln(1.9/0.1) = 1/2 \ln 19 \approx 1.4722$. Further, $(n - 3)^{1/2} = 64^{1/2} = 8$ and z-value $= 1.96$. For the lower confidence bound of $g(\rho)$, we have $g(r) - (z\text{-value})/$　$(n - 3)^{1/2} = 1.4722 - 1.96/8 = 1.2272$. Thus, $g^{-1}(g(r) - (z\text{-value})/(n - 3)^{1/2}) = g^{-1} (1.2272) = (\exp(2(1.2272)) - 1)/(\exp(2(1.2272)) + 1) = (11.6394 -$

$1)/(11.6394 + 1) = 0.8417$ is a lower confidence bound for ρ. Similarly, for the upper confidence bound, we have $g(r) + (z\text{-value})/(n - 3)^{1/2} = 1.7172$ and $g^{-1}(g(r) + (z\text{-value})/(n - 3)^{1/2}) = g^{-1}(1.7172) = 0.9375$. Thus, our point estimate for ρ is $r = 0.90$ and a 95% confidence interval is $(0.8417, 0.9375)$. Note that this interval is not symmetric about the point estimate r.

Regression Model.   We assume that $(x_1, y_1), ..., (x_n, y_n)$ is an i.i.d. sample, that $y_i = \beta_0 + \beta_1 x_i + e_i$ and further that $\{e_i\}$ is independent of $\{x_i\}$. Under this set-up, we have that $E(e \mid x) = 0$ and thus $E(y \mid x) = \beta_0 + \beta_1 x$. That is, the regression function can be interpreted as the expected response *conditional* on a given value of x. In a similar fashion, it can be shown that most of our inferences hold because we can condition on values of $x_1, ..., x_n$. Further, the random explanatory variable set-up provides useful intuition in some applications. For example, in the CAPM model described in Section 3.6, we might use y to represent the returns from a specific firm and x to represent the returns from the market. Then, using equation (TS2.5), we have

$$\text{Var } y = \text{Var}(\beta_0 + \beta_1 x + e) = \beta_1^2 \text{ Var } x + \text{Var } e.$$

In financial economics, we interpret $\text{Var } y$ to be a measure of riskiness of a stock and $\text{Var } x$ to be a measure of the riskiness of the market. Thus, a stock's riskiness can be decomposed into two parts, that due to the market, $\beta_1^2 \text{ Var } x$, and that due to the particular characteristics of a stock, $\text{Var } e$. The latter portion of the variability is often called the "idiosyncratic risk."

TS 3.7 Regression Through the Origin

Least Squares Estimation.   Most applications of regression analysis assume that the expected response is a linear combination of explanatory variables. However, researchers are discovering more and more applications where certain variations provide a more adequate representation than the basic linear model. One of the simplest variations is *regression through the origin*, where the intercept term is taken to be a known quantity, typically 0. By assuming that $\beta_0 = 0$, our model is $y_i = \beta_1 x_i + e_i$ and is sometimes called a *no-intercept model*. For this model, least squares parameter estimates are straightforward. From Section TS 2.6, the least squares estimate of β_1 is that number b_1 that minimizes

$$SS(b_1^*) = \sum_{i=1}^{n} (y_i - b_1^* x_i)^2$$

over all candidate estimates b_1^*. It is easy to verify that

$$b_1 = \frac{\sum_{i=1}^{n} x_i y_i}{\sum_{i=1}^{n} x_i^2}.$$

This is similar to the usual equation for the slope. The difference here is that there is no correction for the mean because it is assumed that the line goes through the origin (the point where both x and y are 0). Additional inferences for this special model can be derived explicitly. In this text, this model is treated as a special case of the general formulation that will be presented in Chapter 4.

Coefficient of Determination. With this model, inference using t-statistics and Analysis of Variance techniques follow directly as a special case of the general formulation in Chapter 4. However, an important summary statistic, the coefficient of determination, R^2, no longer has the same desirable interpretation as in the usual regression model with an intercept term. Because the coefficient of determination is supposed to measure the proportion of variability observed, following the logic in Section 3.3, we might use

$$R_{(0)}^2 = \frac{\sum_{i=1}^{n} \hat{y}_i^2}{\sum_{i=1}^{n} y_i^2}$$

where $\hat{y}_i = b_1 x_i$ is the fitted value. Here, both the numerator and denominator of $R_{(0)}^2$ describe the *variation about zero*. One difficulty with this statistic is that analysts compare this statistic with corresponding statistics for the intercept model, R^2. That is, analysts often need to decide whether or not to include the intercept term, β_0, in the model. Thus, it is natural to compare $R_{(0)}^2$ from the no-intercept model with R^2, the coefficient of determination from the intercept model. However, it is easy to check that even in many situations where the intercept belongs in the model (as justified with a t-test, for example), we may observe $R_{(0)}^2 > R^2$. This is regarded as misleading and thus, it is generally recommended to not cite a coefficient of determination when fitting the no-intercept model. See Kvalseth (1985) for further elaboration of this point.

TS 3.8 Estimation Principles

In applications of linear regression analysis, least squares is by far the most prevalent method of parameter estimation. This is because it is known to be the optimal procedure based on certain models of the data. However, there are alternative estimation procedures that do nearly as well as least squares procedures under routine conditions and that perform much better under slight variants of these routine conditions.

BLUE Estimators. An important justification of the use of least squares estimates is that they are BLUE, an acronym that stands for *best linear unbiased estimator*. This description is due to the following result, known as the

Gauss-Markov Theorem.   Consider the model $y_i = \beta_0 + \beta_1 x_i + e_i$ where $\{e_i\}$ are mean 0 and uncorrelated. Then, the least squares estimates of the regression coefficients have the smallest variance in the class of all linear unbiased estimates.

Recall that an estimate $\hat{\theta}$ is said to be unbiased if $E\,\hat{\theta} = \theta$. A linear estimator $\hat{\theta}$ that depends on random variables $y_1, \ldots, y_n$ is one that can be expressed as a linear combination of the form $\hat{\theta} = \Sigma_{i=1}^{n}\, d_i\, y_i$. For example, to estimate the center of a distribution, the sample mean $\bar{y}$ is a linear estimator although the sample median is not.

UMVU Estimators.   Least squares estimators are also superior to nonlinear alternatives under the following conditions.

Uniform Minimum Variance Unbiased Theorem.   Consider the model $y_i = \beta_0 + \beta_1 x_i + e_i$ where $\{e_i\}$ are i.i.d. $N(0, \sigma^2)$. Then, the least squares estimates of the regression coefficients have the smallest variance in the class of all unbiased estimates.

Because of this result, least squares estimates are said to be UMVU estimates, that is, uniformly minimum variance unbiased estimates. That is, with the normality of the errors $\{e_i\}$, least squares estimates are superior to linear as well as nonlinear alternatives, at least using the variance as the criterion.

Maximum Likelihood Estimation.   Under the assumption of normality of the errors, there is an additional motivation for using least squares estimation. Using the likelihood from the normal curve, it can be shown that maximum likelihood estimators of the regression coefficients are equal to the estimates derived using the least squares principle. Thus, in the special case of normally distributed errors, we get the same estimator based on competing estimation principles. In a sense, this provides an unrelated corroboration of the validity of the resulting estimates.

Ideal Conditions.   The ideal conditions are summarized with the statement that the data follows the model $y_i = \beta_0 + \beta_1 x_i + e_i$, where $\{e_i\}$ are i.i.d. and (possibly) normally distributed. When fitting real data sets to this model, analysts encounter several "violations" of these ideal conditions that need to be addressed in the modeling and estimation. Some of the difficulties come from the fact that the errors are not always from identical distributions. For example, some errors may be outliers or the variance of the errors may depend on the explanatory variables. We also encounter situations where there are mild dependencies among the errors. To address these and related concerns, statisticians have devised alternative ways of estimating regression coefficients. Before introducing these estimators, the following example quantifies the effect on the error sum of squares of using an alternative estimate.

Effect of Alternative Estimates on Error SS.   Recall that the error sum of squares is given by

$$\text{Error SS} = \text{SS}(b_0,b_1) = \sum_{i=1}^{n} (y_i - (b_0 + b_1 x_i))^2.$$

Let $b_1^p = (1 + c)b_1$ be a perturbed value of the least squares regression slope coefficients, where c is a constant to be specified later. So that the fitted regression line goes through the point of averages $(\bar{x}, \bar{y})$, define $b_0^p = \bar{y} - b_1^p \bar{x}$ to be the perturbed intercept estimate. Recall that $(n - 1)s_y^2 = \sum_{i=1}^{n}(y_i - \bar{y})^2$, $(n - 1)s_x^2 = \sum_{i=1}^{n}(x_i - \bar{x})^2$ and that $(n - 1)s_x s_y r = \sum_{i=1}^{n}(y_i - \bar{y})(x_i - \bar{x})$. Thus, we have

$$\text{SS}(b_0^p, b_1^p) = \sum_{i=1}^{n} (y_i - (b_0^p + b_1^p x_i))^2 = \sum_{i=1}^{n} (y_i - \bar{y} - b_1^p(x_i - \bar{x}))^2$$

$$= \sum_{i=1}^{n} (y_i - \bar{y})^2 - 2b_1^p \sum_{i=1}^{n} (x_i - \bar{x})(y_i - \bar{y}) + b_1^{p2} \sum_{i=1}^{n} (x_i - \bar{x})^2$$

$$= (n - 1)s_y^2 - 2(1 + c)b_1((n - 1)s_x s_y r) + (1 + c)^2 b_1^2(n - 1)s_x^2$$

$$= (n - 1)s_y^2(1 - 2(1 + c)r^2 + (1 + c)^2 r^2) = (n - 1)s_y^2(1 - r^2 + c^2 r^2)$$

because $b_1 = r\, s_y/s_x$. Thus, the ratio of $\text{SS}(b_0^p, b_1^p)$ to $\text{SS}(b_0, b_1)$ is $(1 - r^2 + c^2 r^2)/(1 - r^2) = 1 + c^2 r^2/(1 - r^2)$. To interpret this ratio, first consider the case $r = 0$. When there is no linear relationship between x and y, then $r = 0$ and the ratio is 1. We interpret this as saying that it does not matter what type of estimating scheme is used if r is close to zero. Suppose that $r = 0.8$ so that x and y are highly correlated. In this case, the ratio of error sums of squares is $1 + c^2$ $0.64/0.36 = 1 + (1.778)c^2$. To interpret this ratio, suppose that we are willing to live with a 10% increase in error sums of squares in order to enjoy the protection afforded by an alternative estimate. In this case, we would require that $|c|$ $= ((1.10 - 1)/1.778)^{1/2} \approx 0.237$. That is, a slope estimate change of less than 23.7% ensures an error sum of squares change of less than 10%. This flexibility in choice of slopes for a relatively small change in the error sum of squares has led many analysts to consider alternative regression coefficient estimates.

Minimization Estimates.   Minimization estimates of regression coefficients are calculated by minimizing a function of the difference between the response and the fitted regression line. That is, we choose b_0^* and b_1^* to minimize

$$\text{SS}(b_0^*, b_1^*) = \sum_{i=1}^{n} \psi(y_i - (b_0^* + b_1^* x_i)).$$

Here, the function ψ is called a *psi function* (pronounced "sigh"). For example, choosing $\psi(x) = x^2$ yields the traditional least squares estimates. Choosing $\psi(x) = |x|$ yields the so-called *least absolute deviations* estimates. Other choices are also employed in practice. Some of the alternative choices of ψ are presented in Figure TS 3.1.

The basic idea for each of these alternatives is to not allow a residual $\hat{e}_i^* = y_i - (b_0^* + b_1^* x_i)$ to have an undue impact on the choice of parameter estimates. For example, for a large residual $\hat{e}_i^*$, choosing $\psi(x) = |x|$ means that this point provides a smaller portion of $SS(b_0^*, b_1^*)$ than the choice $\psi(x) = x^2$. Similarly, this portion would be smaller still with the choices ψ_1 and ψ_2.

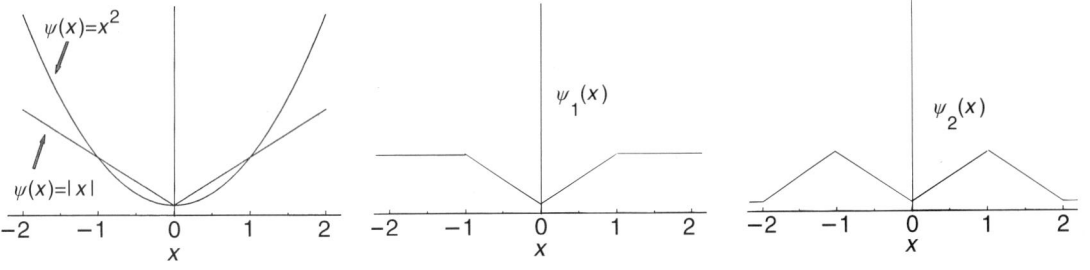

Figure TS 3.1. Plots of several ψ functions

There is a large and emerging literature on the choice of the ψ function. This literature provides a discussion of the relative merits of each choice as well as a discussion of several variants, including weighting by independent variables. A goal of this literature is to produce estimates that work well in the presence of mild violations of the ideal conditions. See Hampel, Ronchetti, et al. (1986), for an introduction to this literature.

Rank Estimates.   A classical way of producing estimates that are *robust*, or "healthy," to mild deviations of the ideal conditions is to use *rank statistics*. For a set of observations $\{y_1, ..., y_n\}$, the rank of each observation is defined to be the number of observations that are less than or equal to that observation. Specifically, we have that the rank of the jth observation is

$$R(y_j) = \text{Rank of } y_j = \text{Number of } y_i's \leq y_j = \sum_{i=1}^{n} I(y_i \leq y_j).$$

Here, I(.) is the indicator of an event. Thus, $I(y_i \leq y_j)$ equals 1 if $y_i \leq y_j$ and equals 0 if $y_i > y_j$. An important example of a rank statistic is *Spearman's correlation coefficient*. This statistic is defined using the usual correlation coefficient but replacing each variable by their rank. That is, y_j is replaced by $R(y_j)$ and similarly for x_j. In the case where there are no ties among the observations, some simplifications of the usual correlation coefficient arise. In this case, the ranks of $\{y_1, ..., y_n\}$ are simply a re-ordering, or permutation, of $\{1, 2, ..., n\}$. Thus, the average rank is $(n + 1)/2$. Similarly, it can be checked that the sum of the squared deviations of the rank is $\sum_{i=1}^{n}(R(y_i) - (n + 1)/2)^2 = \sum_{i=1}^{n}(i - (n + 1)/2)^2 = n(n^2 - 1)/12$. Thus, in the case of no ties, we can express Spearman's correlation coefficient as

$$\textit{Spearman's } r = \frac{\sum_{i=1}^{n}\left(R(x_i) - \frac{n + 1}{2}\right)\left(R(y_i) - \frac{n + 1}{2}\right)}{n(n^2 - 1)/12}.$$

In the regression context, *rank regression* coefficient estimates are defined using the values of b_0^* and b_1^* that minimize

$$SS(b_0^*, b_1^*) = \sum_{i=1}^{n}(y_i - (b_0^* + b_1^*x_i))\psi\{R(y_i - (b_0^* + b_1^*x_i))\}.$$

See, for example, Hettmansperger (1984) for a detailed introduction to this area of investigation.

CHAPTER 4

TS 4.1 Summarizing the Data

Data.   Assume that the data we have available are of the form $(x_{i0}, x_{i1}, x_{i2}, \ldots, x_{ik}, y_i)$, where $i = 1, \ldots, n$. Here, the variable x_{i0} is associated with the "intercept" term. In most applications, we assume that x_{i0} is identically equal to one and thus need not be explicitly represented. However, there are applications where this is not the case and thus, to express the model in general notation, it is included explicitly here. These observations are represented in vector notation using

$$\mathbf{y} = \begin{bmatrix} y_1 \\ y_2 \\ . \\ . \\ y_n \end{bmatrix} \quad \mathbf{X} = \begin{bmatrix} x_{10} & x_{11} & x_{12} & . & . & . & x_{1k} \\ x_{20} & x_{21} & x_{22} & . & . & . & x_{2k} \\ . & . & . & . & . & . & . \\ . & . & . & . & . & . & . \\ x_{n0} & x_{n1} & x_{n2} & . & . & . & x_{nk} \end{bmatrix}.$$

Here $\mathbf{y}$ is the vector of reponses and $\mathbf{X}$ is the matrix of explanatory variables.

Normal Equations.   From Section TS 2.6, under the least squares estimation principle, we choose $b_0^*, b_1^*, \ldots, b_k^*$ to minimize the sum of squares

$$SS(b_0^*, b_1^*, \ldots, b_k^*) = \sum_{i=1}^{n}(y_i - (b_0^*x_{i0} + b_1^*x_{i1} + \ldots + b_k^*x_{ik}))^2.$$

This can be expressed in matrix notation using $\mathbf{b}^* = (b_0^* \, b_1^* \, \ldots \, b_k^*)'$ as

$$SS(\mathbf{b}^*) = (\mathbf{y} - \mathbf{X}\mathbf{b}^*)'(\mathbf{y} - \mathbf{X}\mathbf{b}^*).$$

Taking partial derivatives with respect to each argument and setting these quantities equal to zero yields

$$\frac{\partial}{\partial b_j^*} SS(b_0^*, b_1^*, \ldots, b_k^*) = \sum_{i=1}^{n} (-2x_{ij})(y_i - (b_0^* x_{i0} + b_1^* x_{i1} + \ldots + b_k^* x_{ik}))$$

$$= 0 \qquad j = 0, 1, \ldots, k.$$

In matrix form, this can be expressed as $(\partial/\partial \mathbf{b}^*) SS(\mathbf{b}^*) = \mathbf{0}$ which yields the *normal equations*

$$\mathbf{X}' \mathbf{X} \mathbf{b} = \mathbf{X}' \mathbf{y}.$$

Here, the asterisk notation (*) has been dropped to denote the fact that $\mathbf{b} = (b_0 \, b_1 \, \ldots \, b_k)'$ are the *best* values in the sense of minimizing $SS(\mathbf{b}^*)$ over all choices of $\mathbf{b}^*$.

Least Square Estimates.   The least squares estimates are solutions of the system of equations $\mathbf{X}' \mathbf{X} \mathbf{b} = \mathbf{X}' \mathbf{y}$, called the normal equations. Assuming that $\mathbf{X}' \mathbf{X}$ is invertible, we can write the unique solution as

$$\mathbf{b} = (\mathbf{X}' \mathbf{X})^{-1} \mathbf{X}' \mathbf{y}.$$

As in the case of one independent variable regression, the least squares estimates can be expressed as weighted sums of responses. To see this, use $\mathbf{x}_i = (x_{i0} \, x_{i1} \, x_{i2} \, \ldots \, x_{ik})$ to be the row vector associated with the explanatory variables of the ith observation. With this notation, we have

$$\mathbf{X} = \begin{bmatrix} \mathbf{x}_1 \\ \mathbf{x}_2 \\ . \\ . \\ . \\ \mathbf{x}_n \end{bmatrix} \qquad \text{and} \qquad \mathbf{X}'\mathbf{y} = \sum_{i=1}^{n} \mathbf{x}_i' \, y_i.$$

Thus, define a vector of weights $\mathbf{w}_i = (\mathbf{X}' \mathbf{X})^{-1} \mathbf{x}_i'$, we have

$$\mathbf{b} = \sum_{i=1}^{n} \mathbf{w}_i \, y_i. \tag{TS4.1}$$

Variability Estimates.   Based on the vector of least squares estimates $\mathbf{b}$, we can immediately construct the vector of fitted values

$$\hat{\mathbf{y}} = \mathbf{X} \mathbf{b}.$$

That is, the ith element of $\hat{\mathbf{y}}$ is $\hat{y}_i = b_0 x_{i0} + b_1 x_{i1} + \ldots + b_k x_{ik}$. Similarly, the vector of residuals is $\hat{\mathbf{e}} = \mathbf{y} - \hat{\mathbf{y}}$. This provides the necessary ingredients for the matrix version of the error sum of squares,

$$\text{Error SS} = SS(\mathbf{b}) = (\mathbf{y} - \mathbf{Xb})'(\mathbf{y} - \mathbf{Xb}) = (\mathbf{y} - \hat{\mathbf{y}})'(\mathbf{y} - \hat{\mathbf{y}}) = \hat{\mathbf{e}}'\hat{\mathbf{e}}.$$

An alternative expression for Error SS is

$$\begin{aligned}
\text{Error SS} &= (\mathbf{y} - \hat{\mathbf{y}})'(\mathbf{y} - \hat{\mathbf{y}}) = \mathbf{y}'\mathbf{y} - 2\hat{\mathbf{y}}'\mathbf{y} + \hat{\mathbf{y}}'\hat{\mathbf{y}} \\
&= \mathbf{y}'\mathbf{y} - 2\mathbf{b}'\mathbf{X}'\mathbf{y} + \mathbf{b}'\mathbf{X}'\mathbf{y} = \mathbf{y}'\mathbf{y} - \mathbf{b}'\mathbf{X}'\mathbf{y}.
\end{aligned}$$

(TS4.2)

This expression uses the relationship $\hat{\mathbf{y}}'\hat{\mathbf{y}} = \mathbf{b}'\mathbf{X}'\mathbf{Xb} = \mathbf{b}'\mathbf{X}'\mathbf{X}(\mathbf{X}'\mathbf{X})^{-1}\mathbf{X}'\mathbf{y} = \mathbf{b}'\mathbf{X}'\mathbf{y}$. Thus, our estimate of σ^2 is the mean square error

$$s^2 = \text{Error MS} = \frac{\mathbf{y}'\mathbf{y} - \mathbf{b}'\mathbf{X}'\mathbf{y}}{n - (k + 1)}.$$

TS 4.2 Random Matrices

Expectations.   Consider the matrix of random variables

$$\mathbf{U} = \begin{bmatrix} u_{11} & u_{12} & \cdots & u_{1c} \\ u_{21} & u_{22} & \cdots & u_{2c} \\ \cdot & \cdot & \cdots & \cdot \\ \cdot & \cdot & \cdots & \cdot \\ \cdot & \cdot & \cdots & \cdot \\ u_{n1} & u_{n2} & \cdots & u_{nc} \end{bmatrix}.$$

When we write the expectation of a matrix, this shorthand for the matrix of expectations. Specifically, suppose that the joint probability function of $\{u_{11}, u_{12}, \ldots, u_{1c}, \ldots, u_{n1}, u_{n2}, \ldots, u_{nc}\}$ is available to define the expectation operator. Then

$$\text{E }\mathbf{U} \text{ means } \begin{bmatrix} Eu_{11} & Eu_{12} & \cdots & Eu_{1c} \\ Eu_{21} & Eu_{22} & \cdots & Eu_{2c} \\ \cdot & \cdot & \cdots & \cdot \\ \cdot & \cdot & \cdots & \cdot \\ Eu_{n1} & Eu_{n2} & \cdots & Eu_{nc} \end{bmatrix}.$$

As an important special case, consider the joint probability function for the random variables $y_1, \ldots, y_n$ and the corresponding expectations operator. Then

$$\text{E }\mathbf{y} = \text{E} \begin{bmatrix} y_1 \\ y_2 \\ \cdot \\ \cdot \\ \cdot \\ y_n \end{bmatrix} = \begin{bmatrix} \text{E } y_1 \\ \text{E } y_2 \\ \cdot \\ \cdot \\ \cdot \\ \text{E } y_n \end{bmatrix}.$$

By the linearity of expectations in equation (TS2.2), for a nonrandom matrix $\mathbf{A}$

and vector **B**, we have

$$E(\mathbf{A}\mathbf{y} + \mathbf{B}) = \mathbf{A} \, E \, \mathbf{y} + \mathbf{B}. \tag{TS4.3}$$

Variances.   We can also work with second moments of random vectors. The variance of a vector of random variables is called the *variance-covariance matrix*. It is defined by

$$\text{Var } \mathbf{y} = E((\mathbf{y} - E \, \mathbf{y})(\mathbf{y} - E \, \mathbf{y})').$$

That is, we can express

$$\text{Var } \mathbf{y} = E\left(\begin{bmatrix} y_1 - Ey_1 \\ \cdot \\ \cdot \\ \cdot \\ y_n - Ey_n \end{bmatrix} [(y_1 - Ey_1) \cdots (y_n - Ey_n)]\right)$$

$$= \begin{bmatrix} \text{Var } y_1 & \text{Cov } (y_1, y_2) & \cdots & \text{Cov } (y_1, y_n) \\ \text{Cov } (y_2, y_1) & \text{Var } y_2 & \cdots & \text{Cov } (y_2, y_n) \\ \cdot & & & \cdot \\ \cdot & & & \cdot \\ \cdot & & & \\ \text{Cov } (y_n, y_1) & \text{Cov } (y_n, y_2) & \cdots & \text{Var } y_n \end{bmatrix}$$

because $E((y_i - Ey_i)(y_j - Ey_j)) = \text{Cov}(y_i, y_j)$ and $\text{Cov}(y_i, y_i) = \text{Var } y_i$.

In the case that $y_1, y_2, \ldots, y_n$ are mutually uncorrelated, we have that $\text{Cov}(y_i, y_j) = 0$ for $i \neq j$ and thus

$$\text{Var } \mathbf{y} = \begin{bmatrix} \text{Var } y_1 & 0 & \cdots & 0 \\ 0 & \text{Var } y_2 & \cdots & 0 \\ \cdot & & & \cdot \\ \cdot & & & \cdot \\ \cdot & & & \\ 0 & 0 & \cdots & \text{Var } y_n \end{bmatrix}.$$

Further, if the variances are identical so that $\text{Var } y_i = \sigma^2$, then we can write Var $\mathbf{y} = \sigma^2 \mathbf{I}$, where $\mathbf{I}$ is the $n \times n$ identity matrix. For example, if $y_1, y_2, \ldots, y_n$ are i.i.d., then Var $\mathbf{y} = \sigma^2 \mathbf{I}$.

From equation (TS4.3), it can be shown that

$$\text{Var}(\mathbf{A}\mathbf{y} + \mathbf{B}) = \text{Var}(\mathbf{A}\mathbf{y}) = \mathbf{A}(\text{Var } \mathbf{y})\mathbf{A}'. \tag{TS4.4}$$

For example, if $\mathbf{A} = (a_1 \, a_2 \ldots a_n) = \mathbf{a}'$ and $\mathbf{B} = \mathbf{0}$, then equation (TS4.4) reduces to

$$\text{Var}\left(\sum_{i=1}^{n} a_i y_i\right) = \text{Var}(\mathbf{a'y}) = \mathbf{a'}(\text{Var } \mathbf{y})\mathbf{a} = (a_1 \ldots a_n)\, \text{Var } \mathbf{y} \begin{pmatrix} a_1 \\ \cdot \\ \cdot \\ \cdot \\ a_n \end{pmatrix}$$

$$= \sum_{i=1}^{n} a_i^2 \,\text{Var } y_i + 2 \sum_{i=2}^{n} \sum_{j=1}^{i-1} a_i a_j \,\text{Cov}(y_i, y_j).$$

This is the same result as in equation (TS2.4).

Multivariate Normal Distribution. A vector of random variables $\mathbf{y} = (y_1\, y_2 \ldots y_n)'$ is said to be multivariate normal if all linear combinations of the form $\Sigma_{i=1}^{n} a_i y_i$ are normally distributed. In this case, we write $\mathbf{y} \sim N(\boldsymbol{\mu}, \boldsymbol{\Sigma})$, where $\boldsymbol{\mu} = \text{E } \mathbf{y}$ is the expected value of $\mathbf{y}$ and $\boldsymbol{\Sigma} = \text{Var } \mathbf{y}$ is the variance-covariance matrix of $\mathbf{y}$. From the definition, we have that $\mathbf{y} \sim N(\boldsymbol{\mu}, \boldsymbol{\Sigma})$ implies that $\mathbf{a'y} \sim N(\mathbf{a'}\boldsymbol{\mu}, \mathbf{a'}\boldsymbol{\Sigma}\mathbf{a})$. Thus, if y_i are i.i.d. $N(\mu, \sigma^2)$, then $\Sigma_{i=1}^{n} a_i y_i$ is distributed normally with mean $\mu\Sigma_{i=1}^{n} a_i$ and variance $\sigma^2 \Sigma_{i=1}^{n} a_i^2$ as presented in equation (TS2.8).

TS 4.3 Linear Regression Model

Model Statement. The linear regression model represents the relationship between y and $(x_0, x_1, x_2, \ldots, x_k)$ as

$$y_i = \beta_0 x_{i0} + \beta_1 x_{i1} + \ldots + \beta_k x_{ik} + e_i, \qquad i = 1, \ldots, n.$$

As before, the error terms $\{e_i\}$ are assumed to be i.i.d. random variables with $\text{E } e_i = 0$ and $\text{Var } e_i = \sigma^2$. The independent variables $\{x_{i0}, x_{i1}, x_{i2}, \ldots, x_{ik}\}$ are assumed to be variables, yet non-random. Thus, by the linearity of expectations, the mean response is $\text{E } y_i = \beta_0 x_{i0} + \ldots + \beta_k x_{ik}$. Further, the variance is $\text{Var } y_i = \sigma^2$. We also use the assumption that the error distribution is normal, that is, $e_i \sim N$. By the linearity of normal random variables, we have $y_i \sim N(\beta_0 x_{i0} + \beta_1 x_{i1} + \ldots + \beta_k x_{ik}, \sigma^2)$.

Matrix Notation. In matrix notation, the basic model equation is

$$\mathbf{y} = \mathbf{X}\boldsymbol{\beta} + \mathbf{e}.$$

Here, $\text{E } \mathbf{e} = \mathbf{0}$ and $\text{Var } \mathbf{e} = \sigma^2 \mathbf{I}$. From equations (TS4.3) and (TS4.4), we have that $\text{E } \mathbf{y} = \mathbf{X}\boldsymbol{\beta}$ and $\text{Var } \mathbf{y} = \sigma^2 \mathbf{I}$. Further, in the case that the errors are normally distributed, we have $\mathbf{e} \sim N(\mathbf{0}, \sigma^2 \mathbf{I})$. By the linearity of normal random variables, this means that $\mathbf{y} \sim N(\mathbf{X}\boldsymbol{\beta}, \sigma^2 \mathbf{I})$.

TS 4.4 Finite Sample Properties of Regression Coefficient Estimates

Unbiased Estimates. With the model assumptions in Section TS4.3 and the linearity of expectations in equation (TS4.3), we have

$$\text{E } \mathbf{b} = \text{E}(\mathbf{X'X})^{-1}\mathbf{X'y} = (\mathbf{X'X})^{-1}\mathbf{X'} \text{ E } \mathbf{y} = (\mathbf{X'X})^{-1}\mathbf{X'X}\boldsymbol{\beta} = \mathbf{I}\boldsymbol{\beta} = \boldsymbol{\beta}.$$

Thus, $\mathbf{b}$ is said to be an unbiased estimator of $\boldsymbol{\beta}$. In particular, $\text{E } b_j = \beta_j$ for $j = 0, 1, \ldots, k$.

Variance–Covariance Matrix. With the model assumptions in Section TS4.3, from equation (TS4.4), it is easy to compute

$$\text{Var } \mathbf{b} = \text{Var}((\mathbf{X'X})^{-1}\mathbf{X'y}) = (\mathbf{X'X})^{-1}\mathbf{X'}(\text{Var } \mathbf{y})((\mathbf{X'X})^{-1}\mathbf{X'})'$$
$$= (\mathbf{X'X})^{-1}\mathbf{X'}(\sigma^2\mathbf{I})\mathbf{X}(\mathbf{X'X})^{-1} = \sigma^2(\mathbf{X'X})^{-1}.$$

Thus, for example, $\text{Var } b_j$ is σ^2 times the $(j + 1)$st diagonal of $(\mathbf{X'X})^{-1}$. As another example, $\text{Cov}(b_0, b_j)$ is σ^2 times the element in the first row and $(j + 1)$st column of $(\mathbf{X'X})^{-1}$.

Distribution of Regression Coefficients. Assume, in addition, that the errors are normally distributed. Further, we have $\mathbf{b} = (\mathbf{X'X})^{-1}\mathbf{X'y} = (\mathbf{X'X})^{-1}\mathbf{X'}(\mathbf{X}\boldsymbol{\beta} + \mathbf{e}) = (\mathbf{X'X})^{-1}\mathbf{X'X}\boldsymbol{\beta} + (\mathbf{X'X})^{-1}\mathbf{X'e} = \boldsymbol{\beta} + (\mathbf{X'X})^{-1}\mathbf{X'e}$. Thus, following the logic in equation (TS4.1), we have

$$\mathbf{b} - \boldsymbol{\beta} = \sum_{i=1}^{n} \mathbf{w}_i e_i.$$

Thus, because $\mathbf{b} - \boldsymbol{\beta}$ is a linear combination of normal random variables, it is also normally distributed, that is, $\mathbf{b} - \boldsymbol{\beta} \sim N$. From the expectation and variance calculation, we have $\mathbf{b} \sim N(\boldsymbol{\beta}, \sigma^2(\mathbf{X'X})^{-1})$.

TS 4.5 Inference for Linear Combinations of Estimates

Special Cases. In this subsection, we consider all linear combinations of regression coefficients, $\theta = \mathbf{a}'\boldsymbol{\beta} = \Sigma_{i=0}^{k} a_i\beta_i$. Here, $\mathbf{a} = (a_0 \, a_1 \ldots a_k)'$ is a known vector. We often focus on the two following important special cases. The first case involves choosing $\mathbf{a}$ such that $a_j = 1$ and the other as = 0, that is, $a_0 = a_1 = \ldots = a_{j-1} = a_{j+1} = \ldots = a_k = 0$. With this choice, we have $\theta = \mathbf{a}'\boldsymbol{\beta} = \Sigma_{i=0}^{k} a_i\beta_i = \beta_j$, the regression coefficient for the explanatory variable x_j. The second choice is when we have a known set of explanatory variables in mind of the form $\mathbf{x}_* = (x_{0*}, x_{1*}, \ldots, x_{k*})$. In this case, with $\mathbf{a} = \mathbf{x}_*$, we can interpret $\mathbf{a}'\boldsymbol{\beta} = \mathbf{x}_*'\boldsymbol{\beta}$ as the expected response at $\mathbf{x}_*$.

Means and Variances.   Consider a known vector $\mathbf{a} = (a_0 \, a_1 \, \dots \, a_k)'$ and the linear combination of regression coefficient estimates $\hat{\theta} = \mathbf{a}' \, \mathbf{b} = \Sigma_{i=0}^{k} \, a_i \, b_i$. From equations (TS4.3) and (TS4.4), we have

$$\mathrm{E}\,\hat{\theta} = \mathrm{E}\,\mathbf{a}'\,\mathbf{b} = \mathbf{a}'\,\mathrm{E}\,\mathbf{b} = \mathbf{a}'\,\boldsymbol{\beta} = \theta$$

and

$$\mathrm{Var}\,\hat{\theta} = \mathrm{Var}\,\mathbf{a}'\,\mathbf{b} = \mathbf{a}'\,(\mathrm{Var}\,\mathbf{b})\,\mathbf{a} = \sigma^2\,\mathbf{a}'\,(\mathbf{X}'\mathbf{X})^{-1}\,\mathbf{a}.$$

Thus, for example, we have $\mathrm{E}\,b_j = \beta_j$ and $\mathrm{Var}\,b_j = \sigma^2 \times ((j+1)$st diagonal element of $(\mathbf{X}'\mathbf{X}))$. In addition, if the errors are normally distributed, then $\mathbf{a}'\,\mathbf{b} \sim N(\mathbf{a}'\,\boldsymbol{\beta},\, \sigma^2\,\mathbf{a}'\,(\mathbf{X}'\mathbf{X})^{-1}\,\mathbf{a})$.

Standard Errors.   Replacing σ^2 by s^2 and taking the square root of Var $\hat{\theta}$ yields the standard error of $\hat{\theta}$

$$se(\hat{\theta}) = s\,\sqrt{\mathbf{a}'\,(\mathbf{X}'\mathbf{X})^{-1}\,\mathbf{a}}.$$

Further, if the errors are normally distributed, then it can be checked that

$$\frac{\hat{\theta} - \theta}{se(\hat{\theta})} \sim t_{n-(k+1)}. \tag{TS4.5}$$

Thus, for example, $(b_j - \beta_j)/se(b_j)$ has a t-distribution with $df = n - (k+1)$ degrees of freedom.

Tests of Hypotheses.   Using equation (TS4.5), as in Section TS 3.3 it is straightforward to establish tests of the hypothesis H_0: $\theta = \theta_0$. The following decision making criteria in Table TS 4.5 may be used. Here, the *test statistic* is $(\hat{\theta} - \theta)/se(\hat{\theta})$.

TABLE TS 4.5   Table of Decision Making Procedures for Testing H_0: $\theta = \theta_0$

Alternative hypothesis (H_a)	For the t-value, use $df = n - (k+1)$ and	Procedure: reject H_0 in favor of H_a if
$\theta > \theta_0$	use the significance level	*test statistic* $> t$-value
$\theta < \theta_0$	use the significance level	*test statistic* $< -(t$-value$)$
$\theta \neq \theta_0$	divide the significance level by 2	$|test\ statistic| > t$-value

Confidence Intervals.   From equation (TS4.5), we can immediately write down the corresponding confidence interval. That is, a $100(1 - \alpha)\%$ confidence interval for θ is

$$\hat{\theta} \pm (t\text{-value})\, se(\hat{\theta}),$$

where t-value is a $(1 - \alpha/2)$th percentile from a t-distribution with $df = n -$

$(k + 1)$ degrees of freedom. This immediately yields confidence intervals for partial slopes β_j and for an expected response $x'_* \beta$ as the expected response at x_*.

Predicting Future Values.　Assume we wish to predict a future value, say y_*, at a known set of explanatory variables x_*. Based on the available data, the prediction is $\hat{y}_* = x'_* b$. Using equation (TS2.5), the variance of the prediction error is

$$\text{Var}(y_* - \hat{y}_*) = \text{Var } y_* + \text{Var}(x'_* b) = \sigma^2 + \sigma^2(a' (X'X)^{-1} a),$$

because y_* and $\hat{y}_*$ are independent. Replacing σ^2 by s^2 and taking square roots, we have

$$se(pred) = s \sqrt{1 + a' (X'X)^{-1} a}.$$

It can be checked that

$$\frac{y_* - \hat{y}_*}{se(pred)} \sim t_{n-(k+1)}$$

which leads to our $100(1 - \alpha)\%$ prediction interval

$$\hat{y}_* \pm (t\text{-value}) \, se(pred).$$

Here, t-value is a $(1 - \alpha/2)$th percentile from a t-distribution with $df = n - (k + 1)$ degrees of freedom.

TS 4.6 General Linear Hypothesis

Setup.　Consider the linear regression model $y = \beta_0 x_0 + \beta_1 x_1 + \ldots + \beta_k x_k + e = x' \beta + e$, where $x = (x_0 x_1 \ldots x_k)'$. Many of the ideas about sets of regression coefficients β can be expressed as a special case of the *general linear hypothesis*. This general hypothesis can be stated as $H_0: C \beta = d$. Here, C is a $p \times (k + 1)$ matrix, d is a $p \times 1$ vector and recall that $\beta = (\beta_0 \beta_1 \ldots \beta_k)'$ is a $(k + 1) \times 1$ vector. Both C and d are user specified and depend on the application at hand. Although $k + 1$ is the number of regression coefficients, p is the number of restrictions under H_0 on these coefficients. (For those readers with knowledge of advanced matrix algebra, p is the rank of C.) This null hypothesis is tested against the alternative $H_a: C \beta \neq d$.

Test Procedure.　From the initial, or *full*, model $y = \beta_0 x_0 + \beta_1 x_1 + \ldots + \beta_k x_k + e$, run a regression to get an error sum of squares. To distinguish this from some similar quantities described in the following, call this quantity (Error SS)$_{full}$. Denote s^2_{full} to be the corresponding mean square error, defined by (Error SS)$_{full} / (n - (k + 1))$. Call the model under the hypothesis $H_0: C\beta = d$ to be the *reduced* model. Under this model, run a regression to get an error sum of squares, called (Error SS)$_{reduced}$. From these quantities, compute the test statistic

$$\text{F-ratio} = \frac{\dfrac{(\text{Error SS})_{reduced} - (\text{Error SS})_{full}}{p}}{s^2_{full}}. \tag{TS4.6}$$

Under H_0, it can be shown that the test stastic has an F-distribution with numerator degrees of freedom $df_1 = p$ and denominator degrees of freedom $df_2 = n - (k + 1)$. Thus, we may reject H_0 in favor of H_a if

$$\text{F-ratio} > \text{F-value},$$

where F-value is a $(1 - \alpha)$th percentile from an F-distribution with $df_1 = p$ and $df_2 = n - (k + 1)$ degrees of freedom.

Special Case 1—One Explanatory Variable. In Section TS 4.5, we showed how to use a test based on the t-distribution, or t-test, to investigate H_0: $\beta_j = 0$. This null hypothesis can also be investigated as a special case of the general linear hypothesis, H_0: $\mathbf{C}\boldsymbol{\beta} = \mathbf{d}$, as follows. We choose $p = 1$, $\mathbf{d}$ to be a scalar equal to 0 and $\mathbf{C}$ to be a $1 \times (k + 1)$ vector with a one in the $(j + 1)$th column and zeroes otherwise. Thus, we have

$$\mathbf{C}\boldsymbol{\beta} = [0 \cdots 0\ 1\ 0 \cdots 0] \begin{bmatrix} \beta_0 \\ \vdots \\ \beta_k \end{bmatrix} = \beta_j = 0 = \mathbf{d}.$$

With these choices of p, $\mathbf{d}$, and $\mathbf{C}$, we have that H_0: $\mathbf{C}\boldsymbol{\beta} = \mathbf{d}$ is simply another expression for H_0: $\beta_j = 0$. For the test statistic, we run a full model regression to get $(\text{Error SS})_{full}$ and s^2_{full}. The reduced model is $y = \beta_0 x_0 + \ldots + \beta_{j-1}x_{j-1} + \beta_{j+1}x_{j+1} + \ldots + \beta_k x_k + e$. Run a regression under this model to get $(\text{Error SS})_{reduced}$ and compute

$$\text{F-ratio} = \frac{\dfrac{(\text{Error SS})_{reduced} - (\text{Error SS})_{full}}{1}}{s^2_{full}}.$$

We may then reject H_0 in favor of H_a if F-ratio $>$ F-value, where F-value is a $(1 - \alpha)$th percentile from an F-distribution with $df_1 = 1$ and $df_2 = n - (k + 1)$ degrees of freedom. In this case, the numerator $(\text{Error SS})_{reduced} - (\text{Error SS})_{full}$ is called the extra sum of squares, or Type III Sum of Squares. It is produced automatically by some statistical software packages, thus obviating the need to run separate regressions.

Special Case 2—Adequacy of the Model. Consider the case where $x_{i0} \equiv 1$ and we wish to test H_0: $\beta_1 = \beta_2 = \ldots = \beta_k = 0$. This can be expressed in vector form as

$$
\begin{bmatrix} \beta_1 \\ \beta_2 \\ \cdot \\ \cdot \\ \cdot \\ \beta_k \end{bmatrix} = \begin{bmatrix} 0 \\ 0 \\ \cdot \\ \cdot \\ \cdot \\ 0 \end{bmatrix}.
$$

To express this as a special case of H_0: $\mathbf{C}\boldsymbol{\beta} = \mathbf{d}$, choose $p = k$, $\mathbf{d} = (0\ 0\ \dots\ 0)'$ to be a $k \times 1$ vector of zeroes and $\mathbf{C}$ such that

$$
\mathbf{C}\boldsymbol{\beta} = \begin{bmatrix} 0 & 1 & 0 & 0 & \cdots & 0 \\ 0 & 0 & 1 & 0 & \cdots & 0 \\ \cdot & \cdot & \cdot & \cdot & \cdots & \cdot \\ \cdot & \cdot & \cdot & \cdot & \cdots & \cdot \\ 0 & 0 & 0 & 0 & \cdots & 1 \end{bmatrix} \begin{bmatrix} \beta_0 \\ \beta_1 \\ \cdot \\ \cdot \\ \beta_k \end{bmatrix} = \begin{bmatrix} \beta_1 \\ \beta_2 \\ \cdot \\ \cdot \\ \beta_k \end{bmatrix}.
$$

Now, with H_0, the reduced model is $y = \beta_0 + e$. Running a regression model means that $(\text{Error SS})_{reduced} = \Sigma_{i=1}^{n}(y_i - \bar{y})^2 = \text{Total SS}$. Thus, our test statistic is

$$
F\text{-ratio} = \frac{\dfrac{\text{Total SS} - \text{Error SS}}{k}}{s^2} = \frac{(\text{Regress SS})/k}{s^2} = \frac{\text{Regress MS}}{\text{Error MS}}.
$$

As described in Section 4.3, we reject H_0 if F-ratio $> F$-value, where F-value is a $(1 - \alpha)$th percentile from an F-distribution with $df_1 = k$ and $df_2 = n - (k + 1)$ degrees of freedom.

Special Case 3—Testing Portions of the Model. Suppose that we are interested in comparing a full model

$$
\text{E}\, y = \beta_0 + \beta_1 x_1 + \dots + \beta_k x_k + \beta_{k+1} x_{k+1} + \dots + \beta_{k+p} x_{k+p}
$$

to a reduced model,

$$
\text{E}\, y = \beta_0 + \beta_1 x_1 + \dots + \beta_k x_k.
$$

In this case, we can express H_0: $\beta_{k+1} + \beta_{k+2} = \dots = \beta_{k+p} = 0$ as

$$
\mathbf{C}\boldsymbol{\beta} = \begin{bmatrix} 0 & \cdots & 0 & 1 & 0 & \cdots & 0 \\ 0 & \cdots & 0 & 0 & 1 & \cdots & 0 \\ \cdot & \cdots & \cdot & \cdot & \cdot & \cdots & \cdot \\ \cdot & \cdots & \cdot & \cdot & \cdot & \cdots & \cdot \\ 0 & \cdots & 0 & 0 & 0 & \cdots & 1 \end{bmatrix} \begin{bmatrix} \beta_0 \\ \cdot \\ \cdot \\ \beta_k \\ \beta_{k+1} \\ \cdot \\ \cdot \\ \beta_{k+p} \end{bmatrix} = \begin{bmatrix} \beta_{k+1} \\ \beta_{k+2} \\ \cdot \\ \cdot \\ \beta_{k+p} \end{bmatrix} = \begin{bmatrix} 0 \\ 0 \\ \cdot \\ \cdot \\ 0 \end{bmatrix} = \mathbf{d}.
$$

Thus, with this choice of $\mathbf{C}$ and $\mathbf{d}$, this is another special case of H_0: $\mathbf{C}\boldsymbol{\beta} = \mathbf{d}$. Details of this test are discussed in Section 4.6.

Special Case 4.　As an example of a test that is not described in the main body of the text, first consider the full model $y = \beta_0 + \beta_1 x_1 + \beta_2 x_2 + e$. Suppose we wish to compare this to a reduced model $y = \beta_0 + \beta_1(x_1 + x_2) + e$. For example, y might represent the price of a house, x_1 the square footage that is exposed to sunlight, and x_2 the square footage that is not exposed to sunlight, such as a basement area. Thus, $x_1 + x_2$ represents the total square footage of the house. The reduced model is a special case of the full model under the restriction H_0: $\beta_1 = \beta_2$. It is straightforward to run each model to get the error sums of squares. To write H_0 in matrix form, we have

$$\mathbf{C}\boldsymbol{\beta} = \begin{bmatrix} 0 & 1 & -1 \end{bmatrix} \begin{bmatrix} \beta_0 \\ \beta_1 \\ \beta_2 \end{bmatrix} = \beta_1 - \beta_2 = 0 = \mathbf{d}.$$

Thus, $p = 1$, which gives the final piece of information needed to compute the F-ratio and identify the degrees of freedom needed.

General Expression.　In Section TS 4.4, we discussed the result that $\mathbf{b} \sim N(\boldsymbol{\beta}, \sigma^2, (\mathbf{X}'\mathbf{X})^{-1})$. Using the techniques from Section TS 4.4, it is easy to check that $\mathbf{Cb} \sim N(\mathbf{C}\boldsymbol{\beta}, \sigma^2 \mathbf{C}(\mathbf{X}'\mathbf{X})^{-1}\mathbf{C}')$, that is, $\mathbf{Cb}$ is an unbiased estimator of $\mathbf{C}\boldsymbol{\beta}$, is normally distributed and has variance covariance matrix $\sigma^2 \mathbf{C}(\mathbf{X}'\mathbf{X})^{-1}\mathbf{C}'$. Using the theory of linear models, it can be checked that another expression for the F-ratio in equation (TS4.5) is

$$F\text{-ratio} = \frac{(\mathbf{Cb} - \mathbf{d})'(\mathbf{C}(\mathbf{X}'\mathbf{X})^{-1}\mathbf{C}')^{-1}(\mathbf{Cb} - \mathbf{d})}{ps_{full}^2}, \tag{TS4.7}$$

where s_{full}^2 is the mean square error from the full model.

TS 4.7 Simultaneous Confidence Intervals

Using the F-Distribution.　From Section TS 4.6, we saw that we may express the simultaneous hypothesis H_0: $\boldsymbol{\beta} = \boldsymbol{\beta}_0$ as a special case of the general linear hypothesis H_0: $\mathbf{C}\boldsymbol{\beta} = \mathbf{d}$ with the choice $p = k + 1$, $\mathbf{C}$ a $(k + 1) \times (k + 1)$ identity matrix, and $\mathbf{d} = \boldsymbol{\beta}_0$. Here, $\boldsymbol{\beta}_0 = (\beta_{0,0}\ \beta_{1,0} \ldots \beta_{k,0})'$ is a specified vector of regression coefficients. From equation (TS4.7), the corresponding test statistic,

$$F\text{-ratio} = \frac{(\mathbf{b} - \boldsymbol{\beta}_0)'(\mathbf{X}'\mathbf{X})(\mathbf{b} - \boldsymbol{\beta}_0)}{(k + 1)s^2},$$

has an F-distribution with $df_1 = (k + 1)$ and $df_2 = n - (k + 1)$ degrees of freedom. Similar to the ideas in Section TS 2.8, this hypothesis test may be inverted to yield a confidence region. Thus, a $100(1 - \alpha)\%$ simultaneous confidence region for $\boldsymbol{\beta}$ is all values of $\mathbf{b}^* = (b_0^* \; b_1^* \ldots b_k^*)'$ that satisfy

$$\frac{(\mathbf{b} - \mathbf{b}^*)'(\mathbf{X}'\mathbf{X})(\mathbf{b} - \mathbf{b}^*)}{(k + 1)s^2} \leq F\text{-value} \tag{TS4.8}$$

where F-value is a $(1 - \alpha)$th percentile from an F-distribution with $df_1 = (k + 1)$ and $df_2 = n - (k + 1)$ degrees of freedom. Here, recall that $\mathbf{b} = (\mathbf{X}'\mathbf{X})^{-1}\mathbf{X}'\mathbf{y}$ is the vector of least squares regression estimates.

Using the t-Distribution. From the confidence interval subsection of TS 4.5, we saw that it is straightforward to compute individual confidence intervals for each regression coefficient. For example, a $100(1 - \alpha)\%$ confidence interval for β_j is $b_j \pm (t\text{-value})se(b_j)$, where t-value is a $(1 - \alpha^*/2)$th percentile from a t-distribution with $df = n - (k + 1)$ degrees of freedom. Here α^* is a nominal confidence level. This confidence interval is based on the fact that the set

$$B_j = \{b_j - (t\text{-value})se(b_j) \leq \beta_j \leq b_j + (t\text{-value})se(b_j)\}$$

occurs with probability $1 - \alpha^*$, that is, $\text{Prob}(B_j) = 1 - \alpha^*$. From this, the probability of the complement of this set, B_j^c, occurs with probability α^*, that is, $\text{Prob}(B_j^c) = \alpha^*$.

Suppose that we now wish to establish confidence intervals for $\beta_0, \beta_1, \ldots, \beta_k$ that are jointly, or *simultaneously*, valid. To this end, from probability theory, we have that the probability of B_0 and B_1 and $\ldots$ and B_k joint occurring is

$$\text{Prob}(B_0 \text{ and } B_1 \text{ and } \ldots \text{ and } B_k) = 1 - \text{Prob}(B_0^c \text{ or } B_1^c \text{ or } \ldots \text{ or } B_k^c)$$
$$\geq 1 - (\text{Prob}(B_0^c) + \text{Prob}(B_1^c) + \ldots + \text{Prob}(B_k^c)) = 1 - (k + 1)\alpha^*. \tag{TS4.9}$$

The inequality used is known in probability theory as *Bonferroni's inequality*. Thus, using $\alpha = (k + 1)\alpha^*$, we interpret

$$b_j \pm (t\text{-value})se(b_j) \qquad j = 0, 1, \ldots, k$$

as a $100(1 - \alpha)\%$ joint, or simultaneous, confidence region for $\beta_0, \ldots, \beta_k$. Here, the t-value is a $(1 - \alpha^*/(2(k + 1)))$th percentile from a t-distribution with $df = n - (k + 1)$ degrees of freedom.

Comparison of Methods. The confidence region generated by the method using the F-distribution in equation (TS4.8) can be thought of as an ellipsoid. It is difficult to visualize and tedious to compute. In comparison, the region generated by the t-distribution, sometimes referred to as *Bonferroni confidence regions*, are easy to visualize and compute. Under the assumption of normality, the method using F-distributions is exact. In comparison, the Bonferroni method is a conservative approximation.

Bonferroni Simultaneous Hypothesis Tests. The inequality in equation (TS4.9) can also be used to generate simultaneous hypothesis tests. For example, we could reject H_0: $\boldsymbol{\beta} = \boldsymbol{\beta}_0 = (\beta_{0,0}\ \beta_{1,0} \ldots \beta_{k,0})'$ if any of the test statistics fall in the rejection region. Specifically, we reject H_0 if

$$\frac{|b_j - \beta_{j,0}|}{se(b_j)} > t\text{-value}$$

for $j = 0, 1, \ldots, k$. Here, if the significance level of the test is α, the t-value is a $(1 - \alpha^*/(2(k + 1)))$th percentile from a t-distribution with $df = n - (k + 1)$ degrees of freedom.

CHAPTER 5

TS 5.1 Expressing Models with Categorical Variables in Matrix Form

In Chapter 4, we explored the analysis for models of the form

$$\mathbf{y} = \mathbf{X}\boldsymbol{\beta} + \mathbf{e}$$

where $\mathbf{X}$ is a matrix of explanatory variables such that $\mathbf{X}'\mathbf{X}$ is invertible. In this section, we show how to use this model form for two models with categorical variables. In the next section, we will consider models where $\mathbf{X}'\mathbf{X}$ need not be invertible.

One Categorical Variable Model. Consider the model with one categorical variable introduced in Section 5.2,

$$y_{ij} = \mu_j + e_{ij} \qquad i = 1, \ldots, n_j, \quad j = 1, \ldots, c. \tag{TS5.1}$$

In this model, there are c levels of the categorical variable. As in equation (5.1), this model can be written as

$$y_{ij} = \mu_1 x_{i1} + \mu_2 x_{i2} + \ldots + \mu_c x_{ic} + e_{ij}, \tag{TS5.2}$$

where x_{ij} is an indicator variable that the observation falls in the jth level. Using matrix notation, equation (TS5.2) can be expressed as

$$
\mathbf{y} =
\begin{bmatrix}
y_{11} \\
\cdot \\
\cdot \\
\cdot \\
y_{n_1,1} \\
y_{12} \\
\cdot \\
\cdot \\
\cdot \\
y_{n_2,2} \\
\cdot \\
\cdot \\
\cdot \\
y_{1c} \\
\cdot \\
\cdot \\
\cdot \\
y_{n_c,c}
\end{bmatrix}
=
\begin{bmatrix}
1 & 0 & \cdots & 0 \\
\cdot & \cdot & \cdots & \cdot \\
\cdot & \cdot & \cdots & \cdot \\
\cdot & \cdot & \cdots & \cdot \\
1 & 0 & \cdots & \cdot \\
0 & 1 & \cdots & 0 \\
\cdot & \cdot & \cdots & \cdot \\
\cdot & \cdot & \cdots & \cdot \\
\cdot & \cdot & \cdots & \cdot \\
0 & 1 & \cdots & 0 \\
\cdot & \cdot & \cdots & \cdot \\
\cdot & \cdot & \cdots & \cdot \\
\cdot & \cdot & \cdots & \cdot \\
0 & 0 & \cdots & 1 \\
\cdot & \cdot & \cdots & \cdot \\
\cdot & \cdot & \cdots & \cdot \\
\cdot & \cdot & \cdots & \cdot \\
0 & 0 & \cdots & 1
\end{bmatrix}
\begin{bmatrix}
\mu_1 \\
\mu_2 \\
\cdot \\
\cdot \\
\mu_c
\end{bmatrix}
+
\begin{bmatrix}
e_{11} \\
\cdot \\
\cdot \\
\cdot \\
e_{n_1,1} \\
e_{12} \\
\cdot \\
\cdot \\
\cdot \\
e_{n_2,2} \\
\cdot \\
\cdot \\
\cdot \\
e_{1c} \\
\cdot \\
\cdot \\
\cdot \\
e_{n_c,c}
\end{bmatrix}
= \mathbf{X}\boldsymbol{\beta} + \mathbf{e}. \tag{TS5.3}
$$

For example, with the machine run times example described in Example 5.1, we have $c = 3$ and $n_1 = n_2 = n_3 = 4$. Thus,

$$
\mathbf{y} =
\begin{bmatrix}
1 & 0 & 0 \\
1 & 0 & 0 \\
1 & 0 & 0 \\
1 & 0 & 0 \\
0 & 1 & 0 \\
0 & 1 & 0 \\
0 & 1 & 0 \\
0 & 1 & 0 \\
0 & 0 & 1 \\
0 & 0 & 1 \\
0 & 0 & 1 \\
0 & 0 & 1
\end{bmatrix}
\begin{bmatrix}
\mu_1 \\
\mu_2 \\
\mu_3
\end{bmatrix}
+ \mathbf{e}.
$$

To make the notation more compact, we write $\mathbf{0}$ and $\mathbf{J}$ for a column of zeros and ones, respectively. In cases where the lengths of the columns are variable, a subscript is used. With this convention, another way to express equation (TS5.3) is

$$
\mathbf{y} =
\begin{bmatrix}
\mathbf{J}_1 & \mathbf{0}_1 & \cdots & \mathbf{0}_1 \\
\mathbf{0}_2 & \mathbf{J}_2 & \cdots & \mathbf{0}_2 \\
\cdot & \cdot & \cdots & \cdot \\
\cdot & \cdot & \cdots & \cdot \\
\cdot & \cdot & \cdots & \cdot \\
\mathbf{0}_c & \mathbf{0}_c & \cdots & \mathbf{J}_c
\end{bmatrix}
\begin{bmatrix}
\mu_1 \\
\mu_2 \\
\cdot \\
\cdot \\
\cdot \\
\mu_c
\end{bmatrix}
+ \mathbf{e} = \mathbf{X}\boldsymbol{\beta} + \mathbf{e}. \tag{TS5.4}
$$

Here, $\mathbf{0}_1$ and $\mathbf{J}_1$ stand for vector columns of length n_1 of zeros and ones, respectively, and similarly for $\mathbf{0}_2, \mathbf{J}_2, \ldots, \mathbf{0}_c, \mathbf{J}_c$.

Equation (TS5.4) allows us to apply the machinery developed for the regression model to the model with one categorical variable. As an intermediate calculation, we have

$$(\mathbf{X'X})^{-1} = \left(\begin{bmatrix} \mathbf{J}_1 & \mathbf{0}_2 & \cdots & \mathbf{0}_c \\ \mathbf{0}_1 & \mathbf{J}_2 & \cdots & \mathbf{0}_c \\ \cdot & \cdot & \cdots & \cdot \\ \cdot & \cdot & \cdots & \cdot \\ \cdot & \cdot & \cdots & \cdot \\ \mathbf{0}_1 & \mathbf{0}_2 & \cdots & \mathbf{J}_c \end{bmatrix} \begin{bmatrix} \mathbf{J}_1 & \mathbf{0}_1 & \cdots & \mathbf{0}_1 \\ \mathbf{0}_2 & \mathbf{J}_2 & \cdots & \mathbf{0}_2 \\ \cdot & \cdot & \cdots & \cdot \\ \cdot & \cdot & \cdots & \cdot \\ \cdot & \cdot & \cdots & \cdot \\ \mathbf{0}_c & \mathbf{0}_c & \cdots & \mathbf{J}_c \end{bmatrix} \right)^{-1}$$

$$= \begin{bmatrix} n_1 & 0 & \cdots & 0 \\ 0 & n_2 & \cdots & 0 \\ \cdot & \cdot & \cdots & \cdot \\ \cdot & \cdot & \cdots & \cdot \\ \cdot & \cdot & \cdots & \cdot \\ 0 & 0 & \cdots & n_c \end{bmatrix}^{-1} = \begin{bmatrix} \dfrac{1}{n_1} & 0 & \cdots & 0 \\ 0 & \dfrac{1}{n_2} & \cdots & 0 \\ \cdot & \cdot & \cdots & \cdot \\ \cdot & \cdot & \cdots & \cdot \\ \cdot & \cdot & \cdots & \cdot \\ 0 & 0 & \cdots & \dfrac{1}{n_c} \end{bmatrix}. \qquad \text{(TS5.5)}$$

Thus, the parameter estimates are

$$\mathbf{b} = \begin{bmatrix} \hat{\mu}_1 \\ \cdot \\ \cdot \\ \cdot \\ \hat{\mu}_c \end{bmatrix} = (\mathbf{X'X})^{-1}\mathbf{X'y} = \begin{bmatrix} \dfrac{1}{n_1} & 0 & \cdots & 0 \\ 0 & \dfrac{1}{n_2} & \cdots & 0 \\ \cdot & \cdot & \cdots & \cdot \\ \cdot & \cdot & \cdots & \cdot \\ \cdot & \cdot & \cdots & \cdot \\ 0 & 0 & \cdots & \dfrac{1}{n_c} \end{bmatrix} \begin{bmatrix} \mathbf{J}_1 & \mathbf{0}_2 & \cdots & \mathbf{0} \\ \mathbf{0}_1 & \mathbf{J}_2 & \cdots & \mathbf{0}_c \\ \cdot & \cdot & \cdots & \cdot \\ \cdot & \cdot & \cdots & \cdot \\ \cdot & \cdot & \cdots & \cdot \\ \mathbf{0}_1 & \mathbf{0}_2 & \cdots & \mathbf{J}_c \end{bmatrix} \begin{bmatrix} y_{11} \\ \cdot \\ \cdot \\ y_{n_1,1} \\ y_{12} \\ \cdot \\ \cdot \\ y_{n_2,2} \\ \cdot \\ \cdot \\ y_{1c} \\ \cdot \\ \cdot \\ y_{n_c,c} \end{bmatrix}$$

$$
= \begin{bmatrix} \frac{1}{n_1} & 0 & \cdots & 0 \\ 0 & \frac{1}{n_2} & \cdots & 0 \\ \cdot & \cdot & \cdot & \cdot \\ \cdot & \cdot & \cdot & \cdot \\ \cdot & \cdot & \cdot & \cdot \\ 0 & 0 & \cdots & \frac{1}{n_c} \end{bmatrix} \begin{bmatrix} \sum_{i=1}^{n_1} y_{i1} \\ \cdot \\ \cdot \\ \cdot \\ \sum_{i=1}^{n_c} y_{ic} \end{bmatrix} = \begin{bmatrix} \bar{y}_1 \\ \cdot \\ \cdot \\ \cdot \\ \bar{y}_c \end{bmatrix}.
\tag{TS5.6}
$$

Of course, the fact that $\bar{y}_j$ is the least squares estimate of μ_j could have been obtained directly from equation (TS5.1). However, by rewriting the model in matrix regression notation, we can appeal to Chapter 4 results and need not prove properties of models with categorical variables from first principles. That is, because this model is in regression format, we immediately have all the properties of the regression model.

To illustrate, from equation (TS5.6), the vector of fitted values is

$$
\hat{y} = Xb = \begin{bmatrix} J_1 & 0_1 & \cdots & 0_1 \\ 0_2 & J_2 & \cdots & 0_2 \\ \cdot & \cdot & \cdots & \cdot \\ \cdot & \cdot & \cdots & \cdot \\ \cdot & \cdot & \cdots & \cdot \\ 0_c & 0_c & \cdots & J_c \end{bmatrix} \begin{bmatrix} \bar{y}_1 \\ \bar{y}_2 \\ \cdot \\ \cdot \\ \cdot \\ \bar{y}_c \end{bmatrix} = \begin{bmatrix} J_1 \bar{y}_1 \\ J_2 \bar{y}_2 \\ \cdot \\ \cdot \\ \cdot \\ J_c \bar{y}_c \end{bmatrix}.
$$

This establishes $\hat{y}_{ij} = \bar{y}_j$. Now, using equation (TS4.2), we have

$$
\text{Error SS} = (y - \hat{y})'(y - \hat{y}) = \sum_{j=1}^{c} \sum_{i=1}^{n_j} (y_{ij} - \bar{y}_j)^2,
$$

and $s^2 = \text{Error MS} = (\text{Error SS})/(n - c)$. This yields the one Factor ANOVA table that appears in Section 5.1 of the main body of the text. As another example, from Section 5.2, we have that the standard error of $\hat{\mu}_j$ is

$$
se(\hat{\mu}_j) = s \sqrt{j\text{th diagonal element of } (X'X)^{-1}} = s/\sqrt{n_j} .
$$

One Categorical and One Continuous Variable Model. As another illustration, we now write this model introduced in Section 5.4 in matrix form. Recall from Section 5.4 that the model can be expressed as

$$
y_{ij} = \beta_{0j} + \beta_1 x_{ij} + e_{ij} \qquad i = 1, \ldots, n_j, \ j = 1, \ldots, c.
$$

Similar to equation (TS5.2), this can be expressed as a regression model using indicator variables as

$$
y_{ij} = \beta_{01} z_{i1} + \beta_{02} z_{i2} + \ldots + \beta_{0c} z_{ic} + \beta_1 x_{ij} + e_{ij} .
$$

Here z_{ij} is an indicator variable that the observation falls in the jth level. As in equation (TS5.4), this can be expressed as $\mathbf{y} = \mathbf{X}\boldsymbol{\beta} + \mathbf{e}$ where

$$\mathbf{X} = \begin{bmatrix} \mathbf{J}_1 & \mathbf{0}_1 & \cdots & \mathbf{0}_1 & \mathbf{x}_1 \\ \mathbf{0}_2 & \mathbf{J}_2 & \cdots & \mathbf{0}_2 & \mathbf{x}_2 \\ \cdot & & \cdot & & \cdot \\ \cdot & & \cdot & & \cdot \\ \cdot & & \cdot & & \cdot \\ \mathbf{0}_c & \mathbf{0}_c & \cdots & \mathbf{J}_c & \mathbf{x}_c \end{bmatrix} \quad \text{and} \quad \boldsymbol{\beta} = \begin{bmatrix} \beta_{01} \\ \beta_{02} \\ \cdot \\ \cdot \\ \cdot \\ \beta_{0c} \\ \beta_1 \end{bmatrix}. \tag{TS5.7}$$

As in equation (TS5.4), $\mathbf{0}_j$ and $\mathbf{J}_j$ stand for vector columns of length n_j of zeros and ones, respectively. Further, $\mathbf{x}_j = (x_{1j}, x_{2j}, \ldots, x_{n_j,j})'$ is the column of the continuous variable at the jth level.

Now, straightforward matrix algebra techniques provide the least squares estimates. In particular, the reader will find the reparameterization techniques, to be introduced in Section TS6.3, useful in the calculations.

TS 5.2 General Linear Model

The general linear model is an extension of the linear regression model defined in Section TS 4.2. That is, we begin with

$$y_i = \beta_0 x_{i0} + \beta_1 x_{i1} + \ldots + \beta_k x_{ik} + e_i, \qquad i = 1, \ldots, n,$$

or, in matrix notation,

$$\mathbf{y} = \mathbf{X}\boldsymbol{\beta} + \mathbf{e}. \tag{TS5.8}$$

Here, the error terms $\{e_i\}$ are assumed to be i.i.d. random variables with $\mathrm{E}\, e_i = 0$ and $\mathrm{Var}\, e_i = \sigma^2$. The independent variables $\{x_{i0}, x_{i1}, x_{i2}, \ldots, x_{ik}\}$ are assumed to be variables, yet nonrandom.

To distinguish the regression from the general linear model, in the former we assume that $\mathbf{X}'\mathbf{X}$ is invertible although in the latter this assumption is not made. As we have seen in Chapter 5, an important reason for this generalization relates to handling categorical variables. That is, in order to use categorical variables in the model in equation (TS5.8), the categorical variables are generally re-coded using indicator variables. For this re-coding, generally some type of restrictions need to be made on the set of parameters associated with the indicator variables. However, it is not always clear what type of restrictions are the most intuitive. By expressing the model without requiring that $\mathbf{X}'\mathbf{X}$ be invertible, the restrictions can be imposed after the estimation is done, not before.

Normal Equations.   Even when $\mathbf{X}'\mathbf{X}$ is not invertible, solutions to the normal equations still provide least squares estimates of $\boldsymbol{\beta}$. That is, recall from

Section TS 4.1 that the sum of squares is

$$SS(\mathbf{b}^*) = (\mathbf{y} - \mathbf{Xb}^*)'(\mathbf{y} - \mathbf{Xb}^*),$$

where $\mathbf{b}^* = (b_0^* \; b_1^* \; \ldots \; b_k^*)'$ is a vector of candidate estimates. Solutions of the normal equations are those vectors $\mathbf{b}^\circ$ that satisfy

$$\mathbf{X'Xb}^\circ = \mathbf{X'y}. \tag{TS5.9}$$

We use the notation $^\circ$ to remind ourselves that $\mathbf{b}^\circ$ need not be unique. However, it is a minimizer of the sum of squares. To see this, consider another candidate vector $\mathbf{b}^*$ and note that $SS(\mathbf{b}^*) = \mathbf{y'y} - 2\mathbf{b}^{*\prime}\mathbf{X'y} + \mathbf{b}^{*\prime}\mathbf{X'Xb}^*$. Then, using equation (TS5.9), we have

$$SS(\mathbf{b}^*) - SS(\mathbf{b}^\circ) = -2\mathbf{b}^{*\prime}\mathbf{X'y} + \mathbf{b}^{*\prime}\mathbf{X'Xb}^* - (-2\mathbf{b}^{\circ\prime}\mathbf{X'y} + \mathbf{b}^{\circ\prime}\mathbf{X'Xb}^\circ)$$

$$= -2\mathbf{b}^{*\prime}\mathbf{Xb}^\circ + \mathbf{b}^{*\prime}\mathbf{X'Xb}^* + \mathbf{b}^{\circ\prime}\mathbf{X'Xb}^\circ$$

$$= (\mathbf{b}^* - \mathbf{b}^\circ)'\mathbf{X'X}(\mathbf{b}^* - \mathbf{b}^\circ) = \mathbf{z'z} \geq 0,$$

where $\mathbf{z} = \mathbf{X}(\mathbf{b}^* - \mathbf{b}^\circ)$.

Unique Fitted Values. Despite the fact that there may be (infinitely) many solutions to the normal equations, the resulting fitted values, $\hat{\mathbf{y}} = \mathbf{Xb}^\circ$, are unique. To see this, suppose that $\mathbf{b}_1^\circ$ and $\mathbf{b}_2^\circ$ are two different solutions of equation (TS5.9). Let $\hat{\mathbf{y}}_1 = \mathbf{Xb}_1^\circ$ and $\hat{\mathbf{y}}_2 = \mathbf{Xb}_2^\circ$ denote the vectors of fitted values generated by these estimates. Then,

$$(\hat{\mathbf{y}}_1 - \hat{\mathbf{y}}_2)'(\hat{\mathbf{y}}_1 - \hat{\mathbf{y}}_2) = (\mathbf{b}_1^\circ - \mathbf{b}_2^\circ)'\mathbf{X'X}(\mathbf{b}_1^\circ - \mathbf{b}_2^\circ) = 0,$$

because $\mathbf{X'X}(\mathbf{b}_1^\circ - \mathbf{b}_2^\circ) = \mathbf{X'y} - \mathbf{X'y} = \mathbf{0}$, from equation (TS5.9). This establishes that $\hat{\mathbf{y}}_1 = \hat{\mathbf{y}}_2$ for any choice of $\mathbf{b}_1^\circ$ and $\mathbf{b}_2^\circ$, thus establishing the uniqueness of the fitted values.

Because the fitted values are unique, the residuals are also unique. Thus, the error sum of squares and estimates of variability are also unique.

Generalized Inverses. A generalized inverse of a matrix $\mathbf{A}$ is a matrix $\mathbf{B}$ such that $\mathbf{ABA} = \mathbf{A}$. We use the notation $\mathbf{A}^-$ to denote the generalized inverse of $\mathbf{A}$. In the case that $\mathbf{A}$ is invertible, then $\mathbf{A}^-$ is unique and equals $\mathbf{A}^{-1}$. Although there are several definitions of generalized inverses, the above definition suffices for our purposes. See Searle (1987) for further discussion of alternative definitions of generalized inverses.

With this definition, it can be shown that a solution to the equation $\mathbf{Ab} = \mathbf{c}$ can be expressed as $\mathbf{b} = \mathbf{A}^-\mathbf{c}$. Thus, we can express a least squares estimate of $\boldsymbol{\beta}$ as $\mathbf{b}^\circ = (\mathbf{X'X})^-\mathbf{X'y}$. Statistical software packages can calculate versions of $(\mathbf{X'X})^-$ and thus generate $\mathbf{b}^\circ$.

Estimable Functions. Previously, we saw that each fitted value $\hat{y}_i$ is unique. Because fitted values are simply linear combinations of parameters estimates, it seems reasonable to ask what other linear combinations of parameter estimates are unique. To this end, we say that $C\beta$ is an *estimable function* of parameters if $Cb°$ is invariant to the choice of $b°$. Because fitted values are invariant to the choice of $b°$, we have that $X = C$ produces one type of estimable function. Interestingly, it turns out that all estimable functions are of the form $LXb°$, that is, $C = LX$. See Searle (1987, page 284) for a demonstration of this. Thus, all estimable function are linear combinations of fitted values, that is, $LXb° = L\hat{y}$.

Estimable functions are unbiased and have a variance that does not depend on the choice of the generalized inverse. That is, it can be shown that

$$\mathrm{E}\, Cb° = C\beta$$

and

$$\mathbf{Var}\, Cb° = \sigma^2 C(X'X)^- C' \text{ does not depend on the choice of } (X'X)^-.$$

Testable Hypotheses. As with the linear regression case in Section TS 4.6, it is often of interest to test $H_0: C\beta = d$, where d is a specified vector. This hypothesis is said to be *testable* if $C\beta$ is an estimable function, C is of full row rank, and the rank of C is less than the rank of X. For consistency with the notation of Section TS 4.6, let p be the rank of C and $k + 1$ be the rank of X. Recall that the rank of a matrix is the smaller of the number of linearly independent rows and linearly independent columns. When we say that C has full row rank, we mean that there are p rows in C, so that the number of rows equals the rank.

General Linear Hypothesis. As in Section TS 4.6, the test statistic for examining $H_0: C\beta = d$ is

$$F\text{-ratio} = \frac{(Cb° - d)'(C(X'X)^- C')^{-1}(Cb° - d)}{ps^2_{full}}.$$

If $H_0: C\beta = d$ is a testable hypothesis and the errors e_i are i.i.d. $N(0, \sigma^2)$, the F-ratio has an F-distribution with $df_1 = p$ and $df_2 = n - (k + 1)$. Here, $s^2_{full} = \Sigma_{i=1}^n \hat{e}_i^2 / (n - (k + 1))$ is the full model mean square error.

One Categorical Variable Model. We now illustrate the general linear model by considering a reparameterized version of the model in equations (TS5.1) and (TS5.2) using

$$y_{ij} = \mu + \tau_j + e_{ij} = \mu + \tau_1 x_{i1} + \tau_2 x_{i2} + \ldots + \tau_c x_{ic} + e_{ij}$$

$$i = 1, \ldots, n_j, \quad j = 1, \ldots, c.$$

Unlike Section 5.1 of the main body of the text, at this point we do not impose additional restrictions in the parameters. Similarly to equation (TS5.4), this can be written in matrix form as

$$
\mathbf{y} =
\begin{bmatrix}
\mathbf{J}_1 & \mathbf{J}_1 & \mathbf{0}_1 & \cdots & \mathbf{0}_1 \\
\mathbf{J}_2 & \mathbf{0}_2 & \mathbf{J}_2 & \cdots & \mathbf{0}_2 \\
\mathbf{J}_3 & \mathbf{0}_3 & \mathbf{0}_3 & \cdots & \cdot \\
\mathbf{J}_4 & \mathbf{0}_4 & \mathbf{0}_4 & \cdots & \cdot \\
\cdot & \cdot & \cdot & \cdots & \cdot \\
\mathbf{J}_c & \mathbf{0}_c & \mathbf{0}_c & \cdots & \mathbf{J}_c
\end{bmatrix}
\begin{bmatrix}
\mu \\
\tau_1 \\
\tau_2 \\
\cdot \\
\cdot \\
\tau_c
\end{bmatrix}
+ \mathbf{e} = \mathbf{X}\boldsymbol{\beta} + \mathbf{e}.
$$

Thus, the $\mathbf{X'X}$ matrix is

$$
\mathbf{X'X} =
\begin{bmatrix}
n & n_1 & n_2 & \cdots & n_c \\
n_1 & n_1 & 0 & \cdots & 0 \\
n_2 & 0 & n_2 & \cdots & 0 \\
\cdot & \cdot & \cdot & \cdots & \cdot \\
\cdot & \cdot & \cdot & \cdots & \cdot \\
\cdot & \cdot & \cdot & \cdots & \cdot \\
n_c & 0 & 0 & \cdots & n_c
\end{bmatrix}.
$$

where $n = n_1 + n_2 + \ldots + n_c$. This matrix is not invertible. To see this, note that by adding the last c rows together yields the first row. Thus, the first row is an exact linear combination of the last c rows, meaning that the matrix is not full rank.

The least squares estimates can be expressed as

$$
\mathbf{b}^\circ =
\begin{bmatrix}
\mu^\circ \\
\tau_1^\circ \\
\cdot \\
\cdot \\
\cdot \\
\tau_c^\circ
\end{bmatrix}
= (\mathbf{X'X})^- \mathbf{X'y}.
$$

Estimable functions are linear combinations of fitted values. Because fitted values are $\hat{y}_{ij} = \bar{y}_j$, estimable functions can be expressed as

$$
L = \sum_{i=1}^{c} a_i \bar{y}_i
$$

where $a_1, \ldots, a_c$ are constants. This linear combination of fitted values is an unbiased estimator of

$$
E\,L = \sum_{i=1}^{c} a_i(\mu + \tau_i)
$$

Thus, for example, by choosing $a_1 = 1$, and the other $a_i = 0$, $\mu + \tau_1$ is estimable. As another example, by choosing $a_1 = 1$, $a_2 = -1$, and the other $a_i = 0$, $\tau_1 - \tau_2$ is estimable. It can be shown that μ is not an estimable parameter without further restrictions on $\tau_1, \ldots, \tau_c$.

CHAPTER 6

TS 6.1 Projection Matrix

Fitted Values and Residuals. In Section TS 4.1, we showed that the vector of least squares regression coefficients could be calculated using $\mathbf{b} = (\mathbf{X'X})^{-1}\mathbf{X'}\,\mathbf{y}$. Thus, we can express the vector of fitted values $\hat{\mathbf{y}} = (\hat{y}_1, ..., \hat{y}_n)'$ as

$$\hat{\mathbf{y}} = \mathbf{Xb}. \tag{TS6.1}$$

Similarly, the vector of residuals is the vector of responses minus the vector of fitted values, that is, $\hat{\mathbf{e}} = \mathbf{y} - \hat{\mathbf{y}}$.

Hat Matrix. From equation (TS6.1), we have $\hat{\mathbf{y}} = \mathbf{X}(\mathbf{X'X})^{-1}\mathbf{X'y}$. This equation suggests defining $\mathbf{H} = \mathbf{X}\,(\mathbf{X'X})^{-1}\,\mathbf{X'}$, so that $\hat{\mathbf{y}} = \mathbf{Hy}$. From this, the matrix $\mathbf{H}$ is said to *project* the vector of responses $\mathbf{y}$ into the vector of fitted values $\hat{\mathbf{y}}$. Alternatively, you may think of $\mathbf{H}$ as the matrix that puts the "hat," or carat, on $\mathbf{y}$. From the ith row of the vector equation $\hat{\mathbf{y}} = \mathbf{Hy}$, we have

$$\hat{y}_i = h_{i1}y_1 + h_{i2}y_2 + \ldots + h_{ii}y_i + \ldots + h_{in}y_n.$$

Here, h_{ij} is the number in the ith row and jth column of $\mathbf{H}$. As noted in Section 6.3, because of this relationship, h_{ii} is called the ith *leverage*. Because h_{ii} is the ith diagonal element of $\mathbf{H}$, a direct expression for h_{ii} is

$$h_{ii} = \mathbf{x}'_i(\mathbf{X'\,X})^{-1}\mathbf{x}_i \tag{TS6.2}$$

where $\mathbf{x_i} = (x_{i0}\,x_{i1}\,\ldots\,x_{ik})'$. From this expression, using matrix algebra results, it is easy to calculate the following bounds on h_{ii},

$$n^{-1} \leq h_{ii} \leq 1.$$

Now, because $\mathbf{H'} = \mathbf{H}$, the hat matrix is symmetric. Further, it is also an *idempotent* matrix due to the property that $\mathbf{HH} = \mathbf{H}$. To see this, we have that $\mathbf{HH} = (\mathbf{X}(\mathbf{X'X})^{-1}\mathbf{X'})(\mathbf{X}(\mathbf{X'X})^{-1}\mathbf{X'}) = \mathbf{X}(\mathbf{X'X})^{-1}(\mathbf{X'X})(\mathbf{X'X})^{-1}\mathbf{X'} = \mathbf{X}(\mathbf{X'X})^{-1}\mathbf{X'} = \mathbf{H}$. Similarly, it is easy to check that $\mathbf{I} - \mathbf{H}$ is idempotent. Now, because $\mathbf{H}$ is idempotent, from some results in matrix algebra, it is straightforward to show that $\sum_{i=1}^{n} h_{ii} = k + 1$. As discussed in Section 6.3, we use our bounds and the average leverage, $\bar{h} = (k + 1)/n$, to help identify observations with unusually high leverage.

Variance of Residuals. Using the model equation $\mathbf{y} = \mathbf{X\beta} + \mathbf{e}$, equation (TS6.1) and the hat matrix, we can express the vector of residuals as

$$\hat{\mathbf{e}} = \mathbf{y} - \mathbf{Hy} = (\mathbf{I} - \mathbf{H})(\mathbf{X\beta} + \mathbf{e}) = (\mathbf{I} - \mathbf{H})\mathbf{e}. \tag{TS6.3}$$

The last equality is due to the fact that $(\mathbf{I} - \mathbf{H})\mathbf{X} = \mathbf{X} - \mathbf{HX} = \mathbf{X} - \mathbf{X} = 0$. Using equation (TS4.3), we have

Var $\hat{\mathbf{e}}$

$$= \text{Var}[(\mathbf{I} - \mathbf{H})\mathbf{e}] = (\mathbf{I} - \mathbf{H}) \text{ Var } \mathbf{e} (\mathbf{I} - \mathbf{H}) = \sigma^2(\mathbf{I} - \mathbf{H})\mathbf{I}(\mathbf{I} - \mathbf{H}) = \sigma^2(\mathbf{I} - \mathbf{H}).$$

The last equality comes from the fact that $\mathbf{I} - \mathbf{H}$ is idempotent. Thus, we have that

$$\text{Var } \hat{e}_i = \sigma^2(1 - h_{ii}) \quad \text{and} \quad \text{Cov}(e_i, e_j) = -\sigma^2 h_{ij}. \qquad \text{(TS6.4)}$$

Thus, although the true errors e are uncorrelated, there is a small correlation among residuals $\hat{e}$.

Dominance of the Error in the Residual. Examining the ith row of equation (TS6.3), we have that the ith residual

$$\hat{e}_i = e_i - \sum_{j=1}^{n} h_{ij}e_j \qquad \text{(TS6.5)}$$

can be expressed as a linear combination of independent errors. Taking variances of each side yields

$$\text{Var } \hat{e}_i = \sigma^2(1 - h_{ii}) = \sigma^2\left((1 - h_{ii})^2 + \sum_{j \neq i} h_{ij}^2\right),$$

from equation (TS6.4). Solving for the leverage yields

$$h_{ii} = \sum_{j=1}^{n} h_{ij}^2. \qquad \text{(TS6.6)}$$

Alternatively, equation (TS6.6) may be derived directly from the relation $\mathbf{H} = \mathbf{HH}$. Because h_{ii} is, on average, $(k + 1)/n$, this indicates that each h_{ij} is small relative to 1. Thus, when interpreting equation (TS6.5), we say that most of the information in $\hat{e}_i$ is due to e_i.

Correlations with Residuals. First define $\mathbf{x}^j = (x_{1j}x_{2j} \ldots x_{nj})'$ to be the column representing the jth variable. With this notation, we can partition the matrix of explanatory variables as $\mathbf{X} = (\mathbf{x}^0\mathbf{x}^1 \ldots \mathbf{x}^k)$. Now, examining the jth row of the relation $(\mathbf{I} - \mathbf{H})\mathbf{X} = \mathbf{0}$, we have $(\mathbf{I} - \mathbf{H})\mathbf{x}^j = \mathbf{0}$. With $\hat{\mathbf{e}} = (\mathbf{I} - \mathbf{H})\mathbf{e}$, this yields

$$\hat{\mathbf{e}}'\mathbf{x}^j = \mathbf{e}'(\mathbf{I} - \mathbf{H})\mathbf{x}^j = \mathbf{0}, \qquad \text{for} \quad j = 0, 1, \ldots, k.$$

This result has several implications. If the intercept is in the model, then $\mathbf{x}^0 = (1\ 1\ \ldots\ 1)'$ is a vector of ones. Here, $\hat{\mathbf{e}}'\mathbf{x}^0 = 0$ means that $\sum_{i=1}^{n} \hat{e}_i = 0$ or, the average residual is zero. Further, because $\hat{\mathbf{e}}'\mathbf{x}^j = 0$, it is easy to check that the sample correlation between $\hat{\mathbf{e}}$ and $\mathbf{x}^j$ is zero. Along the same line, we also have that $\hat{\mathbf{e}}'\hat{\mathbf{y}} = \mathbf{e}'(\mathbf{I} - \mathbf{H})\mathbf{Xb} = 0$. Thus, using the earlier argument, the sample correlation between $\hat{\mathbf{e}}$ and $\hat{\mathbf{y}}$ is zero.

Multiple Correlation Coefficient.   For an example of a nonzero correlation, consider $r(\mathbf{y}, \hat{\mathbf{y}})$, the sample correlation between $\mathbf{y}$ and $\hat{\mathbf{y}}$. Because $(\mathbf{I} - \mathbf{H}) \mathbf{x}^0 = \mathbf{0}$, we have $\mathbf{x}^0 = \mathbf{H}\mathbf{x}^0$ and thus, $\hat{\mathbf{y}}'\mathbf{x}^0 = \mathbf{y}' \mathbf{H}\mathbf{x}^0 = \mathbf{y}'\mathbf{x}^0$. Assuming $\mathbf{x}^0 = (1 \; 1 \ldots 1)'$, this means that $\Sigma_{i=1}^{n} \hat{y}_i = \Sigma_{i=1}^{n} y_i$, so that the average fitted value is $\bar{y}$. Thus,

$$r(\mathbf{y},\hat{\mathbf{y}}) = \frac{\sum_{i=1}^{n} (y_i - \bar{y})(\hat{y}_i - \bar{y})}{(n-1)s_y s_{\hat{y}}}.$$

Now, $(n-1) s_y^2 = \Sigma_{i=1}^{n} (y_i - \bar{y})^2 = $ Total SS and $(n-1) s_{\hat{y}}^2 = \Sigma_{i=1}^{n} (\hat{y}_i - \bar{y})^2 = $ Regress SS. Further, with $\mathbf{x}^0 = (1 \; 1 \ldots 1)'$,

$$\sum_{i=1}^{n} (y_i - \bar{y})(\hat{y}_i - \bar{y}) = (\mathbf{y} - \bar{y}\mathbf{x}^0)' \, (\hat{\mathbf{y}} - \bar{y}\mathbf{x}^0) = \mathbf{y}'\hat{\mathbf{y}} - \bar{y}^2\mathbf{x}^{0'}\mathbf{x}^0$$

$$= \mathbf{y}'\mathbf{X}\mathbf{b} - n\bar{y}^2 = \text{Regress SS.}$$

This yields

$$r(\mathbf{y},\hat{\mathbf{y}}) = \frac{\text{Regress SS}}{\sqrt{(\text{Total SS})(\text{Regress SS})}} = \sqrt{\frac{\text{Regress SS}}{\text{Total SS}}} = \sqrt{R^2}.$$

That is, the square root of coefficient of determination, the multiple correlation coefficient, equals the correlation between the observed and fitted responses.

TS 6.2 Leave One Out Statistics

Notation.   To test the sensitivity of regression quantities, there are a number of statistics of interest that are based on the notion of "leaving out," or omitting, one observation. To this end, the subscript notation (i) means to *leave out* the ith observation. For example, omitting the row of explanatory variables $\mathbf{x}_i' = (x_{i0} x_{i1} \ldots x_{ik})$ from $\mathbf{X}$ yields $\mathbf{X}_{(i)}$, a $(n-1) \times (k+1)$ matrix of explanatory variables. Similarly, $\mathbf{y}_{(i)}$ is a $(n-1) \times 1$ vector, based on removing the ith row from $\mathbf{y}$.

Basic Matrix Result.   Suppose that $\mathbf{A}$ is an invertible, $p \times p$ matrix and $\mathbf{z}$ is a $p \times 1$ vector. The following result from matrix algebra provides an important tool for understanding leave one out statistics in linear regression analysis:

$$(\mathbf{A} - \mathbf{z}\mathbf{z}')^{-1} = \mathbf{A}^{-1} + \frac{\mathbf{A}^{-1}\mathbf{z}\mathbf{z}'\mathbf{A}^{-1}}{1 - \mathbf{z}'\mathbf{A}^{-1}\mathbf{z}}. \qquad \text{(TS6.7)}$$

To check this result, simply multiple $\mathbf{A} - \mathbf{z}\mathbf{z}'$ by the right side of equation (TS6.7) to get $\mathbf{I}$, the identity matrix.

Vector of Regression Coefficients. Omitting the ith observation, our new vector of regression coefficients is

$$\mathbf{b}_{(i)} = (\mathbf{X}'_{(i)}\mathbf{X}_{(i)})^{-1}\,\mathbf{X}'_{(i)}\mathbf{y}_{(i)}\,.$$

An alternative expression for $\mathbf{b}_{(i)}$ that is simpler to compute turns out to be

$$\mathbf{b}_{(i)} = \mathbf{b} - \frac{(\mathbf{X}'\mathbf{X})^{-1}\mathbf{x}_i\hat{e}_i}{1 - h_{ii}}\,. \tag{TS6.8}$$

To see equation (TS6.8), first use equation (TS6.7) with $\mathbf{A} = \mathbf{X}'\mathbf{X}$ and $\mathbf{z} = \mathbf{x}_i$ to get

$$(\mathbf{X}'_{(i)}\mathbf{X}_{(i)})^{-1} = (\mathbf{X}'\mathbf{X} - \mathbf{x}_i\mathbf{x}'_i)^{-1} = (\mathbf{X}'\mathbf{X})^{-1} + \frac{(\mathbf{X}'\mathbf{X})^{-1}\mathbf{x}_i\mathbf{x}'_i(\mathbf{X}'\mathbf{X})^{-1}}{1 - h_{ii}}\,,$$

where, from equation (TS6.2), we have $h_{ii} = \mathbf{x}'_i(\mathbf{X}'\mathbf{X})^{-1}\mathbf{x}_i$. Multiplying each side by $\mathbf{X}'_{(i)}\mathbf{y}_{(i)} = \mathbf{X}'\mathbf{y} - \mathbf{x}_i\,y_i$ yields

$$\mathbf{b}_{(i)} = (\mathbf{X}'_{(i)}\mathbf{X}_{(i)})^{-1}\mathbf{X}'_{(i)}\mathbf{y}_{(i)} = \left((\mathbf{X}'\mathbf{X})^{-1} + \frac{(\mathbf{X}'\mathbf{X})^{-1}\mathbf{x}_i\mathbf{x}'_i(\mathbf{X}'\mathbf{X})^{-1}}{1 - h_{ii}}\right)(\mathbf{X}'\mathbf{y} - \mathbf{x}_iy_i)$$

$$= \mathbf{b} - (\mathbf{X}'\mathbf{X})^{-1}\mathbf{x}_iy_i + \frac{(\mathbf{X}'\mathbf{X})^{-1}\mathbf{x}_i\mathbf{x}'_i\,\mathbf{b} - (\mathbf{X}'\mathbf{X})^{-1}\mathbf{x}_i\mathbf{x}'_i(\mathbf{X}'\mathbf{X})^{-1}\mathbf{x}_iy_i}{1 - h_{ii}}$$

$$= \mathbf{b} - \frac{(1 - h_{ii})(\mathbf{X}'\mathbf{X})^{-1}\mathbf{x}_iy_i - (\mathbf{X}'\mathbf{X})^{-1}\mathbf{x}_i\mathbf{x}'_i\mathbf{b} + (\mathbf{X}'\mathbf{X})^{-1}\mathbf{x}_ih_{ii}y_i}{1 - h_{ii}}$$

$$= \mathbf{b} - \frac{(\mathbf{X}'\mathbf{X})^{-1}\mathbf{x}_iy_i - (\mathbf{X}'\mathbf{X})^{-1}\mathbf{x}_i\mathbf{x}'_i\mathbf{b}}{1 - h_{ii}} = \mathbf{b} - \frac{(\mathbf{X}'\mathbf{X})^{-1}\mathbf{x}_i\,\hat{e}_i}{1 - h_{ii}}\,.$$

This establishes equation (TS6.8).

Cook's Distance. To measure the effect, or *influence*, of omitting the ith observation, Cook examined the difference between fitted values with and without the observation. We define Cook's distance to be

$$D_i = \frac{(\hat{\mathbf{y}} - \hat{\mathbf{y}}_{(i)})'(\hat{\mathbf{y}} - \hat{\mathbf{y}}_{(i)})}{(k + 1)s^2}\,,$$

where $\hat{\mathbf{y}}_{(i)} = \mathbf{X}\mathbf{b}_{(i)}$ is the vector of fitted values calculated omitting the ith point.

Using equation (TS6.8) and $\hat{\mathbf{y}} = \mathbf{Xb}$, an alternative expression for Cook's distance is

$$D_i = \frac{(\mathbf{b} - \mathbf{b}_{(i)})'(\mathbf{X}'\mathbf{X})(\mathbf{b} - \mathbf{b}_{(i)})}{(k+1)s^2}$$

$$= \frac{\hat{e}_i^2}{(1-h_{ii})^2} \frac{\mathbf{x}_i'(\mathbf{X}'\mathbf{X})^{-1}(\mathbf{X}'\mathbf{X})(\mathbf{X}'\mathbf{X})^{-1}\mathbf{x}_i}{(k+1)s^2}$$

$$= \frac{\hat{e}_i^2}{(1-h_{ii})^2} \frac{h_{ii}}{(k+1)s^2} = \left(\frac{\hat{e}_i}{s\sqrt{1-h_{ii}}}\right)^2 \frac{h_{ii}}{(k+1)(1-h_{ii})}.$$

This result is not only useful computationally, it also serves to decompose the statistic into the part due to the standardized residual, $(\hat{e}_i/(s(1-h_{ii})^{1/2}))^2$, and due to the leverage, $h_{ii}/((k+1)(1-h_{ii}))$.

Leave One Out Residual. The leave one out residual is defined by $\hat{e}_{(i)} = y_i - \mathbf{x}_i'\mathbf{b}_{(i)}$. It is used in computing the PRESS statistic, described in Section 6.5. A simple computational expression is $\hat{e}_{(i)} = e_i/(1-h_{ii})$. To see this, use equation (TS 6.8) to get

$$\hat{e}_{(i)} = y_i - \mathbf{x}_i'\mathbf{b}_{(i)} = y_i - \mathbf{x}_i'\left(\mathbf{b} - \frac{(\mathbf{X}'\mathbf{X})^{-1}\mathbf{x}_i\hat{e}_i}{1-h_{ii}}\right)$$

$$= \hat{e}_i + \frac{\mathbf{x}_i'(\mathbf{X}'\mathbf{X})^{-1}\mathbf{x}_i\hat{e}_i}{1-h_{ii}} = \hat{e}_i + \frac{h_{ii}\hat{e}_i}{1-h_{ii}} = \frac{\hat{e}_i}{1-h_{ii}}.$$

Leave One Out Variance Estimate. The leave one out estimate of the variance is defined by $s_{(i)}^2 = ((n-1)-(k+1))^{-1}\Sigma_{j\neq i}(y_j - \mathbf{x}_j'\mathbf{b}_{(i)})^2$. It is used in the definition of the *studentized residual,* defined in Section 6.2. A simple computational expression is given by

$$s_{(i)}^2 = \frac{(n-(k+1))s^2 - \dfrac{\hat{e}_i^2}{1-h_{ii}}}{(n-1)-(k+1)}. \tag{TS6.9}$$

To see this, first note that from equation (TS6.3), we have $\mathbf{H}\hat{\mathbf{e}} = \mathbf{H}(\mathbf{I} - \mathbf{H})\mathbf{e} = \mathbf{0}$, because $\mathbf{H} = \mathbf{HH}$. In particular, from the ith row of $\mathbf{H}\hat{\mathbf{e}} = \mathbf{0}$, we have $\Sigma_{j=1}^n h_{ij}\hat{e}_j$

$= 0$. Now, using equations (TS6.6) and (TS6.8), we have

$$\sum_{j \neq i} (y_j - \mathbf{x}'_j \mathbf{b}_{(i)})^2 = \sum_{j=1}^{n} (y_j - \mathbf{x}'_j \mathbf{b}_{(i)})^2 - (y_i - \mathbf{x}'_i \mathbf{b}_{(i)})^2$$

$$= \sum_{j=1}^{n} \left(y_j - \mathbf{x}'_j \mathbf{b} + \frac{\mathbf{x}'_j (\mathbf{X}'\mathbf{X})^{-1} \mathbf{x}_i \hat{e}_i}{1 - h_{ii}} \right)^2 - \hat{e}_{(i)}^2$$

$$= \sum_{j=1}^{n} \left(\hat{e}_j + \frac{h_{ij} \hat{e}_i}{1 - h_{ii}} \right)^2 - \frac{\hat{e}_i^2}{(1 - h_{ii})^2}$$

$$= \sum_{j=1}^{n} \hat{e}_j^2 + 0 + \frac{\hat{e}_i^2}{(1 - h_{ii})^2} h_{ii} - \frac{\hat{e}_i^2}{(1 - h_{ii})^2}$$

$$= \sum_{j=1}^{n} \hat{e}_j^2 - \frac{\hat{e}_i^2}{1 - h_{ii}} = (n - (k + 1))s^2 - \frac{\hat{e}_i^2}{1 - h_{ii}} .$$

This establishes equation (TS6.9).

TS 6.3 Omitting Variables

Notation. To measure the effect on regression quantities, there are a number of statistics of interest that are based on the notion of omitting an explanatory variable. To this end, the superscript notation (j) means to omit the jth variable, where $j = 0, 1, ..., k$. First, recall that $\mathbf{x}^j = (x_{1j} \, x_{2j} \, ... \, x_{nj})'$ is the column representing the jth variable. Further, define $\mathbf{X}^{(j)}$ to be the $n \times k$ matrix of explanatory variables defined by removing $\mathbf{x}^j$ from $\mathbf{X}$. For example, taking $j = k$, we often partition $\mathbf{X}$ as $\mathbf{X} = (\mathbf{X}^{(k)} \mathbf{x}^k)$.

Basic Matrix Result. Suppose that we can partition the $(p + q) \times (p + q)$ matrix $\mathbf{B}$ as

$$\mathbf{B} = \begin{bmatrix} \mathbf{B}_{11} & \mathbf{B}_{12} \\ \mathbf{B}'_{12} & \mathbf{B}_{22} \end{bmatrix},$$

where $\mathbf{B}_{11}$ is a $p \times p$ invertible matrix, $\mathbf{B}_{22}$ is a $q \times q$ invertible matrix, and $\mathbf{B}_{12}$ is a $p \times q$ matrix. Then

$$\mathbf{B}^{-1} = \begin{bmatrix} \mathbf{C}_{11}^{-1} & -\mathbf{B}_{11}^{-1} \mathbf{B}_{12} \mathbf{C}_{22}^{-1} \\ -\mathbf{C}_{22}^{-1} \mathbf{B}'_{12} \mathbf{B}_{11}^{-1} & \mathbf{C}_{22}^{-1} \end{bmatrix}, \qquad (TS6.10)$$

where $\mathbf{C}_{11} = \mathbf{B}_{11} - \mathbf{B}_{12} \mathbf{B}_{22}^{-1} \mathbf{B}'_{12}$ and $\mathbf{C}_{22} = \mathbf{B}_{22} - \mathbf{B}'_{12} \mathbf{B}_{11}^{-1} \mathbf{B}_{12}$. To check this result, simply multiply $\mathbf{B}^{-1}$ by $\mathbf{B}$ to get $\mathbf{I}$, the identity matrix.

Reparameterized Model. Define $\boldsymbol{\beta}^{(k)} = (\beta_0 \beta_1 \ldots \beta_{k-1})'$. With this additional notation, the model $\mathbf{y} = \mathbf{X}\boldsymbol{\beta} + \mathbf{e}$ can be rewritten as

$$\mathbf{y} = \mathbf{X}^{(k)} \boldsymbol{\beta}^{(k)} + \mathbf{x}^k \beta_k + \mathbf{e}. \tag{TS6.11}$$

Now, suppose we run a regression using $\mathbf{x}^k$ as the response vector and $\mathbf{X}^{(k)}$ as the matrix of explanatory variables. Then, the vector of "parameter estimates" is $\mathbf{A} = (\mathbf{X}^{(k)'} \mathbf{X}^{(k)})^{-1} \mathbf{X}^{(k)'} \mathbf{x}^k$. Thus,

$$\hat{\mathbf{e}}_1 = \mathbf{x}^k - \mathbf{X}^{(k)} \mathbf{A} = \mathbf{x}^k - \mathbf{X}^{(k)} (\mathbf{X}^{(k)'} \mathbf{X}^{(k)})^{-1} \mathbf{X}^{(k)'} \mathbf{x}^k$$

can be thought of as the "residuals" of this regression. Substituting $\mathbf{x}^k = \hat{\mathbf{e}}_1 + \mathbf{X}^{(k)} \mathbf{A}$ in equation (TS6.11) yields

$$\mathbf{y} = \mathbf{X}^{(k)} (\boldsymbol{\beta}^{(k)} + \mathbf{A}\beta_k) + \hat{\mathbf{e}}_1 \beta_k + \mathbf{e} = \mathbf{X}^{(k)} \boldsymbol{\alpha}_1 + \hat{\mathbf{e}}_1 \beta_k + \mathbf{e}. \tag{TS6.12}$$

With the new vector of parameters $\boldsymbol{\alpha}_1 = \boldsymbol{\beta}^{(k)} + \mathbf{A}\beta_k$, equation (TS6.12) is called a *reparameterized* version of equation (TS6.11). The reason for introducing this new parameterization is that now the vector of explanatory variables is *orthogonal* to the other explanatory variables, that is, straightforward algebra shows that $\mathbf{X}^{(k)'}\hat{\mathbf{e}}_1 = \mathbf{0}$.

With the notation $\mathbf{X}^* = (\mathbf{X}^{(k)} \ \hat{\mathbf{e}}_1)$ and $\boldsymbol{\alpha} = (\boldsymbol{\alpha}'_1 \ \beta_k)'$, we may now use least squares techniques to estimate the model $\mathbf{y} = \mathbf{X}^* \boldsymbol{\alpha} + \mathbf{e}$. To this end, by equation (TS6.10) and the orthogonality of $\mathbf{X}^{(k)}$ and $\hat{\mathbf{e}}_1$, we have

$$(\mathbf{X}^{*\prime}\mathbf{X}^*)^{-1} = \left([\mathbf{X}^{(k)'} \hat{\mathbf{e}}'_1] \begin{bmatrix} \mathbf{X}^{(k)} \\ \hat{\mathbf{e}}_1 \end{bmatrix} \right)^{-1} = \begin{bmatrix} \mathbf{X}^{(k)'}\mathbf{X}^{(k)} & 0 \\ 0 & \hat{\mathbf{e}}'_1\hat{\mathbf{e}}_1 \end{bmatrix}^{-1}$$

$$= \begin{bmatrix} (\mathbf{X}^{(k)'}\mathbf{X}^{(k)})^{-1} & 0 \\ 0 & (\hat{\mathbf{e}}'_1\hat{\mathbf{e}}_1)^{-1} \end{bmatrix}. \tag{TS6.13}$$

Thus, the vector of least squares estimates is

$$\mathbf{a} = \begin{bmatrix} \mathbf{a}_1 \\ b_k \end{bmatrix} = (\mathbf{X}^{*\prime}\mathbf{X}^*)^{-1}\mathbf{X}^{*\prime}\mathbf{y} = \begin{bmatrix} (\mathbf{X}^{(k)'}\mathbf{X}^{(k)})^{-1} & 0 \\ 0 & (\hat{\mathbf{e}}'_1\hat{\mathbf{e}}_1)^{-1} \end{bmatrix} \begin{bmatrix} \mathbf{X}^{(k)'}\mathbf{y} \\ \hat{\mathbf{e}}'_1\mathbf{y} \end{bmatrix}$$

$$= \begin{bmatrix} (\mathbf{X}^{(k)'}\mathbf{X}^{(k)})^{-1}\mathbf{X}^{(k)'}\mathbf{y} \\ (\hat{\mathbf{e}}'_1\hat{\mathbf{e}}_1)^{-1}\hat{\mathbf{e}}'_1\mathbf{y} \end{bmatrix}. \tag{TS6.14}$$

From equation (TS4.2), the error sum of squares is

$$\text{Error SS} = \mathbf{y}'\mathbf{y} - \mathbf{a}'\mathbf{X}^{*\prime}\mathbf{y} = \mathbf{y}'\mathbf{y} - \begin{bmatrix} (\mathbf{X}^{(k)'}\mathbf{X}^{(k)})^{-1}\mathbf{X}^{(k)'}\mathbf{y} \\ (\hat{\mathbf{e}}'_1\mathbf{y})'/(\hat{\mathbf{e}}'_1\hat{\mathbf{e}}) \end{bmatrix}' \begin{bmatrix} \mathbf{X}^{(k)}\mathbf{y} \\ \hat{\mathbf{e}}'_1\mathbf{y} \end{bmatrix}$$

$$= \mathbf{y}'\mathbf{y} - \mathbf{y}'\mathbf{X}^{(k)}(\mathbf{X}^{(k)'}\mathbf{X}^{(k)})^{-1}\mathbf{X}^{(k)'}\mathbf{y} - \frac{(\hat{\mathbf{e}}'_1\mathbf{y})^2}{\hat{\mathbf{e}}'_1\hat{\mathbf{e}}_1}. \tag{TS6.15}$$

We may now use this expression for the Error SS for computing several quantities of interest.

Variance Inflation Factor. We first would like to establish the relationship between the definition of the standard error of b_j given by

$$se(b_j) = s\sqrt{(j+1)\text{st } \textit{diagonal element of } (\mathbf{X'X})^{-1}}$$

and the relationship involving the variance inflation factor,

$$se(b_j) = s\,\frac{\sqrt{VIF_j}}{s_{x_j}\sqrt{n-1}}\,.$$

By symmetry of the independent variables, we only need consider only the case where $j = k$. Thus, we would like to establish

$$(k+1)\text{st diagonal element of } (\mathbf{X'X})^{-1} = VIF_k/((n-1)\,s_{x_k}^2). \qquad \text{(TS6.16)}$$

First consider the reparameterized model in equation (TS6.12). From equation (TS6.14), we can express the regression coefficient estimate $b_k = (\mathbf{\hat{e}_1' y})/(\mathbf{\hat{e}_1' \hat{e}_1})$. From equation (TS6.13), we have that $\text{Var } b_k = \sigma^2\,(\mathbf{\hat{e}_1' \hat{e}_1})^{-1}$ and thus

$$se(b_k) = s(\mathbf{\hat{e}_1' \hat{e}_1})^{-1/2}. \qquad \text{(TS6.17)}$$

Thus, the $(k+1)$st diagonal element of $(\mathbf{X^{*'}X^{*}})^{-1}$ is $\mathbf{\hat{e}_1' \hat{e}_1}$ which is also the $(k+1)$st diagonal element of $(\mathbf{X'X})^{-1}$. Alternatively, this can be verified directly using equation (TS6.10).

Now, suppose that we run a regression using x^k as the response vector and $\mathbf{X}^{(k)}$ as the matrix of explanatory variables. As noted below equation (TS6.11), $\mathbf{\hat{e}_1}$ represents the "residuals" from this regression and thus $\mathbf{\hat{e}_1' \hat{e}_1}$ represents the error sum of squares. For this regression, the total sum of squares is $\Sigma_{i=1}^{n}\,(x_{ik} - \bar{x}_k)^2 = (n-1)\,s_{x_k}^2$ and the coefficient of determination is R_k^2. Thus,

$$\mathbf{\hat{e}_1' \hat{e}_1} = \text{Error SS} = \text{Total SS}\,(1 - R_k^2) = (n-1)\,s_{x_k}^2/VIF_k.$$

This establishes equation (TS6.16).

Extra Sum of Squares. Suppose that we wish to consider the increase in the error sum of squares going from a *reduced* model

$$\mathbf{y} = \mathbf{X}^{(k)}\boldsymbol{\beta}^{(k)} + \mathbf{e}$$

to a *full* model

$$\mathbf{y} = \mathbf{X}^{(k)}\boldsymbol{\beta}^{(k)} + \mathbf{x}_k\beta_k + \mathbf{e}.$$

For the reduced model, from equation (TS4.2), the error sum of squares is

$$(\text{Error SS})_{reduced} = \mathbf{y'y} - \mathbf{y'X}^{(k)}(\mathbf{X}^{(k)'}\mathbf{X}^{(k)})^{-1}\mathbf{X}^{(k)'}\mathbf{y}. \qquad \text{(TS6.18)}$$

Using the reparameterized version of the full model, from equation (TS6.15), the error sum of squares is

$$(\text{Error SS})_{full} = \mathbf{y'\,y} - \mathbf{y'\,X}^{(k)}(\mathbf{X}^{(k)'}\mathbf{X}^{(k)})^{-1}\mathbf{X}^{(k)'}\mathbf{y} - (\hat{\mathbf{e}}_1'\,\mathbf{y})^2/(\hat{\mathbf{e}}_1'\,\hat{\mathbf{e}}_1). \qquad (\text{TS6.19})$$

Thus, the reduction in the error sum of squares by adding x^k to the model is

$$(\text{Error SS})_{reduced} - (\text{Error SS})_{full} = (\hat{\mathbf{e}}_1'\,\mathbf{y})^2/(\hat{\mathbf{e}}_1'\,\hat{\mathbf{e}}_1). \qquad (\text{TS6.20})$$

As noted in Section TS 4.6, the quantity $(\text{Error SS})_{reduced} - (\text{Error SS})_{full}$ is called the *extra sum of squares*, or Type III Sum of Squares. It is produced automatically by some statistical software packages, thus obviating the need to run separate regressions.

Establishing $t^2 = F$.　For testing the null hypothesis $H_0: \beta_k = 0$, the material in Section 4.3 provides a description of a test based on the t-statistic, $t(b_k) = b_k/se(b_k)$. An alternative test procedure, described in Sections 4.5 and TS 4.6, uses the test statistic

$$F\text{-ratio} = \cfrac{\dfrac{(\text{Error SS})_{reduced} - (\text{Error SS})_{full}}{p}}{(\text{Error MS})_{full}} = \frac{(\hat{\mathbf{e}}_1'\,\mathbf{y})^2}{s^2\,\hat{\mathbf{e}}_1'\,\hat{\mathbf{e}}_1}$$

from equation (TS6.20). Alternatively, from equations (TS6.14) and (TS6.17), we have

$$t(b_k) = \frac{b_k}{se(b_k)} = \frac{(\hat{\mathbf{e}}_1'\,\mathbf{y})/(\hat{\mathbf{e}}_1'\,\hat{\mathbf{e}}_1)}{s/\sqrt{\hat{\mathbf{e}}_1'\,\hat{\mathbf{e}}_1}} = \frac{\hat{\mathbf{e}}_1'\,\mathbf{y}}{s\sqrt{\hat{\mathbf{e}}_1'\,\hat{\mathbf{e}}_1}}\,. \qquad (\text{TS6.21})$$

Thus, $t(b_k)^2 = F\text{-ratio}$.

Partial Correlation Coefficients.　From the full regression model $\mathbf{y} = \mathbf{X}^{(k)}\boldsymbol{\beta}^{(k)} + \mathbf{x}^k\beta_k + \mathbf{e}$, consider two separate regressions. A regression using $\mathbf{x}^k$ as the response vector and $\mathbf{X}^{(k)}$ as the matrix of explanatory variables yields the residuals $\hat{\mathbf{e}}_1$, defined in Section TS 6.2. Similarly, a regression $\mathbf{y}$ as the response vector and $\mathbf{X}^{(k)}$ as the matrix of explanatory variables yields the residuals

$$\hat{\mathbf{e}}_2 = \mathbf{y} - \mathbf{X}^{(k)}(\mathbf{X}^{(k)'}\mathbf{X}^{(k)})^{-1}\mathbf{X}^{(k)'}\,\mathbf{y}.$$

From Section TS 6.1, if $\mathbf{x}^0 = (1\ 1\ \ldots\ 1)'$, then the average of $\hat{\mathbf{e}}_1$ and $\hat{\mathbf{e}}_2$ is zero. In this case, the sample correlation between $\hat{\mathbf{e}}_1$ and $\hat{\mathbf{e}}_2$ is

$$r(\hat{\mathbf{e}}_1, \hat{\mathbf{e}}_2) = \frac{\sum\limits_{i=1}^{n} \hat{e}_{1i}\,\hat{e}_{2i}}{\sqrt{\left(\sum\limits_{i=1}^{n} \hat{e}_{i1}^2\right)\left(\sum\limits_{i=1}^{n} \hat{e}_{i2}^2\right)}} = \frac{\hat{\mathbf{e}}_1'\,\hat{\mathbf{e}}_2}{\sqrt{(\hat{\mathbf{e}}_1'\,\hat{\mathbf{e}}_1)(\hat{\mathbf{e}}_2'\,\hat{\mathbf{e}}_2)}}\,.$$

Because $\hat{\mathbf{e}}_1$ is a vector of residuals using $\mathbf{X}^{(k)}$ as the matrix of explanatory variables, from Section TS 6.1, we have that $\hat{\mathbf{e}}_1' \mathbf{X}^{(k)} = 0$. Thus, for the numerator, we have $\hat{\mathbf{e}}_1' \hat{\mathbf{e}}_2 = \hat{\mathbf{e}}_1' (\mathbf{y} - \mathbf{X}^{(k)} (\mathbf{X}^{(k)'} \mathbf{X}^{(k)})^{-1} \mathbf{X}^{(k)'} \mathbf{y}) = \hat{\mathbf{e}}_1' \mathbf{y}$. From equations (TS6.18) and (TS6.19), we have that

$$(n - (k+1)) s^2 = (\text{Error SS})_{full} = \hat{\mathbf{e}}_2' \hat{\mathbf{e}}_2 - (\hat{\mathbf{e}}_1' \mathbf{y})^2 / (\hat{\mathbf{e}}_1' \hat{\mathbf{e}}_1) = \hat{\mathbf{e}}_2' \hat{\mathbf{e}}_2 - (\hat{\mathbf{e}}_1' \hat{\mathbf{e}}_2)^2 / (\hat{\mathbf{e}}_1' \hat{\mathbf{e}}_1).$$

Thus, from equation (TS6.21)

$$\frac{t(b_k)}{\sqrt{t(b_k)^2 + n - (k+1)}} = \frac{\hat{\mathbf{e}}_1' \mathbf{y} / (s \sqrt{\hat{\mathbf{e}}_1' \hat{\mathbf{e}}_1})}{\sqrt{\dfrac{(\hat{\mathbf{e}}_1' \mathbf{y})^2}{s^2 \hat{\mathbf{e}}_1' \hat{\mathbf{e}}_1} + n - (k+1)}}$$

$$= \frac{\hat{\mathbf{e}}_1' \mathbf{y}}{\sqrt{(\hat{\mathbf{e}}_1' \mathbf{y})^2 + \hat{\mathbf{e}}_1' \hat{\mathbf{e}}_1 s^2 (n - (k+1))}}$$

$$= \frac{\hat{\mathbf{e}}_1' \hat{\mathbf{e}}_2}{\sqrt{(\hat{\mathbf{e}}_1' \hat{\mathbf{e}}_2)^2 + \hat{\mathbf{e}}_1' \hat{\mathbf{e}}_1 \left(\hat{\mathbf{e}}_2' \hat{\mathbf{e}}_2 - \dfrac{(\hat{\mathbf{e}}_1' \hat{\mathbf{e}}_2)^2}{\hat{\mathbf{e}}_1' \hat{\mathbf{e}}_1} \right)}}$$

$$= \frac{\hat{\mathbf{e}}_1' \hat{\mathbf{e}}_2}{\sqrt{(\hat{\mathbf{e}}_1' \hat{\mathbf{e}}_1)(\hat{\mathbf{e}}_2' \hat{\mathbf{e}}_2)}} = r(\hat{\mathbf{e}}_1', \hat{\mathbf{e}}_2).$$

This establishes the relationship between the partial correlation coefficient and the t-ratio statistic.

TS 6.4 Effect of Model Misspecification

Notation. Partition the matrix of explanatory variables $\mathbf{X}$ into two submatrices, each having n rows, so that $\mathbf{X} = (\mathbf{X}_1 \, \mathbf{X}_2)$. For convenience, assume that $\mathbf{X}_1$ is an $n \times p$ matrix. Similarly, partition the vector of parameters $\boldsymbol{\beta} = (\boldsymbol{\beta}_1' \boldsymbol{\beta}_2')'$ such that $\mathbf{X}\boldsymbol{\beta} = \mathbf{X}_1 \boldsymbol{\beta}_1 + \mathbf{X}_2 \boldsymbol{\beta}_2$. We compare the full, or "long," model

$$\mathbf{y} = \mathbf{X}\boldsymbol{\beta} + \mathbf{e} = \mathbf{X}_1 \boldsymbol{\beta}_1 + \mathbf{X}_2 \boldsymbol{\beta}_2 + \mathbf{e}$$

to the reduced, or "short," model

$$\mathbf{y} = \mathbf{X}_1 \boldsymbol{\beta}_1 + \mathbf{e}.$$

This simply generalizes the set-up in Section TS 6.3 to allow for omitting several variables.

Effect of Underfitting. Suppose that the true representation is the long model but we mistakenly run the short model. Our parameter estimates when running the short model are given by $\mathbf{b}_1 = (\mathbf{X}_1' \mathbf{X}_1)^{-1} \mathbf{X}_1' \mathbf{y}$. These estimates are biased because

$$\text{Bias} = \text{E } \mathbf{b}_1 - \boldsymbol{\beta}_1 = \text{E}(\mathbf{X}_1'\mathbf{X}_1)^{-1} \mathbf{X}_1'\mathbf{y} - \boldsymbol{\beta}_1 = (\mathbf{X}_1'\mathbf{X}_1)^{-1} \mathbf{X}_1'\text{E } \mathbf{y} - \boldsymbol{\beta}_1$$

$$= (\mathbf{X}_1'\mathbf{X}_1)^{-1} \mathbf{X}_1'(\mathbf{X}_1\boldsymbol{\beta}_1 + \mathbf{X}_2\boldsymbol{\beta}_2) - \boldsymbol{\beta}_1 = (\mathbf{X}_1'\mathbf{X}_1)^{-1} \mathbf{X}_1'\mathbf{X}_2\boldsymbol{\beta}_2 = \mathbf{A}\boldsymbol{\beta}_2.$$

Here, $\mathbf{A} = (\mathbf{X}_1'\mathbf{X}_1)^{-1} \mathbf{X}_1'\mathbf{X}_2$ is called the *alias*, or bias, matrix. When running the short model, the estimated variance is $s_1^2 = (\mathbf{y}'\mathbf{y} - \mathbf{b}_1'\mathbf{X}_1'\mathbf{y})/(n - p)$. It can be shown that

$$\text{E } s_1^2 = \sigma^2 + (n - p)^{-1} \boldsymbol{\beta}_2'(\mathbf{X}_2'\mathbf{X}_2 - \mathbf{X}_2'\mathbf{X}_1 (\mathbf{X}_1'\mathbf{X}_1)^{-1} \mathbf{X}_1'\mathbf{X}_2)\boldsymbol{\beta}_2. \qquad \text{(TS6.21)}$$

Thus, s_1^2 is an "overbiased" estimate of σ^2.

Let $\mathbf{x}_{1i}'$ and $\mathbf{x}_{2i}'$ be the ith rows of $\mathbf{X}_1$ and $\mathbf{X}_2$, respectively. Using the fitted short model, the ith fitted value is $\hat{y}_{1i} = \mathbf{x}_{1i}'\mathbf{b}_1$. The true ith expected response is $\text{E } y_i = \mathbf{x}_{1i}'\boldsymbol{\beta}_1 + \mathbf{x}_{2i}'\boldsymbol{\beta}_2$. Thus, the bias of the ith fitted value is

$$\text{Bias }(\hat{y}_{1i}) = \text{E } \hat{y}_{1i} - Ey_i = \mathbf{x}_{1i}'\text{ E } \mathbf{b}_1 - (\mathbf{x}_{1i}'\boldsymbol{\beta}_1 + \mathbf{x}_{2i}'\boldsymbol{\beta}_2)$$

$$= \mathbf{x}_{1i}'(\boldsymbol{\beta}_1 + \mathbf{A}\boldsymbol{\beta}_2) - (\mathbf{x}_{1i}'\boldsymbol{\beta}_1 + \mathbf{x}_{2i}'\boldsymbol{\beta}_2) = (\mathbf{x}_{1i}'\mathbf{A} - \mathbf{x}_{2i}')\boldsymbol{\beta}_2.$$

Using this and equation (T6.21), straightforward algebra show that

$$\text{E } s_1^2 = \sigma^2 + (n - p)^{-1}\Sigma_{i=1}^n (\text{Bias}(\hat{y}_{1i}))^2. \qquad \text{(TS6.22)}$$

Effect of Overfitting. Now suppose that the true representation is the short model but we mistakenly use the large model. As in Section TS 6.3, with the alias matrix $\mathbf{A} = (\mathbf{X}_1'\mathbf{X}_1)^{-1}\mathbf{X}_1'\mathbf{X}_2$, we can *reparameterize* the long model

$$\mathbf{y} = \mathbf{X}_1\boldsymbol{\beta}_1 + \mathbf{X}_2\boldsymbol{\beta}_2 + \mathbf{e} = \mathbf{X}_1(\boldsymbol{\beta}_1 + \mathbf{A}\boldsymbol{\beta}_2) + \mathbf{E}_1\boldsymbol{\beta}_2 + \mathbf{e} = \mathbf{X}_1\boldsymbol{\alpha}_1 + \mathbf{E}_2\boldsymbol{\beta}_2 + \mathbf{e}$$

where $\mathbf{E}_1 = \mathbf{X}_2 - \mathbf{X}_2\mathbf{A}$ and $\boldsymbol{\alpha}_1 = \boldsymbol{\beta}_1 + \mathbf{A}\boldsymbol{\beta}_2$. The advantage of this new parameterization is that $\mathbf{X}_1$ is orthogonal to $\mathbf{E}_1$ because $\mathbf{X}_1'\mathbf{E}_1 = \mathbf{X}_1'(\mathbf{X}_2 - \mathbf{X}_1\mathbf{A}) = \mathbf{0}$. Following Section TS 6.3, with $\mathbf{X}^* = (\mathbf{X}_1\mathbf{E}_1)$ and $\boldsymbol{\alpha} = (\boldsymbol{\alpha}_1'\boldsymbol{\beta}_1')'$, the vector of least square estimates is

$$\mathbf{a} = \begin{bmatrix} \mathbf{a}_1 \\ \mathbf{b}_1 \end{bmatrix} = (\mathbf{X}^{*\prime}\mathbf{X}^*)^{-1}\mathbf{X}^{*\prime}\mathbf{y}$$

$$= \begin{bmatrix} (\mathbf{X}_1'\mathbf{X}_1)^{-1} & 0 \\ 0 & (\mathbf{E}_1'\mathbf{E}_1)^{-1} \end{bmatrix}\begin{bmatrix} \mathbf{X}_1'\mathbf{y} \\ \mathbf{E}_1'\mathbf{y} \end{bmatrix} = \begin{bmatrix} (\mathbf{X}_1'\mathbf{X}_1)^{-1}\mathbf{X}_1'\mathbf{y} \\ (\mathbf{E}_1'\mathbf{E}_1)^{-1}\mathbf{E}_1'\mathbf{y} \end{bmatrix}.$$

From the true (short) model, $\text{E } \mathbf{y} = \mathbf{X}_1\boldsymbol{\beta}_1$, we have that $\text{E } \mathbf{b}_2 = (\mathbf{E}_1'\mathbf{E}_1)^{-1}\mathbf{E}_1'\text{E } \mathbf{y} = (\mathbf{E}_1'\mathbf{E}_1)^{-1} \mathbf{E}_1'\text{E}(\mathbf{X}_1\boldsymbol{\beta}_1) = \mathbf{0}$, because $\mathbf{X}_1'\mathbf{E}_1 = \mathbf{0}$. The least squares estimate of $\boldsymbol{\beta}_1$ is $\mathbf{b}_1 = \mathbf{a}_1 - \mathbf{A}\mathbf{b}_2$. Because $\text{E } \mathbf{a}_1 = (\mathbf{X}_1'\mathbf{X}_1)^{-1}\mathbf{X}_1'\text{ E } \mathbf{y} = \boldsymbol{\beta}_1$ under the short model, we have $\text{E } \mathbf{b}_1 = \text{E } \mathbf{a}_1 - \mathbf{A} \text{ E } \mathbf{b}_2 = \boldsymbol{\beta}_1 - 0 = \boldsymbol{\beta}_1$. Thus, even though we mistakenly run the long model, $\mathbf{b}_1$ is still an unbiased estimator of $\boldsymbol{\beta}_1$ and $\mathbf{b}_2$ is an unbiased estimator of $\mathbf{0}$. Thus, there is no bias in the ith fitted value because $\text{E } \hat{y}_i = \text{E } (\mathbf{x}_{1i}'\mathbf{b}_1 + \mathbf{x}_{2i}'\mathbf{b}_2) = \mathbf{x}_{1i}'\boldsymbol{\beta}_1 = \text{E } y_i$.

C_p **Statistic.** Suppose initially that the true representation is the long model but we mistakenly use the short model. The ith fitted value is $\hat{y}_{1i} = \mathbf{x}'_{1i}\mathbf{b}_1$ that has mean square error

$$\text{MSE } \hat{y}_{1i} = \text{E } (\hat{y}_{1i} - \text{E } \hat{y}_{1i})^2 = \text{Var } \hat{y}_{1i} + (\text{Bias } \hat{y}_{1i})^2.$$

For the first part, we have that $\text{Var } \hat{y}_{1i} = \text{Var } (\mathbf{x}'_{1i}\mathbf{b}_1) = \text{Var } (\mathbf{x}'_{1i}(\mathbf{X}'_1\mathbf{X}_1)^{-1}\mathbf{X}'_1\mathbf{y})$ $= \sigma^2 \mathbf{x}_{1i}(\mathbf{X}'_1\mathbf{X}_1)^{-1}\mathbf{x}'_{1i}$. We can think of $\mathbf{x}_{1i}(\mathbf{X}'_1\mathbf{X}_1)^{-1}\mathbf{x}'_{1i}$ as the ith leverage, as in equation (TS6.2). Thus, as noted in Section TS 6.1, we have that $\Sigma_{i=1}^{n} \mathbf{x}_{1i}(\mathbf{X}'_1\mathbf{X}_1)^{-1}\mathbf{x}'_{1i} = p$, the number of columns of $\mathbf{X}_1$. With this, we can define the *standardized total error*

$$\frac{\sum_{i=1}^{n} \text{MSE } \hat{y}_{1i}}{\sigma^2} = \frac{\sum_{i=1}^{n} (\text{Var } \hat{y}_{1i} + (\text{Bias } \hat{y}_{1i})^2)}{\sigma^2}$$

$$= \frac{\sigma^2 \sum_{i=1}^{n} (\mathbf{x}_{1i}(\mathbf{X}'_1\mathbf{X}_1)^{-1}\mathbf{x}'_{1i} + (\text{Bias } \hat{y}_{1i})^2)}{\sigma^2} = p + \sigma^{-2} \sum_{i=1}^{n} (\text{Bias } \hat{y}_{1i})^2.$$

Now, if σ^2 is known, from equation (TS6.22), an unbiased estimate of the standardized total error is

$$p + (n - p)(s_1^2 - \sigma^2)/\sigma^2.$$

Because σ^2 is unknown, it must be estimated. If we are not sure whether the long or short model is the appropriate representation, a conservative choice is to use s^2 from the long, or full, model. Even if the short model is the true model, s^2 from the long model is still an unbiased estimate of σ^2. Thus, we define

$$C_p = p + (n - p)(s_1^2 - s^2)/s^2.$$

If the short model is correct, then $\text{E } s_1^2 = \text{E } s^2 = \sigma^2$ and $\text{E } C_p \approx p$. If the long model is true, then $\text{E } s_1^2 > \sigma^2$ and $\text{E } C_p > p$.

TS 6.5 Maximum Likelihood Estimation and Box-Cox Family of Transformations

Likelihood Functions. In Section TS2.2, we introduced the notion of a joint probability function for a set of random variables $y_1, \ldots y_n$. When this function is evaluated at a set of realizations, we call this a *likelihood function*. In this subsection, we are interested in cases where y is a function of a vector of parameters $\boldsymbol{\theta}$. As an important example, we consider the case where $y_i = \mathbf{x}'_i\boldsymbol{\beta} + e_i$ and $\{e_i\}$ are i.i.d. $N(0, \sigma^2)$. In this case, we have that $y_i \sim N(\mathbf{x}'_i\boldsymbol{\beta},\sigma^2)$ and the $\{y_i\}$ are independent. Thus, the likelihood is

$$\text{Likelihood} = \prod_{i=1}^{n} \frac{1}{\sqrt{2\pi\sigma^2}} \exp\left(-\frac{(y_i - \mathbf{x}'_i\boldsymbol{\beta})^2}{2\sigma^2}\right) \tag{TS6.23}$$

Thus, $\boldsymbol{\theta}$ is made up of $\boldsymbol{\beta}$ and σ^2. In general, we have that

$$\text{Likelihood} = f(y_1, \ldots, y_n; \boldsymbol{\theta}) \tag{TS6.24}$$

where f(.) is either the joint probability mass function or the joint probability density function of $y_1, \ldots, y_n$, depending on whether the random variables are discrete or continuous. The presence of the vector of parameters $\boldsymbol{\theta}$ is explicitly denoted with the notation in equation (TS6.24).

Maximum Likelihood Estimation. The maximum likelihood estimate of $\boldsymbol{\theta}$, denoted by $\hat{\boldsymbol{\theta}}$, is simply that value of $\boldsymbol{\theta}$ that maximizes the likelihood in equation (TS6.24). In the case that $\{y_i\}$ are independent, we can write

$$\text{Log likelihood} = \mathcal{L}(\boldsymbol{\theta}) = \sum_{i=1}^{n} \ln f(y_i; \boldsymbol{\theta}).$$

Finding the maximum of a function is equivalent to finding the maximum of the logarithm of a function. Compared to the likelihood, it is computationally simpler to find the maximum of the log likelihood in many cases. For example, consider the likelihood in equation (TS6.23). Here, we have

$$\mathcal{L}(\boldsymbol{\theta}) = -\frac{n}{2} \ln(2\pi\sigma^2) - \sum_{i=1}^{n} \frac{(y_i - \mathbf{x}_i'\boldsymbol{\beta})^2}{2\sigma^2}$$

with $\boldsymbol{\theta} = (\boldsymbol{\beta}', \sigma^2)'$. After some algebra, we see that maximizing this function yields $\hat{\boldsymbol{\beta}} = (\mathbf{X}'\mathbf{X})^{-1}\mathbf{X}'\mathbf{y}$ and $\hat{\sigma}^2 = n^{-1}\sum_{i=1}^{n}(y_i - \mathbf{x}_i'\hat{\boldsymbol{\beta}})^2$. In particular, the maximum likelihood estimates of the regression coefficients are the same as the ordinary least squares. Note that under the maximum likelihood principle, we assume the normality of the errors, although this assumption was not needed using the least squares estimation principle. In general, maximum likelihood and least squares produce different estimators, even under the normality assumptions. For example, the least squares estimate of σ^2 is $s^2 = (n - (k + 1))^{-1} \sum_{i=1}^{n}(y_i - \hat{y}_i)^2$ although the maximum likelihood estimate is $\hat{\sigma}^2 = n/(n - (k + 1))s^2$.

Box-Cox Family of Transformations. The Box-Cox family of power transformations is defined by

$$y^{(\lambda)} = \begin{cases} \dfrac{y^{\lambda} - 1}{\lambda} & \lambda \neq 0 \\ \ln y & \lambda = 0 \end{cases},$$

for positive values of y. We consider here the model

$$h(y_i, \lambda) = \mathbf{x}_i'\boldsymbol{\beta} + e_i \tag{TS6.25}$$

where h is a function that is known up to the parameter λ. The function h may be in the Box-Cox family or, as another example, may be a member of the family suggested by John and Draper (1980)

$$
h(y,\lambda) = \begin{cases} sign(y)\,\dfrac{(1 + |y|)^\lambda - 1}{\lambda} & \lambda \neq 0 \\[2ex] sign(y)\,\ln(1 + |y|) & \lambda = 0 \end{cases},
$$

that handles responses that may be negative. See Carroll and Ruppert (1988) for further discussion of the choice of the transformation function.

Assume that the errors e_i are i.i.d. $N(0, \sigma^2)$. To discuss the probability density function of $\{y\}$, we first need the *Jacobian* of the transformation that maps y into $h(y, \lambda)$. From, for example, Hogg and Craig (1978, Section 4.3), the Jacobian is $J(y, \lambda) = (\partial/\partial y)\, h(y, \lambda)$. To illustrate, for the Box-Cox family, we have $J(y, \lambda) = y^{\lambda-1}$. Thus, the probability density function of $h(y,\lambda)$ is

$$
g(y_i) = \frac{1}{\sqrt{2\pi\sigma^2}} \exp\left(-\frac{(h(y_i,\lambda) - \mathbf{x}_i'\boldsymbol{\beta})^2}{2\sigma^2}\right) J(y_i, \lambda).
$$

Thus, we can write the log likelihood of $h(y_1,\lambda), \ldots, h(y_n, \lambda)$ as

$$
\mathscr{L}(\boldsymbol{\beta},\sigma^2,\lambda) = -\frac{n}{2}\ln(2\pi\sigma^2) - \frac{1}{2\sigma^2}\sum_{i=1}^{n}(h(y_i,\lambda) - \mathbf{x}_i'\boldsymbol{\beta})^2 + \sum_{i=1}^{n}\ln J_i(\lambda),
$$

where $J_i(\lambda), = J(y_i, \lambda)$. For a fixed $\boldsymbol{\beta}$ and λ, $\mathscr{L}$ is maximized in σ^2 by

$$
\hat{\sigma}^2(\boldsymbol{\beta},\lambda) = \frac{1}{n}\sum_{i=1}^{n}(h(y_i,\lambda) - \mathbf{x}_i'\boldsymbol{\beta})^2.
$$

Putting this is $\mathscr{L}$, we would like to find $\boldsymbol{\beta}$ and λ that maximizes

$$
\mathscr{L}_{\max}(\boldsymbol{\beta},\lambda) = \mathscr{L}(\hat{\sigma}^2(\boldsymbol{\beta},\lambda),\boldsymbol{\beta},\lambda) = -\frac{n}{2}\ln(2\pi\hat{\sigma}^2(\boldsymbol{\beta},\lambda)) - \frac{n}{2} + \sum_{i=1}^{n}\ln J_i(\lambda)
$$

$$
= -\frac{n}{2}\ln\left(\frac{\hat{\sigma}^2(\boldsymbol{\beta},\lambda)}{(\dot{J}(\lambda))^2}\right) - \frac{n}{2}(1 + \log 2\pi)
$$

where $\dot{J} = (\Pi_{i=1}^{n} J(y_i,\lambda))^{1/n}$ is the geometric mean of $J(y_1,\lambda), \ldots, J(y_n, \lambda)$. With the Box-Cox family, we have $J(y_i, \lambda) = \dot{y}_i^{\lambda-1}$. Thus, $\dot{J} = \dot{y}^{\lambda-1}$, where $\dot{y} = (\Pi_{i=1}^{n} y_i)^{1/n}$ is the geometric mean of $y_1, \ldots, y_n$. This yields

$$
\mathscr{L}_{\max}(\boldsymbol{\beta},\lambda) = -\frac{n}{2}\ln\left(\frac{\hat{\sigma}^2(\boldsymbol{\beta},\lambda)}{\dot{y}^{2(\lambda-1)}}\right) - \frac{n}{2}(1 + \ln 2\pi).
$$

Therefore, we choose $\hat{\boldsymbol{\beta}}$ and $\hat{\lambda}$ to minimize

$$\sum_{i=1}^{n} \left(\frac{w_i - \mathbf{x}_i'\boldsymbol{\beta}}{\dot{y}^{\lambda-1}} \right)^2$$

where $w_i = \mathrm{h}(y_i, \lambda)$. This can be accomplished either by using a grid search (over λ) or by using a nonlinear minimization routine. See Myers (1990, page 310) or Draper and Smith (1981, page 225) for further details.

CHAPTER 8

TS 8.1 Weighted and Generalized Least Squares Estimates

Model Statement.   We now extend the model described in Section TS 4.3 to the case where

$$\mathbf{y} = \mathbf{X}\boldsymbol{\beta} + \mathbf{e}, \tag{TS8.1}$$

with $\mathrm{E}\,\mathbf{e} = \mathbf{0}$ and $\mathrm{Var}\,\mathbf{e} = \sigma^2\,\boldsymbol{\Sigma}$. Here, $\sigma^2\boldsymbol{\Sigma}$ is an $n \times n$ variance-covariance matrix. Thus, $\boldsymbol{\Sigma}$ is square and symmetric. Because $\mathbf{a}'\boldsymbol{\Sigma}\mathbf{a} = \mathrm{Var}(\mathbf{a}'\mathbf{e}) \geq 0$ for every vector $\mathbf{a}$, $\boldsymbol{\Sigma}$ is said to be *positive semidefinite*. We will assume that $\mathbf{a}'\boldsymbol{\Sigma}\mathbf{a} > 0$ for every vector $\mathbf{a}$; in this case, $\boldsymbol{\Sigma}$ is said to be *positive definite*. It can be shown (see example, Graybill, 1983, Chapter 12), for a positive definite $\boldsymbol{\Sigma}$, that there exists a matrix, say $\boldsymbol{\Sigma}^{-1/2}$, such that $\boldsymbol{\Sigma}^{-1/2}\,\boldsymbol{\Sigma}\boldsymbol{\Sigma}^{-1/2} = \mathbf{I}$.

Optimal Estimates.   We can premultiply each side of equation (TS8.1) by $\boldsymbol{\Sigma}^{-1/2}$ to get

$$\mathbf{y}^* = \mathbf{X}^*\boldsymbol{\beta} + \mathbf{e}^*, \tag{TS8.2}$$

where $\mathbf{y}^* = \boldsymbol{\Sigma}^{-1/2}\mathbf{y}$, $\mathbf{X}^* = \boldsymbol{\Sigma}^{-1/2}\mathbf{X}$, and $\mathbf{e}^* = \boldsymbol{\Sigma}^{-1/2}\mathbf{e}$. The advantage of this new form is that, because $\mathrm{Var}\,\mathbf{e}^* = \boldsymbol{\Sigma}^{-1/2}\,\mathrm{Var}\,\mathbf{e}\boldsymbol{\Sigma}^{-1/2} = \sigma^2\,\boldsymbol{\Sigma}^{-1/2}\,\boldsymbol{\Sigma}\,\boldsymbol{\Sigma}^{-1/2} = \sigma^2\mathbf{I}$, it satisfies the conditions of the linear regression model described in Section TS4.3. The estimate of $\boldsymbol{\beta}$ is

$$\mathbf{b}_{\mathrm{GLS}} = (\mathbf{X}^{*\prime}\mathbf{X}^*)^{-1}\mathbf{X}^{*\prime}\mathbf{y}^* = (\mathbf{X}'\,\boldsymbol{\Sigma}^{-1}\,\mathbf{X})^{-1}\mathbf{X}'\boldsymbol{\Sigma}^{-1}\,\mathbf{y}.$$

The vector $\mathbf{b}_{\mathrm{GLS}}$ is called the generalized least squares, or GLS, estimate of $\boldsymbol{\beta}$, because it accounts for the variance-covariance structure of $\mathbf{e}$. That is, $\mathbf{b}_{\mathrm{GLS}}$ is the vector $\mathbf{b}^*$ that minimizes the sum of squares

$$\mathrm{SS}(\mathbf{b}^*) = (\mathbf{y} - \mathbf{X}\mathbf{b}^*)'\boldsymbol{\Sigma}^{-1}(\mathbf{y} - \mathbf{X}\mathbf{b}^*). \tag{TS8.3}$$

In cases where $\mathbf{X}'\,\boldsymbol{\Sigma}^{-1}\,\mathbf{X}$ is not invertible, general linear models estimates, described in Chapter 5, can be used. To distinguish this estimate from our usual one, called the *ordinary least squares,* or OLS, estimate, we use the notation

$$\mathbf{b}_{OLS} = (\mathbf{X}'\mathbf{X})^{-1}\mathbf{X}'\mathbf{y}.$$

Finite Sample Properties.   As in Section TS4.4, it is straightforward to check that both $\mathbf{b}_{OLS}$ and $\mathbf{b}_{GLS}$ are unbiased estimates of $\boldsymbol{\beta}$. That is, from equation (TS8.1) and the linearity of expectations in equation (TS4.3), we have

$$\text{E }\mathbf{b}_{OLS} = (\mathbf{X}'\mathbf{X})^{-1}\mathbf{X}' \text{ E } \mathbf{y} = (\mathbf{X}'\mathbf{X})^{-1}\mathbf{X}'\mathbf{X}\boldsymbol{\beta} = \boldsymbol{\beta}$$

and

$$\text{E }\mathbf{b}_{GLS} = (\mathbf{X}'\boldsymbol{\Sigma}^{-1}\mathbf{X})^{-1}\mathbf{X}' \boldsymbol{\Sigma}^{-1} \text{ E } \mathbf{y} = (\mathbf{X}'\boldsymbol{\Sigma}^{-1}\mathbf{X})^{-1}\mathbf{X}'\boldsymbol{\Sigma}^{-1}\mathbf{X}\boldsymbol{\beta} = \boldsymbol{\beta}.$$

Calculation of the variance-covariance matrix is also similar to the development in Section TS4.4. Thus, we have

$$\text{Var }\mathbf{b}_{OLS} = \text{Var}((\mathbf{X}'\mathbf{X})^{-1}\mathbf{X}'\,\mathbf{y}) = \sigma^2(\mathbf{X}'\mathbf{X})^{-1}\mathbf{X}'\boldsymbol{\Sigma}\mathbf{X}(\mathbf{X}'\mathbf{X})^{-1}$$

and

$$\text{Var }\mathbf{b}_{GLS} = \text{Var }((\mathbf{X}'\boldsymbol{\Sigma}^{-1}\mathbf{X})^{-1}\mathbf{X}'\boldsymbol{\Sigma}^{-1}\,\mathbf{y}) = \sigma^2(\mathbf{X}'\boldsymbol{\Sigma}^{-1}\mathbf{X})^{-1}\mathbf{X}'\boldsymbol{\Sigma}^{-1}\boldsymbol{\Sigma}\boldsymbol{\Sigma}^{-1}\mathbf{X}(\mathbf{X}'\boldsymbol{\Sigma}^{-1}\mathbf{X})^{-1}$$

$$= \sigma^2(\mathbf{X}'\boldsymbol{\Sigma}^{-1}\mathbf{X})^{-1}.$$

The variance-covariance matrix of $\mathbf{b}_{OLS}$ is larger than that of $\mathbf{b}_{GLS}$ in the sense that the difference is positive semidefinite, that is, $\mathbf{a}'$ (Var $\mathbf{b}_{OLS}$ − Var $\mathbf{b}_{GLS}$)$\mathbf{a} \geq 0$, for each $\mathbf{a}$. To see this, we have

$$\mathbf{a}'(\text{Var }\mathbf{b}_{OLS} - \text{Var }\mathbf{b}_{GLS})\mathbf{a} = \sigma^2\mathbf{a}'((\mathbf{X}'\mathbf{X})^{-1}\mathbf{X}'\boldsymbol{\Sigma}\mathbf{X}(\mathbf{X}'\mathbf{X})^{-1} - (\mathbf{X}'\boldsymbol{\Sigma}^{-1}\mathbf{X})^{-1})\mathbf{a}$$

$$= \sigma^2\mathbf{a}'(\mathbf{X}'\mathbf{X})^{-1}\mathbf{X}'(\boldsymbol{\Sigma} - \mathbf{X}(\mathbf{X}'\boldsymbol{\Sigma}^{-1}\mathbf{X})^{-1}\mathbf{X}')\mathbf{X}(\mathbf{X}'\mathbf{X})^{-1}\mathbf{a}$$

$$= \sigma^2\mathbf{a}'(\mathbf{X}'\mathbf{X})^{-1}\mathbf{X}'\boldsymbol{\Sigma}^{1/2}(\mathbf{I} - \boldsymbol{\Sigma}^{-1/2}\mathbf{X}(\mathbf{X}'\boldsymbol{\Sigma}^{-1}\mathbf{X})^{-1}\mathbf{X}'\boldsymbol{\Sigma}^{-1/2})$$

$$\times \boldsymbol{\Sigma}^{1/2}\mathbf{X}(\mathbf{X}'\mathbf{X})^{-1}\mathbf{a}$$

$$= \sigma^2\,\mathbf{d}'\mathbf{d} \geq 0,$$

where $\mathbf{d} = (\mathbf{I} - \boldsymbol{\Sigma}^{-1/2}\mathbf{X}(\mathbf{X}'\boldsymbol{\Sigma}^{-1}\mathbf{X})^{-1}\mathbf{X}'\boldsymbol{\Sigma}^{-1/2})\boldsymbol{\Sigma}^{1/2}\mathbf{X}(\mathbf{X}'\mathbf{X})^{-1}\mathbf{a}$.

Because $\mathbf{a}'$ Var $\mathbf{b}_{GLS}$ $\mathbf{a} \leq$ $\mathbf{a}'$ Var $\mathbf{b}_{OLS}$ $\mathbf{a}$, the GLS estimate is a more desirable estimate of $\boldsymbol{\beta}$ than the OLS version. However, computing $\mathbf{b}_{GLS}$ requires knowledge of $\boldsymbol{\Sigma}$.

Two Special Cases.   In the case that $\boldsymbol{\Sigma}$ is diagonal, then $\text{Cov}(e_i, e_j) = 0$ for $i \neq j$, so that the random errors are uncorrelated. Here, elements of the diagonal may vary, thus allowing for the *heteroscedastic* case. That is, the variance of the random errors may vary by observation, denoted by Var $e_i = \sigma_i^2$. In this case, the GLS estimates can be obtained by using the *weighted least squares* procedure described in Section 8.2. That is, define weights proportional to the reciprocal of the variances, $w_i = \sigma^2/\sigma_i^2$. Thus,

$$\Sigma^{-1} = \sigma^2 \begin{bmatrix} \text{Var } e_1 & 0 & \cdots & 0 \\ 0 & \text{Var } e_2 & \cdots & 0 \\ \cdot & \cdot & \cdots & \cdot \\ \cdot & \cdot & \cdots & 0 \\ 0 & 0 & \cdots & \text{Var } e_n \end{bmatrix}^{-1} = \begin{bmatrix} w_1 & 0 & \cdots & 0 \\ 0 & w_2 & \cdots & 0 \\ \cdot & \cdot & \cdots & \cdot \\ \cdot & \cdot & \cdots & \cdot \\ 0 & 0 & \cdots & w_n \end{bmatrix}.$$

It is called the weighted least squares estimate because equation (TS8.3) reduces to

$$SS(\mathbf{b}^*) = (\mathbf{y} - \mathbf{Xb}^*)' \begin{bmatrix} w_1 & \cdots & 0 \\ \cdot & \cdots & \cdot \\ 0 & \cdots & w_n \end{bmatrix} (\mathbf{y} - \mathbf{Xb}^*) = \sum_{i=1}^{n} w_i(y_i - \mathbf{x}_i'\mathbf{b}^*)^2.$$

Section 8.2 describes an application of WLS estimates to binary dependent data. Another important example occurs in survey data where the weights correspond to the number of responses in a category.

A second important case of GLS estimates occur when the data are longitudinal and are correlated over time. We will consider longitudinal data in detail in Chapters 9 through 11. An important special case, described in Chapter 10, is where the data follow an autoregressive model of order one, $AR(1)$. In this case, we have $\text{Cov}(e_i, e_j) = \sigma^2 \rho^{|i-j|}$, where $|\rho| < 1$. Thus, we have

$$\Sigma = \begin{bmatrix} 1 & \rho & \rho^2 & \cdots & \rho^{n-1} \\ \rho & 1 & \rho & \cdots & \rho^{n-2} \\ \cdot & \cdot & \cdot & \cdots & \cdot \\ \cdot & \cdot & \cdot & \cdots & \cdot \\ \rho^{n-1} & \rho^{n-2} & \rho^{n-3} & \cdots & 1 \end{bmatrix}. \tag{TS8.4}$$

We can show, by calculating $\Sigma^{-1/2} \Sigma \Sigma^{-1/2} = \mathbf{I}$, that

$$\Sigma^{-1/2} = \begin{bmatrix} \sqrt{1-\rho^2} & 0 & 0 & \cdots & 0 & 0 \\ -\rho & 1 & 1 & \cdots & 0 & 0 \\ 0 & -\rho & 1 & \cdots & \cdot & \cdot \\ \cdot & \cdot & \cdot & \cdots & \cdot & \cdot \\ \cdot & \cdot & \cdot & \cdots & \cdot & \cdot \\ 0 & 0 & 0 & \cdots & -\rho & 1 \end{bmatrix}.$$

Thus, using equation (TS8.2), the transformed model becomes

$$\mathbf{y}^* = \begin{bmatrix} (1-\rho^2)^{1/2} y_1 \\ y_2 - \rho y_1 \\ y_3 - \rho y_2 \\ \cdot \\ \cdot \\ y_n - \rho y_{n-1} \end{bmatrix} \quad \text{and} \quad \mathbf{X}^* = \begin{bmatrix} (1-\rho^2)^{1/2} \mathbf{x}_1 \\ \mathbf{x}_2 - \rho \mathbf{x}_1 \\ \mathbf{x}_3 - \rho \mathbf{x}_2 \\ \cdot \\ \cdot \\ \mathbf{x}_n - \rho \mathbf{x}_{n-1} \end{bmatrix}$$

General Linear Hypothesis. Because of the rescaling device in equation (TS8.2) to the ordinary linear regression model, all of the inference techniques described in Chapter 4 are available. To illustrate, as in Section TS4.6, the general linear hypothesis can be stated as H_0: $\mathbf{C}\boldsymbol{\beta} = \mathbf{d}$ versus the alternative H_a: $\mathbf{C}\boldsymbol{\beta} \neq \mathbf{d}$. As in Section 4.6, $\mathbf{C}$ is a $p \times (k + 1)$ matrix and $\mathbf{d}$ is a $p \times 1$ vector, both known. The test statistic is

$$F\text{-ratio} = \frac{(\mathbf{Cb}_{\text{GLS}} - \mathbf{d})'(\mathbf{C}(\mathbf{X}'\boldsymbol{\Sigma}^{-1}\mathbf{X})^{-1}\mathbf{C}')^{-1}(\mathbf{Cb}_{\text{GLS}} - \mathbf{d})}{ps_{\text{GLS}}^2},$$

where $s_{\text{GLS}}^2 = (\mathbf{y} - \mathbf{Xb}_{\text{GLS}})'\boldsymbol{\Sigma}^{-1}(\mathbf{y} - \mathbf{Xb}_{\text{GLS}})/(n - (k + 1))$. The procedure is to reject H_0 in favor of H_a if F-ratio $> F$-value, where F-value is a percentile from the F-distribution with $df_1 = p$ and $df_2 = n - (k + 1)$ degrees of freedom.

Feasible Generalized Least Squares. Regression problems are generally centered on estimating parameters associated with the mean, $\mathrm{E}\, y$, which we have denoted by $\boldsymbol{\beta} = (\beta_0, \beta_1, ..., \beta_k)'$. In many problems, parameters associated with the variance, such as $\boldsymbol{\Sigma}$, will also be unknown. In these situations, to determine GLS estimates, we need to estimate $\boldsymbol{\Sigma}$. Parameter estimates with estimated values of $\boldsymbol{\Sigma}$ are called *estimated*, or *feasible, generalized least squares* estimates, and are denoted by $\mathbf{b}_{\text{FGLS}}$.

For a general variance-covariance matrix, there are n variances and $n(n - 1)/2$ covariances. With only n observations available, this is far too many parameters to estimate. We will assume that $\boldsymbol{\Sigma}$ is indexed by an unknown $p \times 1$ vector $\boldsymbol{\theta}$, denoted by $\boldsymbol{\Sigma}(\boldsymbol{\theta})$. Thus, we estimate $\boldsymbol{\theta}$ from the data and, for a given value of $\boldsymbol{\theta}$, $\boldsymbol{\Sigma}(\boldsymbol{\theta})$ can be calculated. To illustrate, consider the $AR(1)$ example in equation (TS8.4), where we have $p = 1$ and $\boldsymbol{\theta} = \rho$. In Chapter 10, we will discuss ways of estimating ρ from the data.

TS 8.2 Logistic Regression

Model Statement. As in Section TS 4.1, we assume that the data are of the form $(x_{i0}, x_{i1}, x_{i2}, ..., x_{ik}, y_i)$, where $i = 1, ..., n$. In this section, y_i are binary, or indicator, variables with mean p_i, that is, $\mathrm{E}\, y_i = p_i$. The expectations are assumed to be a (known) function of a linear combination of explanatory variables, that is, $p_i = \pi(x_i'\boldsymbol{\beta})$. Logistic regression assumes that the logit of the expected value is $x_i'\boldsymbol{\beta}$, or $\text{logit}(p_i) = x_i'\boldsymbol{\beta}$. Thus, $p_i/(1 - p_i) = \exp(x_i'\boldsymbol{\beta})$, so $(1 - p_i)/p_i = 1/p_i - 1 = \exp(-x_i'\boldsymbol{\beta})$. This yields

$$p_i = \pi(x_i'\boldsymbol{\beta}) = \frac{\exp(x_i'\boldsymbol{\beta})}{1 + \exp(x_i'\boldsymbol{\beta})}.$$

Thus, π is the inverse of the logit function. A closely related model, the *probit model*, assumes that the function is $\pi = \Phi$, the cumulative normal distribution function. Although the responses are assumed independent, because they have different means they no longer have identical distributions.

Maximum Likelihood Estimation.   Because y_i are binary, they follow the binomial distribution described in Section TS2.3. That is, $y_i \sim$ Binomial $(1, p_i)$. Because of the independence of $\{y_i\}$, the likelihood can be expressed as

$$L(\boldsymbol{\beta}) = \prod_{i=1}^{n} f_i(y_i, \boldsymbol{\beta}) = \prod_{i=1}^{n} p_i^{y_i}(1 - p_i)^{1-y_i} = \prod_{i=1}^{n} \pi(\mathbf{x}'_i\boldsymbol{\beta})^{y_i}(1 - \pi(\mathbf{x}'_i\boldsymbol{\beta}))^{1-y_i}.$$

Thus, the log likelihood function is

$$\ln L(\boldsymbol{\beta}) = \sum_{i=1}^{n} y_i \ln \pi(\mathbf{x}'_i\boldsymbol{\beta}) + (1 - y_i) \ln (1 - \pi(\mathbf{x}'_i\boldsymbol{\beta})). \qquad \text{(TS8.5)}$$

Using the inverse of the logit function for π, taking partial derivatives with respect to $\boldsymbol{\beta}$ and setting this equal to zero, yields

$$0 = \frac{\partial}{\partial \boldsymbol{\beta}} \ln L(\boldsymbol{\beta}) = \frac{\partial}{\partial \boldsymbol{\beta}} \sum_{i=1}^{n} \left(y_i \ln \frac{\pi(\mathbf{x}'_i\boldsymbol{\beta})}{1 - \pi(\mathbf{x}'_i\boldsymbol{\beta})} + \ln(1 - \pi(\mathbf{x}'_i\boldsymbol{\beta})) \right)$$

$$= \frac{\partial}{\partial \boldsymbol{\beta}} \sum_{i=1}^{n} (y_i\mathbf{x}'_i\boldsymbol{\beta} - \ln(1 + \exp(\mathbf{x}'_i\boldsymbol{\beta}))) = \sum_{i=1}^{n} \left(y_i\mathbf{x}_i - \frac{\mathbf{x}_i \exp(\mathbf{x}'_i\boldsymbol{\beta})}{1 + \exp(\mathbf{x}'_i\boldsymbol{\beta})} \right).$$

Thus, the maximum likelihood estimator **b** is the solution of the $k + 1$ equations

$$\sum_{i=1}^{n} \mathbf{x}_i(y_i - \pi(\mathbf{x}'_i\mathbf{b})) = 0.$$

In particular, if $x_{i0} \equiv 1$, note that the average response, $\sum_{i=1}^{n} y_i/n$, equals the average fitted value $\sum_{i=1}^{n} \pi(\mathbf{x}'_i\mathbf{b})/n$. We saw that this is also true in the linear regression case.

Hypothesis Testing.   Significance of groups of parameters can be examined using a procedure similar to partial F-tests for linear regression, described in Chapter 4. Under the full model, we determine parameter estimates and calculate the log likelihood statistic, denoted by $\ln L_{full}$, from equation (TS8.5). Suppose we are interested in examining the hypothesis H_0: $\mathbf{C}\boldsymbol{\beta} = \mathbf{d}$, where $\mathbf{C}$ is a $p \times (k + 1)$ matrix and $\mathbf{d}$ is a $p \times 1$ vector, both known. Under this restriction, we calculate t he log likelihood statistic, denoted by $\ln L_{reduced}$. Under the null hypothesis, the test statistic

$$G = -2(\ln L_{full} - \ln L_{reduced}),$$

has an asymptotic chi-square distribution with p degrees of freedom. Here, asymptotic refers to a large sample theoretical result as $n \to \infty$. That is, G

$\to_D \chi_p^2$, as $n \to \infty$. Our test procedure is to reject H_0 in favor of H_a: $\mathbf{C}\boldsymbol{\beta} \neq \mathbf{d}$ if G exceeds a percentile from the chi-square distribution with $df = p$ degrees of freedom.

TS 8.3 Generalized Linear Model

Both the linear regression and logistic regression are special cases of a class called *generalized linear models,* denoted by the acronym *GLM.* The main idea behind GLM models is that linear combinations of explanatory variables, $\mathbf{x}_i'\boldsymbol{\beta}$, are useful for predicting expected responses. Under the GLM formulation, the expected response can be transformed and may follow a distribution other than the normal curve.

Under the linear regression model, we used $E\ y_i = \mathbf{x}_i'\boldsymbol{\beta}$. Under the logistic regression model, we used $\text{logit}(E\ y_i) = \mathbf{x}_i'\boldsymbol{\beta}$. Under the GLM formulation, we can use $g(E\ y_i) = \mathbf{x}_i'\boldsymbol{\beta}$. Here, g is a known function called the *link function.* The inverse of g, g^{-1}, yields the regression model, that is, $E\ y_i = g^{-1}(\mathbf{x}_i'\boldsymbol{\beta})$.

Under the linear regression model, we assumed that errors were additive functions of the response and expected response, and could be defined by $y_i = E\ y_i + e_i$. Further, we often used the normal distribution assumption for the errors. Under the GLM formulation, the errors need not be additive nor normal. Rather, the error function is assumed to be from the *exponential family* of distributions. See Bickel and Doksum (1977) for a description of this broad family of distributions. All of the distributions described in Section TS2.3 belong to this family. For example, under the logistic regression model, we used the binomial distribution to determine the error distribution.

CHAPTER 9

TS9.1 Distributions

Collections of Random Variables. As in Section TS2.2, we consider here a collection of random variables, $\{y_1, y_2, ..., y_T\}$. Unlike Section TS2.2, the index $t = 1, 2, ..., T$ refers to the order in which the variable y is observed. We refer to the ordering as time. An ordered collection of random variables is called *stochastic process.* A realization of a stochastic process is called a *time series.* In this text, we do not use the information in the length of time between observations and thus, without loss of generality, assume that observations are equally spaced in time.

Joint Distributions. As in Section TS2.2, our basic building block is

$$F(a_1, a_2, ..., a_T) = \text{Prob}(y_1 \leq a_1, y_2 \leq a_2, ..., y_T \leq a_T),$$

the *joint distribution function* of $\{y_1, y_2, ..., y_T\}$. As described in TS2.2, the joint distribution function allows us to define the expectations operator, E. To illustrate, in the continuous case the *joint probability desnity function* is

$$f(a_1, a_2, ..., a_T) = \frac{\partial}{\partial a_1} \frac{\partial}{\partial a_2} \cdots \frac{\partial}{\partial a_T} F(a_1, a_2, ..., a_T).$$

Thus, the expectations operator is defined as

$$E\ g(y_1, ..., y_T)$$

$$= \int_{all\ occurrences\ of\ y_1} \cdots \int_{all\ occurrences\ of\ y_T} g(y_1, ..., y_T)\ f(y_1, ..., y_T)\ dy_1 \ldots dy_T.$$

As in Section TS2.2, the joint distribution function is sufficient to define the marginal distributions. To illustrate, $F_t(a_t) = F(\infty, ..., \infty, a_t, \infty, ..., \infty)$ is the tth marginal distribution function and $f_t(a_t) = F_t'(a_t)$ is the corresponding density function.

Summary Measures of Probability Functions. As we will see in our definitions under weak stationarity, the most important summary measures for time series data are the mean, variance and covariance. Thus, we define (i) the mean,

$$E\ y_t = \mu_t = \int_{y_t} f_t(y_t)\ dy_t,$$

(ii) the variance,

$$\sigma_t^2 = Var\ y_t = E(y_t - \mu_t)^2 = \int (y_t - \mu_t)^2\ f_t(y_t)\ dy_t,$$

and (iii) the covariance,

$$Cov(y_s, y_t) = E(y_s - \mu_s)(y_t - \mu_t) = E\ y_s y_t - \mu_s \mu_t.$$

Weak Stationarity. Stationarity is the formal, mathematical concept corresponding to the "stability" of a time series of data. There are two definitions of stationarity that are employed in the analysis of time series data, *weak stationarity* and *strict stationarity*. The former is most often used in applications. A series is said to be *weakly stationary* if (i) the mean μ_t does not depend on t and (ii) the covariance between y_s and y_t depends only on the difference between time units, $|t - s|$. Thus, for example, under weak stationarity $E\ y_4 = E\ y_8$ because the means do not depend on time and thus are equal. Further, $Cov(y_4, y_6) = Cov(y_6, y_8)$, because y_4 and y_6 are two time units apart, as are y_6 and y_8. As another implication of condition (ii), note that $\sigma_t^2 = Cov(y_t, y_t) = Cov(y_s, y_s) = \sigma_s^2$. Thus, a weakly stationary series not only has a constant mean, it has a constant variance, that is, homoscedastic.

Strict Stationarity. The concept of weak stationarity quantifies the stability of a stochastic process only through the first two moments, the mean and covariance. In principle, one might be concerned that the entire distribution function is stable over time. A stochastic process is said to be *strictly stationary* if, for each T and integer set $\{i_1, i_2, \ldots, i_T\}$

$$F(a_1, a_2, \ldots, a_T) = \text{Prob}(y_{i_1+s} \leq a_1, y_{i_2+s} \leq a_2, \ldots, y_{i_T+s} \leq a_T), \quad \text{(TS9.1)}$$

for any s. It is not hard to check that strict stationarity implies weak stationarity. In general, the reverse implication is not true. It is true, however, that weak stationary implies strict stationarity when the process $\{y_1, \ldots, y_T\}$ is jointly normally distributed. See Box, Jenkins and Reinsel (1994, Chapter 2) for further discussion of this and related issues.

TS 9.2 Random Walks

Random Processes. A stochastic process $\{y_1, \ldots, y_T\}$ is said to be a *random process* if it is identically and independently distributed, that is, i.i.d. It is easy to see that a random process is weakly stationary. That is, because distributions are identical, we have that $\text{E}\, y_t = \mu_y$ and $\text{Var}\, y_t = \sigma_y^2$ do not depend on t. Because of the independence, we have that $\text{Cov}(y_s, y_t) = 0$ for $|s - t| \neq 0$ and $\text{Cov}(y_s, y_t) = \sigma_y^2$ for $|s - t| = 0$. This is enough to satisfy the two conditions of weak stationarity. Further, it is also easy to check that equation (TS9.1) holds and thus, that a random process is strictly stationary.

Random Walks. Suppose that $\{y_1, \ldots, y_T\}$ is a stochastic process such that the *changes* $u_t = y_t - y_{t-1}$ form a random process with mean μ_u and variance σ_u^2. Then, $\{y_1, \ldots, y_T\}$ is said to be a *random walk process*. Assuming y_0 is known, by the linearity of expectations, equation (TS2.2), we have

$$\text{E}\, y_t = \text{E}\, (y_0 + y_1 - y_0 + y_2 - y_1 + \ldots + y_t - y_{t-1})$$
$$= \text{E}\, (y_0 + u_1 + u_2 + \ldots + u_t)$$
$$= \text{E}\, y_0 + \text{E}\, u_1 + \text{E}\, u_2 + \ldots + \text{E}\, u_t = y_0 + t\, \mu_u.$$

Further, by the independence of the changes, from equation (TS2.6), we have

$$\text{Var}\, y_t = \text{Var}(y_0 + u_1 + u_2 + \ldots + u_t)$$
$$= \text{Var}\, u_1 + \text{Var}\, u_2 + \ldots + \text{Var}\, u_t = t\, \sigma_u^2.$$

This establishes that the random walk process is not stationary, either in the weak or the strict sense.

Estimating Parameters Associated with a Random Walk Process. Because the random walk is nonstationary, there is no single distribution associated with this process and thus no single set of parameters. However, the parameters associated with the changes in the process, μ_u and σ_u^2, are important quantities to estimate. Now, for estimation purposes, the information in a realization of a random walk process $\{y_1, y_2, \ldots, y_T\}$ is equivalent to the information in $\{y_1, u_2, \ldots, u_T\}$, that is, the first observation, y_1, plus subsequent changes, $u_2, \ldots, u_T$. Our estimate of the μ_u can be expressed as

$$\hat{\mu}_u = \frac{\sum_{t=2}^{T} u_t}{T - 1} = \frac{y_T - y_1}{T - 1}.$$

Similarly, our estimate of σ_u^2 can be expressed as

$$\hat{\sigma}_u^2 = \frac{\sum_{t=2}^{T} (u_t - \hat{u}_u)^2}{T - 2} = \frac{\sum_{t=2}^{T} u_t^2 - (T - 1)\hat{\mu}_u^2}{T - 2}$$

$$= \frac{\sum_{t=2}^{T} (y_t - y_{t-1})^2 - (T - 1)\hat{\mu}_u^2}{T - 2}.$$

Forecasting with Random Walks. Based on a realization of a random walk process $\{y_1, \ldots, y_T\}$, suppose that we would like to forecast y_{T+l}, the value of the series l lead time units in the future. Using the changes $u_t = y_t - y_{t-1}$, we can express this future value as

$$y_{T+l} = u_{T+l} + y_{T+l-1} = \ldots = u_{T+l} + u_{T+l-1} + \ldots + u_{T+1} + y_T = y_T + \sum_{k=1}^{l} u_{T+k}.$$

Based on a realization of a random walk, $\{y_1, y_2, \ldots, y_T\}$, we have that the most recent value y_T is known. Thus to forecast y_{T+l}, we need only forecast the sum of future changes $\Sigma_{k=1}^{l} u_{T+k}$. In probability theory, the distribution of a sum of i.i.d. random variables is known as a *convolution*. In mathematical statistics, estimation of this distribution, and corresponding percentiles, has been studied extensively. In practice, the focus is on the estimation of the mean and variance, $E \Sigma_{k=1}^{l} u_{T+k} = l \mu_u$ and $\text{Var}(\Sigma_{k=1}^{l} u_{T+k}) = l \sigma_u^2$. Thus, our point prediction of y_{T+l} is $\hat{y}_{T+1} = y_T + l\hat{\mu}_u$. The corresponding prediction error is $y_{T+l} - \hat{y}_{T+1} = y_T + \Sigma_{k=1}^{l} u_{T+k} - (y_T + l\hat{\mu}_u) = \Sigma_{k=1}^{l} u_{T+k} - l\hat{\mu}_u$. Assuming normality of the changes, we have $\Sigma_{k=1}^{l} u_{T+k} \sim N(l \mu_u, l \sigma_u^2)$ and $\hat{\mu}_u \sim N(\mu_u, \sigma_u^2/(T - 2))$. Because $\Sigma_{k=1}^{l} u_{T+k}$ and $\hat{\mu}_u$ are independent, this yields

$$\sum_{k=1}^{l} u_{T+k} - l \hat{\mu}_u \sim N(0, \sigma_u^2 (l + l^2/(T - 2))).$$

Thus, a $100(1 - \alpha)\%$ prediction interval for y_{T+l} is

$$y_T + l\hat{\mu}_u \pm (t\text{-value})\, \hat{\sigma}_u\, (l + l^2/(T - 2))^{1/2}.$$

Here, t-value is the $(1 - \alpha/2)$th percentile from a t-distribution with $T - 2$ degrees of freedom. An approximate 95% confidence interval is $y_T + l\hat{\mu}_u \pm 2\hat{\sigma}_u\, l^{1/2}$.

Forecasting with Random Processes Having a Trend. Suppose that $\{u_1, u_2, \ldots, u_T\}$ is a random process and that we are interested in forecasting the process

$$y_t = \mathbf{x}_t' \boldsymbol{\beta} + u_t, \qquad (TS9.2)$$

where $\mathbf{x}_t$ is a $(k + 1) \times 1$ vector of explanatory variables and $\boldsymbol{\beta}$ is a $(k + 1) \times 1$ vector of parameters. We assume that $\mathbf{x}_t$ is known for all values of t. In this case, forecasts of future values of the process are the same as predicting future values in the linear regression case, described in Section TS4.5. To illustrate, if we wish to predict y_{T+l}, a l lead time value, then our prediction under the model in equation (TS9.2) is $\hat{y}_{T+l} = \mathbf{x}_{T+l}' \mathbf{b}$, where $\mathbf{b}$ is the least squares estimate of $\boldsymbol{\beta}$. Thus, we have $\mathbf{b} = (\mathbf{X}'\mathbf{X})^{-1}\mathbf{X}'\mathbf{y}$, where $\mathbf{X} = (\mathbf{x}_1 \mathbf{x}_2 \ldots \mathbf{x}_T)'$. Our $100\,(1 - \alpha)\%$ prediction interval is

$$\mathbf{x}_{T+l}' \mathbf{b} \pm (t\text{-value})se(pred),$$

where t-value is a $(1 - \alpha/2)$th percentile from a t-distribution with $df = T - (k + 1)$ degrees of freedom and

$$se(pred) = \hat{\sigma}_u \sqrt{1 + \mathbf{x}_{T+l}'(\mathbf{X}'\mathbf{X})^{-1}\mathbf{x}_{T+l}}\,.$$

Forecasting with Random Walks Having a Trend. Suppose that $\{u_1, u_2, \ldots, u_T\}$ is a random process and that we are interested in forecasting the process

$$y_t - y_{t-1} = \mathbf{x}_t' \boldsymbol{\beta} + u_t. \qquad (TS9.3)$$

To forecast y_{T+l}, we can recursively use equation (TS9.3) to get

$$y_{T+l} = y_{T+l-1} + \mathbf{x}_{T+l}' \boldsymbol{\beta} + u_{T+l} = \ldots = y_T + \left(\sum_{k=1}^{l} \mathbf{x}_{T+k}'\right) \boldsymbol{\beta} + \sum_{k=1}^{l} u_{T+k}.$$

Thus, our point prediction of y_{T+l} is $\hat{y}_{T+l} = y_T + (\sum_{k=1}^{l}\mathbf{x}_{T+k}')\mathbf{b}$. The corresponding prediction error is $y_{T+l} - \hat{y}_{T+l} = \sum_{k=1}^{l}u_{T+k} + (\sum_{k=1}^{l}\mathbf{x}_{T+k}')(\boldsymbol{\beta} - \mathbf{b})$. This is distributed normally with mean 0 and variance

$$\mathrm{Var}\left(\sum_{k=1}^{l} u_{T+k} + \left(\sum_{k=1}^{l} \mathbf{x}_{T+k}'\right)(\boldsymbol{\beta} - \mathbf{b})\right) = \sigma_u^2\left(l + \left(\sum_{k=1}^{l} \mathbf{x}_{T+k}'\right)(\mathbf{X}'\mathbf{X})^{-1}\left(\sum_{k=1}^{l} \mathbf{x}_{T+k}\right)\right).$$

Thus, our $100(1 - \alpha)\%$ prediction interval is

$$y_T + \mathbf{x}_{T+l}' \mathbf{b} \pm (t\text{-value})se(pred),$$

where t-value is a $(1 - \alpha/2)$th percentile from a t-distribution with $df = T - 1 - (k + 1)$ degrees of freedom and

$$se(pred) = \hat{\sigma}_u \sqrt{l + \left(\sum_{k=1}^{l} \mathbf{x}_{T+k}'\right)(\mathbf{X}'\mathbf{X})^{-1}\left(\sum_{k=1}^{l} \mathbf{x}_{T+k}\right)}\,.$$

CHAPTER 10

TS 10.1 Autocorrelations and *AR(p)* Models

Autocorrelations. Assume that $\{y_1, y_2, ..., y_T\}$ is a weakly stationary process with mean $E\, y_t = \mu$ and variance $\mathrm{Var}\, y_t = \sigma_y^2$. Recall, from Section TS 9.1, for a weakly stationary process, that $\mathrm{Cov}(y_t, y_{t-k})$ depends only on k and not on t. For a weakly stationary process, define the lag k *autocorrelation* coefficient to be

$$\rho_k = \mathrm{Corr}(y_t, y_{t-k}) = \mathrm{Cov}(y_t, y_{t-k})/\sigma_y^2,$$

for any integer k. If $k = 0$, then $\rho_0 = \mathrm{Cov}(y_t, y_t)/\sigma_y^2 = 1$. Further, because of the stationarity, we have $\mathrm{Cov}(y_t, y_{t-k}) = \mathrm{Cov}(y_{t+k}, y_t)$ and thus $\rho_{-k} = \rho_k$. Recall from Section 10.1 that the lag k *autocorrelation* statistic is

$$r_k = \frac{\sum_{t=k+1}^{T}(y_t - \overline{y})(y_{t-k} - \overline{y})}{\sum_{t=1}^{T}(y_t - \overline{y})^2}.$$

That is, r_k is the statistic used to estimate the parameter ρ_k.

Standard Errors of Autocorrelations. Because the lag k autocorrelation r_k is a function of the process $\{y_t\}$, the standard error of r_k depends on the model of $\{y_t\}$. To illustrate, for the $AR(1)$ model, it is known (see, for example, Box, Jenkins and Reinsel, 1994, Section 2.1.6) that

$$se(r_k) \approx \frac{1}{\sqrt{T}}\sqrt{\frac{(1 + b_1^2)(1 - b_1^{2k})}{1 - b_1^2} - 2kb_1^{2k}}.$$

For example, with $k = 1$, we have

$$se(r_1) \approx \sqrt{\frac{1 - b_1^2}{T}}.$$

For a random error process, we expect $b_1 \approx 0$, so that $se(r_k) \approx T^{-1/2}$.

AR(p) Model. The lag k autocorrelation ρ_k measures the linear relationship between y_t and y_{t-k}. To model this relationship, we have the *autoregressive model of order p*, or $AR(p)$,

$$y_t = \beta_0 + \beta_1 y_{t-1} + ... + \beta_p y_{t-p} + e_t. \tag{TS10.1}$$

Here, $\{e_1, e_2, ..., e_T\}$ is a mean zero random process such that $\mathrm{Cov}(e_{t+k}, y_t) = 0$

for $k > 0$. This condition is interpreted to mean that future errors are uncorrelated with the current value of a process. By convention, the $AR(p)$ is a model of a stationary, stochastic process. Thus, certain restrictions on the parameters $\beta_1, \beta_2, ..., \beta_p$ are necessary to ensure (weak) stationarity. These restrictions are given in the Backshift Notation subsection below. To illustrate the necessity of the restrictions, note that from equation (TS10.1), using $p = 1$ and $\beta_1 = 1$, we have $y_t = \beta_0 + y_{t-1} + e_t$. This is a representation for a random walk process, a nonstationary model.

Yule-Walker Equations. This set of equations provides insights into the sequential nature of the $AR(p)$ process and provides some useful estimates of the model parameters. By the linearity of covariances (equation TS2.3) and equation (TS10.1), we have

$$\text{Cov}(y_t, y_{t-k}) = \text{Cov}(\beta_0 + \beta_1 y_{t-1} + ... + \beta_p y_{t-p} + e_t, y_{t-k})$$

$$= \text{Cov}(\beta_0, y_{t-k}) + \text{Cov}(\beta_1 y_{t-1}, y_{t-k}) + ... + \text{Cov}(\beta_p y_{t-p}, y_{t-k})$$
$$+ \text{Cov}(e_t, y_{t-k})$$

$$= \beta_1 \text{Cov}(y_{t-1}, y_{t-k}) + ... + \beta_p \text{Cov}(y_{t-p}, y_{t-k}).$$

Dividing each side by σ_y^2 yields

$$\rho_k = \text{Cov}(y_t, y_{t-k})/\sigma_y^2 = \beta_1 \rho_{k-1} + \beta_2 \rho_{k-2} + ... + \beta_p \rho_{k-p}. \quad \text{(TS10.2)}$$

We can use equation (TS10.2) to relate model parameters to autocorrelation parameters. To illustrate, for the $AR(1)$ model, we have $\rho_k = \beta_1 \rho_{k-1}$. With $k = 1$ and using $\rho_0 = 1$, this results in $\rho_1 = \beta_1$ and $\rho_k = \beta_1^k$. More generally, the first p equations in (TS10.2) are called the *Yule-Walker equations:*

$$\rho_1 = \beta_1 + \beta_2 \rho_1 + ... + \beta_p \rho_{p-1}$$

$$\rho_2 = \beta_1 \rho_1 + \beta_2 + ... + \beta_p \rho_{p-2}$$
$$\vdots \qquad \vdots \qquad \vdots$$
$$\rho_p = \beta_1 \rho_{p-1} + \beta_2 \rho_{p-2} + ... + \beta_p.$$

In matrix notation, the Yule-Walker equations can be expressed as

$$\boldsymbol{\rho} = \begin{bmatrix} \rho_1 \\ \rho_2 \\ \cdot \\ \cdot \\ \cdot \\ \rho_p \end{bmatrix} = \begin{bmatrix} 1 & \rho_1 & \rho_2 & \cdots & \rho_{p-1} \\ \rho_1 & 1 & \rho_1 & \cdots & \rho_{p-2} \\ \cdot & \cdot & \cdot & \cdots & \cdot \\ \cdot & \cdot & \cdot & \cdots & \cdot \\ \cdot & \cdot & \cdot & \cdots & \cdot \\ \rho_{p-1} & \rho_{p-2} & \rho_{p-3} & \cdots & 1 \end{bmatrix} \begin{bmatrix} \beta_1 \\ \beta_2 \\ \cdot \\ \cdot \\ \cdot \\ \beta_p \end{bmatrix} = \mathbf{P}\boldsymbol{\beta}^p.$$

Solving for $\boldsymbol{\beta}^p = (\beta_1 \beta_2 ... \beta_p)'$ yields

$$\boldsymbol{\beta}^p = \mathbf{P}^{-1} \boldsymbol{\rho}.$$

Thus, by replacing ρ_k with the estimate r_k for each element in $\mathbf{P}$ and $\boldsymbol{\rho}$, we can get useful estimates of $\boldsymbol{\beta}^p$.

Backshift Notation. The *backshift*, or backwards-shift, operator B is defined by $By_t = y_{t-1}$. The notation B^k means apply the operator k times, that is,

$$B^k y_t = BB \ldots By_t = B^{k-1}y_{t-1} = B^{k-2}y_{t-2} = \ldots = y_{t-k}.$$

This operator is linear in the sense that $B(\alpha_1 y_t + \alpha_2 x_t) = \alpha_1 y_{t-1} + \alpha_2 x_{t-1}$, where α_1 and α_2 are constants. Thus, we can express the AR(p) model as

$$
\begin{aligned}
\beta_0 + e_t &= y_t - (\beta_1 y_{t-1} + \ldots + \beta_p y_{t-p}) \\
&= (1 - \beta_1 B - \beta_2 B^2 - \ldots - \beta_p B^p)\, y_t = \boldsymbol{\phi}(B)y_t.
\end{aligned}
\tag{TS10.3}
$$

If x is a scalar, then $\boldsymbol{\phi}(x) = 1 - \beta_1 x - \beta_2 x^2 - \ldots - \beta_p x^p$ is a pth order polynomial in x. Thus, there exist p roots of the equation $\boldsymbol{\phi}(x) = 0$. These roots, say, $g_1, g_2, \ldots, g_p$, may or may not be complex numbers. It can be shown, see Box, Jenkins and Reinsel (1994), that for stationarity, we need to require that all roots lie strictly outside the unit circle. To illustrate, for $p = 1$, we have $\boldsymbol{\phi}(x) = 1 - \beta_1 x$. The root of this equation is $g_1 = \beta_1^{-1}$. Thus, we require $|g_1| > 1$, or $|\beta_1| < 1$, for stationarity.

Partial Autocorrelations. In Section 4.4 and Section TS 6.3, we considered the partial correlation between y and x_k, after controlling for the effects of $\{x_1, x_2, \ldots, x_{k-1}\}$. Similarly, for time series data, it is of interest to measure the correlation between y_t and y_{t-k}, after controlling for the effects of $\{y_{t-1}, y_{t-2}, \ldots, y_{t-k+1}\}$. To measure this, we write

$$y_t = \beta_{0k} + \beta_{1k}y_{t-1} + \ldots + \beta_{kk}y_{t-k} + u_t.$$

Although we assume that $\{y_t\}$ is a stationary process, we do not assume that y_t follows an $AR(k)$ process. Thus, $\{u_t\}$ need not be a random process. It is stationary because $\{y_t\}$ is stationary and we assume that $Cov(u_{t+k}, y_t) = 0$ for $k > 0$. Following the steps in the Yule-Walker Equation subsection in Section TS 10.1, we have

$$
\begin{aligned}
\rho_1 &= \beta_{1k} + \beta_{2k}\rho_1 + \ldots + \beta_{kk}\rho_{k-1} \\
\rho_2 &= \beta_{1k}\rho_1 + \beta_{2k} + \ldots + \beta_{kk}\rho_{k-2} \\
&\vdots \qquad\qquad \vdots \qquad\qquad \vdots \\
\rho_k &= \beta_{1k}\rho_{k-1} + \beta_{2k}\rho_{k-2} + \ldots + \beta_{kk}.
\end{aligned}
$$

Again, the coefficients $\beta_{1k}, \beta_{2k}, \ldots, \beta_{kk}$ can be solved for in terms of $\rho_1, \rho_2, \ldots, \rho_k$. In particular, the term β_{kk} is a function of $\rho_1, \rho_2, \ldots, \rho_k$ and is called the *lag k partial autocorrelation* coefficient. It has the following three important properties: (1) $\beta_{11} = \rho_1$, (2) for an $AR(p)$ model with $\beta_p \neq 0$, and we have $\beta_{pp} \neq 0$, and (3) for an $AR(p)$ model,

$$\beta_{kk} = 0 \quad \text{for} \quad k > p.$$

Thus, the partial autocorrelation serves as a useful tool for identifying $AR(p)$ models.

TS 10.2 *ARIMA* Models

$MA(q)$ Models.   One interpretation of the model $y_t = \beta_0 + e_t$ is that e_t is the *disturbance* that perturbs our measure of the true, expected value of y_t. Similarly, we can consider the model $y_t = \beta_0 + e_t - \theta_1 e_{t-1}$, where $\theta_1 e_{t-1}$ quantifies the perturbation from the previous time period. Extending this line of thought, we can define the moving average model of order q, or $MA(q)$,

$$y_t = \beta_0 + e_t - \theta_1 e_{t-1} - \ldots - \theta_q e_{t-q}. \tag{TS10.4}$$

As before, $\{e_1, e_2, \ldots, e_T\}$ is a mean zero process such that $\text{Cov}(e_{t+k}, y_t) = 0$ for $k > 0$. With equation (TS 10.4) it is easy to see that $\text{Cov}(y_{t+k}, y_t) = 0$ for $k > q$. Thus, $\rho_k = 0$ for $k > q$. Unlike the $AR(p)$ model, the $MA(q)$ process is stationary for any finite values of the parameters $\beta_0, \theta_1, \ldots, \theta_q$. It is convenient to write the $MA(q)$ using backshift notation, as follows:

$$y_t - \beta_0 = (1 - \theta_1 B - \theta_2 B^2 - \ldots - \theta_q B^q)e_t = \boldsymbol{\theta}(B)e_t \tag{TS10.5}$$

As with $\boldsymbol{\phi}(x)$, if x is a scalar, then $\boldsymbol{\theta}(x) = 1 - \theta_1 x - \theta_2 x^2 - \ldots - \theta_q x^q$ is a qth order polynomial in x. It is unfortunate that the term "moving average" is used for the model defined by equation (TS10.4) and the estimate defined in Section 11.2. We will attempt to clarify each usage as it arises.

ARIMA Model.   Combining the $AR(p)$ and the $MA(q)$ models yields the *autoregressive moving average model* of order p and q, or $ARMA(p,q)$,

$$y_t - \beta_1 y_{t-1} - \ldots - \beta_p y_{t-p} = \beta_0 + e_t - \theta_1 e_{t-1} - \ldots - \theta_q e_{t-q} \tag{TS10.6}$$

which can be represented as

$$\boldsymbol{\phi}(B)y_t = \beta_0 + \boldsymbol{\theta}(B)e_t. \tag{TS10.7}$$

In many applications, the data requires that the differencing filter yield stationarity. We assume that the data is differenced d times to yield

$$
\begin{aligned}
w_t = (1 - B)^d y_t &= (1 - B)^{d-1}(y_t - y_{t-1}) \\
&= (1 - B)^{d-2}((y_t - y_{t-1} - (y_{t-1} - y_{t-2})) = \ldots
\end{aligned}
\tag{TS10.8}
$$

In practice, d is typically zero, one or two. With this filter, the *autoregressive integrated moving average model* of order (p, d, q), denoted by $ARIMA(p,d,q)$, is

$$\boldsymbol{\phi}(B)w_t = \beta_0 + \boldsymbol{\theta}(B)e_t. \tag{TS10.9}$$

where w_t is defined in equation (TS10.8). Often, β_0 is zero for $d > 0$.

Duality between Autoregressive and Moving Average Models. There is a reciprocal relation between autoregressive and moving average models, called a *duality* in mathematics. To begin, recall that for the $AR(p)$ model, we noted that the lag k partial autocorrelation, β_{kk}, is zero for $k > p$. However, we do not have that $\rho_k = 0$, in general. Conversely, for an $MA(q)$ model, we noted that $\rho_k = 0$ for $k > q$. However, we do not have $\beta_{kk} = 0$, in general. Thus, partial autocorrelations help identify autoregressive models and autocorrelations help identify moving average models.

It can be shown that a stationary AR model can be converted to an MA model using

$$y_t = \phi(\mathrm{B})^{-1} \beta_0 + \phi(\mathrm{B})^{-1} e_t$$

because the polynomial $\phi(x)^{-1}$ is well-defined. Similarly, if the roots of $\theta(x)$ lie outside the unit circle, then the $MA(q)$ is said to be *invertible*. In this case, $\theta(x)^{-1}$ is well defined and $y_t \theta(\mathrm{B})^{-1} = \theta(\mathrm{B})^{-1} \beta_0 + e_t$ is an autoregressive representation of the $MA(q)$ model.

An important motivation for combining autoregressive and moving average models is that the resulting $ARMA$ model can be expressed with fewer parameters than may be possible with either an AR or an MA representation. For example, if the AR and MA parts have common roots, then terms can be canceled to yield a simpler model. To illustrate, the $ARMA(1,1)$ model

$$(1 - 0.4\,\mathrm{B})y_t = \beta_0 + (1 - 0.4\,\mathrm{B})e_t$$

can be expressed as

$$y_t = (1 - 0.4\,\mathrm{B})^{-1}\beta_0 + e_t = 1.67\,\beta_0 + e_t$$

which is much simpler.

ψ-Coefficient Representation. The $ARIMA(p,d,q)$ model can be expressed as

$$y_t = \beta_0^* + e_t + \psi_1 e_{t-1} + \psi_2 e_{t-2} + \ldots = \beta_0^* + \sum_{k=0}^{\infty} \psi_k e_{t-k}, \qquad \text{(TS10.10)}$$

called the *ψ-coefficient representation*. That is, the current value of a process can be expressed as a constant plus a linear combination of the current and previous disturbances. Values of $\{\psi_k\}$ depend on the linear parameters of the $ARIMA$ process and can be determined via straightforward recursive substitution. To illustrate, for the $AR(1)$ model, we have

$$y_t = \beta_0 + e_t + \beta_1 y_{t-1}$$
$$= \beta_0 + e_t + \beta_1(\beta_0 + e_{t-1} + \beta_1 y_{t-2}) = \ldots = \beta_0/(1 - \beta_1) + \sum_{k=0}^{\infty} \beta_1^k e_{t-k}.$$

That is, $\psi_k = \beta_1^k$.

TS 10.3 Diagnostic Checking

Estimation. There is a variety of estimation procedures available, including maximum likelihood estimation, and conditional and unconditional least squares estimation. In most cases, these procedures require iterative fitting procedures. See Abraham and Ledolter (1983) for further information.

Residual Autocorrelation.   Residuals from the fitted model should resemble random errors and hence, display few discernible patterns. In particular, we expect $r_k(\hat{e})$, the lag k autocorrelation of residuals, to be approximately zero. To assess this, we have that $se(r_k(\hat{e})) \approx T^{-1/2}$. More precisely, McLeod (1977, 1978) has given approximations for a broad class of *ARMA* models. It turns out that the $T^{-1/2}$ can be improved for small values of k. (These improved values can be seen in the output of most statistical packages.) Surprisingly, the improvement depends on the model that is being fit. To illustrate, suppose that an *AR*(1) model with autoregressive parameter β_1 is fit to the data. Then, the approximate standard error of the lag one residual autocorrelation is $|\beta_1| \, T^{-1/2}$. This standard error can be much smaller than $T^{-1/2}$, depending on the value of β_1.

Testing Several Lags.   To test whether there is significant residual autocorrelation at a specific lag k, we use $r_k(\hat{e})/se(r_k(\hat{e}))$, the test statistic suggested in the preceding paragraph. However, to check whether residuals resemble a random process, we would like to test whether $r_k(\hat{e})$ is close to zero for several values of k. To test whether the first K residual autocorrelation are zero, use the Box and Pierce (1970) chi-square statistic

$$BP = T \sum_{k=1}^{K} r_k(\hat{e})^2.$$

Here, K is a number that is user-specified. If there is no real autocorrelation, then we expect BP to be small; more precisely, Box and Pierce have shown that BP follows an approximate χ^2 distribution with $df = K -$ (number of model linear parameters). For an $ARMA(p,q)$ model, the number of linear parameters is $1 + p + q$. Another widely used statistic is

$$BPL = T(T-2) \sum_{k=1}^{K} \frac{r_k(\hat{e})^2}{T-k} ,$$

due independently to Ljung and Box (1978) and Ansley and Newbold (1979). This statistic performs better in small samples than the BP statistic. Like the BP statistic, under the hypothesis of no residual autocorrelation, BPL follows a χ^2 distribution with $df = K -$ (number of model linear parameters). Thus, for each statistic, we reject H_0: No Residual Autocorrelation if the statistic exceeds *chi-value*, a $1 - \alpha$ percentile from a χ^2 distribution. In practice, a good approximation of *chi-value* is $1.5 \, df$.

TS 10.4 Forecasting

Optimal Point Forecasts.   Similar to forecasts that were introduced in Section TS 9.2, we consider here forecasts that are defined in terms of conditional expectations. Specifically, assume we have available a realization of $\{y_1, y_2, ..., y_T\}$ and would like to forecast y_{T+l}, the value of the series l lead time units in the future. If the parameters of the process were known, then we would use E $(y_{T+l}|y_T, y_{T-1}, y_{T-2}, ...)$, that is, the conditional expectation of y_{T+l} given the value of the series up to and including time T. We use the notation E_T for this conditional expectation. This forecast estimate is optimal in the sense that it minimizes the value of the (conditional) mean square error, $\text{MSE}(b^*) = \text{E}_T(y_{T+l} - b^*)^2$. In practice, values of parameters are replaced by their estimates to yield $\hat{y}_{T+l}$, the estimated value of $\text{E}_T y_{T+l}$.

Forecast Errors.   Using the ψ-coefficient representation in equation (TS10.10), we can express the conditional expectation of y_{T+l} as

$$\text{E}_T\, y_{T+l} = \beta_0^* + \sum_{k=0}^{\infty} \psi_k\, \text{E}_T\, e_{T+l-k} = \beta_0^* + \sum_{k=l}^{\infty} \psi_k\, \text{E}_T\, e_{T+l-k}.$$

This is because, at time T, the errors $e_T, e_{T-1}, ...$, have been realized and hence are known. However, the errors $e_{T+l}, e_{T+l-1}, ..., e_{T+1}$ have not been realized and hence have conditional expectation zero. Thus, the l-step forecast error is

$$y_{T+l} - \text{E}_T y_{T+l} = \beta_0^* + \sum_{k=0}^{\infty} \psi_k e_{T+l-k} - \left(\beta_0^* + \sum_{k=l}^{\infty} \psi_k e_{T+l-k}\right) = \sum_{k=0}^{l-1} \psi_k e_{T+l-k}.$$

As in the Forecasting With Random Walks subsection in Section TS 9.2, we focus on the variability of the forecasts errors. That is, straightforward calculations yield $\text{Var}(y_{T+l} - \text{E}_T y_{T+l}) = \sigma_e^2 \Sigma_{k=0}^{l-1} \psi_k^2$. Thus, assuming normality of the errors, a $100(1-\alpha)\%$ prediction interval for y_{T+l} is

$$\hat{y}_{T+l} \pm (t\text{-value})\hat{\sigma}_e \sqrt{\sum_{k=0}^{l-1} \hat{\psi}_k^2}\,,$$

where t-value is the $(1-\alpha/2)$th percentile from a t-distribution with $df = T -$ (number of linear parameters). If y_t is an $ARIMA(p, d, q)$ process, recall from Section TS 10.2 that ψ_k is a function of $\beta_1, \beta_2, ..., \beta_p, \theta_1, \theta_2, ..., \theta_q$. Thus, the notation $\hat{\psi}_k$ means that we use the same function, with parameter estimates $b_1, b_2, ..., b_k, \hat{\theta}_1, \hat{\theta}_2, ..., \hat{\theta}_q$.

CHAPTER 11

TS 11.1 Relation Between *ARIMA* (0,1,1) and Exponential Smoothing Models

Motivation.   Section 11.2 establishes the relationship between exponential smoothing models and weighted least squares. This relationship provides conditions under which the exponential smoothing forecasts are optimal. Similarly, in this subsection we establish the relationship between exponential smoothing forecasts and $ARIMA(0,1,1)$ forecasts. This relationship will provide us with a method for computing the optimal smoothing parameter.

Relationship. Using equation (TS10.9) the $ARIMA(0,1,1)$ model is $y_t - y_{t-1} = \beta_0 + e_t - \theta_1 e_{t-1}$. Taking β_0 to be zero, and using recursive substitution, we have

$$
\begin{aligned}
e_t &= y_t - y_{t-1} + \theta_1 e_{t-1} = y_t - y_{t-1} + \theta_1(y_{t-1} - y_{t-2} + \theta_1 e_{t-2}) \\
&= y_t - (1 - \theta_1)y_{t-1} - \theta_1 y_{t-2} + \theta_1^2 e_{t-2} \\
&= y_t - (1 - \theta_1)y_{t-1} - \theta_1 y_{t-2} + \theta_1^2(y_{t-2} - y_{t-3} + \theta_1 e_{t-3}) = \dots \\
&= y_t - (1 - \theta_1)(y_{t-1} + \theta_1 y_{t-2} + \theta_1^2 y_{t-3} + \dots).
\end{aligned}
$$

Thus, we have

$$
y_t = e_t + \frac{y_{t-1} + w y_{t-2} + w^2 y_{t-3} + \dots}{\dfrac{1}{1 - w}} \tag{TS11.1}
$$

with $\theta_1 = w$. This is the same as in equation (11.5), apart from the initial starting value. In particular, let $t = T + 1$ and take conditional expectations of both sides of equation (TS11.1) to get

$$
\hat{y}_{T+1} = E_T y_{T+1} = \frac{y_T + w y_{T-1} + w^2 y_{T-2} + \dots}{\dfrac{1}{1 - w}} = \hat{s}_T. \tag{TS11.2}
$$

Further, using the $ARIMA(0,1,1)$ model with $t = T + l$, for $l > 1$, yields

$$
\hat{y}_{T+l} - \hat{y}_{T+l-1} = E_T(y_{T+l} - y_{T+l-1}) = E_T(e_{T+l} - \theta_1 e_{T+l-1}) = 0.
$$

Thus, $\hat{y}_{T+l} = \hat{y}_{T+l-1} = \hat{y}_{T+l-2} = \dots = \hat{y}_{T+1}$. This and equation (TS11.2) establishes the equivalence between the exponential smoothing forecasts and the $ARIMA(0,1,1)$ forecasts.

Conclusions and Extensions. Thus, we have established that an exponential smoothing forecast is a special case of the $ARIMA(0,1,1)$ model, with the smoothing parameter w equal to the moving average parameter θ_1. Because there exists optimal ways of estimating θ_1, this relationship provides an optimal way of selecting the smoothing parameter w. Equation (11.9) specifies this estimation principle. The relationship between exponential smoothing and $ARIMA$ models has been extended to more complex models. It turns out that the kth order exponential smoothing forecasts can be expressed as special cases of $ARIMA(0,k,k)$ forecasts, where k may be 1, 2, 3, ... See Chapter 7 of Abraham and Ledolter (1983) for further discussion of this topic.

TS 11.2 Seasonal ARIMA Models

The seasonal autoregressive model of order P, introduced in equation (11.9) is

$$(1 - \beta_{SB,1}B^{SB} - \beta_{SB,2}B^{SB2} - \ldots - \beta_{SB,P}B^{SBP})y_t = \beta_{SB,0} + e_t. \quad \text{(TS11.3)}$$

Here we use notation $\{\beta_{SB,j}\}$ to distinguish the seasonal autoregressive parameters from the nonseasonal, or consecutive, autoregressive parameters $\{\beta_j\}$. Using the seasonal lag operator $L = B^{SB}$, this can be written more compactly as

$$\boldsymbol{\Phi}(L)y_t = (1 - \beta_{SB,1}L - \ldots \beta_{SB,P}L^P)y_t = \beta_{SB,0} + e_t. \quad \text{(TS11.4)}$$

Similar to equations (TS10.8) and (TS10.5) we can define seasonal differencing and seasonal moving average terms to yield the model

$$\boldsymbol{\Phi}(L)(1 - L)^D y_t = \beta_{SB,0} + \boldsymbol{\Theta}(L)e_t \quad \text{(TS11.5)}$$

where $\Theta(x) = 1 - \theta_{SB,1}x - \ldots - \theta_{SB,Q}x^Q$ and $\{\theta_{SB,j}\}$ are seasonal moving average parameters. Equation (TS11.5) is denoted to be a *SARIMA(P,D,Q)* model. Putting equations (TS10.9) and (TS11.5) yields the multiplicative seasonal autoregressive integrated moving average model of order $(p,d,q)(P,D,Q)$, or *SARIMA(p,d,q)(P,D,Q)*

$$\boldsymbol{\phi}(B)\boldsymbol{\Phi}(L)(1 - B)^d(1 - L)^D y_t = \beta_0 + \boldsymbol{\theta}(B)\boldsymbol{\Theta}(L)e_t. \quad \text{(TS11.6)}$$

Glossary

Added Variable Plot A plot of the response versus an explanatory variable, after controlling for the effects of additional explanatory variables. Also called a partial regression plot.

Aggregation of Data A type of error where different homogeneous subgroups are mistakenly combined to form a heterogeneous group.

Analysis of Variance (ANOVA) Model The acronym stands for analysis of variance. ANOVA models use only categorical quantities as independent variables.

Analysis of Variance (ANOVA) Table The ANOVA table is a bookkeeping device used to keep track of the sources of variability.

Autocorrelation This is a correlation between a variable and its lagged value.

Automatic Variable Selection Procedure A data exploration procedure that allows the analyst to search quickly through a large number of candidate models.

Autoregression A regression of a variable on its lagged value.

Bias The difference between the expected value of an estimator and the parameter being estimated. Bias is an estimation error that often does not become smaller as we take larger sample sizes.

Categorical Variable A numerical label for measurements that fall into distinct groups, or categories.

Causal Models In these models, the explanatory variables have a direct, or causal, effect on the response. This effect is generally established by using the scientific discipline that the data are related to.

Censored Data Data that are constrained to fall within certain boundaries.

Census A complete enumeration of the population.

Characteristic A measurement that is taken on a unit of observation.

Classification An application of regression models that uses binary dependent variables. Rules developed to predict the likelihood of a response being zero or one can be used to classify future observations into groups.

Collection of Entities This is the set of units of observation that are under consideration in the particular problem or area of concern.

Confidence Interval This is another term for interval estimate.

Control Chart A time series plot with reference lines, called control limits, superimposed.

Correlation A statistic that summarizes the strength of the linear relationship between two variables.

Count Data Data that are whole numbers, such as 1, 2, 3 and so on.

Covariate A continuous, that is, noncategorical, explanatory variable.

Cross-Sectional Data Data without an element of time-ordering involved.

Data Criticism For a specified model, examining unusual responses using residuals and examining unusual sets of explanatory variables using leverages.

Data-Snooping The practice of fitting a large number of models to a data set. This practice may lead the analyst to "discover" significant relationship when there are, in fact, none.

Dependent Variable The primary variable of interest; this is the variable that we are trying to predict or explain in terms of auxiliary information. Also called a response variable.

Diagnostic Checking Data criticism and model criticism.

Difference The change in adjacent values of a series.

Explanatory Variable This is another term for an independent, or predictor, variable.

Factor This is a categorical independent variable.

Fixed Seasonal Effects Model Seasonal effects are measured by a combination of parameter estimates plus a deterministic function of time. The time function gives a weight for the season that does not change over time.

Forecasting Predicting future values of a time series.

General Linear Model An extension of the linear regression model. In the general linear model, explanatory variables may be linear combinations of other explanatory variables.

Heteroscedasticity Different scatter, or varying variance, among observations.

High Leverage Point An observation that has an unusually large or small set of explanatory variables.

Histogram A graphical representation of a variable's distribution.

Homoscedasticity Same scatter, or constant variance, among observations.

Idealized Histogram A graphical representation of a variable's distribution that is described by a model.

Impute Missing Data The practice of approximating, or filling in, data values that are not available to the analyst.

Independent Variable The information in this auxiliary variable is used to predict, or explain, the dependent variable. Also called an explanatory, or predictor, variable.

Indicator Variable A categorical variable that has only two groups. The numerical values are usually taken to be one to indicate the presence of an attribute, and zero otherwise.

Interaction Term A variable that is a nonlinear function of two or more explanatory variables; typically, a multiplicative function.

Interval Estimate An interval that contains a point estimate. This interval is constructed to provide a measure of reliability for the point estimate. Also called a confidence interval.

Leading Indicator A predictor variable that depends on time and that becomes available before the response is realized.

Longitudinal Data Data with some element of time-ordering involved.

Logit A special function, defined by $\text{logit}(p) = \ln(p/(1-p))$, where "ln" is the natural logarithm function.

Maximum Likelihood Estimation This is another parameter estimation principle.

Meandering A series is meandering if adjacent values of the series are similar.

Method of Weighted Least Squares A parameter estimation principle that determines estimates by using weights associated with the squared errors. The weights may be specified by the user.

Model Criticism Evaluating the fit of a model to a specific data set.

Multiple Correlation Coefficient The positive square root of the coefficient of determination. It is the correlation between the response and the linear combination of explanatory variables specified by the estimated regression equation.

Normal Curve A specific type of idealized histogram. It is symmetric and is shaped like a bell.

Observational Data Data that are not set nor controlled by the analyst.

Outlier   An observation with an unusually large deviation from the fitted value.

Out-of-Sample Validation   The practice of using one set of data to develop one or more candidate models and another set of data to test, or validate, the best candidate model.

Parameter   A numerical quantity that summarizes an aspect of one or more characteristics of the population.

Partial Correlation Coefficient   The correlation coefficient that summarizes an added variable plot.

Partial Regression Plot   This is another term for an added variable plot.

Point Estimate   A statistic that is used as an approximation of a parameter.

Population   This is the entire collection of entities of interest in the particular problem or area of concern.

Predictor Variable   This is another term for an explanatory, or independent, variable.

Principle of Parsimony   This principle, when applied to model selection, means choosing the simplest model possible. Simpler models are easier to analyze and interpret than more complex models. Also known as "Occam's Razor."

Process   A series of actions or operations that lead to a particular end.

Random Process   A special model of a time series in which there are no patterns through time. This model is also called a "white noise" or an "i.i.d." (identically and independently distributed) process.

Random Sample   A subset of the population chosen so that each draw is selected randomly and the draws are unrelated.

Random Walk Model   Defined as the partial sum of a random process.

Residual Standard Deviation   This is another term for the standard error of the estimate.

Response Variable   This is another term for a dependent variable.

Sample   This is the collection of entities being analyzed. It is a subset of a larger collection, called the population or universe.

Sampling Frame   The list from which the sample is drawn.

Sampling Frame Error   A type of error that occurs when the sampling frame is not an adequate approximation of the universe of interest. This type of error can induce biased estimators.

Scatter Plot   A graphical representation of a bivariate data set.

Standard Error   The estimated standard deviation of a statistic.

Standard Error of the Estimate   This is the square root of the mean square error. Also called the residual standard deviation.

Statistic   A numerical quantity that summarizes an aspect of one or more characteristic of the sample.

Statistical Thinking   The process of locating, organizing and interpreting data to understand or solve a problem.

Statistics   A scientific discipline that is about collecting, summarizing, analyzing and making decisions using data.

Suppressor Variable   An explanatory variable that increases the importance of other explanatory variables when included in the model.

Time Series   A single sequence of data over time; it is often the value of a variable as it evolves over time.

Time Series Plot   A scatter plot of a series versus time. Generally, the series is plotted versus order of occurrence.

Truncated Data   A subset of the full range of potential data. The data in the subset are restricted to fall within certain boundaries.

Unbiased Estimator   An estimator that has no bias, that is, the expected value of an estimator equals the parameter being estimated.

Universe   This is another term for population.

Variable   A measurement that changes. A characteristic that varies over units of observation is a variable.

References

Selected references are given below under the chapter deemed most appropriate. Not all of these references have been cited in the main body of the text.

CROSS-SECTIONAL DATA MODEL TEXTBOOKS

ATKINSON, A. C. (1985). *Plots, Transformations and Regression: An Introduction to Graphical Methods of Diagnostic Regression Analysis.* Clarendon Press, Oxford, England.

BATES, D. M. and WATTS, D. G. (1988). *Nonlinear Regression Analysis and its Applications.* John Wiley & Sons, New York.

CHATTERJEE, S. and HADI, A. S. (1988). *Sensitivity Analysis in Linear Regression.* John Wiley & Sons, New York.

CHATTERJEE, S. and PRICE, B. (1977). *Regression Analysis by Example.* John Wiley & Sons, New York.

COHEN, J. and COHEN, P. (1983). *Applied Multiple Regression/Correlation Analysis for the Behavioral Sciences,* Second Edition, Lawrence Erlbaum Associates, Hillsdale, NJ.

CRYER, J. D. and MILLER, R. B. (1994). *Statistics for Business: Data Analysis and Modelling.* PWS-Kent, Boston.

DIELMAN, T. E. (1991). *Applied Regression Analysis for Business and Economics.* PWS-Kent, Boston.

DRAPER, N. R. and SMITH, H. (1981). *Applied Regression Analysis,* second edition. John Wiley & Sons, New York.

FREEDMAN, D., PISANI, R. and PURVIS, R. (1978). *Statistics.* W. W. Norton, New York.

HAMILTON, L. C. (1992). *Regression with Graphics: A Second Course in Applied Statistics.* Brooks/Cole, Pacific Grove, CA.

HETTMANSPERGER, T. P. (1984). *Statistical Inference Based on Ranks.* John Wiley & Sons, New York.

LITTLE, R. and RUBIN, D. (1987). *Statistical Analysis with Missing Data.* Wiley, New York.

MILLER, R. B. and WICHERN, D. (1977). *Intermediate Business Statistics: Analysis of Variance, Regression and Time Series.* Holt, Rinehart and Winston, New York.

MONTGOMERY, D. C. and PECK, E. A. (1992). *Introduction to Linear Regression Analysis.* Wiley, New York.

MOSTELLER, F. and TUKEY, J. W. (1977). *Data Analysis and Regression.* Addison-Wesley, Reading, MA.

MYERS, R. H. (1990). *Classical and Modern Regression with Applications,* 2nd ed. PWS-Kent, Boston.

NETER, J., WASSERMAN, W. and KUTNER, M. H. (1989). *Applied Linear Regression Models.* Irwin, Homewood, IL.

PEDHAZUR, E. J. (1982). *Multiple Regression in Behavioral Research: Explanation and Prediction.* Holt, Rinehart and Winston, New York.

PLACKETT, R. L. (1960). *Regression Analysis.* Clarendon Press, Oxford, England.

RAO, C. R. (1973). *Linear Statistical Inference and Its Applications,* Second Edition. John Wiley & Sons, New York.

RAWLINGS, J. O. (1986). *Applied Regression Analysis: A Research Tool.* Wadsworth & Brooks/Cole, Pacific Grove, CA.

ROUSSEEUW, P. J. and LEROY, A. M. (1987). *Robust Regression and Outlier Detection.* John Wiley & Sons, New York.

SEARLE, S. R. (1982). *Matrix Algebra Useful for Statistics.* John Wiley & Sons, New York.

SEARLE, S. R. (1987). *Linear Models for Unbalanced Data.* John Wiley & Sons, New York.

SEBER, G. A. F. (1977). *Linear Regression Analysis.* John Wiley & Sons, New York.

TUKEY, J. W. (1977). *Exploratory Data Analysis.* Addison-Wesley, Reading, MA.

WEISBERG, S. (1985). *Applied Linear Regression,* Second Edition. John Wiley & Sons, New York.

WILLIAMS, E. J. (1959). *Regression Analysis.* John Wiley & Sons, New York.

LONGITUDINAL DATA MODEL TEXTBOOKS

ABRAHAM, B. and LEDOLTER, J. (1983). *Statistical Methods for Forecasting.* John Wiley & Sons, New York.

BERNDT, E. R. (1991). *The Practice of Econometrics: Classic and Contemporary.* Addison-Wesley, Reading, MA.

BOX, G. E. P., JENKINS, G. and REINSEL, G. (1994). *Time Series Analysis: Forecasting and Control.* Prentice-Hall, Englewood Cliffs, NJ.

CRYER, J. (1986). *Time Series Analysis.* PWS-Kent, Boston, MA.

CHATFIELD, C. (1991). *The Analysis of Time Series.* Chapman and Hall, New York.

GOLDBERGER, A. (1991). *A Course in Econometrics.* Harvard University Press, Cambridge, MA.

GREENE, W. H. (1993). *Econometric Analysis.* MacMillan, New York.

HARVEY, A. C. (1989). *Forecasting, Structural Time Series Models and the Kalman Filter.* Cambridge University Press, Oxford.

MONTGOMERY, D. C., JOHNSON, L. A. and GARDINER, J. S. (1990). *Forecasting & Time Series Analysis,* McGraw-Hill, New York.

NELSON, C. R. (1983). *Applied Time Series Analysis for Managerial Forecasting.* Holden-Day, San Francisco, CA.

PINDYCK, R. S. and RUBINFELD, D. L. (1991). *Econometric Models and Economic Forecasts,* Third Edition. McGraw-Hill, New York.

ROBERTS, H. V. (1991). *Data Analysis for Managers with MINITAB.* Scientific Press, South San Francisco, CA.

JOURNAL ARTICLES AND OTHER REFERENCES, BY CHAPTER

A reference is given in the chapter for the first citation. If you do not find a reference in a particular chapter, look in the preceding chapter references or in the lists of textbooks.

CHAPTER 1

GALTON, SIR FRANCIS (1885). "Regression towards mediocrity in heredity stature." *Journal of Anthropological Institute* 15, 246–263.

HALLEY, E. (1693). "An estimate of the degrees of the mortality of mankind, drawn from curious tables of the births and funerals at the city of Breslaw; with an attempt to ascertain the price of annuities upon lives." *Phil. Trans.* 17, 596–610.

STIGLER, S. M. (1986). *The History of Statistics: The Meaurement of Uncertainty before 1900.* The Belknap Press of Harvard University Press, Cambridge, MA.

CHAPTER 2

FIENBERG, S. E. (1992). "The history of statistics: A review essay." *Statistical Science* 7, 208–225.

FREES, E. W. (1992). "Forecasting state-to-state migration rates." *Journal of Business and Economic Statistics* 10, 153–167.

FREES, E. W. (1993). "Short-term forecasting of internal migration." *Environment and Planning, Series A,* 25, 1,593–1,606.

FREES, E. W. (1994). "Estimating densities of functions of observations." *Journal of the American Statistical Association,* 89, 517–526.

GRAUNT, J. (1662). *Natural and Political Observations Made Upon the Bills of Mortality.* Martyn, London, England.

STUDENT (W. GOSSET). (1908). "The probable error of a mean." *Biometrika* 6, 1–25.

CHAPTER 3

COHEN, K. J., MAIER, S. F., SCHWARTZ, R. A. and WHITCOMB, D. K. (1986). *The Microstructure of Securities Markets.* Prentice-Hall, Englewood Cliffs, NJ.

KOCH, G. J. (1985). "A basic demonstration of the $[-1, 1]$ range for the correlation coefficient." *American Statistician* 39, 201–202.

LINTNER, J. (1965). "The valuation of risky assets and the selection of risky investments in stock portfolios and capital budgets." *Review of Economics and Statistics*, 13–37.

MARKOWITZ, H. (1959). *Portfolio Selection: Efficient Diversification of Investments,* John Wiley & Sons, New York.

PEARSON, K. (1895). *Royal Society Proceedings* 58, 241.

RODGERS, J. L. and NICEWANDER, W. A. (1988). "Thirteen ways to look at the correlation coefficient." *The American Statistician* 42, 59–65.

SHARPE, W. F. (1964). "Capital asset prices: A theory of market equilibrium under risk." *Journal of Finance,* 425–442.

STIGLER, S. M. (1989). "Galton's account of the invention of correlation." *Statistical Science* 4, 73–86.

CHAPTER 4

BOX, G. E. P. (1980). "Sampling and Bayes inference in scientific modeling and robustness (with discussion)." *Journal of the Royal Statistical Society, Series A,* 143, 383–430.

JOHNSON, R. R. and MESSMER, D. J. (1991). "The effect of advertising on hierarchical stages in vacation destination choice." *Journal of Advertising Research* 31, No. 6, December.

LAGACE, R. R., DAHLSTROM, R. and GASSENGEIMER, J. B. (1991). "The relevance of ethical salesperson behavior on relationship quality: The pharmaceutical industry." *Journal of Personal Selling & Sales Management* 11, No. 4, 39–47.

CHAPTER 5

LEVIN, J. R., SARLIN, R. C. and WEBNE-BEHRMAN, L. (1989). "Analysis of variance through simple correlation." *American Statistician* 43, 32–34.

CHAPTER 6

ANDREWS, D. F. (1971). "Significance test based on residuals." *Biometrika* 58, 139–148.

BECKMAN, R. J. and COOK, R. D. (1983). "Outlier ... s." *Technometrics* 25, 119–145.

BELSEY, D. A., KUH, E. and WELSCH, R. E. (1980). *Regression Diagnostics: Identifying Influential Data and Sources of Collinearity.* John Wiley & Sons, New York.

BENDEL, R. B. and AFIFI, A. A. (1977). "Comparison of stopping rules in forward "stepwise" regression." *Journal of the American Statistical Association* 72, 46–53.

BERK, K. N. (1978). "Comparing subset regression procedures." *Technometrics* 20, 1–6.

BERK, K. N. (1984). "Validating regression procedures with new data." *Technometrics* 26, 331–338.

BERKSON, J. (1950). "Are there two regressions?" *Journal of the American Statistical Association* 45, 164–180.

BOX, G. E. P. (1966). "Use and abuse of regression." *Technometrics* 8, 625–629.

BOX, G. E. P. and COX, D. R. (1964). "An analysis of transformations (with discussion)." *Journal of the Royal Statistical Society, Series B,* 26, 211–246.

BOX, G. E. P. and TIDWELL, P. W. (1962). "Transformation of the independent variables." *Technometrics* 4, 531–550.

CARROLL, R. J. and RUPPERT, D. (1988). *Transformation and Weighting in Regression.* Chapman and Hall, New York.

COOK, R. D. and WEISBERG, S. (1982). *Residuals and Influence in Regression.* Chapman and Hall, New York.

HADI, A. S. (1988). "Diagnosing collinearity-influential observations." *Computational Statistics and Data Analysis* 7, 143–159.

HAMILTON, D. (1987). "Sometimes $R^2 > r_{yx1}^2 + r_{yx2}^2$: Correlated variables are not always redundant." *The American Statistician* 41, 129–132.

HOAGLIN, D. C. and WELCH, R. (1978). "The hat matrix in regression and ANOVA." *The American Statistician.* 32, 17–22.

HOAGLIN, D. C. (1985). "Transformations in everyday experience." *Change* 1, 40–45.

HOCKING, R. R. (1976). "The analysis and selection of variables in linear regression." *Biometrics* 32, 1–49.

HOCKING, R. R. (1983). "Developments in linear regression methodology: 1959–1982 (with discussion)." *Technometrics* 25, 219–249.

KVALSETH, T. O. (1985). "Cautionary note about R^2." *The American Statistician* 39, 279–285.

MALLOWS, C. L. (1973). "Some comments on C_p." *Technometrics* 15, 661–675.

MASON, R. L. and GUNST, R. F. (1985). "Outlier-induced collinearities." *Technometrics* 27, 401–407.

PICARD, R. R. and BERK, K. N. (1990). "Data splitting." *The American Statistician* 44, 140–147.

RENCHER, A. C. and PUN, F. C. (1980). "Inflation of R^2 in best subset regression." *Technometrics* 22, 49–53.

SALL, J. (1990). "Leverage plots for general linear hypotheses." *The American Statistician* 44, 308–315.

SCOTT, A. and WILD, C. (1991). "Transformations and R^2." *The American Statistician* 45, 127–129.

SEARLE, S. R. (1988). "Parallel lines in residual plots." *The American Statistician* 42, 211.

SNEE, R. D. (1977). "Validation of regression models. Methods and examples." *Technometrics* 19, 415–428.

STEWART, G. W. (1987). "Collinearity and least squares regression (with discussion)." *Statistical Science* 2, 68–100.

CHAPTER 7

Box, G. E. P. (1979). "Robustness in the strategy of scientific model building," in R. Launer and G. Wilderson (eds.), *Robustness in Statistics,* page 201–236. Academic Press, New York.

Miller, R. G. (1965). *Simultaneous Statistical Inference.* McGraw-Hill, New York.

Schmit, J. and Roth, K. (1990), "Cost effectiveness of risk management practices." *The Journal of Risk and Insurance,* 57, 455–470.

Tukey, J. W. (1991). "The philosophy of multiple comparisons." *Statistical Science* 6, 100–118.

CHAPTER 8

Christian, C. W., Gupta, S. and Lin, S. (1992). "Determinants of tax preparer usage: Evidence from panel." *National Tax Journal* 46(4), 487–503.

Cox, D. R. (1983). *The Analysis of Binary Data.* John Wiley & Sons, New York.

Cox, D. R. and Wermuth, N. (1992). "A comment on the coefficient of determination for binary responses." *The American Statistician* 46, 1–4.

Hosmer, D. W. and Lemeshow, S. (1989). *Applied Logistic Regression.* John Wiley & Sons, New York.

CHAPTER 9

"Report of the Maturity Guarantees Working Party" (1980). *Journal of the Institute of Actuaries,* 107, 103–213.

Tsay, R. S. (1987), "Conditional heteroscedastic time series models," *Journal of the American Statistical Association* 82, 590–604.

CHAPTER 11

Durbin, J. and Watson, G. S. (1950). "Testing for serial correlation in least squares regression I." *Biometrika* 38, 159–178.

Holt, C. C. (1957). "Forecasting trends and seasonals by exponentially weighted moving averages." *O.N.R. Memorandum,* No. 52, Carnegie Institute of Technology.

Prais, S. J. and Winston, C. B. (1954). "Trend estimators and serial correlation." *Cowles Commission Discussion Paper,* No. 383, Chicago.

Winters, P. R. (1960). "Forecasting sales by exponentially weighted moving averages." *Management Science* 6, 324–342.

CHAPTER 12

CLEVELAND, W. S. (1985). *The Elements of Graphing Data.* Wadsworth, Monterey, CA.

EHRENBERG, A. S. C. (1977). "Rudiments of numeracy." *Journal of the Royal Statistical Society A* 140, 277–297.

LINDEN, D.W. and MACHAN, D. (1992). "Put them at risk." *Forbes Magazine,* May 25, 158.

TUFTE, E. R. (1983). *The Visual Display of Quantitative Information.* Graphics Press, Cheshire, CT.

TUFTE, E. R. (1990). *Envisioning Information.* Graphics Press, Cheshire, CT.

"What 800 Companies Paid for their Bosses." *Forbes Magazine,* May 25, 1992, 182.

CHAPTER 13

ANSCOMBE, F. (1973). "Graphs in statistical analysis." *The American Statistician* 27, 17–21.

BAJGIER, S. M. ATKINSON, M. and PRYBUTOK, V. R. (1989). "Visual fits in the teaching of regression concepts." *The American Statistician* 43, 229–234.

CLEVELAND, W. S., DIACONIS, P. and McGILL, R., (1982). "Variables on scatter plots look more highly correlated when the scales are increased." *Science* 216, 1138–1141.

CLEVELAND, W. S. (1985). *The Elements of Graphing Data.* Wadsworth, Monterey, CA.

CLEVELAND, W. S. (1994). *Visualizing Data.* Hobart Press, Summit, NJ.

CLEVELAND, W. S. and McGILL, R. (1984). "Graphical perception: theory, experimentation, and application to the development of graphical methods." *Journal of the American Statistical Association* 79, 531–554.

DENBY, L. and PREGIBON, D. (1987). "An example of the use of graphics in regression." *The American Statistician* 41, 33–38.

SCHMID, C. F. (1992). *Statistical Graphics: Design Principles and Practices.* Krieger Publishing Company, Krieger Drive, Malabar, FL.

WILK, M. B. and GRANADESIKAN, R. (1968). "Probability plotting methods for the analysis of data." *Biometrika* 55, 1–17.

OTHER

BOX, J. F. (1987). "Guinness, Gosset, Fisher and small samples." *Statistical Science* 2, 45–52.

HOGG, R. V. (1972). "On statistical education." *The American Statistician* 26, 8–11.

HUNTER, W. G. (1981). "The practice of statistics: The real world is an idea whose time has come." *The American Statistician* 35, 72–76.

KHAMIS, H. J. (1991). "Manual computations—a tool for reinforcing concepts and techniques." *The American Statistician* 45, 294–299.

MOORE, T. L. and ROBERTS, R. A. (1989). "Statistics at liberal arts colleges." *The American Statistician* 43, 80–85.

MOSTELLER, F. (1980). "Classroom and platform performance." *The American Statistician* 34, 11–17.

RADKE-SHARPE, N. (1991). "Writing as a component of statistics education." *The American Statistician* 45, 292–293.

ROBERTS, H. V. (1990). "Business and economic statistics (with discussion)." *Statistical Science* 4, 372–402.

ROSE, E. L. MACHAK, J. A. and SPIVEY, W. A. (1988). "A survey of the teaching of statistics in M.B.A. programs." *Journal of Business & Economic Statistics* 6, 273–282.

SINGER, J. D. and WILLETT, J. B. (1990). "Improving the teaching of applied statistics: Putting the data back into data analysis." *The American Statistician* 44, 223–230.

WATTS, D. G. (1981). "A task-analysis approach to designing a regression analysis course." *The American Statistician* 35, 77–84.

TECHNICAL SUPPLEMENTS

ANSLEY, C. F. and NEWBOLD, P. (1979), "On the finite sample distribution of residual autocorrelations in autoregressive moving average models," *Biometrika* 66, 547–553.

BEARD, R. E., PENTIKÄINEN, T. and PESONEN, E. (1984), *Risk Theory: The Stochastic Basis of Insurance*, Chapman and Hall, New York.

BICKEL, P. J. and DOKSUM, K. A. (1977), *Mathematical Statistics*, Holden-Day, San Francisco, CA.

BOX, G. E. P. and PIERCE, D. A. (1970), "Distribution of residual autocorrelations in autoregressive moving average time series models," *Journal of the American Statistical Association* 65, 1509–1526.

GRAYBILL, F. A. (1983). *Matrices with Applications in Statistics*, 2nd ed., Wadsworth, Belmont, CA.

HAMPEL, F. R., RONCHETTI, E. M., ROUSSEEUW, P. J. and STAHEL, W. A. (1986) *Robust Statistics: The Approach Based on Influence Fucntions*, John Wiley & Sons, New York.

HOGG, R. V. and CRAIG, A. T. (1978). *Introduction to Mathematical Statistics*, 4th ed., MacMillan, New York.

JOHN, J. A. and DRAPER, N. R. (1980), "An alternative family of transformations," *Applied Statistics* 29, 190–197.

KVALSETH, T. O. (1985), "Cautionary note about R^2," *American Statistician* 39, 279–285.

LJUNG, G. M. and BOX, G. E. P. (1978), "On a measure of lack of fit in time series models," *Biometrika* 65, 297–303.

McLEOD, A. I. (1977), "Improved Box-Jenkins estimators," *Biometrika* 64, 531–534.

McLEOD, A. I. (1978), "On the distribution of residual autocorrelations in Box-Jenkins models," *Journal of the Royal Statistical Society B* 40, 296–302.

SERFLING, R. J. (1980), *Approximation Theorems of Mathematical Statistics*, John Wiley & Sons, New York.

Probability Tables

STANDARD NORMAL CURVE PROBABILITIES

The numbers in the table give various probabilities for a standard normal distribution. The probabilities can be found by looking at the appropriate row for the lead decimal place and column for the second decimal. For example, the area under the curve to the left of 1.90 is 0.9713. The area under the curve to the left of 1.96 is 0.975. For negative numbers, we get the areas by symmetry. For example, the area under the curve to the left of −1.96 is 0.025. The area between two numbers is determined by subtraction. For example, the area under the curve between −1.96 and 1.96 is 0.95.

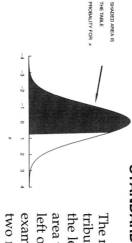

SHADED AREA IS
THE TABLE
PROBABILITY FOR x

Plot for normal table

x	0.00	0.01	0.02	0.03	0.04	0.05	0.06	0.07	0.08	0.09
				Second decimal place in x						
0.0	0.5000	0.5040	0.5080	0.5120	0.5160	0.5199	0.5239	0.5279	0.5319	0.5359
0.1	0.5398	0.5438	0.5478	0.5517	0.5557	0.5596	0.5636	0.5675	0.5714	0.5753
0.2	0.5793	0.5832	0.5871	0.5910	0.5948	0.5987	0.6026	0.6064	0.6103	0.6141
0.3	0.6179	0.6217	0.6255	0.6293	0.6331	0.6368	0.6406	0.6443	0.6480	0.6517
0.4	0.6554	0.6591	0.6628	0.6664	0.6700	0.6736	0.6772	0.6808	0.6844	0.6879
0.5	0.6915	0.6950	0.6985	0.7019	0.7054	0.7088	0.7123	0.7157	0.7190	0.7224
0.6	0.7257	0.7291	0.7324	0.7357	0.7389	0.7422	0.7454	0.7486	0.7517	0.7549
0.7	0.7580	0.7611	0.7642	0.7673	0.7703	0.7734	0.7764	0.7793	0.7823	0.7852
0.8	0.7881	0.7910	0.7939	0.7967	0.7995	0.8023	0.8051	0.8079	0.8106	0.8133
0.9	0.8159	0.8186	0.8212	0.8238	0.8264	0.8289	0.8315	0.8340	0.8365	0.8389
1.0	0.8413	0.8438	0.8461	0.8485	0.8508	0.8531	0.8554	0.8577	0.8599	0.8621
1.1	0.8643	0.8665	0.8686	0.8708	0.8729	0.8749	0.8770	0.8790	0.8810	0.8830
1.2	0.8849	0.8869	0.8888	0.8907	0.8925	0.8943	0.8962	0.8980	0.8997	0.9015
1.3	0.9032	0.9049	0.9066	0.9082	0.9099	0.9115	0.9131	0.9147	0.9162	0.9177

1.4	0.9192	0.9207	0.9222	0.9236	0.9251	0.9265	0.9279	0.9292	0.9306	0.9319
1.5	0.9332	0.9345	0.9357	0.9370	0.9382	0.9394	0.9406	0.9418	0.9429	0.9441
1.6	0.9452	0.9463	0.9474	0.9484	0.9495	0.9505	0.9515	0.9525	0.9535	0.9545
1.7	0.9554	0.9564	0.9573	0.9582	0.9591	0.9599	0.9608	0.9616	0.9625	0.9633
1.8	0.9641	0.9649	0.9656	0.9664	0.9671	0.9678	0.9686	0.9693	0.9699	0.9706
1.9	0.9713	0.9719	0.9726	0.9732	0.9738	0.9744	0.9750	0.9756	0.9761	0.9767
2.0	0.9772	0.9778	0.9783	0.9788	0.9793	0.9798	0.9803	0.9808	0.9812	0.9817
2.1	0.9821	0.9826	0.9830	0.9834	0.9838	0.9842	0.9846	0.9850	0.9854	0.9857
2.2	0.9861	0.9864	0.9868	0.9871	0.9875	0.9878	0.9881	0.9884	0.9887	0.9890
2.3	0.9893	0.9896	0.9898	0.9901	0.9904	0.9906	0.9909	0.9911	0.9913	0.9916
2.4	0.9918	0.9920	0.9922	0.9925	0.9927	0.9929	0.9931	0.9932	0.9934	0.9936
2.5	0.9938	0.9940	0.9941	0.9943	0.9945	0.9946	0.9948	0.9949	0.9951	0.9952
2.6	0.9953	0.9955	0.9956	0.9957	0.9959	0.9960	0.9961	0.9962	0.9963	0.9964
2.7	0.9965	0.9966	0.9967	0.9968	0.9969	0.9970	0.9971	0.9972	0.9973	0.9974
2.8	0.9974	0.9975	0.9976	0.9977	0.9977	0.9978	0.9979	0.9979	0.9980	0.9981
2.9	0.9981	0.9982	0.9982	0.9983	0.9984	0.9984	0.9985	0.9985	0.9986	0.9986
3.0	0.9987	0.9987	0.9987	0.9988	0.9988	0.9989	0.9989	0.9989	0.9990	0.9990

PERCENTILES FOR SEVERAL t-DISTRIBUTIONS

The numbers in the table give various percentiles for a *t*-distribution with *df* degrees of freedom. The percentiles can be found by looking at the appropriate column and row for the probability and the degree of freedom, respectively. For example, for a *t*-curve with *df* = 20, the area under the curve to the left of 2.086 is 0.975. By the symmetry of the *t*-curve, this means that the area between −2.086 and 2.086 is 0.95. The column labeled 'infinity' stands for the theoretical limit of the progression of degrees of freedom which corresponds to the percentile from the *standard normal curve*.

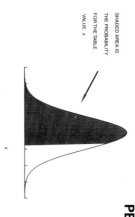

Plot for *t*-table

SHADED AREA IS THE PROBABILITY FOR THE TABLE VALUE *x*

Degrees of freedom (*df*)	Probability																	
	0.500	0.550	0.600	0.650	0.700	0.750	0.800	0.850	0.900	0.950	0.975	0.990	0.995	0.9975	0.999
1	0.000	0.158	0.325	0.510	0.727	1.000	1.376	1.963	3.078	6.314	12.706	31.821	63.657	127.322	318.317
2	0.000	0.142	0.289	0.445	0.617	0.816	1.061	1.386	1.886	2.920	4.303	6.965	9.925	14.089	22.327
3	0.000	0.137	0.277	0.424	0.584	0.765	0.978	1.250	1.638	2.353	3.182	4.541	5.841	7.453	10.215
4	0.000	0.134	0.271	0.414	0.569	0.741	0.941	1.190	1.533	2.132	2.776	3.747	4.604	5.598	7.173
5	0.000	0.132	0.267	0.408	0.559	0.727	0.920	1.156	1.476	2.015	2.571	3.365	4.032	4.773	5.893
6	0.000	0.131	0.265	0.404	0.553	0.718	0.906	1.134	1.440	1.943	2.447	3.143	3.707	4.317	5.208
7	0.000	0.130	0.263	0.402	0.549	0.711	0.896	1.119	1.415	1.895	2.365	2.998	3.499	4.029	4.785
8	0.000	0.130	0.262	0.399	0.546	0.706	0.889	1.108	1.397	1.860	2.306	2.896	3.355	3.833	4.501
9	0.000	0.129	0.261	0.398	0.543	0.703	0.883	1.100	1.383	1.833	2.262	2.821	3.250	3.690	4.297
10	0.000	0.129	0.260	0.397	0.542	0.700	0.879	1.093	1.372	1.812	2.228	2.764	3.169	3.581	4.144
11	0.000	0.129	0.260	0.396	0.540	0.697	0.876	1.088	1.363	1.796	2.201	2.718	3.106	3.497	4.025
12	0.000	0.128	0.259	0.395	0.539	0.695	0.873	1.083	1.356	1.782	2.179	2.681	3.055	3.428	3.930
13	0.000	0.128	0.259	0.394	0.538	0.694	0.870	1.079	1.350	1.771	2.160	2.650	3.012	3.372	3.852
14	0.000	0.128	0.258	0.393	0.537	0.692	0.868	1.076	1.345	1.761	2.145	2.624	2.977	3.326	3.787
15	0.000	0.128	0.258	0.393	0.536	0.691	0.866	1.074	1.341	1.753	2.131	2.602	2.947	3.286	3.733

16	0.000	0.128	0.258	0.392	0.535	0.690	0.865	1.071	1.337	1.746	2.120	2.583	2.921	3.252	3.686
17	0.000	0.128	0.257	0.392	0.534	0.689	0.863	1.069	1.333	1.740	2.110	2.567	2.898	3.222	3.646
18	0.000	0.127	0.257	0.392	0.534	0.688	0.862	1.067	1.330	1.734	2.101	2.552	2.878	3.197	3.611
19	0.000	0.127	0.257	0.391	0.533	0.688	0.861	1.066	1.328	1.729	2.093	2.539	2.861	3.174	3.579
20	0.000	0.127	0.257	0.391	0.533	0.687	0.860	1.064	1.325	1.725	2.086	2.528	2.845	3.153	3.552
21	0.000	0.127	0.257	0.391	0.532	0.686	0.859	1.063	1.323	1.721	2.080	2.518	2.831	3.135	3.527
22	0.000	0.127	0.256	0.390	0.532	0.686	0.858	1.061	1.321	1.717	2.074	2.508	2.819	3.119	3.505
23	0.000	0.127	0.256	0.390	0.532	0.685	0.858	1.060	1.319	1.714	2.069	2.500	2.807	3.104	3.485
24	0.000	0.127	0.256	0.390	0.531	0.685	0.857	1.059	1.318	1.711	2.064	2.492	2.797	3.091	3.467
25	0.000	0.127	0.256	0.390	0.531	0.684	0.856	1.058	1.316	1.708	2.060	2.485	2.787	3.078	3.450
26	0.000	0.127	0.256	0.390	0.531	0.684	0.856	1.058	1.315	1.706	2.056	2.479	2.779	3.067	3.435
27	0.000	0.127	0.256	0.389	0.531	0.684	0.855	1.057	1.314	1.703	2.052	2.473	2.771	3.057	3.421
28	0.000	0.127	0.256	0.389	0.530	0.683	0.855	1.056	1.313	1.701	2.048	2.467	2.763	3.047	3.408
29	0.000	0.127	0.256	0.389	0.530	0.683	0.854	1.055	1.311	1.699	2.045	2.462	2.756	3.038	3.396
30	0.000	0.127	0.256	0.389	0.530	0.683	0.854	1.055	1.310	1.697	2.042	2.457	2.750	3.030	3.385
35	0.000	0.127	0.255	0.388	0.529	0.682	0.852	1.052	1.306	1.690	2.030	2.438	2.724	2.996	3.340
40	0.000	0.126	0.255	0.388	0.529	0.681	0.851	1.050	1.303	1.684	2.021	2.423	2.704	2.971	3.307
60	0.000	0.126	0.254	0.387	0.527	0.679	0.848	1.045	1.296	1.671	2.000	2.390	2.660	2.915	3.232
120	0.000	0.126	0.254	0.386	0.526	0.677	0.845	1.041	1.289	1.658	1.980	2.358	2.617	2.860	3.160
infinity	0.000	0.126	0.253	0.385	0.524	0.674	0.842	1.036	1.282	1.645	1.960	2.326	2.576	2.810	3.090

95TH PERCENTILE FOR SEVERAL F-DISTRIBUTIONS

The numbers in the table give the 95th percentile for an F-distribution with df_1 degrees of freedom in the numerator and df_2 degrees of freedom in the denominator. For example, for an F-curve with $df_1 = 3$ and $df_2 = 20$, the area under the curve to the left of 3.098 is 0.95. The row and column labeled 'infinity' stand for the theoretical limit of the progression of degrees of freedom.

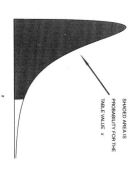

SHADED AREA IS PROBABILITY FOR THE TABLE VALUE x

Plot for F-table

Denominator degrees of freedom (df_2)	Numerator degrees of freedom (df_1)												
	1	2	3	4	5	6	7	8	9	10	15	20	infinity
1	161.448	199.500	215.707	224.583	230.161	233.985	236.768	238.882	240.543	241.881	245.949	248.012	254.314
2	18.513	19.000	19.164	19.247	19.296	19.329	19.353	19.371	19.385	19.396	19.429	19.446	19.496
3	10.128	9.552	9.227	9.117	9.013	8.941	8.887	8.845	8.812	8.786	8.703	8.660	8.526
4	7.709	6.944	6.591	6.388	6.256	6.163	6.094	6.041	5.999	5.964	5.858	5.803	5.628
5	6.608	5.786	5.409	5.192	5.050	4.950	4.876	4.818	4.772	4.735	4.619	4.558	4.365
6	5.987	5.143	4.757	4.534	4.387	4.284	4.207	4.147	4.099	4.060	3.938	3.874	3.669
7	5.591	4.737	4.347	4.120	3.972	3.866	3.787	3.726	3.677	3.637	3.511	3.445	3.230
8	5.318	4.459	4.066	3.838	3.687	3.581	3.500	3.438	3.388	3.347	3.218	3.150	2.928
9	5.117	4.256	3.863	3.633	3.482	3.374	3.293	3.230	3.179	3.137	3.006	2.936	2.707
10	4.965	4.103	3.708	3.478	3.326	3.217	3.135	3.072	3.020	2.978	2.845	2.774	2.538
11	4.844	3.982	3.587	3.357	3.204	3.095	3.012	2.948	2.896	2.854	2.719	2.646	2.404
12	4.747	3.885	3.490	3.259	3.106	2.996	2.913	2.849	2.796	2.753	2.617	2.544	2.296
13	4.667	3.806	3.411	3.179	3.025	2.915	2.832	2.767	2.714	2.671	2.533	2.459	2.206
14	4.600	3.739	3.344	3.112	2.958	2.848	2.764	2.699	2.646	2.602	2.463	2.388	2.131
15	4.543	3.682	3.287	3.056	2.901	2.790	2.707	2.641	2.588	2.544	2.403	2.328	2.066

16	4.494	3.634	3.239	3.007	2.852	2.741	2.657	2.591	2.538	2.494	2.352	2.276	2.010
17	4.451	3.592	3.197	2.965	2.810	2.699	2.614	2.548	2.494	2.450	2.308	2.230	1.960
18	4.414	3.555	3.160	2.928	2.773	2.661	2.577	2.510	2.456	2.412	2.269	2.191	1.917
19	4.381	3.522	3.127	2.895	2.740	2.628	2.544	2.477	2.423	2.378	2.234	2.156	1.878
20	4.351	3.493	3.098	2.866	2.711	2.599	2.514	2.447	2.393	2.348	2.203	2.124	1.843
21	4.325	3.467	3.072	2.840	2.685	2.573	2.488	2.420	2.366	2.321	2.176	2.096	1.812
22	4.301	3.443	3.049	2.817	2.661	2.549	2.464	2.397	2.342	2.297	2.151	2.071	1.783
23	4.279	3.422	3.028	2.796	2.640	2.528	2.442	2.375	2.320	2.275	2.128	2.048	1.757
24	4.260	3.403	3.009	2.776	2.621	2.508	2.423	2.355	2.300	2.255	2.108	2.027	1.733
25	4.242	3.385	2.991	2.759	2.603	2.490	2.405	2.337	2.282	2.236	2.089	2.007	1.711
26	4.225	3.369	2.975	2.743	2.587	2.474	2.388	2.321	2.265	2.220	2.072	1.990	1.691
27	4.210	3.354	2.960	2.728	2.572	2.459	2.373	2.305	2.250	2.204	2.056	1.974	1.672
28	4.196	3.340	2.947	2.714	2.558	2.445	2.359	2.291	2.236	2.190	2.041	1.959	1.654
29	4.183	3.328	2.934	2.701	2.545	2.432	2.346	2.278	2.223	2.177	2.027	1.945	1.638
30	4.171	3.316	2.922	2.690	2.534	2.421	2.334	2.266	2.211	2.165	2.015	1.932	1.622
35	4.121	3.267	2.874	2.641	2.485	2.372	2.285	2.217	2.161	2.114	1.963	1.878	1.558
40	4.085	3.232	2.839	2.606	2.449	2.336	2.249	2.180	2.124	2.077	1.924	1.849	1.509
60	4.001	3.150	2.758	2.525	2.368	2.254	2.167	2.097	2.040	1.993	1.836	1.748	1.389
120	3.920	3.072	2.680	2.447	2.290	2.175	2.087	2.016	1.959	1.910	1.751	1.659	1.254
infinity	3.842	2.996	2.605	2.372	2.214	2.099	2.010	1.938	1.880	1.831	1.667	1.571	*

Answers to Selected Exercises

Chapter 2

2.1 (a) 0.9332   (d) 0.9750
       (b) 0.1587   (e) 0.7994
       (c) 0.1003   (f) 0.8747

2.3 (a) 0.1359
       (b) 0.0230
       (c) 0.0025
       (d) 0.0002, via linear interpolation
       (e) The probability of drawing a number exactly equal to one is zero. This can be seen by calculating a sequence of intervals about zero, where the interval width gets smaller and smaller. Unlike Exercise 2.2 (e), the number need not equal zero and the intervals need not be symmetric about the number.

2.5 (a) 72.8 is the 90th percentile.
       (b) 68.4 is the 80th percentile.
       (c) 57.5 is the approximate 40th percentile.

2.7 We have $\bar{y} = 39/5 = 7.8$ and $s_y^2 = 42.8/4 = 10.7$. The second method is easier.

2.9 (a) The data are cross-sectional.
       (b) The histogram is appended.
       (c) $\bar{y} = 29496$, $s_y = 30454$
       (d) The two largest claims are $(\text{max-}\bar{y})/s_y = 2.17$ standard deviations above the mean.
       (e) The smallest claim is $(\bar{y}\text{-min})/s_y = 0.87$ standard deviations below the mean.
       (f) For the lower end point, use $\bar{y} - 2\, s_y = -31412$. For the upper end point, use $\bar{y} + 2\, s_y = 90409$. The interval is $(-31412, 90409)$. The percentage of claims fall within the interval is $28/30 = 93.3\%$.

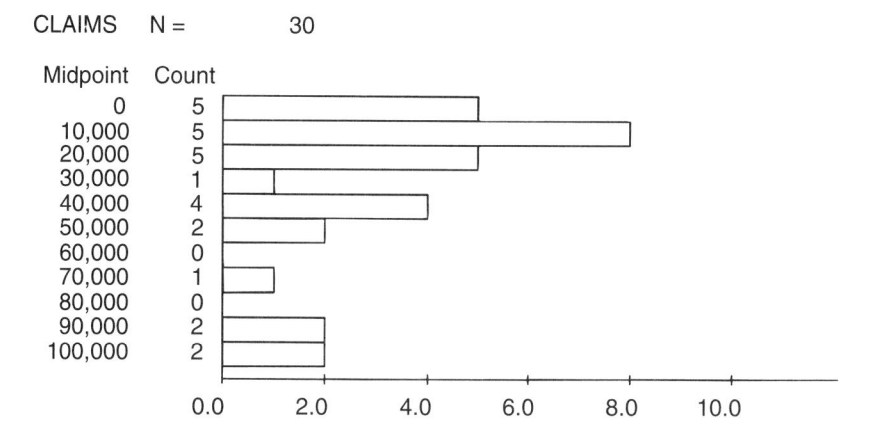

```
CLAIMS    N =            30

Midpoint  Count
      0      5
 10,000      5
 20,000      5
 30,000      1
 40,000      4
 50,000      2
 60,000      0
 70,000      1
 80,000      0
 90,000      2
100,000      2

         0.0    2.0    4.0    6.0    8.0    10.0
```

2.11 (a) The histogram is appended.
     (b) $\bar{y} = 40$ and $s_y = 13.662$.
     (c) (i) 1/4
         (ii) 1/4
         (iii) $\text{Prob}(y \geq 50) = 0.2322$.

```
C1         N =           4

Midpoint  Count
      25     1
      30     0
      35     1
      40     1
      45     0
      50     0
      55     0
      60     1

         0.00   0.20   0.40   0.60   0.80   1.00
```

2.13 (a) 605 is 3.18 standard deviations above the mean.
     (b) $\text{Prob}(y > 605) = \text{Prob}(z > 3.18) \approx 0.001$.
     (c) First, $\Sigma_i y_i = n\bar{y} = 32(416.8) = 13337.6$. Further, $\Sigma_i y_i^2 - n\bar{y}^2 = (n-1)\, s_y^2 = (32-1)(59.1)^2 = 108277.11$. Thus, $\Sigma_i y_i^2 = n\bar{y}^2 + (n-1)\, s_y^2 = 32(416.8)^2 + 108277.11 = 5667388.7$.
     (d) $\Sigma_{i,\text{new}}\, y_i = \Sigma_i y_i - y_{32} = 12732.6$ and $\Sigma_{i,\text{new}}\, y_i^2 = \Sigma_i y_i^2 - y_{32}^2 = 5301363.7$.
     (e) Thus, $\bar{y}_{\text{new}} = 12732.6/31 = 410.73$ and $s_{y,\text{new}} = 48.89$.
     (f) The percentage change is $100(59.1 - 48.89)/59.1 = 17.3\%$. That is, the standard deviation has decreased by 17.3%.

2.15 The t-curve is the one represented by the dashed line. The t-distribution is more variable than the normal and this reflected by the larger values of the t-curve in the tails. Because the area under each is equal to one, the t-curve is smaller in the center.

2.17 **(a)** Via linear interpolation, $\text{Prob}(-2 < t < 2) = 0.703$.
(b) Via linear interpolation, $\text{Prob}(-2 < t < 2) = 0.897$.
(c) Via linear interpolation, $\text{Prob}(-2 < t < 2) = 0.942$.
(d) Via linear interpolation, $\text{Prob}(-2 < t < 2) = 0.944$.
(e) $\text{Prob}(-2 < t < 2) = 0.950$.
(f) $\text{Prob}(-2 < z < 2) = 0.954$.

2.19 **(a)** From the t-table, $(-12.706, 12.706)$ is the interval.
(b) From the t-table, $(-2.571, 2.571)$ is the interval.
(c) From the t-table, $(-2.06, 2.06)$ is the interval.
(d) From the t-table, $(-2.042, 2.042)$ is the interval.
(e) From the t-table, $(-2.00, 2.00)$ is the interval.
(f) From the t-table, $(-1.96, 1.96)$ is the interval.

2.20 **(a)** $\text{Prob}(y > 0.13) = 0.0$.
(b) $\text{Prob}(y > 0.04) = 0.2399$.
(c) $\text{Prob}(y < 0.01) = 0.0787$.

2.22 **(a)** **(i)** A point estimate of μ is $\bar{y} = 30{,}085$.
(ii) The 95% confidence interval is $30{,}085 \pm (2.0)(2{,}024.74) = (26{,}035.5, 34{,}134.5)$.
(b) **(i)** The null hypothesis is: $H_0: \mu = 35000$ and the alternative hypothesis is $H_a:$ $\mu \neq 35000$. This is a two-tailed test. Thus, with $df = n - 1 = 64$, the t-value is 2.0. The test statistic is t-ratio $= (\bar{y} - \mu_0)/(s_y/n^{1/2}) = (30{,}085{-}35{,}000)/(16{,}324/65^{1/2}) = -2.43$. Because the absolute value of t-ratio is larger than t-value, we reject the null hypothesis. Hence, there is not enough evidence to support the claim that your clients have a mean income of 35,000.
(ii) p-value $= \text{Prob}(y \leq 30{,}085) \approx 1\%$.

2.24 **(a)** The 95% prediction interval for the new observed hospital cost is: $2{,}955 \pm (2.037)(1{,}481)(1 + 1/33)^{1/2} = (-107.16, 6{,}017.16)$.
(b) **(i)** From the dotplot, the 97.5th percentile is approximately 7,800.
(ii) From the dotplot, the 2.5th percentile is approximately 1,680.
(iii) Hence, an approximate 95% prediction interval for a new observation is $(1680, 7800)$.

2.25 **(a)** $\bar{y} = 160/4 = 40$ and $s_y = 13.662$.
(b) The 95% confidence interval is $40 \pm 21.736 = (18.264, 61.736)$.
(c) For $H_0: \mu = 35$, the test statistic is $t(\bar{y}) = (40{-}35)/(13.662/(4)^{1/2}) = 0.732$. The t-value with $df = 3$ is 3.182. Thus, we cannot reject H_0 since $|t(\bar{y})| < t$-value. That is, $\bar{y}$ is only 0.732 standard errors above the hypothesized mean of 40. This is not unusual under the reference t-curve.
(d) A 95% prediction interval is $40 \pm 48.6 = (-8.6, 88.6)$.

2.27 **(a)** Because the average assets are $\bar{y} = 3{,}012$ millions of dollars, the total assets are $\Sigma_i y_i = n\bar{y} = 40(3{,}012) = 120{,}480$ millions of dollars.
(b) The new average is $(\text{total assets})/\text{number} = (120{,}480 - 15{,}251)/(40 - 1) = 2{,}698.2$ millions. The new median is the 20th largest mutual fund which is Putnam Growth and Income at 2,395.3 millions of dollars.
(c) The dotplot appears skewed to the right and thus, not normally distributed. One could look at the standard deviations rule or a normal probability plot.

(d) The probability of drawing a no load fund is $14/40 = 35\%$.

(e) The point estimate is $\bar{y} = 0.7607$. The 95% confidence interval is 0.7607 ± 0.0819 $= (0.6788, 8426)$.

(f) For H_0: $\mu = 0.7500$, the test statistic is $t(\bar{y}) = 0.2693$. For H_a: $\mu > 0.7500$, the t-value is 1.684 at $df = 39$. Thus we cannot reject H_0 since $t(\bar{y}) < t$-value.

2.29 (a) (i) 3.315 is the 75th percentile.

     (ii) Using the standard normal curve, 3.315 is at the 0.550 percentile.

(b) (i) Let x_i = net profit of ith firm, z_i = sales of ith firm and x_i/z_i will be the net profit margin of ith firm. From the summary statistics, we have $\bar{x} = 317.8$, $\bar{z} = 5{,}316$, and the average of $(x_i/z_i) = 0.06379 = 6.379\%$.

     (ii) From part (i), we see that $\bar{x}/\bar{z} = 317.8/5{,}316 = 0.05978 = 5.978\%$. This is not equal to 6.379% because, in general, the average of the ratios will not be equal to the ratios of the averages. Stated another way, the ratio of averages is a weighted average of net profit margins, where the weights are given by sales. That is, $\bar{x}/\bar{z} = \sum_{i=1}^{n}(x_i/z_i)z_i/\sum_{i=1}^{n} z_i$.

(c) (i) For the EPS, its maximum and minimum are equal to 12.54 and -4.26, respectively.

     (ii) A 95% prediction interval for EPS is $2.338 \pm (2.126)(2.48)(1 + 1/49)^{1/2} = (-2.7039, 7.3799)$.

(d) The null hypothesis is H_0: $\mu_{\text{EPS}} = 2$ and the alternative hypothesis is H_a: $\mu_{\text{EPS}} \neq 2$. This is a two-tailed test. Thus, with $df = 48$, we use t-value = 2.126, from part c(ii). The test statistic is t-ratio = $t(\bar{y}) = 0.954$. Because $|t(\bar{y})| < t$-value, we do not reject the null hypothesis and say that there is not enough evidence that μ_{EPS} would not be 2.

2.30 (a) Expanding the square, we have

$$\sum_{i=1}^{n}(y_i - \bar{y})^2 = \sum_{i=1}^{n}(y_i^2 - 2\bar{y}y_i + \bar{y}^2) = \sum_{i=1}^{n} y_i^2 - 2\sum_{i=1}^{n} y_i\bar{y} + \sum_{i=1}^{n} \bar{y}^2$$

(b) Because $\bar{y}$ is a constant with respect to the summation and $n\bar{y} = \sum_{i=1}^{n} y_i$, we have

$$\sum_{i=1}^{n} y_i\bar{y} = \bar{y}\sum_{i=1}^{n} y_i = \bar{y}(n\bar{y}) = n\bar{y}^2.$$

Similarly,

$$\sum_{i=1}^{n} \bar{y}^2 = n\bar{y}^2.$$

(c) Putting together the results of part (a) and (b), we have

$$\sum_{i=1}^{n}(y_i - \bar{y})^2 = \sum_{i=1}^{n} y_i^2 - 2n\bar{y}^2 + n\bar{y}^2 = \left(\sum_{i=1}^{n} y_i^2\right) - n\bar{y}^2$$

which yields the desired result.

Chapter 3

3.1 (a) The plot is appended.

(b) (i) We first have $\bar{x} = 2.75$ and $\bar{y} = 3.5$. Thus, $s_x = 2.986$ and $s_y = 3.6968$. Thus, $r = 0.9512$. This yields $b_1 = rs_y/s_x = 1.1776$.

(ii) $b_1 = \{\Sigma_i (x_i - \bar{x})(y_i - \bar{y})\} / \{\Sigma_i (x_i - \bar{x})^2\} = 1.1776.$
(iii) $b_1 = \{\Sigma_i x_i y_i - n\bar{x}\bar{y}\} / \{\Sigma_i x_i^2 - n\bar{x}^2\} = 1.1776.$
(c) Part (c) of Exercise 3.34.

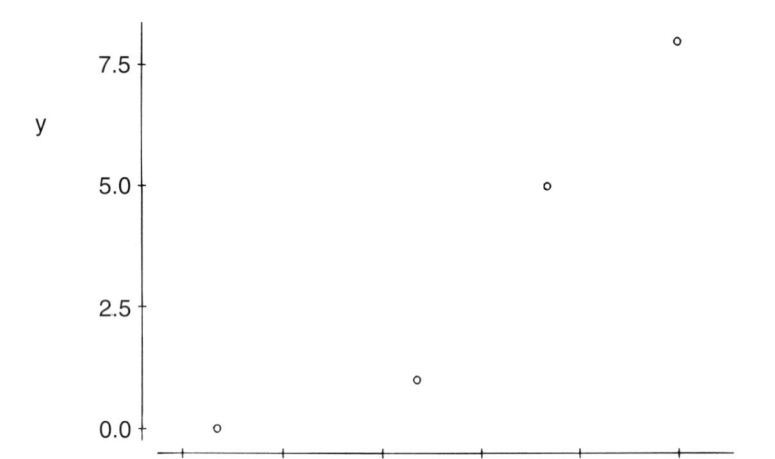

3.3 **(a)** The figure is appended.
(b) See attached figure.
(c) The correlation coefficient will be close to -1 and certainly lower than 0.

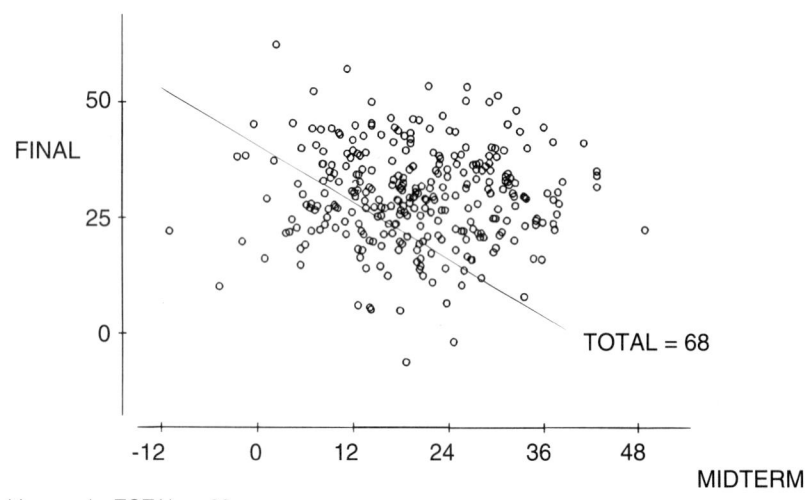

Line marks TOTAL = 68

3.5   (a) The figure is appended.
    (b) (i)   AVG = 65.3 inches.
        (ii)   AVG = 72.95 inches.
    (c) For the children, $\bar{y} = 68.093$ and $s_y = 2.543$ inches. For the midparents, $\bar{x} = 68.303$ and $s_x = 1.812$. The correlation is $r = 0.460$.
        (i)   For the least squares line, we have $b_1 = 0.646$ and $b_0 = 24$. This yields CHILD = 24 + (0.646) MIDPARENT.
        (ii) CHILD = 24 + (0.646) (63.5) = 65.02.
        (iii) CHILD = 24 + (0.646) (73.5) = 71.48.

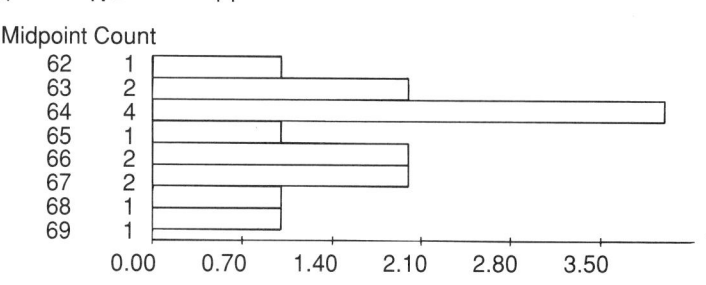

3.7   (a) The figure is appended.
    (b) The correlations coefficient is $r = 0$, because $\bar{x} = 0$, $\bar{y} = 2$, and $\Sigma_i (x_i - \bar{x})(y_i - \bar{y}) = \Sigma_{i=1}^n x_i (y_1 - \bar{y}) = 0$.

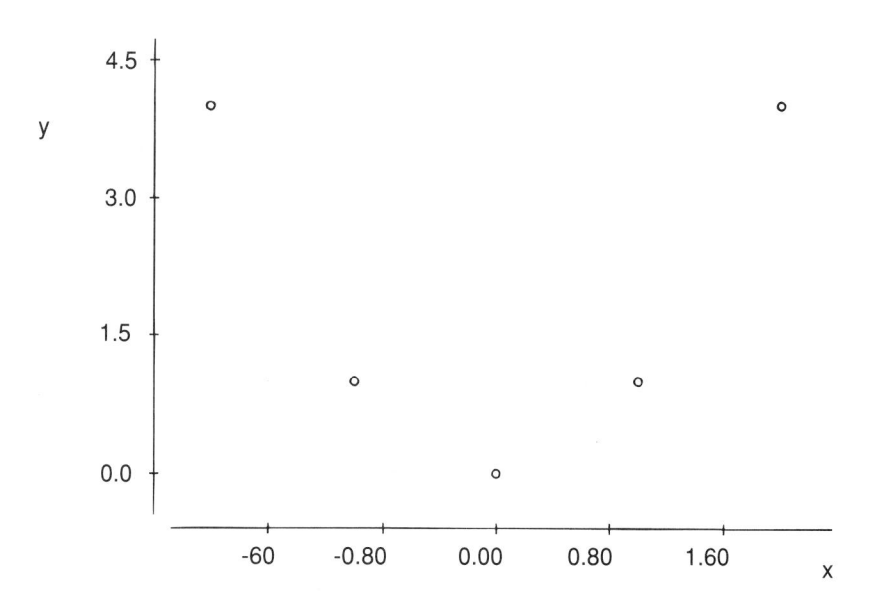

      (c) Because there is a perfect relationship between x and y, one might expect $r = 1$. However, correlation is a measure of linear relationship and thus there may be a less than perfect linear relationship, despite a perfect nonlinear relationship.

3.9   (a) (i)   Different scatter, or varying variance, among observations.

          (ii)   As the level of x increases, the average distance of each observation from the line increases. This growing average spread indicates a growing variability.

      (b) The distance between the upper and lower lines increases as x increases. Because there are a similar number of observations at each level, this increasing distance helps us to visualize the increasing variability. The lines act as reference symbols to compare the individual observations. The lines also visually capture the increasing variability.

      (c) As the level of x increases, the approximate normal curve becomes more disperse. This greater spread indicates a larger variability.

3.10   (a) Percentage due to the 10th observation is $(\hat{e}_{10})^2/\text{SSE} = 64\,s^2/(s^2\,98) \approx 64\%$.

      (b) Percentage due to the 10th observation is $(\hat{e}_{10})^2/\text{SSE} \approx 16\%$.

      (c) Here, $(\hat{e}_{10})^2/\text{SSE} = 88.9\%$.

3.12   (a) The figure is appended.

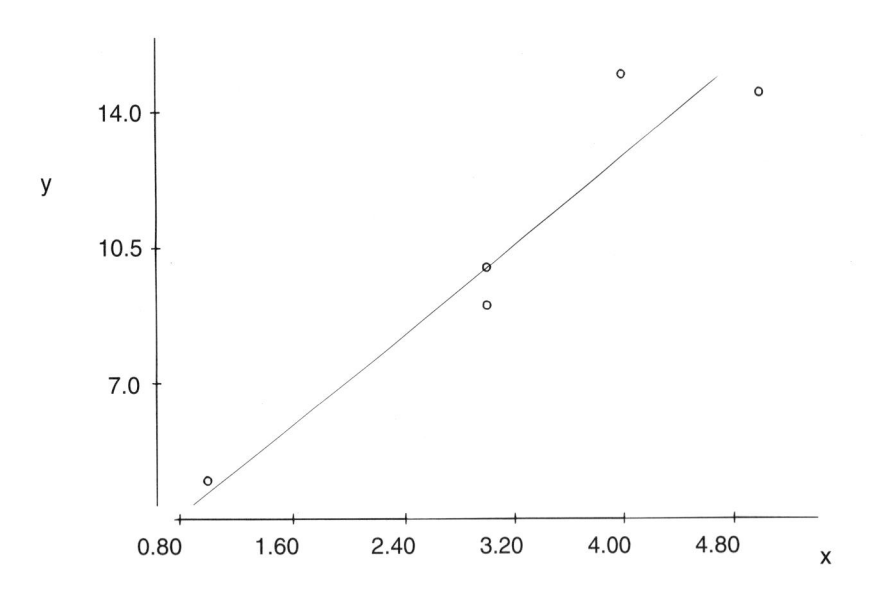

(b)

y	x	$\hat{y}$	$\hat{e}$	$\hat{e}^2$
4.5	1	4	0.5	0.25
9	3	10	−1	1.00
10	3	10	0	0
15	4	13	2	4.00
14.5	5	16	−1.5	2.25
53.0		53	0	7.50

$$s^2 = \sum_{i=1}^{n} \hat{e}^2 / (n-2) = 7.50/3 = 2.5.$$

3.14 $\hat{y}_1 = b_0 + b_1 x_1 = -5$. Because $\hat{e}_1 = 1$, this means $y_1 = -4$. Because $\bar{x} = 6$ and $-1 = b_0$ $= \bar{y} - b_1 \bar{x}$, we have $\bar{y} = 11$. Thus, $y_2 + y_3 = 37$. Because $\sum_{i=1}^{n}(x_i - \bar{x})^2 = 128$, we have $256 = b_1 \sum_{i=1}^{n}(x_i - \bar{x})^2 = \sum_{i=1}^{n} x_i y_i - 3\bar{x}\bar{y}$. Thus, $\sum_{i=1}^{n} x_i y_i = 256 + 3(6)(11) = 454$. That is, $454 = 230 + 8 y_2$. Thus, $y_2 = 28$ and $y_3 = 9$.

3.18 **(a)** The transformations are: $y_{new} = y_{old}/1000$, and $x_{new} = x_{old} - 10$.

(b) By (i), we have $\bar{y}_{new} = \bar{y}_{old}/1000$ and $s_{y,new} = s_{y,old}/1000$. Similarly, we have $\bar{x}_{new}$ $= \bar{x}_{old} - 10$ and $s_{x,new} = s_{x,old}$. Because these are simply linear transformations, the value of r does not change. Hence, $b_{1,new} = r s_{y,new}/s_{x,new} = r\, s_{y,old}/1000/s_{x,old}$ $= 0.002$. Similarly, $b_{0,new} = \bar{y}_{new} - b_{1,new}\bar{x}_{new} = \bar{y}_{old}/1000 - b_{1,old}/1000\,(\bar{x}_{old} - 10) = 0.03$. Finally, because y decreases by a factor of 1000, we have that $s_{new} = s_{old}/1000 = 0.01$.

3.20 Both r and $t(b_1)$ remain the same although b_1 will, in general, be different. The correlation coefficient measures the strength of the relationship between two variables and is unaffected by the choice of independent and dependent variables. However, b_1 measures the slope and the choice does matter.

3.21 $se(pred) = 7.3504$.

3.23 **(a)** **(i)** This yields $\widehat{STKPRICE}_{19} = 30.396 + (4.381)(12.54) = 85.3337$.

(ii) Further, we have the residual = Actual − Fitted = $29.75 - 85.33 = -55.58$.

(b) **(i)** Now, $\bar{y}_{new} = (n\,\bar{y}_{old} - y_{31})/(n-1) = 40.64$.

(ii) We first use the formula $(n-1)\,s_{y,old}^2 = \sum_{old} y_i^2 - n\bar{y}_{old}^2$ to get $\sum_{old} y_i^2 = 103261.3$. Now, we have $\sum_{new} y_i^2 = \sum_{old} y_i^2 - (y_{31})^2 = 102{,}895.4$. With this we can calculate $s_{y,new}^2 = (\sum_{new} y_i^2 - (n-1)\,\bar{y}_{new}^2)/(n-2) = 457.6$. Thus, $s_{new} = 21.4$.

(iii) Let r = correlation coefficient of EPS and STKPRICE. Because $b_1 = r s_y/s_x$, we get $r = b_1\,(s_x/s_y)$. Thus, $r = 0.508$.

3.25 **(a)** Normal scores are percentiles from the standard normal distribution curve.

(b) For the 16th smallest observation, the normal score is -1.0114, corresponding to the 15.586% percentile from the standard normal table.

(c) A normal probability plot is a scatter plot of the normal scores versus the standard residuals.

3.27 **(a)** The confidence interval is $b_1 \pm (t\text{-value})\, se(b_1) = 1.0017 \pm (2)(.2245) = 1.0017 \pm .4490$.

(b) Because $R^2 = r^2 = 0.255$, so $|r| = 0.505$. Because the slope b_1 is positive, we have $r = 0.505$. The correlation coefficient is larger in absolute value since it is the square root of a number between 0 and 1. In this case, it is larger since it is positive.

(c) A point is an outlier if it is unusual in the vertical (y) direction. A point is high leverage if it is unusual in the horizontal (x) direction.

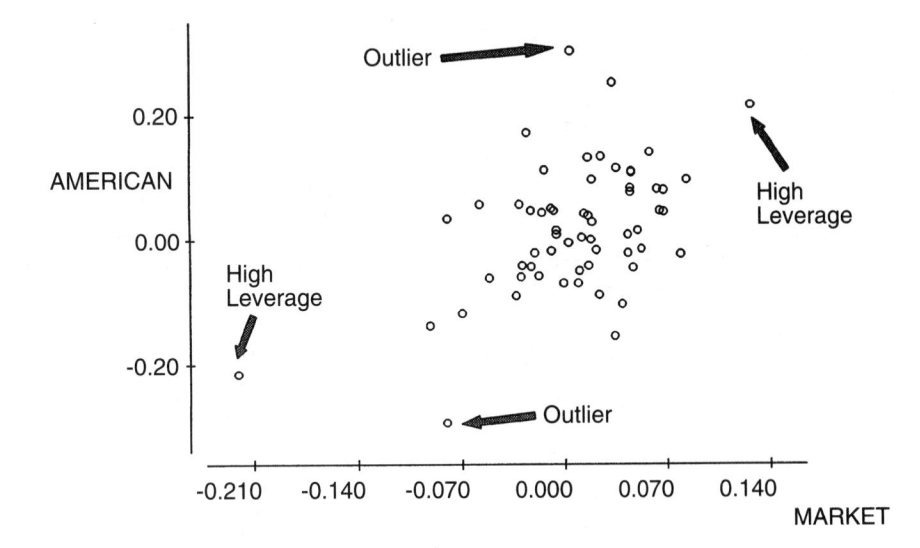

3.29   **(a)** Cross sectional since there is no time ordering of the data.
         (b) We wish to reject the null hypothesis $H_0: \beta_1 = 0$ in favor of the alternative $H_a: \beta_1 \neq 0$. To this end, the test-statistic is $t(b_1) = 1.19$. We compare this test statistic to a t-value $= 2.06$, using $df = 25$ and a 5% level of significance. Thus, we can not reject the null hypothesis in favor of the alternative.
         (c) The coefficient of determination remains unchanged since the correlation coefficient is the same. That is $R^2 = r^2 = 5.4\%$.

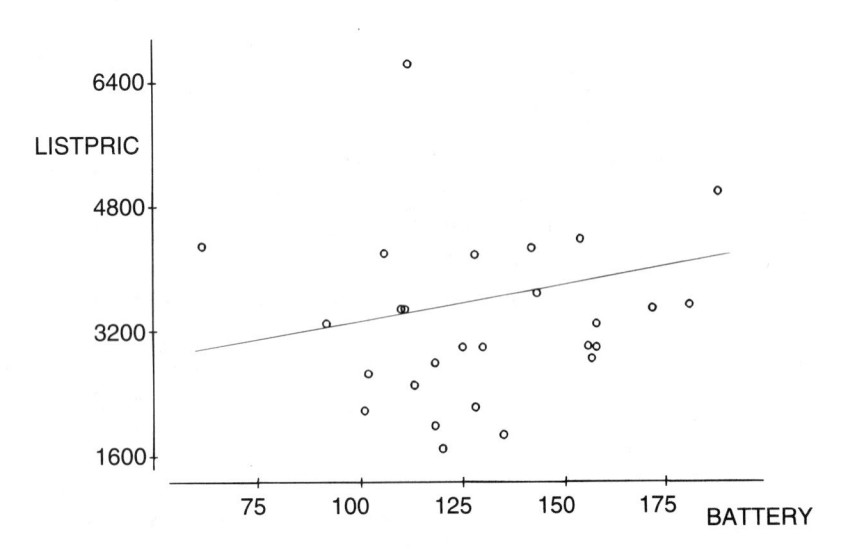

(d) (i) The figure is appended.

  (ii) The correlation is $r = 0.092$. With $s_{\text{LISTPRIC}} = 1{,}070$ and $s_{\text{BATTERY}} = 28.87$, we have $b_1 = 3.4$. With $\bar{y} = 3{,}337$ and $\bar{x} = 130.37$, we have $b_0 = 2{,}890$.

(e) (i) Yes. The t-statistic, $t(b_1)$, is over 3 indicating that the slope is over 3 standard errors from zero. Further, over 30% of the variability in prices is explained by the video benchmark.

  (ii) $\hat{y} = 3{,}352$. Thus, the observed value, $y = 2{,}999$, is 353 less than the fitted value, $\hat{y}$.

  (iii) The expected change is $\frac{1}{2} b_1 = 221.2$ decrease. The 95% confidence interval is $-221.2 \pm \frac{1}{2}(2.060)(129.3) = -221.2 \pm 133.4 = (-354.6, -87.8)$.

  (iv) Eliminating this notebook would lower the regression line and improve the fit.

3.31 (a)

Z	-25	-20	-15	-10	-5	0	5	10	15	20
e_1	-4	-4	-24	-5	1	3	16	7	9	1
e_2	17	9	-6	2	-2	-12	-10	16	-7	-12
x	-8	-11	-21	-8	-7	-12	-5	26	8	8
y	-29	-24	-39	-15	-4	3	21	17	24	21

(b) and (c)

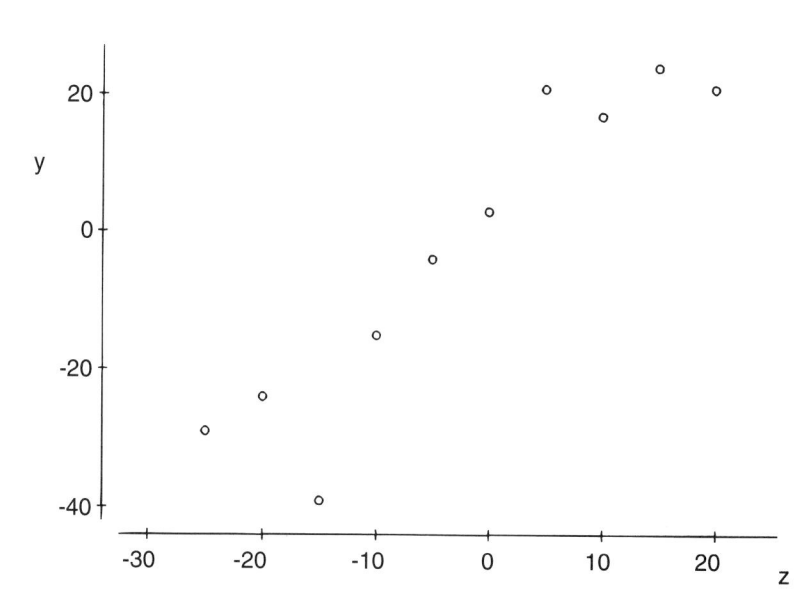

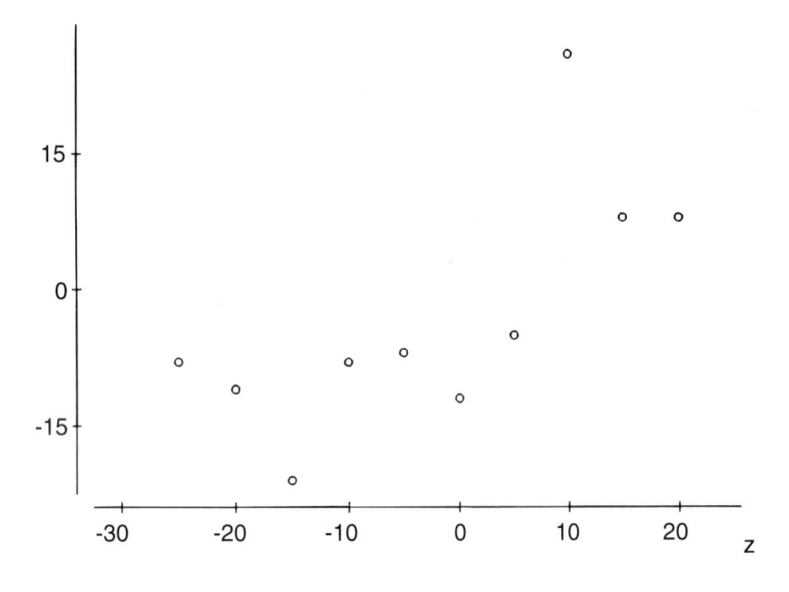

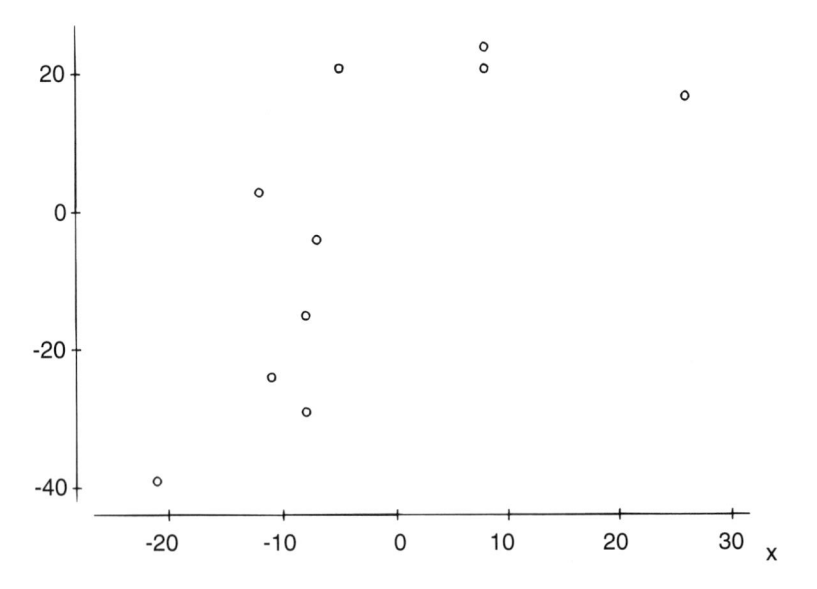

(d) $\hat{y} = 1.29 + 1.26\,x$.

(e) Yes, $t(b_1) = 3.01$, which is large. Further, $R^2 = 53.1\%$ which is large.

(f) $\hat{y} = -5.3 + 1.26\,x$. Here, $t(b_1)$ and R^2 are the same as in part (e).

3.33 **(a) (i)** Because $R^2 = r^2 = 0.873$, the correlation coefficient is $(0.873)^{1/2} = 0.934$.

(ii) The fitted regression line is given by: $\widehat{\text{ASKPRICE}} = 1{,}081 + 1.2 \text{ LOANVAL}$. This is obtained by minimizing the squared deviations of the 212 observations from the line. This line can be used to predict ASKPRICE given the loan value. Although this line is different from the "rule of thumb," the difference of $81 may not be quite significant. The rule of thumb is easy to understand and use.

(iii) This natural variability is estimated by $s = 1{,}495$.

(b) (i) The observations that are likely to have highest leverage are the five points on the very far right of the scatter plot.

(ii) No. This is because if a regression line were fitted on the observations, these "likely" high leverage points will not be very far from the line. For them to be outliers, they have to be unusual in the vertical direction from the line.

(c) (i) ASKPRICE will increase by $b_1(\text{Increase}) = 1.2* 1{,}000 = 1{,}200$.

(ii) A 95% confidence interval for this estimate is $1{,}000* (1.2 \pm (1.96)(0.03167)) = (1{,}137.9, 1{,}262.1)$.

(d) (i) With $x_* = 5{,}175$, the predicted value is $7{,}291.

(ii) The 95% prediction interval for $x_* = 5{,}175$ is $7{,}291 \pm (1.96)(1{,}499.5) = (4{,}352, 10{,}230)$.

3.34 **(a)** $\Sigma_i(x_i - \bar{x})(y_i - \bar{y}) = \Sigma_i(x_i y_i - \bar{x} y_i - x_i \bar{y} + \bar{x}\,\bar{y}) = \Sigma_i x_i y_i - \bar{x} \Sigma_i y_i - \bar{y} \Sigma_i x_i + n\bar{x}\,\bar{y}$
$= \Sigma_i x_i y_i - n\bar{x}\,\bar{y}$ since $\Sigma_i x_i = n\bar{x}$ and $\Sigma_i y_i = n\bar{y}$.

3.36 Recall the relationship $b = r\,(s_y/s_x)$. With this relationship, we have

$$\sqrt{b_{1,y,x}\, b_{1,x,y}} = \sqrt{r\,\frac{s_y}{s_x}\; r\,\frac{s_x}{s_y}} = \sqrt{r^2} = |r|.$$

3.38 **(a)** Because $b_0 = \bar{y} - b_1\bar{x}$, we have $\hat{y} = b_0 + b_1 x_* = \bar{y} - b_1\bar{x} + b_1 x_* = \bar{y} + b_1(x_* - \bar{x})$.

(b) The point prediction is equal to the sample average $\bar{y}$ plus an adjustment for the deviation of x_* from $\bar{x}$. Here, the slope b_1 controls the amount of the adjustment.

3.40 **(c)** Adding and subtracting $\bar{y}$ yields $\Sigma_{i=1}^n \hat{e}_i \hat{y}_i = \Sigma_{i=1}^n ((y_i - \bar{y}) - (\hat{y}_i - \bar{y}))\hat{y}_i = \Sigma_{i=1}^n (y_i - \bar{y})\hat{y}_i - \Sigma_{i=1}^n b_1(x_i - \bar{x})\hat{y}_i = \Sigma_{i=1}^n (y_i - \bar{y})(\bar{y} + b_1(x_i - \bar{x})) - b_1 \Sigma_{i=1}^n (x_i - \bar{x})(\bar{y} + b_1(x_i - \bar{x})) = b_1 \Sigma_{i=1}^n (y_i - \bar{y})(x_i - \bar{x}) - b_1^2 \Sigma_{i=1}^n (x_i - \bar{x})^2 = 0$.

(d) By the definition of residuals, $\Sigma_{i=1}^n \hat{e}_i = \Sigma_{i=1}^n \{y_i - (b_0 + b_1 x_i)\} = n\bar{y} - nb_0 - nb_1\bar{x} = 0$, since $b_0 = \bar{y} - b_1\bar{x}$.

(f) The correlation between the residuals and each of the fitted values and explanatory variable is zero. However, we expect the correlation between the residuals and responses to be non-zero, in general.

3.42 **(a)** $R^2 = (\text{Regression SS})/(\text{Total SS}) = 1 - (\text{Error SS})/(\text{Total SS}) = 1 - ((n-2)s^2)/((n-1)s_y^2)$.

(b) Use $R^2 = r^2$.

(c) Recall that $b_1 = rs_y/s_x$ and $se(b_1) = s/(s_x(n-1)^{1/2})$. Thus, with part (b), we have $t(b_1) = b_1/se(b_1) = rs_y(n-1)^{1/2}/s = ((n-2)\,r^2/(1-r^2))^{1/2}$.

3.44 **(a)** $SS(b_1^*) - SS(b_1) = \Sigma_{i=1}^n \{(y_i - b_1^* x_i)^2 - (y_i - b_1 x_i)^2\} = \Sigma_{i=1}^n \{x_i^2((b_1^*)^2 - (b_1)^2) - 2 x_i y_i (b_1^* - b_1)\} = \Sigma_{i=1}^n \{x_i^2((b_1^*)^2 + (b_1)^2) - 2 x_i y_i b_1^*\} = \Sigma_{i=1}^n \{x_i^2(b_1^* - b_1)^2 - 2 x_i y_i b_1^* + 2 x_i^2 b_1^* b_1\} = (b_1^* - b_1)^2 \Sigma_{i=1}^n x_i^2 \geq 0$.

(b) Let $x_i = z_i^2$ to get $b_1 = \{\Sigma_{i=1}^n z_i^2 y_i\}/\{\Sigma_{i=1}^n z_i^4\}$.

Chapter 4

4.1   **(a)** The 5th and 6th largest observations are at about 3.4. Thus, the 90th percentile is about 3.4. Similarly, since the 2nd largest observation is about 5.2, the 98th percentile is about 5.2.

       (b) From the t-distribution table with $df = 40$, the 95th percentile is 1.684. Because $t^2 = F$, this means that the 90th percentile of the F is $(1.684)^2 = 2.86$. Similarly, since the 99th percentile of the t is 2.423, the 98th percentile of the F is $(2.423)^2 = 5.87$.

4.3   **(a)** $R_a^2 = 1 - s/s_y^2 = 1 - (50)^2/(100)^2 = 1 - 1/4 = .75$.

       (b) We have Total SS $= (n - 1) s_y^2 = 990{,}000$ and Error SS $= (n - (k + 1)) s^2 = 240{,}000$. Thus

Source	SS	df	MS	F
Regression	750,000	3	250,000	100
Error	240,000	96	2,500	
Total	990,000	99		

       (c) $R^2 = (750{,}000)/(990{,}000) = 0.75758$.

4.5   We wish to test H_0: $\beta_{\%REG} = \beta_{MINOR} = 0$ versus the alternative that H_0 is not true. The test statistic is F-ratio $= ((R_{Full}^2 - R_{Reduced}^2)/(\text{change in degrees of freedom}))/(1 - R_{Full}^2)$. The decision-making criterion is to reject H_0 if F-ratio $> F$-value, where the F-value is a percentile from the F-distribution with $df_1 = $ change in degrees of freedom and $df_2 = n - (k + 1)$ degrees of freedom. Here, we have $df_1 = 2$ and $df_2 = 45$ so, at the 5% level, we have F-value $= 3.20$. For the one-variable model, we have $r^2 = R^2 = R_{Reduced}^2$, thus $R_{Reduced}^2 = (0.565)^2 = 0.3192$. Thus, F-ratio $= 56.1$, so we reject H_0.

4.7   **(a) (i)** From the scatter plot, it seems clear that PRICE increases as TOTSQFT increases. Smaller houses have lower prices than larger houses.

            (ii) We can use linear regression with one variable to perform a formal test for the importance of TOTSQFT. The null hypothesis is H_0: $\beta_{TOTSQFT} = 0$, the alternative hypothesis is H_a: $\beta_{TOTSQFT} \neq 0$ and the test statistic is $t(b_1) = 10.14$. Using a 5% level of significance, with $df = n - (k + 1) = 79$, the critical value is t-value $= 1.99$ because the test is two-sided. Because $t(b_1) > t$-value, we reject H_0 and declare TOTSQFT to be statistically significant.

       (b) (i) We can use linear regression to perform a formal test for the importance of TOTSQFT. The null hypothesis is H_0: $\beta_{TOTSQFT} = 0$, the alternative hypothesis is H_a: $\beta_{TOTSQFT} \neq 0$ and the test statistic is $t(b_1) = 0.79$. Using a 5% level of significance, with $df = n - (k + 1) = 78$, the critical value is t-value $= 1.99$ because the test is two-sided. Because $|t(b_1)| < t$-value, we can not reject H_0 and declare TOTSQFT to be statistically insignificant.

            (ii) At first, this result appears unusual because of the high correlation between TOTSQFT and PRICE and, in part a(ii), we declare TOTSQFT to be statistically significant. However, in part b(i) we reached the opposite conclusion.

       (c) (i) The partial correlation between PRICE and TOTSQFT is $r(y, x_2 | x_1) = 0.089$.

            (ii) Although PRICE and TOTSQFT are highly positively correlated, the correlation between PRICE and TOTSQFT after having controlled for EXSQFT is small. This indicates that there is little additional linear information in TOTSQFT when we have already included EXSQFT.

       (d) Because TOTSQFT $=$ UNEXSQFT $+$ EXSQFT, we have $\widehat{PRICE} = 2.24 + 0.0549$ EXSQFT $+ 0.0101$ TOTSQFT $= 2.24 + 0.0650$ EXSQFT $+ 0.0101$ UNEXSQFT.

4.9 (a) Price paid is $y_3 = 140$ (hundreds of dollars), annual income is $x_{31} = 180$ (hundreds of dollars), sex is $x_{32} = 1$ (male) and the educational status is $x_{33} = 1$ (college graduate).

(b) $se(b_2) = s$ (third diagonal element of $(X'X)^{-1})^{1/2} = 55.536$.

(c) (i) $\mathbf{b} = (X'X)^{-1} X'\mathbf{y}$

(ii) $\hat{y} = b_0 + b_1(800) + b_2(0) + b_3(0) = b_0 + b_1(800)$

4.10 (a) F-ratio $= (1/R^2 - 1)^{-1} (n - (k + 1))/k = 58.67$.

(b) Suppose the theoretical model is

$$I = \beta_0 + \beta_A A + \beta_E E + \beta_{AE} AE + \beta_{D(1-W)} D(1 - W) + \beta_{D2(1-W)} D^2(1 - W) + \beta_W W + e$$

The null hypothesis is

$$H_0: \beta_A = \beta_E = \beta_{AE} = \beta_{D(1-W)} = \beta_{D2(1-W)} = \beta_W = 0.$$

The alternative hypothesis is at least one β not equal to 0, excluding β_0. With $df_1 = 6$ and $df_2 = 55 - 7 = 48$, we have that the 95th percentile of the F-distribution is about 2.303. Thus via linear interpolation between the F-value using $df_2 = 40$ and $df_2 = 60$. Alternatively, a conservative approximation is F-value $= 2.336$, using $df_2 = 40$. The decision-making rule is to reject H_0 in favor of the alternative of F-ratio > 2.303. Because F-ratio $= 58.67 > 2.303$, we reject H_0.

(c) $t(b_A) = -3.998$. This says that the partial slope is nearly 4 standard errors below 0, which is clearly important.

(d) If the metropolitan area is more than 900 miles, then W = 1. Thus,

$$\hat{I} = -0.0356 - 0.498A + 0.00326E + 0.0543AE.$$

(e) If $D = 0.300$, this means that W = 0. Thus,

$$\hat{I} = -0.0103 - 0.498A + 0.00326E + 0.0543AE.$$

(f) If $D = 0.300$ and $E = 13.751$, we have $\hat{I} = 0.03453 + 0.2487A$.

(g) If $D = 0.300$ and $E = 8.716$, we have $\hat{I} = 0.01811 - 0.0247A$.

4.12 (a) The number of people per square mile (POP_MILE) is highly skewed. The size of the population (POPLN) is also skewed although the other variables seemed reasonably symmetric.

(b) Nevada is the highest plotting symbol in the vertical direction. Because the number of murders per hundred thousand is 19.992, the number of murders is approximately $19.992 \times 8.00312 = 160$.

(c)

Source	df	SS	MS	F
Regression	7	888.51	126.93	49.58
Error	42	107.51	2.56	
Total	49	996.02		

(d) $R^2 = .892$, $R_a^2 = .874$ and $s = 1.56$. This is a reasonable model in terms of the coefficient of determination.

(e) The null hypothesis is $H_0: \beta_{POVERTY} = \beta_{PCNT\_URB} = \beta_{POPLN} = \beta_{POP\_MILE} = \beta_{HIG\_SCL} = \beta_{PCNT\_PCI} = \beta_{NEVADA} = 0$. The alternative hypothesis is H_a: at least one β is not zero. The F-ratio is 49.58 with $df_1 = 7$ and $df_2 = 42$, at the 5% level of significance, the F-value is approximately 2.247. The decision-making rule is to reject the null in favor of the alternative if the F-ratio exceeds the F-value. We do reject H_0 since $49.58 = F$-ratio $> F$-value $= 2.247$.

(f) It seems reasonable that, other things equal, as POVERTY increases so would the number of murders. Similarly, higher levels of urbanized areas have more murders. The positive sign in POPLN seems correct; larger states have more murders, even on a per capita basis. The negative sign on the POP_MILE indicates that sparsely populated states have more murders. The positive sign on NEVADA is a reflection of the special causes due to Las Vegas. The negative sign associated with HIGHSCL is somewhat surprising.

(g) $t(b_{\text{HIGHSCL}}) = -4.3605$. We wish to test the null hypothesis $H_0: \beta_{\text{HIGHSCL}} = 0$ versus the alternative $H_a: \beta_{\text{HIGHSCL}} \neq 0$. With $df = 42$, at the 10% level of significance we have that the two sided t-value $= 1.683$. We reject H_0 in favor of the alternative since

$$4.3605 = |t(b_{\text{HIGHSCL}})| > t\text{-value} = 1.683.$$

(h) $\hat{y} = 4.9897$. Because $y = 2.9054$, the difference is $\hat{e} = y - \hat{y} = -2.084$. Wisconsin is doing better than predicted under the model.

4.14 **(a)** **(i)** Here, $s = (\text{Error MS})^{1/2} = 1{,}263.19$. This can be taken directly from the computer output.

   (ii) Because $R^2 = (r_{y,\hat{y}})^2$, we have that $r_{y,\hat{y}} = (R^2)^{1/2} = 0.9534$.

(b) **(i)** Fitted ASKPRICE $= 6{,}512.28$.

   (ii) Deviation $=$ (Actual ASKPRICE) $-$ (Fitted ASKPRICE) $= -517.28$.

   (iii) Change in Fitted Value $= -28.3 (76 - 67) = 254.7$ increase.

(c) We want to test the hypothesis: $H_0: \beta_{\text{MILEAGE}} = \beta_{\text{NEWPRICE}} = 0$ against the alternative H_a: at least one of these Beta's is not zero. Using Partial F-test, we compute the Partial F-ratio $= (R^2_{\text{Full}} - R^2_{\text{Reduced}})/p/(1 - R^2_{\text{Full}})/n - (k + p + 1)$. From the computer output, $R^2_{\text{Full}} = 0.909$, $R^2_{\text{Reduced}} = 0.872$, and $n = 212$. Further, $k = 1$ and $p = 2$. Hence, plugging these values to the formula, we get Partial F-ratio $= 42.29$. From the F-table, we have a F-value of 2.996 using $df_1 = 2$, $df_2 = 208$. Since the Partial F-ratio is $>$ than this F-value, we reject the null hypothesis. We therefore conclude that the addition of the variables MILEAGE and NEWPRICE add value to the model.

(d) **(i)** Added variable plots help us to detect relationships (both linear and nonlinear) between the response and an explanatory variable, controlling for the effects of other explanatory variables.

   (ii) The partial correlation is -53.49%.

   (iii) From the correlation matrix, the correlation of ASKPRICE and MILEAGE is -67.10%, a bit higher than that suggested by the partial correlation coefficient. This negative correlation suggest that the larger the MILEAGE, the smaller the ASKPRICE will be. This same trend is suggested by the partial correlation coefficient. In this case, there is little difference between the relationship between y and x and the same relationship after controlling for the effects of other independent variables.

(e) Is c25 important? We test the hypothesis: $H_0: \beta(c25) = 0$ against the alternative hypothesis: $H_a: \beta(c25) \neq 0$. The t-ratio is 2.58 which is larger than 2 (rule of thumb). Hence, we reject the null hypothesis and say that the variable c25 is important.

Chapter 5

5.1 **(a)** The one factor model can be expressed as $y_{ij} = \mu_j + e_{ij}$ over $i = 1, \ldots, 19$ and $j = 1, \ldots, 6$. The null hypothesis is $H_0: \mu_1 = \ldots = \mu_6$ and the alternative is that at least one μ_j is not equal to the others.

(b)

Source	Sum of Squares	df	Mean Square	F-ratio
Regression	25,383	5	5,076.6	0.261
Error	2,096,953	108	19,416.2	
Total	2,122,336	113		

(c) From the ANOVA table, the F-ratio is 0.261. We then compare this against F-value = 2.3, using $df_1 = 5$, $df_2 = 108$ (≈ 120). Because F-ratio is less than F-value, we do not reject H_0, and say that we have no evidence that the time means differ. Hence, TIME is not significant.

(d) From the ANOVA table, the F-ratio is 35.54. We then compare this against F-value ≈ 1.7, using $df_1 = 18$, $df_2 = 95$. Because F-ratio exceeds F-value, we reject H_0, and say that the state means differ. Hence, STATE is significant.

(f) From this plot, we see that (i) average cost varies by state, (ii) the variability is about the same for each state, and (iii) some states around a fitted value of 250 have unusually large filings. The 45-degree line is guaranteed from the algebra.

(g) A two-factor additive model for STATE and TIME is $y_{ij} = \mu + \beta_i + \tau_j + e_{ij}$, where $i = 1, \ldots, 6$ represents TIME effects (β) and $j = 1, \ldots, 19$ represents STATE effects (τ).

(h) The F-ratio for checking TIME effects is $5,077/2,767 = 1.834$. With an F-value = 2.49 ($df_1 = 5$ and $df_2 = 90$), this is not statistically significant. The F-ratio for checking STATE effects is 37.1. With an F-value ≈ 1.7 ($df_1 = 18$ and $df_2 = 90$), this is statistically significant.

5.3 **(a)** To test the significance of TYP, we test equality of means in the analysis of variance model. The null hypothesis is $H_0: \mu_1 = \mu_2 = \mu_3$. The alternative hypothesis is H_a: at least some of the μ's are different. From the ANOVA table, the F-ratio is 5.02. We then compare this against F-value = 3.316, using $df_1 = 2$, $df_2 = 30$. Because F-ratio exceeds F-value, we reject H_0, and say at least one μ differs. Hence, TYP is significant.

(b) **(i)** The point estimate is $\hat{\mu}_1 = \bar{y}_1 = 3,505$.

(ii) The confidence interval for μ_1 is $3,505 \pm (2.042)(1,323.89)/(5)^{1/2} = (2,296, 4,714)$.

(c) **(i)** When fitting a categorical variable with c levels, you need to use only ($c - 1$) indicator variables. This is because once the ($c - 1$) indicators are known, you can easily find out what the indicator value for the cth level will be.

(ii) The t-ratio's appear to be small for each explanatory variable. Taken individually, each explanatory variable is insignificant. However, F-ratio is large enough to say that all the explanatory variables, taken together, significantly affect hospital costs. This is the seeming inconsistency. To explain this, it may be that one or more variables are important determinants of the response. However, when additional variables are entered in the model, the affect of this variable is diluted, to the point that individual variables appear unimportant. This could, for example, be due to the collinarity among variables. High collinearity means high standard errors which in turn means low t-ratios.

(d) (i) The analysis of variance model is $y_{ij} = \mu_j + e_{ij} = \mu + \tau_j + e_{ij}$. In regression format, this is $y = \beta_0 + \beta_{typ1} x_{typ1} + \beta_{typ2} x_{typ2} + e$, where x_{typ1} and x_{typ2} are indicators of admission type 1 and 2, respectively.

(ii) The null hypothesis H_0: $\beta_{src2} = \beta_{src4} = \beta_{pay4} = 0$. The alternative hypothesis is at least one of these β's is not 0. We use partial F-test. Compute the partial F-ratio $= ((R^2_{full} - R^2_{reduced})/p)/((1 - R^2_{full})/(n - (k + p + 1))$. First, we have $R^2_{reduced} = 25.09\%$ and $R^2_{full} = 44.9\%$. Hence, the partial F-ratio $=$ 3.2358. We compare this against F-value ($df_1 = 3$, $df_2 = 27$) $= 2.96$. Because F-ratio exceeds F-value, we reject H_0. Source of admission and payment type are significant.

5.5 (a) (i) The theoretical regression equation is ASSESS92 $= \beta_0 + \beta_1 N_1 + \beta_2 N_2 + \beta_3 N_3 + \beta_4 N_4 + \beta_5 N_5 + \beta_6 N_6 + \beta_7 N_7 + \beta_8 N_8 + \beta_9 N_9 + \beta_{10} N_{10} + e$. Here, N_1 is an indicator variable that indicates the presence of neighborhood 1, N_2 indicates the presence of neighborhood 2, and so on.

(ii) From the ANOVA table, we have $R^2 = 5.380/22.2 = 24.2\%$. Further, the F-ratio $= 2.49$. Using $df_1 = 10$ and $df_2 = 78$, at the 5% level of significance, we have F-value $= 1.96$. This indicates that the neighborhood effect is statistically significant.

(b) (i) The estimated equation is $\widehat{ASSESS92} = -10.28 + 1.09$ ASSESS91. In terms of the basic regression summary statistics, this is very useful. The t-ratio, $=$ 52.66, is highly significant and the coefficient of determination, $R^2 = 97\%$, is large.

(ii) The assessed values in 1992 increased by about 9.3% over the assessed values of 1991.

(iii) A 95% confidence for the slope is 1.0925 ± 0.0409, or $(1.04935, 1.13115)$.

(c) The theoretical regression equation is ASSESS92 $= \beta_0 + \beta_1 N_1 + \beta_2 N_2 + \beta_3 N_3 + \beta_4 N_4 + \beta_5 N_5 + \beta_6 N_6 + \beta_7 N_7 + \beta_8 N_8 + \beta_9 N_9 + \beta_{10} N_{10} + \beta_{11}$ ASSESS91 $+ e$. Here, N_1 is an indicator variable that indicates the presence of neighborhood 1, N_2 indicates the presence of neighborhood 2, and so on. For this full model, the error sum of squares is (Error SS)$_{Full} = 6.0458 \times 10^9$. From the model ASSESS92 $= \beta_0 + \beta_{11}$ ASSESS91 $+ e$, the error sum of squares is (Error SS)$_{reduced} = 6.7522 \times 10^9$. Comparing these two models, we have F-ratio $= 0.8997$. Using $df_1 = 10$ and $df_2 = 77$, at the 5% level of significance, the F-value is 1.9. Hence, after having introduced ASESS91, the effect of neighborhood is statistically insignificant.

Chapter 6

6.1 (a) When predictor variables are added to a model, R^2 always increases, even if the variables added are insignificant. A better measure is R^2_a.

(b) In stepwise regression, a variable is deleted whenever its t-ratio (in absolute value) is less than a specified t-value. In this case, the specified value is 1 and the SALES variable had a t-ratio of 0.44 ($<$1) at the 9th stage of the procedure. Hence, SALES was omitted at the 10th stage. Further a new variable is added if t-ratio exceed the specified value (in absolute value). No new variable was added at the 10th stage because no new variable produced a high enough t-ratio.

(c) Go through each stage and delete the variable with t-ratio that exceeds 1.5 (in absolute value). The resulting model uses the three variables: EPS, ASSETS, and SALES.

6.3   (a) The plot indicates that taller buildings, as measured by the number of floors, command a higher rent. Further, apartment buildings where parking is available also command a higher rent.

(b) $r_{partial} = 0.1362$.

(c) The model including the predictor variables YEAR, NUMFLOORS, ONSITE and RATING seems to be the best. This model has the highest R_a^2 , the lowest s and the coefficient of determination, R^2, is reasonably large. The C_p statistic is small compared to the cut-off value of 5, using four predictor variables. A close alternative is the same model without RATING variable. The R_a^2 is only slightly lower and the s is only slightly higher. The R^2 and C_p statistics are smaller, but that is expected with one fewer variables.

(d) The key thing here is that the two versions of this automatic routine are working with two different data sets. The forward stepwise regression is only using 47 observations, that is, only those observations where we have complete information. The backwards routine is using 77 observations, the number required for the final model. One must be careful when using automatic selection procedures because their performance relies on procedures which may or may not be appropriate for a given data set.

6.5   (a) (i) For small 1991 assessed values, the variability is tight. One can not even visually distinguish the observations from one another. For large assessed values, the variability appears to be greater. This is difficult to see, however.

(ii) The heteroscedasticity is much more evident in Figure E6.5b than Figure E6.5a. In Figure E6.5b, we have controlled for the line, making the changing variability much more apparent.

(b) (i) The point estimate is $\bar{y} = 7.963\%$.

(ii) The estimation procedures are different. In part b(ii), the point estimate is a regression estimate, using ASSESS91 as the independent variable. Here, we have already "controlled for" ASSESS91 by having in the denominator of the ratio.

(iii) Using Section 2.6, the 95% confidence interval is $7.963 \pm (1.99) (5.353/89^{1/2})$ $= 7.963 \pm 1.129$, or $(6.834, 9.092)$.

(c) (i) Figure E6.5c displays less changing variability than Figure E6.5b.

(ii) Because the homoscedasticity assumption seemed more compatible with the data in Figure E6.5c, choose the percentage model. This is 100 $((ASSESS92/ASSESS91) - 1) = \mu + e$.

6.7   (i) *PRESS* is a validation statistic based on the prediction sum of squares. It is defined to be the sum of squares of the *PRESS* residuals, where a *PRESS* residual is the regular residual divided by $1 -$ leverage. Validation implies checking the utility of a model.

(ii) We know that $1/n \le h_{ii} \le 1$, so the quantity $(1 - h_{ii})^2$ is between 0 and 1. Thus, dividing a residual by $(1 - h_{ii})^2$ results in a larger value than the residual alone for each residual. Thus *PRESS* is always larger than Error SS.

(iii) Model 1 *PRESS*: $(3.181/(1 - 0.8333))^2 + (-6.362/(1 - 0.3333))^2 + (3.181/(1 - 0.8333))^2 = 819.319.$

Model 2 *PRESS*: $[1 - \exp(-3)]^2 + [1 - \exp(1.5)]^2 + [20.0855 - \exp(0)]^2 = 379.86.$

6.8   **(a)** **(i)**   *VIF* measures collinearity. It captures linear relationship among the independent variables.

(ii) Severe collinearity exists when $VIF > 10$.

(iii) In case of large collinearity or big *VIF*, possible actions are: (a) recode variables, (b) ignore, but interpret impact or (c) remove variables. This is easy, but difficult when choosing which ones to remove. When removing variables, either: (a) use interpretation, (b) replace them with proxy variables, or (c) use automatic selection procedures (such as stepwise).

(b) **(i)**   A high leverage observation is a point that has an unusual set of explanatory variables. The leverage, denoted by h_{ii}, is our measure to quantify this aspect of the data. An observation is said to have high leverage if h_{ii} exceeds three times the average leverage, that is, $3\bar{h} = 3(k + 1)/n$.

(ii) The ith standardized residual is $\hat{e}_i/se(\hat{e}_i) = \hat{e}_i/(s(1 - h_{ii})^{1/2})$. For the sixth observation, we have $-1.29 = (-12.32)/(14.25(1 - h_{66})^{1/2})$. Solving for h_{66} yields $h_{66} = 0.5508$.

(c) **(i)**   The *PRESS* statistic helps to confirm appropriateness of a model, and is obtained as follows: (a) delete one observation from the sample (one at a time), (b) regress to get parameters, and use this model to predict the deleted data, and (c) compare actual data (y_i) against the predicted data ($\hat{y}_{(i)}$). The *PRESS* statistic is computed as $\Sigma_{i=1}^n (y_i - \hat{y}_{(i)})^2$. We choose the model with the smaller *PRESS* and, hence, pick the five-variable model.

(ii) The five variable model has better R_a^2 (56.3% against 51.0%), a smaller s (14.25 against 15.10), and a smaller *PRESS* (from part i). Four of the five variables have significant t-ratios. The fifth, associated with ASSETS, has a moderate t-ratio, with a p-value close to 10%. Further, a partial F-test can also be used to compare the five-variable against the three-variable model. The resulting partial F-ratio is 3.72, meaning that the addition of SALES and cashflow variables is significant. However, the variables SALES, CASHFLOW and NUMSHARE are highly collinear, as indicated by the *VIF* statistics. Other things equal, we prefer simpler models. They are easier to interpret.

6.10   **(a)**   The dotplot of sales seems to indicate that the distribution is somewhat skewed to the right, with large sellers being farther away from the center of the distribution than small sellers. For example, from the summary statistics, the largest seller is $(416,957 - 123,337)/101,693 = 2.89$ standard deviations above the mean. In contrast, the smallest seller is $(123,337 - 2,743)/101,693 = 1.19$ standard deviations below the mean. Further, the mean is larger than the median.

(b)   From the scatter plot of sales versus price, we see that sales are more variable for small price cars when compared to the variability for high price cars. From the scatter plot of sales versus MPG, we see that sales are more variable for cars with a high MPG rating when compared to the variability for cars with a low MPG rating.

(c)   From the scatter plot of sales versus MPG using type of manufacturer as a plotting code, we see that all cars with high sales are either Fords, GM or Japanese.

This is borne out in the table of sales where we see the low averages for the Chrysler and European types of cars.

(d) Sales seems to be negatively related to Price, although in a nonlinear fashion. The effect of the size of the car is not clear. Sales seem to be positively related to MPG.

(e) With five categories, only four indicator variables are required. Indeed, if the fifth indicator variable were included in the model, perfect collinearity would occur. Most statistical packages would automatically exclude one of the five. Because a perfect relationship among explanatory variables exists, the variance inflation factor would be infinity.

(f) The two observations corresponding to Mitsubishi are clearly unusual, either based solely on Sales or else based on Sales but controlling for MPG, size and type of manufacturer. Having discovered outliers from the preliminary regression fit, we were able to identify specific causes for their unusual behavior. Thus, it seems reasonable to introduce a predictor variable for this cause. Presumably, this variable would be useful in predicting sales for future cars, especially Mitsubishi cars.

(g) The model is a definite improvement. The natural variation s dropped and the adjusted coefficient of determination, R_a^2, increased. Further, the t-ratios of Price and size increased.

(h) The ALTERNATIVE FINAL MODEL that the assistant has run is equivalent to the FINAL REGRESSION MODEL. The basic statistics, including s, R^2, and R_a^2, are all the same. In the final regression model, the indicator variable dropped was for Ford. Thus, when interpreting the regression coefficients associated with the indicator variables, these are estimates of differences between a particular categories and Ford. From the original table of Sales, it is not surprising that there is no significant difference between Japanese and Ford's sales. In contrast, in the alternative final model, the default category is European. Again from the original table of sales, it is not surprising that all the regression coefficients are significantly different from zero.

6.12 **(a)** **(i)** Although many of these variables measure different aspects of health care costs, some of them may really suggest something about the others. For instance, more hospitals may mean more need for nurses and doctors, more hospital beds. This concern is pretty similar to collinearity whereby some of these independent variables may actually be linearly related to some others. If such is the case, some independent variables may become redundant and can therefore be unnecessary to predict life expectancy.

   (ii) The VIF's range from 1.5 to as high as 16.9. A rule of thumb is that there will be serious collinearity if $VIF > 10$. Here, we notice that BEDS_POP and POPDWELL produce the presence of serious collinearity.

(b) **(i)** A total of 40 countries were considered to fit a model. However, 18 countries had some values of the variables that were missing. Hence, only 22 countries were finally considered.

   (ii) By asking for stepwise regression on all variables, only 22 observations were available. More observations would be available for the fitting if certain variables are excluded from the stepwise routine.

   (iii) POPDWELL is initially considered because its t-ratio contribution is large enough. However, later in the process, when more variables come into play, the importance of POPDWELL disappears as indicated by its low t-ratio. Intuitively, other variables are more important predictors than POPDWELL.

(c) (i) When faced with an observation that has unusually large residual, one can:
  (1) include the observation but comment on its possible effects to the model,
  (2) delete the observation if it is believed to be unrepresentative of the sample taken, and
  (3) introduce an indicator variable if able to identify or explain cause for unusually large residual.

(ii) Since the observation is identified as China, and China may be believed to be different from the rest possibly because of its population size, its different form of government, and other factors. The standardized residual associated with China is not extremely large. This suggests that the best course of action is to leave the point in the summary statistics, but comment on the point in the report summary.

6.14 (a) Because $n^{-1} \sum_{i=1}^{n} (1/n) = 1/n$ and $\sum_{i=1}^{n} (x_i - \bar{x})^2 = (n-1) s_x^2$, we have $\bar{h} = n^{-1} \sum_{i=1}^{n} (1/n + (x_i - \bar{x})^2)/((n-1) s_x^2) = n^{-1} + n^{-1} = 2/n$.

(b) By subsitution, we have $(x_i - \bar{x})^2/((n-1) s_x^2) = 5/n$ or $(x_i - \bar{x})^2 = 5(n-1)/n s_x^2 = 5(1 - 1/n) s_x^2$. Thus, $|x_i - \bar{x}| = s_x (5(1 - 1/n))^{1/2}$, or x_i is approximately $2.4 s_x$ above or below $\bar{x}$.

6.16 (a) (i) $\ln 120 - \ln 100 = \ln 1.2 = 0.183232$.

  (ii) $(120/100) - 1 = 0.20000$, slightly larger. The error is $0.2 - 0.183232 = 0.016768$.

(b) (i) $\ln 105 - \ln 100 = \ln 1.05 = 0.048790$.

  (ii) $(105/100) - 1 = 0.05$, slightly larger. The error is $0.05 - 0.04879 = 0.00121$.

Chapter 7

7.1 (a) The null hypothesis is $H_0: \beta_{TAPRE} = \beta_{TAPCE} = 0$ and the alternative hypothesis is that at least one of the β's is not 0. To calculate the F-ratio, we have $n = 35, k = 5, p = 2$, (ERROR SS)$_{reduced} = 2.0967$ and (ERROR SS)$_{full} = 1.9756$. This yields F-ratio $= .8275$. With $df_1 = p = 2$ and $df_2 = n - (k + p + 1) = 27$, at the 5% level of significance, the F-value $= 3.354$. Because F-ratio $< F$-value, we do not reject H_0.

(b) $b_{EPS90} \pm (t\text{-value}) \, se(b_{EPS90}) = 0.27099 \pm (2.045)(0.02243) = 0.27099 \pm 0.04587 = (0.225, 0.317)$.

7.3 (a) The sign of regression coefficient indicates that lower prices do lead to higher sales volume. Formally, we wish to test the null hypothesis $H_0: \beta_{PRICE} = 0$ versus the alternative that $H_a: \beta_{PRICE} < 0$. To this end, we use the t-ratio, $t(b_{PRICE}) = -4.00$. This statistic is compared to a t-value using $df = 48 - (7 + 1) = 40$. Because we are interested in a one-sided alternative, at the 95% level we have t-value $= 1.684$. Because $t(b_{PRICE}) < -t$-value, this tells that the coefficient is significantly smaller than 0 and that we may reject the null hypothesis in favor of the alternative.

(b) The sign of the regression coefficient indicates that lower prices do lead to higher sales volume. Indeed, for a decrease in price of $1,000, based on the model we would expect sales to increase by 0.04858, or roughly 4.9%. A 95% interval estimate is $0.04858 \pm (2.021)(0.01214) = 0.04858 \pm 0.02453 = (0.02405, 0.07311)$, or roughly 2.4% to 7.3%.

(c) No. The regression model does not suggest cause and effect relationships. Instead, interpret the 4.9% increase to mean that, for two "typical" manufacturers that are alike in all ways but price, the one with a price tag that is lower by $1,000 will enjoy sales approximately 4.9% higher than the other.

7.5   **(a)** The null hypothesis is $H_0: \beta_{LIRR} = 0$ and the alternative hypothesis is $H_a: \beta_{LIRR} < 0$. The test statistic is $t(b_{LIRR})$ and the decision making procedure is to reject H_0 in favor of H_a if $t(b_{LIRR}) < -t\text{-value}$. Here, the t-value is calculated using $df = n - (k + 1) = 93$ degrees of freedom, with the significance level 5%. From the t-table, this number is approximately 1.664, interpolating between $df = 60$ and $df = 120$. Because $-1.80 = t(b_{LIRR}) < -1.664$, we reject the null hypothesis in favor of the alternative. Thus, lower life insurance reserve ratios are associated with higher retention levels.

(b) The null hypothesis is $H_0: \beta_{FIRMSIZE} = 1$ and the alternative hypothesis is $H_a: \beta_{FIRMSIZE} \neq 1$. The test statistic is $t(b_{FIRMSIZE})$ and the decision making procedure is to reject H_0 in favor of H_a if $|test\ statistic| > t\text{-value}$. Here, the t-value is calculated using $df = n - (k + 1) = 93$ degrees of freedom, with the significance level 2.5%. From the t-table, this number is approximately 1.990, interpolating between $df = 60$ and $df = 120$. The statistic is $test\ statistic = -4.923$. Because $4.923 = |test\ statistic| > 1.990$, we reject the null hypothesis in favor of the alternative. Thus, there is a significant difference between the true regression coefficient associated with FIRMSIZE and the hypothesized value of 1.

(c) The fitted value in logarithmic units is $loglim = 12.3443$. Thus, the fitted value is $\exp(12.3443) = \$229,650$.

(d) The null hypothesis is $H_0: \beta_{ORG.FORM} = \beta_{LIRR} = 0$ and the alternative hypothesis is that at least one of these betas is not 0. For the full model, we have $(Error\ SS)_{full} = 33.367$, with $n = 97$ and $k = 1$ and $p = 2$. For the reduced model, we have $(Error\ SS)_{reduced} = 35.189$. The test statistic is $F\text{-ratio} = 2.54$. The decision-making procedure is to reject H_0 in favor of H_a if $F\text{-ratio} > F\text{-value}$. Here, the F-value is calculated using $df_1 = p = 2$ and $df_2 = n - (k + p + 1) = 93$ degrees of freedoms, with the significance level 5%. From the F-table, this number is approximately 3.110, interpolating between $df_2 = 60$ and $df_2 = 120$. Because $2.46 = F\text{-ratio} < 3.11$, we can not reject the null hypothesis in favor of the alternative.

7.7   **(a)** Estimate her salary using the regression equation. Compare this estimate against her actual salary. If she's making less than what the regression suggests, then either she is underpaid or is performing below standards. If she's making more than what the regression suggests, then either she is overpaid or is performing above standards.

(b) (i) The t-ratio for the gender parameter is 1.86, which does not suggest a strong argument that the gender variable is a significant one. The argument is that higher male faculty salaries are due to other variables not associated with gender, including years of experience and discipline.

    (ii) The average salary for male is 28% higher than their female counterparts. Even after controlling for years of experience, male faculty salary is still higher than female by 13%. There is some debate as to whether the t-ratio $= 1.86$ is "statistically significant." If we test $H_0: \beta_{GENDER} = 0$ versus $H_a: \beta_{GENDER} > 0$, at the 5% level of significance, the t-value is 1.645. Thus, we would reject H_0 in favor of H_a. This test corresponds to a p-value roughly equal to 3.14%.

    (iii) Use the parameter estimate of the gender variable: 1.62% in this case.

Chapter 8

8.1 When the response variable is a 0 or 1, we expect these types of patterns with the usual residual plots. This is because the residual equals the response (y) minus the fitted value ($\hat{y}$), which is either $1 - \hat{y}$ or $-\hat{y}$, depending on whether y is 1 or 0. Rescaling by the estimated standard error does not change the plot so this is true whether we plot residuals or standardized residuals.

8.3 **(a) (i)** If 2 horses are randomly selected from one race, that means at most 1 horse can win. For example, if the first horse wins, the second can not.

(ii) Because there is a dependence among the dependent variables, there is a dependence among the error terms. This violates a basic assumption of "unrelated draws."

(b) The relationship is standard deviation $\approx (\bar{y}(1 - \bar{y}))^{1/2}$ where $\bar{y}$ is the sample mean.

(c) On average, the crowd has a higher apriori assessment of winners than losers. The crowd is able to predict winners with a certain degree of accuracy.

(d) (i) The t-ratio is $t(b_1) = 7.65$. This is highly significant, indicating that there is little chance that the relationship between FINISH and WIN is due to chance.

(ii) $r = 7.65/((7.65)^2 + 925 - 2)^{1/2} = 0.244$.

(e) The t-ratio, $t(b_1) = 7.65$, indicates that WIN definitely influences FINISH. However, the coefficient of determination, $R^2 = 6\%$, indicates that there is a substantial amount of variability in the variable FINISH that's not explained by the variable WIN. We may label WIN as "statistically significant but practially unimportant." Another interpretation is that the variable WIN is not very useful in predicting the outcome of a single race but may be useful over the long haul.

(f) The estimated model is $\hat{y} = 0.008 + 0.875\,x$. The smallest value of $\hat{y}$ is at $x = 0$, yielding 0.008. The largest value of $\hat{y}$ is at $x = 1$, yielding $0.008 + 0.875\,(1) = .883$. For this fitted model, the fitted values must lie within [0,1].

(g)

x	0	0.01	0.05	0.10	1.0
weighted LS fit	.0083	.0170	.0519	.0955	.8803
logistic regression fit	.0398	.0428	.0572	.0804	.9886

(h) It appears that FINISH is greater than WIN for small values of WIN, that is for long shots. This suggests a strategy of betting on horses that the crowd finds to be a long-shot, say, WIN <0.05. This means that the odds on the tote board should be longer than 15–1.

8.5 **(a)** For the model using FIRMCOST as the dependent variable, we expect the FIRMCOST to be about 5.50 units higher for those firms with a captive insurer, compared to a similar firm without a captive insurer and other variables being held constant.

For the model using CAP as the dependent variable, we expect the probability of having a captive insurer to increase by 0.00546 per unit increase of FIRMCOST, other variables being held constant.

(b) (i) Using the 0.5 cut-off, we would incorrectly misclassify four firms without captive insurers (CAP = 0) and 18 firms with captive insurers (CAP = 1). This yields a total misclassification rate of $22/73 = 30.1\%$.

(ii) A 0.70 cut-off would certainly result in all firms without captive insurers being correctly classified. However, this cut-off would result in 22 firms with captive insurers misclassified, for a total misclassification rate of 30.1%.

(c) The two major drawbacks are: (i) heteroscedastic errors and (ii) fitted values that can be outside [0,1].

Chapter 9

9.1 (a) (i) A stationary time series is one that is stable over time. For stationarity, we require that successive samples of modest size have approximately the same distribution.

(ii) The LONDON index is not stationary. It is clearly nonstationary in the mean. For example, the early part of the series has a much lower level than the latter part of the series.

(b) (i) Both t-ratios for TIME and TIMESQ are much larger than two in absolute value, and are statistically significant. The coefficient of determination, R^2, indicates that the model explains about 84.2% of the variation. The adjusted coefficient of determination, $R_a^2 = 84.1\%$, indicates that the new residual standard deviation, $s = 58.06$, is much lower after the model is fit than before.

(ii) Several observations initially fall below the fitted quadratic curve, and then several fall above, and so on. This pattern of adjacent residuals, the difference between observed and fitted values, indicates residual autocorrelation.

(iii) Using TIME = 255, our two-step forecast is $\widehat{\text{LONDON}} = 2{,}089.87 + 6.3568(255) - 0.0199865(255)^2 = 2{,}411.23$.

9.3 (a) (i) The series seems nonstationary. Although stationary in the variance, there is a slight, yet definite, upward trend in the series. Thus, the mean is increasing, one indication of nonstationary.

(ii) Winter months, including 'A' for January, 'B' for February, 'L' for December, and 'K' for November, have relatively low sales. Summer months, including 'E' for May, 'F' for June, 'G' for July and 'H' for August, have relatively high sales.

(b) (i) The fitted model using MONTH as a categorical variable accommodates fixed seasonality patterns.

(ii) The MONTH factor is important. The F-ratio is 40.12. This is much higher than the corresponding F-value ≈ 1.9, which is the 95th percentile from an F-distribution with $df_1 = 11$ and $df_2 = 180$ degrees of freedom. Further, the corresponding p-value = 0.000, at least to three decimal places. These test statistics indicate a strong statistical significance.

(iii) The plot of residuals versus TIME indicate that there is a linear trend in time. This suggests adding the time variable to the model specified.

9.4 (a) A control chart is a time series plot with control limits superimposed. A time series plot is simply a special kind of scatter plot with the horizontal axis as the order of the observation. Generally, in time series plots and control charts the observations are connected through time in order to display the temporal patterns. The types of temporal patterns that we are searching for including evidence of stationarity, outliers and the meandering nature of the series.

(b) Stationarity is a precise term, although generally it is used to indicate stability. In general, we examine the distribution of the series over time by looking at successive samples of modest size. Some aspects of the distribution that are of particular concern are the mean, or average, level and the volatility, as measured by the variance. This particular series appears stationary, at least through the average level. Some concern may be expressed that the variability is larger in the latter part of the series.

(c) If the series is nonstationary, a histogram provides almost no information. It does tell us approximate values of the largest and smallest observations, but little else of use.

(d) The theoretical random process model for observations is $y_t = \mu + e_t$ where $\{e_t\}$ is itself a random process for the "noise." The estimate of μ is $\hat{\mu} = \bar{y} = 0.04677$, resulting in a fitted model $\hat{y} = 0.04677$.

9.5 (a) (i) A *stationary process* is a process that is stable over time. When examining a stationary process over time, we expect different subsets of successive data points of the same size to behave similarly. When examining processes, we are particularly concerned with the mean level and variation of a process. For a stationary process, both the mean level and variability are constant over time.

(ii) The process is nonstationary in the mean. It is not readily apparent whether it is nonstationary in the variance.

(b) (i) The purposes of transforming the data is to achieve stationarity. By taking away, or filtering out, the main patterns, we can then search for more subtle patterns.

(ii) Based on the figures, the two transformations appear similar. From a statistical perspective, this would argue for taking the differenced series (DIFFBOND) because this is a simpler transformation. From an economic perspective, one could argue that a 1% difference in the bond yield is more important when the average yield is around 9% when compared to periods when the average yield is around 16%. This perspective suggests that percentage changes may be the more useful transformation.

9.6 (a) (i) The IMC Price Series is not cross-sectional data. It is arranged through time and thus is longitudinal data.

(ii) The IMC Price Series is not from a stationary process. There is a clear upward trend in time.

(iii) The IMC Price Series is not from a random process. There is a clear pattern in time, an upward trend. A random process is a process that displays no evident patterns.

(b) (i) The first two weeks of 1992 correspond to $t = 106$ and 107, respectively. Thus, our point forecasts are $27.3 + 0.230(106) = 51.68$ and $27.3 + 0.230(107) = 51.91$, respectively.

(ii) Point forecasts for a random walk model are the most recent time point plus the average difference times the forecast lead time. For this series, the average change is 0.226 and the last time point is 56.75. Thus, the forecasts for the first two weeks of 1992 are $56.75 + (0.226) = 56.976$ and $56.75 + 2(0.226) = 57.202$, respectively.

(iii) The point forecasts for the first two weeks of 1992 for the random walk are close to the last two values of the series. In contrast, there is a major jump between the most recent values of the Price series and the forecast values. This forecast jump would be difficult to defend to a stock investor because it is merely an artifact of the model. This strongly suggests preferring the random walk model.

(c) (i) Under the random process model, the forecast *return* is 0.00632, for each of the first two weeks of 1992. Because the last Price available is 56.75, the forecast price for the first week is 56.75(1 + 0.00632) = 57.109. Similarly, the forecast price for the second week of 1992 is 57.109(1 + 0.00632) = 57.470.

(ii) The graphical feature that we might look for is increasing volatility. If the price difference series displays increasing volatility, one device for dampening this is to consider logarithms. A logarithmic transformation will not take out the increasing trend in time. This could be accounted for by taking differences of logarithmic units which is similar to looking directly at returns.

9.8 (a) (i) The residual standard deviation of the quadratic regression model is $s = 58.06$. The standard deviation of the differences is $s_y = 20.27$. This comparison suggests that the random walk is a preferable model.

(ii) The two-step forecast is $\widehat{\text{LONDON}} = 2{,}493.10 + 2(1.45) = 2{,}496.00$.

(iii) An approximate 95% prediction interval is $2{,}496 \pm 2(20.27)(2)^{1/2} = 2{,}496 \pm 57.33$, or $(2{,}438.67, 2{,}553.33)$.

(b) (i) For a series y_t, the proportional change is $\text{PCHANGE}_t = y_t/y_{t-1} - 1$. The difference of the logarithms is, $\log y_t - \log y_{t-1} = \log(y_t/y_{t-1}) = \log(1 + \text{PCHANGE}_t)$. If the proportional change is fairly small, say, less than 10% in absolute value, then $\log y_t - \log y_{t-1} = \log(1 + \text{PCHANGE}_t) \approx \text{PCHANGE}_t$. In the figure, we see that all proportional changes are small.

(ii) When the proportional changes are large in absolute value, the approximation is no longer adequate.

Chapter 10

10.1 (a) The completed table is:

t	1	2	3	4	5	SUM
y_t	10	6	11	4	9	40
$y_t - \bar{y}$	2	-2	3	-4	1	0
$(y_t - \bar{y})^2$	4	4	9	16	1	34
$y_{t-1} - \bar{y}$	*	2	-2	3	-4	
$(y_{t-1} - \bar{y})(y_t - \bar{y})$	*	-4	-6	-12	-4	-26

Thus, $r_1 = \sum_{t=2}^{T}(y_{t-1} - \bar{y})(y_t - \bar{y})/\sum_{t=1}^{T}(y_t - \bar{y})^2 = -0.765$.

(b) Similarly, $r_2 = 0.500$ and $r_3 = -0.294$.

10.3 (i) See the attached figure.

(ii) As can be seen in the graph, the lag one autocorrelation is approximately $r_1 \approx -1.0$.

(iii) The lag two autocorrelation is approximately $r_2 \approx 1.0$.

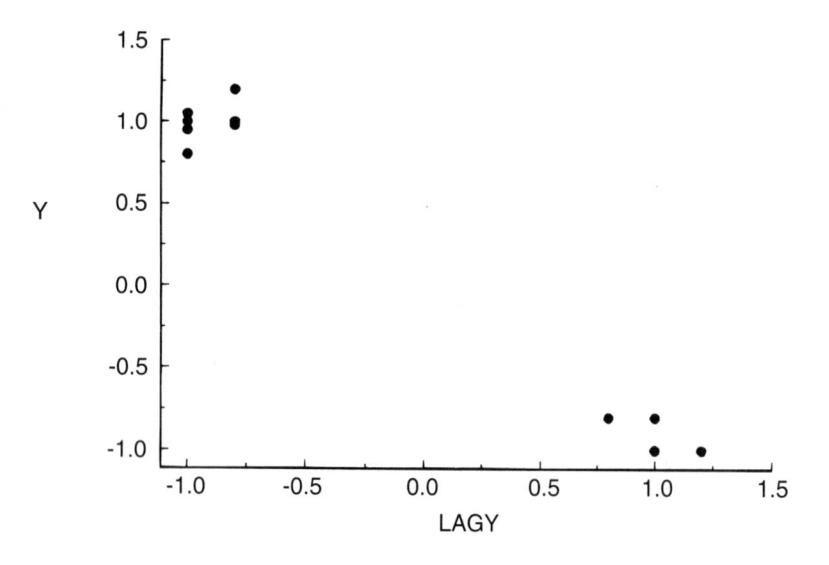

10.5 **(a)** **(i)** This figure shows a strong relationship between the current and immediate past value of %BOND. This is indicative a positively autocorrelated series.

   (ii) From the autocorrelation function, the lag one autocorrelation is $r_1 \approx 0.468$. This correlation is nearly the correlation between the current and immediate past value of %BOND.

(b) The lag one autoregressive parameter is useful. The estimated value is $b_1 = 0.4697$ with a corresponding t-ratio $t(b_1) = 7.06$. This t-ratio is far in excess of 2.00, the usual cut-off for indicating significance.

10.6 **(i)** This plot is one device for checking for further patterns in the residuals. None are apparent from this plot.

   (ii) The fitted $AR(2)$ model is $\hat{y}_t = 0.036 + 0.604\ y_{t-1} - 0.286\ y_{t-2}$, where $y = $ %BOND.

   (iii) We first find $\hat{y}_{181} = 0.036 + 0.604\ (-2.10) - 0.286\ (-0.01) = -1.23$. Thus, $\hat{\text{BOND}}_{181} = \text{BOND}_{180}*(1 + \hat{y}_{181}/100) = 8.75*(1 - 0.0123) = 8.64$.

10.7 **(a)** A meandering series is a sequence where adjacent observations have similar values. The adjective "meandering" is suggested by the leisurely flow of a river. In more technical terms, one can think of a meandering series as one that is positively autocorrelated, at lag one. The series that is plotted appears to be meandering.

(b) For the random process model, the forecast is $\hat{y} = \bar{y} = 3.0105$. This is true for both 1988 and 1989.

(c) The lag 1 autocorrelation, r_1, is nearly equal to the correlation between $\{y_t\}$ and $\{y_{t-1}\}$, the difference is only in how the first value is handled. (Because the first point is missing at $t = 1$ for y_{t-1}.) The fact that the correlation between $\{y_t\}$ and $\{y_{t-1}\}$ is high suggests developing a regression model using y_{t-1} to understand y_t. This is the autoregressive model of order 1.

(d) The total number of observations available for the $AR(1)$ is 12, because we lose one observation by lagging the response. With 2 linear parameters, the degrees of freedom available for error is $12 - 2 = 10$. Thus, $s = (\text{Error SS}/(T - 3))^{1/2} = (\text{Error SS}/10)^{1/2} = 0.1417$.

(e) $\hat{y}_{14} = 2.893$ and $\hat{y}_{15} = 2.926$. Both of these estimates are smaller than the estimate from the random process model, $\hat{y} = \bar{y} = 3.0105$.

(f) For 1988, $k = 1$ and $2.893 \pm 2(0.1417)(1)^{1/2} = 2.893 \pm .283 = (2.610, 3.176)$. For 1989, $k = 2$ and $2.926 \pm 2(0.1417)(1 + (0.6)^2)^{1/2} = 2.926 \pm 0.2834 (1.36)^{1/2} = 2.926 \pm 0.330 = (2.596, 3.256)$.

10.9 **(a)** **(i)**

t	1	2	3	4	5
y_t	207.01	239.83	223.27	224.22	207.65
y_{t-1}	*	207.01	239.83	223.27	224.22

(ii) See the attached figure.

(b) There are no apparent trends in the series, as seen in the control chart. The autocorrelations are reasonably small, compared to an approximate standard error of $1/(T)^{1/2} = 1/30^{1/2} \approx 0.1825$. These facts indicate that the series is stationary.

(c) **(i)** The point forecast is $\bar{y} = 223.37$.

(ii) A 95% forecast interval is $223.37 \pm 2(33.79) = (155.79, 290.95)$.

(d) The correlation coefficient of net sales versus its lagged version is $r_1 = 0.421$.

(e) **(i)** The standard error is $se(r_k) = 1/(T)^{1/2} \approx 0.1825$.

(ii) It is $r_1/se(r_1) = 0.421/0.1825 = 2.222$ standard errors above 0.

(iii) The theoretical value of ρ_2 is $\beta_1^2 = 0.177$.

(iv) $(r_2 - \rho_2)/se(r_2) = -0.526$. Thus, the actual value, r_2, is 0.526 standard errors below the $AR(1)$ model theoretical value, ρ_2.

(f) **(i)** Because the last available data point is $y_{30} = 222.31$, the point forecast is $\widehat{\text{NETSALES}}_{31} = 128.3 + .4245 \text{ NETSALES}_{30} = 222.67$.

(ii) A 95% prediction interval is $222.67 \pm 2s = 222.67 \pm 67.57 = (155.1, 290.24)$.

N* = 1

10.11 **(a)** The correlation between HOMELESS (y) and LAGHOME (x) is given by

$$r = \frac{\sum_{t=1}^{T} (x_t - \bar{x})(y_t - \bar{y})}{(T-1)\, s_x s_y}.$$

The lag one autocorrelation of HOMELESS is given by

$$r_1 = \frac{\sum_{t=2}^{T} (y_t - \bar{y})(y_{t-1} - \bar{y})}{\sum_{t=1}^{T} (y_t - \bar{y})^2}.$$

Note that the average of LAGHOME, $\bar{x}$, is not exactly the same as the average of HOMELESS, $\bar{y}$, because of a single observation. Similarly, the standard deviation of LAGHOME, s_x, is not exactly the same as the standard deviation of HOME-LESS, s_y. Apart from these mild discrepancies, the formulae yield the same result.

(b) **(i)** The standard error of the residual autocorrelations are approximately $se(r_k)$ $\approx 1/(T)^{1/2} \approx 0.1361$. As a rule of thumb, we think that $r_k(\hat{e})$ is statistically significantly different from zero if the ratio $r_k(\hat{e})/se(r_k)$ is larger than two in absolute value. No residual autocorrelation is larger than 0.2722 in absolute value. Hence, all are close to zero.

(ii) The one-step forecast is $\text{HOMELESS}_{56} = 1{,}821.47$. The two-step forecast is $\text{HOMELESS}_{57} = 1{,}781.75$. The three-step forecast is $\text{HOMELESS}_{58} = 1{,}746.32$.

(iii) The 95% prediction interval for the three-step forecast is: $\hat{y}_{T+3} \pm 2s(1 + b_1^2 + b_1^4)^{1/2} = (1{,}197.75,\, 2{,}294.89)$.

(c) **(i)** There is a large lag one residual autocorrelation, $r_1(\hat{e}) = 0.617$. Further, the residual autocorrelations are geometrically decreasing.

(ii) The autoregressive parameter is 0.6218. This is -3.65 standard errors away from one.

(iii) The autoregressive parameter in this case is 0.892. This is -1.58 standard errors away from 1. If the AR parameter is 1, then we have a random walk model.

Chapter 11

11.1 **(a)** **(i)** The square root of the mean square error, s, is $(0.475)^{1/2} \approx 0.689$.

(ii) The autocorrelation function of the residuals displays substantial patterns. For each autocorrelation, the cut-off for statistically different from zero is roughly 2 standard errors. The standard error is approximately $1/(180)^{1/2} \approx 0.0745$. Thus, any autocorrelation more than $2 \times 0.0745 = 0.149$ is significantly far away from zero.

(b) **(i)** Let y be the annual differences and let x be an indicator variable for the 27th point. The least squares estimate of the slope in the equation $y = \beta x + e$ is $b = x_{27}$. Thus, the residuals are $\hat{e} = y - bx$. This residuals can be interpreted as the original data except for the 27th point, which is zero.

(ii) From part a(i), we have $s = 0.689$. The new s is 0.6139. Thus, we have achieved nearly the same "typical error" with a minimal amount of modeling. If we can achieve further reduction by modeling the annual differences, then we will have a better representation of the data than the model arrived at in part a.

(c) (i) The t-ratio of the $AR(1)$ parameter is $t(b_1) = 4.08$. This is much larger than two, indicating that this parameter estimate is significantly different from zero.

(ii) The residuals do not exhibit a random pattern. Under the assumption of randomness, the cut-off is about 0.149, as in part a(ii).

(iii) For a random pattern, we expect about 95% of the autocorrelation estimates to be less than 0.149 in absolute value.

(d) (i) The theoretical model is $\Delta_{12}y_t = \beta_0 + \beta_1 \Delta_{12}y_{t-1} + \beta_2 \Delta_{12}y_{t-12} + \beta_3 \Delta_{12}y_{t-13} + e$, where $\Delta_{12}y_t = y_t - y_{t-12}$.

(ii) The fitted model is $\Delta_{12}\hat{y}_t = 0.154 + 0.289\,\Delta_{12}y_{t-1} - 0.182\,\Delta_{12}y_{t-12} - 0.053\,\Delta_{12}y_{t-13}$, since $(0.289)(0.182) \approx 0.053$.

(iii) With $t = 191$, from part (ii), we have $\Delta_{12}\hat{y}_{193} = 0.154 + 0.289\,\Delta_{12}y_{192} - 0.182\,\Delta_{12}y_{181} - 0.053\,\Delta_{12}y_{180}$. From this table, we have $\Delta_{12}y_{192} = y_{192} - y_{180} = 13.220 - 12.100 = 1.120$, $\Delta_{12}y_{181} = y_{181} - y_{169} = 14.260 - 14.091 = 0.161$, and $\Delta_{12}y_{180} = y_{180} - y_{168} = 12.100 - 12.235 = -0.135$. Thus, $\Delta_{12}\hat{y}_{193} = 0.154 + 0.289(1.120) - 0.182(0.161) - 0.053(-0.135) = 0.456$. Thus, $\hat{y}_{193} = y_{181} + 0.456 = 14.260 + 0.456 = 14.716$.

(iv) For this fitted model, the square root of the mean square error is $s \approx 0.580$. This is much smaller than the estimate in part b(ii), 0.614. Since we have reduced the typical error in the model, this is an argument for choosing the lag one and twelve autoregression model.

11.2 (a) An approximate 95% prediction interval is $579.1 \pm 2(74.9) = (429.3, 728.9)$.

(b) (i) The approximate standard error is $1/T^{1/2} \approx 0.158$. Thus, the first 8 autocorrelations are well below 0.316, the 2 standard errors cut-off. Thus, there are no discernible patterns based on the autocorrelation function.

(ii) The analysis of variance indicates that *quarters* is a significant variable, due to the large F statistic and corresponding p-value. In particular, the table of statistic by quarter indicates that the fourth quarter is much smaller than the other three quarters.

(iii) From the time series plot, we see that the fourth quarter, corresponding to the plotting symbol '4', is generally much lower than the other symbols.

(c) (i) The estimated model is $NEW\hat{I}NC_t = 475.43 + 0.2266\,NEWINC_{t-1} - 102.87\,Q4$, where $Q4$ is an indicator variable for the fourth quarter. For the fourth quarter, the estimated model is $NEW\hat{I}NC_t = 372.56 + 0.2266\,NEWINC_{t-1}$. For other quarters, the estimated model $NEW\hat{I}NC_t = 475.43 + 0.2266\,NEWINC_{t-1}$.

(ii) For the first quarter of 1990, the forecast is 590.54. For the second quarter of 1990, the forecast is 609.25. For the third quarter of 1990, the forecast is 613.49. For the fourth quarter of 1990, the forecast is 511.58.

(d) The estimated model is $NEW\hat{I}NC_t = 442.49 + 0.2729\,NEWINC_{t-1} - 98.18\,Q4 + 187.32\,OBS\ 37$, where $OBS\ 37$ is an indicator variable for the 37th observation. A plausible motivation would be if the first quarter of 1989 were investigaged and it was discovered that the climate for new business was particularly favorable in that quarter. If we were convinced it was a special cause, then an indicator variable is one device to capture the effect of this special event.

Index